Frommer's®

Italy

Here's what the critics say about Frommer's:

"Amazingly easy to use. Very portable, very complete."
—*Booklist*

♦

"The only mainstream guide to list specific prices. The Walter Cronkite of guidebooks—with all that implies."
—*Travel & Leisure*

♦

"Complete, concise, and filled with useful information."
—*New York Daily News*

♦

"Hotel information is close to encyclopedic."
—*Des Moines Sunday Register*

♦

"The best series for travelers who want one easy-to-use guidebook."
—*U.S. Air Magazine*

Other Great Guides for Your Trip:

Frommer's Rome

Frommer's Portable Venice

Frommer's Tuscany & Umbria

Frommer's Italy from $50 a Day

Frommer's Italy's Best-Loved Driving Tours

Frommer's Food Lover's Companion to Italy

Frommer's Europe

Frommer's Europe from $50 a Day

Frommer's Gay & Lesbian Europe

Frommer's Europe's Greatest Driving Tours

The Complete Idiot's Travel Guide to Planning Your Trip to Europe

Frommer's® 99

Italy

by Darwin Porter & Danforth Prince

MACMILLAN • USA

ABOUT THE AUTHORS

A native of North Carolina, **Darwin Porter** was bureau chief for the *Miami Herald* when he was 21 and later worked in television advertising. A veteran travel writer, he wrote Frommer's first-ever guide to Italy and has been a frequent traveler in Italy every since. He is joined by **Danforth Prince,** formerly of the Paris bureau of the *New York Times,* who has lived and traveled in Italy extensively. This team writes a number of best-selling Frommer's guides, notably to England, France, Germany, and the Caribbean.

MACMILLAN TRAVEL

A Simon & Schuster Macmillan Company
1633 Broadway
New York, NY 10019

Find us online at **www.frommers.com**

Copyright © 1999 by Simon & Schuster, Inc.
Maps copyright © by Simon & Schuster, Inc.

MACMILLAN is a registered trademark of Macmillan, Inc.
FROMMER'S is a registered trademark of Arthur Frommer. Used under license.

ISBN 0-02-862273-1
ISSN 1044-2170

Editor: Ron Boudreau
Special thanks to Lisa Renaud, Marie Morris, and Ida McCall
Production Editor: Christy Wagner
Photo Editor: Richard Fox
Design by Michele Laseau
Digital Cartography by John Decamillas and Ortelius Design
Page Creation by Jena Brandt, Ellen Considine, and Laura Goetz

Front cover photo: San Gimignano as seen through grape vines, Tuscany

SPECIAL SALES

Bulk purchases (10+ copies) of Frommer's and selected Macmillan travel guides are available to corporations, organizations, mail-order catalogs, institutions, and charities at special discounts, and can be customized to suit individual needs. For more information write to Special Sales, Macmillan General Reference, 1633 Broadway, New York, NY 10019.

Manufactured in the United States of America

Contents

8   Bologna & Emilia-Romagna   338

9   Venice: La Serenissima   371

10   The Veneto & the Dolomites   435

List of Maps

AN INVITATION TO THE READER

In researching this book, we discovered many wonderful places—hotels, restaurants, shops, and more. We're sure you'll find others. Please tell us about them, so we can share the information with your fellow travelers in upcoming editions. If you were disappointed with a recommendation, we'd love to know that, too. Please write to:

Frommer's Italy '99
Macmillan Travel
1633 Broadway
New York, NY 10019

AN ADDITIONAL NOTE

Please be advised that travel information is subject to change at any time—and this is especially true of prices. We therefore suggest that you write or call ahead for confirmation when making your travel plans. The authors, editors, and publisher cannot be held responsible for the experiences of readers while traveling. Your safety is important to us, however, so we encourage you to stay alert and be aware of your surroundings. Keep a close eye on cameras, purses, and wallets, all favorite targets of thieves and pickpockets.

WHAT THE SYMBOLS MEAN
✪ Frommer's Favorites

Our favorite places and experiences—outstanding for quality, value, or both.

The following abbreviations are used for credit cards:

AE	American Express	DISC	Discover
CB	Carte Blanche	MC	MasterCard
DC	Diners Club	V	Visa

FIND FROMMER'S ONLINE

Arthur Frommer's Outspoken Encyclopedia of Travel (**www.frommers.com**) offers more than 6,000 pages of up-to-the-minute travel information—including the latest bargains and candid, personal articles updated daily by Arthur Frommer himself. No other Web site offers such comprehensive and timely coverage of the world of travel.

The Best of Italy

You've come to Italy to relax and enjoy this beautiful, diverse, and culturally rich country—not to exhaust yourself searching for the best deals and most evocative experiences. So spend your vacation in peace and let us do the work for you.

Though the selections below represent Italy's finest offerings, they by no means exhaust the roster of wonderful things to see and do. Italy is a land of enchanting discoveries, and whether this is your first trip or your 10th, you're bound to come away with your own favorites to add to the list.

1 The Best Travel Experiences

- **Visiting the Art Cities:** When Italy consisted of dozens of principalities, its art treasures were concentrated in many small capitals, each blessed with the patronage of a papal representative or ducal family. Consequently, these cities became treasure troves of exquisite paintings, statues, and frescoes displayed in churches, monasteries, and palaces whose architects are world acclaimed. Though Rome, Florence, and Venice are the best known, you'll find stunning collections in Assisi, Cremona, Genoa, Mantua, Padua, Parma, Palermo, Pisa, Siena, Taormina, Tivoli, Turin, Verona, and Vicenza.

- **Dining Italian Style:** One of the most cherished pastimes of the Italians is eating out. Regardless of how much pizza and lasagne you've had in your life, you'll never have tasted any better than the real thing in Italy. Each region has its own specialties, some handed down for centuries. If the weather is fine and you're dining outdoors with a view of, perhaps, a medieval church or piazza, you'll find it's the closest thing to heaven in Italy. See the end of chapter 2 for a lowdown on Italian cuisine. *Buon appetito!*

- **Celebrating Mass in St. Peter's Basilica:** With the exception of some sites in Jerusalem, St. Peter's in the Vatican is Christendom's most visible and important building. The huge size of the church is daunting. For many visitors, celebrating mass here is a spiritual highlight of their lives. Your co-celebrants are likely to come from every corner of the world. See chapter 5.

- **Attending a Papal Audience:** Many Catholic visitors to Rome eagerly await papal audiences every Wednesday morning, when the pope addresses the general public. If the day is fair, these audiences are sometimes held in St. Peter's Square. All are welcome. See chapter 5.

- **Riding Venice's Grand Canal:** The S-shaped Canal Grande, curving for 2 miles along historic buildings and under ornate bridges, is the most romantic waterway in the world. Most first-timers are stunned by the variety of Gothic and Renaissance buildings, the elaborate styles of which could fill a book on architecture. A ride on the canal will give you ever-changing glimpses of the city's poignant beauty. Your ride doesn't have to be on a gondola; any public *vaporetto* (ferry) sailing between Venice's rail station and Piazza San Marco will provide a heart-stopping view. See chapter 9.

- **Walking in Venice:** The most obvious means of transport in Venice is by boat; an even more appealing method is on foot, traversing hundreds of canals, large and small, and crossing over the arches of medieval bridges. Getting from one point to another can be like walking through a maze—but you won't be hassled by traffic, and the sense of the city's beauty, timelessness, and slow decay is almost mystical. See chapter 9.

- **Spending a Night at the Opera:** More than 2,000 new operas were staged in Italy during the 18th century, and since then Italian opera fans have earned a reputation as the most demanding in the world. Venice was the site of Italy's first opera house, the Teatro di San Cassiano (1637), but it eventually gave way to the fabled La Fenice, which burned down in 1996 and is being restored; in the meantime, opera is presented under a tent at Palafenice. Milan's La Scala is possibly the world's most prestigious opera house, especially for bel canto; however, La Scala will be closed for restoration until sometime in year 2000, so you'll have to check with the Milan tourist office to see what temporary venues are being used. There's also a wide assortment of outdoor settings, like Verona's Arena, one of the largest surviving amphitheaters. Suitable for up to 20,000 spectators and known for its fine acoustics, the Arena presents operas in July and August, when moonlight and the perfumed air of the Veneto add to the charm. See chapters 9, 10, and 11.

- **Shopping Milan:** Milan is one of Europe's most enchanting fashion capitals. You'll find a range of shoes, clothing, and accessories unequaled anywhere else, except perhaps Paris or London. Even if you weren't born to shop, stroll along the streets bordering Via Montenapoleone and check out the elegant offerings from Europe's most famous designers. See chapter 11.

- **Experiencing the Glories of the Empire:** Even after centuries of looting, much remains of the legendary Roman Empire. Of course, Rome boasts the greatest share (the popes didn't tear down everything to recycle into churches)—you'll find everything from the Roman Forum and the Pantheon to the Colosseum and the Baths of Caracalla. And on the outskirts, the long-buried city of Ostia Antica, the port of ancient Rome, has been unearthed and is remarkable. Other treasures are scattered throughout Italy, especially in Sicily. The hordes also descend on Pompeii, buried by volcanic ash from Mt. Vesuvius in A.D. 79, and Herculaneum, buried by lava on that same day. Our favorite spot is Paestum, along Campania's coast; its ruins, especially the Temple of Neptune, are alone worth the trip to Italy. See chapters 5, 14, and 16.

- **Rejuvenating at a Spa:** Though Germany's spas are busier, the *terme* (spas) of Italy enjoy a relaxed charm and thousands of devoted aficionados. Head to Montecatini Terme or the island of Ischia to learn why Italians are so passionate about "the cure." If you're affluent and exhausted, you can opt for a regime of mud baths and immersion in the sulfurous waters bubbling out of geothermal springs. Regardless of how extensively you participate in the spa rituals, you're likely to emerge refreshed and relaxed. See chapters 7 and 14.

- **Reliving the Grand Tour:** During the 18th and 19th centuries, enlightened schoolmasters believed that a tour through Italy was the proper conclusion to a well-rounded education. The sons of prosperous families from France, Britain, and Germany swept southward on grand loops through the Alps; the great art cities of the Veneto, Umbria, and Tuscany; the monuments and churches of Rome; and the ancient ruins of Naples and Sicily. Part of the enchantment of such a tour is stumbling on unexpected charms in the smaller towns as you travel.

2 The Most Romantic Getaways

- **Spoleto:** Spoleto is as ancient as the Roman Empire and as timeless as the music presented there every summer during its world-renowned arts festival. The architecture of this quintessential Umbrian hill town is centered around a core of religious buildings from the 13th century. It's less chic but more romantic during the off-season, when the crowds are less dense. See chapter 7.
- **Portofino:** This is the world's most famous small port, largely because of the well-preserved buildings surrounding its circular harbor. Located 22 miles southeast of Genoa in the heart of the Italian Riviera, Portofino is charming, chic, and cosmopolitan. A cluster of top-notch hotels caters to the very rich and famous. See chapter 13.
- **Capri:** Floating amid azure seas south of Naples, Capri is called the "Island of Dreams." Roman emperors Augustus and Tiberius both went there for R&R, and since the late 1800s celebrities have flocked there for an escape. A boat ride around the island's rugged coastline is one of our favorite things to do. See chapter 14.
- **Ravello:** It's small, sunny, and loaded with notable buildings (such as its 1086 cathedral). Despite its choice position on the Amalfi coast, Ravello manages to retain the aura of an old-fashioned village. Famous residents have included writer Gore Vidal. See chapter 14.
- **Taormina:** This resort, the most charming place in Sicily, is loaded with regional charm, chiseled stonework, and a sense of the ages. Favored by wealthy Europeans and dedicated artists, especially in midwinter, when the climate is delightful, Taormina is a fertile oasis of olive groves, grapevines, and orchards. Visitors will relish the delights of the sun, the sea, and the medieval setting. See chapter 16.

3 The Best Countryside Drives

- **Tuscany and Umbria:** Olive groves, dramatic hill towns, thickly wooded hills often peppered with cypress trees, sun-ripened vineyards, and even snowcapped peaks await you in the provinces of Tuscany and Umbria, often called Italy's land of milk and honey. Much of the scenery was painted by Renaissance artists before your arrival. The drive leaves Florence to visit some of Italy's greatest art cities (like Lucca) or architectural relics (like San Gimignano) and most definitely Siena, Perugia, and Assisi, among Italy's greatest attractions. See chapter 7.
- **Lombardy:** From ancient to modern, Milan, Lombardy, and the Lake District (Maggiore, Como, and Garda) take you from that crucible of chic, Milan, to

alpine vistas and exotic gardens. The Lake District has been called "achingly beautiful," and so it is. This tour also incorporates some of central Italy's most neglected but intriguing art cities, like Cremona (the city of the violin) and Mantua, a former duchy that knew its greatest fame under the Gonzaga dynasty. See chapter 11.

- **The Italian Riviera:** This drive, depicted in countless films, needs little selling from us. This is where the Italians themselves go for *il dolce far niente* (the sweet art of doing nothing). The region is Liguria, and its capital, San Remo, presides over the Riviera di Fiori (Riviera of Flowers). After sampling its turn-of-the-century aura, you can move on to art-filled Genoa, a fitting stopover before plunging into the coastal towns of Rapallo and Portofino, which stand for international chic. See chapter 13.

- **The Amalfi Coast:** The locals defy you to find lovelier towns anywhere. Sorrento, Positano, Amalfi, and Ravello—these names alone suggest carefree days in the sun. Kings, emperors, writers, and artists have all extolled the glories of Campania's sea-wreathed resorts. The drive along the coast is narrow, curvy, and twisting, and while at times you'll feel that seeing the Coasta Amalfitana is a risk to your life, the rewards are worth it. See chapter 14.

- **Sicily:** A drive around this fabled island takes you past majestic ruins, panoramic seascapes, and even a dangerously simmering volcano. You'll be caught in a time warp between Europe and Africa, surrounded by sharp contrasts—from splendid architecture to ghettolike slums. It's a land of prickly cacti, citrus groves, sun-bleached vineyards, Roman amphitheaters, and baroque palaces and churches. Our drive takes you to the highlights, like Agrigento, Catania, Palermo, Segesta, Syracuse, and Trapani. See chapter 16.

4 The Best Museums

- **Musei Vaticani** (the Vatican, Rome): Rambling, disjointed, and unbelievably well stocked with treasures accumulated over the centuries by the popes, this complex contains some of Italy's most famous draws. Among them are the incomparable Sistine Chapel, such sculptures as *Laocoön* and the *Belvedere Apollo,* buildings whose walls were almost completely executed by Raphael, and endless collections of art ranging from (very pagan) Greco-Roman antiquities to Christian art by famous European masters. See chapter 5.

- **Museo Nazionale di Villa Giulia** (Rome): Mysterious and for the most part undocumented, the Etruscans were the ancestors of the Romans. They left a legacy of bronze and marble sculpture, sarcophagi, jewelry, and representations of mythical heroes, some of which were excavated at Cerveteri, a stronghold north of Rome. Most startling about the artifacts is their sophisticated, almost mystical sense of design. The Etruscan collection is housed in a papal villa from the 1500s. See chapter 5.

- **Galleria degli Uffizi** (Florence): This 16th-century Renaissance palace was the administrative headquarters, or *uffizi* (offices), for the Duchy of Tuscany when the Medicis controlled Florence. It's estimated that up to 90% of Italy's artistic patrimony is stored in this building, the crown jewel of Italy's museums. (The Uffizi was the target of a car bomb that caused considerable damage in 1993 but has staged an amazing recovery.) See chapter 6.

- **Museo Nazionale del Bargello** (Florence): The severely angular 13th-century exterior of Il Bargello, in the heart of Florence, is permeated with the raw power of the governing magistrate (*bargello*) who built it. Today its collection of sculpture and decorative accessories is without equal in Italy, including works by Michelangelo and Donatello. See chapter 6.

- **Palazzo Pitti** (Florence): The spheres of influence that dominated Florence during its most creative years revolved around the Medicis and the Pittis, who ruled the city from their respective banks of the Arno. The Pittis moved into this palazzo in 1560, after it was enlarged with two new wings. Today it houses seven museums containing everything from paintings by old masters (like Raphael and Titian) to works by modern artists and a collection of antique silver. See chapter 6.

- **Galleria Nazionale dell'Umbria** (Perugia): Italian Renaissance art has its roots in Tuscan and Umbrian painting from the 1200s. This collection, on the top floor of the Palazzo dei Priori (parts of which date from the 1400s), contains a world-class collection of paintings, most executed in Tuscany or Umbria between the 13th and the 18th centuries. Included are works by Fra Angelico, Piero della Francesco, Perugino, Duccio, and Gozzoli, among others. See chapter 7.

- **Galleria dell'Accademia** (Venice): It's one of the most richly stocked art museums in Italy, boasting hundreds of paintings, many of them Venetian, executed between 1300 and 1790. Among the highlights are works by Bellini, Carpaccio, Giorgione, Titian, and Tintoretto. See chapter 9.

- **Collezione Peggy Guggenheim** (Venice): One of the Western world's most comprehensive and brilliant modern-art collections is housed in an unfinished palazzo along the Grand Canal. The collection is like a cavalcade of 20th-century art, including works by Max Ernest (one of Ms. Guggenheim's former husbands), Picasso, Braque, Magritte, Giacometti, and Moore. See chapter 9.

- **Pinacoteca di Brera** (Milan): Although Milan is usually associated with wealth and corporate power, it contains a worthy assortment of cultural icons as well. Foremost among these is the Brera Picture Gallery, whose collection—shown in a 17th-century palace—is especially rich in paintings from the schools of Lombardy and Venice. See chapter 11.

- **Museo Poldi-Pezzoli** (Milan): In 1881, this museum's namesake donated his extensive art collection to his hometown, thereby creating the base for one of Italy's most influential museums. Included are Persian carpets, portraits by Cranach of Martin Luther and his wife, works by Botticelli and Bellini, and massive amounts of decorative art. See chapter 11.

- **Museo Archeologico Nazionale** (Naples): Naples and the region around it have yielded more sculptural treasures from the Roman Empire than anywhere else. Many of these riches have been accumulated in a rambling building designed as a barracks for the Neapolitan cavalry in the 1500s. Much of the loot excavated from Pompeii and Herculaneum, as well as the Renaissance collections of the Farnese family, is in this museum, which boasts a trove of Greco-Roman antiquities. See chapter 14.

5 The Best Cathedrals

- **Basilica di San Pietro** (the Vatican, Rome): Its roots began with the first Christian emperor, Constantine, in A.D. 324. By 1400 the Roman basilica was in danger of collapsing, prompting the Renaissance popes to commission plans for the largest, most impressive cathedral the world had ever seen. Amid the rich decor of gilt, marble, and mosaics are countless artworks, including Michelangelo's *Pietà*. Other sights here are a small museum of Vatican treasures and the eerie underground grottoes containing the tombs of former popes. An elevator ride (or a rigorous climb) up the tower to Michelangelo's dome provides panoramic views of Rome. See chapter 5.

- **Il Duomo** (Santa Maria del Fiore, Florence): Begun in the late 1200s and consecrated 140 years later, the pink, green, and white marble Duomo was a symbol of Florence's prestige and wealth. It's loaded with world-class art and is one of Italy's largest and most distinctive religious buildings. A view of its red-tiled dome, erected over a 14-year period in what was at the time a radical new design by Brunelleschi, is worth the trip to Florence. Other elements of the Duomo are Giotto's Campanile (bell tower) and the octagonal Baptistery (a Romanesque building with renowned bronze doors). See chapter 6.

- **Basilica di San Francesco** (Assisi): St. Francis, protector of small animals and birds, was long dead when construction began on this double-tiered showcase of the Franciscan brotherhood. Interior decoration, in many cases by Cimabue and Giotto, reached a new kind of figurative realism in Italian art around 1300, long before the masters of the Renaissance carried the technique even further. Consecrated in 1253, the cathedral is one of the highlights of Umbria and the site of many religious pilgrimages. See chapter 7.

- **Il Duomo** (Orvieto): A well-designed transition between the Romanesque and Gothic styles, this cathedral was begun in 1290 and completed in 1600. It sheltered an Italian pope (Clement VII) when Rome was sacked by French soldiers in 1527. Part of the building's mystery derives from Orvieto's role as an Etruscan stronghold long before Italy's recorded history. See chapter 7.

- **Il Duomo** (Milan): Begun in 1386 and finally completed in 1809 on orders of Napoléon, Milan's Duomo is an ornate and unusual building. Gathered around a triangular gable bristling with 135 pointed and chiseled spires, it's both massive and airy. The interior is as severe as its exterior is ornate. See chapter 11.

6 The Best Ruins

- **Ostia Antica** (near Rome): During the height of the Roman Empire, Ostia ("mouth" in Latin) was the harbor town set at the point where the Tiber flowed into the sea. As Rome declined, so did Ostia, and by the early Middle Ages, the town had almost disappeared, its population decimated by malaria. In the early 1900s, archaeologists excavated the ruins of hundreds of ancient buildings, many of which you can view. See chapter 5.

- **Roman Forum** (Rome): Two thousand years ago, most of the known world was directly affected by decisions made in the Roman Forum. Today classicists and archaeologists wander among its ruins, conjuring up the glory that was Rome. What you'll see today is a pale, rubble-strewn version of the site's original majesty—it's now surrounded by modern boulevards packed with whizzing cars. See chapter 5.

- **Palatine Hill** (Rome): According to legend, the Palatine Hill was the site where Romulus and Remus (the orphaned infant twins who survived in the wild by suckling a she-wolf) eventually founded the city. Though Il Palatino is one of the seven hills of ancient Rome, you'll find it hard to distinguish it as such because of the urban congestion rising all around. The site is enhanced by the Farnese Gardens (Orti Farnesiani), laid out in the 1500s on the site of Tiberius's palace. See chapter 5.

- **The Colosseum** (Rome): Rome boasts only a handful of other ancient monuments that survive in such well-preserved condition. A massive amphitheater set incongruously amid a maze of modern traffic, the Colosseum was once the setting for gladiator combat, lion-feeding frenzies, and public entertainment whose cruelty was a noted characteristic of the Empire. All three of the ancient world's classical styles (Doric, Ionic, and Corinthian) are represented, superimposed in tiers one above the other. See chapter 5.

- **Villa Adriana** (near Tivoli): Hadrian's Villa slumbered in rural obscurity until the 1500s, when Renaissance popes ordered its excavation. Only then was the scale of this massive and very beautiful villa from A.D. 134 appreciated. Its builder, Hadrian, who had visited almost every part of his empire, wanted to incorporate the widespread wonders of the world into one fantastic building site. And he succeeded. See chapter 5.
- **Herculaneum** (Campania): Legend says that Herculaneum was founded by Hercules. The historical facts tell us that it was buried under rivers of volcanic mud one fateful day in A.D. 79 after the eruption of Mt. Vesuvius. Seeping into the cracks of virtually every building in town, the scalding mud preserved the timbers of hundreds of structures that would otherwise have rotted over the normal course of time. Devote at least 2 hours to seeing some of the best-preserved houses from the ancient world. See chapter 14.
- **Pompeii** (Campania): Once it was an opulent resort filled with 25,000 wealthy Romans. In A.D. 79, the same eruption that devastated Herculaneum (above) buried Pompeii under at least 20 feet of scalding volcanic ash and pumice stone. Beginning around 1750, Charles of Bourbon ordered the systematic excavation of the ruins—the treasures hauled out of Pompeii sparked a wave of interest in the classical era throughout northern Europe. See chapter 14.
- **Paestum** (Campania): Paestum was discovered by accident around 1750, when local bureaucrats tried to build a road across the heart of what had been a thriving ancient city. Paestum originated as a Greek colony around 600 B.C., fell to the Romans in 273 B.C., and declined into obscurity in the final days of the empire. Today amateur archaeologists can follow a well-marked walking tour through the excavations. See chapter 14.
- **La Valle dei Templi** (Sicily): Though most of it lies in ruins, the Valley of the Temples in Agrigento is one of Europe's most beautiful classical sites, especially in February and March, when the almond trees surrounding it burst into pink blossom. One of the site's five temples dates from as early as 520 B.C.; another (though never completed) ranks as one of the largest temples in the ancient world. See chapter 16.
- **Segesta** (Sicily): Even its site is impressive: a rocky outcropping surrounded on most sides by a jagged ravine. Built around 430 B.C. by the Greeks, Segesta's Doric colonnade is one of the most graceful in the ancient world. The site is stark and mysterious and was believed to have been destroyed by the Saracens (Muslim raiders) in the 11th century. See chapter 16.
- **Selinunte** (Sicily): Its massive columns lie scattered on the ground, as if an earthquake had punished its builders, yet this is one of our favorite ancient ruins in Italy. Around 600 B.C., immigrants from Syracuse built Selinunte into an important trading port. The city was a bitter rival of neighboring Segesta (above) and was destroyed around 400 B.C., then again in 250 B.C. by the Carthaginians. See chapter 16.

7 The Best Castles & Palaces

- **Castel Sant'Angelo** (Rome): Originating as a mausoleum in A.D. 135 for Hadrian and his family, the castle was enlarged in the 500s by Gregory the

Great, who added a Christian chapel to its top floor. After some 900 years, Pope Nicholas V added a brick upper story and angular towers. Later popes added a bridge across the Tiber (complete with stone angels carved by Bernini) and some of the most luxurious apartments in Christendom. See chapter 5.

- **Villa d'Este** (Tivoli): Italian cardinal Hippolyte d'Este decided to retire in the countryside near Tivoli, outside Rome. While building his villa, he created an exquisite garden, where scores of ornate fountains and waterfalls continue to delight visitors. See chapter 5.
- **Palazzo Vecchio** (Florence): Built over a 15-year period beginning in 1299, the Palazzo Vecchio (also called the Palazzo della Signoria) dominates one of Italy's most memorable piazzas. It was intended as an administration building but was transformed 200 years later into the private residence of Cosimo I of the Medici family. Despite its inner luxury and the airy spaciousness of its courtyard, the palazzo has no windows on its ground floor, a reminder of the feudal sense of fortification. See chapter 6.
- **Palazzo Ducale** (Venice): Built in the 1100s and radically upgraded between 1400 and 1550, it functioned as the court, prison, seat of government, and residence for the doge (ruling prince) during the most glorious years of Venetian history. Designed as a massive block of pink and white geometric patterns poised atop 36 delicately carved columns, it's surpassed in grandeur only by the city's cathedral. See chapter 9.
- **Palazzo Ducale** (Mantua): One of Mantua's most impressive showcases, this palazzo was created in the 1500s by joining a newly built palace with a Renaissance chapel and a 200-year-old stone fortress. Inside, many of the walls and ceilings are lavishly adorned with trompe-l'oeil frescoes and carved and gilded plaster, some commissioned by the palace's most legendary occupant, Isabelle d'Este, and some executed by Mantegna. See chapter 11.

8 The Best Wine-Growing Regions

- **Latium** (Lazio): The region around Rome is known for predominantly white wines that include Marino, Est! Est!! Est!!!, Colli Albani, and the widely visible Frascati ("the wine of the popes and the people"). All these are derived almost exclusively from Malvasia and Trebbiano grapes or, in some cases, from combinations of the two. The region's most famous producers of Frascati are **Fontana Candida,** Via di Fontana Candida, 00040 Monte Porzio Catone, Roma (☎ **06/942-0066**), whose winery, 14 miles southwest of Rome, was built around 1900; and **Gotto D'Oro–Cantina Sociale di Marino,** Via del Divino Amore 115, 00040 Frattocchie, Roma (☎ **06/935-6931** and 06/935-6932). To arrange visits, contact the **Gruppo Italiano Vini,** Villa Belvedere, 37010 Calmasino, Verona (☎ **045/626-0600**).
- **Tuscany and Umbria:** Some of Italy's most scenic vineyards lie nestled among the verdant rolling hills of these two stately regions. In fact, the most famous kind of wine in Italy (Chianti) is indelibly associated with Tuscany, while the (usually white) Orivieto and the (usually red) Torgiano are closely associated with Umbria. One of Umbria's most appealing wineries is **Azienda Vallesant di Luigi Barberani,** Azienda Agricola Vallesant, Loc. Cerreto, Baschi, 05023 Terni (☎ **0763/41-820**). One of Tuscany's largest vintners is **Villa Banfi,** Castello Banfi, Sant'Angelo Scalo, Montalcino, 53020 Siena (☎ **0577/840-111**). Near Siena are two other good choices: **Biondi-Santi,** Loc. Greppo, 53024

Montalcino (☎ 0577/847-121), and **Casa Vinicola L. Cecchi,** Loc. Casina dei Ponti, 53011 Castellina in Chianti (☎ 0577/743-024).

- **Emilia-Romagna:** Comprised of two distinct areas (Emilia, to the west of Bologna, around the upriver Po valley; and Romagna, to the east, centered around the delta of the Po), the region is known to gastronomes as the producer of some of Italy's best food, with wines worthy of its legendary cuisine. Emilia's most famous wine is Lambrusco, 50 million bottles of which are produced every year near Modena and Reggio Emilia. Less well known but also highly rated are the Colli Piacentini wines, one of the rising stars for which is **Cantine Romagnoli,** Via Provinciale, Villo di Vigolzone 29020 (☎ 0523/870-129). Wines from Romagna are produced from Sangiovese, Trebbiano, and Albana grapes and are almost universally well respected, cropping up on wine lists throughout the country.

- **The Veneto:** The humid flatlands of the eastern Po Valley have produced memorable reds and whites in great abundance since the days of the Venetian doges. Output includes massive quantities of everything from soft white Soaves and Pinot Grigios to red Valpolicellas and Merlots. Important vineyards in the region are **Azienda Vinicola Fratelli Fabiano,** Via Verona 6, 37060 Sona, near Verona (☎ 045/608-1111), and **Fratelli Bolla,** Piazza Cittadella 3, 37122 Verona (☎ 045/809-0911). Smaller, but well respected because of recent improvements to its vintages, is **Nino Franco** (known for its sparkling prosecco), in the hamlet of Valdobbiadene, Via Garibaldi 177, 31049 Treviso (☎ 0423/972-051). For information on these and the dozens of other producers in the Veneto, contact the **Azienda di Promozione Turistica,** Via Leoncino 61, 37121 Verona (☎ 045/592-828).

- **Trentino–Alto Adige:** The two most important wine-producing regions of northwestern Italy are the Alto Adige (also known as the Bolzano or Sudtirol region) and Trento. The loftier of the two, the Alto Adige, was once part of the Austro-Hungarian province of the South Tyrol. More Germanic than Italian, it clings to its Austrian traditions and folklore and grows an Italian version of the gewürtztraminers (a fruity white) that would more often be found in Germany, Austria, and Alsace. Venerable wine growers include **Alois Lageder** (founded in 1855), Tenuta Loüwengang, Vicolo dei Conti, in the hamlet of Magré (☎ 0471/817-256), and **Schloss Turmhof,** Entiklar, Kurtatsch, 39040 (☎ 0471/880-122). The Trentino area, a short distance to the south, is one of the leading producers of Chardonnay and sparkling wines fermented using methods developed centuries ago. A winery worth a visit is **Cavit Cantina Viticoltori,** Via del Ponte 31, 38100 Trento (☎ 0461/922-055).

- **Friuli–Venezia Giulia:** This region in the cool alpine foothills of northeastern Italy produces a light, fruity vintage that's especially appealing when young. One of the largest and best-respected wineries here is **Livio Felluga,** Via Risorgimento 1, Brazzano di Cormons, 34071 Gorizia (☎ 0481/60203). Another worthy producer known for its high-quality wines is **Eugenio Collavini Vini & Spumanti,** Via della Ribolla Gialla 33040, Corno di Rosazzo, Udine (☎ 0432/753-222).

- **Lombardy** (Lombardia): The Po Valley has always been known for its flat vistas, midsummer humidity, fertile soil, and excellent wines. The region produces everything from dry still reds to sparkling whites with a champagnelike zest. **Guido Berlucchi,** Piazza Duranti 4, Borgonato di Cortefranca, 25040 Brescia (☎ 030/984-451), one of Italy's largest wineries, is especially willing to receive visitors.

- **Piedmont** (Piemonte): Reds with rich and complex flavors make up most of the wine output of this rugged high-altitude region near Italy's border with France. One of the most interesting vineyards is headquartered in a 15th-century abbey near the hamlet of Alba: **Antiche Cantine dell'Annunziata,** Abbazia dell'Annunziata, La Morra, 12064 Cuneo (☎ **0173/50-185**).
- **Campania:** The wines produced in the harsh, hot landscapes of Campania, around Naples in southern Italy, seem stronger, rougher, and in many cases more powerful than those grown in gentler climes. Among the most famous are the Lacryma Christi (Tears of Christ), a white that grows in the volcanic soil near Naples, Herculaneum, and Pompeii; Taurasi, a potent red; and Greco di Tufo, a pungent white laden with the odors of apricots and apples. One of the most frequently visited vineyards is **Mastroberardino,** 75–81 Via Manfredi, Atripalda, 83042 Avellino (☎ **0825/626-123**).
- **Sicily:** Its hot climate and volcanic soil foster the growth of more vineyards than any other region. Most of these are devoted to the production of simple table wines. Of the better vintages, the best-known wine is Marsala, a sweet dessert wine produced in both amber and ruby tones. The production of Marsala got a great boost by the British, whose fleet paid frequent calls in Sicily throughout England's Age of Empire. Lord Nelson himself was an avid connoisseur, encouraging its production and spurring local vintages to produce abundant quantities. One top producer is **Regaleali,** Contrada Regaleali, 93010 Vallelunga, Pratameno Caltanisetta (☎ **0921/542-522**), a historic enterprise near Palermo run by the Tasca d'Almerita family; this winery is also known for its sauvignon-based Nozze d'Oro and such full-bodied reds as Rosso del Conte (whose bouquet has been referred to by connoisseurs as "huge"). Two other names that evoke years of wine-making traditions, thanks to their skill at producing Cerasuolo di Vittoria and Moscato di Pantelleria, are **Cantine Torrevecchia di Favuzza Giuseppe,** Via Ariosto 10A, 90144 Palermo (☎ **0932/989-400**), and **Corvo Duca di Salaparuta,** a 19th-century winery in the hills above Palermo. For information, contact the **Casa Vinicola Duca di Salaparuta,** Via Nazionale, SS113, Casteldaccia, 90014 Palermo (☎ **091/953-988**).

9 The Best Luxury Hotels

- **Hotel de la Ville Inter-Continental Roma** (Rome; ☎ **800/327-0200** in the U.S.): Less stuffy than its neighbor, the Hassler, the Inter-Continental enjoys the same swank location at the top of the Spanish Steps (near an obelisk and a Renaissance church). If you want to splurge in Rome, this is the place to do it. The hotel was built in the 19th century on the site of the ancient gardens of Lucullus. The public rooms boast a 1930s elegance, and the smartly styled guest rooms reflect classic Roman styling. The view from the rooftop terrace is stunning. See chapter 4.
- **Villa San Michele** (Fiesole, near Florence; ☎ **055/59-451**): This former 15th-century monastery is set behind a facade reputedly designed by Michelangelo. Brigitte Bardot once selected it for one of her honeymoons (no one remembers which husband it was). Many visitors consider this hill-town hotel a worthy escape from Florence's often oppressive summer congestion. With a decor that no set designer could ever duplicate, it evokes the charm of an aristocratic private villa. See chapter 6.
- **Hotel Cipriani** (Venice; ☎ **800/992-5055** in the U.S.): This exclusive elegant hotel is in a 3-acre garden on the Isola della Giudecca, one of the calmer islands

that comprise the ancient city of Venice. The grand hotel was built as a cloister in the 15th century and is centered around a large modern pool. See chapter 9.

- **Gritti Palace** (Venice; ☎ **800/325-3535** in the U.S.): Andrea Gritti, a doge who ruled Venice with an iron hand until his death in 1538, is the namesake for this property, gem of one of the world's most elegant hotel chains (CIGA). The exquisite interiors offer a taste of Venice's historic opulence. See chapter 9.

- **Miramonti Majestic Grand Hotel** (Cortina d'Ampezzo; ☎ **0436/4201**): Designed like a massive mountain fortress, this hotel is in the heart of Italy's most glamorous alpine resort. The clientele seems to relish the hotel's Italian panache amid the bracing air of the Dolomites. Despite the modern amenities, there's a 19th-century quality about this place. See chapter 10.

- **Grand Hotel Villa d'Este** (Cernobbio; ☎ **800/223-6800** in North America, 212/838-3110 in New York City, or 031/3481): Built in 1568, this splendid palace in the Lake District is one of the world's most famous Renaissance-era hotels. Step inside and you're surrounded by frescoed ceilings, impeccable antiques, and many other exquisite details. Ten magnificently landscaped acres, parts of which have been nurtured since the 1500s, surround the hotel. Cool breezes are provided by nearby Lake Como and the proximity to the Swiss and Italian Alps. See chapter 11.

- **Albergo Splendido** (Portofino; ☎ **800/237-1236** in the U.S.): Built as a monastery in the 14th century and abandoned because of attacks by North African pirates, this monument was rescued during the 19th century by an Italian baron and converted into a summer home for his family. The posh hillside retreat on the Italian Riviera now accommodates a sophisticated crowd, including many film stars. The scent of mimosas fills the air, and the sea views are blissful. See chapter 13.

- **Grand Hotel Quisisana Capri** (Capri; ☎ **081/837-0788**): This hotel, on a part of the island sheltered from the sometimes annoying winds, was established as a health spa by an English doctor around 1850. It's large, supremely comfortable, and intricately linked to the allure that made Capri popular with the Roman emperors. See chapter 14.

- **Hotel di San Pietro** (near Positano; ☎ **089/875-455**): The only marker identifying this cliffside hotel, in the Campania region, is a 15th-century chapel set beside the winding road. The hotel doesn't advertise, protects the privacy of its guests, and offers frequent transportation into that hub of midsummer glamour, Positano, less than a mile away. Strands of bougainvillea twine around the dramatically terraced white exterior walls; the rooms resemble suites and offer views of the sea. See chapter 14.

- **Palazzo San Domenico** (Taormina, Sicily; ☎ **0942/23-701**): This is one of Europe's great stylish old hotels, a 500-year-old Dominican monastery whose severe lines and dignified bulk are softened with antique tapestries, fragrant gardens, and a sense of the eternal that only Sicily can give. Since its transformation into a hotel in 1896, its guests have included movie legends Dietrich, Garbo, and Loren. See chapter 16.

10 The Best Moderately Priced Hotels

- **Hotel Venezia** (Rome; ☎ **06/445-7101**): Near Rome's main rail terminal, this hotel features Murano glass chandeliers in the guest rooms and public areas, which were recently renovated. Some units have balconies overlooking the street, and everything is well maintained. See chapter 4.

- **Hotel Bellettini** (Florence; ☎ 055/213-561): If you're looking for a place with *A Room with a View* atmosphere, head for this Renaissance palazzo midway between the Duomo and the rail station. It's a family-run affair with an old-time atmosphere evoked by terra-cotta floors and stained-glass windows. The rooms are a bit plain but very comfortable. See chapter 6.
- **Hotel Palazzo Bocci** (Spello, near Assisi; ☎ 0742/301-021): Built in the late 18th century and renovated and transformed into a hotel in 1992, this palace is posh, tasteful, and reasonably priced. Many of the public and private rooms have sweeping views of the valley below. See chapter 7.
- **Hotel Roma** (Modena; ☎ 059/222-218): In the 1700s, this building was among the real-estate holdings of the duca d'Este. Today it's likely to be the temporary home of whatever opera star happens to be singing in Pavarotti's hometown. Flourishing as a hotel since the 1950s, the Roma, in the historic heart of town, is comfortable and uncomplicated. See chapter 8.
- **La Residenza** (Venice; ☎ 041/528-5315): Many of this hotel's guests are art lovers who return to Venice year after year. Built in the 14th century, its interior walls have some of the most charming stucco work in Venice. On the medieval piazza outside, older citizens feed pigeons while younger ones play soccer. See chapter 9.
- **Hotel Menardi** (Cortina d'Ampezzo; ☎ 0436/2400): Built a century ago, this alpine inn exudes Austrian gemütlichkeit (coziness), with blazing fireplaces and windows that overlook a view of alpine meadows and rugged crags. Best of all, it's a short uphill walk from one of Italy's most glamorous resorts. See chapter 10.
- **Hotel Florence** (Bellagio; ☎ 031/950-342): A private villa in the 19th century, this hotel boasts a dignified facade, an arbor with tumbling wisteria, and stone-sided terraces overlooking a lake. A series of renovations in 1990 brought it tastefully up-to-date, and Saturday-night jazz concerts and an American-style bar have made it better than ever. See chapter 11.
- **Albergo Nazionale** (Portofino; ☎ 0185/269-575): This excellent moderately priced choice is in the heart of Italy's most photographed harbor, in the most expensive pocket of posh on the Italian Riviera. Antique furnishings, coved ceilings, and hand-painted Venetian furniture add to the charm and luxury, but nothing equals the view of the harbor from some windows. See chapter 13.
- **Palazzo Murat** (Positano; ☎ 089/875-177): Along the curvy Amalfi drive, the Murat is a reasonably priced retreat in a pricey resort that's big on charm and nostalgia. Jasmine and bougainvillea grow profusely in the garden, and the atmosphere is a bit baroque. This was the former retreat of Napoléon's brother-in-law, the king of Naples. The steep streets are tortuous to climb, but you're following in the footsteps of the rich and famous if you anchor here. See chapter 14.

11 The Best Restaurants

- **Relais Le Jardin** (Rome; ☎ 06/361-3041): The restaurant of the dignified Lord Byron Hotel, in an upscale residential neighborhood a short drive from the center of Rome, the Relais is always on the short list of the country's best. There are places in Rome with better views, but not with such an elegant setting. The service is impeccable, and the menu varies according to what's in season. See chapter 4.
- **La Terraza** (Rome; ☎ 06/478-121): This posh rival of Relais Le Jardin serves some of Rome's finest Italian and international food and also offers a panoramic

view of St. Peter's. Of course, the service is flawless. The "symphony" of seafood for two is perfection. See chapter 4.

- **Don Chisciotte** (Florence; ☎ 055/475-430): This Florentine palazzo near the rail station continues year after year to serve some of the most creative cuisine, with an emphasis on fresh seafood, though this is an inland city. Long before Michelin got around to discovering its allure, we've been dining here on such delights as a risotto of broccoli and baby squid or filet of turbot with radicchio sauce. See chapter 6.

- **San Domenico** (Imola, outside Bologna; ☎ 0542/29-000): Convenient to either Bologna or Ravenna, Italy's undisputed best restaurant is in the unlikely town of Imola. Most deluxe restaurants aspire to yet don't achieve the perfection you'll taste here. The Italian menu declares its dedication to the culinary traditions of the noble families of Italy, offering the most luxurious food and the most elaborate preparations money can buy. The wine list is one of the country's finest. See chapter 8.

- **Harry's Bar** (Venice; ☎ 041/528-5777): It's legendary, it's lighthearted, and it's fun. First made famous by writer Ernest Hemingway, Harry's Bar still serves sublime food in the formal dining room upstairs. The Bellini, peach juice with prosecco (Italian sparkling wine), was born here. See chapter 9.

- **Antico Martini** (Venice; ☎ 041/522-4121): Founded in 1720 as a spot to enjoy the newly developed rage of coffee drinking, this restaurant is one of the very best in Venice. Replete with paneled walls and glittering chandeliers, the Martini specializes in Venetian cuisine. See chapter 9.

- **Ristorante il Desco** (Verona; ☎ 045/595-358): Set in a former palazzo, this restaurant is the best in the Veneto region of northeastern Italy. Its culinary repertoire emphasizes a *nuova cucina* (nouvelle cuisine) that makes use of the freshest ingredients. The wine selections are excellent. See chapter 10.

- **Ristorante Tivoli** (Cortina d'Ampezzo; ☎ 0436/866-400): At this charming and friendly restaurant, a cozy chalet on a hillside above the town, enjoy such flavorful dishes as stuffed rabbit in onion sauce, filet of veal with pine nuts and basil, and a delectable saffron-flavored salmon. See chapter 10.

- **Peck's Restaurant** (Milan; ☎ 02/876-774): In the 19th century, an entrepreneur from Prague moved to Lombardy and founded the most upscale delicatessen (Peck) in Milan. The same management also runs this sumptuously elegant restaurant. You're likely to dine surrounded by the business moguls who run Italy. See chapter 11.

- **Ristorante da Vittorio** (Bergamo; ☎ 035/218-060): On a busy commercial boulevard in a town known for its feudal fortifications, this restaurant stresses regional cuisine with an array of risottos, pastas, and game dishes. See chapter 11.

- **L'Aquila Nigra** (Mantua; ☎ 0376/327-180): To reach this restaurant, which used to be a Renaissance palace, you'll have to meander through a labyrinth of narrow alleyways in the historic heart of Mantua. Inside, the high-ceilinged rooms offer elegant food, served with dignified panache. See chapter 11.

- **Gran Gotto** (Genoa; ☎ 010/583-644): Despite its excellent cuisine, this place manages to remain lighthearted, irreverent, and richly connected to the seafaring life of this ancient Italian port. The zuppa di pesce (a Riviera version of a Marseillaise bouillabaisse) is worth the trip to Genoa. See chapter 13.

- **La Cantinella** (Naples; ☎ 081/764-8684): The only Michelin-starred restaurant in Naples, La Cantinella serves some of the best and most refined seafood in Campania. Opening onto the bay of Santa Lucia, this will be the highlight in your culinary tour of the area. Time-tested Neapolitan classics are served here along with an array of more imaginative dishes. Grilled fish can be prepared as you like it, and chances are you'll like it a lot. See chapter 14.

12 The Best Buys

- **Ceramics:** The town of Faenza, in Emilia-Romagna, has been the center of pottery making, especially majolica, since the Renaissance. Majolica, also known as faïence, is a type of hand-painted, glazed, and heavily ornamented earthenware. Of course, you don't have to go to Faenza to buy it, as shops throughout the country carry it. Tuscany and Umbria are also known for their earthenware pottery, carried by many shops in Rome and Florence.
- **Fashion:** Italian fashion is world-renowned. Pucci and Valentino led the parade, to be followed by Armani, Missoni, Gucci, Versace, and Ferré. Following World War II, Italian design began to compete seriously against the French fashion monopoly. Today Italian designers like Krizia are among the arbiters of the world. Milan dominates the scene with the largest selection of boutiques, followed by Rome and Florence. Ironically, a lot of "French" fashion is now designed and manufactured in Italy, in spite of what the label says.
- **Glass:** Venetian glass, ranging from the delicate to the grotesque, is famous the world over. In Venice you'll find literally hundreds of stores peddling Venetian glass in a wide range of prices. Here's the surprise: A great deal of Venetian glass today isn't manufactured on Murano (an island in the Venetian lagoon) but in the Czech Republic. That doesn't mean the glass is unworthy, though. Many factories outside Italy turn out high-quality glass products that are then shipped to Murano, where many so-called glass factories aren't factories at all but storefronts selling this imported "Venetian" glass.
- **Gold:** The tradition of shaping jewelry out of gold dates from the time of the Etruscans, and this ancient tradition is going strong in Italy today, with artisans still toiling in tiny studios and workshops. Many of the designs they follow are based on ancient Roman originals. Of course, dozens of gold jewelers don't follow tradition at all but design original and often daring pieces. Many shops will even melt down your old gold jewelry and refashion it into something more modern.
- **Lace:** For centuries, Italy has been known for its exquisite and delicate lace—fashioned into everything from women's undergarments to heirloom tablecloths. Florence long ago distinguished itself for the *punto Firenze* (Florentine stitch) made by cloistered nuns, though this tradition has waned over the years. Venetian lace is even more famous, including some of the finest products in the world, especially tombolo (pillow lace), macramé, and an expensive form of lace known as chiacchierino. Of course, the market today is also flooded with cheap machine-made stuff, which a trained eye can quickly spot. Though some pieces, such as a bridal veil, might cost millions of lire, you'll often find reasonably priced collars, handkerchiefs, and doilies in Venice and Florence boutiques.
- **Leather:** The Italians (not just Gucci designers) are the finest leather craftspeople in the world. From boots to luggage, from leather clothing to purses (or wallets), Italian cities—especially Rome, Florence, Venice, and Milan—abound in leather shops selling quality goods. This is one of Italy's best values, in spite of the substandard work that's now appearing. If you shop carefully, you can still find lots of handcrafted Italian leather products.
- **Prints and Engravings:** Ever since the Renaissance, Italy has been a shopping mecca for engravings and prints, especially Rome and Florence. Wood

engravings, woodcuts, mezzotints, copper engravings—you name it and you'll find it. Of course, you have to be a careful shopper. Some prints are genuine antiques and works of rare art, but others are rushed off the assembly line and into the shops. Since you can no longer go to Italy and take home Roman antiques or a crate of Raphaels, you'll have to content yourself with these relatively inexpensive prints and engravings—admittedly reproductions but collectors' items nonetheless.

- **Religious Objects and Vestments:** The religious objects industry in Italy is big and bustling, centered mostly in the Greater Vatican area in Rome. The greatest concentration of shops in Rome is near the ancient Church of Santa Maria Sopra Minerva. They've got it all, from cardinals' birettas and rosary beads to religious art and vestments.

2

Introducing the Land of Leonardo & Michelangelo

Conquerors both noble and notorious, scholars, artistic geniuses, saints and sinners, and millions of others have been born in or drawn to Italy for centuries. Across turbulent seas and rugged mountains the non-natives have come, even risking their lives to see for themselves the riches of this land. Getting there may be considerably easier today—by plane, sea, rail, or car—but the age-old attraction remains.

Some of today's visitors long to get to know the people, as did novelist E. M. Forster, who wrote that the Italians are "more marvellous than the land." Others are drawn to the treasury of artworks by masters like Leonardo, Michelangelo, and Caravaggio and to the treasury of architecture leading from the Etruscans to Palladio. Still others come for the scenery: cypress-studded landscapes, coastal coves, Dolomite peaks, fishing ports, sandy beaches, and charming little hill towns. And there are those lured by the variety of cuisines—nowhere else in the world does Italian food taste so marvelous.

Of course, most travelers to Italy are looking for a little taste of everything above. And Italy, with its cultural heritage and sense of la dolce vita, provides a vast menu from which to choose.

1 The Regions in Brief

Italy is about the size of the U.S. state of Arizona, but the peninsula's shape gives you the impression of a much larger area; the ever-changing seacoast contributes to this feeling, as do the large islands of Sicily and Sardinia. Bordered on the northwest by France, on the north by Switzerland and Austria, and on the east by Slovenia (formerly part of Yugoslavia), Italy is still a land largely surrounded by the sea.

Italy was late in developing a national identity: Only in 1870 were its 20 regions united under a central government. It may be a late bloomer among European nations, but its culture has flourished since antiquity, and no other country boasts as many reminders of its heritage, ranging from Rome's Colosseum to Sicily's Greek ruins.

Two areas within Italy's boundaries aren't under the control of the Italian government: the **State of Vatican City** and the **Republic of San Marino.** Vatican City's 109 acres were established in 1929 by a concordat (formal agreement) between Pope Pius XI and Benito Mussolini, acting as head of the Italian government; the agreement also gave Roman Catholicism special status in the country. The pope is the

The Regions of Italy

sovereign of the State of Vatican City, which has its own legal system and post office. (The Republic of San Marino, with a capital of the same name, strides the top slopes of Mt. Titano, 14 miles from Rimini. It's small and completely surrounded by Italy, so it still exists only by the grace of Italy.)

Here's a brief rundown of the cities and regions covered in this guide:

ROME & LATIUM

The region of **Latium** is dominated by **Rome,** capital of the ancient empire and the modern nation of Italy, and **Vatican City,** the independent papal state. Containing vast lodes of the world's artistic treasures, Latium is a land of myth, legend, grandeur, and ironies. Much of the civilized world was once ruled from here, going back to the days when Romulus and Remus are said to have founded Rome on April 21, 753 B.C. For generations, Rome was justifiably referred to as *caput mundi* (capital of the world). It no longer enjoys such a lofty position, of course, but remains a timeless city, ranking with Paris and London as one of the most visited in Europe. There's no place else with more artistic monuments, not even Venice or Florence. Rome is the country's storehouse of treasures, from the Sistine Chapel to the Roman Forum. It remains the city of la dolce vita. How much time should you budget for the capital? Italian writer Silvio Negro said, "A lifetime is not enough."

FLORENCE, TUSCANY & UMBRIA

Tuscany is one of the most culturally and politically influential provinces—the development of Italy without Tuscany is simply unthinkable. It was the vistas of Tuscany, with the sun-warmed vineyards and towering cypresses, that inspired the artists of the Renaissance. Nowhere in the world does the Renaissance live on more than it does in its birthplace, **Florence,** with its artistic works left by Leonardo and Michelangelo (including the most reproduced statue on earth, his *David*), among others. Since the 19th century, travelers have been flocking to Florence to see the Donatello bronzes, the Botticelli smiles, and all the other preeminent treasures. Alas, it's now an invasion, and so you run the risk of being trampled underfoot as you explore the historic heart of the city. To escape, head for nearby Tuscan hill towns, former stamping ground of the Guelphs and Ghibellines. The main cities to visit are **Lucca, Pisa,** and especially **Siena,** Florence's great historical rival with an inner core that appears to be caught in a time warp. As a final treat, visit **San Gimignano,** northwest of Siena, celebrated for its medieval "skyscrapers" (see the front cover of this guide).

Pastoral, hilly, and fertile, **Umbria** is similar to Tuscany, but with fewer tourists. Its once-fortified network of hill towns is among the most charming in Italy. Crafted from millions of tons of gray-brown rocks, each town is a testament to the masonry and architectural skills of many generations of craftsmen. Cities worth a visit are **Perugia, Gubbio, Assisi, Spoleto** (site of the world-renowned annual arts festival), and **Orvieto,** a mysterious citadel once used as a stronghold by the Etruscans. Called the land of shadows, Umbria is often covered in a bluish haze that evokes an ethereal painted look. Many local artists have tried to capture the province's special glow, with its sun-dappled hills, terraced vineyards, and miles of olive trees. If you're short on time, visit Assisi to check out Giotto's frescoes at the Basilica di San Francesco, and 'igia, the largest and richest of the province's cities.

BOLOGNA & EMILIA-ROMAGNA

Italians seem to agree on only one thing: The food in **Emilia-Romagna** is the best in Italy. The region's capital, **Bologna,** boasts a stunning Renaissance core with plenty of churches and arcades, a fine university with roots in the early Middle Ages, and a populace with a reputation for leftist leanings. The region also has one of the highest standards of living. Though the pluckings are richer in Tuscany and Umbria, Emilia-Romagna has a lot going for it, including tortellini, lasagne, and fettuccine. When not dining in Bologna, you can take time to explore its artistic heritage. Other art cities abound—none more noble than Byzantine **Ravenna,** still living off its past glory as the one-time capital of the declining Roman Empire.

If you can visit only one more city in the region, make it **Parma,** to see the city center with its Duomo and Battistero and to view its National Gallery. This is also the home of parmigiano reggiano cheese (Parmesan) and prosciutto. Also noteworthy is **Modena,** hometown of opera star Pavarotti—known for its cuisine, its cathedral, and its Este Gallery. The crowded Adriatic resort of **Rimini** and the medieval stronghold of **San Marino** are at the periphery of Emilia-Romagna.

VENICE, THE VENETO & THE DOLOMITES

Northeastern Italy is one of Europe's treasure troves, encompassing **Venice** (which could be the world's most beautiful city), the surrounding **Veneto** region, and the mighty **Dolomites** (including the **South Tyrol,** which Italy annexed from Austria after World War I). The Veneto, dotted with rich museums and some of the best architecture in Italy, sprawls across the verdant hills and flat plains between the Adriatic, the Dolomites, Verona, and the edges of Lake Garda. The fortunes of the Veneto revolved, for many generations, around Venice, with its sumptuous palaces, romantic waterways, Palazzo Ducale, and Basilica di San Marco. Aging, decaying, and sinking into the sea, Venice is so alluring we almost want to say visit it even if you have to skip Rome and Florence. As special as Venice and its islands in the lagoon are, we also recommended that you tear yourself away and visit at least three fabled art cities in the "Venetian Arc"—**Verona,** of Romeo and Juliet fame, **Vicenza,** to see the villas of Andrea Palladio where 16th-century aristocrats lived, and **Padua,** ennobled by its Giotto frescoes.

The region of **Trentino–Alto Adige** is far richer in culture, artistic treasures, and activities than the Valle d'Aosta (see below), and its ski resort, **Cortina d'Ampezzo,** is far more fashionable than Courmayeur in the northwestern corridor. Its most interesting bases—especially if you want to see the Austrian version of Italy—are **Bolzano (Bozen)** and **Trent (Trento),** the capital of Trentino. In the extreme northeastern corner of Italy, the region of **Friuli–Venezia Giulia** is, in its own way, one of the most cosmopolitan and culturally sophisticated in Italy. Its capital is the seaport of **Trieste.** The area is filled with art from the Roman, Byzantine, and Romanesque-Gothic eras, and many of the public buildings (especially in Trieste) might remind you more of Vienna.

MILAN, LOMBARDY & THE LAKE DISTRICT

Flat, fertile, prosperous, and politically conservative, **Lombardy** is dominated by **Milan** as Latium is dominated by Rome. Lombardy is one of the world's leading commercial and cultural centers—it has been immersed in the mercantile ethic ever since Milan developed into Italy's gateway to northern German-speaking Europe in the early Middle Ages. Though it's fashionable to belittle Milan for its industrial power and contempt of the poorer regions to the south, its fans compare it to New York. Milan's cathedral is Europe's third largest, its La Scala opera house is the site of some of the finest performances anywhere (though it will be closed for renovation until sometime in 2000), and its museums and churches are world class, containing Leonardo's *Last Supper*. However, Milan is still not in the league of Rome, Florence, and Venice. Work in Milan if you have the time, though you'll find more charm in the neighboring art cities of **Bergamo, Brescia, Pavia, Cremona,** and **Mantua.** Also competing for your time will be the lakes of **Garda** and **Maggiore,** which lie near Lombardy's eastern edge and are the preferred vacation destinations of the Milanese themselves.

PIEDMONT & VALLE D'AOSTA

At Italy's extreme northwestern edge, sharing a set of alpine peaks with France (which in some ways it resembles), **Piedmont** was the district from which Italy's dreams of unification spread in 1861. Long under the domination of the Austro-Hungarian Empire, the Piedmont enjoys a cuisine laced with alpine cheeses and dairy products. It's proud of its largest city, **Turin,** called the "Detroit of Italy" since it's the home of the Fiat empire, as well as vermouth, Asti Spumante, and the Borsalino hat. Though a great cosmopolitan center, it doesn't have the antique charm of Genoa or the sophistication, world-class dining, and chic shopping of Milan. Turin's most controversial sight is the Sacra Sindone (Holy Shroud), which many Catholics believe is the exact cloth in which Christ's body was wrapped when lowered from the cross.

Italy's window on Switzerland and France, **Valle d'Aosta** (the smallest region) often serves as an introduction to the country, especially for those journeying from France through the Mont Blanc tunnel. The introduction is misleading, though, as the Valle d'Aosta stands apart from the rest of Italy, a semiautonomous region of towering peaks and valleys in the northwestern corridor. Known for its alpine sunshine and the ancient French-derived dialect of its citizens, it's more closely linked to France (especially the region of Savoy) than to Italy. An area rich in scenery, dairy products, and wine, its most important city is the ancient Roman city of **Aosta** which, except for some ruins, is rather dull. More intriguing are two of Italy's major ski resorts, **Courmayeur** and **Breuil-Cervinia,** which are rivaled—and topped—only by Cortina d'Ampezzo in the Dolomites. Many of the region's villages are crafted from gray rocks culled from the mountains that rise on all sides. The best time to visit is either in the summer or the deep of winter. Late spring and fall get rather sleepy in this part of the world.

GENOA & THE ITALIAN RIVIERA

Comprising most of the **Italian Riviera,** the unexpected capital of which is the steeply sloping city of **Genoa,** the region of **Liguria** incorporates medieval ports known for their charm (**Portofino, Ventimiglia,** and **San Remo**), a massive naval base (La Spezia), and a quintet of coastal communities (**Cinque Terra**) clinging tenaciously to traditional values. There's also a series of belle epoque seaside resorts (**Rapallo** and **Santa Margherita Ligure**) whose style and nonchalance are reminiscent of resorts along the French Riviera (which eclipses its Italian counterpart). Though overbuilt and overrun, the Italian Riviera is still a land of great beauty. It's actually two Rivieras— the **Riviera di Ponente** to the west, running from the French border to Genoa, and the **Riviera di Levante** to the east. Faced with a choice, make it the more glamorous and cosmopolitan Riviera di Levante. Italy's largest port, Genoa, also merits a visit to learn of its rich culture and history. The historic harbor was given a face-lift for the celebrations honoring Columbus in 1992.

NAPLES, THE AMALFI COAST & CAPRI

More than any other region, **Campania** reverberates with the memories of the ancient Romans, who favored its strong sunlight, fertile soil, and bubbling sulfurous springs.

It manages to incorporate the anarchy of **Naples** with the elegant beauty of **Capri** and the **Amalfi coast.** The district also contains many sites specifically identified in ancient mythology (lakes defined as the entrance to the Kingdom of the Dead, for example) and some of the world's most prolific ancient ruins (including **Pompeii** and **Herculaneum**). No longer the treat of artists, kings, and emperors, Campania is overrun, overcrowded, and over everything, but it still lures visitors. Allow at least a day for Naples, which has amazing museums and the world's worst traffic outside of Cairo. Pompeii and Herculaneum are for the ruin collectors, whereas those seeking Italian sun head for Capri, rivaled only by Portofino for chicdom. The best towns along the Amalfi Drive, even though they're no longer unspoiled, are **Ravello** (not on the sea) and **Positano** (on the sea). **Amalfi** and **Sorrento** are much tackier and more overrun.

APULIA

Sun-drenched and poor, **Apulia** (depending on the dialect, Puglia, Le Puglie, or Apulia) forms the heel of the Italian boot. It's the most frequently visited province of Italy's Deep South; part of its allure lies in its string of coastal resorts. The trulli houses of **Alberobello** are known for their unique cylindrical shapes and conical flagstone-sheathed roofs. Among the region's largest cities are **Bari** (the capital), **Foggia,** and **Brindisi** (gateway to nearby Greece, with which the town shares many characteristics). Each of these is a modern disaster, filled with tawdry buildings, heavy traffic, and rising crime rates (tourists are often the victims). Most visitors pass through Bari at night—it's a favorite with backpackers—and the only reason to spend a night in Brindisi is to catch the ferry to Greece the next morning.

SICILY

The largest Mediterranean island, **Sicily** is a land of beauty, mystery, and world-class monuments. Cynical yet passionate, it's endlessly fascinating, a bizarre mixture of bloodlines and architecture from medieval Normandy, Aragonese Spain, Moorish North Africa, ancient Greece, Phoenicia, and Rome. Since the advent of modern times, part of the island's primitiveness has faded, as thousands of newly arrived cars clog the narrow lanes of its biggest city, **Palermo.** Though poverty remains widespread, the age-old stranglehold of the Mafia seems less certain because of the increasingly vocal protests of an outraged Italian public. On the eastern edge of the island is Mt. Etna, the tallest active volcano in Europe. Many of Sicily's larger cities (**Trapani, Catania,** and **Messina**) are relatively unattractive, but areas of ravishing beauty and eerie historic interest include **Syracuse, Taormina, Agrigento,** and **Selinunte.** Sicily's ancient ruins are rivaled only by those of Rome itself. The Valley of the Temples, for example, is worth the trip here.

2 Italy Today

THE INVADING HORDES

As the new millennium approaches, Italy is scrambling to prepare itself for the crush of visitors who will make pilgrimages to the country for the **Papal Jubilee 2000,** the Holy Year declared by the pope to celebrate the transition into a new era. This onslaught will dwarf the past invasions of the Etruscans, Langobards, or Normans. Venice's mayor, Massimo Cacciari, using metaphors appropriate to his city, said of the oncoming Holy Year, "If the floods are not channeled, we all risk capsizing." His fear was echoed by city authorities in Rome and Florence.

Even the present hordes pouring into the country—the numbers are swollen by millions of Roman Catholics from lands like Poland and Croatia—are flooding Italy's

The Euro & You

As a visitor to Italy, you needn't worry about dealing with the euro for a while. Though slated to take effect on paper on January 1, 1999—at which time the exchange rates of participating countries will be locked in together and will fluctuate against the dollar in sync—this change will apply mostly to financial transactions between businesses in Europe. The euro itself won't be issued as banknotes and coins until January 1, 2002 and won't fully replace national currencies until July 1, 2002.

---

ancient meccas like Venice's *acqua alta*. One Italian politician facetiously suggested placing a NO VACANCY sign at the border.

Those arriving before 2000 will find a friendlier (and even open) Italy—a 15-year closing for repairs wasn't unheard of in the past. There's talk of another renaissance, though we wouldn't go that far. Museums and monuments are being overhauled to be ready for the Jubilee (you'll see lots of scaffolding), museum hours are being streamlined (with a tendency to eliminate 3-hour lunch breaks and to add evening hours), and custodians don't seem as mean when they rush you to the door warning that the museum is closing and you've stared at Pauline Bonaparte long enough.

Even bookshops and cafeterias are opening in museums around Italy, making them more user-friendly. Greater numbers of museums are putting up signs in English (or some other language), not just Italian, offering explanations of what you're actually looking at. And they're installing better lighting—you no longer have to peer at that Caravaggio in a shroud of shadows.

There's a long way to go, of course, and many of the country's treasures still linger almost forgotten in smaller towns. But the present attention devoted to Italy's treasures has been unprecedented in history and is a hopeful welcome sign for upcoming visitors, thousands on thousands of whom will be seeing Italy for the first time.

THE COMING OF THE EURO

There are nascent signs of economic recovery for Italy, but there are also anxieties, especially as the reality of Europe's single currency, the **euro,** sets in. Many Italians fear they may face years of belt-tightening to help reduce the spiraling national debt. Italy signed a stability pact as part of an overall plan to reduce its debt, and the government of prime minister Romano Prodi is pledged to a vigorous program of debt reduction. This has created a somber mood in some quarters, raising fears that Italy will enter a period of fiscal austerity. Deficit reduction measures, totaling perhaps 6.5 million in U.S. dollars, are expected to be unveiled in 1999.

In spite of this, strong forces are actually calling for more government spending, especially trade union leaders, who demand the creation of more jobs and infrastructure investment in the still-depressed south. Prodi is moving ahead with legislation to reduce the work week from 40 to 35 hours.

Though Italy entering the euro circle is a done deal, there are still dire warnings. One Catholic bishop from the south, Don Riboldi, claimed, "This Europe of Maastricht is like the *Divine Comedy* of Dante because for a few rich people it will be paradise, for many it will be purgatory, and for the poor and unemployed it will be an inferno." However, there is hope and signs of rebirth, as reflected by Italy's high trade surplus. Its labor costs remain below that of most other European countries. "Patience," Prodi cautions, "it will take time."

The pro-Europe mood in Italy remains strong, with recent polls showing that 73% of Italians questioned were in favor of a single currency, the highest approval rate of any of the European Union's 15 members. (Only 39% in Germany, for example, approve that country's involvement.) More and more, there is talk of "joining Europe."

One young union leader claimed, "We must remain competitive in a ruthless marketplace, even if it means the temporary loss of jobs while we streamline our operations."

A LAND OF CONTRADICTIONS

Modern Italy is a land of contradictions: a Roman Catholic state ruled by the mores and values of a staunchly religious consciousness that nevertheless is the most corrupt country in Western Europe. It's a land whose sons and daughters emigrated to form large populations around the world, especially in America, but large numbers of its citizens remain viciously opposed to immigrants arriving on their own shore. Because of Italy's long exposed coast, it has long been a prime entry point for illegal immigrants into Europe—German and French officials often refer to it as a "sieve." Even when immigrants are expelled from Italy, they're granted 15 days of legal residence in the country, which is the equivalent of a transit visa to countries in the north (for many of them this is their destination anyway).

"In the course of a century, we've gone from being a land of emigrants to one that takes in immigrants," Luigi Manconi, a Milan sociologist, has stated. "We're just not equipped."

Unemployment, especially in the south, has enhanced racism and prejudice, primarily directed toward the North African or Albanian contingent that has descended on Italy in search of jobs. Despite attempts to turn them back, they continued to arrive in droves in 1998. Most work in the agricultural community as migrant workers, but some are prostitutes in the bustling resorts on the Italian Riviera. These workers aren't accepted into the tight-knit Italian communities.

POLITICS ARE DIRTY

Though the government might try to limit immigration, any attempt to clean up its own image seems hopeless. *La politica e una cosa sporca* (politics are dirty) is an expression often heard in Italy. The charge is certainly justified: Corruption, scandal, and political chaos are part of everyday life. The word *politician* is almost always preceded by the word *corrupt*. It's virtually assumed that anyone entering politics is doing so for personal gain. Italy's precarious modern political system, with 55 governments since World War II, has been compared by many political analysts to the ill-fated First Republic.

THE ECONOMY, THE MAFIA & *IL SORPASSO*

Though Italy ranks fifth among world economic powers and the third largest in Europe, its true economy can't be measured because of the vast underground economy (*economia sommersa*) controlled by the Mafia. Almost every Italian has some unreported income or expenditure. Other global competitors refrain from investing in Italian ventures because of lack of confidence in the government.

Besides soccer (*calcio*), the family, and affairs of the heart, the national obsession is *il sorpasso,* a term describing Italy's surpassing of its archrivals, France and Britain, in economic indicators. Economists disagree about whether or not il sorpasso has happened, and statistics (complicated by the economia sommersa) vary widely. All levels of Italian society are actively engaged to some degree in withholding funds from the government. Complicating the problems for economists, the police, and politicians is the constant interference of the Mafia, whose methods (despite numerous more or less heartfelt crackdowns) continue even more ruthlessly than ever.

An Italian Passion: Soccer

Soccer is one of the all-consuming passions of thousands of Italians, richly inter-twined with their image of the country. Rome boasts two intensely competitive teams, **Lazio** and **Roma,** which tend to play either against each other or against visiting teams from other parts of the country every Sunday afternoon.

Matches are held in Rome at the **Stadio Olimpico,** Foro Italico dei Gladia-tori (☎ **06/36-851**), built by Mussolini. Thousands of tickets are sold during the 2 or 3 hours before each game; they're also sold at the stadium Monday to Friday 9am to 5pm. The players usually take a break from June to August, begin-ning the season with something approaching pandemonium in September.

Florence's home team is **Fiorentina,** and the city's residents take their games very seriously indeed. To watch them, head for the **Stadio Comunale,** Viale Manfredi Fanti 4–6 (☎ **055/587-858**), near Campo di Marte, about 1½ miles northeast of the historic center. Games are usually held on Sunday afternoon September to May, and tickets go on sale at the stadium 2 or 3 hours before game time. Any hotel receptionist can give you details for the upcoming week.

Another complicating factor is the surfeit of laws and their effect on the citizens. Before they get thrown out of office, Italian politicians pass laws and more laws, adding to the millions already on the books. Italy has more laws than any other Western European nation and suffers from a bloated bureaucracy. Something as simple as cashing a check or paying a bill can devour half a day. To escape the bram-bles of red tape, Italians have become marvelous improvisers and corner-cutters. Whenever possible, they bypass the sclerotic public sector and negotiate private deals *fra amici* (among friends).

WHAT THE FUTURE HOLDS

Italy can no longer bask in its glorious past. The country is a land in transition, strug-gling to become a stable, viable contender in the global community. It's probably safe to say, though, that it will continue to be a land of contradictions: Although some view with dread the upcoming invasion for the Jubilee 2000, zillions of trinket ped-dlers are eagerly awaiting the hordes. Even as we write this, factories are busy turning out the souvenirs to be hawked.

3 History 101: Italy Wasn't Built in a Day

Dateline

- Bronze Age Celts, Teutonic tribes, and others from the Mediterranean and Asia Minor inhabit the peninsula.
- 1000 B.C. Large colonies of Etruscans settle in Tuscany and Campania, quickly subjugating many of the Latin inhabitants of the Italian peninsula.
- 800 B.C. Rome begins to take shape, evolving from a

continues

THE ETRUSCANS

Among the early inhabitants of Italy, the most signif-icant were the Etruscans—but who were they? No one knows, and the many inscriptions they left behind (mostly on graves) are of no help, since the Etruscan language has never been deciphered by modern scholars. It's thought they arrived on the eastern coast of Umbria several centuries before Rome was built, around 800 B.C. Their religious rites and architecture show an obvious contact with Meso-potamia; the Etruscans may have been refugees from Asia Minor who traveled westward about 1200 to 1000 B.C. Within 2 centuries, they had subjugated

Tuscany and Campania and the Villanova tribes who lived there.

While the Etruscans built temples at Tarquinia and Caere (present-day Cerveteri), the few nervous Latin tribes who remained outside their sway gravitated to Rome, then little more than a sheepherding village. As its power grew, however, Rome increasingly profited from the strategically important Tiber crossing where the ancient Salt Way (Via Salaria) turned northeastward toward the central Apennines.

From their base at Rome, the Latins remained free of the Etruscans until about 600 B.C. But the Etruscan advance was inexorable, and though the tribes concentrated their forces at Rome for a last stand, they were swept away by the sophisticated Mesopotamian conquerors. The new overlords introduced gold tableware and jewelry, bronze urns and terra-cotta statuary, and the best of Greek and Asia Minor art and culture; they also made Rome the governmental seat of all Latium. Roma is an Etruscan name, and the kings of Rome had Etruscan names: Numa, Ancus, Tarquinius, and even Romulus.

The Estruscans ruled until the Roman revolt around 510 B.C., and by 250 B.C. the Romans and their Campania allies had vanquished the Etruscans, wiping out their language and religion. However, many of the former rulers' manners and beliefs remained, assimilated into the culture. Even today, certain Etruscan customs and bloodlines are believed to exist in Italy, especially in Tuscany.

The best places to see the legacy left by these mysterious people are in Cerveteri and Tarquinia outside Rome. Especially interesting is the Etruscan necropolis, just 4 miles southeast of Tarquinia, where thousands of tombs have been discovered. To learn more about the Etruscans, visit the Museo Nazionale di Villa Giulia in Rome.

THE ROMAN REPUBLIC

After the Roman Republic was established in 510 B.C., the Romans continued to increase their power by conquering neighboring communities in the highlands and forming alliances with other Latins in the lowlands. They gave to their Latin allies, and then to conquered peoples, partial or complete Roman citizenship, with the obligation of military service. Citizen colonies were set up as settlements of Roman farmers, and many of the famous cities of Italy originated as colonies. These colonies were for the most part fortified and linked to Rome by military roads.

The stern Roman republic was characterized by a belief in the gods, the necessity of learning from the

strategically located shepherd village into a magnet for Latin tribes fleeing the Etruscans.

- **600 B.C.** Etruscans occupy Rome, designating it the capital of their empire; the city grows rapidly and a major seaport opens at Ostia.

- **510 B.C.** The Latin tribes, still centered in Rome, revolt against the Etruscans; alpine Gauls attack from the north; Greeks living in Sicily destroy the Etruscan navy.

- **250 B.C.** The Romans, allied with the Greeks, Phoenicians, and native Sicilians, defeat the Etruscans; Rome flourishes and begins the accumulation of a vast empire.

- **49 B.C.** Italy (through Rome) controls the entire Mediterranean world.

- **44 B.C.** Julius Caesar assassinated; his successor, Augustus, transforms Rome from a city of brick to a city of marble.

- **3rd century A.D.** Rome declines under a series of incompetent and corrupt emperors.

- **4th century A.D.** Rome is fragmented politically as administrative capitals are established in such cities as Milan and Trier, Germany.

- **A.D. 395** The empire splits; Constantine establishes a "New Rome" at Constantinople (Byzantium); Goths successfully invade Rome's northern provinces.

- **410–455** Rome is sacked by barbarians.

- **475** Rome falls, leaving only the primate of the Catholic Church in control; the pope slowly adopts many of the powers once reserved for the Roman emperor.

- **800** Charlemagne is crowned Holy Roman

continues

Emperor by Pope Leo III; Italy dissolves into a series of small warring kingdoms.

- **Late 11th century** The popes function like secular princes with private armies.
- **1065** The Holy Land falls to the Muslim Turks; the Crusades are launched.
- **1303–77** The Papal Schism; the pope and his entourage move from Rome to Avignon, France.
- **1377** The papacy returns to Rome.
- **1443** Brunelleschi's dome caps the Duomo in Florence as the Renaissance bursts into full bloom.
- **1469–92** Lorenzo il Magnifico rules in Florence as the Medici patron of Renaissance artists.
- **1499** *The Last Supper* is completed by Leonardo da Vinci in Milan.
- **1508** Michelangelo begins work on the Vatican's Sistine Chapel.
- **1527** Rome is sacked by Charles V of Spain, who is crowned Holy Roman Emperor the following year.
- **1796–97** Napoléon's series of invasions arouses Italian nationalism.
- **1861** The Kingdom of Italy is established.
- **1915–18** Italy enters World War I on the side of the Allies.
- **1922** Fascists march on Rome; Benito Mussolini becomes premier.
- **1929** A concordat between the Vatican and the Italian government is signed, delineating the rights and responsibilities of each party.
- **1935** Italy invades Abyssinia (Ethiopia).
- **1936** Italy signs "Axis" pact with Germany.
- **1940** Italy invades Greece.

continues

past, the strength of the family, education through reading books and performing public service, and—most important—obedience. The all-powerful Senate presided as Rome defeated rival powers one after the other and grew to rule the Mediterranean. The Punic Wars with Carthage in the 3rd century B.C. cleared away a major obstacle, though people said later that Rome's breaking its treaty with Carthage (which led to that city's total destruction) put a curse on Rome.

No figure was more towering during the republic than Julius Caesar, the charismatic conqueror of Gaul. He was called "the wife of every husband and the husband of every wife," among other honors. After defeating the last resistance of the Pompeians in 45 B.C., he came to Rome and was made dictator and consul for 10 years. He was at that point almost a king. Conspirators led by Marcus Junius Brutus stabbed him to death in the Senate on March 15, 44 B.C. Beware the Ides of March.

Marc Antony then assumed control by seizing Caesar's papers and wealth. Intent on expanding the Republic, Antony met with Cleopatra at Tarsus in 41 B.C. She seduced him, and he stayed in Egypt for a year. When Antony eventually returned to Rome, still smitten with Cleopatra, he made peace with Caesar's willed successor, Octavius, and, through the pacts of Brundisium, soon found himself married to Octavius's sister, Octavia. This marriage, however, didn't prevent him from openly marrying Cleopatra in 36 B.C. The furious Octavius gathered western legions and defeated Antony at the Battle of Actium on September 2, 31 B.C. Cleopatra fled to Egypt, followed by Antony, who committed suicide in disgrace a year later. Cleopatra, unable to seduce his successor and thus retain her rule of Egypt, followed suit with the help of an asp.

THE ROMAN EMPIRE

By 49 B.C., Italy ruled all the Mediterranean world either directly or indirectly, with all political, commercial, and cultural pathways leading directly to Rome. The possible wealth and glory to be found in Rome lured many, draining other Italian communities of human resources. Foreign imports, especially agricultural imports, hurt local farmers and landowners. Municipal governments faltered, and civil wars ensued. Public order was restored by the Caesars (planned by Julius but brought to fruition under Augustus). On the eve of the birth of Christ, Rome was a mighty empire whose generals had brought the Western world under the sway of Roman law and civilization.

Born Gaius Octavius in 63 B.C., Augustus, the first Roman emperor, reigned from 27 B.C. to A.D. 14. His reign, called "the golden age of Rome," led to the Pax Romana, or 2 centuries of peace. He had been adopted by, and eventually became the heir of, his great-uncle Julius Caesar. In Rome you can still visit the remains of the Forum of Augustus, built before the birth of Christ, and the Domus Augustana, where the imperial family lived on the Palatine Hill.

The emperors, whose succession started with Augustus's principate after the death of Julius Caesar, brought Rome to new, almost giddy, heights. Augustus transformed the city from brick to marble—much the way that Napoléon III transformed Paris many centuries later. But success led to corruption. The emperors wielded autocratic power, and the centuries witnessed a steady decay in the ideals and traditions on which the empire had been founded. The army became a fifth column of barbarian mercenaries, the tax collector became the scourge of the countryside, and for every good emperor (Augustus, Claudius, Trajan, Vespasian, and Hadrian, to name a few) there were three or four debased heads of state (Caligula, Nero, Domitian, Caracalla, and more).

After Augustus died (by poison?), his widow, Livia—a crafty social climber who had divorced her first husband to marry Augustus—set up her son, Tiberius, as ruler through a series of intrigues and poisonings. A long series of murders ensued, and Tiberius, who ruled during Pontius Pilot's trial and crucifixion of Christ, was eventually murdered in an uprising of landowners. In fact, murder was so common that a short time later Domitian (A.D. 81–96) became so obsessed with the possibility of assassination that he had the walls of his palace covered in mica so he could see behind him at all times. (He was killed anyway.)

Excesses and scandal ruled the day: Caligula (a bit overfond of his sister Drusilla) appointed his horse a lifetime member of the Senate, spent much money on foolish projects, and proclaimed himself a god; Caligula's successor, his uncle Claudius, was deceived and publicly humiliated by one of his wives, the lascivious Messalina (he had her killed), then poisoned by his final wife, his niece Agrippina, to secure the succession of Nero, her son by a previous marriage. Nero's thanks was later to murder not only his mother but also his wife, Claudius's daughter, and his rival, Claudius's son. The disgraceful Nero was removed as emperor while visiting Greece; he committed suicide

- **1943** U.S. Gen. George Patton lands in Sicily and soon controls the island.
- **1945** Mussolini is killed by a mob in Milan; World War II ends.
- **1946** The Republic of Italy is established.
- **1957** The Treaty of Rome, founding the European Community (EC), is signed by six nations.
- **1960s** The country's economy grows under the EC, but the impoverished south lags behind.
- **1970s** Italy is plagued by left-wing terrorism; former premier Aldo Moro is kidnapped and killed.
- **1980s** Political changes in Eastern Europe induce Italy's strong Communist Party to modify its program and even to change its name; the Socialists head their first post-1945 coalition government.
- **1994** A conservative coalition, led by Silvio Berlusconi, wins general elections.
- **1995** Following the resignation of Berlusconi, Lamberto Dini, Treasury minister, is named prime minister.
- **1996** Dini steps down as prime minister, as president dissolves both houses of parliament; in general elections, the center-left coalition known as the Olive Tree sweeps the Senate and the Chamber of Deputies.
- **1997–98** Romano Prodi survives Neo-Communist challenge and continues to press for budget cuts in an effort to "join Europe" in 1999; in May 1998, the Vatican is rocked by the murder of a Swiss Guard and his wife by another Swiss Guard, who then committed suicide.

the cry, "What an artist I destroy." (However, it's doubtful that he ever "fiddled
ile Rome burned.")

By the 3rd century A.D., corruption was so prevalent that there were 23 emperors
in 73 years. How bad had things gotten? So bad that Caracalla, to secure control of
the empire, had his brother Geta slashed to pieces while lying in his mother's arms.
Rule of the empire changed hands so frequently that news of the election of a new
emperor commonly reached the provinces together with a report of his assassination.

The 4th-century reforms of Diocletian held the empire together, but at the expense
of its inhabitants, who were reduced to tax units. He reinforced imperial power while
paradoxically weakening Roman dominance and prestige by dividing the empire into
east and west halves and establishing administrative capitals at outposts like Milan and
Trier, Germany. Diocletian instituted not only heavy taxes but also a socioeconomic
system that made professions hereditary. This edict was so strictly enforced that the
son of a silversmith could be tried as a criminal if he attempted to become a sculptor
instead.

Constantine became emperor in A.D. 306, and in A.D. 330 he made Constantinople (or Byzantium) the new capital of the Empire, moving the administrative functions away from Rome altogether, partly because the menace of possible barbarian
attack in the West had increased greatly. Constantine took the best Roman artisans,
politicians, and public figures with him to the new capital, creating a city renowned
for its splendor, intrigue, jealousies, and passion. Constantine was the first Christian
emperor, allegedly converting after he saw the True Cross in the heavens, accompanied
by the legend, "In This Sign Shall You Conquer." He then defeated the pagan Maxentius and his followers in battle.

THE EMPIRE FALLS

The eastern and western sections of the Roman Empire split in A.D. 395, leaving Italy
without the support it once received from east of the Adriatic. When the Goths moved
toward Rome in the early 5th century, citizens in the provinces, who had grown to
hate and fear the cruel bureaucracy set up by Diocletian and followed by succeeding
emperors, welcomed the invaders. And then the pillage began.

Rome was first sacked by Alaric in August 410. The populace made no attempt to
defend the city (other than trying vainly to buy off the Goth, a tactic that had worked
3 years before); most people simply fled into the hills or headed to their country estates
if they were rich. The feeble Western emperor Honorius hid out in Ravenna the entire
time.

More than 40 troubled years passed until the siege of Rome by Attila the Hun.
Strangely enough, it was the daughter of Honorius's stepsister, Placidia, who sent her
seal ring to the barbarian and precipitated his march on the city. Attila was, however,
dissuaded from attacking thanks largely to a peace mission headed by Pope Leo I in
452. Yet relief was short-lived: In 455, Gaiseric the Vandal carried out a 2-week sack
that was unparalleled in its pure savagery. The empire of the West lasted for only
another 20 years; finally the sacks and chaos ended it in A.D. 476, and Rome was left
to the popes, under the nominal auspices of an exarch from Byzantium (Constantinople).

The last would-be Caesars to walk the streets of Rome were both barbarians: The
first was Theodoric, who established an Ostrogoth kingdom at Ravenna from 493 to
526; and the second was Totila, who held the last chariot races in the Circus Maximus
in 549. Totila was engaged in a running battle with Belisarius, the general of the
Eastern emperor Justinian, who sought to regain Rome for the Eastern Empire. The
city changed hands several times, recovering some of its ancient pride by bravely

resisting Totilla's forces but eventually being entirely depopulated by the continuing battles.

Christianity, a new religion that created a new society, was probably founded in Rome about a decade after Jesus' crucifixion. Gradually gaining strength despite early persecution, it was finally accepted as the official religion of the empire. The best way today to relive the early Christian era is to visit Rome's Appian Way and its Catacombs, along Via Appia Antica, built in 312 B.C. According to Christian tradition, it was here that an escaping Peter encountered the vision of Christ. The Catacombs of St. Callixtus form the first cemetery of the Christian community of Rome.

THE MIDDLE AGES

So a ravaged Rome entered the Middle Ages, her once-proud population scattered and unrecognizable in rustic exile. A modest population started life again in the swamps of the Campus Martius, while the seven hills, now without water since the aqueducts were cut, stood abandoned and crumbling.

After the fall of the Western Empire, the pope took on more and more imperial powers, yet there was no political unity. Decades of rule by barbarians and then Goths were followed by takeovers in different parts of the country by various strong warriors, such as the Lombards. Italy was thus divided into several spheres of control. In 731, Pope Gregory II renounced Rome's dependence on Constantinople and thus ended the twilight era of the Greek exarch who had nominally ruled Rome.

Papal Rome turned toward Europe, where the papacy found a powerful ally in Charlemagne, a king of the barbarian Franks. In 800, he was crowned emperor by Pope Leo III. The capital that he established at Aachen (Aix-la-Chapelle in French) lay deep within territory known to the Romans a half millennium ago as the heart of the barbarian world. Though Charlemagne pledged allegiance to the church and looked to Rome and its pope as the final arbiter in most religious and cultural affairs, he launched northwestern Europe on a course toward bitter political opposition to the meddling of the papacy in temporal affairs.

The successor to Charlemagne's empire was a political entity known as the Holy Roman Empire (962–1806). The new empire defined the end of the Dark Ages but ushered in a period of long and bloody warfare. The Lombard leaders battled Franks. Magyars from Hungary invaded northeastern Lombardy and were in turn defeated by the increasingly powerful Venetians. Normans gained military control of Sicily in the 11th century, divided it from the rest of Italy, and altered forever the island's racial and ethnic makeup and its architecture. As Italy dissolved into a fragmented collection of city-states, the papacy fell under the power of Rome's feudal landowners. Eventually even the process for choosing popes came into the hands of the increasingly Germanic Holy Roman emperors, though this power balance would very soon shift.

Rome during the Middle Ages was a quaint rural town. Narrow lanes with overhanging buildings filled many areas that had been planned as showcases of ancient imperial power, including the Campus Martius. Great basilicas were built and embellished with golden-hued mosaics. The forums, mercantile exchanges, temples, and great theaters of the Imperial Era slowly disintegrated and collapsed. The decay of ancient Rome was assisted by periodic earthquakes, centuries of neglect, and, in particular, the growing need for building materials. Rome receded into a dusty provincialism. As the seat of the Roman Catholic church, the state was almost completely controlled by priests, who had an insatiable need for new churches and convents.

By the end of the 11th century, the popes shook off control of the Roman aristocracy, rid themselves of what they considered the excessive influence of the emperors at Aachen, and began an aggressive expansion of church influence and acquisitions. The deliberate organization of the church into a format modeled on the hierarchies of the ancient Roman Empire put it on a collision course with the empire and the other temporal leaders of Europe, resulting in an endless series of power struggles.

THE RENAISSANCE

The story of Italy from the dawn of the Renaissance in the 15th century to the Age of Enlightenment in the 17th and 18th centuries is as varied and fascinating as that of the rise and fall of the empire. The papacy soon became essentially a feudal state, and the pope was a medieval (later Renaissance) prince engaged in many of the worldly activities that brought criticism on the church in later centuries. The 1065 fall of the Holy Land to the Turks catapulted the papacy into the forefront of world politics, primarily because of the Crusades, many of which the popes directly caused or encouraged (but most of which were judged military and economic disasters). During the 12th and 13th centuries, the bitter rivalries that rocked Europe's secular and spiritual bastions took their toll on the Holy Roman Empire, which grew weaker as city-states buttressed by mercantile and trade-related prosperity grew stronger and as France emerged as a potent nation in its own right. Each investiture of a new bishop to any influential post resulted in endless jockeying for power among many factions.

These conflicts reached their most visible impasse in 1303 during the Great Schism, when the papacy was moved to the French city of Avignon. For more than 70 years, until 1377, viciously competing popes (one in Rome, another under the protection of the French kings in Avignon) made simultaneous claims to the legacy of St. Peter, underscoring as never before the degree to which the church was both a victim and a victimizer in the temporal world of European politics.

The seat of the papacy was eventually returned to Rome, where a series of popes was every bit as interesting as the Roman emperors they replaced. The great families—Barberini, Medici, Borgia—enhanced their status and fortunes impressively when one of their sons was elected pope. For a look at life during this tumultuous period, you can visit Rome's Castel Sant'Angelo, which became a papal residence in the 14th century.

Despite the centuries that had passed since the collapse of the Roman Empire, the age of siege wasn't yet over. In 1527, Charles V, king of Spain, carried out the worst sack of Rome ever. To the horror of Pope Clement VII (a Medici), the entire city was brutally pillaged by the man who was to be crowned Holy Roman Emperor the next year.

During the years of the Renaissance, the Reformation, and the Counter-Reformation, Rome underwent major physical changes. The old centers of culture reverted to pastures and fields, and great churches and palaces were built with the stones of ancient Rome. This construction boom, in fact, did far more damage to the temples of the Caesars than any barbarian sack had done. Rare marbles were stripped from the imperial baths and used as altarpieces or sent to lime kilns. So enthusiastic was the papal destruction of Imperial Rome that it's a miracle anything is left.

This era is best remembered because of its art. The great ruling families, especially the Medicis in Florence, the Gonzagas in Mantua, and the Estes in Ferrara, not only reformed law and commerce but also sparked a renaissance in art. Out of this period arose such towering figures as Leonardo da Vinci and Michelangelo. Many visitors come to Italy to view what's left of the art and glory of that era—everything from Michelangelo's Sistine Chapel at the Vatican to his statue of *David* in Florence, from Leonardo's *Last Supper* in Milan to the Duomo in Florence graced by Brunelleschi's dome.

A UNITED ITALY

The 19th century witnessed the final collapse of the Renaissance city-states, which had existed since the end of the 13th century. These units, eventually coming under the control of a *signore* (lord), were in effect regional states, with mercenary soldiers, civil rights, and assistance for their friendly neighbors. Some had attained formidable power under such signori as the Estes in Ferrara, the Medicis in Florence, and the Viscontis and Sforzas in Milan.

During the 17th, 18th, and 19th centuries, decades of turmoil in Italy had lasted through the many years of succession of different European dynasties; Napoléon made a bid for power in Italy beginning in 1796, fueling his war machines with what was considered a relatively easy victory. During the Congress of Vienna (1814–15), which followed Napoléon's defeat, Italy was once again divided among many factions: Austria was given Lombardy and Venetia, and the Papal States were returned to the pope. Some duchies were put back into the hands of their hereditary rulers, and southern Italy and Sicily went to a Bourbon dynasty. One historic move, which eventually contributed to the unification of Italy, was the assignment of the former republic of Genoa to Sardinia (which at the time was governed by the House of Savoy).

Political unrest became a fact of Italian life, at least some of it encouraged by the rapid industrialization of the north and the almost total lack of industrialization in the south. Despite those barriers, in 1861, thanks to the brilliant efforts of patriots Camillo Cavour (1810–61) and Giuseppe Garibaldi (1807–82), the Kingdom of Italy was proclaimed and Victor Emmanuel (Vittorio Emanuele) II of the House of Savoy, king of Sardinia, became head of the new monarchy.

Garibaldi, the most respected of all Italian heroes, must be singled out for his efforts, which included taking Sicily, then returning to the mainland and marching north to meet Victor Emmanuel II at Teano, and finally declaring a unified Italy (with the important exception of Rome itself). It must have seemed especially sweet to a man whose efforts at unity had caused him to flee the country fearing for his life on four occasions. It's a tribute to the tenacity of this red-bearded hero that he never gave up, even in the early 1850s, when he was forced to wait out one of his exiles as a candlemaker on Staten Island in New York.

Though the hope, pushed by Europe's theocrats and some of its devout Catholics, of attaining one empire ruled by the pope and the church had long ago faded, there was still a fight, followed by generations of hard feelings, when the Papal States—a strategically and historically important principality under the pope's temporal jurisdiction—were confiscated by the new Kingdom of Italy.

The establishment of the kingdom, however, didn't signal a complete unification of Italy because Rome was still under papal control and Venetia still held by Austria. This was partially resolved in 1866, when Venetia joined the rest of Italy after the Seven Weeks' War between Austria and Prussia; in 1871 Rome became the capital of the newly formed country. The Vatican, however, didn't yield its territory to the new order, despite guarantees of nonintervention proffered by the government, and relations between the pope and the country of Italy remained rocky.

THE RISE OF IL DUCE & WORLD WAR II

On October 28, 1922, Benito Mussolini, who had started his Fascist Party in 1919, knew the time was ripe for change. He gathered 50,000 supporters for a march on Rome. Inflation was soaring and workers had just called a general strike, so king Victor Emmanuel II, rather than recognizing a state under siege, recognized Mussolini as the new government leader. In 1929, Il Duce defined the divisions between the Italian government and the Vatican by signing a concordat granting political and fiscal autonomy to Vatican City. It also made Roman Catholicism the official state religion—but that designation was removed in 1978 through a revision of the concordat.

During the Spanish Civil War (1936–39), Mussolini's support of the Falangists, under Franco, helped encourage the formation of the "Axis" alliance between Italy and Nazi Germany. Despite its outdated military equipment, Italy added to the general horror of the era by invading Abyssinia (Ethiopia) in 1935, supposedly to protect Italian colonial interests there. In 1940, Italy invaded Greece through Albania, and in 1942, it sent thousands of Italian troops to assist Hitler in his disastrous campaign along the Russian front. In 1943, Allied forces, under the command of U.S. Gen. George Patton and British Gen. Bernard Montgomery, landed in Sicily and quickly secured the island as they prepared to move north toward Rome.

In the face of likely defeat and humiliation, Mussolini was overthrown by his own cabinet (Grand Council). The Allies made a separate deal with Victor Emmanuel III, who had more or less gracefully collaborated with the Fascists during the previous two decades and now shifted allegiances without much visible fuss. A politically divided Italy watched as battalions of fanatical German Nazis released Mussolini from his Italian jail cell to establish the short-lived Republic of Salò, headquartered on the edge of Lake Garda. Mussolini had hoped for a groundswell of popular opinion in favor of Italian Fascism, but events quickly proved this nothing more than a futile dream.

In April 1945, with almost half a million Italians rising in a mass demonstration against him and the German war machine, Mussolini was captured by Italian partisans as he fled to Switzerland. Along with his mistress, Claretta Petacci, and several others of his intimates, he was shot and strung upside-down from the roof of a Milan gas station.

THE POSTWAR YEARS

Disaffected with the monarchy and its identification with the fallen Fascist dictatorship, Italian voters in 1946 voted for the establishment of a republic. The major political party that emerged following World War II was the Christian Democratic Party, a right-of-center group whose leader, Alcide De Gasperi (1881–1954), served as premier until 1953. The second-largest party was the Communist Party; however, by the mid-1970s it had abandoned its revolutionary program in favor of a democratic form of "Eurocommunism" (in 1991, the Communists even changed their name, to the Democratic Party of the Left).

Though after the war Italy was stripped of all its overseas colonies, it quickly succeeded, in part because of U.S. aid under the Marshall Plan (1948–52), in rebuilding its economy, both agriculturally and industrially. By the 1960s, as a member of the European Community (founded in Rome in 1957), Italy had become one of the leading industrialized nations of the world, prominent in the manufacture of automobiles and office equipment.

But the country continued to be plagued by economic inequities between the prosperous industrialized north and the economically depressed south. It suffered an unprecedented flight of capital (frequently aided by Swiss banks only too willing to accept discreet deposits from wealthy Italians) and an increase in bankruptcies, inflation (almost 20% during much of the 1970s), and unemployment.

During the late 1970s and early 1980s, Italy was rocked by the rise of terrorism, instigated both by neo-Fascists and by left-wing intellectuals from the Socialist-controlled universities of the north.

THE 1990S

In the early 1990s, the Italians reeled as many leading politicians were accused of wholesale corruption. As a result, a newly formed right-wing grouping, led by media magnate Silvio Berlusconi, swept to victory in 1994's general elections. Berlusconi became prime minister at the head of a coalition government. However, in December 1994, he resigned as prime minister after the federalist Northern League Party defected from his coalition and he lost his parliamentary majority. Treasury Minister Lamberto Dini, a nonpolitical banker with international financial credentials, was named to replace Berlusconi.

Dini signed on merely as a transitional player in the topsy-turvy political game. His austere measures enacted to balance Italy's budget, including cuts in pensions and health care, were not popular among the mostly blue-collar workers or the highly influential labor unions. Pending a predicted defeat in a no-confidence vote, Dini stepped down. His resignation in January 1996 left beleaguered Italians shouting "Basta!" (Enough!). This latest shuffling in Italy's political deck prompted President Oscar Scalfaro to dissolve both Italian houses of parliament.

Once again the Italians were faced with forming a new government. April 1996's elections proved a shocker, not only for the defeated politicians but also for the victors. The center-left coalition known as the Olive Tree, led by Romano Prodi, swept both the Senate and the Chamber of Deputies. The Olive Tree, whose roots stem from the old Communist Party, achieved victory by shifting toward the center and focusing their campaign on a strong platform protecting social benefits and supporting Italy's bid to become a solid member of the European Union.

Prodi carried through on his commitment when he announced a stringent budget for 1997 in a bid to be among the first countries to enter the monetary union. That year saw further upheavals in the Prodi government as he continued to push ahead with cuts to the country's generous social-security system. In the autumn Prodi was forced to submit his resignation when he lost critical support in Parliament from the Communist Refounding party, which balked at pension and welfare cuts in the 1998 budget. The party eventually backed off with its demands and Prodi was returned to office, where he pledged to see legislation for a 35-hour work week by 2001.

On a more grisly note, in May 1998 a Papal Swiss Guard committed a brutal act of violence, the worst inside the Vatican walls since the 1981 attempted assassination of Pope John Paul II. Alois Estermann, a Swiss Guard who only hours earlier had been promoted to commander, and his wife, Gladys Meza Romero, were found dead in their Vatican apartment. Lying next to them was the body of their presumed murderer, Vice-Corporal Cedric Tornay, a 3-year veteran of the guards. Just before the murders, Tornay had addressed a letter to his family that was reportedly a suicide note. A Vatican spokesperson has said that Tornay was easily upset and unbalanced— just before the incident he had received a written reprimand for missing a curfew, and he was furious that the previous week he hadn't received a medal of recognition at an awards ceremony for the guards.

4 The Art of Italian Architecture

THE ETRUSCANS & THE ROMANS

The mysterious Etruscans, whose earliest origins lay probably somewhere in Mesopotamia, brought the first truly impressive architecture to mainland Italy. Little remains of their architecture, but historical writings by the Romans record powerful Etruscan **walls, bridges,** and **aqueducts.** As Rome asserted its own identity and over-powered its Etruscan masters, it borrowed heavily from themes already established by Etruscan architects.

Architecture flourished magnificently in Rome, advancing in size and majesty far beyond the examples set by the Etruscans and Greeks. The most important element in this was the fine-tuning of the **arch,** used with a new logic, rhythm, and ease. Monumental buildings were erected, each an embodiment of the strength, power, and careful organization of the Empire itself. Examples are forums and baths scattered across the Mediterranean world (the greatest of which were **Trajan's Forum** and the **Baths of Caracalla,** both in Rome). Equally magnificent were the **Colosseum** and a building that later greatly influenced the Palladians during the Renaissance, Hadrian's **Pantheon,** both erected in Rome.

Of course, these immense achievements were made possible by two major resources: almost limitless funds pouring in from all regions of the empire and an unending supply of slaves captured during military campaigns abroad.

Though it doesn't sound very romantic, the use of **concrete** also had a major influence on Roman architecture, as well as on buildings to come. Concrete, which seemingly lasts forever—as evidenced by the giant concrete dome of Rome's Pantheon and the Baths of Caracalla—made vast buildings possible. *Insulae* (apartment blocks) climbed to seven floors or more, something almost unheard of before. Even though Romans didn't invent the arch or the aqueduct or even concrete, they perfected these building forms, and their methods and styles were to be used throughout Western culture.

THE ROMANESQUE

The art and architecture in the centuries that followed the collapse of Rome became known as **early medieval** or **Romanesque.** In its many variations, it flourished between A.D. 1000 and 1250, though in isolated pockets away from Europe's mainstream it continued for several centuries later.

During the Romanesque period, Italian architects were influenced by the innumerable **Roman ruins**—classical columns, entablatures, vaults, ornamentation, and whole facades were left intact to inspire future generations. Designs at this time were decidedly Italian, as the architecture put emphasis on width and on horizontal lines. Italian buildings, especially churches, were larger and lower to the ground than Romanesque designs from northern Europe. **Churches** were designed in three parts, with a separate **baptistry** and **campanile,** and earlier Romanesque examples took early Christian basilicas as their example, retaining **colonnaded atriums** and **narthex entrances.** After about 1100, the influence of the atrium on overall design declined and the traditional Italian **portico** became more common. **Arcading** (a series of decorative arches—either open or closed with masonry—supported on columns) was commonly used as facade, and **timber roofs** became the norm instead of stone vaults.

Climate also affected the way in which Italian Romanesque designs differed from Romanesque designs found in the rest of Europe. Because snow and heavy rain weren't factors in Italy, architects could design roofs of a lower pitch than was common through much of Europe. Intensive sunlight and heat also led to the incorporation of

smaller windows to exclude rather than trap some of the light. Because of the sunny climate, facades were brightly decorated with **glass mosaics** and **variegated marble,** which would reflect the light in a dramatic and beautiful way. Northern European designs still depended on the more traditional stone sculptural and statuary facades. In addition, stone wasn't as plentiful in Italy as in other parts of Europe. Because of the almost unlimited availability of clay, **brick** became a popular material for structural elements.

Italy, being a series of city-states as opposed to a unified country like many other European nations, also had regional variations of Romanesque design. In the north, with Milan as its center, were found **Lombard Romanesque** designs, which most closely resembled the designs of France and Germany. In central Italy, the **Tuscan** or **Pisan school,** strongly influenced by the Catholic Church, was most closely based on ancient Roman designs. In the south, including Sicily, **Norman Romanesque** was similar to Norman-influenced architecture found in other European nations, but with additional Saracenic, Byzantine, and Greek elements.

Existing examples of Lombard Romanesque date mostly from the 11th and 12th centuries and are most evident in **Milan, Pavia,** and **Verona** and near the lakes and Alps at **Como, Aosta,** and **Ivrea.** Structures are mainly of brick in shades of red, pink, and brown, some decorated with stone or marble. Because the climate was cooler than that of the rest of Italy, buildings here tended to share elements of design, such as more steeply pitched roofs and larger windows, with the rest of Europe. **Stone groin** and **rib vaults** were used extensively, as opposed to the timber roofs favored in the rest of Italy. Arcading was the common external decoration, and **wheel-pattern windows** dominated all other designs. Column designs were in line with the rest of Italy (the columns usually resting on the backs of animals), but the decorations were less classical and introduced a wide range of animals, devils, monsters, flowers, and plants. The most distinctive feature of Lombard Romanesque is the design of tall slender squared **bell towers,** separate from the main body of the church. An excellent example is the bell tower of the **Abbey Church** at Pomposa (ca. 1063). Other fine churches are **San Ambrogio** in Milan; the **cathedral groups** (campanile, cathedral, and baptistery) at Cremona, Ferrara, and Parma; the **Duomo** in Modena; **Sant'Abbondio** at Como; **San Zeno** at Verona; and **San Michele** at Pavia.

Tuscan Romanesque extended from northern Tuscany to Naples, with its center around **Florence, Pisa,** and **Lucca.** This style is known for its brilliant marble facades in intricate patterns, churches built by **basilican plan** (rectangular, with a semicircular apse at one of the short ends and a narthex at the other) with timber roofs and exterior arcading. Columns, capitals, and decoration reflect classical influences. The single outstanding example of Tuscan Romanesque is the **cathedral group at Pisa** (including the famous leaning bell tower). Other examples in the region are **San Martino** (exterior only) and **San Michele** and **San Frediano** at Lucca, **San Miniato al Monte** in Florence, the cathedrals at **Assisi** and **Spoleto, Santa Maria in Cosmedin** at Rome, and the **Amalfi** and **Salerno cathedrals.**

The Norman Romanesque of southern Italy, particularly **Apulia** and **Sicily,** is unique. It blends different cultures and illustrates the turbulent history of the area—colonized by the Greeks, absorbed into the Byzantine Empire, held under Mohammedan domination, and conquered by the Normans in the 11th century. The Normans built the cathedrals here using local craftsmen who incorporated intricate **Byzantine mosaics,** richly carved **Greek sculpture,** and **Saracenic** (rounded) **arches** and **vaults.** Romanesque designs here also share characteristics with cathedrals built by the Normans in England, including massive stonework, brick walls, little or no abutment, solid square towers, and rounded doorways and windows. Of course, the

Knowing Your Apse from Your Ambone:
A Glossary of Architectural Terms

Ambone   A pulpit, either serpentine or simple in form, erected in an Italian church.

Apse   The half-rounded extension behind the main altar of a church; Christian tradition dictates that it be placed at the eastern end of an Italian church, the side closest to Jerusalem.

Atrium   A courtyard, open to the sky, in an ancient Roman house; the term also applies to the courtyard nearest the entranceway of an early Christian church.

Baldacchino (also ciborium)   A columned stone canopy, usually placed above the altar of a church; spelled in English, "baldachin" or "baldaquin."

Baptistery   A separate building or area in a church where the rite of baptism is held.

Basilica   Any rectangular public building, usually divided into three aisles by rows of columns; in ancient Rome, this architectural form was frequently used for places of public assembly and law courts; later, Roman Christians adapted the form for many of their early churches.

Caldarium   The steam room of a Roman bath.

Campanile   A bell tower, often detached, of a church.

Capital   The top of a column, often carved and usually categorized into one of three different orders: Doric, Ionic, or Corinthian.

Castrum   A carefully planned Roman military camp, whose rectangular form, straight streets, and systems of fortified gates quickly became standardized throughout the Empire; modern cities that began as Roman camps and still more or less maintain their original forms include Chester (England), Barcelona (Spain), and such Italian cities as Lucca, Aosta, Como, Brescia, Florence, and Ancona.

Cavea   The curved row of seats in a classical theater; the most prevalent shape was that of a semicircle.

Cella   The sanctuary, or most sacred interior section, of a Roman pagan temple.

Chancel   Section of a church containing the altar.

Cornice   The decorative flange defining the uppermost part of a classical or neoclassical facade.

Cortile   Courtyard or cloisters ringed with a gallery of arches or lintels set atop columns.

Crypt   A church's main burial place, usually below the choir.

Cupola   A dome.

differences were the above-mentioned flatter roofs and smaller windows. Examples of Norman Romanesque include the cathedral at **Cefalu,** the **Monreale Abbey Church** and the **Cappella Palatina** in Palermo, the **Palazzo Farsetti** and **Palazzo Loredan** in Venice, and the town of **San Gimignano** near Siena.

Duomo   Cathedral.

Forum   The main square and principal gathering place of any Roman town, usually adorned with the city's most important temples and civic buildings.

Grotesques   Carved and painted faces, deliberately ugly, used by everyone from the Etruscans to the architects of the Renaissance; they're especially amusing when set into fountains.

Hyypogeium   Subterranean burial chambers, usually of pre-Christian origins.

Loggia   Roofed balcony or gallery.

Lozenge   An elongated four-sided figure that, along with stripes, was one of the distinctive signs of the architecture of Pisa.

Narthex   The anteroom, or enclosed porch, of a Christian church.

Nave   The largest and longest section of a church, usually devoted to sheltering and/or seating worshipers and often divided by aisles.

Palazzo   A palace or other important building.

Piano Nobile   The main floor of a palazzo (sometimes the second floor).

Pietra Dura   Richly ornate assemblage of semiprecious stones mounted on a flat decorative surface, perfected during the 1600s in Florence.

Pieve   A parish church.

Portico   A porch, usually crafted from wood or stone.

Pulvin   A four-sided stone serving as a substitute for the capital of a column, often decoratively carved, sometimes into biblical scenes.

Putti   Plaster cherubs whose chubby forms often decorate the interiors of baroque chapels and churches.

Stucco   Colored plaster composed of sand, powdered marble, water, and lime, either molded into statuary or applied in a thin concretelike layer to the exterior of a building.

Telamone   Structural column carved into a standing male form; female versions are called *caryatids.*

Thermae   Roman baths.

Transenna   Stone (usually marble) screen separating the altar area from the rest of an early Christian church.

Travertine   The stone from which ancient and Renaissance Rome was built, it's known for its hardness, light coloring, and tendency to be pitted or flecked with black.

Tympanum   The half-rounded space above the portal of a church, whose semicircular space usually showcases a sculpture.

THE GOTHIC

What followed was the **Gothic** period (1250 to 1450), with the popes in exile in France and Sicilo-Norman rule giving way to Angevin culture and shifting from Palermo to Naples. During this time, architecture in Lombardy remained essentially

Romanesque; indeed, it has been argued that Italy didn't have a Gothic period of architecture. But it did, with Italian designs differing from the rest of Europe, again, in their continued acknowledgment of Roman culture. What Italy didn't have were the soaring towers and spires, ribbed vaults, slender paneled towers, and quadrangles of similar English designs. What it did have were **timber roofs, brick faced with marble, pointed arches,** and **carved white marble tracery** and **sculpture** (mainly in relief). Ornament and detail remained mainly classical. Towers became less common but when incorporated were still constructed separately.

The best examples of the Gothic in Italy are in **Tuscany,** south toward **Rome,** and in **Venice.** Fine examples of the style include the **Florence, Siena,** and **Orvieto cathedrals.** Many of the churches are less interesting and have largely been altered, but there are numerous exceptions, including **Santa Maria della Spina** at Pisa, **Santi Giovanni e Paolo** and **Santa Maria Gloriosa dei Frari** in Venice, **Santa Croce** in Florence, and **San Francesco** in Assisi. Palaces include the **Ca' d'Oro,** fronting the Grand Canal, and the **Doge's Palace** in Venice. Town halls include the **Palazzo Pubblico** in Siena; the **Palazzo Vecchio** in Florence; the **Palazzo dei Priori** in Perugia; the **Palazzo dei Priori** in Volterra; the **Palazzo Pubblico** in Montepulciano; the **Palazzo dei Consoli** at Gubbio; the **Palazzo Contarini-Fasan, Palazzo Foscari, Palazzo Franchetti,** and **Palazzo Pisani** in Venice; and the **Palazzo Stefano** in Taormina, Sicily.

THE EARLY RENAISSANCE

The **Renaissance** began in Italian art in the 14th century but came relatively late to architecture, first being incorporated in 1420. Designs from this period represent the pinnacle of Italian architecture. Scholars and artists began to question not so much the importance of God but the alleged unimportance of man and turned their gaze to the accomplishments, advancements, and innovations of antiquity, with numerous Roman examples all around (appreciation of all things Greek came much later). All of man's experiences—along with nature in human, animal, and landscape forms—were explored in sculpture, relief, mosaic, and stained glass, without a definitive hierarchy topped by God and religion.

Renaissance architectural style included a return to the incorporation of the **barrel vaults** and **domes** favored by the ancient Romans. In about 1425, Renaissance painters discovered the laws of **perspective,** and **Brunelleschi** was the first to incorporate this in architectural form. As a result, building designs showed control and unity of space and achieved breadth and a feeling of light not found in Gothic churches. Architects became fascinated with Roman and Greek designs of the centrally planned church, which came to be seen as the ultimate classical metaphor. The effect was that design became increasingly concerned with proportion and detail.

During this time, artists became the most important members of the community and, owing to their education and creativity, became more versatile. They embraced multiple forms of expression. Thus, the first Renaissance architect of the Florence Duomo was **Giotto,** the painter. Church builder **Alberti** was first a scholar, writer, and mathematician.

Brunelleschi's masterpiece of the era is the dome of **Florence's Duomo,** which overcame mathematical complications about how to cover an existing 138-foot octagonal span—too great for timber centering—without exterior abutment. Besides being a sculptor, Brunelleschi had studied mathematics and spent time drawing ancient Roman buildings in and around Rome, which had aroused his interest in using large vaults and domed construction in the manner of the Roman baths. His solution for the cathedral was to build a dome on Gothic principles with medieval-style ribs and one that—because of the limitations he was facing—was taller than a true hemisphere (which, being a classicist, he would have preferred). To retain the shape of the dome and reduce the strain of its weight, it was built as two domes, one within the other.

Other examples of Brunelleschi's early Renaissance designs around Florence include **San Spirito** and **San Lorenzo** and the unfinished **Santa Maria degli Angeli,** which, when started in 1437, became the first centrally planned work of the Renaissance. Still other examples are **Santa Maria Novella** in Florence, **Sant'Andrea** in Mantua, and the **Ducal Palace** in Urbino. Florentine palazzi include Alberti's **Rucellai, Medici-Riccardi,** and **Pitti.** Lombardy has few examples because, like Germany and England, its Renaissance was more in decoration than construction.

Perhaps the greatest example of the Renaissance and its marriage of Christian and pagan ideals is the small temple in the courtyard of **San Pietro** in Montorio, which exhibits superb form and simplicity in its undecorated architectural elements, while commemorating a Christian event (the spot where St. Peter was allegedly crucified).

The **Veneto,** under the domination of the Venetian republic, always had different influences because of its close ties with Constantinople, Dalmatia, and the East and its cultural isolation within Italy itself. Here Renaissance designs continued with semi-Gothic facades, and in Venice itself there was no need or room for arcaded courtyards. Examples of the early Venetian Renaissance include the **Scuola di San Rocco** and **Santa Zaccaria.** After the 1527 collapse of Rome, some artists moved north, and the architecture began to reflect southern Renaissance styles. In Venice this can be seen in the **Biblioteca Sansoviniana** (Library of Saint Mark), **Zecca** (Mint), and **Palazzo Cornaro.** Another example is the **Bevilacqua** in Verona.

PALLADIO & THE HIGH RENAISSANCE

The **High Renaissance** was dominated by Bramante, Raphael, and Michelangelo, and its inception is symbolized by Milan falling to the French and Bramante moving to Rome at the beginning of the 16th century. After the French exile of the popes, Pope Sixtus IV began restoring Rome to prominence, with the construction of **St. Peter's Basilica** (below) being the crowning achievement. Other examples are the cloisters at the **Monastery of Sant'Ambrogio,** an exercise in pure classicism, and Michelangelo's **New Sacristy in San Lorenzo** and the **Medici Family Mausoleum,** both in Florence.

Andrea di Pietro (or **Palladio**) became the towering architect of the High Renaissance—the city outside Venice is still called the **Città del Palladio.** Though his designs were adopted around the world, especially in England and America, his native Vicenza remains the best place to view his villas. Palladio arrived in Vicenza in 1523 and worked there until his death in 1580. He wasn't a daring innovator but an academician following the rules of classical Roman architecture. His roofs are tiled and hipped; on each of the four external sides is a pillared rectangular portico. The effect is like a Roman temple. The so-called "attic" in his design was usually surmounted by statues. His most acclaimed building remains the **Villa Rotonda** in Vicenza, a cube with a center circular hall topped by a dome.

THE LATE RENAISSANCE & THE BAROQUE

In 1573, **Giacomo da Vignola** undertook a challenge that was to pave the way for the transition to the **baroque** (1590 to 1780). He was called on to design Rome's **Il Gesu,** the mother church of the Society of Jesus, so every person in a large congregation could hear the service. He responded with a design that included a wide, short barrel-vaulted nave and shallow transepts for good acoustics and the illusion of space. There were no aisles or colonnades, only side chapels, which gave the building a sense of spaciousness and dignity. It was then topped by a large dome with fenestrated drums, flooding the church with dramatic light and unity unknown in Gothic or Renaissance churches.

The church inspired late Renaissance architects, already eager to incorporate more of themselves into their designs, to adapt their classical influences into a **functional unity** that more readily suited the needs of society. The transition wasn't without criticism, and the term *baroque* actually means "misshapen pearl" from the Spanish or Portuguese—a derogatory name stemming from the accentuated curves that evolved.

Still entirely classical in concept, baroque architecture became freer than Renaissance structures with the use of **curves**—not only in ceiling design but in whole walls, which might be alternately concave and convex. The **oval** became the favored building plan, as curves symbolized vitality and movement and were further accented by the use of **dramatic lighting** from only one or two sources.

These changes, as exemplified by the requests made of Vignola in designing Il Gesu, stemmed from a movement away from humanism and back toward the Catholic Church, whose Jesuit visionaries were attempting to reintroduce spiritual values more suited to the modern world. Thus the curve, a more sensual form than the Renaissance rectangle, was used with great exuberance, as the church adopted gaiety and pageantry to try to retain followers who had been seduced by the secular nature of the Renaissance.

One of the great baroque designs is **Bernini's Piazza San Pietro** at St. Peter's Basilica in Rome. The use of vast elliptical colonnade symbolized St. Peter's—the mother church of Christendom—embracing the world. The western ends are joined to the basilica facade by two long corridors, successfully creating space to accommodate vast crowds wanting to witness the pope's blessing of the city. The columns stand four deep, 60 feet high, and are surmounted by an excessive procession of saints starting along the facade and proceeding outward along the piazza.

In addition to St. Peter's Basilica (below), the finest examples of early baroque works are the **New Cathedral** of Brescia, the **San Pietro** in Bologna, and **Santa Susanna** in Rome. The period reached its zenith in such Rome designs as **Sant'Andrea al Quirinale, San Carlo alle Quattro Fontane,** the **Fountain of the Rivers** at Piazza Navona, and the **Triton Fountain** at Piazza Barberini. Other examples are **Santa Maria della Salute** in Venice; the **Sindone Chapel** (home of the shroud), **San Lorenzo,** and the **Basilica di Superga** in Turin; **Santa Maria Egiziaca** in Naples; **Santa Croce** in Lecce; and Sicily's **Cathedral of Palermo.**

ST. PETER'S BASILICA

Behind Bernini's Piazza rises the **Basilica di San Pietro,** the stellar achievement of the late High Renaissance and the early baroque. **Bramante** was only the first in a series of architects to tackle this awesome edifice. Directed by the popes, St. Peter's was built over 120 years. Because of the decades on decades necessary for its construction, St. Peter's is not a towering piece of organized architecture. Therefore, it's almost impossible to discuss it as a harmonious unit. Each piece stands alone, it seems, as exemplified by **Michelangelo's dome.** Even so, the design of the cathedral is truly a feat, being so beautifully proportioned from one part to another as to disguise its huge size. In the classical tradition, it makes use of coffered and paneled barreled vaults, plus vast crossing dome and drum designs.

Michelangelo designed and began the construction of the massive dome from 1547 to 1564. On his death, the work was continued from models, but other architects added their own ideas. The distance you see today, from the top of the lantern over the dome, is 450 feet, a staggering achievement considering building techniques in those days. The sheer mass of the structure—about five times the area of a football field—is the impression you get today. The nave is an enormous barreled vault, coffered and frescoed. No central plan was followed, and little remains of Bramante's original concept, which was that of a dome-topped Greek cross based on Rome's Pantheon. The baroque ornamentation Bernini sumptuously supplied from 1629 onward was certainly not in adherence to Bramante's simpler plan.

THE 18TH & 19TH CENTURIES: A PERIOD OF DECLINE

Around 1780, Italy began to lose the place it had held for several centuries as the leader of architectural innovation. Other nations weren't so directly influenced by the Catholic Church, so the eyes and designs of the world turned to the **French rococo** style, which was freer and more lighthearted and showed an abandonment of order symbolized by its elegant decoration. The rococo style took over as the dominant tradition throughout Europe, and at the same time the Germans, French, and English began to credit the Greeks as originators of the classical style, thus denying the influence of Italy and its Roman heritage.

Perhaps as a result of these snubs of church and history, Italy didn't respond to the rococo movement with the same enthusiasm as the rest of Europe. The Italian designs that came between 1780 and 1920 were for the most part rather lackluster. Rather than responding to a challenge of Italy's role as an architectural innovator, designers began simply to knock off classical models with just a hint of Byzantine decoration or treatment, as evidenced by the facade of **Florence's Duomo.**

In the rest of the world, the Belgian-initiated **art nouveau** movement attempted to challenge the dominance of the rococo, but came and died quickly, springing up in the 1890s and disappearing almost without a trace by 1910. Neither was Italy much inspired by this outside movement, though Milan's **Galleria Vittorio Emanuele II,** with its glass-and-metal roof and iron sculpture, as well as its **Casa Castiglione,** located at 47 Corso Venezia, are good examples of the fleeting art nouveau trend.

THE 20TH CENTURY

Since the beginning of the 20th century, with a few notable exceptions, architecture worldwide has developed a sameness of design and materials that pays little regard to location and culture. In Italy, the marriage of classicism and innovation has given way to large functional squared concrete structures such as the apartment block for the **Societa Novocomum** in Como, the **Santa Maria Novella** rail station in Florence, and the University of Rome's **Instituto Fisico** (Department of Physics).

For a short while, Mussolini attempted to resurrect national pride through the design of **neoclassical structures,** but the result was the construction of pompous buildings like Milan's **Central Rail Station.** Rather than gaining unity through design, the architecture is simply made busy by repeating rectangular arches and windows. Facade decorations were seemingly tacked onto the building just to acknowledge that it's indeed classically inspired. In Rome, the **Foro Italico** stands as one of Mussolini's monumental architectural achievements—it's a large complex of sports arenas, with the name DUCE as a design repeated thousands of times in black-and-white tiles. If Italy produced any great modern architect in the 20th century, it was **Pier Luigi Nervi,** born in 1891 in Milan. He was innovative, creating new buildings in daring styles and shapes best represented by Rome's **Palazzo della Sport,** designed for the 1960 Olympics.

More recently, **steel-and-concrete designs** have attempted the marriage of sharp angles and curves with mixed results, but some examples that work fairly well are the **Palace of Labor** in Turin, the **Church of Sant'Ildefonso** in Milan, and Rome's **Palazzo della Sport, Flaminio Stadium,** and **Termini Station.** But where giants of architecture once trod, men and women with visions less grand rule modern building in Italy today. Instead of creating great architecture, many Italian architects are trying to preserve what already exists. The best example is **Venice.** Though there are those who claim the city of palaces and gondolas may already be dead, few want to give up so easily. There's much talk but little effort to build colossal dikes to protect Venice from the relentless sea. The reason is money—or the lack of it. When money is available, work proceeds to save buildings from imminent collapse, but it's like a bottomless pit. We view it as trying to rebuild ancient Rome in a single day.

5 Mosaics, Frescoes & Other Masterpieces: Italy's Rich History of Art

The wealth and breadth of Italian art is amazing. Italy boasts so much art that some paintings—world masterpieces—that would be the focal point of major museums in other parts of the world are often tucked away in obscure rooms of rarely visited museums. There's too much of a good thing and not enough room to display the bounty, much less maintain the art and protect it from thieves.

ETRUSCAN & ROMAN ART

Though not much Etruscan architecture remains, **Etruscan art** survives in the form of a handful of **murals** discovered in tombs and more numerous examples of finely sculptured **sacrophagi,** many of which rest in Italian museums. The Etruscans were surpassed in the area of sepulchral painting only by the Egyptians. These paintings, most often done as true frescoes right into wet plaster, took as their subject the people and items the deceased would need to live comfortably in the spirit world—servants, horses, chariots, drinking vessels. In coloration, however, Etruscan art moved away from everyday reality—horses might have bright blue or green legs or the coats of animals might be brightened with vivid spots or stripes—in an effort to create a celebratory setting for postlife, as opposed to a grim memorial for grieving survivors. Features of human figures in these works are strongly Oriental, perhaps giving a clue to the origins of the mysterious Estruscans themselves, and the use of line and presentation of figures are strongly influenced by Greek art of the same time period, owing largely to the popularity Greek artists enjoyed among wealthy Etruscan patrons. You can visit several of the most frequently seen of these tombs on day trips from Rome. The best collection of sarcophagi is at the **Museo Nazionale di Villa Giulia** in Rome.

As **Rome** asserted its own identity and overpowered its Etruscan masters, it borrowed heavily from themes already established by Etruscan artists and architects. In time, however, the Romans discovered **Greek art,** fell in love with that country's statuary, and looted much of it.

Eventually, as Rome continued to develop its empire, its artisans began to turn out realistic **portrait sculpture,** which differed distinctly from the more idealized forms of Greek sculpture. Rome was preoccupied with sculpted images—in fact, sculptors made "bodies" en masse and later fitted a particular head on the sculpture on the demand of a Roman citizen. Most Roman painting that survives is in the form of **murals** in the fresco technique, and most of these were uncovered when **Pompeii** and **Herculaneum** were dug up. Basically, Roman art continued the Hellenistic tradition. Rome's greatest artistic expression was in architecture, not in art such as painting.

EARLY CHRISTIAN & BYZANTINE ART

The aesthetic and engineering concepts of the Roman Empire eventually evolved into **early Christian** and **Byzantine art.** More concerned with moral and spiritual values than with the physical beauty of the human form or the celebration of political grandeur, early Christian artists turned to the supernatural and spiritual world for

---

Let There Be Light

Since so much of Italy's art is stuck away in the dark corners of unlighted churches, it's a good idea to carry a pocketful of small coins to drop in boxes to turn on the lights in some churches.

---

their inspiration. Basilicas and churches were lavishly decorated with **mosaics** and **colored marble,** whereas painting depicted the earthly suffering (and heavenly rewards) of **martyrs** and **saints,** with symbols used in the compositions strictly dictated to the artist by the church. Three-dimensional representation was disallowed, following the Eastern tradition that all illusions of action or reality were taboo. In fact, the only freedom the painter enjoyed was in choosing colors and composing shapes.

ROMANESQUE ART

Supported by monasteries or churches, **Romanesque art,** which flourished between A.D. 1000 and 1200, was almost wholly concerned with **ecclesiastical subjects,** often with the intention of educating the worshipers who studied it. Biblical parables were carved in stone or painted into frescoes and became useful teaching aids for a church eager to spread its message. For the most part, **sculpture** from this period, created only as architectural decoration, remained largely Byzantine, with a flatness that disallowed detail. An exception was the sculpture of the **Lombard region,** which was under the influence of Germanic tribes. Here sculpture regained a bulkiness that had been lost since antiquity. One school of Lombard sculpture took the name of its master, **Benedetto Antelami,** and is characterized by stiff posturing that, combined with the dominance of raised features, gives the sculpture its characteristic rigid vigor.

Painting at this time was still limited to church frescoes and illustrations of Christian documents.

GOTHIC ART & THE FORERUNNERS OF THE RENAISSANCE

As the appeal of the Romanesque faded, the **Gothic style,** or **late medieval style,** greatly altered preconceptions of Italian art and encouraged a vast increase in the number of works produced. The Italians were inspired by 14th-century **French art,** because a weakened papacy had fallen under the influence of the French monarchy. French art at the time had an affected sentiment—the pose was everything—and this gradually made itself known in Italian works.

Prior to the Renaissance, Italy's greatest **sculptor** was **Nicola Pisano** (1206–78), whose major work was the pulpit in the baptistery in Pisa, a piece classical in form. The Roman inspiration is evident in the relief figures—relaxed in gesture and lacking individuality—around a high hexagonal box supported on seven Corinthian columns, three of which are propped on the backs of marble lions.

Late in the 13th century, **painting** finally began to break away from its role as architectural adornment, and with the arrival of **Cimabue,** the great age of Italian art was about to dawn. Facts about the life of this towering artist aren't well documented, but he worked, mainly in Tuscany, from 1270 to 1300. He painted a number of frescoes for the upper and lower churches of the **Sacred Convent of San Francesco** at Assisi, but they're in bad condition, his colors obscured over the ages. Cimabue, breaking with the rigidity of Byzantine art, revealed the spirit of his subject, expressing emotion in realistic detail as opposed to the church's symbolic terms. This trail-blazing artist was the harbinger of the greatest art movement in history: the Italian Renaissance.

He was followed by **Giotto** (1266–1336), a painter from Florence, a city where commerce was valued more than an obscure God shrouded in the Catholic Church's increasingly abstract codes and rituals. Giotto was undoubtedly influenced by the rise of **St. Francis,** who arrived in the city preaching that all things were of God and should be loved and treated as God, with no priestly intercession needed. Another person who influenced Giotto was his friend **Dante,** who had just published his *Divine Comedy* "in the volgare," the language of the people. By writing in the language of the people rather than in Latin, the language of the intellectuals, he was the first great poet to embrace the working man rather than alienate him.

Although Giotto's paintings continued to explore Christian themes and stories, they did so figured with people who walked and talked equally with Christ, allowing viewers to equate themselves with the subjects. This was obviously a big step toward the Renaissance, when artists and intellectuals began to strongly question the insignificance of man in the face of God, exploring human feats and accomplishments down through the ages.

THE ITALIAN RENAISSANCE

The Italian Renaissance was born in **Florence** during the 15th century, when members of the powerful Medici family emerged as some of the greatest art patrons in history. The Renaissance began with great artistic events, such as **Ghiberti** defeating **Brunelleschi** in a contest to design bronze doors for the baptistery of Florence's Duomo. (The original doors have been removed to the Duomo Museum for safekeeping and replaced by copies.)

Until the Renaissance, most painters had been viewed as nothing more than stone masons, for example. But in the Renaissance, the artist became an inventor, an architect, an intellectual, a discoverer, and mainly an interpreter of life. Renaissance painting developed mainly in Florence, where it was formal and intellectual, and in **Venice,** where art was designed to create pleasure. **Portraits** began to appear in art—the delight and triumph of the individual personality. Perspective, space composition, and anatomy came into vogue. The plastic and human values in painting were emphasized as never before. An example of that is **Maccio's** *Adam and Eve* in Florence.

The Renaissance gave birth to artists who excelled in both painting and sculpture. Emerging on the scene was **Jacopo della Quercia** (1375–1438), who brought vitality and a robust quality to sculpture, as exemplified by his major work, *Fonte Gaia,* in the Duomo Museum at Siena. His sculpture brought in the new quality of emotion, which would be seen to greater effect later in the works of Michelangelo.

Donatello (1386–1466) emerged as the first great name in Renaissance sculpture, and his *David* became the first important freestanding nude done in Europe since the days of the Romans. His most famous equestrian statue, *Gattamelata,* done in 1444, stands in the piazza of Sant'Antonio in Padua.

Michelangelo Buonarroti (1475–1564) always thought of himself as a sculptor, though his greatness also lies in his skills as an architect and a painter. His early triumph came with a *Pietà,* begun at the age of only 23 and now in St. Peter's in Rome. Working virtually day and night for 2 years, from 1501 to 1503, Michelangelo created the idealized man, his magnificent *David* (now on display in Florence's Accademia), a statue of titanic power and grace. His other legacies include the **Medici tombs,** executed between 1521 and 1534 (next door to San Lorenzo in Florence). The figures of *Night* and *Day* are the best known.

The towering Renaissance painter, of course, was **Leonardo da Vinci** (1452–1519), the epitome of a Renaissance man. Naturalist, anatomist, and engineer, he even conceived of the practicability of mechanical flight. His *Mona Lisa* (now in the Louvre in Paris) is the most famous painting in the world, and his wall painting *The Last Supper* (now in the process of being restored at Santa Maria delle Grazie in Milan) is his most impressive.

Italy had so many great artists during this period that it's mind-boggling, considering that entire centuries have gone by without the emergence of even one great artist. Chief among the lesser lights was **Raphael** (1483–1520). He died early, but not before creating lasting works of art, including his masterpiece, *Madonna del Granduca,* in Florence's Pitti Palace. He painted frescoes in the apartments of Pope Julius II in the Vatican while Michelangelo was painting (very reluctantly) his immortal Sistine Chapel nearby.

The Venetian school was different from the Florentine. In Venice color was crucial, whereas in Florence it was only a decorative note, as most Renaissance artists there were concerned with formal relationships and space through the laws of perspective.

Jacopo Bellini (ca. 1400–70) was the founder of the most celebrated family of artists from the Venetian school. **Giovanni Bellini** (ca. 1430–1516) was the greatest master of Venetian painting in the 1400s. He created rich, serene landscapes to depict mankind's spiritual harmony with nature.

Giorgione (1477–1510) created works of mystical charm and surpassed the Bellini family in his achievements. He's credited with one of the great steps forward in the history of painting as a fine art, the popularization of **easel painting**—a picture existing for its own sake, the purpose of which was simply to give pleasure to the viewer. His *La Tempesta,* for example, was, like many of his paintings, both brooding and tranquil—a painting of haunting, hypnotic beauty, defying interpretation.

The period known as the **High Renaissance** was said to last for only about 25 years, beginning in the early 16th century. This period in art saw more and more emphasis on rich color and subtle variations within forms. Works of great technical mastery emerged. Despite the subtle differences between the stages of the Renaissance, Italy remained Europe's artistic leader for nearly 200 years.

MANNERISM

The transitional period between the Renaissance and the baroque came to be called **Mannerism.** This transition was the result of great turmoil in Europe at the time, with François I of France and Charles V of Spain battling for domination of the continent. Much of the fighting took place in northern Italy, and in 1527 Spain's hired German warriors stormed Rome, the beginning of 3 years of rape and pillage that ended only when the pope crowned Charles an emperor of the Holy Roman Empire. Not surprisingly, artists reacted to the strife that had become everyday life by overturning many of the principles that defined the Renaissance. Painting and sculpture were stripped of balance, stability, and naturalism, which were replaced with **distortion, restlessness,** and **false rigidity.** Out of this period emerged such great artists as **Tintoretto** (1518–94), whose major work was the cycle of **frescoes** for the Scuola di San Rocco in Venice (it took 23 years to finish); Verona-born **Paolo Veronese** (1528–88); and the most sensitive, and some critics say the finest, of the Mannerists, **Parmigianino** (1503–40).

THE BAROQUE & ROCOCO

On the trail of Mannerism, the **baroque movement** swept Italy in the early 1600s and lasted until well into the 1700s. It was a period that attempted to find balance between the spirituality of the Gothic and the secular nature of the Renaissance—a result of the Catholic Counter-Reformation (in response to the Protestant Reformation) and the absolutism that dominated the politics of Europe. Rather than glorifying the universal man, as in the Renaissance, there was exploration of **human ceremony,** a result of a rigid code of courtly behavior. Still the pessimism of the Mannerists was slowly lifting as tight control of kingdoms and the certainty of Jesuit principles allowed a feeling of stability to return to the European nations. Religion continued to play a key role in society, but its expression in the arts was tempered by the worldly scars of the very human conflicts that had occurred. Art responded with an exploration of **depth** and the suggested illusion of **distance,** incorporating a strong sense of **light, color,** and **motion.** It was an age of intensity, drama, and power, which not surprisingly led to a flowering of the dramatic arts as well.

Great artists to emerge during this period were **Giovanni Bernini** (1598–1680), who became renowned both as a sculptor and as a painter, but the two painters who best represented the movement were **Annibale Carracci** (1560–1609), who decorated the Roman palace of Cardinal Farnese, and **Michelangelo da Caravaggio** (1573–1610), one of the pioneers of baroque painting. The even more flamboyant **rococo**—with its increasingly dramatic posturing and use of light—grew out of the baroque style. Much of the work from the baroque period, in fact, is a bit heavy-handed, resulting in an art of unbalanced sentimentality.

THE 19TH CENTURY TO THE PRESENT

By the 19th century, the great light had gone out of art in Italy. (The beacon was picked up by France.) **Neoclassicism**—a return to the aesthetic ideals of ancient Greece and Rome, whose ideals of patriotism were resonant with the growing sense of Pan-Italian patriotism—swept through almost every aspect of the Italian arts. The neoclassicist movement was largely the product of the excitement that resulted from the discovery of **Pompeii** and **Herculaneum. Antonio Canova** (1757–1822) became the most famous of the neoclassical sculptors. But neoclassicism never attained the grandeur in Italy that it did in France.

The 20th century witnessed the birth of several major Italian artists whose works once again captured the imagination of the world. **Giorgio de Chirico** (1888–1978) and **Amedeo Modigliani** (1884–1920; his greatest contribution lay in a new concept of portraiture) were only two among many. **Giorgio Morandi** (1890–1964), the Bolognese painter of bottles and jugs, also became known around the world. The greatest Italian sculptor of the 20th century was **Medardo Rosso** (1858–1928).

Since then Italy has been a European leader in sophisticated and witty interpretations of buildings, paintings, fashion, industrial design, and decor. Many modern Italian artists have infused Italian flair into workaday and utilitarian objects, whose quality, humor, and usefulness have become legendary.

6 A Taste of Italy

Italians are among the world's greatest cooks. Just ask any one of them. Despite the unification of Italy, regional tradition still dominates the various kitchens, ranging from Rome to Lombardy, from the Valle d'Aosta to Sicily. "Italian cuisine" perhaps has little meaning unless it's more clearly defined as Neapolitan, Roman, Sardinian, Sicilian, Venetian, Piedmontese, Tuscan, or whatever. Each region has a flavor and a taste of its own, as well as a detailed repertoire of local dishes.

Italy's cuisine has always been a paramount reason to live. This has been true even from the earliest days: To judge from the lifelike scenes of banquets in their tombs, the Etruscans loved food and took delight in enjoying it. The Romans became famous for their never-ending banquets and for their love of exotic treats, such as flamingo tongues.

Though culinary styles vary, Italy abounds in trattorie specializing in local dishes— some of which are a delight for carnivores, like the renowned *bistecca alla fiorentina*

Impressions

In Italy, the pleasure of eating is central to the pleasure of living. When you sit down to dinner with Italians, when you share their food, you are sharing their lives.

—Fred Plotkin, *Italy for the Gourmet Traveler* (1996)

(cut from flavorful Chianina beef, then charcoal-grilled and served with a fruity olive oil). Other dishes, especially those found at the antipasti buffet, would appeal to every vegetarian's heart: peppers, greens, onions, pastas, beans, tomatoes, and fennel.

Incidentally, except in the south, Italians don't use as much garlic in their food as many foreigners seem to believe. Most Italian dishes, especially those in the north, are butter based. And spaghetti and meatballs isn't an Italian dish, though certain restaurants throughout the country have taken to serving it "for homesick Americans."

CUISINES AROUND THE COUNTRY

Rome is the best place to introduce yourself to Italian cuisine, as it boasts specialty restaurants representing all the culinary centers of the country. Throughout your Roman holiday, you'll encounter such savory viands as *zuppa di pesce* (a soup or stew of various fish, cooked in white wine and flavored with herbs), *cannelloni* (tube-shaped pasta baked with any number of stuffings), *riso col gamberi* (rice with shrimp, peas, and mushrooms, flavored with white wine and garlic), *scampi alla griglia* (grilled prawns, one of the best-tasting, albeit expensive, dishes in the city), *quaglie col risotto e tartufi* (quail with rice and truffles), *lepre alla cacciatore* (hare flavored with tomato sauce and herbs), *zabaglione* (a cream made with sugar, egg yolks, and marsala), *gnocchi alla romana* (potato-flour dumplings with a meat sauce, covered with grated cheese), *abbacchio* (baby spring lamb, often roasted over an open fire), *saltimbocca alla romana* (literally "jump-in-your-mouth"—thin slices of veal with sage, ham, and cheese), *fritto alla romana* (a mixed fry likely to include everything from brains to artichokes), *carciofi alla romana* (tender artichokes cooked with such herbs as mint and garlic, flavored with white wine), *fettuccine all'uovo* (egg noodles with butter and cheese), *zuppa di cozze* (a hearty bowl of mussels cooked in broth), *fritto di scampi e calamaretti* (baby squid and prawns, fast-fried), *fragoline* (wild strawberries, in this case from the Alban Hills), and *finocchio* (fennel, a celerylike raw vegetable with the flavor of anisette, often eaten as a dessert or in a salad).

From Rome, it's on to **Tuscany,** featuring **Florence** and **Siena,** where you'll encounter the hearty cuisine of the Tuscan hills. The main ingredient for most any meal is the superb local olive oil, adored for its low acidity and lovely flavor. In Italy's south, the olives are gathered only after they've fallen off the trees, but here they're hand-picked off the trees so they won't get bruised (this ensures lower acidity and milder aroma). Typical Tuscan pastas are papardelle and penne mingled with a variety of sauces, many of which are tomato based. Tuscans are extremely fond of strong cheeses like gorgonzola, fontina, and parmigiana. Meat and fish are prepared simply and may seem undercooked, though locals would argue that it's better to let the inherent flavor of the ingredients survive the cooking process.

The next major city to visit is **Venice,** where the cookery is typical of the **Venetia** district. It has long ago been called "tasty, straightforward, and homely" by one food critic, and we concur. One of the most typical dishes is *fegato alla veneziana* (liver and onions), as well as *risi e bisi* (rice and fresh peas). Seafood figures heavily in the Venetian diet, and grilled fish is often served with the bitter red radicchio, a lettuce that comes from Treviso.

In **Lombardy,** of which **Milan** is the center, the cookery is more refined and flavorful. No dish here is more famous than *cotoletta alla milanese* (cutlets of tender veal, dipped in egg and bread crumbs, and fried in olive oil until they're a golden brown)— the Viennese called it Wiener schnitzel. *Ossobuco* is the other great dish of Lombardy; this is cooked with the shin bone of veal in a ragoût sauce and served on rice and peas. *Risotto alla milanese* is also a classic—rice that can be dressed in almost any way, depending on the chef's imagination; it's often flavored with saffron and butter, to which chicken giblets have been added, and seemingly always served with heaps of parmagiana reggiano cheese. *Polenta,* a cornmeal mush that's "more than mush," is the staff of life in some parts of northeastern Italy and is eaten in lieu of pasta.

The cooking in the **Piedmont,** of which **Turin** is the capital, and the **Aosta Valley** is different from that in the rest of Italy. Its victuals are said to appeal to strong-hearted men returning from a hard day's work in the mountains. You get such dishes as *bagna cauda,* a sauce made with olive oil, garlic, butter, and anchovies in which you dip uncooked fresh vegetables. *Fonduta* is also celebrated: It's made with melted Fontina cheese, butter, milk, egg yolks, and, for an elegant touch, white truffles.

In the **Trentino–Alto Adige** area, whose chief towns are **Bolzano, Merano,** and **Trent,** the cooking is naturally influenced by the traditions of the Austrian and Germanic kitchens. South Tyrol, of course, used to belong to Austria, and here you get such tasty pastries as strudel.

Liguria, whose chief town is **Genoa,** turns to the sea for a great deal of its cuisine, as reflected by its version of bouillabaisse, a *burrida* flavored with spices. But its most famous food item is *pesto,* a sauce made with fresh basil, garlic, cheese, and walnuts, which is used to dress pasta, fish, and many other dishes.

Emilia-Romagna, with such towns as **Modena, Parma, Bologna, Ravenna,** and **Ferrara,** is one of the great gastronomic centers. Rich in produce, its school of cooking produces many notable pastas now common around Italy: *tagliatelle, tortellini,* and *cappelletti* (larger than tortellini and made in the form of "little hats"). Tagliatelle, of course, are long strips of macaroni, and tortellini are little squares of dough that have been stuffed with chopped pork, veal, or whatever. Equally popular is *lasagne,* which by now everybody has heard of. In Bologna it's often made by adding finely shredded spinach to the dough. The best-known sausage of the area is *mortadella,* and equally famous is a *cotoletta alla bolognese* (veal cutlet fried with a slice of ham or bacon). The distinctive and famous cheese, *parmigiano reggiano,* is a product of Parma and also Reggio Emilia. *Zampone* (stuffed pig's foot) is a specialty of Modena. Parma is also known for its ham, which is fashioned into air-cured prosciutto di Parma. Served in wafer-thin slices, it is deliciously sweet and hailed by gourmets as the finest in the world.

Much of the cookery of **Campania** (spaghetti with clam sauce, pizzas, and so forth), with **Naples** as its major city, is already familiar to North Americans because so many Neapolitans moved to the New World and opened restaurants. *Mozzarella,* or buffalo cheese, is the classic cheese of this area. Mixed fish fries, done a golden brown, are a staple of nearly every table.

Sicily has a distinctive cuisine, with good strong flavors and aromatic sauces. A staple of the diet is *maccheroni con le sarde* (spaghetti with pine seeds, fennel, spices, chopped sardines, and olive oil). Fish is good and fresh in Sicily (try swordfish). Among meat dishes, you'll see *involtini siciliani* on the menu (rolled meat with a stuffing of egg, ham, and cheese cooked in bread crumbs). A *caponata* is a special way of cooking eggplant in a flavorful tomato sauce. The desserts and homemade pastries are excellent, including *cannoli,* cylindrical pastry cases stuffed with ricotta and candied fruit (or chocolate). Their ice creams, called *gelati,* are among the best in Italy.

AND SOME VINO TO WASH IT ALL DOWN

Italy is the largest wine-producing country in the world; as far back as 800 B.C. the Etruscans were vintners. It's said that more soil is used in Italy for the cultivation of grapes than for the growing of food. Many Italian farmers produce wine just for their own consumption or for their relatives in "the big city." However, it wasn't until 1965 that laws were enacted to guarantee regular consistency in wine-making. Wines regulated by the government are labeled DOC (*Denominazione di Origine Controllata*). If you see DOCG on a label (the "g" means *garantita*), that means even better quality control.

THE VINEYARDS OF ITALY   Following traditions established by the ancient Greeks, Italy produces more wine than any other nation. More than 4 million acres of soil are cultivated as vineyards, and recently there has been an increased emphasis on recognizing vintages from lesser-known growers who may or may not be designated as working within a zone of controlled origin and name. (It's considered an honor, and usually a source of profit, to own vines within a DOC. Vintners who are presently limited to marketing their products as unpretentious table wines—*vino di tavola*—often expend great efforts lobbying for an elevated status as a DOC.)

Italy's wine producers range from among the most automated and technologically sophisticated in Europe to low-tech, labor-intensive family plots turning out just a few hundred bottles per year. You can sometimes save money by buying direct from a producer (the signs beside the highway of any wine-producing district will advertise VENDITTA DRETTA). Not only will you avoid paying the retailer's markup, but you also might get a glimpse of the vines that produced the vintage you carry home with you.

Useful vocabulary words for such endeavors are *bottiglieria* (a simple wine shop) and *enoteca* (a more upscale shop where many different vintages, from several different growers, are displayed and sold like magazines in a bookstore). In some cases you can buy a glass of the product before you buy the bottle, and in some cases platters of cold cuts and/or cheeses are available to offset the tang (and alcoholic effects) of the wine.

REGIONAL WINES   Below we've cited only a few popular wines. Rest assured that there are hundreds more you may want to discover for yourself.

Latium: In this major wine-producing region, many of the local wines come from the Castelli Romani, the hill towns around Rome. Horace and Juvenal sang the praises of Latium wines even in imperial times. These wines, experts agree, are best drunk when young, and they're most often white, mellow, and dry (or "demi-sec"). There are seven types, including **Falerno** (straw yellow in color) and **Cecubo** (often served with roast meat). Try also **Colli Albani** (straw yellow with amber tints, served with both fish and meat). The golden-yellow wines of **Frascati** are famous, produced in both a demi-sec and a sweet variety, the latter served with dessert.

Tuscany: Tuscan wines rank with some of the finest reds in France. **Chianti** is the best known, and it comes in several varieties. The most highly regarded is **Chianti Classico,** a lively ruby-red wine mellow in flavor with a bouquet of violets. A good label is Antinori. A less known but remarkably fine Tuscan wine is **Brunello di Montalcino,** a brilliant garnet red that's served with roasts and game. The ruby-red, almost-purple **Vino Nobile di Montepulciano** has a rich, rugged body; it's a noble wine that's aged for 4 years.

Emilia-Romagna: The sparkling **Lambrusco** of this region is by now best known by Americans, but this wine can be of widely varying quality. Most of it is a brilliant ruby red. Be more experimental and try such wines as the dark ruby-red **Sanglovese**

(with a delicate bouquet) and the golden-yellow **Albana,** somewhat sweet. **Trebbiano,** generally dry, is best served with fish.

The Veneto: From this rich breadbasket in northeastern Italy come such world-famous wines as **Bardolino** (a light ruby-red often served with poultry), **Valpolicella** (produced in "ordinary quality" and "superior dry," best served with meats), and **Soave,** so beloved by W. Somerset Maugham, which has a pale amber-yellow color with a light aroma and a velvety flavor. Also try one of the **Cabernets,** either the ruby-red **Cabernet di Treviso** (ideal with roasts and game) or the even deeper ruby-red **Cabernet Franc,** which has a marked herbal bouquet and is served with roasts.

Trentino–Alto Adige: This area produces wine influenced by Austria. Known for its vineyards, the region has some 20 varieties of wine. The straw-yellow, slightly pale-green **Riesling** is served with fish, as is the pale green-yellow **Terlano. Santa Maddalena,** a cross between garnet and ruby, is served with wild fowl and red meats, and **Traminer,** straw yellow, has a distinctive aroma and is served with fish. A **Pinot Bianco,** straw yellow with greenish glints, has a light bouquet and a noble history and is also served with fish.

Friuli–Venezia Giulia: This area attracts those who enjoy a "brut" wine with a trace of flint. From classic grapes come **Merlot,** deep ruby in color, and several varieties of **Pinot,** including **Pinot Grigio,** whose color ranges from straw yellow to gray-pink (good with fish). Also served with fish, the **Sauvignon** has a straw-yellow color and a delicate bouquet.

Lombardy: These wines are justly renowned, and if you don't believe us, would you then take the advice of Leonardo da Vinci, Pliny, and Virgil? These great men have sung the praise of this wine-rich region bordered by the Alps to the north and the Po River to the south. To go with the tasty, refined cuisine of the Lombard kitchen are such wines as **Frecciarossa** (a pale straw-yellow color with a delicate bouquet; order with fish), **Sassella** (bright ruby red; order with game, red meat, and roasts), and the amusingly named **Inferno** (a deep ruby red with a penetrating bouquet; order with meats).

Piedmont: The finest wines in Italy, mostly red, are said to be produced on the vine-clad slopes of the Piedmont. Of course, **Asti Spumante,** the color of straw with an abundant champagnelike foam, is the prototype of Italian sparkling wines. While traveling through this area of northwestern Italy, you'll want to sample **Barbaresco** (brilliant ruby-red with a delicate flavor; order with red meats), **Barolo** (also brilliant ruby-red, best when it mellows into a velvety old age), **Cortese** (pale straw-yellow with green glints; order with fish), and **Gattinara** (an intense ruby-red beauty in youth that changes with age). Piedmont is also the home of **vermouth,** a white wine to which aromatic herbs and spices, among other ingredients, have been added; it's served as an aperitif.

Liguria: This area doesn't have as many wine-producing regions as other parts of Italy yet grows dozens of different grapes. These are made into such wines as **Dolceacqua** (lightish ruby-red, served with hearty food) and **Vermentino Ligure** (pale-yellow with a good bouquet; often served with fish).

Campania: From the volcanic soil of Vesuvius, the wines of Campania have been extolled for 2,000 years. Homer praised the glory of **Falerno,** straw-yellow in color. Neapolitans are fond of ordering a wine known as **Lacrima Christi** ("tears of Christ") to accompany many seafood dishes. It comes in amber, red, and pink. With meat dishes, try the dark mulberry-colored **Gragnano,** which has a faint bouquet of faded violets. The reds and whites of Ischia and Capri are also justly renowned.

Apulia: The heel of the Italian boot, Apulia produces more wine than any other part of Italy. Try **Castel del Monte,** which comes in shades of pink, white, and red.

Sicily: The wines of Sicily, called a "paradise of the grape," were extolled by the ancient poets, including Martial. Caesar himself lavished praise on Mamertine when it was served at a banquet honoring his third consulship. **Marsala,** of course, an amber-yellow wine served with desserts, is the most famous wine of Sicily; it's velvety and fruity and sometimes used in cooking, as in veal marsala. The wines made from grapes grown in the volcanic soil of Etna come in both red and white varieties. Also try the **Corvo Bianco di Casteldaccia** (straw yellow, with a distinctive bouquet) and the **Corvo Rosso di Casteldaccia** (ruby-red, almost garnet, full-bodied and fruity).

OTHER DRINKS

Italians drink other libations as well. Their most famous drink is **Campari,** bright red in color and flavored with herbs; it has a quinine bitterness to it. It's customary to serve it with ice cubes and soda.

Limoncello, a bright yellow drink made by infusing pure alcohol with lemon zest, has become Italy's second most popular drink. It has long been a staple in the lemon-producing region along the Amalfi Coast in Capri and Sorrento, and recipes for the sweetly potent concoction have been passed down by families there for generations. About a decade ago, restaurants in Sorrento, Naples, and Rome started making their own versions. Visitors to those restaurants as well as the Sorrento peninsula began singing limoncello's praises and requesting bottles to go. Now it's one of the most up-and-coming liqueurs in the world, thanks to heavy advertising promotions.

Beer, once treated as a libation of little interest, is still far inferior to wines produced domestically, but foreign beers, especially those of Ireland and England, are gaining great popularity with Italian youth, especially in Rome. This popularity is mainly because of atmospheric pubs, which now number more than 300 in Rome alone, where young people will linger over a pint and a conversation. Most pubs are in the Roman center, and many are licensed by Guinness and its Guinness Italia operations. In a city with 5,000 watering holes, 300 pubs may seem like a drop, but since the clientele is young, the wine industry is trying to devise a plan to keep that drop from becoming a steady stream of Italians who prefer grain to grapes.

High-proof **grappa** is made from the "leftovers" after the grapes have been pressed. Many Italians drink this before or after dinner (some put it into their coffee). It's an acquired taste—to an untrained foreign palate, it often seems rough and harsh.

Italy has many **brandies** (according to an agreement with France, Italians aren't supposed to use the word *cognac* in labeling them). A popular one is **Vecchia Romagna.**

Besides limoncello, there are several popular liqueurs to which the Italians are addicted. Try herb-flavored **Strega** or perhaps an **amaretto** tasting of almonds. One of the best known is **Maraschino,** taking its name from a type of cherry used in its preparation. **Galliano** is also herb flavored, and **Sambucca** (anisette) is made of aniseed and often served with a "fly" (coffee bean) in it. On a hot day, an Italian orders a vermouth, **Cinzano,** with a twist of lemon, ice, and a squirt of soda water.

7 Recommended Reading

GENERAL & HISTORY

Luigi Barzini's *The Italians* (Simon & Schuster, 1996) should almost be required reading for anyone contemplating a trip to Italy—even though it was written in 1964, the insights it gives into what makes modern Italy tick are surprisingly relevant today. The section on Sicily alone is worth the price of the book. William Murray's *The Last Italian: Portrait of a People* (Prentice Hall, 1991) is his second volume of essays on the subject of Italy, its people and its civilization. The *New York Times* called it "a lover's keen, observant diary of his affair."

Edward Gibbon's 1776 *The History of the Decline and Fall of the Roman Empire* is published in six volumes, but Penguin issues a manageable abridgement. This work has been hailed as one of the greatest histories ever written. No one has ever captured the saga of the glory that was Rome the way Gibbon did.

Florence, Biography of a City (Norton, 1993) is Christopher Hibbert's overview on the city of the Renaissance, written in his extremely accessible prose. Hibbert also wrote the most readable group biography of Florence's famous rulers in *The House of Medici: Its Rise and Fall* (Morrow Quill Paperbacks, 1980).

ART & ARCHITECTURE

The Renaissance seems to capture the public's imagination more than any other era, and one of the best accounts is Peter Murray's *The Architecture of the Italian Renaissance* (Schocken, 1986). Giorgio Vasari's *Lives of the Artists Vol. I and II* (Penguin Classics, 1987) is a collection of biographies of the great artists from Cimabue up to Vasari's 16th-century contemporaries. It's an interesting read full of anecdotes and Vasari's theories on art practice. For a more modern art history take, the indispensable tome is Frederick Hartt's *History of Italian Renaissance Art* (Abrams, 1994). For an easier and more colorful introduction, get Michael Levey's *Early Renaissance* (Penguin, 1967) and *High Renaissance* (Penguin, 1975).

Michelangelo, a Biography by George Bull (St. Martin's, 1995) is a well-written scholarly take on the life of the artist penned by one of the most respected translators of Italian classic literature and a Renaissance expert.

FICTION

Many writers have tried to capture the peculiar nature of Italy. Notable works include Italo Calvino's *The Baron in the Trees,* Umberto Eco's *The Name of the Rose,* E. M. Forster's *Where Angels Fear to Tread* and *A Room with a View,* Henry James's *The Aspern Papers,* Giuseppe di Lampedusa's *The Leopard,* Carlo Levi's *Christ Stopped at Eboli,* Thomas Mann's *Death in Venice,* Susan Sontag's *The Volcano Lover,* and Irving Stone's *The Agony and the Ecstasy.*

For a truly juicy read about just how depraved those first emperors were, nothing can beat Robert Graves's *I, Claudius* and *Claudius the God.* They're fabulous, even if you've already seen the BBC miniseries.

TRAVELOGUE

Mark Twain first became nationally famous for his report on a package tour of Europe and Palestine called *The Innocents Abroad* (Oxford University Press, 1996), a good quarter of which is about Italy. Henry James's *Italian Hours* (Penguin Classics, 1995) pulls together several essays painting vivid pictures of places and moments.

D. H. Lawrence and Italy (Penguin Travel Library, 1985) is a collection of three of the author's books set in Italy, including *Etruscan Places,* published posthumously. *A Traveller in Italy* (Dodd, Mead, 1982/Methuen, 1985) is the informed account H. V. Morton wrote of his trip through the peninsula in the 1930s.

Poet/professor Frances Mayes can make us all jealous with *Under the Tuscan Sun* (Chronicle Books, 1996), gleaned from her journals and chronicles about buying and renovating a Tuscan dream house outside Cortona with her husband. They grow grapes, learn traditional recipes, hop in the car to go on a wine-buying spree, visit the unexplored corners of Tuscany, press their first olive oil, and discover the rhythms of the Italian lifestyle.

Planning a Trip to Italy 3

This chapter is devoted to the where, when, and how of your trip—the advance planning required to get it together and take it on the road.

1 Visitor Information, Entry Requirements & Customs

VISITOR INFORMATION

TOURIST BOARD OFFICES For information before you go, contact the **Italian National Tourist Board**—however, Frommer's readers have noted that the office isn't really helpful. For the tourist board's Web site, see below.

In the United States: 630 Fifth Ave., Suite 1565, New York, NY 10111 (☎ **212/245-4822;** fax 212/586-9249); 500 N. Michigan Ave., Suite 2240, Chicago, IL 60611 (☎ **312/644-0990;** fax 312/644-3109); 12400 Wilshire Blvd., Suite 550, Los Angeles, CA 90025 (☎ **310/820-0098;** fax 310/820-6357).

In Canada: 1 place Ville-Marie, Suite 1914, Montréal, PQ H3B 2C3 (☎ **514/866-7667;** fax 514/392-1429).

In the United Kingdom: 1 Princes St., London W1R 8AY (☎ **0171/408-1254;** fax 0171/493-6695).

You can also write directly (in English or Italian) to the provincial or local tourist boards of areas you plan to visit. Provincial tourist boards (**Ente Provinciale per il Turismo**) operate in the principal towns of the provinces. Local tourist boards (**Azienda Autonoma di Soggiorno e Turismo**) operate in all places of tourist interest; you can get a list from the Italian National Tourist Office. However, as we said above, readers have complained that these offices are of little help—but you can try.

THE INTERNET Now that Europe is rushing to get online to keep up with the rest of the electronic world, Italy is delivering a reliable and expansive network of Web sites. However, be aware that the larger networks are often difficult to navigate, especially when you're searching for something specific.

Two good general places to start are the **European Travel Commission**'s site at **www.visiteurope.com/italy** and **Travel Europe**'s site at **www.traveleurope.it**. The **Italian National Tourist Board** sponsors **www.itwg.com**, which goes a bit further than the previous two by providing the most detailed information, including the latest rail timetables. More savvy travelers with tougher questions should seek out **www.tour-web.com**, which has everything from sports to apartment rentals to business opportunities.

Internet city guides are a good way to navigate without getting lost in the virtual countryside. You can visit Venice at **www.doge.it**, where you'll find everything from the latest happenings to the most affordable hotel rooms. Rome boasts the most sites of any Italian city (no surprise): For example, you can search for general info at **www.romeguide.it** or download the latest issue of *Time Out Rome* at **www.timeout.co.uk**.

ENTRY REQUIREMENTS

U.S., Canadian, U.K., Australian, New Zealand, and Irish citizens with a **valid passport** don't need a visa to enter Italy if they don't expect to stay more than 90 days and don't expect to work there. Those who, after entering Italy, find that they'd like to stay more than 90 days can apply for a permit for an extra 90 days, which as a rule is granted immediately. You can apply for the permit at the nearest *questura* (police headquarters).

CUSTOMS

Overseas visitors can bring along most items for personal use duty-free, including fishing tackle, a sporting gun and 200 cartridges, a pair of skis, two tennis racquets, a baby carriage, two hand cameras with 10 rolls of film, and 400 cigarettes (two cartons) or a quantity of cigars or pipe tobacco not exceeding 500 grams (1.1 lb). There are strict limits on importing alcoholic beverages. However, limits are much more liberal for alcohol bought tax-paid in other countries of the European Union.

For U.S. Citizens: Returning U.S. citizens who have been away for 48 hours or more are allowed to bring back, once every 30 days, $400 worth of merchandise duty-free. You'll be charged a flat rate of 10% duty on the next $1,000 worth of purchases. Be sure to have your receipts handy. On gifts, the duty-free limit is $100. For more specific guidance, contact the **U.S. Customs Service,** P.O. Box 7407, Washington, DC 20044 (☎ **202/927-6724**), to request the free pamphlet *Know Before You Go.* You can download it from the Internet at **www.customs.ustreas.gov/travel/kbygo.htm**. If you make purchases in Italy, it's important to keep your receipts. For refunds of the value-added tax (IVA in Italy), see "Fast Facts: Italy" at the end of this chapter.

For EU Citizens: On January 1, 1993, the borders between European countries were relaxed as the European markets united. When you're traveling within the EU, this will have a big impact on what you can buy and take home for personal use.

If you buy your goods in a duty-free shop, then the old rules still apply—you're allowed to take home 200 cigarettes and 2 liters of table wine, plus 1 liter of spirits or 2 liters of fortified wine. But if you buy your wine, spirits, or cigarettes in an ordinary shop in Italy, for example, you can take home almost as much as you like. (U.K. Customs and Excise doesn't set theoretical limits.) If you're returning from a non-EU country, the allowances are the standard ones from duty-free shops. You must declare any goods in excess of these. British Customs tends to be strict and complicated in its requirements. For details, get in touch with **Her Majesty's Customs and Excise Office,** Dorset House, Stamford Street, London, SE1 9PY (☎ **0171/202-4510**).

The Italian Lira, the U.S. Dollar & the U.K. Pound

For American Readers   At this writing, $1 U.S. = approximately 1,720L (or 100L = 6¢), and this was the rate of exchange used to calculate the dollar values given throughout this book, rounded to the nearest dollar. The rate fluctuates from day to day and might not be the same when you travel to Italy.

For British Readers   The ratio of the British pound to the lira fluctuates constantly. At press time, £1 = approximately 2,960L (or 100L = 3.4p).

Lire	U.S.$	U.K.£	Lire	U.S.$	U.K.£
50	0.03	0.02	15,000	8.70	5.10
100	0.06	0.03	20,000	11.60	6.80
300	0.17	0.10	25,000	14.50	8.50
500	0.29	0.17	30,000	17.40	10.20
700	0.41	0.24	35,000	20.30	11.90
1,000	0.58	0.34	40,000	23.20	13.60
1,500	0.87	0.51	45,000	26.10	15.30
2,000	1.16	0.68	50,000	29.00	17.00
3,000	1.74	1.02	100,000	58.00	34.00
4,000	2.32	1.36	150,000	87.00	51.00
5,000	2.90	1.70	200,000	116.00	68.00
7,500	4.35	2.55	500,000	290.00	170.00
10,000	5.80	3.40	1,000,000	580.00	340.00

2 Money

CURRENCY

There are no restrictions as to how much foreign currency you can bring into Italy, though you should declare the amount. This proves to the Italian Customs office that the currency came from outside the country and therefore the same amount or less can be taken out. Italian currency taken into or out of Italy may not exceed 200,000L in denominations of 50,000L or lower.

The basic unit of Italian currency is the **lira** (plural: **lire**), abbreviated **L** in this guide. Coins are issued in denominations of 10L, 20L, 50L, 100L, 200L, and 500L, and bills come in denominations of 1,000L, 2,000L, 5,000L, 10,000L, 50,000L, 100,000L, and 500,000L. Coins for 50L and 100L come in two sizes each, the newer ones both around the size of a dime. The most common coins are the 200L and 500L ones, and the most common bills are the 1,000L, 5,000L, and 10,000L.

For the **best exchange rate,** go to a bank, not to hotels or shops. Currency and traveler's checks (for which you'll receive a better rate than cash) can be changed at the airport and some travel agencies, such as American Express and Thomas Cook. Note the exchange rates offered—it can sometimes pay to shop around.

If you need a check drawn on an Italian bank (for example, to pay a deposit on a hotel room), this can be arranged by a large commercial bank or by a currency specialist like **Ruesch International,** 700 11th St. NW, Washington, DC 20001 (☎ 800/424-2923 or 202/408-1200), which can perform a wide variety of conversion-related transactions for you.

What Things Cost in Rome	U.S.$
Taxi from airport to city center	42.00
Taxi (from central rail station to Piazza di Spagna)	6.80
Subway or public bus (to any destination)	0.95
Local telephone call	0.13
Double room at the Hassler (very expensive)	403.10
Double room at Hotel Columbus (moderate)	214.60
Double room at Hotel Corot (inexpensive)	92.80
Continental breakfast (cappuccino and croissant standing at most cafes and bars)	3.75
Lunch for one at Ristorante da Pancrazio (moderate)	26.10
Dinner for one, without wine, at Relais Le Jardin (expensive)	58.00
Dinner for one, without wine, at Girarrosto Toscano (moderate)	30.00
Dinner for one, without wine, at Otello alla Concordi (inexpensive)	18.00
Pint of beer	3.30
Glass of wine	3.80
Coca-Cola	1.50–2.40
Cup of coffee	1.30
Roll of color film, 36 exposures	7.00
Admission to Vatican Museums and Sistine Chapel	9.00
Movie ticket	7.50

CREDIT CARDS

Using your credit card for most of your purchases is a great way to avoid carrying a large amount of cash and to ensure that you'll get a good exchange rate. **Visa** and **MasterCard** are now almost universally accepted (and in many places preferred) at most hotels, restaurants, and shops in Italy. The majority also accept **American Express,** and **Diners Club** is gaining some ground, especially in more expensive places. The only places that don't accept credit cards are the small mom-and-pop joints, be they one-star hotels, cheap dining spots, or neighborhood shops.

ATM NETWORKS

ATMs are becoming more and more common in Italy. If your bank card has been programmed with a PIN, it's likely you can use it at ATMs abroad to withdraw money from your account or as a cash advance on your credit card—just look for ATMs displaying your network's (Plus, Cirrus, whatever) symbol. But it's still smart to check with your bank to see if your PIN must be reprogrammed for usage in Italy (if you have a six-digit PIN, you'll need to get a new four-digit code). It's also a good idea to determine the frequency limits for withdrawals and cash advances on your credit card.

American Express cardholders have access to the ATMs of Banco Popolare di Milano; the transaction fee is 2% with a minimum charge of $2.50 and a maximum of $20. ATMs give a better exchange rate than banks, but some ATMs exact a service charge on every transaction. For **Cirrus** locations abroad, call ☎ **800/424-7787** or check out MasterCard's Web site at **www.mastercard.com/atm**. For **Plus** usage abroad, call ☎ **800/843-7587** or visit Visa's Web site at **www.visa.com/atms**.

What Things Cost in Florence	U.S.$
Taxi (from the train station to Piazza Signoria)	9.00
Public bus (to any destination)	.95
Local telephone call	.13
Double room at the Excelsior (deluxe)	696.00
Double room at Villa Azalee (moderate)	145.00
Double room at Hotel Elite (budget)	81.20
Continental breakfast (cappuccino and croissant standing at a cafe)	3.50
Lunch for one at Le Fonticine (budget)	16.00
Dinner for one, without wine, at Sabatini (expensive)	45.00
Dinner for one, without wine, at Trattoria Antellesi (moderate)	20.00
Dinner for one, without wine, at Vecchia Firenze (inexpensive)	14.00
Pint of beer	4.60
Glass of wine	2.00-3.60
Coca-Cola	1.30-2.40
Cup of coffee	1.05-1.65
Roll of color film, 36 exposures	9.50
Admission to Uffizi Galleries	6.90
Movie ticket	8.00

TRAVELER'S CHECKS

It's getting easier all the time to just use ATMs to access your checking account while you're on the road. But some people still prefer the security of using traveler's checks. If they're stolen, the value of your checks will be refunded if you've kept a record of the serial numbers. Most large banks sell traveler's checks, charging fees that average 1% to 2% of the value of the checks, though some out-of-the-way banks, in rare instances, have charged as much as 7%. If your bank wants more than a 2% commission, it sometimes pays to call the traveler's check issuers directly for the address of outlets where this commission will be less.

American Express (☎ 800/221-7282 in the United States and Canada; www.americanexpress.com) is one of the leading issuers of traveler's checks. No commission is charged to holders of certain types of American Express cards or members of the Automobile Association of America (AAA). For questions or problems that arise outside the United States and Canada, contact any of the company's many regional representatives.

Other issuers are **Citicorp** (☎ 800/645-6556 in the United States and Canada, or 813/623-1709, collect, from other parts of the world; www.citicorp.com); **Thomas Cook** (☎ 800/223-7373 in the United States and Canada; www.thomascook.com), which issues MasterCard traveler's checks; and **Interpayment Services** (☎ 800/221-2426 in the United States and Canada, or 212/858-8500, collect, from other parts of the world), which sells Visa checks that are issued by a consortium of member banks and the Thomas Cook organization.

Most Italian banks and cambi prefer traveler's checks denominated in either U.S. dollars or Swiss francs.

MONEYGRAMS

American Express's **MoneyGram,** Wadsworth St., Englewood, CO 80155 (☎ 800/ 926-9400), will allow friends back home to wire you money in an emergency in less than 10 minutes. Senders should call AMEX to learn the address of the closest outlet that handles MoneyGrams. Cash, credit card, and the occasional personal check (with ID) are acceptable forms of payment. AMEX's fee is $40 for the first $500, with a sliding scale for larger sums. The service includes a short telex message and a 3-minute phone call from sender to recipient. The beneficiary must present a photo ID at the outlet where the money is received.

3 When to Go

April to June and September and October are the best months for touring Italy— temperatures are usually mild and the hordes not quite so intense. Starting in mid-June, the summer rush really picks up, and from July to mid-September the country teems with visitors. August is the worst month: Not only does it get uncomfortably hot, muggy, and crowded, but the entire country goes on vacation at least from August 15 to the end of the month, and a good percentage of Italians take off the entire month. Many hotels, restaurants, and shops are closed—except at the spas, beaches, and islands, which are where 70% of the Italians head. From late October to Easter, most attractions go on shorter winter hours or are closed for renovation, many hotels and restaurants take a month or two off between November and February, spa and beach destinations become padlocked ghost towns, and it can get much colder than you'd expect (it may even snow).

   High season on most airlines' routes to Rome usually stretches from June to the beginning of September. This is the most expensive and most crowded time to travel. **Shoulder season** is from April to May, early September to October, and December 15 to 24. **Low season** is November 1 to December 14 and December 25 to March 31.

WEATHER

It's warm all over Italy in summer; it can be very hot in the south, especially inland. The high temperatures (measured in Italy in degrees Celsius) begin in Rome in May, often lasting until sometime in October. Winters in the north of Italy are cold with rain and snow, but in the south the weather is warm all year, averaging 50°F in winter.

   For the most part, it's drier in Italy than in North America. High temperatures, therefore, don't seem as bad since the humidity is lower. In Rome, Naples, and the south, temperatures can stay in the 90s for days, but nights are most often comfortably cooler.

   The average high temperatures in **Rome** are 82°F in June, 87°F in July, and 86°F in August; the average lows are 63°F in June and 67°F in July and August. In **Venice,** the average high temperatures are 76°F in June, 81°F in July, and 80°F in August; the average lows are 63°F in June, 66°F in July, and 65°F in August.

HOLIDAYS

Offices and shops in Italy are closed on the following **national holidays:** January 1 (New Year's Day), Easter Monday, April 25 (Liberation Day), May 1 (Labor Day), August 15 (Assumption of the Virgin), November 1 (All Saints' Day), December 8 (Feast of the Immaculate Conception), December 25 (Christmas Day), and December 26 (Santo Stefano).

   Closings are also observed in the following cities on **feast days** honoring their patron saints: Venice, April 25 (St. Mark); Florence, Genoa, and Turin, June 24

(St. John the Baptist); Rome, June 29 (Sts. Peter and Paul); Palermo, July 15 (Santa Rosalia); Naples, September 19 (St. Gennaro); Bologna, October 4 (St. Petronio); Cagliari, October 30 (St. Saturnino); Trieste, November 3 (San Giusto); Bari, December 6 (St. Nicola); and Milan, December 7 (St. Ambrose).

ITALY CALENDAR OF EVENTS

For more information about these and other events, contact the various tourist offices throughout Italy. Dates often vary from year to year.

January

- **Carnival,** Piazza Navona, Rome. Marks the last day of the children's market and lasts until dawn of the following day. Usually January 5.
- **Epiphany celebrations,** nationwide. All cities, towns, and villages in Italy stage Roman Catholic Epiphany observances. One of the most festive celebrations is the Epiphany Fair at Rome's Piazza Navona. Usually January 5 to 6.
- **Festa di Sant'Agnese,** Sant'Agnese Fuori le Mura, Rome. An ancient ceremony in which two lambs are blessed and shorn. Their wool is used later for palliums. Usually January 17.
- **Festival della Canzone Italiana (Festival of Italian Popular Song),** San Remo, the Italian Riviera. A 3-day festival with major artists performing the latest Italian song releases. Late January.
- **Foire de Saint Ours,** Aosta, Valle d'Aosta. Observing a tradition that has existed for 10 centuries, artisans from the mountain valleys display their wares—often made of wood, lace, wool, or wrought iron—created during the long winter. Late January.

February

- ✪ **Carnevale,** Venice. At this riotous time, theatrical presentations and masked balls take place throughout Venice and on the islands in the lagoon. The balls are by invitation, but the street events and fireworks are open to everyone. Contact the **Venice Tourist Office,** San Marco, Giardinetti Reali, Palazzo Selva, 30124 Venezia (☎ 041/522-6356). The week before Ash Wednesday, the beginning of Lent.

March

- **Festa di Santa Francesca Romana,** Piazzale del Colosseo near Santa Francesco Romana in the Roman Forum. A blessing of cars. Usually March 9.
- **Festa di San Giuseppe,** the Trionfale Quarter, north of the Vatican, Rome. The heavily decorated statue of the saint is brought out at a fair with food stalls, concerts, and sporting events. Usually March 19.

April

- **Holy Week observances,** nationwide. Processions and age-old ceremonies—some from pagan days, some from the Middle Ages—are staged. The most notable procession is led by the pope, passing the Colosseum and the Roman Forum up to Palatine Hill; a torchlit parade caps the observance. Sicily's observances are also noteworthy. Beginning 4 days before Easter Sunday; sometimes at the end of March but often in April.
- **Scoppio del Carro (Explosion of the Cart),** Florence. An ancient observance in which a cart laden with flowers and fireworks is drawn by three white oxen to the Duomo, where at noon mass a mechanical dove detonates it from the altar. Easter Sunday.

- **Festa della Primavera,** Rome. The Spanish Steps are decked out with banks of flowers, and later orchestral and choral concerts are presented in Trinità dei Monti. Dates vary.
- **Easter Sunday,** Piazza di San Pietro, Rome. In an event broadcast around the world, the pope gives his blessing from the balcony of St. Peter's.

May

✪ **Maggio Musicale Fiorentino (Musical May Florentine),** Florence. Italy's oldest and most prestigious music festival, with an emphasis on music from the 14th to the 20th century and with a calendar peppered with ballet and opera as well. Some concerts and ballets are presented free in Piazza della Signoria; ticketed events (concerts 30,000 to 100,000L/$17 to $58, operas 45,000 to 200,000L/$26 to $116, ballet 35,000L/$21) are held at the Teatro Comunale, Via Solferino 16, and the Teatro della Pergola, Via della Pergola 18. For schedules and tickets, contact the **Maggio Musicale Fiorentino/Teatro Comunale,** Corso Italia 16, 50123 Firenze (☎ **055/27-791** or 055/211-158). Late April to June.

- **Concorso Ippico Internazionale (International Horse Show),** Piazza di Siena in the Villa Borghese, Rome. Usually May 1 to 10, but the dates can vary.

June

- **Son et Lumière,** Rome. The Roman Forum and Tivoli areas are dramatically lit at night. Early June to end of September.
- **San Ranieri,** Pisa. The town honors its patron saint with candlelit parades, followed the next day by eight rower teams competing in 16th-century costumes. June 16.
- **Gioco del Ponte,** Pisa. Teams in Renaissance costume take part in a much-contested tug-of-war contest on the Ponte di Mezzo, which spans the Arno River. Last Sunday in June.

✪ **Festival dei Due Mondi/Festival di Spoleto,** Spoleto. Dating from 1958, this festival was the artistic creation of Maestro and world-class composer Gian Carlo Menotti, who continues to be very visible and still presides over the event. International performers convene for 3 weeks of dance, drama, opera, concerts, and art exhibits in this Umbrian hill town north of Rome. The main focus is to highlight music composed from 1300 to 1799. For tickets and details, contact the **Festival dei Due Mondi,** Piazza Duomo 7, 06049 Spoleto (☎ **0743/220-320** or 0743/45-028; fax 0743/220-321). During the festival, information is also available at the box office of the Teatro Nuovo, Piazza Belli (☎ **0743/40-265**). June 26 to July 12.

- **Festa di San Pietro,** St. Peter's Basilica, Rome. The most significant Roman religious festival, observed with solemn rites. Usually around June 29.
- **Biennale d'Arte (International Exposition of Modern Art),** Venice. One of the most famous art events in Europe, taking place during alternate (odd-numbered) years. June to October.

July

✪ **Il Palio,** Siena. Palio fever grips this Tuscan hill town for a wild and exciting horse race from the Middle Ages. Pageantry, costumes, and the celebrations of the victorious contrada mark the well-attended spectacle. It's a "no rules" event: Even a horse without a rider can win the race, which takes place on Piazza del Campo. For details, contact the **Azienda di Promozione Turistica,** Piazza del Campo 56, 53100 Siena (☎ **0577/280-551**). July 2 and August 16.

- **Arena di Verona (Arena Outdoor Opera Season),** Verona. Culture buffs flock to the 20,000-seat Roman amphitheater. Early July to mid-August.
- **Festa di Nolantri,** Rome. Trastevere, the most colorful quarter, becomes a gigantic outdoor restaurant, with tables lining the streets and merrymakers and musicians providing the entertainment. After reaching the quarter, find the first empty table and try to get a waiter—but keep a close eye on your valuables. For details, contact **Ente Provinciale per il Turismo,** Via Parigi 11, 00185 Roma (☎ 06/4889-9253). Mid-July.
- **Festa del Redentore (Feast of the Redeemer),** Venice. Marks the lifting of the plague in July 1578, with fireworks, pilgrimages, and boating on the lagoon. Third Saturday and Sunday in July.
- **Festival Internazionale di Musica Antica,** Urbino. A cultural extravaganza, as international performers converge on Raphael's birthplace. It's the most important Renaissance and baroque music festival in Italy. For details, contact the **Azienda di Promozione Turistica,** Piazza del Rinascinento 1, I-61092 Urbino (☎ 0722/2613). Ten days in late July.

August

- **Festa delle Catene,** San Pietro in Vincoli, Rome. The relics of St. Peter's captivity go on display in this church. August 1.

September

○ **Venice International Film Festival.** Ranking after Cannes, this festival brings together stars, directors, producers, and filmmakers from all over the world. Films are shown more or less constantly between 9am and 3am in various areas of the Palazzo del Cinema on the Lido. Though good numbers of the seats are reserved for international jury members, the public can attend virtually whenever they want, pending available seats. For information, contact the **Venice Film Festival,** c/o the La Biennale office, Ca' Giustinian, Calle del Ridotto 1364A, 30124 Venezia. Call ☎ 041/521-8838 for details on how to acquire tickets, or check out the Web site at **www.labiennale.it.** September 3 to 13.
- **Regata Storica,** the Grand Canal, Venice. A maritime spectacular; many gondolas participate in the canal procession, though gondolas don't race in the regatta itself. First Sunday in September.
- **Sagra dell'Uva,** Basilica of Maxentius, the Roman Forum, Rome. At this harvest festival, musicians in ancient costumes entertain and grapes are sold at reduced prices. Dates vary, usually early September.

October

- **Sagra del Tartufo,** Alba, Piedmont. Honors the expensive truffle in Alba, the truffle capital of Italy, with contests, truffle-hound competitions, and tastings of this ugly but very expensive and delectable fungus. For details, contact the **Azienda di Promozione Turistica,** Piazza Medford, 12051 Alba (☎ 0173/ 35-833). October 12 to 26.

December

- **Christmas Blessing of the Pope,** Piazza di San Pietro, Rome. Delivered at noon from the balcony of St. Peter's Basilica. It's broadcast around the world. December 25.
- **New Year's Eve 1999.** At press time, no official festivities for the turn of the millennium have been announced, but you can be assured of major parties all over Italy, particularly in Rome, which will become one huge street party. And of course they'll be a special mass at St. Peter's.

4 Health & Insurance

STAYING HEALTHY

You'll encounter few health problems traveling in Italy. The tap water is generally safe to drink, the milk is pasteurized, and health services are good.

If you take prescription medicine, it's a good idea to bring along copies of your prescriptions (written in the generic not brand-name form). If you need a doctor, your hotel can recommend one, or you can contact your embassy or consulate. Before you leave, you can obtain a list of English-speaking doctors from the **International Association for Medical Assistance to Travelers (IAMAT),** in the United States at 417 Center St., Lewiston, NY 14092 (☎ **716/754-4883**), or in Canada at 40 Regal Rd., Guelph, ON N1K 1B5 (☎ **519/836-0102**). Its Web site is at **www.sentex.net/~iamat**.

If you suffer from a chronic illness or special medical condition, consider purchasing a Medic Alert identification bracelet or necklace, which will immediately alert any doctor to your condition and provide Medic Alert's 24-hour hot-line number so foreign doctors can obtain your vital medical facts at no charge. The initial membership is $35, and there's a $15 yearly fee. Contact the **Medic Alert Foundation,** 2323 Colorado Ave., Turlock, CA 95382 (☎ **800/825-3785;** www.medicalert.org).

INSURANCE

Travelers' insurance needs are (1) health and accident, (2) trip cancellation, and (3) lost luggage. Before buying extra insurance, check your homeowner's, automobile, and medical policies, as well as the insurance provided by your credit-card companies and auto and travel clubs. You may already have adequate off-premises theft coverage. Note that to submit any insurance claim you must always have thorough documentation, including all receipts, police reports, medical records, and such. Remember, Medicare covers U.S. citizens traveling only in Mexico and Canada.

If you're prepaying for your vacation or taking a charter or any other flight that has cancellation penalties, look into cancellation insurance. Some credit-card companies, however, provide trip-cancellation coverage if you purchase your tickets with their card.

Some companies offering travel insurance—ranging from trip cancellation, trip interruption, lost luggage, and accident and medical coverage—are **Travel Guard International,** 1145 Clark St., Stevens Point, WI 54481 (☎ **800/826-1300**); **Travel Insured International, Inc.,** P.O. Box 280568, East Hartford, CT 06128-0568 (☎ **800/243-3174** in the United States, 203/528-7663 outside the United States 7:45am to 7pm EST); **Healthcare Abroad (MEDEX),** c/o Wallach & Co., 107 W. Federal St. (P.O. Box 480), Middleburg, VA 20118-0480 (☎ **800/237-6615** or 703/687-3166); and **Access America,** 6600 W. Broad St., Richmond, VA 23230 (☎ **800/284-8300**).

British companies offering traveler's insurance are **Columbus Travel Insurance Ltd.** (☎ **0171/375-0011** in London) or, for students, **Campus Travel** (☎ **0171/730-3402** in London). Columbus Travel will sell travel insurance only to people who have been official residents of Britain for at least a year. Britain's Consumers' Association recommends you insist on seeing the policy and reading the fine print before buying travel insurance.

5 Tips for Travelers with Special Needs

FOR TRAVELERS WITH DISABILITIES

If you're flying around Europe, the airlines and ground staff will help you on and off planes and reserve seats for you with sufficient legroom, but it's essential to arrange for this in advance by contacting your airline.

Recent laws in Italy have compelled rail stations, airports, hotels, and most restaurants to follow a stricter set of regulations about **wheelchair accessibility** to rest rooms, ticket counters, and the like. Even museums and other attractions have conformed to the regulations, which mimic many of those presently in effect in the United States. Always call ahead to check on the accessibility in hotels, restaurants, and sights you wish to visit.

With overcrowded streets, more than 400 bridges, and difficult-to-board vaporetti, Venice has never been accused of being too user-friendly for those with disabilities. Nevertheless, some improvements have been made. The Venice tourist office distributes a free map called *Veneziapertutti,* or "Venice for all." The map illustrates what part of Venice is accessible by the use of different color-coded references, and it also outlines a list of accessible churches, monuments, gardens, public offices, hotels, and lavatories with facilities for the handicapped. According to various announcements, Venice in the future will pay even more attention in its efforts to allow persons with disabilities to get around with greater ease—possibly retractable ramps operated by magnetic cards.

Before you go, there are several agencies that can provide advance-planning information. One is the **Travel Information Service** of Philadelphia's Industrial Rehab Program (☎ **215/456-9600,** or 215/456-9602 for TTY). You may also want to join a tour for visitors with disabilities. For the names and addresses of operators offering such tours—as well as other miscellaneous travel information—contact the **Society for the Advancement of Travel for the Handicapped,** 347 Fifth Ave., Suite 610, New York, NY 10016 (☎ **212/447-7284**). Annual membership dues are $45 but $30 for seniors and students.

You can obtain a copy of **"Air Transportation of Handicapped Persons"** from the Distribution Unit, U.S. Department of Transportation, Publications Division, M-4332, Washington, DC 20590. Write for Free Advisory Circular No. AC12032.

For the blind or visually impaired, the best source of advice is the **American Foundation for the Blind,** 11 Penn Plaza, Suite 300, New York, NY 10001 (☎ **800/ 232-5463** for ordering information kits and supplies, or 212/502-7600). Another good organization is **Flying Wheels Travel,** 143 W. Bridge (P.O. Box 382), Owatonna, MN 55060 (☎ **800/525-6790**), which offers various escorted tours, cruises, and private tours.

For a $25 annual fee, **Mobility International USA,** P.O. Box 10767, Eugene, OR 97440 (☎ **541/343-1284** voice and TDD; fax 541/343-6182), provides members with information on various destinations and offers discounts on videos, publications, and programs it sponsors.

For U.K. travelers, the **Royal Association for Disability and Rehabilitation (RADAR),** Unit 12, City Forum, 250 City Rd., London EC1V 8AF (☎ **0171/ 250-3222**), publishes three holiday "fact packs" for £2 each or £5 for all three. The first one provides general information, including planning and booking a holiday, insurance, and finances; the second outlines transportation available when going abroad and equipment for rent; the third deals with specialized accommodations. Another good resource is the **Holiday Care Service,** Imperial Building, 2nd Floor, Victoria Road, Horley, Surrey RH6 7PZ (☎ **01293/774-535;** fax 01293/784-647), a national charity advising on accessible accommodations for the elderly and persons with disabilities. Annual membership is £30.

FOR GAY & LESBIAN TRAVELERS

Since 1861, Italy has had liberal legislation regarding homosexuality, but that doesn't mean it has always been looked on favorably in a Catholic country. Homosexuality is much more accepted in the north than in the south, especially in Sicily, though Taormina has long been a gay mecca. However, all major towns and cities have an active gay life, especially Florence, Rome, and Milan, which considers itself the "gay capital" of Italy and is the headquarters of **ARCI Gay,** the country's leading gay organization with branches throughout Italy. Capri is the gay resort of Italy, rivaled only by the gay beaches of Venice.

PUBLICATIONS   Men can order *Spartacus,* the international gay guide ($32.95), or *Odysseus 1999, The International Gay Travel Planner,* a guide to international gay accommodations ($27). Both lesbians and gays might want to pick up a copy of *Gay Travel A to Z* ($16), which specializes in general information, as well as listings of bars, hotels, restaurants, and places of interest for gay travelers throughout the world. The *Ferrari Guides* (www.q-net.com) is another very good series of gay and lesbian guidebooks.

However, in early 1999 Macmillan Travel will publish its first guide especially for gays and lesbians, ✪*Frommer's Gay & Lesbian Europe,* which includes Rome, Florence, Venice, and Milan among its offerings. These books and others are available from **A Different Light,** 151 W. 19th St., New York, NY 10011 (☎ **800/343-4002** or 212/989-4850; www.adlbooks.com), and **Giovanni's Room,** 1145 Pine St., Philadelphia, PA 19107 (☎ **215/923-2960;** fax 215/923-0813).

Our World, 1104 N. Nova Rd., Suite 251, Daytona Beach, FL 32117 (☎ **904/ 441-5367;** fax 904/441-5604), is a magazine devoted to options and bargains for gay and lesbian travel worldwide. It costs $35 for 10 issues. The upscale *Out & About,* 8 W. 19th St., Suite 401, New York, NY 10011 (☎ **800/929-2268;** fax 800/ 929-2215), has been hailed for its "straight" reporting about gay travel. At $49 per year for 10 information-packed issues, it profiles the best gay or gay-friendly hotels, gyms, clubs, and other places throughout the world. Both publications are also available at most gay and lesbian bookstores.

ORGANIZATIONS   The **International Gay Travel Association (IGTA),** 4331 N. Federal, Suite 304, Fort Lauderdale, FL 33308 (☎ **800/448-8550** for voice mailbox, or 954/776-2626; www.iglta.com), encourages gay and lesbian travel worldwide. With around 1,200 member travel agencies, it specializes in networking travelers with the appropriate gay-friendly service organization or tour specialist. It offers a quarterly newsletter, marketing mailings, and a membership directory that's updated four times a year.

FOR SENIOR TRAVELERS

Many senior discounts are available, but note that some may require membership in a particular association.

PUBLICATIONS   For information before you go, obtain the free booklet "101 Tips for the Mature Traveler" from **Grand Circle Travel,** 347 Congress St., Suite 3A,

Boston, MA 02210 (☎ **800/221-2610** or 617/350-7500; fax 617/350-6206; www. gct.com).

ORGANIZATIONS   The **American Association of Retired Persons (AARP),** 601 E St. NW, Washington, DC 20049 (☎ **202/434-AARP;** www.aarp.org), is the nation's leading organization for people 50 and older. It serves their needs and interests through advocacy, research, informative programs, and community services provided by a network of local chapters and experienced volunteers throughout the country. The organization also offers members a wide range of special membership benefits, including *Modern Maturity* magazine and the monthly *Bulletin*.

Information is also available from the **National Council of Senior Citizens,** 8403 Colesville Rd., Suite 1200, Silver Spring, MD 20910 (☎ **301/578-8800**), charging $13 per person or per couple. You receive a bimonthly magazine, part of which is devoted to travel tips, as well as discounts on hotel and auto rentals.

Mature Outlook, P.O. Box 9390, Des Moines, IA 50306-9519 (☎ **800/ 336-6330;** fax 515/252-7855), is a travel organization for people over 50. Members are offered discounts at ITC-member hotels and a bimonthly magazine. The $14.95 to $19.95 annual membership fee entitles members to coupons for discounts at Sears. Savings are also offered on selected auto rentals and restaurants.

TRAVEL SERVICES   If you need a companion in your age range with whom to share your travel and leisure, consider contacting **Travel Companion Exchange,** P.O. Box 833, Amityville, NY 11701 (☎ **516/454-0880**). This helpful service has found companions for hundreds of travelers from all over the United States and Canada. Members meet through a confidential mail network based on newsletters that allow members to place their listing as well as respond to others. Membership costs are $99 for 6 months or $159 for a year. **SAGA International Holidays,** 222 Berkeley St., Boston, MA 02116 (☎ **800/343-0273;** fax 617/375-5951), runs inclusive tours and cruises for travelers 50 years or older.

DISCOUNT RAIL CARD   For information on the various special rail discounts available for senior travelers, see "Getting to Italy from the United Kingdom," "Getting to Italy from Within Europe," and "Getting Around Italy" later in this chapter.

FOR STUDENT TRAVELERS

Council Travel Service (CTS) (a subsidiary of the Council on International Educational Exchange) is America's largest student, youth, and budget travel group, with more than 60 offices worldwide. The main office is at 205 E. 42nd St., New York, NY 10017 (☎ **800/226-8624** in the United States to find your local branch, or 212/ 822-2700; www.ciee.org). Council Travel can issue the **International Student Identity Card (ISIC),** available to all bona fide students for $19; it entitles holders to generous travel and other discounts and provides a basic health and life insurance plan and a 24-hour help line. If you're no longer a student but are still under 25, you can get a **GO 25,** which will get you the insurance and some of the discounts as well (but not student admission prices in museums). CTS also sells **Eurail** and **YHA (Youth Hostel Association) passes** and can book hostel or hotel accommodations.

CTS's **U.K. office** is at 28A Poland St. (Oxford Circus), London W1V 3DB (☎ 0171/437-7767); the **Italy office** is in Rome, near the train station at Via Genova 16, 00184 Roma (☎ 06/46791). In Canada, **Travel CUTS,** 187 College St., Toronto, Ont. M5T 1P7 (☎ **416/798-2887**), offers similar services.

Campus Travel, 52 Grosvenor Gardens, London SW1W OAG (☎ **0171/ 730-3402**), opposite Victoria Station, is Britain's leading specialist in student and youth travel worldwide. It provides a comprehensive travel service specializing in low rail, sea, and airfares, holiday breaks, and travel insurance, plus student discount cards.

YOUTH HOSTELS   Students on a budget can also join **Hostelling International** (or IYHF as it's known abroad). For $25 annually ($10 for those under 18, $15 for those over 54), you get a card entitling you to a discount at official IYH/AIG hostels (of which there are more than 50 in Italy), but not at most private hostels (of which there are a few). In the **United States,** the address is 733 15th St. NW, Suite 840, Washington, DC 20005 (☎ **202/783-6161**). In the **United Kingdom,** you can get a card at Covent Garden, 14 Southampton St., London WC23 7HY (☎ **0171/ 836-8541**). For more information in Britain, contact the **Youth Hostels Association of England and Wales,** 8 St. Stephen's Hill, St. Albans, Hertfordshire AL1 2DY (☎ **01727/855-215**).

DISCOUNT RAIL CARD   For information on special student/youth rail discounts, see "Getting to Italy from the United Kingdom," "Getting to Italy from Within Europe," and "Getting Around Italy" later in this chapter.

6 Getting to Italy from North America

BY PLANE

High season on most airlines' routes to Rome usually is June to the beginning of September. This is the most expensive and most crowded time to travel. **Shoulder season** is April to May, early September to October, and December 15 to 24. **Low season** is November 1 to December 14 and December 25 to March 31.

Fares to Italy are constantly changing, but you can expect to pay somewhere in the range of $400 to $800 for a direct round-trip ticket from New York to Rome in coach class.

Flying time to Rome from New York, Newark, and Boston is 8 hours, from Chicago 10 hours, and from Los Angeles 12½ hours. Flying time to Milan from New York, Newark, and Boston is 8 hours, from Chicago 9¼ hours, and from Los Angeles 11½ hours.

American Airlines (☎ **800/433-7300;** www.americanair.com) offers daily nonstop flights from Chicago's O'Hare Airport, with flights from all parts of American's vast network making connections into Chicago. **TWA** (☎ **800/221-2000;** www.twa.com) offers daily nonstop flights from New York's JFK to both Rome and Milan. **Delta** (☎ **800/241-4141;** www.delta-air.com) also flies from New York's JFK to both Milan and Rome; separate flights depart every evening for both destinations. For a few months in midwinter, service to one or both of these destinations might be reduced to six flights a week. **United** (☎ **800/538-2929;** www.ual.com) has service to Milan only from Dulles Airport in Washington, D.C. **US Airways** (☎ **800/ 428-4322;** www.usairways.com) offers one flight daily to Rome out of Philadelphia (you can connect through Philly from most major U.S. cities). And **Continental** (☎ **800/525-0280;** www.flycontinental.com) flies twice daily to Rome from its hub in Newark.

Canadian Airlines International (☎ **800/426-7000;** www.cdnair.ca) flies daily from Toronto to Rome. Two of the flights are nonstop; the others touch down en route in Montréal, depending on the schedule.

British Airways (☎ **800/AIRWAYS;** www.british-airways.com), **Virgin Atlantic Airways** (☎ **800/862-8621;** www.fly.virgin.com), **Air France** (☎ **800/237-2747;** www.airfrance.com), **KLM** (☎ **800/374-7747;** www.klm.nl), and **Lufthansa** (☎ **800/645-3880;** www.lufthansa-usa.com) offer some attractive deals for anyone

Travel Deals on the Internet

Those hooked up to the Internet can find excellent travel deals online. Increasingly, travel agencies and companies are using the Web as a medium to offer everything from vacations to plane reservations to budget airline tickets on major carriers. To save you time and effort searching out worthwhile sites, we suggest the following.

A good place to start is Macmillan Travel's site, **Arthur Frommer's Outspoken Encyclopedia of Travel** (**www.frommers.com**), where you'll find lots of up-to-the-minute travel information—including the latest bargains and candid articles updated daily by Arthur Frommer himself. Most **major airlines** maintain their own sites—see above for their Web addresses. These sites are the best to check for day-to-day fares to get the very best deal on the flight of your choice.

There are many travel sites maintained by travel services and agencies offering basically the same service as the airline sites, except on a much wider scale. A few of the better-respected ones are **Travelocity** (www.travelocity.com), which also advertises last-minute deals; **Microsoft Expedia** (www.expedia.com), which will e-mail you weekly with the best fares for a chosen destination; and **Yahoo's Flifo Global** (travel.yahoo.com/travel), whose "Fare Beater" compares airlines to find the best going rate. For most, just enter your dates and cities and the computer looks for the lowest fares.

Great last-minute deals are often available directly from many airlines through a free service called **E-Savers.** Each week, the airline sends you an e-mail list of discounted flights, usually leaving the upcoming Thursday to Saturday and returning the following Monday to Wednesday. Of course, this is mainly for the person who can drop everything and take a long weekend in Italy. You can sign up at any airline's Web site (see above).

Promoting itself as a travel service and not an agency, **www.momentsnotice.com** provides a vacation bargain hunter's dream. Updated each morning, many of the deals are snapped up by the end of the day. A drawback is that many of these vacations require you to drop everything and go almost immediately. At **www.180096hotel.com** you'll find budget reservations at prestigious hotels all over the world, many accommodations up to 65% off. You can book online, cutting out travel agents.

interested in combining a trip to Italy with a stopover in, say, Britain, Paris, Amsterdam, or Germany along the way.

Alitalia (☎ 800/223-5730 in the United States, 514/842-8241 in Canada; www.alitalia.it/english/index.html) is the Italian national airline, with nonstop flights to Rome from different North American cities, including New York (JFK), Newark, Boston, Chicago, and Miami. Nonstop flights into Milan are from New York (JFK), Newark, and Los Angeles. From Milan or Rome, Alitalia can easily book connecting domestic flights if your final destination is elsewhere in Italy. Alitalia participates in the frequent-flyer programs of other airlines, including Continental and US Airways. *A word to the wise:* Don't expect the same kind of service and comfort from Alitalia that you'd get from other major European airlines—and unlike other carriers, Alitalia doesn't forbid smoking. Unless it's offering an irresistible deal or you just can't get a seat on a U.S. carrier, we advise choosing another airline.

For the latest on airline Web sites, check **airlines-online.com** or **www.itn.com**.

OTHER GOOD-VALUE CHOICES   In its purest sense, a **bucket shop,** or **consolidator,** acts as a clearinghouse for blocks of tickets that airlines discount and consign during normally slow periods of air travel. Tickets are sometimes priced at up to 35% less than the full fare. Perhaps your reduced fare will be no more than 20% off the regular fare. Terms of payment can vary—anywhere from 45 days prior to departure to last-minute sales offered in a final attempt by an airline to fill an empty aircraft.

One of the biggest U.S. consolidators is **Travac,** 989 Ave. of the Americas, New York, NY 10018 (☎ 800/TRAV-800 or 212/563-3303), which offers discounted seats throughout the United States to most cities in Europe on airlines like TWA, United, and Delta. Another branch office is at 2601 E. Jefferson St., Orlando, FL 32803 (☎ 407/896-0014).

We've also had good service and good deals by using ☎ 1-800-FLY-4-LESS.

Since dealing with unknown bucket shops might be a little risky, it's wise to call the Better Business Bureau in your area to see if complaints have been filed against the company from which you plan to purchase a ticket.

You might also check into **charter flights.** Before paying, check the restrictions on your ticket or contract and do some comparison shopping to make sure you're really saving over the cost of a regularly scheduled flight. You may be asked to purchase a tour package and pay far in advance. You'll pay a stiff penalty (or forfeit the ticket) if you cancel. Charters are sometimes canceled when the plane doesn't fill up. In some cases, the charter-ticket seller will offer you an insurance policy for your own legitimate cancellation (hospitalization, death in the family, whatever).

One reliable charter-flight operator is **Council Charter,** run by the Council on International Educational Exchange, 205 E. 42nd St., New York, NY 10017 (☎ 800/2-COUNCIL or 212/822-2900); It arranges charter seats on regularly scheduled aircraft. One of the biggest New York charter operators is **Travac,** 989 Ave. of the Americas, New York, NY 10018 (☎ 800/TRAV-800 or 212/563-3303).

BY ORGANIZED TOUR

Some people love escorted tours: They free you from spending lots of time behind the wheel; they take care of all the details; and they tell you what to expect at each attraction. You know your costs up front and don't get many surprises. Escorted tours can take you to the maximum number of sights in the minimum amount of time with the least amount of hassle.

Other people need more freedom and spontaneity and prefer to discover a destination by themselves—they don't mind getting caught in a thunderstorm without an umbrella or finding that a recommended restaurant is no longer in business. That's just the adventure of travel.

If you do choose an escorted tour, ask a few simple questions before you buy:

1. What is the cancellation policy? Do you have to put a deposit down? Can they cancel the trip if they don't get enough people? How late can you cancel if you're unable to go? When do you pay? Do you get a refund if you cancel? If *they* cancel?

2. How jam-packed is the schedule? Do they try to fit 25 hours into a 24-hour day, or is there ample time for relaxing and shopping? If you don't enjoy getting up at 7am every day and not returning to your hotel until 6 or 7pm at night, certain escorted tours may not be for you.

3. How big is the group? The smaller the group, the more flexible and the less time you'll spend waiting for people to get on and off the bus. Tour operators may be evasive about this, because they may not know the exact size of the

group until everybody has made their reservations, but they should be able to give you a rough estimate. Some tours have a minimum group size and may cancel the tour if they don't book enough people.

4. What's included? Don't assume anything. How much choice do you have? Can you opt out of certain activities, or does the bus leave once a day, with no exceptions? Are all your meals planned in advance? Can you choose your entree at dinner, or does everybody get the same chicken cutlet?

If you choose an escorted tour, think strongly about purchasing travel insurance, especially if the tour operator asks to you pay up front. But don't buy insurance from the tour operator! If they don't fulfill their obligation to provide you with the vacation you've paid for, there's no reason to think they'll fulfill their insurance obligations either. Get travel insurance through an independent agency, some of which are recommended earlier in this chapter.

The biggest tour operator is **Perillo Tours,** 577 Chestnut Ridge Rd., Woodcliff Lake, NJ 07675-9888 (☎ **800/431-1515** in the United States or 201/307-1234; www.perillotours.com), family operated for three generations—perhaps you've seen the TV commercials featuring "Mr. Italy," Mario Perillo, and his son. Since it was founded in 1945, it has sent more than a million travelers to Italy. Perillo's tours cost much less than you'd spend if you arranged a comparable trip yourself. Accommodations are in first-class hotels, and guides tend to be well qualified, well informed, and sensitive to the needs of participants. Perillo has hundreds of departures year-round. From April to October, nine itineraries are offered, ranging from 8 to 15 days and covering broadly different regions. From November to April, the "Off-Season Italy" tour covers three of Italy's premier cities (Rome, Florence, Venice) during a season when they're likely to be less crowded.

Another contender is **Italiatour,** a company of the Alitalia Group (☎ **800/ 845-3365** or 212/765-2183; www.italiatour.com), offering a wide variety of tours through all parts of Italy. It specializes in tours for independent travelers who ride from one destination to another by train or rental car. In most cases, the company sells prereserved accommodations, which are usually less expensive than if you had reserved them yourself. Because of the company's close link with Alitalia, the prices quoted for air passage are sometimes among the most reasonable on the retail market.

Trafalgar Tours, 11 E. 26th St., New York, NY 10010 (☎ **800/854-0103;** www.trafalgartours.com), is one of Europe's largest tour operators, offering affordable packages with lodgings in unpretentious hotels. The 14-day "Best of Italy" tour begins and ends in Rome, with five stops, including Sorrento, Venice, and Florence. Some meals and twin-bed accommodations in first-class hotels are part of the package. The 12-day "Bellissimo" tour also begins and ends in Rome and includes Capri, Assisi, Venice, and Montecatini. Check with your travel agent for more information on these tours. Trafalgar only takes calls from agents.

One of Trafalgar's leading competitors, known for offering roughly equivalent affordable tours, is **Globus/Cosmos Tours,** 5301 S. Federal Circle, Littleton, CO 80123-2980 (☎ **800/221-0090;** www.globusandcosmos.com). Globus has first-class escorted coach tours of various regions lasting from 8 to 16 days. Cosmos, a budget branch of Globus, sells escorted tours of about the same length. Tours must be booked through a travel agent, but you can call the 800 number for brochures. Another competitor is **Insight International Tours,** 745 Atlantic Ave., #720, Boston, MA 02111 (☎ **800/582-8380**), which books superior first-class, fully escorted motor-coach tours lasting from 1 week to a 36-day grand tour.

Finally, **Abercrombie & Kent,** 1520 Kensington Rd., Oak Brook, IL 60523 (☎ **800/323-7308**) and Sloane Square House, Holbein Place, London SW1W 8NS

(☎ **0171/730-9600**), offers a variety of luxurious premium packages. Your overnight stays will be in meticulously restored castles and exquisite Italian villas, most of which are four- and five-star accommodations. Several trips are offered, including tours of the Lake Garda region and the southern territory of Calabria. The company's Web site is **www.abercrombiekent.com**.

7 Getting to Italy from the United Kingdom

BY PLANE

If a special air-travel promotion from a travel agent isn't available or feasible at the time of your visit, then an **APEX ticket** might be the way to keep costs trimmed. These tickets must be reserved in advance. However, an APEX ticket offers a discount without the usual booking restrictions. You might also ask the airlines about a **Eurobudget ticket,** which imposes restrictions or length-of-stay requirements.

British newspapers are always full of classified ads touting "slashed" fares to Italy. One good source is *Time Out,* a magazine published in London. London's *Evening Standard* has a daily travel section, and the Sunday editions of almost any newspaper will run many ads. Though competition is fierce, one well-recommended company that consolidates bulk ticket purchases and then passes the savings on to its consumers is **Trailfinders** (☎ **0171/937-5400** in London). It offers access to tickets on such carriers as SAS, British Airways, and KLM.

CEEFAX, a British TV information service included on many home and hotel TVs, runs details of package holidays and flights to Italy and beyond. Just switch to your CEEFAX channel and you'll find a menu of listings that includes travel information.

Both **British Airways** (☎ **0345/222-111** in the U.K.; www.british-airways.com) and **Alitalia** (☎ **0171/602-7111;** www.alitalia.it/english/index.html) have frequent flights from London's Heathrow Airport to Rome, Milan, Venice, Pisa (the gateway to Florence), and Naples. Flying time from London to these cities is from 2 to 3 hours. BA also has one direct flight a day from Manchester to Rome.

Virgin Airlines (☎ **01293/747-747** in London or 800/862-8621 in North America) does not serve Italy in any capacity.

BY TRAIN

Many rail passes are available in the United Kingdom for travel in Europe. For details, stop in at or contact the **International Rail Centre,** Victoria Station, London SW1V 1JZ (☎ **0990/848-848**). The staff can help you find the best option for the trip you're planning. Some of the most popular are the **Inter-Rail** and **EuroYouth** passes, entitling you to unlimited second-class travel in 26 European countries.

Route 26 tickets are a worthwhile option for travelers under 26. They allow you to move leisurely from London to Rome, with as many stopovers en route as you want, using a different route southbound (through Belgium, Luxembourg, and Switzerland) from the return route northbound (exclusively through France). All travel must be completed within 2 months of the departure date. Route 26 tickets from London to Rome cost from £173 for the most direct route or from £198 for a roundabout route through the south of France.

Wasteels, adjacent to Platform 2 in Victoria Station, London SW1V 1JZ (☎ **0171/834-6744**), will sell a **Rail Europe Senior Pass** to U.K. residents for £5. With it, a British resident over 60 can buy discounted tickets on many of Europe's rail lines. To qualify, you must present a valid British Senior Citizen rail card, available for £16 at any BritRail office on presentation of proof of age and British residency.

BY BUS

Eurolines, 52 Grosvenor Gardens (opposite Victoria Rail Station), Victoria, London SW1 (☎ **0990/143219** for information and reservations by credit card), is the leading operator of scheduled coach service across Europe. Its comprehensive network of services includes regular departures to destinations throughout Italy, including Turin, Milan, Bologna, Florence, and Rome; plus summer services to Verona, Vicenza, Padua, and Venice.

Eurolines' services to Italy depart from London's Victoria Coach Station and are operated by modern coach, with reclining seats and a choice of smoking or non-smoking areas. Return tickets are valid for up to 6 months, and for added flexibility you may leave the return date open.

A round-trip ticket from London to Rome using as direct a route as possible is £125 or from £88 one-way, depending on the season. Travelers under 26 pay around £10 less each way; children are allowed a 30 to 40% discount. Departures in either direction are daily, and the trip takes around 37 hours each way. Tickets are for direct travel to Rome only.

BY PACKAGE TOUR

The oldest travel agency in Britain, **Cox & Kings** (☎ **0171/873-5006**) specializes in unusual, if pricey, holidays. Their Italy offerings include organized tours through the country's gardens and sites of historic or aesthetic interest, opera tours, pilgrimage-style visits to sites of religious interest, and food- and wine-tasting tours. The staff is noted for their focus on tours of ecological and environmental interest.

If your interests are more varied, call the London headquarters of the **International Association of Travel Agencies (IATA)** (☎ **0181/607-9080**) for the names and addresses of tour operators that specialize in travel relating to your interest.

8 Getting to Italy from Within Europe

BY TRAIN

If you plan to travel heavily on the European and/or British rails, you'll do well to secure the latest copy of the *Thomas Cook European Timetable of Railroads.* This 500-plus-page timetable accurately documents all of Europe's mainline passenger rail services. It's available exclusively in North America from **Forsyth Travel Library,** 226 Westchester Ave., White Plains, NY 10604 (☎ **800/367-7984**), for $27.95 (plus $4.50 shipping in the U.S. and $5.50 in Canada), or at travel specialty stores.

New electric trains have made travel between France and Italy faster and more comfortable than ever before. **France's TGVs** travel at speeds of up to 185 miles per hour and have cut travel time between Paris and Turin from 7 to 5½ hours and between Paris and Milan from 7½ hours to 6¾ hours. **Italy's ETRs** travel at speeds of up to 145 miles per hour and currently run between Milan and Lyon (5 hours), with a stop in Turin.

EUROPEAN-WIDE RAILPASSES Eurailpass Many travelers to Europe take advantage of one of the greatest travel bargains, the **Eurailpass,** which permits unlimited first-class rail travel in any country in Western Europe (except the British Isles) and Hungary in Eastern Europe. Oddly, it doesn't include travel on the rail lines of Sardinia, which are organized independently of the rail lines of the rest of Italy.

The advantages are tempting: There are no tickets; simply show the pass to the ticket collector, then settle back to enjoy the scenery. Seat reservations are required on some trains. Many of the trains have couchettes (sleeping cars), for which an extra fee is charged. Obviously, the 2- or 3-month traveler gets the greatest economic advantages. To obtain full advantage of a 15-day or 1-month pass, you'd have to spend a great deal of time on the train.

Eurailpass holders are entitled to considerable reductions on certain buses and ferries as well. You'll get a 20% reduction on second-class accommodations from certain companies operating ferries between Naples and Palermo or for crossings to Sardinia and Malta.

A **consecutive-day Eurailpass** lets you travel first-class only on unlimited trains for a set period ranging from 15 days to 3 months. The cost is $538 for 15 days, $698 for 21 days, $864 for 1 month, $1,224 for 2 months, and $1,512 for 3 months. Children 3 and under travel free providing they don't occupy a seat (otherwise, they're charged half fare); children under 12 pay half fare.

The **Eurail Saverpass,** valid all over Europe for first class only, offers discounted 15-day travel for groups of three or more people traveling together from April to September or two people traveling together from October to March. The price is $458 for 15 days, $594 for 21 days, and $712 for 1 month.

The **Eurail Flexipass,** valid in first class and offering the same privileges as the Eurailpass, allows passengers to visit Europe with more flexibility. However, it provides a number of individual travel days that can be used over a much longer period of consecutive days—making it possible to stay over in a city or town without losing a day of travel. There are two passes: 10 days of travel within 2 months for $634 and 15 days of travel within 2 months for $836.

If you're under 26, you can purchase a **Eurail Youthpass,** entitling you to unlimited second-class travel wherever the Eurailpass is honored. The pass is $376 for 15 consecutive days, $605 for 1 month, or $857 for 2 months. There's also a **Eurail Youth Flexipass** for travelers under 26.

Europass   The **Europass** is more limited than the Eurailpass but may offer better value for visitors traveling over a smaller area. It's good for 2 months and allows 5 days of rail travel within three to five European countries (Italy, France, Germany, Switzerland, and Spain) with contiguous borders.

For travel in three of the countries (Italy plus two others), the fare for adults in first class is $416 for 5 days of travel. For travel in four, the adult fare is $436 for 5 days of travel. For travel in all five, the adult fare is $446 for 5 days of travel. If two adults travel together, the second one receives a 40% discount. You can add extra days to your Europass by paying a surcharge of $42 per extra day, maximum of 10. The 40% companion discount also applies here.

For travelers under 26, a **Europass Youth** is available. The fares are 35 to 55% off those quoted above, and the pass is good only for second-class travel. Unlike the adult Europass, there's no discount for a companion.

WHERE TO BUY A EURAILPASS OR EUROPASS   You can buy these passes from travel agents or from railway agents in major cities like New York, Montréal, and Los Angeles. Eurailpasses are also available from the North American offices of CIT Tours (see "Getting Around Italy," below) or through **Rail Europe** (☎ 800/ 4-EURAIL). No matter what everyone tells you, you can buy Eurailpasses in Europe as well as in America (at the major train stations) but they're more expensive. Rail Europe can also give you information on the rail/drive versions of the passes.

HOW TO USE A EURAILPASS OR EUROPASS   In addition to saving you money, these easy-to-use passes can save you time. In most cases, you won't have to wait in line at the ticket window at the train station—you just need to scribble the date on the pass as you hop on the train. You will, however, need to go to the ticket window if the train you want to take requires you to reserve a seat (such as the Pendolino) or if you want a spot in a sleeping couchette. The Eurailpass gets you only a 33% discount on the TGV through the Chunnel from London to Paris. To allow you to take night trains without using 2 days on your pass, a Eurail day begins at 7pm and runs until midnight of the following night.

BY CAR

If you're already on the Continent, particularly in a neighboring country such as France or Austria, you may want to drive to Italy. However, you should make arrangements in advance with your car-rental company.

It's also possible to drive from London to Rome, a distance of 1,124 miles, via Calais/Boulogne/Dunkirk, or 1,085 miles via Oostende/Zeebrugge, not counting channel crossings by either Hovercraft ferry or the Chunnel. Milan is some 400 miles closer to Britain than is Rome. If you cross over from England and arrive at one of the continental ports, you still face a 24-hour drive. Most drivers play it safe and budget 3 days for the journey.

Most of the roads from Western Europe leading into Italy are toll-free, with some notable exceptions. If you use the Swiss superhighway network, you'll have to buy a special tax sticker at the frontier. You'll also pay to go through the St. Gotthard Tunnel into Italy. Crossings from France can be through the Mont Blanc Tunnel, for which you'll pay, or you can leave the French Riviera at Menton and drive directly into Italy along the Italian Riviera toward San Remo.

If you don't want to drive such distances, ask a travel agent to book you on a Motorail arrangement where the train carries your car. This service, however, is good only to Milan, as there are no car and sleeper expresses running the 400 miles south to Rome.

9   Getting Around Italy

BY PLANE

Italy's domestic air network on **Alitalia** (☎ **800/223-5730** in the United States or 0171/602-7111 in the U.K.; www.alitalia.it/english/index.html) is one of the largest and most complete in Europe. There are some 40 airports serviced regularly from Rome, and most flights are under an hour. Fares vary, but some discounts are available. Tickets are discounted 50% for passengers 2 to 11 years old; for passengers 12 to 22, there's a youth fare. And anyone can get a 30% reduction by taking domestic flights departing at night.

BY TRAIN

Trains provide a medium-priced means of transport, even if you don't buy the Eurailpass or one of the special Italian Railway tickets (below). As a rule of thumb, second-class travel usually costs about two-thirds the price of an equivalent first-class trip. A *couchette* (a private fold-down bed in a communal cabin) requires a supplement above the price of first-class travel. In a land where *mamma* and *bambini* are highly valued, children 4 to 11 receive a discount of 50% off the adult fare and children 3 and under travel free with their parents.

An **Italian Railpass** (known in Italy as a **BTLC Pass**) allows non-Italian citizens to ride as much as they like on Italy's entire rail network. Buy the pass in the United States or at main train stations in Italy, have it validated the first time you use it at any rail station, and ride as frequently as you like within the time validity. An 8-day pass is $266 first class and $177 second, a 15-day pass $332 first class and $221 second, a

Travel Times Between the Major Cities

Cities	Distance	Air Travel Time	Train Travel Time	Driving Time
Florence to Milan	298km/185 mi	55 min	2½ hrs	3½ hrs
Florence to Venice	281km/174 mi	2 hrs, 5 min	4 hrs	3¼ hrs
Milan to Venice	267km/166 mi	50 min	3½ hrs	3 hr, 10 min
Rome to Florence	277km/172 mi	1 hr, 10 min	2½ hrs	3⅓ hrs
Rome to Milan	572km/355 mi	1 hr, 5 min	5 hrs	6½ hrs
Rome to Naples	219km/136 mi	50 min	2½ hrs	2½ hrs
Rome to Venice	528km/327 mi	1 hr, 5 min	5¼ hrs	6 hrs
Rome to Genoa	501km/311 mi	1 hr	6 hrs	5¾ hrs
Rome to Turin	669km/415 mi	1 hr, 5 min	9–11 hrs	7¾ hrs

21-day pass $386 first class and $257 second, and a 30-day pass $465 first class and $310 second. All passes have a $15 issuing fee per class.

With the Italian Railpass and each of the other special passes, a supplement must be paid to ride on certain rapid trains, designated **ETR-450** or **Pendolino trains.** The rail systems of Sardinia are administered by a separate entity and aren't included in the Railpass or any of the other passes.

Another option is the **Italian Flexirail Card,** which entitles you to a predetermined number of days of travel on any rail line in a certain time period. It's ideal for passengers who plan in advance to spend several days sightseeing before boarding a train for another city. A pass giving 4 possible travel days out of a block of 1 month is $209 first class and $139 second, a pass for 8 travel days stretched over a 1-month period $293 first class and $195 second, and a pass for 12 travel days within 1 month $375 first class and $250 second.

In addition, the **Kilometric Ticket** is valid for 2 months' worth of travel on regular trains. (You can use it on special train rides if you pay a supplement.) The ticket is valid for 20 trips, providing that the total distance covered doesn't exceed 1,875 miles. The price is $264 first class and $156 second. The issuing fee is $25 per pass.

You can buy any of these passes from a travel agent or at **CIT Tours,** the official representative of Italian State Railway, with offices at 15 W. 44th St., Suite 104, New York, NY 10036 (☎ **800/243-8687** or 212/730-2121; fax 212/730-4544); at 6033 W. Century Blvd., Suite 980, Los Angeles, CA 90045 (☎ **800/248-8687** or 310/338-8616; fax 310/670-4269); or at 9501 W. Devon Ave., Suite 502, Rosemont, IL 60018 (☎ **800/223-7987** or 847/318-1031). For price information, call ☎ **800/248-8687.**

BY BUS

Italy has an extensive and intricate bus network, covering all regions. However, because rail travel is inexpensive, the bus is not the preferred method of travel. Besides, drivers seem to go on strike every 2 weeks.

One of the leading bus operators is **SITA,** Viale del Cadorna 105, Florence (☎ 055/47821). SITA buses serve most parts of the country, especially the central belt, including Tuscany, but not the far frontiers. Among the largest of the other companies, with special emphasis in the north and central tiers, is **Autostradale,** Piazzale Castello, Milan (☎ 02/801-161). **Lazzi,** Via Mercadante 2, Florence (☎ 055/363-041) goes through Tuscany, including Siena, and much of central Italy.

Where these nationwide services leave off, **local bus companies** operate in most regions, particularly in the hill sections and the alpine regions where rail travel isn't possible. For more information, see "Getting There" in the various city, town, and village sections.

BY CAR

U.S. and Canadian drivers must carry an **International Driver's License** when touring Italy or obtain a declaration from the **Automobile Club d'Italia (ACI)** entitling them to drive on Italian roads. The declaration is available from any ACI frontier or provincial office; to obtain the declaration, U.S. or Canadian drivers must present a valid driver's license from their home country with an Italian translation. (Several organizations, including AAA, can provide translations.) The possession of such a translation is intended to facilitate procedures with Italian police personnel, who don't necessarily understand English text. In practice, however, the translation is often not even looked at. But if you're respecting the letter of the Italian law, it's necessary to have it.

Apply for an International Driver's License at any **American Automobile Association (AAA)** branch. You must be at least 18 and have two 2- by 2-inch photographs, a $10 fee, and a photocopy of your U.S. driver's license with a AAA application form. To find the AAA office nearest you, check the local telephone directory or contact AAA's national headquarters at 1000 AAA Dr., Heathrow, FL 32746-5063 (☎ 800/222-4357 or 407/444-7000). Remember that an International Driver's License is valid only if physically accompanied by your original driver's license and is signed on the back. In Canada, you can get the address of the Canadian Automobile Association closest to you by calling ☎ 613/247-0117.

The **Automobile Club d'Italia (ACI)** is the equivalent of the American Automobile Association. It has offices throughout Italy, including the head office at Via Marsala 8, 00185 Roma (☎ 06/4998-2389), open Monday to Friday 8am to 2pm. The ACI's 24-hour **Information and Assistance Center (CAT)** is at Via Magenta 5, 00185 Roma (☎ 06/4477). Both offices are near the main rail station (Stazione Termini).

RENTALS Many of the most charming landscapes in Italy lie away from the main cities, far away from the train stations. For that, and for sheer convenience, renting a car is usually the best way to explore the country. But you have to be a pretty aggressive and alert driver who won't be fazed by super-high speeds on the autostrada or narrow streets in the cities and towns. Italian drivers have truly earned their reputation as bad but daring.

However, the legalities and contractual obligations of renting a car in Italy (where accident and theft rates are very high) are more complicated than in almost any other European country. To rent a car here, a driver must have nerves of steel, a sense of humor, a valid driver's license, and a valid passport and (in most cases) be over 25. Payment and paperwork are simpler if you present a valid credit card with your completed rental contract. If that isn't possible, you'll almost surely be required to pay a substantial deposit, sometimes in cash. Insurance on all vehicles is compulsory, though any reputable rental firm will arrange it in advance before you're even given the keys.

The three major car-rental companies in Italy are **Avis** (☎ 800/331-2112; www.avis.com), **Budget** (☎ 800/472-3325; www.budgetrentacar.com), and **Hertz** (☎ 800/654-3001; www.hertz.com). U.S.-based companies specializing in European car rentals are **Auto-Europe** (☎ 800/223-5555; www.autoeurope.com); **Europe by Car** (☎ 800/223-1516, 800/252-9401 in California, or 212/581-3040 in New York; www.europebycar.com); and **Kemwel** (☎ 800/678-0678; www.kemwel.com).

In some cases, slight discounts are offered to members of the American Automobile Association (AAA) or the American Association of Retired Persons (AARP). Be sure to ask.

Each company offers a **collision-damage waiver (CDW)** at $14 to $21 per day (depending on the car's value). Some companies include CDWs in the prices they quote; others don't. This extra protection will cover all or part of the repair-related costs if you have an accident. (In some cases, even if you buy the CDW, you'll pay $200 to $300 per accident. Ask questions before you sign.) If you don't have CDW and have an accident, you'll usually pay for all damages, up to the car's replacement cost. Because most newcomers aren't familiar with local driving customs and conditions, we highly recommend you buy the CDW, though certain credit-card issuers will compensate you for any accident-related liability to a rented car if the imprint of their card appears on the rental contract. In addition, because of Italy's rising theft rate, all three of the major U.S.-based companies offer theft and break-in protection policies (Avis and Budget require it). For pickups at most Italy airports, all three companies must impose a 10% government tax. To avoid that charge, consider picking your car up at an inner-city location. There's also an unavoidable 19% government tax, though more and more companies are including this in the rates they quote.

GASOLINE   Gasoline (known as *benzina*) is expensive in Italy, as are *autostrade* tolls. Carry enough cash if you're going to do extensive motoring and be prepared for sticker shock every time you fill up even a medium-sized car with "super benzina," which has the octane rating appropriate for most of the cars you'll be able to rent. It's priced throughout the country at around 2,000L ($1.15) per liter (about 7,400L/ $4.30 per gallon). Filling up the tank of a medium-sized car can set you back around 78,000L ($45).

Gas stations on autostrade are open 24 hours, but on regular roads gas stations are rarely open on Sunday, many close noon to 3pm for lunch, and most shut down after 7pm. Make sure the pump registers zero before an attendant starts refilling your tank. A popular scam, particularly in the south, is to fill your tank before resetting the meter so you pay not only your bill but the charges run up by the previous motorist.

DRIVING RULES   The Italian Highway Code follows the Geneva Convention and Italy uses international road signs. Driving is on the right, passing on the left. Violators of the highway code are fined; serious violations may also be punished by imprisonment. In cities and towns, the speed limit is 50 kilometers per hour (kmph) or 31 miles per hour (mph). For all cars and motor vehicles on main roads and local roads, the limit is 90 kmph or 56 mph. For the autostrade (national express highways), the limit is 130 kmph or 81 mph. Use the left lane only for passing. If a driver zooms up behind you on the autostrade with his or her lights on, that's your sign to get out of the way! Use of seat belts is compulsory.

ROAD MAPS   The best touring maps are published by the **Automobile Club d'Italia (ACI)** and the **Italian Touring Club,** or you can purchase the maps of the **Carta Automobilistica d'Italia,** covering Italy in two maps on the scale of 1:800,000 (1cm = 8km). These two maps should fulfill the needs of most motorists. If you plan to explore one region of Italy in depth, consider one of 15 regional maps (1:200,000; 1cm = 2km), published by **Grande Carta Stradale d'Italia.**

All maps mentioned above are sold at certain newsstands and at all major bookstores in Italy, especially those with travel departments. Many travel bookstores in the United States also carry them. If U.S. outlets don't have these maps, they often offer **Michelin's red map of Italy** (no. 988), on a scale of 1:1,000,000 (1cm = 10km).

BREAKDOWNS & ASSISTANCE   In case of car breakdown or for any tourist information, foreign motorists can call ☎ **116** (nationwide telephone service). For road information, itineraries, and all sorts of travel assistance, call ☎ **06/4477** (ACI's information center located near the Automobile Club d'Italia). Both services operate 24 hours.

BY FERRY

Ferries are used primarily in the south. Driving time from Naples to Sicily is cut considerably by taking one of the vessels operated by **Tirrenia Lines,** Molo Angioino, Stazione Marittima, in Naples (☎ **081/720-1111;** fax 081/720-1297). Departures are daily at 8pm for the 10-hour trip from Naples to Palermo. With slight variations for the season, expect to pay around 80,000L ($46) for a one-way pedestrian fare and around 140,000L ($81) for one-way passage with a car and up to two passengers, plus any supplements if you want to rent a cabin. Arrival time in Palermo is 7am the next day. Naples is also the site of frequent ferry and hydrofoil departures for the offshore islands of Capri and Ischia.

10 Tips on Accommodations

Italy controls the prices of its hotels, designating a minimum and a maximum rate. The difference between the two may depend on the season, the room's location, or even its size. Italian hotels are **classified by stars,** indicating their category of comfort: five stars for deluxe, four for first class, three for second, two for third, and one for fourth. Government ratings don't depend on the decoration or on frescoed ceilings but rather on facilities, such as elevators and the like. Many of the finest hostelries in Italy are rated second class because they serve only breakfast (a blessing for those seeking to escape the board requirements).

   Reservations are advised, even in the so-called slow months of November to March. Travel to Italy peaks from May to October, when moderate and budget hotels are full.

APARTMENTS, VILLAS & PALAZZI

For information on renting villas or apartments, you may write directly to the local tourist board or provincial tourist office in the city or town where you expect to stay. For addresses, refer to "Essentials" in the individual city or town listings. Information on villas and apartments is also available in daily newspapers or through local real-estate agents in Italy.

   These organizations rent villas or apartments: **Hideaways International,** 767 Islington St., Portsmouth, NH 03801 (☎ **800/843-4433** or 603/430-4433; www.hideaways.com); **At Home Abroad, Inc.,** 405 E. 56th St., Suite 6H, New York, NY 10022-2466 (☎ **212/421-9165;** fax 212/752-1591); **Rent a Vacation Everywhere, Inc. (RAVE),** 135 Meigs St., Rochester, NY 14607 (☎ **716/256-0760;** fax 716/256-2676); **Hometours International, Inc.,** P.O. Box 11503, Knoxville, TN

A Note on Bathrooms & Garages

All accommodations listed in this guide have a **private bathroom** unless specified otherwise. Hotel bathrooms in Italy have either a **shower stall** or a **tub/shower combination;** your chances of getting either are 50/50. Most hotels in Italy don't have **parking garages;** for those that do, we have indicated any charges.

37939 (☎ **800/367-4668**); **Grand Luxe International, Inc.,** 165 Chestnut St., Allendale, NJ 07401 (☎ **201/327-2333;** www.grandluxe.com); and **Rentals in Italy,** 1742 Calle Corva, Camarillo, CA 93010 (☎ **800/726-6702** or 805/987-5278; fax 805/482-7976; www.rentvillas.com).

If you're looking to stay in a historic palazzo or castello, you may be interested in the deluxe accommodations provided by **Abitare la Storia,** Località L'Amorosa, 53048 Sinalunga (Siena) (☎ **0577/632-256;** fax 0577/632-160). This nonprofit organization represents owner-managed hotels, residences, restaurants, and conventions centers around Italy, in the city and the country.

FARMHOUSES

Another option is to stay in a house, an apartment, or a bedroom on an Italian farm as part of a program known as *agriturismo*. Most of the farms lie in rural areas outside the town centers.

Italy Farm Holidays, 547 Martling Ave., Tarrytown, NY 10591 (☎ **914/ 631-7880;** fax 914/631-8831), represents about 50 working farms scattered for the most part in the Piedmont, Tuscany, Umbria, Veneto, and Puglia, any of which would be suitable as a base for touring the region's art cities.

Each farm or cooperative has passed inspection, and some of the most desirable ones lie just a few miles from the heart of Florence and Siena. Most properties require minimum stays of 3 to 7 days and payment in full in advance. Many offer meals (usually breakfast) as part of the arrangement; others provide amenities like free use of bikes or optional horseback riding. Only a few of the places contain more than seven rentable accommodations, most have private bathrooms, and many contain kitchens of their own.

Weekly rates for two begin at around $600 in low season in a modest apartment or B&B, rising to around $5,000 in high season for an elegant villa or a historic castle suitable for up to 10 occupants. House cleaning or maid service isn't provided unless it's specifically arranged as a supplement or when you stay for more than 1 week in an apartment or house.

RELIGIOUS INSTITUTIONS

Convents, monasteries, and other religious institutions in Italy offer accommodations, generally of the fourth-class hotel or *pensioni* category. Some are just for men; others are for women only. Many, however, accept married couples. Italian tourist offices generally have abbreviated listings of these places, or you can write directly to the archdiocese (Archidiocesi di Roma, for example) in cities in which you desire such an accommodation.

Accommodations can range from rather luxurious convents to bone-bare monastic cells. One of the main reasons to stay in a religious institution is economy, as the rooms are invariably cheaper than those in hotels or pensioni.

11 Tips on Dining

For a quick bite, go to a *bar*—while it does serve alcohol, it functions mainly as a cafe. Prices here have a split personality: *al banco* is standing at the bar, while *à tavola* means sitting at a table where they'll wait on you and charge two to four times as much. In bars you can find *panini* sandwiches on various rolls and *tramezzini* (giant triangles of white-bread sandwiches with the crusts cut off). These both run 2,000L to 6,000L ($1.35 to $4) and are traditionally stuck in a kind of tiny press to flatten and toast them so the crust is crispy and the filling hot and gooey; microwaves have unfortunately invaded and are everywhere, turning *panini* into something resembling a soggy hot tissue.

Pizza a taglio or *pizza rustica* indicate a place where you can order pizza by the slice—though Florence is infamous for serving some of Italy's worst pizza this way. Florentines fare somewhat better at *pizzerie,* casual sit-down restaurants that cook large, round pizzas with very thin crusts in wood-burning ovens. A *tavola calda* (literally "hot table") serves ready-made hot foods you can either take away or eat at one of the few small tables often available. The food is usually very good, and you can get away with a full meal at a *tavola calda* for well under 25,000L ($17). A *rosticceria* is the same type of place with some chickens roasting on a spit in the window.

Full-fledged restaurants go by the names *osteria, trattoria,* or *ristorante.* Once upon a time, these terms meant something—*osterie* were basic places where you could get a plate of spaghetti and a glass of wine; *trattorie* were casual places serving simple full meals of filling peasant fare; and *ristoranti* were fancier places, with waiters in bowties, printed menus, a wine list, and hefty prices. Nowadays, fancy restaurants often go by the name of trattoria to cash in on the associated charm factor, trendy spots use osteria to show they're hip, and simple inexpensive places sometimes tack on ristorante to ennoble themselves.

You'll find at many restaurants, especially larger ones and in cities, a *menu turistico* (tourists' menu), costing anywhere from 10,000L ($7) to 40,000L ($27), sometimes called *menu del giorno* (menu of the day).This set-price menu usually covers all meal incidentals—including table wine, cover charge, and 15% service charge—along with a first course (*primo*) and second course (*secondo*), but it almost always offers an abbreviated selection of pretty bland dishes: spaghetti in tomato sauce and slices of pork. Sometimes better is a *menu à prezzo fisso* (fixed-price menu). It usually doesn't include wine but sometimes covers the service and *coperto* and often offers a wider selection of better dishes, occasionally house specialties and local foods. Ordering à la carte, however, offers you the best chance for a memorable meal. Even better, forego the menu entirely and put yourself in the capable hands of your waiter.

It's also possible to go into one of hundreds of general food stores (*alimentari*) throughout the country and have sandwiches prepared on the spot or buy the makings for a picnic lunch to be enjoyed in a park.

FAST FACTS: Italy

American Express   Offices are found in Rome at Piazza di Spagna 38 (☎ 06/ 67-641), in Florence on Via Dante Alighieri (☎ 055/50-981), in Venice at San Marco 1471 (☎ 041/167-87-20-00), and in Milan at Via Brera 3 (☎ 02/ 72-00-36-93). All offices are now open Monday to Friday 9am to 5:30pm and Saturday 9am to 12:30pm. The money transactions section of the Venice office is open Monday to Saturday 8am to 8pm.

Business Hours   Regular business hours are generally Monday to Friday 9am (sometimes 9:30am) to 1pm and 3:30 (sometimes 4) to 7 or 7:30pm. In July or August, **offices** may not open in the afternoon until 4:30 or 5pm. **Banks** are open Monday to Friday 8:30am to 1 or 1:30pm and 2 or 2:30 to 4pm and are closed all day Saturday, Sunday, and national holidays. The midafternoon closing (*riposo*) is often observed in Rome, Naples, and most southern cities; however, in Milan and other northern and central cities the custom has been abolished by some merchants. Most shops are closed on Sunday, except for certain barbershops that are open on Sunday morning and tourist-oriented stores that are now permitted to remain open on Sunday during the high season. If you're in Italy in summer and the heat is intense, we suggest you learn the custom of the riposo too.

Drug Laws　Penalties are severe and could lead to either imprisonment or deportation. Selling drugs to minors is dealt with particularly harshly.

Drugstores　At every drugstore (*farmacia*) there's a list of those that are open at night and on Sunday.

Electricity　The electricity in Italy varies considerably. It's usually alternating current (AC), varying from 42 to 50 cycles. The voltage can be anywhere from 115 to 220. It's recommended that any visitor carrying electrical appliances obtain a transformer. Check the exact local current with the hotel where you're staying. Plugs have prongs that are round, not flat; therefore, an adapter plug is also needed.

Embassies/Consulates　In case of an emergency, embassies have a 24-hour referral service.

The **U.S. Embassy** is in Rome at Via Vittorio Veneto 119A (☎ **06/46-741;** fax 06/488-2672). **U.S. consulates** are in Florence at Lungarno Amerigo Vespucci 46 (☎ **055/239-8276;** fax 055/284-088) and Milan at Via Principe Amedeo 2–10 (☎ **02/29-03-51-41**). The embassy and consulates are open Monday to Friday 8:30am to noon and 2 to 5:30pm. There's also a consulate in Naples on Piazza della Repubblica (☎ **081/583-8111**), open Monday to Friday 8am to 1pm and 2 to 5pm. The consulate in Genoa is at Via Dante 2 (☎ **010/ 58-44-92**), open Monday only noon to 2pm.

The **Canadian Consulate** and passport service is in Rome at Via Zara 30 (☎ **06/445-981**). The **Canadian Embassy** in Rome is at Via G. B. de Rossi 27 (☎ **06/445-981;** fax 06/445-98754). Both offices are open Monday to Friday 8:30am to 12:30pm.

The **U.K. Embassy** is in Rome at Via XX Settembre 80A (☎ **06/482-5441;** fax 06/487-3324), open Monday to Friday 9:15am to 1:30pm. The **U.K. Consulate** in Florence is at Lungarno Corsini 2 (☎ **055/284-133**), open Monday to Friday 9:30am to 12:30pm and 2:30 to 4:30pm. The **Consulate General** in Naples is at Via Francesco Crispi 122 (☎ **081/663-511**), open Monday to Friday 9am to 12:30pm and 2 to 4:30pm. In Milan, contact the office at Via San Paolo 7 (☎ **02/723-001**), open Monday to Friday 9:15am to 12:15pm and 2:30 to 4:30pm.

The **Australian Embassy** is in Rome at Via Alessandria 215 (☎ **06/852-721;** fax 06/852-723-00), open Monday to Thursday from 8:30am to 12:30pm and 1:30 to 5:30pm and Friday 8:30am to 1:15pm. The **Australian Consulate** is in Rome at Corso Trieste 25 (☎ **06/852-721**), open Monday to Thursday 9am to noon and 1:30 to 5pm and Friday 9am to 1pm.

The **New Zealand Embassy** is in Rome at Via Zara 28 (☎ **06/440-2928;** fax 06/440-2984), open Monday to Friday from 8:30am to 12:45pm and 1:45 to 5pm. The **Irish Embassy** in Rome is at Piazza di Campitelli 3 (☎ **06/ 697-9121;** fax 06/679-2354), open Monday to Friday 9:30am to 12:30pm and 2 to 4pm. For consular queries, dial ☎ **06/697-91211.**

Emergencies　Dial ☎ **113** for an ambulance, police, or fire. In case of a breakdown on an Italian road, dial ☎ **116** at the nearest telephone box; the nearest Automobile Club of Italy (ACI) will be notified to come to your aid.

Legal Aid　The consulate of your country is the place to turn, though offices can't interfere in the Italian legal process. They can, however, inform you of your rights and provide a list of attorneys. You'll have to pay for the attorney out of your pocket—there's no free legal assistance. If you're arrested for a drug offense, about all the consulate will do is notify a lawyer about your case and perhaps inform your family.

Liquor Laws   Wine with meals has been a normal part of family life for hundreds of years in Italy. Children are exposed to wine at an early age, and consumption of alcohol isn't anything out of the ordinary. There's no legal drinking age for buying or ordering alcohol. Alcohol is sold day and night throughout the year, as there's almost no restriction on the sale of wine or liquor in Italy.

Mail   Mail delivery in Italy is notoriously bad. One letter from a soldier, postmarked in 1945, arrived in his home village in 1982. Letters sent from New York, say, in November, are often delivered (if at all) the following year. Don't trust the mail for your hotel reservations and deposits; fax your hotel if possible and try to put deposits on your credit card instead of sending a check. Your family and friends back home may receive your postcards in a week, or it might take 8 weeks (sometimes longer). Postcards, aerogrammes, and letters weighing up to 20 grams to the United States and Canada cost 1,300L (75¢), to the United Kingdom and Ireland 800L (45¢), and to Australia and New Zealand 1,400L (80¢). You can purchase stamps at all post offices and at *tabacchi* (tobacco) stores.

Newspapers/Magazines   In major cities, it's possible to find the *International Herald Tribune* or *USA Today* as well as other English-language newspapers and magazines, including *Time* and *Newsweek*, at hotels and news kiosks. The *Rome Daily American* is published in English.

Police   Dial ☎ **113,** the all-purpose number for police emergency assistance in Italy.

Rest Rooms   All airport and rail stations, of course, have rest rooms, often with attendants, who expect to be tipped. Bars, nightclubs, restaurants, cafes, gas stations, and all hotels have facilities as well. Public toilets are also found near many of the major sights. Usually they're designated as *WC* (water closet) or *donne* (women) or *uomini* (men). The most confusing designation is *signori* (gentlemen) and *signore* (ladies), so watch that final *i* and *e!* Many public toilets charge a small fee or employ an attendant who expects a tip, so always keep a few 200L and 500L coins on hand. It's also a good idea to carry some tissues in your pocket or purse—they often come in handy!

Safety   The most common menace, especially in large cities, particularly Rome, is the plague of pickpockets and roving gangs of Gypsy children who virtually surround you, distract you in all the confusion, and steal your purse or wallet. Never leave valuables in a car and never travel with your car unlocked. A U.S. State Department travel advisory warns that every car (whether parked, stopped at a traffic light, or even moving) can be a potential target for armed robbery.

Taxes   As a member of the European Union, Italy imposes a **value-added tax** (called **IVA** in Italy) on most goods and services. The tax most affecting visitors is the one imposed on hotel rates, which ranges from 9% in first- and second-class hotels to 19% in deluxe hotels.

Non-EU (European Union) citizens are entitled to a **refund of the IVA** if they spend more than 300,000L ($174) at any one store, before tax. To claim your refund, request an invoice from the cashier at the store and take it to the Customs office (*dogana*) at the airport to have it stamped before you leave. *Note:* If you're going to another EU country before flying home, have it stamped at the airport Customs office of the last EU country you will be in (for example, if you're flying home via Britain, have your Italian invoices stamped in London). Once back home, mail the stamped invoice (keeping a photocopy for your records) back to the original vendor within 90 days of the purchase. The vendor will, sooner or later, send you a refund of the tax you paid at the time of your original purchase. Reputable stores view this as a matter of ordinary paperwork and are businesslike about it. Less honorable stores might lose your dossier. It pays to deal with established vendors on large purchases. You can also request that the refund be credited to the credit card with which you made the purchase; this is usually a faster procedure.

Many shops are now part of the **"Tax Free for Tourists"** network (look for the sticker in the window). Stores participating in this network issue a check along with your invoice at the time of purchase. After you have the invoice stamped at Customs, you can redeem the check for cash directly at the Tax Free booth in the airport—in Rome, it's past Customs; in Milan's airports the booth is inside the Duty Free shop—or mail it back in the envelope provided within 60 days.

Telephone/Fax/Telegrams   A **local phone call** in Italy costs 200L (10¢). **Public phones** accept coins, precharged phone cards (*scheda* or *carta telefonica*), or both. You can buy a carta telefonica at any tabacchi (tobacconists; most display a sign with a white *T* on a brown background) in increments of 5,000L ($2.90), 10,000L ($6), and 15,000L ($9). To make a call, pick up the receiver and insert 200L or your card (break off the corner first). Most phones have a digital display that will tell you how much money you've inserted (or how much is left on the card). Dial the number, and don't forget to take the card with you after you hang up.

To **call from one city code to another,** dial the city code, complete with initial zero, then the number. To **dial direct internationally,** dial 00, then the country code, the area code, and the number. Country codes are as follows: the United States and Canada 1, the United Kingdom 44, Ireland 353, Australia 61, New Zealand 64. Make international calls from a public phone if possible, because hotels almost invariably charge ridiculously inflated rates for direct dial, but bring plenty of schede to feed the phone. Calls dialed directly are billed on the basis of the call's duration only. A reduced rate is applied 11pm to 8am on Monday to Saturday and all day Sunday. Direct-dial calls from the United States to Italy are much cheaper, so arrange for whomever to call you at your hotel.

To ring free, **national telephone information** (in Italian) in Italy, dial ☎ **12.** **International information** is available at ☎ **176** but costs 1,200L (70¢) a shot.

To **make collect or calling card calls,** drop in 200L (10¢) or insert your card (don't worry—the call's free and you get the money back when you're done), dial one of the numbers below, and an American operator will be on shortly to assist you (as Italy has yet to discover the joys of the touch-tone phone, you'll have to wait for the operator to come on). The following calling-card numbers work all over Italy: **AT&T** 172-1011, **MCI** 172-1022, **Sprint** 172-1877. To make collect calls to a country besides the United States, dial ☎ **170** (free) and practice your Italian counting in order to relay the number to the Italian operator. Tell him or her you want it *al carico del destinatario.*

Don't count on all Italian phones having touch-tone service! You may not be able to access your voice mail or answering machine if you call home from Italy.

Your hotel will most likely be able to send or receive **faxes** for you, sometimes at inflated prices, sometimes at cost. Otherwise, most *cartolerie* (stationery stores), *copisti* or *fotocopie* (photocopy shops), and some *tabacchi* (tobacconists)

Calling Italy

To call Italy from the United States, dial the **international prefix, 011;** then Italy's **country code, 39;** then the **city code** (for example, **06** for Rome and **055** for Florence); then the actual **phone number.**

Note that numbers in Italy do indeed range from four to eight digits in length. Also note that, when calling from outside Italy, you must now include the zero in the city code (previously you had to drop the zero). This also applies when you call anywhere within Italy—even when you're calling within the town you're visiting.

---

offer fax services. For **telegrams,** ITALCABLE operates services abroad, transmitting messages by cable or satellite. Both internal and foreign telegrams may be dictated over the phone by calling ☎ **186.**

Time   In terms of standard time zones, Italy is 6 hours ahead of eastern standard time in the United States. Daylight saving time goes into effect in Italy each year from the end of March to the end of September.

Tipping   This custom is practiced with flair in Italy—many people depend on tips for their livelihoods. In **hotels,** the service charge of 15% to 19% is already added to a bill. In addition, it's customary to tip the chambermaid 1,000L (60¢) per day; the doorman (for calling a cab) 1,000L (60¢); and the bellhop or porter 3,000L to 5,000L ($1.75 to $2.90) for carrying your bags to your room. A concierge expects about 15% of his or her bill, as well as tips for extra services performed, which could include help with long-distance calls. In expensive hotels these lire amounts are often doubled.

In **restaurants and cafes,** 15% is usually added to your bill to cover most charges. An additional tip isn't expected, but it's nice to leave the equivalent of an extra couple of dollars if you've been pleased with the service. Checkroom attendants expect 1,500L (85¢), and washroom attendants should get 200L to 500L (10¢ to 25¢). Restaurants are required by law to give customers official receipts. **Taxi drivers** expect at least 15% of the fare.

Water   Though most Italians take mineral water with their meals, tap water is safe everywhere, as are public drinking fountains. Unsafe sources will be marked ACQUA NON POTABILE. If tap water comes out cloudy, it's only the calcium or other minerals inherent in a water supply that often comes untreated from fresh springs.

4 Settling into Rome: The Eternal City

Rome is a city of images, vivid and unforgettable. You can see one of the most striking at dawn—ideally from Janiculum Hill—when the city's silhouette, with its bell towers and cupolas, gradually comes into focus. Rome is also a city of sounds, beginning early in the morning with the peal of church bells calling the faithful to mass. The streets quickly fill with cars, taxis, and motor scooters, blaring their horns as they weave in and out of traffic. The sidewalks become overrun with office workers rushing off to their desks, but not before stealing into cafes for their first cappuccino of the day. Shop owners throw up the metal grilles protecting their stores as loudly as possible, seeming to delight in their contribution to the general din. The fruit-and-vegetable stands buzz with activity, as an eclectic group of Romans arrives to buy the day's supply of fresh produce, haggling over prices and caviling over quality.

Around 10am the tourists take to the streets, battling the crowds and traffic as they wend from Renaissance palaces and baroque buildings to the Colosseum and the Forum, symbols of a once-great empire whose heart was Rome, the Eternal City. Indeed, Rome often appears to have two populations: one of Romans and one of visitors (during summer especially). Of course, if you visit in August, you may not see many true Romans—the locals flee the heat at that time. Or as one Roman woman once told us, "Even if we're too poor to go on vacation, we close the shutters and pretend we're away so neighbors won't find out we couldn't afford to leave the city."

The traffic, alas, is worse than ever, and in many places the car exhaust has left a layer of grime coating buildings, fountains, and statues that were gleaming white in decades past. Restoration programs are underway all over the city, but this is Italy, so everything proceeds at a leisurely pace.

But in spite of all the crowds and chaos, Romans still live the good life. After you've wandered through the Colosseum, marveled at the Pantheon, traipsed through St. Peter's, and thrown a coin in the Trevi Fountain, you can pause to experience the charm of Rome at dusk. Find a cafe at summer twilight and watch the shades of pink and rose turn to gold and copper before night finally falls. That's when a new Rome awakens. The cafes and restaurants grow more animated and more fun, especially if you've found one on an antique piazza or along a narrow alley deep in Trastevere. After dinner, you can stroll by the lighted fountains or through Piazza Navona and have a gelato—and the night is yours.

As the city prepares for Roma 2000 and the millennium, it will be upgrading its urban landscape with better traffic signals, trees along the roads, flower beds in traffic islands, small public gardens in various areas, and restoration of ancient monuments, among many other improvements. That's on the horizon and in the works, but it doesn't have to dampen your visit in the meantime—though you may see lots of scaffolding.

In chapter 5 we'll tell you all about the historic sites, great museums, and cultural highlights. These are important ingredients in the appreciation of this centuries-old city, the key to its fascinating past. But Rome is also a vibrant modern metropolis, pulsing with all kinds of activities day and night. As you take part in them, you'll find yourself embracing the city's life with intensity, like a Roman.

1 Essentials

ARRIVING

BY PLANE   Chances are you'll arrive in Italy at Rome's **Leonardo da Vinci International Airport** (☎ 06/65-951 or 06/6595-3640 for information), popularly known as **Fiumicino,** 18½ miles from the city center. (If you're flying by charter, you might wing into Ciampino Airport; see below.)

After you leave Passport Control, you'll see two information desks (one for Rome, one for Italy). At the Rome desk you can pick up a general (not detailed) map and some pamphlets Monday to Saturday 8:30am to 7pm; the staff here can also help you find a hotel room if you haven't reserved ahead. A *cambio* (money exchange) operates daily 7:30am to 11pm and offers surprisingly good rates. Luggage storage is available 24 hours in the main arrivals building daily, costing 5,000L ($2.90) per bag.

There's a **train station** in the airport. To get into the city, follow the signs marked TRENI for the 30-minute shuttle service running to the main station, **Stazione Termini** (arriving on Track 22). It runs 7am to 10pm for 15,000L ($9) one-way. On the way you'll pass a machine dispensing tickets automatically, or you can buy them in person near the tracks if you don't have small bills on you yet. When you arrive at Termini, get out of the train as quickly as possible and grab a baggage cart. It's a long schlepp from Track 22 to the exit or to the other train connections, and there never seem to be enough baggage carts available.

Should you arrive on a charter flight at **Ciampino** (☎ 06/794-941), take a COTRAL bus, departing every 30 minutes or so, which will deliver you to the Anagnina stop of Metropolitana Line A. Take Line A to Stazione Termini, where you can make your final connections. Trip time is about 45 minutes, costing 2,000L ($1.15).

Taxis from Fiumicino (da Vinci) to the city are expensive—70,000L ($41) and up. From Ciampino, the rate is the same but the trip shorter. Call ☎ 06/6645, 06/3570, or 06/4994 for information.

BY TRAIN OR BUS   Trains and buses arrive in the center of old Rome at the silver **Stazione Termini,** Piazza dei Cinquecento (☎ 1478/880-881); this is the train, bus, and subway transportation hub for all Rome and is surrounded by many hotels (especially cheaper ones).

If you're taking the **Metropolitana** (Rome's subway network), follow the illuminated red-and-white M signs. To catch a **bus,** go straight through the outer hall and enter the sprawling bus lot of Piazza dei Cinquecento. You'll also find taxis there.

The station is filled with services. At a branch of the Banca San Paolo di Torino (between Tracks 8 to 11 and Tracks 12 to 15) you can exchange money. Informazioni Ferroviarie (in the outer hall) dispenses information on rail travel to other parts of

A Few Train Station Warnings

In Stazione Termini, you'll almost certainly be approached by touts claiming to work for a tourist organization. They really work for individual hotels (not always the most recommendable) and will say almost anything to sell you a room. Unless you know something about Rome's layout and are savvy, it's best to ignore them.

Be aware of all your belongings at all times and be sure to keep your wallet and purse away from professionally experienced fingers. Never ever leave your bags unattended for even a second, and while making phone calls or waiting in line, make sure your attention doesn't wander from any bags you've set by your side or on the ground. Be aware if someone asks *you* for directions or information—it's meant to distract you and easily will.

Ignore the taxi drivers soliciting passengers right outside the terminal; they can charge unaware travelers as much as triple the normal amount. Instead, line up in the taxi queue in Piazza dei Cinquecento.

Italy. There's also a tourist information booth here, along with baggage services, newsstands, and snack bars.

BY CAR   From the north, the main access route is the **Autostrada del Sole (A1),** cutting through Milan and Florence, or you can take the coastal route, **SSI Aurelia,** from Genoa. If you're driving north from Naples, you take the southern lap of the **Autostrada del Sole (A2).** All the autostrade join with the **Grande Raccordo Anulare,** a ring road encircling Rome, channeling traffic into the congested city. Long before you reach this road, you should study a map carefully to see what part of Rome you plan to enter and mark your route accordingly. Route markings along the ring road tend to be confusing.

Return your rental car immediately, or at least get yourself to a hotel, park your car, and leave it. We don't recommend driving in Rome at all. The traffic is just too nightmarish.

VISITOR INFORMATION

Information is available at three locations maintained by the Aziebda Provinciale di Turismo (APT). They include a kiosk at **Leonardo da Vinci Airport** (☎ 06/6595-6074); a kiosk in **Stazione Termini** (☎ 06/487-1270); and a kiosk and **administrative headquarters** at Via Parigi 5 (☎ 06/4889-9255). All of these are open Monday to Friday 8:15am to 7:15pm (Saturday to 2pm). However, don't expect much from these offices.

More helpful, and stocking maps and brochures, are the offices maintained by the **Commune di Roma** at half a dozen sights around the city. You can identify them because they have red-and-orange or yellow-and-black signs saying COMMUNE DI ROMA—PUNTI DI INFORMAZIONE TURISTICA. They're staffed daily 9am to 6pm, except the one at Termini, which is open daily 8am to 9pm. Here are the addresses and phone numbers: in Stazione Termini (☎ 06/4890-6300); in Piazza Pia, near the Castelo Sant'Angelo (☎ 06/6880-9707); in Piazza San Giovanni in Laterano (☎ 06/7720-3598); along Largo Carlo Goldoni, near the intersection of Via del Corso and Via Condotti (☎ 06/6813-6061); on Via Nazionale, near the Palazzo delle Esposizioni (☎ 06/4782-4525); on Largo Corrado Ricci, near the Colosseum (☎ 06/6992-4307); and in Trastevere on Piazza Sonnino (☎ 06/5833-3457).

Enjoy Rome, Via Varese 39 (☎ 06/445-1843; fax 06/445-0734; E-mail fulang@flashnet.it; www.enjoyrome.com), was begun by a wonderful young couple, Fulvia and Pierluigi, with a simple but bright idea, and it's the answer to many travelers' dreams. In their English-speaking, visitor-friendly office near the station, they dispense information about just about everything in Rome and are far more pleasant and organized than the government-run Board of Tourism. They also find hotel rooms at rock-bottom to moderate prices (hostels to three-star hotels) free of charge. Summer hours are Monday to Friday 8:30am to 7pm and Saturday 8:30am to 1:30pm; winter hours are Monday to Friday 8:30am to 1:30pm and 3:30 to 6pm.

For information on the Web, try **www.informaroma.it**.

CITY LAYOUT

Arm yourself with a detailed street map, not the general overview handed out free at tourist offices. Most hotels hand out a pretty good version at their front desks.

The bulk of ancient, Renaissance, and baroque Rome (as well as the train station) lies on the east side of the **Tiber River (Fiume Tevere),** which meanders through town. However, several important landmarks are on the other side: **St. Peter's Basilica** and the **Vatican,** the **Castel Sant'Angelo,** and the colorful **Trastevere** neighborhood.

The city's various quarters are linked by large boulevards (large at least in some places) that have mostly been laid out since the late 19th century. Starting from the **Vittorio Emanuele monument,** a controversial pile of snow-white Brescian marble that's often compared to a wedding cake, there's a street running practically due north to **Piazza del Popolo** and the city wall. This is **Via del Corso,** one of the main streets of Rome—noisy, congested, always crowded with buses and shoppers, called simply "Il Corso." To its left (west) lie the Pantheon, Piazza Navona, Campo de' Fiori, and the Tiber. To its right (east) you'll find the Spanish Steps, the Trevi Fountain, the Borghese Gardens, and Via Veneto.

Back at the Vittorio Emanuele monument, the major artery going west (and ultimately across the Tiber to St. Peter's) is **Corso Vittorio Emanuele.** Behind you to your right, heading toward the Colosseum, is **Via del Fori Imperiali,** laid out in the 1930s by Mussolini to show off the ruins of the imperial forums he had excavated, which line it on either side. Yet another central conduit is **Via Nazionale,** running from **Piazza Venezia** (just in front of the Vittorio Emanuele monument) east to **Piazza della Repubblica** (near Stazione Termini). The final lap of Via Nazionale is called **Via Quattro Novembre.**

FINDING AN ADDRESS This can be a problem because of the narrow streets of old Rome and the little, sometimes hidden *piazze* (squares). Numbers usually run consecutively, with odd numbers on one side of the street and evens on the other. However, in the old districts the numbers will sometimes run up one side to the end, then run back in the opposite direction on the other side. Therefore, no. 50 could be opposite no. 308.

TRAFFIC For the 2½ millennia before Rome's wide boulevards were built, the citizens had to make their way through narrow byways and curves that defeated all but the best senses of direction. These streets—among the city's most charming aspects— still exist, mostly still cobblestoned and unspoiled by the advances of modern construction. However, this tangled street plan has one troublesome element: cars. Rome traffic is awful! When the claustrophobic street plans of the Dark Ages open unexpectedly onto a vast piazza, every driver accelerates full throttle, while pedestrians flatten themselves against marble fountains for protection or stride with firm jaws right into the thick of the howling mess.

Sometimes it's actually faster to walk than to take a bus, especially during any of Rome's four daily rush hours (that's right, four: to work, home for lunch/ *riposo,* back to work, home in the evening). The hectic crush of urban Rome is considerably less during August, when many Romans are out of town on vacation.

NEIGHBORHOODS IN BRIEF

This section will give you some idea of where you may want to stay and where the major attractions are.

Near Stazione Termini   The main train station, **Stazione Termini,** adjoins **Piazza della Repubblica,** and most likely this will be your introduction to Rome. Much of the area is seedy and filled with gas fumes from all the buses and cars, but it has been improving. If you stay here, you may not get a lot of atmosphere, but you'll have a lot of affordable options and a very convenient location, near the transportation hub of the city and not too far from ancient Rome. There's a lot to see here, including the **Basilica di Santa Maria Maggiore** and the **Baths of Diocletian.** There are some high-class hotels sprinkled in the area, including the **Grand,** but many are long past their heyday.

The neighborhoods on either side of Stazione Termini have improved greatly recently and some streets are now attractive. The best-looking area is ahead and to your right as you exit the station on the Via Marsala side. Most budget hotels here occupy a floor or more of a palazzo, and the entries are often drab, though upstairs they're often charming or at least clean and livable. In the area to the left of the station, as you exit, the streets are wider, the traffic is heavier, and the noise level is higher. This area off Via Giolitti is being redeveloped, and now most streets are in good condition. There are a few that still need improvement, and caution at night is a given.

Via Veneto & Piazza Barberini   In the 1950s and early 1960s, **Via Veneto** was the haunt of the *dolce vita* set, as the likes of King Farouk and Swedish actress Anita Ekberg paraded up and down the boulevard to the delight of the paparazzi. The street is still here, still the site of luxury hotels and elegant cafes and restaurants, though it's no longer the happening place to be. It's lined with restaurants catering to those tourists who've heard of this famous boulevard from decades past, but they're mostly overpriced and overcrowded. Rome city authorities would like to restore this legendary street to some of its former glory by banning vehicular traffic on the top half. It makes for a pleasant stroll in any case.

To the south, Via Veneto comes to an end at **Piazza Barberini,** dominated by the 1642 **Triton Fountain (Fontana del Triton),** a baroque celebration with four dolphins holding up an open scallop shell in which sits a triton blowing into a conch. Overlooking the square is the **Palazzo Barberini.** In 1623, when Cardinal Maffeo Barberini became Pope Urban VIII, he ordered Carlo Maderno to build a palace here; it was later completed by Bernini and Borromini.

Ancient Rome   Most visitors explore this area first, taking in the **Colosseum, Palatine Hill,** the **Roman Forum,** the **Imperial Forums,** and the **Circus Maximus.** It forms part of the *centro storico* (historic district)—along with **Campo de' Fiori** and **Piazza Navona** and the **Pantheon** described below. Because of its narrow streets, airy piazzas, antique atmosphere, and great location, visitors enjoy staying here instead of in the less attractive, duller, and rather seedier districts like the section around the train station (though that neighborhood has improved a lot). If you base yourself here, you can walk to the monuments and avoid the hassle of Rome's inadequate public transportation. But room prices are often 30 to 50% higher than those in other less desirable areas. So if you want atmosphere, you've got to pay for it.

Campo de' Fiori & the Jewish Ghetto   South of Corso Vittorio Emanuele and centered around **Piazza Farnese** and the market square of **Campo de' Fiori,** many buildings in this area were constructed in Renaissance times as private homes. Stroll along **Via Giulia**—Rome's most fashionable street in the 16th century—with its antiques stores, interesting hotels, and modern art galleries.

West of Via Arenula lies one of the city's most intriguing districts, the old **Jewish Ghetto,** where the dining options far outnumber the hotel options. In 1556, Pope Paul IV ordered the Jews, about 8,000 at the time, to move into this area. The walls weren't torn down until 1849. Though we think ancient and medieval Rome have a lot more atmosphere, this area is close to many attractions and makes a great place to stay. Nevertheless, hoteliers still sock it to you on prices.

Piazza Navona & the Pantheon   One of the most desirable areas of Rome, this district is a maze of narrow streets and alleys dating back to the Middle Ages and is filled with churches and palaces built during the Renaissance and baroque eras, often with rare marbles and other materials stripped from ancient Rome. The only way to explore it is on foot. Its heart is **Piazza Navona,** built over Emperor Domitian's stadium and bustling with sidewalk cafes, palazzi, street artists, musicians, and pickpockets. There are several hotels in the area and plenty of trattorie. Rivaling it—in general activity, the cafe scene, and nightlife—is the area around the **Pantheon,** which remains from ancient Roman times surrounded by a district built much later (this "pagan" temple was turned into a church and rescued, but the buildings that once surrounded it are long gone). If you'd like to stay in medieval Rome, you face the same 30 to 50% increase in hotel prices as you do for ancient Rome.

Piazza del Popolo & the Spanish Steps   At press time undergoing a major facelift, **Piazza del Popolo** was laid out by Giuseppe Valadier and is one of Rome's largest squares. It's characterized by an obelisk brought from Heliopolis in lower Egypt during the reign of Augustus. At the end of the square is the **Porta del Popolo,** the gateway in the 3rd-century Aurelian wall. In the mid-16th century this was one of the major gateways into the old city. If you enter the piazza along Via del Corso from the south, you'll see twin churches, **Santa Maria del Miracoli** and **Santa Maria di Montesanto,** flanking the street. But the square's major church is **Santa Maria del Popolo** (1442–47), one of the best examples of a Renaissance church in Rome.

Ever since the 17th century, the **Spanish Steps** (former site of the Spanish ambassador's residence) has been a meeting place for visitors. Keats lived in a house opening onto the steps, and some of Rome's most upscale shopping streets fan out from it, including **Via Condotti.** The elegant **Hassler,** one of Rome's grandest hotels, lies at the top of the steps. If you want to sleep in the hippest part of town, you must be willing to part with a lot of extra lire. This area charges some of the capital's highest prices, not only for hotels but also for restaurants, designer silk suits, and leather loafers.

Around Vatican City   Across the Tiber, **Vatican City** is a small city-state, but its influence extends around the world. The **Vatican Museums** and **St. Peter's** take up most of the land area, and the popes have lived here for 6 centuries. Though the neighborhood contains some good hotels (and several bad ones), it's somewhat removed from the more happening scene of ancient and Renaissance Rome, and getting to and from it can be time-consuming. And the area is rather dull at night and contains few if any of Rome's finest restaurants. Vatican City and its surrounding area are best for exploring during the day.

Trastevere   The most authentic district of Rome, **Trastevere** is a place to see how real people live away from the touristy areas. It lies across the Tiber, and its people are of mixed ancestry, including Jewish, Roman, and Greek, and they speak their own dialect. The area centers around the ancient churches of **Santa Cecilia** and **Santa Maria in Trastevere.** Home to many young expats, the district became a gathering

Rome Orientation

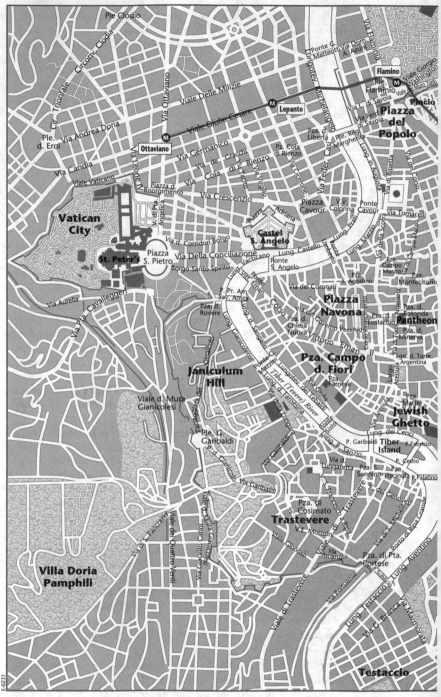

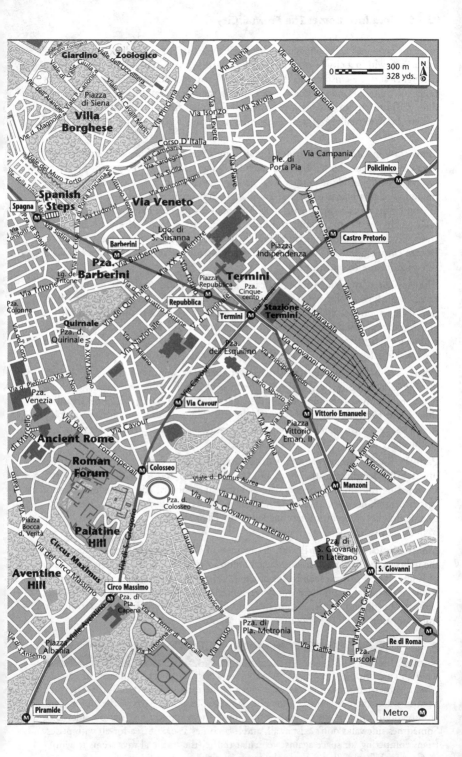

91

place for hedonists and bohemians after World War II. There are those who speak of it as a "city within a city"—or at least a village within a city. It's said that the language is rougher and the cuisine spicier, and though Trastevere doesn't have the glamorous hotels of central Rome, it does have some of the last remaining authentic Roman dining. Trastevere used to be a great hunting ground for budget travelers, but foreigners from virtually everywhere have been buying real estate en masse here, so change is in the air.

Testaccio   In A.D. 55, Nero ordered that Rome's thousands of broken amphoras and terra-cotta roof tiles be stacked in a carefully designated pile to the east of the Tiber, just west of Pyramide and today's Ostia Railway Station. Over the centuries, the mound grew to a height of around 200 feet, then compacted to form the centerpiece for one of the city's most unusual neighborhoods, **Testaccio.** Eventually, houses were built on the terra-cotta mound and caves dug into its mass to store wine and foodstuffs. Bordered by the Protestant cemetery, Testaccio is home to restaurants with very Roman cuisine. However, don't wander around here alone at night; the area still has a way to go before regentrification.

The Appian Way   **Via Appia Antica** is a 2,300-year-old road that has witnessed much of the history of the ancient world. By 190 B.C. it extended from Rome to Brindisi on the southeast coast, and its most famous sight today is the **catacombs,** the graveyards of patrician families (despite what it says in *Quo Vadis?* they weren't used as a place for Christians to hide out while fleeing persecution). This is one of the most historically rich areas of Rome to explore but not a viable place to stay.

Prati   The little-known **Prati** district is a middle-class suburb north of the Vatican. It's been discovered by budget travelers because of its affordable pensioni, though it's not conveniently located for much of the sightseeing you'll want to do. The **Trionfale flower-and-food market** itself is worth the trip. The area also abounds in shopping streets less expensive than those found in central Rome, and street crime isn't much of a problem.

Parioli   Rome's most elegant residential section, **Parioli** is framed by the green spaces of the **Villa Borghese** to the south and the **Villa Glori** and **Villa Ada** to the north. It's a setting for some of the city's finest restaurants, hotels, and nightclubs. It's not exactly central, however, and can be a hassle if you're dependent on public transportation. Parioli lies adjacent to Prati but across the Tiber to the east, and, like Prati, is one of the safer districts.

Monte Mario   On the northwestern precincts of Rome, **Monte Mario** is the site of the deluxe **Cavalieri Hilton,** an excellent stop to take in a drink and the panorama of Rome. If you plan to spend a lot of time shopping and sightseeing in the heart of Rome, it's a difficult and often expensive commute. The area lies north of Prati, away from the hustle and bustle of central Rome. Bus no. 913 runs from Piazza Augusto Imperator near Piazza del Popolo to Monte Mario.

2 Getting Around

Though large, Rome is excellent for walking—you'll find sites of interests often clustered together rather than spread out. Much of the inner core is traffic-free—so you'll need to walk whether you like it or not. However, in many parts of the city it's hazardous and uncomfortable because of the crowds, heavy traffic, and narrow sidewalks. Sometimes sidewalks don't exist at all, and it becomes a sort of free-for-all with pedestrians competing for space against vehicular traffic (the traffic always seems to win).

Caution: When walking, always be on your guard for speeding traffic.

Rome Metropolitana

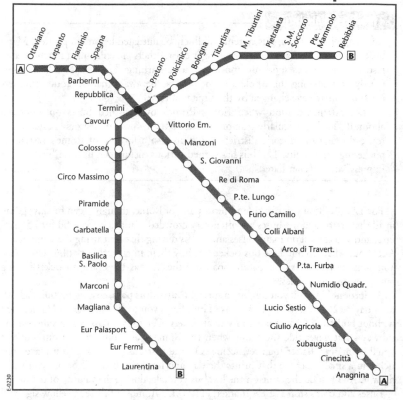

BY SUBWAY

The **Metropolitana,** or **Metro** for short, is the fastest means of transportation, operating daily 5:30am to 11:30pm. It has two underground lines: **Line A** goes between Via Ottaviano (near St. Peter's) and Anagnina, stopping at Piazzale Flaminio (near Piazza del Popolo), Piazza di Spagna, Piazza Vittorio Emanuele, and Piazza San Giovanni in Laterano. **Line B** connects the Rebibbia District with Via Laurentina, stopping at Via Cavour, Stazione Termini, the Colosseum, the Circus Maximus, the Pyramid, St. Paul's Outside the Walls, and E.U.R. A big red letter "M" indicates the entrance to the subway.

Tickets are 1,500L (85¢) and are available from *tabacchi* (tobacco shops), many newsstands, and vending machines at all stations. These machines accept 50L, 100L, and 200L coins, and some of them will take 1,000L notes. Some stations have managers, but they won't make change. Booklets of tickets are available at *tabacchi* and in some terminals. You can also purchase a tourist pass on either a daily or a weekly basis (see below).

Building a subway system for Rome hasn't been easy, since every time workers start digging they discover an old temple or other archaeological treasure and heavy earth-moving has to cease for a while.

BY BUS & TRAM

Roman buses and trams are operated by an organization known as **ATAC (Azienda Tramvie e Autobus del Commune di Roma),** Via Volturno 65 (☎ **06/4695-4444** for information).

Two Bus Warnings

Any map of the Roman bus system will likely be outdated before it's printed. Many buses listed on the "latest" map no longer exist; others are enjoying a much-needed rest, and new buses suddenly appear without warning. There's also talk of completely renumbering the whole system soon, so be aware that the route numbers listed here may have changed by the time you travel.

Take extreme caution when riding Rome's overcrowded buses—pickpockets abound! This is particularly true on bus no. 64, a favorite of visitors because of its route through the historic districts and thus also a favorite of Rome's vast pickpocketing community. This bus has earned various nicknames, like the "Pickpocket Express" and "Wallet Eater."

For 1,500L (85¢) you can ride to most parts of Rome, though it can be slow going in all that traffic and the buses are often very crowded. Your ticket is valid for 75 minutes, and you can get on many buses and trams during that time using the same ticket. Ask about where to purchase bus tickets, or buy them in tabacchi or at bus terminals. You must have your ticket before boarding the bus, as there are no ticket-issuing machines on the vehicles.

At Stazione Termini, you can buy a special **tourist bus pass,** costing 6,000L ($3.50) for a day or 24,000L ($14) for a week. This allows you to ride on the ATAC network without bothering to purchase individual tickets. The tourist pass is also valid on the subway—but never ride the trains when the Romans are going to or from work or you'll be mashed flatter than fettuccine. On the first bus you board, you place your ticket in a small machine that prints the day and hour you boarded before you withdraw it. And you do the same on the last bus you take during the validity of the ticket.

Buses and trams stop at areas marked FERMATA. At most of these, a yellow sign will display the numbers of the buses that stop there and a list of all the stops along each bus's route in order, so you can easily search out your destination. In general they're in service daily 6am to midnight. After that and until dawn, you can ride on special night buses (they have an "N" in front of their bus number), which run only on main routes. It's best to take a taxi in the wee hours—if you can find one.

At the **bus information booth** at Piazza dei Cinquecento, in front of the Stazione Termini, you can purchase a directory complete with maps summarizing the routes.

Though routes change often, a few old reliable routes have remained valid for years, such as **no. 27** from Stazione Termini to the Colosseum, **nos. 75** and **170** from Stazione Termini to Trastevere, and **no. 492** from Stazione Termini to the Vatican. But if you're going somewhere and are dependent on the bus, be sure to carefully check where the bus stop is and exactly what bus goes there—don't assume it'll be the same bus the next day.

BY TAXI

If you're accustomed to hopping a cab in New York or London, then do so in Rome. If not, take less expensive means of transport or walk. Avoid paying your fare with large bills—invariably, taxi drivers claim they don't have change, hoping for a bigger tip (stick to your guns and give only about 10%). Don't count on hailing a taxi on the street or even getting one at a stand. If you're going out, have your hotel call one. At a restaurant, ask the waiter or cashier to dial for you. If you want to phone for yourself, try one of these numbers: ☎ **06/6645,** 06/3570, or 06/4994.

The meter begins at 4,500L ($2.60) for the first 3 kilometers, then increases 200L (10¢) per 150 meters. Every suitcase is 2,000L ($1.15), and on Sunday a 2,000L

($1.15) supplement is assessed. There's another 5,000L ($2.90) supplement 10pm to 7am.

BY BICYCLE, MOTOR SCOOTER & MOTORCYCLE

Bichi & Bachi, Via dei Viminale 5 (☎ 06/4828-8443), maintains an inventory of about 50 motor scooters and motorcycles you can rent as a means of zipping through the dense traffic. (We recommend this only if you're an experienced urbanite with nerves of steel.) Open daily 8am to 7pm, it charges 40,000L to 80,000L ($23 to $46) per day, depending on the model you select. Another agency that provides mopeds is **Happy Rent,** Via Farimi 3 (☎ 06/481-8185), 300 yards from Stazione Termini. Most mopeds cost 20,000L ($12) for 1 hour or 60,000L ($35) for the entire day. Happy Rent also offers several guided moped tours of Rome and the surrounding area. It's open Monday to Saturday 9am to 7pm.

You'll find many places to rent bikes throughout Rome. Ask at your hotel for the nearest rental location or go to **I Bike Rome,** Via Vittorio Veneto 156 (☎ 06/322-5240), which rents bicycles from the underground parking garage at the Villa Borghese. Most bikes cost 4,000L ($2.30) per hour or 10,000L ($6) per day. Mountain bikes rent for 7,000L ($4.05) per hour or 18,000L ($10) per day. It's open daily 9am to 7pm.

Bike riders are permitted anywhere in the city, including pedestrian-only zones and traffic-free areas such as St. Peter's Square, where you can ride within the arcaded confines of what's been called the world's most magnificent oval. Also appealing is a 18½-mile bike lane beside the Tiber extending from central Rome north to the industrial suburb of Castel Jubileo.

BY CAR

All roads may lead to Rome, but you don't want to drive once you get here. Plan on walking and using public transport. Since the reception desks of most Roman hotels have at least one English-speaking person, call ahead to find out the best route into Rome from wherever you're starting out. You're usually allowed to park in front of the hotel long enough to unload your luggage. You'll want to get rid of your rental car as soon as possible or park in a garage.

To the neophyte, Roman driving will appear like the chariot race in *Ben-Hur.* When the light turns green, go forth with caution. Many Roman drivers at the other part of the intersection will still be going through the light even though it has turned red. Roman drivers in traffic gridlock move bravely on, fighting for every inch of the road until they can free themselves from the tangled mess. To complicate matters, many zones, such as that around Piazza di Spagna, are traffic-free.

As you're leaving Rome, if you want to rent a car to drive around the rest of Italy, **Hertz** has its main office near the parking lot of the Villa Borghese, at Via Vittorio Veneto 156 (☎ 06/321-6831). The **Budget** headquarters is at Via Ludovisi 60 (☎ 06/482-0966). **Avis** is at Via Sardegna 38A (☎ 06/41-999 or 06/428-24-728). **Maggiore,** an Italian company, has an office at Via di Tor Cervara 225 (☎ 06/229-351). There are also branches of the major rental agencies at the airport.

FAST FACTS: Rome

American Express   The Rome offices are at Piazza di Spagna 38 (☎ 06/67-641). The travel service is open Monday to Friday 9am to 5:30pm and Saturday 9am to 12:30pm. Hours for the financial and mail services are Monday to Friday 9am to 5pm. The tour desk is open during the same hours as those for travel services and also Saturday 2 to 2:30pm (May to October).

Business Hours In general, **banks** are open Monday to Friday 8:30am to 1:30pm and 3 to 4pm. Some banks keep afternoon hours ranging from 2:45 to 3:45pm. There's a branch of **Citibank** at Via Abruzzi 2 (☎ **06/478-171**). The bank office is open Monday to Friday 8:30am to 1:30pm. Shopping hours are governed by the *riposo* (siesta). Most **stores** are open year-round Monday to Saturday 9am to 1pm and then 3:30 or 4pm to 7:30 or 8pm. Most are closed Sunday.

Currency Exchange There are exchange offices located throughout the city, and they're also at all major rail and air terminals, including Stazione Termini, where the cambio (exchange booth) beside the rail information booth is open daily 8am to 8pm. At some cambi you'll have to pay commissions, often 1½%. Banks, likewise, often charge commissions.

Dentists To find a dentist who speaks English, call the **U.S. Embassy** in Rome (☎ **06/46-741**). You may have to call around in order to get an appointment. There's also the 24-hour **G. Eastman Dental Hospital,** Viale Regina Elena 287 (☎ **06/844-831**).

Doctors For a doctor, call the U.S. Embassy (above), which will provide a list of doctors who speak English. All big hospitals have a 24-hour first-aid service (go to the emergency room). You'll find English-speaking doctors at the privately run **Salvator Mundi International Hospital,** Viale delle Mura Gianicolensi 67 (☎ **06/588-961**). For medical assistance, the **International Medical Center** is on 24-hour duty at Via Giovanni Amendola 7 (☎ **06/488-2371**). You could also contact the **Rome American Hospital,** Via Emilio Longoni 69 (☎ **06/22-551**), with English-speaking doctors on duty 24 hours. A more personalized service is provided 24 hours a day by **MEDI-CALL,** Studio Medico, Via Salaria 300, Palazzina C, interno 5 (☎ **06/884-0113**). It can arrange for qualified doctors to make a call to your hotel or anywhere in Rome. In most cases, the doctor will be a GP who can refer you to a specialist if needed. Fees begin at around $100 per visit and can go higher if a specialist or specialized treatments are necessary. Frankly, paying this fee and waiting for a doctor to arrive at your hotel room is usually a lot more convenient than waiting in a hospital emergency room.

Drugstores A reliable pharmacy is **Farmacia Internazionale,** Piazza Capranica 96 (☎ **06/679-4680**). Most pharmacies are open 8:30am to 1pm and 4 to 7:30pm. In general, they follow a rotation system so that several are always open on Sunday (the rotation schedule is posted outside each one).

Embassies/Consulates See "Fast Facts: Italy" in chapter 3.

Emergencies The police hot-line number is ☎ **21-21-21**. Usually, however, dial ☎ **112** for the police, to report a fire, or summon an ambulance.

Hospitals See "Doctors," above.

Luggage Storage This is available at **Stazione Termini** along Tracks 1 and 22, open daily 5am to 1am. The charge is 5,000L ($2.90) per piece per 12-hour period.

Mail Post office boxes in Italy are red and attached to walls. The left slot is only for letters intended for the city; the right is for all other destinations. Vatican post office boxes are blue, and you can buy special stamps at the **Vatican City Post Office,** adjacent to the information office in St. Peter's Square; it's open Monday to Friday 8:30am to 7pm and Saturday 8:30am to 6pm. Letters mailed at

Vatican City reach North America far more quickly than does mail sent from within Rome for the same cost.

Rome's **main post office** is at Piazza San Silvestro 19, 00186 Roma (☎ 06/ 6771), between Via del Corso and Piazza di Spagna, open Monday to Friday 9am to 6pm and Saturday 9am to 2pm. Mail addressed to you at this central office, with *fermo posta* written after the name and address of the post office, will be given to you on identification by passport. Stamps (*francobolli*) can be purchased at *tabacchi* (tobacconists).

Newspapers/Magazines You can get the *International Herald Tribune, USA Today,* the *New York Times,* and *Time* and *Newsweek* magazines at most newsstands. The expat magazine (in English) *Wanted in Rome* comes out monthly and lists current events and shows. If you want to try your hand at reading Italian, the Thursday edition of the newspaper *La Repubblica* contains Trova Roma, a magazine supplement full of cultural and entertainment listings, and *Time Out* now has a Rome edition.

Police See "Emergencies," above.

Rest Rooms Facilities are found near many of the major sights, often with attendants, as are those at bars, nightclubs, restaurants, cafes, and hotels, plus the airports and the railway station. (There are public rest rooms near the Spanish Steps, or alternatively, you can stop into the McDonald's there—one of the nicest branches of the golden arches you'll ever see!) You're expected to leave 200L to 500L (10¢ to 30¢) for the attendant. It's not a bad idea to carry some tissues in your pocket when you're out and about.

Safety Pickpocketing is the most common problem. Men should keep their wallets in their front pocket or inside jacket pocket. Purse-snatching is also commonplace, with young men on Vespas who will ride past you and grab your purse. To avoid trouble, stay away from the curb and keep your purse on the wall side of your body and the strap across your chest. Don't lay anything valuable on tables or chairs where it can be grabbed up. Gypsy children have long been a particular menace, though the problem isn't as severe as in years past. If they completely surround you, you'll often virtually have to fight them off. They'll often approach you with pieces of cardboard hiding their stealing hands. Just keep repeating a firm "no!"

Taxes A **value-added tax** (called **IVA** in Italy) is added to all consumer products and most services, including restaurants and hotels. The tax is not the same for all goods and services. The tax is 12% on clothing and 19% on most luxury goods.

Telephone There are two types of **public pay phones** in regular service. The first accepts coins or special grooved tokens (*gettoni*), which you'll sometimes (rarely these days) receive in change. The second operates with a **phonecard** (to buy one, ask for a *scheda* or *carta telefonica*), available at *tabacchi* and bars in 5,000L ($2.90) and 10,000L ($6) denominations; break off the perforated

Country & City Codes

The **country code** for Italy is **39**. The **city code** for Rome is **06**; you must now use this code every time you call Rome: if you're calling from outside Italy, if you're calling from another city within Italy, and even if you're calling within Rome.

corner of the card before using it and insert arrow end first. Local phone calls cost 200L (12¢). To make a call, lift the receiver, insert a coin or card (arrow first), and dial.

To make collect calls to the United States, or with your calling card, phone AT&T's USA Direct at ☎ 06/172-10-11, MCI's Call USA at ☎ 06/172-10-22, or US Sprint at ☎ 06/172-18-77. You can also call ☎ 06/172-10-01 for Canada, ☎ 06/172-10-61 for Australia, and ☎ 06/172-00-44 for the United Kingdom.

Transit Information Leonardo da Vinci International Airport (☎ 06/65-951); Ciampino Airport (☎ 06/794-941); bus information (☎ 06/46-951); rail information (☎ 1478/880-881).

3 Accommodations

The good news is that Roman hoteliers are sprucing up for the Papal Jubilee 2000 visitors who are expected to flood the city at the millennium. The bad news is that some of that construction and renovation may be going on when you visit in 1999. See the "Neighborhoods in Brief" section, earlier in this chapter, to get an idea of where you may want to base yourself.

Among the luxury leaders, there has been no earthshaking news since the 1994 opening of the **Hotel Eden,** now a market leader. After all, it's almost impossible to open a five-star palace hotel in Rome today because real estate isn't available. However, a new four-star choice, the **Hotel dei Mellini,** has opened between Piazza del Popolo and St. Peter's and is making a splash. A number of small hotels—like the **Hotel Nerva**—have either opened or undergone renovations, making them worthy contenders. We've reviewed the best of these newly discovered or rediscovered candidates, some of which we couldn't recommend only a short time ago.

Rome is a year-round tourist destination, so you'll need to make reservations well in advance no matter what the season. Because of its importance as a religious center, some groups book hundreds of rooms in the winter "low season" to take advantage of the better discounts. Many hotels grant winter discounts (usually no more than 10%), and you may have to negotiate this at the reception desk. If you happen to arrive without a reservation, stop by the Rome desk at Stazione Termini and the staff will help you book a room (see "Visitor Information" earlier in this chapter).

NEAR STAZIONE TERMINI
VERY EXPENSIVE

Hotel Mediterraneo. Via Cavour 15, 00184 Roma. ☎ **800/223-9832** in the U.S. or 06/488-4051. Fax 06/474-4105. www.italyhotel.com/home/roma/mediterraneo/mediterraneo. html. E-mail: mediterraneo@venere.it. 271 units. A/C MINIBAR TV TEL. 480,000L ($278) double; 575,000–1,140,000L ($334–$661) suite. Rates include buffet breakfast. AE, DC, MC, V. Parking 35,000L ($20). Metro: Termini.

The Mediterraneo sports vivid Italian art-deco styling. Because it's beside what Mussolini planned as his triumphant passageway through Rome, the local building codes were deliberately violated and approval was granted for the creation of an unprecedented 10-floor hotel. Its height, coupled with its position on one of Rome's hills, provides panoramic views from the most expensive rooms on the highest floors (some of which have lovely terraces) and from its roof garden and bar (open May to October), which is especially charming at night.

Mario Loreti, one of Mussolini's favorite architects, designed an interior sheathing of gray marble, the richly allegorical murals of inlaid wood, and the art-deco friezes ringing the ceilings of the enormous public rooms. The lobby is also decorated with antique busts of Roman emperors.

Our only quibble with this otherwise award-winning hotel is over a few jarring notes—like the 1960s-style orange elevators and the furniture (rustic and slightly battered, if still solid and dependable) in some of the guest rooms. A slight imperfection in an otherwise marvelous and historically evocative setting.

Dining: The gracefully curved bar is crafted from illuminated cut crystal. Another artful touch is the ships' figureheads adorning the ceiling of the breakfast room, where a generous buffet is served. Though unheralded, the hotel restaurant serves excellent and affordable Roman and Italian cuisine, including beef tenderloin with a sauce of green peppercorns and cognac and roast baked duck breast with muscadet grapes.

Amenities: Car-rental desk, concierge, room service, dry cleaning/laundry, baby-sitting.

Le Grand Hotel. Via Vittorio Emanuele Orlando 3, 00185 Roma. ☎ **800/325-3589** in the U.S. and Canada, or 06/47-091. Fax 06/474-7307. 170 units. A/C MINIBAR TV TEL. 610,000–670,000L ($354–$389) double; from 1,000,000L ($580) suite. Continental breakfast 56,000L ($34). AE, DC, MC, V. Parking 50,000–60,000L ($29–$35). Metro: Piazza della Repubblica.

When Cesar Ritz founded the Grand in 1894, it struck a note of elegance the hotel has tried to maintain ever since. The service is first-rate. The location, near the rail station, isn't the most charming, but it's certainly convenient and only a few minutes from Via Veneto. The Grand looks like a large late-Renaissance palace, its facade covered with carved loggias, lintels, quoins, and cornices. Inside, the floors are marble, with Oriental rugs, and the walls a riot of baroque plasterwork and crystal chandeliers. Louis XVI furniture, antique clocks, and wall sconces complete the picture.

The spacious guest rooms are conservatively decorated with matching curtains and carpets and come with a dressing room and fully tiled bath. Each room is unique: Most are traditional and the rest modern; some are less grand than you might expect from the impressive lobby. Every room is soundproof.

Dining: Le Grand Bar is an elegant meeting place where tea is served every afternoon, sometimes accompanied by a harpist or pianist. You can enjoy quick meals at the Salad Bar or try Le Restaurant, the more formal dining room. Dietetic and kosher foods can be arranged with advance notice.

Amenities: 24-hour room service, baby-sitting, laundry/valet.

Mecenate Palace Hotel. Via Carlo Alberto 3, 00185 Roma. ☎ **06/4470-2024.** Fax 06/446-1354. www.venere.it/home/roma/mecenate/mecenate.html. E-mail: mecenate@venere.it. 62 units. A/C MINIBAR TV TEL. 500,000L ($290) double; 1,000,000L ($580) suite. Rates include continental breakfast. AE, DC, MC, V. Parking 40,000L ($23). Metro: Termini.

One of Rome's newest four-star hotels opened on the site of what was once a private villa built in the Liberty (art nouveau) style around 1900. It rises five floors above a neighborhood near the main rail station. The pastel-colored rooms, where traces of the original detailing mix with contemporary furnishings, overlook such monuments

Hotel Notes

All the hotels listed serve breakfast (often a buffet with coffee, fruit, rolls, and cheese), but it's not always included in the room rate, so check the listing carefully.

Nearly all hotels are heated in the cooler months, but not all are air-conditioned in summer, which can be vitally important during July and August. The deluxe and first-class ones are, but after that it's a toss-up. Be sure to check the listing carefully before you book a stay in the dog days of summer!

Rome Accommodations

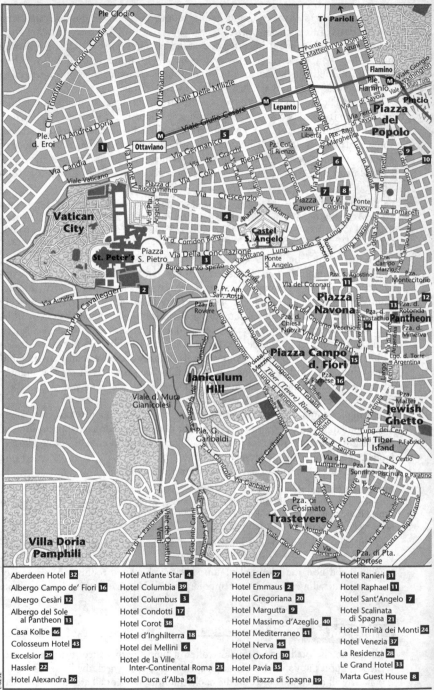

Aberdeen Hotel **32**
Albergo Campo de' Fiori **16**
Albergo Cesàri **12**
Albergo del Sole
  al Pantheon **13**
Casa Kolbe **46**
Colosseum Hotel **43**
Excelsior **29**
Hassler **22**
Hotel Alexandra **26**

Hotel Atlante Star **4**
Hotel Columbia **39**
Hotel Columbus **3**
Hotel Condotti **17**
Hotel Corot **38**
Hotel d'Inghilterra **18**
Hotel dei Mellini **6**
Hotel de la Ville
  Inter-Continental Roma **23**
Hotel Duca d'Alba **44**

Hotel Eden **27**
Hotel Emmaus **2**
Hotel Gregoriana **20**
Hotel Margutta **9**
Hotel Massimo d'Azeglio **40**
Hotel Mediterraneo **41**
Hotel Nerva **45**
Hotel Oxford **30**
Hotel Pavia **35**
Hotel Piazza di Spagna **19**

Hotel Ranieri **31**
Hotel Raphael **11**
Hotel Sant'Angelo **7**
Hotel Scalinata
  di Spagna **21**
Hotel Trinità dei Monti **24**
Hotel Venezia **37**
La Residenza **28**
Le Grand Hotel **33**
Marta Guest House **8**

E-0232

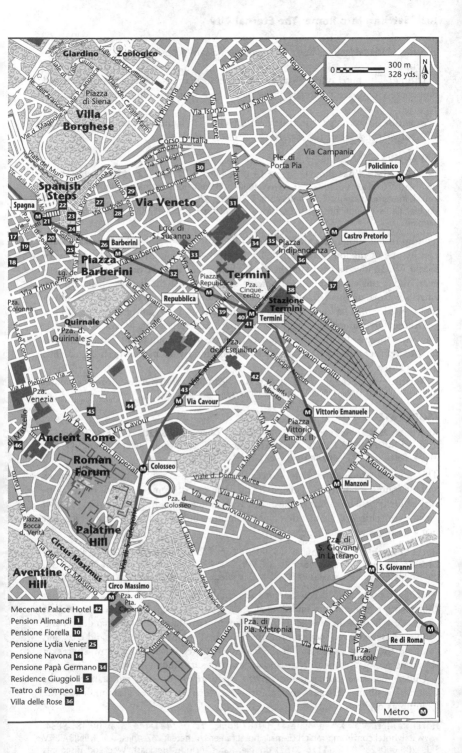

Mecenate Palace Hotel **42**
Pension Alimandi **1**
Pensione Fiorella **10**
Pensione Lydia Venier **25**
Pensione Navona **14**
Pensione Papà Germano **34**
Residence Giuggioli **5**
Teatro di Pompeo **15**
Villa delle Rose **36**

Metro **M**

as Santa Maria Maggiore. Each room contains a safe-deposit box and multilanguage satellite TV.

Dining: The hotel offers a bar and a rather formal restaurant serving lunch and dinner every day except Sunday, plus a roof garden with sweeping views over Roman rooftops.

Amenities: Concierge, room service, dry cleaning/laundry, twice-daily maid service, baby-sitting, secretarial services.

EXPENSIVE

Hotel Massimo d'Azeglio. Via Cavour 18, 00184 Roma. ☎ **800/223-9832** in the U.S., or 06/487-0270. Fax 06/482-7386. www.italyhotel.com/home/roma/azeglio/azeglio.html. E-mail: massimo.d'azeglio@italyhotel.com. 200 units. A/C MINIBAR TV TEL. 430,000L ($249) double. Rates include breakfast. DC, MC, V. Parking 35,000–45,000L ($20–$26). Metro: Termini.

This up-to-date hotel near the train station and opera was opened as a small restaurant by one of the founders of an Italian hotel dynasty more than a century ago. In World War II, it was a refuge for the king of Serbia and also a favorite with Italian generals. Today this centrally located hotel is the flagship of the Bettoja chain. Run by Angelo Bettoja and his charming wife, it offers comfortable accommodations, plus a well-trained staff. The hotel boasts one of the area's most elegant neoclassical facades.

Dining/Diversions: For many decades the hotel restaurant, Massimo d'Azeglio, was a neighborhood fixture. It's no longer *the* place to go around here, but if you're too tired to venture out, it's still a safe bet for good food with market-fresh ingredients. There's also a bar.

Amenities: Concierge, room service, dry cleaning/laundry, baby-sitting, car-rental desk.

MODERATE

Aberdeen Hotel. Via Firenze 48, 00184 Roma. ☎ **06/482-3920.** Fax 06/482-1092. 26 units. A/C MINIBAR TV TEL. 260,000L ($151) double. Rates include buffet breakfast. AE, DC, MC, V. Parking 30,000–40,000L ($17–$23). Metro: Termini.

This completely renovated hotel is near the opera house, central to both landmarks and the train station. It's in a quiet and fairly safe area of Rome—in front of the Ministry of Defense. The rooms are furnished with rather anonymous modern styling and include conveniences like hair dryers. The breakfast buffet is the only meal served, but many inexpensive trattorie lie nearby.

Hotel Columbia. Via del Viminale 15, 00184 Roma. ☎ **06/474-4289.** Fax 06/474-0209. E-mail: columbia@flashnet.it. 45 units. A/C MINIBAR TV TEL. 211,000–240,000L ($122–$139) double. Rates include breakfast. AE, DC, MC, V. Metro: Piazza della Repubblica.

Near the train station, this is one of the neighborhood's newest hotels, a three-star choice with a hardworking multilingual staff. It's a very well-done radical renovation (1997) of a hotel built around 1900. The interior contains Murano chandeliers and simple, conservatively modern furniture. The guest rooms are compact and cozy and can hold their own with some of the best of the three-star hotels nearby. There's an appealing roof garden, with a bar and a view over surrounding rooftops.

Under the same management, on the opposite side of the rail station, is the Columbia's sibling, **Hotel Venezia** (below), which sometimes accommodates the Columbia's overflow.

Hotel Ranieri. Via XX Settembre 43, 00187 Roma. ☎ **06/481-4467.** Fax 06/481-8834. www.italyhotel.com/roma/ranieri. E-mail: hotel.ranieri@venere.it. 47 units. A/C MINIBAR TV TEL. 200,000–280,000L ($116–$162) double. Rates include breakfast. Weekend discounts

Accommodations Near Stazione Termini & Via Veneto

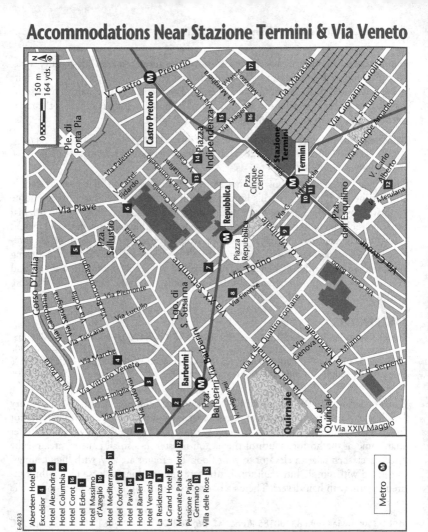

Aberdeen Hotel **8**
Excelsior **4**
Hotel Alexandra **9**
Hotel Columbia **16**
Hotel Corot **16**
Hotel Eden **1**
Hotel Massimo d'Azeglio **10**
Hotel Mediterraneo **11**
Hotel Oxford **5**
Hotel Pavia **14**
Hotel Ranieri **6**
Hotel Venezia **17**
La Residenza **3**
Le Grand Hotel **7**
Mecenate Palace Hotel **12**
Pensione Papà Germano **13**
Villa delle Rose **15**

Metro **Ⓜ**

E-0233

available Dec–Feb; daily discount rates in Aug. AE, MC, V. Parking 28,000–35,000L ($16–$20). Metro: Piazza della Repubblica.

The Ranieri is a winning three-star hotel in an old but restored building. The guest rooms received a substantial renovation in 1995, complete with new furniture, carpets, wall coverings, and even new bathrooms. The location is good—from here you can easily stroll to the opera, Piazza della Repubblica, and Via Vittorio Veneto. The public rooms, the lounge, and the dining room are attractively decorated, in part with contemporary art. You can arrange for a home-cooked meal in the dining room.

✪ **Hotel Venezia.** Via Varese 18 (near Via Marghera), 00185 Roma. ☎ **06/445-7101.** Fax 06/495-7687. E-mail: venezia@flashnet.it. 61 units. A/C MINIBAR TV TEL. 248,000L ($149) double; 336,000L ($202) triple. Rates include breakfast. AE, DC, MC, V. Metro: Termini.

Just when you've decided the whole city was full of overpriced hotels, the Venezia will restore your faith in affordable rooms. The location is good—3 blocks from the rail station, in a relatively quiet, part-business, part-residential area dotted with a few old villas and palms. The Venezia is a good-looking and cheerful choice with charming public rooms. In some cases, the guest rooms are furnished in 17th-century style, though some are beginning to look worn (the last renovation was in 1991). All units are spacious and boast Murano chandeliers and conveniences like hair dryers; some have balconies for surveying the street action. The housekeeping is superb—the management really cares and the helpful staff speaks English.

Villa delle Rose. Via Vicenza 5, 00185 Roma. ☎ **06/445-1788.** Fax 06/445-1639. 38 units. A/C TV TEL. 220,000–275,000L ($128–$160) double. Rates include breakfast. AE, DC, MC, V. Metro: Termini or Castro Pretorio.

Less than 2 blocks north of the rail station, behind a dignified cut-stone facade inspired by the Renaissance, this hotel was built in the late 1800s as a private home for a wealthy family. Despite many renovations, the ornate trappings of the original are still visible, including a set of Corinthian-capped marble columns in the lobby and a flagstone-covered terrace that fills part of a verdant back garden. Much of the interior has been redecorated with traditional wall coverings and new carpets. Morning breakfasts in the garden, where rows of pink and red roses bloom, do a lot to add country flavor to an otherwise very urban and noisy location. The English-speaking staff is helpful and tactful.

INEXPENSIVE

Hotel Corot. Via Marghera 15–17, 00185 Roma. ☎ **06/4470-0900.** Fax 06/4470-0905. 20 units. A/C MINIBAR TV TEL. 160,000–190,000L ($93–$110) double; 180,000–230,000L ($104–$133) triple; 210,000–260,000L ($122–$151) quad. Rates include breakfast. 15% weekend discounts for multiple-night stays. AE, DC, MC, V. Parking 25,000–35,000L ($15–$20). Metro: Termini.

This modernized hotel occupies the second and third floors of a turn-of-the-century building that contains a handful of private apartments and another, somewhat inferior hotel. The Corot is a safe if not thrilling bet north of the train station; it's far better than some of the horrors south of there. You register in a small paneled area on the street level, then take an elevator to your floor. The rooms are airy, with high ceilings, and filled with simple but traditional furniture and soothing colors. The bathrooms are modern, with hair dryers. There's a bar near a sunny window in one of the public rooms.

Hotel Pavia. Via Gaeta 83, 00185 Roma. ☎ **06/483-801.** Fax 06/481-9090. 25 units. A/C MINIBAR TV TEL. 170,000–225,000L ($99–$131) double. Rates include breakfast. AE, DC, MC, V. Parking 15,000–20,000L ($9–$12). Metro: Termini.

The Pavia, in a much-renovated 100-year-old villa, is a popular choice on this quiet street near the gardens of the Baths of Diocletian. You'll pass through a wisteria-covered passage that leads to the recently modernized reception area and the tasteful public rooms, where the staff is attentive and friendly. The front rooms tend to be noisy, but that's the curse of all Termini hotels. Nevertheless, the rooms are comfortable and fairly attractive. It's a safe haven in an area where you can't always be sure of quality.

Pensione Papà Germano. Via Calatafimi 14A, 00185 Roma. ☎ **06/486-919.** 16 units, 6 with bathroom. TEL. 65,000L ($38) double without bathroom, 85,000L ($49) double with bathroom; 75,000L ($44) triple without bathroom; 100,000L ($58) triple with bathroom. 10% discount Nov–Mar. AE, MC, V. Metro: Termini.

This is about as basic as anything in this book, but it's clean and decent. This 1892 building has undergone some recent renovations yet retains its modest ambience. Chances are that your fellow travelers will arrive, backpack in tow, directly from the train station 4 blocks south. Located on a block-long street immediately east of the Baths of Diocletian, this pensione has clean accommodations with plain furniture, hair dryers, well-maintained showers, and a high-turnover crowd of European and North American students. The energetic English-speaking owner, Gino Germano, offers advice on sightseeing. No breakfast is served, but dozens of cafes nearby open early.

NEAR VIA VENETO & PIAZZA BARBERINI
VERY EXPENSIVE

✪ **Excelsior.** Via Vittorio Veneto 125, 00187 Roma. ☎ **800/325-3589** in the U.S. and Canada, or 06/47-081. Fax 06/482-6205. 365 units. A/C MINIBAR TV TEL. 671,000–737,000L ($389–$427) double; 1,265,000–2,035,000L ($734–$1,180) suite. Breakfast 35,000L ($21). AE, MC, V. Metro: Piazza Barberini.

If money is no object, here's a top contender. The Excelsior (Ess-*shell*-see or) is far livelier and better than its sibling, the Grand. It has a lot more style, with guests like Arab princesses and international financiers. This limestone palace's baroque corner tower, looking right over the U.S. Embassy, is a landmark in Rome. You enter a string of cavernous reception rooms with thick rugs, marble floors, gilded garlands decorating the walls, and Empire furniture. Everything looks just a little bit dowdy today, but the Excelsior endures, seemingly as eternal as Rome itself. In no small part that's because of the exceedingly hospitable staff.

The guest rooms come in two varieties: new (the result of a major renovation) and traditional. The old ones are a bit worn, while the newer rooms have more imaginative color schemes and plush carpeting. They're spacious and elegantly furnished, often with antiques and silk curtains. Most of the rooms are unique, though many have sumptuous Hollywood-style marble bathrooms with separate tubs and showers, sinks, and bidets.

Dining: The Excelsior Bar (daily 10:30am to 1am) is the most famous on Via Vittorio Veneto, and La Cupola is known for its national and regional cuisine, with spa cuisine and kosher food prepared on request.

Amenities: Room service, baby-sitting, laundry/valet, beauty salon, barbershop.

✪ **Hotel Eden.** Via Ludovisi 49, 00187 Roma. ☎ **800/225-5843** in the U.S., or 06/478-121. Fax 06/482-1584. www.forte-hotels.com. 112 units. A/C MINIBAR TV TEL. 810,000–950,000L ($470–$551) double; from 2,100,000L ($1,218) suite. Breakfast 54,000L ($32). AE, DC, MC, V. Parking 50,000L ($29). Bus: 119.

For several generations after it opened in 1889, this ornate hotel, near the top of the Spanish Steps, reigned over one of the world's most stylish shopping neighborhoods. Hemingway, Callas, Ingrid Bergman, Fellini—all checked in during its heyday. In 1989 it was bought by Trusthouse Forte, and it reopened in 1994 after 2 years (and $20 million) of renovations that enhanced its grandeur and added the amenities its five-star status calls for. The hotel's hilltop position guarantees a panoramic view over the city from most rooms. You expect a lovely room at these prices, and that's what you get, including a marble-sheathed bathroom, draperies worthy of *Architectural Digest*, and decor that harks back to the late 19th century. Understated elegance is the rule.

Dining/Diversions: There are a piano bar and a glamorous restaurant, La Terrazza (see "Dining," later in this chapter).

Amenities: Concierge, 24-hour room service, dry cleaning/laundry, newspaper delivery on request, secretarial service (prior notification necessary), valet parking, gym and health club.

EXPENSIVE

Hotel Alexandra. Via Vittorio Veneto 18, 00187 Roma. ☎ **06/488-1943.** Fax 06/487-1804. www.venere.it/roma/alexandra. E-mail: alexandra@venere.it. 45 units. A/C MINI-BAR TV TEL. 350,000L ($203) double; 430,000L ($249) triple; 470,000L ($273) suite. Rates include buffet breakfast. AE, DC, MC, V. Parking 35,000L ($20). Metro: Piazza Barberini.

This is one of your few chances to stay on Via Veneto without going broke (though it's not exactly cheap). Set behind the dignified stone facade of what was a 19th-century mansion, this hotel offers immaculate rooms filled with antique furniture and modern conveniences. Rooms facing the front are exposed to the roaring traffic and animated street life of Via Veneto; those in back are quieter but with less of a view. Breakfast is the only meal served, though a staff member can carry drinks to you in the reception area. The breakfast room is especially appealing: Inspired by an Italian garden, it was designed by noted architect Paolo Portoghesi.

MODERATE

Hotel Oxford. Via Boncompagni 89, 00187 Roma. ☎ **06/4282-8952.** Fax 06/4281-5349. www.italyhotel.com/roma/oxford/oxford.html. E-mail: oxford@star.flashnet.it. 59 units. A/C MINIBAR TV TEL. 290,000L ($168) double; 340,000L ($197) triple; 390,000L ($226) suite. Rates include buffet breakfast. 20% reductions Jan–Mar 15, Aug, and Nov–Dec. AE, DC, MC, V. Parking 35,000–45,000L ($20–$26). Bus: 56 or 58.

The Oxford is a decent, though not spectacular, choice adjacent to the Borghese Gardens. Recently renovated, it's now centrally heated and fully carpeted throughout. There's a pleasant lounge and Tony's bar (serving snacks), plus a dining room offering good Italian cuisine. The guest rooms, which were recently renovated, contain simple modern furnishings; they're a bit sterile and functional but well maintained.

La Residenza. Via Emilia 22–24, 00187 Roma. ☎ **06/488-0789.** Fax 06/485721. www.italyhotel.com/roma/la_residenza. E-mail: hotel.la.residenza@italyhotel.com. 29 units. A/C MINIBAR TV TEL. 295,000–305,000L ($171–$177) double; 335,000–355,000L ($194–$206) suite. Rates include buffet breakfast. AE, MC, V. Parking (limited) 10,000L ($6). Metro: Piazza Barberini.

La Residenza, in a superb but noisy location, successfully combines the intimacy of a generously sized town house with the elegant appointments of a four-star hotel. It's a bit old-fashioned and homelike but still a favorite among international travelers. The converted villa has an ivy-covered courtyard and a labyrinthine series of upholstered public rooms with Empire divans, oil portraits, and cushioned rattan chairs. A series of terraces is scattered strategically throughout.

NEAR ANCIENT ROME
MODERATE

Colosseum Hotel. Via Sforza 10, 00184 Roma. ☎ **06/482-7228.** Fax 06/482-7285. www.venere.it/home/roma/colosseum/colosseum.html. E-mail: colosseum@venere.it. 47 units. A/C TV TEL. 180,000–215,000L ($104–$125) double. Rates include breakfast. AE, DC, MC, V. Parking 30,000L ($17). Metro: Cavour.

Two short blocks southwest of Santa Maria Maggiore, this hotel offers affordable and comfortable (though small) rooms. Someone with flair and lots of lire designed the public areas and upper hallways, which have a hint of baronial grandeur. The drawing room, with its long refectory table, white walls, red tiles, and provincial armchairs, invites lingering. The guest rooms are furnished with well-chosen antique reproductions (beds of heavy carved wood, dark-paneled wardrobes, leatherwood chairs), and all have stark white walls and sometimes old-fashioned plumbing.

Hotel Duca d'Alba. Via Leonina 14, 00184 Roma. ☎ **06/484-471.** Fax 06/488-4840. www.venere.it/home/duca_dalba/duca_dalba.html. E-mail: duca.d'alba@venere.it. 27 units,

11 with shower only, 16 with bathroom. A/C MINIBAR TV TEL. 190,000L ($110) double with shower only, 270,000L ($157) double with bathroom. Rates include breakfast. AE, DC, MC, V. Parking 40,000L ($23). Metro: Cavour.

A bargain near the Roman Forum and the Colosseum, this hotel lies in the Suburra neighborhood, which was once pretty seedy but is being gentrified. Though completely renovated, the hotel still retains an old-fashioned air (it was built in the 19th century). The rooms are tasteful, even a bit decorated, with soothing colors, light wood pieces, personal safes, and hair dryers. The most desirable rooms are the four with private balconies.

Hotel Nerva. Via Tor di Conti 3–5, 00184 Roma. ☎ **06/678-1835.** Fax 06/699-22204. 19 units. AC MINIBAR TV TEL. 200,000–340,000L ($116–$197). Rates include breakfast. AE, DC, MC, V. Metro: Colosseo.

Some of its walls and foundations date from the 1500s, others from a century later, but the modern amenities date back only to 1997. The site, on a terrace above and a few steps from the Roman Forum, would appeal to any student of archaeology and literature. The welcome from the Cirulli brothers is warm and accommodating. The decor is accented with wood panels and terra-cotta tiles; some rooms even have the original ceiling beams. Otherwise, the furniture is serviceable, contemporary, and comfortable.

INEXPENSIVE

Casa Kolbe. Via San Teodoro 44, 00186 Roma. ☎ **06/679-4974.** 65 units. TEL. 130,000L ($75) double. Breakfast 7,000L ($4.20). AE, DC, MC, V. Metro: Circo Massimo.

This three-story hotel often caters to tour groups from North America and Germany, who arrive en masse by bus. The rooms, painted in old-fashioned tones of deep red and brown, are deliberately very simple. They're well scrubbed, even if some are a bit battered from frequent use. Many overlook a small garden, and the hotel's location, underneath the Palatine, is convenient to the archaeological treasures of Old Rome. The hotel dining room, open only to guests, serves set menus for 25,000L ($15).

NEAR CAMPO DE' FIORI
MODERATE

✪ **Teatro di Pompeo.** Largo del Pallaro 8, 00186 Roma. ☎ **06/6830-0170.** Fax 06/6880-5531. 12 units. A/C TV TEL. 300,000L ($174) double. Rates include breakfast. AE, DC, MC, V. Parking 30,000L ($17). Bus: 46, 62, or 64.

Built on top of the ruins of the Theater of Pompey, from about 55 B.C., this small charmer lies near the spot where Julius Caesar met his end on the Ides of March. Intimate and refined, it's on a quiet piazzetta near the Palazzo Farnese and Campo de' Fiori. The rooms are decorated in an old-fashioned Italian style with hand-painted tiles, and the beamed ceilings date from the days of Michelangelo. Reserve as early as possible.

INEXPENSIVE

✪ **Albergo Campo de' Fiori.** Via del Biscione 6, 00186 Roma. ☎ **06/6880-6865.** Fax 06/687-6003. 27 units, 9 with bathroom; 1 honeymoon suite. 140,000L ($81) double without bathroom, 160,000L ($93) double with shower only, 200,000L ($116) double with bathroom; 175,000L ($102) triple without bathroom, 200,000L ($116) triple with shower only, 250,000L ($145) triple with bathroom; 200,000L ($116) honeymoon suite. Rates include breakfast. MC, V. Bus: 46, 62, or 64 from Stazione Termini to Museo di Roma; then arm yourself with a good map for the walk.

A wonderful budget hideaway right in the historic center of Rome, this cozy hotel offers rustic rooms, many quite tiny and sparsely adorned, others with a lot of character. The first-floor rooms have been renovated. Yours might have a ceiling of clouds and blue skies along with mirrored walls. Best is the sixth-floor honeymoon suite, with a canopied queen-size bed. (Honeymooners beware: There's no elevator.) Since it costs the same as a regular double with bath, it's often booked well in advance. You can enjoy the panorama from the terrace overlooking the vegetable-and-flower market and, in the distance, St. Peter's.

NEAR PIAZZA NAVONA & THE PANTHEON
VERY EXPENSIVE

Albergo del Sole al Pantheon. Piazza della Rotonda 63, 00186 Roma. ☎ **06/678-0441.** Fax 06/6994-0689. E-mail: hotsole@flashnet.it. 30 units. A/C MINIBAR TV TEL. 500,000L ($290) double; 600,000–700,000L ($348–$406) suite. Rates include breakfast. AE, DC, MC, V. Parking 35,000L ($20). Bus: 119.

You're obviously paying for the million-dollar view and the location, but you may find it's worth it to be across from the Pantheon, one of antiquity's greatest surviving architectural relics. (Okay, so you're above a McDonald's, but one look at the Pantheon at sunrise and you won't think about burgers.) This is one of the oldest hotels in the world; the first records of it as a hostelry appear in 1467. The hotel is amazingly eccentric in its layout and built on various levels—prepare to walk up and down a lot of three- or four-step staircases. The guest rooms vary greatly in decor, none award-winning and much of it hit or miss. Windows are double glazed but, even so, those opening onto Piazza della Rotonda tend to be noisy at all hours. The quieter accommodations overlook the courtyard but are sans the view.

Dining: Breakfast is the only meal served, but there are dozens of trattorie in the neighborhood.

Amenities: Only laundry/dry cleaning, baby-sitting (not always available).

Hotel Raphael. Largo Febo 2, 00186 Roma. ☎ **06/682-831.** Fax 06/687-8993. www. raphaelhotel.com. E-mail: info@raphaelhotel.com. 73 units. A/C MINIBAR TV TEL. 495,000–595,000L ($287–$345) double; 660,000–760,000L ($383–$441) suite. Breakfast 31,000L ($19). AE, DC, MC, V. Parking 40,000L ($23). Bus: 70, 81, 87, or 115.

Adjacent to Piazza Navona, this hotel is within easy walking distance of many attractions. Its rooftop garden terrace boasts a panorama of the ancient city. The charming ivy-covered facade invites you to enter the lobby, which is decorated with antiques that might rival local museums. Some of the suites have private terraces, and all the well-appointed guest rooms have direct-dial phones and satellite TV. Some are quite small, however.

Dining: The elegant restaurant/bar, Café Picasso, serves a French/Italian hybrid cuisine.

Amenities: Room service, fitness room, baby-sitting, laundry, currency exchange.

MODERATE

Albergo Cesàri. Via di Pietra 89A, 00186 Roma. ☎ **06/679-2386.** Fax 06/679-0882. www.venere.it/home/roma/cesari/cesari.html. E-mail: cesari@venere.it. 50 units. A/C TV TEL. 230,000–300,000L ($133–$174) double; 270,000–340,000L ($157–$197) triple; 390,000L ($226) quad. Rates include breakfast. AE, DC, MC, V. Parking 45,000L ($26). Bus: 492 from Stazione Termini.

The Cesàri, on an ancient street in the old quarter, has occupied its desirable location between the Trevi Fountain and the Pantheon since 1787. Its well-preserved exterior harmonizes with the Temple of Neptune and many little antiques shops nearby. The rooms have mostly functional modern pieces, but there are a few traditional trappings as well to maintain character. In 1998, all guest rooms and the breakfast room were completely renovated.

🕐 Family-Friendly Hotels

Cavalieri Hilton *(see p. 116)* This hotel is like a resort, with a pool, gardens, and plenty of grounds for children to run and play. It's only 15 minutes from the center of Rome, which you can reach by the hotel shuttle bus.

Hotel Massimo d'Azeglio *(see p. 102)* Near Stazione Termini, this place has long been a family favorite. The rooms are large, well kept, and comfortable, and the well-trained staff is great with kids.

Hotel Ranieri *(see p. 102)* This hotel offers a family-style atmosphere, with some rooms that are large enough to house families of three or four. Baby cots are on hand as well.

Hotel Venezia *(see p. 103)* At this good moderately priced family hotel near Stazione Termini, the rooms have been renovated and most are large enough to hold extra beds for children.

INEXPENSIVE

Pensione Navona. Via dei Sediari 8, 00186 Roma. ☎ **06/686-4203.** Fax 06/6880-3802. 30 units, 22 with bathroom. 130,000L ($75) double without bathroom, 140,000L ($81) double with bathroom; 210,000L ($122) triple with bathroom. Rates include breakfast. No credit cards. Bus: 70, 81, 87, or 115.

The pensione is on a small street radiating from Piazza Navona's southeastern tip. The rooms aren't as glamorous as the exterior, but the Navona offers decent accommodations, many of which have been renovated and some of which open to views of the central quiet courtyard. Run by an Australian-born family of Italian descent, the place boasts tiled bathrooms, ceilings high enough to help relieve the midsummer heat, and an array of architectural oddities (the legacy of the continual construction this palace has undergone since 1360). You can get an air-conditioned room by request for 40,000L ($23) extra per night (only in the doubles with bath).

NEAR PIAZZA DEL POPOLO & THE SPANISH STEPS
VERY EXPENSIVE

The Hassler. Piazza Trinità dei Monti 6, 00187 Roma. ☎ **800/223-6800** in the U.S., or 06/699-340. Fax 06/678-9991. E-mail: hasselroma@maclink.it. 100 units. A/C MINIBAR TV TEL. 695,000L–1,030,000L ($403–$597) double; from 2,250,000L ($1,305) suite. Breakfast 55,000L ($33). AE, DC, MC, V. Parking 40,000L ($23) in nearby garage. Metro: Piazza di Spagna.

The Hassler uses the Spanish Steps as its grand entrance. The original 1885 Hassler was rebuilt in 1944. Its crown has become a bit tarnished, but it has such a mystique from tradition and the one-of-kind location that it can get away with charging astronomical rates. The lounges and the guest rooms, with their "Italian Park Avenue" trappings, all strike a faded if still glamorous 1930s note. The rooms, some of which are small, have a personalized look—Oriental rugs, tasteful draperies at the French windows, brocade furnishings, comfortable beds, and (the nicest touch of all) bowls of fresh flowers. Some have balconies with views of the city. Despite all this, you can get better rooms elsewhere in Rome for this kind of money.

Dining/Diversions: The Hassler Roof Restaurant is a favorite with visitors and Romans alike for its fine cuisine and view. Its Sunday brunch is a popular rendezvous time. The Hassler Bar is ideal, if a little formal, for cocktails; in the evening it has piano music.

Amenities: Room service, telex and fax, limousine, in-room massages, laundry, nearby fitness center, tennis court (summer), free bicycles available.

✪ **Hotel de la Ville Inter-Continental Roma.** Via Sistina 67–69, 00187 Roma. ☎ **800/ 327-0200** in the U.S. and Canada, or 06/67-331. Fax 06/678-4213. www.interconti.com. E-mail: rome@interconti.com. 215 units. A/C MINIBAR TV TEL. 560,000–730,000L ($325– $423) double; from 990,000L ($574) suite. Rates include continental breakfast. AE, DC, MC, V. Parking 35,000L ($20). Metro: Piazza di Spagna or Barberini.

We prefer this place to the overpriced glory of the Hassler next door. The hotel looks deluxe (it's officially rated first class) from the minute you walk through the revolving door, where a smartly uniformed doorman greets you. Once inside this palace, built in the 19th century on the site of the ancient Gardens of Lucullus, you'll find Oriental rugs, marble tables, brocade furniture, and an English-speaking staff. There are end-less corridors leading to what at first seems a maze of ornamental lounges. Some of the public rooms have a sort of 1930s elegance, others are strictly baroque, and in the middle of it all is an open courtyard.

The guest rooms and the public areas have been renovated in a beautifully classic and yet up-to-date way. The higher rooms with balconies have wonderful views of Rome, and you're free to use the roof terrace with the same view.

Dining/Diversions: La Piazzetta de la Ville Restaurant, on the second floor over-looking the garden, serves an Italian and international cuisine. The hotel also has an American bar with a pianist during cocktail hours.

Amenities: 24-hour room service, baby-sitting, laundry/valet.

Hotel d'Inghilterra. Via Bocca di Leone 14, 00187 Roma. ☎ **06/69-981.** Fax 06/ 6992-2243. www.charminghotels.it/inghilterra. E-mail: hir@charminghotel.it. 98 units. A/C MINIBAR TV TEL. 660,000L ($383) double; 825,000L ($479) triple; 1,133,000L ($657) suite. Rates include breakfast. AE, DC, MC, V. Parking 40,000L ($23). Metro: Piazza di Spagna.

The Inghilterra holds onto its traditions and heritage, even though it has been reno-vated. If you're willing to spend a king's ransom, Rome's most fashionable small hotel is up there with the Hassler and Inter-Continental. It has hosted big names from Ernest Hemingway and Franz Liszt to Alec Guinness. The rooms have mostly old pieces (gilt and lots of marble, mahogany chests, and glittery mirrors) complemented with modern conveniences. Some, however, are just too small. The preferred rooms are higher up, opening onto a tile terrace, with a balustrade and a railing covered with flowering vines and plants.

Dining: The Roman Garden serves excellent Roman dishes. The English-style bar with its paneled walls, tip-top tables, and old lamps is a favorite gathering spot in the evening. The Roman Garden Lounge offers light lunches and snacks.

Amenities: Concierge, room service, dry cleaning/laundry, baby-sitting, car-rental desk, secretarial services, gym.

EXPENSIVE

✪ **Hotel Scalinata di Spagna.** Piazza Trinità dei Monti 17, 00187 Roma. ☎ **06/ 679-3006.** Fax 06/6994-0598. www.italyhotel.com/home/roma/scalinata/scalinata.html. 16 units. A/C MINIBAR TV TEL. 450,000L ($261) double; 500,000L ($290) triple; 700,000L ($406) suite. Rates include breakfast. AE, MC, V. Parking 40,000L ($23). Metro: Piazza di Spagna.

This hotel near the Spanish Steps has always been one of Rome's top choices. Think of it as an intimate inn or boutique hotel rather than a full-service hotel. It's at the top of the steps, across from the Hassler, in a delightful little building—only two floors are visible from the outside—nestled between much larger structures, with four relief

Accommodations Near the Spanish Steps

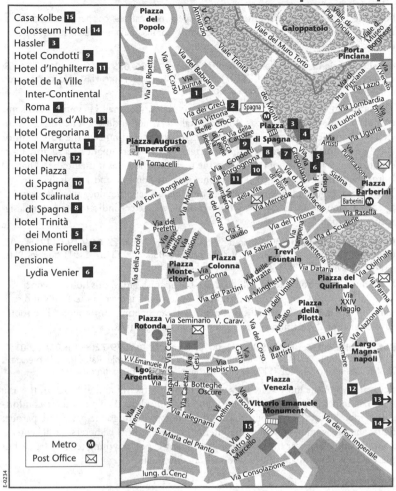

Casa Kolbe **15**
Colosseum Hotel **14**
Hassler **3**
Hotel Condotti **9**
Hotel d'Inghilterra **11**
Hotel de la Ville
    Inter-Continental
    Roma **4**
Hotel Duca d'Alba **13**
Hotel Gregoriana **7**
Hotel Margutta **1**
Hotel Nerva **12**
Hotel Piazza
    di Spagna **10**
Hotel Scalinata
    di Spagna **8**
Hotel Trinità
    dei Monti **5**
Pensione Fiorella **2**
Pensione
    Lydia Venier **6**

Metro **Ⓜ**
Post Office ✉

columns across the facade and window boxes with bright blossoms. The recently redecorated interior is like an old inn's—the public rooms are small with bright print slipcovers, old clocks, and low ceilings.

The decorations vary radically from one guest room to the next. Some have low beamed ceilings and ancient-looking wood furniture; others have loftier ceilings and more run-of-the-mill furniture. Everything is spotless and pleasing to the eye.

Dining: Breakfast is the only meal served, but you'll enjoy it on one of the most panoramic terraces in all Rome.

Amenities: Concierge, dry cleaning/laundry, baby-sitting.

MODERATE

Hotel Condotti. Via Mario de' Fiori 37, 00187 Roma. ☎ **06/679-4661.** Fax 06/679-0484. 16 units. A/C MINIBAR TV TEL. 230,000–320,000L ($133–$186) double; 290,000–350,000L ($168–$203) minisuite. Rates include breakfast. AE, DC, MC, V. Metro: Piazza di Spagna.

Small, choice, and terrific for shoppers intent on being near the toniest boutiques, this hotel is chic, intimate, and comfortable. It's small-scale (no bar, no restaurant, though breakfast is served). The mostly English-speaking staff is cooperative and hard-working. The modern, mostly blue-and-white rooms may not have much historic charm, but they're comfortable and soothing.

Hotel Gregoriana. Via Gregoriana 18, 00187 Roma. ☎ **06/679-4269.** Fax 06/678-4258. 19 units. A/C TV TEL. 340,000L ($197) double. Rates include breakfast. No credit cards. Parking 35,000L ($20). Metro: Piazza di Spagna.

Though surrounded by much more expensive places, the small Gregoriana has some fans of its own, including guests from the Italian fashion industry. The ruling matri-arch of an aristocratic family left the building to an order of nuns in the 19th century, but they eventually retreated to other quarters. (Today there might be a slightly more elevated spirituality in Room C than in the rest of the hotel, as it used to be a chapel.) Throughout the hotel, the smallish rooms provide comfort and fine Italian design. The elevator cage is a black-and-gold art-deco fantasy, and the door to each room has a reproduction of an Erté print whose fanciful characters indicate the letter desig-nating that room.

Hotel Piazza di Spagna. Via Mario de' Fiori 61, 00187 Roma. ☎ **06/679-6412.** Fax 06/679-0654. 16 units. A/C MINIBAR TV TEL. 270,000–330,000L ($157–$191) double. Rates include breakfast. AE, MC, V. Metro: Piazza di Spagna. Bus: 590.

Set about a block from the downhill side of the Spanish Steps, this hotel was once just an unknown run-down pensione until new owners took it over in the 1990s and sub-stantially upgraded it. It's small but classic, with an inviting atmosphere. The rooms have a functional streamlined decor; some even have Jacuzzis.

Hotel Trinità dei Monti. Via Sistina 91, 00187 Roma. ☎ **06/679-7206.** Fax 06/699-0111. 23 units. MINIBAR TV TEL. 220,000–290,000L ($128–$168) double. Rates include breakfast. AE, MC, V. Parking 30,000L ($17). Metro: Barberini or Piazza di Spagna.

Between two of the most-visited piazzas in Rome (Barberini and di Spagna), this is a well-maintained friendly hotel. The rooms come in subdued colors and are comfort-able if not flashy. They're outfitted with elaborate herringbone-patterned parquet floors and big windows flooding the interior with sunlight. The hotel's social center is a simple coffee bar near the reception desk. Don't expect anything terribly fancy, but the welcome is warm and the location ultra-convenient.

INEXPENSIVE

Hotel Margutta. Via Laurina 34, 00187 Roma. ☎ **06/322-3674.** Fax 06/320-0395. 21 units. 165,000L ($96) double; 220,000L ($128) triple. Rates include breakfast. AE, DC, MC, V. Metro: Flaminio.

The Margutta, on a cobblestone street near Piazza del Popolo, offers attractively dec-orated rooms, a helpful staff, and a simple breakfast room. The best guest rooms are the three on the top floor, offering a great view. Two of these three (nos. 50 and 51) share a terrace, and the larger room has a private terrace. (There's usually a 20 to 35% supplement for these.) Drawbacks? No air-conditioning, no room phones.

Pensione Fiorella. Via del Babuino 196, 00187 Roma. ☎ **06/361-0597.** 7 units, none with bathroom. 110,000L ($64) double. Rates include breakfast. No credit cards. Metro: Flaminio.

A few steps from Piazza del Popolo is this utterly basic but comfortable pensione. Antonio Albano and his family are one of the best reasons to stay here—they speak little English, but their humor and warm welcome make renting one of their very clean rooms a lot like visiting a lighthearted Italian relative. Logistical drawbacks: The doors of the Fiorella shut at 1am, and reservations can be made only a day before you check in.

Pensione Lydia Venier. Via Sistina 42, 00187 Roma. ☎ **06/679-1744.** Fax 06/679-7263. 28 units, 17 with shower only, 10 with bathroom. TV TEL. 180,000L ($104) double without bathroom, 220,000L ($128) double with shower only, 240,000L ($139) double with bathroom. Rates include breakfast. AE, DC, MC, V. Metro: Piazza Barberini or Piazza di Spagna.

This respectable pensione is on one of the upper floors of a gracefully proportioned apartment building on a street jutting out from the top of the Spanish Steps. The rooms are utterly simple, with understated furnishings—a dignified combination of slightly battered modern and antique and an occasional reminder of an earlier era (like a ceiling fresco). The service here is wonderful, and the staff go out of their way to be helpful, especially to those who don't speak Italian.

NEAR VATICAN CITY
VERY EXPENSIVE

✪ **Hotel Atlante Star.** Via Vitelleschi 34, 00193 Roma. ☎ **06/687-3233.** Fax 06/ 687-2300. www.atlantehotels.com. E-mail: atlante.star@atlantehotels.com. 65 units. A/C MINIBAR TV TEL. 540,000L ($313) double; from 600,000L ($348) suite. Rates include breakfast. AE, DC, MC, V. Parking 40,000L ($23). Metro: Ottaviano. Tram: 19 or 30.

The Atlante Star is a first-class hotel near the Vatican, with striking views of St. Peter's. The tastefully renovated lobby is covered with dark marble, chrome trim, and exposed wood; the upper floors give the impression of being inside a luxurious ocean liner. This stems partly from the lavish use of curved and lacquered surfaces, walls upholstered in printed fabrics, modern bathrooms, and wall-to-wall carpeting. Even the door handles are deco. The rooms are small but posh, with all the modern comforts. There's also a royal suite with a Jacuzzi. If there's no room at this inn, the owner will try to accommodate you in his less expensive **Hotel Atlante Garden** nearby.

Dining: Les Etoiles is an elegant roof-garden choice at night, with a 360° view of Rome and an illuminated St. Peter's in the background. The flavorful cuisine is inspired in part by Venice.

Amenities: 24-hour room service, laundry/valet, baby-sitting, express checkout, foreign-currency exchange, secretarial services in English, translation services.

EXPENSIVE

Hotel Columbus. Via della Conciliazione 33, 00193 Roma. ☎ **06/686-5435.** Fax 06/ 686-4874. 92 units. MINIBAR TV TEL. 370,000L ($215) double. Rates include buffet breakfast. AE, DC, MC, V. Free parking. Bus: 62.

An impressive 15th-century palace, the Columbus was once the home of the wealthy cardinal who became Pope Julius II and tormented Michelangelo into painting the Sistine Chapel. The building looks much as it must have centuries ago—a severe time-stained facade, small windows, and heavy wooden doors leading from the street to the colonnades and arches of the inner courtyard. The cobbled entranceway leads to a reception hall with castlelike furniture, then on to a series of baronial public rooms. Note the main salon with its walk-in fireplace, oil portraits, battle scenes, and Oriental rugs.

The guest rooms are considerably simpler than the tiled and tapestried salons, done in soft beiges and furnished with comfortable modern pieces. All the accommodations are spacious, but a few are enormous and still have such original details as decorated wood ceilings and frescoed walls. However, only some are air-conditioned.

Dining: Many guests like La Veranda so much they prefer to dine here at night instead of roaming the streets looking for a trattoria. Standard Italian cuisine is served: time-tested recipes made with fresh ingredients rather than anything too innovative.

Amenities: Concierge, room service, dry cleaning/laundry, car-rental desk.

Hotel dei Mellini. Via Muzio Clementi 81, 00193 Roma. ☎ **06/324771.** Fax 06/3247-7801. www.benere.it/roma/dei-mellini. E-mail: dei.mellini/net.it. 80 units. A/C MINIBAR TV TEL. 410,000L ($238) double; 500,000–600,000L ($290–$348) suite. Rates include breakfast. AE, DC, MC, V. Metro: Lepanto or Flaminio. Parking 35,000L ($20).

Built in the neoclassical style as a town house in the early 1900s, this hotel remained a private home until 1970, when it was abandoned and stood as an empty shell. In 1995, it opened after a radical transformation into a four-star winner that has become one of the neighborhood's most desirable hotels. It consists of two interconnected buildings, one with four floors and one with six; the top is graced with a terrace overlooking the baroque cupolas of at least three churches. A small staff, headed by the highly capable Roberto Altezza, maintains comfortable, carefully decorated guest rooms whose decor includes art deco touches, Italian marble, heavy draperies, and mahogany furniture. One of the best points about the hotel is its location in a quiet neighborhood without a lot of traffic.

Dining: Other than a simple platter of food that the staff might rustle up on short notice, breakfast is the only meal served. The breakfast room is extremely pleasant, adjoining a small green courtyard. There's also a hospitable American bar.

Amenities: Concierge, room service, dry cleaning/laundry, courtesy car, car-rental desk, nearby gym.

INEXPENSIVE

Hotel Emmaus. Via delle Fornaci 23, 00165 Roma. ☎ **06/638-0370.** Fax 06/635-658. 26 units. MINIBAR TV. 150,000–180,000L ($87–$104) double. Rates include breakfast. AE, DC, MC, V. Metro: Ottaviano. Bus: 65.

Because of its relatively low prices and location a short walk west of the Vatican, you might share this hotel with Catholic pilgrims from all over the world. Occupying an older building last renovated and upgraded in 1992, it offers unpretentious and basic but comfortable accommodations. There's an elevator and a breakfast area.

Hotel Sant'Angelo. Via Mariana Dionigi 16, 00193 Roma. ☎ **06/322-0758.** Fax 06/320-4451. 25 units. AC TV TEL. 150,000–220,000L ($87–$128) double; 210,000–250,000L ($122–$145) triple. Rates include continental breakfast. AE, DC, MC, V. Parking 35,000L ($20). Metro: Cavour.

Right off Piazza Cavour (northeast of the Castel Sant'Angelo) and a 10-minute walk from St. Peter's, this hotel is in a relatively untouristy area. Maintained and operated by several members of the Torre family, it occupies the second and third floors of an imposing 200-year-old building whose other floors house offices and private apartments. The rooms are simple, modern, and clean, with wooden furniture and views of either the street or of a rather bleak but quiet courtyard.

Marta Guest House. Via Marianna Dionigi 17, 00193 Roma. ☎ **06/32-40-428.** Fax 06/323-0184. 9 units, 1 with bathroom. 95,000L ($55) double without bathroom, 130,000L ($75) double with bathroom. AE, DC, MC, V. Bus: 492 to Piazza Cavour.

Named after one of its owners, Marta Balbi, this is a friendly and well-scrubbed but simple pensione with a good location near Piazza Cavour, not far from the Spanish Steps. It fills the entire second floor of a 10-story apartment house built around 1900. Take an elevator upstairs to the unassuming reception area, where a staff member will lead you to one of the airy and high-ceilinged but utterly plain and unassuming rooms. No breakfast is served, but the neighborhood is filled with cafes where you can get your morning cappuccino.

Pension Alimandi. Via Tunisi 8, 00192 Roma. ☎ **06/3972-6300.** Fax 06/3972-3943. 35 units. TV TEL. 175,000L ($102) double. Breakfast 15,000L ($9). AE, DC, MC, V. Parking 25,000L ($15). Metro: Ottaviano.

Named after the three brothers who run it (Luigi, Enrico, and Paolo), this friendly, well-managed guesthouse was built as an apartment house in 1908. It's in a bland residential neighborhood very close to the Vatican. The rooms are comfortable, albeit a bit small, with unremarkable contemporary furniture and cramped but modern-looking bathrooms. Each of the three upper floors is serviced by two elevators leading down to a simple lobby. The social center and most appealing spot is the roof garden, with potted plants, a bar, and views toward the dome of St. Peter's. Breakfast is available.

Residence Giuggioli. Via Germanico 198, 00192 Roma. ☎ **06/324-2113.** 5 units, 1 with bathroom. 110,000L ($64) double without bathroom, 130,000L ($75) double with bathroom. No credit cards. Parking 25,000–40,000L ($15–$23) in nearby garage. Metro: Ottaviano.

The force behind this place is Sra. Gasparina Giuggioli, whose family founded this guesthouse in the 1940s. It occupies most of the second floor of a five-story apartment house from the 1870s, with accommodations in high-ceilinged rooms that were originally much grander than they are today but whose noble proportions are still obvious. Three of the five rooms have balconies overlooking the street; the one with the private bathroom is no. 6. Residence Giuggioli is always popular and crowded, partly because the owner is so convivial and partly because the rooms are larger-than-expected and have a scattering of antiques and reproductions. There's no breakfast or other meal service, but there are cafes nearby.

If this place is full, walk a few flights to the similar **Pensione Lady** (☎ **06/ 324-2112**), where up to seven rooms might be available at about the same rates.

IN PARIOLI
VERY EXPENSIVE

✪ **Hotel Lord Byron.** Via G. de Notaris 5, 00197 Roma. ☎ **06/322-0404.** Fax 06/ 322-0405. www.italyhotel.com/roma/lord-byron. E-mail: lord.byron@italyhotel.com. 37 units. A/C MINIBAR TV TEL. 470,000–620,000L ($273–$360) double; from 800,000L ($464) suite. Rates include buffet breakfast. AE, DC, MC, V. Metro: Flaminio. Bus: 26 or 52.

Lots of sophisticated travelers with hefty wallets are forgetting about the old landmarks (the Grand and Excelsior) and choosing to check into this chic boutique hotel. The Lord Byron exemplifies modern Rome—an art-deco villa set on a residential hilltop in Parioli, an area of embassies and exclusive town houses at the edge of the Villa Borghese. From the curving entrance steps off the staffed parking lot in front, you'll notice striking design touches. Flowers are everywhere, the lighting is discreet, and everything is on an intimate scale—it seems more like a private home than a hotel. Each of the guest rooms is unique, but most have lots of mirrors, upholstered walls, a spacious bathroom with gray marble accessories, a big dressing room/closet, and all the amenities. Check into room no. 503, 602, or 603 for the most panoramic views.

Dining: Relais Le Jardin is one of Rome's best restaurants (see "Dining," later in this chapter).

Amenities: Concierge, 24-hour room service, laundry/valet.

MODERATE

Hotel degli Aranci. Via Barnaba Oriani 9–11, 00197 Roma. ☎ **06/808-5250.** Fax 06/ 807-0202. 57 units. A/C MINIBAR TV TEL. 300,000L ($174) double; 350,000L ($203) suite. Rates include breakfast. AE, DC, MC, V. Free parking. Bus: 3 or 53.

This former villa is on a tree-lined street, surrounded by similar villas now used, in part, as consulates' and diplomats' homes. Most of the accommodations have tall windows opening onto city views and are filled with provincial furnishings or English-style reproductions. The public rooms have memorabilia of ancient Rome scattered about, like medallions of soldiers in profile, old engravings of ruins, and classical vases. A marble-topped bar in an alcove off the sitting room adds a relaxed touch. From the glass-walled breakfast room at the rear, you can see the tops of orange trees.

INEXPENSIVE

Hotel delle Muse. Via Tommaso Salvini 18, 00197 Roma. ☎ **06/808-8333.** Fax 06/808-5749. E-mail: hmuse@flashnet.it. 61 units. TV TEL. 160,000–200,000L ($93–$116) double; 220,000–260,000L ($128–$151) triple. Rates include buffet breakfast. AE, CB, DC, DISC, MC, V. Parking 30,000L ($17). Bus: 4. Tram: 19.

This three-star hotel, half a mile north of the Villa Borghese, is a winning but undiscovered choice. It's run by the efficient English-speaking Giorgio Lazar. Most rooms have been renovated but remain rather spartan and minimalist. In summer, Sr. Lazar operates a restaurant in the garden. A bar is open 24 hours in case you get thirsty at 5am. There's also a TV room, a writing room, and a dining room.

IN MONTE MARIO
VERY EXPENSIVE

Cavalieri Hilton. Via Cadlolo 101, 00136 Roma. ☎ **800/445-8667** in the U.S. and Canada, or 06/35091. Fax 06/3509-2241. 393 units. A/C MINIBAR TV TEL. 625,000–825,000L ($375–$495) double; from 1,350,000L ($810) suite. AE, CB, DC, DISC, MC, V. Parking 5,000–35,000L ($2.90–$21). Free shuttle bus to/from city center.

The Cavalieri Hilton combines all the advantages of a resort hotel with the convenience of being a 15-minute drive from the city center. Overlooking Rome and the Alban Hills from atop Monte Mario, it's set among 15 acres of trees, flowering shrubs, and stonework. Its facilities are amazingly complete. The entrance leads into a lavish red-and-gold lobby, whose sculpture and winding staircases are usually flooded with sunlight from the massive windows.

The guest rooms and suites, many with panoramic views, are contemporary and stylish. Soft furnishings in pastels are paired with Italian furniture in warm-toned woods. Each unit has a keyless electronic lock, individually controlled heating and air-conditioning, a color TV with in-house movies, a radio, and a bedside control for all the gadgets, as well as a spacious balcony. The bathrooms, sheathed in Italian marble, come with large mirrors, a hair dryer, international electric sockets, a vanity mirror, piped-in music, and a phone. There are facilities for the disabled.

Dining/Diversions: The stellar La Pergola restaurant boasts one of the best views in Rome; its light Mediterranean menu emphasizes seafood like tagliolini with tiger prawns in pesto. In summer, Il Giardino dell'Uliveto, with a pool veranda, is an ideal choice.

Amenities: Concierge, room service, laundry/valet, tennis courts, jogging paths, indoor arcade of shops, outdoor pool. The hotel's health and fitness center could be the setting for a film on late Empire decadence, with its triple-arched Turkish bath, marble, and mosaics; there's a 55-foot indoor pool and a state-of-the-art weight room.

4 Dining

Rome remains one of the world's great capitals for dining, with even more diversity today than ever before. Most of its trattorie haven't changed their menus in a quarter of a century (except to raise the prices, of course), but there's an increasing number of chic upscale spots with chefs willing to experiment as well as a growing handful of Chinese, Indian, and other ethnic spots for those days when you just can't face another plate of pasta. The great thing about Rome is that you don't have to spend a fortune to eat really well.

Rome's cooking isn't subtle, but its kitchen rivals anything the chefs of Florence or Venice can turn out. A feature of Roman restaurants is skill at borrowing—and sometimes improving on—the cuisine of other regions. Throughout the capital you'll come across Neapolitan (*alla neapolitana*), Bolognese (*alla bolognese*), Florentine (*alla fiorentina*), and even Sicilian (*alla siciliana*) specialties. One of the city's oldest sections, Trastevere, is a gold mine of colorful streets and restaurants with time-tested recipes.

In general, lunch is served 1 to 3pm and dinner 8 to around 10:30pm. August is a popular month for Romans to leave on vacation and so many restaurants will be closed.

NEAR STAZIONE TERMINI
MODERATE
Scoglio di Frisio. Via Merulana 256. ☎ 06/487-2765. Reservations recommended. Main courses 18,000–32,000L ($10–$19). AE, DC, MC, V. Mon–Fri 12:30–3pm; daily 7:30–11pm. Metro: Manzoni. Bus: 714 or 16 from Stazione Termini. NEAPOLITAN/PIZZA.

Scoglio di Frisio is the choice suprême to introduce yourself to the Neapolitan kitchen. Get reacquainted with a genuine plate-sized Neapolitan pizza (crunchy, oozy, and excellent) with clams and mussels. Or perhaps start with a medley of stuffed vegetables and antipasti before moving on to chicken cacciatore or veal scaloppine. Scoglio di Frisio also makes for an inexpensive night of slightly hokey but still charming entertainment, as cornball "O Sole Mio" renditions and other Neapolitan songs spring forth from a guitar, mandolin, and strolling tenor (who's Mario Lanza reincarnate). The nautical decor (in honor of the top-notch fish dishes) is complete with a high-ceilinged grotto of fisher's nets, crustaceans, and a miniature three-masted schooner.

INEXPENSIVE
Il Dito e La Luna. Via dei Sabelli 47–51, San Lorenzo. ☎ 06/494-0726. Reservations recommended. Main courses 18,000–22,000L ($10–$13). No credit cards. Mon–Sat 8pm–midnight. Metro: Termini. SICILIAN/ITALIAN.

This charming small-scale restaurant has a menu that's equally divided between traditional Sicilian and more creative and up-to-date recipes prepared with gusto and flair. Il Dito e La Luna is an unpretentious bistro, with counters and service areas accented with the fruits of a bountiful harvest. The menu includes fresh orange-infused anchovies served on orange segments, creamy flan of mild onions and mountain cheese, and seafood couscous loaded with shellfish. Pastas like square-cut spaghetti (*tonnarelli*) prepared with mussels, bacon, tomatoes, and exotic mushrooms are succulent. Even those not particularly enamored with fish might like the *baccalà mantecato* (baked and pulverized salt cod) with lentils.

Trimani Wine Bar. Via Cernaia 37b. ☎ 06/446-9630. Salads and platters 10,000–35,000L ($6–$20); glass of wine (depending on vintage) 5,000–12,000L ($2.90–$7). AE, DC, MC, V.

A Dining Note

At rock-bottom restaurants you may be charged a *pane e coperto* ("bread and cover charge"), from 1,000L to 3,000L (60¢ to $1.75) per person. Also note that a *servizio* (tip) of 10 to 15% will often be added to your bill or included in the price, though patrons often leave an extra 1,000L to 3,000L (60¢ to $1.75) as a token.

Rome Dining

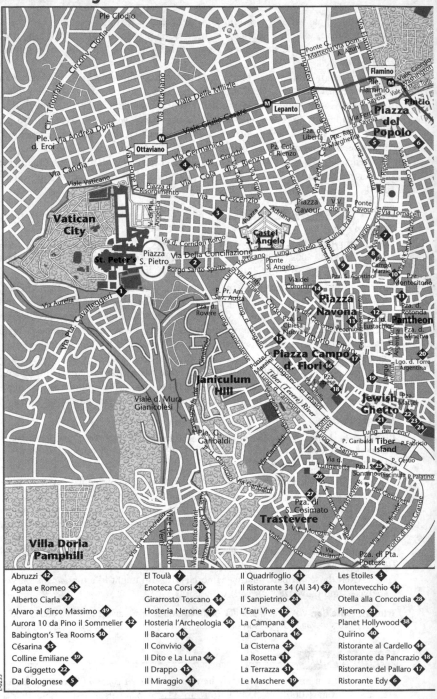

Abruzzi **42**
Agata e Romeo **45**
Alberto Ciarla **27**
Alvaro al Circo Massimo **49**
Aurora 10 da Pino il Sommelier **32**
Babington's Tea Rooms **30**
Césarina **35**
Colline Emiliane **39**
Da Giggetto **22**
Dal Bolognese **5**

El Toulà **7**
Enoteca Corsi **20**
Girarrosto Toscano **34**
Hosteria Nerone **47**
Hosteria l'Archeologia **50**
Il Bacaro **10**
Il Convivio **9**
Il Dito e La Luna **46**
Il Drappo **15**
Il Miraggio **41**

Il Quadrifoglio **43**
Il Ristorante 34 (Al 34) **37**
Il Sanpietrino **24**
L'Eau Vive **12**
La Campana **8**
La Carbonara **16**
La Cisterna **25**
La Rosetta **11**
La Terrazza **31**
Le Maschere **19**

Les Etoiles **3**
Montevecchio **14**
Otella alla Concordia **28**
Piperno **21**
Planet Hollywood **38**
Quirino **40**
Ristorante al Cardello **44**
Ristorante da Pancrazio **18**
Ristorante del Pallaro **17**
Ristorante Edy **6**

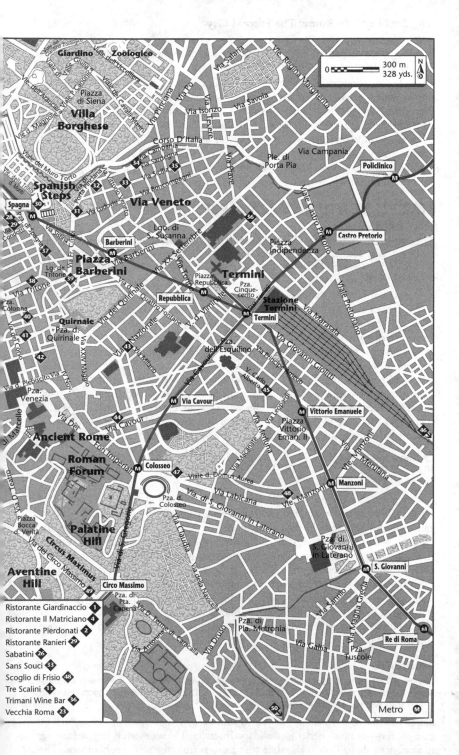

Ristorante Giardinaccio ❶
Ristorante Il Matriciano ❹
Ristorante Pierdonati ❷
Ristorante Ranieri ㉙
Sabatini ㉖
Sans Souci ㉝
Scoglio di Frisio ㊽
Tre Scalini ⓭
Trimani Wine Bar ㊱
Vecchia Roma ㉓

Mon–Sat 11:30am–3pm and 5:30pm–midnight. Closed several weeks in Aug. Metro: Piazza della Repubblica or Castro Pretorio. CONTINENTAL.

Opened as a tasting center for French and Italian wines, spumantis, and liqueurs, this elegant wine bar has a lovely decor (stylish but informal) and comfortable seating. More than 30 wines are available by the glass, and to accompany them you can choose from a bistro-style menu, with light dishes like salade niçoise, vegetarian pastas, herb-laden bean soups (fagiole), quiche, Hungarian goulash, and platters of French and Italian cheeses and pâtés. Trimani also maintains a well-stocked shop about 40 yards from its wine bar, at Via Goito 20 (☎ 06/446-9661), where an astonishing array of Italian wines is for sale.

NEAR VIA VENETO & PIAZZA BARBERINI
VERY EXPENSIVE

✪ **La Terrazza.** In the Hotel Eden, Via Ludovisi 49. ☎ 06/478-121. Reservations recommended. Main courses 42,000–72,000L ($24–$42); fixed-price menu 120,000L ($70). AE, DC, MC, V. Daily 12:30–2:30pm and 7:30–10:30pm. Metro: Barberini. ITALIAN/INTERNATIONAL.

This restaurant serves the city's finest cuisine (a distinction shared with Relais Le Jardin, below) and offers a sweeping view over St. Peter's from the fifth floor of the Eden. The service manages to be formal and flawless, yet not at all intimidating. Chef Enrico Derfligher, the wizard behind about a dozen top-notch Italian restaurants around Europe, prepares a menu that varies with the seasons and is among the most polished in Rome. Selections might include a warm salad of grilled vegetables lightly toasted with greens in balsamic vinegar, red tortelli (whose pink coloring comes from tomato mousse) stuffed with mascarpone cheese and drizzled with lemon, or grilled tagliata of beef with eggplant and tomatoes. On our last visit, we shared a superb "symphony" of seafood—artfully arranged and prepared only for two or more, it includes perfectly seasoned Mediterranean sea bass, turbot, gilthead, and prawns.

✪ **Sans Souci.** Via Sicilia 20. ☎ 06/482-1814. Reservations required. Main courses 40,000–70,000L ($23–$41). AE, DC, MC, V. Tues–Sun 8pm–1am. Closed Aug 10–30. Metro: Barberini. FRENCH/ITALIAN.

Not long ago, Sans Souci was getting a little tired but now has bounced back, and Michelin has restored its coveted star. If you want to splurge on a big night out, it's a great place for glitz and old-time glamour. As you step into the dimly lit lounge, the maître d' will present you with the menu, which you can peruse while sipping a drink amid tapestries and glittering mirrors. The menu is ever changing, though the classics never disappear. A great beginning is the goose-liver terrine with truffles, one of the chef's signatures. The fish soup is, according to one Rome restaurant critic, "a legend to experience." The soufflés are also popular (including artichoke, asparagus, and spinach), or perhaps you'll choose ravioli filled with truffles, homemade foie gras, or Normandy lamb. Save room for a special soufflé (prepared for two), such as chocolate and Grand Marnier.

MODERATE

Aurora 10 da Pino Il Sommelier. Via Aurora 10. ☎ 06/474-2779. Reservations recommended. Main courses 20,000–30,000L ($12–$17). AE, DC, MC, V. Tues–Sun noon–3pm and 7–11:15pm. Metro: Barberini. ITALIAN.

Skip those tourist traps along Via Veneto and walk another block or two—you'll be glad you did—or much better food and lovely service. The wait staff is very welcoming to foreigners, though you'll also dine with regulars from the chic neighborhood. The place is noted for its awesome array of more than 250 wines, representing every

Dining Near Stazione Termini & Via Veneto

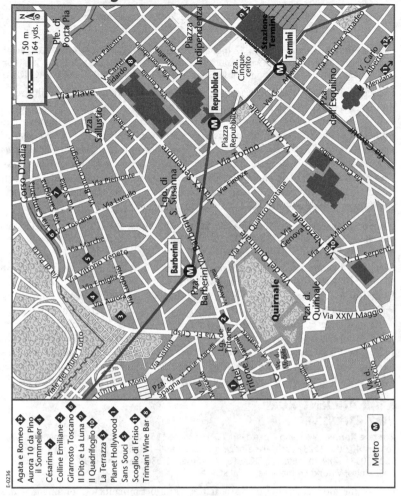

Agata e Romeo ◆12
Aurora 10 da Pino il Sommelier ◆4
Césarina ◆7
Colline Emiliane ◆2
Girarrosto Toscano ◆6
Il Dito e La Luna ◆9
Il Quadrifoglio ◆10
La Terrazza ◆3
Planet Hollywood ◆1
Sans Souci ◆5
Scoglio di Frisio ◆11
Trimani Wine Bar ◆8

Metro: Ⓜ

E-0236

province. Dishes may include linguine with lobster, a Sicilian-style fish fry, swordfish in herb sauce, beef filet with porcini mushrooms, risotto with asparagus, and beef stew flambé. The cookery is savory and first-rate, using top-quality ingredients, and several dishes are prepared tableside with a flourish.

Césarina. Via Piemonte 109. ☎ **06/488-0828.** Reservations recommended. Main courses 17,000–45,000L ($10–$26). AE, DC, MC, V. Mon–Sat 12:30–3pm and 7:30–11pm. Metro: Barberini. EMILIANA-ROMAGNOLA/ROMAN.

Specializing in the cuisines of Rome and the region around Bologna, this former hole-in-the-wall has grown since matriarch Césarina Masi opened it around 1960 (many Rome veterans fondly remember Ms. Masi's strict supervision of her kitchen and how she'd lecture regulars who didn't finish their tagliatelle). Though Césarina died in the mid-1980s, the restaurant keeps her traditions going. The tactful and polite staff roll an excellent *bollito misto* (an array of well-seasoned boiled meats) from table to table on a trolley and often follow with misto Césarina—four kinds of handmade pasta, each served with a different sauce. Equally appealing is the saltimbocca and the *cotoletta alla bolognese*, a veal cutlet baked with ham and cheese. A dessert specialty is semifreddo Césarina with hot chocolate. The food is excellent and the selection of fresh antipasti is very appealing.

Colline Emiliane. Via Avignonesi 22 (right off Piazza Barberini). ☎ **06/481-7538.** Reservations highly recommended. Main courses 16,000–25,000L ($9–$15). MC, V. Sat–Thurs 12:45–2:45pm and 7:45–10:45pm. Closed Aug. Metro: Barberini. EMILIANA-ROMAGNOLA.

Colline Emiliane is a small place serving the *classica cucina bolognese*. It's family-run—the owner is the cook and his wife makes the pasta (about the best you'll encounter in Rome). The house specialty is an inspired *tortellini alla panna* (with cream sauce and truffles), but the less expensive pastas are excellent as well, such as *maccheroni al funghetto* and *tagliatelle alla bolognese*. As an opener for your meal, we suggest *culatello di Zibello*, a delicacy from a small town near Parma known for having the finest prosciutto in the world. Main choices include *braciola di maiale* (boneless rolled pork cutlets that have been stuffed with ham and cheese, breaded, and sautéed) and *giambonnetto* (roast veal Emilian style with roast potatoes).

Girarrosto Toscano. Via Campania 29. ☎ **06/482-3835.** Reservations required. Main courses 22,000–55,000L ($13–$32). AE, DC, MC, V. Thurs–Tues 12:30–2:30pm and 7:30–11pm. Bus: 95, 116. Metro: Barberini, then a long stroll. TUSCAN.

Girarrosto Toscano, facing the walls of the Borghese Gardens, draws large crowds, so you may have to wait. Under the vaulted ceilings of a cellar, it serves some of Rome's finest Tuscan fare. Begin by enjoying an enormous selection of antipasti, from succulent little meatballs and melon with prosciutto to *frittate* (omelets) and an especially delicious Tuscan salami. You're then given a choice of pasta, like fettuccine in cream sauce. Although expensive, *bistecca alla fiorentina* (grilled steak seasoned with oil, salt, and pepper) is worth every lire if you're in the mood to splurge. Fresh fish from the Adriatic is served daily. Order with care if you're on a budget—both meat and fish are priced according to weight and can run considerably higher than the prices above.

NEAR ANCIENT ROME
VERY EXPENSIVE

Agata e Romeo. Via Carlo Alberto 45. ☎ **06/446-6115.** Reservations recommended. Main courses 40,000L ($23) each; fixed-price menus 85,000–100,000L ($49–$58) without wine, 150,000L ($87) with wine. AE, DC, MC, V. Mon–Sat 12:30–3pm and 7:30–11:15pm. Closed Aug. Metro: Vittorio Emmanuele. NEW ROMAN.

One of the most charming places near the Vittorio Emmanuele monument is this striking duplex restaurant in turn-of-the-century Liberty style. You'll enjoy the creative cuisine of Romeo Caraccio (who manages the dining room) and his wife, Agata Parisella, who prepares her own version of sophisticated Roman food. Look for pasta garnished with broccoli and cauliflower and served in skate broth as well as a crisp version of *sformato* loaded with eggplant, parmagiana, mozzarella, and Italian herbs. Swordfish might be served thin-sliced as *roulade* and loaded with capers and olives; beans will probably be studded with mussels, clams, and pasta. Carnivores, fish lovers, and vegetarians will all find something on the menu. If you're feeling flush and are interested in sampling a wide array of dishes, go all the way by ordering the 150,000L ($87) fixed-price menu, which includes at least four courses and a glass of wine to accompany each. For dessert, consider Agata's succulent version of *millefoglie*, a puff pastry stuffed with almonds and sweetened cream.

EXPENSIVE

Alvaro al Circo Massimo. Via dei Cerchi 53. ☎ **06/678-6112.** Reservations required. Main courses 20,000–60,000L ($12–$35). AE, CB, DC, DISC, MC, V. Tues–Sun 11am–3pm; Tues–Sat 7–11pm. Closed Aug. Metro: Circo Massimo. ITALIAN.

Take a Gelato Break

If you're craving addictively tasty gelato, our top choice is ✪ **Giolitti,** Via Uffici del Vicario 40 (☎ 06/699-1243), the city's oldest ice-cream shop. Some of the sundaes look like Vesuvius about to erupt. It's open daily 7am to 2am. They stock flavors you might not have heard of in most North American ice-cream parlors, such as gianduia (chocolate hazelnut). The selection also includes an array of the relatively predictable strawberry, chocolate, coffee, and vanilla flavors, as well as cassata Siciliana and a custard-based rich concoction known as "zabaiglone." There's also a selection of sometimes preposterously oversized showpiece-style sundaes with names like Copa Olimpico di Roma and Copa Mondiale, which contain slightly different portions of absolutely everything. And if you want at least the illusion you're eating healthy, you might opt for the Copa Primanata, which contains ice cream plus lots of cut-up fresh fruit. Depending on what you order, prices here and at each of the establishments noted below range from 2,500L ($1.50) to 16,000L ($10).

Close behind is **Tre Scalini,** Piazza Navona 28 (☎ 06/880-1996; see full entry below), celebrated for its tartufo. It's said that you haven't really experienced Rome until you've enjoyed a tartufo at Tre Scalini. Another favorite is the **Palazzo del Freddo Giovanni Fassi,** Via Principe Eugenio 65–67 (☎ 06/446-4740). More than 100 years old, this ice-cream outlet (part of a gelato factory) turns out delectable concoctions and specializes in rice ice cream. Hours are Tuesday to Sunday noon to 12:30am.

If you're fond of these frothy frulatti frappes for which Italy is famous, head to **Pascucci,** Via Torre Argentina 20 (☎ 06/686-4816), where blenders work all day grinding fresh fruit into delectable drinks. They're open Monday to Saturday noon to 1am. And if you're in the mood for some frozen yogurt, try Yogofruit, P. G. Travani Arquati 118 (☎ 587-972), near Piazza San Sonnino. It's especially popular with young Romans, who line up to sample the tart frozen yogurt concoctions blended with fruit from the Latium countryside. It's open daily noon to 1:30pm.

Alvaro al Circo Massimo, at the edge of the Circus Maximus, is the closest thing in Rome to a genuine provincial inn, right down to the corncobs hanging from the ceiling and rolls of fat sausages. The antipasti and pasta dishes are fine, the meat courses are well prepared, and there's an array of fresh fish that's never overcooked. Other specialties are tagliolini with mushrooms and truffles and roasted turbot with potatoes. They're especially well stocked with exotic seasonal mushrooms, including black truffles rivaling the ones you'd find in Spoleto. A basket of fresh fruit rounds out the meal. The atmosphere is comfortable and mellow. Summer features patio dining.

MODERATE

Il Quadrifoglio. 19 Via del Boschetto. ☎ 06/482-6096. Reservations recommended. Main courses 20,000–25,000L ($12–$15). AE, DC, MC, V. Mon–Sat 7pm–midnight. Metro: Cavour. NEAPOLITAN.

In a grandiose palace, this likable, well-managed restaurant lets you sample the flavors and herbs of Naples and southern Italy. You'll find a tempting selection of antipasti, featuring anchovies, peppers, capers, onions, and breaded and fried eggplant, all garnished with herbs and olive oil. Pastas are made daily, usually with tomato- or oil-based sauces, always with herbs and usually aged crumbling cheeses, and perhaps garnished with squid or octopus. Try a rice dish (one of the best is *sartù di riso,* studded with vegetables, herbs, and meats), followed by grilled octopus or a simple but savory *granatine* (meatballs, usually of veal, bound together with mozzarella). Dessert anyone? A longtime favorite is torta caprese, with hazelnuts and chocolate.

INEXPENSIVE

Abruzzi. Via del Vaccaro 1. ☎ **06/679-3897.** Reservations recommended. Main courses 9,000–22,000L ($5–$13). DC, MC, V. Sun–Fri 12:30–3pm and 7:30–10:30pm. Closed Aug. Bus: 46. ABRUZZESE/ROMANA.

Abruzzi, which takes its name from the region east of Rome, is at one side of Piazza SS. Apostoli, just a short walk from Piazza Venezia. The good food and reasonable prices make it a big draw for students. The chef offers a satisfying assortment of cold antipasti. With your starter, we suggest a liter of garnet-red wine; we once had one whose bouquet was suggestive of Abruzzi's wildflowers. If you'd like a soup as well, you'll find a good *stracciatella* (egg-and-Parmesan soup). A typical main dish is *vitella tonnata con capperi* (veal in tuna sauce with capers).

Hostaria Nerone. Via Terme di Tito 96. ☎ **06/474-5207.** Reservations recommended. Main courses 14,000–22,000L ($8–$13). AE, DC, MC, V. Mon–Sat noon–3pm and 7–11pm. Metro: Colosseo. ROMAN/ITALIAN.

Built atop the ruins of the palace that used to belong to Nero, this is a well-managed trattoria run by the energetic De Santis family, who cook, serve, and handle the large crowds of hungry locals and visitors. Opened in 1929 at the edge of the Colle Oppio Park, it contains two compact dining rooms, plus a terrace lined with flowering shrubs that offers a view over the Colosseum and the majestic ruins of the Baths of Trajan. The copious antipasti buffet represents the bounty of Italy's fields and seas. The pastas include a savory version of spaghetti with clams and steaming bowlfuls of *pasta fagioli* (with beans). There's also grilled crayfish and swordfish; Italian sausages garnished with polenta; veal and chicken dishes; and traditional rich desserts like *zuppe inglese* and *panna cotta.*

Ristorante al Cardello. Via del Cardello 1 (at the corner of Via Cavour). ☎ **06/474-5259.** Reservations recommended. Main courses 10,000–14,000L ($6–$8). AE, DC, MC, V. Mon–Sat 12:30–3:30pm and 7:30–10:45pm. Closed Aug. Metro: Cavour. ROMAN/ABRUZZI.

Charming and conveniently close to the Colosseum, this restaurant has thrived since the 1920s, when it was opened in the semicellar of an 18th-century building. We always love the antipasti buffet, where the flavorful marinated vegetables reveal the bounty of the Italian harvest; at 10,000L ($6) per person for a reasonable serving, it's a great deal. Then you might follow with *bucatini* (thick spaghetti) *alla matriciana;* roast lamb with potatoes, garlic, and mountain herbs; or a thick hearty stew.

NEAR CAMPO DE' FIORI & THE JEWISH GHETTO
EXPENSIVE

Il Drappo. Vicolo del Malpasso 9. ☎ **06/687-7365.** Reservations required. Main courses 22,000–28,000L ($13–$16); fixed-price menu (including Sardinian wine) 65,000–70,000L ($38–$41). AE, CB, DC, V. Mon–Sat 8pm–midnight. Closed 2 weeks in Aug. SARDINIAN.

Il Drappo, a favorite of the local artsy crowd, is on a narrow street near the Tiber and run by a woman known to her regulars only as "Valentina." You'll have your choice of two tastefully decorated dining rooms festooned with yards of patterned cotton draped from the ceiling. Flowers and candles are everywhere. Fixed-price dinners may include a wafer-thin appetizer called *carte di musica* (sheet-music paper), topped with tomatoes, green peppers, parsley, and olive oil, which is followed by fresh spring

ⓘ Family-Friendly Restaurants

Césarina *(see p. 121)* A longtime family favorite, this restaurant offers the most kid-pleasing pastas in town, each handmade and presented with a different sauce. You can request a selection of three kinds of pasta on one plate so finicky young diners can try a little taste of each.

Otello alla Concordia *(see p. 133)* This place is as good as any to introduce your child to hearty Roman cuisine. If your child doesn't like the spaghetti with clams, then maybe the eggplant parmigiana will do. Families can dine in an arbor-covered courtyard.

Tre Scalini *(see p. 129)* All families visit Piazza Navona at some point, and this is the best choice if you'd like a dining table overlooking the square. Perhaps a juggler or a fire eater will come by to entertain the crowds. The cookery is Roman and the menu is wide enough to accommodate most palates—including children's. The tartufo (ice cream with a coating of bittersweet chocolate, cherries, and whipped cream) at the end of the meal is a classic bound to please.

Planet Hollywood, Via del Tritone 118 (☎ 06/4282-8012). If the kids absolutely insist they can't take another day without a burger or a taco, then head to Rome's Planet Hollywood. Behind its stately neoclassical facade, you'll find all the usual suspects on the menu, as well as a souvenir stand if you want to bring some Americana back to America with you.

lamb in season, a fish stew made with tuna caviar, or a changing selection of strongly flavored regional specialties that are otherwise difficult to find in Rome. For dessert, try the *seadas* (cheese-stuffed fried cake in a special dark honey). The service is first-rate.

Piperno. Via Monte de'Cenci 9. ☎ 06/6880-6629. Reservations recommended. Main courses 30,000–40,000L ($17–$23). AE, DC, MC, V. Tues–Sun noon–2:30pm and Tues–Sat 8–10:30pm. Bus: 23. ROMAN.

This longtime favorite, opened in 1856 and now run by the Mazzarella and Boni families, celebrates the Jerusalem artichoke, incorporating it into a number of recipes. You'll be served by a uniformed crew of hardworking waiters, whose advice and suggestions are worth considering. You might begin with *fritto misto vegetariano,* consisting of artichokes, cheese-and-rice croquettes, mozzarella, and stuffed squash blossoms, before moving on to a fish filet, veal, succulent beans, or a pasta creation. Many of the foods are fried or deep-fried and benefit from a technique that leaves them flaky and dry, not at all greasy. (The deep-fried artichokes, when submerged in hot oil, open their leaves into a form that's akin to a lotus's and infinitely more delicious.)

MODERATE

Da Giggetto. Via del Portico d'Ottavia 21–22. ☎ 06/686-1105. Reservations recommended. Main courses 16,000–22,000L ($9–$13). AE, DC, MC, V. Tues–Sun 12:30–3pm and 7:30–11pm. Closed Aug 1–15. Bus: 23. ROMAN/JEWISH.

Da Giggetto is right next to the Theater of Marcellus; old Roman columns extend practically to its doorway. Romans flock to this bustling trattoria for its special traditional dishes. None is more typical than *carciofi alla giudia,* baby-tender fried artichokes—a true delicacy. The cheese concoction called *mozzarella in carrozza* is another delight, as are the zucchini flowers stuffed with mozzarella and anchovies. You could also sample shrimp sautéed in garlic and olive oil or saltimbocca.

Il Sanpietrino. Piazza Costaguti 15. ☎ **06/6880-6471.** Reservations recommended. Main courses 22,000–34,000L ($13–$20). AE, DC, MC, V. Mon–Fri 12:30–2:30pm; Mon–Sat 8–11pm. Metro: Colosseo or Circo Massimo. ROMAN.

This Jewish Ghetto restaurant, with three formal dining rooms, is stylish but affordable, with a sophisticated selection of both traditional and modern dishes. Chef Marco Cardio uses market-fresh ingredients to prepare a seasonal cuisine that's varied and inventive at any time of the year. His combinations are often a surprise but generally delightful—the *pasta fagiole* (bean soup) comes not only with the traditional ingredients but also with mussels and even octopus. The medley of fish antipasti is so tempting you might want to make a meal of it, enjoying items like fresh anchovies baked between layers of well-seasoned eggplant. Main courses (if you still have room after all that antipasti) include ravioli stuffed with sea bass or a *bignolini*, pastry baked with porcini mushrooms and a cheese fondue. We always go for the crème brûlée for dessert, but if you want something lighter, the fresh tangerine sorbet is wonderful.

La Carbonara. Piazza Campo de' Fiori 23. ☎ **06/686-4783.** Reservations recommended. Main courses 16,000–30,000L ($9–$17). AE, MC, V. Wed–Mon noon–2:30pm and 6:30–11:30pm. Closed 3 weeks in Aug. Bus: 46, 62, or 64. ROMAN.

In an antique palazzetto at the edge of the market square, this amiable trattoria claims to be the home of the original spaghetti carbonara. According to a much-disputed legend, the owner's ancestors devised the recipe in the final days of World War II, when American GIs donated to the chef their K-rations of powdered eggs and salted bacon. The result was the pasta dish enriched with egg yolks, cheese, and bacon that's world famous. A cholesterol festival, for sure, but it's worth the calories. The menu also features succulent antipasti, grilled meats, fresh and intelligently prepared seasonal vegetables, and several other kinds of pasta, including tagliolini with porcinis. Another specialty is bucatini al'Amatriciana, with a sauce of tomato, bacon, and hot peppers.

Ristorante da Pancrazio. Piazza del Biscione 92. ☎ **06/686-1246.** Reservations recommended. Main courses 18,000–32,000L ($10–$19); fixed-price menu 45,000L ($26). AE, DC, MC, V. Thurs–Tues noon–3pm and 7:30–11:15pm. Closed 2 weeks in Aug (dates vary). Bus: 46, 62, or 64. ROMAN.

This place is popular as much for its archaeological interest as for its food. One of its two dining rooms is gracefully decorated in the style of an 18th-century tavern; the other occupies the premises of Pompey's ancient theater and is lined with marble columns, carved capitals, and bas-reliefs. In this historic setting, you can enjoy traditional Roman dishes like *risotto alla pescatora* (with seafood), several kinds of scampi, saltimbocca, *abbacchio al forno* (roast lamb with potatoes), and ravioli stuffed with artichoke hearts. No one gets innovative around here—these dishes are prepared according to time-tested recipes.

✪ **Ristorante del Pallaro.** Largo del Pallaro 15. ☎ **06/6880-1488.** Reservations recommended. Fixed-price menu 32,000L ($19). No credit cards. Tues–Sun 1–3pm and 7:30pm–1am. Bus: 46, 62, or 64. ROMAN.

The cheerful woman in white who emerges with clouds of steam from the bustling kitchen is owner Paola Fazi. She runs two simple dining rooms where value-conscious Romans go for good food at bargain prices. (She also claims—though others dispute it—that Julius Caesar was assassinated on this very site.) No à la carte meals are served, but the fixed-price menu has made the place famous. As you sit down, your antipasto, the first of eight courses, appears. Then comes the pasta of the day, followed by roast veal, white meatballs or (Friday only) dried cod, along with potatoes and eggplant. For

Dining Near Campo de' Fiori & Piazza Navona

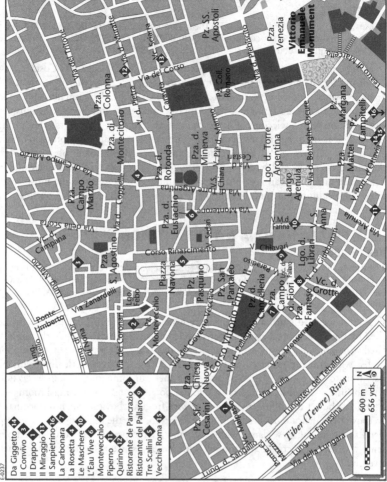

Da Giggetto 14
Il Convivo 3
Il Drappo 13
Il Miraggio 16
Il Sanpietrino 7
La Carbonara 4
La Rosetta 1
Le Maschere 10
L'Eau Vive 6
Montevecchio 2
Piperno 11
Quirino 12
Ristorante de Pancrazio 8
Ristorante del Pallaro 9
Tre Scalini 5
Vecchia Roma 15

your final courses, you're served mozzarella, cake with custard, and fruit in season. The meal also includes bread, mineral water, and half a liter of the house wine. This is the type of hearty food you might be served if you were invited to the home of a prosperous Roman family.

Vecchia Roma. Via della Tribuna di Campitelli 18. ☎ **06/686-4604.** Reservations recommended. Main courses 23,000–28,000L ($13–$16). AE. Thurs–Tues 1–3:30pm and 8–11pm. Closed 15 days in Aug. Bus: 64, 90, 90b, 97, or 774. ROMAN/ITALIAN.

Vecchia Roma is a charming moderately priced trattoria in the heart of the Ghetto. Movie stars have frequented the place, sitting at the crowded tables in one of the four small dining rooms (the back room is the most popular). The owners are known for their "fruits of the sea," a selection of fresh seafood. The minestrone is made with fresh vegetables, and an interesting selection of antipasti, including salmon or vegetables, is always available. The pastas and risottos are savory, including linguine alla marinara with calamari— the "green" risotto with porcini mushrooms is reliably good. The chef prepares excellent cuts of meat, including his specialty, lamb and *la spigola* (a type of white fish).

INEXPENSIVE

Le Maschere. Via Monte della Farina 29 (near Largo Argentina). ☎ **06/687-9444.** Reservations recommended. Main courses 12,000–20,000L ($7–$12). AE, DC, MC, V. Tues–Sun 7:30pm–midnight. Closed Aug. Bus: 46, 62, or 64. CALABRESE.

Le Maschere specializes in the fragrant, often-fiery cookery of Calabria's Costa Viola—lots of fresh garlic and wake-up-your-mouth red peppers. In a cellar from the 1600s decorated with regional artifacts of Calabria, it has enlarged its kitchen and added three dining rooms, all festooned with fantastic medieval- and Renaissance-inspired murals. Begin with a selection of *antipasti calabresi*. For your first course, you can try one of their many preparations of eggplant or a pasta—perhaps with broccoli or with devilish red peppers, garlic, bread crumbs, and more than a touch of anchovy. The chef also grills meats and fresh swordfish caught off the Calabrian coast. If you don't want a full meal, you can visit just for pizza and beer and listen to the music at the piano bar, beginning at 8pm. In summer, you can dine at a small table outside overlooking a tiny piazza.

NEAR PIAZZA NAVONA & THE PANTHEON
VERY EXPENSIVE

Il Convivio. Via dell'Orso 44. ☎ **06/686-9432.** Reservations recommended. Main courses 42,000–44,000L ($24–$26); fixed-price *menu degustazione* 100,000L ($58). AE, DC, MC, V. Tues–Sat 1–2:30pm; Mon–Sat 8–10:30pm. Closed 1 week in Aug. Metro: Spagna, then a long stroll. ITALIAN/ROMAN.

The well-conceived pan-Italian menu here is definitely daring. The creativity is supplied by the Troiani brothers, who cook, welcome visitors, and compile the sophisticated wine list. We love to begin with *ricotta romanda calda,* warm ricotta dumplings stuffed with crunchy *guanciale* and bits of salt pork and served with sliced porcinis; zesty tomato sauce gives it an extra zing. The chef can sometimes be a little *too* bold, as with his roast rabbit, stuffed with mashed potatoes and porcini mushrooms—he intensifies the act by adding a sauce made with fresh anchovies, which unfortunately overpower the delicate truffles topping the creation. But the seafood salad is a happy blend of squid, mussels, clams, white fish, and a large prawn, placed on a bed of al dente carrots and zucchini and topped with lemony sauce. The desserts are equally inventive.

✪ **La Rosetta.** Via della Rosetta 8. ☎ **06/686-1002.** Reservations recommended. Main courses 60,000–100,000L ($35–$58). AE, DC, MC, V. Mon–Fri 1–3:30pm and Mon–Sat 8–11:30pm. Closed the last 3 weeks of Aug. Bus: 70 to Largo Argentina. Metro: Spagna, then a long stroll. SEAFOOD.

You won't find any meat on the menu at this sophisticated and ultra-expensive choice near Piazza Navona, where members of the Riccioli family have been directing operations since the late 1960s. If money is no object, there's no better seafood in Rome. You'll likely be seated amid the arches and paneling of the soothingly decorated main dining room, though there's an alcove off to the side that's a bit more private. An excellent start to any meal, especially as the temperature begins to soar, is an *insalata di frutti di mare*, studded with squid, lobster, octopus, and shrimp. Menu items include just about every fish that's native to the Mediterranean, as well as a few from the Atlantic coast of France. There's even a sampling of lobster imported from Maine, which can be boiled with drawn butter or served Catalan style, with tomatoes, red onions, and wine sauce. Hake, monkfish, and sole can be grilled or roasted in rock salt and served with potatoes, and calamari is available deep-fried (breaded or unbreaded) or stewed. Everyone at our table agreed that the homemade spaghetti garnished with shrimp, squash blossoms, and pecorino cheese—with a drizzling of olive oil and herbs adding a savory zing—was tops among the pasta dishes.

MODERATE

Montevecchio. Piazza Montevecchio 22. ☎ **06/686-1319.** Reservations required. Main courses 22,000–32,000L ($13–$19). AE, MC, V. Tues–Sat 1–3pm; Tues–Sun 8pm–midnight. Closed Aug 10–25 and Dec 26–Jan 9. Bus: 44, 46, 55, 60, 61, 62, 64, or 65. Metro: Spagna, then a long stroll. ROMAN/ITALIAN.

To visit, you must negotiate the winding streets of one of Rome's most confusing neighborhoods, near Piazza Navona. The heavily curtained restaurant on this Renaissance piazza is where both Raphael and Bramante had studios and where Lucrezia Borgia spun many of her intrigues. The entrance opens onto a high-ceilinged room filled with rural mementos and bottles of wine. Your meal might begin with a strudel of porcini mushrooms followed by the invariably good pasta of the day, perhaps a bombolotti stuffed with prosciutto and spinach. Then you might choose roebuck with polenta, roast Sardinian goat, or veal with salmon mousse. Many of these traditional recipes are impossible to find on Roman menus anymore.

Tre Scalini. Piazza Navona 30. ☎ **06/687-9148.** Reservations recommended. Main courses 20,000–38,000L ($12–$22). AE, DC, MC, V. Daily 12:15–3pm and 7–11pm. Closed Dec–Feb. Bus: 44, 46, 55, 60, 61, 62, 64, or 65. Metro: Spagna, then a long stroll. ROMAN.

Opened in 1882, this is the most famous restaurant on Piazza Navona—a landmark for ice cream as well as more substantial meals. Yes, it's crawling with tourists, but its waiters are a lot friendlier and more helpful than those at the nearby Passetto, and the setting can't be beat. There's a cozy bar on the upper floor with a view over the piazza, but most visitors opt for the ground-floor cafe or restaurant. During warm weather, try to snag a table on the piazza, where the people-watching is extraordinary.

House specialties are risotto with porcinis, spaghetti with clams, roast duck with prosciutto, a carpaccio of sea bass, saltimbocca, and roast lamb Roman style. No one will object if you order just a pasta and salad, unlike at other restaurants nearby. Their famous tartufo (ice cream disguised with a coating of bittersweet chocolate, cherries, and whipped cream) and other ice creams cost 10,000L ($6) each.

INEXPENSIVE

Il Miraggio. Vicolo Sciarra 59. ☎ **06/678-0226.** Reservations recommended. Main courses 12,000–20,000L ($7–$12). AE, MC, V. Thurs–Tues 12:30–3:30pm and 7:30–11pm. Closed Feb 5–20. Bus: 56, 60, 62, 81, 85, 95, 160, 175, 492, or 628. Metro: Barberini, then a long stroll. ROMAN/SARDINIAN/SEAFOOD.

You may want to want to escape the roar of traffic along Via del Corso by ducking into this informal spot on a crooked side street (about midway between Piazza Venezia and Piazza Colonna). It's a cozy neighborhood setting with good food. House specialties are *tortellini alla papalina, spaghetti alla bottarga* (with roe sauce), and *spigola alla vernaccia* (sea bass sautéed in butter and vernaccia wine from Tuscany). The meat dishes are well prepared, and there's an array of fresh fish. For dessert try the typical Sardinian *seadas,* thin-rolled pastry filled with fresh cheese, fried, and served with honey.

✪ **L'Eau Vive.** Via Monterone 85. ☎ **06/6880-1095.** Reservations recommended. Main courses 10,000–30,000L ($6–$17); fixed-price menus 15,000, 22,000, and 30,000L ($9, $13, and $17). AE, MC, V. Mon–Sat 12:30–2:30pm and 8–10:30pm. Closed Aug 1–20. Bus: 70, 81, 87, or 115. Metro: Barberini, then a long stroll. FRENCH/INTERNATIONAL.

This offbeat spot is run by lay missionaries who wear the dress or costumes of their native countries. The restaurant occupies the cellar and ground floor of the

17th-century Palazzo Lantante della Rovere and is filled with monumental paintings under vaulted ceilings. In this formal atmosphere, at 10pm each night the waitresses sing religious hymns and Ave Marias. Pope John Paul II used to dine here when he was still archbishop of Krakow, and today some jet-setters have adopted it as their favorite spot. The tasteful place settings include fresh flowers and good glassware, and the cellar is well stocked with French wines. Main dishes range from beef filet flambéed with cognac to lighter selections like couscous, perhaps with homemade pâté or a salad niçoise to begin. The chocolate mousse is a smooth finish. Your tip will be turned over for religious purposes.

Quirino. Via delle Muratte 84. ☎ **06/679-4108.** Main courses 15,000–30,000L ($9–$17); fish dishes 35,000L ($20). AE, MC, V. Mon–Sat 12:30–3:30pm and 7–11pm. Closed 3 weeks in Aug. Metro: Barberini. ROMAN/ITALIAN/SICILIAN.

Quirino is a good place to dine after you've tossed your coin into the Trevi Fountain. The atmosphere is typical Italian, with hanging chianti bottles, a beamed ceiling, and muraled walls. The food is strictly home-cooking. We're fond of a mixed fry of tiny shrimp and squid rings that resemble onion rings. Specialties include vegetarian antipasti, homemade pasta with clams and porcini mushrooms, *pasta alla Norma* (a typical Sicilian plate), and a variety of fresh tasty fish. For dessert there's chestnut ice cream with hot chocolate sauce or homemade cannoli.

NEAR PIAZZA DEL POPOLO & THE SPANISH STEPS
VERY EXPENSIVE

✪ **El Toulà.** Via della Lupa 29B. ☎ **06/687-3498.** Reservations required for dinner. Main courses 40,000–55,000L ($23–$32); fixed-price menus 100,000–120,000L ($58–$70). AE, DC, MC, V. Tues–Sat 1–3pm; Mon–Sat 8–11pm. Closed Aug. Bus: 81, 115, 492, 590, or 628. Metro: Spagna, then walk west on Via Font. Borghese. ROMAN/VENETIAN.

El Toulà, offering sophisticated haute cuisine, is the glamorous flagship of an upscale chain that's now gone international. The setting is elegant, with vaulted ceilings, large archways, and a charming bar. The impressive always-changing menu has one section devoted to Venetian specialties, in honor of the restaurant's origins. Items include *fegato* (liver) *alla veneziana*, vegetable-stuffed calamari, *baccala* (codfish mousse with polenta), and *broetto*, a fish soup made with monkfish and clams. Save room for the seasonal selection of sorbets and sherbets (the cantaloupe and fresh strawberry are celestial)—you can request a mixed plate if you'd like to sample several. El Toulà usually isn't crowded at lunchtime.

MODERATE

Babington's Tea Rooms. Piazza di Spagna 23. ☎ **06/678-6027.** Main courses 20,000–38,000L ($12–$22); brunch 45,000L ($26). AE, MC, DC, V. Daily 9am–8:30pm. Metro: Spagna. ENGLISH/MEDITERRANEAN.

When Victoria was on the throne in 1893, an Englishwoman named Anne Mary Babington arrived in Rome and couldn't find a place for "a good cuppa." With stubborn determination, she opened her own tearooms near the foot of the Spanish Steps, and the rooms are still going strong, though prices are terribly inflated because of its fabulous location. You can order everything from Scottish scones and Ceylon tea to a club sandwich and American coffee. Brunch is served at all hours. Pastries cost 4,000 to 13,000L ($2.30 to $8); a pot of tea (dozens of varieties available) goes for 12,000L ($7).

Dal Bolognese. Piazza del Popolo 1–2. ☎ **06/361-1426.** Reservations required. Main courses 22,000–28,000L ($13–$16); fixed-price menu 65,000L ($38). AE, MC, V. Tues–Sun 12:30–3pm and 8:15pm–1am. Closed 2 weeks in Aug. Metro: Flaminio. BOLOGNESE.

Dining Near the Spanish Steps

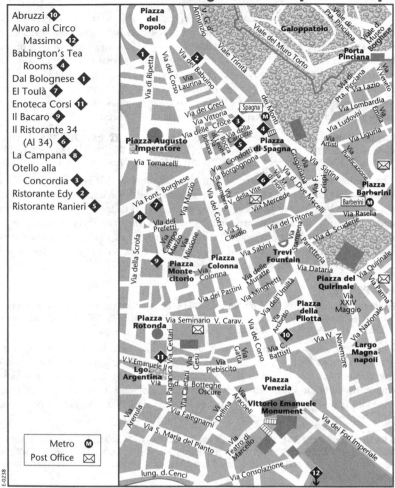

Abruzzi ⑩
Alvaro al Circo Massimo ⑫
Babington's Tea Rooms ④
Dal Bolognese ①
El Toulà ⑦
Enoteca Corsi ⑪
Il Bacaro ⑨
Il Ristorante 34 (Al 34) ⑥
La Campana ⑧
Otello alla Concordia ③
Ristorante Edy ②
Ristorante Ranieri ⑤

Metro Ⓜ
Post Office ✉

This is one of those rare dining spots that's chic but actually lives up to the hype with truly noteworthy food. Young actors, shapely models, artists from nearby Via Margutta, and even corporate types on expense accounts show up, trying to land one of the few sidewalk tables. To begin, we suggest a *misto de pasta*—four pastas, each with a different sauce, arranged on the same plate. A worthy substitute would be thin, savory slices of Parma ham or perhaps the prosciutto and melon (try a little freshly ground pepper on the latter). For your main course, specialties include lasagne verde, tagliatelle alla bolognese, and a recommendable *cotolette alla bolognese* (veal cutlet topped with cheese). They're not inventive, but they're simply superb.

You may want to cap your evening by calling on the **Rosati** cafe next door (or its competitor, the **Canova,** across the street), to enjoy one of the tempting pastries—that is, if the renovation on the piazza is ever finished, making this a lovely spot again.

Il Bacaro. Via degli Spagnoli 27, near Piazza delle Coppelle. ☎ **06/686-4110.** Reservations recommended. Main courses 18,000–30,000L ($10–$17). DC, MC, V. Mon–Sat 8pm–midnight. Metro: Spagna. ITALIAN.

Unpretentious and very accommodating to foreigners, this restaurant contains only about half a dozen tables and operates from an ivy-edged hideaway alley near Piazza di Spagna. Long ago, the site was a palazzo from the 1600s, and some vestiges of the building's former grandeur remain intact, despite an impossibly cramped kitchen where the efforts of the staff to keep the show moving are nothing short of heroic. The offerings are time-tested and flavorful: homemade ravioli stuffed with mushrooms and parmagiana (in season); grilled beef filet with roasted potatoes; radicchio stuffed with Gorgonzola; and an unusual version of warm carpaccio of beef.

Ristorante Ranieri. Via Mario de' Fiori 26 (off Via Condotti). ☎ **06/678-6505.** Reservations required. Main courses 22,000–32,000L ($13–$19). AE, DC, MC, V. Mon–Sat 12:30–3pm and 7:30–11pm. Metro: Spagna. INTERNATIONAL/ITALIAN.

The Ranieri is well into its second century (it opened in 1843). Neapolitan-born Giuseppe Ranieri was the chef to Queen Victoria, and his namesake restaurant still maintains its Victorian trappings. Nothing ever seems to change. Start with prosciutto and melon or that classic Roman soup, *stracciatella* (made with eggs and cheese). Another starter might be crêpes alla Ranieri, with eight types of cheese; we've enjoyed it for years. Beefsteak from Florence is meltingly tender, as is the veal liver. You might also try the osso bucco Lombardy style.

INEXPENSIVE

Enoteca Corsi. 89 Via del Gesú. ☎ **06/679-0821.** Reservations not necessary. Main courses 10,000L ($6) each; vegetable side dishes 4,000L ($2.30). AE, DC, MC, V. Mon–Sat noon–2:30pm. Closed Aug. Metro: Spagna. ROMAN.

This is a breath of unpretentious fresh air in a pricey neighborhood—an informal wine tavern open for lunch only. Both dining rooms are usually packed and full of festive din, just as they've always been since 1943. The wine list includes affordable choices from around Italy, and the platters of straightforward cuisine will go with your selection perfectly. It's nothing fancy, just hearty fare like spaghetti matriciana, gnocchi, Roman tripe, and roasted codfish with garlic and potatoes.

Il Ristorante 34 (Al 34). Via Mario de' Fiori 34. ☎ **06/679-5091.** Reservations required. Main courses 17,000–28,000L ($10–$16); fixed-price menu 55,000L ($32). AE, DC, MC, V. Tues–Sun 12:30–3pm and 7:30–10:30pm. Closed 1 week at Easter and 3 weeks in Aug. Metro: Spagna. ROMAN.

Il Ristorante 34, very good and increasingly popular, is close to Rome's most famous shopping district. Its long, narrow interior is sheathed in scarlet wallpaper, ringed with modern paintings, and capped with a vaulted ceiling. In the rear, stop to admire a display of dolce proudly exhibited near the entrance to the bustling kitchen. The kitchen is highly reliable; the chef might whip caviar and salmon into the noodles to enliven a dish or add generous chunks of lobster into the risotto. He also believes in rib-sticking fare like pasta lentil soup or meatballs in a sauce with "fat" mushrooms. One of his most interesting pastas comes with a pumpkin-flavored cream sauce, and his spaghetti with clams is among the best in Rome.

La Campana. Vicolo della Campana 18. ☎ **06/686-7820.** Reservations recommended. Main courses 18,000–25,000L ($10–$15). AE, DC, MC, V. Tues–Sun 12:30–2:30pm and 7:30–11pm. Metro: Spagna. ROMAN.

If you opt for a meal in this comfortable not-particularly-innovative restaurant, you won't be alone. The place has been dishing up traditional Roman specialties since it began welcoming locals and religious pilgrims in 1518 (unlike those folks, you'll enjoy air-conditioning in summer). Look for a well-stocked antipasti buffet, rich pastas, juicy herb-laden roast lamb with potatoes, roast hen with roasted vegetables, and grilled fish or squid. The welcome is always warm, after all those years and all those thousands of diners.

Otello alla Concordia. Via della Croce 81. ☎ **06/679-1178.** Main courses 12,000–25,000L ($7–$15); fixed-price menu 36,000L ($21). AE, DC, MC, V. Mon–Sat 12:30–3pm and 7:30–11pm. Closed 2 weeks in Feb. Metro: Spagna. ROMAN.

On a side street amid the glamorous boutiques near the northern edge of the Spanish Steps, this is one of Rome's most popular and consistently reliable restaurants. A stone corridor from the street leads into the dignified Palazzo Povero. Choose a table in the arbor-covered courtyard or the cramped but convivial dining rooms. Displays of Italian bounty decorate the interior, where you're likely to rub elbows with many of the shopkeepers from the surrounding fashion district. The *spaghetti alle vongole veraci* (with clams) is excellent, as are Roman-style saltimbocca, *abbacchio arrosto* (roast baby lamb), eggplant parmigiana, a selection of grilled or sautéed fish dishes (including swordfish), and several preparations of veal.

Ristorante Edy. Vicolo del Babuino 4. ☎ **06/3600-1738.** Reservations recommended. Main courses 15,000–27,000L ($9–$16). AE, DC, MC, V. Mon–Sat noon–3pm and 7pm–midnight. Closed 1 week in Aug. Metro: Spagna or Flaminio. ROMAN/ABRUZZESE.

Named after the nickname (Edy) of Abruzzi-born owner Edmondo Campricotti, this likable and unpretentious family-run restaurant is midway between the Spanish Steps and Piazza del Popolo. You'll feel very Roman here, since the place is usually packed with an animated crowd of locals. Though it's in the heart of Rome, it enjoys a tranquil setting with a few tables on the street. Tried-and-true menu items that the kitchen produces with gusto include spaghetti with artichokes, fettuccine with mushrooms and ricotta, and a mixed seafood grill with calamari, shrimp, and (if available) turbot. But we can never resist the grilled roast lamb surrounded with roast potatoes in the Abruzzese style.

NEAR VATICAN CITY
VERY EXPENSIVE

✪ **Les Etoiles.** In the Hotel Atlante Star, Via Vitelleschi 34. ☎ **06/689-3434.** Reservations required. Main courses 36,000–58,000L ($21–$34). AE, DC, MC, V. Daily 12:30–2:30pm and 7:30–11pm. Metro: Ottaviano, then a long stroll. MEDITERRANEAN/INTERNATIONAL.

Les Etoiles ("The Stars") deserves all the stars it receives. At this garden in the sky you'll have an open window over Rome's rooftops—a 360° view of landmarks, especially the floodlit dome of St. Peter's. A flower terrace contains a trio of little towers named Michelangelo, Campidoglio, and Ottavo Colle. In summer, everyone wants a table outside, but in winter almost the same view is available near the picture windows. Savor the textures and aromas of sophisticated Mediterranean cuisine with perfectly balanced flavors, perhaps choosing quail in a casserole with mushrooms and herbs, artichokes stuffed with ricotta and pecorino cheese, Venetian-style risotto with squid ink, and roast suckling lamb with mint. The creative chef is justifiably proud of his many regional dishes, and the service is refined, with an exciting French and Italian wine list.

MODERATE

Ristorante Il Matriciano. Via dei Gracchi 55. ☎ **06/321-2327.** Reservations required, especially for dinner. Main courses 20,000–30,000L ($12–$17). AE, DC, MC, V. Daily 12:30–3pm and 8–11:30pm. Closed Aug 5–25, Wed in Nov–Apr, and Sat in May–Oct. Metro: Ottaviano. ROMAN.

Il Matriciano is a family restaurant with a devoted following and a convenient location near St. Peter's. The food is good, but it's mostly country fare. Appropriately, the decor is kept to a minimum. In summer, try to get one of the sidewalk tables behind a green hedge and under a shady canopy. For openers you might enjoy *zuppa di verdura* (vegetable soup) or ravioli di ricotta. From many dishes, we recommend *scaloppa alla valdostana* or *abbacchio* (suckling lamb) *al forno*. The specialty, *bucatini matriciana*, is a variation on the favorite sauce in the Roman repertoire, amatriciana, richly flavored with bacon, tomatoes, and basil. Dining at the homelike convivial tables, you're likely to see an array of Romans, including prelates and cardinals ducking out of the nearby Vatican for a meal.

Ristorante Pierdonati. Via della Conciliazione 39. ☎ 06/6880-3557. Reservations not necessary. Main courses 12,000–40,000L ($7–$23); fixed-price menu 25,000L ($15). AE, MC, V. Fri–Wed noon–3:30pm and 7–10:30pm. Closed Aug. Bus: 62. ROMAN.

Ristorante Pierdonati has been serving wayfarers to the Vatican since 1868. In the same building as the Hotel Columbus, this restaurant was the former home of Cardinal della Rovere. Today it's the headquarters of the Knights of the Holy Sepulchre of Jerusalem and is the best choice for a sit-down lunch after touring St. Peter's. Try the calves' liver Venetian style, stewed veal with tomato sauce, or ravioli bolognese. It's robust and filling fare. Given this location, expect a crowd. Tuesday and Friday are fresh fish days.

INEXPENSIVE
Ristorante Giardinaccio. Via Aurelia 53. ☎ 06/631-367. Reservations recommended, especially on weekends. Main courses 10,000–16,000L ($6–$9). AE, DC, MC, V. Wed–Mon 12:15–3:30pm and 7:15–11pm. Bus: 46. ITALIAN/MOLISIAN/INTERNATIONAL.

This popular restaurant, operated by Nicolino Mancini, is only a stone's throw from St. Peter's. Unusual for Rome, it offers Molisian specialties from southeastern Italy. It's rustically decorated in the country-tavern style with dark wood and exposed stone. Flaming grills provide succulent versions of perfectly done quail, goat, and other dishes, but perhaps the mutton goulash would be more adventurous. You can order many versions of pasta, including *taconelle*, a homemade pasta with lamb sauce, which is often served. Vegetarians will like the large self-service selection of antipasti. This is robust "peasant" fare, a perfect introduction to the cuisine of an area rarely visited by Americans.

IN TRASTEVERE
EXPENSIVE
Alberto Ciarla. Piazza San Cosimato 40. ☎ 06/581-8668. Reservations required. Main courses 26,000–46,000L ($15–$27); fixed-price menus 80,000–90,000L ($46–$52). AE, DC, MC, V. Mon–Sat 8:30pm–12:30am. Bus: 44, 75, or 710. SEAFOOD.

Alberto Ciarla is the best and one of Trastevere's most expensive restaurants. In an 1890 building, set into an obscure corner of an enormous square, it serves truly elegant fish dishes. You'll be greeted with a cordial reception and a lavish display of seafood on ice. A dramatically modern decor plays shades of brilliant light against patches of shadow for a Renaissance chiaroscuro effect. Specialties include a handful of ancient recipes subtly improved by Signor Ciarla (an example is the soup of pasta and beans with seafood). Original dishes include a delectable fish in orange sauce, spaghetti with clams, and a full array of shellfish. The filet of sea bass is prepared in at least three ways, including an award-winning version with almonds.

Sabatini. Piazza Santa Maria in Trastevere 13. ☎ 06/581-2026. Reservations recommended. Main courses 40,000–80,000L ($23–$46). AE, DC, MC, V. Daily noon–3pm and 8pm–midnight. Closed 2 weeks in Aug (dates vary). Bus: 45, 75, 170, 181, or 280. ROMAN/SEAFOOD.

This is one of the most popular dining spots in Rome, a real neighborhood spot in a lively location. (You may have to wait for a table even if you have a reservation.) In summer, tables are placed out on the charming piazza and you can look across at the floodlit golden frescoes of the church. Inside, the dining room sports beamed ceilings, stenciled walls, lots of paneling, and framed oil paintings. The spaghetti with seafood is excellent, and fresh fish and shellfish, especially grilled scampi, may tempt you as well. For a savory treat, try *pollo con pepperoni*, chicken cooked with red and green peppers. (Order carefully, though; your bill can skyrocket if you choose grilled fish or the Florentine steaks.) Accompany it all with a frascati or a chianti classico in a hand-painted pitcher.

MODERATE

La Cisterna. Via della Cisterna 13. ☎ **06/581-2543.** Reservations recommended. Main courses 20,000–35,000L ($12–$20). AE, DC, MC, V. Mon–Sat 7pm–midnight. Bus: 45, 75, 170, 181, or 280. ROMAN.

If you'd like traditional home cooking based on the best regional ingredients, head here. La Cisterna, named for an ancient well from imperial times discovered in the cellar, lies deep in the heart of Trastevere. For more than 75 years it has been run by the Simmi family, who are genuinely interested in serving only the best as well as providing a good time for all. In good weather you can dine at sidewalk tables. If it's rainy or cold you'll be in rooms decorated with murals. In summer you can inspect the antipasti right out on the street before going in. Specialties include Roman-style suckling lamb (abbacchio), *rigatoni a l'amatriciana, pappallini romana* (wide noodles flavored with prosciutto, cheese, and eggs), shrimp, and fresh fish (especially sea bass baked with herbs).

IN TESTACCIO

Checchino dal 1887. Via di Monte Testaccio 30. ☎ **06/574-3816.** Reservations recommended. Main courses 13,000–35,000L ($8–$20). AE, DC, MC, V. Tues–Sat 12:30–3pm and 8–11pm. Closed Aug and 1 week around Christmas. Bus: 713. ROMAN.

During the 1800s, a local wine shop flourished here, selling drinks to the butchers working in the nearby slaughterhouses. In 1887, the ancestors of the present owners began serving food too, giving birth to the restaurant you'll find today. Slaughterhouse workers in those days were paid part of their meager salaries with the *quinto quarto* (fifth quarter) of each day's slaughter (the tail, feet, intestines, and other parts not for the squeamish). Following centuries of Roman traditions, Ferminia, the wine shop's cook, somehow transformed these products into the tripe and oxtail dishes that form an integral part of the menu. Many Italian diners come here to relish these dishes, which might not be for you unless you're truly adventurous. They include *rigatone con pajata* (pasta with small intestines), *coda alla vaccinara* (oxtail stew), *fagiole e cotiche* (beans with intestinal fat), and other examples of *la cocina povera* (food of the poor). Safer and possibly more appetizing is the array of well-prepared salads, soups, pastas, steaks, cutlets, grills, and ice creams. The English-speaking staff is helpful and kind, tactfully proposing alternatives if you're not ready for Roman soul food.

ON THE APPIAN WAY

Hostaria l'Archeologia. Via Appia Antica 139. ☎ **06/788-0494.** Reservations recommended, especially on weekends. Main courses 15,000–30,000L ($9–$17); fixed-price menu from 26,000L ($15). AE, DC, MC, V. Fri–Wed 12:30–3:30pm and 8–10:40pm. Bus: 218 from San Giovanni or 660 from colli Albani. ROMAN/ITALIAN.

Hostaria l'Archeologia is only a short walk from the catacombs of St. Sebastian. The family-run restaurant is like an 18th-century village tavern with lots of atmosphere, strings of garlic and corn, oddments of copper hanging from the ceiling, earth-brown beams, and sienna-washed walls. In summer, you can dine in the garden out back under the wisteria. The Roman fare is first-rate; you can glimpse the kitchen from behind a partition in the exterior garden parking lot. Many Roman families visit on the weekend, sometimes in giant groups. Of special interest is the wine cellar, excavated in an ancient Roman tomb, with bottles dating to 1800. (You go through an iron gate, down some stairs, and into the underground cavern. Along the way, you can still see the holes once occupied by funeral urns.)

IN PARIOLI
VERY EXPENSIVE

✪ **Relais Le Jardin.** In the Hotel Lord Byron, Via G. de Notaris 5. ☎ **06/361-3041.** Reservations required. Main courses 45,000–55,000L ($26–$32). AE, DC, MC, V. Mon–Sat 1–3pm and 8–10:30pm. Closed Aug. Bus: 26 or 52. ITALIAN/TRADITIONAL.

Relais Le Jardin is one of the best places to go for both traditional and creative cuisine, and a chichi crowd with demanding palates patronizes it nightly. There are places in Rome with better views, but not with such an elegant setting, inside one of the capital's most exclusive small hotels. The lighthearted decor combines white lattice with bold colors and flowers. The service is impeccable.

The pastas and soups are among the finest in town. We were particularly taken by the tonnarelli pasta with asparagus and smoked ham served with concassé tomatoes. The chef can take a dish once served only to the plebes in ancient times, bean soup with clams, and make it something elegant. For your main course you can choose from roast loin of lamb with artichoke romana or grilled beef sirloin with hot chicory and sautéed potatoes. The chef also creates a fabulous risotto with pheasant sauce, asparagus, black truffle flakes, and a hint of fresh thyme—it gets our vote as the best risotto around.

MODERATE

Al Ceppo. Via Panama 2. ☎ **06/841-9696.** Reservations recommended. Main courses 18,000–28,000L ($10–$16). AE, DC, MC, V. Tues–Sun 12:30–3pm and 8–11pm. Closed the last 3 weeks of Aug. Bus: 53 or 168. ROMAN.

Because the place is somewhat hidden (though only 2 blocks from the Villa Borghese, near Piazza Ungheria), you're likely to rub elbows with more Romans than tourists here. This is a longtime favorite, and the cuisine is as good as it ever was. "The Log" features an open wood-stoked fireplace on which the chef roasts lamb chops, liver, and bacon to charcoal perfection. The beefsteak, which hails from Tuscany, is also succulent. Other dishes are linguine monteconero (with clams and fresh tomatoes); a savory spaghetti with peppers, fresh basil, and pecorino cheese; a swordfish filet filled with grapefruit, parmagiana, pine nuts, and dry grapes; and a fish carpaccio (raw sea bass) with a green salad, onions, and green pepper. Save room for dessert, especially the apple cobbler, pear-and-almond tart, or chocolate meringue hazelnut cake.

Exploring Rome 5

With the imminent approach of Papal Jubilee 2000, its turn-of-the-millennium celebration, Rome has been working hard to spruce up. The grime of car exhaust and other pollution is being scrubbed from many facades, revealing the original glory of the Eternal City (though Rome could stand even more work on this front), and ancient treasures like the Colosseum are being shored up. Work will continue frantically until the very dawn of the millennium—there's a new vitality in the air. You may see scaffolding here and there, but you'll also get the benefit of viewing some newly restored monuments. Many of the popular areas (such as the Trevi Fountain and Piazza Navona) are sparkling and inviting again. The Frommer's prize for cleanup goes to the "artists" who transformed dingy Piazza di Sant'Ignazio into the rococo gem it was always meant to be. Even the churches along Via del Corso, including that jewel of the baroque era, San Marcello, shine again along the streets of this magnificently historic city.

Whether they're time-blackened or newly gleaming, the ancient monuments dotted throughout the city are a constant reminder that Rome was of one of the greatest centers of Western civilization. In the heyday of the Empire, all roads led to Rome with good reason. It was one of the first cosmopolitan cities, importing slaves, gladiators, great art—even citizens—from the far corners of the world. Despite its carnage and corruption, Rome left a legacy of law; a heritage of great art, architecture, and engineering; and an uncanny lesson in how to conquer enemies by absorbing their cultures.

But ancient Rome is only part of the spectacle. The Vatican has had a tremendous influence on making the city a tourism center. Though Vatican architects stripped down much of the glory of the past, looting ancient ruins for their precious marble, they created great Renaissance treasures and even occasionally incorporated the old into the new—as Michelangelo did when turning the Baths of Diocletian into a church. And in the years that followed, Bernini adorned the city with the wonders of the baroque, especially his glorious fountains.

Today, besides being the Italian capital, Rome, in a larger sense, belongs to the world.

1 St. Peter's & the Vatican

In 1929, the Lateran Treaty between Pope Pius XI and the Italian government created the **Vatican,** the world's smallest sovereign

Millennium Milestones: Roma 2000

In A.D. 1000, at the dawn of Christendom's second millennium, thousands of devoutly religious Romans gathered on the city's hilltops, anxiously awaiting the return of Christ the Majesty to judge the living and the dead. Despite the fanatical predictions of many mystics and visionaries that the world would end a thousand years after the arrival of Christ, nothing particularly eventful happened. The dejected masses of the Roman faithful returned to their homes, churches, and workday rituals to continue their lives in the Eternal City.

This time around, they may simply be waiting for the government to finish the many proposed work projects that are supposed to make the end of the second millennium more event-filled than its dawn. Since 1997, locals and visitors alike have had a sense of the fuss being raised. Renovation of neighborhood squares has created hectic street detours and reduced the amount of available parking. The work is continuing throughout 1999; whether everything will be ready or not is anyone's guess. The dawn of the millennium is threatening to arrive at Greenwich Mean Time whether Rome is ready or not.

Consequently, this urban chaos has left a question in many minds as to whether the benefits of these restoration projects will outweigh the inconvenience. Progress is being made very slowly through a path of governmental red tape, a lack of definitive central planning, and archaeological projects that almost daily uncover new difficulties or setbacks in meeting projected completion deadlines.

Indeed, broad-based powers and funds have been allocated for these improvements. Yet, the initiation—let alone progress—of many projects has proved to be as frustrating as driving the city's streets. Alas, civic-mindedness gives way

independent state. It has only a few hundred citizens and is protected (theoretically) by its own militia, the curiously uniformed (some say by Michelangelo) Swiss guards.

The only entrance to the Vatican for the casual visitor is through one of the glories of the Western world—Bernini's **St. Peter's Square (Piazza San Pietro).** As you stand in the huge piazza, you'll be in the arms of an ellipse partly enclosed by a majestic **Doric-pillared colonnade.** Atop it stands a gesticulating crowd of some 140 saints. Straight ahead is the facade of **St. Peter's Basilica** (Sts. Peter and Paul are represented by statues in front, Peter carrying the Keys to the Kingdom), and to the right, above the colonnade, are the dark brown buildings of the **papal apartments** and the **Vatican Museums.** The grand view as you approach was marred as of this writing by the scaffolding that covers the basilica's facade, but work should be completed before 2000. In the center of the square is an **Egyptian obelisk,** brought from the ancient city of Heliopolis on the Nile delta. Flanking the obelisk are two 17th-century **fountains**—the one on the right (facing the basilica) by Carlo Maderno, who designed the facade of St. Peter's, was placed here by Bernini himself; the other is by Carlo Fontana.

On the left side of the piazza is the **Vatican Tourist Office** (☎ **06/6988-4466** or 06/6988-4866), open Monday to Saturday 8:30am to 7pm. It sells maps and guides, accepts reservations for tours of the Vatican Gardens, points you in the right direction for papal-audience tickets, and tries to answer any questions you might have. A **shuttle bus** leaves from in front of this office for the entrance to the Vatican Museums daily every 30 minutes 8:45am to 1:45pm in summer and 8:45am to 12:45pm in

to businesses vying for their slice of the pie, and groundbreaking just about any-where exposes multiple layers of history that require new plans of exploration and protection. Inconveniences are also evident in more contemporary struc-tures, as many museums and restaurants have limited their hours of operation, decreased the space accessible to customers, or even closed their doors to enlarge gallery and dining space or renovate rest rooms. There's a rush to transform churches, schools, homes, and abandoned buildings into lodgings as well, causing pedestrian detours and increased levels of noise pollution.

The plans sound good: banning vehicular traffic in whole neighborhoods, transforming inner-city parking lots into open squares for socialization, opening new parking areas closer to the autostrada and rail lines at the outskirts of the city, scheduling high-speed trains and bus connections to depart every 5 minutes toward the core historic district, and planting scores of trees and flower beds to beautify the city. Anxiety and speculation rise as individual links in the master plan fall apart or simply remain ignored. There's fear in some quarters that ini-tial plans were too ambitious. Dozens of small projects envisioned hardly had seemed to get off the ground by 1998.

Perhaps the city's cultural program series, begun in 1997 to focus attention on the role of Rome as a crucible of civilization, will provide the impetus needed to get its politicos and engineers in gear during 1999, as the clock rapidly ticks toward that long-awaited midnight. But then again, the success of that program has been largely tied to the enthusiasm of outsiders, as musicians and artists from around the world have responded to the city's call to honor the spirit of Western Civilization—a decidedly easier feat than altering the concrete structure from which it sprang.

winter; the fare is 2,000L ($1.20). (Take it: It's a long and generally uninteresting walk to the museum entrance; from the bus's route you'll pass through some of the Vatican's lovely gardens.) The post office and rest rooms are adjacent.

✪ **St. Peter's Basilica (Basilica di San Pietro).** Piazza San Pietro. ☎ **06/6988-4466** (06/6988-5518 for reservations to see excavation sites). Basilica (including treasury and grot-toes) free. Guided tour of excavations around St. Peter's tomb 10,000L ($6). Dome 5,000L ($2.90) adults, 2,000L ($1.15) students; or 6,000L ($3.50) to take elevator partway. Sacristy (with Historical Museum) 8,000L ($4.80). Basilica (including treasury) Mar–Sept daily 7am–7pm (to 6pm Oct–Feb). Grottoes daily 8am–5pm. Dome Mar–Sept daily 8am–5:45pm (to 4:45pm Oct–Feb). Sacristy Apr–Sept daily 9am–6pm (to 5pm Oct–Mar). Bus: 46. Metro: Ottaviano/San Pietro, then a long stroll.

In ancient times, the Circus of Nero, where St. Peter is said to have been crucified, was slightly to the left of where the basilica is now located. Peter was buried here in A.D. 64 near the site of his execution, and in 324 Constantine commissioned a basilica to be built over Peter's tomb. The original structure stood for more than 1,000 years, until it verged on collapse. The present basilica, mostly completed in the 1500s and

A St. Peter's Warning

A dress code for men and women prohibiting shorts, bare arms and shoulders, and skirts above the knee is strictly enforced at all times in the basilica. You *will* be turned away. In addition, you must remain silent and cannot take photographs.

Rome Attractions

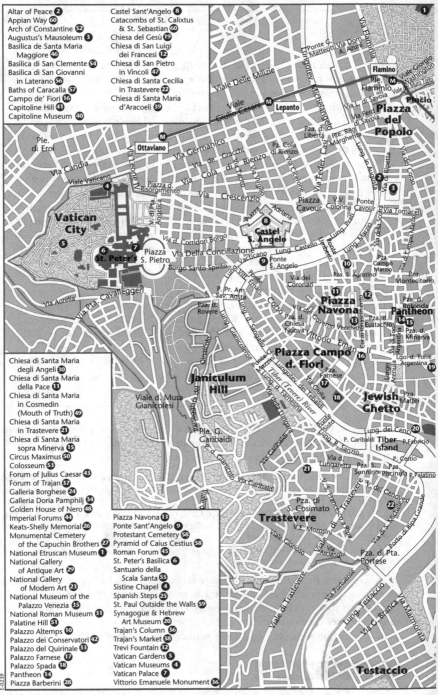

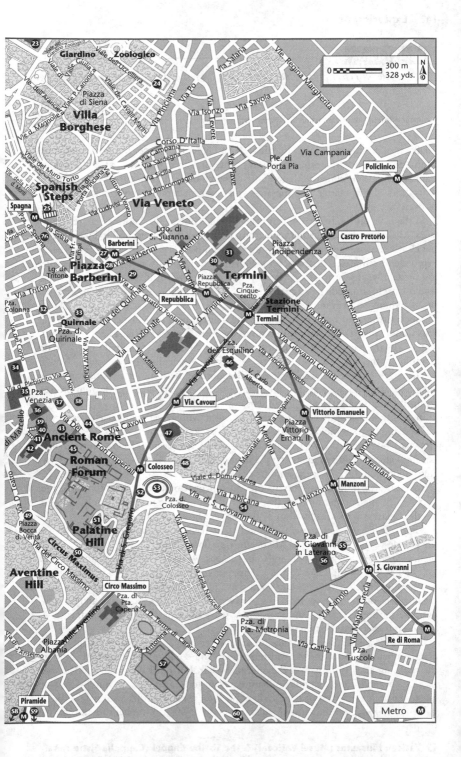

1600s, is predominantly High Renaissance and baroque. Inside, the massive scale is almost too much to absorb, showcasing some of Italy's greatest artists: Bramante, Raphael, Michelangelo, and Maderno. In a church of such grandeur—overwhelming in its detail of gilt, marble, and mosaic—you can't expect much subtlety. It's meant to be overpowering.

In the nave on the right (the first chapel) stands one of the Vatican's greatest treasures: Michelangelo's exquisite *Pietà,* created while the master was still in his early 20s but clearly showing his genius for capturing the human form. (The sculpture has been kept behind reinforced glass since a madman's act of vandalism in the 1970s.) Note the incredibly lifelike folds of Mary's robes and her youthful features (though she would have been middle-aged at the time of the Crucifixion, Michelangelo portrayed her as a young woman to convey her purity).

Much farther on, in the right wing of the transept near the Chapel of St. Michael, rests Canova's neoclassic **sculptural tribute to Pope Clement XIII.** The truly devout stop to kiss the feet of the **13th-century bronze of St. Peter,** attributed to Arnolfo di Cambio (at the far reaches of the nave, against a corner pillar on the right). Under Michelangelo's dome is the celebrated **baldacchino** by Bernini, resting over the papal altar. The canopy was created in the 17th century—in part, so it's said, from bronze stripped from the Pantheon, though that's up for debate.

In addition, you can visit the **treasury,** filled with jewel-studded chalices, reliquaries, and copes. One robe worn by Pius XII strikes a simple note in these halls of elegance. The sacristy now contains a **Historical Museum (Museo Storico)** displaying Vatican treasures, including the large 1400s bronze tomb of Pope Sixtus V by Antonio Pollaiuolo and several antique chalices.

You can also head downstairs to the **Vatican grottoes,** with their tombs of the popes, both ancient and modern (Pope John XXIII gets the most adulation). Behind a wall of glass is what's assumed to be the tomb of St. Peter himself.

After you leave the grottoes, you'll find yourself in a courtyard and ticket line for the grandest sight: the climb to **Michelangelo's dome,** which towers about 375 feet high. (*Warning:* Though you can walk up the steps, we recommend taking the elevator for as far as it goes—it'll save you 171 steps, but you'll still have 320 to go. The climb isn't recommended if you're not in good shape or are claustrophobic—and there's no turning back once you've started.) After you've made it, you'll have an astounding view over the rooftops of Rome and even the Vatican Gardens and papal apartments. A photo op if ever there was one.

To go even farther down, to the area around St. Peter's tomb, you must apply several days beforehand to the **excavations office** (you could also stop by first thing in the morning and try to get on the afternoon tour, but don't count on it). You can make your applications Monday to Saturday 9am to noon and 2 to 5pm by passing under the arch to the left of the facade of St. Peter's. For 10,000L ($6), you'll take a guided tour of the tombs that were excavated in the 1940s, 23 feet beneath the church floor.

✪ **Vatican Museums (Musei Vaticani) & the Sistine Chapel (Cappella Sistina).** Vatican City, Viale Vaticano (a long walk around the Vatican walls from St. Peter's Square or take

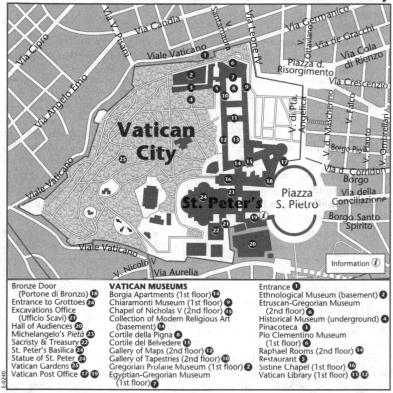

Vatican City

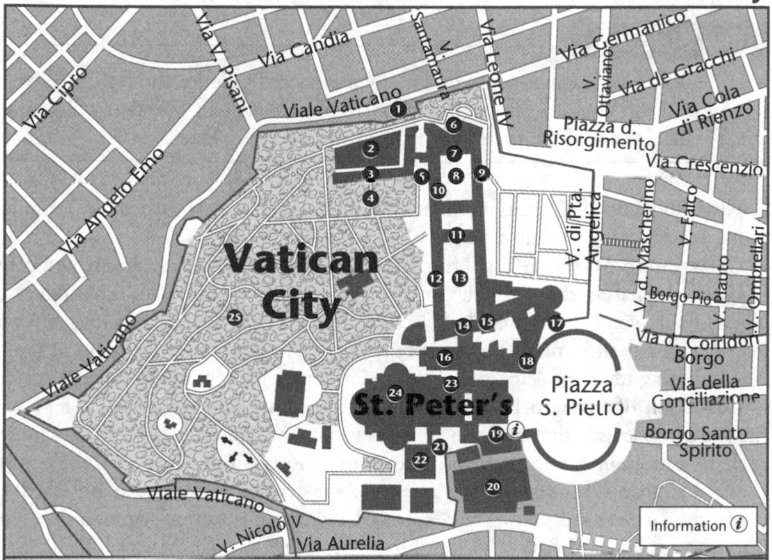

Bronze Door (Portone di Bronzo) 18
Entrance to Grottoes 24
Excavations Office (Ufficio Scavi) 21
Hall of Audiences 20
Michelangelo's *Pietà* 23
Sacristy & Treasury 22
St. Peter's Basilica 24
Statue of St. Peter 24
Vatican Gardens 25
Vatican Post Office 17 19

VATICAN MUSEUMS
Borgia Apartments (1st floor) 14
Chiaramonti Museum (1st floor) 9
Chapel of Nicholas V (2nd floor) 15
Collection of Modern Religious Art (basement) 14
Cortile della Pigna 8
Cortile del Belvedere 13
Gallery of Maps (2nd floor) 12
Gallery of Tapestries (2nd floor) 10
Gregorian Profane Museum (1st floor) 2
Egyptian-Gregorian Museum (1st floor) 7
Entrance 1
Ethnological Museum (basement) 2
Etruscan-Gregorian Museum (2nd floor) 6
Historical Museum (underground) 4
Pinacoteca 3
Pio Clementino Museum (1st floor) 6
Raphael Rooms (2nd floor) 14
Restaurant 5
Sistine Chapel (1st floor) 16
Vatican Library (1st floor) 11 12

E-0240

the shuttle bus—see above). ☎ **06/6988-3333.** Admission 18,000L ($10) adults; 12,000L ($7) children; free for everyone the last Sun of each month (be ready for a crowd). Mid-Mar to late Oct Mon–Fri and final Sun of the month 8:45am–4:45pm, Sat 8:45am–1:45pm. Off-season Mon–Sat 8:45am–1:45pm. Closed all national and religious holidays (except Easter week) and first 3 Sun of the month. Metro: Ottaviano/San Pietro.

The Vatican Museums comprise one of the world's greatest art collections. You'll see a gigantic repository of treasures from antiquity and the Renaissance, all housed in a labyrinthine series of lavishly adorned palaces, apartments, and galleries leading you to the real gem: the Sistine Chapel. The Vatican Museums occupy a part of the papal palaces built from the 1200s onward. From the former papal private apartments, the museums were created over a period of time to display the vast treasure trove of art acquired by the Vatican.

You'll climb a magnificent spiral ramp to get to the ticket windows. After you're admitted, you can choose your route through the museum from **four color-coded itineraries**—A, B, C, D—according to the time you have (from 1½ to 5 hours) and your interests. You determine your choice by consulting large-size panels on the wall and then following the letter/color of your choice. All four itineraries culminate in the Sistine Chapel. Obviously, 1, 2, or even 20 trips will not be enough to see the wealth of the Vatican, much less to digest it. With that in mind, we've previewed only a representative sampling of the masterpieces on display (in alphabetical order).

Borgia Apartments: Frescoed with biblical scenes by Pinturicchio of Umbria and his assistants, these rooms were designed for Pope Alexander VI (the infamous Borgia pope). They may be badly lit but boast great splendor and style. At the end of the

Buy the Book

In the Vatican Museums you'll find many overpacked galleries and few labels on the works. At the Vatican tourist office you can buy a detailed guide that will help you make more sense of the incredible riches you'll be seeing here.

Raphael Rooms is the Chapel of Nicholas V, an intimate room frescoed by Dominican monk Fra Angelico, the most saintly of all Italian painters.

Chiaramonti Museum: You'll find a dazzling array of Roman sculpture and copies of Greek originals in these galleries. In the Braccio Nuovo, built as an extension of the Chiaramonti, you can admire *The Nile,* a magnificent reproduction of a long-lost Hellenistic original and one of the most remarkable pieces of sculpture from antiquity. The imposing statue of Augustus of Prima Porta presents him as a regal commander.

Collection of Modern Religious Art: This museum, opened in 1973, represents the American artists' first invasion of the Vatican (the church had previously limited itself to European art from before the 18th century). But Pope Paul VI's hobby changed all that. Of the 55 rooms, at least 12 are devoted to American artists. All the works chosen were judged on their "spiritual and religious values." Among the American works is Leonard Baskin's 5-foot bronze sculpture of *Isaac.* Modern Italian artists like De Chirico and Manzù are also displayed, and there's a special room for the paintings of the Frenchman Georges Rouault.

Egyptian-Gregorian Museum: Experience the grandeur of the Pharaohs by studying sarcophagi, mummies, statues of goddesses, vases, jewelry, sculptured pink-granite statues, and hieroglyphics.

Ethnological Museum: This is an assemblage of works of art and objects of cultural significance from all over the world. The principal route is a half-mile walk through 25 geographical sections, displaying thousands of objects covering 3,000 years of world history. The section devoted to China is especially interesting.

Etruscan-Gregorian Museum: With sarcophagi, a chariot, bronzes, urns, jewelry, and terra-cotta vases, this gallery affords remarkable insights into an ancient civilization. One of the most acclaimed exhibits is the Regolini-Galassi tomb, unearthed in the 19th century at Cerveteri (see "Side Trips from Rome," later in this chapter). It shares top honors with the *Mars of Todi,* a bronze sculpture probably dating from the 5th century B.C.

Historical Museum: This museum, founded by Pope Paul VI, was established to tell the history of the Vatican. It exhibits arms, uniforms, and armor, some dating back to the early Renaissance. The carriages displayed are those used by the popes and cardinals in religious processions. Among the showcases of dress uniforms are the colorful outfits worn by the Pontifical Army Corps, which was discontinued by Pope Paul VI.

Pinacoteca (Picture Gallery): The Pinacoteca houses paintings and tapestries from the 11th to the 19th century. As you pass through room 1, note the oldest picture at the Vatican, a keyhole-shaped wood panel of the *Last Judgment* from the 11th century. In room 2 is one of the finest pieces—the *Stefaneschi Triptych* (six panels) by Giotto and his assistants. Bernardo Daddi's masterpiece of early Italian Renaissance art, *Madonna del Magnificat,* is also here. And you'll see works by Fra Angelico, the 15th-century Dominican monk who distinguished himself as a miniaturist (his *Virgin with Child* is justly praised—check out the Madonna's microscopic eyes).

In the Raphael salon (room 8) you can view three paintings by that Renaissance giant: the *Coronation of the Virgin, the Virgin of Foligno,* and the massive *Transfiguration* (completed shortly before his death). There are also eight tapestries made by Flemish weavers from cartoons by Raphael. In room 9, seek out Leonardo da Vinci's

Papal Audiences

When he's in Rome, the pope gives public audiences every Wednesday beginning at 10:30am (sometimes at 10am in the hot summer). It takes place in the Paul VI Hall of Audiences, though sometimes St. Peter's Basilica and St. Peter's Square are used to accommodate a large attendance. Anyone is welcome, but you must obtain a **free ticket** first from the office of the Prefecture of the Papal Household, accessible from St. Peter's Square by the Bronze Door, where the right-hand colonnade (as you face the basilica) begins. The office is open Monday to Saturday 9am to 1pm. Tickets are readily available on Monday and Tuesday, but sometimes you won't be able to get into the office on Wednesday morning. Occasionally, if there's enough room you can attend without a ticket.

You can also write ahead to the **Prefecture of the Papal Household,** 00120 Città del Vaticano (☎ **06/6988-3017**), indicating your language, the dates of your visit, the number of people in your party, and, if possible, the hotel in Rome to which the cards should be sent the afternoon before the audience. American Catholics, armed with a letter of introduction from their parish priest, should apply to the **North American College,** Via dell'Umiltà 30, 00187 Roma (☎ **06/690-011**).

At noon on Sunday, the pope speaks briefly from his study window and gives his blessing to the visitors and pilgrims gathered in St. Peter's Square. From about mid-July to mid-September, the Angelus and blessing take place at the summer residence at Castelgandolfo, some 16 miles outside of Rome and accessible by metro and bus.

masterful—but uncompleted—*St. Jerome with the Lion,* as well as Giovanni Bellini's *Pietà,* and one of Titian's greatest works, the *Virgin of Frari.* Finally, in room 10, feast your eyes on one of the masterpieces of the baroque, Caravaggio's *Deposition from the Cross.*

Pio Clementino Museum: Here you'll find Greek and Roman sculptures, many of which are immediately recognizable. The rippling muscles of the *Belvedere Torso,* a partially preserved Greek statue (1st century B.C.) much admired by the artists of the Renaissance, especially Michelangelo, reveal an intricate knowledge of the human body. In the rotunda is a large gilded bronze of *Hercules* dating from the late 2nd century. Other major sculptures are under porticoes opening onto the Belvedere courtyard. From the 1st century B.C., one sculpture shows Laocoön and his two sons locked in an eternal struggle with the serpents. The incomparable *Apollo of Belvedere* (a late Roman reproduction of an authentic Greek work from the 4th century B.C.) has become the symbol of classic male beauty.

Raphael Rooms: While still a young man, Raphael was given one of the greatest assignments of his short life: the decoration of a series of rooms in the apartments of Pope Julius II. The decoration was carried out by Raphael and his workshop from 1508 to 1524. In these works, Raphael achieves the Renaissance aim of blending classic beauty with realism. In the first chamber, the Stanza dell'Incendio, you'll see much of the work of Raphael's pupils but little of the master—except in the fresco across from the window. The figure of the partially draped Aeneas rescuing his father (to the left of the fresco) is sometimes attributed to Raphael, as is the surprised woman with a jug balanced on her head to the right.

Raphael reigns supreme in the next and most important salon, the Stanza della Segnatura, the first room decorated by the artist, where you'll find the majestic *School*

A Sistine Chapel Tip

To get the best view of the Sistine Chapel's ceiling, bring along binoculars.

---

of Athens, one of the artist's best-known works, depicting such philosophers from the ages as Aristotle, Plato, and Socrates. Many of these figures are actually portraits of some of the greatest artists of the Renaissance, including Bramante (on the right as Euclid, bent over and balding as he draws on a chalkboard), Leonardo da Vinci (as Plato, the bearded man in the center pointing heavenward), even Raphael himself (looking out at you from the lower-right corner). While he was painting this masterpiece, Raphael stopped work to walk down the hall for the unveiling of Michelangelo's newly finished Sistine Chapel ceiling. He was so impressed that he returned to his *School of Athens* and added to his design a sulking Michelangelo sitting on the steps. Another well-known masterpiece here is the *Disputà del Sacramento.*

The Stanza d'Eliodoro, also by the master, manages to flatter Raphael's papal patrons (Julius II and Leo X) without compromising his art (though one rather fanciful fresco depicts the pope driving Attila from Rome). Finally, there's the Sala di Constantino, which was completed by his students after Raphael's death. The loggia, frescoed with more than 50 scenes from the Bible, was designed by Raphael, but the actual work was done by his loyal students.

✪ **Sistine Chapel:** Michelangelo considered himself a sculptor, not a painter. While in his 30s, he was commanded by Julius II to stop work on the pope's own tomb and to devote his considerable talents to painting ceiling frescoes—an art form of which the Florentine master was contemptuous. Michelangelo labored for 4 years (1508 to 1512) over this epic project, which was so physically taxing it permanently damaged his eyesight. All during the task he had to contend with the pope's incessant urgings to hurry up; at one point Julius threatened to topple Michelangelo from the scaffolding—or so Vasari relates.

It's ironic that a project undertaken against the artist's wishes would form his most enduring legend. Glorifying the human body as only a sculptor could, Michelangelo painted nine panels, taken from the pages of Genesis, and surrounded them with prophets and sibyls. The most notable panels detail the expulsion of Adam and Eve from the Garden of Eden and the creation of man (where God's outstretched hand imbues Adam with spirit). The Florentine master was in his 60s when he began the masterly *Last Judgment* on the altar wall. Again working against his wishes, Michelangelo presents a more jaundiced view of people and their fate; God sits in judgment and sinners are plunged into the mouth of hell.

A master of ceremonies under Paul III, Monsignor Biagio da Cesena, protested to the pope about the "shameless nudes" painted by Michelangelo. Michelangelo showed he wasn't above petty revenge by painting the prude with the ears of a jackass in hell. When Biagio complained to the pope, Paul III maintained he had no jurisdiction in hell. However, Daniele de Volterra was summoned to drape clothing over some of the bare figures—thus earning for himself a dubious distinction as a haberdasher.

On the side walls are frescoes by other Renaissance masters, like Botticelli, Perugino, Luca Signorelli, Pinturicchio, Cosimo Roselli, and Ghirlandaio. We'd guess that if these paintings had been displayed by themselves in other chapels, they would be the object of special pilgrimages. But since they have to compete unfairly with the artistry of Michelangelo, they're virtually ignored by the average visitor.

The restoration of the Sistine Chapel in the 1990s touched off a worldwide debate among art historians. The chapel was on the verge of collapse, from both its age and the weather, and restoration has taken years, as restorers used advanced computer analyses in their painstaking and controversial work. They reattached the fresco and repaired the ceiling, ridding the frescoes of their dark and shadowy look. Critics claim that in addition to removing centuries of dirt and grime—and several of the added "modesty" drapes—the restorers removed a vital second layer of paint as well. Purists argue that many of the restored figures seem flat compared to the original, which had more shadow and detail. Others have hailed the project for saving Michelangelo's masterpiece for future generations to appreciate and for revealing the vibrancy of his color palette.

Vatican Library: The library is richly decorated, with frescos created by a team of Mannerist painters commissioned by Sixtus V.

THE VATICAN GARDENS

Separating the Vatican from the secular world on the north and west are 58 acres of lush gardens filled with winding paths, brilliantly colored flowers, groves of massive oaks, and ancient fountains and pools. In the midst of this pastoral setting is a small summer house, Villa Pia, built for Pope Pius IV in 1560 by Pirro Ligorio. The gardens contain medieval fortifications from the 9th century to the present. Profuse waters sprout from a variety of fountains.

You can visit the gardens only on a guided tour, which must be arranged in advance and is limited to 33 people; so reserve as far in advance as possible during the busy summer. (*Note:* You cannot get tickets by phone.) Tours in English run Monday and Tuesday and Thursday to Saturday at 10am. Tickets are 18,000L ($10) and are available at the Vatican Tourist Office (see above).

NEAR VATICAN CITY

✪ **Castel Sant'Angelo.** Lungotevere Castello 50. ☎ **06/687-5036.** Admission 8,000L ($4.65) adults; children 17 and under and seniors 60 and over free. Daily 9am–3pm. Closed 2nd and last Tues of each month. Bus: 23, 46, 49, 62, 87, 98, 280, or 910. Metro: Ottaviano/ San Pietro or Lepanta, then a long stroll.

This overpowering castle, in a landmark position on the Tiber, was built in the 2nd century as a tomb for Emperor Hadrian; it continued as an imperial mausoleum until the time of Caracalla. If it looks like a fortress, it should—that was its function in the Middle Ages, built over the Roman walls and linked to the Vatican by an underground passage that was much used by the fleeing papacy, who escaped from unwanted visitors like Charles V during his 1527 sack of the city. In the 14th century, it became a papal residence, enjoying various connections with Boniface IX, Nicholas V, and Julius II, patron of Michelangelo and Raphael. But its legend rests largely on its link with Pope Alexander VI, whose mistress bore him two children—Cesare and Lucrezia Borgia.

The highlight here is a trip through the Renaissance apartments with their coffered ceilings and lush decoration. Their walls have witnessed some of the most diabolical plots and intrigues of the High Renaissance. Later, you can go through the dank cells that once echoed with the screams of Cesare's victims of torture. The most famous figure imprisoned here was Benvenuto Cellini, the eminent sculptor and goldsmith, remembered chiefly for his candid *Autobiography.* Now an art museum, the castle halls display the history of the Roman mausoleum, along with a wide-ranging selection of ancient arms and armor. You can climb to the top terrace for another one of those dazzling views of the Eternal City.

2 The Colosseum, the Roman Forum & Highlights of Ancient Rome

✪ **Colosseum (Colosseo).** Piazza del Colosseo, Via dei Fori Imperiali. ☎ **06/700-4261.** Street level free; upper levels 8,000L ($4.65) or free if you're under 18 or over 60. Audio tours in English 7,000L ($4.05) (leave ID as a deposit, but it's really not worth it). Guided tours in English with archaeologist 3 times per morning on Sun and holidays 6,000L ($3.50). Tickets to Palatine Hill also sold at box office for 12,000L ($7). Apr–Sept Mon–Tues and Thurs–Sat 9am–7pm, Wed and Sun 9am–1pm; Oct–Mar Mon–Tues and Thurs–Sat 9am–3pm, Wed and Sun 9am–1pm. Metro: Colosseo.

Though it's a mere shell, the Colosseum remains the greatest architectural inheritance from ancient Rome. Vespasian ordered the construction of the elliptical bowl, called the Amphitheatrum Flavium, in A.D. 72; it was inaugurated by Titus in A.D. 80 with a many-weeks-long bloody combat between gladiators and wild beasts. At its peak, under the cruel Domitian, the Colosseum could seat 50,000. The vestal virgins from the temple screamed for blood, as more and more exotic animals were shipped in from the far corners of the Empire to satisfy jaded tastes (lion vs. bear, two humans vs. hippopotamus, or whatever). Not-so-mock naval battles were staged (the canopied Colosseum could be flooded), and the defeated combatants might have their lives spared if they put up a good fight. Many historians now believe that one of the most enduring legends about the Colosseum—that Christians were fed to the lions here—is unfounded.

Long after it ceased to be an arena to amuse sadistic Romans, the Colosseum was struck by an earthquake. Centuries later it was used as a quarry, its rich marble facing stripped away to build palaces and churches. On one side, part of the original four tiers remains; the first three levels were constructed in Doric, Ionic, and Corinthian styles to lend variety. Efforts are currently under way to restore and shore up the Colosseum, but they seem to be dragging. However, scaffolding covers only one section, so the renovations needn't interfere with your visit—they mar a photo angle or two.

A highly photogenic memorial next to the Colosseum, the **Arch of Constantine** was erected by the Senate in A.D. 315 to honor Constantine's defeat of the pagan Maxentius (306). Many of the reliefs have nothing whatever to do with Constantine or his works but tell of the victories of earlier Antonine rulers—they were apparently lifted from other, long-forgotten memorials.

Historically, the arch marks a period of great change in the history of Rome and thus the history of the world. Converted to Christianity by a vision on the battlefield, Constantine ended the centuries-long persecution of the Christians (during which many devout followers of the new religion had often been put to death in a most gruesome manner). While Constantine didn't ban paganism (which survived officially until the closing of the temples more than half a century later), he espoused Christianity himself and began the inevitable development that culminated in the conquest of Rome by the Christian religion.

After visiting the Colosseum, it's convenient to look at the site of the **Domus Aurea (Golden House of Nero)** on Via Labicana on the Esquiline Hill; it faces the Colosseum and is adjacent to the Forum. This was one of the most sumptuous palaces of all time, built by Nero after a disastrous fire swept over Rome in A.D. 64 (contrary to legend, he didn't fiddle while Rome burned). Not much remains of its former glory, but once the floors were made of mother-of-pearl and the furniture of gold. The area that's the Colosseum today was an ornamental lake reflecting the glitter of the Golden

(say yes)

You pop the question in Paris, you better have an **AT&T Direct**® Service wallet guide in your pocket. It's a list of access

numbers you need to call home fast and clear from around the world, using an AT&T Calling Card or credit card.

So you can give everyone back home a ring.

For a list of **AT&T Access Numbers,** take the attached wallet guide.

I t ' s   a l l   w i t h i n   y o u r   r e a c h .

For Travelers
who want more than
the Official Line

For Travelers Who Want More Than the Official Line

the
Unofficial
Guide® to
New Orleans

The Guides with More Than 2.5 Million Copies in Print!

the
Unofficial
Guide® to
Walt Disney World®

The Series with More Than 2.5 Million Copies Sold!

♦ Save Time & Money
♦ Hotels & Restaurants
Candidly Rated & Ranked
Insider Tips & Warnings

Eve Zibart with Bob Sehlinger

♦ Tips & Warnings
♦ Save Money & Time
♦ All Attractions Ranked & Rated
♦ Plus Disney's New Animal Kingdom

Bob Sehlinger

For Travelers Who Want More Than the Official Line

the
Unofficial
Guide® to
Las Vegas

The Series with More Than 2.5 Million Copies Sold!

♦ Save Time & Money
♦ Insider Gambling Tips
♦ Casinos & Hotels
Candidly Rated & Ranked

Bob Sehlinger

Also Available:

- The Unofficial Guide to Branson
- The Unofficial Guide to Chicago
- The Unofficial Guide to Cruises
- The Unofficial Disney Companion
- The Unofficial Guide to Disneyland
- The Unofficial Guide to the Great Smoky & Blue Ridge Mountains
- The Unofficial Guide to Miami & the Keys
- Mini-Mickey: The Pocket-Sized Unofficial Guide to Walt Disney World
- The Unofficial Guide to New York City
- The Unofficial Guide to San Francisco
- The Unofficial Guide to Skiing in the West
- The Unofficial Guide to Washington, D.C.

Macmillan Publishing USA

Ancient Rome & Attractions Nearby

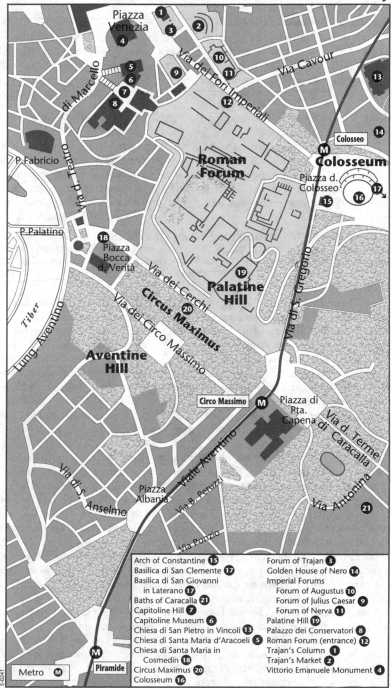

149

The Ruins Before & After

To appreciate the Colosseum, Roman Forum, and other ruins more fully, buy a copy of the small red book called *Rome Past and Present* (Vision Publications), sold in bookstores or on stands near the Forum. Its plastic overleafs show you the elaborate way things were 2,000 years ago.

House. The hollow ruins—long stripped of their lavish decorations—lie near the entrance to Oppius Park.

During the Renaissance, painters like Raphael chopped holes in the long-buried ceilings of the Domus Aurea to gain admittance. Once here, they were inspired by the frescoes and the small "grotesques" of cornucopia and cherubs. The word *grotto* came from this palace, as it was believed to have been built underground. Remnants of these almost-2,000-year-old frescoes and fragments of mosaics remain. All interiors have been closed for years.

✪ **Roman Forum (Foro Romano) and Palatine Hill (Palatino).** Via dei Fori Imperiali. ☎ **06/699-0110.** Admission 12,000L ($7) adults; children 17 and under and seniors 60 and over free. Apr–Sept Mon–Sat 9am–6pm, Sun 9am–1pm; Oct–Mar Mon–Sat 9am–sunset, Sun 9am–1pm. Last admission 1 hour before closing. Closed holidays. Metro: Colosseo. Bus: 27, 81, 85, 87, or 186.

When it came to cremating Caesar, purchasing a harlot for the night, or sacrificing a naked victim, the Roman Forum was the place to be. Traversed by Via Sacra (Sacred Way), it was built in the marshy land between the Palatine and Capitoline hills. It flourished as the center of Roman life in the days of the Republic, before it gradually lost prestige to the Imperial Forums.

You'll see only ruins and fragments, an arch or two, and lots of overturned boulders, but with some imagination you can feel the rush of history here. That any semblance of the Forum remains today is miraculous, as it was used for years (like the Colosseum) as a quarry. Eventually it reverted to what the Italians call a *campo vaccino* (cow pasture). But excavations in the 19th century began to bring to light one of the world's most historic spots.

By day, the columns of now-vanished temples and the stones from which long-forgotten orators spoke are mere shells. Bits of grass and weed grow where a triumphant Caesar was once lionized. But at night, when the Forum is silent in the moonlight (you can get a dramatic view of the floodlit ruins from the Campidoglio), it isn't difficult to imagine vestal virgins still guarding the sacred temple fire. (*Historical footnote:* The maidens were assigned to keep the temple's sacred fire burning—but to keep their own passions under control. Failure to do the latter sent them to an early grave . . . alive!)

You can spend at least a morning wandering alone through the ruins of the Forum. If you're content with just looking at the ruins, you can do so at your leisure. But if you want the stones to have some meaning, purchase a detailed plan at the gate (the temples are hard to locate otherwise).

A long walk up from the Roman Forum leads to the **Palatine Hill** (which you can visit on the same ticket and at the same hours as the Forum), one of Rome's seven hills. The Palatine, tradition tells us, was the spot on which the first settlers built their huts, under the direction of Romulus. In later years, the hill became a patrician residential district that attracted such citizens as Cicero. In time, however, the area was gobbled up by imperial palaces and drew a famous and infamous roster of tenants, like Livia (some of the frescoes in the House of Livia are in miraculous condition), Tiberius, Caligula (he was murdered here by members of his Praetorian Guard), Nero, and Domitian.

Only the ruins of its former grandeur remain today, and you really need to be an archaeologist to make sense of them, as they're more difficult to understand than those in the Forum. But even if you're not interested in the past, it's worth the climb for the panoramic view of both the Roman and the Imperial forums, as well as the Capitoline Hill and the Colosseum.

Imperial Forums (Fori Imperiali). Via de Fori Imperiali. Free admission. Metro: Colosseo. Bus: 27, 85, 87, or 186. Keep to the right side of the street.

It was Mussolini who issued the controversial orders to cut through centuries of debris and junky buildings to carve out Via dei Fori Imperiali, thereby linking the Colosseum to the grand 19th-century monuments of Piazza Venezia. Excavations under his Fascist regime began at once, and many archaeological treasures were revealed.

Begun by Julius Caesar as an answer to the overcrowding of Rome's older forums during the days of the empire, the Imperial Forums were at the time of their construction flashier, bolder, and more impressive than the buildings in the Roman Forum. This site conveyed the unquestioned authority of the emperors at the height of their absolute power. On the street's north side you'll come to a large outdoor restaurant, where Via Cavour joins the boulevard. Just beyond the small park across Via Cavour are the remains of the **Forum of Nerva,** built by the emperor whose 2-year reign (A.D. 96–98) followed that of the paranoid Domitian. You'll be struck by just how much the ground level has risen in 19 centuries. The only really recognizable remnant is a wall of the Temple of Minerva with two fine Corinthian columns. This forum was once flanked by that of Vespasian, which is now gone. It's possible to enter the Forum of Nerva from the other side, but you can see it just as well from the railing.

The next forum you approach is the **Forum of Augustus,** built before the birth of Christ to commemorate the emperor's victory over the assassins Cassius and Brutus in the Battle of Philippi (42 B.C.). Like the Forum of Nerva, you can enter this forum from the other side (cut across the wee footbridge).

Continuing along the railing, you'll see the vast semicircle of **Trajan's Market,** Via Quattro Novembre 94 (☎ 06/679-0048), whose teeming arcades stocked with merchandise from the far corners of the Roman world long ago collapsed, leaving only a few cats to watch after things. The shops once covered a multitude of levels, and you can still wander around many of them. In front of the perfectly proportioned facade—designed by Apollodorus of Damascus at the beginning of the 2nd century—are the remains of a great library, and fragments of delicately colored marble floors still shine in the sunlight between stretches of rubble and tall grass. Trajan's Market is worth the descent below street level. To get there, follow the service road you're on until you reach the monumental Trajan's Column on your left, where you turn right and go up the steep flight of stairs leading to Via Nazionale. At the top, about half a block farther on the right, you'll see the entrance. It's open Tuesday to Sunday 9am to 4:30pm. Admission is 3,750L ($2.15) adults and 2,500L ($1.45) students; children 17 and under and seniors 60 and over are free.

Before you head down through the labyrinthine passages, you might like to climb the **Tower of the Milizie,** a 12th-century structure that was part of the medieval headquarters of the Knights of Rhodes. The view from the top (if it's open) is well worth the climb.

You can enter the **Forum of Trajan** on Via Quattro Novembre near the steps of Via Magnanapoli. Once through the tunnel, you'll emerge into the newest and most beautiful of the Imperial Forums, built between A.D. 107 and 113 and designed by Greek architect Apollodorus of Damascus (who laid out the adjoining market). There are many statue fragments and pedestals bearing still-legible inscriptions, but more interesting is the great Basilica Ulpia, whose gray marble columns rise roofless into the sky. This forum was once regarded as one of the architectural wonders of the world.

Beyond the Basilica Ulpia is **Trajan's Column,** in magnificent condition, with intricate bas-relief sculpture depicting Trajan's victorious campaign (though from your vantage point you'll be able to see only the earliest stages). The next stop is the **Forum of Julius Caesar,** the first of the Imperial Forums. It lies on the opposite side of Via dei Fori Imperiali. This was the site of the Roman stock exchange, as well as of the Temple of Venus.

After you've seen the wonders of ancient Rome, you might continue up Via dei Fori Imperiali to Piazza Venezia, where the white Brescian marble **Vittorio Emanuele Monument** dominates the scene. (You can't miss it.) Italy's most flamboyant landmark, it was built in the late 1800s to honor the first king of Italy. It has been compared to everything from a frosty wedding cake to a Victorian typewriter and has been ridiculed because of its harsh white color in a city of honey-gold tones. An eternal flame burns at the Tomb of the Unknown Soldier. The interior of the monument has been closed for many years, but you'll come to use it as a landmark as you figure your way around the city.

Circus Maximus (Circo Massimo). Between Via dei Cerchi and Via del Circo Massimo. Metro: Circo Massimo.

The Circus Maximus, with its elongated oval proportions and ruined tiers of benches, will remind you of the setting for *Ben-Hur.* Today a formless ruin, the once-grand circus was pilfered repeatedly by medieval and Renaissance builders in search of marble and stone. At one time, 250,000 Romans could assemble on the marble seats, while the emperor observed the games from his box high on the Palatine Hill.

The circus lies in a valley formed by the Palatine Hill on the left and the Aventine Hill on the right. Next to the Colosseum, it was the most impressive structure in ancient Rome, located certainly in one of the most exclusive neighborhoods. For centuries, the pomp and ceremony of imperial chariot races filled this valley with the cheers of thousands.

When the dark days of the 5th and 6th centuries fell, the Circus Maximus seemed a symbol of the complete ruination of Rome. The last games were held in 549 on the orders of Totilla the Goth, who had seized Rome in 547 and established himself emperor. He lived in the still-glittering ruins on the Palatine and apparently thought that the chariot races in the Circus Maximus would lend credence to his charade of empire. It must have been a pretty miserable show, since the decimated population numbered something like 500 when Totilla recaptured the city. The Romans of these times were caught between Belisarius, the imperial general from Constantinople, and Totilla the Goth, both of whom fought bloodily for control of Rome. After the travesty of 549, the Circus Maximus was never used again, and the demand for building materials reduced it, like so much of Rome, to a great dusty field.

✪ Capitoline Museum (Museo Capitolino) and Palazzo dei Conservatori. Piazza del Campidoglio. ☎ **06/6710-2071.** Admission (to both) 10,000L ($6) adults, 5,000L ($2.90) children under 18. Free on last Sun of each month. Tues–Sun 9am–7pm. Bus: 44, 85, 87, 170, 175, 181, 628, 640, or 810.

Of Rome's seven hills, the **Capitoline (Campidoglio)** is the most sacred—its origins stretch way back into antiquity (an Etruscan temple to Jupiter once stood on this spot). The approach is dramatic as you climb the long sloping steps by Michelangelo. At the top is a perfectly proportioned square, **Piazza del Campidoglio,** also laid out by the Florentine artist. Michelangelo positioned the bronze equestrian statue of

Marcus Aurelius in the center, but it has now been moved inside to be protected from pollution (a copy was placed out on the pedestal in 1997). The Campidoglio is dramatic at night (walk around to the back for a regal view of the floodlit Forum). The other steps adjoining Michelangelo's approach will take you to Santa Maria d'Aracoeli.

One side of the piazza is open; the others are bounded by the **Senatorium (Town Council),** the statuary-filled **Palace of the Conservatori (Curators),** and the **Capitoline Museum.** These museums house some of the greatest pieces of classical sculpture in the world.

The **Capitoline Museum** was built in the 17th century based on an architectural sketch by Michelangelo. In the first room is *The Dying Gaul,* a work of majestic skill that's a copy of a Greek original dating from the 3rd century B.C. In a special gallery all her own is the *Capitoline Venus,* who demurely covers herself. This statue was the symbol of feminine beauty and charm down through the centuries (also a Roman copy of a 3rd century B.C. Greek original). *Amore* (Cupid) and *Psyche* are up to their old tricks near the window.

The famous equestrian statue of Marcus Aurelius, whose years in the piazza made it a victim of pollution, has recently been restored and is now kept in the museum for protection. This is the only bronze equestrian statue to have survived from ancient Rome, mainly because it was thought for centuries that this was a statue of Constantine the Great and papal Rome respected the memory of the first Christian emperor. It's beautiful, though the perspective is rather odd. The statue is housed in a glassed-in room on the street level, the Cortile di Marforio; it's a kind of Renaissance greenhouse, surrounded by windows.

The **Palace of the Conservatori,** across the way, was also based on a Michelangelo architectural plan and is rich in classical sculpture and paintings. One of the most notable bronzes—a work of incomparable beauty—is *Lo Spinario* (a little boy picking a thorn from his foot), a Greek classic dating from the 1st century B.C. In addition, you'll find *Lupa Capitolina* (the *Capitoline Wolf*), a rare Etruscan bronze that may go back to the 5th century B.C. (Romulus and Remus, the legendary twins the wolf suckled, were added at a later date). The palace also contains a Pinacoteca (Picture Gallery)—mostly works from the 16th and 17th centuries. Notable canvases are Caravaggio's *Fortune-Teller* and his curious *John the Baptist, The Holy Family* by Dosso Dossi, *Romulus and Remus* by Rubens, and Titian's *Baptism of Christ.* The entrance courtyard is lined with the remains (head, hands, foot, and a kneecap) of an ancient colossal statue of Constantine the Great.

Baths of Caracalla (Terme di Caracalla). Via delle Terme di Caracalla 52. ☎ **06/ 575-8626.** Admission 8,000L ($4.65) adults; children 11 and under free. Tues–Sat 9am–1pm. Bus: 628.

Named for the emperor Caracalla, the baths were completed in the early 3rd century. The richness of decoration has faded and the lushness can be judged only from the shell of brick ruins that remain. In their heyday, they sprawled across 27 acres and could handle 1,600 bathers at one time. A circular room, the ruined caldarium for very hot baths, had been the traditional setting for operatic performances in Rome, until it was discovered that the ancient structure was being severely damaged.

OTHER ATTRACTIONS NEAR ANCIENT ROME
Chiesa di Santa Maria d'Aracoeli. Piazza d'Aracoeli. ☎ **06/679-8155.** Free admission. Daily 7am–noon and 4–7pm. Bus: 44, 46, or 75.

On the Capitoline Hill, this landmark church was built for the Franciscans in the 13th century. According to legend, Augustus once ordered a temple erected on this spot, where a sibyl, with her gift of prophecy, forecast the coming of Christ. In the interior are a coffered Renaissance ceiling and a mosaic of the Virgin over the altar in the Byzantine style. If you're enough of a sleuth, you'll find a tombstone carved by the great Renaissance sculptor Donatello. The church is known for its **Bufalini Chapel,** a masterpiece by Pinturicchio, who frescoed it with scenes illustrating the life and death of St. Bernardino of Siena. He also depicted St. Francis receiving the stigmata. These frescoes are a high point in early Renaissance Roman painting. You have to climb a long flight of steep steps to reach the church, unless you're already on the neighboring Piazza del Campidoglio, in which case you can cross the piazza and climb the steps on the far side of the Museo Capitolino.

National Museum of the Palazzo Venezia (Museo Nazionale del Palazzo Venezia). Via del Plebiscito 118. ☎ **06/679-8865.** Admission 8,000L ($4.65) adults; children under 18 and adults over 60 free. Tues–Sat 9am–2pm, Sun 9am–1pm. Bus: 57, 65, 70, or 75.

The Museum of the Palazzo Venezia, in the geographic heart of Rome, served as the seat of the Austrian Embassy until the end of World War I. During the Fascist regime (1928 to 1943), it was the seat of the Italian government. The balcony from which Mussolini used to speak to the people was built in the 15th century. You can now visit the rooms and halls containing oil paintings, porcelain, tapestries, ivories, and ceramics. No one particular exhibit stands out—it's the sum total that adds up to a major attraction. The State Rooms occasionally open to host temporary exhibits.

Chiesa di Santa Maria in Cosmedin. Piazza della Bocca della Verità 18. ☎ **06/678-1419.** Free admission. Daily 9am–1pm and 2:30–6pm. Bus: 81 or 175. Metro: Circo Massimo.

This little church was begun in the 6th century but subsequently rebuilt—and a Romanesque campanile was added in the 12th century. People come not for great art treasures but to see the **"Mouth of Truth,"** a large disk under the portico. As Gregory Peck demonstrated to Audrey Hepburn in the film *Roman Holiday,* the mouth is supposed to chomp down on the hand of liars who insert their paws. (According to local legend, a former priest used to keep a scorpion in back to bite the fingers of anyone he felt was lying.)

Basilica di San Clemente. Via San Giovanni in Laterano at Piazza San Clemente, Via Labicana 95. ☎ **06/7045-1018.** Basilica free; grottoes 4,000L ($2.30). Mon–Sat 9am–12:30pm and 3–6pm, Sun 10am–noon and 3–6pm. Metro: Colosseo.

From the Colosseum, head up Via San Giovanni in Laterano to this basilica. It isn't just another Roman church—far from it! In this church-upon-a-church, centuries of history peel away. In the 4th century, a church was built over a secular house from the 1st century, beside which stood a pagan temple dedicated to Mithras (god of the sun). Down in the eerie grottoes (which you can explore on your own—unlike the catacombs on the Appian Way), you'll discover well-preserved frescoes from between the 9th and 11th century. The Normans destroyed the lower church, and a new one was built in the 12th century. Its chief attraction is the bronze-orange mosaic (from that period) adorning the apse, as well as a chapel honoring St. Catherine of Alexandria with frescoes by Masolino.

Basilica di San Giovanni in Laterano. Piazza San Giovanni in Laterano 4. ☎ **06/ 6988-6433.** Basilica free; cloisters 4,000L ($2.30). Summer daily 7am–6:45pm (off-season to 6pm). Metro: San Giovanni.

This church—not St. Peter's—is the cathedral of the diocese of Rome, where the pope comes to celebrate mass on certain holidays. Built in A.D. 314 by Constantine, it has suffered the vicissitudes of Rome, forcing it to be rebuilt many times. Only fragmented parts of the baptistery remain from the original.

The present building is characterized by its 18th-century facade by Alessandro Galilei (statues of Christ and the Apostles ring the top). A 1993 terrorist bomb caused severe damage, especially to the facade. Borromini gets the credit (some say blame) for the interior, built for Innocent X. It's said that in the misguided attempt to redecorate, frescoes by Giotto were destroyed (remains believed to have been painted by Giotto were discovered in 1952 and are now on display against a column near the entrance on the right inner pier). In addition, look for the unusual ceiling and the sumptuous transept and explore the 13th-century cloisters with twisted double columns.

The popes used to live next door at the **Palazzo Laterano** before the move to Avignon in the 14th century. Across the street is the **Santuario della Scala Santa (Palace of the Holy Steps),** Piazza San Giovanni in Laterano (☎ 06/7049-4619). It's alleged that the 28 marble steps here (now covered with wood for preservation) were originally at Pontius Pilate's villa in Jerusalem and that Christ climbed them the day he was brought before Pilate. According to a medieval tradition, the steps were brought from Jerusalem to Rome by Constantine's mother, Helen, in 326, and they've been in this location since 1589. Today pilgrims from all over the world come here to climb the steps—on their knees. This is one of the holiest sites in Christendom, though some historians say the stairs may date only to the 4th century.

Chiesa di San Pietro in Vincoli (St. Peter in Chains). Piazza San Pietro in Vincoli 4A (off Via degli Annibaldi). ☎ 06/488-2865. Free admission. Spring/summer daily 7am–12:30pm and 3:30–7pm (autumn/winter to 6pm). Metro: Via Cavour, then cross the boulevard and walk up the flight of stairs. Turn right and you'll head into the piazza; the church will be on your left.

This church was founded in the 5th century to house the chains that bound St. Peter in Palestine—they're preserved under glass. But the drawing card is the tomb of Julius II, with one of the world's most famous sculptures: ○ **Michelangelo's** *Moses.* As readers of Irving Stone's *The Agony and the Ecstasy* know, Michelangelo was to have carved 44 magnificent figures for the tomb. That didn't happen, of course, but the pope was given one of the greatest consolation prizes—a figure intended to be "minor" that's now numbered among Michelangelo's masterpieces. In the *Lives of the Artists,* Vasari wrote about the stern father symbol of Michelangelo's *Moses:* "No modern work will ever equal it in beauty, no, nor ancient either." The church is currently undergoing restoration, but *Moses* is still on view. It's badly lit, though, so bring 500L coins to turn on the light box.

3 The Pantheon & Attractions Near Piazza Navona & Campo de' Fiori

THE PANTHEON & NEARBY ATTRACTIONS

The Pantheon stands on **Piazza della Rotunda,** a lively square with cafes, vendors, and great people-watching.

○ **Pantheon.** Piazza della Rotonda. ☎ 06/6830-0230. Free admission. Mon–Sat 9am–6pm, Sun 9am–1pm. Bus: 70, 81, 119, 170.

Of all ancient Rome's great buildings, only the Pantheon ("All the Gods") remains intact. It was built in 27 B.C. by Marcus Agrippa and reconstructed by Hadrian in the early 2nd century A.D. This remarkable building, once ringed with white marble statues of Roman gods in its niches, is among the architectural wonders of the world because of its dome and its concept of space. Animals were sacrificed and burned in the center, and the smoke escaped through the only means of light, an opening at the top 27 feet in diameter. The Pantheon is 142 feet wide and 142 feet high. Michelangelo came here to study the dome before designing the cupola of St. Peter's (whose dome is 2 feet smaller than the Pantheon's). The walls are 25 feet thick, and the bronze doors leading into the building weigh 20 tons each. About 125 years ago, the tomb of Raphael was discovered here (fans still bring him flowers). Victor Emmanuel II, king of Italy, and his successor, Umberto I, are interred here as well.

Chiesa di Santa Maria Sopra Minerva. Piazza della Minerva 42. ☎ **06/679-3926.** Free admission. Daily 7am–noon and 4–7pm. Bus: 44, 46, or 116.

Beginning in 1280, early Christian leaders ordained that the foundation of an ancient temple dedicated to Minerva (goddess of wisdom) be reused as the base for Rome's only Gothic church. Architectural changes and redecorations in the 1500s and 1900s stripped it of some of its magnificence, but it still includes an awe-inspiring collection of medieval and Renaissance tombs. You'll find a beautiful chapel frescoed by Fillipino Lippi and, to the left of the apse, a muscular *Risen Christ* carrying a rather small marble cross carved by Michelangelo (the bronze drapery covering Christ's nudity was added later). Under the altar lie the remains of St. Catherine of Siena, and in the passage to the left of the choir, surrounded by a small fence, is the floor tomb of the great monastic painter Fra Angelico. The amusing baby elephant carrying a small obelisk in the piazza outside was designed by Bernini.

Chiesa del Gesù. Piazza del Gesù, Via degli Astalli 16. ☎ **06/697-001.** Free admission. Apr–Sept daily 6am–12:30pm and 4–7pm; Oct–Mar daily 6am–12:30pm and 4:30–7:15pm. Bus: 44, 46, or 116.

Built from 1568 to 1584 with donations from a Farnese cardinal, this was for several centuries the most potent and powerful church in the Jesuit order. It was conceived as a bulwark against the perceived menace of the Protestant Reformation and is an important legacy from the Catholic Counter-Reformation. The yellow marble sheathing part of the interior was added in the 1800s.

Galleria Doria Pamphilj. Piazza del Collegio Romano 2 (off Via del Corso). ☎ **06/ 679-7323.** Gallery 13,000L ($8) adults, 10,000L ($6) students/seniors; apartments 5,000L ($2.90). Fri–Wed 10am–5pm. Private visits can be arranged. Metro: Colosseo or Cavour, then a long stroll.

This museum offers a look at what it's really like to live in an 18th-century palace—it has been restored to its former splendor and expanded to include four rooms long closed to the public. It's partly leased to tenants (on the upper levels) and there are shops on the street level—but you'll overlook all this after entering the grand apartments of the Doria Pamphilj family, which traces its lines to before the great 15th-century Genoese admiral Andrea Doria. The apartments surround the central court and gallery. The ballroom, drawing rooms, dining rooms, and family chapel are open and full of gilded furniture, crystal chandeliers, Renaissance tapestries, and family portraits. The Green Room is especially rich, with a 15th-century Tournay tapestry, paintings by Memling and Filippo Lippi, and a seminude portrait of Andrea Doria by Sebastiano del Piombo. The Andrea Doria Room, dedicated to the admiral and to the ship of the same name, contains a glass case with mementos of the great 1950s maritime disaster.

Skirting the central court is a picture gallery with a memorable collection of frescoes, paintings, and sculpture. Most important are the portrait of Innocent X by Velázquez, *Salome* by Titian, works by Rubens and Caravaggio, the *Bay of Naples* by Pieter Brueghel the Elder, and a copy of Raphael's portrait of Principessa Giovanna d' Aragona de Colonna (who looks remarkably like Leonardo's *Mona Lisa*). Most of the

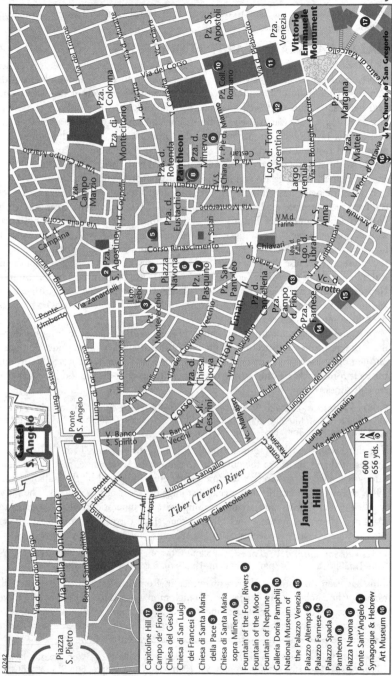

The Pantheon & Attractions Nearby

Capitoline Hill 17
Campo de' Fiori 13
Chiesa del Gesù 12
Chiesa di San Luigi dei Francesi 5
Chiesa di Santa Maria della Pace 3
Chiesa di Santa Maria sopra Minerva 9
Fountain of the Four Rivers 6
Fountain of the Moor 7
Fountain of Neptune 4
Galleria Doria Pamphilj 10
National Museum of the Palazzo Venezia 11
Palazzo Altemps 2
Palazzo Farnese 14
Palazzo Spada 15
Pantheon 8
Piazza Navona 6
Ponte Sant'Angelo 1
Synagogue & Hebrew Art Museum 16

157

sculpture came from the Doria country estates: marble busts of Roman emperors, bucolic nymphs, and satyrs.

PIAZZA NAVONA & NEARBY ATTRACTIONS

✪ **Piazza Navona,** one of the most beautifully baroque sites in all Rome, is an ocher-colored gem, unspoiled by new buildings or even by traffic. Its shape results from the ruins of the Stadium of Domitian, lying underneath. Great chariot races were once held here (some rather unusual—such as the one in which the head of the winning horse was lopped off as it crossed the finish line and carried by runners to be offered as a sacrifice by the vestal virgins on top of the Capitoline Hill). In medieval times, the popes used to flood the piazza to stage mock naval encounters. Today the piazza is packed with vendors and street performers and lined with (pricey) cafes where you can enjoy a cappuccino or gelato and indulge in unparalleled people-watching.

Besides the twin-towered facade of 17th-century Santa Agnes, the piazza boasts several baroque masterpieces. The best known, in the center, is Bernini's **Fountain of the Four Rivers (Fontana dei Fiumi),** whose four stone personifications symbolize the world's greatest rivers—the Ganges, Danube, della Plata, and Nile. It's fun to try to figure out which is which. (*Hint:* The figure with the shroud on its head is the Nile, so represented because the river's source was unknown at the time.) At the south end is the **Fountain of the Moor (Fontana del Moro),** also by Bernini. The **Fountain of Neptune (Fontana di Neptuno),** which balances that of the Moor, is a 19th-century addition; it has been restored after a demented 1997 attack by two men who broke off the tail of one of its sea creatures.

In summer, there are outdoor art shows in the evening, but visit during the day—that's the best time to inspect the fragments of the original stadium under a building on the north side of the piazza. If you're interested, walk out at the northern exit and turn left for a block. It's astonishing how much the level of the ground has risen since ancient times.

Palazzo Altemps. Piazza S. Apollinare 8. ☎ **06/68337-59.** Admission (includes entrance to National Roman Museum and Palazzo Massimo alle Terme) 12,000L ($7). Tues–Sat 9am–2pm and Sun 9am–1pm. Bus 70, 87, 119, or 186.

The third branch of the National Roman Museum (below), this 15th-century palace was restored and opened to the public in December 1997. It houses part of the fabled Ludovisi Collection of Greek and Roman sculpture, acquired by the Italian state in 1901; many of these works have been in storage for most of this century. The palace is filled with Venuses and nymphs along with homoerotic works like Pan and Daphnis. Many frescoes were uncovered in the palace, the earliest from the 12th century. A frescoed chapel is dedicated to St. Anicetus, the 2nd-century pope.

Chiesa di San Luigi dei Francesi. Via Santa Giovanna d'Arco. ☎ **06/688-271.** Fri–Wed 8am–12:30pm and 3:30–7pm, Thurs 8am–12:30pm. Bus: 70, 81, or 87.

This has been the national church of France in Rome since 1589, and a stone salamander (the symbol of the Renaissance French monarch François I) was subtly carved into its facade. Inside, in the last chapel on the left, is a noteworthy series of frescoes by Caravaggio—the celebrated *Calling of St. Matthew* on the left, *St. Matthew and the Angel* in the center, and the *Martyrdom of St. Matthew* on the right.

Chiesa di Santa Maria della Pace. Vicolo del Arco della Pace 5 (off Piazza Navona). ☎ **06/686-1156.** Free admission. Tues–Sat 10am–noon and 4–6pm, Sun 9–11am. Bus: 70, 81, or 87.

According to legend, blood flowed from a statue of the Virgin above the altar here after someone threw a pebble at it. This legend motivated Pope Sixtus to rebuild the church in the 1500s on the foundations of an even older sanctuary. For generations after that, its curved porticos, cupola atop an octagonal base, cloisters by Bramante, and frescoes by Raphael helped make it one of the most fashionable churches for aristocrats residing in the surrounding palazzos. Before you go, check to make sure the church is open because it was undergoing renovations at press time.

CAMPO DE' FIORI & THE JEWISH GHETTO

During the 1500s, **Campo de' Fiori** was the geographic and cultural center of secular Rome, site of dozens of inns that would almost certainly have been reviewed by this guidebook. From its center rises a statue of severe-looking monk Giordano Bruno, whose presence is a reminder that religious heretics were occasionally burned at the stake here. Today, ringed with venerable houses, the campo is the site of an **open-air food market** held Monday to Saturday from early in the morning until around noon, or whenever the food runs out.

Built from 1514 to 1589, **Palazzo Farnese,** on Piazza Farnese, was designed by Sangallo and Michelangelo, among others, and was an astronomically expensive project for the time. Its famous residents have included a 16th-century member of the Farnese family, Pope Paul III, Cardinal Richelieu, and the former Queen Christina of Sweden, who moved to Rome after abdicating. During the 1630s, when the heirs couldn't afford to maintain it, the palazzo became the site of the French Embassy, as it still is (it's closed to the public). For the best view of it, cut west from Via Giulia along any of the narrow streets—we recommend Via Mascherone or Via dei Farnesi.

The **Palazzo Spada,** Capo di Ferro 3 (☎ 06/686-1158), built around 1550 for Cardinal Gerolamo Capo di Ferro and later inhabited by the descendants of several other cardinals, was sold to the Italian government in the 1920s. Its richly ornate facade, covered in high-relief stucco decorations in the Mannerist style, is the finest of any building from 16th-century Rome. Though the State Rooms are closed, the richly decorated courtyard and a handful of galleries of paintings are open. Admission is 4,000L ($2.30) adults; children 17 and under and seniors 60 and over are free. Hours are Tuesday to Saturday 9am to 7pm and Sunday 9am to 1pm.

The best way to see the **Jewish Ghetto** is to go on a free walking tour offered by **Service International de Documentation Judeo-Chrétienne,** Via Plebiscito 112 (☎ 06/679-5307). An interesting remnant from the era of the ghetto is **San Gregorio,** Ponte Quattro Capi, at the end of Via del Portico d'Ottavia; it bears an inscription in both Hebrew and Latin asking Jews to convert to Catholicism.

Across from the church stands the **Sinagoga Ashkenazita** (☎ 06/6840-061), open only for services. Trying to avoid all resemblance to a Christian church, the building (1874–1904) evokes Babylonian and Persian details. The synagogue was attacked by terrorists in 1982 and since then has been heavily guarded by *carabinieri* (a division of the Italian army) armed with machine guns. It houses the **Jewish Museum (☎ 06/6840-061),** open Monday to Thursday 9am to 5pm, Friday 9am to 2pm, and Sunday 9am to 12:30pm. Admission is 8,000L ($4.65). Many rare and even priceless treasures are here, including a Moroccan prayer book from the early 14th century and ceremonial objects from the 17th-century Jewish Ghetto.

4 The Spanish Steps, the Trevi Fountain & Attractions Nearby

✪ **Spanish Steps (Scalinata della Trinità dei Monti).** Piazza di Spagna. Metro: Spagna.

The steps—filled in spring with flower vendors, jewelry dealers, and photographers snapping pictures of visitors—and the square take their names from the Spanish

A Trevi Tip

Of course you have to toss a coin in the Trevi Fountain. To do things properly, hold your lira coin in the right hand, turn your back to the fountain, and toss the coin over your shoulder (being careful not to bean anyone behind you). Then the spirit of the fountain will see to it that you return to Rome one day—or that's the tradition, at least.

Embassy, which used to be headquartered here. Designed by Italian architect Francesco de Sanctis and built from 1723 to 1725, they were funded almost entirely by the French as a preface to Trinità dei Monti at the top.

At the foot of the steps is a **boat-shaped fountain** designed by Pietro Bernini (not to be confused with his son, Giovanni Lorenzo Bernini, a far greater sculptor). About 2 centuries ago, when the foreign art colony was in its ascendancy, the 136 steps were covered with young men and women who wanted to pose for the painters—men with their shirts unbuttoned to show off what they hoped was a *David*-esque physique and women consistently draped like Madonnas.

The steps and the piazza below are always packed with a crowd: strolling, reading in the sun, browsing the vendors' carts, and people-watching. Near the steps, you'll also find an American Express office, public rest rooms (near the Metro stop), and the most sumptuous McDonald's we've ever seen.

Keats-Shelley Memorial. Piazza di Spagna 26. ☎ **06/678-4235.** Admission 5,000L ($2.90). May–Sept Mon–Fri 9am–1pm and 3–6pm; Oct–Apr Mon–Fri 9am–1pm and 2:30–5:30pm. Guided tours by appointment. Metro: Spagna.

At the foot of the Spanish Steps is this 18th-century house where Keats died of consumption on February 23, 1821, at age 25. Since 1909, when it was bought by well-intentioned English and American literary types, it has been a working lib-rary established in honor of Keats and the poet Shelley, who drowned off the coast of Viareggio with a copy of Keats in his pocket. Mementos range from the kitsch to the immortal and are laden with nostalgia. The apartment where Keats spent his last months, carefully tended by his close friend Joseph Severn, shelters a strange death mask of Keats as well as the "deadly sweat" drawing by Severn.

✪ Trevi Fountain (Fontana dei Trevi). Piazza di Trevi. Metro: Piazza Barberini.

As you elbow your way through the summertime crowds around the Trevi Fountain, you'll find it hard to believe that this little piazza was nearly always deserted before the film *Three Coins in the Fountain* brought the stampede of tour buses. Today this newly restored gem is a must on everybody's itinerary.

Supplied by water from the Acqua Vergine aqueduct and a triumph of the baroque style, it was based on the design of Nicolo Salvi (who's said to have died of illness contracted during his supervision of the project) and was completed in 1762. The design centers around the triumphant figure of Neptunus Rex, standing on a shell chariot drawn by winged steeds and led by a pair of tritons. Two allegorical figures in the side niches represent good health and fertility.

On the southwestern corner of the piazza is a somber, not particularly spectacular-looking church, **Chiesa SS. Vincenzo e Anastasio,** with a strange claim to fame. Within it survive the hearts and intestines of several centuries of popes. According to legend, the church was built on the site of a spring that burst from the earth after the beheading of St. Paul, at one of three sites where his head is said to have bounced off the ground.

Palazzo del Quirinale. Piazza del Quirinale. Free admission (but a passport or similar ID is required for entrance). Sun 9am–1pm. Metro: Barberini.

Until the end of World War II, this palace was the home of the king of Italy, and before that it was the residence of the pope. Despite its Renaissance origins (nearly every important architect in Italy worked on some aspect of its sprawling premises), it's rich in associations with ancient emperors and deities. The colossal statues of the dioscuri Castor and Pollux, which now form part of the fountain in the piazza, were found in the nearby great baths of Constantine, and in 1793 Pius VI had the ancient Egyptian obelisk moved here from the Mausoleum of Augustus. The sweeping view of Rome from the piazza, which crowns the highest of the seven ancient hills of Rome, is itself worth the trip.

AROUND VIA VENETO & PIAZZA BARBERINI

Piazza Barberini lies at the foot of several Roman streets, among them Via Barberini, Via Sistina, and Via Vittorio Veneto. It would be a far more pleasant spot were it not for the heavy traffic swarming around its principal feature, Bernini's **Fountain of the Triton (Fontana del Tritone).** For more than 3 centuries, the strange figure sitting in a vast open clam has been blowing water from his triton. Off to one side of the piazza is the aristocratic side facade of the **Palazzo Barberini,** named for one of Rome's powerful families; inside is the **Galleria Nazionale d'Arte Antica** (below). The Renaissance Barberini reached their peak when a son was elected pope as Urban VIII; he encouraged Bernini and gave him great patronage.

As you go up Via Vittorio Veneto, look for the small fountain on the right corner of Piazza Barberini—it's another Bernini, the small **Fountain of the Bees (Fontana delle Api).** At first they look more like flies, but they're the bees of the Barberini, the crest of that powerful family complete with the crossed keys of St. Peter above them (the keys were always added to a family crest when a son was elected pope).

National Gallery of Antique Art (Galleria Nazionale d'Arte Antica). Via Quattro Fontane 13. ☎ 06/481-4430. Admission 8,000L ($4.65) adults; children 17 and under/ seniors 60 and over free. Mon–Fri 10am–2pm, Sat 9am–7pm, Sun and holidays 9am–1pm. Metro: Barberini.

The **Palazzo Barberini,** right off Piazza Barberini, is one of the most magnificent baroque palaces in Rome. It was begun by Carlo Maderno in 1627 and completed in 1633 by Bernini, whose lavishly decorated rococo apartments, the Gallery of Decorative Art, are on view.

The bedroom of Princess Cornelia Costanza Barberini and Prince Giulio Cesare Colonna di Sciarra stands just as it was on their wedding night, and many household objects are displayed in the decorative art gallery. In the chambers, boasting frescoes and hand-painted silk linings, you can see porcelain from Japan and Bavaria, canopied beds, and a wooden baby carriage.

On the first floor is a splendid array of paintings from the 13th to the 16th century, most notably *Mother and Child* by Simone Martini and works by Filippo Lippi, Andrea Solario, and Francesco Francia. Il Sodoma has some brilliant pictures here, like *The Rape of the Sabines* and *The Marriage of St. Catherine.* One of the best known paintings is Raphael's beloved *La Fornarina,* the baker's daughter who was his mistress and who posed for his Madonna portraits. Titian is represented by his *Venus and Adonis.* Also here are Tintorettos and El Grecos. Many visitors come just to see the magnificent Caravaggios, including *Narcissus.*

Monumental Cemetery of the Capuchin Brothers (Cimitero Monumentale dei Padri Cappuccini). Beside the Church of the Immacolate Conception, Via Vittorio Veneto 27. ☎ 06/487-1185. Donation required. Fri–Wed 9am–noon and 3–6pm. Metro: Barberini.

One of the most horrifying sights in all Christendom, this is a series of chapels with hundreds of skulls and crossbones woven into mosaic "works of art." To make this allegorical dance of death, the bones of more than 4,000 Capuchin brothers were used. Some of the skeletons are intact, draped with Franciscan habits. The creator of this chamber of horrors? The tradition of the friars is that it was the work of a French Capuchin. Their literature suggests that you should visit the cemetery keeping in mind the historical moment of its origins, when Christians had a rich and creative cult for their dead and great spiritual masters meditated and preached with a skull in hand. Those who have lived through the days of crematoriums and other such massacres may view the graveyard differently, but to many who pause to think, this sight has a message. It's not for the squeamish, however. The entrance is halfway up the first staircase on the right of the church.

NEAR PIAZZA DEL POPOLO

✪ **Piazza del Popolo** is haunted with memories. According to legend, the ashes of Nero were enshrined here, until 11th-century residents began complaining to the pope about his imperial ghost. The **Egyptian obelisk** dates from the 13th century B.C., removed from Heliopolis to Rome during Augustus's reign (it stood at the Circus Maximus). The piazza was designed in the early 19th century by Valadier, Napoléon's architect. The lovely **Santa Maria del Popolo** (with two Caravaggios) is at its northern curve, and opposite are almost-twin baroque churches, overseeing the never-ending traffic. Note that at press time the piazza was a mess of scaffolding at it receives a sprucing up—hopefully the job will be done by the time you get to Rome.

Altar of Peace (Ara Pacis). Via di Ripetta. ☎ **06/671-02-071.** Admission 10,000L ($6). Tues–Sat 9am–7pm, Sun 9am–6:45pm. Bus: 81.

In an airy glass-and-concrete building beside the eastern banks of the Tiber at Ponte Cavour rests a reconstructed treasure from the reign of Augustus. It was built by the Senate as a tribute to that emperor and the peace he had brought to the Roman world. You can see portraits of the imperial family—Augustus, Livia (his second wife), Tiberius (Livia's son from her first marriage and Augustus's successor), even Julia (Augustus's unfortunate daughter, who divorced her first husband to marry Tiberius and then was exiled by her father for her sexual excesses)—on the marble walls. The altar was reconstructed from literally hundreds of fragments scattered in museums for centuries. A major portion came from the foundations of a Renaissance palace on the Corso. The reconstruction—quite an archaeological adventure story in itself—took place during the 1930s.

Augustus's Mausoleum (Mausoleo Augusteo). Via di Ripetta and Piazza Augusteo Imperatore. Bus: 81, 115, or 590. Metro: Spagna.

This seemingly indestructible pile of bricks has been here for 2,000 years and will probably remain for another 2,000. Like the larger tomb of Hadrian across the river, this was once a circular marble-covered affair with tall cypresses, symmetrical groupings of Egyptian obelisks, and some of Europe's most spectacular ornamentation. Many of the 1st-century emperors had their ashes deposited in golden urns inside, and it was probably because of this crowding that Hadrian decided to construct an entirely new tomb (the Castel Sant'Angelo) for himself in another part of Rome. The imperial remains stayed intact here until the 5th century, when invading barbarians smashed the bronze gates and stole the golden urns, emptying the ashes on the ground outside. After periods when it functioned as a Renaissance fortress, a bullfighting ring, and a private garden, the tomb was restored in the 1930s by Mussolini, who might have envisioned it as a burial place for himself. You can't enter, but you can walk along the four streets encircling it.

5 In the Villa Borghese

The **Villa Borghese,** in the heart of Rome, is 3½ miles in circumference. One of Europe's most elegant parks, it was created by Cardinal Scipione Borghese in the 1600s. Umberto I, king of Italy, acquired it in 1902 and presented it to the city of Rome. With lovely landscaped vistas, the greenbelt is crisscrossed by roads, but you can escape from the traffic and seek a shaded area—usually pine or oak—to enjoy a picnic or simply relax. On a sunny weekend afternoon, it's a pleasure to stroll here and see Romans at play, relaxing or in-line skating. There are a few casual cafes and some food vendors throughout; you can also rent bikes here. In the northeast of the park is a small zoo; the park is also home to a few outstanding museums.

✪ **Galleria Borghese.** Piazza Scipione Borghese, off Via Pinciano, in the Villa Borghese. ☎ 06/854-8577 for reservations, 06/841-7645 for information. Admission 10,000L ($6). Tues–Sun 9am–7pm; July 10–Sept 14 also Tues–Sun 8:30–11:30pm.

This legendary art gallery shut its doors in 1984 and appeared virtually to have closed forever. However, in early 1997, after a complete restoration, it returned in all its fabulous glory. The bad news is that it's hard to get in because of limited access (see below). The Italian state purchased the museum in 1902, but, as it turned out, it was resting on an unstable honeycomb of subterranean grottos and watercourses.

A whole new generation has come into adulthood in Rome without sampling this treasure trove, which includes such masterpieces as Bernini's *Apollo and Daphne,* Titian's *Sacred and Profane Love,* and Raphael's *Deposition,* even Caravaggio's *Jerome.* The collection began with the gallery's founder, Scipione Borghese, who by the time of his death in 1633 had accumulated some of the greatest art of all time, even managing to acquire Bernini's early sculptures. Some paintings were spirited out of Vatican museums and even confiscated when their rightful owners were hauled off to prison until they became "reasonable" about turning over their art. The great collection suffered at the hands of Napoléon's notorious sister Pauline, who married Prince Camillo Borghese in 1807 and sold most of the ancient collection (many works are now in the Louvre in Paris). One of the most popular pieces of sculpture in today's gallery, ironically, is Canova's life-size sculpture of Pauline in the pose of *Venus Victorious.* (When Pauline was asked if she felt uncomfortable posing in the nude, she replied, "Why should I? The studio was heated.")

Note: No more than 300 visitors are allowed on the ground floor at one time, no more than 90 on the upper floor. You must make a reservation ahead of time. You can call for a reservation, but the number invariably seems to be busy. For those who do get through and are able to make an appointment, the chance to see works like Bernini's *David* and *Rape of Persephone* are worth the effort. If you'll be in Rome for a few days, try stopping by on your first day in person to reserve tickets for a later day.

✪ **National Etruscan Museum (Museo Nazionale di Villa Giulia).** Piazzale di Villa Giulia 9, in the Villa Borghese. ☎ 06/322-6571. Admission 8,000L ($4.65) adults; children 18 and under/seniors 60 and over free. Tues–Sat 9am–7pm, Sun 9am–2pm. Metro: Flaminio, then a long stroll through the park.

This 16th-century papal palace shelters a priceless collection of art and artifacts from the mysterious Etruscans, who predated the Romans. Known for their sophisticated art and design, they left a legacy of sarcophagi, bronze sculptures, terra-cotta vases, and jewelry, among other items. If you have time for only the masterpieces, head for

Beneath It All: Touring Roma Sotteranea

Talk about the "underground" and a growing legion of Romans will excitedly take up the story, offering tidbits about where to go, who to talk to, what's been seen, and what's allegedly awaiting discovery around the next bend in the sewer. The sewer? That's right. **Roma Sotteranea (Subterranean Rome)** is neither subway nor trendy arts movement but the vast historic ruins of a city that has been occupied for nearly 3,000 years, the first 2 millenniums of which are now largely buried by natural sediment and man-made landfills. In fact, archaeologists estimate that these processes have left the streets of ancient Rome as much as 20 yards beneath the surface.

A little to deep for you? Consider this: Each year, an inch of dust in the form of pollen, leaves, pollution, sand, and silt from disintegrating ruins settles over Rome. That silt has really taken a toll in its own right. Archaeologists estimate that the ruins of a one-story Roman house will produce debris 6 feet deep over its entire floor plan. When you multiply that by more than 40,000 apartment buildings, 1,800 palaces, and numerous giant public buildings, a real picture of the burial of the ancient city presents itself. You should also take note of the centuries-old Roman tradition of burying old buildings in landfills, which can raise the level of the earth up to several yards all at once. In fact, past builders have often filled up massive stone ruins with dirt or dug down through previous landfills to the columns and vaults of underlying structures, then laid a foundation for a new layer of Roman architecture.

As a result, many buildings on the streets today actually provide direct access to Rome's inner world. Doorways lead down to hidden crypts and shrines—the existence of which are closely guarded secrets. Nondescript locked doors in churches and other public buildings often open on whole blocks of the ancient city, streets still intact. For example, take **San Clemente,** the 12th-century basilica east of the Colosseum, where a staircase in the sacristy leads down to the original 4th-century church. Not only that, but a staircase near the apse goes down to an earlier Roman apartment building and temple, which in turn leads down to a giant public building dating back to the Great Fire (A.D. 64). Another interesting doorway to the past is in the south exterior wall of **St. Peter's,** leading down to an intact necropolis. That crumbling brick entry in the gardens on the

room 7, with a remarkable 6th-century B.C. *Apollo from Veio* (clothed, for a change). The other two widely acclaimed statues in this gallery are *Dea con Bambino* (*Goddess with a Baby*) and a greatly mutilated but still powerful *Hercules* with a stag. In room 8, you'll see the lions' sarcophagus from the mid-6th century B.C., which was excavated at Cerveteri, north of Rome.

Finally, one of the world's most important Etruscan art treasures is the bride and bridegroom coffin from the 6th century B.C., also dug out of the tombs of Cerveteri (in room 9). Near the end of your tour, another masterpiece of Etruscan art awaits you in room 33: the Cista Ficoroni, a bronze urn with paw feet, mounted by three figures, dating from the 4th century B.C.

National Gallery of Modern Art (Galleria Nazionale d'Arte Moderna). Viale delle Belle Arti 131, in the Villa Borghese. ☎ **06/322-981.** Admission 8,000L ($4.65) adults; children 17 and under/seniors 60 and over free. Tues–Sun 9am–10pm. Bus: 56 or 910.

This gallery of modern art is a short walk from the Etruscan Museum. With its neoclassic and Romantic paintings and sculpture, it makes a dramatic change from the

east side of Esquiline Hill carries you into the vast **Domus Aurea (Golden House),** Nero's residence, built on the ruins left by the Great Fire (see the entry for the Colosseum).

Don't expect a coherent road map of this subterranean world, as the nuggets you'll find will be interspersed with views of buildings on the surface. Likewise, there's no coherent labyrinth meandering from one point to another beneath the city streets. A guided tour can be useful, especially those focusing on Roman excavations and anything to do with church crypts. Several tour companies now offer selected subterranean views. One of the most appealing is **Genti e Paesi** (☎ **06/8350-1755**), which offers a 90-minute tour of many crypts beneath San Clemente for 12,000L ($7). Other tours last 90 to 120 minutes and cost 12,000L to 18,000L ($7 to $11). One giving a vivid sense of the layers of artifact-laden debris beneath Rome involves tours through the Castello Sant'Angelo. Two competitors of Genti e Paesi, with roughly equivalent tours, are **Itinera** (☎ **06/275-7323**) and **LUPA** (☎ **06/7135-6027**), both run by trained archaeologists. **Città Nascosta** (☎ **06/321-6059**) offers offbeat tours to less-visited churches and monuments and advertises the week's schedule via a recorded phone announcement that changes every week.

For those who want still more access to this world, the Italian monthly magazine *Forma Urbis* features the photos of Carlo Pavia, who (armed with lights, camera, hip boots, and oxygen mask) slogs through ancient sewage and hordes of jumping spiders, giant rats, and albino insects to record part of the ancient city that has never been seen before. Pavia's most bizarre discovery was a series of plants from North Africa and the Arab world growing in rooms beneath the Colosseum. The theory is they grew from seeds that fell from the coats of exotic animals sent into the arena to battle gladiators.

It's probably true that much of the underground will remain inaccessible to the general public. However, influential citizens such as Emanuele Gattis, a retired government archaeologist who oversaw more than 30 years' worth of construction projects in Rome, are urging government leaders to seize their opportunity and direct part of the billions of lire being spent to beautify Rome for Papal Jubilee 2000 into opening up more of the city's buried past.

---

glories of the Renaissance and ancient Rome. Its 75 rooms also house the largest collection in Italy of 19th- and 20th-century works by Balla, Boccioni, De Chirico, Morandi, Manzù, Marini, Burri, Capogrossi, and Fontana. Look for Modigliani's *La Signora dal Collaretto* and large *Nudo.* There are also many works of Italian optical and pop art and a good representation of foreign artists, including Degas, Cézanne, Monet, and van Gogh. Surrealism and expressionism are well represented by Klee, Ernst, Braque, Miró, Kandinsky, Mondrian, and Pollock. You'll also find sculpture by Rodin. Several other important sculptures, including one by Canova, are on display in the museum's gardens. You can see the collection of graphics, the storage rooms, and the Department of Restoration by appointment Tuesday to Friday.

6 The Appian Way & the Catacombs

Of all the roads that led to Rome, **Via Appia Antica**—built in 312 B.C.—was the most famous. It eventually stretched all the way from Rome to the seaport of Brindisi, through which trade with the colonies in Greece and the East was funneled. According to Christian tradition, it was along the Appian Way that an escaping Peter encountered the vision of Christ, causing him to go back into the city to face subsequent martyrdom.

Of the monuments on the Appian Way, the most impressive is the **Tomb of Cecilia Metella,** within walking distance of the catacombs. The cylindrical tomb honors the wife of one of Julius Caesar's military commanders from the Republican era. Why such an elaborate tomb for such an unimportant person in history? Cecilia Metella happened to be singled out for enduring fame because her tomb has remained and the others have decayed.

Along the Appian Way, patrician Romans built great monuments above the ground and Christians met in the catacombs beneath. You can visit the remains of both. In some dank, dark grottoes (never stray too far from your party or one of the exposed lightbulbs), you can still discover the remains of early Christian art. Of those open to the public, the catacombs of St. Callixtus and St. Sebastian are the most important.

Catacombs of St. Callixtus (Catacombe di San Callisto). Via Appia Antica 110. ☎ **06/ 513-6725.** Admission 8,000L ($4.65) adults, 4,000L ($2.30) children 6–15; children 5 and under free. Thurs–Tues 8:30am–noon and 2:30–5pm (to 5:30pm in summer). Bus: 218 from Piazza San Giovanni in Laterano to Fosse Ardeatine; ask driver to let you off at Catacombe di San Callisto.

"The most venerable and most renowned of Rome," said Pope John XXIII of these funerary tunnels. The founder of Christian archaeology, Giovanni Battista de Rossi (1822–94), called them "catacombs par excellence." They're the first cemetery of the Christian community of Rome, burial place of 16 popes in the 3rd century. They bear the name of St. Callixtus, the deacon Pope St. Zephyrinus put in charge of them and who was later elected pope (217–22) in his own right. The complex is a network of galleries stretching for nearly 12 miles, structured in five levels and reaching a depth of about 65 feet. There are many sepulchral chambers and almost half a million tombs. Paintings, sculptures, and epigraphs (with such symbols as the fish, anchor, and dove) provide invaluable material for the study of the life and customs of the ancient Christians and the story of their persecutions.

Entering the catacombs, you see at once the most important crypt, that of the nine popes. Some of the original marble tablets of their tombs are still preserved. The next crypt is that of St. Cecilia, the patron of sacred music. This early Christian martyr received three ax strokes on her neck, the maximum allowed by Roman law, which failed to kill her outright. Farther on, you'll find the famous Cubicula of the Sacraments with its 3rd-century frescoes.

Catacombs of St. Sebastian (Catacombe di San Sebastiano). Via Appia Antica 136. ☎ **06/785-0350.** Admission 8,000L ($4.65) adults, 4,000L ($2.30) children 6–15; children 5 and under free. Fri–Wed 8:30am–noon and 2:30–5:30pm (to 5pm in winter). Bus: 218 from San Giovanni or 660 from the Colli Albani Metro stop.

Today the tomb of St. Sebastian is in the basilica, but his original tomb was in the catacombs under it. From the reign of Valerian to the reign of Constantine, the bodies of St. Peter and St. Paul were hidden in the catacombs, which were dug from tufo, a soft volcanic rock. The big church was built in the 4th century. The tunnels here, if stretched out, would reach a length of 7 miles. In the tunnels and mausoleums are mosaics and graffiti, along with many other pagan and Christian objects from centuries even before the time of Constantine.

7 More Attractions

AROUND STAZIONE TERMINI

Basilica di Santa Maria Maggiore (St. Mary Major). Piazza di Santa Maria Maggiore. ☎ 06/488-1094. Free admission. Daily 7am–7pm. Metro: Termini.

This great church, one of Rome's four major basilicas, was built by Pope Liberius in A.D. 358 and rebuilt by Pope Sixtus III from 432 to 440. Its 14th-century campanile is the loftiest in the city. Much doctored in the 18th century, the church's facade is not an accurate reflection of the treasures inside. Restoration of the 1,600-year-old church has begun and is scheduled for completion in 2000. The basilica is especially noted for the 5th-century Roman mosaics in its nave, as well as for its coffered ceiling, said to have been gilded with gold brought from the New World. In the 16th century, Domenico Fontana built a now-restored "Sistine Chapel." In the following century, Flaminio Ponzo designed the Pauline (Borghese) Chapel in the baroque style. The church also contains the tomb of Bernini, Italy's most important baroque sculptor and architect. Ironically, the man who changed the face of Rome with his elaborate fountains is buried in a tomb so simple it takes a sleuth to track it down (to the right near the altar).

✪ National Roman Museum (Museo Nazionale Romano). Via Enrico de Nicola 79. ☎ 06/488-0856. Admission (includes entrance to Palazzo Massimo alle Terme and Palazzo Altemps) 12,000L ($7). Tues–Sat 9am–2pm, Sun and holidays 9am–1pm. Metro: Repubblica.

Near Piazza dei Cinquecento, which fronts the rail station, this museum occupies part of the 3rd-century A.D. Baths of Diocletian and part of a convent that may have been designed by Michelangelo. It houses one of Europe's finest collections of Greek and Roman sculpture and early Christian sarcophagi.

The Ludovisi Collection is the highlight, particularly the statue of the Gaul slaying himself after he has done in his wife (a brilliant copy of a Greek original from the 3rd century B.C.). Another prize is a one-armed Greek *Apollo.* A galaxy of other treasures includes *The Discus Thrower of Castel Porziano* (an exquisite copy), *Aphrodite of Cirene* (a Greek original), and the so-called *Hellenistic Ruler,* a Greek original of an athlete with a lance. A masterpiece of Greek sculpture, *The Birth of Venus* is in the Ludovisi Throne room. *The Sleeping Hermaphrodite (Ermafrodito Dormiente)* is an original Hellenistic statue. You can stroll through the cloister, filled with statuary and fragments of antiquity, including a fantastic mosaic.

For the same ticket, you can visit an extension of the collection at the **Palazzo Massimo alle Terme,** Largo di Villa Peretti (☎ 06/489-03-500). This branch contains ancient treasures unearthed in excavations in and around Rome and keeps the same hours as the parent museum above. The third and final branch of the museums is at the **Palazzo Altemps,** which finally opened in 1997 (above). This is also included in the ticket.

Chiesa di Santa Maria degli Angeli. Piazza della Repubblica 12. ☎ 06/488-0812. Free admission. Daily 7:30am–12:30pm and 4–6:30pm. Metro: Repubblica.

On this site, adjoining the National Roman Museum, once stood the "tepidarium" of the Baths of Diocletian. But in the 16th century Michelangelo (nearing the end of his life) converted the grand hall into one of Rome's most splendid churches. (Though surely the artist wasn't responsible for "gilding the lily"—putting trompe-l'oeil columns in the midst of the genuine pillars.) The church is filled with tombs and paintings, but its crowning treasure is the statue of *St. Bruno* by the great French sculptor Jean-Antoine Houdon. It's larger than life and about as real.

IN THE TESTACCIO AREA & SOUTH

Protestant Cemetery. Via Caio Cestio 6. ☎ **06/574-1900.** Free admission (but a 1,000L/60¢ offering is customary). Apr–Sept Tues–Sun 9am–6pm (Oct–Mar to 5pm). Metro: Piramide. Bus: 23 or 27.

Near Porta San Paola, in the midst of cypress trees, lies the old cemetery where John Keats is buried. In a grave nearby, Joseph Severn, his "deathbed" companion, was interred beside him 6 decades later. Dejected and feeling his reputation as a poet diminished by the rising vehemence of his critics, Keats asked that the following epitaph be written on his tombstone: "Here lies one whose name was writ in water." A great romantic poet Keats certainly was, but a prophet, thankfully not. Percy Bysshe Shelley, author of *Prometheus Unbound,* drowned off the Italian Riviera in 1822, before his 30th birthday, and his ashes rest beside those of Edward John Trelawny, fellow romantic and man of the sea.

Pyramid of Caius Cestius. Piazzale Ostiense. Metro: Piramide.

From the 1st century B.C., the Pyramid of Caius Cestius, about 120 feet high, looks as if it belongs to the Egyptian landscape. It was constructed during the "Cleopatra craze" in architecture that swept across Rome. You can't enter the pyramid, but it's a great photo op. And who was Caius Cestius? He was a rich magistrate in imperial Rome whose tomb is more impressive than his achievements. You can visit at any time.

St. Paul Outside the Walls (Basilica di San Paolo Fuori le Mura). Via Ostiense 184. ☎ **06/541-0341.** Free admission. Basilica, daily 7am–6:30pm; cloisters, daily 9am–1pm and 3–6pm. Metro: San Paolo Basilica.

The Basilica of St. Paul, whose origins go back to the time of Constantine, is Rome's fourth great patriarchal church; it's believed to have been erected over the tomb of St. Paul, was burned in 1823, and was subsequently rebuilt. From the inside, its windows may appear to be stained glass, but they're actually translucent alabaster. With its forest of single-file columns and mosaic medallions (portraits of the various popes), this is one of the most streamlined and elegantly decorated churches in Rome. Its most important treasure is a 12th-century candelabra by Vassalletto, who's also responsible for the remarkable cloisters, containing twisted pairs of columns enclosing a rose garden. The Benedictine monks and students sell a fine collection of souvenirs, rosaries, and bottles of Benedictine every day except Sunday and religious holidays.

IN TRASTEVERE

From many vantage points in the Eternal City, the views are panoramic, but one of the best spots for a memorable vista is the ✪ **Gianicolo (Janiculum Hill),** across the Tiber, not one of the "Seven Hills" but certainly one of the most visited (and a stop on many bus tours). The view is at its best at sundown or at dawn, when the skies are often fringed with mauve. The Janiculum was the site of a battle between Giuseppe Garibaldi and the forces of Pope Pius IX in 1870—an event commemorated with statuary. Take bus no. 41 from Ponte Sant'Angelo.

Chiesa di Santa Cecilia in Trastevere. Piazza Santa Cecilia. ☎ **06/589-9289.** Church free; Cavallini frescoes free (but a donation is requested); excavations 2,000L ($1.15). Main church daily 10am–noon and 4–6pm; frescoes Tues and Thurs 10–11:30am. Bus: 44, 75, 170, or 181.

A cloistered and still-functioning convent with a fine garden, Santa Cecilia contains a difficult-to-visit fresco by Cavallini in its inner sanctums and a late 13th-century baldacchino by Arnalfo di Cambio over the altar. The church is built on the reputed site of Cecilia's long-ago palace, and for a small fee you can descend under the church to inspect the ruins of some Roman houses as well as peer through a gate at the stuccoed grotto beneath the altar.

Chiesa di Santa Maria in Trastevere. Piazza Santa Maria in Trastevere. ☎ **06/581-4802.** Free admission. Daily 7am–7pm. Bus: 44, 75, 170, or 181.

This Romanesque church at the colorful center of Trastevere was built around A.D. 350 and is one of the oldest in Rome. The body was added around 1100, and the portico in the early 1700s. The restored mosaics on the apse date from around 1140, and below them are the 1293 mosaic scenes depicting the life of Mary done by Pietro Cavallini. The faded mosaics on the facade are 12th or 13th century, and the octagonal fountain in the piazza is an ancient Roman original restored and added to in the 17th century by Carlo Fontana.

PONTE SANT'ANGELO

The trio of arches in the river's center has been basically unchanged since the **Ponte Sant'Angelo** was built around A.D. 135; the arches abutting the river's embankments were added late in the 19th century as part of a flood-control program. On December 19, 1450, so many pilgrims gathered on this bridge (which at the time was lined with wooden buildings) that about 200 of them were crushed to death. Since the 1960s, the bridge has been reserved for pedestrians who can stroll across and admire the statues designed by Bernini. On the southern end is the site of one of the most famous executions of the Renaissance, **Piazza Sant'Angelo.** In 1599, Beatrice Cenci and several members of her family were beheaded on orders of Pope Clement VIII. Their crime? Plotting the successful death of their rich and brutal father. Their tale later inspired a tragedy by Shelley and a novel by a 19th-century Italian politician named Francesco Guerrazzi.

8 Organized Tours

Because of the sheer number of sights to see, some first-time visitors like to start out with an organized tour. While few things can really be covered in any depth on these overview tours, they're sometimes useful for getting your bearings.

One of the leading operators is **American Express,** Piazza di Spagna 38 (☎ 06/67-641), open Monday to Friday 9am to 5:30pm and Saturday 9am to 12:30pm. Its tours, all in English, are the most closely geared to Americans. One of the most popular is a 4-hour orientation tour of Rome and the Vatican, departing most days at 9:30am for 70,000L ($41) per person. Another 4-hour tour, focusing on ancient Rome (including visits to the Colosseum, the Roman Forum, the ruins of the Imperial Palace, and San Pietro in Vincoli), goes for the same price. Of the many excursions offered outside the city limits, the most popular is a 5-hour bus tour to Tivoli, where you'll see the Villa d'Este and its spectacular gardens and the ruins of the Villa Adriana for 70,000L ($41) per person.

If your time in Italy is rigidly limited, you might opt for 1-day excursions to points farther afield on tours marketed (but not conducted) by American Express. Though rushed and far too short to expose the many-layered majesty of these destinations, a series of 1-day tours is offered to Pompeii, Naples, and Sorrento for 160,000L ($93) per person; to Florence for 190,000L ($110); and to Capri for 210,000L ($122). Lunch is included, but to participate you'll need a lot of stamina, as each tour departs around 7am and returns sometime after 9 or 10pm to your hotel.

The agency **Enjoy Rome,** Via Varese 39 (☎ 06/445-18-43; fax 06/445-07-34; E-mail fulang@flashnet.it; www.enjoyrome.com), makes the 1-day sprint from Rome to Pompeii as inexpensive and painless as possible with an 8:30am-to-5:30pm round-trip daily tour by air-conditioned minivan (fitting eight passengers), costing 60,000L ($35). The trip is 3 hours one-way, and an English-speaking driver and loads of maps and materials help you bone up on the ancient wonders that await. You're on your own once you reach the archaeological site and there's no imposed restaurant lunch: That's what keeps their prices the lowest around. During the high season, be ready for crowds and temperatures at a consistent high.

Another option is **Scala Reale,** Via Varese 52 (☎ **888/467-1986** in the United States, or 06/4470-0898), a cultural association founded by American architect Tom Rankin. He offers small-group tours and excursions focusing on the architectural and artistic significance of Rome. Tours include visits to monuments, museums, and piazzas as well as to neighborhood trattorie. In addition, custom-designed tours are available. Tours begin at 60,000L ($35). Children 12 and under are admitted free to walking tours. Tour discounts are available for a group of four.

9 Shopping

Rome offers temptations of every kind, but here we focus on the urge to shop that sometimes overcomes even the most stalwart of visitors. You might find hidden oases of charm and value in unpublicized streets and districts, but what follows is a listing and description of certain streets known throughout Italy for their shops. The monthly rent on these famous streets is very high, and those costs are passed on to you. Nonetheless, a stroll down some of these streets presents a cross section of the most desirable wares in Italy.

Cramped urban spaces and a well-defined sense of taste have encouraged most Italian stores to elevate the boutique philosophy to its highest levels. The theory is that if you like what you see in a shop window, you'll find it duplicated, in spirit and style, inside. Lack of space and definition of a merchandising program usually restrict a store's merchandise to one particular style, degree of formality, or mood.

Shopping hours are generally Monday 3:30 to 7:30pm and Tuesday to Saturday 9:30 or 10am to 1pm and 3:30 to 7 or 7:30pm. Some shops are open on Monday mornings, however, and some don't close for the afternoon break.

THE TOP SHOPPING STREETS

VIA BORGOGNONA   This street begins near Piazza di Spagna, and both the rents and the merchandise are chic and very expensive. Like its neighbor, Via Condotti, Via Borgognona is a mecca for wealthy well-dressed women from around the world. Its storefronts have retained their baroque or neoclassical facades.

VIA COLA DI RIENZO   Bordering the Vatican, this long, straight street runs from the Tiber to Piazza Risorgimento. Since the street is wide and clogged with traffic, it's best to walk down one side and then up the other. Via Cola di Rienzi is known for stores selling a wide variety of merchandise at reasonable prices—from jewelry to fashionable clothes and shoes.

VIA CONDOTTI   Easy to find because it begins at the base of the Spanish Steps, this is Rome's poshest and most visible upper-bracket shopping street. Even the recent incursion of some less elegant stores hasn't diminished the allure of Via Condotti as a consumer's playground for the rich and super rich. For us mere mortals, it's a great place for window-shopping and people-watching.

VIA DEL CORSO   Not attempting the stratospheric image or prices of Via Condotti or Via Borgognona, Via del Corso boasts styles aimed at younger consumers. There are, however, some gems scattered amid the shops selling jeans and sporting

A Shopping Caveat

We won't pretend that Rome is Italy's finest shopping center (Florence, Milan, and Venice are) or that its shops are unusually inexpensive (most aren't). But even on the most elegant of Rome's thoroughfares, there are values mixed in with the costly boutiques.

equipment. The most interesting stores are nearest the fashionable cafes of Piazza del Popolo (however, at press time Piazza del Popolo was a mess of scaffolding).

VIA FRANCESCO CRISPI   Most shoppers reach this street by following Via Sistina (below) one long block from the top of the Spanish Steps. Near the intersection of these streets are several shops well suited for unusual and less expensive gifts.

VIA FRATTINA   Running parallel to Via Condotti, it begins, like its more famous sibling, at Piazza di Spagna. Part of its length is closed to traffic. Here the concentration of shops is denser, though some aficionados claim that its image is slightly less chic and prices are slightly lower than at its counterparts on Via Condotti. It's usually thronged with shoppers who appreciate the lack of motor traffic.

VIA NAZIONALE   The layout recalls 19th-century grandeur, but the traffic is horrendous; crossing Via Nazionale requires a good sense of timing and a strong understanding of Italian driving patterns. It begins at Piazza della Repubblica and runs down almost to the 19th-century monuments of Piazza Venezia. You'll find an abundance of leather stores (more reasonable in price than those in many other parts of Rome) and a welcome handful of stylish boutiques.

VIA SISTINA   Beginning at the top of the Spanish Steps, Via Sistina runs to Piazza Barberini. The shops are small, stylish, and based on the tastes of their owners. The pedestrian traffic is less dense than on other major streets.

VIA VITTORIO VENETO & VIA BARBERINI   Evocative of *La Dolce Vita* fame, Via Veneto is filled these days with expensive hotels and cafes and an array of relatively expensive stores selling shoes, gloves, and leather goods.

SHOPPING A TO Z

ANTIQUES   Some visitors to Italy consider the trove of antiques for sale the country's greatest treasure. The value of almost any antique has risen to alarming levels as increasingly wealthy Europeans outbid one another frenziedly. You might remember that any antique dealer who risks the high rents of central Rome is acutely aware of the value of almost everything ever made and will probably recognize anything of value long before his or her clients.

Beware of fakes; remember to insure anything you have shipped home; and for larger purchases—anything more than 300,000L ($174) at any one store—keep your paperwork in order to obtain your tax refund (see "Fast Facts: Italy" in chapter 3).

Via dei Coronari, buried in a colorful section of the Campus Martius, is lined with stores offering magnificent vases, urns, chandeliers, chaises, refectory tables, and candelabra. To find the street's entrance, turn left out of the north end of Piazza Navona and pass the excavated ruins of Domitian's Stadium—it will be just ahead. There are more than 40 antiques stores in the next 4 blocks. Bring your pocket calculator and keep in mind that stores are frequently closed between 1 and 4pm.

Italian furniture from the days of Caesar through the 19th century is for sale at **Ad Antiqua Domus,** Via Paola 25–27 (☎ **06/686-1530**). It's as much a museum of Italian furniture design through the ages as it is a shop. A second location is at Via dei Coronari 227 (☎ **06/686-1186**). An antiquer's mecca, **ArtImport,** Via del Babuino

150 (☎ 06/322-13-30), always has something for sale that's intriguing and tasteful—that is, if you can agree on a price. The store's motto is, "In the service of the table," so there's an emphasis on silver, though the objects used to decorate a table are broader than that. The goblets, elegant bowls, candlesticks, and candelabra here are almost without equal in Rome.

BOOKSTORES   Catering to the English-speaking communities of Rome, the **Economy Book and Video Center,** Via Torino 136 (☎ 06/474-6877), sells only English-language books (new and used, paperback and hardcover), greeting cards, and videos. Staffed by British, Australian, and American workers, it's about a block from the Piazza della Repubblica Metro station, and bus lines no. 64, 70, and 170. The **Lion Bookshop,** Via del Greci 33 (☎ 06/3265-4007), is the oldest English-language bookshop in town, specializing in literature, both American and English. It also sells children's books and photographic volumes on both Rome and Italy. A vast choice of English-language videos is for sale or rent. It's closed in August.

The collection of Italian-language books at **Rizzoli,** Largo Chigi 15 (☎ 06/679-6641), is one of the largest in Rome, but if your native language is French, English, German, or Spanish, the interminable shelves of this large store have a section to amuse, enlighten, and entertain you.

The gay bookstore **Libreria Babele,** Via Paola 44 (☎ 06/687-66-28), sells a gay map of Rome. For women, the **Virginia Woolf Center,** Via Lungara 1a in Trastevere (☎ 06/686-42-01), is a main clearinghouse for information.

DEPARTMENT STORES   In Piazza Colonna, **La Rinascente,** Via del Corso 189 (☎ 06/679-7691), is an upscale store offering clothing, hosiery, perfume, cosmetics, housewares, and furniture. It also has its own line of clothing (Ellerre) for men, women, and children. This is the largest of the Italian department-store chains, with another branch at Piazza Cavour. One of Rome's six branches of **Standa** is at Corso Francia 124 (☎ 06/333-8719). They couldn't be called stylish by any stretch of the imagination, but you may find it enlightening to wander (just once) through the racks of department-store staples to see what an average Italian household might accumulate. Other branches are at Corso Trieste 200, Via Cola di Rienzo 173, Viale Regina Margherita 117, and Viale Trastevere 62–64.

A DISCOUNTER   Certain stores that can't move their merchandise at any price often consign these goods to discounters. In Italy, the original labels are usually still inside the garments, and you'll find some chic ones strewn in with other garments. Why wouldn't they sell at higher prices in more glamorous shops? Some are the wrong size, some have gone out of fashion, and some are a stylistic mistake the designer wishes had never been produced.

Discount System, Via del Viminale 35 (☎ 06/482-3917), sells menswear and womenswear by many of the big names (Armani, Valentino, Nino Cerruti, Fendi, and Krizia). Even if an item isn't from a famous designer, it often came from a factory that produces some of the best quality of Italian fashion. However, don't give up hope: If you find something you like, know that it will be priced at around 50% of its original price tag, and it just might be a cut-rate gem well worth your effort. To get here, take the Metro to Repubblica and walk.

FASHION   The exclusive **Angelo,** Via Bissolati 34 (☎ 06/474-1796), is a custom tailor for discerning men and has been featured in publications like *Esquire* and *Gentleman's Quarterly.* Angelo employs the best cutters and craftspeople, and his taste is impeccable. Custom shirts, dinner jackets, and even casualwear can be made on short notice. If you don't have time to wait, he'll ship anywhere. The outlet also sells ready-made items like cardigans, cashmere pullovers, evening shirts, suits, and overcoats.

Battistoni, Via Condotti 61A (☎ 06/678-6241), is known for the world's finest men's shirts. As Marlene Dietrich once noted, "With that said, you don't need to sell the shop anymore." It also hawks a cologne, Marte (Mars), for the "man who likes to conquer." ✪ **Emporio Armani,** Via del Babuino 119 (☎ 06/3600-2197), stocks relatively affordable menswear crafted by the designer who has dressed perhaps more stage and screen stars than any other in Italy. If these prices aren't high enough for you, try the more expensive line a short walk away at **Giorgio Armani,** Via Condotti 77 (☎ 06/699-1460). The merchandise here is sold at sometimes staggering prices that are still often 30% less than what you'd pay in the United States.

Dating to 1870, **Schostal,** Via del Corso (☎ 06/679-1240), is for men who like their garments (everything from underwear to cashmere overcoats) conservative and well crafted. The prices are more reasonable than you might think, and the staff is courteous and attentive. Behind all the chrome mirrors is swank **Valentino,** Via Condotti 13 (☎ 06/678-3656), where you can become the most fashionable man in town—if you can afford to. Valentino's women's haute couture is sold around the corner at Via Bocca di Leone 15 (☎ 06/679-5862).

The prices at **Benetton,** Via Condotti 18 (☎ 06/679-7982), are about the same as those at less glamorous addresses. Famous for woolen sweaters, tennis wear, blazers, and the kind of outfits you'd want to wear on a private yacht, this company has suffered (like every other clothier) from inexpensive Asian copies of its designs. The original, however, is still the greatest. Their men's line is worth a look, and across the street at Via Condotti 19 (☎ 06/679-7982), you'll find its outlet for children's clothes (infants to age 12). At **Gianfranco Ferré,** Via Borgognona 6 (☎ 06/679-7445), you can find the women's line of this famous designer whose clothes have been called "adventurous."

Givenchy, Via Borgognona 21 (☎ 06/678-4058), is the Roman headquarters of one of the great designer names of France. Here you'll find ready-to-wear garments for stylish women with warm Italian weather in mind. It also features tasteful shirts and pullovers for men. **Max Mara,** Via Frattina 28 (☎ 06/679-3638), is one of the best outlets in Rome for womenswear if you like to look chic. The fabrics are appealing and the alterations are free. Rapidly approaching the stratospheric upper levels of Italian fashion is ✪ **Renato Balestra,** Via Sistina 67 (☎ 06/679-5424), whose women's clothing attains standards of lighthearted elegance at its best. This branch carries a complete line of the latest ready-to-wear. The administrative headquarters and center of its couture department are nearby at Via Ludovisi 35 (☎ 06/482-1723), though appointments are recommended there. It's advisable to stop into the Via Sistina branch for an idea of the designer's style before contacting the couture department, if only to save costs.

Baby House, Via Cola di Rienzo 117 (☎ 06/321-4291), offers what might be Italy's most label-conscious collection of children's and young people's clothing. With an inventory of clothes suitable for children and adolescents to age 15, it sells clothing by Valentino, Bussardi, and Biagiotti, whose threads are usually reserved for adult playtime. **The College,** Via Condotti 47 (☎ 06/678-4036), has everything you'll need to make adorable children more adorable. Part of the inventory is reserved for adult men and women, but the majority is intended for the infant and early adolescent. A vast women's line is also featured.

A FLEA MARKET   On Sundays 7am to 1pm, every peddler from Trastevere and the surrounding Castelli Romani sets up a temporary shop at the sprawling **Porta Portese open-air flea market,** near the end of Viale Trastevere (catch bus no. 75 to Porta Portese, then take a short walk to Via Portuense). The vendors are likely to sell merchandise ranging from secondhand paintings of Madonnas and termite-eaten Il Duce wooden medallions, to pseudo-Etruscan hairpins, bushels of rosaries, 1947 TVs, and books printed in 1835. Serious shoppers can often ferret out a good buy. If you've ever been impressed with the bargaining power of the Spaniard, you haven't seen anything till you've viewed an Italian. By 10:30am the market is full of people. As at any street market, beware of pickpockets.

FOOD & FOOD MARKETS   At old-fashioned ✪ **Castroni,** Via Cola di Rienzo 196 (☎ 06/687-4383), you'll find an amazing array of unusual foodstuffs from around the Mediterranean. If you want herbs from Apulia, pepperoncino oil, cheese from the Valle d'Aosta, or that strange brand of balsamic vinegar whose name you can never remember, Castroni will have it. Filled to the rafters with the abundance of agrarian Italy, it also carries foods that are exotic in Italy but commonplace in North America, like taco shells, corn curls, and peanut butter.

Near Santa Maria Maggiore, Rome's largest market takes place Monday to Saturday 7am to noon at **Piazza Vittorio Emanuele.** Most of the vendors at the gigantic market sell fresh fruit, vegetables, and other foodstuff, though some stalls are devoted to cutlery, clothing, and the like. There's probably little to tempt the serious shopper, but the insight into Roman life is invaluable. A market of even greater charm is held Monday to Saturday 6am to noon at **Campo de' Fiori.** This is Rome's most picturesque food market—but it's also the costliest.

GIFTS   **Grispigni,** Via Francesco Crispi 59 (☎ 06/679-0290), has a large assortment of leather-covered boxes, women's purses, compacts, desk sets, and cigarette cases. There's also a constantly changing array of gifts if you're searching for some "small item" to take back. **Anatriello Argenteria Antica E Moderna Roma,** Via Frattina 123 (☎ 06/678-9601), is known for stocking new and antique silver, some of it among the most unusual in Italy. All the new items are made by Italian silversmiths, in designs ranging from the whimsical to the dignified. Also displayed are antique pieces of silver from England, Germany, and Switzerland.

JEWELRY   Rome's most prestigious jeweler for more than a century, ✪ **Bulgari,** Via Condotti 10 (☎ 06/679-3876), boasts a shop window that's a visual attraction in its own right. Bulgari designs combine classical Greek aesthetics with Italian taste, changing in style with the years yet clinging to tradition. Prices range from "affordable" to "the sky's the limit." At **E. Fiore,** Via Ludovisi 31 (☎ 06/481-9296), you can choose a jewel and have it set to your specifications. Or you can make your selection from a rich assortment of charms, bracelets, necklaces, rings, brooches, corals, pearls, and cameos. Also featured are elegant watches, silverware, and goldware. Fiore does expert repair work on jewelry and watches.

One of the city's best gold- and silversmiths, **Frederico Buccellati,** Via Condotti 31 (☎ 06/679-0329), specializes in neo-Renaissance creations. The designs of the handmade jewelry and holloware recall those of Renaissance goldmaster Benvenuto Cellini. **Siragusa,** Via delle Carrozze 64 (☎ 06/679-7085), is more like a museum than a shop, specializing in unusual jewelry based on ancient carved stones or archaeological pieces. Handmade chains, for example, often hold coins and beads from the 3rd and 4th centuries B.C. discovered in Asia Minor.

LEATHER   Italian leather is among the very best in the world; it can attain buttersoft textures more pliable than cloth. You'll find hundreds of leather stores in Rome, many of them excellent.

At **Alfieri,** Via del Corso 2 (☎ 06/361-1976), you'll find virtually any garment you can think of (except for the blatantly erotic) fashioned in leather. Opened in the 1960s, with a somewhat more funky and counterculture slant than Casagrande or Campanile, it prides itself on leather jackets, boots, bags, belts, shirts, hats, pants for men and women, short shorts that might remind you of Austrian lederhosen, and skirts that come in at least 10 (sometimes neon-inspired) colors. Though everything is made in Italy, be alert that the virtue of this place is the reasonable prices rather than the ultra-high quality. You'll find whimsy, an amazingly wide selection, and affordable prices, but be sure to check the stitching and operability of zippers, or whatever, before you invest.

Despite the postmodern sleekness of its premises, **Campanile,** Via Condotti 58 (☎ 06/678-3041), bears a pedigree going back to the 1870s and an impressive inventory of well-crafted leather jackets, belts, shoes, bags, and suitcases. The quality is high. If famous names in leatherware appeal to you, you'll find most of the biggies at **Casagrande,** Via Cola di Rienzo 206 (☎ 06/687-4610), like Fendi and its youth-conscious offspring, Fendissime, Cerruti, Mosquino, and Valentino. This is a well-managed store that has developed an impressive reputation for quality and authenticity since the 1930s. The prices are more reasonable than those for equivalent merchandise in some other parts of town.

Fendi, Via Borgognona 36A–39 (☎ 06/679-7641), is mainly known for its avant-garde leather goods, but it also has furs, stylish purses, ready-to-wear clothing, and a new men's line of clothing and accessories. Fendi also carries gift items, home furnishings, and sports accessories. Of course, **Gucci,** Via Condotti 8 (☎ 06/679-0405), has been as a legend since 1900. Its merchandise consists of high-class leather goods, like suitcases, handbags, wallets, shoes, and desk accessories. It also has elegant menswear and womenswear, including beautiful shirts, blouses, and dresses, as well as ties and neck scarves. *La bella figura* is alive and well here, and the prices have never been higher. **Saddlers Union,** Via Condotti 26 (☎ 06/679-8050), is a great place to look for well-crafted leather accessories. The wide selection of bags might lure you here, but there's plenty more—belts, wallets, shoes, briefcases, and other finely crafted items.

LINGERIE At **Brighenti,** Via Frattina 7–8 (☎ 06/679-1484), amid several famous neighbors on Via Frattina, you might run across a "seductive fantasy." Here it's strictly lingerie di lusso or, perhaps better phrased, haute corseterie. **Tomassini di Luisa Romagnoli,** Via Sistina 119 (☎ 06/488-1909), offers delicately beautiful lingerie and negligees, all original designs of Luisa Romagnoli. Most of the merchandise is of shimmery Italian silk; other items, to a lesser degree, are of fluffy cotton or frothy nylon. Highly revealing garments are sold either ready-to-wear or are custom-made. **Vanità,** Via Frattina 70 (☎ 06/679-1743), features underthings in *all* colors—no rainbow can match the selection. Yes, you can get black or white, but take the time to browse and you'll discover hues you've never dreamed of.

MOSAICS Mosaics are an art form as old as the Roman Empire. Many of the objects displayed at **Savelli,** Via Paolo VI 27 (☎ 06/6830-7017), were inspired by ancient originals discovered in thousands of excavations, including those at Pompeii and Ostia. Others, especially the floral designs, depend on the whim and creativity of the artist. Objects include tabletops, boxes, and vases. The cheapest mosaic objects begin at around $125 and are unsigned products crafted by students at an art school partially funded by the Vatican. Objects made in the Savelli workshops that are signed by the individual artists (and that tend to be larger and more elaborate) range from $500 to $25,000. The outlet also contains a collection of small souvenir items like keychains and carved statues.

PORCELAIN One of the most prestigious retail outlets for porcelain in the city, ✪ **Richard Ginori,** Via de Tritone 177 (☎ 06/679-3836), contains a roster of the impeccably crafted porcelain of Richard Ginori. Founded in 1735, it offers porcelain that's almost sure to spark the acquisitive interest of the grand bourgeois and their wanna-bes. Anything you buy can be shipped, or—if you prefer to acquire your porcelain at Ginori's outlets in North America (which include Tiffany's in New York)—you can at least check out the dozens of patterns produced by Italy's most glamorous manufacturer. The outlet on Via de Tritone opened in 1912.

PRINTS & ENGRAVINGS   At ✪ **Alberto di Castro,** Via del Babuino 71 (☎ **06/ 361-3752**), you'll find Rome's largest collection of antique prints and engravings. There are rack after rack of depictions of everything from the Colosseum to the Pantheon, each evocative of the best architecture in the Mediterranean world, priced from $25 to $1,000 depending on the age and rarity of the engraving. **Alinari,** Via d'Alibert 16A (☎ **06/679-2923**), takes its name from the famed 19th-century Florentine photographer. Original prints and photos of Alinari are almost as prized as paintings in national galleries, and you can pick up your own here.

   Giovanni B. Panatta Fine Art Shop, Via Francesco Crispi 117 (☎ **06/679-5948**), sells excellent color and black-and-white prints covering a variety of subjects, from 18th-century Roman street scenes to astrological charts. There's also a selection of reproductions of medieval and Renaissance art that's attractive and reasonably priced. **Fava,** Via del Babuino 180 (☎ **06/361-0807**), recaptures the era when Neapolitans sold 17th- and 18th-century pictures of the eruptions of Vesuvius, once highly sought by collectors. Many of these "volcanic paintings" of yesteryear can still cause a conflagration today. This is really unusual art from the attics of the days of yore.

RELIGIOUS OBJECTS   In a neighborhood loaded with purveyors of religious art and icons, **Anna Maria Gaudenzi,** Piazza delle Minerva 69A (☎ **06/679-0431**), claims to be the oldest of its type in Rome. If you collect depictions of the Madonna, paintings of the saints, exotic rosaries, chalices, small statues, or medals, you can feel secure in knowing that thousands of pilgrims have spent their money here before you. Whether you view its merchandise as a devotional aid or as bizarre kitsch, this shop has it all.

SHOES   At **Dominici,** Via del Corso 14 (☎ **06/361-0591**), a few steps from Piazza del Popolo, you'll find an amusing collection of men's and women's shoes in a pleasing variety of vivid colors. The style is aggressively young at heart and the quality good. **Ferragamo,** Via Condotti 73–74 (☎ **06/679-8402**), sells elegant footwear, plus women's clothing and accessories and ties, in an atmosphere full of Italian style. There are always many customers waiting to enter the shop; management allows them to enter in small groups. Figure on a 30-minute wait.

   Fragiacomo, Via Condotti 35 (☎ **06/679-8780**), sells shoes for men and women in a champagne-colored showroom with gilt-painted chairs and big display cases. **Lily of Florence,** Via Lombardia 38 (☎ **06/474-0262**), has a shop in Rome, with the same merchandise that made the outlet so well known in the Tuscan capital. The colors come in a wide range, the designs are stylish, and the leather texture is of good quality. Lily sells shoes for both men and women and features American sizes with prices 30% to 40% less than in the States.

WINE & LIQUOR   At the historic **Buccone,** Via Ripetta 19 (☎ **06/361-2154**), the selection of wines and gastronomic specialties is among the finest in Rome. **Trimani,** Via Goito 20 (☎ **06/446-9661**), opened in 1821, sells wines and spirits from Italy, among other offerings. Purchases can be shipped to your home. Trimani collaborates with the Italian wine magazine *Gambero Rosso*, organizing some lectures about wine where devotees can improve their knowledge and educate their tastebuds. **Ai Monasteri,** Piazza delle Cinque Lune 76 (☎ **06/6880-2783**), is a treasure trove of liquors (including liqueurs and wines), honey, and herbal teas made in Italian monasteries and convents. You can buy excellent chocolates and other candies as well. You make your selections in a quiet atmosphere reminiscent of a monastery, just 2 blocks from Bernini's Fountain of the Four Rivers in Piazza Navona. The shop will ship some items home for you.

10 Rome After Dark

When the sun goes down, Rome's palaces, ruins, fountains, and monuments are bathed in a theatrical white light. There are actually few evening occupations quite as pleasurable as a stroll past the solemn pillars of old temples or the cascading torrents of Renaissance fountains glowing under the blue-black sky.

The **Fountain of the Naiads (Fontana delle Naiadi)** on Piazza della Repubblica, the **Fountain of the Tortoises (Fontana della Tartarughe)** on Piazza Mattei, and the **Trevi Fountain (Fontana dei Trevi)** are particularly beautiful at night. The **Capitoline Hill** is magnificently lit after dark, with its measured Renaissance facades glowing like jewel boxes. Behind the **Senatorial Palace** is a fine view of the illuminated Roman Forum. If you're across the Tiber, **Piazza San Pietro** (in front of St. Peter's) is impressive at night without the tour buses and crowds. And a combination of illuminated architecture, Renaissance fountains, and sidewalk shows and art expos enliven **Piazza Navona.** If you're ambitious and have a good sense of direction, try exploring the streets to the west of the piazza, which look like a stage set when lit at night.

Even if you don't speak Italian, you can generally follow the listings of special events and evening entertainment featured in *La Repubblica,* a leading Italian newspaper. *Trova Roma,* a special weekly entertainment supplement (good for the coming week) is published in this paper on Thursday. The minimagazines *Metropolitan* and *Wanted in Rome* have listings of jazz, rock, and such and give an interesting look at expatriate Rome. The daily *Il Messaggero* lists current cultural news, especially in its Thursday magazine supplement, *Metro.* And *Un Ospite a Roma,* available free from the concierge desks of top hotels, is full of details on what's happening.

THE PERFORMING ARTS

CLASSICAL MUSIC   Concerts given by the orchestra of the **Academy of St. Cecilia,** Via della Conciliazione 4 (☎ **06/688-01044**), usually take place at Piazza Villa Giulia, site of the Etruscan Museum, from late June to late July; in winter they're held in the academy's concert hall on Via della Conciliazione. Sometimes other addresses are used for its concerts, including a handful of historic churches. Performance nights are Saturday, Sunday, Monday, or Tuesday; Fridays feature chamber music. Tickets run 25,000L to 80,000L ($15 to $46).

A Few Nightlife Warnings

During the peak of summer, usually in August, all nightclub proprietors seem to lock their doors and head for the seashore, where they operate alternate clubs. Some close at different times each year, so it's hard to keep up-to-date. Always have your hotel check to see if a club is operating before you make a trek to it.

Be aware that there are no inexpensive nightclubs in Rome. Many of the legitimate nightclubs, besides being expensive, are highlighted by hookers plying their trade. Younger people fare better than some more sedate folk, as the dance clubs open and close with freewheeling abandon.

Large and well publicized, the **Teatro Olimpico,** Piazza Gentile da Fabriano (☎ 06/323-4890), hosts a widely divergent collection of singers, both classical and pop, who perform according to a schedule that sometimes changes at the last minute. Occasionally the space is devoted to chamber orchestras or visiting foreign orchestras. Tickets run 20,000L to 80,000L ($12 to $46).

Check the daily papers for **free church concerts** given around town, especially near Easter and Christmas.

OPERA   If you're in the capital for the opera season, usually late December to June, you may want to attend the historic **Teatro dell'Opera,** Piazza Beniamino Gigli 1, off Via Nazionale (☎ 06/481-601). Nothing is presented in August; in summer, the venue usually switches elsewhere. Call ahead or ask your concierge before you go. Tickets are 20,000L to 260,000L ($12 to $151).

DANCE   Performances of the Rome Opera Ballet are given at the **Teatro dell'Opera** (above). The regular repertoire of classical ballet is supplemented by performances of internationally acclaimed guest artists, and Rome is on the major agenda for troupes from around the world, including the Alvin Ailey dancers. Watch for announcements in the weekly entertainment guides about other venues, including the Teatro Olimpico, or even open-air ballet performances.

A MEAL & A SONG

Da Ciceruacchio, Piazza dei Mercanti, at Via del Porto 1, in Trastevere (☎ 06/580-6046), was once a sunken jail (the vine-covered walls date from the 18th century). Folkloric groups appear throughout the evening, especially singers of Neapolitan songs, accompanied by guitars and harmonicas—a rich repertoire of old-time favorites, some with bawdy lyrics. Charcoal-broiled steaks and chops are served along with lots of local wine, and bean soup is a specialty. The grilled mushrooms are another good opening, as is the spaghetti with clams. You can dine Tuesday to Sunday 8pm to midnight for 40,000L to 60,000L ($23 to $35).

Da Meo Patacca, Piazza dei Mercanti 30, in Trastevere (☎ 06/5833-1086), serves bountiful "Roman country" meals to flocks of tourists. The atmosphere is one of extravaganza—primitive and colorful in a carnival sense—good fun if you're in the mood. Downstairs is a vast cellar with strolling musicians and singers. Many menu offerings are as adventurous as the decor (wild boar, wild hare, quail), but you'll also find corn on the cob, pork and beans, thick-cut sirloins, and chicken on a spit. Expect to spend 70,000L ($41) and up for a meal, though don't expect fine cuisine. In summer, you can dine at outdoor tables. It's open daily 8 to 11:30pm.

Roman rusticity is combined with theatrical flair at **Fantasie di Trastevere,** Via di Santa Dorotea 6, in Trastevere (☎ 06/588-1671), where the famous actor Petrolini made his debut. In the 16th century, this restaurant was an old theater built for Queen Cristina of Sweden and her court. The cuisine isn't subtle but is bountiful. Such dishes as the classic saltimbocca (ham with veal) are preceded by tasty pasta, and everything is aided by Castelli Romani wines. Accompanying the main dishes is a big basket of warm country herb bread. Expect to pay 75,000L to 90,000L ($44 to $52) for a full meal. If you visit for a drink, the first one will be 35,000L ($20). Some two dozen folk singers and musicians in regional costumes perform, making it a festive affair. Meals begin daily at 8pm, with piano bar music 8:30 to 9:30pm, followed by the show, lasting to 10:30pm.

BARS & CAFES

Unless you're dead set on making the Roman nightclub circuit, try what might be a far livelier and less expensive scene—sitting late at night on **Via Veneto, Piazza della**

Rotonda, Piazza del Popolo (at least after the scaffolding comes down), or one of Rome's other piazzas, all for the cost of an espresso, cappuccino, or Campari.

If you're looking for some scrumptious **ice cream,** see Café Rosati and Giolitti below as well as the box "Take a Gelato Break" in chapter 4.

ON VIA VENETO   Back in the 1950s (a decade *Time* magazine gave to Rome, in the way it conceded the 1960s to London), **Via Vittorio Veneto** rose in fame as the choicest street in Rome, crowded with aspiring and actual movie stars, their directors, and a fast-rising group of card-carrying members of the jet set. Today the *bella gente* (beautiful people), movie stars, and directors wouldn't be caught dead on Via Veneto—the street has moved into the mainstream of world tourism. Nevertheless, you may want to spend some time there.

✪ **Harry's Bar,** Via Vittorio Veneto 150 (☎ **06/484-643**), is a perennial favorite. Every major Italian city (like Florence and Venice) seems to have one, and Rome is no exception, though this one has no connection with the others. This haunt of IBFs (International Bar Flies) at the top of Via Veneto is chic and sophisticated. In summer, tables are placed outside. For those who wish to dine outdoors but want to avoid the scorching sun, a new air-conditioned sidewalk cafe is open May to November. Meals inside cost about double what you'd pay outside. In back is a small dining room serving some of the finest food in central Rome, with meals going for 90,000L to 100,000L ($52 to $58). The restaurant inside is open Monday to Saturday 12:30 to 3pm and 7:30pm to 1am, while outside you can eat noon to midnight. The bar is open Monday to Saturday 11am to 2am (closed August 1 to 10), and the piano bar is open nightly from 11pm.

Caffè de Paris, Via Vittorio Veneto 90 (☎ **06/488-5284**), rises and falls in popularity depending on the decade. In the 1950s it was a haven for the fashionable, and now it's a popular restaurant in summer, when the tables spill right out onto the sidewalk and the passing crowd walks through the maze.

ON PIAZZA DEL POPOLO   At the center of **Piazza del Popolo** is a 13th-century B.C. Egyptian obelisk, and around it are Santa Maria del Popolo and almost-twin baroque churches. Note that at press time the piazza was filled with scaffolding at it receives a sprucing up—hopefully the job will be done by the time you get to Rome.

Café Rosati, Piazza del Popolo 5A (☎ **06/322-5859**), has been around since 1923 and attracts a crowd of all persuasions who drive up in Maseratis and Porsches. It's really a sidewalk cafe/ice-cream parlor/candy store/confectionery/ristorante that has been swept up in the fickle world of fashion. The later you go, the more interesting the action will be. It serves lunch and dinner daily noon to 11pm.

Though the management has filled it with boutiques selling expensive gift items, like luggage and cigarette lighters, many Romans still consider **Canova Café,** Piazza del Popolo 16 (☎ **06/361-2231**), *the* place on the piazza. The Canova has a sidewalk terrace for people-watching, plus a snack bar, a restaurant, and a wine shop. In summer, you'll have access to a courtyard whose walls are covered with ivy and where flowers grow in terra-cotta planters. A buffet meal is 20,000L ($12) and up. Food is served daily noon to 3:30pm and 7 to 11pm, but the bar is open 8am to midnight or 1am.

It sounds like an old Cole Porter song, but **Night & Day,** 50 Via Dell'Oca (☎ **06/ 320-2300**), is actually one of the most patronized Irish pubs in the vicinity of Piazza de Popolo. Open daily 5pm to 5am, it doesn't really get hot until 2am, when many dance clubs close for the evening. American music is played as you down your Harps & Guinness. Amazingly, foreigners are issued drink cards, making all their drinks 5,000L ($2.90) instead of the 8,000L ($4.65) usually charged. There's never a cover.

NEAR THE PANTHEON Many visitors to the Eternal City now view **Piazza della Rotonda,** across from the Pantheon and reconstructed by Hadrian in the early 2nd century, as the "living room" of Rome. This is especially true on summer nights.

Di Rienzo, Piazza della Rotonda 8–9 (☎ **06/686-9097**), the most desirable cafe on this piazza, is open daily 7am to 1 or 2am. In fair weather, you can sit at one of the sidewalk tables (if you can find one free). In cooler weather, you can retreat inside, where the walls are inlaid with the type of marble found on the Pantheon's floor. Many types of pastas appear on the menu, as does risotto alla pescatora (fisherman's rice) and several meat courses. You can also order pizzas. **Taza d'Oro,** Piazza della Rotonda, Via degli Orfani 84 (☎ **06/678-9792**), is known for serving its own brand of espresso. Another specialty—ideal on a hot summer night—is granità di caffè (coffee that has been frozen, crushed into a velvety slushlike ice, and placed in a glass between layers of whipped cream). They're open daily from 7:30am to 1am.

Strongly brewed coffee is one of Italy's elixirs, and many Romans will walk blocks and blocks for what they consider a superior brew. **Caffè Sant'Eustachio,** Piazza Sant'Eustachio 82 (☎ **06/686-1309**), is one of Rome's most celebrated espresso shops, where the water supply is funneled into the city by an aqueduct built in 19 B.C. Rome's most experienced espresso judges claim the water plays an important part in the coffee's flavor, though steam forced through ground Brazilian coffee roasted on the premises has a significant effect as well. Purchase a ticket from the cashier for as many cups as you want, then leave a small tip (about 200L/10¢) for the counterperson when you present your receipt. It's open Tuesday to Friday and Sunday 8:30am to 1am and Saturday 8:30am to 1:30am.

IN TRASTEVERE Piazza del Popolo once lured the sophisticated from Via Veneto, and now several cafes in **Trastevere,** across the Tiber, threaten to attract the same from Popolo. Fans who saw Fellini's *Roma* know what **Piazza Santa Maria in Trastevere** looks like at night. The square—filled with milling throngs in summer—is graced with an octagonal fountain and a 12th-century church. Children run and play on the piazza, and occasional spontaneous guitar fests break out when the weather's good.

The **Café-Bar di Marzio,** Piazza Santa Maria in Trastevere 15 (☎ **06/581-6095**), is a warmly inviting place. It's strictly a cafe (not a restaurant), offering both indoor and outdoor tables at the edge of the square with the best view of its fountain. Marzio is open Tuesday to Sunday 7am to 2am.

NEAR THE SPANISH STEPS Since 1760, the ✪ **Antico Caffè Greco,** Via Condotti 84 (☎ **06/679-1700**), has been Rome's poshest coffee bar, the gathering place of the literati. Previous sippers have included Stendhal, Goethe, and even D'Annunzio. Keats would also sit here and write. Today, you're more likely to see dowagers on a shopping binge and American tourists, but there's plenty of atmosphere. In front is a wooden bar and beyond a series of small salons. You sit at marble-topped tables of Napoleonic design, against a backdrop of gold or red damask, romantic paintings, and antique mirrors. The house specialty is paradisi, made with lemon and orange. It's open Monday to Saturday 8am to 9pm (closed for 10 days in August).

The fermented fruits of the vine have played a prominent role in Roman life since the word *bacchanalian* was first invented (and that was very early indeed), and one of the best places to taste Italian wines, brandies, and grappa is at **Enoteca Fratelli Roffi Isabelli,** Via della Croce 76B (☎ **06/679-0896**). A stand-up drink in its darkly antique confines is the perfect ending to a visit to the nearby Spanish Steps. You can opt for a postage-stamp table in back or stay at the bar.

NEAR PIAZZA COLONNA The center of Rome's government, **Piazza Colonna** stands at the meeting point of two major arteries, Via Tritone and Via del Corso. The prime minister resides at Palazzo Chigi, at the corner of Via del Corso near La Rinascente. In the center of the square is the Colonna di Marco Aurelio (column of Marcus Aurelius), dedicated to the emperor in A.D. 193. A statue of Marcus Aurelius stood atop the column until 1589, when Pope Sixtus V replaced it with the present statue of St. Paul.

For devotees of gelato (addictively tasty ice cream), **Giolitti,** Via Uffici del Vicario 40 (☎ **06/699-1243**), is one of the city's most popular nighttime gathering spots and the oldest ice-cream shop. Some of the sundaes look like Vesuvius about to erupt. Many people take gelato out to eat on the streets; others enjoy it in the postempire splendor of the salon inside. You can have your "cuppa" daily 7am to 2am. There are many excellent, smaller gelaterie throughout Rome, wherever you see the cool concoction advertised as *produzione propria* (homemade). See the box "Take a Gelato Break" in chapter 4.

LIVE-MUSIC CLUBS

At **Alexanderplatz,** Via Ostia 9 (☎ **06/3974-2171**), you can hear jazz (not rock) Monday to Saturday 9pm to 2am, with live music beginning at 10:15pm. The good restaurant here serves everything from gnocchi alla romana to Japanese. There's no cover, but a 3-month membership is 12,000L ($7). **Big Mama,** Vicolo San Francesco a Ripa 18 (☎ **06/581-2551**), is a hangout for jazz and blues musicians where you're likely to meet the up-and-coming stars of tomorrow and sometimes even the big names. It's open Monday to Saturday 9pm to 1:30am (closed July to September). For big acts, the cover is 20,000L to 30,000L ($12 to $17), plus 10,000L to 20,000L ($6 to $12) for a 30-day or 1-year membership fee.

Fonclea, Via Crescenzio 82A (☎ **06/689-6302**), offers live music every night—Dixieland, rock, r&b. This is basically a cellar jazz place and crowded pub that attracts patrons from all walks of Roman life. The music starts at 9:15pm and usually lasts until 12:30am. The club is open nightly 7pm to 2am (on Friday and Saturday to 3:30am). There's also a restaurant featuring grilled meats, salads, and crêpes. A meal starts at 35,000L ($20), but if you want dinner it's best to reserve a table. On Saturday there's a 10,000L ($6) cover. **Music Inn,** Largo dei Fiorentini 3 (☎ **06/6880-2220**), is among Rome's leading jazz clubs. Some of the biggest names in jazz, both European and American, have performed here. It's open Thursday to Sunday 8pm to 2am (closed July and August). The cover is 15,000L ($9).

St. Louis Music City, Via del Cardello 13A (☎ **06/474-5076**), is another jazz venue, but it doesn't necessarily attract the big names. What you get are young and sometimes very talented groups beginning their careers. Many celebrities patronize the place. Soul and funk are performed on occasion. You can dine at a restaurant on the premises, where meals are 35,000L ($20) and up. It's open Tuesday to Sunday 9pm to 2am, and the 7,000L ($4.05) cover includes club membership. ✪ **Arciliuto,** Piazza Monte Vecchio 5 (☎ **06/687-9419**), is a romantic candlelit spot that was reputedly once the studio of Raphael. Monday to Saturday 10pm to 2am, you can enjoy a music salon ambience, with a pianist, guitarist, and violinist. The presentation also includes live Neapolitan songs and new Italian madrigals, even current hits from Broadway or

A Nightlife Note

A neighborhood with an edge, Testaccio is radical chic—don't wander around alone at night. The area still has a way to go before regentrification. However, Testaccio is the place to ask about what's hot in Rome when you arrive, as crowds are fickle.

London's West End. This place is hard to find, but it's within walking distance of Piazza Navona. The cover is 35,000L ($20), including the first drink; it's closed July 20 to September 3.

NIGHTCLUBS & DANCE CLUBS

In a setting of high-tech futuristic rows of exposed pipes and ventilation ducts, **Alien,** Via Velletri 13–19 (☎ 06/841-2212), provides a bizarre space-age view of future shock, bathed in strobe lights and house/techno music. Dull moments in any evening are punctuated with a cabaret-esque master or mistress of ceremonies with brief interludes of cabaret or comedy. It's open Tuesday to Saturday 11pm to 4am, with a 30,000L to 35,000L ($17 to $20) cover that includes the first drink.

✪ **Gilda,** Via Mario dei Fiori 97 (☎ 06/678-4838), is an adventurous nightclub/disco/restaurant known for its glamorous acts. In the past it has hosted Diana Ross and splashy Paris-type revues. The artistic direction assures first-class shows, a well-run restaurant, and disco music played between the live acts. The restaurant and pizzeria open at 9:30pm and occasionally present shows. An international cuisine is featured, with meals beginning at 45,000L ($26). The disco (midnight to 4am) presents music of the 1960s as well as modern recordings. The attractive piano bar, Swing, features Italian and Latin music. The cover is 40,000L ($23) and includes the first drink.

Notorious, Via San Nicola de Tolentino 22 (☎ 06/474-6888), really isn't. It's one of Rome's most popular discos, open Tuesday to Saturday 11pm to 4am. The music is always recorded. The beautiful people crowd in here, often in their best finery. Show up late—it's more fashionable. The cover is 40,000L ($23). One of Rome's largest and most energetic nightclubs, **Alpheus,** Via del Commercio 36 (☎ 06/574-7826), contains three sprawling rooms, each with a different musical sound and an ample number of bars. You'll find areas devoted to Latin music, other areas playing rock, and an area devoted to jazz. Live bands come and go, and there's enough cultural variety in the crowd to keep virtually anyone amused throughout the evening. It's open Friday and Saturday 10:30pm to 4am and charges 15,000L ($9) cover.

Counterculture, blasé, and clinging to the punk-rock and UK-indie music culture, **Black Out,** Via Saturnia 18 (☎ 06/7049-6791), occupies an industrial-looking site open only Friday and Saturday 10:30pm to 4am. Whenever it can manage, a live band is presented on Thursday—very late. The recorded music includes punk, retro, r&b, grunge, and whatever else happens to be in fashion. There's always one room (with an independent sound system) set aside as a lounge. The 10,000L ($6) cover includes the first drink. Everything about **Club Picasso,** Via Monte di Testaccio 63 (☎ 06/574-2975), was inspired by L.A.-style nightclubs, where r&b, rock, and funk blare out across a crowd that loves to dance, dance, dance. Don't expect a crowd full of only teeny-boppers, as patrons ranges from their 20s to 40s, with lots of people-watchers in between. The door bouncer maintains strict provisions against anyone who looks like troublemaking is part of his or her entertainment. It's open Tuesday to Saturday 10pm to 4am. On Friday and Saturday there's a 15,000L ($9) cover that includes the first drink.

Close to the American Embassy and Via Veneto, **Jackie O,** Via Boncompagni 11 (☎ 06/4288-5457), succeeds at capturing the glittery flashiness of *La Dolce Vita.* The crowd tends to be affluent and over 30. If you opt to go dancing here (it's not as frenzied as some might like), you might begin your evening with a drink at the piano bar, then perhaps end it with a meal at the restaurant, where meals average 50,000L ($29), without wine. It's open Tuesday to Sunday 10:30pm to 4am, and the cover of 40,000L

($23) includes the first drink. **Magic Fly,** Via Bassanello 15, Cassia-Grottarossa (☎ **06/3326-8956**), is somewhat cramped when it really begins to rock; this disco/piano bar, more elegant than the norm, lies outside the ring road encircling Rome's center, about 3 miles northeast. It changes its sound depending on the night of the week and might include Latin salsa and merengue, American-style rock, or British new wave. The sense of poshness encourages many men to wear ties. Magic Fly is open Wednesday to Sunday 10:30pm to dawn, with a cover of 25,000L to 30,000L ($15 to $17), including the first drink. It's best to take a taxi here and back.

Radio Londra, Via Monte Testaccio 67 (no phone), revels in the counterculture ambience of punk rock, inspired, as its name implies, by the chartreuse-haired, nose-pierced devotees common in London. Everyone here tries to look and act as freaky as possible. Since Radio Londra is near the popular gay L'Alibi (see below), the down-stairs club attracts many brethren, though the crowd is mixed. Upstairs is a pub/pizzeria where bands often appear; you can even order a veggie burger with a Bud. The club is open Wednesday to Monday 11:30am to 4am, and the pub/pizzeria serves Sunday, Monday, and Wednesday to Friday 9pm to 3am (to 4am on Saturday). The cover is 15,000L ($9), including the first drink.

GAY & LESBIAN CLUBS

Opened in 1984 by a Louisiana-born expatriate, John, and his Italian partner, Gianni, the **Hangar,** Via in Selci 69 (☎ **06/488-1397**), is the premier gay venue. It's on one of Rome's oldest streets, adjacent to the Forum, on the site of the palace once inhab-ited by Claudius's deranged wife Messalina. (If you're familiar with *I, Claudius,* you might remember that among her more blatant acts was challenging a prostitute to see who could take on more men and marrying her lover while still married to Claudius—she was beheaded for the latter. Her ghost is rumored to inhabit the premises here.) Each of the Hangar's two bars has an independent sound system. Women are welcome any night except Monday, when the club features videos and entertainment for men. The busiest nights are Saturday, Sunday, and Monday, when as many as 500 people cram inside. It's open Wednesday to Monday 10:30pm to 2:30am (closed for 3 weeks in August). There's no cover.

L'Alibi, Via Monte Testaccio 44 (☎ **06/574-3448**), in Testaccio, is a year-round venue on many a gay man's agenda. The crowd, however, tends to be mixed, both Roman and international, straight and gay, male and female. One room is devoted to dancing. It's open Tuesday to Sunday 11pm to 4am, and the cover is 20,000L ($12). **Angelo Azzuro,** Via Cardinal Merry del Val 13 (☎ **06/580-0472**), is a gay "hot spot" deep in the heart of Trastevere, open Friday, Saturday, and Sunday 11pm to 4am. There's no food—men dance with men to recorded music. Women are also invited, and Friday is for women only. On Friday and Sunday, the cover is 10,000L ($6), including the first drink; it's 12,000L ($7) on Saturday.

A fixture on the lesbian nighttime scene, **Joli Coeur,** Via Sirte 5 (☎ **06/8621-6240**), attracts women from around Europe during its very limited hours—only Saturday and Sunday 11pm to 5am. Saturday is reserved for women only, though on Sunday the crowd can be mixed. The cover is 20,000L ($12) and includes the first drink. The **Time Cafe,** Via di Monte Giordano, near Piazza Navona (☎ **06/6830-7051**), seems to have a Sunday appeal.

Two English-speaking gay and lesbian organizations can be found in Rome: **ARCI-Gay,** Via Primo Acciaresi 7 (☎ **06/4173-0752**), and **Circolo Mario Mieli,** Via Ostiense 202 (☎ **06/54-13-985**). Both are helpful with political and social information.

11 Side Trips from Rome: Tivoli, Ostia Antica & More

Most European capitals are ringed with a number of worthwhile attractions, but for sheer variety Rome tops them all. Just a few miles away, you can go back to the dawn of Italian history and explore the dank tombs the Etruscans left as their legacy or drink the golden wine of the towns in the Alban Hills (Castelli Romani). You can wander the ruins of Hadrian's Villa, the "queen of villas of the ancient world," or be lulled by the music of the baroque fountains in the Villa d'Este. You can turn yourself bronze on the beaches of Ostia di Lido or explore the remarkable ruins of Ostia Antica, Rome's ancient seaport.

Unless you're rushed beyond reason, allow at least 3 days to take a look at the attractions in the environs. We've highlighted the best of the lot below.

TIVOLI & THE VILLAS

Tivoli, known as Tibur to the ancient Romans, is 20 miles east of Rome on Via Tiburtina—about an hour's drive with traffic. If you don't have a car, take Metro Line B to the end of the line, the Rebibbia station. After exiting the station, board an Acotral bus the rest of the way to Tivoli. Generally, buses depart about every 20 minutes during the day. For information about the town, check with **Azienda Autonoma di Turismo,** Largo Garibaldi (☎ 0774/334-522), Tivoli.

EXPLORING THE VILLAS

Tivoli was the playground of emperors. Today its reputation continues unabated: It's the most popular half-day jaunt from Rome. The ruins of **Hadrian's Villa** as well as the **Villa d'Este,** with their fabulous fountains and gardens, remain the two chief attractions—and both are major attractions, even if you must curtail your sightseeing in Rome. Right inside the town, you can look at two villas before heading to the environs of Tivoli and the ruins of Hadrian's Villa.

✪ **Villa d'Este.** Piazza Trento, Viale delle Centro Fontane. ☎ **0774/312-070.** Admission 8,000L ($4.65) adults when the water jets are at full power, 5,000L ($2.90) adults at other times; children 17 and under and seniors 60 and over free. Nov–Feb daily 9am–4pm; Mar to mid-Apr daily 9am–4:30pm; mid-Apr to mid-Sept daily 9am–6:30pm; mid-Sept to Oct daily 9am–4:30pm. The bus from Rome stops right near the entrance.

Like Hadrian centuries before, Cardinal Ippolito d'Este of Ferrara believed in heaven on earth, and in the mid-16th century, he ordered this villa built on a hillside. The dank Renaissance structure, with its second-rate paintings, is hardly worth the trek from Rome, but the gardens below (designed by Pirro Ligorio) dim the luster of those at Versailles.

You descend the cypress-studded slope to the bottom and on the way are rewarded with everything from lilies to gargoyles spouting water, torrential streams, and waterfalls. The loveliest fountain is the **Fontana del'Ovato,** by Ligorio. But nearby is the most spectacular achievement: the **hydraulic organ fountain,** dazzling with its water jets in front of a baroque chapel, with four maidens who look tipsy. The work represents the genius of Frenchman Claude Veanard. The moss-covered **Fountain of**

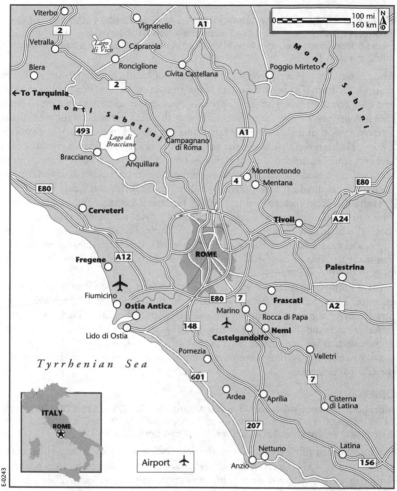

Dragons, also by Ligorio, and the so-called **Fountain of Glass** by Bernini are the most intriguing. The best walk is along the promenade, with 100 spraying fountains. The garden is worth hours of exploration, but you'll need frequent rests after those steep climbs.

Villa Gregoriana. Largo Sant'Angelo. No phone. Admission 2,500L ($1.45) adults, 1,000L (60¢) children 11 and under. May–Aug daily 10am–7:30pm; Sept daily 9:30am–6:30pm; Oct–Mar daily 9:30am–4:30pm; Apr daily 9:30am–6pm. The bus from Rome stops near the entrance.

Villa d'Este dazzles with artificial glamour, but Villa Gregoriana relies more on nature. The gardens were built by Pope Gregory XVI in the 19th century. At one point on the circuitous walk carved along a slope, you can stand and look out onto the most panoramic waterfall (Aniene) at Tivoli. The trek to the bottom on the banks of the Anio is studded with grottoes and balconies that open onto the chasm. The only problem is that if you do make the full journey, you may need a helicopter to pull you up again (the climb back is fierce). From one of the belvederes there's a panoramic view of the Temple of Vesta on the hill.

✪ **Hadrian's Villa (Villa Adriana).** Via di Villa Adriana. ☎ **0774/530-203.** Admission 8,000L ($4.65) adults; children 17 and under and seniors 60 and over free. Daily 9am–sunset (about 6:30pm in summer, 4pm Nov–Mar). Closed Christmas, New Year's Day, and May Day. Bus: 2 or 4 from Tivoli.

The globe-trotting Hadrian spent the last 3 years of his life in the grandest style. Less than 4 miles from Tivoli, he built one of the greatest estates ever erected in the world and filled acre after acre with some of the architectural wonders he'd seen on his many travels. A preview of what he envisioned in store for himself, the emperor even created a representation of hell centuries before Dante got around to recording its horrors in a poem. Hadrian was a patron of the arts, a lover of beauty, and even something of an architect, and he directed the staggering feat of building much more than a villa: It was a self-contained world for a vast royal entourage and the hundreds of servants and guards they required to protect them, feed them, bathe them, and satisfy their libidos.

Hadrian erected theaters, baths, temples, fountains, gardens, and canals bordered with statuary throughout his estate. He filled the palaces and temples with sculpture, some of which now rests in the museums of Rome. In later centuries, barbarians, popes, and cardinals, as well as anyone who needed a slab of marble, carted off much that made the villa so spectacular. But enough of the fragmented ruins remain for us to piece together the story.

For a glimpse of what the villa used to be, see the plastic reconstruction at the entrance. Then, following the arrows around, look in particular for the **Marine Theater** (ruins of the round structure with Ionic pillars); the **Great Baths,** with some intact mosaics; and the **Canopus,** with a group of caryatids whose images are reflected in the pond, as well as a statue of Mars. For a closer look at some of the items excavated, you can visit the museum on the premises and a museum and visitor center near the villa parking area.

DINING

Albergo Ristorante Adriano. Via di Villa Adriana 194. ☎ **0774/535-028.** Main courses 14,000–32,000L ($8–$19); fixed-price menu 75,000L ($44). AE, DC, MC, V. Mon–Sat 12:30–2:30pm and 8–10pm, Sun 12:30–2:30pm. Bus: 2 or 4 from Tivoli. ITALIAN.

In a stucco-sided villa a few steps from the ticket office sits an idyllic stop either before or after you visit Hadrian's Villa. It offers terrace dining under plane trees or indoor dining in a high-ceilinged room with terra-cotta walls, neoclassical moldings, and white Corinthian pilasters. The food is home-style cooking, and the menu includes roast lamb, saltimbocca (veal cooked with ham), a variety of veal dishes, deviled chicken, salads and cheeses, and simple desserts—everything homemade. They're especially proud of their homemade pastas.

Le Cinque Statue. Via Quintillio Varo 8. ☎ **0774/335-366.** Reservations recommended. Main courses 12,000–25,000L ($7–$15). AE, DC, MC, V. Sat–Thurs 12:30–3pm and 7:30–10pm. Closed Aug 15–30. The Acotral bus from Rome stops nearby. ROMAN.

This restaurant takes its name from the quintet of old carved statues (like Apollo Belvedere and gladiators) decorating the place. Today this comfortable restaurant is maintained by a hardworking Italian family who prepares an honest, unpretentious cuisine. Everything is accompanied by the wines of the hill towns of Rome. Begin with a pastiche of mushrooms or make a selection from the excellent antipasti. Try the rigatoni with fresh herbs, tripe fried Roman style, or mixed fry of brains and vegetables. All the pasta is freshly made. They also have a wide array of ice creams and fruits.

OSTIA ANTICA: ROME'S ANCIENT SEAPORT

Ostia Antica is one of the area's major attractions, particularly interesting to those who can't make it to Pompeii. If you want to see both ancient and modern Rome, grab your swimsuit, towel, and sun block and take the Metro Line B from Stazione Termini to the Magliana stop. Change here for the Lido train to Ostia Antica, about 16 miles from Rome. Departures are about every half hour, and the trip takes only 20 minutes. The Metro lets you off across the highway that connects Rome with the coast. It's just a short walk to the excavations.

Later, board the Metro again to visit the **Lido di Ostia,** the beach. Italy may be a Catholic country, but the Romans don't allow religious conservatism to affect their bathing attire. This is the beach where the denizens of the capital frolic on the seashore and at times create a merry carnival atmosphere, with dance halls, cinemas, and pizzerias. The Lido is set off best at Castelfusano, against a backdrop of pinewoods. This stretch of shoreline is referred to as the Roman Riviera.

✪ **Ostia Antica's Ruins.** Vlale dei Romagnoli 717. ☎ **06/5635-8099.** Admission 8,000L ($4.65) adults; children 18 and under free. Apr–Sept daily 9am–7pm (Oct–Mar to sunset). Metro: Ostia Antica Line Roma–Ostia–Lido.

Ostia, at the mouth of the Tiber, was the port of ancient Rome, serving as the gateway for all the riches from the far corners of the empire. It was founded in the 4th century B.C. and became a major port and naval base primarily under two later emperors, Claudius and Trajan.

A prosperous city developed, full of temples, baths, theaters, and patrician homes. Ostia flourished for about 8 centuries before it began to wither away. Gradually it became little more than a malaria bed, a buried ghost city that faded into history. Though a papal-sponsored commission launched a series of digs in the 19th century, the major work of unearthing was carried out under Mussolini's orders from 1938 to 1942 (the work had to stop because of the war). The city is only partially dug out today, but it's believed that all the chief monuments have been uncovered.

These principal monuments are clearly labeled. The most important spot is **Piazzale delle Corporazioni,** an early version of Wall Street. Near the theater, this square contained nearly 75 corporations, the nature of their businesses identified by the patterns of preserved mosaics. Greek dramas were performed at the **ancient theater,** built in the early days of the empire. The classics are still aired here in summer (check with the tourist office for specific listings), but the theater as it looks today is the result of much rebuilding. Every town the size of Ostia had a forum, and during the excavations a number of pillars of the ancient **Ostia Forum** were uncovered. At one end is a 2nd-century B.C. temple honoring a trio of gods—Minerva, Jupiter, and Juno (little more than the basic foundation remains). In addition, in the enclave is a well-lit **museum** displaying Roman statuary along with some Pompeii-like frescoes. There are perfect picnic spots beside fallen columns or near old temple walls.

THE CASTELLI ROMANI & THEIR WINES

For the Roman emperor and the wealthy cardinal in the heyday of the Renaissance, the **Castelli Romani (Roman Castles)** exerted a powerful lure, and they still do. The Castelli aren't castles but hill towns—many of them with an ancient history. The wines from the Alban Hills will add a little *feu de joie* to your life.

The ideal way to explore the hill towns is by car. But you can get a limited review by taking one of the buses that leaves every 20 minutes from Rome's Subaugusta stop on Metro Line A.

CASTELGANDOLFO

Since the early 17th century, the resort of **Castelgandolfo** on Lake Albano, 16 miles from Rome, has been the summer retreat of the popes. It attracts thousands of pilgrims yearly, though the papal residence, **Villa Barberini,** and its surrounding gardens are private and open only on special occasions. Interestingly, the pope's summer place incorporates part of the notoriously despotic emperor Domitian's palace (but the pastimes have changed).

On days the pope grants a mass audience, thousands of visitors (many of whom arrive on foot) stream into the audience hall. Pope Pius XII, worried about the thousands who waited out in the rain to see him, built this air-conditioned structure to protect the faithful from the elements. On a summer Sunday the pope usually appears on a small balcony in the palace courtyard, reciting with the crowd the noon Angelus prayers.

The seat of the papacy opens onto a little square in the center of the town, where vacationers sip their wine—nothing pontifical here. A chairlift transports you from the hillside town to the lake, where some of the aquatic competitions were held in the 1960 Olympics. Bernini's hand is evident in the church of **San Tomaso di Villanova** and the fountainon the main square, **Piazza della Libertà.** If you need to be sold more on visiting Castelgandolfo, remember that it was praised by eminent guidebook writer Goethe.

NEMI

The Romans flock to **Nemi** in droves, particularly from April to June, for the succulent **strawberries** of the district—acclaimed by some gourmets as Europe's finest. In May, there's a strawberry festival. Nemi was also known to the ancients. A temple to the huntress Diana was erected on **Lake Nemi,** which was said to be her "looking glass." In A.D. 37, Caligula built luxurious barges to float on the lake. Mussolini, much later, drained Nemi to find the barges, but it was a dangerous time to excavate them from the bottom. They were senselessly destroyed by the Nazis during the infamous retreat.

At the **Roman Ship Museum (Museo delle Navi),** Via di Diana 15 (☎ 06/ 939-8040), you can see two scale models of the ships destroyed by the Nazis. The major artifacts on display are mainly copies, as the originals now rest in world-class museums. The museum is open daily: April to September 9am to 6:30pm (October to March to 1:30pm). Admission is 4,000L ($2.30) adults; children 18 and under and seniors 60 and over are free. To reach the museum, head from the center of Nemi toward the lake.

The 15th-century **Palazzo Ruspoli,** a private baronial estate, is the focal point of Nemi, but the town itself invites exploration—particularly the alleyways the locals call streets and the houses with balconies jutting out over the slopes. While darting like Diana through the Castelli Romani, try to time your schedule to have lunch here.

Dining

✪ **Ristorante Il Castagnone.** In the Diana Park Hotel, Via Nemorense 44. ☎ 06/ 936-4041. Reservations recommended. Main courses 16,000–35,000L ($9–$20). AE, DC, MC, V. Daily noon–3pm and 8–10pm. ROMAN/SEAFOOD.

This well-managed dining room of the town's best hotel takes a definite pride in a Roman-based cuisine featuring seafood above meat and attentive formal service usually delivered with a kind of gentle humor. Amid neoclassical accessories and marble, you can order delectable veal, chicken, beef, and fish dishes like fried calamari, spaghetti with shellfish in garlicky tomato-based sauce, and roasted lamb with potatoes and Mediterranean herbs. As you dine, expect a sweeping view from the restaurant's windows of the lake.

FRASCATI

About 13 miles from Rome on Via Tuscolana and some 1,073 feet above sea level, **Frascati** is one of the most beautiful of the hill towns. It's known for the wine to which it lends its name as well as its villas, which luckily bounced back from the severe destruction caused by World War II bombers. To get there, take one of the Cotral buses leaving from the Anagina stop of Metro Line A. From there take the blue Cotral bus to Frascati. Again, the transportation situation in Italy is constantly in a state of flux, so check your route at the station.

Though Frascati wine is exported—and served in many of Rome's restaurants and trattorie—tradition holds that it's best near the vineyards from which it came. Romans drive up on Sunday just to drink it. To sample some of the golden white wine, head for **Cantina Comandini,** Via F. Filiberto 1 (☎ **06/942-0915**), right off Piazza Roma. The Comandini family welcomes you to the wine cellar, a regional tavern in which they sell Frascati from their own vineyards. You can drink the wine on the spot for 6,000L ($3.50) per liter or 1,500L (85¢) per glass and can buy sandwiches to go with your vino. The tavern is open Monday to Saturday 4 to 8pm. Reservations are recommended.

Stand in the heart of Frascati, at Piazza Marconi, to see the most important of the estates: **Villa Aldobrandini,** Via Massala. The finishing touches to this 16th-century villa were added by Maderno, who designed the facade of St. Peter's in Rome, but you can visit only the gardens. Still, with its grottoes, yew hedges, statuary, and splashing fountains it makes for an exciting outing. The gardens are open daily 9am to 1pm and 3 to 5pm, but you must go to the **Azienda di Soggiorno e Turismo,** Piazza Marconi 1 (☎ **06/942-0331**), to ask for a free pass. The office is open Monday to Friday 8am to 2pm and 3:30 to 6:40pm and Saturday 8am to 2pm.

If you have a car, you can continue about 3 miles past the Villa Aldobrandini to **Tuscolo,** an ancient spot with the ruins of an amphitheater dating from about the 1st century B.C. It offers what may be one of Italy's most panoramic views. You may also want to visit the bombed-out **Villa Torlonia,** adjacent to Piazza Marconi. Its grounds have been converted into a public park whose chief treasure is the "Theater of the Fountains," designed by Maderno.

Dining

Cacciani Restaurant. Via Armando Diaz 13. ☎ **06/942-0378.** Reservations required on weekends. Main courses 19,000–32,000L ($11–$19). AE, DC, MC, V. Tues–Sun 12:30–3pm and 7:30–10:30pm. Closed Jan 7–19 and Aug 18–27. ROMAN.

Cacciani is the choicest restaurant in Frascati, where the competition has always been tough. A modern restaurant in the town center, it boasts a terrace commanding a view of the valley. The kitchen is exposed to the public, and it's fun just to watch the women wash the sand off the spinach. To get you started, we recommend the pasta specialties, such as fettuccine or rigatoni alla vaccinara (oxtail in tomato sauce). For a main course, the baby lamb with a sauce of white wine and vinegar is always reliable. There is, of course, a large choice of wines, which are kept in a cave under the restaurant. If you call ahead, the Cacciani family will arrange a combined visit to several of Frascati's wine-producing villas along with a memorable meal at their restaurant.

PALESTRINA

If you go out of Rome through the Porta Maggiore and travel on Via Prenestina for about 24 miles, you'll eventually come to **Palestrina,** a medieval hill town overlooking a wide valley. When U.S. airmen flew over in World War II and bombed part of the town, they scarcely realized their actions would launch Palestrina as an important tourist attraction. After the debris was cleared, a pagan temple (once one of the greatest in the world) emerged: the **Fortuna Primigenia,** rebuilt in the days of the empire but dating from centuries before.

Palestrina predates the founding of Rome by several hundred years. It resisted conquest by the early Romans and later took the wrong side in the civil war between Marius and Sulla. When Sulla won, he razed every stone in the city except the Temple of Fortune and then built a military barracks on the site. Later, as a favorite vacation spot for the emperors and their entourages, it sheltered some of the empire's most luxurious villas. During medieval feuds, the city was repeatedly destroyed. Its most famous child was Pier Luigi da Palestrina, recognized as the father of polyphonic harmony.

The **Colonna-Barberini Palace** (☎ 06/481-4591), high on a hill overlooking the valley, today houses Roman statuary found in the ruins, plus Etruscan artifacts like urns the equal of those in Rome's Villa Giulia. But worth the trip itself is the **Nile Mosaic,** a well-preserved ancient Roman work, the most remarkable one ever uncovered. The mosaic details the flooding of the Nile, a shepherd's hunt, mummies, ibises, and Roman warriors, among other things. The museum is open Tuesday to Sunday 9am to an hour before sunset. Admission is 8,000L ($4.65) adults; children 17 and under and seniors 60 and over are free.

In Palestrina you'll also find a **Duomo** dating from 1100, with a mostly intact bell tower. It rests on the foundation of a much earlier pagan temple.

Accommodations

Albergo Ristorante Stella (Restaurant Coccia). Piazza della Liberazione 3, Palestrina, 00036 Roma. ☎ **06/953-8172.** Fax 06/957-3360. 29 units. AC TV TEL. 100,000L ($58) double; 160,000L ($93) suite. AE, DC, V.

The buff-colored Albergo Ristorante Stella, in the commercial center of town, is on a cobblestone square with parked cars, trees, and a small fountain. It was renovated in 1995, though the rooms remain rather basic but comfortable. The simple lobby is filled with warm colors, curved leather couches, and autographed photos of local sports heroes. In the small lounge you might have an aperitif before lunch, and in the sunny restaurant meals begin at 40,000L ($23); it's open daily noon to 3pm and 7 to 9pm.

FREGENE

The fame of **Fregene**—a coastal city north of the Tiber and 24 miles from Rome—dates to the 1600s, when the land belonged to the Rospigliosi, a powerful Roman family. Pope Clement IX, a member of that family, planted a forest of pines that extends along the shoreline for 2½ miles and stands half a mile deep to protect the land from the strong winds of the Mediterranean. Today the pines make a dramatic backdrop for the resort's golden sands and luxurious villas. You can take a Civitavecchia-bound train from Rome's Stazione Termini to Fregene, the first stop. Or you can take the bus, which leaves from the Lepanto Metro stop and carries you to the center of Fregene.

Accommodations & Dining

La Conchiglia. Lungomare di Ponente 4, Fregene, 00050 Roma. ☎ **06/668-5385.** Fax 06/668-5385. 36 units. A/C MINIBAR TV TEL. 160,000–180,000L ($93–$104) double. Rates include breakfast. AE, DC, MC, V.

La Conchiglia means "The Shellfish"—an appropriate name for this hotel and restaurant right on the beach with views of the water and the pines. Built in 1934, the hotel features a circular lounge with built-in curving wall banquettes facing a cylindrical fireplace with a raised hearth. A resort aura is created by the large green plants. The bar in the cocktail lounge, which faces the terrace, is also circular. The guest rooms are comfortable and well furnished.

It's also possible to stop by just for a meal, and the food is good. Try, for example, spaghetti with lobster and grilled fish or one of many excellent meat dishes. Meals start at 50,000L ($29). The restaurant is in the garden and open daily 1 to 3pm and 8 to 10pm.

ETRUSCAN HISTORICAL SIGHTS
CERVETERI (CAERE)

As you walk through Rome's Etruscan Museum (Villa Giulia), you'll often see *Caere* written under a figure vase or sarcophagus. This is a reference to the nearby town known today as **Cerveteri,** one of Italy's great Etruscan cities, whose origins may go as far back as the 9th century B.C.

Of course, the Etruscan town has long since faded, but not the **Necropolis of Cerveteri** (☎ 06/994-0001). The effect is eerie; Cerveteri is often called a "city of the dead." When you go beneath some of the mounds, you'll discover the most striking feature—the tombs are like rooms in Etruscan homes. The main burial ground is the Necropolis of Banditacca. Of the graves thus far uncovered, none is finer than the **Tomba Bella** (or the Reliefs' Tomb), the burial ground of the Matuna family. Articles like utensils and even house pets were painted in stucco relief. Presumably these paintings were representations of items the dead family would need in the world beyond. The necropolis is open Tuesday to Sunday: May to September 9am to 6pm (October to April to 3:30pm). Admission is 8,000L ($4.65).

Relics from the necropolis are displayed at the **Museo Nazionale Cerite,** Piazza Santa Maria Maggiore (☎ 06/994-1354). The museum, housed within the ancient walls and crenellations of Ruspoldi Castle, is open Tuesday to Sunday 9am to 7pm. Admission is free.

You can reach Cerveteri by bus or car. If you're driving, head out Via Aurelia, northwest of Rome, for 28 miles. By public transport, take Metro Line A in Rome to the Lepanto stop; from Via Lepanto you can catch a Cotral bus (☎ 06/324-4724) to Cerveteri; the trip takes about an hour and costs 4,900L ($2.85). Once you're at Cerveteri, it's a 1¼-mile walk to the necropolis—follow the signs pointing the way.

TARQUINIA

If you wish to see tombs even more striking and more recently excavated than those at Cerveteri, go to **Tarquinia.** The medieval turrets and fortifications atop the rocky cliffs overlooking the sea seem to contradict the Etruscan name of Tarquinia. Actually, Tarquinia is the adopted name of the old medieval community of Corneto, in honor of the major Etruscan city that once stood nearby.

The main attraction in the town is the **Tarquinia National Museum,** Piazza Cavour (☎ 0776/856-036), devoted to Etruscan exhibits and sarcophagi excavated from the necropolis a few miles away. The museum is housed in the Palazzo Vitelleschi, a Gothic palace from the mid-15th century. Among the exhibits are gold jewelry, black vases with carved and painted bucolic scenes, and sarcophagi decorated with carvings of animals and relief figures of priests and military leaders. But the biggest attraction is in itself worth the ride from Rome—the almost life-size pair of winged horses from the pediment of a Tarquinian temple. The finish is worn here and there and the terra-cotta color shows through, but the relief stands as one of the greatest Etruscan masterpieces ever discovered. The museum is open Tuesday to Sunday 9am to 7pm and charges 8,000L ($4.65) admission.

A 5,000L ($2.90) admission admits you to the ✪ **Etruscan Necropolis** (☎ **0766/ 856-308**), covering more than 2½ miles of rough terrain near where the ancient Etruscan city once stood. Thousands of tombs have been discovered, some of which haven't been explored even today. Others, of course, were discovered by looters, but many treasures remain even though countless pieces were removed to museums and private collections. The paintings on the walls of the tombs have helped historians reconstruct the life of the Etruscans—a heretofore impossible feat without a written history. They depict feasting couples in vivid colors mixed from iron oxide, lapis lazuli dust, and charcoal. One of the oldest tombs (from the 6th century B.C.) depicts young men fishing while dolphins play and colorful birds fly high above. Many of the paintings convey an earthy, vigorous, sex-oriented life among the wealthy Etruscans. The tombs are generally open Tuesday to Sunday 9am to an hour before sunset (to 2pm November to March). You can reach the grave sites by taking a bus from the Barriera San Giusto to the Cimitero stop. Or try the 20-minute walk from the museum. Inquire at the museum for directions.

To reach Tarquinia by car, take Via Aurelia outside Rome and continue on the autostrada toward Civitavecchia. Bypass Civitavecchia and continue another 13 miles north until you see the exit signs for Tarquinia. As for public transport, going by train is preferred: A diretto train from Roma Ostiense station takes 50 minutes. Eight buses a day leave from the Via Lepanto stop in Rome for the 2-hour trip to the town of Barriera San Giusto, 1½ miles from Tarquinia. Bus schedules are available at the **tourist office** in Barriera San Giusto (☎ **0766/856-384**), open Monday to Saturday 8am to 2pm.

Florence: Birthplace of the Renaissance

6

Except for Venice, no other European city lives off its past the way Florence (Firenze) does. After all, it was the birthplace of the Renaissance, an amazing outburst of activity from the 14th to the 16th century that completely changed the Tuscan town. Under the benevolent eye (and purse) of the Medicis, Florence blossomed into an unrivaled repository of art and architecture treasures by geniuses like Botticelli, Brunelleschi, Cellini, Donatello, Fra Angelico, Ghiberti, Giotto, Leonardo, Michelangelo, and Raphael. Since the 19th century, it has been visited by seemingly half the world—wanting to see Michelangelo's *David*, Botticelli's "Venus on the Half Shell" (*Birth of Venus*), and Brunelleschi's dome.

At first glance, Florence may seem a bit foreboding and architecturally not the Gothic fantasy of lace Venice is. Many of its palazzi look like severe fortresses, as was the Medici style. They were built, after all, to keep foreign enemies at bay. These facades, though, however uninviting, mask treasures within, as the thousands of visitors who overrun the too-narrow streets know and appreciate. The locals both bemoan this crush and at the same time welcome it, because they know it puts food on the table. "It's the price we pay for fame," laments a local merchant. "The visitors have crowded our city and strained our facilities, but they make it possible for me to own a villa in Fiesole and take my children on vacation to San Remo every year."

The city fathers or mothers have been wise to keep the inner Renaissance core relatively free of modern architecture and polluting industry. Florence has industry, but it has been sent to the suburbs. The city is relatively clean and safe as Italian cities go, with far less crime than Rome and certainly far less than Naples. You can generally walk the narrow cobblestone streets at night unmolested, though caution is always advised.

A myth you mustn't believe—and it's heard more and more frequently—is that Florence is becoming the "Los Angeles of Italy." Perhaps the rumor got started because Florentines own the highest per capita number of cellular phones in Europe. That's because they're trying to keep up with the changing world, not to impress you with their current achievements. They know the only reason you're coming is to pay homage to their glorious past.

May and September are the ideal times to visit. The worst times are the week before and including Easter and June until the first week of September—Florence is literally overrun during these times, and the streets weren't designed for mass tourism. Temperatures in July and August hover in the 70s, dropping to a low of 45°F in December and January.

1 Essentials

ARRIVING

BY PLANE   If you're flying from North America, the best air connection is Rome, where you can board a domestic flight to the **Galileo Galilei Airport** at Pisa (☎ 050/500-707), 58 miles west of Florence. (You cannot fly directly from the States to this airport.) There's a shuttle train every hour or two (10 or 11am to 5 or 6pm) between the airport and Florence's Santa Maria Novella station; the trip takes a little over an hour and costs 8,000L ($4.65) one-way.

Florence's small airport, **Amerigo Vespucci** (☎ 055/30-615), is about 3 miles northwest of the city on Via del Termine, near the A11 autostrada. Many of the European airlines serve this airport, and it receives domestic flights from cities like Rome and Milan and international flights from cities like Brussels, Frankfurt, London, Munich, Nice, and Paris. ATAF bus no. 62 runs between the airport and the Santa Maria Novella rail station every 20 minutes, costing 1,500L ($9). The 15-minute taxi ride from the airport to the city should cost about 35,000L ($20).

Domestic air service is provided by **Alitalia,** Lungarno degli Acciaiuoli 10–12 in Florence (☎ 055/27-881).

BY TRAIN   Florence lies in the heart of Italy and is a major stop for Eurailpass holders. If you're coming north from Rome, count on a 2- to 3-hour trip, depending on your connection. Bologna is just an hour away by train and Venice 4 hours. The **Stazione Santa Maria Novella (S.M.N.),** on Piazza della Stazione (☎ 01478/88-088 for railway information), adjoins Piazza Santa Maria Novella, which boasts one of Florence's great churches. From here, most of the major hotels are within easy reach, either on foot or by taxi or bus. Facilities in the station include a currency exchange (open Monday to Saturday 8:20am to 6:30pm), a hotel booking service (see "Accommodations" later in this chapter), and a 24-hour luggage storage at the top of Track 16.

Some trains into Florence stop at the **Stazione Campo di Marte,** on the eastern side of Florence—however, it's worth avoiding. A 24-hour bus service (no. 91) runs between the two terminals.

BY BUS   Two long-distance bus lines service Florence: **SITA,** Viale Cadorna 103–105 (☎ 055/214-457), and **Lazzi Eurolines,** Piazza della Stazione 4–6 (☎ 055/215-155). SITA connects Florence with such Tuscan hill towns as Siena, Arezzo, Pisa, and San Gimignano, and Lazzi Eurolines provides service from such cities as Rome and Naples.

BY CAR   Florence, because of its central location, enjoys good autostrada connections with the rest of Italy, especially Rome and Bologna. Autostrada A1 connects Florence with both the north and the south. Florence lies 172 miles north of Rome, 65 miles west of Bologna, and 185 miles south of Milan. Bologna is about an hour away by car, and Rome is 3 hours away. The Tyrrhenian coast is only an hour from Florence on A11 heading west.

Use a car only to get to Florence. Don't even contemplate using it once here, as most of central Florence is closed to all vehicles except those of local residents.

VISITOR INFORMATION

Contact the **Azienda Promozione Turistica,** Via A. Manzoni 16 (☎ 055/234-6284; fax 055/234-6286), open Monday to Saturday 8:30am to 1:30pm. Another helpful office handling data about Florence and Tuscany is at Via Cavour 1R (☎ 055/290-832; fax 055/276-0383), open Monday to Saturday 8:15am to 7:15pm and Sunday 8:15am to 1:45pm. Yet another helpful information office is just south of Piazza Santa Croce at Borgo Santa Croce 29R (☎ 055/23-40-444), open Monday to Saturday 8:15am to 7:15pm; Sunday hours hadn't been decided at press time. There's also a small visitor (Uffizio Informazioni Turistiche) office inside the main train terminal.

CITY LAYOUT

Florence is a city designed for walking, with all the major sights in a concentrated area. The only problem is that the sidewalks in summer are almost unbearably crowded.

The *centro storico* (historic center) is split by the **Arno River,** which usually is serene but can at times turn ferocious with floodwaters. The major part of Florence, certainly its historic core with most of the monuments, lies on the north ("right") side of the river. But the "left" side isn't devoid of attractions. Many visitors frequent the **Oltrarno** ("across the Arno") for its tantalizing trattorie; they also maintain that the shopping there is less expensive. Even the most hurried of you will surely want to cross the Arno to see the Pitti Palace with its many art treasures and walk through the Giardini di Boboli, a series of formal gardens, the most impressive in Florence. In addition, you'll want to cross over to check out the panoramic views of the city from Piazzale Michelangiolo—especially breathtaking at sunset; to reach it, follow Viale Michelangiolo up the flank of the hill (one easy way to go is to take bus no. 13 from the train station).

The Arno is spanned by eight bridges, of which the **Ponte Vecchio (Old Bridge),** lined with overhanging jewelry stores, is the most celebrated and most central. Many of these bridges were ancient structures until the Nazis, in a hopeless last-ditch effort, senselessly destroyed them in their "defense" of Florence in 1944. With tenacity, Florence rebuilt its bridges, using pieces from the destroyed structures whenever possible. The **Ponte Santa Trínita** is the second-most important bridge. It leads to **Via dei Tornabuoni,** the right bank's most important shopping street (don't look for bargains, however). At the Ponte Vecchio you can walk, again on the right bank of the Arno, along Via por Santa Maria, which becomes Via Calimala. This leads you into **Piazza della Repubblica,** a commercial district known for its cafes.

From here, you can take Via Roma, which leads directly into **Piazza di San Giovanni,** where you'll find the baptistery and its neighboring sibling, the larger **Piazza del Duomo,** with the world-famous cathedral and Giotto bell tower. From the far western edge of Piazza del Duomo you can take Via del Proconsolo south to **Piazza della Signoria,** to see the landmark Palazzo Vecchio and its sculpture-filled Loggia della Signoria.

High in the olive-planted hills overlooking Florence is the ancient town of **Fiesole,** with Etruscan and Roman ruins and a splendid cathedral.

FINDING AN ADDRESS   Florence has two street-numbering systems—red (*rosso*) or blue or black (*blu* or *nero*) numbers. Red numbers identify commercial enterprises, such as shops and restaurants. Blue or black numbers identify office buildings, private homes, apartment houses, or hotels. Renumbering without the color system is on the horizon, though no one seems exactly certain when it will be implemented. In this chapter, red-numbered addresses are indicated by an "R" following the building number, as in "39R."

Since street numbers are chaotic, it's better to get a cross street or some landmark if you're looking for an address along a long boulevard.

STREET MAPS   At the very least, arm yourself with a map from the tourist office (see "Visitor Information"). But if you'd like to see Florence in any depth—particularly those little side streets—buy a **Falk map** (indexes are included), which gives all the streets. Falk maps are available at all bookstores and at most newsstands.

NEIGHBORHOODS IN BRIEF

Florence isn't divided into neighborhoods the way many cities are. Most locals refer to either the left bank or the right bank of the Arno and that's about it, unless they head out of town for the immediate environs, such as Fiesole. The following selection of "neighborhoods"—most grouped around a palace, church, or square—is therefore rather arbitrary.

This section will give you some idea of where you may want to stay and where the major attractions are.

Centro   Called simply that by Florentines, **Centro** could include all the historic heart of Florence, but mostly the term is used to describe the area southwest of the Duomo. This district isn't as important as it used to be, as Piazza della Signoria (below) now attracts more visitors. Centro's heyday was in the 1800s, when it was filled with narrow medieval streets that were torn down to make a grander city center. Lost forever were great homes of the Medicis and the Sacchettis, among others. **Piazza della Repubblica,** though faded, is still lively day and night with its celebrated cafes, like **Giubbe Rosse** (1888) and **Caffè Gilli** (1733). Centro's most fashionable artery is **Via dei Tournabuoni,** the city's most elegant shopping street. Pause on this street at no. 83, **La Giacosa,** for a *battistero* (pastry) before continuing to survey the palazzi and the high-quality but lethally priced merchandise.

Piazza del Duomo   In the heart of Florence, **Piazza del Duomo** and its surrounding area are dominated by the tricolored **Duomo,** site of the former local grain and hay markets. One of the largest buildings in the Christian world, this cathedral is exceeded only by St. Peter's in Rome. You come on it unexpectedly because the surrounding buildings weren't torn down to give it breathing room. Capped by Brunelleschi's dome—an amazing architectural feat—the structure now dominates the skyline. Every visitor flocks here to see not only the Duomo but also the neighboring *campanile* (bell tower), one of Italy's most beautiful, and the **baptistery** across the way. Now consecrated to St. John the Baptist, the baptistery was originally a pagan temple honoring Mars. Its doors are among the jewels of Renaissance sculpture. Also in this neighborhood is the **Museo dell'Opera del Duomo,** a sculpture haven that includes some of the most important works of Donatello. A few touristy hotels and trattorie are found around the Duomo.

Piazza della Signoria   The core of pre-Renaissance Florence, this section—**Piazza della Signoria** in particular—has been the site of many dramatic moments, including Savonarola's "bonfire of the vanities," in which Florentines burned precious items like jewelry and paintings to purify themselves. The surrounding narrow streets from the Middle Ages were the former stamping ground of Dante and other legendary Florentines. Today this heavily visited square is home to the **Loggia dei Lanzi,** with Cellini's *Perseus* holding up a beheaded Medusa, Florence's most photographed original statue still outside. Michelangelo's *David* on the square is a copy, the original having been moved inside to protect it from the elements. To the south are the **Galleria degli Uffizi** and the **Palazzo Vecchio.**

Piazza Santa Maria Novella & the Train Station   On the northwestern edge of central Florence is the large Piazza Santa Maria Novella, with its church of the same name, founded in the 13th century by the Dominicans. Completed in 1360, it's filled with admirable frescoes by Domenico Ghirlandaio and a crucifix by Brunelleschi. Donatello allegedly was so taken with the crucifix that on seeing it he dropped a basket of eggs he was carrying. This area isn't all art and culture, however. Northwest of Santa Maria Novella is the city's busiest section, centered at **Piazza della Stazione,** where the **Stazione della Santa Maria Novella** is located. Like all rail stations in Italy, it's surrounded by budget hotels, some of dubious quality. Leading off of **Piazza dell'Unita Italiana,** Via del Melarancio goes a short distance east to **San Lorenzo,** the first cathedral of Florence. Beyond San Lorenzo is **Piazza Madonna degli Aldobrandini,** one of the more forgettable squares were it not the entrance to the **Medici Chapels.** Because it is, thousands can be seen flocking here to see Michelangelo's tombs, whose allegorical figures of *Day* and *Night* are among the most famous sculptures of all time. Southwest of Piazza Santa Maria Novella, toward the Arno, is **Piazza Ognissanti,** a fashionable (albeit car-clogged) Renaissance square opening onto the river. On this square are two of the city's most legendary hotels: the **Grand** and the **Excelsior.**

Piazza San Marco   Though it has none of the grandeur of the square of the same name in Venice, **Piazza San Marco** and its surroundings on the northern fringe of Centro are nevertheless one of the most important in Florence—centered around its church, now the **Museo di San Marco.** Located in a former Dominican monastery, the museum houses a collection of the greatest works of Fra Angelico, who decorated the walls of the monks' cells with edifying scenes. This quarter is also overrun by visitors, most rushing to the **Galleria dell'Accademia** on Via Ricasoli to see the monumental figure of *David* (1501 to 1504) by Michelangelo. A perfect example of the sculptor's humanism, it's the most reproduced statue in the world. Other area highlights are **Piazza della Santissima Annunziata,** Florence's most beautiful, graced by an equestrian statue of Ferdinand I de' Medici by Bologna. The square is also the setting for **Santanissima Annunziata,** the church of the Servite Order, built by Michelozzo in the 15th century.

Piazza Santa Croce   This section and its **Piazza Santa Croce** is in the southeastern part of the old town, near the Arno, and is dominated by the Gothic church of **Santa Croce** (or Holy Cross), completed in 1442. Once the scene of jousts and festivals, even *calcio* (a local game of football), the piazza in time became the headquarters of the Franciscans, who established a firm base there in 1218. The area retains little of its former prestige but remains a much-visited part of Florence, though not as trodden as the areas above. Today the church is the virtual Pantheon of Florence, containing the tombs of Michelangelo and Machiavelli, among others. A little distance to the north of Santa Croce is **Casa Buonarroti,** on Via Ghibellina, which Michelangelo acquired for his nephew. Today it's a museum with a collection of works by Michelangelo, mainly drawings, gathered by his nephew. From here you can follow Via Buonarroti to **Piazza dei Ciompi,** a lively square unknown to many visitors; it's filled with stalls peddling secondhand goods. Look for old coins, books, and even antique Italian uniforms.

Ponte Vecchio   Southwest of Piazza della Signoria is the **Ponte Vecchio (Old Bridge)** area. The oldest of Florence's bridges, it's flanked by jewelry stores and will carry you to the Oltrarno. This has always been a strategic crossing place, even when it was a stone bridge. In the Middle Ages it was the center for leather craftspeople, fishmongers, and butchers, but over the years jewelers' shops have replaced these lessglamorous industries. **Corridoio Vasariano** runs the length of the bridge above the shops—built by Vasari in just 5 months. Actually, the Ponte Vecchio was almost destroyed on the night of August 4, 1944, when the Nazi hierarchy gave orders to blow up all the bridges along the Arno. Even though mined, the Ponte Vecchio was miraculously spared. Though one of the most congested parts of Florence, this area is on every visitor's itinerary.

Across the Arno   The "left bank" of the Arno River, known as the **Oltrarno,** is home to the **Palazzo Pitti,** with its picture gallery and **Giardini di Boboli,** Massacio's frescoes in the church of **Santa Maria del Carmine,** artisans' workshops, some good restaurants, and the postcard panorama of Florence and its dome from **Piazzale Michelangiolo.** Even those visitors who stay glued to the right bank cross the Arno to visit the Pitti Palace. It's outranked only by the Uffizi in its treasure trove of art. When the crowds at the Pitti get you down, you can always escape to the lush greenery of the Boboli. At the top of the gardens is an elegant fortress known as **Forte Belvedere,** built between 1590 and 1595. It affords one of the most panoramic views of Florence and is well worth the climb. The center of this district is **Piazza Santo Spirito,** an animated square shaded by trees and a former stamping ground of the Brownings, who lived there after their secret marriage in 1847 until the death of Elizabeth in 1861.

Fiesole   Though a town in its own right, medieval **Fiesole** is treated by some as a suburb of Florence. An ancient Etruscan town on a hill overlooking Florence, it has panoramic views of the city of the Renaissance and of the Arno Valley. It was founded by the Etruscans, perhaps as early as the 7th century B.C. Its center is the large **Piazza Mino da Fiesole.** The fresh, clean air of Fiesole makes it an ideal retreat when the heart of Florence is sultry and overrun with visitors. There are hotels here, as well as trattorie, or you can visit to see the sights, including the **Convent of San Fancesco** and the **Duomo,** or to just take in the view.

2 Getting Around

Because Florence is so compact, walking is the ideal way—and at times the only way, because of numerous pedestrian zones—to get around. In theory at least, pedestrians have the right of way at uncontrolled zebra crossings, but don't count on that should you encounter a speeding Vespa.

Beware: Some of the sidewalks are less than 3 feet wide, summer brings dense crowds, and traffic is hazardous. Though the general public can't drive in Florence, taxis, locals with parking permits, and endless motor scooters can and do. Also wear strong, sturdy shoes before facing the cobbled or flagstone streets.

BY BUS

If you plan to use public buses, you must buy your ticket before boarding, but for 1,500L (90¢) you can ride on any public bus for a total of 70 minutes. A 24-hour pass is 6,000L ($3.50). You can buy bus tickets at *tabacchi* (tobacconists) and newsstands. Once on board, you must validate your ticket in the box near the rear door or you stand to be fined 76,000L ($44), no excuses accepted. The local **bus station** (which serves as the terminal for ATAF city buses) is at Piazza della Stazione (☎ 055/ 5650-222), behind the train station.

Bus routes are posted at bus stops, but the numbers of routes can change overnight, because of sudden repair work going on at one of the ancient streets—perhaps a water main broke overnight and caused flooding. We recently found that a bus route map printed only 1 week prior was already out of date. Therefore, if you're dependent on bus transport, you'll need to inquire that day for the exact number of the vehicle you wish to board.

BY TAXI

You can find taxis at stands at nearly all the major squares. Rates are expensive, so you should avoid them if you can. The charge is 1,350L (80¢) per kilometer, with a 6,000L ($3.50) minimum. If you need a **radio taxi,** call ☎ **055/4390** or 055/4798.

BY BICYCLE & MOTOR SCOOTER

Bicycles and motor scooters, if you avoid the whizzing traffic, are two other practical ways of getting around. **Alinari,** near the rail station at Via Guelfa 85R (☎ **055/ 280-500**), rents bikes for 4,000L to 5,000L ($2.30 to $2.90) per hour or 20,000L to 30,000L ($12 to $17) per day, depending on the model. Also available are small-engined, rather loud motor scooters renting for 9,000L ($5) per hour or 45,000L ($26) per day. Renters must be 18 or over and must leave a passport, driver's license, and the number of a valid credit card. Alinari is open Monday to Saturday 9am to 1pm and 3 to 7:30pm and Sunday (March to October) 10am to 1pm and 3 to 7:30pm.

BY GUIDED TOUR

If you have a limited amount of time or want to get an overall view before exploring on your own, many companies run guided bus tours of the main sights. The two virtually indistinguishable big names are **American Express** (☎ 055/50-981) and **SitaSightseeing** (☎ 055/214-721). They run morning tours of the major sights and separate afternoon tours of the top secondary sights, costing 55,000L ($32) per person for each half-day tour, museum admissions included. Both companies also run afternoon tours to Pisa (50,000L/$29) and the Chianti (60,000L/$35) and an all-day trip combining Siena and San Gimignano (86,000L/$50). To arrange any other kind of guided tour, visit the **Ufficio Guide Turistiche** (☎ 055/2302-283) at Via Roma 4.

BY CAR

Driving a car in Florence is hopeless—not only because of the snarled traffic and the maze of one-way streets but also because much of what you've come to see is in a pedestrian zone. If you arrive by car, don't even think of parking aboveground. Instead, look for prominently posted blue signs with the letter *P* that will lead you to the nearest garage. If your hotel doesn't have its own, someone on the staff will direct you to the nearest one or will arrange valet parking. Garage fees average 35,000L to 40,000L ($20 to $23), though vans or large luxury cars may cost as much as 50,000L ($29).

The most centrally located garages are the **International Garage,** Via Palazzuolo 29 (☎ 055/282-386); **Garage La Stazione,** Via Alamanni (☎ 055/284-768); **Auto-parking SLL,** Via Fiesolana 19 (☎ 055/247-7871); and **Garage Anglo-Americano,** Via dei Barbadori 5 (☎ 055/214-418). If these are full, you can almost always find a space at the **Garage Porte Nuova,** Via Portenuove (☎ 055/333-355).

You will, however, need a car to explore the surrounding countryside of Tuscany in any depth. Car-rental agencies include **Avis,** Borgo Ognissanti 128R (☎ 055/ 213-629); **Budget,** Via Finiguerra 31R (☎ 055/287-161); and **Hertz,** at the Amerigo Vespucci Airport (☎ 055/307-370).

FAST FACTS: Florence

American Express   The office is at Via Dante Alighieri 20–22R (☎ 055/ 50-981), open Monday to Friday 9am to 5:30pm and Saturday 9am to 12:30pm.

Business Hours   Mid-June to mid-September, most **shops** and **businesses** are open Monday to Friday 9am to 1pm and 4 to 8pm. Off-season hours, in general, are Monday 3:30 to 7:30pm and Tuesday to Saturday 9am to 1pm and 3:30 to 7:30pm.

Consulates   The **U.S. Consulate** is at Lungarno Amerigo Vespucci 38 (☎ 055/239-8276), open Monday to Friday 9am to 12:30pm. The **U.K. Consulate** is at Lungarno Corsini 2 (☎ 055/284-133), near Piazza Santa Trínita, open Monday to Friday 9:30am to 12:30pm and 2:30 to 4:30pm. Citizens of other English-speaking countries, including **Canada, Australia,** and **New Zealand,** should contact their diplomatic representatives in Rome (see chapter 4).

Currency Exchange   Local banks in Florence grant the best rates. Most banks are open Monday to Friday 8:30am to 1:30pm and 2:45 to 3:45pm. The tourist office (see "Visitor Information," earlier in this chapter) exchanges money at official rates when banks are closed and on holidays, but a commission is often charged. You can also go to the Ufficio Informazione booth at the rail station, open daily 7:30am to 7:40pm. American Express (above) also exchanges money. One of the best places to exchange currency is the post office (below).

Dentists/Doctors   For a list of English-speaking doctors or dentists, consult your consulate or contact **Tourist Medical Service,** Via Lorenzo il Magnifico 59 (☎ 055/475-411). Visits without an appointment are possible only Monday to Friday 11am to noon and 5 to 6pm and Saturday 11am to noon. After hours, an answering service gives names and phone numbers of dentists and doctors who are on duty.

Emergencies   For fire, call ☎ **115;** for an ambulance, call ☎ **118;** for the police, ☎ **113;** and for road service, ☎ **116.**

Hospitals   Call the **General Hospital of Santa Maria Nuova,** Piazza Santa Maria Nuova 1 (☎ 055/27-581).

Luggage Storage   This is available at **Stazione Santa Maria Novella,** in the center of the city on Piazza della Stazione (☎ 055/23-52-190). It's open daily 4:15am to 1:30am. The cost is 5,000L ($2.90) per bag per 12 hours.

Pharmacies   **Farmacia Molteni,** Via Calzaiuoli 7R (☎ 055/215-472), is open 24 hours.

Police   Dial ☎ **113** in an emergency. English-speaking foreigners who want to see and talk to the police should go to the **Ufficio Stranieri station** at Via Zara 2 (☎ 055/49-771), where English-speaking personnel are available daily 9am to 2pm.

Post Office   The **Central Post Office** is at Via Pellicceria 3, off Piazza della Repubblica (☎ 055/277-4322 for English-speaking operators, or 055/ 277-4282 or 055/277-4283), open Monday to Saturday 8:15am to 7pm. You can buy stamps and telephone cards at Windows 21 and 22. If you want your mail sent to Italy general delivery (*fermo posta*), have it sent in care of this post office (use the 50100 Firenze postal code). You can pick mail up at Windows 23 and 24. A telegram, telex, and fax office on the second floor is open Monday to Saturday 8:15am to 7pm (you can also send telegrams 24 hours a day by phoning ☎ 186). A foreign exchange office is open Monday to Friday 8:15am to 6pm; you can also exchange money (notes only) at ATMs on the ground floor daily

Country & City Codes

The **country code** for Italy is **39**. The **city code** for Florence is **055;** you must now use this code every time you call Florence: if you're calling from outside Italy, if you're calling from another city within Italy, and even when you're calling within Florence.

8:15am to 7pm. If you want to send packages of up to 20kg, go to the rear of the building and enter at Piazza Davantati 4.

Rest Rooms   Public toilets are found in most galleries, museums, bars and cafes, and restaurants, as well as bus, train, and air terminals. Usually they're designated as *WC* (water closet) or *donne* (women) or *uomini* (men). The most confusing designation is *signori* (gentlemen) and *signore* (ladies), so watch that final *i* and *e!*

Safety   Violent crimes are rare in Florence; most crime consists mainly of pickpockets who frequent crowded tourist centers, such as corridors of the Uffizi Galleries. Members of group tours who cluster together are often singled out as victims. Car thefts are relatively common: Don't leave your luggage in an unguarded car, even if it's locked in the trunk. Women should be especially careful in avoiding purse snatchers, some of whom grab a purse while whizzing by on a Vespa, often knocking the woman down. Documents like passports and extra money are better stored in safes at your hotel if available.

Taxes   A **value-added tax (IVA)** is added to all consumer products and most services, including those at hotels and restaurants. The tax is refundable if you spend more than 300,000L ($174) at any one store.

Telephone   Public pay phones accept either coins (100L, 200L, or 500L coins) or a phonecard (sometimes only one or the other). The latter, a *carta telefonica* (or scheda telefonica), is available at tabacchi and bars in 5,000L ($2.80), 10,000L ($6), and 15,000L ($9) denominations and can be used for local or international calls. Break off the perforated corner of the card before using it. Local phone calls cost 200L (12¢), enough to put you in contact with AT&T, MCI, or Sprint's direct-dialing international operators (below). To make a call, lift the receiver, insert a coin or card, and dial. You may find old pay phones that still accept special tokens, gettoni, which you'll sometimes receive in bars in exchange for change, though by now the system is rather extinct.

You can place long-distance and international phone calls at the Telecom office north of the Duomo at Via Cavour 21R (open daily 8am to 9:45pm). Several countries also have direct operator service, allowing callers to use AT&T or MCI calling cards or call collect (reverse charges) from almost any phone including pay phones.

To make collect calls to the United States, or with your calling card, phone AT&T's USA Direct at ☎ **06/172-10-11,** MCI's Call USA at ☎ **06/172-10-22,** or US Sprint at ☎ **06/172-18-77.** You can also call ☎ **06/172-10-01** for Canada, ☎ **06/172-10-61** for Australia, and ☎ **06/172-00-44** for the United Kingdom.

Transit Information   For international flights from Galileo Galilei Airport, call ☎ **050/500-707;** for domestic flights at Amerigo Vespucci Airport, call ☎ **055/30-615;** for rail information, dial ☎ **055/278-785;** for long-distance bus information, call ☎ **055/483-651;** and for city buses, dial ☎ **055/56-501.**

3 Accommodations

For sheer charm and luxury, Florence's hotels are among the finest in Europe, and many of the grand old villas and palaces have been converted into hotels. There aren't too many cities where you can find a 15th- or 16th-century palace—tastefully decorated and most comfortable—rated a second-class pensione. Florence is equipped with hotels in all price ranges and with widely varying standards, comfort, service, and efficiency.

However, during summer there simply aren't enough rooms to meet the demand, and if you arrive without a reservation you may not find a place for the night and will have to drive to nearby Montecatini, where you'll always stand a good chance of securing accommodations.

In Florence, the most desirable—and often most expensive—place to stay in terms of shopping, nightlife, sightseeing, and restaurants is the historic heart on the Arno's right bank, especially in Centro and around the Duomo and Piazza della Signoria. Yes, this area is much too touristy, but staying here is a lot better than staying on the outskirts—inadequate public transport makes commuting difficult. Driving into the center is impossible, because of the heavy traffic and because major districts are pedestrian-only zones.

The cheapest lodgings in Centro are around the rail station; these are also the least desirable, of course—with a few notable exceptions. The area directly around the Termini and Santa Maria Novella, though generally safe during the day, is the center of major drug dealing late at night and should be avoided then. This area isn't all budget lodgings, however; also here is Piazza Ognissanti—south of Piazza Santa Maria Novella toward the Arno—one of Florence's most fashionable squares and the home of the city's two most famous hotels.

Also in the historic center, but less tourist trodden and a bit more tranquil, is the area around Piazza San Marco and the University quarter.

Once you cross the Arno, lodgings are much scarcer, though there are places to stay, including some *pensioni*. In general, prices are lower across the Arno, and you'll be near one of the major attractions, the Pitti Palace.

Many luxury hotels exist on the outskirts of Florence, as do cheaper boardinghouses. Again, these are acceptable alternatives if you don't mind the commute. As a final option, consider lodging in Fiesole, where it's cooler and much more tranquil. Bus no. 7 runs back and forth between Fiesole and Centro.

If you should arrive without a reservation and don't want to wander around town on your own looking for a room, go in person (instead of calling) to the **Consorizio ITA office** (☎ 055/282-893) in the rail terminal at Piazza della Stazione, open daily 9am to 9pm. The Consorizio ITA charges a small fee for the service and collects the first night's room charge.

IN CENTRO
VERY EXPENSIVE

✪ **Hotel Helvetia & Bristol.** Via dei Pescioni 2, 50123 Firenze. ☎ **055/287-814.** Fax 055/288-353. 65 units. A/C MINIBAR TV TEL. 420,000L–540,000L ($244–$313) double; 680,000–1,400,000L ($394–$812) suite. Breakfast 34,100L ($20). AE, DC, MC, V. Parking 40,000L ($23). Bus: 6, 11, 36, 37, or 68.

This hotel is in the most elegant part of Florence, a few steps from the Duomo between Via dei Tornabuoni and Via degli Strozzi and near Piazza Santa Trinita. It was built in the late 19th century and once attracted the likes of Luigi Pirandello, Giorgio De Chirico, and Enrico Fermi, a well as Eleonora Duse and her lover,

Gabriele D'Annunzio. Following a massive restoration, it reopened in 1989 and has reclaimed a lot of that old glory; it's rivaled only by the Regency (below). The Helvetia & Bristol lacks the Regency's modern flair, however, and is somber, with draped windows, tasseled chairs, 15th-century paintings, and regal period furnishings. Strict attention was paid to preserving its original architectural details. The guest rooms come in about three sizes—from extremely generous to cramped. Some of the better rooms have whirlpool tubs.

Dining: The first-class Giardino d'Inverno (Winter Garden) was a gathering spot for Florentine intellectuals in the 1920s, with an 18th-century–style open gallery. It's now a cocktail bar serving light food. The main dining room, the Bristol, serves deluxe Tuscan cuisine (dinner only).

Amenities: Room service, baby-sitting, laundry, valet, car-rental desk, secretarial service, facilities for the disabled.

Savoy Hotel. Piazza della Repubblica 7, 50123 Firenze. ☎ **055/283-313.** Fax 055/ 284-840. www.Italyhotel.com/hotelm/3839.html. E-mail: savoy@florenceallegro.it. 98 units. A/C MINIBAR TV TEL. 450,000–530,000L ($261–$307) double; from 1,030,000L ($597) suite. Rates include breakfast. AE, DC, MC, V. Parking 45,000–55,000L ($26–$32). Bus: 22, 36, or 37.

Ranking after (a long way after) both the Grand and the Excelsior (below), the five-star Savoy stands in the clamorous commercial center/historic district, an area filled with fine stores and just a 5-minute walk from the rail station. The dignified Savoy, built in 1890, has a buff-colored facade with neoclassical trim. The predictably upper-class interior includes potted plants, period art, patterned carpeting, and coffered ceilings. The guest rooms boast traditional Italian styling, though the pink-and-black marble baths have more style than the rather somber rooms.

Dining: The hotel's elegant Tuscan restaurant features both a regional and an international cuisine. There's also a bar area with frescoed walls reminiscent of a trompe-l'oeil view from an 18th-century balcony.

Amenities: Room service, baby-sitting, laundry, valet, limited facilities for the disabled.

MODERATE

Hotel Calzaiuoli. Via dei Calzaiuoli, 50122 Firenze. ☎ **055/212-456.** Fax 055/268-310. 45 units. A/C MINIBAR TV TEL. 300,000L ($174) double. Rates include breakfast. AE, DC, MC, V. Parking 45,000L ($26). Bus: 22, 36, or 37.

Midway between the Duomo and the Uffizi, this hotel has one of the city's most desirable locations, as the major attractions lie virtually on its doorstep. Though the building is old (it was a home in the 1800s) and the location historic, the interior has been completely modernized in a severe contemporary style. Its Pietra Serena staircase remains, however. The rooms are simple but comfortable, with functional and efficient pieces. Some of the furnishings are a bit tattered, but grace notes include the patterned carpeting and painted friezes (lucky guests get a room with a view of the Duomo's cupola).

Pensione Pendini. Via degli Strozzi 2, 50123 Firenze. ☎ **055/211-170.** Fax 055/281-807. www.italyhotel.com/firenze/pendini/pendini.html. E-mail: pendini@dada.it. 42 units. TEL. 250,000L ($145) double. AE, DC, MC, V. Rates include breakfast. Parking 35,000–40,000L ($20–$23). Bus: 22, 36, or 37.

Opened in 1879, the family-owned and -run Pendini offers a distinguished but faded setting on the fourth floor of an arcaded building. Your room may overlook the active Piazza della Repubblica or front an inner courtyard (more peaceful). Brothers David and Emmanuele Abolaffio have brought renewed vitality here since their takeover in 1994. They're even rejuvenating the once stale bathrooms. The all-purpose lounge is

Florence Accommodations

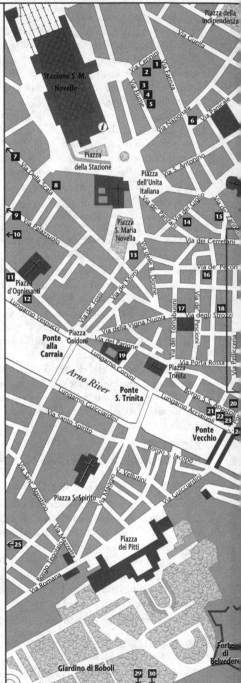

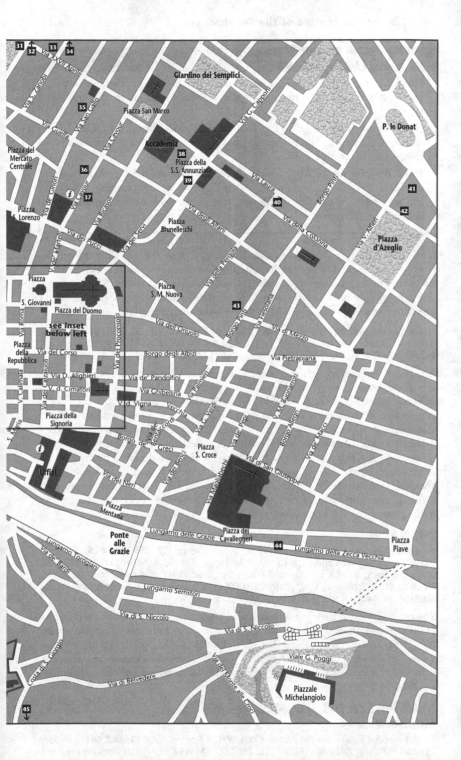

ⓗ Family-Friendly Hotels

Hotel Casci *(see p. 212)*   This inexpensive gem has a great location in the historic district, and many of its rooms are rented as triples and quads, ideal for families.

Hotel Nuova Italia *(see p. 210)*   Families get special discounts at this 17th-century building near the rail station, and the hotel offers some very spacious rooms suitable for large broods.

Hotel Belletini *(see p. 209)*   Young sisters Marzia and Gina and their family provide a cozy historic atmosphere at the Belletini, which is centrally located and reasonably priced. The staff is also very helpful with newcomers who are unfamiliar with Florence.

furnished family style with a piano and card tables. The breakfast salon, a redecorated large room inside one of the arcades, offers a view of the whole of Via degli Strozzi. All the rooms are soundproof, and some have quite a lot of character, with reproduction antiques. The bar/lounge is open 24 hours. The Pendini isn't for everyone, but it's one of our long-enduring favorites. Breakfast is the only meal served.

Hotel Tornabuoni Beacci. Via dei Tornabuoni 3, 50123 Firenze. ☎ **055/212-645.** Fax 055/283-594. 28 units. A/C MINIBAR TV TEL. 250,000–300,000L ($145–$174) double. Rates include breakfast. AE, DC, MC, V. Parking 38,000L ($22). Bus: 6, 11, 36, 37, or 68.

The Tornabuoni Beacci, near the Arno and Piazza Santa Trínita on the principal shopping street, occupies the three top floors of a 16th-century Strozzi family palazzo. All its public rooms have been furnished in an old Florentine style, with bowls of flowers, parquet floors, a formal fireplace, old paintings, murals, and rugs. Though it still has an aura of old-fashioned gentility, the hotel was recently renovated, with more air-conditioning added. The roof terrace is for late-afternoon drinks or breakfast; in summer, dinner, typically Florentine and Italian dishes, is also served here. The view of the nearby Bellosguardo hills, churches, towers, and rooftops is worth experiencing. The guest rooms are moderately well furnished but worn. Top-floor rooms, though a bit cramped, open onto views of the rooftops. The grace note of the whole place is a cozy reading room with a 1600s tapestry.

INEXPENSIVE

Pensione Bretagna. Lungarno Corsini 6, 50123 Firenze. ☎ **055/289-618.** Fax 055/289-619. www.dbweb.agora.stm.it/market/bretagna. E-mail: hotelpens.bretagna@agora.stm.it. 18 units, 9 with bathroom. TV TEL. 145,000L ($84) double without bathroom, 155,000L ($90) double with bathroom; 210,000L ($122) triple with bathroom. Rates include breakfast. AE, MC, V. Parking 30,000L ($17). Bus: B, C, or 9.

The centrally located Bretagna is in an early Renaissance palace that was the residence of Louis Napoléon in the 1820s, though it's rather basic and simply furnished today. It's a good cost-conscious choice, though, and is run by a helpful staff, most of whom speak English. The guest rooms are rather plain, but the public rooms are impressive, with gilded stucco work, painted ceilings, fireplaces, and a balcony overlooking the Arno.

NEAR PIAZZA DEL DUOMO
MODERATE

Grand Hotel Cavour. Via del Proconsolo 3, 50122 Firenze. ☎ **055/282-461.** Fax 055/218-955. 92 units. A/C MINIBAR TV TEL. 260,000L ($151) double. Rates include breakfast. AE, DC, MC, V. Parking from 40,000L ($23). Bus: 14, 23, or 71.

Opposite the Bargello Museum, between Via del Corso and Via Dante Alighieri, this 13th-century palace stands on one of Florence's busiest and noisiest streets, which even double-glazed windows can't blot out. It once belonged to the Cerchi family, and in the lounge you can see where the courtyard was laid out. The coved main lounge, with its frescoed ceiling and crystal chandelier, is of special interest, as is the old chapel, now used as a dining room (the altar and confessional are still there). The guest rooms are traditionally styled and comfortable but a little too claustrophobic. The roof terrace offers a panoramic sweep over the Duomo, Palazzo Vecchio, and more. A refined Tuscan cuisine is served in the hotel's rather staid restaurant honoring Beatrice in its name. Laundry and baby-sitting are available, as are facilities for the disabled.

NEAR PIAZZA SANTA MARIA NOVELLA & THE TRAIN STATION
VERY EXPENSIVE

Grand Hotel. Piazza Ognissanti 1, 50123 Firenze. ☎ **800/325-3589** in the U.S. and Canada, or 055/288-781. Fax 055/217-400. 107 units. A/C MINIBAR TV TEL. 750,000–825,000L ($435–$479) double; from 1,200,000–2,420,000L ($696–$1,404) suite. Breakfast 34,000L ($20). AE, DC, MC, V. Parking from 50,000L ($29). Bus: B, C, or 9.

The Grand is a bastion of luxury, with elaborate belle epoque lounges. After a long slumber, the hotel was restored to some of its former grandeur when ITT Sheraton purchased the CIGA chain. It's across from the Excelsior (below), which is more luxurious with more facilities. Neither the Grand nor the Excelsior, though among Florence's top three or four hotels, is as exclusive as the Regency (below). A hotel of history and tradition, the Grand was once one of the greatest hotels of Europe when it was known as Grand Hotel Royal de la Paix. Its rooms and suites have a refined elegance, the most desirable overlooking the Arno. Each contains silks, brocades, and real or reproduction antiques. All rooms are meant—at least vaguely—to evoke 15th-century Florence.

Dining/Diversions: A highlight is the restored Winter Garden, an enclosed court lined with arches where regional and seasonal specialties are served along with an array of international dishes. Guests gather at night in the Fiorino Bar to listen to piano music.

Amenities: Room service, baby-sitting, laundry/valet, currency exchange, facilities for the disabled.

Grand Hotel Villa Medici. Via il Prato 42, 50123 Firenze. ☎ **055/238-1331.** Fax 055/238-1336. www.venere.it/firenze/villa_medici.html. E-mail: sina@italyhotel.com. 99 units. A/C MINIBAR TV TEL. 490,000–680,000L ($284–$394) double; 950,000–1,050,000L ($551–$609) suite. Breakfast 33,000L ($20). AE, CB, DC, MC, V. Parking 45,000–60,000L ($26–$35). Bus: 9, 13, 16, 17, or 26.

This old-time favorite is an 18th-century Medici palace 2 blocks southwest of the train station. In general, this hotel appeals more to tradition-oriented Europeans than to Americans, who may want more up-to-date facilities. Out back is a private garden (not Florence's finest), with a modest pool. The most peaceful rooms front the garden; however, during the day there's noise from the convent school next door. The rooms are traditionally and often handsomely furnished, yet rather cramped. The bathrooms boast thick towels and hair dryers. We prefer the accommodations on the sixth floor, as they open onto terraces. The staff is one of the best trained in Florence.

Dining: The Lorenzo de' Medici serves both international and Florentine cuisine. The restaurant is graced with marble pilasters and illuminated by Murano chandeliers, but the cuisine is only standard.

Amenities: Room service, baby-sitting, laundry/valet, cleaning/pressing facilities, pool.

✪ **Hotel Excelsior.** Piazza Ognissanti 3, 50123 Firenze. ☎ **800/325-3535** in the U.S. and Canada, or 055/264-201. Fax 055/210-278. 168 units. A/C MINIBAR TV TEL. 750,000–825,000L ($435–$479) double; 1,200,000–2,500,000L ($696–$1,450) suite. Breakfast 34,000L ($20). AE, DC, MC, V. Parking 50,000L ($29). Bus: B, C, or 9.

The Excelsior is the ultimate in well-ordered luxury in Florence. Cosmopolitan and sophisticated, it boasts the best-trained staff in town, but in recent years more tranquil and less commercial establishments, like the Regency and Helvetia & Bristol, have been attracting some of its guests. But if you like glamour and glitz, check into the Excelsior (but be sure to make reservations well in advance). Part of the hotel was once owned by Carolina Bonaparte, Napoléon's sister. The opulent guest rooms have 19th-century Florentine antiques and sumptuous fabrics. They offer lots of comfortable chairs and baths with heated racks, thick terry-cloth towels, and high ceilings. All reflect a heavy-handed style of decorating, and some are much more luxurious than others. In these old palaces, expect accommodations to come in a variety of configurations. Naturally, the rooms on the top floor with balconies overlooking the Arno and the Ponte Vecchio are the best and most sought after.

Dining/Diversions: Il Cestello is a deluxe restaurant serving elegantly prepared international cuisine. The Donatello Bar is reviewed in "Florence After Dark," later in this chapter.

Amenities: Room service, baby-sitting, laundry/valet, express checkout, translation services, currency exchange, facilities for the disabled.

EXPENSIVE

Hotel Albani Firenze. Via Fiume 12, 50123 Firenze. ☎ **055/26-030.** Fax 055/211-045. www.italyhotel.com/hotelm/3809.html. 80 units. A/C MINIBAR TV TEL. 350,000–460,000L ($203–$267) double; from 800,000L ($464) suite. Rates include breakfast. AE, DC, MC, V. Valet parking 35,000L ($21). Bus: 10, 12, 25, 31, or 32.

In 1993, a respected nationwide chain transformed a run-down pensione, a 10-minute walk from the Duomo, into one of Florence's most appealing four-star luxury hotels. The setting is the august premises of what was built around 1900 as a villa. Today, you'll find a up-to-date comforts and *House & Garden*–style draperies, artwork, and architectural embellishments. The formal high-ceilinged interiors sometimes verge on the theatrical but are never forbidding.

Dining/Diversions: A restaurant serves traditional Italian and international food at lunch and dinner every day except Sunday. Adjacent to the restaurant is the hotel's bar, a brown and wood-paneled affair staffed by waiters who aren't otherwise on duty within the restaurant. Open daily from 11am to 11pm, it serves wine by the glass and the usual array of American-style spirits and European brandies, cognacs, and liqueurs.

Amenities: Concierge, 24-hour room service, dry cleaning/laundry, newspaper delivery.

Hotel Astoria Palazzo Gaddi. Via del Giglio 9, 50123 Firenze. ☎ **055/239-8095.** Fax 055/214-632. 112 units. A/C MINIBAR TV TEL. 470,000L ($273) double; 860,000L ($499) suite. Rates include buffet breakfast. AE, DC, MC, V. Parking 40,000L ($23) nearby. Bus: 1, 2, 12, 16, 17, 22, 29, or 30.

Despite its location in a setting of cheap hotels, this is an impressive Renaissance palace. In the 17th century John Milton wrote parts of *Paradise Lost* in one of the rooms. This 16th-century palace has been renovated and turned into a serviceable choice, with a helpful staff and experienced management. From the rooms on the upper floors you'll have a view over the terra-cotta rooftops. The rooms have stylish and traditional furnishings for the most part, though some are decorated in a more sterile modern manner. The bathrooms are first-rate, with fluffy towels and hair dryers. The front rooms, overlooking a traffic-clogged avenue, are noisiest.

Dining: The garden-style Palazzo Gaddi restaurant serves a Tuscan cuisine.

Amenities: Room service, laundry, baby-sitting, car-rental desk, shopping boutique, currency exchange.

MODERATE

Hotel Malaspina. Piazza della Indipendenza 24, 50129 Firenze. ☎ **055/489-869.** Fax 055/474-809. 32 units. A/C MINIBAR TV TEL. 280,000L ($162) double. Rates include buffet breakfast. AE, DC, MC, V. Bus: 10, 12, 25, 31, 32, or 91.

A 10-minute walk north of the Duomo, this hotel opened in 1993 in the 19th-century premises of what was a dorm for students at a nearby dentistry school. The inviting interior has been carefully renovated and outfitted with traditional furniture that fits gracefully into the high-ceilinged public rooms and guest rooms. The windows are big, and the floors tend to be covered in either glazed or terra-cotta tiles. Each room contains a safe. Breakfast is the only meal served.

Villa Azalée. Viale Fratelli Rosselli 44, 50123 Firenze. ☎ 055/214-242. Fax 055/268-264. E-mail: villaazalee@fi.flashnet.it. 24 units. A/C MINIBAR TV TEL. 250,000L ($145) double; 336,000L ($195) triple. Rates include buffet breakfast. AE, DC, MC, V. Parking 35,000L ($20). Bus: 1, 2, 9, 13, 16, 17, 26, 27, 29, 30, or 35.

Handsome Villa Azalée, on a street corner with a big flowery garden, is a remake of an 1870s home. The personal touch of the owners is reflected in the atmosphere and the tasteful decor, which features tall white-paneled doors with ornate brass fittings, parquet floors, crystal chandeliers, and antiques intermixed with credible reproductions. The soundproof Laura Ashley–style guest rooms are distinctive (one boasts a flouncy canopy bed). Former stables out back were converted into some of the most charming rooms in Florence, if you opt for the rustic British style, with wood floors, heavy beamed ceilings, and sleigh beds. The hotel is a 5-minute walk from the rail station. You can rent bikes here for 5,000L ($2.90) per day.

INEXPENSIVE

Hotel Ariele. Via Magenta 11, 50123 Firenze. ☎ **055/211-509.** Fax 055/268-521. 40 units. AC TV TEL. 215,000L ($124.70) double; 250,000L ($145) triple. Rates include breakfast. AE, DC, MC, V. Parking 20,000L ($12). Bus: B, C, or 9.

Located just a block from the Arno, the Ariele, an old corner villa that has been converted into a roomy pensione, bills itself as "Your Home in Florence." The building is architecturally impressive, with large salons and lofty ceilings. The furnishings, however, combine antique with functional. The rooms are a grab bag of comfort.

✪ Hotel Bellettini. Via de Conti 7, 50123 Firenze. ☎ **055/213-561.** Fax 055/283-551. www.firenze.net/hotelbellettini. E-mail: hotel.bellettini@dada.it. 27 units, 22 with bathroom. A/C TEL. 150,000L ($87) double without bathroom, 180,000L ($104) double with bathroom. Rates include buffet breakfast. AE, DC, MC, V. Parking 30,000L ($17). Bus: 36 or 37.

For the kind of historic ambience you'll find here (not to mention the location in the heart of town, midway between the Duomo and the rail station), this hotel charges refreshingly reasonable rates. The palazzo was built in the 1300s, with a history of innkeeping that goes back at least 300 years, and is maintained by Tuscany-born sisters Marzia and Gina, who, along with their helpful staff, are well versed in explaining the labyrinth of Florence's streets to newcomers. This place is so traditional—with terra-cotta floors, beamed ceilings, and touches of stained glass—that you expect Henry James or Elizabeth Barrett Browning to check in at any minute. The rooms are plain (occasionally somewhat ascetic) but comfortable. About half have TVs, and many have sweeping views of Florence that could turn you into E. M. Forster.

Hotel Berkleys. Via Fiume 11, 50123 Firenze. ☎ **055/212-302.** Fax 055/238-2147. 9 units. TV TEL. 140,000L ($81) double; 180,000L ($104) triple; 215,000L ($125) quad. Rates include breakfast. MC, V. Bus: 10, 12, 25, 31, 32, or 91.

This pleasant but modest hotel, about a block east of the rail station, occupies the top floor of a 19th-century apartment building whose lower floors contain two less desirable two-star hotels. The owners, the Andreoli family, are polite and friendly, and there's an employee on duty throughout the day and night. The simple lobby leads into a breakfast nook and a bar area, where drinks are served on request. The rooms are simple but clean. Of course, you stay here for the prices, not for any grandeur.

Hotel Elite. Via della Scala 12, 50123 Firenze. ☎ **055/215-395.** 8 units, 3 with shower only, 5 with bathroom. TV TEL. 120,000L ($70) double with shower only, 140,000L ($81) double with bathroom. Breakfast 10,000L ($6). No credit cards. Parking from 30,000L ($17). Bus: 1, 2, 12, 16, 17, 22, 29, or 30.

The Elite is an attractive little pensione worthy of being better known, located two floors above street level in a 19th-century apartment building about 2 blocks from the rail station. It's also convenient for exploring most of the major monuments. Owner Maurizio Maccarini speaks English and is a welcoming host. The small hotel rents light and airy rooms, divided equally between singles and doubles. Some singles have only a shower (no toilet).

Hotel Le Vigne. Piazza S. Maria Novella 24, 50123 Firenze. ☎ **055/294-449.** Fax 055/230-2263. 19 units, 16 with bathroom. A/C TEL. 150,000–190,000L ($87–$110) double with bathroom; 255,000L ($148) triple with bathroom; 320,000L ($186) suite for four. Rates include buffet breakfast. AE, DC, MC, V. Parking 30,000L ($17). Bus: 1, 2, 12, 16, 17, 22, 29, or 30.

Le Vigne offers comfortably furnished rooms and enjoys a prime location on one of the most central squares (the sitting room overlooks the square). An Italian family took over this 15th-century building and restored it in the early 1990s, preserving the old features, including frescoes, whenever possible. The small hotel is on the first floor (second to Americans) of this old-fashioned building. Six of the units are air-conditioned, and a few singles don't have baths. Breakfast, a generous self-service buffet, is the only meal served.

Hotel Mario's. Via Faenza 89, 50123 Firenze. ☎ **055/216-801.** Fax 055/212-039. 16 units. A/C TV TEL. 150,000–250,000L ($87–$145) double; 200,000–320,000L ($116–$186) triple. Rates include breakfast. AE, DC, MC, V. Parking 27,000L ($16). Bus: 10, 12, 25, 31, 32, or 91.

Two blocks from the rail station and close to San Lorenzo Market, this winning choice on the first floor of an old Florentine building has been a hotel since 1872 when the *Room with a View* crowd started arriving in search of the glory of the Renaissance. The spotless place has been completely restored and furnished in a typical Florentine style. Mario Noce is a gracious host, and he and his staff speak English. Though you'll find cheaper inns in Florence, the service and hospitality make Mario's worth your lire. Some of the rooms open onto a small garden, and furnishings are often antique reproductions, including armoires and wrought-iron headboards. Fresh flowers and fresh fruit are put out daily. Some of the beams in the public areas are 300 years old.

Hotel Nuova Italia. Via Faenza 26, 50123 Firenze. ☎ **055/287-508.** Fax 055/210-941. 20 units. A/C TEL. 180,000–195,000L ($104–$113) double; 230,000–280,000L ($133–$162) triple; 280,000–320,000L ($162–$186) quad. Rates include breakfast. AE, MC, V. Parking 35,000–40,000L ($20–$23) nearby. Bus: 10, 12, 25, 31, 32, or 91.

This little hotel, in a renovated 17th-century building only a block from the rail station, near the San Lorenzo Market, has been welcoming Frommer's readers since 1958, the first ones showing up with copies of *Europe on $5 a Day*. A Canadian, Eileen, met and fell in love with Luciano Viti, then a bellboy. Today they own the hotel and are grandparents with a new generation of Vitis waiting to take over one day. The rooms are pleasantly furnished and decorated with paintings and posters. Some large rooms are suitable for families, to whom the management grants special discounts. The Vitis, who happen to serve a fantastic cappuccino, will help you figure out how to get around Florence and offer tips on where to shop and what to do.

Hotel Vasari. Via B. Cennini 9–11, 50123 Firenze. ☎ **055/212-753.** Fax 055/294-246. 30 units. A/C MINIBAR TV TEL. 150,000–230,000L ($87–$133) double. Rates include breakfast. AE, DC, MC, V. Parking 15,000L ($9). Bus: 10, 12, 25, 31, 32, or 91.

The Vasari has ties to some of Florence's most prestigious literary associations, thanks to the fact that for several years it was the home of 19th-century French poet Alphonse de la Martine. Built in the 1840s as a home, it was a run-down two-star hotel until 1993, when its owners poured money into its renovation and upgraded it to one of the most reasonably priced three-star hotels in town. Its three stories are connected by elevator, and the rooms are comfortable, albeit somewhat spartan. Some of the public areas retain their elaborate vaulting.

Stella Mary Hotel. Via Fiume 17, 50123 Firenze. ☎ **055/215-694.** Fax 055/264-206. 7 units. TV TEL. 65,000–145,000L ($38–$84) double; 105,000–175,000L ($61–$102) triple. Breakfast 10,000L ($6). AE, MC, V. Parking 30,000L ($17). Bus: 10, 12, 25, 31, 32, or 91.

This small pensione is 12 blocks from the rail station and around the corner from a busy bus station. The English-speaking owners, Mrs. Vittoria and her son, personally operate a comfortable "home in Firenze." The rooms are cozy and full of light, and a sitting room with a TV is reserved for guests. Though breakfast is the only meal served, the staff can recommend several restaurants nearby. The hotel, in a classic Florentine-style building with an elevator, is only a short walk from the San Lorenzo Church and the San Lorenzo Market.

NEAR PIAZZA SAN MARCO
EXPENSIVE

Loggiato dei Serviti. Piazza SS. Annunziata 3, 50122 Firenze. ☎ **055/289-592.** Fax 055/289-595. 30 units. A/C MINIBAR TV TEL. 310,000L ($180) double; 365,000–495,000L ($212–$287) suite. Rates include breakfast. AE, DC, MC, V. Parking 35,000–45,000L ($20–$26). Bus: 6, 31, or 32.

The amazing thing about this hotel is that it accepts paying guests at all—equally antique buildings throughout Europe are usually reserved as museums or showcases for local bureaucracies. But here you can wander through the premises of what was built in 1527 as a monastery (a symmetrical foil for the Ospedale degli Innocenti across the square) and has been a hotel since the early 1900s. In 1997, it was transformed from a run-down student place into a carefully restored three-star hotel. The guest rooms are artfully designed to emphasize the building's antique origins, usually with beamed or vaulted ceilings and terra-cotta floors. There's a bar on the premises, breakfast is the only meal served.

MODERATE

Hotel Cellai. Via 27 Aprile, 14, 50129 Firenze. ☎ **055/489-291.** Fax 055/470-387. www.italyhotel.com/hotelm/3873.html. 45 units. A/C MINIBAR TV TEL. 250,000L ($145) double. Rates include breakfast. AE, DC, MC, V. Bus: 6, 31, or 32.

In the 1930s, the Cellai family began renting a handful of rooms. Eventually the enterprise grew into the large-scale place you see today. Two blocks east of the landmark Piazza della Indipendenza, a 10-minute walk north of the Duomo, it boasts dignified public rooms with terra-cotta floors and architectural details. The guest rooms are individually decorated, some with appealing contemporary paintings. Try to ask for one with a varnished wooden ceiling supported by very old beams—these rooms seem more appealing and a bit warmer.

Hotel Le Due Fontane. Piazza della SS, Annunziata 14, 50122 Firenze. ☎ **055/210-185.** Fax 055/294-461. 56 units. A/C MINIBAR TV TEL. 260,000L ($151) double; 400,000L ($232) suite. Rates include breakfast. AE, CB, DC, DISC, MC, V. Parking 20,000L ($12). Bus: 6, 31, or 32.

This hotel is a small palace on Florence's best-known Renaissance square, right in the heart of the artistic center, within an easy walk of the Duomo. Though the building dates to the 14th century, the hotel has been completely renovated and modernized and offers simply but tastefully furnished rooms that are well kept if a bit uninspired. The upper-floor rooms offer the most tranquil night's sleep. Services and facilities include a concierge, laundry, personal hotel-bus service, car-rental facilities, boutiques, a business center, baby-sitting, and a bar.

Hotel Rapallo. Via Santa Caterina d'Alessandria 7, 50129 Firenze. ☎ **055/472-412.** Fax 055/470-385. www.dinonet.it/rapallo. E-mail: rapallo@dinonet.it. 30 units. MINIBAR TV TEL. 190,000–273,000L ($110–$158) double; 256,000–381,000L ($149–$221) triple. Rates include breakfast. AE, DC, MC, V. Parking 20,000L ($12). Bus: 10, 12, 25, 31, 32, or 91.

Though the Rapallo isn't typical of Florence, it's nevertheless completely revamped and inviting. The small lounge is brightened by planters, Oriental rugs, and barrel stools set in the corners for drinking and conversation. The guest rooms are furnished mostly with blond-wood furniture, and all have a safe and, on request, a TV. The hotel is within walking distance of the rail station.

INEXPENSIVE

Hotel Casci. Via Cavour 13, 50129 Firenze. ☎ **055/211-686.** Fax 055/239-6461. www.traveleurope.it/h4/htm. E-mail: casci@pn.itnet.it. 25 units. TV TEL. 110,000–170,000L ($64–$99) double; 140,000–225,000L ($81–$131) triple; 170,000–280,000L ($99–$162) quad. Rates include breakfast. AE, DC, MC, V. Parking 35,000–40,000L ($20–$23). Bus: 1, 6, 7, 11, 17, 33, 67, or 68.

The Casci is a well-run little hotel 200 yards from the main rail station and 100 yards from Piazza del Duomo. As one reader wrote, "For location, location, location, there's nothing better in Florence." It dates from the 15th century, and some of the public rooms (like the breakfast room) feature the original frescoes. Giacchino Rossini, the famous composer of *The Barber of Seville* and *William Tell,* lived here from 1851 to 1855. The hotel is both traditional and modern, and the English-speaking reception staff looks after you very well. The rooms are comfortably furnished, each with a hair dryer. Every year four or five are upgraded and renovated. The few units overlooking the street are soundproof.

Hotel Cimabue. Via B. Lupi 7, 50129 Firenze. ☎ **055/471-989.** Fax 055/475-601. 16 units. TV TEL. 155,000–185,000L ($90–$107) double. Rates include buffet breakfast. AE, DC, MC, V. Parking 22,000L ($13). Bus: 6, 31, or 32.

This was built in 1904 as a Tuscan-style palazzo, and the most charming rooms are the five with original frescoed ceilings. Four of these are one floor above street level and the other on the ground floor. The hotel was last renovated in 1991 but contains turn-of-the-century antiques that correspond to the building's age. Its Belgian-Italian management extends a warm multicultural welcome.

Hotel Europa. Via Cavour 14, 50129 Firenze. ☎ and fax **055/210-361.** 13 units. TV TEL. 170,000L ($99) double. Rates include breakfast. AE, MC, V. Bus: 1, 6, 7, 11, 17, 33, 67, or 68.

Two long blocks north of the Duomo, this 16th-century building has been a family-run hotel since 1925. Despite the antique appearance of the simple exterior, much of the interior has been modernized, though it contains plenty of homey touches. All but four of the rooms overlook the back, usually opening onto a view of Giotto's campanile; those facing the street are noisier but benefit from double glazing. Breakfast is the only meal served.

Hotel Morandi alla Crocetta. Via Laura 50, 50121 Firenze. ☎ **055/234-4747.** Fax 055/248-0954. www.dada.it/hotel.morandi. 10 units. A/C MINIBAR TV TEL. 240,000L ($139) double; 320,000L ($186) triple. Breakfast 18,000L ($11). AE, DC, MC, V. Parking 18,000L ($10). Bus: 6, 31, or 32.

This charming small hotel 2 blocks from the Accademia is run by one of Florence's most experienced hoteliers, the sprightly octogenarian Katherine Doyle, who came here from her native Ireland when she was 12. Though built in 1511 as a convent, it contains everything needed for a pensione and is on a backstreet near a university building. The rooms have been tastefully restored, filled with framed examples of 19th-century needlework, beamed ceilings, and antiques. In the best Tuscan tradition, the tall windows are sheltered from the sun with heavy draperies. You register in an austere salon filled with Persian carpets.

Hotel Splendor. Via S. Gallo 30, 50129 Firenze. ☎ **055/483-427.** Fax 055/461-276. 31 units, 25 with bathroom. TV TEL. 165,000L ($96) double without bathroom, 220,000L ($128) double with bathroom; 290,000L ($168) triple with bathroom. Rates include buffet breakfast. AE, MC, V. Parking 30,000L ($17). Bus: 1, 6, 7, 11, 17, 33, 67, or 68.

Though the Splendor is within a 10-minute walk of the Duomo, the residential neighborhood it occupies is a world away from the milling hordes of the tourist district. The hotel occupies three high-ceilinged floors of a 19th-century apartment building, and its elegantly faded public rooms evoke the kind of family-run pensione that early in the century attracted the *Room with a View* crowd. This is the domain of the Masoero family, whose homelike rooms contain an eclectic array of semiantique furniture. There's no restaurant, but room service is available.

NEAR PIAZZA SANTA CROCE
VERY EXPENSIVE

✪ **Hotel Monna Lisa.** Borgo Pinti 27, 50121, Firenze. ☎ **055/247-9751.** Fax 055/247-9755. 34 units. A/C MINIBAR TV TEL. 480,000–550,000L ($278–$319) double. Rates include breakfast. AE, DC, MC, V. Parking 20,000L ($12). Bus: B 14, 23, or 71.

This hotel (yes, it's Monna with two *n*'s) once appeared in *Frommer's Europe from $5 a Day,* but its prices have skyrocketed and it can't be included even in the current *Europe from $50 a Day.* However, for old-world elegance in the setting of a 14th-century Tuscan palazzo, it's virtually unbeatable. The palazzo once belonged to the Neri family, whose most famous member, St. Philip Neri, was born in room no. 19. The facade is forbiddingly severe, in keeping with the architectural style of its heyday. But when you enter the reception rooms, you'll find an inviting atmosphere like that of an aristocratic private home. Most of the great old rooms overlook either an inner patio or a rear garden. Each room is handsomely furnished with fine antiques and oil paintings, including Giambologna's original competition piece for the *Rape of the Sabines.* There are other works by Giovanni Dupré (1817 to 1882), the neoclassical sculptor (the hotel is still owned by member of this artist's family). Painted wood and coffered ceilings are still found in many rooms. The baths have recently been renovated, and some of them have a Jacuzzi. The rooms vary greatly in style and decor—some are quite spacious, others a bit cramped.

Dining: Breakfast in the only meal served, but there's an American-style bar.

Amenities: Concierge, baby-sitting, laundry.

EXPENSIVE

Plaza Hotel Lucchesi. Lungarno della Zecca Vecchia 38, 50122 Firenze. ☎ **800/223-9832** in the U.S., or 055/26-236. Fax 055/248-0921. E-mail: hplaza@dada.it. 107 units. A/C MINIBAR TV TEL. 350,000–520,000L ($203–$302) double; 480,000–640,000L ($278–$371) suite. Rates include breakfast. AE, DC, MC, V. Parking 25,000–40,000L ($15–$23). Bus: B, 13, 14, or 23.

This hotel (often a favorite with tour groups) was built in 1860 but has been renovated many times since. It lies along the banks of the Arno, a 10-minute walk from the Duomo and a few paces from the imposing Santa Maria della Croce. Its interior decor includes lots of glossy mahogany, acres of marble, and masses of fresh flowers. Though the guest rooms have up-to-date equipment (like trouser presses) and are comfortable and well maintained, they seem dated. About 20 open onto private terraces or balconies, some with enviable views over historic Florence.

Dining/Diversions: A large breakfast buffet and dinner are served in the sunny La Serra. The food is only average, however; you'll do better at one of the restaurants nearby. There's also a bar.

Amenities: 24-hour room service, baby-sitting, laundry/valet, car-rental desk.

NEAR THE PONTE VECCHIO
EXPENSIVE

Hotel Augustus. Vicolo del'Oro 5, 50123 Firenze. ☎ **055/27263.** Fax 055/268-557. www.lungarnohotels.it. E-mail: lungarnohotels@lungarnohotels.it. 70 units. A/C MINIBAR TV TEL. 425,000L ($247) double; 565,000L ($328) suite. Rates include buffet breakfast. AE, DC, MC, V. Parking 30,000–40,000L ($17–$23). Bus: 23 or 71.

The Augustus is for those who require modern comforts while enjoying a historic setting. The Ponte Vecchio is just a short stroll away, as is the Uffizi. The exterior is rather pillbox modern, but the interior seems light, bright, and comfortable. Some of the rooms open onto little private balconies with garden furniture. The decor consists of relatively simple provincial pieces, and the overall effect is rather lackluster but well maintained. Views of the Arno are often blocked by neighboring buildings.

Dining/Diversions: The expansive lounge and drinking area is like an illuminated cave, with a curving ceiling and built-in conversation areas. Regrettably, there's no view from the bar. Snacks are served, however, 8am to 11:30pm. Even though there's no restaurant, dozens are literally at your doorstep.

Amenities: Concierge, room service, dry cleaning/laundry, car-rental desk.

Hotel Continental. Lungarno Acciaiuoli 2, 50123 Firenze. ☎ **055/27262.** Fax 055/283-139. 49 units. A/C MINIBAR TV TEL. 350,000–450,000L ($203–$261) double; 530,000–760,000L ($307–$441) suite. Rates include continental breakfast. AE, DC, MC, V. Valet parking 35,000–40,000L ($20–$23). Bus: 23 or 71.

At the Ponte Vecchio's entrance, the Continental occupies some select real estate and is a better choice than its sibling, the Augustus. Through the lounge windows and from some of the rooms you can see the little jewelry and leather shops flanking the much-painted bridge. The hotel was created in the 1960s, so its style of accommodation is utilitarian, with functional furniture softened by decorative accessories. You reach your room by the elevator or by a wrought-iron staircase (note that parts of the old stone structure have been retained). The management likes to put up

North Americans, knowing they'll be attracted to the roof terrace, a vantage point for viewing Piazzale Michelangiolo, the Pitti Palace, the Duomo and campanile, and Fiesole. Artists fight to get the penthouse suite up in the Torre Guelfa dei Consorti (tower).

Dining/Diversions: There's a small bar but no restaurant.

Amenities: Concierge (7am to midnight), room service, dry cleaning/laundry, baby-sitting.

MODERATE

Hermitage Hotel. Vicolo Marzio 1, Piazza del Pesce I, 50122 Firenze. ☎ **055/287-216.** Fax 055/212-208. www.italyhotel.com/firenze/hermitage. E-mail: hermitage@italyhotel.com. 29 units. AC TV TEL. 260,000–330,000L ($151–$191) double; 390,000L ($226) triple; 470,000L ($273) family room. Rates include breakfast. MC, V. Parking 30,000–40,000L ($17–$23). Bus: 23 or 71.

On the Arno, the offbeat Hermitage is a charming place that has been recently renovated. It boasts a rooftop sun terrace offering a view of much of Florence, including the nearby Uffizi and the Duomo. You can take your breakfast under a leafy arbor surrounded by potted roses and geraniums. The success of this hotel has much to do with its English-speaking owner, Vincenzo Scarcelli, who has made the Hermitage an extension of his home, furnishing it in part with antiques and well-chosen reproductions. Best of all is his warmth toward guests, many of whom keep coming back. The extremely small rooms are pleasantly furnished, many with 17th- to 19th-century Tuscan antiques, rich brocades, and good beds, plus double-glazed windows. The tiled baths are superb, with lots of gadgets. The rooms overlooking the Arno have the most scenic view and have been fitted with double-glass windows that reduce the traffic noise by 40%. Breakfast is served in a dignified beam-ceilinged room.

INEXPENSIVE

✪ **Hotel Torre Guelfa.** Borgo SS. Apostoli 8, 50123 Firenze. ☎ **055/239-63-38.** Fax 055/239-85-77. 11 units. A/C MINIBAR TV TEL. 170,000L ($99) single; 250,000L ($145) double. Rates include continental breakfast. AE, MC, V. Bus: 6, 11, 36, 37, or 68.

To experience the 360° view from this hotel's 13th-century tower is breathtaking. This is the tallest privately owned tower in Florence's *centro storico*, and its view is only one reason to stay in this landmark hotel before it applies for three-star status and raises its rates. Though you're just two steps from the Ponte Vecchio (and equidistant from the Duomo), you'll want to put sightseeing on hold and linger in your canopied iron bed, your room made even more inviting by warm-colored walls and paisley carpeting (for a view similar to the medieval tower's, ask for room no. 15 with a huge private terrace).

The Torre Guelfa's young owners have created the **Relais Uffizi** (see phone number above), a sibling hotel a few cobbled lanes away in an evocative alley opening onto the Uffizi and Piazza della Signora. Similar in spirit, decor, price, and size (11 rooms), it isn't blessed with a tower, but it does have a lounge with an unmatched view of the piazza, all housed in a handsome 14th-century refurbished palazzo.

Pensione Alessandra. Borgo SS. Apostoli 17, 50123 Firenze. ☎ **055/283-438.** Fax 055/210-619. 25 units, 16 with bathroom. TV TEL. 120,000L ($70) double without bathroom, 180,000L ($104) double with bathroom. Rates include breakfast. AE, MC, V. Parking 30,000–35,000L ($17–$20). Bus: 6, 11, 36, 37, or 68.

Near the Ponte Vecchio and Piazza Trinita, this is a completely unpretentious two-star pensione. It's an old-fashioned kind of place, the type that unmarried Victorian ladies might have found a safe haven on their Grand Tour. Though the facade has retained some of its 15th-century severity, the rooms have been modernized into efficient, if not particularly luxurious, accommodations; almost all have air-conditioning. Some of the units are quite spacious, others are of medium size, but none is really cramped. Parquet floors and a scattering of antiques add to the Tuscan charm of the place. The bathrooms have been rejuvenated, and, even if shared, are in ample supply. Breakfast is the only meal served.

ON OR NEAR PIAZZA MASSIMO D'AZEGLIO

Piazza Massimo d'Azeglio is a 12-minute walk northeast of the historic core.

EXPENSIVE

✪ **Hotel Regency.** Piazza Massimo d'Azeglio 3, 50121 Firenze. ☎ **055/245-247.** Fax 055/ 234-6735. www.regency-hotel.com. E-mail: info@regency-hotel.com. 34 units. A/C MINIBAR TV TEL. 400,000–620,000L ($232–$360) double; 800,000–950,000L ($464–$551) suite. Rates include breakfast. AE, DC, MC, V. Parking 45,000L ($26). Bus: 6, 31, or 32.

Much less overtly commercial than the Grand or the Excelsior, the Regency is an intimate villa of taste and exclusivity, a member of Relais & Châteaux. It lies a bit apart from the shopping and sightseeing center but is only a 15-minute stroll from the cathedral. And though its location isn't central (a blessing for tranquillity seekers), it's quickly reached by taxi or bus. This luxurious hideaway, filled with stained glass, paneled walls, and reproduction antiques, offers exquisite accommodations, including some special rooms on the top floor with terraces.

Dining: The attractive Relais Le Jardin is renowned for its *alta cucina.* You can also take your meals in the well-lit winter garden or on an inner courtyard in summer.

Amenities: Concierge, room service, baby-sitting, laundry/valet.

INEXPENSIVE

Albergo Losanna. Via Vittorio Alfieri 9, 50121 Firenze. ☎ and fax **055/245-840.** 11 units, 4 with bathroom. TEL. 105,000L ($61) double without bathroom, 130,000L ($75) double with bathroom; 220,000L ($128) suite. Rates include breakfast. AE, MC, V. Parking 30,000–35,000L ($17–$20). Bus: 6, 31, or 32.

A good inexpensive choice, the Losanna is a family-run place off Viale Antonio Gramsci, between Piazzale Donatello and Piazza Massimo d'Azeglio. It offers utter simplicity and cleanliness as well as insight into a typical Florentine atmosphere—the hotel seemingly belongs in the 1800s, when English people venturing abroad often preferred to stay in a family home rather than a hotel. The rooms are homey and well kept, but the furnishings are simple and a bit tired.

ACROSS THE ARNO
EXPENSIVE

Hotel Villa Carlotta. Via Michele di Lando 3, 50125 Firenze. ☎ **055/220-530.** Fax 055/ 233-6147. 32 units. A/C MINIBAR TV TEL. 280,000–410,000L ($162–$238) double. Rates include breakfast. AE, DC, MC, V. Free parking. Bus: B or C.

This hotel was built during the Edwardian age as a villa and bought in the 1950s by Carlotta Schulmamm. The lavish renovations she poured into it transformed it into one of Florence's most charming smaller hotels. The aura is still very much like that of a private home, and it's located in a residential section. In 1985, all the rooms were upgraded, with the addition of silk wallpaper and bedspreads, reproduction antiques, private safety-deposit boxes, and crystal chandeliers; each also has a view of the surrounding garden. The hotel is only a 10-minute walk from the Ponte Vecchio; by taxi, it's a 5-minute ride.

Dining: Il Bobolino serves meals ranging from fresh salads to full culinary regalias. **Amenities:** Room service, baby-sitting, laundry/valet, car-rental desk.

MODERATE

Pensione Annalena. Via Romana 34, 50125 Firenze. ☎ **055/222-402.** Fax 055/222-403. 20 units. TV TEL. 250,000L ($145) double. Rates include breakfast. AE, DC, MC, V. Parking 20,000L ($12). Bus: B or C.

Built in the 15th century, the Annalena has had many owners, including the Medicis. In the past three-quarters of a century it has been a haven for artists and writers (Mary McCarthy once wrote of its importance as a cultural center). During most of that time it was the domain of the late sculptor Olinto Calastri, but now it's owned by Claudio Salvestrini. Most of the simply furnished and rather severe rooms overlook a garden. Don't be put off by the lack of air-conditioning, as the high ceilings and thick masonry walls almost guarantee a relatively comfortable temperature in summer. During World War II, the Annalena was the center of the underground, and many Jews and rebel Italians found safety hidden away in an underground room behind a secret door. The pensione is about a 5-minute walk from the Pitti and 10 minutes from the Ponte Vecchio.

INEXPENSIVE

Classic Hotel. Viale Machiavelli 25, 50125 Firenze. ☎ **055/229-3512.** Fax 055/229-353. 22 units. 210,000L ($122) double; 330,000L ($191) suite. Breakfast 12,000L ($7). AE, DC, MC, V. Bus: C.

Within a 15-minute walk south of the Duomo, this hotel occupies the stately pink-walled premises of what was built in the 19th century as a private villa. It has its own garden, where vines climb over a network of arbors and trellises. You'll find cool interiors with high ceilings and either glazed tile or terra-cotta floors and comfortable rooms painted in pale colors with a medley of conservatively modern or traditional furniture. Don't expect opulence—instead, you'll find an appealing low-key place.

ON THE OUTSKIRTS
EXPENSIVE

✪ **Torre di Bellosguardo.** 2 Via Roti Michelozzi, 50124 Firenze. ☎ **055/229-8145.** Fax 055/229-008. 16 units. TEL. 450,000L ($261) double; from 550,000L ($319) suite. Breakfast 30,000L ($18). AE, V. Free valet parking. Bus: 12 or 13 to Piazza Tasso, where a taxi will take you up the hill.

On a hilltop near the south bank of the Arno, less than 2 miles southwest of the Duomo, this hotel occupies the palatial premises of what in the 1300s was a private villa. A medieval aura lingers in its long halls and alfresco loggias. Framed by an avenue of timeless cypresses, the mansion was built by Guido Cavalcanti, a Florentine nobleman and friend of Dante. You'll register under the frescoed ceiling of what used to be a ballroom, and the high-ceilinged guest rooms evoke the grandeur (though simplified) of another age. If you can afford the price, opt for the romantic tower suite with its panoramic sweep. Plumbing fixtures are up-to-date and stylish, in vivid contrast to the otherwise antique setting. The rooms aren't air-conditioned, but because of the building's site atop of a breezy hilltop, it isn't really missed. A pool is set in a sprawling park and garden.

Dining: Breakfast is the only meal served, but the sunny veranda or cool dining room seems to make up for this lack. The veranda is so tempting you might linger like Elizabeth Barrett Browning, placing your soul "in a state of trance."

Amenities: Concierge, 24-hour room service.

4 Dining

The Florentine table has always been set with the abundance of the Tuscan countryside. That means the region's best olive oil and wine, like chianti; wonderful fruits and vegetables; fresh fish from the coast; and game in season. Meat-lovers all over Italy sing the praise of *bistecca alla fiorentina,* an inch-thick juicy steak on the bone often served with white Tuscan beans.

The Tuscan cuisine (except for some of its hair-raising specialties) should please most North Americans, as it's simply flavored, without rich spices, and based on the hearty produce from the hills. Florentine restaurants aren't generally as acclaimed by gourmets as those of Rome, though good moderately priced places abound. Florentines often assert that the cooking in the other regions of Italy "offends the palate."

IN CENTRO
MODERATE

Al Lume di Candela. Via delle Terme 23R. ☎ **055/294-566.** Reservations required. Main courses 28,000–40,000L ($16–$23). AE. Tues–Sat noon–2:30pm and 7:30–11pm; Mon 7:30–11pm. Closed 1 week in Aug. Bus: C. TUSCAN/INTERNATIONAL.

Opened in 1948, Al Lume di Candela is in a 13th-century tower that was partially leveled when its patrician family fell from grace (the prestige of Tuscan families was once reflected in how high their family towers soared). It offers typical Florentine cuisine in an elegant candlelit decor of English-style furnishings and De Chirico paintings. The food is precise, combining rich tastes and unusual flavors, but stick to the Tuscan dishes (avoid the bland international fare). Menu choices include taglierini with sage and porcini mushrooms; a light house-smoked salmon; veal chops stuffed with white beans (cannellini) and arugula; entrecôte (sirloin) of beef grilled with pepper, olive oil, and Tuscan herbs; maccheroncini with thyme; and calamari seared in sherry with pecorino cheese. The desserts are made daily, and the spongecake covered in fresh raspberry cream is a summer delight. From the cellar emerges at least 200 wines, with Chianti Classici the wine of choice. One old-timer still remembers when Bing Crosby (then one of the world's richest entertainers) arrived here carrying a dog-eared copy of *Frommer's Europe on $5 a Day.* Bing is long gone and so are those cheap prices.

✪ **Cantinetta Antinori.** Piazza Antinori 3. ☎ **055/292-234.** Reservations recommended. Main courses 25,000–32,000L ($15–$19). AE, DC, MC, V. Mon–Fri 12:30–2:30pm and 7–10:30pm. Closed Aug and Dec 24–Jan 6. Bus: 6, 11, 36, 37, or 68. FLORENTINE/TUSCAN.

Behind the severe stone facade of the 15th-century Palazzo Antinori is one of Florence's most popular restaurants and one of the city's few top-notch wine bars. It's no small wonder that the cellars are supremely well stocked since this is a showplace for the vintages of the oldest (600 years) and most distinguished wine company in Tuscany, Umbria, and Piedmont. You can sample these by the glass at the stand-up bar or by the bottle as an accompaniment to the Italian meals served at wooden tables on Richard Ginori China. The not especially large room is decorated with floor-to-ceiling racks of aged and undusted wine bottles. You can eat a full meal or just snacks. The cookery is standard but satisfying, especially the sausages with white haricot beans and the fresh Tuscan ewe's cheese. Many of the ingredients come direct from the Antinori merchesi farms. Tripe in the Florentine style is for the traditionalist, though you may opt for fettuccine in duck sauce instead. Nothing is finer to the Florentine palate than a thick slab of oven-roasted Chiana beef, even if it is a bit pricey.

Oliviero. Via delle Terme 51R. ☎ **055/287-643.** Reservations required. Main courses 32,000L ($19). AE, CB, DC, DISC, MC, V. Mon–Sat 7–11pm. Closed Aug. Bus: 14, 23, or 71. TUSCAN.

ⓒ Family-Friendly Restaurants

Da Pennello *(see p. 222)*   This family-style trattoria near Dante's house offers filling, tasty, and inexpensive dishes.

Gelateria Vivoli *(see p. 224)*   After tasting the ice cream here—in virtually every known flavor—your child might agree that this place was worth the trip to Florence.

La Nandina *(see p. 229)*   Florentine families frequent this place off the Arno, a 4-mile walk from the Uffizi.

This is a small but smart and luxurious dining room. The finest traditions of Tuscan cookery are maintained; highly select fresh ingredients are used in the seasonal menu. You may, for example, savor appetizers like octopus salad with basil, string beans, and tomatoes; fried mussels and squash blossoms; or Tuscan ham with figs and bread coated with virgin olive oil. Main courses usually include fresh fish; grilled boned rabbit and young cock with shell beans; or ravioli stuffed with chopped liver and served with a delicate white onion sauce. For dessert, try the green fig mousse with almonds and chocolate.

NEAR PIAZZA DEL DUOMO
INEXPENSIVE

Le Mossacce. Via del Proconsolo 55R. ☎ **055/294-361.** Main courses 9,000–15,000L ($5–$9). AE, MC, V. Mon–Fri noon–2:30pm and 7–9:30pm. Closed Aug. Bus: 14, 23, or 71. TUSCAN/FLORENTINE.

The 35-seat Le Mossacce, patronized by a long list of faithful Tuscans, is midway between the Bargello and the Duomo. It opened at the turn of the century, and within its 300-year-old walls hardworking waiters serve a wide range of excellent Florentine and Tuscan specialties, like ribollita (a thick vegetable soup), baked lasagne, and heavily seasoned baked pork. Bistecca alla fiorentina is a favorite—and you'll be hard-pressed to find it for less. We advise you to throw yourself on the mercy of a kindly waiter: On our last visit, the waiter rejected our first two food suggestions, preferring to serve us what he viewed as good and fresh that day. He was right!

Vecchia Firenze. Borgo degli Albizi 18. ☎ **055/234-0361.** Main courses 12,000–22,000L ($7–$13); fixed-price menu 20,000L ($12). AE, DC, MC, V. Tues–Sun 11am–3pm and 7pm–midnight. Bus: 14, 23, or 71. FLORENTINE/TUSCAN.

Vecchia Firenze, housed in a 14th-century palace with an elegant entrance, combines atmosphere and budget meals. Some tables are in the courtyard; others are in the vaulted dining rooms or the stone-lined cantina downstairs. The place caters to students and the working people of Florence, who eat here regularly and never seem to tire of its simple but good-tasting offerings. You might begin with tagliatelle Vecchia Firenze (there's a different version every day), then follow with a quarter of a roast chicken or sole in butter. If you're out with a Florentine, he or she might opt for the grilled rabbit, the Florentine beefsteak, or grilled sea bass.

NEAR PIAZZA DELLA SIGNORIA
MODERATE

Da Ganino. Piazza dei Cimatori 4R. ☎ **055/214-125.** Reservations recommended. Main courses 16,000–30,000L ($9–$17). AE, DC, MC, V. Mon–Sat 1–3pm and 8–11pm. Bus: 14, 23, or 71. FLORENTINE/TUSCAN.

Florence Dining

 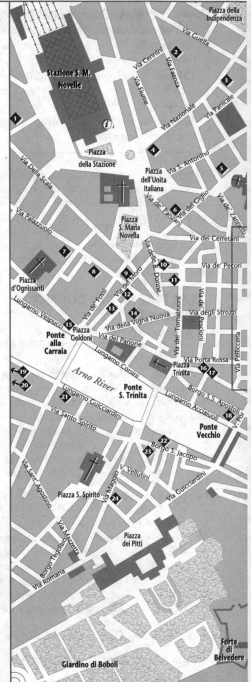

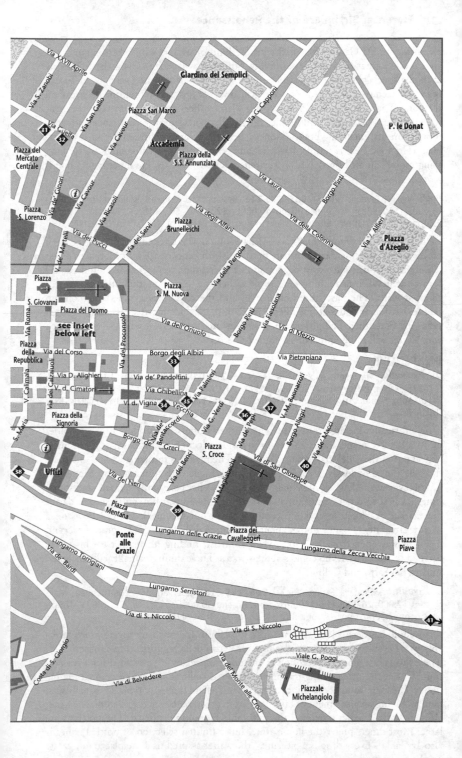

Via XXVII Aprile
Giardino dei Semplici
Via S. Zanobi
Via San Gallo
Via Cavour
Piazza San Marco
Via G. Capponi
P. le Donat
Via Guelfa
31
32
Piazza del Mercato Centrale
Accademia
Piazza della S.S. Annunziata
Via de' Ginori
Via Cavour
i
Via Laura
Borgo Pinti
Via Ricasoli
Piazza S. Lorenzo
Via degli Alfani
Via della Colonna
Via V. Alfieri
Piazza d'Azeglio
Via dei Pucci
Via de' Martelli
Piazza Brunelleschi
Via dei Servi
Piazza
S. Giovanni
Piazza del Duomo
Piazza S. M. Nuova
Via della Pergola
S. Giovanni
see inset below left
Via del Proconsolo
Via dell'Oriuolo
Borgo Pinti
Via Fiesolana
Via di Mezzo
Via Roma
Piazza della Repubblica
Via del Corso
Borgo degli Albizi
Via Pietrapiana
33
Via D. Alighieri
Via de' Pandolfini
Via Calimala
Via dei Calzaiuoli
V. d. Cimatori
Via Ghibellina
Via Palmieri
35
34 Vecchia
Vi d. Vigna
36
37
V. M. Buonarroti
Piazza della Signoria
Via de' Benci
Via G. Verdi
Borgo de' Greci
Via de' Bentaccordi
Via de' Pepi
Borgo Allegri
Via de' Macci
S. Maria
i
Piazza S. Croce
Via di San Giuseppe
40
38
Uffizi
Via del Neri
Via Magliabechi
Piazza Mentana
39
Piazza dei Cavalleggeri
Piazza Piave
Ponte alle Grazie
Lungarno delle Grazie
Lungarno della Zecca Vecchia
Lungarno Torrigiani
Via de' Bardi
Lungarno Serristori
Via di S. Niccolo
Via di S. Niccolo
41
Costa di S. Giorgio
Viale G. Poggi
Via di Belvedere
Via del Monte alle Croci
Piazzale Michelangiolo

The intimate Da Ganino is staffed with the kind of waiters who take the quality of your meal as their personal responsibility. Someone will recite to you the frequently changing specialties of the day, which might include well-seasoned versions of Tuscan beans, spinach risotto, grilled veal liver, grilled veal chops, and Florentine beefsteak on the bone. The tagliatelle con tartufi (pasta with truffles) makes an excellent if expensive appetizer. Also worthwhile is the chicken filet with lemon-cream sauce and fritto misto of meats, including brains, kidneys, beef filets, lamb chops, and grilled vegetables. "The food here is simple, flavorful, and reasonable, and who could ask for anything more?" an art historian from Lawrence, Kansas, told us. He dines here 3 nights a week.

Paoli. Via dei Tavolini 12R. ☎ **055/216-215.** Reservations required. Main courses 18,000–35,000L ($10–$20); fixed-price menu 40,000L ($23). AE, DC, MC, V. Wed–Mon noon–2:30pm and 7–10:30pm. Closed 3 weeks in Aug. Bus: 14, 23, or 71. TUSCAN/ITALIAN.

Paoli, between the Duomo and Piazza della Signoria, was opened in 1824 by the Paoli brothers in a building dating in part from the 13th century. One of Florence's finest restaurants, it turns out a host of specialties but could be recommended almost solely for its medieval-tavern atmosphere, with arches and ceramics stuck into the fresco-adorned walls. The pastas are homemade, and the chef does a superb rognoncino (kidney) trifolato and sole meunière. A recommendable side dish is piselli (garden peas) alla fiorentina. The ultra-fresh vegetables are often served with olive oil, which your waiter will loudly proclaim as the world's finest.

INEXPENSIVE

Da Pennello. Via Dante Alighieri 4R. ☎ **055/294-848.** Main courses 12,000–22,000L ($7–$13); fixed-price menu 30,000L ($17). AE, MC, V. Tues–Sat noon–2:30pm and 7–10:15pm, Sun noon–2:30pm. Closed Aug 1–30 and Dec 25–Jan 3. Bus: 14. FLORENTINE/ ITALIAN.

This informally operated trattoria ("The Painter") offers many Florentine specialties on its à la carte menu and is known for its wide selection of antipasti; you can make a meal out of these delectable hors d'oeuvres. The ravioli is homemade, and one pasta specialty (loved by locals) is spaghetti carrettiera, made with tomatoes and pepperoni. To follow, you can have deviled roast chicken. The chef posts daily specials, and sometimes it's best to order one of these, as the food offered was bought fresh that day at the market. A Florentine cake, zuccotto, rounds out the meal. Da Penello is on a narrow street near Dante's house, about a 5-minute walk from the Duomo. As legend has it, it was opened in the 1500s when an artist, finding no market for his work, decided to feed artists who could sell their wares. These dining pals allegedly included Andrea del Sarto and Cellini.

Il Cavallino. Via della Farine 6R. ☎ **055/215-818.** Reservations recommended. Main courses 12,000–26,000L ($7–$15); fixed-price menu 30,000L ($17). AE, DC, MC, V. Thurs–Tues noon–2:30pm and 7–10pm. Bus: 14, 23, or 71. TUSCAN/ITALIAN.

Il Cavallino has been a local favorite since the 1930s. It's on a tiny street (which probably won't even be on your map) leading off Piazza della Signoria at its northern end. There's usually a gracious reception at the door, especially if you called for a reservation. Two of the three dining rooms have vaulted ceilings and peach-colored marble floors. The main room looks out over the piazza. Menu items are typical hearty Tuscan fare, including an assortment of boiled meats in green herb sauce, grilled filet of steak, chicken breast Medici style, and the inevitable Florentine spinach. The portions are large. Most diners prefer the house wine, but a limited selection of bottled wines is also available. "Every drop is a pleasure," the waiter assured us as he placed our carafe on the well-set table.

NEAR PIAZZA SANTA MARIA NOVELLA & THE TRAIN STATION
VERY EXPENSIVE

✪ **Harry's Bar.** Lungarno Vespucci 22R. ☎ **055/239-6700.** Reservations recommended. Main courses 19,000–34,000L ($11–$20). AE, MC, V. Mon–Sat noon–3pm and 7–11pm. Closed Dec 18–Jan 8 and 1 week in Aug. Bus: C, 6, 9, 11, 36, 37, or 68. ITALIAN/AMERICAN.

Harry's Bar, in an 18th-century building in a prime position on the Arno, has been an enclave of expats and well-heeled visiting Yankees since 1953, when it attracted the *Three Coins in the Fountain* set after they'd tossed their coins in the Trevi, said goodbye to Roma, and headed for Florence. Those days are gone forever and with them the memories of heady times when an Italian princess might arrive with a white rat perched on her shoulder (with which she'd exchange kisses). The international menu is select and beautifully prepared, including risotto or tagliatelle with ham, onions, and cheese and a tempting gamberetti (crayfish) cocktail. Harry has created his own tortellini, but his hamburger and his club sandwich are the most popular items. The chef also prepares about a dozen specialties every day: breast of chicken "our way," grilled giant-sized scampi, and lean broiled sirloin. An apple tart with cream nicely finishes off a meal. This remains the only place in Florence to get a perfect martini.

I Quattro Amici. Via degli Orti Oricellari 29. ☎ **055/215-413.** Reservations recommended. Main courses 43,000–70,000L ($25–$41). AE, DC, MC, V. Daily noon–3pm and 7–10:30pm. Bus: 10, 12, 25, 31, 32, or 91. SEAFOOD.

Run by four Tuscan entrepreneurs who had known each other since childhood, this restaurant occupies the street level of a modern building near the rail station. With a vaguely neoclassical decor, it serves endless quantities of fish to a landlocked crowd eager for memories of the sea. Specialties include pasta with shrimp and grappa, fish soup, fried shrimp, and squid Livorno style, and grilled, stewed, or baked versions of all the bounty of the Mediterranean. The roast sea bass and roast snapper, flavored with Mediterranean herbs, are among the finest dishes. The vegetables are fresh and flavorful. Every Thursday, Friday, and Saturday evening, diners are treated to live music.

MODERATE

Buca Lapi. Via del Trebbio 1R. ☎ **055/213-768.** Reservations required for dinner. Main courses 22,000–35,000L ($13–$20). AE, DC, MC, V. Tues–Sat 12:30–2:30pm and 7:30–10:30pm. Closed 2 weeks in Aug. Bus: 6, 9, 11, 36, 37, or 68. TUSCAN/INTERNATIONAL.

This cellar restaurant (under the Palazzo Antinori) opened in 1880 and is big on glamour, good food, and fun. The vaulted ceilings are covered with travel posters from all over the world. The cooks know how to turn out the classic dishes of the Tuscan kitchen with finesse, and there's a long table of interesting fruits, desserts, and vegetables. Skip the international fare. Specialties include scampi giganti alla griglia (super-sized shrimp) and bistecca alla fiorentina (local beefsteak). In season, the fagioli toscani all'olio (Tuscan beans in native olive oil) are a delicacy. For dessert, try crêpes Suzette or the local choice, zuccotto, a dome-shaped ice-cream cake studded with almonds and rich in chocolate. The wine list is full of reasonably priced Tuscan and Chianti wines.

✪ **Don Chisciotte.** Via Ridolfi 4R. ☎ **055/475-430.** Reservations recommended. Main courses 26,000–32,000L ($15–$19). AE, DC, MC, V. Mon 8–10:30pm, Tues–Sat 1–2:30pm and 8–10:30pm. Bus: 10, 12, 25, 31, 32, or 91. TUSCAN/SEAFOOD.

One floor above street level in a venerable Florentine palazzo, this restaurant is known for its creative cuisine and changing array of fresh fish. We feel we discovered this place, as we were touting its glory long before Michelin got around to discovering it.

Take a Gelato Break

Opened in the 1930s and today run by the third generation of the Vivoli family, the ✪ **Gelateria Vivoli,** Via Isola delle Stinche 7R (☎ 055/292-334), on a backstreet near Santa Croce, produces some of Italy's finest ice cream and provides the gelati for many of Florence's restaurants. Buy a ticket first and then select your flavor. Choose from blueberry, fig, melon, and other fruits in season, as well as chocolate mousse or coffee ice cream flavored with espresso. A special ice cream is made from rice. You can also choose from a number of semifreddi— an Italian ice cream using cream as a base instead of milk. The most popular flavors are almond, marengo (a type of meringue), and zabaglione (eggnog). Others are limoncini alla crema (candied lemon peels with vanilla ice cream) and aranciotti al cioccolate (candied orange peels with chocolate ice cream). Prices range from 3,000L to 16,000L ($1.75 to $9), and it's open Tuesday to Sunday 8am to 1am (closed 3 weeks in August; dates vary).

Of all the centrally located gelaterie, **Festival del Gelato,** Via del Corso 75R, just off Via dei Calzaiuoli (☎ **055/239-4386**), has been the only serious contender to Vivoli, offering about 50 flavors along with pounding pop music and colorful neon. It's open Tuesday to Sunday: summer 8am to 1am and winter 11am to 1am.

The soft pink dining room reflects the colors of the menu items, which are produced with a flourish from the kitchens. The cuisine is creative, based on flavors that are often enhanced by an unusual assortment of fresh herbs, vegetables, and fish stocks. Choose from risotto of broccoli and baby squid; red taglierini with clams, pesto, and cheese; black ravioli colored with squid ink and stuffed with a purée of shrimp and crayfish; and filet of turbot with radicchio sauce.

✪ **Sabatini.** Via de' Panzani 9A. ☎ **055/211-559.** Reservations recommended. Main courses 26,000–38,000L ($15–$22). AE, DC, MC, V. Tues–Sun 12:30–2:30pm and 7:30–10:30pm. Bus: 6, 9, 11, 36, 37, or 68. FLORENTINE.

Despite the less-than-chic location near the rail station, Florentines and visitors alike have long extolled Sabatini as the finest of the restaurants characteristic of the city. You'll get better food here than at the highly touted Enoteca Pinchiorri, which Michelin gives two stars but which has consistently drawn more reader disapproval (and we concur) than any other restaurant in Florence. To celebrate our annual return to Sabatini, we order the same main course we had on our first visit—boiled Valdarno chicken with a savory green sauce. Back then we complained to the waiter that the chicken was tough. He replied, "But, of course!" Florentines like chicken with muscle, not the hothouse variety so favored by Americans. Having eaten a lot of Valdarno chicken since then, we're now more appreciative of Sabatini's dish. But on subsequent visits we've found some of the other main courses more delectable, especially the veal scaloppine with artichokes, sole meunière, or classic beefsteak Florentine. Another specialty is spaghetti Sabatini, a cousin of spaghetti carbonara but enhanced with fresh tomatoes. American-style coffee is served, following the Florentine cake, called zuccotto.

✪ **Trattoria Garga.** Via del Moro 48R. ☎ **055/239-8898.** Reservations required. Main courses 30,000–50,000L ($17–$29). AE, DC, MC, V. Tues–Sat 7:30pm–midnight, Sun 7:30pm–midnight. Bus: 6, 9, 11, 36, 37, or 68. TUSCAN/FLORENTINE.

Some of the most creative cuisine in Florence is served here, between the Ponte Vecchio and Santa Maria Novella. The thick Renaissance walls contain paintings by both Florentine and American artists, including those painted by the owners, Giuliano Gargani and his Canadian wife, Sharon. Both operatic arias and heavenly odors emerge from a postage-stamp–sized kitchen. Many of the Tuscan menu items are so unusual that Sharon's bilingual skills are put to good use: octopus with peppers and garlic, boar with juniper berries, grilled marinated quail, and "whatever strikes the mood" of Giuliano. One dish has earned a lot of publicity—tagliarini magnifico, made with angel-hair pasta, orange and lemon rind, mint-flavored cream, and Parmesan cheese.

INEXPENSIVE

Buca Mario. Piazza Ottaviani 16R. ☎ **055/214-179.** Reservations recommended. Main courses 15,000–30,000L ($9–$17). AE, DC, MC, V. Fri–Tues 12:15–2:30pm and 7:15–10:30pm. Closed Aug. Bus: 6, 9, 11, 36, 37, or 68. FLORENTINE.

Buca Mario, in business for a century, is one of Florence's most famous cellar restaurants, located in the 1886 Palazzo Niccolini. While diners sit at tables beneath the vaulted ceilings, the waiters (some of whom have worked in the States) will suggest an array of fine-textured homemade pastas, grilled T-bone, Dover sole, or beef carpaccio, followed by a tempting selection of desserts, like "grandmother cake," a lemon-and-almond cake. We always like to begin with a medley of cured pork specialties called affettati toscani—the tastiest selection of "cold cuts" you're likely to encounter in Florence. There's a wonderful exuberance about the place, but in the enigmatic words of one longtime patron: "It's not for the fainthearted."

La Carabaccia. Via Palazzuolo 190R. ☎ **055/214-782.** Main courses 15,000–30,000L ($9–$17). AE, MC, V. Tues–Sat 12:30–2:30pm; daily 7:30–10:30pm. Closed 15 days in Aug. Bus: 6, 9, 11, 36, 37, or 68. FLORENTINE.

Two hundred years ago, a carabaccia was a workaday boat, shaped like a hollowed-out half onion and used on the Arno to dredge silt and sand from the bottom. This restaurant still features the favorite onion soup of the Medici, zuppa carabaccia, a creamy white onion soup served with croutons (not in the French style, the chef rushes to tell you). You can, of course, eat more than onions here. "It's always a delight," said one habitué, "to come by every day to see what inspired the chef at the market." The menu changes daily and is based on whatever fresh ingredients are available. There's always one soup, followed by four or five pastas, including crespelle (crêpe) of such fresh vegetables as asparagus or artichokes. Our savory swordfish baked in parchment with essence of fresh tomato was perfectly prepared, especially when served with the house wine, a white Galestro. You'll find the homemade breads irresistible (especially the onion variety).

Le Fonticine. Via Nazionale 79R. ☎ **055/282-106.** Reservations required for dinner. Main courses 14,000–28,000L ($8–$16). AE, DC, MC, V. Tues–Sat noon–3pm and 7:30–10pm. Closed Aug and Dec 24–Jan 6. Bus: 10, 12, 25, 31, 32, or 91. TUSCAN/BOLOGNESE.

Le Fonticine was part of a convent until owner Silvano Bruci converted both it and its adjoining garden into this hospitable restaurant close to the San Lorenzo food market. Today the richly decorated interior contains all the abundance of an Italian harvest, as well as the second passion of Signor Bruci's life, his collection of original modern paintings. The first passion, as a meal here reveals, is the cuisine he and his wife produce from recipes she collected from her childhood in Bologna.

Proceed to the larger of the two dining areas; along the way you can admire dozens of portions of fresh pasta decorating the table of an exposed grill. At the far end of the room a wrought-iron gate shelters the wine collection Mr. Bruci has amassed, like his paintings, over many years. The food, served in copious portions, is both traditional and delectable. Begin with a platter of fresh antipasti or with samplings of three of the most excellent pasta dishes of the day. You might follow with fegatina di pollo (chicken), veal scaloppine, or one of the other main dishes.

Osteria Numero Uno. Via del Moro 18–20R. ☎ **055/284-897.** Reservations recommended. Main courses 18,000–35,000L ($10–$20). AE, DC, MC, V. Mon 7pm–12:30am, Tues–Sat 11am–3pm and 7pm–12:30am. Closed 2 weeks in Aug. Bus: C, 6, 9, 11, 36, 37, or 68. INTERNATIONAL/FLORENTINE.

This restaurant derives its name from its original location at no. 1 (numero uno) on a street near its present location on Via del Moro. In 1985, it moved to its new premises in a 15th-century palazzo a 3-minute walk from the rail station. The cuisine is a well-prepared, well-presented blend of international foods and Italian dishes. Many patrons (often lawyers, civil servants, and reporters) prefer the main dining room, with its vaulted ceiling and oversized fireplace, though two adjacent dining rooms contain the spillover. Menu choices include taglierini with mushrooms (with or without truffles); ravioli stuffed with ricotta and basil or fresh artichokes; risotto with asparagus or sweet peppers; carpaccio of beef or salmon; chicken with marsala or Parmesan; turbot baked with artichokes, herbs, and potatoes; and Florentine-style beefsteak, usually prepared for two. The atmosphere is often rushed, with rather hysterical waiters darting about.

Ristorante Otello. Via degli Orti Oricellari 36R. ☎ **055/216-517.** Reservations recommended. Main courses 12,000–30,000L ($7–$17). AE, DC, MC, V. Daily noon–3pm and 7:30–11pm. Bus: 10, 12, 25, 31, 32, or 91. FLORENTINE/TUSCAN.

Next to the train station, the Otello serves an animated crowd in comfortably renovated surroundings. Its antipasto Toscano is one of the best in town, an array of appetizing hors d'oeuvres that practically becomes a meal in itself. The waiter urges you to "Mangi, mangi, mangi!" ("Eat, eat, eat!") and that's what diners do. You might want to try one of the wonderful pasta dishes, such as spaghetti with baby clams or pappardelle with garlic sauce. The meat and poultry dishes are equally delectable, including sole meunière and veal pizzaiola with lots of garlic.

Sostanza. Via del Porcellana 25R. ☎ **055/212-691.** Reservations recommended. Main courses 15,000–28,000L ($9–$16). No credit cards. Mon–Fri noon–2:10pm and 7:30–9:30pm. Closed Aug and 2 weeks at Christmas. Bus: C, 6, 9, 11, 36, 37, or 68. FLORENTINE.

Sostanza is the city's oldest (opened in 1869) and most revered trattoria. It has long been where working people have gone for excellent moderately priced food. In recent years, however, it has begun attracting a more sophisticated set too, despite its somewhat raffish atmosphere. Florentines call the place Troia, which means "the trough" but also suggests a woman of easy virtue. The small dining room has crowded family tables, but when you taste what comes out of that kitchen, you'll know that fancy decor would be superfluous. Specialties include breaded chicken breast and a succulent T-bone. You might also want to try tripe in the Florentine way: cut into strips, then baked in a casserole with tomatoes, onions, and Parmesan cheese.

Trattoria Antellesi. Via Faenza 9R. ☎ **055/216-990.** Reservations recommended. Main courses 15,000–25,000L ($9–$15). AE, DC, MC, V. Daily noon–3pm and 7–10:30pm. Bus: 1, 6, 7, 11, 17, 33, 67, or 68. TUSCAN.

Occupying a 15th-century historic monument, steps from the Medici Chapels, this place is devoted almost exclusively to well-prepared versions of time-tested Tuscan recipes. Owned by Enrico Verrecchia and his Arizona-born wife, Janice, the restaurant prepares at least seven *piatti del giorno* (daily specials) that change according to the market's ingredients. Dishes might include tagliatelle with porcini mushrooms or braised arugula, crespelle alla fiorentina (cheesy spinach crêpe introduced to France by Catherine de' Medici's kitchen staff), pappardelle with wild boar, market-fresh fish (generally on Friday), Valdostana chicken, and properly grilled bistecca alla fiorentina. The array of quality Italian wines (with an emphasis on Tuscany) has for the most part been selected by Janice herself.

NEAR PIAZZA SAN MARCO
INEXPENSIVE

Cafaggi. Via Guelfa 35R. ☎ **055/294-989.** Reservations recommended. Main courses 12,000–30,000L ($7–$17); fixed-price menu 24,000L ($14). AE, MC, V. Mon–Sat noon–3pm and 7–10pm. Bus: 1, 6, 7, 11, 17, 33, 67, or 68. TUSCAN.

Atmospheric and charming, this 100 seat trattoria has flourished in this modestly proportioned palazzo since 1922. The tables are scattered throughout two old-fashioned dining rooms. The menu features Tuscan dishes, including Florentine beefsteak, steaming bowls of vegetarian soup, and grilled fish accompanied with rice, potatoes, or a medley of very fresh salads and vegetables. Forget the calories and try the millefoglie alle creme for dessert—it positively overflows with cream.

l'Toscano. Via Guelfa 70R. ☎ **055/215-475.** Reservations recommended at dinner. Main courses 12,000–35,000L ($7–$20); fixed-price menu 27,000L ($16). AE, DC, MC, V. Wed–Mon noon–2:30pm and 7:30–10:30pm. Closed Aug 1–15. Bus: 12 or 91. TUSCAN.

Bouquets of flowers liven up this restaurant's mostly beige interior, but despite the understated setting, the place is a magnet for gastronomes who appreciate the all-Tuscan specialties that emerge from its kitchens. Menu items change with the seasons but are often at their best in late autumn and winter, when mixed platters with slices of wild boar, venison, partridge, and (when available) pheasant are a worthy substitute for the antipasti that tempt visitors the rest of the year. Ravioli, made on the premises and stuffed with spinach, is always popular, as well as any of several forms of gnocchi or tagliatelle. Fish (usually sea bass or monkfish, pan-fried or grilled) is most prominent on Friday, but veal, turkey, pork, and Florentine beefsteaks are also offered.

NEAR PIAZZA SANTA CROCE
MODERATE

✪ **Cibreo.** Via dei Macci 118R. ☎ **055/234-1100.** Reservations recommended in restaurant, not accepted in trattoria. Main courses 45,000L ($26) in restaurant, 20,000L ($12) in trattoria. AE, DC, MC, V (restaurant only). Tues–Sat 12:45–2:30pm and 7:30–11:15pm. Closed late July–early Sept. Bus: 13 or 14. TUSCAN.

The unpretentious Cibreo consists of a restaurant, a less formal tavern-style trattoria, and a cafe/bar across the street. The impossibly old-fashioned small kitchen is noteworthy for neither containing a grill nor serving pastas. Cibreo is the brainchild of the inventive Fabio Picchi and Benedetta Vitali. Menu items include a sformato (a soufflé made from potatoes and ricotta, served with Parmesan cheese and tomato sauce), inzimmino (Tuscan-style squid stewed with spinach), and a flan of Parmesan cheese, veal tongue, and artichokes. The cicina is high spirited, flavored with garlic and spice—one Florentine reviewer even called it "lusty."

Some of the staff are expatriate New Yorkers who excel at explaining the culinary themes. The restaurant takes its name from (and serves) an old Tuscan dish (cibreo) that was allegedly so delectable it nearly killed Catherine de' Medici. (She consumed so much she was overcome with near-fatal indigestion.) The dish is prepared only on request, and usually for specially catered meals ordered in advance. It combines the organs, meat, and crest (or comb) of a chicken with tons of garlic, rosemary, sage, and wine. Chocoholics can finish off with the flourless chocolate cake, so sinfully good it should be outlawed.

Del Fagioli. Corso dei Tintori 47R. ☎ **055/244-285.** Reservations recommended. Main courses 25,000–45,000L ($15–$26). No credit cards. Mon–Fri noon–2:30pm and 7:30–10:30pm. Closed Aug. Bus: 23 or 71. FLORENTINE/TUSCAN.

Devoted to the pleasures of country-style Tuscan cuisine, this restaurant (whose name translates as "beans") occupies a pair of dining rooms lined with old engravings of Florence's monuments. It serves a choice of locally made affettati toscani (sausages, pâtés, and dried or salted meats), hearty ribollita (cabbage and bread soup), several types of spaghetti and tagliatelle, sliced turkey breast, Florentine beefsteak, and game dishes in season. Fish might include oven-roasted sea bass or monkfish, its flavor enhanced with herbs.

La Baraonda. Via Ghibellina 67R. ☎ **055/234-1171.** Reservations recommended. Lunch main courses 15,000L ($9); dinner main courses 25,000L ($15). AE, DC, MC, V. Tues–Sat 1–2:30pm; Mon–Sat 7:30–10pm. Bus: 14. TUSCAN.

Locals (many of them merchants and hotel employees) make up about 80% of the crowd at this bustling trattoria serving Tuscan cuisine flavored with seasonal local ingredients. Some members of the staff speak fluent English and in many cases will propose carefully assembled fixed-price meals. Examples from the ever-changing menu are sformato di verdure (vegetable soufflé made with artichokes or whatever else is in season), risotto with fresh greens, and a savory meat loaf (polpettone in umido) made with veal and tomatoes. At the end of the meal, complimentary sweets and grappa are served.

INEXPENSIVE

Ristorante Dino. Via Ghibellina 51R. ☎ **055/241-452.** Reservations recommended. Main courses 18,000–22,000L ($10–$13). AE, DC, MC, V. Tues–Sat noon–3pm and 7:30–10:30pm, Sun noon–2:30pm. Bus: 14. TUSCAN.

In a 14th-century building near the Casa Buonarroti, this animated restaurant has vaulted ceilings and a cuisine inspired by members of the Casini family. Specialties include spaghetti alla Dino, flavored with carrots, celery, chiles, and aromatic herbs; risotto della Renza, rich with aromatic herbs and fresh tomatoes; and ribollita, the cabbage, bean, and bread soup of Tuscany. Tuscan purists often flash back to their childhoods at the mention of one ever-present dish: garetto Ghibellino, a historic recipe made from pork shanks with celery and sage. The excellent wine list features vintages from around Italy, especially Tuscany.

Trattoria Pallottino. Via Isola della Stinche 1R. ☎ **055/289-573.** Reservations recommended at dinner. Main courses 13,000–26,000L ($8–$15). AE, DC, MC, V. Tues–Sun 12:30–2:30pm and 7:30–11pm. Bus: 14, 23, or 71. TUSCAN/FLORENTINE.

On a narrow street less than a block from Piazza Santa Croce, this distinctive restaurant contains only two sometimes cramped dining rooms. Flickering candles illuminate a timeless Italian scene where the staff works hard, usually with humor and style. Menu specialties include succulent antipasti, tagliolini with cream and herbs, and ravioli with spinach or pine nuts and cream sauce, as well as peposa (a slab of beef marinated for at least 4 hours in a rich broth of ground black pepper, olive oil, and tomatoes) and spaghetti fiacchiraia (spaghetti laden with spicy red chiles, olive oil, and tomatoes). Dessert might be vanilla custard drizzled with a compôte of fresh fruit.

NEAR THE PONTE VECCHIO
MODERATE

La Nandina. Borgo SS. Apostoli 64R. ☎ **055/213-024.** Reservations recommended. Main courses 20,000–35,000L ($12–$20). AE, DC, MC, V. Mon 7–10:30pm, Tues–Sat noon–3pm and 7–10:30pm. Closed 2 weeks in Aug. Bus: 23 or 71. TUSCAN/INTERNATIONAL.

This family-run restaurant is just off the Arno, about a 4-minute walk from the Uffizi. Opened in 1924, this elegant restaurant is an old favorite with both Florentines and visitors. You can have an apéritif in the plushly upholstered cocktail lounge and dine in the 14th-century cellar. The cuisine consists of dishes from the provinces as well as from Rome and Venice and might include ravioli with flap mushrooms, spinach crêpes, curried breast of capon, veal piccatina, several kinds of beefsteak, and a changing array of daily specials. All the food is high quality but not fussy.

INEXPENSIVE

Buca dell'Orafo. Via Volta dei Girolami 28R. ☎ **055/213-619.** Main courses 15,000–30,000L ($9–$17). No credit cards. Tues–Sat 12:30–2:30pm and 7:30–10:30pm. Closed Aug and 2 weeks in Dec. Bus: 23 or 71. FLORENTINE.

This is an authentic neighborhood restaurant whose cuisine is firmly rooted in Tuscan traditions and whatever happens to be in season. Accessible via an alley stretching beneath a vaulted arcade adjacent to Piazza del Pesce, it's named after the *orafo* (goldsmith shop) that used to occupy its premises throughout the Renaissance. The place is usually stuffed with regulars, who appreciate the fact that the chef has made almost no concessions to international palates. Your pasta (usually taglierini) will probably be garnished with a seasonal vegetable, like asparagus, broccoli rabe, mushrooms, peas, or asparagus. Florentine tripe and beefsteak are enduring favorites, as is *stracotto e fagioli* (beef braised in a sauce of chopped vegetables and red wine), served with beans in tomato sauce.

NEAR PIAZZA TRINITA
MODERATE

✪ **Il Latini.** Via del Palchetti 6R (off Via dei Vigna Nuova). ☎ **055/210-916.** Reservations recommended. Main courses 12,000–25,000L ($7–$15). AE, DC, MC, V. Tues–Sun 12:30–2:30pm and 7:30–10:30pm. Closed 15 days in Aug and 2 weeks around Christmas and New Year's. Bus: C, 6, 11, 36, 37, or 68. TUSCAN/FLORENTINE.

It's loud and claustrophobic and service borders on hysterical, but this is an enduringly popular place, with long lines. Diners spend about 50,000L ($29) per person for a vast amount of food. A waiter will arrive to recite a list of items corresponding to antipasti, pasti, main course, and dessert. If you insist on seeing a printed menu, someone will probably find one, but it's a lot more fun just to go with the flow. Don't expect decorative subtleties: The paintings are garish, and nobody is shy about displaying each and every framed award the place has ever earned; even the ceiling is festooned with hanging ham hocks, cheeses, and salamis. You can enjoy heaping portions of pastas like penne with meat and cream sauce, deep-fried zucchini flowers or artichokes, and grilled meats that include veal, chicken, beef, and pork.

ACROSS THE ARNO
EXPENSIVE

La Capannina di Sante. Piazza Ravenna, adjacent to the Ponte Giovanni da Verrazzano. ☎ **055/68-8345.** Reservations recommended. Main courses 25,000–65,000L ($15–$38); fixed-price menu 90,000L ($52). AE, DC, MC, V. Mon–Sat 7:30pm–1am. Closed 1 week in Aug. SEAFOOD.

This simple and unpretentious restaurant, featuring a riverview terrace, has functioned in more or less the same way on and off since 1935. It serves only the best and freshest seafood, prepared in a healthy manner, usually with olive oil or butter and Mediterranean seasonings. Examples are filet of sea bass or turbot, mixed seafood grill, and an occasional portion of veal or steak. For an appetizer, we recommend the sampling of hot seafood—there's none finer in Florence. The wines are simple and straightforward, and the greeting is warm and friendly. You can take a taxi to reach this place.

Trattoria Vittoria. Via della Fonderia 52R. ☎ **055/225-657.** Reservations recommended. Main courses 20,000–45,000L ($12–$26). AE, DC, MC, V. Thurs–Tues noon–3:30pm and 7:30–10:30pm. Bus: C, 6, 11, 36, 37, or 68. SEAFOOD.

This unheralded place serves some of the finest fish in Florence. It's a big and bustling trattoria, with frenetic service. Most of the fresh fish dishes of the day are priced according to weight, making a main dish considerably higher than the prices above. Sole is the most expensive. Two savory choices to begin your meal are risotto alla marinara and spaghetti alla vongole (clams). The mixed fish fry gives you a little bit of everything. The desserts are homemade and extremely rich.

MODERATE

Mamma Gina. Borgo Sant' Jacopo 37R. ☎ **055/239-6009.** Reservations required for dinner. Main courses 20,000–30,000L ($12–$17). AE, DC, MC, V. Mon–Sat noon–2:30pm and 7–10pm. Closed Aug 7–21. Bus: C, 6, 11, 36, 37, or 68. TUSCAN.

Mamma Gina is a rustic restaurant that prepares fine foods in the traditional bustling manner. Though run by a corporation that operates other restaurants around Tuscany, this place is named after its founding matriarch, whose legend has continued despite her death in the 1980s. A few of the savory menu items are cannelloni Mamma Gina (stuffed with a purée of minced meats, spices, and vegetables), tagliolini with artichoke hearts or mushrooms and whatever else is in season, and chicken breast Mamma Gina, baked in the northern Italian style with prosciutto and Emmenthaler cheese. This is an ideal spot for lunch after visiting the Pitti Palace.

Trattoria Cammillo. Borgo Sant' Jacopo 57R. ☎ **055/212-427.** Reservations required. Main courses 16,000–40,000L ($9–$23). AE, DC, MC, V. Thurs–Tues noon–2:30pm and 7:30–10:30pm. Closed mid-Dec to Jan and Aug 1–21. Bus: C, 6, 11, 36, 37, or 68. TUSCAN.

On the ground floor of a former Medici palace, the Cammillo is one of the most popular (and perhaps the finest) of the Oltrarno dining spots. Its most serious rival is Mamma Gina. Snobbish boutique owners cross the Arno regularly to feast here; they know they'll get specialties like tagliatelle flavored with fresh peas and truffles. This sounds like such a simple dish, but when it's prepared right, it's a real treat. You'll also find excellent assortments of fried or grilled vegetables, superfresh scampi and sole, fried deboned pigeon with artichokes, and chicken breast with truffles and Parmesan. The trattoria is between the Ponte Vecchio and Ponte Santa Trínita. Because of increased business, you're likely to be rushed through a meal.

INEXPENSIVE

La Baruciola. Via Maggio 61R. ☎ **055/281-906.** Reservations recommended. Main courses 9,000–18,000L ($5–$10). AE, DC, MC, V. Mon–Sat 12:30–2:30pm and 7–10:30pm. Bus: B or C. TUSCAN.

In a 16th-century building adjacent to the Pitti Palace, this restaurant celebrates the art of *cucina casalinga* (home cooking) and draws a busy crowd of Tuscans searching for the cuisine of their childhoods. In a pair of white dining rooms whose decor is understated you can enjoy pastas like homemade ravioli with butter and sage;

mushroom soup; penne with mushrooms and cream; ribollita, the heady soup of Tuscany; and a mixed platter of fish or smoked meat. The place appeals to those who like simple well-prepared dishes, brimming with flavor but low in price.

Pierot. Piazza Tadeo Gaddi 25R. ☎ **055/702-100.** Reservations recommended. Main courses 10,000–20,000L ($6–$12). AE, DC, MC, V. Mon–Sat noon–3pm and 7–11pm. Closed July 15–31. Bus: 9, 11, or 36. SEAFOOD/TUSCAN.

Pierot, which has been a fixture here since 1955, is housed in a 19th-century building constructed during the reign of Vittorio Emanuel. Though a few other places also specialize in seafood, this is a bit of an oddity in landlocked Florence. The seasonal menu varies with the availability of ingredients but may include linguine with frutti di mare (fruits of the sea), pasta with lobster sauce, and a choice of traditional Tuscan steaks, soups, and vegetables. Seafood risotto is deservedly a favorite. The wine list features some 120 choices.

Trattoria Angiolino. Via San Spirito 36R. ☎ **055/239-8976.** Reservations recommended. Main courses 13,000–20,000L ($8–$12). AE, DC, MC, V. Tues–Sun 12:30–1:30pm and 7–10:30pm. Bus: C, 6, 11, 36, 37, or 68. ITALIAN/TUSCAN.

This restaurant has thrived in this 14th-century building since the 1920s and has fed a friend or relative of virtually everyone in Florence. The decor is old-timey and warm, with a potbellied stove and brick floors, and the menu includes Tuscan and Italian dishes that many visitors remember from their childhood. Choose from an array of antipasti, steaming bowls of pasta e fagioli (beans), a roster of homemade pastas like ravioli and taglioni, veal and chicken cutlets prepared either Milanese or parmigiana style, and rich homemade cakes and pastries.

5 Seeing the Sights

Florence was the fountainhead of the Renaissance, the city of Dante and Boccaccio. Florentines are noted for their cunning, as represented by Machiavelli; however, they're not noted for their religious zeal, as evoked by Savonarola, who might've found a better reception in Geneva. For 3 centuries the city was dominated by the Medici family, patrons of the arts and masters of assassination. But it is chiefly through Florence's incomparable artists that we know of the apogee of the Renaissance: Ghiberti, Fra Angelico, Donatello, Brunelleschi, Botticelli, Leonardo da Vinci, and Michelangelo.

In Florence we can trace the transition from medievalism to the age of "rebirth." For example, all modern painters owe a debt to an ugly, unkempt man named Masaccio (Vasari's "Slipshod Tom") who died at 27. Modern painting began with his frescoes in the Brancacci Chapel in Santa Maria del Carmine, which you can see today. Years later, Michelangelo painted a more celebrated Adam and Eve in the Sistine Chapel, but even this great artist never realized the raw humanity of Masaccio's Adam and Eve fleeing from the Garden of Eden.

Group tourism has so overwhelmed this city that in 1996 officials demanded organized tour groups to book visits in advance and pay an admission fee. No more than 150 tour buses are allowed into the center at one time—considering the smallness of the place, that's still a large amount. Today, there are more than seven tourists for each native Florentine. And that doesn't even count the day-trippers, who rush off to Venice in the late afternoon. But despite all its traffic and inconveniences, Florence is still one the world's greatest art cities. Those tour buses are here for a reason.

For information on specialized sightseeing tours of Florence and the surrounding countryside, see the "Tuscan Tours" box in chapter 7.

Getting Tickets to the Uffizi

As tourism to Italy increases, so do the lines to get into the major museums. Much of the problem behind the Uffizi's often alarming wait is the security policy regulating the number of visitors inside at any one time. Now you can buy tickets in advance for a designated time and day, eliminating an often 3-hour wait in peak season. You can stand (and stand) in line at the museum or try the following:

- Call ☎ **055/471-960** Monday to Friday 8am to 6:30pm. You'll receive information (there's always an English speaker) on how to send an international bank draft (this is the expensive and complicated option for non-credit card holders), or you'll be given the fax number to authorize payment by Master-Card or Visa only. They permit groups of 40 reserved ticket holders to enter every 15 minutes: In high season be flexible with alternative days you want to request; requests must be made a minimum of 5 days in advance (some exceptions will be made). Cost is the usual museum admission of 12,000L ($7) plus a 2,400L ($1.40). It'll be the best 2,400L you ever spend.

- On arrival in Florence, you must pick up the tickets at the train station's tourist office (see "Visitor Information"); at the I.T.A. office, Viale Gramsci 9A (not a terribly convenient address); or at the Uffizi's ticket-sales booth on the designated day and time your visit has been approved. Show up 5 minutes early and walk directly past the hours-long line of those who didn't read this book.

THE TOP MUSEUMS

✪ **Uffizi Galleries (Galleria degli Uffizi).** Piazzale degli Uffizi 6. ☎ **055/238-8651.** Admission 12,000L ($7). Tues–Sat 8:30am–6:50pm, Sun and holidays 8:30am–1:50pm (last entrance 30 minutes before closing). Bus: 23 or 71.

On the 1737 death of Anna Maria Ludovica, the last Medici grand duchess, she bequeathed to the people of Tuscany a wealth of Renaissance and even classical art. The paintings and sculptures had been accumulated by the powerful grand dukes during 3 centuries of rule that witnessed the height of the Renaissance. All this is housed in an impressive palazzo commissioned by Duke Cosimo de' Medici in 1560 and initiated by Giorgio Vasari to house the Duchy of Tuscany's administrative offices (*uffizi* means "offices").

To see and have time to absorb all the Uffizi's paintings would take at least 2 weeks, so we'll present only the sketchy highlights. The Uffizi is nicely grouped into periods or schools to show the development and progress of Italian and European art.

Room 2: Here you'll meet up with those rebels from Byzantium, Cimabue and his pupil Giotto, with their Madonnas and bambini. Since the Virgin and Child seem to be the overriding theme of the earlier Uffizi artists, it's enlightening just to follow the different styles over the centuries, from the ugly, almost midget-faced babies of the post-Byzantine works to the red-cheeked chubby cherubs that glorified the baroque. One of the great works in the center of the salon is Giotto's masterful *Ognissanti Maestà* (1310). Dante wrote in *Purgatory,* "Cimabue thought that he held the field in painting, but now Giotto is acclaimed and his fame obscured."

Room 3: Look for Simone Martini's *Annunciation,* full of grace; the halo around the head of the Virgin doesn't conceal her pouty mouth. Fra Angelico of Fiesole, a 15th-century painter lost in a world peopled with saints and angels, makes his Uffizi debut with (naturally) *Madonna and Bambino.* A special treasure is the *Santa Trinita Madonna* by Masaccio, who died at an early age but is credited as the father of modern painting: In his Madonnas and bambini we see the beginnings of the use of perspective in painting. Fra Angelico's *Coronation of the Virgin* is also in this salon.

Room 8: Here you'll find Friar Filippo Lippi's far-superior *Coronation of the Virgin,* as well as a galaxy of charming Madonnas. He was a rebel among the brethren.

Rooms 10 to 14: These are the Botticelli rooms, with his finest works. Botticelli ("little barrels") was the nickname of the great master of women in flowing gowns, Sandro Filipepi. Many come to contemplate his "Venus on the Half Shell": This supreme conception of life—the *Birth of Venus*—really packs 'em in. But before being captured by Venus, check out *Minerva Subduing the Centaur,* which brought about renewed interest in mythological subjects. Botticelli's *Allegory of Spring* or *Primavera* is a gem; it's often called a symphony because you can listen to it. Set in a citrus grove, it depicts Venus with Cupid hovering over her head; Mercury looks out of the canvas to the left. Before leaving the room, look for Botticelli's *Adoration of the Magi,* in which you'll find portraits of the Medici (the vain man at the far right is Botticelli with golden curls and a yellow robe), and his allegorical *Calumny.* The rooms also contain the *Adoration of the Shepherds,* a superbly detailed triptych commissioned for a once-important Tuscan family and painted by Hugo van der Goes, a 15th-century artist.

Room 15: Here you'll come across one of Leonardo da Vinci's unfinished paintings, the brilliant *Adoration of the Magi,* and Verrocchio's *Baptism of Christ,* not a very important painting but noted because Leonardo painted one of the angels when he was 14. Also here hangs Leonardo's *Annunciation,* reflecting the early years of his genius with its twilight atmosphere and each leaf painstakingly in place. The splendid Renaissance palace he designed is part of the background.

Room 18: The most beautiful room in the gallery, with its dome of pearl shells, contains the *Venus of the Medici* at center stage; it's one of the most reproduced of all Greek sculptural works, a 1st-century copy of a Greek original.

Room 19: This room is devoted to Perugino, especially his *Madonna* and his *Portrait of Francesco delle Opere,* and to Luca Signorelli's *Holy Family.* Signorelli was taught by his master, Piero della Francesca, to convey depth and perspective, as illustrated by this work.

Room 20: This room takes you into the world of German artists who worked in Florence—notably Lucas Cranach and Dürer, both intrigued with the Adam and Eve theme.

Room 21: You'll see the beginnings of important Venetian painting here, as exemplified by Giovanni Bellini's *Sacred Allegory.*

Room 22: It contains a calvacade of northern Europeans, especially Hans Holbein the Younger's *Portrait of Sir Richard Southwell.*

Room 23: Correggio's *Rest on the Flight to Egypt* (1515) dominates this room, but the finest pieces are by Andrea Mantegna (1489)—*Epiphany, Circumcision,* and *Ascension.*

On May 27, 1993, a terrorist bomb (presumably planted by the Mafia) blasted through a section of the Uffizi. Though paintings were destroyed, many masterpieces, including works by Botticelli and Michelangelo, were spared, some because they were protected by shatterproof glass. In all, 200 works of art were damaged but only 3 completely destroyed.

In early 1998, the Uffizi reopened nine rooms damaged by the blast. In seven of these, paintings by Veronese, Tintoretto, and non–Italian Renaissance masters are displayed, and the other two feature Titians. The Uffizi owns two Titian interpretations of Venus (one depicted with Cupid). When it came to representing voluptuous

A Tip on Seeing *David*

The wait to get in to see *David* can be up to an hour. Try getting to the Accademia before the museum opens in the morning or an hour or two before closing.

females on canvas, Titian had no rival. In other rooms are important Mannerists: Parmigianino, Veronese, and Tintoretto (*Leda and the Swan*). Works by Rubens, Caravaggio (*Bacchus*), and Rembrandt are also displayed. The masterpieces are Michelangelo's *Holy Family* (1506 to 1508) and Raphael's Leonardoesque *Madonna of the Goldfinch* (1505) and his portraits of Pope Julius II and Pope Leo X. Final adjustments to the placement of these works may be made before the Uffizi assigns them permanent positions.

✪ Academy Gallery (Galleria dell'Accademia). Via Ricasoll 60. ☎ **055/238-8609.** Admission 12,000L ($7) adults; ages 17 and under free. Tues–Sat 8:30am–6:50pm, Sun 8:30am–1:50pm. Bus: 1, 6, 7, 11, 17, 33, 67, or 68.

This museum boasts many paintings and sculptures, but they're completely overshadowed by one work: Michelangelo's colossal *David,* unveiled in 1504 and now the world's most fabled sculpture. It first stood in Piazza della Signoria but was moved to the Academy in 1873 (a copy was substituted). One of the most sensitive accounts we've ever read of how Michelangelo turned the 17-foot "Duccio marble" into *Il Gigante* (the Giant) is related in Irving Stone's *The Agony and the Ecstasy.* Stone describes a Michelangelo "burning with marble fever" who set out to create a *David* who "would be Apollo, but considerably more; Hercules, but considerably more; Adam, but considerably more; the most fully realized man the world had yet seen, functioning in a rational and humane world."

How well Michelangelo succeeded is much in evidence today. Spawning controversy down through the years and even attacked with a hammer in 1991, *David* is also the world's most reproduced statue with or without a fig leaf. However, it hasn't always met with admirers. A 19th-century visitor, William Hazlitt, claimed the masterpiece was but "an awkward overgrown actor at one of our minor theaters, without his clothes." Over the centuries, *David* has also become a symbol of homosexual camp, its reproductions (often bad) adorning gay restaurants, bars, hotels, and certainly apartments around the world. There's even a restaurant in Las Vegas where the statue's rhinestone-studded fig leaf is raised and lowered every 5 minutes.

David is so overpowering in his majesty that many visitors head here just to see him and leave immediately after. However, the hall leading up to him is lined with other Michelangelos, notably his quartet of celebrated nonfiniti *Prisoners* or *Slaves.* "With my mother's milk, I sucked in the hammer and chisels I use for my statues," wrote Michelangelo. The statues are presumably unfinished, though art historians have found them more dramatic in their current state as they depict the struggles of figures to free themselves from stone. Originally intended for the tomb of Pope Julius II, these statues were worked on for 40 years by Michelangelo, who was never pleased with them. The gallery also displays Michelangelo's statue of St. Matthew, which he began carving in 1504.

The Academy also owns a gallery of paintings, usually considered to be of minor importance (works by Santi di Tito, Granacci, and Albertinelli, for example). Yet there are masterpieces as well, notably Lo Scheggia's 1440s *Cassone Adimari,* a panel from a wedding chest.

✪ Pitti Palace (Palazzo Pitti) and Boboli Gardens (Giardini di Boboli). Piazza dei Pitti. ☎ **055/238-85** for palace, ☎ **055/238-85** for gardens. Admission to palace: Palatina,

12,000L ($7); Galleria d'Arte Moderna, 8,000L ($4.65); Argenti, 4,000L ($2.30). Admission to gardens: 4,000L ($2.30). Palace: Tues–Sat 8:30am–6:50pm, Mon 8:30am–1:50pm. Gardens: Apr–May and Oct daily 9am–6:30pm; June–Sept daily 9am–7:30pm; Nov–Feb daily 9am–4:30pm; Mar daily 9am–5:30pm. Last admission 1 hour before closing. Bus: B or C.

The massive bulk of the **Palazzo Pitti** is one of Europe's greatest artistic treasure troves, with the city's most extensive coterie of museums embracing a painting gallery second only to the Uffizi. It's a virtual calvacade of the works of Titian, Rubens, Raphael, and Andrea del Sarto. The Pitti, built in the mid-15th century (Brunelleschi was probably the original architect), was once the residence of the powerful Medici family. It's located across the Arno (a 5-minute walk from the Ponte Vecchio).

There are actually several museums in this complex, the most important of which is the first-floor **Galleria Palatina,** housing one of Europe's great art collections, with masterpieces hung one on top of the other as in the days of the Enlightenment. If for no other reason, you should come for its Raphaels. After passing through the main door, proceed to the Sala di Venere (Venus), where you'll find Titian's *La Bella,* of rich and illuminating color (entrance wall), and portrait of Pietro Aretino, one of his most distinguished works. On the opposite wall are Titian's *Concert of Music,* often attributed to Giorgione, and his portrait of Julius II.

In the Sala di Apollo (on the opposite side of the entrance door) are Titian's *Man with Gray Eyes*—an aristocratic handsome romanticist—and his luminously gold *Mary Magdalene,* covered only with her long hair. On the opposite wall are van Dyck portraits of Charles I of England and Henrietta of France. This salon also contains some of the grandest works of Andrea del Sarto, notably his *Holy Family* and his *Deposition.*

In the Sala di Marte (entrance wall) is an important *Madonna and Child* by Murillo of Spain and the Pitti's best-known work by Rubens, *The Four Philosophers.* Rubens obviously had so much fun with this rather lighthearted work that he painted himself in the far left (that's his brother, Filippo, seated). On the left wall is one of Ruben's most tragic and moving works, *Consequences of War*—an early *Guernica,* painted in his declining years.

In the Sala di Giove (entrance wall) are Andrea del Sarto's idealized *John the Baptist* in his youth and Fra Bartolomeo's *Descent from the Cross.* On the third wall (opposite the entrance wall) is the Pitti's second famous Raphael, *La Velata,* the woman under the veil, known as La Fornarina, his bakery-girl mistress.

In the following gallery, the Sala di Saturno, look to the left on the entrance wall to see Raphael's *Madonna of the Canopy.* On the third wall near the doorway is the greatest Pitti prize, Raphael's *Madonna of the Chair,* his best-known interpretation of the Virgin and what's probably one of the six most celebrated paintings in all Europe. In the Sala dell'Iliade (to your left on the entrance wall) is a work of delicate beauty, Raphael's rendition of a pregnant woman. On the left wall is Titian's *Portrait of a Gentleman,* which he was indeed. (Titian is the second big star in the Palatine Gallery.) Other masterpieces are in the smaller rooms that follow, notably the Sala dell'Educazione di Giove, home to the 1608 *Sleeping Cupid* that "the divine" Caravaggio painted in Rome while escaping charges of murder in Malta.

The **Appartamenti Reali** boasts lavish reminders of when the Pitti was a private residence. This was once the home of the Kings of Savoy, when they presided over a unified Italy. Reopened in 1993 after restoration, these apartments in all their baroque sumptuousness, including a flamboyant decor and works of art by del Sarto and Caravaggio, can be viewed only on a guided tour, usually Tuesday and Saturday (also on an occasional Thursday) 9 to 11am and 3 to 5pm. Tours leave every hour. Reservations are needed, so call ☎ **051/238-8614.**

Florence Attractions

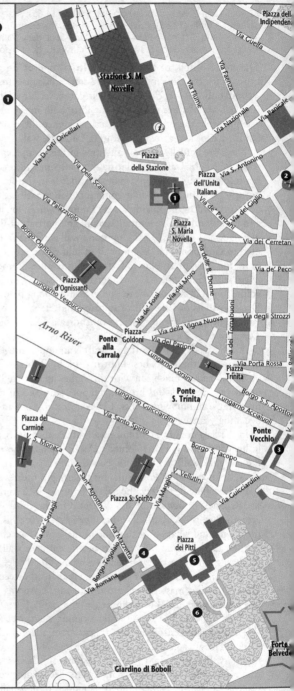

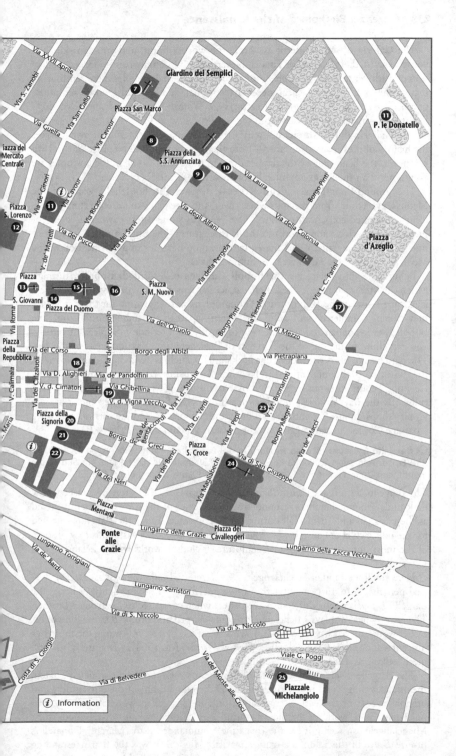

The **Galeria d'Arte Moderna** is hardly the world's finest, and you can skip it if you're exhausted after all those Titians. Nevertheless, it contains an important collection of 19th-century proto-Impressionist works of the Macchiaioli school, embracing many romantic and neoclassical pieces. Exceptional are Giovanni Dupré's sculptural group *Cain and Abel* and Giovanni Fattori's *The Tuscan Maremma*. Even if you don't like the art, the panoramic view from the top floor is worth the visit.

The **Galleria del Costume,** housed in the Palazzina della Meridiana wing, traces the history of dress over 2 centuries—from the tight corsets and panniers of the 18th century to the beginning of the flapper dress in the 1920s. Some of the costumes are even older than this, as exemplified by one worn by Eleonora of Toledo.

The ground-floor **Museo degli Argenti** displays the household wares of the Medicis, everything from precious ivory, silver, and rare gems to Lorenzo the Magnificent's celebrated collection of vases. These precious stone vases spawned a vogue for *pietra dura* (precious stone work) in the 19th century—the English called it "Florentine mosaic." One writer called the entire collection here "a camp glorification of the Medici." Many of the exhibits are in dubious taste.

Behind the Pitti Palace are the **Boboli Gardens (Giardini di Boboli),** through which the Medicis romped. These Renaissance gardens were laid out by Triboli, a great landscape artist, in the 16th century. Though plans were drawn up for them in 1549, they weren't completed until 1656 and weren't open to the public until 1766. The Boboli is ever-popular for a promenade or an idyllic interlude in a pleasant setting. You can climb to the top of the Fortezza di Belvedere for a dazzling view of the city. The gardens are filled with fountains and statuary, such as *Venus* by Giambologna in the "Grotto" of Buontalenti. Our favorite? An absurd Mannerist piece depicting Cosimo I's court jester posing as a chubby Bacchus riding a turtle, next to Vasari's Corridor. (By the way, **Vasari's Corridor** runs the length of the Ponte Vecchio above the jewelry shops. In just 5 months Vasari built and designed it, and the corridor was once a passage Cosimo I used to get from the Palazzo Vecchio to the Palazzo Pitti.)

✪ **Bargello Museum (Museo Nazionale del Bargello).** Via del Proconsolo 4. ☎ **055/ 238-8606.** Admission 8,000L ($4.65). Tues–Sat 8:30am–1:50pm; 2nd and 4th Sun of the month 9am–2pm, 1st and 3rd Mon of the month 8:30am–1:50pm. Bus: 14 or 23.

The Bargello, a short walk from Piazza della Signoria, is a 1255 fortress palace whose dark underground chambers resounded with the cries of the tortured when it served as the city's jail and Town Hall during the Renaissance. Today the Bargello—named for the police chief or constable (*bargello*) who ruled here—is a vast repository of some of the most important Renaissance sculpture, including works by Michelangelo and Donatello.

Here you'll see another Michelangelo *David* (referred to in the past as *Apollo*), chiseled perhaps 25 to 30 years after the statuesque figure in the Academy Gallery. The Bargello *David* is totally different—even effete when compared to its stronger brother. The armory here displays Michelangelo's grape-capped and drunk *Bacchus* (one of his earlier works, carved when he was 22), who's tempted by a satyr. Among the more significant sculptures is Giambologna's *Winged Mercury* (ca. 1564), a Mannerist masterpiece looking as if it's ready to take flight.

The Bargello displays two versions of Donatello's *John the Baptist*—one emaciated, the other a younger and much kinder man. Donatello was one of the outstanding and original talents of the early Renaissance, and in this gallery you'll learn why. His *St. George* is a work of heroic magnitude. According to an oft-repeated story, Michelangelo, on seeing it for the first time, commanded it to "March!" Donatello's bronze *David* in this salon is a truly remarkable figure—it was the first freestanding nude since the Romans stopped chiseling. As depicted, David is narcissistic (a stunning contrast to Michelangelo's latter-day virile interpretation). For the last word, however, we'll have to call back our lady of the barbs, Mary McCarthy, who wrote: "His *David* . . . wearing nothing but a pair of fancy polished boots and a girlish bonnet, is a transvestite's and fetishist's dream of alluring ambiguity."

Look for at least one more work, another *David*—this one by Andrea del Verrocchio, one of the finest of the 15th-century sculptors. The Bargello also contains a large number of terra-cottas by the della Robbia clan.

Museum of St. Mark (Museo di San Marco). Piazza San Marco 3. ☎ 055/238-8608. Admission 8,000L ($4.65). Daily 8:30am–1:50pm. Closed 1st, 3rd, and 5th Sun of the month; 2nd and 4th Mon of the month; Jan 1, May 1, and Christmas. Bus: 1, 6, 7, 10, 11, 17, or 20.

This state museum is a handsome Renaissance palace whose cell walls are decorated with frescoes by the mystical Fra Angelico, one of Europe's greatest 15th-century painters. In the days of Cosimo de' Medici, San Marco was built by Michelozzo as a Dominican convent. It contained bleak, bare cells, which Angelico and his students brightened considerably with some of the most important works of this pious artist of Fiesole, who portrayed recognizable landscapes in vivid colors.

After buying a ticket, you enter the **Cloister of St. Anthony (Chiostro di Sant'Antonio),** designed by Michelozzo. Turn right in the cloister to enter the **Ospizio dei Pellegrini,** virtually a Fra Angelico gallery filled with painted panels and altarpieces. Here you'll see one of his better-known paintings, *The Last Judgment* (1431), depicting people with angels on the left dancing in a circle and lordly saints towering overhead. Hell, as it's depicted on the right, is naive (Dante-esque)—infested with demons, reptiles, and sinners boiling in a stew. Much of hell was created by Angelico's students; his brush was inspired only by the Crucifixion, Madonnas, and bambini—or landscapes, of course. Henry James claimed that Angelico "never received an intelligible impression of evil; and his conception of human life was a perpetual sense of sacredly loving and being loved." Here also are his *Deposition* (ca. 1440), an altarpiece removed from Santa Trinita, and his *Madonna dei Linaiuoli,* commissioned by the flax workers' guild. Other works to look for are Angelico's panels from the life of Christ.

Now you can enter the courtyard, where a sign points the way to the **Chapter House (Capitolaire),** to the right of a large convent bell. Here you can see a large *Crucifixion and Saints* painted in 1442 by Fra Angelico. Returning to the courtyard, follow the sign into the **Refectory (Refettorio)** to see a *Last Supper* by Domenico Ghirlandaio, who taught Michelangelo how to fresco. This work is rather realistic, the saints with tragic faces evoking a feeling of impending doom.

From the courtyard you can go up to the second floor to view the highlight of the museum: Fra Angelico's *The Annunciation.* The rest of the floor is taken up with Dormitory Cells, 44 small cells once used by the Dominicans (cells 12 to 14 were once occupied by Savonarola and contain portraits of the reformer by Bartolomeo, who was plunged into acute melancholy by the jailing and torturing of his beloved teacher). Most of the cells were frescoed by Angelico and his students from 1439 to 1445 and depict scenes from the Crucifixion.

THE DUOMO, CAMPANILE & BAPTISTERY

In the heart of Florence, at **Piazza del Duomo** and **Piazza San Giovanni** (named after John the Baptist), is a complex of ecclesiastical buildings that form a triumvirate of top sights.

✪ **Cathedral of Santa Maria del Fiore (Il Duomo).** Piazza del Duomo. ☎ 055/ 230-2885. Cathedral, free; excavations, 5,000L ($2.90); cupola, 10,000L ($6). Apr–Oct daily 9am–6:50pm (Nov–Mar to 6:20pm). Bus: B, 14, 23, 36, 37, or 71.

The Duomo, graced by Brunelleschi's red-tiled dome, is the crowning glory of Florence and the star of the skyline. Before entering, take time to view the exterior with its geometrically patterned bands of white, pink, and green marble. The Duomo is one of the world's largest churches and represents the flowering of the "Florentine Gothic" style. As is typical with cathedrals, construction stretched over centuries: Begun in 1296, it was finally consecrated in 1436, though finishing touches on the facade were applied as late as the 19th century. The cathedral was designed by Arnolfo di Cambio in the closing years of the 13th century, and the funds were raised in part by a poll tax.

Brunelleschi's efforts to build the dome (1420 to 1436) could be the subject of a film, as were Michelangelo's vexations over the Sistine Chapel. At one time before his plans were accepted, the architect was tossed out on his derrière and denounced as an idiot. He eventually won the commission by a clever "egg trick," as related in Giorgio Vasari's *Lives of the Painters,* written in the 16th century: The architect challenged his competitors to make an egg stand on a flat piece of marble. Each artist tried to make the egg stand but failed. When it was Brunelleschi's turn, he took the egg and cracked its bottom slightly on the marble and thus made it stand upright. Each of the other artists said he could've done the same thing, if he'd known he could crack the egg. Brunelleschi retorted that they also would've known how to vault the cupola if they had seen his model or plans.

His dome—a "monument for posterity"—was erected without supports. When Michelangelo began to construct a dome over St. Peter's, he paid tribute to Brunelleschi's earlier cupola in Florence: "I am going to make its sister larger, yes, but not lovelier."

Inside, the overall effect of the cathedral is bleak, except when you stand under the cupola, frescoed in part by Vasari. Some of the stained-glass windows in the dome were based on designs by Donatello (Brunelleschi's friend) and Ghiberti (Brunelleschi's rival). You can climb 463 spiraling steps to Brunelleschi's ribbed dome for a view that's well worth the trek (however, you can climb only 414 steps and get the same view from Giotto's campanile, below).

Also in the cathedral are some terra-cottas by Luca della Robbia. In 1432 Ghiberti, taking time out from his "Gates to Paradise," designed the tomb of St. Zenobius. Excavations in the depths of the cathedral have brought to light the remains of the ancient Cathedral of Santa Reparata (tombs, columns, and floors), which was probably founded in the 5th century and transformed in the following centuries until it was demolished to make way for the present cathedral. The entrance to the excavations is via a stairway near the front of his cathedral, to the right as you enter.

Incidentally, during some 1972 excavations Brunelleschi's tomb of was discovered, and new discoveries indicate the existence of a second tomb nearby. Giotto's tomb, which has never been found, may be in the right nave, beneath the campanile that bears his name.

✪ Giotto's Bell Tower (Campanile di Giotto). Piazza del Duomo. ☎ **055/230-2885.** Admission 10,000L ($6). Apr–Oct daily 9am–6:50pm (Nov–Mar to 4:20pm). Closed Jan 1, Easter, Sept 8, and Christmas. Bus: B, 14, 23, 36, 37, or 71.

If we can believe the accounts of his contemporaries, Giotto was the ugliest man ever to walk the streets of Florence. It's ironic, then, that he left to posterity Europe's most beautiful campanile (bell tower), rhythmic in line and form. That Giotto was given the position of *capomastro* and grand architect (and pensioned for 100 gold florins for his service) is remarkable in itself, as he's famous for freeing painting from the confinements of Byzantium. He designed the campanile in the last 2 or 3 years of his life and died before its completion.

The final work was admirably carried out by Andrea Pisano, one of Italy's greatest Gothic sculptors (see his bronze doors on the baptistery). The "Tuscanized" Gothic tower, with bands of the same colored marble as the Dumomo, stands 274 feet, and you can climb 414 steps to the top for a panorama of the sienna-colored city. The view will surely rank among your most memorable—it encompasses the enveloping hills and Medici villas. If a medieval pageant happens to be passing underneath (likely in spring), so much the better. After Giotto's death, Pisano and Luca della Robbia did some fine bas-relief and sculptural work, now in the Museo dell'Opera del Duomo (below).

☼ Baptistery (Battistero San Giovanni). Piazza S. Giovanni. **☎ 055/230-2885.** Admission 5,000L ($2.90). Mon–Sat 1:30–6:30pm, Sun 8:30am–1:30pm. Bus: B, 14, 23, 36, 37, or 71.

Named after the city's patron saint, Giovanni (John the Baptist), the octagonal baptistery dates from the 11th and 12th centuries. It's the oldest structure in Florence and is a highly original interpretation of the Romanesque style, with bands of pink, white, and green marble to match the Duomo and campanile.

Visitors from all over the world come to gape at its three sets of bronze doors. In his work on two sets of the doors (the east and the north), Lorenzo Ghiberti reached the pinnacle of his artistry in quattrocento Florence. To win his first commission on the north doors, the 23-year-old sculptor had to compete against formidable opposition like Donatello, Brunelleschi (architect of the Duomo's dome), and Siena-born Jacopo della Quercia. On seeing Ghiberti's work, Donatello and Brunelleschi conceded defeat. By the time he'd completed the work on the north doors, Ghiberti was around 44. The gilt-covered panels—representing scenes from the New Testament, including the Annunciation, the Adoration, and Christ debating the elders in the temple—make up a flowing rhythmic narration in bronze. To protect them from the elements, the originals were removed to the Museo dell'Opera del Duomo (below), but the copies are works of art unto themselves.

After his long labor, the Florentines gratefully gave Ghiberti the task of sculpting the east doors (directly opposite the Duomo entrance). Given carte blanche, Ghiberti designed his masterpiece, choosing as his subject familiar scenes from the Old Testament, like Adam and Eve at the creation. This time Ghiberti labored over the rectangular panels from 1425 to 1452 (he died in 1455). On seeing the finished work, Michelangelo is said to have exclaimed, "These doors are fit to stand at the gates of Paradise," and so they're nicknamed the "Gates of Paradise." Ghiberti apparently agreed: He claimed he personally planned and designed the Renaissance—all on his own.

Shuttled off to adorn the south entrance and to make way for Ghiberti's "Gates of Paradise" were the baptistery's oldest doors, by Andrea Pisano, mentioned earlier for his work on Giotto's bell tower. For his subject, the Gothic sculptor represented the "Virtues" as well as scenes from the life of John the Baptist, whom the baptistery honors. The door was completed in 1336. On the interior (just walk through Pisano's door—no charge), the dome is adorned with 13th-century mosaics, dominated by a figure of Christ. Mornings are reserved for worship.

Museum of the Duomo (Museo dell'Opera del Duomo). Piazza del Duomo 9. **☎ 055/ 230-2885.** Admission 10,000L ($6). Apr–Oct Mon–Sat 9am–6:50pm (Nov–Mar to 5:20pm). Bus: B, 14, 23, 36, 37, or 71.

This museum, across from the Duomo but facing the apse of Santa Maria del Fiore, is beloved by connoisseurs of Renaissance sculpture. It houses the sculpture removed from the campanile and the Duomo—to protect the pieces not only from the weather but also from visitors who want samples. A major attraction here is an unfinished *Pietà* by Michelangelo, in the middle of the stairs. It was carved between 1548 and 1555, when the artist was in his 70s. In this vintage work, a figure representing Nicodemus (but said to have Michelangelo's face) is holding Christ. The great Florentine intended it for his own tomb, but he's believed to have grown disenchanted with it and to have attempted to destroy it. The museum has a Brunelleschi bust, as well as della Robbia terra-cottas. The premier attraction is the restored panels of Ghiberti's "Gates of Paradise" removed from the baptistery. In gilded bronze, each is a masterpiece of Renaissance sculpture, perhaps the finest low-relief perspective in all Italian art.

You'll see bits and pieces from what was the old Gothic-Romanesque fronting of the cathedral, with ornamental statues, as conceived by the original architect, Arnolfo di Cambio. One of Donatello's early works, *St. John the Evangelist,* is here—not his finest hour certainly, but anything by Donatello is worth looking at. One of his most celebrated works, the *Magdalene,* is in the room with the *cantorie* (below). This wooden statue once stood in the baptistery and had to be restored after the 1966 flood. Dating from 1454 to 1455, it's stark and penitent.

A good reason for coming here is to see the marble choirs (cantorie) of Donatello and Luca della Robbia (the works face each other and are in the first room you enter after climbing the stairs). The della Robbia choir is more restrained, but it still "Praises the Lord" in marble—with clashing cymbals and sounding brass that constitute a reaffirmation of life. In contrast, all restraint breaks loose in the cantoria of dancing cherubs in Donatello's choir—it's a romp of chubby bambini. Of all Donatello's works, this one is the most lighthearted. But, in total contrast, lavish your attention on Donatello's *Zuccone,* one of his masterpieces, created for Giotto's bell tower.

ON PIAZZA DELLA SIGNORIA

The L-shaped ✪ **Piazza della Signoria,** though never completed, is one of Italy's most beautiful; it was the center of secular life in the days of the Medici and is today a virtual sculpture gallery. Through it pranced church robbers, connoisseurs of entrails, hired assassins seeking employment, chicken farmers from Valdarno, book burners, and many great men (including Machiavelli, on a secret mission to the Palazzo Vecchio, and Leonardo da Vinci, trailed by his inevitable entourage).

On the square is the controversial **Fountain of Neptune (Fontana dei Neptuno;** 1560 to 1575), with the sea god surrounded by creatures from the deep, as well as frisky satyrs and nymphs. It was designed by Ammannati, who later repented for chiseling Neptune in the nude. But Michelangelo, to whom Ammannati owed a great debt, judged the fountain inferior. Florentines used to mock it as *Il Biancone* ("big whitey"). Actually, the Mannerist bronzes around the basin aren't at all bad; many may have been designed by a young Giambologna.

Near the fountain is a **small disk** in the ground, marking the spot where Savonarola was executed. This zealous monk was a fire-and-brimstone reformer who rivaled Dante in conjuring up the punishment hell would inflict on sinners. His chief targets were Lorenzo the Magnificent and the Borgia pope, Alexander VI, who excommunicated him. Savonarola whipped the Florentine faithful into an orgy of religious fanaticism but eventually fell from favor. Along with two other friars, he was hanged in the square in 1498. Afterward, as the crowds threw stones, a pyre underneath the men consumed their bodies. It's said that the reformer's heart was found whole and grabbed up by souvenir collectors. His ashes were tossed into the Arno.

For centuries, Michelangelo's *David* stood in this square, but it was moved to the Academy Gallery in the 19th century. The work you see on the square today is an inferior copy, commonly assumed by many first-timers to be Michelangelo's original. Near the towering statue stands Baccio Bandinelli's *Heracles* from 1534. Bandinelli, however, was no Michelangelo, and his statue has been denounced through the centuries, Cellini himself dismissing it as a "sack of melons."

The 14th-century ✪ **Loggia della Signoria** (sometimes called the **Loggia dei Lanzi**) houses a gallery of sculpture often depicting violent scenes. The most famous piece is a rare work by Benvenuto Cellini, the goldsmith and tell-all autobiographer: Critics have said that his exquisite but ungentlemanly *Perseus*, holding up the severed head of Medusa, is the most significant Florentine sculpture since Michelangelo's *Night* and *Day*. What you see is actually a copy. The original Perseus stood here from 1545 to 1996, when he was removed for restoration. The future of the original statue remains uncertain. Three other well-known pieces are Giambologna's bronze statue of **Duke Cosimo de' Medici** on horseback, celebrating the man who subjugated all Tuscany under his military rule; his *Rape of the Sabines,* an essay in three-dimensional Mannerism; and his *Hercules with Nessus the Centaur,* a chorus line of half a dozen Roman vestal wallflowers.

✪ **Palazzo Vecchio (Palazzo della Signoria).** Piazza della Signoria. ☎ **055/276-8465.** Admission 10,000L ($6). Mon–Wed and Fri–Sat 9am–7pm, Sun 8am–1pm. Last admission 1 hour before closing. Bus: 23 or 71.

The secular "Old Palace" is Florence's most famous and imposing palazzo. Gothic master builder Arnolfo di Cambio constructed it from 1299 to 1302, though it wasn't until 1540 that Cosimo I and the Medicis called it home. It's most remarkable architectural feature is the 308-foot tower, an engineering feat that required supreme skill at the time. Today the palazzo is occupied by city employees but much is open to the public.

The 16th-century **Hall of the 500 (Salone dei Cinquecento),** the most outstanding part of the palace, is filled with Vasari & Co. frescoes as well as sculpture. A tragic loss to Renaissance art, the frescoes originally done by Leonardi da Vinci in 1503 melted when braziers were brought in to speed up the drying process. The ever-inventive Leonardo had used wax in his pigments, and of course the frescoes melted under the heat. As you enter the hall, look for Michelangelo's *Victory,* depicting an insipid-looking young man treading on a bearded older man (it has been suggested that Michelangelo put his own face on that of the trampled man). This 1533 to 1534 statue was originally intended for the tomb of Pope Julius but later acquired by the Medicis.

Later you can stroll through the rest of the palace, examining its apartments and main halls. You can also visit the private apartments of Eleanor of Toledo, the Spanish wife of Cosimo I, and a chapel that was begun in 1540 and frescoed by Bronzino. The palace displays the original of Verrocchio's bronze putto (1476) from the courtyard fountain, called both *Winged Cherub Clutching a Fish* and *Boy with a Dolphin.* You'll also find a 16th-century portrait of Machiavelli that's attributed to Santi di Tito. Donatello's famous bronze group *Judith Slaying Holofernes* (1455) once stood on Piazza della Signoria but was brought inside. The salons, such as a fleur-de-lis apartment, have their own richness and beauty.

Following his arrest, Savonarola was taken to the Palazzo Vecchio for more than a dozen torture sessions, including "twists" on the rack. The torturer pronounced Savonarola his "best" customer.

NEAR PIAZZA SAN LORENZO

Piazza San Lorenzo and its satelline, **Piazza Modonna degli Aldobrandini,** are lively and colorful. A huge market, the **Mercato Centrale,** forms around the church of

The Good Old Ponte Vecchio

Spared by the Nazis in their bitter retreat from the Allied advance in 1944, the "Old Bridge" at Via Por Santa Maria and Via Guicciardini is the last remaining medieval ponte spanning the Arno (the Germans blew up the rest). It was again threatened in the 1966 flood, when the waters of the Arno swept over it and washed away a fortune in jewelry from the goldsmiths' shops flanking the bridge.

The Ponte Vecchio was built in 1220, probably on the Roman site of a bridge for the Via Cassia, the ancient road running through Florence on its way to Rome. Vasari claims that Taddeo Gaddi reconstructed it in 1354, and Vasari himself designed the corridor running over it. Once home to butchers, it was cleared of this stench by Ferdinand de' Medici, who allowed these "vile arts" to give way to goldsmiths and jewelers who have remained ever since.

Today the restored Ponte Vecchio is closed to vehicular traffic. The little shops continue to sell everything from the most expensive of Florentine gold to something simple—say, a Lucrezia Borgia poison ring.

San Lorenzo, continuing all the way to the area of San Marco. For details, see "Shopping" later in this chapter.

✪ **Medici Chapels (Cappelle Medicee).** Piazza Madonna degli Aldobrandini 6. ☎ **055/ 238-8602.** Admission 10,000L ($6). Tues–Sat 8:30am–3pm, Sun 8:30am–2pm. Bus: 1, 6, 7, 11, 17, 33, 67, or 68.

A mecca for all pilgrims, the Medici tombs are adjacent to the Basilica of San Lorenzo (below). You enter the tombs, housing the "blue-blooded" Medici, in back of the church by going around to Piazza Madonna degli Aldobrandini. First you'll pass through the baroque **Chapel of the Princes (Cappella dei Principi),** that octagon of death often denounced for its "trashy opulence." In back of the altar is a collection of Italian reliquaries.

The real reason you come here is to see the **New Sacristy,** designed by Michelangelo as a gloomy mausoleum. "Do not wake me; speak softly here," Michelangelo wrote in a bitter verse. Working from 1521 to 1534, he created the Medici tombs in a style that foreshadowed the baroque. Lorenzo the Magnificent—a ruler who seemed to embody the qualities of the Renaissance itself, and one of the greatest names in the history of the Medici family—was buried near Michelangelo's uncompleted *Madonna and Child* group, a simple monument evoking a promise unfulfilled.

Ironically, the finest groups of sculpture were reserved for two Medici "clan" members, who (in the words of Mary McCarthy) "would better have been forgotten." Both are represented by Michelangelo as armored, idealized princes of the Renaissance. In fact, Lorenzo II, duke of Urbino, depicted as "the thinker," was a deranged young man (just out of his teens before he died). Clearly, Michelangelo wasn't working to glorify these two Medici dukes. Rather, he was chiseling for posterity. The other two figures on Lorenzo's tomb are most often called *Dawn* and *Dusk,* with morning represented as woman and evening as man.

The two best-known figures—Michelangelo at his most powerful—are *Night* and *Day* at the feet of Giuliano, the duke of Nemours. *Night* is chiseled as a woman in troubled sleep and *Day* as a man of strength awakening to a foreboding world. These figures weren't the works of Michelangelo's innocence.

Discovered in a sepulchral chamber beneath the Medici Chapels was Michelangelo's only group of mural sketches, with access via a trap door and a winding staircase.

Apparently, he had used the walls as a giant doodling sheet. Drawings include a sketch of the legs of Duke Giuliano, Christ risen, and the Laocoön, the Hellenistic figure group. Fifty drawings, done in charcoal on plaster walls, were found. You can ask for a free ticket to view the sketches at the ticket office for the chapels.

Basilica di San Lorenzo. Piazza San Lorenzo. ☎ **055/216-634.** Free admission. Library Mon–Sat 9am–1pm; study room Mon–Sat 8am–2pm. Bus: 1, 6, 7, 11, 17, 33, 67, or 68.

This is Brunelleschi's 1426 Renaissance church, where the Medicis used to attend services from their nearby palace on Via Larga, now Via Camillo Cavour. Critic Walter Pater found it "great rather by what it designed or aspired to do, than by what it actually achieved." Most visitors flock to see Michelangelo's **New Sacristy** with his *Night* and *Day* (see the Medici Chapels, above), but Brunelleschi's handiwork deserves some time too.

Built in the style of a Latin cross, the church is distinguished by harmonious grays and rows of Corinthian columns. The **Old Sacristy** (walk up the nave, then turn left) was designed by Brunelleschi and decorated in part by Donatello (see his terra-cotta bust of St. Lawrence). This is often cited as the first and finest work of the early Renaissance. Even more intriguing are the two bronze 1460 pulpits of Donatello, among his last works, a project carried out by students following his death in 1466. Scenes depict Christ's passion and resurrection.

After exploring the Old Sacristy, go through the first door (unmarked) on your right and you'll emerge outside. A sign will point to the entrance of the **Biblioteca Medicea Laurenziana** (☎ 055/210-760), which you enter at Piazza San Lorenzo 9. Designed by Michelangelo to shelter the expanding collection of the Medicis, the library is a brilliant example of Mannerist architecture, its chief attraction a *pietra serna* flight of curving stairs. Michelangelo worked on it in 1524, but the finishing touches were completed in 1578 by Vasari and Ammannati. Michelangelo, however, designed the reading benches. The library is filled with some of Italy's greatest manuscripts—many of which are handsomely illustrated. In the rare-book collection are autographs by Petrarch, Machiavelli, Poliziano, and Napoléon. You're kept at a distance by protective glass, but it's well worth the visit.

Palazzo Medici-Riccardi. Via Camillo Cavour 1. ☎ **055/276-0340.** Admission 6,000L ($3.50). Mon–Tues and Thurs–Sat 9am–12:30pm and 3–6pm, Sun 9am–noon. Bus: 1, 6, 7, 11, 17, 33, 67, or 68.

This palace, a short walk from the Duomo, was the home of Cosimo de' Medici before he took his household to the Palazzo Vecchio. In the apogee of the Medici power, it was once adorned with some of the world's greatest masterpieces, such as Donatello's *David*. Built by Michelozzo in the mid-15th century, the brown stone building was also the scene, at times, of the court of Lorenzo the Magnificent. Art lovers visit today chiefly to see the mid-15th-century frescoes by Benozzo Gozzoli in the **Medici Chapel** (not to be confused with the Medici Chapels above). Gozzoli's frescoes, depicting the journey of the Magi, form his masterpiece—they're a hallmark in Renaissance painting. Though taking a religious theme as his subject, the artist turned it into a gay romp, a pageant of royals, knights, and pages, with fun mascots like greyhounds and even a giraffe. It's a fairy-tale world come alive, with faces of the Medicis along with local celebrities who were as famous as Madonna in their day but are known only to scholars today.

Another gallery, which you enter via a separate stairway, was frescoed by Luca Giordano in the 18th century, but his work seems merely decorative. The apartments, where the prefect lodges, aren't open to the public. The gallery, incidentally, may also be viewed free.

ON OR NEAR PIAZZA DELLA SANTISSIMA ANNUNZIATA

Lovely **Piazza della Santissima Annunziata** is surrounded on three sides by arcades. In the center is an equestrian statue of Grand Duke Ferdinand I by Giambologna. The **Hospital of the Innocents** stands on the eastern side. Once Brunelleschi wanted to create a perfectly symmetrical square here, but he died before his plans could be realized. The piazza is a popular student hangout.

Hospital of the Innocents (Ospedale degli Innocenti). Piazza della Santissima Annunziata 12. ☎ **055/249-1723.** Admission 5,000L ($2.90). Thurs–Tues 8:30am–2pm. Bus: 6, 31, or 32.

Opened in 1445, this was the world's first hospital for foundlings, though the Medici and Florentine bankers weren't known for welfare benefits. The building and the loggia with its Corinthian columns were conceived by Brunelleschi and marked the first architectural bloom of the Renaissance in Florence. On the facade are terra-cotta medallions done in blues and opaque whites by Andrea della Robbia depicting babes in swaddling clothes.

Still used as an orphanage, the building no longer has its "lazy Susan," where Florentines used to deposit unwanted bambini, ring the bell, and then flee. It does contain an art gallery, and notable among its treasures is a terra-cotta *Madonna and Child* by Luca della Robbia, plus works by Sandro Botticelli. One of its most important paintings is *Adoration of the Magi* by Domenico Ghirlandaio (the chubby bambino looks a bit pompously at the Wise Man kissing his foot).

Archaeological Museum (Museo Archeologico). Via della Colonna 38. ☎ **055/ 23-575.** Admission 8,000L ($4.65). Tues–Sat 9am–2pm, Sun 9am–1pm. Closed 1st, 3rd, and 5th Sunday of each month (open Mon following a 5th Sun). Bus: 6, 31, or 32.

This museum, a short walk from Piazza della Santissima Annunziata, houses one of Europe's most outstanding Egyptian and Etruscan collections in a palace built for Grand Duchess Maria Maddalena of Austria. The Etruscan-loving Medicis began that collection, though the Egyptian loot was first acquired by Leopold II in the 1830s. Its Egyptian mummies and sarcophagi are on the first floor, along with some of the better-known Etruscan works. Pause to look at the lid to the coffin of a fat Etruscan (unlike the blank faces staring back from many of these tombs, this man's countenance is quite expressive).

One room is graced with three bronze Etruscan masterpieces, among the rarest objets d'art of these relatively unknown people. They include the *Chimera,* a lion with a goat sticking out of its back. This was an Etruscan work of the 5th century B.C., found near Arezzo in 1555. The lion's tail—in the form of a venomous reptile—lunges at the trapped beast. The others are *Minerva* and an *Orator,* ranging from the 5th to the 1st century B.C. Another rare find is a Roman bronze of a young man, the so-called *Idolino* fished from the sea at Pesaro. The statue has always been shrouded in mystery; it may have been a Roman statue sculpted around the time of Christ. The François vase on the ground floor, from 570 B.C., is celebrated. A prize in the Egyptian department is a wood-and-bone chariot, beautifully preserved, that astonishingly dates back to a tomb in Thebes from the 14th century B.C.

ON PIAZZA SANTA MARIA NOVELLA

Hardly the most beautiful or tranquil square, **Piazza Santa Maria Novella** overflows with traffic from the rail station. Vendors, backpackers, beggars, and buses and taxis vie for precious space. Visitors will want to tolerate this furor for only one reason—to see the basilica.

Catching the View from Piazzale Michelangiolo

For a view of the wonders of Florence below and Fiesole above, climb aboard bus no. 12 or 13 at the Ponte alla Grazie (the first bridge east of the Ponte Vecchio) for a 15-minute ride to ✪ **Piazzale Michelangiolo,** an 1865 belvedere over-looking a view seen in many a Renaissance painting and on many a modern-day postcard. It's reached along Viale Michelangiolo. It's best at dusk, when the purple-fringed Tuscan hills form a frame for Giotto's bell tower, Brunelleschi's dome, and the towering hunk of stones that stick up from the Palazzo Vecchio. Another copy of Michelangelo's *David* dominates the square and gives the piaz-zale ("wide piazza") its name (but note the spelling difference). Crown your trip with a gelato at the **Gelateria Michelangiolo** (☎ **055/234-2705**), open daily 10am to 1am.

Warning: At certain times during the day, the square is overrun with tour buses and peddlers selling trinkets and cheap souvenirs. If you go at these times, often midday in summer, you'll find the view of Florence is still intact—but you may be struck down by a Vespa or crushed in a crowd if you try to enjoy it.

Basilica di Santa Maria Novella. Piazza Santa Maria Novella. ☎ **055/215-918.** Church, free; Spanish Chapel and cloisters, 5,000L ($2.90) seniors/children 12–20; children 11 and under free. Church, Mon–Fri 7am–12:15pm and 3–6pm; Sat 7am–12:15pm and 3–5pm; Sun 3–5pm. Spanish Chapel and cloisters, Mon–Thurs and Sat 9am–2pm; Sun 8am–1pm. Bus: 6, 9, 11, 36, 37, or 68.

Near the rail station is one of Florence's most distinguished churches, begun in 1278 for the Dominicans. Its geometric facade, with bands of white and green marble, was designed in the late 15th century by Leon Battista Alberti, an aristocrat and true Renaissance man (philosopher, painter, architect, poet). The church borrows from and harmonizes the Romanesque, Gothic, and Renaissance styles.

In the left nave as you enter, the third large painting is the great Masaccio's *Trinità,* a curious work that has the architectural form of a Renaissance stage setting but whose figures (in perfect perspective) are like actors in a Greek tragedy. If you view the church at dusk, you'll see the stained-glass windows in the fading light cast kaleidoscope fan-tasies on the opposite wall.

Head straight up the left nave to the **Gondi Chapel** for a look at Brunelleschi's wooden *Christ on the Cross,* said to have been carved to compete with Donatello's same subject in Santa Croce (below). According to Vasari, when Donatello saw Brunelleschi's completed Crucifix, he dropped his apron full of eggs intended for their lunch. "You have symbolized the Christ," Donatello is alleged to have said. "Mine is an ordinary man." (Some art historians reject this story.)

In 1485, Ghirlandaio contracted with a Tornabuoni banker to adorn the sanctuary behind the main altar with frescoes illustrating scenes from the lives of Mary and John the Baptist. Michelangelo, a teenager at the time, is known to have studied under Ghirlandaio (perhaps he even worked on this cycle).

In the north transept a staircase leads to the remarkable **Strozzi Chapel,** honoring St. Thomas Aquinas. Decorated between 1350 and 1357 by Nardo di Cione and Andrea Orcagna, it depicts Dante's *Purgatorio* and *Inferno.* On the left wall is *Paradiso.*

If time remains, you may want to visit the **cloisters,** going first to the Green Cloister and then to the splendid Spanish Chapel frescoed by Andrea di Bonaiuto in the 14th century (one panel depicts the Dominicans in triumph over heretical wolves).

ON OR NEAR PIAZZA SANTA CROCE

Every street leading to the famed **Piazza Sante Croce** thrives on tourism, usually packed with shops selling leather goods. The square has been an integral part of Florentine life for centuries, beginning when Franciscan friars used to preach here. The piazza used to be the playing field for calcio (a kind of football that's no longer played), and a marble disk in the center marks the center line of pitch. Today it's still devoted to popular gatherings, like games, events, and jousts.

Basilica di Santa Croce. Piazza Santa Croce 16. ☎ **055/244-619.** Church, free; cloisters and church museum, 4,000L ($2.40). Church, daily 8am–12:30pm and 3–6:30pm. Museum and cloisters, Mar–Sept Thurs–Tues 10am–12:30pm and 2:30–6:30pm; Oct–Feb daily 10am–12:30pm and 3–5pm. Bus: B, 13, 23, or 71.

Florence's Pantheon or Tuscany's Westminster Abbey, this church shelters the tombs of everyone from Michelangelo to Machiavelli, from Dante (he was actually buried at Ravenna) to Galileo, who at the hands of the Inquisition "recanted" his concept that the earth revolves around the sun. Just as Santa Maria Novella was the church of the Dominicans, Santa Croce, said to have been designed by Arnolfo di Cambio, was the church of the Franciscans. Believe us, you can brave a visit here better than Stendhal, who, after seeing Santa Croce, gushed: "I had attained to that supreme degree of sensibility where the divine intimations of art merge with the impassioned sensuality of emotion. As I emerged, I was seized with a fierce palpitation of the heart; I walked in constant fear of falling to the ground."

In the right nave (first tomb) is the Vasari-executed monument to Michelangelo, whose 89-year-old body was smuggled back to his native Florence from its original burial place in Rome, where the pope wanted the corpse to remain. Along with a bust of the artist are three allegorical figures representing the arts. In the next memorial, a prune-faced Dante, a poet honored belatedly in the city that exiled him, looks down. Farther on, still on the right, is the tomb of Niccolo` Machiavelli, whose *The Prince* (about Cesare Borgia) became a virtual textbook in the art of wielding power. Nearby is Donatello's lyrical bas-relief *The Annunciation.*

The Trecento frescoes are reason enough for visiting Santa Croce—especially those by Giotto to the right of the main chapel. Once whitewashed, the Bardi and Peruzzi chapels were "uncovered" in the mid-19th century in such a clumsy fashion that they had to be drastically restored. Though badly preserved, the frescoes in the **Bardi Chapel** are most memorable, especially the deathbed scene of St. Francis. The cycles in the **Peruzzi Chapel** are of John the Baptist and St. John. In the left transept is Donatello's once-controversial wooden Crucifix—too gruesome for some Renaissance tastes, including that of Brunelleschi, who is claimed to have said: "You [Donatello] have put a rustic upon the cross." (For Brunelleschi's "answer," go to Santa Maria Novella.) Incidentally, the **Pazzi Chapel,** entered through the cloisters, was designed by Brunelleschi, with terra-cottas by Luca della Robbia.

Inside the monastery of this church the Franciscan fathers established the **Leather School** at the end of World War II. The purpose of the school was to prepare young boys technically to specialize in Florentine leather work. The school has flourished and produced many fine artisans who continue their careers here. Stop in and see the work when you visit the church.

Casa Buonarroti. Via Ghibellina 70. ☎ **055/241-752.** Admission 10,000L ($6) adults, 7,000L ($4.05) students/children. Wed–Mon 9:30am–1:30pm. Bus: 14.

Only a short walk from Santa Croce stands the house Michelangelo managed to buy for his nephew, Lionardo. But it was Lionardo's son, named after Michelangelo, who turned the house into a virtual museum to his great uncle, hiring artists and painters to adorn it with frescoes. Turned into a museum by his descendants, the house was restored in 1964. It contains some fledgling work by the great artist, as well as some models by him. Here you can see his *Madonna of the Stairs,* which he did when he was 16 (maybe younger), as well as a bas-relief he did later, the *Battle of the Centaurs.* The casa is enriched by many of Michelangelo's drawings and models, shown to the public in periodic exhibits. A curiosity among them is the wooden model for the San Lorenzo facade that Michelangelo designed but never constructed.

LITERARY LANDMARKS

Dante's House (Casa di Dante). Via Santa Margherita 1. ☎ 055/219-416. Admission 5,000L ($2.90) adults, 3,000L ($1.75) children 9 and under. Mon and Wed–Sat 10am–4pm, Sun 10am–2pm. Bus: B, C, or 9.

For those of us who were spoon-fed hell but spared purgatory, a pilgrimage to this rebuilt medieval house may be of passing interest, though it contains few specific exhibits of note. Most likely this isn't the actual house where Dante lived, but it's typical of residences of that time in his neighborhood. It was restored and turned into a museum dedicated to the poet laureate in 1911. Dante was exiled from his native Florence in 1302 for his political involvements. He never returned and thus wrote his *Divine Comedy* in exile, conjuring up fit punishment in the Inferno for his Florentine enemies. Dante certainly had the last word. You reach the house by walking down Via Dante Alighieri.

Casa Guidi. Piazza S. Felice Felice 8. ☎ 055/284-393. Free admission. Apr–Nov Mon, Wed, and Fri 2–4pm (but call first to verify). Closed Dec–Mar. Bus: B or C.

Across from the Pitti Palace and not far from the Arno is the former residence of Elizabeth Barrett and Robert Browning. They chose this location less than a year after their clandestine marriage in London, and it became their home for the remaining 14 years of their life together. Casa Guidi is where their son was born and where they wrote some of their best-known works.

Elizabeth died here in 1861, and you can visit her tomb at the English cemetery in Florence (though it really isn't worth the schlepp). After her death, a heart-broken Browning left Florence, never to return (he died in Venice in 1889 and is buried in Westminster Abbey in London). The poets' son, Pen, acquired the residence in 1893, intending to make a memorial to his parents; however, he died before completing his plans. The rooms were first opened to the public in 1971, when the Browning Institute, an international charitable organization, acquired the apartment. "White doves in the ceiling" and frescoes of "angels looking down from a cloud," both of which Elizabeth wrote about, will interest Browning aficionados.

In a more cynical age, there's the possibility of rejecting the Brownings' life in Florence as "sentimental." Regardless, it's admirable what the institute has done to pay homage to the two 19th-century poets who were the center of the Anglo-Florentine community, much as Keats and Shelley were the stars in "English Rome." Elizabeth Barrett Browning wrote regarding Casa Guidi that "the charm of a home is a home to come back to."

FOR VISITING AMERICANS

Florence American Cemetery and Memorial. Via Cassia, 50023 Impruneta. ☎ 055/202-0020. Free admission. May 15–Sept 15 daily 8am–6pm (Sept 16–May 14 to 5pm). The SITA city bus stops at the cemetery entrance every 2 hours, except on holidays, when there's usually no service; the bus follows Via Cassia.

The Florence American Cemetery and Memorial is on a 70-acre site about 7½ miles south of the city on the west side of Via Cassia. One of 14 permanent American World

War II military cemetery memorials built on foreign soil by the American Battle Monuments Commission, it's on a site that was liberated on August 3, 1944, and later became part of the zone of the U.S. Fifth Army. Most of the 4,402 servicemen and -women interred here died in the fighting after the capture of Rome in June 1944.

A SYNAGOGUE

La Sinagoga di Firenze. Via Farini 4. ☎ **055/234-6654.** Admission 6,000L ($3.50) adults, 4,000L ($2.30) children 15–18, free for children 14 and under. Apr–Sept Sun–Thurs 10am–1pm and 2–5pm, Fri 10am–1pm; Oct–Mar Sun–Thurs 10am–1pm and 2–4pm, Fri and Sun 10am–1pm. Closed Jewish holidays. Bus: 6, 31, or 32.

The synagogue is in the Moorish style, inspired by Constantine's Byzantine church of Hagia Sophia. Completed in 1882, it was badly damaged by the Nazis in 1944 but has been restored to its original splendor. A museum is upstairs, exhibiting, among other displays, a photographic record of the history of the ghetto that remained in Florence until 1859.

6 Shopping

THE SHOPPING SCENE

Skilled craftsmanship and traditional design unchanged since the days of the Medicis have made this a serious shopping destination. Florence is noted for its hand-tooled **leather goods** and various **straw merchandise,** as well as superbly crafted **gold jewelry.** Its reputation for fashionable custom-made clothes is no longer what it was, having lost its position to Milan.

The whole city strikes many visitors as a gigantic department store. Entire neighborhoods on both sides of the Arno offer good shops, though those along the medieval Ponte Vecchio (with some exceptions) strike most people as too touristy.

Florence isn't a city for bargain shopping, though. Most visitors interested in gold or silver jewelry head for the **Ponte Vecchio** and its tiny shops. It's difficult to tell one from another, but you really don't need to since the merchandise is similar. If you're looking for a charm or souvenir, these shops are fine. But the heyday of finding gold jewelry bargains on the Ponte Vecchio is long gone.

The street for antiques is **Via Maggio;** some of the furnishings and objets d'art here are from the 16th century. Another major area for antiques shopping is **Borgo Ognissanti.** Florence's Fifth Avenue is **Via dei Tornabuoni**—the place to head for the best-quality leather goods, for the best clothing boutiques, and for stylish but costly shoes. Here you'll find everyone from Giorgio Armani to Salvatore Ferragamo.

The better shops are for the most part along Tornabuoni, but there are many on **Via Vigna Nuova, Via Porta Rossa,** and **Via degli Strozzi.** You might also stroll on the lungarno along the Arno. For some of the best buys in leather, check out **Via del Parione,** a short narrow street off of Tornabuoni.

Shopping hours are generally Monday 4 to 7:30pm and Tuesday to Saturday 9 or 10am to 1pm and 3:30 or 4 to 7:30pm. During summer, some shops are open Monday morning. However, don't be surprised if some shops are closed for several weeks in August or for the entire month.

SHOPPING A TO Z

ANTIQUES　There are many outlets for antiques in Florence (but those high prices!). If you're in the market for such expensive purchases or if you just like to browse, try the following.

The chic **Adriana Chelini,** Via Maggio 28A (☎ **055/213-471**), specializes in 16th- and 17th-century furniture, from small to large pieces. It also carries some paintings and porcelain and glass items from later periods. **Bottega San Felice,** Via Maggio 39R (☎ 055/215-479), offers many intriguing items from the 19th century, sometimes in the style known as Charles X. The shop also sells more modern pieces. Many art-deco items are for sale, as are many Biedermeier pieces.

   Gallori Turchi, Via Maggio 10–12–14R (☎ 055/282-279), is one of Florence's best antiques stores for the serious well-heeled collector. Some of its rare items date to the 16th century. They range from polychrome figures to gilded Tuscan pieces, from Majolica to ceramics. The shop is closed from August 1 to 25. The Bartolozzis have been doing business at **Guido Bartolozzi,** Via Maggio 18R (☎ 055/215-602), since 1887, when they were here to greet those on the Grand Tour. Their specialty is European antiques from the 16th to the 19th century. Furniture, tapestries, china, glassware, and many other items are on display. The eclectic **Paolo Romano,** Borgo Ognissanti 20 (☎ 055/293-294), carries furniture, accessories, and objets d'art from the 16th to the 19th century. Many pieces are small and demure; others are more suitable to the place you'll move to when you become the next Bill Gates.

ART   Opened in 1870 and thus Florence's oldest art gallery, **Galleria Masini,** Piazza Goldoni 6R (☎ 055/294-000), is a few minutes' walk from the Excelsior and other leading hotels. The selection of modern and contemporary paintings by top artists is extensive, representing more than 500 Italian painters. Even if you're not a collector, this is a good place to select a picture that'll be a lasting reminder of your visit to Italy—you can take it home duty-free.

BOOKSTORES   The oldest English bookstore in Florence devoted to American and British books and one of the finest bookstores in Europe, **BM Bookshop,** Borgo Ognissanti 4R (☎ 055/294-575), carries an excellent selection of paperbacks, travel guides, art and architecture books, history, Italian interest, fashion, design, and children's books, plus the city's largest collection of Italian cookbooks in English. **Libreria il Viaggio,** Borgo degli Albizi 41R (☎ 055/240-489), is a specialty bookstore selling maps and guidebooks from all over the world, in a wide variety of languages, including English. It's one of the finest bookstores of its type in Italy, with a tempting variety of titles and merchandise.

FABRIC   In business for more than half a century, ✪ **Casa di Tessuti,** Via de' Pecori 20R (☎ 055/215-961), is for fabric connoisseurs, with some of the nation's largest and highest-quality selections of linen, silk, wool, and cotton. The Romoli family are the longtime proprietors. Though Florentine embroidery was once considered a dying art, **Cirri,** Via por Santa Maria (☎ 055/239-6593), keeps it alive, with literally hundreds of beautiful designs in linen, cotton, and silk.

FASHION   Italian clothing from lesser-known designers like Caractere is available at **Glamour,** Borgo Sant' Jacopo 49 (☎ 055/210-334). Though the style is first rate, the prices are more affordable than at most fashion houses in Florence. You'll find good-quality sweaters as well as blouses and skirts in various materials. At **Loretta Caponi,** Piazza Antinori 4 (☎ 055/213-668), the arched ceiling and gold-and-turquoise trim create a perfect atmosphere in which to browse through a wonderful selection of slip dresses, robes, linens, and children's wear in luxurious silks, velvets, and cottons.

   Mariposa, Lungarno Corsini 2 (☎ 055/284-259), offers women's and men's fashions from such famous designers as Krizia, Fendi, Rocco Barocco, Missoni, and Mimmina. Foreign customers are often granted a 20% discount on tax-free items. Featured at **Max Mara,** Via del Pecori 23 (☎ 055/239-6590), are high-quality women's clothes designed and produced by Max Mara, synonymous with classic elegance and even a touch of flamboyance. The selection covers everything from hats and coats to suits and slacks. You won't find the big names, but many of the "unknowns" are getting better known every day. In the center of town near the Duomo is **Romano,** Piazza della Repubblica (☎ **055/239-6890**), a glamorous clothing store for both women and men. The owners commissioned a curving stairwell to be constructed under the high ornate ceiling. But even more exciting are leather and suede goods, along with an assortment of stylish dresses, shoes, and handbags—the prices are high, but so is the quality.

GIFTS   Among the many treasures found at ✪ **Balatresi Gift Shop,** Lungarno Acciaiuoli 22R (☎ **055/287-851**), are Florentine mosaics created by Maestro Metello Montelatici, one of the greatest mosaicists alive. The store also sells original ceramic figurines by the sculptor Giannitrapani and a fine selection of hand-carved alabaster, enamel ware, and Tuscan glass. The wide inventory at **Menegatti,** Piazza del Pesce, Ponte Vecchio 2R (☎ **055/215-202**), includes pottery from Florence, Faenza, and Deruta. There are also della Robbia reproductions made in red clay like the originals. Items can be sent home if you arrange it at the time of your purchase.

GLASS   The small **Cose del '900,** Borgo Sant' Jacopo 45 (☎ **055/283-491**), is full of glass items of every description from 1900 to 1950—shot glasses, drinking glasses, centerpieces, and many art deco pieces. Dating back to the era of the grand dukes, the art of grinding and engraving glass is still carried out at ✪ **Paola Locchi,** Via Burchiello 10 (☎ **055/229-8371**), with exquisite skill and craftsmanship. Every kind of engraved object seemingly is sold, some of it of stupendous size. You can even find engraved goblets that decorated the banqueting tables of the ancients.

HERBALISTS   **Antica Farmacia del Cinghiale,** Piazza del Mercato Muovo 4R (☎ **055/282-128**), in business for some 3 centuries, is an *erboristeria,* dispensing herbal teas and fragrances, along with herbal potpourris. A pharmacy is also here. The ✪ **Officina Profumo Farmaceutica di Santa Maria Novella,** Via della Scala 16N (☎ **055/216-276**), is the most fascinating pharmacy in Italy. Northwest of Santa Maria Novella, it opened in 1612, offering a selection of herbal remedies that were created by friars of the Dominican order. Those closely guarded secrets have been retained, and many of the same elixirs are still sold today. You've heard of papaya as an aid to digestion, but what about elixir of rhubarb? A wide selection of perfumes, scented soaps, shampoos, and potpourris, along with creams and lotions, is also sold. The shop is closed Saturday afternoon in July and August.

JEWELRY   Buying jewelry is almost an art in itself, so proceed with caution. Florence is known for its jewelry. You'll find some stunning antique pieces, and, if you know how to buy, some good values.

   Befani e Tai, Via Vacchereccia 13R (☎ **055/287-825**), is one of the most unusual jewelry stores in Florence—some of its pieces date from the 19th century. The store was opened after World War II by expert goldsmiths who were childhood friends. Some of their clients even design their own jewelry for special orders. **Faraone-Settepassi,** Via dei Tornabuoni 25R (☎ **055/215-506**), one of the most distinguished jewelers of the Renaissance city, draws a well-heeled patronage.

   Located away from the Ponte Vecchio, **Mario Buccellati,** Via dei Tornabuoni 69–71R (☎ **055/239-6579**), a branch of the Milan store that opened in 1919, specializes in exquisite handcrafted jewelry and silver. A large selection of intriguing pieces at high prices is offered. Modern 18-carat gold jewelry is the specialty at **Elisabetta Fallaci,** Ponte Vecchio 10 and 22 (☎ **055/294-981**), all made in Florence. Look also for the beautiful enameled 18K gold boxes from the 1800s.

LEATHER   Universally acclaimed, Florentine leather is still the fine product it always was—smooth, well shaped, and often in vivid colors.

The Art of Marbleizing

The city that prides itself as the literary cradle of Italy has always known how best to present its folios and manuscripts.

The brilliantly colored marbleized end pages decorating the inside covers of books and photo albums use techniques that were developed in Persia and Turkey and imported to Italy during the 1400s by Florentine and Venetian merchants. The technique was improved and kept alive in Florence throughout the 19th and 20th centuries.

How do they do it? The "marbleizing" technique takes advantage of the relative densities of water and oil-based pigments to "float" layers of ink above the basins of water. By jiggling sheets of paper through multicolored brew, teams of trained artisans create the peacock-feathered effect that has been so popular throughout the ages. Part of the expense of marbleized paper involves the need to discard large amounts of ink, as the basin of pigment is usually thrown away after the treatment of each piece of paper.

The well-known Beltrami leather goods are sold at **Beltrami,** Via del Tornabuoni 48 (☎ 055/287-779), as well as expensive evening clothes, heavyweight silk scarves, and fashions of the best quality. This is one of several Beltrami shops in the area. High fashion, high prices, and high quality are what you'll find here, but prices are significantly lower than what you'll pay for Beltrami in the States. **Beltrami Spa,** Via del Panzani 1 (☎ 055/212-661), offers last season's fashions at discounts of 20 to 50%. There are further discounts for multiple purchases, and since the original prices are still on the items, you can tell how much you're saving.

Sergio Bojola, Via dei Rondinelli 25R (☎ 055/211-155), a leading name in leather, has distinguished himself in Florence by the variety of his selections, in both synthetic materials and beautiful leathers. You'll find first-class quality and craftsmanship. ✪ **Cellerini,** Via del Sole 37 (☎ 055/282-533), is one of the city's master leathersmiths. Silvano Cellerini has been called a genius in Florentine leather. Original purses, shoulder bags, suitcases, accessories, wallets, and even a limited number of shoes (for both women and men) are sold here.

This branch of **Gucci,** Via del Tornabuoni 73 (☎ 055/264-011), is the mother of all Gucci shops. Though much imitated around the world, this Gucci product is real. In general, prices are a bit cheaper here than in Milan and a lot less expensive than in the United States. There's every Gucci item imaginable—belts to shoes to shawls to the chic Gucci scarf.

Leonardo Leather Works, Borgo dei Greci 16A (☎ 055/292-202), concentrates on two of the oldest major crafts of Florence: leather and jewelry. Leather goods include wallets, bags, shoes, boots, briefcases, clothing, travel bags, belts, and gift items, with products by famous designers. No imitations are permitted. The jewelry department has a large assortment of gold chains, bracelets, rings, earrings, and charms. **Pollini,** Via Calimala 12R (☎ 055/214-738), offers a wide array of stylized merchandise, like shoes, suitcases, clothing, and belts. It's in the historic heart of Florence, near the Ponte Vecchio.

MARKETS   Intrepid shoppers head for the **Mercato Nuovo (Straw Market** or **New Market),** 2 blocks south of Piazza della Repubblica. (It's called "Il Porcellino" by the Italians because of the bronze statue of a reclining wild boar here—a copy of the one in the Uffizi.) Tourists pet its snout (which is well worn) for good luck. The market stands in the monumental heart of Florence, an easy stroll from the Palazzo Vecchio. It sells not only straw items but also leather goods, along with typical Florentine merchandise—frames, trays, hand-embroidery, table linens, and hand-sprayed and -painted boxes in traditional designs. The market is open Monday to Saturday 9am to 7pm.

However, even better bargains await those who make their way through the push-carts to the stalls of the open-air **Mercato Centrale** (**Mercato San Lorenzo**), in and around Borgo San Lorenzo, near the rail station. If you don't mind bargaining, which is imperative, you'll find an array of merchandise like raffia bags, Florentine leather purses, sweaters, gloves, salt-and-pepper shakers, straw handbags, and art reproductions. It's open Monday to Saturday 9am to 7pm.

MOSAICS   Florentine mosaics are universally recognized. Bruno Lastrucci, the director of **Arte Musiva,** Largo Bargellini 2–4 (☎ **055/241-647**), is one of the most renowned exponents of this art form. In the workshop you can see artisans—including some of the major mosaicists of Italy—plying their craft, creating both traditional Florentine and modern designs. A selection of the most significant works is permanently displayed in the gallery.

PAPER & STATIONERY   **Giulio Giannini & Figlio,** Piazza Pitti 37R (☎ **055/ 212-621**), has been a family business for more than 140 years and is the leading stationery store in Florence. Foreigners often snap up the exquisite merchandise for gift-giving later in the year. The specialty at **Il Papiro,** Via Cavour 55R (☎ **055/ 215-262**), is party-colored marbleized paper that's skillfully incorporated into objects ranging from bookmarks to photo albums. (Have a favorite relative who's getting married soon? These make great wedding albums.) More unusual are the marbleized wood (like music boxes) and leather (couture-style purses and bags) items, as well as the marbleized fabric. The staff is charming, and the prices are reasonable, considering the high quality. There are branches at Piazza del Duomo 24R and Lugarno Acciaiuoli 42R (☎ **055/215-262** for both branches).

Opened in 1774 and maintained today by descendants of the original founders, ✪ **Pineider,** Piazza della Signoria 13R (☎ **055/284-655**), is the oldest store in Florence specializing in printing and engraving. The most aristocratic-looking greeting cards, business cards, stationery, and formal invitations come from this outfit. Because most orders take between 2 and 3 weeks to fill, many clients place their orders here, then arrange to have the final product shipped home. The store also stocks a wide range of gifts, like beautifully crafted diaries, stationery, the kinds of desk sets you'd offer your favorite CEO, portfolios, address books, photo albums, and etchings of vistas unique to Florence. A less extensive branch (it doesn't take custom engraving orders) is at Via dei Tornbuoni 76 (☎ **055/211-605**).

PRINTS & ENGRAVINGS   **Ducci,** Lungarno Corsini 24 (☎ **055/214-550**), hawks the best selection of historical prints and engravings covering the history of Florence from the 13th century. Also available are Florentine boxes covered with gold leaf, marble fruit, and wooden items. **Giovanni Baccani,** Via della Vigna Nuova 75R (☎ **055/214-467**), has long been a specialist in this field. Everything it sells is old. "The Blue Shop," as it's called, offers a huge array of prints and engravings, often of Florentine scenes. Tuscan paper goods are also sold.

SHOES   **Casadei,** Via del Tornabuoni 33R (☎ **055/287-240**), is an interesting shop painted white with pillars, making the room look like a small colonnade; it's one of four Casadei shops in Italy (others are in Rome and Ferrara and near Bologna). Locally produced women's shoes, boots, and handbags are sold, all with the Casadei label. Prices begin at 300,000L ($174). **Lily of Florence,** Via Guicciardini 2R (☎ **055/294-748**), offers both men's and women's shoes in American sizes. For women, Lily distributes both her own creations and those of other well-known designers. The stylish shoes come in a wide range of colors and are made of high-quality leather.

⊙ **Salvatore Ferragamo,** Via dei Tornabuoni 14R (☎ **055/292-123**), has long been one of the most famous names in shoes. Though he started in Hollywood just before World War I, the headquarters of this famed manufacturer were installed here in the Palazzo Ferroni, on the most fashionable shopping street of Florence, before World War II broke out. Ferragamo sells shoes for both men and women, along with elegant boutique items, like men's and women's clothing, scarves, handbags, ties, and luggage. But chances are you'll want to visit it for its stunning shoes, known for their durability and style. If you're really interested, check out the **Ferragamo Museum** at Via dei Tornabuoni 2 (☎ **055/336-0456**), open Monday, Wednesday, and Friday 9am to 1pm and 2 to 6pm. This free museum, on the second floor of a block devoted completely to the Ferragamo aesthetic, chronicles the family-run empire from its beginnings. There's also a display of exquisite shoes from other eras.

SILVER   Pampaloni, Borgo Santi Apostoli 47R (☎ **055/289-094**), is headed by Gianfranco Pampaloni, a third-generation silversmith. He often bases designs on past achievements—for example, a 1604 goblet by the Roman artist Giovanni Maggi. The business was launched in 1902, and some of the classic designs turned out back then are still being made.

A fabled name among world-class shoppers, **Brandimartre,** Via Bartolini 19–21 (☎ **055/238-1557**), is Florence's best-stocked workshop and silver showcase. This semi-precious metal is exquisitely handcrafted into a number of dazzling items, including signature goblets. They even do frivolous designs for the man or women who has everything—a silver cheese grater, for example.

WINES   Though this restaurant is self-described as presenting a typical Florentine menu, the emphasis at **Il Cantinone,** Via Santo Spirito 6 (☎ **055/218-898**), is on wine—principally the wines of Tuscany, such as Black Label, Santo Cristo, and Villa Antinori. Purchase your choice by the glass or by the bottle to take with you. And don't forget to try the Vin Santo, a Tuscan dessert wine, with almond cookies. If you want a little more substance, their fixed-price menus are 14,000L to 40,000L ($8 to $23).

7 Florence After Dark

Evening entertainment in Florence isn't an exciting prospect, unless you simply like to walk through the narrow streets or head toward Fiesole for a truly spectacular view of the city at night. The typical Florentine begins an evening early at one of the cafes listed below.

For theatrical and concert listings pick up a free copy of *Welcome to Florence,* available at the tourist office. This handy publication contains information on recitals, concerts, theater productions, and other cultural offerings.

From late April to July, the city welcomes classical musicians for its ⊙ **Maggio Musicale** festival of cantatas, madrigals, concertos, operas, and ballets, many of which are presented in Renaissance buildings. Schedule and ticket information is available from **Maggio Musicale Fiorentino/Teatro Comunale,** Via Solferino 15, 50123 Firenze (☎ **055/27-791**). Tickets cost 20,000 to 200,000L ($12 to $116).

THE PERFORMING ARTS

The ❂ **Teatro Comunale di Firenze/Maggio Musicale Fiorentino,** Corso Italia 16 (☎ 055/211-158), is Florence's main theater, with opera and ballet seasons presented September to December and concert season January to April. This theater is also the venue for the Maggio Musicale, Italy's oldest and most prestigious festival that takes place in Florence from late April to July and offers opera, ballet, concerts, recitals, cinema, and meetings. The box office is open Tuesday to Friday 11am to 5:30pm, Saturday 9am to 1pm, and 1 hour before the curtain. Tickets run 40,000L to 200,000L ($23 to $116) for the opera, 35,000L to 100,000L ($20 to $58) for concerts, and 24,000L to 50,000L ($14 to $29) for the ballet.

The **Teatro della Pergola,** Via della Pergola 18 (☎ 055/247-9651), is Florence's major legitimate theater, but you'll have to understand Italian to appreciate most of its plays. Plays are performed year-round except during the Maggio Musicale, when the theater becomes the setting for many of the festival events. Performances are Tuesday to Saturday at 8:45pm. The box office is open Tuesday to Saturday 9:30am to 1pm and 3:30 to 6:45pm and Sunday 10am to noon. Tickets run 18,500L to 42,500L ($11 to $25).

Recently renovated, the **Teatro Verdi,** Via Ghibellina 101 (☎ 055/212-320), is a venue for prestigious dance and classical music events. Major operatic and ballet performances are often presented here as well, including "big name" performers. Even a leading pop star has been known to dominate the stage. You really have to inquire locally when you're here, as you never know what the presentation is going to be. In such a situation, ticket prices can vary greatly, perhaps 10,000L to 35,000L ($6 to $20).

LIVE-MUSIC CLUBS

In Dante's former neighborhood, **Chiodo Fisso,** Via Dante Alighieri 16R (☎ 055/238-1290), is the best venue for Italian folk music. The owners refer to it as a "guitar club," and acoustic guitar sets are a regular feature. Drinks are a bit pricey: You can order a bottle of Chianti (hardly the best) for 25,000L ($15). Except for 2 weeks in August, the club opens daily 9pm to 3am and the cover is 3,000L ($1.75). In the cellar of an antique building in the historic heart of town, **Full-Up,** Via della Vigna Vecchia 23–25R (☎ 055/293-006), attracts college students who appreciate the club's two-in-one format. One section contains a smallish dance floor and recorded dance music; the other is a somewhat more restrained piano bar. The place can be fun, and even older patrons feel at ease. It's open Monday to Saturday 11pm to 4am, with a 15,000L to 25,000L ($9 to $15) cover that includes the first drink.

Nothing could be more unexpected in this city of Donatello and Michelangelo than a club called the **Red Garter,** Via de' Benci 33R (☎ 055/234-4904), right off Piazza Santa Croce. The club, which has an American Prohibition–era theme, attracts young people from all over the world and features everything from rock to bluegrass. A mug of Heineken lager on tap goes for 7,000L ($4.05), and most tall drinks, made from "hijacked hootch," as it's known here, begin at 10,000L ($6). The club is open Monday to Thursday 8:30pm to 1am and Friday to Sunday 9pm to 1:30am. "Happy Hour" is every evening until 9:30pm. There's no cover. Set within a 10-minute bus ride from the Piazza del Duomo (take bus no. 29 or 30 to a point near Florence's airport), **Tenax,** Via Pratese 46A (☎ 055/308-160), is Florence's premier venue for everything from live rock to hip-hop and rap. The bands come from throughout Italy and the rest of Europe. This place used to be a garage and is appropriately battered and grungy. Shows begin nightly except Monday at 10pm and continue until around 4am. The cover is 20,000L to 30,000L ($12 to $17), including the first drink.

Church Concerts

Many cultural presentations are performed in churches. These might include open-air concerts in the cloisters of the Badia Fiesolana in Fiesole or at the Ospedale degli Innocenti, on summer evenings only. Orchestral offerings—performed by the Regional Tuscan Orchestra—are often presented at Santo Stefano al Ponte Vecchio.

CAFES

Café Rivoire, Piazza della Signoria 5R (☎ 055/214-412), offers a classy and amusing old-world ambience with a direct view of the statues of one of our favorite squares in the world. You can sit at one of the metal tables on the flagstones outside or at one of the wooden tables in a choice of inner rooms filled with marble detailing and unusual oil renderings of the piazza outside. If you don't want to sit at all, try the bar, where many colorful characters talk, flirt, or gossip. There's also a selection of small sandwiches, omelets, and ice creams. The cafe is noted for its hot chocolate.

Giacosa, Via dei Tornabuoni 83R (☎ 055/239-6226), is a deceptively simple-looking cafe whose stand-up bar occupies more space than its limited number of tables. Behind three Tuscan arches on a fashionable shopping street in the center of the old city, it has a warmly paneled interior, a lavish display of pastries and sandwiches, and a reputation as the birthplace of the Negroni. That drink, as you probably know, is a combination of gin, Campari, and red vermouth. You can also wet your whistle with Singapore slings, Italian and American coffee, and a range of aperitifs. Light meals are also served, and the cafe is famous for its ice cream.

The oldest and most beautiful cafe in Florence, **Gilli,** Piazza della Repubblica 39R, via Roma 1 (☎ 055/213-896), occupies a desirable position in the center of the city, a few minutes' walk from the Duomo. It was founded in 1789, when Piazza della Repubblica had a different name. You can sit at a brightly lit table near the bar or retreat to an intricately paneled pair of rooms to the side and enjoy the flattering light from the Venetian-glass chandeliers. Daily specials, sandwiches, toasts, and hard drinks are sold, along with an array of "tropical" libations.

The waiters at ✪ **Giubbe Rosse,** Piazza della Repubblica 13–14R (☎ 055/212-280), still wear the Garibaldi red coats as they did when it was founded in 1888. Originally a beer hall and later a meeting place of Florentine futurists, today it's an elegantly paneled cafe/bar/restaurant filled with turn-of-the-century chandeliers and polished granite floors. You can enjoy a drink or cup of coffee at one of the small tables near the zinc-top bar. An inner dining room has a soaring vaulted ceiling of reddish brick. Light lunches and full American breakfasts are specialties.

BARS & PUBS

Donatello Bar, in the Hotel Excelsior, Piazza Ognissanti 3 (☎ 055/264-201), is the city's most elegant watering hole. Named in honor of the great Renaissance artist, this bar and its adjoining restaurant, Il Cestello, attract well-heeled international visitors along with the Florentine cultural and business elite. The ambience is enlivened by a marble fountain and works of art. Piano music is featured daily 7pm to 1am. If you ask whether the **Dublin Pub,** Via Faenza 27R (☎ 055/293-049), is an Italian pub, the all-Italian staff will respond rather grandly that such a concept doesn't exist and pubs are by definition Irish. And once you get beyond the fact that virtually no one on the staff has ever been outside Tuscany and there's very little to do here except drink and perhaps practice your Italian, you might settle down and have a rollicking old (very Latin) time. Beers, at least, are appropriately Celtic and include Harp, Guinness,

Kilkenny, and Strong's on tap. You'll find it near the Santa Maria Novella railway station.

After an initial success in Rome, **Fiddler's Elbow,** Piazza Santa Maria Novella 7R (☎ 055/215-056), an Irish pub, has now invaded this city and quickly became one of the most popular watering holes. An authentic pint of Guinness is the most popular item to order. The location is in the vicinity of the rail station.

DANCE CLUBS

Meccanò, Viale degli Olmi 1 (☎ 055/331-371), is Florence's best, biggest, and most international disco. Within a 20-minute bus ride from Piazza del Duomo, near the Parco della Cascine, it's one of the few discos in Italy to offer an indoor/outdoor setting that includes century-old trees, a terrace, and three dance floors. The musical venue includes everything from punk to rock to funk to garage. Gays mix with the mostly straight crowd with ease, and the average age is 18 to 35. There's no real dress code, but if you opt to dine at the restaurant, you'll find that the crowd there is better dressed. Set menus are 35,000L ($20) and served beginning at 9pm. Don't be surprised if someone decides to dance on your table after you've finished eating. Dancing reigns supreme every night except Sunday, Monday, and Wednesday, 11:30pm to 4am. The cover runs 15,000L to 30,000L ($9 to $17), including the first drink.

Space Electronic, Via Palazzuolo 37 (☎ 055/293-082), is the only club with karaoke. The decor consists of gigantic carnival heads, wall-to-wall mirrors, and an imitation space capsule that goes back and forth across the dance floor. If karaoke doesn't thrill you, head to the new ground-floor pub, which stocks an ample supply of imported beers. On the upper level is a large dance floor with a wide choice of music and the best sound-and-light show in town. This place attracts a lot of foreign women who want to hook up with Florentine men on the prowl. The disco opens nightly at 11pm and usually goes until 4am. The 25,000L ($15) cover includes the first drink.

Much of the popularity of **Yab Yum,** Via Sassetti 5R (☎ 055/215-160), derives from its location in the heart of the historic core. Owned and operated by the same entrepreneurs who maintain the larger, more fun, and less inhibited Meccanò, it offers much the same kind of music, albeit in a smaller and more cramped setting. Partly because its interior is less well air-conditioned, it closes between May and October. Otherwise, hours are Monday to Saturday 11pm to 4am. The cover runs 15,000L to 30,000L ($9 to $17) and includes the first drink.

GAY & LESBIAN CLUBS

Florence's leading gay bar, **Crisco,** Via S. Egidio 43R (☎ 055/248-0580), caters only to men and is located in an 18th-century building containing a bar and a dance floor. Classified as a club privato, it's open on Wednesday, Thursday, Sunday, and Monday 10:30pm to 3:30am and Friday and Saturday 10:30pm to 5 or 6am. The cover can be 12,000L to 20,000L ($7 to $12), depending on the night of the week.

Many of Tuscany's gay and lesbian community consider **Santanassa Bar,** Via del Pandolfini 26 (☎ 055/243-356), a Saturday-night staple. In summer, the crowd gets international. There's a crowded bar on the street level, sometimes with a live piano player, where many of the patrons seem to have known one another for years. On Friday and Saturday the cellar is transformed into a disco. It's open Sunday to Thursday 10pm to 3:30am and Friday and Saturday 10pm to 5am. The bar and disco are open year-round. The cover, including the first drink, is 12,000L ($7) Sunday to Thursday and 15,000L to 20,000L ($9 to $12) Friday and Saturday.

Tabasco, Piazza Santa Cecelia 3 (☎ 055/213-000), is one of Florence's leading gay bars, a tradition since 1974 near Piazza della Signoria. The club offers a bar, along with video games and X-rated male-action movies, plus music like retro-rock and techno. You must be 18 to be admitted. It's open Tuesday to Sunday 10pm to at least 4am or later on weekends. The cover runs 15,000L to 25,000L ($9 to $15) and includes the first drink.

8 A Side Trip to Fiesole

For more extensive day trips, you can refer to the next chapter. But Fiesole is a virtual suburb of Florence.

When the sun shines too hot on Piazza della Signoria and tourists try to prance bare-backed into the Uffizi, Florentines are likely to head for the hills—usually to Fiesole. But they'll encounter more tourists, as this town (once an Etruscan settlement) is the most popular outing from the city. Bus no. 7, leaving from Piazza San Marco, will take you here in 25 minutes and give you a panoramic view along the way. You'll pass fountains, statuary, and gardens strung out over the hills like a scrambled jigsaw puzzle.

EXPLORING THE TOWN

In Fiesole you won't find anything as dazzling as the Renaissance treasures of Florence—the town's charms are more subtle. Fortunately, all major sights branch out within walking distance of the main piazza, **Piazza Mino da Fiesole,** beginning with the **Cattedrale di San Romolo (Duomo).** At first this cathedral may seem austere, with its concrete-gray Corinthian columns and Romanesque arches. But it has its own beauty. Dating from A.D. 1000, it was much altered during the Renaissance. In the Salutati Chapel are important sculptural works by Mino da Fiesole. It's open daily 7:30am to noon and 4 to 7pm.

Bandini Museum (Museo Bandini). Via Dupre 1. ☎ 055/59-477. Admission (includes admission to Teatro Romano e Museo Civico, below) 10,000L ($6) adults, 5,000L ($2.90) children 6–16/students; children 5 and under free. Jan–Feb and Nov–Dec daily 9:30am–5pm; Mar and Oct daily 9am–6pm; Apr–Sept daily 9am–7pm.

This ecclesiastical museum, around to the side of the Duomo, belongs to the Fiesole Cathedral Chapter, established in 1913. On the ground floor are della Robbia terra-cotta works, as well as art by Michelangelo and Pisano. On the top floors are paintings by the best Giotto students, which reflect ecclesiastical and worldly themes, most of them the work of Tuscan artists of the 14th century.

Roman Theater and Civic Museum (Teatro Romano e Museo Civico). Via Portigiani 1. ☎ 055/59-477. Admission (includes admission to Bandini museum, above) 10,000L ($6) adults, 5,000L ($2.90) children 6–16/students; children 5 and under free. Jan–Feb and Nov–Dec daily 9:30am–5pm; Mar and Oct daily 9am–6pm; Apr–Sept daily 9am–7pm.

On this site is the major surviving evidence that Fiesole was an Etruscan city 6 centuries before Christ and later a Roman town. In the 1st century B.C. a theater was built, the restored remains of which you can see today. Near the theater are the skeletonlike ruins of the baths, which may have been built at the same time. Try to visit the Etruscan-Roman museum, with its many interesting finds that date from the days when Fiesole—not Florence—was supreme (a guide is on hand to show you through).

Museum of the Franciscan Missionaries (Museo Missionario Francescano Fiesole). Via San Francesco 13. ☎ 055/59-175. Free admission (but a donation is expected). Church daily 8am–noon and 3–6pm. Museum Mon–Sat 9:30am–12:30pm and 3–6pm, Sun 9–11am and 3–6pm (to 7pm daily in summer). Bus: 7.

The hardest task you'll have in Fiesole is to take the steep goat-climb up to the Convent of San Francesco. You can visit the Gothic-style Franciscan church, built in the first years of the 1400s and consecrated in 1516. Inside are many paintings by well-known Florentine artists. In the basement of the church is the ethnological museum. Begun in 1906, the collection has a large section of Chinese artifacts, including ancient bronzes. An Etruscan-Roman section contains some 330 archaeological pieces, and an Egyptian section also has numerous objects.

ACCOMMODATIONS

Hotel Villa Aurora. Piazza Mino da Fiesole 39, Fiesole, 50014 Firenze. ☎ **055/59-100.** Fax 055/59-587. 27 units. A/C MINIBAR TV TEL. 227,000–335,000L ($132–$194) double. Rates include breakfast. AE, DC, MC, V. Bus: 7.

On Fiesole's main square, behind a facade of green shutters and ocher-colored stucco, the Aurora occupies a structure built in the 18th century as a private house. In 1890 it became a hotel that catered almost exclusively to arts-conscious English people making their Grand Tour. The hotel continues to rent rooms, which have been modernized and simplified and even include Jacuzzis. Views over faraway Florence are visible from the back rooms, which cost more than those overlooking the piazza. On the premises are a back terrace with hanging vines, a pergola, and views of the city. Connecting doors can be opened between some rooms to create suites, which cost around 550,000L ($319). Though a continental breakfast is included, you'll be billed separately for extras like eggs and cereal. This is true, of course, all over Italy.

Pensione Bencista. Via Benedetto de Maiano 4, Fiesole, 50014 Firenze. ☎ and fax **055/59-163.** 44 units, 32 with bathroom. TEL. 120,000L ($70) per person without bathroom, 140,000L ($81) per person with bathroom. Rates include half board. No credit cards. Bus: 7.

The Bencista has been the family villa of the Simoni family for years. One guest found it was like E. M. Forster's "*A Room with a View* gone to the country." It was built around 1300, with additions made about every 100 years after that. In 1925, Paolo Simoni opened the villa to paying guests. Today it's run by his son, Simone Simoni. Its position, high up on the road to Fiesole, is commanding, with an unmarred view of the city and the hillside villas. The spread-out villa has many lofty old rooms furnished with family antiques. They vary in size and interest; many are without bath and have hot and cold running water only. In chilly weather, guests meet each other in the evening in front of a huge fireplace. The Bencista is suitable for parents who might want to leave their children in the country while they take jaunts into the city. It's a 10-minute bus ride from the heart of Florence.

✪ **Villa San Michele.** Via Doccia 4, Fiesole, 50014 Firenze. ☎ **800/237-1236** in the U.S., or 055/59-451. Fax 055/598-734. www.orient-expresshotels.com. E-mail: villasanmichele@firenze.net. 40 units. A/C MINIBAR TV TEL. 1,100,000–1,430,000L ($638–$829) double; 2,600,000L ($1,508) suite. Rates include half board. AE, DC, MC, V. Closed mid-Nov to mid-Mar. Bus: 7.

The San Michele is an ancient monastery of unsurpassed beauty in a memorable setting on a hill below Fiesole, a 15-minute walk south of the center. It was built in the 15th century, and after being damaged in World War II, it was carefully restored. The facade and loggia were reportedly designed by Michelangelo. A curving driveway, lined with blossoming trees and flowers, leads to the entrance. A 10-arch covered loggia continues around the view side of the building to the Italian gardens at the rear. Most of the rooms open onto the view; the others face the inner courtyard. Each room is unique, some with iron or wooden canopy beds, antique chests, Savonarola chairs, formal draperies, old ecclesiastical paintings, candelabra, and statues. Poets and artists have stayed at the San Michele and sung its praises.

   Dining/Diversions: Chairs and tables are set out on the loggia for moonlit dinners, at which a refined Tuscan cuisine is served. Guests also enjoy the frescoed Cenacolo piano bar.

   Amenities: Concierge, room service, secretarial services, baby-sitting, shuttle bus to town, heated outdoor pool, solarium, facilities for the disabled.

DINING

Trattoria le Cave di Maiano. Via delle Cave 16. ☎ **055/59-133.** Reservations required. Main courses 18,000–28,000L ($10–$16); fixed-price lunch 50,000L ($29). AE, DC, MC, V. Tues–Sun 12:30–3:30pm; daily 7:30pm–midnight. Closed Aug 10–20. TUSCAN.

This former farmhouse is at Maiano, a 15-minute ride east from the heart of Florence and just a short distance south of Fiesole. It's a family-run place. The rustically decorated trattoria is a garden restaurant, with stone tables and large sheltering trees. We recommend highly the antipasto and homemade green tortellini. For a main course, there's a golden grilled chicken or savory herb-flavored roast lamb. For side dishes, we suggest fried polenta, Tuscan beans, and fried potatoes. As a final treat, the waiter will bring you homemade ice cream with fresh raspberries.

7

Tuscany & Umbria

Rome may rule Italy, but **Tuscany** presides over its heart. The Tuscan landscapes, some little changed since the days of the Medicis, look just like Renaissance paintings, with cypress trees and olive groves and evocative hill towns and those fabled Chianti vineyards.

Tuscany was the place where the Etruscans first appeared in Italy. The Romans followed, absorbing and conquering them, and by the 11th century the region had evolved into a collection of independent city-states, such as Florence and Siena, each trying to dominate the others. Many of the cities we'll visit knew the apogee of their economic and political power in the 13th century. The Renaissance was immensely popular in Florence, but it was slow to come to Siena, which remains a gem of Gothic glory.

In time, however, the Renaissance did arrive with its titans of art, like Giotto, Michelangelo, and Leonardo. Ever since these geniuses "invented" the Renaissance (it wasn't called that at the time), the world has flocked to Tuscany to see not just the land but also some of the world's greatest art. Critics claim, without much exaggeration, that Western civilization was "rediscovered" in Tuscany. According to D. H. Lawrence, Tuscany became "the perfect center of man's universe."

Art flourished under the tutelage of the powerful Medicis, and the legacy remains of Masaccio, della Francesca, Signorelli, Raphael, Donatello, Botticelli, and countless others, including the engineering feats of architects like Brunelleschi. This first Renaissance is well known. Lesser known is the second Renaissance that came to Tuscany long after the Medici dynasty expired in 1737. Drawn to the region to write about its art, history, and landscapes was a stellar literary brigade headed by Gorky, Twain, Shelley, Stedhal, Dostoyevsky, the Brownings, and even Dylan Thomas.

Tuscany became known for its men of letters, such as Dante, Petrarch, and Boccaccio (who put the seal of approval on the Tuscan dialect by writing in the vernacular rather than Latin), and its Renaissance artists, but **Umbria,** a small region at the heart of the Italian peninsula, is associated mainly with saints. Christendom's most beloved saints were born here, foremost of whom was St. Francis of Assisi, founder of the Franciscans. Also born here were St. Valentine, a 3rd-century bishop of Terni, and St. Clare, founder of the Order of Poor Clares.

However, Umbrian painters also contributed to the glory of the Renaissance, like Il Perugino, whose lyrical works you can see in the

Driving Through Tuscany & Umbria

Here's how to link together the region's highlights if you have a car.

Day 1: From Florence, take the autostrada west toward Lucca and Pisa, but, if time permits, consider an overnight stop in the most fashionable spa in Italy, **Montecatini Terme,** signposted off the autostrada. Here you can get in some R&R after having drained yourself experiencing all the Renaissance glories of Florence.

Day 2: Back on the autostrada west, you can be in **Lucca** within the hour—enough time for a full day of sightseeing. In the center of a fertile plain, Lucca is known for its foodstuff, so in addition to seeing its major sights, especially its Duomo with a green-and-white marble facade, you can enjoy wonderful eating. After a night in Lucca, the trail heads south.

Day 3: From Lucca, your next destination on the autostrada is **Pisa.** Though it's too dangerous to climb the Leaning Tower anymore, Pisa is a great art city, known especially for its architecture. In addition to its Duomo, chief attractions are the Baptistery, the Camposanto, and the Museo dell'Opera del Duomo.

Day 4: Travel southeast for a visit to **San Gimignano,** ringed by three sets of historic walls and known for its medieval towers. No cars are allowed inside the city walls. You can cover most of the sights in a day, and San Gimignano is one of the most romantic stopovers in the province.

Day 5: Go in the direction of Poggibonsi and cut south to **Siena,** the highlight of this driving tour, one of the world's best-preserved medieval cities. Visit the Duomo, the Battistero, the Cathedral Museum, and most definitely the Pinacoteca Nazionale. Siena is rich in many other sights, and you may not have time for everything if you're limited to only one night.

Day 6: Head southeast along E78, crossing the autostrada between Florence and Rome, and follow the signs to the ancient city of **Perugia,** where you'll want to overnight. The regional capital of Umbria is rich in sights—notably its piazza IV Novembre and Galleria Nazionale dell'Umbria.

Day 7: Head southeast to **Assisi** to see some of its major attractions, including the Temple of Minerva and the Basilica di San Francesco. However, instead of anchoring there for the night, as most visitors do, head south to **Spoleto** for the night. Have a good dinner (with truffles) and wander at leisure that night around this often-neglected art city (except at festival time).

Galleria Nazionale dell'Umbria in Perugia. Umbria's landscapes, also the subject of countless paintings, are as alluring as ever: You'll pass through a hilly chestnut-wooded terrain interspersed with fertile plains of olive groves and vineyards (Pliny the Elder was among the first to rhapsodize over the vino of Umbria).

In September 1997, twin earthquakes (5.7 and 5.6 on the Richter scale), with an epicenter just outside Assisi, struck within hours of each other. Umbria sustained considerable damage, especially in Acciano and Assisi, where 11 people were killed and another 13,000 forced to take refuge in tents. The following 11 days of aftershocks and tremors hindered the recovery effort by the Italian government and relief organizations and poured salt in the wounds of those left wondering what to do. The tremors were felt as far south as Rome and as far north as Florence. For more on this, see the box "Umbria Shakes, Rattles & Rolls" later in this chapter.

The serious wine connoisseur may want to call ahead and make appointments to view some of Italy's best wineries lying in this area. For a list of the places to visit with

Tuscany & Umbria

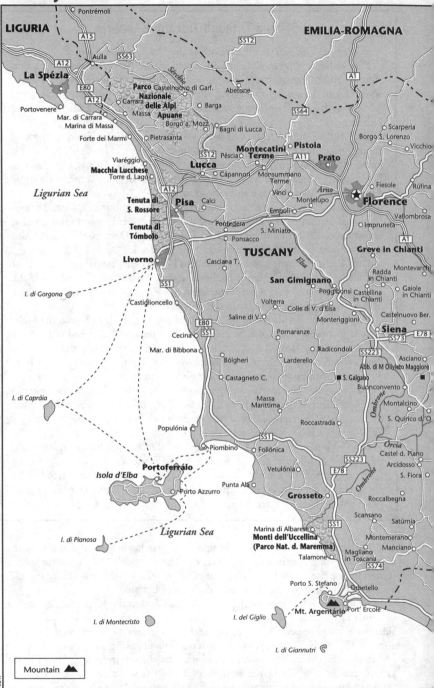

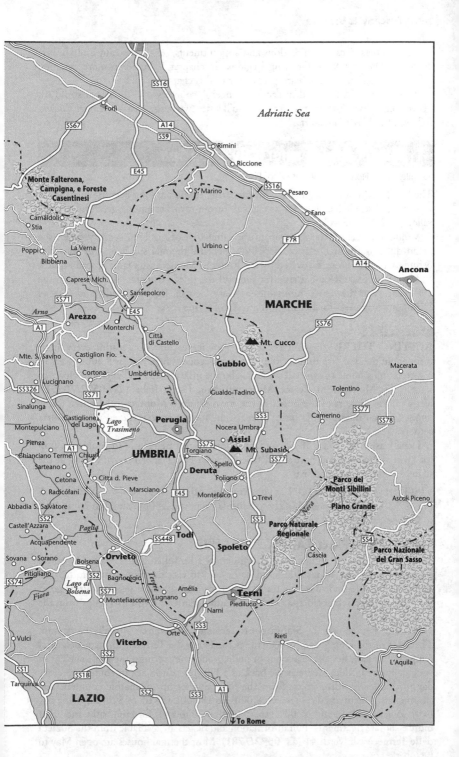

phone numbers to call for directions and appointments, see the Tuscany and Umbria entry in "The Best Wine-Growing Regions" in chapter 1. For even more wineries, refer to the section on La Chiantigiana later in this chapter.

How much time to spend in each province? A countess at a Tuscan villa told us: "Give each a year. Who knows? Perhaps you'll write two bestsellers—*A Year in Tuscany,* followed by *A Year in Umbria.*"

1 Montecatini Terme: Italy's Top Spa

19 miles NE of Florence, 26 miles NE of Pisa

The best known of all Italian spas, **Montecatini Terme** has long been frequented for its cures and scenic location. It's a peaceful Tuscan town set among green hills of the valley called Valdinievole.

Montecatini Terme's fame began in the latter part of the 18th century, when the grand duke of Tuscany, Pietro Leopoldo, opened a thermal spa here. But centuries before that it had been discovered by the Romans. Montecatini's fame spread rapidly, and by 1890 it was a regular stop for some of the titled aristocrats of Europe. In the 20th century, it drew such luminaries as Gary Cooper, Rose Kennedy, and Gabriel D'Annunzio and was further immortalized in Fellini's *8½.*

ESSENTIALS

GETTING THERE   From Florence a **train** leaves for Montecatini every hour throughout the day. Trip time is 50 minutes, and a one-way passage is 8,500L ($4.95). Montecatini is home to two rail stations, about a mile apart. The larger and closer to Florence is **Montecatini Terme Monsummano,** Piazza Italia (☎ 0572/78551). More central to most of the hotels of the town center is **Montecatini Centro** (same phone), which might save a bit of transit time for passengers headed to the resort's center.

Lazzi buses (☎ 0583/584-877) from Florence run frequently to Montecatini in less than an hour. If you have a **car,** take All from Florence or Pistoia, exiting at the signposted turnoffs to the spa.

VISITOR INFORMATION   The **tourist office** is at 66–68 Viale Verdi (☎ 0572/772-244), open Monday to Saturday 9am to 12:30pm and 3 to 7pm (April to October, also Sunday 9am to noon).

SEEING THE SPA & TAKING THE CURE

Many visitors are just regular tourists who enjoy a restful stop in a spa town; others come to lose weight, to take the mud baths, and to visit the sauna-cum-grotto. The mineral waters are said to be the finest in Europe, and the most serious visitors go to the 19th-century **Tettuccio spa,** with its beautiful gardens, to fill their cups from the curative waters.

Modern thermal centers, **Stabilimenti Termali,** await you at virtually every turn. The focus of the long grand promenade is the **Parco dei Termi,** with its neoclassical temples. The park lies above a series of underground hot springs, the most ancient of which appears in documents as far back as 1370. It's customary to come here every day to drink a healthful tonic from the fountains set up on marble counters. Spa treatments at the thermal centers are 8,000L to 18,000L ($4.65 to $10) for half a day (with tonics to drink) and 35,000L to 75,000L ($20 to $44) for mud baths and other more elaborate treatments. Full information and tickets are available from the **Società delle Terme,** Viale Verdi 41 (☎ 0572/7781). Most thermal houses are open May to October.

Montecatini is filled with dozens of hotels and pensiones, mostly art nouveau buildings from the beginning of this century, and many would-be visitors to Florence—unable to find a room in that overcrowded city—journey east to Montecatini instead. The spa has a season lasting from April to October, and the town really shuts down in the off-season.

When you tire of all that rest, you can take a funicular from Viale Diaz up to **Montecatini Alto** to enjoy its panoramic view. This town was important in the Middle Ages, containing about two dozen towers that were demolished in 1554 on orders of Cosimo de' Medici. You can walk along narrow streets to the ruins of a fortress, paying a short visit to St. Peter's Church. You'll invariably come across the main square, named for poet Giuseppe Giusti. From the hillside town, you can see Florence on a clear day.

Today Montecatini attracts some of the world's most fashionable people on the see-and-be-seen circuit, especially during the horse-racing season from April to October. It's filled with some of Europe's most expensive boutiques, so don't come looking for bargains.

ACCOMMODATIONS

Grand Hotel Croce di Malta. Viale IV Novembre 18, 51016 Montecatini Terme. ☎ **0572/ 9201.** Fax 0572/767-516. 140 units. A/C MINIBAR TV TEL. 280,000L ($162) double; 370,000L ($215) suite. Rates include breakfast. Half board 25,000L ($15) per person. AE, DC, MC, V. Parking 20,000L ($12).

Built in 1920 in a residential neighborhood near the spa, the imposing facade of this hotel rises from behind a screen of shrubbery and an outdoor terrace. It's the most accommodating and attractive of the upper-middle-bracket hotels, with a vaguely modernized interior renovated in 1995 and touches of polished marble scattered throughout the guest rooms and public areas. A helpful staff and affordable prices make it a perennial favorite. In 1997, the hotel was enlarged with the addition of a four-story wing (rooms in this wing have bathtubs with Jacuzzis).

✪ Grand Hotel e la Pace. Via della Toretta 1, 51016 Montecatini Terme. ☎ **0572/ 75-801.** Fax 0572/78-451. www.traveleurope.it/h114.htm. 150 units. A/C MINIBAR TV TEL. 550,000L ($319) double; 750,000-850,000L ($435-$493) suite. Breakfast 20,000L ($12). AE, DC, MC, V. Closed Nov-Apr 1. Free parking.

This gilded-age bastion has maintained its white-glove formality since 1869. Rivaled only by the Bella Vista (it doesn't have the Grand Hotel's panache), the hotel is outfitted with frescoes, elaborate ceilings, flowered sun terraces, soaring columns, lots of gilt, and all the ornate detailing you'd expect. A renovation upgraded the premises in 1994. The guest rooms are less lavish than the public areas but are discreetly comfortable. Anyone who wants full access to Montecatini's health and beauty treatments must leave the hotel and go into the nearby park. However, the hotel offers a limited array of supervised spa facilities on its premises, one of the few hotels in town that does.

Dining/Diversions: The adequate Michelangelo is a formal and elegant venue for Tuscan meals. An informal pool restaurant is also available, plus two bars, one with piano music. Musical presentations and cuisine theme nights are highlights of the summer season.

Amenities: Concierge, room service, health club with Jacuzzi and sauna, outdoor pool, laundry/dry cleaning, baby-sitting, secretarial services, business center, children's center, various shops and salons nearby.

Grand Hotel Vittoria. Viale della Libertà, 51016 Montecatini Terme. ☎ **0572/ 79-271.** Fax 0572/910-520. www.traveleurope.it/h89.htm. 84 units. A/C MINIBAR TV TEL.

Tuscan Tours

It's believed that Tuscany's grandeur is best viewed from a bike. Responding to this, Florence-based ○ **I Bike Italy** (☎ **055/234-2371** or 0347/419-8288), staffed with Americans, Brits, Danes, New Zealanders, and Australians, offers professionally guided single-day rides in the Tuscan countryside. The rides are deliberately designed to meander past olive groves, vineyards, artfully crumbling castles, and vine-covered estates whose pedigrees originated during the Renaissance.

Pending demand, tours begin daily in Florence at 9am with a rendezvous on the north end (closest to the Duomo) of Ponte alle Grazie (one bridge upriver from Ponte Vecchio). The company provides a shuttle service to carry participants in and out of the city, use of a 21-speed bicycle, helmets, water bottles, and a bilingual bike guide to show you the way, fix any flats, and generally maneuver the way around any problems that might arise. All tours cover from 15 to 20 scenic miles (the average speed is a leisurely 3.2 mph) and return the same day to Florence between 4:30 and 5pm. The cost is 95,000L ($55) per person, with lunch and equipment included. The same company leads less extensive walking tours in Tuscany, beginning and ending at the above-mentioned bridge in Florence. Priced at 75,000L ($44) for a 3-hour walk, they end in Fiesole, a scenic hill town near Florence, and include 4 to 5 miles of trekking with supervision by a British, American, Italian, or Danish guide.

If biking doesn't appeal but you value a tour guide whose focus is customized to your interests, consider the offerings of **Custom Tours in Tuscany,** 206 Ivy Lane, Highland Park, IL 60035 (☎ **847/432-1814;** fax 847/432-1889), with up to 10 well-trained bilingual staff members, each intimately familiar with Tuscany's art and culture. The company listens carefully to what you want to see and

---

100,000–150,000L ($58–$87) per person double. Rates include half board. AE, DC, MC, V. Parking 10,000L ($6).

Despite a 1994 renovation, this cost-conscious hotel retains a pleasantly old-fashioned aura. Away from the center of town amid dignified homes, it's one of the best of the reasonably priced hotels. Semiantique touches abound, like a double travertine stairway flanked by masses of flowers. Verdi stayed here shortly after the hotel opened, before it went through other transitions, including a brief stint as a monastery. It served as headquarters for the Nazis and then for the Americans during World War II. On the premises are a small pool, tranquil garden, tennis court, and covered terrace. There's now a large-scale convention center as well as a "beauty farm" for spa-related rejuvenation.

Hotel Manzoni. Viale Manzoni 28, 51016 Montecatini Terme. ☎ **0572/70-175.** Fax 0572/911-012. www.traveleurope.it/h109.htm. 49 units. A/C MINIBAR TV TEL. 200,000–240,000L ($120–$144) double. Rates include half board. AE, DC, MC, V. Free parking.

In a building more than 600 years old, the Simoncini-Greco family has run this comfortable hotel since 1921. They offer the best of both worlds, with 17th- to 19th-century furnishings and modern amenities. There's also a landscaped garden, a pool, a lounge, a recreation room, a bar, a formal dining room, and two elevators. You can make use of free 18-speed touring bikes to better enjoy the green parks and olive-covered hills. The restaurant's fine Mediterranean cuisine is rich in local seafood,

do, then tailors a day-long guided tour for you. Its staff can help you visit Florence's important monuments, guide you through labyrinths of less-often-visited alleyways, and show you where to buy antiques, gold jewelry, leather, extra-virgin olive oil, or bed and table linens at a fraction of the regular prices.

Day tours in Tuscany include visits to Lucca, Siena, San Gimignano, and Pietrasanta, with an emphasis on the cultural quirks and architecture that make each site unique. They begin and end in Florence but may be expanded into longer countryside trips. In Florence, plan to do a lot of walking; outside of Florence, the guides will accompany you in your own rented car or arrange for a car and driver. Fees are $325 per day for Florence tours or $425 for tours in the Tuscan countryside (6 to 7 hours) for up to two. Extra persons are $25 each. Transportation, meals, highway tolls, museum admissions, and gratuities aren't included.

Other options for touring Tuscany are offered by **Mountain Travel/Sobek,** 6420 Fairmount Ave., El Cerrito, CA 94530 (☎ **888/687-6235** or 510/527-8100)—a company known for adventure trips to some of the most exotic and/or inaccessible areas of Asia, Europe, Africa, and the two Americas. One of its most popular offerings is a guided 9-day walking tour across the hills and valleys of Tuscany and the Cinque Terre. You explore medieval towns like Siena, Pisa, Radda in Chianti, and Volterra on foot. Though not exactly easy, these walks are geared to a relatively leisurely pace for maximum appreciation of the grandeur around you. Accommodations are in two- and three-star hotels, some from the 1400s. Departures are in May, June, September, and October. Land prices (without airfare) begin at a relatively pricey $2,890 to $3,090 per person, double occupancy, with most meals included.

meats, poultry, and homemade pastas, along with a delectable selection of fresh vegetables and recently prepared desserts.

Hotel Villa Ida. Viale G. Marconi 55, 51016 Montecatini Terme. ☎ **0572/78-201.** Fax 0572/772-008. 21 units. A/C MINIBAR TV TEL. 110,000L ($64) double with breakfast, 170,000L ($99) double with half board. AE, DC, MC, V.

Bargain-hunting spa devotees gravitate to this 19th-century building that was radically upgraded in the late 1980s. It offers simple comforts, but everything is cozy and refined in a genteel sort of way. A modern decor now graces the place and the rooms are immaculately maintained. The hotel also offers such extras as a library, TV lounge, and tavern for wine tasting. Two terraces are ideal for an alfresco breakfast or dinner. The food is well prepared, though not necessarily aimed at the diet conscious.

DINING

Gourmet. Via Amendola 6. ☎ **0572/771-012.** Reservations recommended. Main courses 28,000–42,000L ($16–$24). AE, DC, MC, V. Wed–Mon noon–2pm and 8–11pm. Closed Jan 7–20 and Aug 1–20. ITALIAN.

In a 19th-century building with a Liberty-style interior, this is the best independent restaurant in town. It prides itself on formal service and a cuisine that's more unusual than the run-of-the-mill pastas and veal dishes of lesser competitors. Menu items change seasonally and with the availability of ingredients, but you'll often find a spectacular array of antipasti ("antipasti fantasia") with seafood and fresh vegetables, ravioli stuffed with pulverized sea bass and herbs, risotto with scampi, and a medley of fruit garnishes (melon slices with lobster and honey-vinegar sauce, for example). Most items are delicious, impeccably fresh, and beautifully presented. The desserts are made fresh daily and might include a Grand Marnier soufflé.

Ristorante Pietre Cavate. Via Pietre Cavate 11. ☎ **0572/95-42-58.** Reservations recommended. Main courses 20,000–30,000L ($12–$17). AE, DC, MC, V. Daily 7pm–midnight. TUSCAN.

The Bertini family, headed by its ebullient spokesman, Doriano Bertini, are the creative force behind this warmly hospitable farmhouse less than a mile north of the town center. Travelers who have appreciated its charms have included journalists from *Forbes* magazine, whose circa 1995 articles are proudly displayed in the trio of rustic-looking dining rooms. The cuisine is a celebration of Tuscany, with special emphasis on maccheroni with tomato and parmigiano sauce, pappardelle with chunks of rabbit, stuffed onions, savory stews, and chunky cuts of veal, pork, and beef. Come here with an appetite and an appreciation for the view that extends out over the rooftops of nearby Montecatini.

2 Lucca

45 miles W of Florence, 13 miles E of Pisa, 209 miles N of Rome

In 56 B.C., Caesar, Crassus, and Pompey met in **Lucca** and agreed to rule Rome as a triumvirate. By the time of the Roman Empire's collapse, it was virtually the capital of Tuscany. Periodically in its valiant, ever-bloody history, Lucca was an independent principality, similar to Genoa. This autonomy attests to the fame and prestige it enjoyed. Now, however, Lucca is largely bypassed by time and travelers, rewarding the discriminating few.

By the late 1600s, Lucca had gained its third and final set of city walls. This girdle of ramparts is largely intact and is one of the major reasons to visit the town, with its medley of architecture ranging from Roman to Liberty (the Italian term for art nouveau). Lucca was the birthplace of Giacomo Puccini, whose favorite watering hole, the Antico Caffè di Simo (below), still stands.

Today, Lucca is best known for its *olio d'oliva lucchese,* the quality olive oil produced in the region outside the town's walls, and shoppers will be delighted to find a number of upscale boutiques here, testimony to an affluence not dependent on the tourist trade. Thriving, cosmopolitan, and perfectly preserved, Lucca is a sort of Switzerland of the south: the banks have latticed Gothic windows, the shops look like well-stocked linen cupboards, children play in landscaped gardens, and geraniums bloom from the roofs of medieval tower houses.

ESSENTIALS

GETTING THERE At least 20 **trains** travel daily between Florence and Lucca. The trip takes 1¼ hours and costs 7,000L ($4.05) each way. The rail station lies about a quarter-mile south of Lucca's historic core, a short walk from the city's ramparts. For rail information in Lucca, call ☎ **0583/47-013.** If you don't have a lot of luggage, you can walk into the center; otherwise, most of the city's buses (most notably nos. 3 and 6) and long queues of taxis stand ready to take you there.

The **Lazzi bus** company (☎ **0583/584-877**) operates buses traveling between Florence and Lucca. They take less time than the train (50 minutes to an hour), and unlike the train, they carry passengers to a point within the city walls. Bus transit between Florence and Lucca, however, costs a bit more than the train—10,000L ($6)

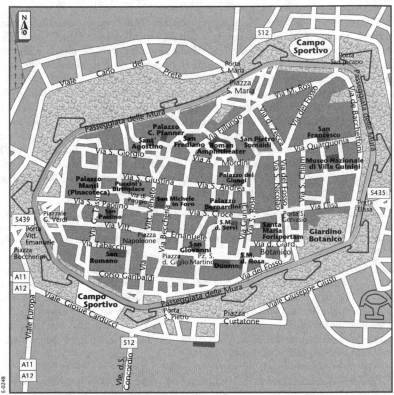

each way. Buses pick up passengers in front of the rail station in Florence and drop them off in Lucca at both the rail station and the historic core at Piazzale Verdi, near the tourist office.

If you've got a **car,** leave Florence and take A11 through Prato, Pistoia, and Montecatini (above) before reaching the outskirts of Lucca. If you're in Pisa, take SS12.

VISITOR INFORMATION The Lucca **tourist office** is on Piazzale Verdi (☎ **0583/419-689**), open daily 9:30am to 6:30pm April to October (off-season to 3:30pm).

EXPLORING THE TOWN

✪ **Le Mura** enclose the old town, the zone of the most visitor interest. The Lucchesi are fiercely proud of these city walls, the best-preserved Renaissance defense ramparts in Europe. The present walls, measuring 115 feet at the base and soaring 40 feet high, replaced crumbling ramparts built during the Middle Ages. If you'd like to join in one of the grand promenades of Tuscany, you can gain access to the ramparts from one of 10 bastions, the most frequently used of which is in back of the tourist office at **Piazzale Verdi.** For orientation, you may want to walk completely around the city on the tree-shaded ramparts, a distance of 2½ miles.

Besides the major sights below, worth seeking out is the **Roman Amphitheater (Anfiteatro Romano),** at Piazza Anfiteatro, reached along Via Fillungo. You can still see the outlines of its arches in its outer walls, and within the inner ring only the rough form remains to evoke what must have been. Once the theater was adorned with many-hued Tuscan marble, but greedy builders hauled off its materials to create some of the many churches of Lucca, including San Michele and the Duomo. The foundations of the former grandstands, which once rang with the sound of Tuscans screaming for gladiator blood, now support an ellipse of houses from the Middle Ages. The theater is from the 2nd century A.D.

Napoléon's widow, Marie Louise, ordered the clearing of the medieval buildings, for which Lucca's boys playing soccer on the asphalt today can be thankful. Lucca was given later to Marie Louise following its rule by Elisa, the French dictator's sister. Marie Louise became Lucca's favorite ruler, and the Lucchesi erected a statue to her that's still **Piazza Napoleone** (her son sold Lucca to Leopold II of Tuscany in 1847). If you want to catch a glimpse at Lucca life, find a chair at one of the sleepy cafes and pass the day away. In July and August, you can come to the **Piazza Guidiccioni** nearby and see a screening of the latest Italian and U.S. hits in the open air.

Cattedrale di San Martino (Duomo). Piazza San Martino. ☎ **0583/494-726.** Admission: Cathedral, free; sacristy and inner sanctum, 3,000L ($1.75) adults, 1,500L (85¢) children under 14; children under 6 are free. Church and sacristy: Apr–Oct daily 10am–6pm; Nov–Mar Mon–Fri 10am–2, Sat–Sun 10am–5pm.

On Piazza San Martino, the Duomo is the town's most visible monument, dating back to 1060, though the present structure was mainly rebuilt during the following centuries. The facade is exceptional, evoking the Pisan-Romanesque style but with enough originality and idiosyncrasies to distinguish it from the Duomo at Pisa. Designed mostly by Guidetto da Como in the early 13th century, the west front contains three wide ground-level arches, surmounted by three scalloped galleries with taffy-like twisting columns tapering in size.

The main relic inside—in some ways the religious symbol of Lucca itself—is the *Volto Santo*, a crucifix carved by Nicodemus (so tradition has it) from the Cedar of Lebanon. The face of Christ was supposedly chiseled onto the statuary. The main art treasure lies in the sacristy: It was sculpted by Jacopo della Quercia as a tomb for local aristocrat Ilaria del Carretto, who died in 1405 while still young, the wife of Paolo Guinigi. The marble effigy of the young lady, in regal robes and guarded by chubby bambini, rests atop the sarcophagus—the cathedral's diffused mauve afternoon light casts a ghostly glow on her face.

Duomo Museum (Museo della Catedrale). Piazza Antelmenelli. ☎ **0583/490-530.** Admission 5,000L ($2.90) adults, 3,000L ($1.75) ages 6–18; children under 6 free. Same hours as for Duomo, above.

Adjacent to the Duomo is this museum, with somewhat dusty-looking memorabilia. It's filled with mostly minor artworks, except Matteo Civitali's late 15th-century choir screen (removed from the cathedral in 1987) and Jacopo della Quercia's majestic early 15th-century *St. John the Evangelist*, a sculpture.

Chiesa San Frediano. Piazza San Frediano. ☎ **0583/493-627.** Free admission. Mon–Sat 7:30am–noon and 3–6pm, Sun 9am–1pm and 3–6pm.

Romanesque in style, this is one of Lucca's most important and famous churches, built when the town enjoyed its greatest glory, in the 12th and 13th centuries. The severe white facade is relieved by a 13th-century mosaic of Christ ascending, and the campanile rises majestically. The interior is dark, and visitors often speak in whispers. But the bas-reliefs on the Romanesque font add a note of comic relief: Supposedly depicting the story of Moses, among other themes, they show Egyptians in medieval armor chasing after the Israelites. Two tombs in the basilica (in the fourth chapel on the left) were the work of Jacopo della Quercia, the celebrated Sienese sculptor.

San Michele in Foro. Piazza San Michele. ☎ **0583/48-459.** Free admission. Daily 7:30am–12:30pm and 3–6pm.

This church often surprises first-timers to Lucca, who mistake it for the Duomo. Begun in 1143, it's the most memorable example of the style and flair the Lucchese brought to the Pisan-Romanesque school of architecture. The exquisite west front, employing the scalloped effect, is spanned by seven ground-level arches, then surmounted by four tiers of galleries, utilizing imaginatively designed columns. Dragon-slaying St. Michael, wings outstretched, rests on the friezelike peak of the final tier. Inside, seek out a Filippo Lippi painting, *Saints Sebastian, Jerome, Helen, and Roch,* on the far wall of the right transept. If you're here in September, the piazza outside, which was the old Roman forum, holds a daily colorful open market selling everything from olive oil to souvenirs of Tuscany.

National Picture Gallery and Palazzo Mansi Museum (Pinacoteca Nazionale e Museo di Palazzo Mansi). Via Galli Tassi 43. ☎ **0593/55-570.** Admission 8,000L ($4.65) adults, 4,000L ($2.30) children 6–18; children 5 and under free. Tues–Sat 9am–7pm, Sun 9am–2pm.

The Lucchesi horde their art treasures in this palace built for the powerful Mansi family, whose descendants are still some of the movers and shakers in town. Though Tuscany has far greater preserves of art, there are some treasures here, notably a portrait of Princess Elisa by Marie Benoist. Elisa Bonaparte (1777 to 1820), who married into a local wealthy family, the Bacceocchis, was "given" the town by her brother Napoléon in 1805 when he made her princess of Lucca and Piombino. Unlike her profligate sister Pauline Borghese in Rome, Elisa was a strong woman with a remarkable aptitude for public affairs. A patron of the arts and letters, she laid out Piazza Napoleone and achieved other accomplishments, earning her the nickname "semiramis of Lucca." The collection is enriched by works from Lanfranco, Luca Giordano, and Tintoretto, among others, though not their greatest works. There's a damaged Veronese, but Tintoretto's *Miracle of St. Mark Freeing the Slave* is amusing—the patron saint of Venice literally dive-bombs from heaven to save the day.

Puccini's Birthplace (Casa Natale di Puccini). Via di Poggio 9. ☎ **0583/58-40-28.** Admission 5,000L ($2.90) adults, 3,000L ($1.75) children under 10. Mar 15–June Tues–Sun 10am–1pm and 3–6pm, July–Aug Tues–Sun 10am–1pm and 3–7pm, Sept–Nov 15 Tues–Sun 10am–to 1pm and 3–6pm, Nov 16–December Tues–Sun 10am–1pm.

This was the birthplace of one of Italy's greatest operatic composers, Giacomo Puccini (1858 to 1924). More than any other Italian town (except Milan, where opera is viewed with passion), Lucca celebrates the memory and achievements of Puccini, whose operas are enthusiastically performed every September during the Festival of Santa Croce. This is an unpretentious house near Piazza San Michele that contains the piano at which he composed *Turnadot,* several of his librettos, letters, objets d'art, and mementos.

SHOPPING

The rolling and sometimes sunblasted hills around Lucca have been famous since the days of the Romans for their gnarled olive trees and scenic beauty. They produce an amber-colored oil prized by gastronomes throughout the world as the finest anywhere.

You won't have to look far for access to the product, as every supermarket, butcher shop, and delicatessen in Lucca sells a baffling variety, in glass or metal containers ranging from pocketbook-sized to megadrums suitable for institutional kitchens. But if you want to travel into the surrounding hills to check out the production of this heart-healthy product, two of the best-known companies sell their products on premises evoking early 20th-century Tuscan farmhouse life: **Maionchi,** in the hamlet of Tofori (☎ **0583/978-194**), 11 miles northeast of Lucca; and **Camigliano,** Via per Sant'Andrea 49 (☎ **0583/490-420**), 6 miles northeast of Lucca.

Looking for souvenirs of your stop in Lucca? A promenade along the town's best shopping streets, **Via Fillungo** and **Via del Battistero** (Lucca's less prestigious answer to Milan's Via Montenapoleone), can satisfy most materialistic cravings. The best gift/souvenir shops are **Insiene,** Via Vittorio Emanuele 9 (☎ **0583/419-649**), and **Incontro,** Via Buia (☎ **0583/491-225**), which places a special emphasis on Lucca's rustically appealing porcelain, pottery, tiles, and crystal.

ACCOMMODATIONS

Hotel Villa La Principessa. Strada Statale del Brennero 1616, 55050 Mass Pisana (Lucca). ☎ **0583/370-037.** Fax 0583/379-136. 40 units. A/C MINIBAR TV TEL. 340,000–390,000L ($197–$226) double; 430,000L ($249) suite. Breakfast 24,000L ($14). AE, DC, MC, V. Closed Nov–Mar. Bus: 2 from center of Lucca. Free parking.

Across the highway from Locanda l'Elisa (below), this is a well-managed four-star hotel—less luxurious than its competitor but also less expensive. It's 2 miles south of the city walls, beside a meandering highway with sharp turns and limited visibility. The hotel is sheltered with hedges, flowering trees, and the best kinds of architectural detailings from other eras. It was built in 1320 as the home of one of the dukes of Lucca, Castruccio Castracani, who was later depicted by Machiavelli as the "Ideal Prince." Later, when the hills around Lucca were dotted with the homes of members of the Napoleonic court, the house was rebuilt in dignified 18th-century style. The guest rooms are comfortably renovated with everything you'll need.

Dining: The refined continental breakfast, elegantly served, is the only meal offered.

Amenities: Concierge, room service, outdoor pool, nearby health club, jogging track and nature trails nearby, business center, laundry, in-room massage, baby-sitting.

✪ **Locanda l'Elisa.** Strada Statale del Brennaro 1952, 55050 Mass Pisana (Lucca). ☎ **0583/379-737.** Fax 0583/379-019. E-mail: elisa@relaischateaux.fr. 10 units. A/C MINIBAR TV TEL. 450,000L ($261) double; 550,000L ($319) junior suite for two. Breakfast 32,000L ($19). AE, DC, MC, V. Bus: 2 from center of Lucca. Free parking.

This Relais & Châteaux member is the region's most elegant hotel, 2 miles south of the city walls. During the mid-19th century, it was the home of an army officer who was the preferred escort and intimate companion of Napoléon's sister Elisa, who lived in the larger villa across the road. Today, both lovers' villas are upscale hotels (Elisa's is now the Hotel Villa La Principessa, above, though the two are no longer under the same management). Behind a dignified neoclassical facade, Locanda l'Elisa has verdant gardens, a worthy collection of antiques, discreet and charming service, and guest rooms larger and more plushly decorated than those in its sibling. All but two of the rooms are skillfully decorated junior suites, with views of either gardens or a park and furnishings the Bonapartes might've lived with comfortably.

Dining: Il Gazebo is recommended under "Dining," below.

Amenities: Room service, large pool, baby-sitting, laundry/dry cleaning.

✪ **Piccolo Hotel Puccini.** Via di Poggio 9, 55100 Lucca. ☎ **0583/55-421.** Fax 0583/53-487. 14 units. TV TEL. 128,000L ($74) double. Breakfast 5,000L ($3). AE, MC, V. Free parking nearby.

Your best bet in the center is this palace built in the 1400s, across from the house where Puccini was born. The classical music played in the lobby area (often Puccini) commemorates the long-ago association. Right off Piazza San Michele, one of the most enchanting in Lucca, this little hotel is better than ever now that an energetic couple, Raffaella and Paolo, has taken it over, breathing new life into the property. Intimate and comfortable, the rooms are beautifully maintained with freshly starched curtains, good beds, crisp linens, and tasteful furnishings. Some windows open onto the small square in front with a bronze statue of the great Puccini.

DINING

✪ **Buca di Sant'Antonio.** Via della Cervia 1. ☎ **0583/55-881.** Reservations recommended. Main courses 20,000–22,000L ($12–$13). AE, DC, MC, V. Tues–Sun noon–3pm; Tues–Sat 7:30–10:30pm. Closed 2 weeks in July. TUSCAN.

On a difficult-to-find alleyway near Piazza San Michele, this is Lucca's finest restaurant. The 1782 building was constructed on the site of a chapel (Buca di Sant'Antonio) that was believed to be favorable for invoking the protective powers of St. Anthony. The cuisine is refined and inspired, respecting the traditional ways but also daring to innovative. Menu items include homemade ravioli stuffed with ricotta and pulverized zucchini, grilled meat and fish dishes, codfish, and roast Tuscan goat with roast potatoes and braised greens. Many visitors make it a point to order the house special dessert—a *semifreddo Buccellato* that combines partially melted ice cream with local red berries.

Da Giulio in Pelleria. Via della Conce 45.☎ **0583/55-948.** Reservations recommended. Main courses 8,000–12,500L ($4.65–$7); fixed-price menus 28,000–32,000L ($16–$19). AE, DC, MC, V. Tues–Sat and 3rd Sun of the month noon–2:30pm and 7:15–10:15pm. Closed Aug. LUCCHESE.

Less expensive than many of its competitors, this restaurant occupies a 200-year-old building near the Porta San Donato and attracts lots of habitués with uncompromising allegiance to local traditions and time-honored recipes. Under its present management since 1991, it presents dishes like great minestrones, pastas, veal, hearty soups, and chicken dishes served in robust portions. Some regional dishes might be a little too ethnic for most North American tastes, such as *cioncia* (veal snout and herbs).

Giglio. Piazza del Giglio 2. ☎ **0583/494-058.** Reservations recommended. Main courses 20,000–25,000L ($12–$15). AE, DC, MC, V. Thurs–Tues noon–3pm; Thurs–Mon 7–10pm. Closed Feb. REGIONAL/TUSCAN.

In regional appeal and popularity, this place is rivaled only by the Buca di Sant' Antonio (above). The secret to its appeal might be its rustic decor (including 15th-century architectural detailing), its attentive staff, and its fine interpretations of time-honored Tuscan and regional recipes. Menu items usually include steaming bowls of *minestre di farro,* homemade tortellini with meat sauce, roasted codfish with olive oil, stewed rabbit with olives, and *tortes* made from vegetables like carrots or with a base of cream and chocolate.

Il Gazebo. In the Locanda l'Elisa, Strada Statale del Brennero 1952. ☎ **0583/379-737.** Reservations recommended. Main courses 30,000–35,000L ($17–$20); fixed-price menu 85,000L ($49). AE, DC, MC, V. Mon–Sat 12:30–2:30pm and 8–10pm. Bus: 2 from center of Lucca. ITALIAN/TUSCAN.

Some patrons from the region chose to dine here so they can visit one of Tuscany's most elegant hotels. Set in the Locanda l'Elisa, 2 miles south of Lucca's center, the restaurant is a re-creation of an English conservatory. The wraparound windows in the almost circular room offer views over a garden replanted at great expense in the early 1990s. The service, as you'd expect in a Relais & Châteaux, is impeccable. Menu items include upscale versions of local Luccan recipes, including farro Lucchese, red-bean soup with locally grown greens. Less ethnic dishes are steamed scampi with fresh tomato sauce, smoked swordfish with grilled eggplant, and ravioli stuffed with herbed eggplant and served with prawn sauce. Each is prepared with refinement and skill.

Trattoria da Leo. Via Tegrimi 1. ☎ **0583/49-22-36.** Reservations recommended. Main courses 18,000–25,000L ($10–$15). No credit cards. Mon–Sat noon–2:30pm and 7:30–10:30pm. TUSCAN.

Known for its unpretentious approach to Tuscan cuisine and family administration (almost no one speaks English, but there's a menu in English), this is a pleasant trattoria close to Piazza San Michele. The food is earthy and savory, with few newfangled ideas. Though the building containing it is medieval, the decor of the dining rooms (one large, one very small) is vaguely 1930s. Menu items include an array of pastas, most made fresh; *ministre di Farro;* fried chicken with fresh seasonal greens; steamed chicken with polenta; and at least three versions of codfish. The allure here is its authenticity, its ethnicity, and the goodwill of the hardworking staff.

LUCCA AFTER DARK

Sleepy Lucca comes to life during July and August at the time of the classical music festival, **Estate Musicale Lucchese.** Venues spring up everywhere, and the tourist office keeps a list. The town also comes alive on July 12, when residents don medieval costumes and parade through the city, the revelry continuing late into the night.

In Puccini's hometown you'll find a devotion to opera, and in October and November his work is showcased at the **Teatro Comunale del Giglio,** Piazza di Giglio (☎ **0583/47521**). More classical musical performances fill the town in September during the **Septembre Lucchese Festival,** highlighted by Volto Santo feast day on September 13. The crucifix bearing the "face" of Christ (normally housed in a chapel in the Duomo) is hauled through town to commemorate its miraculous journey to Lucca. The rest of the year, presentations usually revolve around a small-scale roster of genteel concerts and musical comedies. Cafes at night fill up with wine-drinking revelers.

If you're not in Lucca during one of these special events, follow in the footsteps of Puccini and head to **Antico Caffè di Simo,** Via Fillungo 58 (☎ **0583/46-234**), where the composer used to come to eat and drink and perhaps dream about his next opera. At this historic cafe you can order the best gelato (ice cream) in town while taking in the old-time aura of faded mirrors, brass, and marble. It's open Tuesday to Sunday 8am to 8pm. A bar/cafe especially popular with young people is **Guibileo,** Piazza San Tommaso (☎ **0583/312-914**), open daily 8pm to midnight.

3 Pisa & Its Perpendicularly Challenged Tower

47 miles W of Florence, 207 miles NW of Rome

One of Katherine Anne Porter's best short stories is "The Leaning Tower," in which there's a memorable scene dealing with a German landlady's sentimental attachment to a 5-inch plaster replica of the Leaning Tower of Pisa, a souvenir whose ribs caved in at the touch of a prospective tenant. "'It cannot be replaced,' said the landlady, with a severe, stricken dignity. 'It was a souvenir of the Italian journey.'" Ironically, the year (1944) Miss Porter's story was published, a bomb fell near the real campanile, but the original wasn't damaged.

Few buildings in the world have captured imaginations as much as the **Leaning Tower of Pisa**—the single most instantly recognizable building in all the Western world, except for the Eiffel Tower. Perhaps visitors are drawn to it as a symbol of the fragility of people or at least the fragility of their work. The Leaning Tower is a powerful landmark.

There's more to Pisa than meets the usual tourist's eye, however. There are other historic sights. And there's also the present: Go into the busy streets surrounding the

Pisa

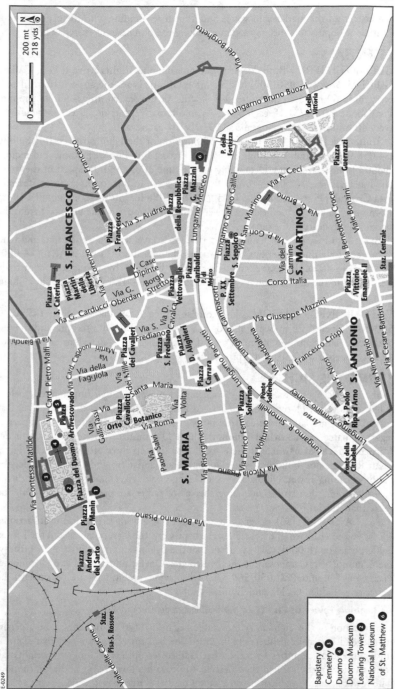

Bapistery ①
Cemetery ③
Duomo ④
Duomo Museum ⑤
Leaning Tower ②
National Museum of St. Matthew ⑥

0   200 mt
    218 yds

S. FRANCESCO

Via S. Francesco

Via del Borghetto

Lungarno Bruno Buozzi

P. della Vittoria

P. della Fortezza

Piazza Guerrazzi

Piazza G. Mazzini

Piazza della Repubblica

Lungarno Mediceo

Via A. Ceci

Via G. Bruno

Piazza S. Francesco

Via S. Andrea

Via S. Lorenzo

Lungarno Galileo Galilei

Via G. Bruno

Staz. Centrale

Piazza S. Caterina

Piazza Martiri della Libertà

V. Case Dipinte

Borgo Stretto

Via G. Carducci

Oberdan

Via Cardi Capponi

Via della Faggiola

Via Card. Pietro Maffi

Piazza del Duomo

Via L. Bianchi

Via Contessa Matilde

Via Galli-Tassi

Via Cavalca

Via S. Frediano

Piazza dei Cavalieri

Piazza Vettovaglie

Piazza Garibaldi

P. di Mezzo

Piazza Dante Alighieri

Piazza D. Alighieri

Piazza S. Frediano

Piazza F. Carrara

Piazza XX Settembre

S. Sepolcro

Piazza S. Paolo

Lungarno Gambacorti

Via P. Gori

Via San Martino

S. MARTINO

Via del Carmine

Corso Italia

Piazza Vittorio Emanuele II

Via Benedetto Croce

Viale Bonaini

Via Giuseppe Mazzini

Via Francesco Crispi

S. ANTONIO

Via E. Nicola

Via Nino Bixio

Via Cesare Battisti

Ripa d'Arno

Lungarno Sonnino Sidney

Ponte della Cittadella

Arno

Lungarno Simonelli R.

Lungarno Pacinotti

Lungarno Mediceo

Via Madalena

Ponte Solferino

Piazza Solferino

Via Enrico Fermi

Via Volturno

Via Roma

A. Volta

Via Risorgimento

S. MARIA

Via Paolo Salvi

Via Nicola Pisano

Via Bonanno Pisano

Piazza D. Manin

Piazza del Duomo

Archivescovado

Piazza Cavallotti

Via dei Mille

Santa Maria

Orto Botanico

Piazza Andrea del Sarto

Via Card. Pietro Maffi

Piazza Martiri

Staz. Pisa-S. Rossore

Viale delle Cascine

277

university and the market and you'll find a town resounding with the exuberance of its student population and its residents making the purchases of everyday life.

ESSENTIALS

GETTING THERE   Both domestic and international **flights** arrive at Pisa's **Galileo Galilei Airport** (☎ 050/500-707 for information). From the airport, trains depart every 30 to 60 minutes, depending on the time of the day, for the 5-minute trip into Pisa (about 2,000L/$1.15 each way). As an alternative, bus no. 7 leaves the airport every 40 minutes for the city (about 1,200L/70¢ each way).

   Trains link Pisa and Florence every 30 minutes for the 1-hour trip, costing 8,000L ($4.65) one-way. Trains running along the seacoast link Pisa with Rome and require about 3 hours travel time. Depending on the time of day and the speed of the train, one-way fares are 37,000L to 100,000L ($21 to $58). In Pisa, trains arrive at **Stazione Pisa Centrale,** Piazza Stazione (☎ 050/1478-88088 for information), about a 10- to 15-minute walk from the Leaning Tower. Otherwise, you can take bus no. 1 from the station to the heart of the city.

   Buses into Pisa are less frequent and a lot less convenient than the trains and tend to be used only during periods of rail strikes. The local bus carrier is APT (☎ 050/505-511 in Pisa). If you've got a **car,** leave Florence by taking the autostrada west (A11) to the intersection (A12) going south to Pisa. Travel time is about an hour each way.

VISITOR INFORMATION   The **tourist office** is at Via Cammeo (☎ 050/560-464), open April to September daily 9:30am to 1pm and 3 to 7pm and the rest of the year daily 9am to 5:30pm. A second branch is at Piazza della Stazione (☎ 050/42291), open daily 9:30am to 1pm and 3 to 6:30pm.

SEEING THE SIGHTS

In the Middle Ages, Pisa reached the apex of its power as a maritime republic before it fell to its rivals, Florence and Genoa. As is true of most cities at their zenith, Pisa turned to the arts and made contributions in sculpture and architecture. Its greatest legacy remains at **Piazza del Duomo,** which D'Annunzio labeled the **Campo dei Miracoli (Field of Miracles).** Here you'll find the top three attractions, all original Pisan-Romanesque buildings—the Duomo; the baptistery; and the campanile, the famous Leaning Tower. Nikolaus Pevsner, in his classic *An Outline of European Architecture,* wrote: "Pisa strikes one altogether as of rather an alien character—Oriental more than Tuscan."

   Note: A 10,000L ($6) ticket (you can buy it at any of the included attractions) allows you to visit two of these sights: the baptistery, the Camposanto, and the Museo dell'Opera. For 18,000L ($10) you can visit the five major attractions: the baptistery; the Duomo; the Camposanto; the Museo dell'Opera; and the Museo di Sinopie, Piazza del Duomo (☎ 050/560-547), displaying preliminary fresco sketches by Veneziano, Taddeo Gaddi, and Traini.

✪ **Leaning Tower of Pisa (Campanile).** Piazza del Duomo. Bus: 1.

Construction of this eight-story campanile began in 1174 by Bonanno, and a persistent legend is that he deliberately intended the bell tower to lean (but that claim is undocumented). Another legend is that Galileo let objects of different weights fall from the tower, then timed their descent to prove his theories on bodies in motion. The tower is said to be floating on a sandy base of water-soaked clay; it leans at least 14 feet from perpendicular. If it stood straight, it would measure about 180 feet tall.

   Alas, this icon is in serious danger of collapse. The government is taking various measures to keep it from falling, including clamping five rings of half-inch steel cable around its lower stones and stacking tons of lead around its base to keep it stabilized. At press time, the latest brainstorm was to secure it with industrial-strength cables attached to the closest structure, rather than blocking off the entire visitor-clogged area should it topple without notice (this is one of the world's most closely watched buildings, but the 1997 earthquakes in Umbria have put all Tuscany on the alert). Try to see it from all angles: It definitely appears more exaggerated from certain angles.

In 1990, visits inside the tower were suspended. In years gone by, one of the major attractions in Europe was to climb the Tower of Pisa—taking all 294 steps. But that's too dangerous today, and you must be content to observe it from the outside. If you want to do what everyone else will be doing, find the right position and have someone photograph you as you attempt to hold up the tower.

Il Duomo. Piazza del Duomo 17. ☎ **050/560-547.** Admission 3,000L ($1.75). Apr–Sept daily 7:45am–8pm (Nov–Mar to 7pm). Visits for sightseeing purposes are discouraged during masses and religious rites. Bus: 1.

This cathedral was designed by Buschetto in 1063, though in the 13th century Rainaldo erected the unusual facade with its four layers of open-air arches diminishing in size as they ascend. It's marked by three bronze doors, rhythmic in line, that replaced those destroyed in a disastrous 1595 fire. The most artistic is the original south Door of St. Ranieri, the only one to survive the fire; it was cast by Bonnano Pisano in 1180.

In the restored interior, the chief treasure is the polygonal pulpit by Giovanni Pisano, finished in 1310. It was damaged in the fire and finally rebuilt (with bits of the original) in 1926. It's held up by porphyry pillars and column statues symbolizing the Virtues, and the relief panels depict biblical scenes. The pulpit is similar to an earlier one by Giovanni's father, Nicola Pisano, in the baptistery across the way.

There are other treasures too, like Galileo's lamp (which, according to unreliable tradition, the Pisa-born astronomer used to formulate his laws of the pendulum). At the entrance to the choir pier is a painting that appears to be the work of Leonardo but is in fact *St. Agnes and Lamb,* in the High Renaissance style by the great Andrea del Sarto. In the apse you can view a 13th-century mosaic, *Christ Pancrator,* finished in 1302 by Cimabue (it survived the great fire).

✪ Baptistery (Battistero). Piazza del Duomo. ☎ **050/560-547.** Admission (including entry to the Duomo Museum or the Camposanto) 10,000L ($6). Nov–Feb daily 9am–4:40pm; Mar and Oct daily 9am–5:40pm; Apr–Sept daily 8am–7:40pm. Closed Dec 31–Jan 1. Bus: 1.

Begun in 1153, the baptistery is like a Romanesque crown. Though its most beautiful feature is the exterior, with its arches and columns, you should visit the interior to see the hexagonal pulpit made by Nicola Pisano from 1255 to 1260. Supported by pillars resting on the backs of three marble lions, the pulpit contains bas-reliefs of the Crucifixion, the Adoration of the Magi, the presentation of the Christ child at the temple, and the Last Judgment (many angels have lost their heads over the years). Column statues represent the Virtues. At the baptismal font is a contemporary John the Baptist by a local sculptor. The echo inside the baptistery shell has enthralled visitors for years.

Duomo Museum (Museo dell'Opera del Duomo). Piazza Arcivescovado. ☎ **050/560-820.** Admission (including entry to the baptistery or the Camposanto) 10,000L ($6). Apr–Sept daily 8am–7:30pm, Oct–Mar daily 9am–5pm. Bus: 1.

This museum exhibits works of art removed from the monumental buildings on the piazza. The heart of the collection, on the ground floor, consists of sculptures spanning the 11th to the 13th century. A notable treasure is an Islamic griffin from the 11th century, a bronze brought back from the Crusades as booty. For decades it adorned the cupola of the cathedral before brought here for safekeeping. The most famous exhibit is the *Madonna and the Crucifix* by Giovanni Pisano, carved from an ivory tusk in 1299. Also exhibited is the work of French goldsmiths, presented by Maria de' Medici to Archbishop Bonciani in 1616.

Upstairs are paintings from the 15th to the 18th century. Some of the textiles and embroideries date from the 15th century; another section of the museum is devoted to Egyptian, Etruscan, and Roman works. In the 19th century, Carlo Lasinio restored the Camposanto frescoes (below) and made a series of etchings of each. These etchings were widely published, influencing the pre-Raphaelite artists of the time. When the Camposanto was bombed in 1944, the etchings were destroyed, but Lasinio's legacy provided an enduring record of what they were like.

Cemetery (Camposanto). Piazza del Duomo. ☎ **050/560-547.** Admission (including admission to the baptistery or the Duomo Museum) 10,000L ($6). Nov–Feb daily 9am–4:40pm; Mar and Oct daily 9am–5:40pm; Apr–Sept daily 8am–7:40pm. Bus: 1.

This cemetery was designed by Giovanni di Simone in 1278, but a bomb hit it in 1944 and destroyed most of the famous frescoes that once covered the inside. Recently it has been partially restored. It's said that earth from Calvary was shipped here by the Crusaders on Pisan ships (the city was a great port before the water receded). The cemetery is of interest because of its sarcophagi, statuary, and frescoes. One room contains three of the frescoes from the 14th century that were salvaged from the bombing: *The Triumph of Death, The Last Judgment,* and *The Inferno,* with the usual assortment of monsters, reptiles, and boiling caldrons. *The Triumph of Death* is the most interesting, with its flying angels and devils. In addition, you'll find lots of white-marble bas-reliefs, including Roman funerary sculpture.

National Museum of St. Matthew (Museo Nazionale di San Matteo). Piazzetta San Matteo 1 (near Piazza Mazzini). ☎ **050/541-865.** Admission 8,000L ($4.65) adults; children 17 and under/seniors 60 and over free. Tues–Sat 9am–7pm, Sun 9am–2pm. Bus: 1.

This well-planned museum contains a good assortment of paintings and sculptures, many dating from the 13th to the 16th century. You'll find statues by Giovanni Pisano; Simone Martini's *Madonna and Child with Saints,* a polyptych; Nino Pisano's *Madonna del Látte* (Madonna of the Milk), a marble sculpture; Masaccio's *St. Paul,* painted in 1426; Domenico Ghirlandaio's two *Madonna and Saints* depictions; and works by Strozzi and Alessandro Magnasco.

SHOPPING

On the second weekend of every month, an **antiques fair** fills the Ponte di Mezzo. Virtually everything from the Tuscans hills is for sale, from virgin fresh olive oil to what one dealer told us was the "original" *Mona Lisa* (not the one hanging in the Louvre).

If you're not in town for the antiques fair, head for **Piazza Vettovaglie,** just off Via Borgo Stretto, which has a market daily 7am to 1:30pm. You'll find everything from old clothing to fresh Tuscan food products. The market sprawls outside its boundaries, spilling onto Via Domenio Cavalca. You can skip the restaurants for lunch and eat here, as there's an array of little trattorie that will fill you up—all at an affordable price. You can also pick up the makings for a picnic to enjoy later in the Tuscan hillsides.

A horde of intriguing stores lines **Via Borgo Stretto,** an arcaded street evocative of the ones in Bologna. Mimes and street performers often entertain the shoppers.

ACCOMMODATIONS

Grand Hotel Duomo. Via Santa Maria 94, 56126 Pisa. ☎ **050/561-894.** Fax 050/560-418. 96 units. A/C MINIBAR TV TEL. 290,000L ($168) double; 340,000L ($197) suite. Rates include breakfast. AE, DC, MC, V. Parking 30,000L ($17). Bus: 1.

This hotel isn't as grand as its name implies and the staff not as well-trained or cooperative as you'd hope, but its dignified facade and high-ceilinged interior evoke the early 20th century better than many of its competitors. Its location in the heart of town makes it convenient, and the rooms at the front are the most desirable, opening onto the monuments of Piazza del Duomo. It has a covered roof garden for great city views and comfortable room, most of which were renovated in 1997. The dining room boasts tall murals and serves relatively standard Italian specialties; it's often filled with tour groups. The hotel provides room service (7am to 2am) and laundry service.

Hotel d'Azeglio. Piazza Vittorio Emanuele II 18B, 56125 Pisa. ☎ **050/500-310.** Fax 050/ 28-017. 29 units. A/C MINIBAR TV TEL. 200,000L ($116) double. AE, DC, MC, V. Parking 15,000L ($9). Bus: 1.

This is an unremarkable first-class hotel near the rail station and the air terminal, in the commercial center. It's viewed as the best hotel in town, at least by Michelin, but don't expect too much, as competition in innkeeping isn't too keen in Pisa. There's an American bar and a roof garden with a panoramic city view. The standard rooms are well maintained and reasonably comfortable. It's a good safe nest for the night but not a lot more.

Jolly Hotel Cavalieri. Piazza della Stazione 2, 56125 Pisa. ☎ **800/221-2636** or 050/ 43-290. Fax 050/502-242. 100 units. A/C MINIBAR TV TEL. 320,000L ($186) double. Rates include breakfast. AE, DC, MC, V. Parking 36,000L ($21). Bus: 1.

A bland chain-run property, this seven-story hotel opens onto a view of the train station and its piazza. The rooms are filled with time-worn furniture, paneling, and large expanses of glass. The Cavalieri hosts dozens of business travelers, who appreciate the tranquil bar and restaurant for meetings. The Restaurant Cavalieri, with an adjacent piano bar, serves lunch and dinner daily. Parking is often possible in the square in front of the station or in a nearby garage.

✪ **Royal Victoria.** Lungarno Pacinotti 12, 56126 Pisa. ☎ **050/940-111.** Fax 050/ 940-180. E-mail: rvh@csinfo.it. 48 units, 40 with bathroom. TV TEL. 100,000L ($58) double without bathroom, 160,000L ($93) double with bathroom; 175,500L ($102) triple with bathroom; 185,000L ($107) quad with bathroom. Rates include breakfast. Discounts of 12% available Sun night and for stays of 4 days or more. AE, DC, MC, V. Parking 30,000L ($17). Bus: 1, 2, 3, 4, 5, 7, or 13.

This isn't Pisa's most luxurious hotel, but it's our undisputed favorite, thanks to its deeply rooted sense of history and staff that's vastly more accommodating that the ones in some of its more expensive (and often blander) competitors. Adjacent to the Arno and within walking distance of most of the jewels in Pisa's crown, it was built in 1839 by ancestors (five generations ago) of the genteel manager, Nicola Piegaja, who runs the place with his brother. The rooms are comfortable and clean, though a bit old-fashioned. There's no room service, but a bar near the lobby is open 24 hours.

DINING

✪ **Al Ristoro dei Vecchi Macelli.** Via Volturno 49. ☎ **050/20-424.** Reservations required. Main courses 16,000–35,000L ($9–$20); fixed-price menu 50,000–90,000L ($29– $52). AE, DC. Mon–Tues and Thurs–Sat noon–3pm and 8–10:30pm. Closed 2 weeks in Aug. Bus: 1. INTERNATIONAL/PISAN.

This is Pisa's best and most formal restaurant, in a comfortably rustic 1930s building near Piazzetta di Vecchi Macelli. Residents of Pisa claim that the cuisine is prepared with something akin to love, and they prove their devotion by returning frequently. After selecting from a choice of two dozen seafood antipasti, you can enjoy homemade pasta with scallops and zucchini, fish-stuffed ravioli in shrimp sauce, gnocchi with pesto and shrimp, or roast veal with velvety truffle-flavored cream sauce.

Da Bruno. Via Luigi Bianchi 12. ☎ **050/560-818.** Reservations recommended for dinner. Main courses 20,000–28,000L ($12–$16); fixed-price menu 30,000L ($17). AE, DC, MC, V. Mon noon–2:30pm, Wed–Sun noon–3pm and 7–10:30pm. Bus: 2, 3, or 4. PISAN.

For around half a century, Da Bruno has survived in its location 400 yards from the Leaning Tower. It's one of Pisa's finest restaurants, though it charges moderate tabs. The locals are particularly fond of this place. Many in-the-know diners prefer the old-fashioned but market-fresh dishes of the Tuscan kitchen, including hare with pappardelle (a wide noodle), a thick regional vegetable soup (zuppa alla paesana), and codfish with leeks and tomatoes (baccalà con porri).

Emilio. Via del Cammeo 44. ☎ **050/562-141.** Fax 050/562-096. Reservations recommended. Main courses 20,000–35,000L ($12–$20); fixed-price menu 18,000–26,000L ($10–$15). AE, DC, MC, V. Sat–Thurs noon–3:30pm and 7–10:30pm. Bus: 1. PISAN/ITALIAN.

Partly because of its well-prepared food and partly because of its proximity to Piazza del Duomo, this restaurant attracts more foreign tourists than almost any other in Pisa. Built in the 1960s and renovated in 1991 in a style some visitors compare to a South American hacienda, it contains a large high window similar to what you'd expect in a church—it filters light down on the brick-walled interior. The menu features a fresh assortment of antipasti, spaghetti with clams, risotto with mushrooms, fish dishes like branzini à l'Isolana oven-baked with tomatoes and vegetables, and Florentine-style beefsteaks. "You come a stranger, but you leave a friend," the waiter said as we were leaving, forgetting he'd used that same line only a year ago.

La Grotta. Via San Francesco 103. ☎ **050/578-105.** Reservations recommended. Main courses 15,000–22,000L ($9–$13). No credit cards. Mon–Sat 7:30–11:30pm (last order). Closed Aug. Bus: 2, 3, 4, or 7. TUSCAN/ITALIAN.

Cramped and convivial, this papier-mâché faux grotto fits the cliché of a hysterical, warm-hearted trattoria. Part of its charm derives from old-fashioned scenes you won't see elsewhere—like the presentation to children of an age-old candied treat, bread smeared with red wine and sugar, and the presentation to adults of wine from a local vineyard called Venerosso. Menu items include many traditional Tuscan dishes, presented with a lack of pretension. Expect pappardelle with rabbit, gnocchi stuffed with ricotto and spinach, roasted fowl or lamb with herb-encrusted potatoes, and high-calorie desserts like tiramisu and assorted pastries and ice creams. The rustic-looking dining room fits only 40 diners, so reservations and a willingness to wait for a table are important.

PISA AFTER DARK

After dinner, Pisans seem to go to bed. But on summer evenings **free classical music concerts** are presented on the steps of the Duomo. Music aficionados from all over the world can be seen sprawled out on the lawn. Concerts are also presented in the Duomo, which is known for its phenomenal acoustics. The tourist office has details. The best time to be in Pisa is the last Sunday in June, when Pisans stage their annual tug-of-war, the **Gioco del Ponte,** which revives some of their pomp and ceremony from the Middle Ages. Each quadrant of the city presents richly costumed parades.

4 San Gimignano: The Manhattan of Tuscany

26 miles NW of Siena, 34 miles SW of Florence

This golden lily of the Middle Ages is called the Manhattan of Tuscany since it preserves 13 of its noble towers, giving it a skyscraper skyline (see the front cover of this guide). The approach to the walled town is dramatic today, but once it must've been fantastic, as **San Gimignano** in the heyday of the Guelph and Ghibelline conflict had as many as 72 towers. Its fortresslike severity is softened by the subtlety of its harmonious squares, and many of its palaces and churches are enhanced by Renaissance frescoes, as San Gimignano could afford to patronize major painters.

But despite its beauty and authenticity, the town can seem like a made-to-order tourist mecca during the day, with large groups shuffling through the sites and in and out of the numerous restaurants and gift shops. Wait until late afternoon or early evening and you can get a sense of the town without so many distractions. Go to one of the tasting rooms for a sample of the famous Vernaccia, the light white wine bottled in the region, or if you've seen the film of E. M. Forster's *Where Angels Fear to Tread,* starring Helen Mirren and Helena Bonham-Carter, try to identify locations (one was La Cisterna, below).

ESSENTIALS

GETTING THERE   The **rail** station nearest to San Gimignano is the station at Poggibonsi, serviced by regular trains from Florence and Siena. At Poggibono, buses depart from in front of the rail station at frequent intervals, charging 2,600L ($1.50) each way to the center of San Gimignano. For information, call ☎ **0577/204-111.**

Buses operated by TRA-IN (☎ **0577/204-111**) service San Gimignano from Florence with a change at Poggibonsi (trip time: 75 minutes); the one-way fare is 10,000L ($6). The same company also operates service from Siena, with a change at Poggibonsi (trip time: 50 minutes); the one-way fare is 7,900L ($4.60). In San Gimignano, buses stop at Piazzale Montemaggio, outside Porta San Giovanni, the southern gate. You'll have to walk into the center, as vehicles aren't allowed in most of the town's core.

If you've got a **car,** leave Florence (1½ hours) or Siena (1 hour and 10 minutes) by the Firenze-Siena autostrada and drive to Poggibonsi, where you'll need to cut west along a secondary route (S324) to San Gimignano.

VISITOR INFORMATION   The **Associazione Pro Loco,** Piazza del Duomo 1 (☎ **0577/940-008**), is open November to February daily 9am to 1pm and 2 to 6pm (March to October to 7pm).

EXPLORING THE TOWN

In the town center is the palazzo-flanked **Piazza della Cisterna,** so named because of the 13th-century cistern in its heart. Connected with the irregularly shaped square is its satellite, **Piazza del Duomo,** whose medieval architecture—towers and palaces—is almost unchanged. It's the most beautiful spot in town. On the square, the **Palazzo del Popolo** was designed in the 13th century, and its **Torre Grossa,** built a few years later, is believed to have been the tallest "skyscraper" (about 178 feet high) in town—see the entry for the Civic Museum below for how to climb this tower.

Note: One ticket, available at any of the sites below, allows admission to all of them for 16,000L ($9) adults, and 12,000L ($7) students under 18 and children.

Duomo Collegiata o Basilica di Santa Maria Assunta. Piazza del Duomo. ☎ **0577/ 940-316.** Church, free; chapel, 3,000L ($1.75) adults, 2,000L ($1.15) students 6–18; children 5 and under free. Daily 9:30am–12:30pm and 3–5:30pm.

Residents of San Gimignano still call this a Duomo (cathedral), even though it was demoted to a "Collegiata" once the town lost its bishop. Don't judge this book by its cover (facade). Plain and austere on the outside, dating from the 12th century, it's richly decorated inside. Actually, the facade for some reason was never finished.

Escaping from the burning Tuscan sun, retreat inside to a world of tiger-striped arches and a galaxy of gold stars. Head for the north aisle, where in the 1360s Bartolo di Fredi depicted scenes from the Old Testament. Two memorable ones are *The Trials of Job* and *Noah with the Animals*. Other outstanding works by this artist are in the lunettes off the north aisle, including a medieval view of the cosmography of the Creation. In the right aisle, panels trace scenes from the life of Christ—the kiss of Judas, the Last Supper, the Flagellation, and the Crucifixion. As a bizarre curiosity, seek out Bartolo's horrendous *Last Judgment,* one of the most perverse in Italy. Abandoning briefly his rosy-cheeked Sienese madonnas, he depicted distorted and suffering nudes, shocking at the time.

The chief attraction here is the **Chapel of Santa Fina,** designed by Giuliano and Benedetto da Maiano. Michelangelo's fresco teacher, Domenico Ghirlandaio, frescoed it with scenes from the life of a local girl, Fina, who became the town's patron saint. Her deathbed scene is memorable. According to accounts of the day, the little girl went to the well for water and accepted an orange from a young swain. When her mother scolded her for her wicked ways, she was so mortified that she prayed for the next 5 years, until St. Anthony called her to heaven.

Civic Museum (Museo Civico). In the Palazzo del Popolo, Piazza del Duomo 1. ☎ **0577/ 940-340.** Admission 7,000L ($4.05) adults, 5,000L ($3) students, and 3,500L ($2.10) children. Apr–Oct daily 9:30am–7pm; Nov–Mar Tues–Sun 9:30am–1pm and 2:30–4:30pm.

This museum is installed upstairs in the Palazzo del Popolo (town hall). Most notable is the **Sala di Dante,** where the White Guelph-supporting poet spoke out for his cause in 1300. Look for one of the masterpieces of San Gimignano—the *Maestà* (Madonna enthroned) by Lippo Memmi (later touched up by Gozzoli). The first large room upstairs contains the other masterpiece: a *Madonna in Glory,* with Sts. Gregory and Benedict, painted by Pinturicchio. On the other side of it are two depictions of the *Annunciation* by Filippino Lippi. On the opposite wall, note the magnificent Byzantine Crucifix by Coppo di Marcovaldo.

Passing through the Museo Civico, you can scale the **Torre Grossa** and be rewarded with a bird's-eye view of this most remarkable town. The tower, the only one in town you can climb, is open March to October daily 9:30am to 7:30pm; off-season, Tuesday to Saturday 9:30am to 1:30pm and 2:30 to 4:30pm. Admission is 8,000L ($4.65) adults and 6,000L ($3.50) students under 18/children.

Around to the left of the cathedral on the little Piazza Luigi Pecori is the **Museum of Sacred Art (Museo d'Arte Sacra)** (☎ 0577/942-226), an unheralded museum of at least passing interest for its medieval tombstones and wooden sculpture. It also has an illustrated-manuscript section and an Etruscan section. It keeps the same hours as the Museo Civico.

Museum of Medieval Crimiology (Museo di Criminologia Medioevale). Via di Castello 1. ☎ **0577/942-243.** Admission 12,000L ($7) adults, 5,000L ($3) children. Apr– Oct daily 10am–1pm and 2–7pm; off-season Sat–Sun 11am–1pm and 2–6pm.

The Marquis de Sade would have taken delight here. In this Tuscan chamber of horrors, some of the most horrendous instruments of torture are on display. For torture in the style of the Middle Ages, this chamber has the cutting edge. In case you don't know just how the devices worked, descriptions are provided in English. As the curator explained, the museum has a political agenda even today. The exhibits like cast-iron chastity belts inherently reveal some of the sexism involved in torture devices with the revelation that many have been updated for use around in the world today, from Africa to South America. These include the garrote, that horror of the Inquisition trials of the 1400s. Fittingly enough, this bizarre sight is housed in what locals call the Torre del Diavolo (devil's tower).

ACCOMMODATIONS

Hotel Bel Soggiorno. Via San Giovanni 91, 53037 San Gimignano. ☎ **0577/940-375.** Fax 0577/943-149. web.tin.it/san_gimignano. 22 units. A/C TV TEL. 150,000–160,000L ($87–$93) double; from 210,000L ($122) suite. Breakfast 12,000L ($7). AE, DC, MC, V. Closed Jan–Feb. Parking 15,000L ($9).

Though no longer the town's best, having bowed to the Relais Santa Chiara and La Cisterna, this hotel is still the best value. The Gigli family has run it since 1886. The rear guest rooms and dining room open on the lower pastureland and the bottom of the village. The rooms are small and pleasantly revamped, and some have antiques and terraces. About half open onto views of the Val d'Elsa. All were designed in High Tuscan style by an architect from Milan; eight have air-conditioning and four offer minibars. In summer you'll be asked to have your meals at the hotel (no great hardship, as the cuisine is excellent). Medieval style, the dining room boasts murals depicting a wild boar hunt (see "Dining," below, for a full review).

Hotel La Cisterna. Piazza della Cisterna 24, 53037 San Gimignano. ☎ **0577/940-328.** Fax 0577/942-080. E-mail: LACISTERNA@10L.IT. 52 units. TV TEL. 150,000–190,000L ($87–$110) double; 215,000L ($125) suite. Rates include breakfast. AE, DC, MC, V. Closed Jan–Feb. Parking 20,000L ($12).

Opened in 1919, the ivy-covered La Cisterna is modernized but still retains its medieval lines (it was built at the base of some 14th-century patrician towers). For years, it was the only hotel in town, and it's still one of the leading inns. Many people visit it just to patronize Ristorante Le Terrazze (see "Dining," below). The rooms are generally large; some of the best ones open onto terraces with views of the Val d'Elsa. Because of the narrow cobble-covered streets surrounding the inn, guests may drop off their luggage at the hotel entrance, then drive a short distance outside the city's medieval walls to park their cars.

Hotel Leon Bianco. Piazza della Cisterna, 53037 San Gimignano. ☎ **0577/941-294.** Fax 0577/942-123. E-mail: leonbianco@see.it. 21 units. A/C TV TEL. 160,000–180,000L ($93–$104) double. Breakfast 13,000L ($8). AE, DC, MC, V. Parking 19,000L ($11).

This restored 14th-century villa offers San Gimignano at its best—the front rooms look out over the stark medieval Piazza della Cisterna and the rear rooms have a sweeping view of the Elsa Valley. Features include vaulted ceilings, terra-cotta floors, and rooms individualized by the quirks and construction of an ancient dwelling (one is rustically romantic with vaulted ceilings and alcoves composed entirely of rough brick). The sunny roof terrace is a good place to order breakfast or a drink or just to lounge and relax. There's no restaurant on the premises, but several are a short stroll away.

Hotel Pescille. Località Pescille, 53037 San Gimignano. ☎ **0577/940-186.** Fax 0577/943-165. http://hotelinfoplus.com/sangimignano/pescille.htm. 50 units. TV TEL. 150,000–230,000L ($87–$133) double. Breakfast 15,000L ($9). AE, DC, MC, V. Closed Nov to mid-Mar. Head 2 miles north of San Gimignano, following the signs to Volterra.

Few other hotels in the region convey as strong a sense of sleepy rural Tuscany, and though the blasé staff has sometimes drawn complaints, you might appreciate the spot's tranquillity after too strong a dose of big-city tourism. About 2 miles from town, it's surrounded by vineyards and groves of olive trees. The rooms are outfitted in an old-time style influenced by rustic Tuscany, often with countryside views. Though all rooms are comfortable and charming, the most striking is the Tower Room, an eagle's-nest eyrie overlooking San Gimignano's towers in the distance. Breakfast is the only meal served, but a bar serves coffee and drinks.

✪ **Relais Santa Chiara.** Via Matteotti 15, 53037 San Gimignano. ☎ **0577/940-701.** Fax 0577/942-096. www.cybermarket.it/rsc. E-mail: RSC@cyber.dada.it. 41 units. A/C MINIBAR TV TEL. 220,000–320,000L ($128–$186) double; 280,000–390,000L ($162–$226) suite. Rates include buffet breakfast. AE, DC, MC, V.

This solid comfortable hotel lies in a residential neighborhood about a 10-minute walk south of the medieval ramparts. It's the prestigious place to stay, far superior to either La Cisterna or the Bel Soggiorno. It's surrounded with elegant gardens and a pool, and its spacious public rooms contain Florentine terra-cotta floors and mosaics. The comfortable guest rooms are furnished in precious brierwood and walnut and include a Jacuzzi, radio, and hair dryer. Though the hotel is relatively new, the furnishings and ambience blend in harmoniously with the Tuscan countryside. There's no restaurant, but the hotel serves a buffet breakfast and snacks at lunch in summer.

DINING

Ristorante Bel Soggiorno. In the Hotel Bel Soggiorno, Via San Giovanni 91. ☎ **0577/940-375.** Reservations recommended. Main courses 20,000–28,000L ($12–$17); fixed-price menu 45,000L ($27). AE, DC, MC, V. Thurs–Tues 12:30–2:30pm and 7:30–10pm. TUSCAN.

Thanks to windows overlooking the countryside and a devoted use of fresh ingredients from nearby farms, at this restaurant you'll get a strong sense of Tuscany's agrarian bounty. Two of the most appealing specialties (available only late summer to late winter) are roasted wild boar with red wine and mixed vegetables and pappardelle pasta garnished with a savory ragout of pheasant. Other pastas are pappardelle with roasted hare and risotto with herbs and seasonal vegetables. Main courses stress vegetable garnishes and thin-sliced meats that are simply but flavorfully grilled over charcoal.

Ristorante Le Terrazze. In La Cisterna, Piazza della Cisterna 24. ☎ **0577/940-328.** Reservations required. Main courses 20,000–24,000L ($12–$14). AE, DC, MC, V. Wed 7:30–10pm, Thurs–Mon 12:30–2:30pm and 7:30–10pm. Closed Nov–Feb. TUSCAN.

One of this restaurant's two dining rooms boasts stones laid in the 1300s. The newer dining room (added in 1969) has lots of rustic accessories and large windows overlooking the old town and the Val d'Elsa. The setting is one of a country inn, and the food features an assortment of produce from the surrounding Tuscan farms. The soups and pastas make fine beginnings, and specialties of the house include delectable items like sliced filet of wild boar with polenta and Chianti, breast of goose with walnut sauce, suppe San Gimignanese (a hearty minestrone), vitello (veal) alla Cisterna with buttered beans, Florence-style steaks, and risotto con funghi porcini (with mushrooms). A superb dessert that's about as regional as it gets is a local sweet wine, Vin Santo, accompanied by an almond biscuit.

SAMPLING THE VINO

San Gimignano produces its own white wine, Vernaccia, one of Italy's relatively esoteric (at least to foreigners) vintages. One of the widest selections in town, as well as samplings of Chianti from throughout Tuscany, is displayed and sold at **Da Gustavo,** Via San Matteo 29 (☎ **0577/940-057**). Small but select, it's run by the Beccuci family and has been thriving here since 1946. Don't think you'll have to select a vintage based solely on the recommendation of the salespeople: There's an informal stand-up bar where glasses are 2,500L to 10,000L ($1.45 to $6). If you don't see what you're looking for on the shelves, ask—someone will probably haul it out from a storeroom the moment you mention its name.

A worthy competitor, with a similar format, is **Bar Enoteca il Castello,** Via di Castello 20 (☎ **0577/940-878**), maintained by members of the Rainieri and Salvestrini families. A bar at one end dispenses generous doses of bread, cheese, salami, and simple platters designed as flavorful foils to glasses of wine priced from 3,000L ($1.75) each. There are views over the nearby hills, tables to sit at (a fact you'll appreciate after a glass or two), and take-away bottles of most of the vintages produced in the San Gimignano region. Set menus are 28,000L to 32,000L ($16 to $19).

EN ROUTE TO SIENA

Traveling from San Gimignano to Siena, you can take S324 east from San Gimignano to Poggibonsi, then turn south on S2, following the path of the ancient Roman highway Via Cassia, now a little traveled byway into Siena. Not only will you avoid the heavily trafficked autostrada but also you'll absorb more of the history, architecture, and geography of the region, taking in the sight of its hillside vineyards, ancient walled villages, and historic tales of struggle. On SS323, 9 miles north of Siena, is the town of **Monteriggioni,** built as a Sienese lookout fortress to guard against attack by the Florentines in 1213. The original walls are still intact and contain the 14 towers that once gave it an imposing skyline, looming up out of the wild, a symbol of Sienese might. A stop here will take you back in time, wandering the streets of a village little changed after more than 700 years of civilization.

5 Siena & the Palio delle Contrade

21 miles S of Florence, 143 miles NW of Rome

After visiting Florence, it's altogether fitting, and certainly bipartisan, to call on what has been labeled in the past its natural enemy. In Rome you see classicism and the baroque and in Florence the Renaissance, but in the walled city of **Siena** you stand solidly planted back in the Middle Ages. On three sienna-colored hills in Tuscany's center, Sena Vetus lies in Chianti country. Perhaps preserving its original character more markedly than any other city in Italy, it's even today a showplace of the Italian Gothic.

American novelist William Dean Howells (*The Rise of Silas Lapham*) called Siena "not a monument but a light." Though it's regrettably too often visited on a quick day trip, Siena is a city of contemplation and profound exploration, characterized by Gothic palaces, almond-eyed Madonnas, aristocratic mansions, letter-writing St. Catherine (patron saint of Italy), narrow streets, and medieval gates, walls, and towers.

Such a point of view may be heretical, but one can almost be grateful Siena lost its battle with Florence. Had it continued to expand and change after reaching the zenith of its power in the 14th century, chances are it would be markedly different today, influenced by the rising tides of the Renaissance and the baroque (represented here only in a small degree). But Siena retained its uniqueness—certain Sienese painters were still showing the influence of Byzantium in the late 15th century.

The university (founded 1240) is still a leading industry, and the conversation you'll overhear between locals in the streets is the purest Italian dialect in the country. But you may have to wait until evening, since most residents retreat into the seclusion of their homes during the days full of tour buses. They emerge to reclaim the cafes and squares at night, when most visitors have gone. In a nod to its reputation as a commercial leader during the Middle Ages, you can convert your dollars to lire at the **Monte dei Paschi,** the oldest bank in the world.

ESSENTIALS

GETTING THERE   The **rail** link to Florence is sometimes inconvenient, since you often have to change and wait at other stations, like Empoli. But trains run every hour from Florence, costing 8,000L ($4.65) one-way. You arrive at the **station** at Piazza Fratelli Rosselli (☎ **0577/280-115**). This is an awkward half-hour climb uphill to the monumental heart; however, bus no. 2, 4, 6, or 10 will take you to Piazza Gramsci near the center.

Headquartered in Siena, **TRA-IN,** Piazza San Domenico 1 (☎ **0577/204-245**), offers bus service to all Tuscany in air-conditioned coaches. The one-way fare between Florence and Siena is 10,500L ($6). The trip takes 1¼ hours. If you've got a **car,** head south from Florence along the Firenze-Siena autostrada, a superhighway linking the two cities, going through Poggibonsi.

VISITOR INFORMATION   The **tourist office** is at Piazza del Campo 56 (☎ **0577/280-551**), open Monday to Saturday 8:30am to 7:30pm (April, May, September, and October also Sunday 8:30am to 2pm).

EXPLORING THE MEDIEVAL CITY

There's much to see here. We'll start in the heart of Siena, the shell-shaped **Piazza del Campo,** described by Montaigne as "the finest of any city in the world." Pause to enjoy the **Fonte Gaia,** which locals sometimes call the "fountain of joy" because it was inaugurated to great jubilation througout the city, with embellishments by Jacopo della Quercia (the present sculptured works are reproductions; the badly beaten original ones are found in the town hall).

Civic Museum (Museo Civico). In the Palazzo Pubblico, Piazza del Campo. ☎ **0577/ 292-263.** Admission 8,000L ($4.65) adults, 4,000L ($2.30) students; children under 12 free. May–Sept daily 9:30am–6:30pm; Nov–Apr Mon–Sat 10am–5pm, Sun and holidays 9:30am– 1:30pm. Bus: A, B, or N.

The Palazzo Pubblico dates from 1288 to 1309 and is filled with important artworks by some of the leaders in the Sienese school of painting and sculpture. This collection is the Museo Civico.

In the **Sala del Mappomondo** is Simone Martini's earliest-known work (ca. 1315), *La Maesta,* the Madonna enthroned with her Child, surrounded by angels and saints. The other remarkable Martini fresco (on the opposite wall) is the equestrian portrait of Guidoriccio da Fogliano, general of the Sienese Republic, in ceremonial dress.

The next room is the **Sala della Pace,** frescoed from 1337 to 1339 by Ambrogio Lorenzetti; the allegorical frescoes show the idealized effects of good government and bad government. In this depiction, the most notable figure of the Virtues surrounding the king is *La Pace* (Peace). To the right of the king and the Virtues is a representation of Siena in peaceful times. On the left Lorenzetti showed his opinion of "ward heelers," but some of the sting has been taken out of the frescoes, as the evil-government scene is badly damaged. Actually, these were propaganda frescoes in their day, commissioned by the party in power, but they're now viewed as among the most important of all secular frescoes to come down from the Middle Ages.

Accessible from the courtyard of the Palazzo Pubblico is the **Torre del Mangia,** the most characteristic architectural landmark on the skyline of Siena. Dating from the 14th century, it soars to a height of 335 feet. The tower takes its name from a former bell-ringer, a sleepy fellow called *mangiagaudagni* ("eat the profits"). Surprisingly, it has no subterranean foundations. If you climb this needlelike tower, which Henry

Siena

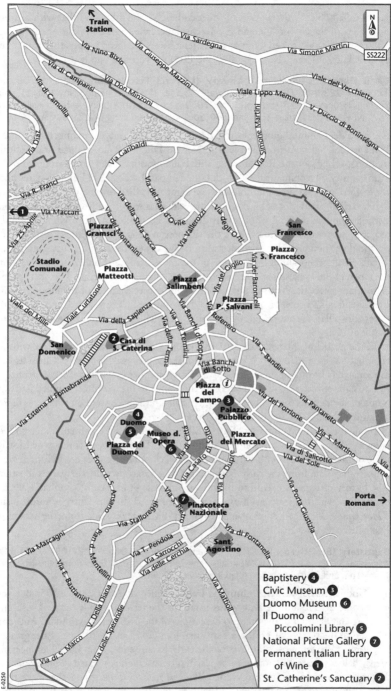

Baptistery ④
Civic Museum ③
Duomo Museum ⑥
Il Duomo and
    Piccolimini Library ⑤
National Picture Gallery ⑦
Permanent Italian Library
    of Wine ①
St. Catherine's Sanctuary ②

James called "Siena's declaration of independence," you'll be rewarded with a drop-dead view of the city skyline and the Tuscan landscape. In the Middle Ages, this was Italy's second-tallest tower; Cremona has Siena beat. The tower is open the same hours as the Civic Museum, charging 7,000L ($4.05) for you to climb it.

✪ **Il Duomo & Piccolimini Library (Libreria Piccolomini).** Piazza del Duomo. ☎ **0577/283-048.** Duomo, free; library, 2,000L ($1.15). Duomo, Nov–Mar 15 daily 7:30am–1:30pm and 2:30pm–5pm (Mar 16–Oct to 7:30pm). Library, Apr–Oct daily 9am–7pm; Nov–Mar daily 10am–1pm and 2:30–5pm. Closed Jan 1 and Dec 25. Bus: A.

At Piazza del Duomo, southwest of Piazza del Campo, stands an architectural fantasy. With its colored bands of marble, the Sienese **Duomo** is an original and exciting building, erected in the Romanesque and Italian Gothic styles and dating from the 12th century. The dramatic facade—designed in part by Giovanni Pisano—dates from the 13th century, as does the Romanesque campanile (bell tower).

The zebralike interior of black-and-white stripes is equally stunning. The floor consists of various embedded works of art depicting both biblical and mythological subjects (many are roped off to preserve the richness in design). Numerous artists worked on the floor, notably Domenico Beccafumi. The octagonal 13th-century pulpit is by Nicola Pisano (Giovanni's father), one of the most significant Italian sculptors before the dawn of the Renaissance (see his pulpit in the baptistery at Pisa). The Siena pulpit is his masterpiece; it reveals in relief such scenes as the slaughter of the innocents and the Crucifixion. The elder Pisano finished the pulpit in 1268, aided by his son and others. Its pillars are supported by four marble lions, again reminiscent of the Pisano pulpit at Pisa.

In the chapel of the left transept (near the library) is a glass-enclosed box with an arm that tradition maintains is the one John the Baptist used to baptize Christ as well as Donatello's bronze of John the Baptist. To see another Donatello work in bronze (a bishop's gravemarker) look at the floor in the chapel to the left of the pulpit's stairway. Some of the designs for the inlaid wooden stalls in the apse were by Riccio. A representational blue starry sky twinkles overhead.

Inside the Duomo is the **Piccolimini Library,** founded by Cardinal Francesco Piccolomini (later Pius III) to honor his uncle (Pius II); the library is renowned for its cycle of frescoes by the Umbrian master Pinturicchio. His frescoes are well preserved, though they date from the early 16th century. In Vasari's words, the panels illustrate "the history of Pope Pius II from birth to the minute of his death." Raphael's alleged connection with the frescoes, if any, is undocumented. In the center is an exquisite *Three Graces,* a Roman copy of a 3rd-century B.C. Greek work from the school of Praxiteles.

Baptistery (Battistero). Piazza San Giovanni (behind the Duomo). ☎ **0577/283-048.** Admission 3,000L ($1.75). Mar–Sept daily 9am–7:30pm; Oct daily 9am–6pm; Nov–Mar daily 10am–1pm and 2:30–5pm. Closed Jan 1 and Dec 25. Bus: A.

The Gothic facade was left unfinished by Domenico di Agostino in 1355. But you don't come here to admire that—you come for the frescoes inside, many lavish and intricate and devoted in the main to depictions of the lives of Christ and St. Anthony. The star of the place, however, is a baptismal font (1417 to 1430), one of the greatest in all Italy. The foremost sculptors of the early Renaissance, from both Florence and Siena, helped create this masterpiece. Jacopo della Quercia created *Annunciation to Zacharias,* Giovanni di Turino crafted *Preaching of the Baptist* and the *Baptism of Christ,* and Lorenzo Ghiberti worked with Giuliano di Ser Andrea on the masterful *Arrest of St. John.* Our favorite is Donatello's *Feast of Herod,* a work of profound beauty and deep perspective.

The Palio: Spectacle of Violence

The best time to visit Siena is usually on July 2 or August 16, the occasions of the ✪ **Palio delle Contrade,** a historical pageant and tournament known throughout Europe that draws thousands annually. In the horse race, each bare-back-riding jockey represents a *contrada* (one of the 17 wards into which the city is divided), each district identified by its characteristic colors. The race, which requires tremendous skill, takes place on Piazza del Campo in the historic heart. Before the race, much pageantry evoking the 15th-century parades by, with colorfully costumed men and banners. The flag-throwing ceremony, depicted in so many travelogue films, takes place at this time. And just as enticing is the victory celebration.

But like the Spanish bullfight, Siena's major event is coming under increasing fire for its brutality. For the event, the temperature in town rises higher than the blistering Tuscan sun. All the pomp and ritual of the Middle Ages live again, as heralds, child drummers, flag-bearers, and Renaissance costumes evoke the pomp of the festival.

Three days before the big race, trial races are held, the final trial on the morning of the event. There are 17 contrade in Siena, but because Piazza del Campo holds only 10 contrade, the wards are chosen by lot. Young partisans, flaunting the colors of their contrada, race through the medieval streets in packs. Food and wine are bountiful on the streets of each contrada on the eve of the race.

The event could easily be considered all in good fun, except that some partisans take it far too seriously. There have been kidnappings of the most skilled jockeys before the race. Bribery has been reported as commonplace. So fiercely competitive is the race that all that seems to remain taboo is the sabotaging of the horse's reins. During the race, jockeys have been known to unseat the competition, though a riderless horse is allowed to win. The event has been cited for its cruelty to animals, as horses are sometimes impaled by guardrails along the track. TV cameras move in on the gore, capturing live the spurting blood as a horse collides with the rail. Jockeys have been caught on camera kicking the horses. In theory, riders are supposed to alternate whip strokes between their mounts and their competitors'.

One Sienese who has attended 30 Palios has said, "Winning, not sportsmanship, is the only thing that's important. There are rules, but we Italians never bother to worry about rules. Instead of a horse race, you might call the event a rat race."

Note: Don't buy expensive tickets for the day of the Palio. It's free to stand in the middle—and a lot more fun. Just get to Piazza del Campo very early and bring a book and a Thermos. The square becomes almost impossibly crowded, and the temperature can range from rainy and cold to blistering hot. If it's a sunny day, it's a good idea to bring some sort of head covering, since most of the viewing area isn't shaded. For a memorable dinner and a lot of fun, join one of the 17 contrade holding a *cena* (supper) outdoors the night before the race.

Duomo Museum (Museo dell'Opera Metropolitana). Piazza del Duomo 8. ☎ **0577/ 42309.** Admission 6,000L ($3.50). Apr–Sept daily 9am–7:30pm; Oct daily 9am–6pm; Nov–Mar daily 9am–1:30pm. Closed Dec 25–Jan 1. Bus: A.

This museum houses paintings and sculptures created for Il Duomo. On the ground floor is much interesting sculpture, including works by Giovanni Pisano and his assistants. But the real draw hangs on the next floor in the **Sala di Duccio:** his fragmented *La Maestà,* a Madonna enthroned, painted from 1308 to 1311 and one of Europe's greatest late medieval paintings. The majestic panel was an altarpiece by Duccio di Buoninsegna for the cathedral, filled with dramatic moments illustrating the story of Christ and the Madonna. A student of Cimabue, Duccio was the first great name in the school of Sienese painting. Upstairs are the collections of the treasury, and on the top floor is a display of paintings from the early Sienese school.

○ **National Picture Gallery (Pinacoteca Nazionale).** In the Palazzo Buonsignori, Via San Pietro 29. ☎ **0577/281-161.** Admission 8,000L ($4.65) adults; children 17 and under free. Mon 8:30am–1:30pm, Tues–Sat 8:30am–2pm, Sun 8am–1pm. Bus: A.

Housed in a 14th-century palazzo near Piazza del Campo is the national gallery's collection of the Sienese school of painting, which once rivaled that of Florence. Displayed here are some of the giants of the pre-Renaissance. Most of the paintings cover the period from the late 12th century to the mid-16th century.

The principal treasures are on the second floor, where you'll contemplate the artistry of Duccio in **rooms 3 and 4.** Duccio was the first great Sienese master. **Rooms 5 to 8** are rich in the art of the two Lorenzetti brothers, Ambrogio and Pietro, who painted in the 14th century. Ambrogio is represented by an *Annunciation* and a *Crucifix,* but one of his most celebrated works, carried out with consummate skill, is an almond-eyed *Madonna and Bambino* surrounded by saints and angels. Pietro's most important entry is an altarpiece, *Madonna of the Carmine,* made for a Siena church in 1329. Simone Martini's *Madonna and Child* (1321) is damaged but one of the best-known paintings here.

In the salons to follow—often rearranged—are works by Giovanni di Paolo (*Presentation at the Temple*), Sano di Pietro, and Giovanni Antonio Bazzi (called Il Sodoma, allegedly because of his sexual interests). Of exceptional interest are the cartoons of mannerist master Beccafumi, from which many of the panels in the cathedral floor were created.

St. Catherine's Sanctuary (Santuario e Casa di Santa Caterina). Costa di S. Antonio. ☎ **0577/44177.** Free admission (an offering is expected). Mon–Sat and holidays 9am–12:30pm and 3:30–6:30pm. Bus: A.

Of all the personalities associated with Siena, the most enduring legend surrounds St. Catherine, acknowledged by Pius XII in 1939 as Italy's patron saint. Born in 1347 to a dyer, the mystic was instrumental in persuading the papacy to return to Rome from Avignon. The house where she lived, between Piazza del Campo and San Domenico, has now been turned into a sanctuary—it's really a church and an oratory, with many artworks, located where her father had his dyeworks. On the hill above is the 13th-century **Basilica of San Domenico,** where a chapel dedicated to St. Catherine was frescoed by Il Sodoma.

Permanent Italian Library of Wine (Enoteca Italica Permanente). Fortezza Medicea. ☎ **0577/288-497.** Free admission. Mon noon–8pm, Tues–Sat noon–1am. Bus: C.

Owned and operated by the Italian government, the Enoteca Italica Permanente, a showcase for the finest wines of Italy, would whet the palate of even the most demanding wine lover. An unusual architectural setting is designed to show bottles to their best advantage. The place lies just outside the entrance to an old fortress, at the bottom of an inclined ramp, behind a massive arched doorway. Marble bas-reliefs and wrought-iron sconces, along with regional ceramics, are set into the high brick walls of the labyrinthine corridors, the vaults of which were built for Cosimo de' Medici in 1560. There are several sunny terraces for outdoor wine tasting, an indoor stand-up bar, and voluminous lists of available vintages, for sale by the glass or the bottle. Special wine tastings for groups may be booked for 15,000L ($9) for two wines and 17,500L ($10) for three. Count yourself lucky if the bartender will agree to open an iron gate for access to the subterranean wine exposition. Here, in the lowest part of the fortress, carpenters have built illuminated display racks containing bottles of recent vintages.

SHOPPING

Though Siena's shopping scene has always paled when compared to that of its larger rival, Florence, you'll still find a selection of stores and boutiques. The best of the lot is **Arcaico,** Via di Citta 81 (☎ 0577/280-551), the centerpiece of three almost-adjacent shops stocking Siena's richest trove of ceramics and souvenir items. Examples of the merchandise are cachepots for dressing up a potted plant, religious figurines, decorative tiles, dinnerware painted in pleasing floral patterns, and wine and water jugs.

A worthy competitor is **Martini Marisa,** Via del Capitano 5 and 11 (☎ 0577/ 288-177), purveyor of gift items, local stoneware, and porcelain. Also try the nearby premises **of Zina Proveddi,** Via del Citta 96 (☎ 0577/286-078), smaller than either of its competitors but with a cozier feel and an emphasis on rustic and affordable pottery and painted tiles set into wood. Proud of its role as the oldest (ca. 1920) purveyor of ceramic souvenirs in Siena, it displays a wide variety of handmade ceramics, each manufactured in Umbria or Tuscany. **Ceramiche Santa Caterina,** Via di Città 51 (☎ 0577/283-098), offers sculpture, dishes, and tile among the items for sale, but custom orders are available on request—and the owners say they can make anything you can describe in their Siena-based factories.

Specializing in older jewelry, **Antichita Saena Vetus,** Via di Città 53 (☎ 0577/ 42-395), handles furniture and paintings from the 1700s and 1800s and always has smaller pieces reasonably priced for the bargain hunter. There's also a small assortment of oil paintings, art objects, and small-scale furniture, though the emphasis is on estate jewelry. If you're looking for old or old-fashioned engravings, out-of-print books, and art objects, head for **La Balzana,** Piazza del Campo 55 (☎ 0577/ 285-380), an appealingly dusty venue that also includes an assortment of local pottery and souvenirs.

Utilizing the colors and designs of Renaissance Siena, **Siena Ricama,** Via di Città 61 (☎ 0577/288-339), is the place to order custom-made hand-embroidered table and bed linens, each of which is laboriously stitched, entirely by hand, in Siena. More contemporary in its appeal is the intricately crafted knitware at **Il Telaio,** Chiasso del Bargello 2 (☎ 0577/47-065). Though there's a small collection of pullovers for men, most of the stock includes artfully tailored women's jackets, scarves, and jumpers. Focusing on smaller leather goods, **Mercatissimo della Calzatura e Pelletteria,** Viale Curtatone 1 (☎ 0577/2813-05), is the largest store of its type in Siena. Although there's an inventory of tennis and basketball sneakers imported from Asia, most of the allure is from the discounted prices on upscale Italian-made leather goods (handbags, suitcases, briefcases, and men's and women's shoes).

Don't overlook Siena as an outlet for some of Tuscany's finest wines. There's an outlet for local Chianti—sold in individual bottles and sometimes four-packs and six-packs—on virtually every street corner. Many of the finer bottles are wrapped in the distinctive straw sheathing. For the largest selection, head to the **Enoteca Italiana Permanente** (see above). A Tuscan gourmet's delight, the **Enoteca San Domenico,**

Via del Paradiso 56 (☎ 0577/271-181), sells regional wines and grappa by the bottle, and also hawks pasta, virgin olive oils, sauces, jams, and assorted sweets.

ACCOMMODATIONS

You'll definitely need hotel reservations if you're here for the Palio. Make them far in advance and secure your room with a deposit.

VERY EXPENSIVE

✪ **Certosa di Maggiano.** Strada di Certosa 82, 53100 Siena. ☎ **0577/288-180.** Fax 0577/288-189. 17 units. A/C MINIBAR TV TEL. 600,000–700,000L ($348–$406) double; 900,000–1,300,000L ($522–$754) suite. Rates include breakfast. AE, DC, MC, V. Parking 50,000L ($29).

This early 13th-century Certosinian monastery lay in dusty disrepair until 1975, when Anna Grossi Recordati renovated it and began attracting some of the world's social luminaries to its 700-year-old interior. It lacks the facilities and formal service of the Park Hotel Siena, but many guests prefer the intimacy of this cozy retreat. The stylish public rooms fill the spaces between what used to be the ambulatory of the central courtyard, and the complex's medieval church still holds mass on Sunday. Most guest rooms are spacious and filled with antiques mixed with art objects; one has a private walled garden. The hotel isn't easy to find, set away from the center of town on a narrow road. There are some signs, but you may want to phone ahead for directions.

Dining: The small vaulted dining room contains a marble fireplace and entire walls of modern ceramics. It's open to nonguests who make a reservation. The cuisine is excellent.

Amenities: Room service, guide service, massages, baby-sitting, heliport, tennis courts, pool.

EXPENSIVE

Jolly Hotel Excelsior. Piazza La Lizza, 53100 Siena. ☎ **800/221-2626** in the U.S. or 0577/288-448. Fax 0577/41-272. www.tradetours.com/italia/siena/joexce.htm. 126 units. A/C MINIBAR TV TEL. 280,000–400,000L ($162–$232) double; 350,000–600,000L ($203–$348) suite. Rates include breakfast. AE, DC, MC, V. Parking 45,000L ($26). Bus: C.

In the commercial center of the newer section of Siena, near the sports stadium, this hotel is a distinguished member of a nationwide chain, though it lacks the ambience and beauty of either the Certosa di Maggiano or the Park Hotel Siena. It was built as the Excelsior in the 1880s and completely renovated about a century later. The high-ceilinged lobby is stylishly Italian, with terra-cotta accents and white columns. The guest rooms have modern but uninspired furniture, a trim monochromatic color scheme, and many conveniences.

Dining: The hotel's restaurant features both Tuscan and international dishes.

Amenities: Concierge, room service, laundry/dry cleaning, baby-sitting.

Park Hotel Siena. Via di Marciano 18, 53100 Siena. ☎ **0577/44-803.** Fax 0577/49-020. www.charminghotels.it/parkhotel. E-mail: reservation_phs@charminghotels.it. 69 units. A/C MINIBAR TV TEL. 320,000–430,000L ($186–$249) double; 650,000–900,000L ($377–$522) suite. Breakfast 28,000L ($17). AE, DC, MC, V. Closed Dec 3–Feb. Free parking. About a 12-minute drive (1½ miles) southwest of the city center.

This building was commissioned in 1530 by one of Siena's most famous Renaissance architects. It was transformed into a luxury hotel around the turn of the century and has remained the leading hotel in Siena ever since. It doesn't have the antique charm of the Certosa di Maggiano but is more professionally run. A difficult access road leads around a series of hairpin turns (watch the signs carefully) to a buff-colored villa set with a view over green trees and suburbanite houses. The landscaped pool, double-glazed windows, upholstered walls, and plush carpeting have set new standards around here. The hotel is well tended, with stylish modern decoration and comfortably furnished public salons. Several famous golf courses are nearby; golf packages are offered through the hotel, which has its own six-hole course.

Dining: Meals in the hotel restaurant may include wild mushroom salad with black truffles, tortellini with spinach and ricotta, and a regularly featured series of dishes from Tuscany, Umbria, or Emilia-Romagna.

Amenities: Room service, laundry/valet, pool, two tennis courts, six-hole golf course.

Villa Scacciapensieri. Via di Scacciapensieri 10, 53100 Siena. ☎ **0577/41-441.** Fax 0577/ 270-854. E-mail:villasca@tin.it. 32 units. A/C MINIBAR TV TEL. 270,000–360,000L ($157– $209) double; 440,000L ($255) suite. Rates include breakfast. AE, DC, MC, V. Closed Jan–Feb. Free parking. About 2 miles from Siena.

This is one of Tuscany's lovely old villas, where you can stay in a personal, if timeworn, atmosphere. Standing on the crest of a hill, the villa is approached by a private driveway under shade trees. Although it's not as state-of-the-art as it once was, it's still preferred by many tradition-minded Europeans, who seem to appreciate its antiquated charms. The rooms vary widely in style and comfort, and your opinion of this hotel may depend on your room assignment.

Dining: The informal restaurant serves Tuscan and Italian cuisine. You can dine here Thursday to Tuesday (reserve ahead).

Amenities: Room service, laundry/valet, baby-sitting, pool, tennis courts.

MODERATE

Garden Hotel. Via Custoza 2, 53100 Siena. ☎ **0577/47-056.** Fax 0577/46-050. www.tin. it/compgarden. E-mail: gardenh@tin.it. 125 units. TV TEL. 190,000–250,000L ($110–$145) double. Rates include breakfast. AE, DC, MC, V. Bus: 6 or 10. Less than a mile north of Siena's fortifications.

One of the really pleasant places to stay outside Siena boasts an 18th-century core built as a villa by a Sienese aristocrat and expanded in the 1970s with a modern annex. High up on the ledge of a hill, it commands a view of Siena and the countryside that has been the subject of many a painting. The hotel stands formal and serene, with a long avenue of clipped hedges. Its outstanding features are its garden and its reasonable prices. The core villa contains 25 rooms, each high-ceilinged but less luxurious than the 100 in the modern annex. The annex rooms, air-conditioned and very comfortable, are conservatively modern. The breakfast room has a flagstone floor, decorated ceiling, and view of the hills. The restaurant, open daily for lunch and dinner, includes some of the showrooms in the villa and sprawls onto a flowering terrace during clement weather. The pool is open June to September.

Hotel Duomo. Via Stalloreggi 38, 53100 Siena. ☎ **0577/289-088.** Fax 0577/43-043. 23 units. A/C TV TEL. 210,000L ($122) double. 20–40% less in slow periods. AE, DC, MC, V. Rates include breakfast. Parking 16,000L ($9) nearby. Bus: A.

The Hotel Duomo, excellently located just south of its namesake, is in a 12th-century palazzo that once was barracks for medieval troops, though the only reminders of that time are the Renaissance central staircase and the brickwork in the basement breakfast room. Most carpeted accommodations are of a modest size but not cramped, and the modern furnishings are as tasteful as functional gets. The baths are tiny, but the mattresses lie on wood-slat orthopedic frames. If you want to secure one of the 13 rooms with Duomo views, be sure ask when booking. The friendly staff is polished and professional.

Hotel Santa Caterina. Via Enea Silvio Piccolomini 7, 53100 Siena. ☎ **0577/221-105.** Fax 0577/271-087. www.sienanet.it/hsc. E-mail: hsc@sienanet.it. 19 units. A/C MINIBAR TEL. 220,000L ($128) double. Rates include breakfast. AE, DC, MC, V. Parking 15,000L ($9) nearby. Bus: 2, A, or N.

This 18th-century villa is beautifully preserved, featuring original terra-cotta floors, sculpted marble fireplaces and stairs, arched entryways, beamed ceilings, and antique wooden furniture. Its grounds include a terraced rear garden overlooking the valley south of Siena. When booking, you may want to specify one of the 12 rooms overlooking the garden and valley beyond it. Each room is well furnished and tasteful, and the hotel features a bar and breakfast veranda. There's no restaurant, but several good eateries are a short walk away.

Villa Belvedere. Belvedere, 53034 Colle di Val d'Elsa Siena. ☎ **0577/920-966.** Fax 0577/924-128. 15 units. TV TEL. 170,000–243,000L ($99–$141) double. Rates include buffet breakfast. AE, DC, MC, V. Exit the autostrada from Florence at Colle di Val d'Elsa Sud and follow the signs.

Villa Belvedere, about 7½ miles from Siena and halfway to San Gimignano, occupies a 1795 building. In 1820 it was the residence of Ferdinand III, archduke of Austria and grand duke of Tuscany, and in 1845 Grand Duke Leopold II lived there. Surrounded by a large park with a pool, the hotel has bar service, a garden with a panorama, and elegant dining rooms where typical Tuscan and classic Italian dishes are served. The old-fashioned guest rooms, furnished in part with antiques, overlook the park. There's also a tennis court.

INEXPENSIVE

Albergo Chiusarelli. Viale Curtatone 9, 53100 Siena. ☎ **0577/280-562.** Fax 0577/271-177. 50 units. TV TEL. 160,000L ($93) double; 220,000L ($128) triple. Rates include breakfast. AE, MC, V. Free parking. Bus: C.

Near Piazza San Domenico, the three-star Chiusarelli is in an ocher-colored 1870 building with Ionic columns and Roman caryatids supporting a second-floor loggia. The interior has been almost completely renovated, and each functional, albeit lackluster, room contains a modern bath and a hair dryer. Ask for a room in back to escape the street noise. The hotel is just at the edge of the old city and is convenient to the parking areas at the sports stadium a 5-minute walk away. The basement-level Ristorante Chiusarelli serves standard full meals—often to tour groups. The cuisine is Tuscan, but it's hardly memorable.

Castagneto Hotel. Via del Cappuccini 39, 53100 Siena. ☎ **0577/45-103.** Fax 0577/283-266. 11 units. TV TEL. 180,000L ($104) double. Breakfast 15,000L ($9). No credit cards. Closed Dec 15–Mar 15. Bus: 1.

On a low hill commanding a view over Siena, about a mile northwest of the center, this modestly proportioned brick villa was built in the 1700s. Today it's a hotel maintained by the Francioni brothers and is set behind a gravel-covered parking lot near a garden with birds, vines, and trees. It contains simple rooms in clean and functional working order. Only doubles are available, though single travelers are often accepted at the rate above. The Castagneto is way down the scale from the hostelries above but is an acceptable choice because of its prices.

✪ **Piccolo Hotel Etruria.** Via Donzelle 3, 53100 Siena. ☎ **0577/288-088.** Fax 0577/288-461. 13 units. TV TEL. 110,000L ($64) double. AE, DC, MC, V. Breakfast 6,000L ($4). Parking 10,000–15,000L ($6–$9) nearby. Closed around Dec 10–27. Bus: A, B, or N.

This small family-run hotel could veritably thumb its nose at the big corporate chains, as it offers equally comfortable modernity with twice the character and at one-fourth the price. In both the main building and the annex across the street, the rooms have tiled floors, wood-toned built-in furnishings with stone-topped desks and end tables, and leather strap chairs. The baths are immaculate. Book early. The only real drawback is the 12:30am curfew.

NEARBY ACCOMMODATIONS

Locanda dell'Amorosa. Località Amorosa, 53048 Sinalunga. ☎ **0577/679497.** Fax 0577/ 632001. E-mail: locanda.amorosa@interbusiness.it. 17 units. A/C MINIBAR TV TEL. 360,000–420,000L ($209–$244) double; 490,000–550,000L ($284–$319) suite. Rates include breakfast. AE, DC, MC, V. Closed Jan 6–Mar 5. From Siena, drive southeast for 28 miles along SS326, following the signs first for Arezzo and then for Perugia.

Until the 1960s, this compound of agrarian buildings was a working farm, with its own school, priest (who conducted masses out of the chapel), and rich traditions of winemaking and olive-oil production. In the 1980s, the compound was transformed into a hotel resembling a small Tuscan village, with 14th-century stonework. Today, thanks to substantial investments by local entrepreneur Carlo Citterio, few other hotels in the region evoke rural Tuscany with as much historic charm or finesse.

The guest rooms are formal, with tasteful furnishings that go well with the rich tapestry of Tuscan life unfolding around the hotel. The upscale restaurant serves main courses at about 30,000L ($17). Open for lunch and dinner daily except Sunday and lunch on Monday, it's supplemented with the less formal platters served in what used to be a storage cellar and is now a wine bar.

There are still about 200 acres of farmland associated with this hotel, about 20 of which are devoted to winemaking for the robust table wines (Sangioveto de Borgo) that continue to be produced here. What used to be the granary is now a convention center, favored for weekend rendezvous of some of the region's corporations.

DINING
MODERATE

Al Mangia. Piazza del Campo 43. ☎ **0577/281-121.** Reservations recommended. Main courses 28,000–48,000L ($16–$28); set-price *menu touristica* 60,000L ($35). AE, DC, MC, V. Daily noon–3:30pm and 7–10pm. Closed Wed Nov–Feb. Bus: A. TUSCAN/INTERNATIONAL.

Al Mangia, one of the most appealing restaurants in the center, has outside tables overlooking the town hall. The building was constructed more or less continuously between 1100 and the late 1600s. The food is artfully cooked and presented by a relatively formal well-trained staff. Menu items change with the seasons but usually include *pici alla Siennese* (thick noodles made only with flour and water) with a sauce of fresh tomatoes, tarragon, and cheese; spicy spaghetti with baby spring onions and sausages; *filetto alla terra di Siena* (grilled steak with a Chianti-and-tarragon sauce); and boneless T-bone steak with rosemary and olive oil, garnished with white beans. The other excellent choices are osso bucco with artichokes and roasted boar *cacciatore* (hunter's style, with mushrooms and onions, available only in season). The homemade desserts include *panforte*, a cake enriched with almonds and candied fruits.

INEXPENSIVE

Al Marsili (Ristorante Enoteca Gallo Nero). Via del Castoro 3. ☎ **0577/47-154.** Reservations recommended. Main courses 15,000–30,000L ($9–$17). AE, DC, MC, V. Tues–Sun 12:30–2:30pm and 7:30–10:30pm. Bus: A. SIENESE/ITALIAN.

This beautiful restaurant stands between the Duomo and Via di Città. You dine beneath crisscrossed ceiling vaults whose russet-colored brickwork was designed centuries ago. The antipasti offer some unusual treats, like polenta with chicken liver sauce; a medley of the best of Siena's cold cuts; and smoked venison, wild boar, and goose blended into a delectable pâté. You can even order sturgeon flavored with fresh herbs. The wide selection of pastas ranges from the typical vegetable soup of Siena (ribollita alla senese) to a risotto with four cheeses. For your second piatti, you might opt for guinea fowl with prunes, pine seeds, and almonds or the wild boar with tomato sauce. The panna cotta is a cream pudding with fresh berries and the dolce Marsili a soft cake flavored with coffee and mascarpone cream.

Da Guido. Vicolo Pier Pettinaio 7. ☎ **0577/280-042.** Reservations required. Main courses 14,000–22,000L ($8–$13). AE, DC, MC, V. Thurs–Tues 12:30–3pm and 7:30–10pm. Bus: A. SIENESE/INTERNATIONAL.

Da Guido is a medieval Tuscan restaurant about 100 feet off the promenade near Piazza del Campo. It's decked out with crusty old beams, aged brick walls, arched ceilings, and iron chandeliers. Our approval is backed up by the public testimony of more than 300 prominent people who've left autographed photos to adorn the walls of the three dining rooms. Meals seem to taste best when preceded with selections from the antipasti table. Pastas that appeal to anyone who loves the taste of spring vegetables include *rustici alla Guido* (spaghetti laced with mushrooms, truffles, and fresh asparagus). Some of the best meat dishes are grilled over the kitchen's charcoal grill and include spicy chicken breast with rosemary, sage, garlic, and Tabasco sauce and beefsteak alla Guido, grilled simply with a sauce of olive oil and rosemary.

La Taverna di Nello (Nello La Taverna). Via del Porrione 28–30. ☎ **0577/289-043.** Reservations required. Main courses 16,000–28,000L ($9–$16). AE, DC, MC, V. Mar–Nov daily noon–3pm and 7–10pm; Dec and Feb Tues–Sat noon–3pm and 7–10pm. Closed Jan. Bus: A, B, or N. TUSCAN/VEGETARIAN.

Here you'll find an ambience that's about as typical of the Sienese region as anything you'll find. On a narrow stone-covered street half a block from Piazza del Campo, the restaurant, as its name implies, offers a tavern decor with brick walls, hanging lanterns, racks of wine bottles, and sheaves of corn hanging from the ceiling. Best of all, you can view the forgelike kitchen with its crew of uniformed cooks busily preparing your dinner from behind a row of hanging copper utensils. Specialties include a salad of fresh radicchio, green lasagne ragoût style, and lamb cacciatore with beans. Freshly made pasta is served every day. Your waiter will gladly suggest a local vintage.

SIENA AFTER DARK

Though Siena doesn't contain many nightclubs, you can mingle with your nocturnal counterparts at **Blue Eyes Pub,** Via Giovanni Duprè 64 (☎ **0577/42-650**), offering an indulgently permissive setting that's neither completely English nor completely Italian. There are touches of marble, battered Formica tables, and five kinds of beer on tap. Mugs begin at 6,500L ($3.75). It's open Wednesday to Monday 6pm to 3am.

6 La Chiantigiana: The Aroma of the Grape

La Chiantigiana, as SS222 is known, twists and turns narrowly through the hilly terrain of Tuscany's famous wine region. **Chianti,** once associated with cheap, sweet Italian wines, has finally captured the attention of connoisseurs with well-crafted *classicos* and *riservas*. This is the result of improved attention to growth and vinification techniques over the last 2 decades. The year 1990 proved to be a landmark, producing a vintage that quickly disappeared from world markets, some labels of which are highly prized by collectors. The area is also home to *vin santo,* a dessert wine something like old sherry that's difficult to find elsewhere.

The entire area is only 30 miles north to south and 20 miles at its widest point. You could rent a bike or scooter for your tour, but you'd have to cope with hills, dust, and

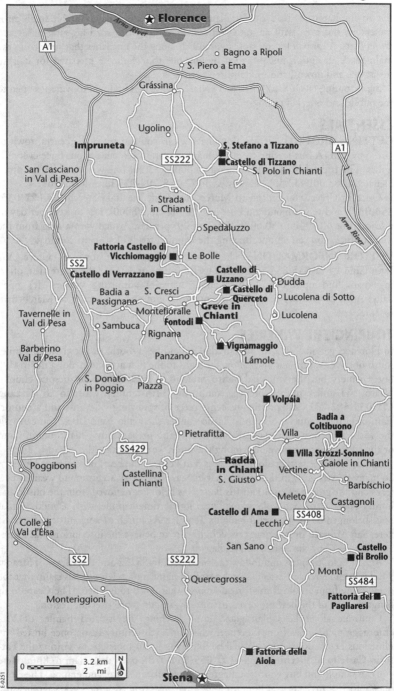

The Chianti Region

Florence

Arno River

A1

Bagno a Ripoli
S. Piero a Ema

Grássina

Ugolino

Impruneta

SS222

S. Stefano a Tizzano
Castello di Tizzano
S. Polo in Chianti

A1

San Casciano
in Val di Pesa

Strada
in Chianti

Spedaluzzo

Arno River

Fattoria Castello di
Vicchiomaggio
Le Bolle

SS2

Castello di Verrazzano

Badia a
Passignano

Tavernelle in
Val di Pesa

Sambuca

Barberino
Val di Pesa

S. Cresci

Montefioralle

Castello di
Uzzano

Castello di
Querceto

Greve in
Chianti

Fontodi

Rignana

Panzano

Dudda

Lucolena di Sotto

Lucolena

Vignamaggio

Lámole

S. Donato
in Poggio

Piazza

Volpaia

Badia a
Coltibuono

SS429

Pietrafitta

Villa

Villa Strozzi-Sonnino

Poggibonsi

Castellina
in Chianti

Radda
in Chianti
S. Giusto

Vertine

Gaiole in Chianti

Barbíschio

Meleto

Castagnoli

Colle di
Val d'Elsa

Castello di Ama

Lecchi

SS408

SS2

SS222

Quercegrossa

San Sano

Castello
di Brolio

Monti

SS484

Monteriggioni

Fattoria dei
Pagliaresi

0   3.2 km
0   2   mi

N

Fattoria della
Aiola

Siena

E-0251

the driving habits of "road king" Italians. Renting an easily maneuverable small car is preferable, but even with an auto you still must deal with road-hogging buses and flying Fiats. A car will let you stop at vineyards along the dirt lanes that stray from the main road, an option not provided by any bus tour. Still, be prepared for hairpin turns, ups and downs, and unidentified narrow lanes.

Signs touting DEGUSTAZIONE or VENDITÀ DIRETTA lead you to wineries open to the public and offering tastings.

ESSENTIALS

GETTING AROUND   If you don't have a car, you can reach the central town of Greve by a **SITA bus** leaving from the main station in Florence about once every 1½ hours. The trip takes an hour and costs 5,000L ($2.90) one-way. A SITA bus from Siena costs 6,000L ($3.50) one-way. Call ☎ **055/294-955** for information.

Once in Greve, you can go to **Marco Ramuzzi,** Via Italo Stecchi 23 (☎ **055/ 853-037**), and rent a mountain bike for 15,000L to 20,000L ($9 to $12) per day or a scooter for 40,000L to 50,000L ($23 to $29) per day. Armed with a map from the tourist office, you can set out, braving the winding roads of Chianti country.

VISITOR INFORMATION   The **tourist office** in the town of Greve, Via Luca Cino 1 (☎ **055/854-5243**), is a useful source of data for the entire area, offering maps and up-to-date listings about wineries admitting visitors. It's open daily: April to October 8am to 1pm and 3 to 6pm and November to March 8am to 2pm.

TOURING THE WINERIES

In Florence, get on SS222 off autostrada E35 and head south. At Petigliolo, 2½ miles south of the city, turn left and follow the signs to the first attraction along the road— not a winery but the vine-clad **Santo Stefano a Tizzano,** a Romanesque church. Nearby, 11 miles from Florence, stands the 11th-century **Castello di Tizzano** (☎ 055/482-737), the prestigious centerpiece of sprawling vineyards and a consortium of farms producing Chianti Classico under the Gallo Nero label. You can visit the 15th- and 16th-century cellars and sample and perhaps buy Chianti or vin santo or the award-winning olive oil, among the finest we've ever tasted.

About 1¼ miles farther along SS222 is **San Polo,** at the heart of Italy's iris industry. So many flowers grow in this region that in May (dates vary according to weather patterns and the growing season) an Iris Festival is held. Far removed from the bustle and hordes of Florence, San Polo seems like a lonely time capsule, with a building that once belonged to the powerful Knights Templar. A church of ancient origins stands here, **San Miniato in Robbiana,** which, if we're to believe the inscription, was consecrated in 1077 by the bishop of Fiesole.

At San Polo, turn left and follow the signs back to SS222 and the village of **Strada,** 9 miles from Florence. "Street" seems a strange name for a town—locals claim that the name came from an old Roman road (*strada*) that ran through here. The **Castello di Mugano,** one of the best preserved in Tuscany, stands guard over the region.

Continue along La Chiantigiana until reaching the isolated hamlet of **Vicchiomaggio,** 12 miles from Florence, where an 11th-century castle once hosted the illustrious Leonardo da Vinci. You'll be following in his footsteps by visiting the **Fattorio Castello di Vicchiomaggio** (☎ 055/854-078), open daily 8am to 8pm. Here you can sample and buy wines, homegrown olive oil, vin santo, and grappa. The estate once sold Tuscany's greatest honey, though that was stopped several years ago because of stiff competition. Overall, the estate controls more than 300 acres, 70 of which are devoted to vineyards.

Nearby, about a mile north of the hamlet of Greve, lies the hamlet of **Verrazzano,** a name that's more familiar to New Yorkers than to Tuscans because of the famous bridge bearing the name of Giovanni da Verrazzano (though the bridge's name is spelled Verrazano—go figure). He left the land of the grape and set to sea in the service of François I of France. In 1524, he was the first European colonial to sail into the harbor of New York and the island of Manhattan before disappearing without a trace on his second voyage to Brazil.

His birthplace still stands on a hilltop overlooking Greve. The **Castello di Verrazzano** (☎ 0577/854-243) is centered around a 10th-century tower surrounded by other buildings from the 15th and 16th centuries. If you call ahead to make a reservation, the castle is open Monday to Friday 8am to 5pm. (Individual tourists are most sincerely welcomed when they show up on either Thursday or Saturday at 11am or 3pm, when tours are geared specifically for them.) Visits through the antique caves usually include a sampling of the estate's well-recommended red and white wines, as well as complimentary platters of salami, cheese, and almond-scented biscuits. You can buy bottles of any of the wines. Unless the staff is rushed, you might even get instruction about how to become a wine snob. If you didn't make reservations, on SS222 heading south toward Greve is a *punto vendita* (sales outlet) open during daylight hours on Saturday and Sunday.

About a mile north of Greve, you come to one of the region's premier attractions, the stunning ✪ **Castello di Uzzano,** Via Uzzano 5 (☎ 0577/854-032), built for the bishop of Florence sometime in the 1200s. Today it's the centerpiece of a 700-acre estate containing 5,500 olive trees, richly stocked stables, and almost 60 acres of vineyards. You can visit in summer merely by dropping in, but in winter you need a reservation. Visitors are welcome Monday to Friday 8am to noon and 1 to 6pm. The castle charges 8,000L ($4.65) to visit its cellars and 12,000L ($7) to explore its 6 acres of award-winning gardens, a holdover from the Renaissance. Later, you can buy wine, olive oil, and honey from the land around the estate.

At one time the castle was the home of Niccolò da Uzzano, a philanthropist/humanist who was a great patron of the arts. For the highlight of your Chianti tour, ask the hardworking and very sophisticated French/Dutch owner, Marion de Jacobert, to prepare one of her picnic lunches, which you can enjoy in the gardens. Meals include prosciutto, the finest Tuscan salami, vine-ripened tomatoes, an assortment of cheeses, country fresh bread, and fruity Chianti, of course. You can even stroll over here in about an hour from the Greve bus station (below).

If your schedule allows you to visit only one Tuscan winery, make it this one, especially if you're dependent on public transport. On the premises are six apartments, with a kitchen, a TV, a phone, a minibar, an air-conditioner, and a stereo, priced at 300,000L ($174) double, without breakfast. Since the owner is an interior decorator, they're stylishly furnished, with antiques like Empire beds resting under wooden ceilings. The kitchens are marvelously equipped with such luxuries as Richard Ginori china. Riding lessons from the stables can be arranged.

The road continues to **Greve in Chianti,** the region's unofficial capital, lying on the banks of the Greve River. The grandest wine fair in Tuscany takes place here every September. Its heartbeat square is the funnel-shaped **Piazza del Mercatale,** with a statue honoring Giovanni da Verrazzano. Greve's castle long ago burned to the ground, but on Piazzetta Santa Croce you can visit the parish church, **Santa Croce,** containing a triptych depicting the Annunciation by Bicci di Lorenzo. Greve is filled with wine shops (*enoteche*), yet we find it far more adventurous to buy from the wineries themselves.

Four miles from Greve, along the road signposted Figline Val d'Arno, you'll find a tranquil estate, the **Castello di Querceto,** Via Dudda 61 (☎ 055/854-9064). It boasts more than 125 acres of vineyards producing several grades of red Chianti and La Corte (made, like Chianti, from the same Sangiovese grapes) and at least two whites (especially Le Giuncaie de Vernaccia). It's centered around a verdant park with an 11th-century castle that's visible only from the outside. The staff is proud to show off their winery and cellars and sell wine, olive oil, and regional produce.

Six miles south of Greve is **Fontodi,** Via San Leonino (☎ 055/852-005), accessible via SS222, near the village of Panzano, half a mile southeast of the hamlet of Sant' Eufrosino. Here you'll find 155 acres of vineyards radiating from a stone villa built in stages between the 18th and 19th century, plus wine-tastings and sales of several grades of Chianti and a reputable table wine known as Flaccianello della Pieve.

Immediately south of Greve on SS222 is another highlight: ✪ **Vignamaggio,** boasting a beautiful Renaissance villa (☎ 055/853-559) that was once the residence of La Gioconda (Lisa Gherardini). With her enigmatic smile, she sat for the most famous portrait of all time, Leonardo da Vinci's *Mona Lisa,* now in Paris's Louvre. You can tour the gardens—some of the most beautiful in Tuscany—Monday to Friday for 15,000L ($9) if you call in advance for a reservation. If the classical statues and towering hedges seem familiar, it means you saw Kenneth Branagh's 1993 *Much Ado About Nothing,* which was shot here. After a tour of the gardens, you can enjoy a wine tasting in the front office. In 1404, the wine of this estate became the first red to be referred to as "Chianti."

From Greve, continue 3½ miles south along the winding Chiantigiana to one of the most enchanting spots in the Chianti, the little agricultural village of **Panzano.** It's worth a walk around, and parts of its medieval castle—which once witnessed battles between Florence and Siena—remain. The village women make the finest embroidery around, and you may want to acquire some from the locals.

Farther south is the delightful hilltop town of **Castellina in Chianti,** with a population of only 3,000. Once a fortified Florentine outpost against the Sienese, it fell to Sienese-Aragonese forces in 1478. But when Siena collapsed in 1555 to Florentine forces, sleepy little Castellina was left to slumber for centuries. That's why the town has preserved its quattrocento look, with its once fortified walls virtually intact. Little houses were constructed into the walls and also nesting on top of them. The covered walkway, Via della Volte, is the most historic in town. Though bottegas here sell Chianti and olive oils, you're better off delaying your purchases until later, because you're on the doorstep of some of the finest wineries in Italy.

After Castellina, detour from SS222 and head east along a tortuous winding road to **Radda in Chianti,** with a population of 1,700. Radda is surrounded by the rugged region of Monti del Chianti and was the ancient capital of Lega del Chianti. The streets of the village still follow their original plan from the Middle Ages. The main square with its somber **Palazzo Comunale,** bearing a fresco from the 1400s, is like walking back into a time capsule.

From Radda, continue along the winding road, signposted Gaiole in Chianti. Along the way you'll come on ✪ **Tenuta Badia a Coltibuono** (☎ 0577/749-498), a wine estate/restaurant (see "Dining" below). Try to time your arrival for lunch, as the Tuscan food is excellent and most typical of the region. Called "the abbey of the good harvest," this place was founded by Vallombrosian monks in 770, and they were the first vine growers of Chianti. For around a century and a half, the Stucchi Prinetti family has been linked to the property. You should call for a reservation to visit. In summer, there are guided tours 10:30am to 1pm, including a wine tasting for 5,000L

($2.90). A shop on site sells the wines of the region, Coltibuono olive oil, wine vinegars aged in casks, strongly scented balsamic vinegar, and exquisite acacia, chestnut, heather, and manna honey.

After a meal, continue 6 miles east to the market town of **Gaiole in Chianti,** with a population of 5,000. You'll come to a local cooperative, the **Agricoltori Chianti Geografico,** Via Mulinaccio 10 (☎ 0577/749-489), a branch of one of the region's largest associations of wine growers (more than 200). About 1¼ miles north of Gaiole in Chianti, it contains a modern winepressing facility with prodigious output of (red) Chianti Classico and (white) Valdarbia. The local *vin santo* is made of trebbiano and malvasia grapes left to dry before pressing and fermented in small oak barrels for about 4 years. The cooperative sells wine by the glass or bottle, as well as olive oil and the Chianti Colli Senesi and the (white) Gallestro wines produced on its lands near Siena. Know in advance that though you won't get a particularly intense dose of antique architecture, the insights you'll gain into the production and marketing of wines make the visit worthwhile.

Use Gaiole as a starting point for interesting wine tours in the area, notably to the towering ✪ **Castello di Brolio** (☎ 0577/7301), 6 miles south along SS484. This is home of the Barone Ricasoli Wine House, famous since the 19th century for Ricasoli's experiments aimed at improving the quality of Chianti. Known as the Iron Baron, he inherited the property in 1829 and in time became one of the creators of a unified Italy and was elected its second prime minister. The property's history goes back to 1141, when Florentine monks came here to live at a site whose vineyards go back to 1005. Caught up many times in the bombardments between the warring forces of Florence and Siena, the castle was later torn down, but then authorities in Florence ordered that it be reconstructed. Visiting hours are Monday to Saturday 9am to noon and 2:30 to 5:30pm; admission is 5,000L ($2.90). A cantina sells the award-winning wines.

If you're a true devotee, you'll find many other wineries in the area—all easily reached by car from Gaiole.

Among the most interesting is **Fattoria dei Pagliaresi,** in the hamlet of Castelnuovo in Berardenga (☎ 0577/359-070), about 7½ miles southeast of Gaiole on SS484. In the mid-1990s, the charming English-speaking owner, Chiara Sanguineti, sold the cellars and vineyards to other growers, but the 300-year-old farmhouse she maintains sits in the middle of vineyards, near ancient olive groves. You can tour the farm; taste or buy wine, grappa, honey, and olive oil; visit lovely gardens; and (if you reserve in advance) enjoy a well-prepared Tuscan farmhouse lunch for 30,000L to 40,000L ($17 to $23).

Another possibility for fruitful and educational visits is 3 miles east, in the hamlet of Rentennano, near the village of Monti. Here **Fattoria San Giusto** (☎ 0577/747-121) is the site of a 12th-century cellar, atop of which later architects built a villa in the 15th century. Centerpiece of 430 acres of farmland, 76 of which are devoted to vineyards, it produces two grades of Chianti as well as a simple table wine (Percarlo) connoisseurs find surprisingly flavorful.

If you backtrack, taking SS408 to Siena, you can follow the signposts about 6 miles north to **Fattoria della Aiola,** near the hamlet of Vagliagli, 12½ miles southwest of Gaiole. Site of a ruined medieval castle (only a wall and moat remain) and a 19th-century villa (not open to the public), it features 90 acres of vineyards that produce Chianti, Sangiovese, grappa, and Spumante "Aioli Brut" (a sparkling wine similar to champagne). The winery even produces olive oil and vinegar. This place receives a lot of visitors, sometimes arriving by bus, so advance reservations or at least a phone call before arriving are a good idea.

ACCOMMODATIONS ALONG LA CHIANTIGIANA

The atmospheric Tuscan inns along the Chianti road are fabled, and many motorists like to break up a visit between Florence and Siena with a night at one of these hotels. The best centers for overnighting are Greve in Chianti, Radda, Gaiole, and Castellina in Chianti (our favorite). Many of these inns are also noted for their good food and wine. Even if you're not a guest, you might visit for a meal.

Albergo del Chianti. Piazza Matteotti 86, 50022 Greve in Chianti. ☎ and fax **055/ 85-37-63.** 22 units. A/C MINIBAR TV TEL. 150,000L ($90) double. Rate includes breakfast. Half-board 35,000L ($20) per person. AE, MC, V.

At the edge of Greve's main square, with a facade and foundation as old (more than 1,000 years) as the square itself, this is a charming small inn whose accommodations look out over a microcosm of rural Italy. Each of the cozy rooms is painted in a different color (blue, red, pink, whatever) and has some kind of wrought-iron bedstead. Aside from breakfast, dinner is the only meal served, and only to hotel residents; it's always accompanied by a selection of regional wines.

Castello di Spaltenna. Pieve di Spaltenna, 53013 Gaiole in Chianti. ☎ **0577/749-483.** Fax 0577/749-269. 26 units. A/C MINIBAR TV TEL. 310,000–395,000L ($180–$229) double; 450,000–490,000L ($261–$284) junior suite for two. Rates include American breakfast. AE, DC, MC, V. Closed mid-Nov to mid-Mar.

One of the region's most idiosyncratic and historic hotels is on a hill above the wine-producing village of Gaiole. Opened during the Middle Ages as a monastery, it retains some of its medieval flair, despite several enlargements and modifications. In the compound are a small medieval chapel, two soaring towers, and several stone-sided annexes, one housing some of the junior suites. The rooms are cozy and traditionally furnished, with all the modern conveniences. Some have fireplaces, and each enjoys some kind of view over the surrounding landscapes. Look for wrought-iron or wooden headboards and terra-cotta floors whose tiles, in some cases, are as much as a thousand years old. The restaurant serves lunch and dinner daily noon to 2pm and 7:30 to 9:30pm, with main courses at 29,000L to 36,000L ($17 to $21). Tuscan specialties include Florentine beefsteak, homemade pastas, steaming minestrone, and fresh vegetables from nearby suppliers. There's also a pool.

Hotel Il Girarrosta. Via Roma 41, 53107 Radda in Chianti. ☎ **0577/738-010.** 9 units. 60,000L ($35) double. Rates include breakfast. No credit cards.

Smaller and more informal than Villa Miranda (below), this hotel is the bargain of Chianti. It has been a family-run inn since 1927 at the center of Radda village. The rooms are simple but neat and comfortable. A lot of the owners' energy is funnelled into the wholesome-looking trattoria, which operates daily at both lunch and dinner. Serving Tuscan specialties redolent with Mediterranean herbs and olives, it charges 25,000L ($15) for a set-price meal any day except Wednesday. The building is very old (no one is quite sure how old) but has been renovated.

Hotel Salivolpi. Via Fiorentina 89, 53011 Castellina in Chianti. ☎ and fax **0577/740-484.** www.vol.it/colline_verdi. E-mail: colverd@mbox:vol.it. 19 units. TEL. 140,000–150,000L ($81–$87) double. Rates include breakfast. AE, DC, MC, V.

The good living continues at this farm setting against a backdrop that looks like a Renaissance painting in the Uffizi. After it was turned from farm to hotel in 1984, Salivolpi has been visited by some of the world's most discriminating travelers, drawn to its setting and ambience. The rooms are spread across three buildings, each decorated with Tuscan antiques and beautifully maintained. There's a pool and garden but no restaurant (some good ones are a short drive away).

⭐ **Hotel Tenuta di Ricavo.** Ricavo, 53011 Castellina in Chianti (2 miles north of town). ☎ **0577/740-221.** Fax 0577/741-014. www.romantikhotels.com/rhcaste. E-mail: ricavo@ chiantinet.it. 23 units. MINIBAR TV TEL. 265,000–420,000L ($154–$244) double; 370,000– 463,000L ($215–$269) suite. Rates include breakfast. MC, V. Closed early Nov–Apr 30.

Our favorite in the district, this place is a fantasy of what a Tuscan inn should look like. In fact, it's like a medieval hamlet of stone-built houses, complete with a pool. On nippy nights guests gather in the public lounge with its blazing fireplace. The innkeepers rent beautifully furnished and maintained rooms. The restaurant, La Pecora Nera, run by Alessandro Lobrano, serves an excellent Tuscan cuisine, accompanied by the delectable wines of the Chianti country. Surrounding the compound are 445 acres of woodlands, composed mainly of holm oak and cypress. The area is threaded through with paths, ideal for excursions on foot or a mountain bike.

La Villa Miranda. Loc. Villa, 53107 Radda in Chianti. ☎ **0577/738-021.** Fax 0577/ 738-668. 60 units. 130,000–150,000L ($75–$87) double. Breakfast 15,000L ($9). MC, V.

Villa Miranda, .6 miles east of Radda, was built on the site of a posthouse and became a small inn in 1842. The reigning duenna is Donna Miranda herself, somewhat of a local legend. Nowadays, most of the antiques-filled rooms in the outbuildings have amenities like minibars, air-conditioning, TVs, and phones, while those in the main structure are rather basic. The restaurant is one of the finest in the area, specializing in regional fare like wild boar cooked in white wine. Mamma Miranda claims her ribollita is the best vegetable soup in Tuscany and no one disagrees! Her homemade ravioli is equally delectable, as is her tender and well-flavored Florentine beefsteak. If you've always resisted ordering mutton, try Mamma Miranda's. You might become a convert. There are two pools and a tennis court.

Villa Casalecchi. Casalecchi 18, 53001 Castellina in Chianti. ☎ **0577/740-240.** Fax 0577/ 741-111. 19 units. TV TEL. 300,000–380,000L ($174–$220) double; 400,000L ($232) suite. Rates include breakfast. AE, DC, MC, V. Closed Nov to 1 week before Easter.

Almost as elegant as the Tenuta di Ricavo, this four-star hotel is built against a hill. You arrive on the hilltop and enter into what's actually the top floor. Though the building is quite old, it was remodeled extensively in 1984 and boasts a refined Tuscan ambience with beautifully furnished rooms. The restaurant is used for catering to some of the world's finest palates and serves a perfect Tuscan cuisine, with extremely fresh ingredients. In summer, it's possible to dine in the evergreen garden. You can swim in a panoramic pool or play tennis on the court (there's even a bowling alley). It's also possible to go on excursions into the Chianti country on a mountain bike or on horseback (there are various stables in the area).

DINING ALONG LA CHIANTIGIANA

Some of the best food in Italy is served in Chianti—all dishes accompanied by the wine of the region. Many visitors view a stop at one of these restaurants almost as important as touring the wineries. We've selected the places that serve the finest food in the area—all at affordable prices.

GREVE & ENVIRONS

Borgo Antico. Via Case Sparse 15, Lucolena. ☎ **055/851-024.** Reservations recommended. Set-price menus 40,000–60,000L ($23–$35) without wine, 50,000–80,000L ($29–$46) with wine. AE, MC, V. Mar–Sept daily noon–3pm and 7–9:30pm, Oct–Feb Fri 7–9:30pm, Sat noon–3pm, and 7–9:30pm, Sun noon–3pm. Nov–Jan, Fri 7–9:30pm, Sat noon–3pm and 7–9:30pm, Sun noon–3pm. AE, MC, V. Drive 10 miles northeast of Greve along SS222. TUSCAN.

Charming and hospitable and opened 30 years ago in a 200-year-old compound of farmhouses and barns, this country inn is more upscale than you might think, thanks to the hardworking efforts of the Marunti family, who haul in ultrafresh produce from nearby farms every morning. The pastas are always made fresh on the premises, and the desserts, especially such relatively simple concoctions as crema cotta and tiramisu, are wonderful. Don't expect fish, as it doesn't appear on any menu. Florentine-style beefsteaks are among the best in the region, tender and succulent and loaded with Mediterranean herbs and olive oil. Filets of turkey grilled with olive oil and veal scallops with lemon juice or wine are worth the drive. As you dine, you'll enjoy views of the nearby slopes of Monte San Michele.

On the premises are a trio of simple guest rooms. None has a TV or phone, but the solid stone walls and old-time setting more than compensate. Each has a private bathroom, though in one case it's outside the bedroom. Doubles are 80,000L to 90,000L ($46 to $52). Because the owners spend their mornings out buying supplies for the days' cooking, no breakfast is served.

Bottega del Moro. Piazza Trieste 14R, Greve in Chianti. ☎ **055/853-753.** Reservations required. Main courses 17,000–27,000L ($10–$16). AE, DC, MC, V. Thurs–Tues 12:15–2:15pm and 7:15–9:30pm. Closed Nov and the 1st week of June. TUSCAN.

Our favorite restaurant in the center of Greve occupies an early 20th-century stone-sided building that was a blacksmith's shop for many years. (Locals referred to the blacksmith, because of the charcoal that blackened his face, as "The Moor," and ever since the nickname "Lair of the Moor" has been associated with this restaurant.) Maintained by English-speaking Elizabeth Tassi and her husband, Sergio, who runs the kitchen, it specializes in a lightened, less oily version of Tuscan cuisine. Menu items include homemade ravioli with butter and sage; Florentine-style tripe, beefsteaks, and roasted rabbit from nearby fields; and skewered meat grilled to perfection. The unusual modern paintings ringing the two dining rooms are by a well-known local artist, Alvaro Baralie, a friend of the owners. A flowering terrace provides limited extra seating on the square during clement weather.

La Cantinetta. Via Mugnano 93, Spedaluzzo (1½ miles north of Greve). ☎ **055/857-2000.** Reservations recommended. Main courses 12,000–23,000L ($7–$13). AE, DC, MC, V. Daily noon–2:30pm and 7:30–10:30pm. Closed Tues Nov–Mar. From Greve, follow S93 toward Firenze for 1½ miles. TUSCAN.

To experience rural Tuscany, consider a meal in the garden of this stone-sided restaurant built around 1800 as a farmhouse. It's been serving generous portions of pastas, risottos, and *peposo* (chunks of beef stewed in red wine with tomatoes and peppers) since the 1970s, usually to residents of the surrounding region who sometimes drive long distances to reach it. Tagliata with truffles or porcinis is a sure winner, as is chicken cooked with Tuscan vegetables. Adventurous palates sometimes enjoy the stuffed rabbit or stuffed pigeon. Thanks to the setting ringed with the agrarian bounty of Tuscany, the food actually seems to taste better than if it had been served in a more urban venue.

Montagliari. Via di Montagliari 27, Panzano (between Montagliari and Greve, a half-mile north of Panzano). ☎ **055/852-184.** Reservations recommended. Main courses 24,000–27,000L ($14–$16). MC, V. Tues–Sun 1–3pm and 7:30–9pm. TUSCAN.

Associated with a local vineyard, this is a representative of agrarian Tuscan charm and culinary authenticity. Tables are set out in a garden, and the place is decorated like an old Tuscan farmhouse. The specialty here is wild boar cacciatora, which deserves a star. You can also order roasted pork or rabbit with potatoes, tortellini stuffed with minced meat, or roasted lamb In the age-old style of the Tuscan hills. A plate of penne with raw chopped tomatoes and homegrown basil disappears quickly.

CASTELLINA & ENVIRONS

Albergaccio di Castellina. Via Fiorentina 35, Castellina (on road to San Donato). ☎ **0557/ 741-042.** Reservations suggested. Main courses 22,000–27,000L ($13–$16); fixed-price menu 65,000L ($38). No credit cards. Mon, Fri, and Sat 12:30–2pm; Mon–Sat 7:30–9:30pm. Closed Nov 1–20. TUSCAN.

With rough stone walls and beamed ceilings, this restaurant is a Tuscan cliché of charm, noted for its regional fare prepared with very fresh ingredients deftly handled by a local staff. A winning combination is the platter of gnocchi and ricotta with white truffles, or you can order a dish of wide noodles cooked with wild boar or ravioli stuffed with shredded pork and chestnuts. The tender herb-flavored Tuscan lamb is a dish to savor.

Antica Trattoria La Torre. Piazza del Comune 15, Castellina in Chianti. ☎ **0577/ 740-236.** Reservations required in summer. Main courses 12,000–20,000L ($7–$12). AE, DC, MC, V. Sat–Thurs noon–2:30pm and 7:30–9:30pm. Closed Sept 1–15. TUSCAN.

This old family-run dining room on the principal square depends on the harvest from the field, stream, and air to keep its good cooks busy. The Tuscan game, the birds (like pigeons and guinea fowl), and the local beef are the finest in the area. The Florentine beefsteak alone is worth the trip. The surroundings may be simple, but the food is sublime and reasonably priced.

Il Vignale. Via XX Settembre 23, Radda in Chianti. ☎ **0577/738-094.** Reservations recommended. Main courses 30,000–45,000L ($17–$26). AE, DC, MC, V. Daily 1–2:30pm and 7:30–9:30pm. Closed Jan–Feb. TUSCAN.

This rustic yet elegant place is the best family-run dining room in the area, turning out a Tuscan cuisine that's flavorful and prepared with the freshest of ingredients. A habitué told us, "This is as close as you can get to being served food that you might be offered in a local home." It's popular with residents and visitors alike. Every day something new appears, and the cuisine is quite creative.

Tenuta Badia a Coltibuono. ☎ **0577/749-031.** Reservations required. Main courses 22,000–26,000L ($13–$15); fixed-price menus 30,000–40,000L ($17–$23); platters from 22,000L ($13). MC, V. Apr–Oct daily 12:30–3pm and 7–9pm. Closed Nov–Mar. MC, V. TUSCAN.

This restaurant occupies a medieval building adjacent to the winery recommended above. It's very much a family affair, with owner Paolo Stucchi Prinetti the host in the dining room and the chef preparing food from recipes given a touch of originality by the mistress of the domain, Lorenza de' Medici. Dishes are based on simple seasonal ingredients whose flavors are accented by fresh herbs and greens. Fresh pasta is made daily, and regional meat specialties include rabbit, lamb, and the extraordinary Chianina beef of Tuscany. Local goat and sheep's milk cheese are served, and homemade desserts conclude the meals. The wine list highlights the vintages of Coltibuono.

7 Arezzo

50 miles SE of Florence

The most landlocked of all towns or cities of Tuscany, Arezzo was originally an Etruscan settlement and later a Roman center. The city flourished in the Middle Ages before its capitulation to Florence.

The walled town grew up on a hill, but large parts of the ancient city, including native son Petrarch's house, were bombed during World War II before the area fell to the Allied advance in the summer of 1944. Apart from Petrarch, famous sons of Arezzo have included Vasari, the painter/architect remembered chiefly for his history of the Renaissance artists, and Guido of Arezzo (sometimes known as Guido Monaco), who gave the world the modern musical scale before his death in the mid-11th century.

Today, Arezzo looks a little rustic, as if the glory of the Renaissance has long past it by. But this isn't surprising when you consider that it lost its prosperity when Florence annexed it in 1348. Arezzo might look a bit down at the heel, but it really isn't. The city today has one of the biggest jewelry industries in Western Europe. Little firms on the outskirts turn out an array of rings and chains, and bank vaults are overflowing with gold ingots. However, the inner core, which most visitors want to explore, didn't share in this gold and looks as if it needs a rehab.

ESSENTIALS

GETTING THERE   A **train** comes from Florence at intervals of 20 to 60 minutes throughout the day. The trip takes between 40 and 60 minutes, costing 7,500 to 13,000L ($4.35 to $8) one-way, depending on its speed. In Arezzo, trains depart and arrive at the **Stazione Centrale,** Piazza della Repubblica (☎ 0575/22-663). Because there are no direct trains from Siena to Arezzo, rail passengers from Siena are required to make hot, prolonged, and tiresome rail transfers in the junction of Chiusi. Therefore, unless it happens to be Sunday (see below), it's better to opt for travel by bus if your point of origin is Siena.

Because of complicated transfers required en route and travel time of as much as 2½ hours each way, trips by **bus** from Florence to Arezzo isn't a good idea. Bus routes from Siena to Arezzo, however, are preferable to the bothersome train transfers. Monday to Saturday, five buses per day travel from Siena directly to Arezzo. On Sunday, however, you'll have to take the train. For information on bus routes, in Arezzo, call **ATAM Point** at ☎ 0575/38-26-51.

If you have a **car** and are in Rome, head north on A1; from Florence, head south on A1. In both directions, the turn-off for Arezzo is clearly marked.

VISITOR INFORMATION   The **tourist office,** at Piazza della Repubblica 28 (☎ 0575/377-678), is open April to September every Monday to Saturday 9am to 1:15pm and 3 to 7pm and Sunday 9am to 1pm; October to May, it's open Monday to Saturday 9am to 1:15pm and 3 to 7pm and Sunday 9am to 1pm.

EXPLORING THE TOWN

The biggest event on the Arezzo calendar is the **Giostra del Saraceno,** staged the third Sunday of June and the first Sunday of September on Piazza Grande. Horsemen in medieval costumes reenact the lance-charging joust ritual—with balled whips cracking in the air—as they have since the 13th century. But you should visit **Piazza Grande** at any time of the year for the medieval and Renaissance palaces and towers that flank it, including the 16th-century loggia by Vasari.

If you have only an hour for Arezzo, race to the ✪ **Basilica di San Francesco,** Piazza San Francesco (☎ 0575/20-630), a Gothic church finished in the 14th century for the Franciscans. Inside is a Piero della Francesca masterpiece, a fresco cycle called *Legend of the True Cross.* His frescoes are remarkable for their grace, clearness, dramatic light effects, well-chosen colors, and ascetic severity. Vasari credited della Francesca as a master of the laws of geometry and perspective, and Sir Kenneth Clark called Piero's frescoes "the most perfect morning light in all Renaissance painting." The frescoes depict the burial of Adam, Solomon receiving the queen of Sheba at the court (the most memorable scene), the dream of Constantine with the descent of an angel, and the triumph of the Holy Cross with Heraclius, among other subjects. You can visit daily 8:30am to noon and 2 to 6:30pm. Admission is free. *Warning:* The frescoes are being restored until 2000 and only limited sightseeing is possible.

Santa Maria della Pieve, Corso Italia (☎ **0575/22-629**), is a Romanesque church with a front of three open-air loggias (each pillar designed uniquely). The 14th-century bell tower is known as "the hundred holes," as it's riddled with windows. Inside, the church is bleak and austere, but there's a notable polyptych, *The Virgin with Saints,* by one of the Sienese Lorenzetti brothers (Pietro), painted in 1320. The church is open Monday to Saturday 8am to 1pm and 3 to 7pm and Sunday 8am to 1pm and 3 to 6:30pm. Admission is free.

A short walk away is **Petrarch's House,** Via dell'Orto 28A (☎ **0575/24-700**), which has been rebuilt after war damage. Born at Arezzo in 1304, Petrarch was a great Italian lyrical poet and humanist who immortalized his love, Laura, in his sonnets. His house is open Monday to Saturday 10am to noon and Monday to Friday 3 to 5pm; admission is free. Ring the bell to enter.

Also notable is the **House of Vasari,** Via XX Settembre 55 (☎ **0575/300-301**), purchased by the artist—and the first art history writer—in 1540. There are works by Visari himself, but it's apparent that his fame rests on his *Lives of the Artists* more than it does on his actual artwork. His best works are *Virtue, Envy, and Fortune* and *Deposition.* Other works displayed are by Santi di Tito, Alessandro Allori, and Il Poppi. Admission is free, and the house is open daily 9am to 7pm.

You might also want to check out **Il Duomo,** Piazza del Duomo (☎ **0575/ 23-991**), built in the pure Gothic style—rare for Tuscany. The cathedral was begun in the 13th century, but the final touches (the facade) weren't applied until the outbreak of World War I. Its art treasures include stained-glass windows (1519 to 1523) by Guillaume de Marcillat and a main altar in the Gothic style. Its main treasure, though, is *Mary Magdalene,* a Piero della Francesca masterpiece. It's open daily 7am to 12:30pm and 3 to 6:30pm. Admission is free.

SHOPPING

Arezzo hosts one of Europe's biggest gold jewelry industries. In the very center of town, around **Piazza Grande,** are dozens of antiques shops that have earned for Arezzo the title of "ye olde curiosity shop of Tuscany." These spill out onto the piazza during the **Antiques Fair,** held the first weekend of every month.

ACCOMMODATIONS

There are no outstanding hotels that'll induce you to linger, the way you might in San Gimignano or Siena. They're comfortable and affordable but usually attract people in Arezzo on "gold business."

Hotel Continentale. Piazza Guido Monaco 7, 52100 Arezzo. ☎ **0575/20-251.** Fax 0575/ 350-485. 74 units. MINIBAR TV TEL. 160,000L ($93) double. Breakfast 15,000L ($9). AE, DC, MC, V. Parking 18,000L ($10).

This modern geometric hotel is certainly different from the more antique architecture characterizing most of the town's core. However, less than 200 yards from the town's rail station, the Continentale offers affordable accommodations in an early 1950s setting. Renovations have kept the place up-to-date. About 70% of the rooms (scattered over five efficiently decorated floors) have air-conditioning, and since the price is the same for all rooms, it pays to request one specifically in advance.

DINING

✪ **Buca di San Francesco.** Via San Francesco 1. ☎ **0575/23-271.** Reservations recommended. Main courses 16,000–36,000L ($9–$21). AE, DC, MC, V. Wed–Sun 12:30–3pm and 7–11pm. ITALIAN.

In the historic core, this admirable restaurant—the city's finest—is in the cellar of a building from the 1300s; it's decorated with medieval references and strong Tuscan colors of sienna and blue. Menu items include pollo del Valdarno arrosto (roast chicken from the valley of the Arno) flavored with anise, homemade tagliolini with tomatoes and ricotta, and calves' liver with onions. A popular first course is green noodles with a rich meat sauce, oozing with creamy cheese and topped with a hunk of fresh butter. All ingredients are fresh, many of the staples are produced in-house, and even the olive oil is from private sources not shared by other restaurants.

8 Gubbio: A Center for Ceramics

25 miles NE of Perugia, 135 miles N of Rome, 57 miles SE of Arezzo, 34 miles N of Assisi

Gubbio is one of the best-preserved medieval towns in Italy. It has modern apartments and stores on its outskirts, but once you press through that, you're firmly back in the Middle Ages. The best-known streets of its medieval core are **Via XX Settembre, Via dei Consoli, Via Galeotti,** and **Via Baldassini.** All these are in the old town (Città Vecchia), set against the steep slopes of Monte Ingino.

Since Gubbio is off-the-beaten track, it remains a fairly sleepy backwater today except for intrepid shoppers who drive here to shop for ceramics (see below). Gubbio is almost as well known for ceramics as is Deruta. The last time Gubbio entered the history books was in 1944, when 40 hostages were murdered by the Nazis. Today, the central **Piazza dei Quaranta Martiri** is named for and honors those victims.

ESSENTIALS

GETTING THERE   Gubbio doesn't have a rail station of its own, so **train** passengers headed for Gubbio from other parts of Italy get off at the nearby rail station of Fossato di Vico, 12 miles away, then transfer to one of the frequent buses that make the short trip on to Gubbio. Fossato di Vico lies astride the rail lines stretching between Rome and Ancona. One-way bus transfers to Gubbio from Fossato di Vico cost 3,700L ($2.15).

There are about eight **buses** a day into Gubbio from Perugia (see below). Trip time takes about 65 minutes, and a one-way ticket is 7,400L ($4.30). Buses arrive and depart from Piazza 40 Martiri (☎ 075/922-0066) in the heart of town.

If you've got a **car** and are coming from Rome, follow A1 to Orte, then take SS3 north 88 miles to its intersection with SS298 at Schéggia. Go southwest on SS298 for 8 miles to Gubbio. From Florence, take A1 south to Orte, then follow the directions above. From Perugia, this turnoff is 25 miles northeast on the SS298.

VISITOR INFORMATION   The **tourist office,** at Piazza Oderisi 6 (☎ 075/922-0693), is open Monday to Saturday 8:30am to 1:30pm and 3:30 to 6:30pm and Sunday 9:30am to 12:30pm.

EXPLORING THE OLD TOWN

If the weather is right, you can take a cable car up to **Monte Ingino,** at a height of 2,690 feet, for a panoramic view of the area. Service is daily: June to August 8:30am to 8pm (to 7:30pm April, May, and September to March). A round-trip ticket is 6,500L ($3.75).

Back in Gubbio, you can set about exploring a town that knew its golden age in the 1300s. Begin at **Piazza Grande,** the most important square. Here you can visit the **Palazzo dei Consoli** (☎ 075/927-4298), a Gothic edifice housing the famed bronze *tavole eugubine,* a series of tablets as old as Christianity, discovered in the 15th century. The tablets contain writing in the mysterious Umbrian language. The museum has a display of antiques from the Middle Ages and a collection of not very worthwhile paintings. It's open daily: April to September 10am to 1pm and 3 to 6pm and October to March 10am to 1pm and 2 to 5pm. Admission is 5,000L ($2.90) adults; children under 12 are free.

The other major sight is the **Ducal Palace (Palazzo Ducale),** Via Ducale (☎ 075/ 927-5872). This palace is associated with the memories (not always good ones) of the ruling dukes of Urbino. It was built for Federico of Montefeltro and is open Monday to Saturday 9am to 1pm and 2:30 to 7pm and Sunday 9am to 1pm; admission is 4,000L ($2.30). After visiting the palace, you can go inside **Il Duomo,** Via Ducale (☎ 075/927-3980), across the way. The cathedral is a relatively unadorned pink Gothic building with some stained-glass windows from the 12th century. It has a single nave. It's open daily 9am to 12:30pm and 3:30 to 8:30pm, and admission is free.

Gubbio has some minor attractions as well, including the **Chiesa di San Francesco,** Piazza Quaranta Martiri (☎ 075/927-3460), built in the Gothic style with three apses and one of the earliest churches to honor St. Francis. The interior walls of the north apse are covered with a set of stunning frescoes executed in the early 1400s. The name of local painter Ottaviano Nelli is relatively unknown, but reproductions of his work often appear in Italian art books. Admission is free, and it's open daily 9am to 1pm and 2 to 7pm.

You can also visit the **Teatro Romano,** Via del Teatro Romano, open daily 9am to 1pm. Dating from the time of Augustus, this theater is now a ruin. Admission is free.

SHOPPING

This is the major reason many visitors flock here. Gubbio's fame as a ceramics center had its beginnings to the 14th century. In the 1500s, the industry rose to the height of its fame. Sometime during this period, a Mastro Giorgio pioneered a particularly intense, iridescent ruby red that awed his competitors. Today, pottery workshops are found all over town, the beautiful flowery plates lining walls of shop doorways. You can't miss them.

Two of the best outlets are in the town center. Head for **Ceramica Rampini,** Via Leonardo da Vinci 94 (☎ 075/927-2963), or its largest competitor, **La Mastro Giorgio,** 3 Piazza Grande (☎ 075/927-1574). La Mastro Giorgio opens its factory, at Via Tifernate 10 (☎ 075/927-3616), about half a mile from the center, to well-intentioned visitors who phone in advance for a convenient hour.

Gubbio is known for more than pots and vases: Its replicas of medieval crossbows (*balestre*) are prized as children's toys and macho decorative ornaments by aficionados of such things. If you want to add a touch of medieval authenticity to your den or office (costing from 20,000L/$12 for a cheap version to as much as 150,000L/$87 for something much more substantial), head for **Negocio Medioevo,** Ponte d'Assi (☎ 075/927-2596), or **Rafael & Giuliani Morelli,** Ponte d'Assi (☎ 075/ 927-2934).

ACCOMMODATIONS

Hotel Gattapone. Via Beni 6, 06024 Gubbio. ☎ **075/927-2417.** Fax 075/927-1269. 18 units. MINIBAR TV TEL. 140,000–160,000L ($81–$93) double. Rates include breakfast. AE, DC, MC, V. Closed Jan. Parking 5,000L ($2.90).

Originally a palazzo, this is a pleasant but not particularly plush hotel at the bottom of a narrow alleyway whose flagstone pavement is spanned with soaring medieval buttresses. What it lacks in luxuries it makes up for in low prices. Although the furniture throughout is modern and relatively uninspired, there are a few handcrafted details, such as timbered ceilings and arches of chiseled stone. Breakfast, the only meal served, is offered in a sun-flooded breakfast room where large windows offer glimpses of a tiny garden. For other meals, the staff refers guests to the Taverna del Lupo (below). In 1997, the hotel received a full refurbishment.

Hotel San Marco. Via Perugino 5, 06024 Gubbio. ☎ **075/922-0234.** Fax 075/927-3716. 63 units. TV TEL. 140,000L ($81) double. Rates include breakfast. AE, DC, MC, V. Parking 15,000L ($9) in nearby garage.

Its unpromising location on the busiest corner in town is the San Marco's only drawback. Other than that, this is a worthwhile, not particularly expensive hotel near a municipal parking lot. Built in stone-sided stages between 1300 and the 1700s, it contains an arbor-covered terrace and traditionally furnished rooms that are comfortable and well maintained. The Restaurant San Marco serves Italian food beneath russet-colored brick vaulting.

Palace Hotel Bosone. Via XX Settembre 22, 06024 Gubbio. ☎ **075/922-0698.** Fax 075/922-0552. 30 units. MINIBAR TV TEL. 125,000–140,000L ($73–$81) double; 220,000–295,000L ($128–$171) suite. Breakfast 10,000L ($6). AE, DC, MC, V. Closed 3 weeks in Feb. Free self-parking nearby.

This hotel is in the town's most scenic location, and it's also one of the most historic, having once housed Dante Alighieri when it was owned by a patrician Gubbian family, the Bosone clan. Set at the meeting point of an almost endless flight of stone steps and a narrow street in the upper regions of town, it was built in the 1300s and enlarged during the Renaissance. The three-story stone building was converted from a private home into a hotel in 1974, welcoming guests ever since into cozy rooms trimmed with stone. Breakfast is the only meal served; for other meals, the staff directs guests to the Taverna del Lupo (below).

✪ Villa Montegranelli. 2 miles SW of Gubbio (reached along Via Buozzi). ☎ **075/922-20-185.** Fax 075/927-33-72. 20 units. TV TEL. 175,000L ($102) double. Breakfast 25,000L ($15). DC, MC, V.

The area's most tranquil retreat isn't in Gubbio itself but in this lovely restored 18th-century manor house in a panoramic setting with a distant view of Gubbio. The rooms are beautifully furnished, often with antiques, and the full baths are completely modern and kept in perfect condition. The public rooms have been restored in keeping with their original architecture of wood ceilings and stone walls. The mattresses are new and firm, and the staff is among the most helpful and efficient in the area, providing such thoughtful extras as placing a basket of fresh fruit in your room every day.

Even if you can't stay here, consider calling ahead and visiting for a refined meal. A full dinner starts at 50,000L ($29). Meals begin with market-fresh antipasti, a superb selection, following with one of the superb homemade pastas, especially those with fresh asparagus. Veal in beet sauce is a classic and ancient dish.

DINING

Ristorante Federico de Montefeltro. Via della Repubblica 35. ☎ **075/927-3949.** Reservations recommended. Main courses 16,000–25,000L ($9–$15). AE, DC, MC, V. Fri–Wed noon–3pm and 7–10:30pm; July–Aug daily noon–3pm and 7–10:30pm. Closed Feb. ITALIAN/UMBRIAN.

Named after the feudal lord who built the ducal palace, this restaurant stands beside steeply inclined flagstones in the oldest part of the city. Inside is a pair of tavern-style dining rooms ringed with exposed stone and pinewood planking. Many of the specialties are based on ancient regional recipes, though the selection of tasty antipasti covers the traditions of most of the Italian peninsula. Menu items include platters garnished with truffles, roast suckling pig, several preparations of polenta, and spaghetti with mushrooms and tomato. Fresh fish is visible and available on Friday. You'll also be served a local version of unleavened bread fried in oil as part of the meal. The dessert specialty is a Chantilly torte.

Taverna del Lupo. Via Giovanni Ansidei 21. ☎ **075/927-4368.** Reservations recommended. Main courses 18,000–30,000L ($10–$17). AE, DC, MC, V. Tues–Sun 12:15–3pm and 7pm–midnight. Closed Jan. ITALIAN/UMBRIAN.

This is the most authentically medieval of the many competing restaurants in Gubbio. Built in the 1200s, with unusual rows of tiles, it contains ceilings supported by barrel vaults and ribbing of solid stone, from which hang iron chandeliers. For such a relatively modest place, the menu is sophisticated and filled with the rich bounty from this part of Italy, each dish deftly prepared by a talented kitchen staff. Menu items include a terrine of duck studded with truffles, suprême of pheasant, rich minestrones, and many of the pork, veal, and beef dishes that are distinctly Tuscan.

9 Perugia: Capital of Umbria

50 miles SE of Arezzo, 117 miles N of Rome, 96 miles SE of Florence

Perugia was one of a dozen major cities in the mysterious Etruscan galaxy, and here you can peel away the epochs. For example, one of the town gates is called the **Arco di Augusto (Arch of Augustus).** The loggia spanning the arch dates from the Renaissance, but the central part is Roman. Builders from both periods used the reliable Etruscan foundation, which was the work of architects who laid stones to last.

Today the city—home to luscious Perugina chocolate—is the capital of Umbria; it has retained much of its Gothic and Renaissance charm, though it has been plagued with wars and swept up in disastrous events. The city is one of universities and art academies, attracting a young, vibrant crowd—some of whom can be seen in one of the zillions of local bars, pizzerias, music shops, and cafes enjoying the famous chocolate *baci* (kisses). To capture the essence of the Umbrian city, you must head for **Piazza IV Novembre** in the heart of Perugia. During the day, the square is overrun, so try to go late at night when the old town is sleeping. That's when the ghosts come out to play.

ESSENTIALS

GETTING THERE   Perugia has **rail** links with Rome and Florence, but connections can be awkward. About 2 trains per day from Rome often connect in Foligno, where, if you miss a train, there can be a wait up to an hour or more. If possible, try to get one of the infrequent direct trains that take only 3 hours or even an IC train that cuts the trip down to 2½ hours. A one-way ticket from Rome is 18,000L to 26,000L ($10 to $15). Most trains from Florence connect in Terontola, though there are 5 daily direct trains as well. A one-way fare is 14,000L ($8), but direct trains impose a supplement of about 8,500L ($4.95). For information and schedules, call ☎ 075/500-7467. Arrivals are at the train station lying away from the town's monumental core at Piazza Vittorio Veneto. Bus nos. 6, 7, 9, 11, and 12 run to Piazza Italia, as close as you get to the center.

A daily **bus** arrives in Perugia, pulling into Piazza Partigiani, a short walk from the city's historic core. One-way fares from Rome are 22,000L ($13) for a transit that takes 2½ hours. The several buses that pull into Perugia from Florence charge 19,000L ($11) each way, for a trip that takes 2 hours. For information and schedules, call ☎ 075/500-9641. Buses that operate exclusively in Perugia use Piazza Italia as their central base, departing and arriving there.

If you have a **car** and are coming from either Rome or Florence, Autostrada del Sole (A1) takes you to the cutoff east to Perugia. Just follow the signs. From Siena, SS73 winds its way to Perugia and connects with the autostrada. If you arrive by car, you can drive to your hotel to unload your baggage; after that, you'll be directed to a parking lot on the outskirts.

VISITOR INFORMATION   The **tourist office** is at Piazza IV Novembre 3 (☎ 075/573-6458), open Monday to Saturday 8:30am to 1pm and 2 to 6pm and Sunday and holidays 9am to 1pm (closed January 1 and December 25 and 26).

EXPLORING THE CITY

As the villages of England compete for the title of most picturesque, so the cities of Italy vie for the honor of having the most beautiful square. As you stand on the central ✪ **Piazza IV Novembre,** you'll know Perugia is among the top contenders for that honor.

In the heart of the piazza is the **Grand Fountain (Fontana Maggiore),** built sometime in the late 1270s by a local architect, a monk named Bevignate. A major restoration that's returning it to some of its former glory should be done by the end of 1999. The fountain's artistic triumph stems from the sculptural work by Nicola Pisano and his son, Giovanni. Along the lower basin is statuary symbolizing the arts and sciences, Aesop's fables, the months of the year, the signs of the zodiac, and scenes from the Old Testament and Roman history. On the upper basin (mostly the work of Giovanni) is allegorical sculpture, such as one figure representing Perugia, as well as saints, biblical characters, and even 13th-century local officials.

After viewing the marvels of the fountain, you'll find that most of the other major attractions either open onto Piazza IV Novembre or lie only a short distance away (see below).

An escalator will take passengers from the older part of Perugia at the top of the hill and the upper slopes to the lower city. During construction, the old **Rocca Paolina** fortress, Via Marzia, was rediscovered, along with buried streets. The fortress had been covered over to make the gardens and viewing area at the end of Corso Vannucci in the last century. The old streets and street names have been cleaned up, and the area is well lighted, with an old wall exposed and modern sculpture added. The fortress was built in the 1500s by Sangallo. The Etruscan gate, **Porta Marzia,** is buried in the old city walls and can be viewed from Via Baglioni Sotterranea. This street lies in the fortress and is lined with houses, some dating from the 1400s. The escalator to the Rocca operates daily 6am to 1am; the Rocca is open daily 8am to 7pm.

Il Duomo (Cathedral of San Lorenzo). Piazza IV Novembre. ☎ 075/572-3832. Free admission. Daily 7am–noon and 4–7pm.

The exterior of the cathedral is rather raw-looking, as if the builders had suddenly been called away and never returned. The basilica is built in the Gothic style and dates from the 14th and 15th centuries. In the **Cappella di San Bernardino,** you'll find *Descent from the Cross* by Frederico Barocchio. And in the **Capella del Sacremento** hangs Luca Signorelli's *Madonna,* an altarpiece created in 1484. Signorelli was a pupil of della Francesca.

Perugia

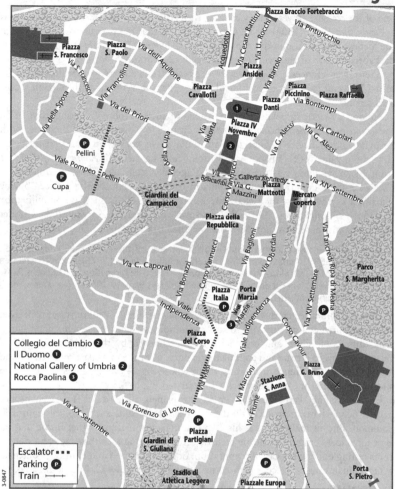

Collegio del Cambio ②
Il Duomo ①
National Gallery of Umbria ②
Rocca Paolina ③

Escalator ▪▪▪
Parking Ⓟ
Train ┣━━━┫

3-0847

○ **National Gallery of Umbria (Galleria Nazionale dell'Umbria).** Third floor of the Palazzo dei Priori, Corso Vannucci 19. ☎ **075/574-1257.** Admission 8,000L ($4.65) adults; children 17 and under/seniors free. Mon–Sat 9am–7pm, Sun 9am–1pm. Closed the first Mon of every month.

Opposite Il Duomo is the **Palace of the Priors (Palazzo dei Priori),** one of the finest secular buildings in Italy, dating from the 13th century and containing both the National Gallery and the Collegio del Cambio (below). Its facade is characterized by a striking row of mullioned windows. Over the main door is a Guelph (member of the papal party) lion and a griffin of Perugia, which hold chains once looted from a defeated Siena. You can walk up the stairway (the Vaccara) to the pulpit. By all means explore the interior, especially the vaulted Sala dei Notari, frescoed with stories of the Old Testament and from Aesop. October to May, it's open Tuesday to Sunday 9am to 1pm and 3 to 7pm (June to September, it's open daily the same hours).

On the palazzo's third floor is the **National Gallery of Umbria,** containing the most comprehensive collection of Umbrian art from the 13th to the 19th century. It's one of the treasure troves of Italy. Among the earliest paintings of interest (room 4) is a *Virgin and Child* (1304) by Duccio di Buoninsegna, the first important master of the Sienese school. Also in this room is a small *Madonna and Child* (1405) by Gentile da Fabriano, one of the gems of the collection. In room 5 you'll see a masterpiece by Piero della Francesca, the *Polyptych of Sant'Antonio,* a massive altarpiece from the mid-15th century. Guarded by a medley of saints, the Virgin is enthroned in a classical setting.

No one is exactly sure who painted the eight panels in room 8. Dating from 1473, the *Miracles of St. Bernardino of Siena* was created in a workshop of the time. Both Perugino and Francesco di Giorgio Martini may have worked on these panels.

In room 9 are works of native-son Perugino, among them his *Adoration of the Magi* from 1475. Perugino was the master of Raphael. Often accused of sentimentality, Today Perugino doesn't enjoy the popularity he did at the peak of his career, but he remains a key painter of the Renaissance, noted for his landscapes, as exemplified by the 1517 *Transfiguration.* You'll also find art by Pinturicchio, who studied under Perugino and whose most notable work was the library of Siena's Duomo.

Collegio del Cambio. Corso Vannucci 25. Street level of the Palazzo dei Priori (above). ☎ 075/572-8599. Admission 5,000L ($2.90) adults, 3,000L ($1.75) students; children under 12 free. Mar–Oct Mon–Sat 9am–12:30pm and 2:30–5:30pm, Sun and holidays 9am–12:30pm; Nov–Feb Mon–Sat 8am–2pm, Sun and holidays 9am–12:30pm. Closed New Year's Day, May Day, and Christmas.

During the Middle Ages, this section of the sprawling Palazzo dei Priori was conceived and maintained as a precursor of today's commodities exchanges, where grains, cloth, foodstuffs, gold, silver, and currencies were exchanged by the savvy merchants of Perugia. Today, its artistic and architectural appeal is for the most part centered around the **Hall of the Audience,** a meeting room whose frescoes were painted by Perugino and his assistants, one of whom was a 17-year-old Raphael.

On the ceiling, Perugino represented the planets allegorically. The Renaissance master peopled his frescoes with the Virtues, sybils, and such biblical figures as Solomon. But his masterpiece is his own countenance. It seems rather ironic that (at least for once) Perugino could be realistic, even depicting a chubby face and double chins resting under a red cap. Another room of interest is the **Chapel of S. J. Battista,** which contains many frescoes painted by a pupil of Perugino, G. Nicola di Paolo.

SHOPPING

The most famous foodstuff in town comes from one of Italy's best-loved manufacturers of chocolates and bon-bons, **Perugina.** Don't expect a high-glam, high-profile outlet: Displays of the foil-wrapped chocolates crop up at tobacco shops, supermarkets, newspaper kiosks, and sometimes gas stations throughout the city. Confused about the product? The selection includes *cioccolato al latte* (milk chocolate), and its darker counterpart, *cioccolato fondente,* both sold in everything from mouth-sized morels (*baci*) to romance-sized decorative boxes. One always-reliable outlet for the product is the **Bar Ferrari,** Corso Vannucci 43 (☎ 075/575-6197), which stockpiles Perugina products prominently amid the workaday bustle of one of the most popular bars/cafes in town. Chocoholics who want even stronger doses of the stuff sometimes opt to visit the factory itself, which offers tours to those who phone in advance: The **Fabrica Perugina** (☎ 075/52-761), 3 miles west of Perugia's historic core, forms the centerpiece of the hamlet of San Sisto.

Looking for ceramics and souvenirs that are more enduring than your hunger pangs? Head for Perugia's most interesting shops—**La Bottega dei Bassai,** Via Baglioni (☎ 075/572-3108), and **Ceccucci,** Corso Vannucci 38 (☎ 075/573-5143). If you're searching for fashion, particularly the cashmere garments that are

Shopping for Ceramics in Deruta

One of the highlights of a trip to this part of Italy is shopping for a product that has been associated with Umbria since the days of the Renaissance painters. The manufacturing town of **Deruta,** 12½ miles south of Perugia off Via Flaminia (beside E45 in the direction of Rome), has more than 300 manufacturers lining both sides of the town's main street. If you're not driving, you can catch one of six daily buses marked "Perugia–Deruta" at Perugia's Piazza Partigiana.

By the way, don't even think of saying the word *porcelain* within earshot of anyone in town. (*Stoneware* or, even better, *glazed terra-cotta* is preferred.) The process involves forming the region's terra-cotta clay into sturdy-looking bowls, umbrella stands, plates, cups, and art objects; firing them; glazing them with distinctive arabesques and bright colors; and firing them again. Especially popular is a design associated with the region since the Renaissance (when Raphael commissioned some of this ceramicware here): a motif of dragons cavorting amid flowers and vines.

The largest manufacturer, with some of the most reliable shipping services and the biggest sampling of wares, is **Ubaldo Grazie,** Via Tiberina 181 (☎ 075/971-0201). Look for sophisticated marketing programs, authentic copies of antique pieces, and more contemporary interpretations based on style-conscious Italian modernism. Many pieces of their colorfully painted stoneware are featured in Tiffany's, Bergdorf Goodman, and upscale mail-order catalogs like Williams Sonoma. Their specialties include cachepots, vases, and dinnerware. Anything you buy on site can be shipped via UPS to any destination in the world. The factory outlet is open Monday to Friday 9am to 1pm and 2:30 to 6:30pm and Saturday 9am to 1pm only. Free factory tours, lasting about half an hour, are sometimes offered to those who phone and reserve in advance.

A less comprehensive nearby competitor is **Antonio Margaritelli,** Via Tiberina 214 (☎ 075/971-1572). Founded in 1975, this factory outlet stocks material that's roughly equivalent to that at the Ubaldo Grazie factories but in a less diverse selection.

What should you look for in your Deruta ceramics? You can get a fast education in the town's ceramic traditions from the **Museo della Ceramica Umbra,** Palazzo del Comune, Piazza dei Consoli (☎ 075/971-1143). It's open Tuesday to Sunday 10am to 1pm and 3 to 6pm, charging 5,000L ($2.90) per person for a view of ceramics produced in the region between the 1500s and today. The museum was enlarged and expanded in 1997, almost as a gesture of civic pride.

tailored and often designed in Perugia, consider a jaunt 4 miles south to the village of Ponta San Giovanni, where one of the largest inventories of cashmere garments (coats, suits, dresses, and sweaters) for men and women is stockpiled at **Big Bertha,** Ponta San Giovanni (☎ 075/599-7572).

ACCOMMODATIONS

Hotel Brufani. Piazza Italia 12, 06100 Perugia. ☎ **075/573-2541.** Fax 075/572-0210. www.venere.com/home/perugia/brufani/brufani.html. E-mail: Brufani@italyhotel.com. 27 units. A/C MINIBAR TV TEL. 400,000–517,000L ($232–$300) double; 500,000–770,000L ($290–$447) suite. Breakfast 33,000L ($20). AE, CB, DC, MC, V. Parking 30,000L ($17).

At the top of the city, this five-star hotel was built by Giacomo Brufani in 1884 on the ruins of the ancient Rocca Paolina, a site known to the ancient Romans that later served as the home of one of the Renaissance popes. It's placed on a cliff edge, only a

few yards from Corso Vannucci. Most of the rooms offer a view of the Umbrian landscape so beloved by painters. Recent renovations have upgraded most of the rooms
and added new bathrooms. The first-floor rooms are grander, with antiques and frescoed ceilings. The good cafe/restaurant, Collins, is named for the great-grandfather of
Mr. Bottelli, who succeeded the original owner, Mr. Brufani, nearly a century ago. The
hotel is now split from the Palace Hotel Bellavista (below), which shares the same
building.

Hotel Fortuna Perugia. Via Bonazzi 19, 06123 Perugia. ☎ **075/572-2845.** Fax 075/
573-5040. 33 units. MINIBAR TV TEL. 140,000–180,000L ($81–$104) double. Breakfast
12,000L ($7). AE, DC, MC, V. Free parking.

Here's a chance to stay at a four-star hotel that deliberately "downgraded" itself in
1996 to three-star status and then lowered its prices. In the heart of town, it dates from
the 14th century but has been extensively reconstructed over the years. Today, arched
leaded glass doors lead to an interior of hardwood floors, tasteful art, and a welcoming
atmosphere. The guest rooms boast sleek contemporary styling—often blond woods
and flamboyant fabrics—and are filled with modern amenities. Even better than the
rooms are the views, some of which might've inspired Perugino himself. The hotel has
a reading room, a cozy bar, and a rooftop terrace opening onto the tile roofs of the
town and the Umbrian landscape. When the weather's right, guests take their cap-
puccinos and croissants here. There's no restaurant, but many trattorie are almost literally outside the door.

Hotel La Rosetta. Piazza Italia 19, 06121 Perugia. ☎ and fax **075/572-0841.** 96 units.
MINIBAR TV TEL. 199,000L ($115) double; 285,000L ($165) suite. Rates include breakfast.
AE, DC. Parking 30,000L ($17).

Since this Perugian landmark opened in 1927, it has expanded from a seven-room
pensione to a labyrinthine complex. La Rosetta is one of the leading inns in town,
though not quite as desirable as the Locanda della Posta. With its frescoed ceiling,
Suite 55 has been declared a national treasure. (The bullet holes that papal mercenaries
shot into the ceiling in 1848 have been artfully preserved.) The less grandiose rooms
include decors ranging from slickly contemporary to Victorian to 1960s style. Each
unit is peaceful, clean, and comfortable. The restaurant is recommended under
"Dining," below.

Locanda della Posta. Corso Vannucci 97, 06121 Perugia. ☎ **075/572-8925.** Fax 075/
573-2562. www.assind.perugia.it/hotel/locanda. E-mail: locanda@assind.perugia.it. 41 units.
A/C MINIBAR TV TEL. 200,000–295,000L ($116–$171.10) double; 300,000–350,000L ($174–
$203) suite. Rates include breakfast. AE, DC, MC, V. Parking 20,000L ($12) in nearby garage.

Goethe and Hans Christian Andersen slept here—in fact, this used to be the only
hotel in Perugia. It sits on the main street of the oldest part of town, behind an impressive ornate facade sculpted in the 1700s. We prefer this luxuriously decorated small
hotel to the Brufani, which is five stars only in the rating eyes of the local government.
The della Posta's views may not be as grand, but it's better run and has more comfortable and better-kept rooms.

Palace Hotel Bellavista. Piazza Italia 12, 06100 Perugia. ☎ **075/572-0741.** Fax 075/
572-9092. 74 units. MINIBAR TV TEL. 190,000L ($110) double; 280,000L ($162) suite. Rates
include breakfast. AE, DC, MC, V. Parking 25,000L ($15) in public lot nearby. Bus: 36.

This is the less glamorous and less expensive of the two hotels occupying the dignified
premises of what was built in the late 1800s as a home for a prominent English family,
the Collinses, who eventually married into an aristocratic local family, the Brufanis.
The Brufani (above) and the Bellavista fill the entire premises but have separate

entrances, managements, and staffs. Despite the Bellavista's three-star status, its public rooms are grander than those in its five-star counterpart. The rooms are simple, clean, and functional, some with wallpaper and either ceramic tile or wooden floors. There's a bar but no restaurant.

DINING

✪ **Il Falchetto.** Via Bartolo 20. ☎ **075/573-1775.** Main courses 30,000–60,000L ($17–$35). AE, DC, MC, V. Tues–Sun noon–2:30pm and 7:30–10:30pm. UMBRIAN/ITALIAN.

This restaurant a short walk from Piazza Piccinino (where you'll be able to park) has flourished in this 19th-century building since 1941. The dining room in the rear has the most medieval ambience, its stone walls from the 1300s still intact. In summer you might opt for a table outside. Many of the dishes adhere to traditional themes and have a certain zest that has won critical approval. Menu items include tagliatelle with truffles, grilled trout from the Nera River, prosciutto several ways, pasta with chick-peas, grilled filet of goat, and filet steak with truffles. One special dish, of which the chef is justly proud, is falchetti (gnocchi with ricotta and spinach). Some of the best Umbrian wines are served.

La Rosetta. In the Hotel La Rosetta, Piazza Italia 19. ☎ **075/572-0841.** Reservations recommended, especially in summer. Main courses 14,000–29,000L ($8–$17). AE, DC, MC, V. Daily 12:30–3pm and 7:30–10pm. UMBRIAN.

La Rosetta has gained more fame than the hotel containing it. Every politician from the region uses the restaurant, and during the Perugia jazz festival (10 days in mid-summer) virtually every star stays and dines here. You'll find three dining areas: an intimate wood-paneled salon, a main dining area divided by Roman arches and lit by brass chandeliers, and a courtyard enclosed by the walls of the villa-style hotel. Under shady palms you can have a leisurely meal that's both simple and reliable. The menu choice is vast, but a few specialties stand out: To begin, the finest dishes are spaghetti alla Norcina (with a truffle sauce) and vol-au-vent di tortellini Rosetta. Among the main dishes, the outstanding entry is scaloppine alla Perugina; other notables are Florentine beefsteak with Marsala wine, grilled swordfish with truffled-stuffed tortellini, and a regional specialty you either love or you don't, scallopine Perugina (filet of veal drenched in a sauce concocted from chicken livers).

La Taverna. Via delle Streghe 8. ☎ **075/572-4128.** Reservations recommended. Main courses 15,000–25,000L ($9–$15). AE, DC, MC, V. Tues–Sun 12:30–2:30pm and 7:30–11pm. UMBRIAN.

One of the finest and most innovative restaurants in Umbria, La Taverna is in a medieval house. Its entrance is at the bottom of one of the narrowest alleyways in town, in the heart of Perugia's historic center. (Prominent signs indicate its position off Corso Vannucci at the bottom of a flight of stairs.) Three dining rooms—filled with exposed masonry, oil paintings, and a polite staff—radiate from the high-ceilinged vestibule. The cuisine is inspired by Claudio Brugalossi, an Umbrian chef who spent part of his career in Tampa, Florida, working for the Hyatt chain. Menu choices include truffle-stuffed ravioli, tagliata with arugula, veal filet with black truffles, and grilled red snapper.

✪ **Osteria del Bartolo.** Via Bartolo 30. ☎ **075/573-1561.** Reservations recommended. Main courses 16,000–30,000L ($9–$17); fixed-price all-Umbrian menu 60,000L ($35); *menu degustazione* 100,000L ($58); *menu vegetariano* 40,000L ($23). AE, DC, MC, V. Mon–Sat 1–2:45pm and 8–10:30pm. Closed Jan. UMBRIAN.

At the historic center of town in a palazzo with 14th-century foundations, this family-run restaurant is known for its fresh ingredients, culinary flair, and elegant presentations.

It's the pacesetter in Perugia. Many dishes are traditional. Straight from the cookbooks of the 1600s, botaccio is made with farmer's bread stuffed with sausage, vegetables, and a sharp pecorino cheese and then baked in the oven. Also tempting are fresh tortelli with porcini mushrooms, ricotta di pecora, steamed tomatoes, and olive oil. The restaurant makes its own butter twice a day, its own bread once a day, and its own pasta with every order. The chef also makes his own desserts. There's enough distance between tables to allow discreet conversations.

Trattoria Ricciotto. Piazza Danti 19. ☎ and fax **075/572-1956.** Reservations recommended. Main courses 18,000–30,000L ($10–$17); fixed-price menus 30,000–50,000L ($17–$29). AE, DC, MC, V. Mon–Sat 12:30–3pm and 7:30–10pm. UMBRIAN.

Since 1888, this rustically elegant restaurant has been owned and operated by members of the Betti family, who cook, serve, uncork the wine, and welcome you to Perugia. In a building dating in part from the 14th century, it offers well-prepared specialties like fettuccine with truffles, maccheroni arrabbiata (pasta with tomatoes and red and green peppers), spring lamb chasseur, and fagotti Monte Bianco (turkey with parmigiano, ham, and cream sauce). One of the most satisfying meals in town is a platter containing two cuts of veal, served with a spinach soufflé and roasted potatoes. What's a good preface? Consider tagliatelle with green olives or maccheroni with mushrooms and cream sauce.

PERUGIA AFTER DARK

Begin your evening by joining in Italy's liveliest *passeggiata* (a promenade at dusk) along Corso Vannucci, a pedestrian strip running north to south. Everyone, especially the students of Perugia, seems to stroll here. Many drop into one of the little cafes or enoteche for an aperitivo. If you cafe hop or wine-bar crawl, you can sample as many as 150 wines from 60 Umbrian vineyards—providing you can keep on your feet.

Two cafes outshine the rest: The better is chandelier-lit **Sandri Pasticceria,** Corso Vannucci 32 (☎ 075/572-4112), offering drinks, cakes, pastries, and sandwiches. You can also order full meals, including eggplant parmagiana and veal cutlet Milanese. It's another outlet for the city's famous chocolates. Sandri's main competitor is **Caffè del Cambio,** Corso Vannucci 29 (☎ 075/572-4165), a favorite of university students. The first room is most impressive—with a vaulted ceiling, it contains racks of pastries, cones of ice cream, a long stand-up bar, and a handful of tiny tables. The low-ceilinged room in back is smoky, more crowded, and much livelier.

The hottest time to visit Perugia is for Italy's foremost jazz festival, **Umbria Jazz,** which sprawls over a 10-day period in early or mid-July (dates vary). Jazz heavies like Sonny Rollins and Keith Jarrett have shown up here to perform. For ticket sales and schedules, call ☎ 075/573-2432. Tickets are 20,000L to 80,000L ($12 to $46).

Perugia has a good number of pubs where you can sit around and chew on more than just the town's famous chocolates. Foremost among them is the **Australian Pub,** Via del Verzaro 39 (☎ 075/572-0206), where four kinds of beer (including Heineken) are served on tap from 7,000L ($4.05) per mug. There's no music or dancing, only an ambience that's more southern hemisphere than southern Mediterranean. It's open Tuesday to Sunday 7pm to 2am. The **Hostaria del Lupo Mannaro,** Via Guardabassi 4, near Piazza Morlacchi (☎ 075/573-6827), functions as an affordable Umbrian restaurant to 10pm, then transforms into a wine bar from 10:15pm to 1am. The setting is raffish, irreverent, and loud; later in the evening, recorded music reverberates off the old stones of the very old vaulting. Main courses range from 12,000 to 22,000L ($7 to $13) and are served Tuesday to Friday 12:30 to 3pm and Tuesday to Sunday 8pm to midnight.

10 Assisi

110 miles N of Rome, 15 miles SE of Perugia

Ideally placed on the rise to Mt. Subasio, watched over by the medieval **Rocca Maggiore,** this purple-fringed Umbrian hill town retains a mystical air. The site of many a pilgrimage, Assisi is forever linked in legend with its native son, St. Francis. The gentle saint founded the Franciscan order and shares honors with St. Catherine of Siena as the patron saint of Italy. But he's remembered by many, even non-Christians, as a lover of nature (his preaching to an audience of birds is one of the legends of his life). Dante compared him to John the Baptist.

St. Francis put Assisi on the map, and making a pilgrimage here is one of the highlights of a visit to Umbria. Today, Italy's Catholic youth flock here for religious conferences, festivals, and reflection. But even without St. Francis, the hill town merits a visit for its interesting sights and architecture. Sightseers and pilgrims mingling together get a little thick in summer, and at Easter or Christmas you're likely to be trampled underfoot. We've found it best and less crowded in spring or fall.

ESSENTIALS

GETTING THERE   Although there's no **rail** station in Assisi, the city lies within a 30-minute bus or taxi ride from the rail station in the nearby hamlet of Santa Maria degli Angeli. From Santa Maria degli Angeli, buses depart at 30-minute intervals for Piazza Matteotti, in the heart of Assisi. One-way fares are 2,500L ($1.45). If you're coming to Assisi from Perugia by train, expect to pay around 5,000L ($2.90) one-way. If you're coming from Rome, expect to pay around 20,000L ($12) each way. From either of those points of origin, expect a transfer en route in Foligno. Rail fares between Florence and Assisi are about 24,000L ($14) each way and usually require a transfer in the junction of Terontola.

Frequent **buses** connect Perugia (above) with Assisi, the trip taking 1 hour and costing 5,000L ($2.90) one-way. One bus a day arrives from Rome. Requiring about 3 hours, it costs 30,000L ($17) one-way. Two buses pull in from Florence, taking 2½ hours and costing 25,000L ($15) one-way.

If you have a **car,** in 30 minutes from Perugia you can be in Assisi by taking S3 southwest. At the junction of Route 147, just follow the signs toward Assisi. But you'll have to park outside the town's core, as those neighborhoods are usually closed to traffic. (*Note:* The police officer guarding the entrance to the old town will usually let motorists drop off luggage at a hotel in the historic zone, with the understanding that you'll eventually park in a lot on the outskirts of town. Likewise, delivery vehicles are allowed to drop off supplies in the town's pedestrian zones daily 10am to noon and 4 to 6pm.)

VISITOR INFORMATION   The **tourist office** is at Piazza del Comune 12 (☎ 075/812-534), open Monday to Friday 8am to 2pm and 3:30 to 6:30pm, Saturday 9am to 1pm and 3:30 to 6:30pm, and Sunday 9am to 1pm.

EXPLORING THE TOWN

Piazza del Comune, in the heart of Assisi, is a dream for a lover of architecture from the 12th to the 14th century. On the square is a pagan structure, with six Corinthian columns, called the **Temple of Minerva (Tampeo di Minerva),** from the 1st century B.C. With Minerva-like wisdom, the people of Assisi turned it into a baroque church inside so as not to offend the devout. Adjoining the temple is the 13th-century **Tower (Torre),** built by Ghibelline supporters. The site is open daily 7am to noon and 2:30pm to dusk.

Umbria Shakes, Rattles & Rolls

In September 1997, twin earthquakes (5.7 and 5.6 on the Richter scale), with an epicenter just outside Assisi, struck within hours of each other. Umbria sustained considerable damage, especially in the towns of Acciano and Assisi, where a total of 11 people were killed and another 13,000 Umbrians forced to take refuge in tents. The following 11 days of aftershocks and tremors hindered the recovery effort by the Italian government and relief organizations and only poured salt in the wounds of those left wondering what to do. The tremors were felt as far south as Rome and as far north as Florence.

Considerable damage was suffered in Assisi—the quakes released most of their fury on the Basilica di San Francesco. Frescoes and bricks from the vaulted inner roof crashed down after the initial quake, killing two Fransican friars and two surveyors from the Italian Culture Ministry there accessing the damage. Additional tremors caused extra stones from the roof to fall, and the tympanum of the left transept was almost completely destroyed as most of the outside stones of the upper part of the tympanum have fallen. The cloister was the least affected. Despite the damage, the burial service for the two fallen friars was held in the basilica to throngs who mourned the friars and what was left of their homes. Authorities claim the restoration of all the quake-affected buildings in the region could cost more than $1 billion, and no date for completion has been announced. A restoration program for the basilica has already begun.

These quakes and aftershocks were the first major rumblings sustained in Italy since 1980, when a devastating 6.8 quake struck near Naples, killing 2,570; a smaller, minor quake struck this same region in 1984. The geological culprit is the Apennine mountain range, running down the center of Italy, and has been the source of documented seismic activity since 1349.

✪ **Basilica di San Francesco.** Piazza San Francesco. ☎ **075/819-001.** Free admission. Apr–Oct daily 8:30am–7pm (Nov–Mar to 6pm).

This important church, with both an upper and a lower church, houses some of the most important cycles of frescoes in Italy, including works by such pre-Renaissance giants as Cimabue and Giotto. The lower basilica is from 1228 to 1230 and the upper basilica from 1230 to 1253. The basilica and its paintings form the most significant monument to St. Francis. You can still visit the lower basilica, but the upper basilica, the site of the Giotto frescoes, is regrettably closed because of quake damage. However, the staff presents a short video showing the frescoes. Currently, restoration work is racing against the clock, as Herculean efforts are being made to save the church, which looks like a giant Gulliver strapped to an operating table. Parts of it are wrapped in metal scaffolding. Normally, it might take years to complete the work, but Pope John Paul III wants it done for 2000, when millions of pilgrims are expected to come to this hilltown.

Until the restoration is done, you can enjoy Giotto's most celebrated frescoes, of St. Francis preaching to the birds, only on video. In the nave are the cycle of 27 additional frescoes, some by Giotto, though the authorship of the entire cycle is a subject of controversy. Many frescoes are almost surrealistic (in architectural frameworks), like a stage set that strips away the walls and allows you to see the actors inside. In the cycle you can see pictorial evidence of the rise of humanism that led to Giotto's and Italy's split from the rigidity of Byzantium.

Assisi

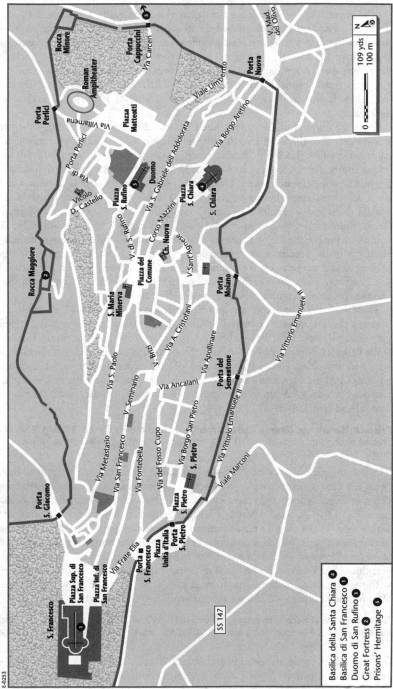

Basilica della Santa Chiara ❹
Basilica di San Francesco ❶
Duomo di San Rufino ❸
Great Fortress ❷
Prisons' Hermitage ❺

323

The upper church also contains the damaged masterpiece by Cimabue, his *Crucifixion*. Time and quakes have robbed the fresco of its former radiance, but its power and ghostlike drama remain at least on video. The cycle of badly damaged frescoes in the transept and apse are other works by Cimabue and his helpers. Rather tragically, art experts spend hours daily sorting through boxes of rubble, trying to piece together the jigsaw puzzle caused by the quakes. There's a debate about whether the Cimbaue and Giotto frescoes will ever be in good-enough condition to be restored to their historic place.

From the transept of the upper church, proceed down the stairs through the two-tiered cloisters to the lower church; this will put you in the south transept, which is open to the public. Look for Cimabue's faded but masterly *Virgin and Child* with four angels and St. Francis looking on from the far right; it's often reproduced in detail as one of Cimabue's greatest works. On the other side of the transept is *Deposition from the Cross*, a masterpiece by Sienese artist Pietro Lorenzetti, plus a *Madonna and Child* with St. John and St. Francis (stigmata showing). In a chapel honoring St. Martin of Tours, Simone Martini of Siena painted a cycle of frescoes, with great skill and imagination, depicting the life and times of that saint. Finally, under the lower church is the crypt of St. Francis, with some relics of the saint. In the past, visitors weren't allowed access to the vaults containing these highly cherished articles, only scholars and clergymen were. Some of the items displayed are the saint's tunic, cowl, and shoes and the chalice and communion plate used by him and his followers.

From the lower church you can also visit the **Treasury** and **Perkins Collection.** The Treasury shelters precious church relics, often in gold and silver, and even the original gray sackcloth worn by St. Francis before the order adopted the brown tunic. Here also is the Perkins Collection, a limited but rich exhibit donated by a U.S. philanthropist who had assembled a masterful collection of Tuscan/Renaissance works, including paintings by Luca Signorelli and Fra Angelico. The Treasury and the Perkins Collection are open daily 9:30am to noon and 2 to 6pm (closed Sunday and November to March) and cost 3,000L ($1.75).

Prisons' Hermitage (Eremo delle Carceri). Via Eremo delle Carceri. ☎ **075/812-301.** Free admission (donations accepted). Daily 8am–6pm. About 2½ miles east of Assisi (out Via Eremo delle Carceri).

The Eremo delle Carceri dates from the 14th and 15th centuries. The "prison" isn't a penal institution but rather a spiritual retreat. It's believed that St. Francis retired to this spot for meditation and prayer. Out back is a moss-covered gnarled ilex (live oak) more than 1,000 years old, where St. Francis is believed to have blessed the birds, after which they flew in the four major compass directions to symbolize that Franciscans, in coming centuries, would spread from Assisi all over the world. The friary contains some faded frescoes. One of the handful of friars who still inhabit the retreat will show you through. Donations are accepted to defray the cost of maintenance. In keeping with the Franciscan tradition, the friars at Le Carceri are completely dependent on alms for their support. Visitation has been unaffected by the quakes.

Great Fortress (Rocca Maggiore). ☎ **075/815-292.** Reached by an unmarked stepped street opposite the basilica. Admission 5,000L ($2.90) adults, 3,500L ($2.05) children under 18. Daily 10am–dusk.

The Great Fortress sits astride a hill overlooking Assisi. You should visit if for no other reason than the panoramic view of the Umbrian countryside from its ramparts. The present building (now in ruins but spared by the earthquakes' wrath) dates from the 14th century, and the origins of the structure go back beyond time. The dreaded

Cardinal Albornoz built the medieval version to establish papal domination over the town. A circular rampart was built in the 1500s by Pope Paul III.

Basilica della Santa Chiara (Clare). Piazza della Santa Chiara. ☎ **075/812-282.** Basilica, free; however, the custodian turns away visitors in shorts, miniskirts, plunging necklines, and backless or shoulderless attire. Nov–Mar daily 6:30am–noon and 2–6pm; Apr–Oct daily 6:30am–12:05pm and 2–6:55pm.

The basilica is dedicated to "the little plant of Blessed Francis," as St. Clare liked to describe herself. Born in 1193 into one of the noblest families of Assisi, Clare gave all her wealth to the poor and founded, together with St. Francis, the Order of the Poor Clares. She was canonized by Pope Alexander IV in 1255. Pope Pius XII declared her Patroness of Television in 1958. It was decided to entrust to her this new means of social communication based on a vision she had on Christmas Eve 1252 while bedridden in the Monastery of San Damiano: She saw the manger and heard the friars sing in the Basilica of St. Francis.

Though many of the frescoes that once adorned the basilica have been completely or partially destroyed (not as a result of the quakes), much remains that's worthy of note. On entering, your attention will be caught by the striking *Crucifix* behind the main altar, a painting on wood dating from the time of the church itself (ca. 1260). The work is by "the Master of St. Clare," who's also responsible for the beautiful icons on either side of the transept. In the left transept is an oft-reproduced fresco of the Nativity from the 14th century. The basilica houses the remains of St. Clare as well as the crucifix under which St. Francis received his command from above.

The closest bus stop is near Porta Nuova, the eastern gate to the city at the beginning of Viale Umberto I. The bus doesn't have a number; it departs from the depot in Piazza Matteotti for its first run to the train station at 5:35am and concludes its final run at 11:59pm. Buses arrive at half-hour intervals. There was little damage to the basilica as a result of the quakes, and it should be operating at full steam during the lifetime of this edition.

Duomo di San Rufino. Piazza San Rufino. ☎ **075/812-285.** Church, free; crypt, 3,000L ($1.75). Mar–Nov 4 daily 10am–noon and 2:30–6pm (to 5pm Nov 5–Feb).

Built in the mid-12th century, the Duomo is graced with a Romanesque facade, greatly enhanced by rose windows. This is one of the finest churches in the hill towns, as important as the one at Spoleto. Adjoining it is a bell tower (campanile). Inside, the church has been baroqued, an unfortunate decision that lost the purity the front suggests. St. Francis and St. Clare were both baptized here. The church was spared damage during the quakes.

ACCOMMODATIONS

Space in Assisi tends to be tight—so reservations are vital. For such a small town, however, it has a good number of accommodations.

Albergo Ristorante del Viaggiatore. Via San Antonio 14, 06081 Assisi. ☎ **075/816-297** or 075/812-424. Fax 075/813-051. 16 units. TEL. 90,000L ($52) double. Half board 80,000L ($46) per person. Rates include breakfast. MC, V.

In Michelin's lineup of the hotel properties of Assisi, this one is at the bottom of the totem pole, yet it's among the tops for value. This ancient town house has been totally renovated, though the stone walls and arched entryways of the lobby hint at its age. The high-ceilinged rooms are spacious and very contemporary. The restaurant has been operated by the same family for years and offers excellent local and regional fare and wines.

Hotel dei Priori. Corso Mazzini 15, 06081 Assisi. ☎ **075/812-237.** Fax 075/816-804. www.assind.perugia.it/hotel/dpriori. E-mail: deipriori@assind.perugia.it. 39 units. TEL. 145,000–190,000L ($84–$110) double; 214,000–254,000L ($124–$147) suite. Rates include breakfast. AE, DC, MC, V. Free parking.

Opened in 1923, this hotel has been continuously renovated. It occupies one of the town's most historic buildings, dating back to the 17th century, when it was known as the Palazzo Nepis. A homelike, somewhat old-fashioned Umbrian atmosphere prevails. Marble staircases and floors, terra-cotta, vaulted ceilings, and stone-arched doorways remain from its seigniorial palazzo heyday. Antiques and tasteful prints in both the rooms and the public areas add grace notes, along with a collection of Oriental rugs. Many of the rooms are a bit small, however. The hotel also has a bar and serves Umbrian specialties only to hotel guests and only April to October.

Hotel Giotto. Via Fontebella 41, 06082 Assisi. ☎ **075/812-209.** Fax 075/816-479. 72 units. TV TEL. 204,000L ($118) double; 325,000L ($189) suite. Rates include breakfast. AE, DC, MC, V. Closed Nov–Mar. Free parking.

The Giotto is up-to-date and well run, built at the edge of town on several levels and opening onto panoramic views. Some of the foundations are 500 years old, but because of frequent modernizations it's hard to tell. Though targeted by tour groups, the Giotto is the best hotel in Assisi (the Subasio, its major competitor, is disappointing). It has spacious modern public rooms and comfortable guest rooms; bright colors predominate, though many rooms look tatty. The Giotto offers small formal gardens and terraces for meals or sunbathing.

Hotel Sole. Corso Mazzini 35, 06081 Assisi. ☎ **075/812-373** or 075/812-922. Fax 075/813-706. 35 units. TV TEL. 100,000L ($58) double; 130,000L ($75) triple. Breakfast 18,000L ($11). Half board 80,000L ($46) per person. AE, DC, MC, V.

For Umbrian hospitality and a general down-home feeling, the Sole is a winner in the heart of medieval Assisi—comfortable but traditional, a bit tattered but affordable. The severe beauty of rough stone walls and ceilings, terra-cotta floors, and marble staircases pay homage to the past, balanced by big-cushioned chairs in the TV lounge and contemporary wrought-iron bed frames and well-worn furnishings in the guest rooms. The rooms, some of which are across the street in an annex, are rather basic for the most part and feature aging baths. The family owners also offer one of the town's best cuisines under the 15th-century vaults of their restaurant. The food is so savory you might want to take half board. This would be a good choice for dining even if you aren't a guest.

Hotel Umbra. Via degli Archi 6 (Piazza del Commune), 06081 Assisi. ☎ **075/812-240.** Fax 075/813-653. 30 units. TEL. 170,000L ($99) double; 235,000L ($136) suite. Breakfast 15,000L (9). AE, DC, MC, V. Closed mid-Jan to Mar 15. Parking 15,000L ($9).

With origins going back to the 1400s, the Umbra is the most centrally located hotel in Assisi, right off Piazza del Comune. The outdoor terraced dining room is a local favorite (see "Dining," below). You enter through old stone walls covered with vines and walk under a leafy pergola. The lobby is compact and functional. The guest rooms are arranged as small apartments, with comfortable beds; some have a tiny balcony overlooking the crusty old rooftops and the Umbrian countryside. All are graced with at least one or two antiques from the 18th or 19th century.

St. Anthony's Guest House. Via Galeazzo Alessi 10, 06081 Assisi. ☎ and fax **075/812-542.** 20 units. 72,000–76,000L ($42–$44) double. Rates include breakfast. No credit cards. Closed Nov–Mar 15. Parking 5,000L ($2.90).

This special place offers economical, comfortable accommodations in a medieval villa turned guesthouse. Operated by the Franciscan Sisters of the Atonement (an order that originated in Graymoor, New York) and located on the upper ledges of Assisi, it offers the pilgrim/traveler hospitality and a peaceful atmosphere. In all, 35 people can be accommodated. For an extra 20,000L ($12), a midday meal is served at 1pm in a restored 12th-century dining room. The sisters and their co-workers welcome you, showing you their library with English-language books but always reminding you this is not a hotel but a religious guesthouse.

NEARBY ACCOMMODATIONS

✪ **Hotel Palazzo Bocci.** Via Cavour 17, 06038 Spello. ☎ **0742/301-021.** Fax 0742/ 301-464. 23 units. A/C MINIBAR TV TEL. 200,000–240,000L ($116–$139) double; 260,000– 320,000L ($151–$186) suite. Rates include breakfast. AE, DC, MC, V. Head 6½ miles south-east of Assisi along S147.

In the historic center of Spello, this palace dates from the late 18th century. The owner bought it in 1989, renovated it, and opened it as a hotel in 1992. Inside is a courtyard with a view of the valley, a beautiful fountain, and two age-old palms. Taste and restraint went into designing the public rooms and the guest rooms, some of which open onto panoramic views. Each soundproof room has hydromassage, a safe, a writing desk with two chairs, a hair dryer. There's a nice bar and a lush garden with a panoramic view where drinks are served. A buffet breakfast is offered, and a well-known restaurant, Il Molino, is in front of the hotel. The village has a pool (7,500L/$4.35 per hour) and tennis courts (15,000L/$9 per hour) within a 5-minute walk.

DINING

Il Medioevo. Via dell'Arco dei Priori 4B. ☎ **075/813-068.** Reservations recommended. Main courses 16,000–22,000L ($9–$13). AE, DC, MC, V. Thurs–Tues noon–2:30pm and 7:30– 9:45pm. Closed Jan 7–Feb 7 and July 1–20. UMBRIAN/INTERNATIONAL.

Assisi's best restaurant is one of the architectural oddities of the town's historic center, with foundations that are at least 1,000 years old. During the Middle Ages and again in Renaissance times, the structure was successively enlarged and modified until today it's an authentic medieval gem. Alberto Falsinotti and his family prepare superb versions of Umbrian recipes whose origins are as old as Assisi itself. Specialties are tortelloni stuffed with minced turkey, veal, and beef and served with butter and parmigiano reggiano; gnocchi stuffed with ricotta and spinach and sprinkled with parmigiano reggiano; roasted rabbit with red-wine sauce and truffles; roast lamb with rosemary, potatoes, and herbs; homemade pasta stuffed with black truffles; and grilled filet of veal with herb sauce.

Ristorante Buca di San Francesco. Via Brizi 1. ☎ **075/812-204.** Reservations recommended. Main courses 25,000–40,000L ($15–$23). AE, DC, MC, V. Tues–Sun noon–2:30pm and 7:30–9:30pm. Closed July 1–15. UMBRIAN/ITALIAN.

Hospitable and evocative of the Middle Ages, this restaurant occupies the premises of a cave near the foundation of a 12th-century palace. Menu items change frequently, based on the availability of ingredients, but what you're likely to find are *spaghetti alla buca,* with exotic mushrooms and meat sauce; *umbricelli* (big noodles) with asparagus sauce; *cannelloni* (crêpes) with ricotta, spinach, and tomatoes; *carlacca* (baked crêpes stuffed with cheese, prosciutto, and roasted veal), and *piccione alla sisana* (roasted pigeon with olive oil, capers, and aromatic herbs). There are about a hundred seats in the dining room and another 60 in the garden, overlooking the buildings in Assisi's historic center.

Umbra. Via degli Archi 6 (Piazza del Commune). ☎ **075/812-240.** Reservations recommended. Main courses 15,000–26,000L ($9–$15). AE, DC, MC, V. Mon–Sat noon–2pm and 7:45–9:30pm. Closed Jan 10–Mar 15. UMBRIAN.

Though most of the building containing this venerable restaurant dates from the Middle Ages, the walls of the laundry and the kitchens (in the basement) are from the final days of the Roman Empire. The restaurant, previously recommended for its hotel rooms, was opened as an inn in 1926 or 1928 (the owners can't remember exactly), and its shaded garden is charming enough to have pleased even St. Francis. This is the personal statement of the owner and his capable staff. The Umbrian menu items range from the fanciful to the classical. In many dishes, flavorful use is made of truffles, as in spaghetti, capellati pasta, or gnocchi. Other winners are *crespelle à l'Umbra,* a cheesy herb-laden appetizer, or one of our favorites, *agnello alla cacciatore* (hunter's-style lamb, with mushrooms, onions, and peppers). The most "typico" dessert is *rocciata,* a cigar-shaped pastry made from egg yolks, flour, and honey.

11 Spoleto & the Festival of Two Worlds

80 miles N of Rome, 30 miles SE of Assisi, 130 miles S of Florence, 40 miles SE of Perugia

Hannibal couldn't conquer it, but Gian-Carlo Menotti did—and how! Before Maestro Menotti put Spoleto on the tourist map in 1958, it was known mostly to art lovers, teachers, and students. Today the chic and fashionable and the artistic and arty flood the Umbrian hilltown to attend performances of the world-famous **Festival dei Due Mondi (Festival of Two Worlds),** most often held in June and July. Menotti searched and traveled through many towns of Tuscany and Umbria before making a final choice. When he saw Spoleto, he fell in love with it. And quite understandably.

ESSENTIALS

GETTING THERE **Trains** arrive several times a day from Rome, the fastest of which are IC (Inter-City) trains, a bit more expensive than ordinary trains, some of which might require a transfer. The one-way fare from Rome to Spoleto is 16,000L to 23,000L ($9 to $13), depending on the train speed. The fastest will take about 90 minutes; those requiring connections can take 2½ hours. Trains also run several times a day between Perugia and Spoleto, a distance of about an hour, charging 6,000L to 12,000L ($3.50 to $7) each way. The **rail station** in Spoleto (☎ 0743/48-516) is at Piazza Polvani, just outside the historic heart. Notice the gigantic statue in front by Philadelphia-born artist Alexander Calder. Circolare bus A, B, C, or D will take you from the rail station into Piazza della Libertà in the town center, for a one-way fee of 1,200L (70¢). Buy your ticket for the Circolare at the bar, perhaps along with an espresso, in the rail station.

At least two **buses** arrive every day from Perugia, taking 1½ hours and costing 10,400L ($6) one-way. For information, call ☎ 0743/212211. Bus routes to Spoleto from Rome are a lot less convenient, in some cases requiring complicated transfers, and priced at from 13,000L ($8) each way. For information about bus transfers from Rome, call the tourist office in Spoleto, **Marozzi SNC** (☎ 06/474-2801), or **Bucci SNC** (☎ 0721/32401).

If you have a **car** and are coming from either Assisi or Perugia (above), continue along S3, heading south to the junction of Foligno, where you can pick up Hwy. 75 for the rest of the route into Spoleto. Driving time from Assisi is about 30 minutes.

VISITOR INFORMATION The **tourist office** is at Piazza della Libertà 7 (☎ 0743/220-311), open April to September daily 9:30am to 1pm and 4:30 to

---

The Spoleto Festival

Since the late 1950s, the artistic world has shown up here for the ✪ **Festival dei Due Mondi (Festival of Two Worlds)**, an internationally acclaimed event. It's held annually most often in June and July and attracts the elite of the operatic, ballet, and theatrical worlds from Europe and America. Tickets for most events are 10,000L to 50,000L ($6 to $29), plus a 15% handling charge.

For tickets in advance, write to the **Associazione Festival dei Due Mondo,** Biglietteria Festival dei Due Mondi, Teatro Nuovo, Piazza Belli 06049 Spoleto. Once in Spoleto, you can get tickets at the **Teatro Nuovo** (☎ **0743/44-325** or 0743/222-367). Another contact is the **Associazione Festival dei Due Mondi,** Via Cesare Beccaria 18, 00196 Roma (☎ **06/321-0288**).

7:30pm and November to March daily (except Sunday afternoon) 9am to 1pm and 3:30 to 6:30pm.

SEEING THE TOWN

Long before Tennessee Williams arrived to premiere a new play, Thomas Schippers to conduct the opera *Macbeth,* or Shelley Winters to do three one-act plays by Saul Bellow, Spoleto was known to St. Francis and Lucrezia Borgia (she occupied the 14th-century castle towering over the town, the Rocca dell'Albornoz). The town is filled with palaces of Spoletan aristocracy, medieval streets, and towers built for protection at the time when visitors weren't as friendly as they are today. There are churches, churches, and more churches—some of which, like San Gregorio Maggiore, were built in the Romanesque style in the 11th century.

The tourist center of town is **Piazza del Duomo,** with its **Duomo.** The cathedral is a hodgepodge of Romanesque and medieval architecture, with a 12th-century campanile. Its facade is of exceptional beauty, renowned for its 1207 mosaic by Salsterno. You should visit the interior if for no other reason than to see the cycle of frescoes (1467 to 1469) in the chancel by Filippo Lippi. His son, Filippino, designed the tomb for his father, but a mysterious grave robber hauled off the body one night about 2 centuries later. The keeper of the apse will be happy to unlock it for you. These frescoes, believed to have been carried out largely by students, were the elder Lippi's last work; he died in Spoleto in 1469. As friars went in those days, Lippi was a bit of a swinger; he ran off with a nun, Lucrezia Buti, who later posed as the Madonna in several of his paintings. The Duomo is open daily 8am to 1pm and 3 to 6:30pm (to 5:30pm off-season). Admission is free.

If time remains, you might want to visit other churches here, notably the 11th-century **Sant'Eufemia** on Via Saffi, between Piazza del Duomo and Piazza del Mercanto. Note the gallery above the nave, where women were required to sit, a holdover from the Eastern Church; it's one of the few such galleries in Italy. In the courtyard, double stairs lead to the **Museo Diocesano** (☎ **0743/223-2450**), noted for its Madonna paintings, one from 1315. Room 5 contains Filippino Lippi's 1485 *Madonna and Child with Sts. Montano and Bartolomeo.* The church and museum are open daily 10am to 12:30pm and 3:30 to 7pm (to 6pm November to February). Admission to both is 5,000L ($3).

You can reach the remains of the **Teatro Romano** (☎ **0743/223-277**) along Via Apollinare. It dates from the 1st century A.D., and excavations here began in 1891. It's a setting for performances during the Spoleto Festival. For 4,000L ($2.30) you can visit Monday to Saturday 9am to 1:30pm and 2:30 to 7pm and Sunday 9am to 1:30pm. For the same ticket you can also visit the **Archaeological Museum (Museo Archeologico)** nearby, with a warrior's tomb dating from the 7th century B.C. Among the exhibits are Les Poletina, two tablets inscribed after 241 B.C.

A walk along Via del Ponte will bring you to the ✪ **Ponte delle Torri,** with nine towering pylons separating stately arches. The bridge is 264 feet high and 760 feet long, spanning a gorge. It's believed to date from the 13th century and is one of the most photographed sights in Spoleto. Even Goethe praised it when he passed this way in 1786.

Motorists wanting a view can continue up the hill from Spoleto around a winding road (about 5 miles) to **Monteluco,** an ancient spot 2,500 feet above sea level. Monteluco is peppered with summer villas. The monastery here was once frequented by St. Francis of Assisi.

ACCOMMODATIONS

Spoleto offers an attractive range of hotels, but when the "two worlds" crowd in at festival time, the going's rough (one year a group of students bedded down on Piazza del Duomo). In an emergency, the **tourist office** (above) can arrange a list of where to stay in a private home at a moderate price—it's imperative to phone in advance for a reservation. Many of the private rooms are often rented well ahead to artists appearing at the festival. Innkeepers are likely to raise all the prices below to whatever the market will bear.

Albornoz Palace Hotel. Viale Matteotti, 06049 Spoleto. ☎ **0743/221-221.** Fax 0743/221-600. www.assind.perugia.it/hotel/albornoz. E-mail: albornoz@assind.perugia.it. 96 units. A/C MINIBAR TV TEL. 160,000–370,000L ($93–$215) double; 350,000–590,000L ($203–$342) suite. Rates include breakfast. AE, DC, MC, V. Free parking.

In a residential neighborhood half a mile south of town, this five-story modern building is the largest and best equipped in Spoleto. However, the tiny Gattapone (below) is more luxurious and more tranquil. A small garden in back contains a pool. The marble-trimmed lobby is decorated with large modern paintings by American-born artist Sol Lewitt, and on the premises are two restaurants and a bar. The rooms are painted in cool tones of blue-gray and contain modern baths and views over either Spoleto, Monteluco, or the surrounding hills.

Hotel Charleston. Piazza Collicola 10, 06049 Spoleto. ☎ **0743/220-052.** Fax 0743/222-010. 18 units. MINIBAR TV TEL. 155,000L ($90) double; 190,000L ($110) triple. Rates include breakfast. AE, DC, MC, V. Parking 15,000L ($9).

This tile-roofed, sienna-fronted building is from the 17th century. Today it serves as a pleasantly accessorized hotel in the historic center. It's a solid and reliable choice, with wood-beamed ceilings, terra-cotta floors, and open fireplaces. Each of the rooms has a ceiling accented with beams of honey-colored planking and comfortable mattresses. Many rooms have been updated with new furnishings and baths. There's a sauna, as well as a bar, a library, and a sitting room with a writing table.

Hotel Clarici. Piazza della Vittoria 32, 06049 Spoleto. ☎ **0743/223-311.** Fax 0743/222-010. 24 units. A/C MINIBAR TV TEL. 150,000L ($87) double; 170,000L ($99) triple. Rates include breakfast. AE, DC, MC, V. Parking 10,000L ($6).

The Clarici is rated only third class, but it's airy and modern, the best of the budget bets in Spoleto. Each accommodation has a private balcony that opens onto a view. The hotel doesn't emphasize style but rather the creature comforts: soft low beds, built-in wardrobes, steam heat, and an elevator. There's a large terrace for sunbathing or sipping drinks.

Spoleto

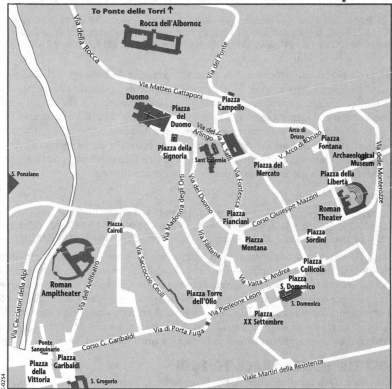

Hotel dei Duchi. Viale Giacomo Matteotti 4, 06049 Spoleto. ☎ **0743/44-541.** Fax 0743/44-543. 53 units. MINIBAR TV TEL. 180,000L ($104) double; 350,000L ($203) suite. Rates include breakfast. Half board 120,000L ($72) per person. AE, DC, MC, V. Free parking.

This bare-brick modern hotel is within walking distance of the major sights yet perches on a hillside with views and terraces. It lacks the style of the Gattapone and Albornoz Palace and seems more geared to commercial travelers. Dei Duchi is graced with brick walls, open-to-the-view glass, and lounges with modern furnishings and original paintings. Some rooms have balconies, plus bland bed coverings, wood-grained furniture, and built-in cupboards—in all, a bit drab. Half board is required in high season. In summer, you have a choice of two dining rooms, each airy and roomy.

✪ **Hotel Gattapone.** Via del Ponte 6, 06049 Spoleto. ☎ **0743/223-447.** Fax 0743/223-448. 16 units. MINIBAR TV TEL. 230,000L ($133) double; 330,000L ($191) suite. Rates include continental breakfast. AE, DC, MC, V. Free parking.

The Gattapone is more a spectacle than a hotel, and we'd rank it as the finest choice for the discriminating traveler, with a lot more personality and style than the Albornoz Palace. Probably the only 16-room hotel in Italy to be rated first class, it's among the clouds, high on a twisting road leading to the ancient castle and the 13th-century Ponte delle Torri. The hotel occupies two side-by-side stone 17th-century cottages. The view side has a two-story picture window and an open spiral stairway leading from the intimate lounge to the guest rooms. Each room is uniquely furnished, with comfortable beds, antiques, and plenty of space. Breakfast is the only meal served.

⊙ **Hotel San Luca.** Via Interna della Mura 21, 06049 Spoleto. ☎ **0743/223-399.** Fax 0743/223-800. www.assind.perugia.it/hotel/sanluca. E-mail: hotelsanluca@mail.caribusiness.it. 35 units. A/C TV TEL. 210,000L ($122) double; from 250,000L ($145) suite. AE, DC, MC, V. Parking 25,000L ($15).

In a restored building from the 19th century, this hotel is the most up-to-date in town, filled with ambience and style. Wherever you turn there's a grace note of the past, like a roof garden and a spacious courtyard with a 1602 fountain. All the elegant rooms are spacious and furnished in a sober yet comforting style, with all the amenities. The baths are particularly welcoming, with such extras as a hair dryer, phone, and towel warmer. Many rooms are also fitted with a massage bath. The public rooms respect the style of the building, with period furniture. A garden solarium and a good restaurant serving Umbrian specialties make this hotel even more alluring.

DINING

Il Tartufo. Piazza Garibaldi 24. ☎ **0743/40-236.** Reservations required. Main courses 18,000–26,000L ($10–$15); fixed-price menus 30,000–60,000L ($17–$35). AE, DC, MC, V. Tues–Sat noon–3pm and 7:30–10:30pm; Sun noon–3pm. Closed July 15–31. UMBRIAN.

At Il Tartufo, outside the heart of town near the amphitheater, you may be introduced to the Umbrian *tartufo* (truffle)—if you can afford it. It's served in the most expensive appetizers and main courses at Spoleto's oldest restaurant. This excellent tavern serves at least nine regional specialties using the black tartufo. A popular dish (and a good introduction for neophyte palates) is strengozzi al tartufo, a pasta dish with truffles. Or you may want to start with an omelet like frittata al tartufo. Main dishes of veal and beef are also excellently prepared. For such a small restaurant, the menu is large.

OFF THE BEATEN TRACK TO TODI

For years, **Todi** lay slumbering in the Umbrian sun. Then the world moved in. Visa used it as a backdrop for a commercial, and the University of Kentucky keeps consistently voting it "the most livable town in the world." This has brought a monied class from America rushing in to buy decaying castles and villas, hoping to convert them into holiday homes. And Todi has imitated Spoleto and now stages a **Festival di Todi,** attracting ballet, theatrical, and operatic stars during the first 10 days of each September.

Taking Route 418 out of Spoleto for 28 miles northwest will lead you to what the excitement is all about. At Acquasparta, get on autostrada 3 northwest. Soon you'll come to this well-preserved medieval village, today a retreat for wealthy artists and diplomats. The setting with its Etruscan, Roman, and medieval past has been likened to a long-ago fairy tale.

On arriving, you'll enter the triangularly walled town through one of its three gates, named for the destinations of the roads leading away: **Rome** in the southwest wall, **Perugia** in the north, and **Orvieto** in the southeast. The remains of original Roman and Etruscan walls are also evident just inside the Rome gate. The central square, **Piazza del Popolo,** was built over a Roman forum and is as harmonious as any in Italy. It contains the 12th-century Romanesque-Gothic **cathedral** and three beautiful palaces—the **Palazzo del Popolo,** built in 1213; the **Palazzo del Capitano,** dating from 1292; and the 14th-century **Palazzo dei Priori,** with its trapezoidal tower. Each summer, all three are filled with the wares of the **National Exhibit of Crafts (Mostra Nazionale dell'Artigianato).**

Also on view are **Santa Maria della Consolazione,** standing guard over Todi with its domes and exquisite stained glass, and the 13th-century **San Fortunato,** in the **Piazza della Repubblica,** burial site of the town's most famous citizen, the monk/

medieval poet Jacopone. To the right of the church, a path leads uphill to the ruins of a 14th-century castle known as **La Rocca.** From here, a walk up the twisting Viale della Serpentina will reward you with a bird's-eye view of the surrounding valley—fitting in a town allegedly founded on the spot where an eagle used a stolen Umbrian tablecloth to line its aerie. If the climb seems a bit much, check the view from **Piazza Garibaldi.**

Today, the artisans of Todi are particularly renowned for their woodwork. Examples of historical as well as contemporary craft are available for perusal or purchase, especially during the **summer craft exhibition** along Piazza del Popolo.

12 Orvieto

75 miles N of Rome, 47 miles SW of Perugia, 70 miles SW of Assisi

Built on a pedestal of volcanic rock above vineyards in a green valley, **Orvieto** is the hill town closest to Rome and is often visited by those who don't have the time to explore other spots in Umbria. It lies on the Paglia, a tributary of the Tiber, and sits on an isolated rock some 1,035 feet above sea level. Crowning the town is its world-famed cathedral. A road runs from below up to Piazza del Duomo.

The most spectacularly sited hill town in Umbria (but not the most spectacular town), Orvieto was founded by the Etruscans, who were apparently drawn to it because of its good defensive possibilities. Likewise, long after its days as a Roman colony, it became a papal stronghold. It was a natural fortress, as its cliffs rise starkly from the valley below, even though Orvieto, when you finally reach it, is relatively flat. Although the tall, sheer cliffs on which the town stands saved it from the incursion of railroads and superhighways, time and traffic vibrations have caused the soft volcanic rock to disintegrate so that work is imminently necessary to shore up the town.

Orvieto is known for its white wine—the best place to enjoy it is at a wine cellar at Piazza del Duomo 2 as you contemplate the cathedral's facade.

ESSENTIALS

GETTING THERE   Three **trains** a day arrive in Orivieto from Perugia. Because of frequent stops, the trip takes 1½ hours. A one-way ticket is 10,000L ($6). From Florence, the handful of trains making the trip require 2 hours, with a one-way ticket at 16,500L ($10). From Rome, the train takes 1½ hours and costs 12,100L ($7) each way. Don't expect a particularly convenient arrival if you opt for the train, as the Orvieto's rail station lies below the town in the valley. Transit between the station and the town center is accessible via Bus A, which departs at intervals of 40 minutes or less, throughout the day and most of the night, or via a small-scale funicular operating daily 7:15am and 8:30pm. One-way transit from the rail station to the town by either bus or funicular is 1,500L (85¢). For information, call ☎ 0763/300-434 or the tourist office (below).

From Perugia, you can take an **ATC bus** to Orvieto for 12,000L ($7) each way, but the only departure is early in the morning (usually around 5:55am) Monday to Saturday. You can buy tickets on the bus. For information, call ☎ 0763/301-224. If you've got a **car** and are coming from Rome, drive for about 90 minutes (a distance of around 75 miles north along A1) to Orvieto. From Perugia, head 26 miles south on SS3bis to Todi, then take SS448 for 15½ miles southwest to the intersection of SS205 and drive 5½ miles to Orvieto.

VISITOR INFORMATION   The **tourist office,** at Piazza del Duomo 24 (☎ 0763/341-772), is open Monday to Friday 8:15am to 2pm and 4 to 7pm, Saturday 10am to 1pm and 4 to 7pm, and Sunday 10am to noon and 4 to 7pm.

EXPLORING THE TOWN

✪ **Il Duomo.** Piazza del Duomo. ☎ **0763/341-167.** Admission 3,000L ($1.75). Apr–Sept daily 7am–1pm and 2:30–7:30pm; Nov–Feb to 5:30pm, Mar and Oct to 6:30pm.

Erected on the site of two older churches and dedicated to the Virgin, the Duomo was begun in 1288 (maybe even earlier) to commemorate the Miracle of Bolsena. This alleged miracle came out of the doubts of a priest who questioned the transubstantiation (the incarnation of Jesus Christ in the Host). However, so the story goes, at the moment of consecration, the Host started to drip blood. The priest doubted no more, and the Feast of Corpus Christi was launched.

The cathedral is known for its elaborately adorned facade, rich statuary, marble bas-reliefs, and mosaics. Pope John XXIII once proclaimed that on Judgment Day, God would send his angels down to earth to pick up this Duomo's facade and transport it back to heaven. The modern bronze portals are controversial, and many art historians journey from around the world to see them. Installed in 1970, they were the work of eminent sculptor Emilio Greco, who took as his theme the Misericordia, the seven acts of corporal charity. One panel depicts Pope John XXIII's famous visit to the prisoners of Rome's Queen of Heaven jail in 1960. Some critics have called the doors "outrageous"; others have praised them as "one of the most original works of modern sculpture." You decide.

The west facade, divided into three gables, boasts richly sculptured marble based on designs of Lorenzo Maitani of Siena. Four wall surfaces around the three doors were adorned with bas-reliefs, also based on Maitani designs. He worked on the facade until his death in 1330. The bas-reliefs depict scenes from the Bible, including the Last Judgment. After Maitani's death, Andrea Pisano took over, but the actual work carried on until the dawn of the 17th century.

For decades, every guidebook writer has suggested that the cathedral facade is best viewed at sunset. However, there's nothing wrong with dawn's early light.

Inside, the nave and aisles were constructed in alternating panels of black and white stone. You'll want to seek out the **Cappella del Corporale,** with its mammoth silver shrine based on the design of the cathedral facade. This 1338 masterpiece, richly embellished with precious stones, was the work of Ugolino Vieri of Siena and designed to shelter the Holy Corporal from Bolsena (the cloth in which the bleeding Host was wrapped). The most celebrated chapel is the **Cappella di San Brizio,** which contains newly restored frescoes of the Last Judgment and the Apocalypse by Luca Signorelli. Michelangelo was said to have been inspired by the frescoes at the time he was contemplating the Sistine Chapel. The masterpiece was produced between 1499 and 1503 and cost $4.4 million to renovate. Signorelli was called to complete the frescoes, which were begun in 1447 by Fra Angelico.

Pozzo di San Patrizio (St. Patrick's Well). Viale Sangallo, off Piazza Cahen. ☎ **0763/343-768.** Admission 6,000L ($3.50) adults, 4,000L ($2.30) students; children 12 and under free. Apr–Sept daily 9:30am–7pm; Oct–Mar daily 10am–7pm.

St. Patrick's Well is an architectural curiosity, and in its day it was an engineering feat. Pope Clement VII ordered the well built when he feared that Orvieto might come under siege and its water supply be cut off. The well was entrusted to the design of Antonio da Sangallo the Younger in 1527. It's some 200 feet deep and about 42 feet in diameter, cut into volcanic rock. Two spiral staircases, with about 250 steps, lead into the wells. These spiral ramps never meet.

Museum of Archaeology and Civic Museum (Musei Archeologici Faina e Civico). In the Palazzo Faina, Piazza del Duomo 29. ☎ **0763/341-511** or 0763/341-216. Admission 7,000L ($4.05) adults, 4,000L ($2.30) students; children 12 and under free. Apr–Sept Tues–Sun 10am–1pm and 3–7pm; Oct–Mar Tues–Sun 10am–1pm and 2:30–7pm.

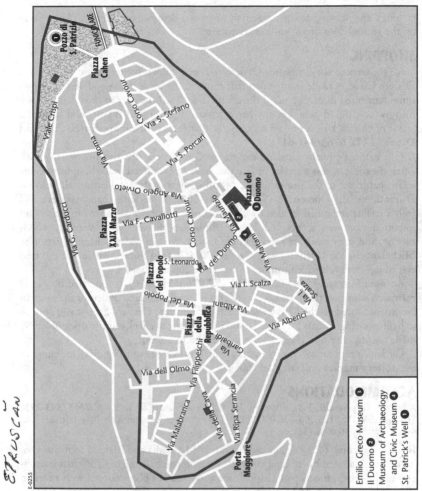

Orvieto

CITY ETRUSCAN

Originally a private collection, this museum across from the cathedral contains many Etruscan artifacts found in and around Orvieto. In addition to the stone sarcophagi, terra-cotta portraits, and vials of colored glass left by the Etruscans, it exhibits many beautiful Greek vases. Three of the most important objects are amphorae attributed to one of the finest of the Attic vase painters, Exekias (550–540 B.C.). They were found in a necropolis near Orvieto and are a gauge as to the richness reached by the city-state of Velzna, as Orvieto used to be known.

Emilio Greco Museum (Museo Emilio Greco). In the Palazzo Soliano, Piazza del Duomo. ☎ **0763/344-605.** Admission 5,000L ($2.90) adults, 3,000L ($1.75) students; children 12 and under free. Apr–Sept Mon–Sat 10:30am–1pm and 3–7pm (to 6pm off-season).

This museum opened in 1991 to house an important art collection donated to the city by eminent sculptor Emilio Greco. A devoted advocate of civic pride and an internationally recognized sculptor best remembered in Orvieto for his sculpting of the bronze doors in the front of the Duomo (see above), he died in 1996 during his mid-80s. You'll find 32 Greco sculptures and 60 graphic works (including lithographs, etchings, and drawings). The modern museum was designed by architect Giulio Savio on the ground floor of a 14th-century palazzo.

SHOPPING

Since the days of the Etruscans, Orvieto has been known for its limpid white wine, Orvieto Classico, made from grapes that thrive in the local chalky soil and are sometimes fermented in caves around the countryside. You'll be able to buy glasses of the fruity wine ("liquid gold") at any bar or tavern in town, but if you want to haul a bottle or two back to your own digs, try the town's best wine shop, **Foresi,** Piazza del Duomo 2 (☎ **0763/341-611**).

Gift items, especially lace and carved wooden objects, are also noteworthy local enterprises. For access to styles of lace that have embroidered everything from courtesan's petticoats to the sleeves of priests during mass at the local cathedral, head for **Duranti,** Via del Duomo 13 (☎ **0763/344-606**). Tablecloths, handkerchiefs, and frilly curtains are available, along with an occasional baptismal robe. You'll also find imported European scents and locally distilled perfumes. Woodworking, woodcarving, and inlay work are specialties of Orvieto. For the widest selection, patronize **Michelangeli,** Via Gualverio Michelangeli (☎ **0763/342-660**), where you can find everything from full-scale furniture to an ornate cup and bowl.

Antonia Carraro, Corso Cavour 101 (☎ **0763/342-870**), is operated by a local matriarch who gave the place her name. This is a well-respected outlet for the agrarian bounty produced on the hillsides and fields surrounding Orvieto. Even if you opt not to haul away ingredients for a picnic, you might want to check out the stock of locally made breads, olive oils, cheeses, salamis, wines, and biscotti.

Orvieto is also known for its pottery, which is best seen on Saturday mornings at the **pottery market** on Piazza del Popolo.

ACCOMMODATIONS

Albergo Filippeschi. Via Filippeschi 19, 05019 Orvieto. ☎ and fax **0763/343-275.** 16 units. TV TEL. 125,000–130,000L ($73–$75) double. Rates include breakfast. AE, DC, MC, V. Parking 10,000L ($6).

If you're searching for a bargain and the rates of La Badia and Maitani aren't for you, head here. Managed by its family owners, the Filippeschi is the most affordable property in the center. It occupies a historic mansion and has been restored with a certain style and grace by gutting a decaying structure and modernizing it. The rooms are generally spacious, and though lacking style, they contain modern amenities like a small refrigerator. There's a cozy bar but no restaurant, and a generous breakfast is served in a tasteful room.

✪ **Hotel La Badia.** S.N.C. Località La Badia 8, 05019 Orvieto Terni. ☎ **0763/90-359.** Fax 0763/92-796. 26 units. A/C MINIBAR TV TEL. 240,000–270,000L ($139–$157) double; 394,000–477,000L ($229–$277) suite. Half board 70,000L ($41) per person. AE, MC, V. Closed Jan–Feb. Free parking. Located 3 miles east of town center.

This is one of the most memorable of the country inns in this part of Italy, set atop a hill facing the rocky foundations of Orvieto. This was the site of a Benedictine abbey (Badia, in local dialect) in the 8th century and was upgraded to a monastery in the 12th, when a church was built nearby. In the 19th century, the buildings were renovated by an aristocratic family who did what they could to preserve the irreplaceable stonework. Today the hotel is the finest, most historic, and most charming in Orvieto, with tennis courts, a pool, a well-chosen collection of antiques, and luxurious guest rooms (sizes vary greatly, though). Views extend over the surrounding countryside, and a restaurant provides elegant meals with discreet service.

Hotel Maitani. Via Maitani 5, 05018 Orvieto. ☎ and fax **0763/342-011.** 40 units. A/C TV TEL. 210,000L ($122) double; 250,000–290,000L ($145–$168) suite. Breakfast 18,000L ($11). AE, DC, MC, V. Closed Jan 7–22. Parking 20,000L ($12).

The stone-sided building that houses this family-run hotel was built as a palazzo around 600 years ago. It was transformed into a hotel in 1966. The rooms, scattered over four floors, are mostly modernized but do retain some reminders of their medieval origins. They're small but cozy and comfortable. Breakfast is the only meal served, though several restaurants are nearby. Both the hotel and the street it sits on were named after the architect who designed Orvieto's famous cathedral. If you have a car, it's best to try to check in early, as the hotel has parking space for only eight vehicles.

✪ **Villa Ciconia.** Via dei Tigli 69, 05019 Orvieto. ☎ **0763/305-582.** Fax 0763/302-097. 10 units. MINIBAR TV TEL. 170,000–220,000L ($99–$128) double. Rates include breakfast. AE, DC, MC, V. Bus: 3. The villa is 4km from Orvieto.

This beautiful 16th-century villa (the best hotel in the environs) sits in an 8-acre park at the confluence of the Chain and Paglia rivers. It has the thick walls, terra-cotta floors, and beamed ceilings typical of its era. Huge chestnut beams run more than 13 yards along the ceiling of the lobby, and the main dining room features a great stone fireplace and a lacuna ceiling with ornate molding and frescoes around the walls. The spacious rooms have park views and period furnishings. A room with air-conditioning is an extra 20,000L ($12) per night. Guests can use a nearby public sports center with an indoor Olympic pool, indoor and outdoor red-clay tennis courts, and horseback riding. The restaurant features a wide variety of tasty regional dishes and a large selection of local and national wines. Truffles figure prominently on the menu.

DINING

La Grotto del Funeral. Via Ripper Ceramic 41. ☎ **0763/343-276.** Reservations recommended. Main courses 16,000–27,000L ($9–$16). AE, DC, MC, V. Tues–Sun noon–2:30pm and 7pm–1am. UMBRIAN/PIZZA.

The cuisine is the type of traditional fare Umbrian grandmothers have served their families for generations—fresh, flavorful, and nutritious, with no attempt to be creative. The setting, however, is a surprisingly dry cave below the city center that includes many eerie references to other days and other times. No one seems to have any idea how long the cave has been in everyday use (the staff believes it was part of the storerooms used by the ancient Etruscans). Menu items include an array of grilled meats (like grilled lamb, grilled pork with potatoes and vegetables), pastas flavored with local mushrooms and truffles, and very fresh vegetables. From a wood-burning oven emerge the most savory pizzas in town.

8

Bologna & Emilia-Romagna

In the northern reaches of central Italy, **Emilia-Romagna** is known for its gastronomy and for its art cities, Modena and Parma. Here families like the Renaissance dukes of Ferrara rose in power and influence, creating courts that attracted painters and poets, notably Tasso and Ariosto.

Bologna, the capital, stands at the crossroads between Venice and Florence and is linked by express highways to Milan and Tuscany. By basing yourself in this ancient university city, you can branch out in all directions: north for 32 miles to Ferrara; southeast for 31 miles to the ceramics-making town of Faenza; northwest for 25 miles to Modena with its Romanesque cathedral; or 34 miles farther northwest to Parma, the legendary capital of the Farnese family duchy in the 16th century. Ravenna, famed for its mosaics, lies 46 miles east of Bologna on the Adriatic Sea.

Most of our stops in this region lie on the ancient Roman **Via Emilia,** which began in Rimini and stretched to Piacenza, a Roman colony that often attracted invading barbarians. This ancient land—known to the Romans as Æmilia, and to the Etruscans before them—is rich in architecture (Parma's cathedral and baptistery) and in scenic beauty (the green plains and the slopes of the Apennines). Emilia is one of Italy's most bountiful farming districts and sets a table highly praised in Europe—both for its wines and for its imaginatively prepared pasta dishes.

The serious wine connoisseur may want to visit one of the region's outstanding wineries. To call for an appointment, refer to the Emilia-Romagna entry under "The Best Wine-Growing Regions" in chapter 1.

1 Bologna: Capital of Emilia-Romagna

32 miles S of Ferrara, 94 miles SW of Venice, 235 miles N of Rome

The manager of a hotel in Bologna once lamented: "The Americans! They spend a week in Florence, a week in Venice. Why not 6 days in Florence, 6 days in Venice, and 2 days in Bologna?" That's a good question. **Bologna** is one of the most sadly overlooked cities in Italy—we've found cavernous accommodation space here in July and August, when the hotels in Venice and Florence were packed as tightly as a can of Progresso clam sauce.

"But what is there to see?" is also a common question. True, Bologna boasts no Uffizi or Doge's Palace, but it does offer a beautiful

Emilia-Romagna

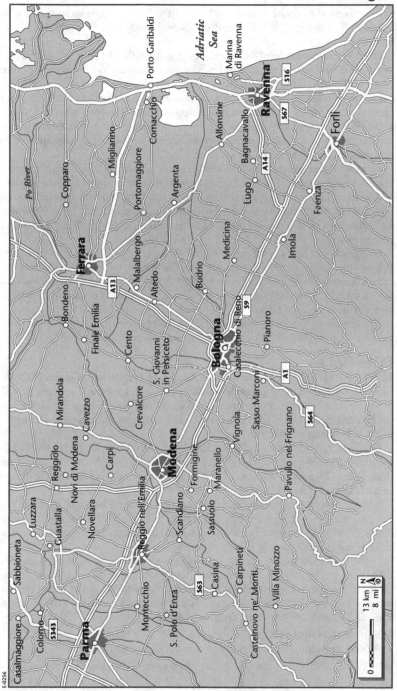

E-0256

city that's one of the most architecturally unified in Europe—a panorama of marbled sidewalks and porticos that, if spread out, would surely stretch all the way to the border.

Filled with sienna-colored buildings, Bologna is Emilia's leading city. Its rise as a commercial power was almost assured by its strategic location as the geographic center between Florence and Venice. And its university, the oldest in Europe (founded 1088), has for years generated a lively interest in art and culture. It features the nation's best medical school as well as one of its top business schools. The bars, cafes, and squares of the city fill up with young people drawn to its academy, and an eclectic mix of concerts, art exhibits, and avant-garde ballet and theater are booked to keep up with the demand for cultural activity.

Perhaps because the student population is so large, Bologna is a center of great tolerance, with the national gay alliance and several student organizations making their headquarters here. Politically, communism and socialism figure prominently in the voter profile, which may be why the region has been largely unscathed by the scandal and corruption of neighboring precincts, where blatant capitalism has led to Mafia-corrupted activity.

Bologna is also Italy's gastronomic capital. Gourmets flock here just to sample the cuisine—the pastas (tortellini, tagliatelle, lasagne verde), the meat and poultry specialties (zampone, veal cutlet bolognese, tender turkey breasts in sauce supreme), and the mortadella, Bologna's incomparable sausage, as distant a cousin to baloney as porterhouse is to the hot dog.

The city seems to take a vacation in August, becoming virtually dead. You'll notice signs proclaiming CHIUSO ("closed") almost everywhere you look.

ESSENTIALS

GETTING THERE   The international **Aeroporto Guglielmo Marconi** (☎ 051/ 312-336 for information) is 4 miles north of the town center and serviced by such domestic carriers as Aermediterranea and ATI; all the main European airlines have connections through this airport. A frequent bus runs from the airport to the air terminal at Bologna's rail station.

Bologna's **rail station** is at Piazza delle Medaglie d'Oro (☎ 051/630-2111 or 1478/88-088 toll-free in Italy only). Trains arrive hourly from Rome (3½ hours) and from Milan (2½ hours). Bus nos. 25 and 30 run between the station and the historic core of Bologna, Piazza Maggiore.

Because of its role as an important rail junction, Bologna isn't well served by **bus** companies. So even though there's a **bus station** at Piazza XX Settembre 6 (☎ 051/ 290-290), most of its focus is on local city buses. Here, more than in most other large cities in Italy, it really pays to stick to the train.

If you have a **car** and are coming from Florence, continue north along Autostrada del Sole A1 until you reach the outskirts of Bologna, where signs direct you to the city center. Coming over the Apennines, A1 runs northwest to Milan just before the outskirts of Bologna. A13 cuts northeast to Ferrara and Venice, and A14 dashes east to Rimini, Ravenna, and the towns along the Adriatic.

VISITOR INFORMATION   The **tourist office** is at Piazza Maggiore 6 (☎ 051/ 239-660), open Monday to Saturday 9am to 7pm and Sunday 9am to 12:30pm.

GETTING AROUND   Bologna is easy to cover on foot; most of the major sights are in and around Piazza Maggiore. However, if you don't want to walk, **city buses** leave for most points from either Piazza Nettuno or Piazza Maggiore. Free maps are available at the storefront office of the **AT (Azienda Trasporti)** at Piazza Galvani 4, behind San Petronio. You can buy tickets at one of many booths and tobacconists in

Bologna. Once on board, you must have your ticket validated. **Taxis** are on radio call at ☎ **051/372-727** or 051/534-141.

SEEING THE SIGHTS

On Piazza del Nettuno (adjacent to Piazza Maggiore) stands the ✪ **Neptune Fountain (Fontana del Nettuno).** Characteristic of the pride and independence of Bologna, this fountain has gradually become a symbol of the city, but it was designed in 1566 by a Frenchman named Giambologna by the Italians (his fame rests largely on his work in Florence). Viewed as irreverent by some, "indecent" by the Catholic Church, and magnificent by those with more liberal tastes, this 16th-century fountain depicts Neptune with rippling muscles, a trident in one arm and a heavy foot on the head of a dolphin. The church forced Giambologna to manipulate Neptune's left arm to cover his monumental endowment. Giambologna's defenders denounced this as "artistic castration." Around his feet are four highly erotic cherubs, also with dolphins. At the base of the fountain, four very sensual sirens spout streams of water from their breasts.

Basilica di San Petronio. Piazza Maggiore. ☎ **051/225-442.** Free admission. Apr–Sept daily 7:15am–1:30pm and 2:30–6:30pm; Oct–Mar daily 7:15am–1pm and 2–6pm.

Sadly, the facade of this enormous Gothic basilica honoring the patron saint of Bologna was never completed. Legend has it that the construction was greatly curtailed by papal decree when the Vatican learned that Bologna city fathers had planned to erect a basilica larger than St. Peter's. Though the builders went to work in 1390, after 3 centuries the church was still not finished (though Charles V was crowned emperor here in 1530). However, Jacopo della Quercia of Siena did grace the central door with a masterpiece Renaissance sculpture. Inside, the church could accommodate the traffic of New York's Grand Central Terminal. The central nave is separated from the aisles by pilasters shooting up to the flying ceiling arches. Of the 22 art-filled chapels, the most interesting is the **Bolognini Chapel,** the fourth on the left as you enter, embellished with frescoes representing heaven and hell. The purity and simplicity of line represent some of the best of the Gothic in Italy.

Palazzo Comunale. Piazza Maggiore 6. ☎ **051/203-526.** Each museum separately, 8,000L ($4.65) adults, 4,000L ($2.30) children 14–18/seniors 60 and over; children 13 and under free. Combined ticket to both museums, 12,000L ($7) adults, 6,000L ($3.50) children 14–18; children 13 and under free. Tues–Sat 10am–6pm, Sun guided tour at 4pm. Closed holidays.

Built in the 14th century, this town hall has seen major restorations but happily retains its splendor. Enter through the courtyard, then proceed up the steps on the right to the **Comunal Collection of Fine Arts (Collezioni Comunali d'Arte),** which includes many paintings from the 14th- and 19th-century Emilian school. Another section comprises the **Museum of Giorgio Morandi (Museo di Giorgio Morandi),** devoted to the works of this famed painter of Bologna (1890–1964). His subject matter (a vase of flowers or a box) might've been mundane, but he transformed these objects into works of art of startling intensity and perception. Some of his finest works are landscapes of Grizzana, a village where he spent many a lazy summer working and drawing. There's also a reconstruction of his studio.

Basilica di San Domenico. Piazza San Domenico 13. ☎ **051/640-0411.** Free admission. Daily 7am–1pm and 2:15–7pm.

The basilica dates from the 13th century but has undergone many restorations. It houses the beautifully crafted tomb of St. Domenico, in front of the Capella della Madonna. The sculptured tomb—known as an *area*—is a Renaissance masterpiece, a joint enterprise of Niccolò Pisano, Guglielmo (a friar), Niccolò dell'Arca, Alfonso

Lombardi, and the young Michelangelo. Observe the gaze and stance of Michelangelo's *San Procolo,* which appears to be the "rehearsal" for his later *David.* The choir stalls, the basilica's second major artistic work, were carved by Damiano da Bergamo, another friar, in the 16th century.

Tower of the Asinelli (Torre degli Asinelli) and Tower of the Garisenda (Torre degli Garisenda). Piazza di Porta Ravegnanna. Admission 3,000L ($1.75). May–Sept daily 9am–6pm (Oct–Apr to 5pm).

These leaning towers, the virtual symbol of Bologna, keep defying gravity year after year. Stendhal observed that a Bolognese far from home is likely to burst into tears at the thought of his beloved two towers. In Canto 31 of the *Inferno,* Dante wrote that when the giant Antaeus picked him up, along with Virgil, and lowered him into a well, he likened the experience to the dizzy sensation of looking up at the Garisenda Tower as a cloud drifts "over against the slant of it, swimming low."

These towers were built by patricians in the 12th century. In the Middle Ages, Bologna contained dozens of these skyscraper towers, ahead of Manhattan by several centuries. They were status symbols: The more powerful the family, the taller their tower was. The smaller one, the **Garisenda,** is only 162 feet tall and leans about 10½ feet from the perpendicular. The family who built this tower didn't prepare a solid foundation, and it sways tipsily to the south. When the Garisenda clan saw what they'd done, they gave up. In 1360, part of the tower was lopped off as it was viewed as a threat to public safety. The taller one, the **Asinelli** (334 feet tall, a walk up of nearly 500 steps), inclines almost 7½ feet. Those who scale the Asinelli should be awarded a medal, but instead they're presented with a panoramic view of the red-tile roofs of Bologna and the green hills beyond.

After visiting the towers, take a walk up what must be the most architecturally elegant street in Bologna, **Via Strada Maggiore,** with its colonnades and mansions.

Santo Stefano. Via Santo Stefano 24. ☎ 051/223-256. Free admission to church and museum. Daily 9am–1pm and 3:30–5:30pm.

From the leaning towers (above), head up Via Santo Stefano to see a quartet of churches linked together. A church has stood on this site since the 5th century, which even then was a converted Temple of Isis. Charlemagne stopped here to worship on his way to France in the 8th century.

The first church you enter is the 11th-century **Church of the Crucifix (Chiesa di Crocifisso),** relatively simple with only one nave and a crypt. To the left is the entrance to **Santo Sepolcro,** a polygonal temple dating principally from the 12th century. Under the altar is the tomb of San Petronio (St. Petronius), modeled after the Holy Sepulchre in Jerusalem and adorned with bas-reliefs. Continuing left, you enter the churches of **Santi Vitale e Agricola.** The present buildings, graced with three apses, also dates from the 11th century. To reenter Santo Sepolcro, take the back entrance this time into the **Courtyard of Pilate,** onto which several more chapels open. Legend has it that the basin in the courtyard was the one in which Pontius Pilate washed his hands after condemning Christ to death. (Actually, it's a Lombard bathtub from the 8th century.) Through the courtyard entrance to the right, proceed into the Romanesque **cloisters,** dating from the 11th and 12th centuries. The names on the wall of the lapidary honor Bolognese war dead.

Chiesa di San Giacomo Maggiore (St. James). Piazza Rossini or Via Zamboni 15. ☎ 051/225-970. Free admission. Daily 8am–noon and 3:30–6pm.

This church was a Gothic structure in the 13th century but, like so many others, was altered and restored at the expense of its original design. Still, it's one of Bologna's most interesting churches, filled with art treasures. The **Bentivoglio Chapel** is the

Archaelogical Museum **7**
Basilica di San Domenico **9**
Basilica di San Petronio **6**
Chiesa di San Giacomo Maggiore **2**
National Picture Gallery **1**

Neptune Fountain **4**
Palazzo Comunale **5**
Santo Stefano **8**
Tower of the Asinelli and
    Tower of the Garisenda **3**

most sacred haunt, though time has dimmed the luster of its frescoes. Near the altar, seek out a *Madonna and Child* enthroned, one of the most outstanding works of Francesco Erancia. The holy pair are surrounded by angels and saints, as well as by a half-naked Sebastian to the right. Nearby is a sepulchre of Antonio Bentivoglio, designed by Jacopo della Quercia, who labored so long over the doors to the Basilica of San Petronio. In the **Chapel of Santa Cecilia** you'll discover important frescoes by Francia and Lorenzo Costa.

Archaeological Museum (Museo Civico Archeologico). Via dell'Archiginnasio 2. ☎ **051/233-849.** Admission 8,000L ($4.65) adults, 4,000L ($2.30) students/seniors over 60; children under 14 free. Tues–Fri 9am–2pm, Sat–Sun 9am–1pm and 3:30–7pm.

This museum houses one of Italy's major Egyptian collections, as well as important discoveries dug up in Emilia. As you enter, look to the right in the atrium to see a decapitated marble torso, said to be Nero's. One floor below street level, a new Egyptian section presents a notable array of mummies and sarcophagi. The chief attraction in this collection is a cycle of bas-reliefs from Horemheb's tomb. On the ground floor, a new wing contains a gallery of casts, displaying copies of famous Greek and Roman sculptures. On the first floor, reached through a gallery of casts, two exceptional burial items from Verucchio (Rimini) are exhibited. Note the wood furnishings, footrests, and the throne of tomb 89, which is decorated with scenes from everyday life and ceremonial parades.

Upstairs are cases of prehistoric objects, tools, and artifacts. Etrusan relics comprise the best part of the museum, especially the highly stylized Askos Benacci, depicting a man on a horse that's perched on yet another animal. Also displayed are terra-cotta urns, a vase depicting fighting Greeks and Amazons, and a bronze Certosa jar from the 6th century B.C. The museum's greatest single treasure is Phidias's head of Athena Lemnia, a copy of the 5th-century B.C. Greek work.

National Picture Gallery (Pinacoteca Nazionale di Bologna). Via delle Belle Arti 56. ☎ **051/243-222.** Admission 8,000L ($4.65) adults; children 18 and under free. Tues–Sat 9am–2pm, Sun 9am–1pm. Closed holidays.

The most significant works of the school of painting that flourished in Bologna from the 14th century to the heyday of the baroque have been assembled under one roof in this second-floor pinacoteca. The gallery also houses works by other major Italian artists, such as Raphael's *St. Cecilia in Estasi.* Guido Reni (1575 to 1642) of Bologna steals the scene with his *St. Sebastian* and his *Pietà*, along with his penetrating *St. Andrea Corsini, The Slaying of the Innocents,* and idealized *Samson the Victorious.* Other Reni works are *The Flagellation of Christ, The Crucifixion,* and his masterpiece, *Ritratto della Madre* (a revealing portrait of his mother that must surely have inspired Whistler). Then seek out Vitale de Bologna's (1330 to 1361) rendition of St. George slaying the dragon—a theme in European art that parallels Moby Dick in America. Also displayed are works by Francesco Francia, and especially noteworthy is a polyptych attributed to Giotto.

SHOPPING

Collectors of art deco and art nouveau will find a variety of objets d'art at **Art Decorativi,** Via Santo Stefano 12/A (☎ **051/222-758**). Obviously the stock changes, but expect to find items like Murano glass, dish sets, furniture, and lamps. If you call puppeteer **Demitrio Presini** (☎ **051/649-1837**) you might catch him and set up an appointment to see his creations, but your chances are better if you show up at his workshop at Via Rizzoli 17 (no phone) between 1:30 and 6:30pm. Here you can tour the facilities and see how his puppets (including *burratini,* wooden puppets in handmade costumes) are made. You can't buy anything on the premises, but you can order a puppet that'll be made and shipped to you within 1 to 3 months. Presini specializes in local and regional characters but is capable of any custom work you may want.

   Galleria Marescalchi, Via Mascarela 116/B (☎ **051/240-368**), features more traditional art, offering paintings and prints for view or sale by native son Morandi, Italian modern master De Chirico, and such foreigners as Chagall and Magritte. Fans of musical mastery should head to **Bongiovanni,** Via Rizzoli 28/E (☎ **051/225-722**), which stocks rare and popular recordings of operatic and classical scores on cassette, CD, and even vinyl.

   A number of shops more than adequately illustrate the city's nickname Bologna la Grassa (Bologna the Fat). An array of breads, pasta, and pastries make **Atti,** with locations at Via Caprarie 7 (☎ **051/220-425**) and Via Drapperie 6 (☎ **051/233-369**), tempting whether you're hungry or not. Among the pastries is the Bolognese specialty *certosino,* a heavy loaf resembling fruitcake. Available at the Via Caprarie location is an assortment of *gastronomie*—delectable heat-and-serve starters and main courses made fresh at the shop. If you want chocolate, **Majani,** Via Carbonesi 5 (☎ **051/234-302**), claims to be Italy's oldest sweets shop, having made and sold confections since 1796. A wide assortment of chocolates awaits you, accompanied by several types of biscuits, and at Easter they also make eggs, "rabbits," and "lambs." A stop at **Tamburini,** Via Caprarie 1 (☎ **051/234-726**), lends credence to claims that it's Italy's most lavish food shop. You can choose from an incredible array of gastronomie, including meats and fish, soups and salads, vegetables, and sweets, as well as fresh pasta to prepare at

---

The World's Greatest China Shop

Faenza, 36 miles southeast of Bologna, has lent its name to a form of ceramics called faïence, which originated on the island of Majorca, off Spain's coast. Faenza potters found inspiration in the work coming out of Majorca and in the 12th century began to produce their own designs—characterized by brilliant colors and floral decorations. The art reached its pinnacle in the 16th century, when the "hot-fire" process was perfected, during which ceramics were baked at a temperature of 1,742°F.

The legacy of this fabled industry is preserved today at the **International Museum of Ceramics (Museo Internazionale delle Ceramiche),** Via Campidoro 2 (☎ **0546/21-240**), called "the world's greatest china shop." Housed here are works not only from the artisans of Faenza but also from around the world, including pre-Columbian pottery from Peru. Of exceptional interest are Etruscan and Egyptian ceramics and a wide-ranging collection from the Orient, even from the days of the Roman Empire.

Deserving special attention is the section devoted to modern ceramic art, including works by Matisse and Picasso. On display are Picasso vases and a platter with his dove of peace, a platter in rich colors by Chagall, a "surprise" from Matisse, and a framed ceramic plaque of the Crucifixion by Georges Rouault. Another excellent work, the inspiration of a lesser-known artist, is a ceramic woman by Dante Morozzi. Even the great Léger tried his hand at ceramics.

June to September, the museum is open Tuesday to Saturday 9am to 7pm and Sunday 9:30am to 1pm and 3 to 7pm; October to May, hours are Tuesday to Friday 9:30am to 1:30pm, Saturday 3 to 6pm, and Sunday 9:30am to 1pm and 3 to 7pm. Admission is 10,000L ($6) adults and 4,000L ($2.30) children 17 and under. It's closed New Year's Day, May Day, August 15, and Christmas.

---

home. If you don't have anything to cook or serve your pasta in, **Schiavina,** Via Clavature 16 (☎ **051/223-438**), sells every kitchen utensil you might need, like cookware, silverware, glasses, dinnerware, and knives.

If you have hard-to-fit feet, head to **Piero,** Via delle Lame 56 (☎ **051/558-680**), with attractive footwear for men and women in large sizes, ranging up to European size 53 for men (American size 20) and size 46 for women. Bruno Magli quickly made a name for himself after opening his first shoe factory in 1934. Today, **Bruno Magli** shops selling leather bags, jackets, and coats for men and women—in addition to shoes—are at Galeria Cavour 9 (☎ **051/266-915**) and Piazza della Mercanzia 2 (☎ **051/231-126**). With styles ranging from elegant to casual, **Marisell,** Via Farini 4 (☎ **051/234-670**), offers womenswear by some of today's best Italian designers. A range of men's and women's clothes is available at **Paris, Texas,** Via Altabella 11 (☎ **051/225-741**), including (but not limited to) designer eveningwear; the location at Via dell'Indipendenza 67/B (☎ **051/241-994**) focuses more on casuals like jeans and T-shirts. A third location is at Via Strada Maggiore (☎ **051/225-724**).

The Veronesi family has been closely tied to the jewelry trade for centuries. Now split up and competing among themselves, the various family factions are represented by **Arrigo Veronesi,** Via dell'Archiginnasio 4/F (☎ **051/230-811**), which sells modern jewelry and watches; **F. Veronesi & Figli,** Piazza Maggiore 4 (☎ **051/224-835**), which offers contemporary jewelry, watches, and silver using ancient designs; and **Giulio Veronesi,** with locations at Piazza di Re Enzo 1 (☎ 051/ 234-237) and Galleria Cavour (☎ 051/234-196), which sells modern jewelry and Rolex watches.

ACCOMMODATIONS

Bologna hosts four to six trade fairs a year, during which hotel room rates rise dramatically. Some hotels announce their prices in advance; others prefer to wait until bookings are actually being accepted, perhaps to see what the market will bear.

Be duly warned: At trade fair times (dates vary yearly; check with the tourist office) business clients from throughout Europe book the best rooms, and you'll be paying a lot of money to visit Bologna.

VERY EXPENSIVE

Grand Hotel Baglioni. Via dell'Indipendenza 8, 40121 Bologna. ☎ 051/225-445. Fax 051/234-840. www.italyhotel.com/emilia_romagna/bologna/baglioni. 125 units. A/C MINIBAR TV TEL. 510,000–675,000L ($296–$392) double; 900,000–2,050,000L ($522–$1,189) suite. Rates include breakfast. AE, DC, MC, V. Parking 45,000L ($26).

Far better and more atmospheric than its chief rival, the Carlton, the Baglioni boasts a desirable location in the center of Bologna, near the main square. Its four-story facade is crafted of the same reddish brick that distinguishes many of the city's older buildings, and the interior is noted for its wall and ceiling frescoes. Each soundproof room contains reproductions of antique furniture as well as all the modern conveniences you'd expect in a grand hotel. They're generally spacious, the fourth-floor units being the largest of all.

Dining: Good-tasting Bolognese cooking is served in the elegant I Carracci (see "Dining," below).

Amenities: Room service, baby-sitting, laundry/valet, hairdresser.

EXPENSIVE

Grand Hotel Elite. Via Aurelio Saffi 36, 40131 Bologna. ☎ 051/649-1432. Fax 051/ 649-2426. www.hotelinfoplus.com/bologna/elite.htm. 173 units. A/C MINIBAR TV TEL. 370,000L ($215) double; 430,000L ($249) suite. Rates include breakfast. AE, DC, MC, V. Parking 18,000–35,000L ($10–$20).

Located on the city's northwestern edge, a 12-minute walk from the center, this eight-story hotel was built in the 1970s as a combination of private apartments and hotel rooms. In 1993, the entire structure was transformed into a hotel. The guest rooms are comfortable but lackluster.

Dining/Diversions: Even if you're not staying here, you may want to patronize the Cordon Bleu, which features international food and the classic cuisine of Emilia-Romagna (closed Sunday). Also popular is a bar with comfortable banquettes and a good selection of whisky and regional wines.

Amenities: Concierge, room service, dry cleaning/laundry, conference room, baby-sitting, health club, bike and car rental nearby, 36-hole golf course within 5 miles.

Royal Hotel Carlton. Via Montebello 8, 40121 Bologna. ☎ 051/249-361. Fax 051/ 249-724. www.hotelinfoplus.com/bologna/royalcarlton.htm. 273 units. A/C MINIBAR TV TEL. 440,000L ($255) double; 630,000–750,000L ($365–$435) suite. Rates include breakfast. AE, DC, MC, V. Parking 25,000–35,000L ($15–$20).

Some claim that the Carlton, only a few minutes' walk from many of the national monuments, is the best hotel in Bologna, but we feel that honor goes to the Baglioni. The Hilton-style Carlton is a rather austere commercial place with a triangular garden, catering mainly to business travelers. It's in the modern style, with a balcony and picture window for each room, though the views aren't particularly inspiring.

Dining: One of Bologna's most dramatic staircases sweeps from the second floor to a point near the comfortable American Bar, a grill restaurant serving decent regional and international food.

Amenities: Room service, baby-sitting, laundry/valet, limited facilities for the disabled.

MODERATE

Hotel Corona d'Oro 1890. Via Oberdan 12, 40126 Bologna. ☎ **051/236-456.** Fax 051/262-679. www.hotelinfoplus.com/bologna/coronadoro1890.htm. 35 units. A/C MINIBAR TV TEL. 300,000–460,000L ($174–$267) double. Rates include breakfast. AE, DC, MC, V. Parking 40,000L ($23).

This fine palazzo, the home of the noble Azzoguidi family in the 15th century, still preserves the architectural features of various periods, from the art nouveau in the hall to the medieval severity of the coffered ceiling in the meeting room to the frescoes, depicting coats-of-arms and landscapes, in the rooms. Though the rooms are decorated according to various periods, they have fax and computer hookups and safes. The hotel is a short distance from Piazza Maggiore.

Hotel dei Commercianti. Via de'Pignattari 11, 40124 Bologna. ☎ **051/233-052.** Fax 051/224-733. www.italyhotel.com/hotelm/4769.html. 35 units. A/C MINIBAR TV TEL. 280,000–460,000L ($162–$267) double, 600,000L ($348) suite. Rates include breakfast. AE, DC, MC, V. Parking 35,000–40,000L ($20–$23).

This hotel is near the site of the "Domus" (the first seat of the town hall) for the commune of Bologna in the 12th century. Recent restorations uncovered original wooden features you can see in the hall and the rooms in the old tower. Despite the centuries-old history, the atmosphere is bright and all modern amenities are offered. The rooms, decorated with antique furniture, feature safes. The hotel is beside San Petronio in the pedestrian area of Piazza Maggiore.

Hotel Milano Excelsior. Viale Pietramellara 51 (near Piazza Medaglie d'Oro), 40121 Bologna. ☎ **051/246-178.** Fax 051/249-448. www.hotelinfoplus.com/bologna/starhotelmilano.htm. 76 units. A/C MINIBAR TV TEL. 245,000L ($142) double; 335,000L ($194) suite. During trade fairs, 430,000L ($249) double; 520,000L ($302) suite. Rates include breakfast. AE, DC, MC, V. Parking 10,000L ($6).

The Excelsior is a first-class hotel and has all the associated trappings, including an American bar as well as a restaurant decorated with crystal chandeliers. The location is particularly convenient for motorists because of its proximity to the approach roads to many other Italian cities. However, the nearby rail station is equally attractive to travelers without cars. It has a completely modern decor, though a number of its rooms contain more traditional furnishings. The hotel offers excellent service and an attentive staff, and the Ristorante il Vasgello serves tasty Emilian food (closed on Sunday).

Hotel Orologio. Via IV Novembre 10, 40123 Bologna. ☎ **051/231-253.** Fax 051/260-552. Www.venere.com/hotelm/4781.html. 35 units. A/C MINIBAR TV TEL. 210,000–400,000L ($122–$232) double. Rates include breakfast. AE, DC, MC, V. Parking 35,000–40,000L ($20–$23).

This charming small hotel faces the clock (*orologio*) on the civic center and is in the historical center of medieval Bologna, with a view of Piazza Maggiore and the Podestà Palace. The rooms are decorated with modern furnishings and have safes. This is the ideal place for those who wish to steep themselves in the past without forfeiting modern comforts.

Hotel Tre Vecchi. Via dell'Indipendenza 47, 40121 Bologna. ☎ **051/231-991.** Fax 051/ 224-143. 96 units. A/C MINIBAR TV TEL. 270,000L ($157) double. During trade fairs, 400,000L ($232) double. Rates include breakfast. AE, DC, MC, V. Parking 25,000–30,000L ($15–$17) in garage; 8,000L ($4.65) on street.

This hotel opened in the 1970s in a century-old building on a much-traveled street a 5-minute walk from the train station. The rooms are clean, bright, and relatively quiet, thanks to the soundproofing. The gentle humor in the name ("Three Geriatrics") was the idea of the trio of aging entrepreneurs who founded the hotel, which contains two elevators and several lounges where guests can relax and watch TV. Breakfast is the only meal served.

INEXPENSIVE

Albergo Al Cappello Rosso. Via de Fusari 9, 40123 Bologna. ☎ **051/261-891.** Fax 051/ 227-179. www.hotelinfoplus.com/bologna/cappellorosso.htm. 33 units. A/C MINIBAR TV TEL. 345,000L ($200) double. During trade fairs and congresses, 460,000L ($267) double. Rates include breakfast. AE, DC, MC, V.

In the 14th century, "The Red Hat" of the name referred to the preferred headgear of the privileged tradesmen who stayed at this inn. More than 600 years later, the hotel has been revamped into an ultramodern place with no hint of its past. It's in the heart of Bologna, in a busy shopping district. If modern comfort is what you want or if you need a break from the more rustic charms of many Italian lodges, this is the place for you. The rooms tend to be rather modular, but the staff is gracious and willing to help. A sleek brass-topped bar is in the hotel, and excellent meals are available steps away in a selection of restaurants.

Hotel Alexander. Viale Pietramellara 47, 40121 Bologna. ☎ **051/247-118.** Fax 051/ 247-248. 108 units. A/C MINIBAR TV TEL. 225,000–295,000L ($131–$171) double. Rates include breakfast. AE, DC, MC, V. Parking 18,000L ($10) outside.

The Alexander is the best hotel buy near Piazza Medaglie d'Oro, the main hub of car and trail traffic in the city. Perched near the more expensive Excelsior, the Alexander features desirable rooms, with brightly painted foyers, compact furnishings, and tidy baths. The double-glass windows help blot out street noise. The main lounge is crisp and warm, with wood paneling and lounge chairs placed on Turkish rugs.

DINING
EXPENSIVE

Diana. Via dell'Indipendenza 24. ☎ **051/231-302.** Reservations recommended. Main courses 20,000–40,000L ($12–$23). AE, DC, MC, V. Tues–Sun noon–2:30pm and 7–10:30pm. Closed Jan 1–10 and Aug. REGIONAL/INTERNATIONAL.

Occupying a late medieval building in the heart of town, this well-recommended restaurant has been popular since 1920. It offers three gracefully decorated dining rooms and a verdant terrace. The Diana was named in honor of the goddess of the hunt because of the many game dishes it served when it first opened. In recent years, though game is still featured in season, the restaurant opts for a staple of regional and international cuisine, all competently prepared. Begin with one of the city's most delicious appetizers—spuma di mortadella, a pâté made of mortadella sausage served with dainty white toast. You'll never eat baloney again.

I Carracci. In the Grand Hotel Baglioni, Via dell'Indipendenza 8. ☎ **051/225-445.** Reservations required. Main courses 25,000–32,000L ($15–$19). AE, DC, MC, V. Mon–Sat 12:30– 2:30pm and 7:30–10:30pm. Closed Aug 1–25. ITALIAN/INTERNATIONAL.

Bologna's most fashionable dining spot, the Carracci is named after the family of artists who decorated the premises with frescoes. Its cuisine equals that of the Notai (below), and the service is impeccable. The elegant dining room dates from the 16th century. The ceiling frescoes were painted in the 1700s by the Carracci brothers, and their interpretation of the seasons is richly allegorical and mythical. The seasonally adjusted menu features the freshest produce and highest-quality meat, poultry, and fish. A few dishes we've enjoyed are tortellini in brodo, tagliatelle in ragoût, veal scallop alla bolognese, wild boar cacciatore, and grilled salmon filet. The wine list is among the finest of any restaurant in the province.

✪ Nuovi Notai. Via de' Pignattari 1. ☎ **051/228-694.** Reservations required. Main courses 18,000–26,000L ($10–$15); fixed-price menus 48,000–65,000L ($28–$38). AE, DC, MC, V. Mon–Sat 12:30–2:30pm and 8–11pm. ITALIAN/TUSCAN/UMBRIAN.

Behind a lattice- and ivy-covered facade next to the cathedral, within view of one of Italy's most beautiful squares, this sublime restaurant draws a loyal crowd. In summer, tables are placed outside. Music lovers and relaxing businesspeople appreciate the piano bar. The decor combines the belle epoque with Italian flair and includes artwork, hanging Victorian lamps, and clutches of beautifully arranged flowers on each table.

The fine cooking is based on the best local products. An attachment to culinary traditions doesn't preclude a modern approach to the cuisine. Menu items include a flan of cheese fondue, gratin of gnocchi with truffles, beef filet cooked in a cartoccio (a paper bag) and garnished with porcini mushrooms, and deboned breast of wild goose. Dessert might be suprême of almonds with ricotta cheese and coffee sauce.

Ristorante al Pappagallo. Piazza della Mercanzia 3C. ☎ **051/232-807.** Reservations recommended. Main courses 32,000–34,000L ($19–$20). AE, DC, MC, V. Mon–Sat 12:30–2:30pm and 7:30–10:30pm. BOLOGNESE.

This restaurant has a faithful following that has included Einstein, Hitchcock, and Toscanini. It's still going strong, but it's no longer the finest in Italy. "The Parrot" is on the ground floor of a Gothic mansion across from the landmark 14th-century Merchants' Loggia (a short walk from the leaning towers). For the best introduction, begin with lasagne verde al forno (baked lasagne that gets its green color from minced spinach). For the main course, try the specialty of the house: filetti di tacchino, superb turkey breasts baked with white wine, parmigiano cheese, and truffles. Modern low-calorie offerings also appear on today's menu. The restaurant boasts an impressive wine list and serves amber-colored Albana wine and sparkling red Lambrusco, two of the best-known wines of Emilia.

MODERATE

Montegrappa da Nello. Via Montegrappa 2. ☎ **051/236-331.** Reservations recommended for dinner. Main courses 15,000–40,000L ($9–$23). AE, DC, MC, V. Tues–Sun noon–3pm and 7–11:30pm. Closed Aug. BOLOGNESE/INTERNATIONAL.

Montegrappa da Nello, one of the few restaurants still doing classic Bolognese cuisine, has a faithful following that swears by its pasta dishes. Franco and Ezio Bolini are the hosts, and they insist that all the produce be fresh. The menu offers tortellina Montegrappa (a pasta favorite served in cream-and-meat sauce) and graminia (a very fine white spaghetti presented with mushrooms, cream, and pepper). The restaurant is also known for its fresh white truffles and mushrooms. A sublime salad is made with truffles, mushrooms, parmigiano cheese, and artichokes. For a main course, misto del cuoco is a mixed platter of the chef's specialties, including zampone, cotoletta alla bolognese, and scaloppine with fresh mushrooms.

INEXPENSIVE

Antica Osteria Romagnola. Via Rialto 13. ☎ **051/263-699.** Reservations recommended for dinner. Main courses 20,000–30,000L ($12–$17). AE, DC, MC, V. Tues 7:30–11pm; Wed–Sat 12:30–2:30pm and 7:30–11pm; Sun 12:30–2:30pm and 7:30–11pm. Closed Jan 7–16 and Aug. ITALIAN.

Unlike many of its competitors, this place offers cuisines from throughout Italy, including the distant south. You might begin with one of the unusual and well-flavored risottos or choose from a savory selection of antipasti. The variety of pastas is also impressive, like ravioli with essence of truffles, garganelli pasta with zucchini, and pasta whipped with asparagus tips. You might also select a terrine of ricotta and arugula (the latter was considered an aphrodisiac by the ancient Romans). For your main course you might try a springtime specialty, capretto (roast goat) with artichokes and potatoes, or filet mignon with aromatic basil.

Grassilli. Via del Luzzo 3. ☎ **051/237-938** or 051/222-961. Reservations required. Main courses 20,000–25,000L ($12–$15). AE, DC, MC, V. Thurs–Sat 12:30–2:30pm and Mon–Tues 8–10:30pm, Sun 12:30–2:30pm. Closed July 20–Aug 15, Dec 24–Jan 6, and for dinner on holidays. BOLOGNESE/INTERNATIONAL.

Grassilli is a good bet for conservative regional cooking with few deviations from time-tested recipes. It's in a 1750s building across from an antiques store, on a narrow cobblestone alley a short block from the leaning towers. There's also a street-side canopy for outdoor dining. At night the place can be festive, and your good time will be enhanced if you order a specialty like tortellini in mushroom-cream sauce, the chef's special tournedos, tortellini alla Bologna, or grilled or roasted meat.

Rosteria da Luciano. Via Nazario Sauro 19. ☎ **051/231-249.** Reservations recommended. Main courses 18,000–28,000L ($10–$16); fixed-price lunch 20,000–40,000L ($12–$23). AE, DC, MC, V. Thurs–Tues noon–2pm and 7:30–10:30pm. Closed Aug. BOLOGNESE.

For moderate prices, this restaurant within walking distance of the city center serves some of Bologna's best food. It has an art-deco style and contains three large rooms with a real Bolognese atmosphere. We prefer the front room, opening onto the kitchen. As a novelty, on the street is a window looking directly into the kitchen. To begin your gargantuan repast, request the tortellini in rich cream sauce. Well-recommended main dishes are the fritto misto all'Italiana (mixed fry) and the scaloppe con porcini (veal with mushrooms). One savory offering is cotoletta alla bolognese, veal layered with ham and parmigiano cheese, then baked. A dramatic dessert is crêpes flambés.

INEXPENSIVE

Osteria dell'Orsa. 1/F Via Mentana. ☎ **051/231-576.** Reservations recommended. Main courses 10,000–16,000L ($6–$9). AE, MC, V. Daily noon–2am. ITALIAN.

In the 1970s, this restaurant moved from another part of town into this 15th-century building near the university and (thanks to some of the best ragú bolognese in town) has continued to thrive. Most diners opt for the high-ceilinged, medieval-looking main floor, though an informal cantinalike room in the cellar is open for additional seating. You won't go wrong if you preface a meal with any kind of pasta labeled "bolognese." Other options include homemade tagliolini (with the above-mentioned ragú) or tortelloni with cheese, ham, and mushroom sauce. Veal cutlet fiorentina (with spinach) is always worthwhile, and if you feel adventurous, you can always opt for grilled donkeymeat (*samarino*) that for the regulars is a culinary staple.

Osteria del Moretto. 5 Via di San Mamolo. ☎ **051/580-284.** Main courses 10,000–13,000L ($6–$8). No credit cards. Mon–Sat 8pm–2:30am. BOLOGNESE.

This simple trattoria/bar has operated with few obvious changes in the duet of rooms and on the simple menu since around 1900. Built as a convent in the 13th century, it lies near the Porto San Mamolo, in the historic core of Bologna. Most of the stand-up patrons drink wine and, in some cases, segue from drinks into a working-class meal. This might include selections from a platter of local cheese as an antipasto, steaming bowls of pasta e fagiole (with beans), spaghetti bolognese, a cold salad of meat and vegetables known as salata Trentino, eggplant parmigiana, and chicken—but no fish of any kind.

NEARBY DINING

✪ **San Domenico.** Via Gaspara Sacchi 1, Imola. ☎ **0542/29-000.** Reservations recommended. Main courses 45,000–60,000L ($26–$35); fixed-price lunch Tues–Sun 60,000–65,000L ($35–$38); fixed-price dinner Tues–Sat (including wine) 100,000L ($58); menu degustazione 135,000L ($78). AE, DC, MC, V. Tues–Sun 12:30–2:30pm; Tues–Sat 8–10:30pm. Closed Jan 1–10 and July 27–Aug 25. In Imola, 21 miles southeast of Bologna. ITALIAN.

Gastronomes from all over Europe and America travel to the unlikely village of Imola to savor the offerings of what some food critics (ourselves included) consider the best restaurant in Italy. The restaurant can also be easily reached from Ravenna.

The cuisine is sometimes compared to France's modern cuisine creations. However, owner Gian Luigi Morini claims his delectable offerings are nothing more than adaptations of festive regional dishes, except they're lighter, more subtle, and served in manageable portions. He was born in this rambling stone building whose simple facade faces the courtyard of a neighboring church. For 25 years, Signor Morini worked at a local bank, returning home every night to administer his restaurant. Now his place is among the primary attractions of Emilia-Romagna.

A tuxedo-clad member of his talented young staff will escort you to a table near the tufted leather banquettes. Meals include heavenly concoctions made with the freshest ingredients. You might select goose-liver pâté studded with white truffles, fresh shrimp in creamy sweet bell-pepper sauce, roast rack of lamb with fresh rosemary, stuffed chicken suprême wrapped in lettuce leaves, or fresh handmade spaghetti with shellfish. Signor Morini has collected some of the best vintages in Europe for the past 30 years, with some bottles of cognac dating to the time of Napoléon.

BOLOGNA AFTER DARK

Since the Middle Ages, in both politics and art, Bologna has been noted for a wild, sometimes self-indulgent side. This, coupled with a large population of students and persons under 35, contributes to a burgeoning night scene and some of the most diverse nightclubs of any city its size in Italy.

During July and August, the city authorities transform the **parks** along the town's northern tier into an Italian version of a German biergarten complete with disco music under colored lights. Vendors sell beer and wine from indoor/outdoor bars set up on the lawns and merchants hawk food and souvenirs from raffish-looking stands. Events range from live jazz to classical concerts. Ask any hotelier or the tourist office for the schedule of midsummer events, or try your luck by taking either a taxi or (much less convenient) bus no. 25 or 91A from the main station to Arena Parco Nord.

The **Teatro Comunale,** Via Largo Respighi (☎ **051/529-999**), is the venue for major cultural presentations, including opera, ballet, and orchestral presentations. The **Circolo della Musica di Bologna,** Via Galleria 11 (☎ **051/227-032**), presents free classical music concerts in summer. For the rest of the year, there's always a cafe, bar, or pub nearby. Counterculture wanna-bes head to the **Piccolo Bar,** Piazza Giuseppe Verdi 4 (☎ **051/227-147**), where you'll get a whiff of Gen-X's hopes and dreams as interpreted by Italy.

Another hot spot is the **Cantina Bentivoglio,** Via Mascarella 4/B (☎ **051/ 265-416**), lying off Via delle Belle Arti. This is a fairly upmarket joint serving reasonably priced food and wine. Nightclubbers know it offers some of the best live jazz Tuesday to Sunday after 10:30pm, when there's less emphasis on food. The cover is 4,000L ($2.30). The club is open Tuesday to Sunday 8pm to 2am but closes for about 6 weeks every summer (dates vary). If a piano bar is your style, head for the **Cabala American Bar,** Via Strada Maggiore (☎ **051/265-445**), a chic rendezvous open daily 7pm to 2am.

Bologna's most popular gay bar is **Cassero,** Piazza Porta Saragozza 2 (☎ **051/ 644-6902**), located in a venerable medieval building that opens onto a third-floor terrace with a view of the stars. Open daily 9:30pm to at least 2:30am, it's transformed into a disco Thursday to Sunday. Thursday is for lesbians only; Friday to Sunday is mostly for *uomini* (men).

As a university city, Bologna has many student cafes. One of the most central and popular is **Mocambo,** Via d'Azaglio 1/E (☎ **051/229-516**), near the Duomo. Its major competitor, also facing the Duomo, is **Bar Giuseppe,** Piazza Maggiore 1 (☎ **051/264-444**), serving some of the best espresso in town.

2 Ferrara: Fabled Domain of the Estes

259 miles N of Rome, 32 miles N of Bologna, 62 miles SW of Venice

When Papa Borgia (Pope Alexander VI) was shopping for a third husband for the apple of his eye, darling Lucrezia, his gaze fell on the influential house of Este. From the 13th century, this great Italian family had dominated **Ferrara,** building up a powerful duchy and a reputation as patrons of the arts. Alfonse d'Este, son of the shrewd but villainous Ercole I, the ruling duke of Ferrara, was an attractively virile candidate for Lucrezia's much-used hand. (Her second husband was murdered, perhaps by her brother, Cesare, who was the apple of nobody's eye—with the possible exception of Machiavelli. Her first marriage, a political alliance, was to Giovanni Sforza, but it was annulled in 1497.)

Though the Este family may have had reservations (after all, it was common gossip that the pope "knew" his daughter in the biblical sense), they finally consented to the marriage. As the duchess of Ferrara, a position she held until her death, Lucrezia bore seven children. But one of her grandchildren, Alfonso II, wasn't as prolific, even though he had a reputation as a roué: He left the family without a male heir. The greedy eye of Pope Clement VIII took quick action, gobbling up the city as his fief in the waning months of the 16th century. The great house of Este went down in history, and Ferrara sadly declined under the papacy.

Incidentally, Alfonso II was a dubious patron of Torquato Tasso (1544 to 1595), author of the epic *Jerusalem Delivered,* a work that was to make him the most celebrated poet of the Late Renaissance. The legend of Tasso—who's thought to have been insane, paranoid, or at least tormented—has steadily grown over the centuries. It didn't need any more boosting, but Goethe fanned the legend through the Teutonic lands with his late 18th-century drama *Torquato Tasso.* It's said that Alfonso II at one time made Tasso his prisoner.

Ferrara today is still relatively undiscovered, especially by globe-trotting North Americans. The city is richly blessed, with much of its legacy intact. Among the historic treasures remaining are a great cathedral and the Este Castle, along with enough ducal palaces to make for a fast-paced day of sightseeing. Its palaces, for the most part, have long been robbed of their lavish furnishings, but the faded frescoes, the paintings that weren't carted off, and the palatial rooms are reminders of the vicissitudes of power.

Modern Ferrara is one of the most health-conscious places in all Italy. Bicycles outnumber the automobiles on the road, and more than half the citizens get exercise by jogging. In fact, it's almost surreal: Enclosed in medieval walls under a bright sky, everywhere you look, you'll find the people of Ferrara engaged in all sorts of self-powered locomotion.

ESSENTIALS

GETTING THERE   Getting to Ferrara by **train** is fast and efficient, as it's on the main train line between Bologna and Venice. A total of 33 trains a day originating in Bologna pass through. Trip time is 40 minutes, and the fare is 4,300L ($2.50) oneway. Some 24 trains arrive from Venice (1½ hours); the one-way fare is 10,100L ($6). For information and schedules, call ☎ **0532/770-340** or 1478/88-088 (toll free in Italy only).

From most destinations the train is best, but if you're in Modena (below), you'll find 11 **bus** departures a day for Ferrara. Trip time is between 1½ and 2 hours, and a oneway ticket is 8,500L ($4.95). In Ferrara, bus information for the surrounding area is available by calling ☎ **0532/599-490.** If you've got a **car** and are coming from Bologna, take A13 north. From Venice, take A4 southwest to Padua and continue on A13 south to Ferrara.

VISITOR INFORMATION   The **tourist office** is at Castello Estense, Piazza delle Castello (☎ **0532/209-370**), open Monday to Saturday 9am to 1pm and 2 to 6pm and Sunday 9am to 1pm.

EXPLORING THE TOWN

Castello Estense. Piazza delle Castelo. ☎ **0532/299-233.** Admission 8,000L ($4.65) adults; children 10 and under free. Tues–Sun 9:30am–5:30pm.

A moated four-towered castle (lit at night), this proud fortress began as a bricklayer's dream near the end of the 14th century, though its face has been lifted and wrenched about for centuries. It was home to the powerful Este family, where the dukes went about their ho-hum daily chores—trysting with their own lovers, murdering their wives' lovers, beheading or imprisoning potential enemies, whatever. Today it's used for the provincial and prefectural administration offices, and you can view many of its once-lavish rooms—notably the **Salon of Games,** the **Salon of Dawn,** and a **Lombardesque chapel** that once belonged to Renata di Francia, daughter of Louis XII. Parisina d'Este, wife of Duke Nicolò d'Este III, was murdered with her lover, Ugolino (the duke's illegitimate son), in the dank prison below the castle, creating the inspiration for Browning's "My Last Duchess."

Il Duomo and Museo del Duomo. Piazza Cattedrale. ☎ **0532/207-449.** Free admission, but donation appreciated. Oct–Dec and Mar Tues–Sun 10am–noon and 3–5pm; Apr–Sept Tues–Sun 10am–noon and 4–6pm. Closed Jan–Feb.

Only a short stroll from the Este castle, the 12th-century **Duomo** weds the delicate Gothic with the more virile Romanesque. The offspring is an exciting pink marble facade. Behind the cathedral is a typically Renaissance **campanile (bell tower).** Inside, the massive structure is heavily baroqued, as the artisans of still another era festooned it with trompe l'oeil.

The entrance to the **Museo del Duomo** is to the left of the atrium as you enter. It's worth a visit just to see works by Ferrara's most outstanding 15th-century painter, Cosmé Tura. Aesthetically controversial, the big attraction here is Tura's St. George slaying the dragon to save a red-stockinged damsel in distress. Opposite is an outstanding work by Jacopo della Quercia depicting a sweet, regal Madonna with a pomegranate in one hand and the Child in the other. Also from the Renaissance heyday of Ferrara are some bas-reliefs, notably a Giano bifronte (a mythological figure looking at the past and the future), along with some 16th-century arazzi (tapestries) woven by hand.

Civic Museum of Ancient Art (Museo Civico d'Arte Antica). In the Palazzo Schifanoia, Via Scandiana 23. ☎ **0532/64-178.** Admission 6,000L ($3.50) adults, 3,000L ($1.75) students; children 17 and under free. Daily 9am–7pm. Closed major holidays.

The Schifanoia Palace was built in 1385 for Albert V d'Este and enlarged by Borso d'Este (1450 to 1471). The Ancient Art Museum was founded in 1758 and transferred to its present site in 1898. First exhibited were only coins and medals, but then the collection was enhanced by donations of archaeological finds, antique bronzes, small Renaissance plates and pottery, and other collections.

Art lovers are lured to the **Salon of the Months** to see the astrological cycle. Humanist Pellegrino Prisciani conceived the subjects of the cycle, though Cosmé Tura, the official court painter, was probably the organizer of the works. Tura was the founder of the Ferrarese School, to which belonged, among others, Ercole de' Roberti and Francesco del Cossa, who painted the March, April, and May scenes. In the wall cycle, which represents the 12 months, each month is subdivided into three horizontal bands: The lower band shows scenes from the daily life of courtiers and people, the middle displays the relative sign of the zodiac, and the upper presents the triumph of the classical divinity for that particular myth. The frescoes form a complex presentation, leading to varying interpretations as to their meaning.

Palazzo dei Diamanti. Corso Ercole d'Este 21. ☎ **0532/205-844.** Admission 12,000L ($7), 8,000L ($4.65) children under 18. Daily 9am–7pm.

The Palazzo dei Diamanti, another jewel of Este splendor, is so named because of the 9,000 diamond-shaped stones on its facade. Of the handful of museums sheltered here, the **National Picture Gallery (Pinacoteca Nazionale)** is the most important. It houses the works of the Ferrarese artists—notably the trio of old masters, Tura, del Cossa, and Roberti. The collection covers the chief period of artistic expression in Ferrara from the 14th to the 18th century. The next important is the **Civic Gallery of Modern Art (Museo Civico d'Arte Moderne),** which sponsors the most important contemporary art exhibits in town. The other three museums in the palazzo aren't really worth your time. The same ticket admits you to the entire complex.

Casa Romei. Via Savonarola 30. ☎ **0532/240-341.** Admission 4,000L ($2.30) adults; children under 18/seniors over 60 free. Daily 8:30am–2pm.

This 15th-century palace near the Este tomb was the property of John Romei, a friend and confidant of the fleshy Duke Borso d'Este, who made the Este realm a duchy. John (Giovanni) was later to marry one of the Este princesses, though we don't know if it was for love or power or both. In later years, Lucrezia and her gossipy coterie—riding in the ducal carriage drawn by handsome white horses—used to descend on the Romei house, perhaps to receive Borgia messengers from Rome. Its once-elegant furnishings have been carted off, but the chambers (many with terra-cotta fireplaces) remain, and the casa has been filled with frescoes and sculpture.

SHOPPING

Ferrara has a rich tradition of artisanship dating back to the Renaissance. You can find some of the best, albeit expensive, products in the dozen or so antiques stores that dot the town's historic center. A particularly appealing dealer is **Antichita San Michele,** Via del Turco 22 (☎ 0532/211-055). Newer goods, often fashioned in Renaissance style, include ceramics whose designs are etched directly into the clay. Examples of the craft are displayed, sold, and shipped from **Ceramica Artistica Ferrarese,** Via Baluardi 125 (☎ 0532/66-093), and **La Marchesana,** Via Cortevecchia 38A (☎ 0532/240-535).

More unusual is an outfit specializing in wrought iron, **Chierici,** Via Bartoli 17 (☎ 0532/67-057), near the Ponte San Giorgio. Some of the smaller pieces, such as decorative brackets or fireplace tools, make good souvenirs.

Food products? **Antica Salumeria Polesinati,** Via Mazzini 78 (☎ 0532/206-833), and **Enoteca Al Brindisi,** Via Adelardi 11 (☎ 0532/209-142), stockpile the fruits of the Ferrarese harvest in historically evocative settings. Outdoor markets? Every month except August, on the first Saturday and first Sunday of every month, the **open-air antiques and handcraft markets** feature lots of junk amid the increasingly rare treasures. They're conducted 8am to 7pm in both Piazza Municipale (mostly antiques and bric-a-brac) and Piazza Savonarola (mainly handcrafts and bric-a-brac).

ACCOMMODATIONS

✪ **Hotel Duchessa Isabella.** Via Palestro 70, 44100 Ferrara. ☎ 0532/202-121. Fax 0532/202-638. 28 units. A/C MINIBAR TV TEL. 480,000L ($278) double; from 650,000L ($377) suite. Rates include breakfast. AE, DC, MC, V. Bus: 1, 2, 3, or 9.

This was the home of the head of one of the region's most respected Jewish organizations until the late 1980s. In 1990, it opened as a five-star hotel with a spectacular decor, named after the Este family's most famous ancestor, Isabella. Today it's a member of the illustrious Relais & Châteaux chain. The rooms are each decorated in a different color scheme and identified by the names of the flowers whose colors they most closely resemble. Each boasts a sense of history, is outfitted with all the modern amenities, and is very comfortable.

Dining: The elegant restaurant is set beneath lavishly gilded and painted ceilings. (In summer, the venue moves outside into the garden.) The cuisine is based on the traditional recipes of Emilia-Romagna, though a wide choice of less esoteric dishes is also available.

Amenities: Room service, laundry/valet service, conference facilities, free use of bicycles. A horse-drawn landau takes guests on excursions around Ferrara's historic center.

Hotel Europa. Corso della Giovecca 49, 44100 Ferrara. ☎ 0532/205-456. Fax 0532/212-120. 40 units. A/C MINIBAR TV TEL. 175,000L ($102) double; 220,000L ($128) suite. Rates include breakfast. Parking 12,000L ($7). AE, DC, MC, V. Bus: 1, 2, 3, or 9.

In the 1600s, this palace was built near the Castello d'Estense. In 1880, it was transformed into one of the most prestigious hotels in town, but during World War II portions of the rear were bombed and then repaired in a less grandiose style. Today, the three-star place continues in a worthy but less spectacular version, offering a well-trained staff, relatively reasonable prices, and a handful of rooms overlooking the corso (they retain ceiling frescoes from the building's original construction). The other rooms are clean and comfortable, with antique furnishings and modern comforts. There's a bar but no restaurant; breakfast is the only meal served.

✪ **Locanda Borgonuovo.** Via Cairoli 29. 44100 Ferrara. ☎ **0532/211-100.** Fax 0532/248-000. www.4net.com/business/borgonuovo. 4 units. A/C MINIBAR TV TEL. 140,000–160,000L ($81–$93) double. Rates include breakfast. AE, MC, V. Bus: 1, 2, 3, or 9.

This is the kind of pensione containing so many aspects of a private home that loyal clients sometimes reserve their rooms a full year in advance. It occupies the two lower floors of a four-story medieval palazzo that belonged to the owner's father. The rooms are outfitted with family antiques and mementos, containing bathrooms that were upgraded in 1994—the year the site began accepting paying guests. Breakfasts are appealingly personable, directed by either Signora Adele Orlandini or her charming son Filippo. Though it lies in a traffic-free pedestrian zone about a hundred yards from the Castello d'Estense, rented cars can still park for free on the street outside.

Ripagrande Hotel. Via Ripagrande 21, 44100 Ferrara. ☎ **0532/765-250.** Fax 0532/764-377. www.4net.com/busness/ripa. E-mail: ripa@mbox.4net.it. 40 units. A/C MINIBAR TV TEL. 310,000L ($180) double; from 330,000L ($191) junior suite. Rates include breakfast. AE, DC, MC, V. Parking 20,000L ($12). Bus: 1, 2, 3, or 9.

The Ripagrande, one of the most unusual hotels in town, occupies a Renaissance palace. Rich coffered ceilings, walls in Ferrarese brickwork, 16th-century columns, and a wide staircase with a floral cast-iron handrail characterize the broad entrance hall. Inside the hotel are two Renaissance courtyards decorated with columns and capitals. Half of the 40 rooms are junior suites with sleeping areas connected to an internal stairway. The rooms are spacious, with modern and tasteful furnishings, often antique reproductions. Some of the accommodations are trilevel, with a garretlike bedroom above. The most desirable rooms are on the top floor, opening onto terraces overlooking the red-tile roofs of Ferrara. Laundry and room service are provided.

DINING

Grotta Azzurra. Piazza Sacrati 43. ☎ **0532/209-152.** Reservations recommended. Main courses 13,000–25,000L ($8–$15); fixed-price menus 25,000–50,000L ($15–$29). AE, DC, MC, V. Mon–Tues and Thurs–Sat 12:30–2:30pm and 7:30–9:30pm, Sun 12:30–2:30pm. Closed July 5–31. Bus: 1, 2, 3, or 9. FERRARESE/SEAFOOD.

Behind a classic brick facade on a busy square, Grotta Azzurra seems like a restaurant you might encounter on the sunny isle of Capri, not in Ferrara. However, the cuisine is firmly entrenched in the northern Italian kitchen. It's best to visit in autumn, when favorite dishes include wild boar and pheasant, usually served with polenta. Many sausages, served as antipasti, are made with game as well. More esoteric dishes include a boiled calf's head and tongue, while a local favorite is boiled stuffed pork leg. The chef is also an expert at grilled meats, especially pork, veal, and beef.

La Provvidenza. Corso Ercole I d'Este 92. ☎ **0532/205-187.** Reservations required. Main courses 18,000–38,000L ($10–$22). AE, DC, MC, V. Tues–Sun noon–2:30pm and 8–10pm. Closed Aug 11–17. Bus: 1, 2, 3, or 9. FERRARESE/ITALIAN.

La Provvidenza, whose building is from around 1750, stands on the same street as the Palazzo dei Diamanti. It has a farm-style interior, with a little garden where the regulars request tables in fair weather. The antipasti table is the finest we've seen (or sampled) in Ferrara. Really hearty eaters should order a pasta, such as fettuccine with smoked salmon, before tackling the main course, perhaps perfectly grilled and seasoned veal chops. Other specialties are pasticchio alla Ferrarese (macaroni mixed with a mushroom-and-meat sauce laced with creamy white sauce) and fritto misto di carne (mixed grill). The dessert choice is wide and luscious. Take a large appetite to this local favorite.

FERRARA AFTER DARK

During July and August, concerts and temporary art exhibits are offered as part of the **Estate a Ferrara** program. The tourist office will provide a schedule of events and dates, which vary from year to year. During the rest of the year, you can rub elbows with fellow drinkers, and usually lots of students, at a refreshingly diverse collection of bars, pubs, and discos. **Osteria Al Brindisi,** Via Adelardi 11 (☎ 0532/209-142), claims, with some justification, to be the oldest wine bar in the world, with a tradition of uncorking bottles that goes back to the early 1400s. Wine begins at around 1,500L (85¢) per glass and seems to taste best when accompanied by a few of the dozen kinds of panini (sandwiches).

The hottest dance club is **Giardini Sonori** (☎ 0532/466-333), Via della Ricostruzione, open Monday, Wednesday, Friday, and Saturday, but show up after 10pm. North of the historic center, **Pelledoca,** Via Arianuova 21 (☎ 0532/248-952), is another hot club, luring the town's youth along with any foreign visitors. Hours depend on the crowd.

3 Ravenna & Its Mosaics

46 miles E of Bologna, 90 miles S of Venice, 81 miles NE of Florence, 227 miles N of Rome

Ravenna is one of the most unusual towns in Emilia-Romagna. Today, you'll find a sleepy town with memories of a great past, luring hordes of tourists to explore what remains. As the capital of the Western Roman Empire (from A.D. 402), the Visigoth Empire (from A.D. 473), and the Byzantine Empire under Emperor Justinian and Empress Theodora (A.D. 540–752), Ravenna became one of the greatest cities on the Mediterranean.

Having achieved its cultural peak as part of the Byzantine Empire between the 6th and the 8th century, Ravenna is known for the many well-preserved mosaics created during that time—the finest in all Western art and the most splendid outside Istanbul. Although it now looks much like any other Italian city, the low Byzantine domes of its churches still evoke its Eastern past.

ESSENTIALS

GETTING THERE   With frequent **train** service and only 1¼ hours by train from Bologna, Ravenna can be easily visited on a day trip; one-way fare is 7,400L ($4.30). There's also frequent service to Ferrara; one-way fare is 6,700L ($3.90). At Ferrara, you can make connections to Venice. The train station is a 10-minute walk from the center at Piazza Fernini (☎ 01478/88-088). The train is better than the **bus.** Once at Ravenna, however, you'll find both a regional (ATR) system and a municipal (ATM) bus network serving the area. Buses depart from outside the train station at Piazza Fernini. The tourist office (below) has bus or rail schedules and more details; or you can call ☎ 0544/35-288 or 01478/88-099 (toll free in Italy only). If you've got a **car** and are coming from Bologna, head east along A14 or southeast of Ferrara on S309.

VISITOR INFORMATION   The **tourist office** is at Piazza Mameli 4 (☎ 0544/35-404), open Monday to Saturday 8:30am to 6pm (in summer, also Sunday 9am to noon and 3 to 6pm).

EXPLORING THE TOWN

You can actually see all the sights in 1 busy day. The center of Ravenna is **Piazza del Popolo,** which has a Venetian aura to it. To the south, off the colonnaded Piazza San Francesco, you can visit the **Tomba di Dante** on Via Dante Alighieri. After crossing

---

The Leaning Towers of Ravenna

North of Piazza del Popolo is a 12th-century leaning tower, the **Torre Pubblica.** This tower (which you can't visit) leans even more than the Tower of Pisa. Nearby along Viale Farini is another leaning tower, the 12th-century **Campanile di San Giovanni Evangelista,** even tipsier than the Torre Pubblica. When Allied bombs struck the church in World War II, its apse was destroyed, but the mighty tower wasn't toppled.

Piazza dei Caduti and heading north along Via Guerrini, you can reach the **Battistero della Neoniano** at Piazza del Duomo. Directly southeast and opening onto Piazza Arcivescovado is the **Museo Arcivescovile** and the **chapel of San Andrea.**

Then you can head back to the tourist office, cutting west along Via San Vitale. This will take you to the **Basilica di San Vitale** and the **Mausoleum of Gallo Placidia** behind the basilica. Nearby is the **Museo Nazionale di Ravenna** along Via Fiandrini (adjacent to Via San Vitale). To cap off your day, you can take bus no. 4 or 44 from the rail station or Piazza Caduti to visit the **Basilica of Sant'Appollinare in Classe,** reached along Via Romeo Sud.

If you're planning on seeing more than one sight, the most economical choice is to buy a **combination ticket** to visit these six monuments for 10,000L ($6): the Battistero della Neoniano, Archepiscopal Museum/Chapel of San Andrea, Church of San Vitale, Mausoleum of Galla Placidia, Adrian Baptistry, and Basilica of Sant'Apollinare. The ticket is available at the tourist office.

Battistero della Neoniano. Piazza del Duomo. Admission (including admission to Museo Arcivescovile) 5,000L ($2.90). Apr–Oct daily 9:30am–6:30pm (to 4:30pm off-season). Closed Christmas and New Year's Day.

This octagonal baptistery was built in the 5th century, and in the center of the cupola is a tablet showing John the Baptist baptizing Christ. The circle around the tablet depicts in dramatic mosaics of deep violet-blues and sparkling golds the 12 crown-carrying Apostles. The baptistery originally serviced a cathedral that no longer stands (the present-day Duomo was built around the mid-18th century and is of little interest except for some unusual pews). Beside it is a campanile from the 11th century, perhaps earlier.

Archepiscopal Museum and Chapel of San Andrea (Museo Arcivescovile e Capella di San Andrea). In the Archbishop's Palace, Piazza Arcivescovado. ☎ 0544/39-196. Admission 5,000L ($2.90). Tues–Sat 9am–7pm (to 4:30pm in winter), Sun 9am–1pm.

This twofold attraction is housed in the 6th-century Archbishop's Palace. In the **museum,** the major exhibit is an ivory throne carved for Archbishop Maximian, from around the mid-6th century. In the **chapel** (oratory) dedicated to St. Andrea are brilliant mosaics. Pause in the antechamber to look at an intriguing mosaic above the entrance—an unusual representation of Christ as a warrior, stepping on the head of a lion and snake; tough haloed, he wears partial armor, evoking "Onward, Christian Soldiers." The chapel—built in the shape of a cross—contains other mosaics that are "angelic," both figuratively and literally. Busts of saints and apostles stare down at you with the ox-eyed look of Byzantine art.

Museo e Basilica di San Vitale. Via San Vitale 17. ☎ 0544/34-424. Admission 6,000L ($3.50). Daily 9am–6:30pm.

This octagonal domed church dates from the mid–6th century. The mosaics inside— in brilliant greens and golds, lit by light from translucent panels—are among the most celebrated in the Western world. Covering the apse is a mosaic of a clean-shaven Christ astride the world, flanked by saints and angels. To the right is a mosaic of Empress Theodora and her court, and to the left the man who married this courtesan/actress, Emperor Justinian, and his entourage. If you can tear yourself away from the mosaics long enough, you might admire the church's marble decoration. Seven large arches span the temple, but the frescoes of the cupola are unimaginative.

✪ **Mausoleum of Galla Placidia.** Via San Vitale. ☎ **0544/34-266.** Admission 6,000L ($3.50). Apr–Sept daily 9am–7pm (Oct–Mar to 4:30pm).

This 5th-century chapel is so unpretentious you'll think you're at the wrong place. But inside it contains some exceptional mosaics dating back to antiquity, though they may not look it. Translucent panels bring the mosaics alive in all their grace and harmony—vivid with peacock blue, moss green, Roman gold, eggplant, and burnt orange. The mosaics in the cupola literally glitter with stars. Popular tradition claims that the cross-shaped structure houses the tomb of Galla Placidia, sister of Honorius, Rome's last emperor. Galla, who died in Rome in A.D. 450, is one of history's most powerful women. She became virtual ruler of the Western world after her husband, Ataulf, king of the Visigoths, died—only a virtual ruler because she became a regent for Valentinian III, who was only 6 at the time of his father's death.

National Museum of Ravenna (Museo Nazionale di Ravenna). Via Fiandrini (adjacent to Via San Vitale). ☎ **0544/34-424.** Admission 8,000L ($4.65) adults; children 17 and under/seniors 60 and over free. Tues–Sat 8:30am–6:30pm, Sun 8:30am–1:30pm.

This museum contains archaeological objects from the early Christian and Byzantine periods—icons, fragments of tapestries, medieval armaments and armory, sarcophagi, ivories, ceramics, and bits of broken pieces from the stained-glass windows of San Vitale.

Basilica of Sant'Apollinare in Classe. Via Romeo Sud. ☎ **0544/527-004.** Free admission. Daily 8:30am–noon and 2–5:30pm (to 6:30pm in summer). Bus: 4 or 44 from the rail station (every 20 minutes) or Piazza Caduti.

About 3½ miles south of the city (you can stop by on the way to Ravenna if you're heading north from Rimini), this church dates from the 6th century and was consecrated by Archbishop Maximian. Dedicated to St. Apollinare, the bishop of Ravenna, the early basilica stands side-by-side with a campanile—symbols of faded glory now resting in a lonely low-lying area. Inside is a central nave flanked by two aisles, the latter containing tombs of ecclesiastical figures in the Ravenna hierarchy. The floor (once carpeted with mosaics) has been rebuilt. Along the central nave are frescoed tablets. Two dozen marble columns line the approach to the apse, where you'll find the major reason for visiting the basilica: The mosaics here are exceptional, rich in gold and turquoise, set against a background of top-heavy birds nesting in shrubbery. St. Apollinare stands in the center, with a row of lambs on either side lined up as in a processional, the 12 lambs symbolizing the Apostles, of course.

Tomba di Dante. Via Dante Alighieri. Free admission. Daily 8am–7pm.

Right off Piazza Garibaldi, the final monument to Dante Alighieri, "the divine poet," isn't much to look at—graced as it is with a marble bas-relief. But it's a far better place than he assigned to some of his fellow Florentines. The author of the *Divine Comedy*, in exile from his hometown of Florence, died in Ravenna on September 14, 1321. To the right of the small temple is a mound of earth in which Dante's urn went "underground" from March 1944 to December 1945 because it was feared his tomb might suffer from the bombings. Near the tomb is the 5th-century church of **San Francesco,** the site of the poet's funeral.

A DAY AT THE BEACH

By taking bus no. 70 from Ravenna, in just 20 minutes you can enjoy **white-sand beaches** set against a backdrop of pine forests. Lined with beach clubs, snack shops, and ice-cream stands, these beaches are extremely overcrowded during the sultry summer. The most beautiful beaches are found along a stretch called **Punta Marina di Ravenna.** Marina di Ravenna is also lively at night with pubs and discos open until the early hours.

SHOPPING

No one can enter or leave Ravenna without being influenced by the severely dignified mosaics adorning the interiors of the most important churches. One of the best places to admire (and buy) examples of the art form is **Studio Acomena,** Via di Roma 60 (☎ **0544/37-119**). Replicas of Christ, the Madonna, the saints, and penitent sinners appear in all their majesty amid more secular forms whose designs were inspired by Roman gladiators or floral and geometric motifs. Virtually anything can be shipped. **Scianna,** Via di Roma 30 (☎ **0544/37-556**), and **Luciana Notturni,** Via Arno 13 (☎ **0544/63-002**), are two worthy competitors.

ACCOMMODATIONS

Hotel Bisanzio. Via Salara 30, 48100 Ravenna. ☎ **0544/217-111.** Fax 0544/32-539. www.bestwestern.com. 38 units. A/C MINIBAR TV TEL. 165,000–210,000L ($96–$122) double. Rates include breakfast. AE, DC, MC, V. Parking 25,000L ($15).

A few minutes' walk from many of Ravenna's treasures in the heart of town, the Bisanzio is cheaper and has more personality than the Jolly (below). It's a pleasantly coordinated and completely renovated modern hotel. The guest rooms have attractive Italian styling, some with mottled batik wall coverings. The uncluttered breakfast room has softly draped windows, and guests have use of a garden.

Hotel Centrale Byron. Via IV Novembre 14, 48100 Ravenna. ☎ **0544/212-225.** Fax 0544/34-114. 54 units. A/C TV TEL. 105,000–130,000L ($61–$75) double. Rates include breakfast. AE, DC, MC, V. Parking 20,000L ($12).

This art deco–inspired hotel is a few steps from Piazza del Popolo. The lobby is an elegantly simple combination of white marble and brass detailing. The long, narrow public rooms, arranged "railroad style," include an alcove sitting room and a combination TV room, bar, and snack and breakfast-room area. The guest rooms are simply but comfortably furnished. Why Lord Byron and not the literary legend of the city, Dante? Dante may have died here, but Lord Byron and his mistress of the moment (both happened to be married) once shared a nearby palace.

Jolly Hotel. Piazza Mameli 1, 48100 Ravenna. ☎ **800/221-2626** in the U.S. or 0544/ 35-762. Fax 0544/216-055. 84 units. A/C MINIBAR TV TEL. 220,000–250,000L ($128–$145) double; from 300,000L ($174) suite. Rates include breakfast. AE, DC, MC, V. Parking 20,000– 30,000L ($12–$17).

This hotel, built in 1950 in the postwar crackerbox style with a bunkerlike facade, contains two elevators and a conservative decor of stone floors and lots of paneling. As Ravenna suffers from a dearth of first-class accommodations, the Jolly has become a favorite of business travelers. However, it's too sterile for our tastes. Its La Matta restaurant serves a standard local and international cuisine. Services include room service, baby-sitting, and laundry.

DINING

Bella Venezia. Via IV Novembre 16. ☎ **0544/212-746.** Reservations required. Main courses 16,000–24,000L ($9–$14); fixed-price menu 28,000L ($16). AE, DC, MC, V. Mon–Sat noon–2:30pm and 7–10pm. Closed Dec 23–Jan 15. ROMAGNOLA/ITALIAN.

The Bella Venezia is a few steps from Piazza del Popolo and next to the Hotel Centrale Byron. Despite the name, the only Venetian dish prepared is delicious fegato alla veneziana (liver fried with onions). The repertoire is almost exclusively regional, with such dishes as risotto, cappelletti alla romagnola (cap-shaped pasta stuffed with a mix of ricotta, roasted pork loin, chicken breast, and nutmeg, served with meat sauce), and garganelli pasta served with whatever happens to be in season (baby asparagus, mushrooms, or peas). All pastas are made by hand, and the place is very family run, very warm, and very old Italy.

Ristorante La Gardèla. Via Ponte Marino 3. ☎ **0544/217-147.** Reservations recommended. Main courses 10,000–20,000L ($6–$12). AE, DC, MC, V. Fri–Wed noon–2:30pm and 7–10pm. Closed Feb 10–20 and Aug 10–20. EMILIA-ROMAGNA/SEAFOOD.

La Gardèla, a few steps from one of Ravenna's most startling leaning towers, is spread out over two levels with paneled walls lined with racks of wine bottles. The waiters bring out an array of typical but savory dishes. Specialties are tortelloni della casa (made with ricotta, cream, spinach, tomatoes, and herbs) and spezzatino alla contadina (roast veal with potatoes, tomatoes, and herbs). Ravioli is stuffed with truffles, and one of their past best pasta dishes, tagliatelle, is offered with porcini mushrooms. The chefs prepare more fresh fish than ever before, most often from the Adriatic. Considering the quality of the food and the first-rate ingredients, this is Ravenna's best restaurant buy.

Ristorante Tre Spade. Via Faentina 136. ☎ **0544/500-522.** Reservations recommended. Main courses 18,000–30,000L ($10–$17); fixed-price menu 65,000L ($38). AE, DC, MC, V. Tues–Sat 12:30–2:30pm and 7:30–10:30pm, Sun 12:30–2:30pm. Closed first 3 weeks of Aug. INTERNATIONAL/EMILIAN/SEAFOOD.

This appealing spot has been serving good cuisine since 1980. Ristorante Tre Spade keeps prices under control while magically combining solid technique and inventiveness. Specialties include an asparagus parfait accompanied by a zesty sauce of bits of green peppers and black olives and seafood that's creative and tasteful. This might be followed by taglioni with smoked-salmon sauce, veal cooked with sage, spaghetti with fruits of the sea (including clams in their shells), green gnocchi in Gorgonzola sauce, or roast game in season, plus a good collection of wines. The menu changes frequently, and daily specials are offered according to the market.

RAVENNA AFTER DARK

Some of the most spontaneous good times here unfold beside the **Marina di Ravenna,** where a roster of pubs and dance bars combine big-city glitter with the charm and idiosyncrasies of this very ancient city. The best club here for socializing and drinking is **Santa Fe,** Via delle Nazione 180 (☎ **0544/530-239).**

If you're here in July and August, you can enjoy the **Ravenna Festival Internazionale.** Even Pavarotti and other greats might show up to perform. Tickets begin at 25,000L ($15) but go much higher. For information, call ☎ **0544/213-895;** for tickets, call ☎ **0544/325-77.** A **Dante Festival** takes place the second week in September, sponsored by the church of San Francesco. Call ☎ **0544/332-56** for details. Further entertainment is offered by the **Ravenna Teatro** (☎ **0544/302-27),** which sponsors free summer concerts in the various squares and churches around town.

4 Modena: Home to Ferrari & Maserati

25 miles NW of Bologna, 250 miles NW of Rome, 81 miles N of Florence

After Ferrara fell to Pope Clement VIII, the Este family established a duchy at **Modena** in the closing years of the 16th century. This city in the Po Valley possesses many great art treasures evoking its more glorious past. On the food front, Modena's chefs enjoy an outstanding reputation in hard-to-please gastronomic circles. And traversed by the ancient Roman Via Emilia, Modena is a hot spot for European art connoisseurs.

Modena is an industrial zone blessed with Italy's highest per-capita income and can seem as sleek as the sports cars it produces. This is partially because of its 20th-century face-lift, the result of the city being largely rebuilt following the destructive World War II bombings. These factors create a stark contrast to both the antiquity and the poverty so noticeable in other regions. It's best known abroad as home to automobile and racing giants Ferrari, Maserati, and De Tomaso, as well as for its production of Lambrusco wine and balsamic vinegar. Locals also proudly claim opera star Luciano Pavarotti as one of their greatest exports.

Many visitors who care little about antiquities come here to do business with the Ferrari or Maserati car plant (both off-limits to the general public). However, you can visit a showroom, the **Galleria Ferrari,** Via Dino Ferrari 43 in Maranello (☎ **0536/ 943-204**), a suburb of Modena. The showroom displays engines, trophies, and both antique and the latest Ferrari cars. It's open Tuesday to Sunday 9:30am to 12:30pm and 3 to 6pm, charging an admission of 15,000L ($9). From the bus station on Via Bacchini in Modena, a bus marked MARANELLO departs hourly during the day. Ask at the tourist office (below) for details and a map.

ESSENTIALS

GETTING THERE   There are good **train** connections to and from Bologna (one train every 30 minutes); trip time is 20 minutes, and a one-way fare is 3,400L ($1.95). Trains arrive from Parma once per hour (trip time: 40 minutes); the one-way fare is 5,100L ($2.95). For information and schedules, call ☎ **059/218-226** or 1478/ 88-088 toll free in Italy only. The train is better, but if you're in Ferrara, one local ATCM **bus** (no. 7) leaves for Modena every hour; trip time is 1½ hours and a one-way fare is 8,400L ($4.85). In Modena, call ☎ **059/308-801** for information. If you've got a **car** and are coming from Bologna, take A1 northeast until you see the turnoff for Modena.

VISITOR INFORMATION   The **tourist office** is on Via Canalgrande (☎ **059/ 206-660**), open Monday, Tuesday, and Thursday to Saturday 8:30am to 1pm and 3 to 7pm; Wednesday 8:30am to 1pm; and Sunday 9:30am to 12:30pm.

SEEING THE SIGHTS

✪ **Il Duomo.** Piazza del Duomo. ☎ **059/216-078.** Free admission. Daily 7am–noon and 3:30–7pm.

One of the glories of the Romanesque in northern Italy, Modena's cathedral was built in a style that'll be familiar to anyone who has been to Lombardy. It was founded in closing year of the 11th century and designed by an architect named Lanfranco, with Viligelmo as decorator. The work was carried out by Campionesi masons from Lake Lugano. The cathedral, consecrated in 1184, was dedicated to St. Geminiano, the patron saint of Modena, a 4th-century Christian and defender of the faith. Towering from the rear is the **Ghirlandina,** a 12th- to 14th-century campanile, 285 feet tall. Leaning slightly, the bell tower guards the replica of the Secchia Rapita (stolen bucket), garnered as booty from a defeated Bolognese.

The facade of the Duomo features a 13th-century rose window by Anselmo da Campione. It also boasts Viligelmo's main entryway, with pillars supported by lions, as well as Viligelmo bas-reliefs depicting scenes from Genesis. But don't confine your look to the front. The south door, the so-called Princes' Door, was designed by Viligelmo in the 12th century and is framed by bas-reliefs illustrating scenes in the saga of the patron saint. You'll find an outside pulpit from the 15th century, with emblems of Matthew, Mark, Luke, and John.

Inside, there's a vaulted ceiling, and the overall effect is gravely impressive. The Modenese wisely restored the cathedral during the first part of the 20th century, so that its present look resembles the original design. The gallery above the crypt is an outstanding piece of sculpture, supported by four lions. The pulpit is held up by two hunchbacks. And the crypt, where the body of the patron saint was finally taken, is a forest of columns; here you'll find Guido Mazzoni's *Holy Family* group in terra-cotta, completed in 1480.

✪ **Galleria Estense and Biblioteca Estense.** In the Palazzo del Musei, Largo Sant'Agostino 48 (off Via Emilia). ☎ **059/222-145.** Gallery, 8,000L ($4.65) adults; children 17 and under/seniors 60 and over free. Gallery, Tues and Fri–Sat 9am–7pm, Wed–Thurs 9am–2pm, Sun 9am–1pm; library, Mon–Thurs 9am–7pm, Fri–Sat 9am–1pm.

The **Galleria Estense** is noted for its paintings from the Emilian or Bolognese school from the 14th to the 18th century. The nucleus of the collection was created by the Este family in the heyday of their duchies in Ferrara and then Modena. Some of the finest work is by Spanish artists, including a miniature triptych by El Greco of Toledo and a portrait of Francesco I d'Este by Velázquez. Other works are Bernini's bust of Francesco I and paintings by Correggio, Veronese, Tintoretto, Carracci, Reni, and Guercino.

One of the greatest libraries in southern Europe, the **Biblioteca Estense** (☎ **059/222-248**) contains around 500,000 printed works and 13,000 manuscripts. An assortment of the most interesting volumes is kept under glass for visitors to inspect. Of these, the most celebrated is the 1,200-page *Bible of Borso d'Este,* bordered with stunning miniatures.

SHOPPING

If you want to go shopping, you can always cruise the car lots of the city (which has more Fiat factories than anywhere else in the world), looking for the best deal and hinting for invitations to one of the Agnelli family's cocktail parties. But if a car isn't in your budget, consider a bottle or two of the item that changed the face of salad making forever—balsamic vinegar.

Until the advent of nouvelle cuisine, which fundamentally changed many of the tenets of how North Americans ate, few people outside Italy had ever heard of balsamic vinegar. Today, gastronomes tend to panic in a kitchen without a good supply of the stuff, and Modena produces Italy's largest and most aromatic. A shop in the town center that sells esoteric food products, as well as bottles of the aromatic vinegar from virtually every producer in the region, is **Fini,** Piazza San Francesco (☎ **059/223-314**). **Justi,** Via Capitani 47 (☎ **059/441-203**) exports crates of the vinegar throughout Europe, as well as bottles on the premises.

ACCOMMODATIONS

Canalgrande Hotel. Corso Canalgrande 6, 41100 Modena. ☎ **059/217-160.** Fax 059/221-674. www.hotelinfoplus.com/modena/canalgrande.htm. 72 units. A/C MINIBAR TV TEL. 275,000L ($160) double; from 432,000L ($251) suite. Rates include breakfast. AE, DC, MC, V. Parking 15,000L ($9). Bus: 7, 12, or 14.

In the old town, the Canalgrande is housed in a 300-year-old stucco palace and has more atmosphere and charm than the more highly rated Hotel Real Fini. The Canalgrande boasts elaborate mosaic floors, Victorian-era furniture, carved and frescoed ceilings, and chandeliers. The rooms are not large yet not cramped, decorated in muted pastels. Some of the best rooms open onto balconies, and these (no surprise) are grabbed up first. If you want a quieter room, ask for one on the garden side. Under the basement's vaulted ceiling is a tavern, La Secchia Rapita (the Stolen Bucket), serving modest lunches and dinners Thursday to Tuesday. The garden's central flowering tree seems filled with every kind of bird in Modena.

Hotel Daunia. Via del Pozzo 159, 41100 Modena. ☎ **059/371-182.** Fax 059/374-807. 46 units. A/C MINIBAR TV TEL. 162,000L ($94) double. Rates include breakfast. AE, DC, MC, V. Parking 25,000L ($15). Bus: 7, 12, or 14.

Away from the city center, this recently built hotel boasts an exterior in a modified 18th-century design. Inside, however, it's modern Italian all the way, with gleaming brass, polished woods, eclectic contemporary furniture, and marble and tiled floors. The pleasant bar features a curved wood surface and sleek black wood and leather. But the breakfast room has a rather claustrophobic cafeteria feel. The guest rooms are comfortable but seem rather bare, with light-colored walls and neutral fabrics contrasted by dark wood furnishings. In an unusual arrangement, the hotel restaurant, L'Aragosta, is on the far side of the city center, and a free taxi service shuttles hungry lodgers back and forth. It serves numerous variations of pizzas, antipasti, and Italian wines along with traditional regional dishes. A private guarded parking lot ensures the safety of your vehicle.

Hotel Libertà. Via Blasia 10, 41100 Modena. ☎ **059/222-365** or 059/222-305. Fax 059/222-502. www.hotelinfoplus.com/modena/liberta.htm. 51 units. A/C MINIBAR TV TEL. 190,000L ($110) double; 280,000L ($162) suite. Rates include breakfast. AE, DC, MC, V. Parking 25,000L ($15). Bus: 7, 12, or 14.

A modern hotel wrapped in an aged exterior, this lodge is mere steps away from the cathedral and the Palazzo Ducale. Marble and terra-cotta floors run throughout, and a large sleek bar features plush leather chairs and couches. The guest rooms favor floral wallpapers and blond-wood furniture with plaid and other geometric fabrics; some top-floor rooms are made cozy by sloping ceilings with skylights. The hotel has a breakfast room, a TV lounge, a meeting room, and two garages (one on-site and the other nearby). Several restaurants are close by, and the staff particularly recommends Da Enzo (below), only 25 yards away.

○ **Hotel Roma.** Via Farini 44, 41100 Modena. ☎ **059/222-218.** Fax 059/223-747. www. hotelinfoplus.com/modena/roma.htm. 55 units. MINIBAR TV TEL. 135,000L ($78) double; 150,000L ($87) suite. Rates include breakfast. AE, DC, MC, V. Parking 15,000L ($9). Bus: 7, 12, or 14.

The Roma is a buff-and-white neoclassical building about 2 blocks from the cathedral. The building dates from the 17th century, when it belonged to the duke of Este. It's one of our favorite hotels in its category and is also the preferred hotel of many of the opera stars who come to Pavarotti's hometown for concerts and auditions. The windows and doors are soundproof, presumably so anyone can privately imitate his or her favorite diva. The guest rooms have high ceilings, tasteful colors, and comfortable and attractive furnishings. The lobby is a long skylit room with an arched ceiling, a bar, and a snack bar.

DINING

○ **Fini.** Rue Frati Minori 54. ☎ **059/223-314.** Reservations recommended. Main courses 30,000–50,000L ($17–$29). AE, DC, MC, V. Wed–Sun 12:30–2:30pm and 8–10:30pm. Closed July 25–Aug 25 and Dec 22–Jan 3. Bus: 6 or 11. MODENESE/INTERNATIONAL.

A visit to this restaurant is well worth making the trip to Modena. Proudly maintaining the high reputation of the city's kitchens, Fini is one of the best restaurants you'll encounter in Emilia-Romagna and is Pavarotti's favorite when he's in town.

Despite its modernized art nouveau decor, including Picasso-esque murals and banquettes, it opened in 1912. For an appetizer, try the creamy green lasagne or the tortellini (prepared in six ways—for example, with truffles). For a main dish, the gran bollito misto reigns supreme. A king's feast of boiled meats, accompanied by a selection of four sauces, is wheeled to your table. The meat board includes zampone (a specialty of Modena, stuffed pigs' trotters boiled with beef), a calf's head, an ox tongue, chicken, and ham. After all this rich fare, you may settle for the fruit salad for dessert. Lambrusco is the superb local wine choice.

Ristorante Da Enzo. Via Coltellini 17 (off Piazza Mazzini). ☎ **059/225-177.** Reservations recommended. Main courses 16,000–30,000L ($10–$17); fixed-price menus 35,000–50,000L ($20–$29). AE, DC, MC, V. Tues–Sun noon–3pm and 7–10:30pm. Closed 3 weeks in Aug. Bus: 7, 12, or 14. MODENESE.

Clean, conservative, and well known in Modena, this restaurant is one floor above street level in an old building in the historic center's pedestrian zone. Specialties of the house include all the classic dishes, such as pappardelle (wide noodles) with rabbit meat, lasagne verde, several kinds of tortellini, and an array of grilled meats liberally seasoned with herbs and balsamic vinegar. Zampone (stuffed pigs' trotters) is another specialty.

MODENA AFTER DARK

This bustling powerhouse of Italy's industrial machine offers enough evening diversion to amuse an entire assembly line of factory workers and enough culture to absorb an entire theater of Pavarotti fans. Opera arrives in winter at the **Teatro Comunale,** Corso Canal Grande 85 (☎ 059/225-663). At press time the theater was closed for renovations but should reopen sometime in 1999; check with the tourist office. Culture doesn't sleep all summer. In July and August, Modena presents a series of theater, ballet, opera, and musical performances called **Sipario in Piazza.** You might even get to see Pavarotti perform. For details, contact the **Ufficio Sipario in Palazzo Comunale,** Piazza Grande (☎ 059/206-460). Tickets are 15,000L to 50,000L ($9 to $29).

You can always stroll through the neighborhood where everyone seems to gravitate on long hot evenings, the **Parco Amendola,** to the south of Modena's historic core, filled with ice-cream stands, cafes, and bars.

5 Parma: Parmigiano Reggiano, Prosciutto & More

284 miles NW of Rome, 60 miles NW of Bologna, 75 SE of Milan

Parma, straddling Via Emilia, was the home of Correggio, Il Parmigianino, Bodoni (of type fame), and Toscanini and is the home of Parma ham (prosciutto) and parmigiano (Parmesan) cheese. It rose in influence and power in the 16th century as the seat of the Farnese duchy.

On the extinction of the male Farnese line, Parma came under the control of the French Bourbons. Its most loved ruler, Marie-Louise, widow of Napoléon and niece of Marie Antoinette, arrived in 1815 after the Congress of Vienna awarded her this duchy. Marie-Louise became a great patron of the arts, and much of the collection she acquired is on display at the Galleria Nazionale (below). Rising unrest in 1859 forced her abdication, and in 1860, following a plebiscite, Parma was incorporated into the kingdom of Italy.

It has also been a mecca for opera lovers such as Verdi, the great Italian composer whose works include *Il Trovatore* and *Aïda.* He was born in the small village of Roncole, north of Parma, in 1813. In time, his operas echoed through the Teatro Regio, the opera house that was built under the orders of Marie-Louise. Because of Verdi,

Parma became a center of music, and even today the opera house is jam-packed in season. It's said that the Teatro Regio is the most "critical Verdi house" in Italy.

Today, Parma, one of Italy's most prosperous cities, is known for its production of parmigiano and prosciutto, as well as the graciousness of its citizens, considered the most polite in all Italy.

ESSENTIALS

GETTING THERE   Parma is conveniently served by the Milan-Bologna **rail** line, with 20 trains a day arriving from Milan (trip time: 80 minutes); the one-way fare is 11,700L ($7). From Bologna, 34 trains per day arrive in Parma (trip time: 1 hour); the one-way fare is 7,200L ($4.20). There are seven connections a day from Florence (trip time: 3 hours); a one-way fare is 15,500L ($9). For information and schedules, call ☎ 1478/88-088 toll free in Italy only.

From major towns or cities in Italy, trains are usually more efficient than the buses because of faster connections. However, the **bus** comes into play if you're planning on visiting provincial towns in the Parma area. Information and schedules are available at the bus terminal at Piazzale Carlo Alberto della Chiesa 7 near the train station (☎ 0521/21-41). If you've got a **car** and are in Bologna, head northwest along A1.

VISITOR INFORMATION   The **tourist office** is at Via Melloni (☎ 0521/218-889), open Monday to Saturday 9am to 7pm and Sunday 9am to 12:30pm.

SEEING THE CITY

✪ **Il Duomo.** Piazza del Duomo. ☎ 0521/235-886. Free admission. Daily 7am–12:30pm and 3–7pm.

Built in the Romanesque style in the 11th century, with 13th-century Lombard lions guarding its main porch, the dusty pink Duomo stands side-by-side with a **campanile (bell tower)** constructed in the Gothic-Romanesque style and completed in 1294. The facade of the cathedral is highlighted by three open-air loggias. Inside, two darkly elegant aisles flank the central nave. The octagonal cupola was frescoed by a master of light and color, Correggio (1494 to 534), one of Italy's greatest painters of the High Renaissance. His fresco here, *Assumption of the Virgin,* foreshadows the baroque. The frescoes were painted from 1522 to 1534. In the transept to the right of the main altar is a Romanesque bas-relief, *The Deposition from the Cross* by Benedetto Antelami, which is somber, each face bathed in tragedy. Made in 1178, the bas-relief is the best-known work of the 12th-century artist, who was the most important sculptor of the Romanesque in northern Italy.

✪ **Battistero.** Piazza del Duomo 7. ☎ 0521/235-886. Admission 3,000L ($1.75). Daily 9am–12:30pm and 3–7pm.

Among the greatest Romanesque buildings in northern Italy, the baptistery was the work of Antelami. The project was begun in 1196, though the date it was actually completed is unclear. Made of salmon-colored marble, it's spanned by four open tiers (the fifth is closed off). Inside, the baptistery is richly frescoed with biblical scenes: a *Madonna Enthroned* and a *Crucifixion.* But it's the sculpture by Antelami that's the most worthy treasure and provides the basis for that artist's claim to enduring fame.

Abbey of St. John (San Giovanni Evangelista). Piazzale San Giovanni 1. ☎ 0521/235-592. Free admission to church and cloisters; 4,000L ($2.30) for pharmacist's shop. Daily 8:30am–noon and 3–6:30pm; pharmacist's shop daily 9am–1:45pm.

Behind the Duomo is this church of unusual interest. After admiring the baroque front, pass into the interior to see yet another cupola by Correggio. Working from 1520 to 1524, the High Renaissance master depicted the *Vision of San Giovanni.*

Vasari liked it so much he became completely carried away in his praise, suggesting the "impossibility" of an artist conjuring up such a divine work and marveling it could actually have been painted "with human hands." Correggio also painted a St. John with pen in hand, in the transept (over the door to the left of the main altar). Il Parmigianino, the second Parmesan master, did some frescoes in the chapel at the left of the entrance. You can visit the **abbey,** the **school,** the **cloister,** and a **pharmacist's shop** where monks made potions for some 6 centuries, a practice that lasted until the closing years of the 19th century. Mortars and jars, some as old as the Middle Ages, line the shelves.

Arthur Toscanini Birthplace and Museum (Casa Natale e Museo di Arturo Toscanini). Via Rodolfo Tanzi 13. ☎ **0521/285-499.** Admission 3,000L ($1.75). Tues–Sun 10am–1pm; Tues–Sat 3–6pm.

This is the house where the great musician/conductor was born in 1867. Toscanini was unquestionably the greatest orchestral conductor of the first half of the 20th century and one of the most astonishing musical interpreters of all time. He spent his childhood and youth in this house, which has been turned into a museum with interesting relics and a record library, containing all the recorded works he conducted.

✪ **National Gallery (Galleria Nazionale) and National Archaeological Museum (Museo Archeologico Nazionale).** In the Palazzo della Pilotta, Piazza della Pace, Via della Pilotta 5. ☎ **0521/233-309** (National Gallery) or 0521/233-718 (Archaeological Museum). National Gallery, 12,000L ($7) adults. Archaeological Museum, 4,000L ($2.30) adults; children under 18 free. National Gallery, daily 9am–2pm. Archaeological Museum, Tues–Sun 9am–7pm.

The Palazzo della Pilotta once housed the Farnese family in Parma's heyday as a duchy in the 16th century. Badly damaged by bombs in World War II, it has been restored and turned into a palace of museums.

The **National Gallery** offers a limited but well-chosen selection of the works of Parma artists from the late 15th to the 19th century—notably paintings by Correggio and Parmigianino. In one room is an unfinished head of a young woman attributed to Leonardo. Correggio's *Madonna della Scala* (of the stairs), the remains of a fresco, is also displayed. But his masterpiece is *St. Jerome with the Madonna and Child.* Imbued with delicacy, it represents age, youth, love—a gentle ode to tenderness. In the next room is Correggio's *Madonna della Scodella* (with a bowl), with its agonized faces. You'll also see Correggio's *Coronation,* a golden fresco that's a work of great beauty, and his less successful *Annunciation.* One of Parmigianino's best-known paintings is *St. Catherine's Marriage,* with its rippling movement and subdued colors.

You can also view **St. Paul's Chamber,** which Correggio frescoed with mythological scenes, including one of Diana. The chamber faces onto Via Macedonio Melloni. On the same floor as the National Gallery is the **Farnese Theater,** a virtual jewel box, evocative of Palladio's theater at Vicenza. Built in 1618, the structure was bombed in 1944 and has been restored. Admission to the theater is included in the admission to the gallery; however, should you wish to visit it and not the gallery, there's a separate charge of 4,000L ($2.30).

Also in the palazzo is the **National Archaeological Museum.** It houses Egyptian sarcophagi, Etruscan vases, Roman- and Greek-inspired torsos, Bronze Age relics, and its best-known exhibit, the Tabula Alimentaria, a bronze-engraved tablet dating from the reign of Trajan and excavated at Velleia in Piacenza.

SHOPPING

Parma's most famous food product—Parmesan (parmigiano) cheese—or one of its non-Italian clones, is savored all over the world. Virtually every corner market sells thick wedges of the stuff, but if you're looking to buy your cheese in a setting that's both historic and redolent with herbs and spices, head for the **Salumerí Garibaldi,** Via Garibaldi 42 (☎ **0521/235-606**), or its nearby competitor, the **Specialitá di Parma,** Via Farini 9 (☎ **0521/233-591**).

Hoping to learn more about the region's famous hams and cheeses? There are well-funded bureaucracies in Parma whose sole functions are to encourage the world to use greater quantities of the city's tastiest products. They can arrange tours and visits to the region's most famous producers. For information about Parma cheeses, contact the **Consorzio del Parmigiano Reggiano,** Via Gramsci 26 (☎ **0521/292-700**). For insights into the dressing and curing of Parma hams, contact the **Consorzio del Prosciutto di Parma,** Via M. dell' Arpe 8B (☎ **0521/243-987**).

If the idea of a spectacular inventory of wine, sold by folk who really know their product, appeals to you, try the **Enoteca Fontana,** Via Farina 24a (☎ **0521/286-037**), which sells bottles from virtually every vineyard in the region.

Looking for a souvenir of Parma that's more durable? Head to **Palma,** Burgo Angelo Massa 9 (☎ **0521/284-939**), for a selection of locally made handcrafts, including ceramics, wood carvings, and textiles.

ACCOMMODATIONS

Hotel Button. Strada San Vitale 7 (off Piazza Garibaldi), 43100 Parma. ☎ **0521/208-039.** Fax 0521/238-783. 41 units. TV TEL. 165,000L ($96) double. Rates include continental breakfast. AE, DC, MC, V. Closed July 5–31.

The Button is a local favorite, one of the best bargains in the town center. This is a family-owned and -run hotel, and you're made to feel welcome. Perhaps you'll even join the locals in the lounge gathered around the TV to watch soccer games. The rooms are simple but comfortably furnished and generally spacious, though the decor is dull. The hotel doesn't have a restaurant.

Hotel Farnese International. Via Reggio 51A, 43100 Parma. ☎ **0521/994-247.** Fax 0521/992-317. www.hotelinfoplus.com/parma/farneseinternat.htm. 76 units. A/C MINIBAR TV TEL. 179,000–210,000L ($104–$122) double. Rates include buffet breakfast. AE, DC, MC, V. Free parking outdoors, 12,000L ($7) indoors.

This hotel isn't up to the standards of the Stendhal (below) but makes for a good overnight stop. It's located in a quiet area that's convenient to the town center, airport, and fairs. Parma specialties are served in the hotel restaurant, Il Farnese. The rooms are comfortably furnished in Italian marble. Laundry and room service are provided.

Hotel Verdi. Via Pasini 18, 43100 Parma. ☎ **0521/293-539** or 0521/293-549. Fax 0521/293-559. 20 units. A/C MINIBAR TV TEL. 255,000–290,000L ($148–$168) double; 285,000–330,000L ($165–$191) suite. Breakfast 18,000L ($11). AE, DC, MC, V. Free parking.

Facing the expansive beauty of the Ducal Gardens, this art nouveau hotel has preserved the elegance of its era while meeting the needs of today's visitors. In the public areas, sheer draperies warm the sunlight to a golden glow reflected off the black-and-gold marble floors. The guest rooms feature parquet floors, briarwood furnishings, fine linens, and safes. The baths are lined in marble and include luxurious soaps and body oils as well as hair dryers. The adjacent Santa Croce restaurant offers a refined yet cordial atmosphere resplendent with period art, furnishings, and lighting in which to savor traditional cuisine and fine Italian wines. In summer, a brick courtyard alive with greenery allows you to dine outdoors. To ensure vehicle safety, a guarded parking garage is at the rear of the hotel.

During the day you can walk through the **Parco Ducale** (Ducal Gardens), which was landscaped by the French architect Petitot and decorated with statues by another

Frenchman, Boudard. With its splashing fountains, wide expanses of greenery, and gravel paths, it makes for a nice stroll and is a place to relax. Free admission to walk through the gardens.

Palace Hotel Maria Luigia. Viale Mentana 140, 43100 Parma. ☎ **0521/281-032.** Fax 0521/231-126. www.venere.com/home/emilia_romagna/parma/maria_luigia/maria_luigia. html. E-mail: maria.luigia@italyhotel.com. 107 units. A/C MINIBAR TV TEL. 400,000L ($232) double; 600,000L ($348) suite. Rates include breakfast. AE, CB, DC, MC, V. Parking 20,000L ($12).

This hotel, built of brick in 1974 and located near the station, was and still is a welcome addition to the Parma hotel scene. It caters especially to business travelers and is still superior to the Stendhal (below). Bold colors and molded-plastic built-ins set the up-to-date mood, and the comfortable modern rooms feature soundproof walls as well as other amenities. There's an Italian-looking American bar on the premises. The hotel also has one of the best restaurants in Parma, Maxim's, which serves excellent Italian and international specialties daily. Room service is available around the clock.

Park Hotel Stendhal. Piazzetta Bodini 3, 43100 Parma. ☎ **0521/208-057.** Fax 0521/ 285-655. www.travelweb.com/travelweb/init.htm or www.bestwestern.com. E-mail: stendhal. htl@rsadvnet.it. 66 units. A/C MINIBAR TV TEL. 280,000L ($162) double. Rates include breakfast. AE, DC, MC, V. Parking 20,000L ($12).

The Stendhal sits on a square near the opera house, a few minutes' walk from many of the important sights and 6 blocks south of the station. The rooms are well maintained and furnished with contemporary pieces that are reproductions of various styles, ranging from rococo to provincial. Try for one of the traditional-looking rooms where the furnishings are classic with matching fabrics and patterned carpets. There's a traditional American bar and lounge, with comfortable armchairs for before- and after-dinner drinks. La Pilotta, the hotel restaurant, serves a cuisine typical of Parma, with a medley of international dishes. Laundry service and room service are provided.

DINING

The chefs of Parma are known throughout Italy for the quality of their cuisine. Of course, parmigiano reggiano has added just the right touch to millions of Italian meals, and the word *parmigiana* is quite familiar to American diners.

Croce di Malta. Borgo Palmia 8. ☎ **0521/235-643.** Reservations recommended. Main courses 10,000–22,000L ($6–$13). AE, DC, MC, V. Mon–Sat 12:30–2:30pm and 7:30–11pm. PARMIGIANA.

Local legend has it that angry citizens plotted to assassinate the last duke of Parma while he was drowning in vino at this tavern. All the dishes for which Parma is famous are served, even some esoteric ones, like cappelletti (a pasta that turns magenta because it's made with beets) and tortelli (made a golden amber with the addition of pumpkin, though another version is made with potatoes). Tagliatelle is served in almost any style. Other savory dishes are roast veal stuffed with cheese and chicken flavored with wine and Gorgonzola.

✪ La Greppia. Strada Garibaldi 39A. ☎ **0521/233-686.** Reservations required. Main courses 25,000–40,000L ($15–$23). AE, DC, MC, V. Wed–Sun 12:30–3:30pm and 7:30–10:30pm. Closed July. PARMIGIANA.

La Greppia has an unpretentious decor, yet it's near the top of every gourmet's list. The competition is keen in Parma, but its only serious rival is Parizzi (below). Through a plate-glass window at one end of the dining room you can see the all-woman staff at work in the kitchen. Leading the team is the co-owner, Paola Cavassini, and her good-natured husband, Maurizio Rossi, who presides over the dining room. The chefs adjust their menus depending on the season. Likely dishes are veal kidneys sautéed with fines herbes and demi-glacé sauce, chicken breast with orange sauce, pappardella alla Greppia (with cream and dried porcinis), and roast rack of rabbit flavored with thyme. Many dishes are flavored with fresh thyme or mushrooms or even cherries. The fresh fruit tarts are succulent, but the kitchen is known for its compelling chocolate cake, which one reviewer claimed was much better than the famed Sachertorte of Vienna's Hotel Sacher.

✪ **Parizzi.** Strada della Repubblica 71. ☎ **0521/285-952.** Reservations required. Main courses 20,000–35,000L ($12–$20). Tues–Sat noon–2:30pm and 7–9:30pm. Closed Dec 24–25. AE, DC, MC, V. PARMIGIANA.

In the historic core, the building that houses Parizzi dates to 1551, when it first opened as an inn; the present restaurant was opened in 1958 by the father of the present owner. Seated under the skylit patio, the people of Parma, known for their exacting tastes and demanding palates, enjoy the rich cuisine for which their town is celebrated. This restaurant is among the two best in Parma, comparable to La Greppia. Both richly deserve their Frommer's stars. After you're shown to a table in one of the good-sized dining rooms, a trolley cart filled with antipasti is wheeled before you, containing shellfish, stuffed vegetables, and marinated salmon. After the antipasti, you might be tempted by *culatelo*, cured ham made from sliced haunch of wild boar; a pasta served with a sauce of herbs and parmigiano reggiano; a parmigiano soufflé with white truffles; roasted guinea fowl with Fonseca wine; stracotta of beef with red-wine sauce; or veal scaloppine layered with Fontina cheese and ham.

PARMA AFTER DARK

Life in Parma extends beyond munching on strips of salty ham and cheese. The **Teatro di Reggio,** Via Garibaldi, near Piazza della Pace (☎ **0521/218-910**), is the site of concerts throughout the year as well as the annual midsummer **Concerti Nei Chiostri.**

If you're looking for a glass or two of some alarmingly esoteric wines, head for the bar section of a spot recommended in the shopping section, the **Enoteca Fontana,** Via Farina 24A (☎ **0521/286-037**).

The city's most appealing American-style bar, with an admittedly heavy Italian accent, is **La Corriere Stravagante,** Via C. Prati 4 (☎ **0521/964-318**), where stiff drinks are served in a setting accented by stonework, wooden tables, and lots of animated dialogues. At **Bacco Verde,** Via Cavalloti (☎ **0521/230-487**), sandwiches, glasses of beer, and a wide selection of Italian wines are dispensed in a cramped but convivial setting ringed with antique masonry.

Are you in the mood for dancing? The town's most interesting and successful disco is **Dadaumpa,** Via Emilio Este 48 (☎ **0521/483-802**), a stylish and light-hearted venue for European and New World dance tunes. More oriented toward students and persons under 25 is **Astrolabio,** Via Zarotta 86A (☎ **0521/460-538**).

Venice: La Serenissima 9

One rainy morning as we were leaving our hotel—a converted palazzo—a decorative stone fell from the lunette, narrowly missing us. For a second it looked as if we were candidates for a gondola funeral cortège to the island of marble tombs, San Michele. In dismay, we looked back at the owner, a woman straight from a Modigliani portrait. From the doorway, she leaned like the Tower of Pisa, mocking the buildings of her city. Throwing up her hands, she sighed, "Venezia, Venezia," then went inside.

That woman had long ago surrendered to the inevitable decay embracing this city like the moss at the base of the pilings. **Venice** (La Serenissima—the Serene Republic) is a preposterous monument to both the folly and the obstinacy of humankind. It shouldn't exist . . . but it does, much to the delight of thousands of visitors, gondoliers, lacemakers, hoteliers, restaurateurs, and glassblowers.

Centuries ago, in an effort to flee barbarians, Venetians left drydock and drifted out to a flotilla of "uninhabitable" islands in the lagoon. Survival was difficult enough, but no Venetian has ever settled for mere survival. The remote ancestors of the present inhabitants created the world's most beautiful city. To your children's children, however, Venice may be nothing more than a legend. It's sinking at a rate of about 2½ inches per decade. Estimates are that if no action is taken soon, one-third of the city's art will deteriorate hopelessly within the next decade or so. Clearly, Venice is in peril. One headline proclaimed, "The Enemy's at the Gates."

But for however long it lasts, Venice, decaying or not, will be one of the highlights of your trip through Italy. It lacks the speeding cars and roaring mopeds of Rome; instead, you make your way through the city either by boat or on foot. It would be ideal were it not for the tourist hordes—far more than any barbarian invasion—who descend, creating a virtual emergency for those who need space to walk and air to breathe. These masses overwhelm the squares and make the streets almost impossible to navigate. In the sultry summer heat of the Adriatic, the canals become a smelly stew. Steamy and overcrowded July and August are the worst times to visit; May, June, September, and October are much more ideal.

Though it's one of the world's most enchantingly lovely and evocative cities, you do pay a price, literally and figuratively, for all this beauty. Venice is virtually selling its past to the world, even more so

---

Impressions

When I went to Venice—my dream became my address.

—Marcel Proust, letter to Mme Strauss (May 1906)

---

than Florence, and anybody who has been here leaves complaining of the outrageous prices, which can be double what they are elsewhere in the country. Since the 19th century, Venice has thrived on its visitors, including the likes of Lord Byron and Thomas Mann, but these high prices have forced out many locals. They have fled across the lagoon to dreary Mestre, an industrial complex launched to help boost the regional economy.

Today the city is trying belatedly to undo the damage its watery environs and tourist-based economy have wrought. In 1993, after a 30-year hiatus, the canals were once again dredged in an attempt to reduce water loss and reduce the stench brought in with the low tides. In an effort to curb the other 30-year-old problem of residential migration to Mestre, state subsidies are now being offered to the citizens of Venice as an incentive to not only stay but also to renovate their crumbling properties.

Despite all its problems and relatively modest plans (so far) for saving itself, Venice still endures.

But for how long? That is the question.

1 Essentials

ARRIVING

All roads lead not necessarily to Rome but, in this case, to the docks on mainland Venice. The arrival scene at the unattractive Piazzale Roma is filled with nervous expectation; even the most veteran traveler can become confused. Whether arriving by train, bus, car, or airport limo, everyone walks to the nearby docks (less than a 5-minute walk) to select a method of transport to his or her hotel. The cheapest way is by *vaporetto* (public motorboat), the more expensive by gondola or motor launch (see "Getting Around," later in this chapter).

Warning: If your hotel is near one of the public vaporetto stops, you can sometimes struggle with your own luggage until you reach the hotel's reception area. In any event, the one time-tested piece of advice for Venice-bound travelers is that excess baggage is bad news, unless you're willing to pay dearly to have it carried for you to the docks. Porters can't accompany you and your baggage on the vaporetto.

BY PLANE   You can now fly from North America to Venice via Rome on Alitalia. You'll land at the **Aeroporto Marco Polo** (☎ 041/260-6111) at Mestre, north of the city on the mainland. The **Cooperativa San Marco** (☎ 041/522-2303) operates a *motoscafo* (shuttle boat) service departing from the airport and taking visitors to Piazza San Marco in about an hour (with a stop at the Lido after about 45 minutes). The fare is 17,000L ($10). If you've got some extra lire to spend, you can arrange for a **private water taxi** by calling ☎ 041/541-5084. The cost to ride to the heart of Venice is 130,000L ($78).

It's less expensive, however, to take a bus from the airport to the public hookup for transport into Venice. Run by **Azienda Trasporti Veneto Orientale** (☎ 041/520-5530), a shuttle bus links the airport with Piazzale Roma for 5,000L ($2.90). The trip takes about half an hour, and departures are usually on the hour. Even cheaper is a local bus company, **ACTV** (☎ 041/528-7886), whose bus no. 5 makes the run for 1,400L (80¢). The ACTV buses depart every half hour and take about half an hour to reach Piazzale Roma. From Piazzale Roma, you can hook up with a vaporetto to take you to (or near) your hotel.

BY TRAIN Trains pull into the **Stazione di Santa Lucia,** at Piazzale Roma (☎ 041/788-8088 in Italy only for information). Travel time from Rome is about 5¼ hours, from Milan 3½, from Florence 4, and from Bologna 2. The best—and least expensive—way to get from the station to the rest of town is taking a vaporetto that departs near the station's main entrance. There's also a **tourist office** at the station (☎ 041/592-8727).

Anyone between 16 and 29 is eligible for a **"Rolling Venice" pass,** entitling you to discounts in museums, restaurants, stores, language courses, hotels, and bars. Valid for 1 year, it costs 5,000L ($2.90) and can be picked up at a special "Rolling Venice" office set up in the train station during summer.

BY BUS Buses from mainland Italy arrive at Piazzale Roma. For schedules, call **ACTV** at Piazzale Roma (☎ 041/528-7886). If you're coming from a distant city in Italy, it's better to take the train. But Venice has good bus connections with nearby cities like Padua, and a one-way fare from Padua to Venice (or vice versa) is 5,000L ($2.90). The cheapest way to reach the heart of Venice from the bus station is by vaporetto.

BY CAR Venice has autostrada links with the rest of Italy, with direct routes from such cities as Trieste (driving time: 1½ hours), Milan (3 hours), and Bologna (2 hours). Bologna is 94 miles southwest of Venice, Milan 165 miles west, and Trieste 97 miles east. Rome is 327 miles southwest.

If you arrive by car, there are several multitiered parking areas at the terminus where the roads end and the canals begin. One of the most visible is the **Garage San Marco,** Piazzale Roma (☎ 041/523-5101 or 041/523-2213), near the vaporetto, gondola, and motor launch docks. You'll be charged 34,000L to 46,000L ($20 to $27) per day or maybe more, depending on the car size, and from 22,000L to 33,000L ($13 to $19) for 12 hours. From spring to fall this municipal car park is nearly always filled. You can fax a reservation for a space however at **041/52-89969.** You're more likely to find parking on **Isola del Tronchetto** (☎ 041/520-7555), costing 25,000L ($15) per day. From Tronchetto, take vaporetto no. 82 to Piazza San Marco. If you have heavy luggage, you'll need a water taxi. Parking is also available at Mestre.

VISITOR INFORMATION

Visitor information is available at the **Azienda di Promozione Turistica,** Palazzetto Selva–Giardinetti Reali (Molo S. Marco) (☎ 041/522-6356). Summer hours are daily 9:30am to 6:30pm; off-season, it's open Monday to Saturday 9:30am to 3:30pm. The staff is generally unwelcoming and most helpful if you need specific questions answered. Posters around town with exhibit and concert schedules are more helpful. Ask for a schedule of the month's special events and an updated list of museum and church hours, as these can change erratically and often.

CITY LAYOUT

MAIN ARTERIES & STREETS Venice lies 2½ miles from the Italian mainland (connected to Mestre by the Ponte della Libertà) and 1¼ miles from the open seas of the Adriatic. It's an archipelago of 118 islands. Most visitors, however, concern themselves only with **Piazza San Marco** and its vicinity. In fact, the entire city has only one piazza, which is San Marco. Venice is divided into six quarters (*sestieri*): **San Marco** (the most frequented), **Santa Croce, San Polo, Castello, Cannaregio,** and **Dorsoduro.**

A Note on Street Designations

Be prepared for a lot of unfamiliar street designations. A broad street running along a canal is a *fondamenta,* a narrower street running along a canal is a *calle,* and a paved road is a *salizzada, ruga,* or *calle larga.* A *rio terra* is a filled canal channel now used as a walkway and a *sottoportego* a passage beneath buildings. And you'll often encounter the word *campo* when you come to an open-air area—that's a reference to the fact that such a place was once grassy, and in days of yore cattle grazed there.

Many of Venice's so-called streets are actually canals (*rios*), somewhere around 150 in all, spanned by a total of 400 bridges. Venice's version of a main street is the **Grand Canal (Canal Grande),** which snakes through the city like an inverted S and is spanned by three bridges—the white marble **Ponte Rialto,** the wooden **Ponte Accademia,** and the stone **Ponte degli Scalzi.** The Grand Canal splits Venice into two unequal parts.

South of Dorsoduro, which is south of the Grand Canal, is the **Canele della Guidecca,** a major channel separating Dorsoduro from the large island of La Guidecca. At the point where Canale della Guidecca meets the **Canale di San Marco,** you'll spot the little **Isola di San Giorgio Maggiore,** with a church by Palladio. The most visited islands in the lagoon, aside from the **Lido,** are **Murano, Burano,** and **Torcello.**

FINDING AN ADDRESS   A maniac must've numbered Venice's buildings at least 6 centuries ago. The system is completely illogical. Before you set out for a specific place, get detailed instructions and have someone mark the place on your map. Instead of depending on street numbers, try to locate the nearest cross street. Since old signs and numbers have decayed over time, it's best to look for signs posted outside rather than for a number.

Even with all the directions and signposts in the world, getting lost in Venice is inevitable and a great way to explore the city. Still, a little background can't hurt—you can at least try to understand why you're lost.

A helpful hint: Every building has a street address and a mailing address, which are never the same thing. For example, a business at Calle delle Botteghe 3150 (Botteghe Street) will have a mailing address of San Marco 3150, since it's in the San Marco sestiere (district) and all buildings in an individual district are numbered continuously from 1 to 6,000. In this chapter, we give the street name first, followed by the mailing address. With this system, landmarks become important, and one of the biggest is the Grand Canal. This inverted S of a waterway splits the city into two and can actually appear on more than one side of you at once. And the sun and other navigational devices are valuable resources that can help lead you in the right direction.

Squares also take on their own Venetian character, with only San Marco actually having the piazza designation used in other Italian communities (all the other squares are *campos*). Now that everything is as clear as the sludgy water filling a summertime canal at low tide, realize that asking directions and maintaining good humor while being thoroughly disoriented are the most important factors in getting around Venice. It's no wonder so many visitors stick to the sights immediately around Piazza San Marco—but press on, get lost, and explore the charming nooks and crannies unspoiled by the crowds.

STREET MAPS   If you really want to tour Venice and experience that hidden, romantic trattoria on a nearly forgotten street, don't even think about using a map that doesn't detail every street and have an index on the back. The best of the lot is the **Falk**

map of Venice. It details everything (well, almost), and since it's pocket size, you can open it in the Adriatic winds without fear of it blowing away. It's sold at many news kiosks and at all bookstores.

NEIGHBORHOODS IN BRIEF

This section will give you some idea of where you may want to stay and where the major attractions are.

San Marco   Welcome to the center of Venice. Napoléon called it the drawing room of Europe, and it's one crowded drawing room today. The heart of Venetian life for more than a thousand years, it's here that you'll find the major attractions: **Piazza San Marco (St. Mark's Square),** dominated by **St. Mark's Basilica.** Just outside the basilica is the **campanile (bell tower),** a reconstruction of the one that collapsed in 1902. Around the corner is the **Palazzo Ducale (Doge's Palace),** with its **Bridge of Sighs.** In spite of these stellar attractions, this is basically a gaudy tourist belt filled with some of the most overpriced coffee shops in the world, including **Florian's,** founded in 1720, and **Quadri,** which opened in 1775. The most celebrated watering hole, however, is away from the square—**Harry's Bar,** founded by Giuseppe Cipriani but made famous by Hemingway. In and around the square are some of the most convenient hotels in Venice (though not necessarily the best) and an array of expensive shops and trattorie catering to the Yankee dollar, the British pound, the German mark, or whatever.

Castello   The shape of Venice is often likened to that of a fish. If so, Castello is the tail. The largest and most varied of the six sestieri, Castello is home to many attractions, such as the **Arsensale,** and some of the city's plushest hotels, such as the **Danieli.** One of the district's most notable attractions is the Gothic **Santa Giovanni e Paolo (Zanipolo),** the Pantheon of the doges. Cutting through the sestiere is **Campo Santa Maria Formosa,** one of Venice's largest open squares. The most elegant and frequented street is **Riva degli Schiavoni,** running along the Grand Canal—this is the site of some of the finest hotels and restaurants and one of the city's favorite promenades.

Cannaregio   This is Venice's gateway, the first of the six sestieri. It lies away from the rail station at the northwest side of Venice and shelters about a third of the population, some 20,000 residents. At its heart is the **Santa Lucia Station,** from 1955. The area also embraces the old **Jewish Ghetto,** the first one on the continent. Jews began to move here at the beginning of the 16th century, when they were segregated from the rest of the city. From here, the word *ghetto* later became a generic term all over the world. Attractions in this area include the **Ca' d'Oro,** the finest example of the Venetian Gothic style; the **Madonna dell'Orto,** a 15th-century church known for its Tintorettos; and **Santa Maria dei Miracoli,** with a Madonna portrait supposedly able to raise the dead. Unless you're coming to view some church or palace or even the ghetto, this area doesn't offer much else, as its hotels and restaurants aren't the best. Some of the cheapest lodging is found along **Lista di Spagna,** immediately to the left as you exit the train station.

San Polo   This is the heart of commercial Venice and the smallest of the six sestieri. It's reached by crossing the **Ponte di Rialto (Rialto Bridge)** spanning the Grand Canal. The shopping here is much cheaper than in the boutiques around Piazza San Marco. One of the major attractions is the **Erberia,** which Casanova wrote about in his 18th-century biography. Both wholesale and retail markets still pepper this

Impressions

Wonderful city, streets full of water, please advise.

—Robert Benchley

ancient site. At its center is **San Giacomo di Rialto,** the city's oldest church. The district also encloses the **Scuola Grande di San Rocco,** a repository of the works of Tintoretto. **Campo San Polo** is one of the oldest and widest squares and one of the principal venues for Carnevale. San Polo is also filled with moderately priced hotels and a large number of trattorie, many specializing in seafood. In general, the hotels and restaurants are cheaper here than along San Marco but not as cheap as those around the train station in Cannaregio.

Santa Croce   This district, which takes its name from a church that was long ago destroyed, generally follows the snakelike curve of the Grand Canal from Piazzale Roma to a point just short of the Ponte di Rialto. It's split into two rather different neighborhoods. The eastern part is in the typically Venetian style and is one of the least crowded parts of Venice, though it has some of the Grand Canal's loveliest palazzi. The western side is more industrialized and isn't very interesting to explore.

Dorsoduro   This district is compared to New York's Greenwich Village or London's Chelsea, though in truth it doesn't resemble either very much. The least populated of the sestieri, it's filled with old homes and half-forgotten churches. Dorsoduro is the southernmost section of the historic district, and its major attraction is the **Galleria dell'Accademia.** Its second-most-visited attraction is the **Peggy Guggenheim Foundation.** It's less trampled than the areas around the Rialto Bridge and Piazza San Marco. Its most famous church is **La Salute,** whose first stone was laid in 1631. The **Zattere,** a broad quay built after 1516, is one of the favorite promenades in Venice. Cafes, trattorie, and pensiones abound in the area.

THE LAGOON ISLANDS

The Lido   This slim sandy island (7½ miles long and about half a mile wide, though reaching 2½ miles at its broadest point) cradles the Venetian lagoon, offering protection against the Adriatic. The Lido is Italy's most fashionable bathing resort and site of the fabled **Venice Film Festival.** It was the setting for many famous books, like Thomas Mann's *Death in Venice* and Evelyn Waugh's *Brideshead Revisited.* Some of the most fashionable and expensive hotels are found along the Lido Promenade. The most famous are the **Grand Hotel Excelsior** and **Grand Hotel des Bains,** but there are cheaper places as well. The best way to get around is by bike or tandem, which you can rent at Via Zara and Gran Viale.

Torcello   Lying 5½ miles northeast of Venice, Torcello is called "the mother of Venice," having been settled in the 9th century. It was once the most populous of the islands in the lagoon, but since the 18th century it has been nearly deserted. If you ever hope to find solitude in Venice, you'll find it here, following in the footsteps of Hemingway. It's visited today chiefly by those wishing to see its **Cattedrale di Torcello,** with its stunning Byzantine mosaics, and to lunch at **Locanda Cipriani.**

Burano   Perched 5½ miles northeast of Venice, Burano is the most populous of the lagoon islands. In the 16th century, it produced the finest lace in Europe. Lace is still made here, but it's nothing like the product of centuries past. Inhabited since Roman times, Burano is different from either Torcello or Murano. Forget lavish palaces. The

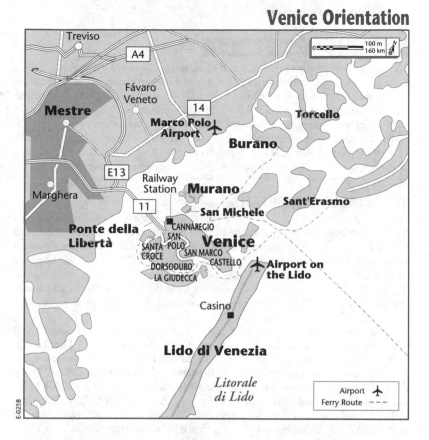

Treviso
A4
Fávaro
Veneto
14
Marco Polo
Airport
Mestre
Torcello
Burano
E13
Railway
Station
Murano
Marghera
11
Sant'Erasmo
San Michele
Ponte della
Libertà
CANNAREGIO
SAN
POLO
Venice
SANTA
CROCE
SAN MARCO
DORSODURO
CASTELLO
Airport on
the Lido
LA GIUDECCA
Casino
Lido di Venezia
Litorale
di Lido
Airport
Ferry Route
0   100 m
           160 km
E-0258

houses are often simple and small and painted in deep blues, strong reds, and striking yellows. The island is still peopled by fisherfolk, and one of the reasons to visit is to dine in one of its trattorie, where, naturally, the specialty is fish.

Murano   This island, three-quarters of a mile northeast of Venice, has been famed for its glassmaking since 1291. Today Murano is the most visited island in the lagoon. Once a closely guarded secret, Murano glassmaking is now clearly visible to any tourist who wants to observe the technique on a guided tour. You can also visit a glass museum, the **Museo Vetrario di Murano,** and see two of the island's notable churches, **San Pietro Martire** and **Santi Maria e Donato.** You'll likely be on the island for lunch, and there are a number of moderately priced trattorie to be found here as well.

2 Getting Around

Since you can't hail a taxi, at least not on land, get ready to walk and walk and walk. Of course, you can break up your walks with vaporetto or boat rides—great respites from dealing with the packed (and we mean *packed*) streets in summer.

However, note that in autumn, the high tide (*acqua alta*) is a real menace. The squares often flood—beginning with Piazza San Marco, one of the city's lowest points. Many visitors and locals wear knee-high boots to navigate their way. In fact, some hotels maintain a storage room full of boots in all sizes for their guests.

A Few Notes on Getting Around

Time and again while exploring, you'll think you know where you're going, only to wind up on a dead-end street or at the side of a canal with no bridge to get to the other side. Just remind yourself that Venice's physical complexity is an integral part of its charm and of the memorable experience it guarantees.

Fortunately, around the city are yellow signs whose arrows direct you toward one of five major landmarks: Ferrovia (the train station), Piazzale Roma, the Rialto (Bridge), (Piazza) San Marco, and the Accademia (Bridge). You'll often find these signs grouped together, their arrows pointing off in different directions.

BY PUBLIC TRANSPORTATION

Much to the chagrin of the once-ubiquitous gondoliers, Venice's **motorboats (vaporetti)** provide inexpensive and frequent, if not always fast, transportation in this canal city. The service is operated by **ACTV (Azienda del Consorzio Trasporti Veneziano),** Calle Fisero, San Marco 1810 (☎ 041/528-7886). An *accelerato* is a vessel that makes every stop and a *diretto* only express stops. The average fare is 4,000L ($2.30). Note that in summer the vaporetti are often fiercely crowded. Pick up a map of the system at the tourist office. The vaporetti run daily, with frequent service 7am to midnight, then hourly midnight to 7am.

If you'd like to ride more than walk around Venice, several discount tickets—sold at the stations—are available. The most popular is the **Biglietto 24 Ore,** costing 15,000L ($9) and offering 24 hours of unlimited travel on any ACTV vaporetto. For 3 full days of unlimited travel, opt for the **Biglietto 3 Giorni,** costing 30,000L ($17); if you plan to be in Venice for 1 week, the **Biglietto 7 Giorni** costs 55,000L ($32) and allows 7 days of unlimited travel. Another bargain is the 5,000L ($2.90) **Biglietto Isole,** good for unlimited travel for 1 day in one direction on line 12, serving the more remote islands in the lagoon and the most visited, Murano, Burano, and Torcello.

The Grand Canal is long and snakelike and can be crossed via only three bridges, including the one at Rialto. If there's no bridge in sight, the trick in getting across is to use one of the **traghetti gondolas** strategically placed at key points. Look for them at the end of any passage called Calle del Traghetto. Under government control, the fare is only 1,000L (60¢).

BY MOTOR LAUNCH (WATER TAXI)

It costs more than the public vaporetto, but you won't be hassled as much when you arrive with your luggage if you hire one of the city's many private **motor launches (taxi acquei).** You may or may not have the cabin of one of these sleek vessels to yourself, since the captains fill their boats with as many passengers as the law allows before taking off. Your porter's uncanny radar will guide you to one of the inconspicuous piers where a water taxi waits.

The price of a transit by water taxi from Piazzale Roma (the road/rail terminus) to Piazza San Marco is 80,000L ($46) for up to four passengers and 100,000L ($58) for more than four. The captains adroitly deliver you, with luggage, to the canalside entrance of your hotel or on one of the smaller waterways within a short walking distance of your destination. You can also call for a water taxi—try the **Cooperativa San Marco** at ☎ 041/522-2303.

BY GONDOLA

If you wish to ride in a gondola, you and your gondolier have two major agreements to reach: the price of the ride and the length of the trip. If you aren't careful, you're likely to be taken on both counts. It's a common sight to see a gondolier huffing and puffing to take his passengers on a "quickie," often reducing the hour to 15 minutes. The gondolier, with his eye on his watch, is anxious to dump you and pick up the next batch of passengers. His watch almost invariably runs fast.

There *is* an accepted official rate schedule (100,000L/$58), but we've never known anyone to honor it. The actual fare depends on how well you stand up to the gondolier's attempt to get more money. Prices *begin* at 150,000L ($87) for up to 50 minutes. One gondolier confided to us that he settled for that amount in 1972. Today most gondoliers will ask at least double the official rate and reduce your time aboard to 30 to 40 minutes or even less. Prices go up after 8pm. In fairness to the gondoliers, we must say that they have an awful job, which is romanticized out of perspective by the world. They row boatloads of tourists across hot, smelly canals with such endearments screamed at them as "No sing! No pay!" And these fellows must make plenty of lire while the sun shines, as their work ends when the first cold winds blow in from the Adriatic.

Two major gondola stations at which you can rent gondolas are **Piazza San Marco** (☎ 041/520-0685) and **Ponte di Rialto** (☎ 041/522-4904).

BY CAR

Obviously you won't need a car in Venice, but you might want one as a means of exploring nearby cities like Padua. Most of the car-rental agencies lie near the rail station in the traffic-clogged Piazzale Roma. You can make arrangements at **Hertz,** Piazzale Roma 496E (☎ **800/654-3131** or 041/528-4091), open Monday to Friday 8am to 12:30am and 3 to 5:30pm and Saturday 8am to 1am. Two of its most viable competitors are **Europcar** (associated with National in the U.S.), Piazzale Roma 496H (☎ **800/328-4567** or 041/523-8616), and **Avis,** Piazzale Roma 496G (☎ **800/331-2112** or 041/522-5825). The latter contenders are open Monday to Friday 8:30am to 12:30pm and 2:30 to 6pm and Saturday 8:30am to 1am.

FAST FACTS: Venice

American Express   The office is Salizzada San Moisè, San Marco 1471 (☎ **041/520-0844**). City tours and mail handling can be obtained here. May to October, hours are Monday to Saturday 8am to 8pm for currency exchange and 9am to 5:30pm for all other transactions; November to April, hours are Monday to Friday 9am to 5:30pm and Saturday 9am to 12:30pm.

Baby-sitters   In lieu of a central booking agency, arrangements have to be made individually at various hotels. Obviously, the more advanced your notice, the better your chances of getting an English-speaking sitter.

Consulates   The **U.K. Consulate** is at Dorsoduro 1051, at the foot of the Accademia Bridge (☎ **041/522-7207**), open Monday to Friday 10am to noon and 2 to 3pm. The **United States, Canada,** and **Australia** have consulates in Milan, about 3 hours away by train (see "Fast Facts: Milan" in chapter 11). The **U.S. Consulate** in Milan is at Via Principe Amedeo 2/10 (☎ **02/2903-5141**).

Currency Exchange   There are many banks in Venice where you can exchange money. You might try the **Banco Commerciale Italiana,** Via XXII Marzo, San Marco 2188 (☎ **041/529-6811**), or **Banco San Marco,** Calle Larga S. Marco, San Marco 383 (☎ **041/529-3711**).

Dentist/Doctor   Your best bet is to have your hotel call and set up an appointment with an English-speaking dentist or doctor. The American Express office and the British Consulate also have lists. Also see "Hospitals," below.

Country & City Codes

The **country code** for Italy is **39**. The **city code** for Venice is **041;** you must now use this code every time you call Venice: if you're calling from outside Italy, if you're calling from another city within Italy, and even if you're calling within Venice.

Drugstores   If you need a drugstore in the middle of the night, call ☎ **192** for information about which is open. Pharmacies take turns staying open late. A well-recommended central pharmacy is **International Pharmacy,** Via XXII Marzo, San Marco 2067 (☎ **041/522-2311**).

Emergencies   Call ☎ **113** for the police, ☎ **118** for an ambulance, or ☎ **115** to report a fire.

Hospitals   Get in touch with the **Civili Riuniti di Venezia,** Campo Santi Giovanni e Paolo (☎ **041/529-4111**), staffed with English-speaking doctors 24 hours a day.

Laundry/Dry Cleaning   One of the most convenient coin-operated Laundromats and dry-cleaning enterprises is **Lavanderia Gabriella,** Calle Fiubera, San Marco 985 (☎ **041/522-1758**). Set behind Piazza San Marco, its washing machines are available daily 8am to 7pm and its dry-cleaning facilities Monday to Saturday 8am to 12:30pm and 3 to 7pm.

Newspapers/Magazines   The *International Herald Tribune* and *USA Today* are sold at most newsstands and in many first-class and deluxe hotels, as are the European editions (in English) of *Time* and *Newsweek*.

Police   See "Emergencies," above.

Post Office   The **main post office** is at Salizzada Fontego dei Tedeschi, San Marco 5554 (☎ **041/271-7111**), in the vicinity of the Rialto Bridge. It's open Monday to Saturday 8:15am to 7pm.

Rest Rooms   These are available at Piazzale Roma and various other places but aren't as plentiful as they should be. A truly spotless one is at the foot of the Accademia Bridge (be sure to have some 500L coins). Often you'll have to rely on the rest room in a cafe, though you should purchase something, perhaps a light coffee, as in theory the toilets are for customers only. Most museums and galleries have public toilets. You can also use the public toilets at the Albergo Diurno, on Via Ascensione, just behind Piazza San Marco. Remember, *signori* means men and *signore* women.

Safety   The curse of Venice is the pickpocket artist. Violent crime is rare. But because of the overcrowding in vaporetti and even on the small narrow streets, it's easy to pick pockets. Purse snatchers are commonplace as well. A purse snatcher can dart out of nowhere, grab a purse, and disappear in seconds down some narrow dark alley. Keep valuables locked in a safe in your hotel, if one is provided.

Taxes   A 19% **value-added tax (called IVA)** is added to the price of all consumer goods and products and most services, such as those in hotels and restaurants.

Telephone   See "Fast Facts: Rome" in chapter 4.

Transit Information   For flight information, call ☎ **041/260-6111;** for rail information, ☎ **1478/88-088** toll free in Italy only; and for bus schedules, ☎ **041/528-7886.**

3 Accommodations

Venice has some of the most expensive hotels in the world, like the Gritti Palace and the Cipriani. But there are also dozens of unheralded moderately priced places, often on hard-to-find narrow streets. Venice has never been known, however, as an inexpensive destination.

Because of their age and lack of uniformity, Venice's hotels offer widely varying rooms. For example, it's entirely possible to stay in a hotel generally considered "expensive" while paying only a "moderate" rate—that is, if you'll settle for a less desirable room. Many "inexpensive" hotels and boardinghouses have two or three rooms in the "expensive" category. Usually these accommodations are more spacious and open onto a view. Also, if an elevator is essential for you, always inquire in advance when booking a room.

The cheapest way to visit Venice is to book into a *locanda* (small inn), rated below the *pensioni* (boardinghouses). Standards are highly variable in these places, many of which are dank, dusty, and dark. The rooms even in many second- or first-class hotels are often cramped, as space has always been a problem in Venice. It's estimated that in this "City of Light," at least half the rooms in any category are dark, so be duly warned. Those with lots of light opening onto the Grand Canal carry a hefty price tag.

The most difficult times to find rooms are during the February Carnevale, Easter, and from June to September. Because of the tight hotel situation, it's advisable to make reservations as far in advance as possible. After those peak times, you can virtually have your pick of rooms. Most hotels, if you ask at the reception desk, will grant you a 10 to 15% discount in winter (November to March 15). But getting this discount may require a little negotiation. A few hotels close in January if there's no prospect of business.

Should you arrive without a reservation, go to one of the **AVA (Hotel Association) reservations booths** throughout the area at the train station, the municipal parking garage at Piazzale Roma, the airport, and the information point on the mainland where the highway comes to an end. The main office is at Piazzale Roma (☎ **041/ 522-8640**). To secure a room you're required to post a deposit that's then rebated on your hotel bill. Depending on the hotel classification, deposits are 20,000L to 90,000L ($12 to $52) per person. All hotel booths are open daily 9am to 8 or 9pm.

See the "Neighborhoods in Brief" section, earlier in this chapter, to get an idea of where you may want to base yourself, whether it be in less touristy San Polo or Dorsoduro or amid the crowds in and around Piazza San Marco (where hotels tend to be expensive).

NEAR PIAZZA SAN MARCO
VERY EXPENSIVE

✪ **Gritti Palace.** Campo Santa Maria del Giglio, San Marco 2467, 30124 Venezia. ☎ **800/ 325-3535** in the U.S. and Canada, or 041/794-611. Fax 041/520-0942. www.italyhotel.com/ hotelm/653.html. 99 units. A/C MINIBAR TV TEL. 847,000–1,100,000L ($491–$638) double; 2,090,000–4,180,000L ($1,212–$2,424) suite. Breakfast 38,5000L ($23). AE, DC, MC, V. Vaporetto: Santa Maria del Giglio.

The Gritti, in a stately setting on the Grand Canal, is the renovated palazzo of the 15th-century doge Andrea Gritti. Even after its takeover by Sheraton ITT, it's still a bit starchy, but in terms of prestige only the Cipriani tops it. The place has a bit of a museum aura (some of the original furnishings are roped off, for example). For Hemingway it was his "home in Venice," and for years it has drawn a some of the world's greatest theatrical, literary, political, and royal figures. The range and variety of rooms seem almost limitless, from elaborate suites to relatively small singles. But in every case, the glamour is evident. For a splurge, ask for Hemingway's old suite or the Doge Suite, once occupied by W. Somerset Maugham.

Dining: Ristorante Club del Doge is among the best in Venice but also egregiously priced.

Amenities: 24-hour room service, baby-sitting, laundry/valet; use of the Hotel Excelsior's facilities on the Lido.

EXPENSIVE

Hotel Casanova. Frezzeria, San Marco 1284, 30124 Venezia. ☎ **041/520-6855.** Fax 041/520-6413. 49 units. A/C MINIBAR TV TEL. 340,000L ($197) double; 420,000L ($244) triple; 370,000L ($215) suite. Rates include breakfast. AE, DC, MC, V. Vaporetto: San Marco.

This former home is a few steps from Piazza San Marco. Though the name Casanova sounds romantic, the hotel doesn't have a lot of character; it does, however, contain a collection of church art and benches from old monasteries (sitting on flagstone floors near oil portraits). The modernized guest rooms are for the most part devoid of charm yet well maintained. The accommodations vary considerably in size—some are quite small. The most intriguing units are on the top floor, with exposed brick walls and sloping beam ceilings.

Dining: Breakfast is the only meal served, but there are many dining choices outside your door.

Amenities: Concierge, room service (drinks only, no food), laundry, newspaper delivery on request, twice-daily maid service.

Hotel Concordia. Calle Larga, San Marco 367, 30124 Venezia. ☎ **041/520-6866.** Fax 041/520-6775. www.italyhotel.com/home/venezia/concordia/concordia.html. E-mail: veniceitaly@hotelconcordia.com. 58 units. A/C MINIBAR TV TEL. 310,000–590,000L ($180–$342) double. Rates include buffet breakfast. AE, DC, MC, V. Vaporetto: San Marco.

The four-star Concordia, in a russet-colored building with stone-trimmed windows, is the only hotel with rooms overlooking St. Mark's Square. A series of gold-plated marble steps takes you to the lobby, where you'll find a comfortable bar area, good service, and elevators to whisk you to the labyrinthine halls. All guest rooms are decorated in a Venetian antique style and contain, among other amenities, an electronic safe and a hair dryer.

Dining: Breakfast is the only meal served, but light meals and Italian snacks are available in the bar.

Amenities: 24-hour room service, baby-sitting, laundry/valet.

Hotel Saturnia International. Calle Larga XXII Marzo, San Marco 2398, 30124 Venezia. ☎ **041/520-8377.** Fax 041/520-7131. www.italyhotel.com/venezia/saturnia. E-mail: saturnia@doge.it. 95 units. A/C MINIBAR TV TEL. 336,000–630,000L ($195–$365) double. Rates include breakfast. AE, DC, MC, V. Vaporetto: San Marco.

The Saturnia International was skillfully created from a 14th-century palazzo near Piazza San Marco. You're surrounded by richly embellished beauty here—a grand hallway with a wooden staircase, heavy iron chandeliers, fine paintings, and beamed ceilings. The individually styled guest rooms are spacious and furnished with chandeliers, Venetian antiques, tapestry rugs, gilt mirrors, and ornately carved ceilings. Many overlook the hotel's quiet courtyard.

Dining: La Caravella is recommended under "Dining," later in this chapter.

Amenities: Room service, baby-sitting, laundry/valet.

Hotel Scandinavia. Campo Santa Maria Formosa, Castello 5240, 30122 Venezia. ☎ **041/522-3507.** Fax 041/523-5232. 39 units. A/C MINIBAR TV TEL. 370,000–500,000L ($215–$290) double. Rates include breakfast. AE, MC, V. Vaporetto: San Zaccaria or Rialto.

⊕ Family-Friendly Hotels

American Hotel *(see p. 391)* This secluded hotel is across the Grand Canal away from the tourist hordes. It's a solid moderately priced choice where many rooms are rented as triples.

Pensione Accademia *(see p. 391)* The best of Venice's pensioni, this villa has a garden and large rooms. This former Russian Embassy was the fictional home of Katharine Hepburn in the film classic *Summertime.*

Hotel Quattro Fontane *(see p. 393)* Long a Lido family favorite, this hotel guarantees summertime fun. It's somewhat like staying in the big chalet of a Venetian family. There's a private beach too.

This hotel isn't in San Marco (it's in neighboring Castello), but it has a convenient location not far from Piazza San Marco, so we've placed it in this section. A radical overhaul in 1992 added a third star to its rating. The palace boasts a dark-pink facade just off one of the most colorful squares in Venice. The public rooms are filled with copies of 18th-century Italian chairs, Venetian-glass chandeliers, and a re-created rococo decor. The guest rooms are decorated in the Venetian style, but modern comforts have been added. A lobby lounge overlooks Campo Santa Maria Formosa.

MODERATE

Hotel do Pozzi. Corte do Pozzi, San Marco 2373, 30124 Venezia. ☎ **041/520-7855.** Fax 041/522-9413. 35 units. MINIBAR TV TEL. 260,000L ($151) double. Rates include breakfast. AE, DC, MC, V. Vaporetto: Santa Maria del Giglio.

Small, modernized, and just a short stroll from the Grand Canal and Piazza San Marco, this place is more like a country tavern than a hotel. Its original structure is 200 years old, opening onto a paved courtyard with potted greenery. You can arrive via water taxi, boat, gondola, or vaporetto. The sitting and dining rooms are furnished with antiques (and near antiques) intermixed with utilitarian modern decor. Baths have been added, and a major refurbishing has given everything a fresh touch. Laundry and baby-sitting are available.

Hotel La Fenice et des Artistes. Campiello de la Fenice, San Marco 1936, 30124 Venezia. ☎ **041/523-2333.** Fax 041/520-3721. 69 units. TV TEL. 310,000–340,000L ($180–$197) double; 390,000–440,000L ($226–$255) suite. Rates include breakfast. AE, DC, MC, V. Vaporetto: San Marco.

This hotel offers widely varying accommodations in two connected buildings, each at least 100 years old. One is rather romantic, though a bit timeworn, with an impressive staircase leading to the overly decorated rooms (one was once described as "straight out of the last act of *La Traviata,* enhanced by small gardens and terraces"). Your satin-lined room may have an inlaid desk and a wardrobe painted in the Venetian manner to match a baroque bed frame. The carpets might be thin, however, and the fabrics aging. The rooms in the other building are far less glamorous, with modern sterile furniture. All but about three of the rooms are air-conditioned.

Hotel Montecarlo. Calle dei Specchieri, San Marco 463, 30124 Venezia. ☎ **800/ 528-1234** or 041/520-7144. Fax 041/520-7789. www.italyhotel.com/venezia/montecarlo or www.bestwestern.com. E-mail: mocarlo@doge.it. 48 units. A/C TV TEL. 190,000–450,000L ($110–$261) double. Rates include breakfast. AE, DC, MC, V. Vaporetto: San Marco.

A 2-minute walk from Piazza San Marco, this hotel opened some years ago in a 17th-century building but was recently renovated to include modern baths. The upper halls

Venice Accommodations & Dining

ACCOMMODATIONS
Alloggi ai do Mori **37**
American Hotel **57**
Boston Hotel **42**
Danieli Royal Excelsior **62**
Doni Pensione **64**
Gritti Palace **48**
Hotel Abbazia **1**
Hotel Bernardi-
 Semenzato **13**
Hotel Bisanzio **66**
Hotel Campiello **63**
Hotel Carpaccio **4**
Hotel Casanova **43**
Hotel Cipriani **59**
Hotel Concordia **38**
Hotel do Pozzi **50**
Hotel Geremia **6**
Hotel Giorgione **15**
Hotel La Calcina **11**
Hotel La Fenice
 et des Artistes **47**
Hotel Marconi **23**
Hotel Montecarlo **36**
Hotel Rialto **25**
Hotel San Cassiano
 Ca' Favretto **12**
Hotel Saturnia
 International **51**
Hotel Savoia & Jolanda **61**
Hotel Scandinavia **30**
La Residenza **67**
Locanda Montin **10**
Locanda Remedio **32**
Locanda Sturion **21**
Londra Palace **65**
Pensione Accademia **7**

DINING
Ai Tre Spiedi **17**
Al Covo **68**

Alfredo, Alfredo **41**
"Al Graspo de Uva" **24**
Al Mascaron **29**
Antico Martini **46**
Da Ivo **34**
Do Forni **35**
Do Leoni **60**
Favorita **56**
Fiaschetteria Toscana **19**
Harry's Bar **53**
Il Milion **20**
La Caravella **52**
La Furatola **5**
Le Chat Qui Rit **39**
Linea d'Ombra **8**
Locanda Montin **9**
Nuova Rivetta **40**
Osteria da Fiore **3**
Poste Vecchie **14**
Quadri **54**
Restaurant da Bruno **28**
Ristorante à la Vecia
 Cavana **16**
Ristorante al
 Mondo Novo **27**
Ristorante Belvedere **55**
Ristorante Cipriani **58**
Ristorante Corte
 Sconta **69**
Ristorante da Raffaele **49**
Rôsticceria
 San Bartolomeo **26**
Sempione **31**
Taverna La Fenice **45**
Tiziano Bar **18**
Trattoria alla Madonna **22**
Trattoria Antica Besseta **2**
Trattoria La Colomba **44**
Vini da Arturo **43**

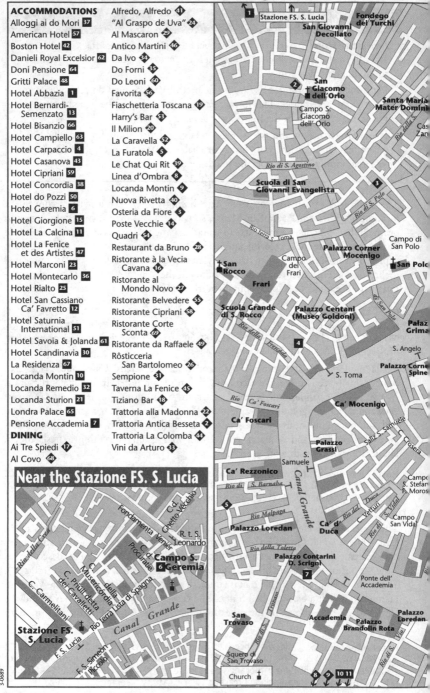

384

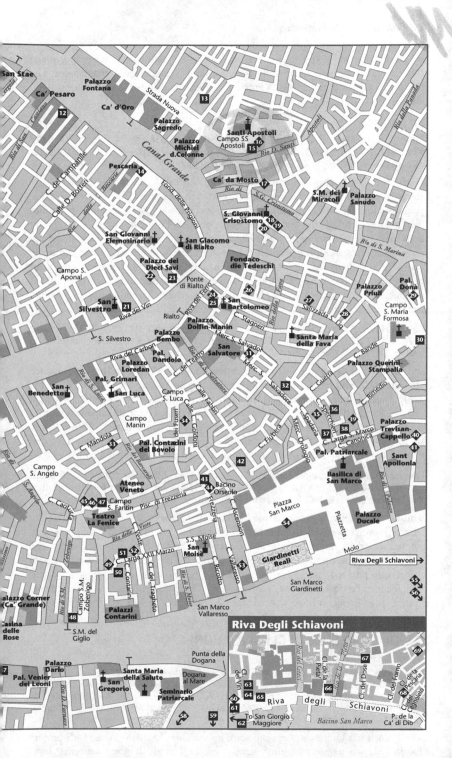

San Stae

Palazzo
Fontana

Ca' Pesaro

12

Ca' d'Oro

Strada Nuova

13

Palazzo
Sagredo

Canal Grande

Palazzo
Michiel
d.Colonne

Campo SS
Apostoli

Santi Apostoli

15 16

Rio D. Santi

Pescaria 14

Ca' da Mosto 17

Rio di

S.M. dei
Miracoli

Palazzo
Sanudo

San Giovanni
Elemosinario

San Giacomo
di Rialto

S. Giovanni
Crisostomo

18 19

20

Rio di S. Marina

Campo S.
Aponal

Palazzo dei
Dieci Savi

22 23

Ponte
di Rialto

Fondaco
die Tedeschi

26

Palazzo
Priuli

Pal.
Dona

29

Campo
S. Maria
Formosa

San
Silvestro

21

Riva del Vin

24

25

San
Bartolomeo

Stagneri

27

Salizzada S. Liq

28

30

Rialto

S. Silvestro

Palazzo
Dolfin-Manin

Palazzo
Bembo

Pal.
Dandolo

Riva del Carbon

Merc. S. Salvador

San
Salvatore

31

Santa Maria
della Fava

C. Bande

Palazzo Querini-
Stampalia

Palazzo
Loredan

Pal. Grimani

San
Benedetto

San Luca

Campo
S. Luca

C. del Teatro di S. Salvatore

Merc. Salvadore

32

C. Guerra

Rimedio

Campo
Manin

dei Fuseri

34

Calle Cortoni

C. Fiubera

Salvadore

Merc. Orologio

35

36

Pal. Specchieri

39

37

38

Larga S. Marco

C. Canonica

Palazzo
Trevisan-
Cappello

40

41

C. Mandola

33

Rio dei Barcaroli

Pal. Contarini
del Bovolo

42

Pal. Patriarcale

Sant
Apollonia

Campo
S. Angelo

43

Bacino
Orseolo

Basilica di
San Marco

Ateneo
Veneto

44

C. Caotorta

45 46 47

Campo
S. Fantin

Teatro
La Fenice

Pisc. di Frezzeria

Frezzeria

C. Ascension

Piazza
San Marco

54

Piazzetta

Palazzo
Ducale

49

Rio delle Veste

51 52

C. Larga XXII Marzo

50

C. dei Fuseri

C. del Traghetto

S.S. Moise

San
Moise

C. Vallaresso

53

Molo

Giardinetti
Reali

Riva Degli Schiavoni →

Palazzo Corner
(Ca' Grande)

Campo S.M.
Zobenigo

48

S.M. del
Giglio

Palazzi
Contarini

San Marco
Vallaresso

San Marco
Giardinetti

55

56

Casina
delle
Rose

7

Palazzo
Dario

Pal. Venier
dei Leoni

San
Gregorio

Santa Maria
della Salute

Seminario
Patriarcale

Punta della
Dogana

Dogana
al Mare

58

59

Riva Degli Schiavoni

67

69

C. del Vin

C. de la
Pieta

Cl. de la Dose

66

Cl. del Forno

63

64

65

Riva

degli

Schiavoni

68

60

61

62

To San Giorgio
Maggiore

Bacino San Marco

P. de la
Ca' di Dio

are lined with paintings by Venetian artists. The double rooms are nicely proportioned and decorated with Venetian-style furniture and Venetian-glass chandeliers. The restaurant, Antico Pignolo, serves lunch and dinner and features both Venetian and international dishes.

INEXPENSIVE

Alloggi ai do Mori. Calle Larga San Marco, San Marco 658, 30124 Venezia. ☎ 041/520-4817. Fax 041/520-5328. 11 units, 7 with bathroom. TV TEL. 130,000L ($75) double without bathroom, 160,000L ($93) double with bathroom. MC, V. Vaporetto: San Marco.

Don't expect an obscure corner of Venice if you check into this small-scale hotel—it's about 10 paces from Europe's densest concentration of tourists. You'll have to balance your need for space with your love of panoramas (and your ability to climb stairs since there's no elevator), as the lower-level rooms of this 1450 town house are larger but don't have any decent views while the rooms on the third and fourth floors are cramped but have sweeping panoramas over the basilica's domes. The site is frequently upgraded, rewallpapered, and repainted by the owner, Antonella Bernardi. The furniture in the rooms is simple and modern, and most of the street noise is muffled thanks to double-paned windows. The dozens of cafes in the neighborhood make up for the fact that no meals are served.

Boston Hotel. Ponte dei Dai, San Marco 848, 30124 Venezia. ☎ 041/528-7665. Fax 041/522-6628. 42 units. TEL. 200,000–290,000L ($116–$168) double. Rates include buffet breakfast. AE, DC, MC, V. Closed Nov–Feb. Vaporetto: San Marco.

Built in 1962, the Boston is just a whisper away from St. Mark's. The hotel was named after an uncle who left to seek his fortune in Boston and never returned. The little living rooms combine the old and the new, containing many antiques and Venetian ceilings. For the skinny guest, there's a tiny self-operated elevator and a postage-stamp-sized street entrance. Most of the rooms, with parquet floors, have built-in features, snugly designed beds, chests, and wardrobes. Several even have tiny balconies that open onto canals. Twenty rooms are air-conditioned and 20 equipped with TVs.

Locanda Remedio. Calle del Remedio, Castello 4412, 30122 Venezia. ☎ 041/520-6232. Fax 041/521-0485. 13 units. A/C MINIBAR TV TEL. 150,000–230,000L ($87–$133) double. Rates include breakfast. MC, V. Vaporetto: San Zaccharia.

This hotel isn't actually in San Marco but in nearby Castello; it's so close to Piazza San Marco, however, we've included it here. This hotel was built around 1500, in a gray-fronted style that's not as intricate as the many nearby buildings. From the street-level reception area, you climb a narrow flight of stairs up to the public salons that have been turned into private rooms. Each has simple but durable furniture but none a particularly memorable view. Breakfast is served in a room graced with faded ceiling frescoes overlooking a neighborhood that (despite its proximity to San Marco) is calm and quiet.

ON OR NEAR RIVA DEGLI SCHIAVONI
VERY EXPENSIVE

✪ **Danieli Royal Excelsior.** Riva degli Schiavoni, Castello 4196, 30122 Venezia. ☎ 800/325-3535 in the U.S. and Canada, or 041/522-6480. Fax 041/520-0208. www.ittsheraton.com (click on "luxury collection"). 240 units. A/C MINIBAR TV TEL. 670,000–850,000L ($389–$493) double; 950,000–3,700,000L ($551–$2,146) suite. Rates include buffet breakfast. AE, DC, MC, V. Vaporetto: San Zaccaria.

The Danieli was built as a grand showcase by the Doge Dandolo in the 14th century and in 1822 was transformed into a deluxe "hotel for kings." It's the most ornate hotel in Venice, surpassed only by the Cipriani and Gritti Palace. Placed in a most spectacular position, right on the Grand Canal, it has sheltered not only kings but princes, cardinals, ambassadors, and such literary figures as George Sand and Charles Dickens.

You enter into a four-story stairwell, with Venetian arches and balustrades. The atmosphere is luxurious throughout—even the balconies opening off the main lounge are illuminated by stained-glass skylights. The rooms range widely in price, dimension, decor, and vistas, and those opening onto the lagoon cost a lot more. Alfred de Musset and Ms. Sand made love in room no. 10, the most requested accommodation at the Danieli.

Dining/Diversions: From the rooftop Terrazza Danieli, you have an unblocked view of the canals and "crowns" of Venice. There's also an intimate cocktail lounge and a bar offering piano music.

Amenities: Room service, baby-sitting, laundry/valet; hotel launch to the Lido in summer.

EXPENSIVE

Hotel Bisanzio. Calle della Pietà, Castello 3651, 30122 Venezia. ☎ **800/528-1234** in the U.S., or 041/520-3100. Fax 041/520-4114. www.bisanzio.com. E-mail: email@bisanzio.com. 47 units. A/C MINIBAR TV TEL. 350,000L ($203) double. Rates include buffet breakfast. AE, DC, MC, V. Vaporetto: San Zaccaria.

A few steps from St. Mark's Square, this hotel in the former home of sculptor Alessandro Vittoria offers hospitality and good service. It has an elevator and terraces, plus a little bar and a mooring for gondolas and motorboats. The rooms are generally quiet, each decorated in a Venetian antique style. The lounge opens onto a traditional courtyard. Amenities include 24-hour room service, baby-sitting, and laundry.

Hotel Savoia & Jolanda. Riva degli Schiavoni, Castello 4187, 30122 Venezia. ☎ **041/520-6644.** Fax 041/520-7494. 83 units. TEL. 300,000–350,000L ($174–$203) double; from 450,000L ($261) suite. Rates include breakfast. AE, DC, MC, V. Vaporetto: San Zaccaria.

The Savoia & Jolanda occupies a prize position on Venice's main street, with a lagoon at its front yard. It opened at the turn of the century as one of the most prominent hotels along Riva degli Schiavoni, transformed from a palazzo. Though its exterior reflects much of old Venice, the interior is somewhat spiritless; the staff, however, make life comfortable. Most of the modern rooms have a view of the boats and the Lido; they contain desks and armchairs. An addition holds 20 units with air-conditioning, phones, minibars, and TVs. The Principessa restaurant is open daily for lunch and dinner, serving specialties like spaghetti Bragozo with mussels and clams.

✪ **Londra Palace.** Riva degli Schiavoni, Castello 4171, 30122 Venezia. ☎ **041/520-0533.** Fax 041/522-5032. www.italyhotel.com/venezia/londrapalace. 70 units. A/C MINIBAR TV TEL. 320,000–620,000L ($186–$360) double; 520,000–780,000L ($302–$452) junior suite. Rates include breakfast. AE, DC, MC, V. Vaporetto: San Zaccaria.

The Londra is a gabled manor with 100 windows on the lagoon, a few yards from Piazza San Marco. The hotel's most famous patron was arguably Tchaikovsky, who wrote his Fourth Symphony in room no. 108 in December 1877; he also composed several other works here. The cozy reading room off the main lobby is reminiscent of an English club, boasting leaded windows and paneled walls with framed blowups of some of Tchaikovsky's sheet music. The guest rooms are luxurious, often with lacquered Venetian furniture. Romantics ask for one of the two attic rooms decorated in the Regency style with beamed ceilings. The courtyard rooms are quieter and cheaper, opening onto rooftop views instead of the Grand Canal.

Dining/Diversions: The hotel has a popular piano bar and an excellent restaurant, Do Leoni (see "Dining," below for separate review).

Amenities: Room service, baby-sitting, laundry/valet, conference hall.

MODERATE

Hotel Campiello. Campiello del Vin, Castello 4647, 30122 Venezia. ☎ **041/520-5764.** Fax 041/520-5798. www.hcampiello.com. 16 units. A/C TV TEL. 200,000–250,000L ($116–$145) double. Rates include breakfast. AE, MC, V. Closed Jan. Vaporetto: San Zaccaria.

This pink-fronted Venetian town house dates to the 1400s, but today you'll find cost-conscious Venetian-style accommodations last renovated in the mid-1990s. Though rated only two stars by the tourist office, it's better than its status implies, because of a spectacular location nearly adjacent to the more expensive hotels and because of such Renaissance touches as marble mosaic floors and carefully polished hardwoods. Elderly or infirm guests sometimes opt for the only room with a separate entrance, a ground-floor hideaway that fortunately has been flooded by high tides only once during the previous century. Breakfast is the only meal served.

INEXPENSIVE

Doni Pensione. Calle de Vino, Castello 4656, 30122 Venezia. ☎ **041/522-4267.** Fax 041/522-4267. 15 units, 3 with bathroom. 110,000L ($64) double without bathroom, 150,000L ($87) double with bathroom. Rates include breakfast. No credit cards. Vaporetto: San Zaccaria.

The Doni sits in a tranquil position, about a 3-minute walk from St. Mark's. Most of its very basic rooms overlook either a little canal, where four or five gondolas are usually tied up, or a garden with a tall fig tree. Simplicity and cleanliness prevail, especially in the down-to-earth guest rooms.

✪ **La Residenza.** Campo Bandiera e Moro, Castello 3608, 30122 Venezia. ☎ **041/528-5315.** Fax 041/523-8859. 16 units. A/C MINIBAR TV TEL. 150,000–230,000L ($87–$133) double. Rates include breakfast. MC, V. Vaporetto: Arsenale.

La Residenza is in a 14th-century building that looks a lot like a miniature Doge's Palace. It's on a residential square where children play soccer and older people feed the pigeons. After gaining access (press the button outside the entrance), you'll pass through a stone vestibule lined with ancient Roman columns before ringing another bell at the bottom of a flight of stairs. First an iron gate and then a door will open into an enormous salon filled with elegant antiques, 300-year-old paintings, and some of the most marvelously preserved walls in Venice. The guest rooms are far less opulent than the public salons, furnished with contemporary pieces and functional accessories. The choice ones are usually booked far in advance, especially for Carnevale.

NEAR THE PONTE DI RIALTO
EXPENSIVE

Hotel Rialto. Riva del Ferro, San Marco 5149, 30124 Venezia. ☎ **041/520-9166.** Fax 041/523-8958. www.nettuno.it/fiera/hotelrialto. E-mail: hotelrialto@ve.nettuno.it. 77 units. A/C MINIBAR TV TEL. 250,000–400,000L ($145–$232) double. Rates include breakfast. AE, DC, MC, V. Vaporetto: Rialto.

The Rialto opens right onto the Grand Canal at the foot of the Ponte di Rialto, the famous bridge flanked with shops. Its rooms are quite satisfactory, combining modern or Venetian furniture with ornate Venetian ceilings and wall decorations. The hotel has been considerably upgraded to second class, and private baths have been installed. The most desirable and expensive double rooms overlook the Grand Canal—these go first.

Dining: The dining room and its adjacent bar are open daily April to October.

Amenities: Concierge, room service, newspaper delivery on request.

MODERATE

Hotel Marconi. Riva del Vin, San Polo 729, 30125 Venezia. ☎ **041/522-2068.** Fax 041/522-9700. www.italyhotel.com/hotelm/705.html. 26 units. A/C MINIBAR TV TEL. 173,000–344,000L ($100–$200) double. Rates include breakfast. AE, MC, V. Vaporetto: Rialto.

The Marconi, less than 50 feet from the Rialto Bridge, was built in 1500 when Venice was at the height of its supremacy. The drawing-room furnishings would be appropriate for visiting archbishops, and the Maschietto family operates everything efficiently. Only four of the lovely old rooms open onto the Grand Canal, and these, of course, are the most eagerly sought. Meals are usually taken in an L-shaped room with Gothic chairs, but in fair weather the sidewalk tables facing the Grand Canal are preferred by many.

✪ **Locanda Sturion.** Calle del Sturion, San Polo 679, 30125 Venezia. ☎ **041/523-6243.** Fax 041/522-8378. E-mail: sturion@tin.it. 11 units. A/C MINIBAR TV TEL. 200,000–310,000L ($116–$180) double. Rates include continental breakfast. AE, DC, MC, V. Vaporetto: Rialto.

In the early 1200s, the Venetian doges commissioned a site where foreign merchants, who traded goods at the time near the Rialto Bridge, could stay for the night after a hard day's bargaining. After long stints as a private residence, the site continues its tradition of catering to foreign visitors. A private entrance leads up four steep flights of marble steps, past apartments on the lower floors, to a labyrinth of cozy, clean, but not overly large guest rooms. Most have views over the terra-cotta rooftops of this congested neighborhood; two, however, open onto views of the Grand Canal. The intimate breakfast room is a honey—almost like a parlor with red brocaded walls, a Venetian chandelier, and a trio of big windows opening onto the Grand Canal.

IN CANNAREGIO
EXPENSIVE

Hotel Giorgione. Campo SS. Apostoli, Cannaregio 4587, 30131 Venezia. ☎ **041/522-5810.** Fax 041/523-9092. www.hotelgiorgione.com. E-mail: giorgione@hotelgiorgione.com. 78 units. A/C MINIBAR TV TEL. 190,000–380,000L ($110–$220) double; 390,000–420,000L ($226–$244) suite. Rates include buffet breakfast. AE, DC, MC, V. Vaporetto: Ca' d'Oro.

Despite modernization, the decor here is traditionally Venetian. The lounges and public rooms are equipped with fine furnishings and decorative accessories, and the comfortable and stylish guest rooms are designed to coddle guests. The hotel also has a typical Venetian garden. It's rated second class by the government, but the Giorgione maintains higher standards than many of the first-class places.

Dining: Breakfast is the only meal served, but many trattorie lie nearby.

Amenities: Concierge, room service, dry cleaning/laundry, baby-sitting, twice-daily maid service, small pool, business center, conference rooms, secretarial services.

MODERATE

Hotel Geremia. Campo San Geremia, Cannaregio 290A, 30121 Venezia. ☎ **041/716-245.** Fax 041/524-2342. 20 units, 14 with bathroom. TV TEL. 125,000L ($73) double without bathroom, 190,000L ($110) double with bathroom. Rates include breakfast. Discounts of 20% in winter. AE, MC, V. Vaporetto: Ferrovie.

For years, the small Geremia survived as a low-cost, one-star hotel many guests considered worthy of two-star status. In 1997, the government finally raised it to two stars, justifying an almost immediate increase in rates. In a modernized turn-of-the-century setting, this hotel is a 5-minute walk from the railway station. Inside, you'll find well-maintained pale-green rooms (none with water views but all with safes). There's no elevator, but no one can deny that the price is appealing.

INEXPENSIVE

✪ **Hotel Bernardi-Semenzato.** Calle de l'Oca, Cannaregio 4366, 30121 Venezia. ☎ **041/522-7257.** Fax 041/522-2424. Hotel, 18 units, 10 with bathroom; annex, 8 units, 1 with bathroom. A/C TV TEL. 75,000L ($44) double without bathroom, 120,000L ($70) double with bathroom; 105,000L ($61) triple without bathroom, 130,000L ($76) triple with bathroom. Breakfast 6,000L ($3.50). MC, V. Closed Nov 20–Dec 10. Vaporetto: Ca' d'Oro.

From the outside, this weather-worn palazzo doesn't hint of its full 1995 renovation, which left hand-hewn ceiling beams exposed, air-conditioned rooms with coordinated headboard/spread sets, and baths modernized and brightly retiled. The enthusiastic English-speaking owners, Maria Teresa and Leonardo Pepoli, aspire to three-star style and had just received a two-star rating at press time, but they offer one-star rates (which are even less off-season). The addition of an annex 3 blocks away offers the chance to feel as if you've rented an aristocratic apartment. Most of the annex's large bathless rooms should have baths added by the time you arrive. (To get the rates above, be sure to mention you're a Frommer's reader when you're booking.)

IN SAN POLO
MODERATE

Hotel Carpaccio. San Tomà, San Polo 2765, 30125 Venezia. ☎ **041/523-5946.** Fax 041/524-2134. 20 units. MINIBAR TV TEL. 310,000L ($180) double. Rates include breakfast. MC, V. Closed mid-Nov to Feb. Vaporetto: San Tomà.

Don't be put off by the narrow, winding alleys that lead to the wrought-iron entrance of this second-class hotel—the building was meant to be approached by gondola. Once inside, you'll realize that your location in the heart of the oldest part of the city justifies the confusing arrival. This used to be the Palazzo Barbarigo della Terrazza, and part of it is still reserved for private apartments. The tasteful and spacious guest rooms are filled with serviceable furniture. The salon is decorated with gracious pieces, marble floors, and an arched window overlooking the Grand Canal. Breakfast is the only meal served.

IN SANTA CROCE
MODERATE

Hotel San Cassiano Ca' Favretto. Calle della Regina, Santa Croce 2232, 30135 Venezia. ☎ **041/524-1768.** Fax 041/721-033. www.italyhotel.com/hotelm/711.html. E-mail: cassiano@cassiano.it. 36 units. A/C MINIBAR TV TEL. 200,000–344,000L ($116–$200) double. Rates include breakfast. AE, DC, MC, V. Vaporetto: San Stae.

This hotel used to be the studio of 19th-century painter Giacomo Favretto. The gondola pier and the dining room porch both afford views of the lacy facade of the Ca' d'Oro, perhaps the most beautiful building in Venice. The building is a former 14th-century palace, and the present owner has worked closely with Venetian authorities to preserve the original details, like a 20-foot beamed ceiling in the entrance area. Fifteen of the conservatively decorated rooms overlook one of two canals, and many are filled with antiques or high-quality reproductions.

NEAR THE RAIL STATION
MODERATE

Hotel Abbazia. Calle Priulli 68, 30121 Venezia. ☎ **041/717-949.** 39 units. TV TEL. 180,000–310,000L ($104–$180) double. Rates include breakfast. AE, DC, MC, V. Vaporetto: Ferrovia.

Only a handful of other hotels lie closer to the rail station. The benefit for travelers is that there's no need to transfer onto any vaporetto, as the hotel is accessible entirely by bridge and street from the station, which lies within a 10-minute walk. This dignified structure was built in 1889 as a monastery for barefooted Carmelite monks, who established a verdant garden in what's now the courtyard. Some visitors consider the garden the most appealing spot, planted with subtropical plants that seem to thrive almost miraculously thanks to the way they're sheltered from the cold Adriatic winds by the surrounding building. There's no restaurant on the premises and no bar, though drinks can be carried to your spot in the lobby if you request one. You'll find a highly accommodating staff and comfortable but unfrilly rooms that retain some of their original ascetic sobriety. Most of them (25) overlook the courtyard, ensuring quiet in an otherwise noisy neighborhood.

IN DORSODURO
EXPENSIVE

American Hotel. Campo San Vio, Dorsoduro 628, 30123 Venezia. ☎ 041/520-4733. Fax 041/520-4048. E-mail: hotelameri@tin.it. 29 units. A/C MINIBAR TV TEL. 340,000L ($197) double; 400,000L ($232) triple. Rates include buffet breakfast. AE, MC, V. Vaporetto: Accademia.

On a small waterway, the American (there's nothing American about it) lies in an ocher building across the Grand Canal from the most heavily touristed areas. The modest lobby is filled with murals, warm colors, and antiques, and the location is perfect for anyone wanting to avoid the crowds that descend on Venice in summer. The rooms are comfortably furnished in a Venetian style, but they vary in size; some of the smaller ones are a bit cramped. Many rooms with their own private terrace face the canal. On the second floor is a beautiful terrace where guests can relax over drinks. The staff is attentive and helpful.

MODERATE

Hotel La Calcina. Zattere al Gesuati, Dorsoduro 780, 30123 Venezia. ☎ 041/520-6466. Fax 041/522-7045. 29 units. A/C TEL. 170,000–280,000L ($99–$162) double. Rates include buffet breakfast. AE, MC, V. Vaporetto: Zattere.

Recently renovated (and just in time!), La Calcina lies in a secluded and less-trampled district that used to be the English enclave before the area developed a broader base of tourism. John Ruskin, who wrote *The Stones of Venice,* stayed here in 1877, and he charted the ground for his latter-day compatriots. This pensione is absolutely spotless, and the furnishings are well chosen but hardly elaborate. The rooms are cozy and comfortable.

✪ **Pensione Accademia.** Fondamenta Bollani, Dorsoduro 1058, 30123 Venezia. ☎ 041/523-7846. Fax 041/523-9152. 27 units. 190,000–330,000L ($110–$191) double. Rates include breakfast. AE, DC, MC, V. Vaporetto: Accademia.

The Accademia is the most patrician of the pensioni, in a villa whose garden extends into an angle created by the junction of two canals. The interior features Gothic-style paneling, Venetian chandeliers, and Victorian-era furniture. The building served as the Russian Embassy before World War II and as a private house before that. There's an upstairs sitting room flanked by two large windows and a formal rose garden. The spacious guest rooms are decorated with original furniture from the 19th century. Some are air-conditioned and most have been renovated. This was the fictional residence of Katharine Hepburn's character in the film *Summertime.*

INEXPENSIVE

✪ **Locanda Montin.** Fondamenta di Borgo, Dorsoduro 1147, 31000 Venezia. ☎ 041/522-7151. Fax 041/520-0255. 10 units, 3 with bathroom. 90,000L ($52) double without bathroom, 100,000L ($58) double with bathroom. AE, DC, MC, V. Vaporetto: Accademia.

The Montin is an old-fashioned Venetian inn whose adjoining restaurant is one of the most loved in the area. It's officially listed as a fourth-class hotel, but the rooms are considerably larger and better than that rating would suggest. Reservations are virtually mandatory because of its reputation. The inn is a bit difficult to locate—it's marked by only a small carriage lamp etched with the name—but is worth the search.

ON ISOLA DELLA GIUDECCA
VERY EXPENSIVE

✪ **Hotel Cipriani.** Isola della Giudecca 10, 30133 Venezia. ☎ **800/992-5055** in the U.S., or 041/520-7744. Fax 041/520-7745. 104 units. A/C MINIBAR TV TEL. 950,000–1,400,000L ($551–$812) double; from 2,100,000L ($1,218) suite. Rates include breakfast. AE, DC, MC, V. Closed Nov–Mar. Vaporetto: Zitelle.

With its isolated location, haute service, and exorbitant prices, the Cipriani outclasses every other posh contender, including the Danieli and Gritti Palace. Set in a 16th-century cloister on the residential island of Giudecca, this pleasure palace was opened in 1958 by the late Giuseppe Cipriani, the founder of Harry's Bar and the one real-life character in Hemingway's Venetian novel. The guest rooms have different amenities—ranging from tasteful contemporary to an antique design—but all have splendid views. The Cipriani, incidentally, is the only hotel on Giudecca, which otherwise is calm and quiet.

Dining: Lunch is served in the bar, Il Gabbiano, either indoors or on terraces overlooking the water. More formal meals are served at night in the Restaurant.

Amenities: The best in Venice, with two employees for every room. A private launch service ferries guests, at any hour, to and from the hotel's own pier near Piazza San Marco. Room service, baby-sitting, laundry/valet; Olympic-size pool with filtered salt water, tennis courts, sauna, fitness center.

ON THE LIDO
VERY EXPENSIVE

✪ **Excelsior Palace.** Lungomare Marconi 41, 30126 Lido di Venezia. ☎ **800/325-3535** in the U.S. and Canada, or 041/526-0201. Fax 041/526-7276. www.ittsheraton.com (click on the "luxury collection"). 114 units. A/C MINIBAR TV TEL. 605,000–737,000L ($351–$427) double; 1,265,000–2,420,000L ($734–$1,404) suite. Breakfast 38,500L ($23). AE, DC, MC, V. Parking 35,000L ($20). Closed Nov–Mar 15. Vaporetto: Lido, then bus A, B, or C.

When the mammoth Excelsior was built, it was the biggest resort hotel of its kind in the world and did much to make the Lido fashionable. Today it offers the most luxury along the Lido, though it doesn't have the antique character of the Hotel des Bains. Its rooms range in style and amenities from cozy singles to suites. Most of the social life takes place around the angular pool or on the flowered terraces leading up to the cabanas on the sandy beach. All guest rooms (some big enough for tennis games) have been modernized, often with vivid summerlike colors.

Dining/Diversions: The hotel features one of the most elegant dining rooms of the Adriatic, the Tropicana. The Blue Bar has piano music and views of the beach.

Amenities: 24-hour room service, baby-sitting, laundry/valet; six tennis courts, pool, private pier with boat rental are available. A private launch makes hourly runs to the Gritti Palace and the Danieli on the Grand Canal.

EXPENSIVE

✪ **Hotel des Bains.** Lungomare Marconi 17, 30126 Lido di Venezia. ☎ **800/325-3535** in the U.S. and Canada, or 041/526-5921. Fax 041/526-0113. www.ittsheraton.com (click on "luxury collection"). 210 units. A/C MINIBAR TV TEL. 455,000–700,000L ($264–$406) double; 700,000–1,400,000L ($406–$812) suite. Breakfast 33,000L ($20). AE, DC, MC, V. Closed Nov–Mar. Vaporetto: Lido, then bus A, B, or C.

This hotel was built in the grand era of European resort hotels, but its supremacy on the Lido was long ago lost to the Excelsior. It has its own wooded park and beach with individual cabanas. Its confectionery-like facade dates from the turn of the century. Thomas Mann stayed here several times before making it the setting for his *Death in Venice*, and later it was used as a set for the film of the same name. The renovated interior exudes the flavor of the leisurely life of the belle epoque. The guest rooms are well furnished and fairly large.

Dining: Guests can dine in a large veranda room cooled by Adriatic sea breezes. The food is top-rate and the service superior.

Amenities: Room service, baby-sitting, laundry/valet. A motorboat shuttles back and forth between Venice and the Lido. Many resort-type services are available at the Golf Club Alberoni (tennis courts, large pool, private pier).

✪ **Hotel Quattro Fontane.** Via Quattro Fontane 16, 30126 Lido di Venezia. ☎ **041/526-0227.** Fax 041/526-0726. 57 units. A/C TV TEL. 360,000–500,000L ($209–$290) double. Rates include breakfast. AE, DC, MC, V. Closed Easter and Nov–Apr 4. Vaporetto: Lido, then bus A, B, or C.

In its price bracket, the Quattro Fontane is one of the most charming hotels on the Lido. The trouble is, a lot of people know that, so it's likely to be booked. This former summer home of a 19th-century Venetian family is most popular with the British, who seem to appreciate the homelike atmosphere, the garden, the helpful staff, and the rooms with superior amenities, not to mention the good food served at tables set under shade trees. Many of the rooms are furnished with antiques.

Dining: The dining room is open April to October. There's a bar adjacent to the restaurant.

Amenities: Concierge, room service, laundry/dry cleaning, newspaper delivery on request, twice-daily maid service). The hotel maintains changing booths and about a dozen private cabanas on the beach, a short walk away. There's also a tennis court.

MODERATE

Hotel Belvedere. Piazzale Santa Maria Elisabetta 4, 30126 Lido di Venezia. ☎ **041/526-0115.** Fax 041/526-1486. 30 units. A/C TV TEL. 180,000–295,000L ($104–$171) double. Rates include breakfast. AE, DC, MC, V. Vaporetto: Lido.

The restored and modernized Belvedere has been run by the same family since 1857, and its restaurant is justifiably popular (see "Dining," later in this chapter). Right across from the vaporetto stop, the hotel is open all year, which is unusual for the Lido, and offers simply furnished rooms. All have air-conditioning or a view of the lagoon. There's parking in its garden. As an added courtesy, the Belvedere offers guests free entrance to the Casino Municipale, and in summer guests can use the hotel's bathing huts on the Venetian Lido.

Hotel Helvetia. Gran Viale 4–6, 30126 Lido di Venezia. ☎ **041/526-0105.** Fax 041/526-8903. 56 units. TEL. 180,000–310,000L ($104–$180) double. Rates include breakfast. MC, V. Closed Nov–Mar. Vaporetto: Lido, then bus A, B, or C.

The Helvetia is a russet-colored 19th-century building with stone detailing on a side street near the lagoon side of the island, an easy walk from the vaporetto stop. The quieter rooms face away from the street, and rooms in the older wing have belle epoque high ceilings and attractively comfortable furniture. The newer wing is more streamlined and has been renovated in a more conservative style. Breakfast is served, weather permitting, in a flagstone-covered wall garden behind the hotel. Baby-sitting, laundry, and 24-hour room service are available.

4 Dining

Though Venice doesn't grow much foodstuff and is hardly a victory garden, it's bounded by a rich agricultural district and plentiful vineyards in the hinterlands.

The city gets the choicest items on its menus from the Adriatic—but beware that the fish dishes are very expensive. For example, the menu price of fresh grilled fish (*pesce alla griglia*) commonly refers to the *etto* (per 100 grams) and so is a fraction of the real cost. Have the waiter estimate it before you order.

The many specialties prepared in the Venetian kitchen will be surveyed in the restaurant recommendations to follow. For Italy, Venice's restaurants are high priced, yet many trattorie cater to moderate budgets.

Note: For the location of restaurants in this section, see the "Venice Accommodations & Dining" map on p. 384.

NEAR PIAZZA SAN MARCO
VERY EXPENSIVE

✪ **Harry's Bar.** Calle Vallaresso, San Marco 1323. ☎ **041/528-5777.** Reservations recommended. Main courses 80,000–95,000L ($46–$55). AE, DC, MC, V. Daily 10:30am–1am Apr–Oct. Daily 10:30am–11pm Nov–Mar. Vaporetto: San Marco. VENETIAN.

Harry's Bar serves the best food in Venice. A. E. Hotchner, in his *Papa Hemingway*, quoted the writer as saying, "We can't eat straight hamburger in a Renaissance palazzo on the Grand Canal." So he ordered a 5-pound "tin of beluga caviar" to "take the curse off it." Hemingway would probably skip the place today, and the prices would come as a shock even to him. Harry, by the way, is an Italian named Arrigo, son of the late Commendatore Cipriani. Like his father, Arrigo is an entrepreneur extraordinaire known for the standard of his cuisine. His bar is a big draw for martini-thirsty Americans, but Hemingway and Hotchner always ordered a Bloody Mary. The most famous drink is the Bellini (Prosecco and white peach juice). (Off-season, the Bellinis can become watered-down horrors—a gamble at 17,500L/$10.) You can have your choice of dining in the bar downstairs or the room with a view upstairs. We recommend the Venetian fish soup, followed by the scampi Thermidor with rice pilaf or the seafood ravioli. The food is relatively simple but absolutely fresh.

EXPENSIVE

✪ **Antico Martini.** Campo San Fantin, San Marco 1983. ☎ **041/522-4121.** Reservations required. Main courses 36,000–55,000L ($21–$32); fixed-price menus 40,000–55,000L ($23–$32) at lunch, 72,000–98,000L ($42–$57) at dinner. AE, DC, MC, V. Wed 7–11:30pm, Thurs–Mon noon–2:30pm and 7–11:30pm. Vaporetto: San Marco or Santa Maria del Giglio. VENETIAN/INTERNATIONAL.

Antico Martini, the city's leading restaurant, elevates Venetian cuisine to its highest level. Elaborate chandeliers glitter and gilt-framed oil paintings adorn the paneled walls. The courtyard is splendid in summer. An excellent beginning is the risotto di frutti di mare ("fruits of the sea") in a creamy Venetian style with plenty of fresh seafood. For a main dish, try the fegato alla veneziana, tender liver fried with onions and served with polenta, a yellow cornmeal mush. The chefs are better at regional dishes than at international ones. The restaurant has one of the city's best wine lists, featuring more than 350 wines. The yellow Tocai is an interesting local wine and especially good with fish dishes.

La Caravella. In the Hotel Saturnia International, Calle Larga XXII Marzo, San Marco 2398. ☎ **041/520-8901.** Reservations required. Main courses 44,000–80,000L ($26–$46); fixed-price lunch 85,000L ($49). AE, DC, MC, V. Daily noon–3pm and 7pm–midnight. Vaporetto: San Marco. VENETIAN/INTERNATIONAL.

A Note on Fresh Fish

The fish merchants at the Mercato Rialto (Venice's main open-air market) take Monday off, which explains why so many restaurants are closed on Monday. Those that are open on Monday are selling Saturday's goods—beware!

La Caravella has an overblown nautical atmosphere and a leather-bound menu that may make you think you're in a tourist trap. It may be expensive, but it's not a trap: It's a citadel of good food and wine. The restaurant contains four dining rooms and a courtyard for summer. The decor is rustically elegant, with frescoed ceilings, bouquets of flowers, and wrought-iron lighting fixtures. Many of the specialties are featured nowhere else in town. You might begin with an antipasti misto de pesce (fish) with olive oil and lemon juice or prawns with avocado. Two star specialties are granceola (Adriatic sea crab on carpaccio) and chateaubriand for two. The best item to order, however, is one of the poached fish, such as bass—priced according to weight and served with a tempting sauce. The ice cream in champagne is a soothing finish.

Quadri. Piazza San Marco, San Marco 120–124. ☎ **041/522-2105.** Reservations required. Main courses 45,000–69,000L ($26–$40). AE, DC, MC, V. Wed–Sun noon–2:30pm; Tues–Sun 7–10:30pm. Vaporetto: San Marco. INTERNATIONAL.

One of Europe's most famous restaurants, Quadri is even better known as a cafe (see "Venice After Dark" later in this chapter). This deluxe place, with its elegant decor and crowd, overlooks the "living room" of Venice. Many diners come just for the view and are often surprised by the memorable setting, high-quality cuisine, and impeccable service. Harry's Bar and Antico Martini have better food, though the chef's skills are considerable. It's often packed with celebrities during art and film festivals, the world glitterati taking delight in this throwback to the days of La Serenissima. The chef is likely to tempt you with such dishes as scallops with saffron, salt codfish with polenta, marinated swordfish, or sea bass with crab sauce. Dessert specialties are "baked" ice cream and lemon mousse with fresh strawberry sauce.

MODERATE

✪ **Al Covo.** Campiello della Pescaria, Castello 3968. ☎ **041/522-3812.** Reservations recommended for dinner. Main courses 38,000L ($22); fixed-price lunch 48,000L ($28). Fri–Tues 12:45–2:15pm and 7:45–10:15pm. Vaporetto: Arsenale. VENETIAN/SEAFOOD.

The antique setting and sophisticated management and cookery by Cesare Benelli and his Texas-born wife, Diane, create a special charm as well as very fresh and very appealing Venetian dishes. What's their preferred dish? They respond, "That's like asking us, 'Which of your children do you prefer?' since we strongly attach ourselves to the development of each dish." Look for a succulent reinvention of a medieval version of fish soup; potato gnocchi flavored with go (a local whitefish); seafood ravioli; linguine zestly blended with zucchini and fresh peas; and delicious fritto misto with scampi, squid, a bewildering array of fish, and deep-fried vegetables like zucchini flowers. Al Covo prides itself on not having any freezers, guaranteeing that all food is imported fresh every day. As you set out for this place, be alert to the fact that it lies near Piazza San Marco, not near Rialto, as is frequently thought because of a square there with a similar name.

Da Ivo. Calle dei Fuseri, San Marco 1809. ☎ **041/528-5004.** Reservations required. Main courses 30,000–100,000L ($18–$60). AE, DC, MC, V. Mon–Sat noon–2:30pm and 7–11pm. Closed Jan 6–31. Vaporetto: San Marco. TUSCAN/VENETIAN.

Da Ivo has such a faithful crowd you'll think at first you're in a semiprivate club. The rustic atmosphere is cozy and relaxing, and your well-set table is bathed in candlelight.

Florentines head here for fine Tuscan cookery, but regional Venetian dishes are also served. In season, game, prepared according to ancient traditions, is cooked over an open charcoal grill. One cold December day our hearts and plates were warmed by an order of a homemade tagliatelli topped with slivers of tartufi bianchi, the unforgettable pungent white truffle from Piedmont. Dishes change according to the season and the availability of ingredients but are likely to include swordfish, anglerfish, a stewpot of fish, or cuttlefish in its own ink.

Do Forni. Calle dei Specchieri, San Marco 468. ☎ **041/523-2148.** Reservations recommended. Main courses 25,000–40,000L ($15–$23). AE, DC, MC, V. Daily noon–4pm and 6pm–midnight. Vaporetto: San Marco. VENETIAN.

Centuries ago, this was where bread was baked for local monasteries, but today it's the busiest restaurant in Venice—even when the rest of the city slumbers under a wintertime Adriatic fog. It's divided into two sections, separated by a narrow alley. The Venetian cognoscenti prefer the front part, decorated in Orient Express style. The larger section in back is like a country tavern, with ceiling beams and original paintings. The English menu (with at least 80 dishes to choose from, prepared by a team of 14 cooks) is entitled "food for the gods" and lists such specialties as spider crab in its own shell, risotto primavera, linguine with rabbit, and sea bass in papillote (parchment). The food is international in scope.

Ristorante da Raffaele. Calle Larga XXII Marzo (Fondamenta delle Ostreghe), San Marco 2347. ☎ **041/523-2317.** Reservations recommended Sat–Sun. Main courses 20,000–35,000L ($12–$20). AE, DC, MC, V. Fri–Wed noon–3pm and 7–11pm. Closed Dec 10 to mid-Feb. Vaporetto: San Marco or Santa Maria del Giglio. ITALIAN/VENETIAN.

The Raffaele, a 5-minute walk from Piazza San Marco, has long been a favorite canalside restaurant. It's often overrun with tourists, but the veteran kitchen staff handles the onslaught well. Dating from 1953, the restaurant offers the kind of charm and atmosphere unique to Venice. The huge inner sanctum has a high-beamed ceiling, 17th- to 19th-century pistols and sabers, exposed brick, wrought-iron chandeliers, a massive fireplace, and copper pots (hundreds of them). The food is excellent, beginning with a choice of tasty antipasti or well-prepared pastas. Seafood specialties include scampi, squid, and deep-fried fish from the Adriatic. The grilled meats are wonderful. Finish with a tempting dessert. The crowded conviviality is part of the experience.

Taverna La Fenice. Campiello de la Fenice, San Marco 1939. ☎ **041/522-3856.** Reservations required. Main courses 18,000–32,000L ($10–$19). AE, DC, MC, V. Aug–Apr Mon 7–10:30pm, Tues–Sat noon–2:30pm and 7–10:30pm; May–July daily noon–2:30pm and 7–10:30pm. Closed 2nd week in Jan. Vaporetto: San Marco. ITALIAN/VENETIAN.

Opened in 1907, when Venetians were flocking in record numbers to hear the bel canto performances in nearby La Fenice opera house (which burned down a few years ago), this restaurant is one of Venice's most romantic dining spots. The interior is suitably elegant, but the preferred spot in clement weather is outdoors beneath a canopy. The service is smooth and efficient. The most appetizing beginning is the selection of seafood antipasti. The fish is fresh from the Mediterranean. You might enjoy the risotto con scampi e arugula, tagliatelle with cream sauce and exotic mushrooms, John Dory filets with butter and lemon, turbot roasted with potatoes and tomato sauce, scampi with tomatoes and rice, or carpaccio alla Fenice.

Trattoria La Colomba. Piscina Frezzeria, San Marco 1665. ☎ **041/522-1175.** Reservations recommended. Main courses 40,000–75,000L ($23–$44). AE, DC, MC, V. Daily noon–2:30pm and 7–11:30pm. Closed Wed from June 19–Aug, and Nov–Apr. Vaporetto: San Marco or Rialto. VENETIAN/INTERNATIONAL.

ⓘ Family-Friendly Restaurants

Alfredo, Alfredo *(see p. 397)*   This is a great spot for the family on a sightseeing run. Short-order items are served quickly, including spaghetti with a number of sauces and freshly made salads.

Le Chat Qui Rit *(see p. 398)*   This is a self-service cafeteria where children are allowed to select what they want. Lots of pasta dishes.

Tiziano Bar *(see p. 401)*   You can order hot pasta dishes and sandwiches, consumed standing at the counter or seated on one of the high stools.

This is one of the most distinctive trattorie in town, with a history going back at least a century and a legendary association with some of Venice's leading painters. In 1985, a $2-million restoration improved the place, making it a more attractive foil for the modern paintings adorning its walls (they change seasonally and are for sale). Menu items are likely to include at least five daily specials based on Venice's time-honored cuisine as well as risotto di funghi del Montello (risotto with mushrooms from the local hills of Montello) and baccalà alla vicentina (milk-simmered dry cod seasoned with onions, anchovies, and cinnamon and served with polenta). The fruits and vegetables used in the dishes are for the most part grown on the lagoon islands.

Vini da Arturo. Calle degli Assassini, San Marco 3656. ☎ **041/528-6974.** Reservations recommended. Main courses 28,000–43,000L ($16–$25). No credit cards. Mon–Sat noon–2:30pm and 7–10:30pm. Closed Aug. Vaporetto: San Marco or Rialto. VENETIAN.

Vini da Arturo attracts many devoted regulars to its seven tables, including artists and writers. You get delectable local cooking—not just the standard clichés and not seafood, which may be unique for a Venetian restaurant. One restaurant owner, who likes to dine here occasionally instead of at his own place, explained, "The subtle difference between good and bad food is often nothing more than the amount of butter and cream used." Instead of ordering plain pasta, try the tantalizing spaghetti alla Gorgonzola. The beef is also good, especially when prepared with a cream sauce flavored with mustard and pepper. The salads are made with fresh ingredients, often in unusual combinations; particularly interesting is the pappardelle radicchio.

INEXPENSIVE

Alfredo, Alfredo. Campo San Filippo e Giacomo, Castello 4294. ☎ **041/522-5331.** Main courses 17,000–28,000L ($10–$16); 2-course fixed-price menu 22,000L ($13). AE, DC, MC, V. Thurs–Tues 11am–2am. Vaporetto: San Zaccaria. VENETIAN/INTERNATIONAL.

Alfredo, Alfredo might be classified as a coffee shop. You can order any number of items prepared in short order, like spaghetti with a number of sauces, freshly made salads, crêpes, various grilled meats, and omelets. The food isn't always first-rate and the atmosphere is a bit hysterical at times, but its long hours make it a convenient spot for a light meal at almost any time of day.

Al Mascaron. Calle Lunga Santa Maria Formosa, Castello 5225. ☎ **041/522-5995.** Reservations recommended. Main courses 15,000–40,000L ($9–$23). No credit cards. Mon–Sat 12:30–3pm and 7–11pm. Vaporetto: Rialto or an Marco. VENETIAN.

Loud and unpretentious, offering three dining rooms decorated with Venetian artifacts, this is the type of restaurant that encourages patrons to sit next to strangers at long trestle tables on which are slammed copious portions. These are likely to include deep-fried calamari, spaghetti with lobster, monkfish in a salt crust, pastas, savory risottos, and Venetian-style calves' liver (which locals prefer rather pink), plus the best

Take a Gelato or Pastry Break

If you're in the mood for some tasty gelato (ice cream), head to the **Gelateria Paolin,** Campo San Stefano, Dorsoduro 2962A (☎ **041/522-5576**), offering 18 flavors. It has stood on the corner of this busy square since the 1930s, making it Venice's oldest ice-cream parlor. You can order your ice cream to go or eat it at one of the sidewalk tables (it costs more if you eat it at a table). June to September, it's open daily 7:30am to midnight; October to May, hours are Tuesday to Sunday 7:30am to 8:30pm.

One of the city's best-respected pastry shops is the **Pasticceria Marchini,** Ponte San Maurizio, San Marco 2769 (☎ **041/522-9109**), whose cakes, muffins, and pastries figure prominently in the childhood memories of many of the city's residents. The high-caloric output of the busy kitchens is displayed behind glass cases and sold by the piece for eating at the bar (there are few tables) or by the kilogram for eating elsewhere. The pastries include traditional versions of *torte del Doge,* made from almonds and pine nuts; *zalleto,* made from a mix of cornmeal and eggs; and *bigna,* akin to zabaglione, concocted from chocolate and cream. It's open daily 8:30am to 8:30pm.

seafood of the day made into salads. There's also a convivial bar, where locals drop in to spread the gossip of the day, play cards, have a glass of vino, and order snacks.

Le Chat Qui Rit. Calle Frezzeria, San Marco 1131. ☎ **041/522-9086.** Main courses 10,000–16,000L ($6–$9); pizzas 9,000–14,000L ($5–$8). No credit cards. Nov–Aug Sun–Fri 11am–9:30pm; Sept–Oct daily 11am–9:30pm. Vaporetto: San Marco. VENETIAN/PIZZA.

This self-service cafeteria/pizzeria offers food prepared "just like mama made." It's very popular because of its low prices. Dishes might include cuttlefish simmered in stock and served on a bed of yellow polenta or various fried fish. You can also order a steak grilled very simply, flavored with oil, salt, and pepper or a little garlic and herbs if you prefer. Main-dish platters are served rather quickly after you order them.

Nuova Rivetta. Campo San Filippo, Castello 4625. ☎ **041/528-7302.** Reservations recommended. Main courses 16,000–28,000L ($9–$16). AE, MC, V. Tues–Sun 10am–10pm. Closed July 23–Aug 20. Vaporetto: San Zaccaria. VENETIAN/SEAFOOD.

Nuova Rivetta is an old-fashioned trattoria where you get good food at a good price. Many find it best for lunch during a stroll around Venice. The most representative dish is frittura di pesce, a mixed fish fry from the Adriatic that includes squid or various other "sea creatures" that turned up at the day's market. Other specialties are gnocchi stuffed with Adriatic spider crab, pasticcio of fish (a main course), and spaghetti flavored with squid ink. The most typical wine is Prosecco, whose bouquet is refreshing and fruity with a slightly sharp flavor; for centuries it has been one of the most celebrated wines of the Veneto.

Restaurant da Bruno. Calle del Paradiso, Castello 5731. ☎ **041/522-1480.** Main courses 12,000–25,000L ($7–$15); fixed-price menu 24,000L ($14). AE, DC, MC, V. Wed–Mon noon–3pm and 7–11pm. Closed 1 week in Jan. Vaporetto: San Marco or Rialto. VENETIAN.

On a narrow street about halfway between the Rialto Bridge and Piazza San Marco, this is like a country taverna and attracts its crowds by grilling meats on an open-hearth fire. You get your antipasti at the counter and watch your prosciutto order being prepared—paper-thin slices of spicy flavored ham wrapped around breadsticks (grissini). In the right season, da Bruno does some of the finest game dishes in Venice; if featured, try its capriolo (roebuck) and its fagiano (pheasant). A typical Venetian dish prepared well here is the zuppa di pesce (fish soup). Other specialties are filet of beef with pepper sauce, veal scaloppine with wild mushrooms, scampi and calamari, and squid with polenta. After that rich fare, you may settle for a macedonia of mixed fruit for dessert.

Sempione. Ponte Beretteri, San Marco 578. ☎ **041/522-6022.** Reservations recommended. Main courses 17,600–31,000L ($10–$18). AE, DC, MC, V. Daily 11:30am–3pm and 6:30–10pm. Closed Jan. Vaporetto: Rialto. VENETIAN.

This restaurant has done an admirable job of feeding locals and visitors for almost 90 years. Set adjacent to a canal in a 15th-century building near Piazza San Marco, it contains three dining rooms done in a soothingly traditional style, a well-trained staff, and a kitchen focusing on traditional Venetian cuisine. Examples are grilled fish, spaghetti with crabmeat, risotto with fish, fish soup, and a delectable version of Venetian calf's liver that hasn't been significantly changed since the restaurant was founded. Try for a table by the window so you can watch the gondolas glide by.

○ Trattoria alla Madonna. Calle della Madonna, San Polo 594. ☎ **041/522-3824.** Reservations recommended but not always accepted. Main courses 18,000–22,000L ($10–$13). AE, MC, V. Thurs–Tues noon–3pm and 7:15–10pm. Closed Jan 7–Feb 7 and Aug 1–15. Vaporetto: Rialto. VENETIAN/ITALIAN.

No, this place has nothing to do with *that* Madonna. It opened in 1954 in a 300-year-old building and is one of Venice's most popular and characteristic trattorie, specializing in traditional Venetian recipes and grilled fresh fish. A good beginning might be the antipasto frutti di mare (fruits of the sea). Pastas, polentas, risottos, meats (including *fegato alla veneziana,* liver with onions), and many kinds of irreproachably fresh fish are widely available. Many creatures of the sea are displayed in a refrigerated case near the entrance.

ON OR NEAR RIVA DEGLI SCHIAVONI
EXPENSIVE
Do Leoni. In the Londra Palace, Riva degli Schiavoni, Castello 4171. ☎ **041/520-0533.** Reservations recommended. Main courses 30,000–60,000L ($17–$35); 3-course lunch (without drinks) 42,000L ($24). Guests of the Londra Palace receive 20% off (excludes fixed-price menu). AE, DC, MC, V. Restaurant, daily noon–3pm and 7:30–11pm; bar, daily 10am–1am. Vaporetto: San Zaccaria. VENETIAN/INTERNATIONAL.

For years, this restaurant was known by the French version of its name, Les Deux Lions. In the elegant Londra Palace, it offers a panoramic view of a 19th-century equestrian statue ringed with heroic women taming—you guessed it—lions. The restaurant is filled with scarlet and gold, a motif of lions patterned into the carpeting, and reproductions of English furniture. Lunches are brief buffet-style affairs, where patrons serve themselves from a large choice of hot and cold Italian and international food. The appealing candlelit dinners are more formal, emphasizing Venetian cuisine. The chef's undeniable skill is reflected in such dishes as chilled fish terrine, baked salmon in champagne sauce, and baby rooster with green-pepper sauce. Depending on the weather, you can dine out on the piazza overlooking the lions and their masters.

NEAR THE ARSENALE
MODERATE
Ristorante Corte Sconta. Calle del Pestrin, Castello 3886. ☎ **041/522-7024.** Reservations required. Main courses 20,000–35,000L ($12–$20); fixed-price menu 70,000–85,000L ($41–$49). AE, DC, MC, V. Tues–Sat 12:30–2:30pm and 7:30–9:30pm. Closed Jan 7–Feb 7 and July 15–Aug 15. Vaporetto: Arsenale. SEAFOOD.

Corte Sconta is behind a narrow storefront you'd probably ignore if you didn't know about this place. On a narrow alley whose name is shared by at least three other streets in Venice (this one is near Campo Bandiere e Moro and San Giovanni in Bragora), this modest restaurant has a multicolored marble floor, plain wooden tables, and no serious attempt at decoration. It has become well known, however, as a sophisticated gathering place for artists, writers, and filmmakers. As the depiction of the satyr chasing the mermaid above the entrance implies, it's a fish restaurant, serving a variety of grilled creatures (much of the "catch" is largely unknown in North America). The fresh fish is flawlessly grilled and flawlessly fresh—the gamberi, for example, is placed live on the grill. A great start is marinated salmon with arugula and pomegranate seeds in rich olive oil. If you don't like fish, a tender beef filet is available. The big stand-up bar in an adjoining room seems to be almost a private fraternity of the locals.

NEAR THE PONTE DI RIALTO
EXPENSIVE

Fiaschetteria Toscana. Campo SS. San Giovanni Crisostomo, Cannaregio 5719. ☎ **041/ 528-5281.** Reservations required. Main courses 18,000–35,000L ($10–$20). AE, DC, MC, V. Wed–Mon 12:30–2:30pm and 7:30–10:30pm. Vaporetto: Rialto. VENETIAN.

Though this purports to be a rather stylish restaurant, there may be some rough points in the service (the staff is hysterically busy) and presentations. Nonetheless, this is the preferred choice of many food-savvy Venetians who often regard it as a venue for a celebration. Despite the high prices and the closely packed tables, this is a hot spot for trendoids who appreciate the see-and-be-seen ambience, offering a vaguely permissive aura where filmmakers and models can feel comfortable. The dining rooms are on two levels, the upstairs of which is somewhat more claustrophobic. In the evening, the downstairs is especially appealing with its romantic candlelit ambience. Menu items include frittura della Serenissima (mixed platter of fried seafood with vegetables), veal scallops with lemon-marsala sauce and mushrooms, ravioli stuffed with whitefish and herbs, and several kinds of Tuscan-style beefsteak.

MODERATE

✪ **"Al Graspo de Uva."** Calle Bombaseri, San Marco 5094. ☎ **041/520-0150.** Reservations required. Main courses 26,000–35,000L ($15–$20). AE, DC, MC, V. Tues–Sun 12:15–3pm and 7:15–10:45pm. Closed Jan 2–17. Vaporetto: Rialto. SEAFOOD/VENETIAN.

"Al Graspo de Uva" is one bunch of grapes you'll want to pluck: It's a winner for that special meal. Decorated in the old taverna style, it offers several air-conditioned dining rooms. One has a beamed ceiling, hung with garlic and copper bric-a-brac. Among the best fish restaurants in Venice, "Al Graspo de Uva" has been patronized by Elizabeth Taylor, Jeanne Moreau, and even Giorgio de Chirico. You can help yourself to all the hors d'oeuvres you want—known on the menu as "self-service mammoth." Next try the gran fritto dell'Adriatico, a mixed treat of deep-fried fish from the Adriatic. The desserts are also good, especially the peach Melba.

Poste Vechie. Pescheria Rialto, San Polo 1608. ☎ **041/721-822.** Reservations recommended. Main courses 21,000–45,000L ($12–$26). AE, DC, MC, V. Wed–Mon noon–3pm and 7–10:30pm. Vaporetto: Rialto. SEAFOOD.

This charming restaurant is near the Rialto fish market and connected to the rest of the city by a small privately owned bridge. It opened in the early 1500s as a post office—when they used to serve food to fortify the mail carriers for their deliveries. Today it's the oldest restaurant in Venice, with a pair of intimate dining rooms (both graced with paneling, murals, and 16th-century mantelpieces) and a courtyard that evokes the countryside. Menu items include superfresh fish from the nearby markets; a salad of shellfish and exotic mushrooms; tagliolini flavored with squid ink, crabmeat, and fish sauce; and the pièce de résistance, seppie (cuttlefish) à la veneziana with polenta. If you don't like fish, calves' liver or veal shank with ham and cheese are also well prepared. The desserts come rolling to your table on a trolley and are usually delicious.

Ristorante à la Vecia Cavana. Rio Terà SS. Apostoli, Cannaregio 4624. ☎ **041/ 528-7106.** Main courses 35,000–60,000L ($20–$35); fixed-price menu 35,000–100,000L ($20–$58). AE, DC, MC, V. Fri–Wed noon–2:30pm and 7:30–10:30pm. Vaporetto: Ca' d'Oro. SEAFOOD.

Ristorante à la Vecia Cavana is off the tourist circuit and well worth the trek through the winding streets to find it. A cavana is a place where gondolas are parked, a sort of liquid garage, and the site of this restaurant was such a place in the Middle Ages. When you enter, you'll be greeted by brick arches, stone columns, terra-cotta floors, framed modern paintings, and a photo of 19th-century fishermen relaxing after a day's work. It's an appropriate introduction to a menu specializing in seafood, like a mixed grill from the Adriatic, fried scampi, fresh sole, squid, three types of risotto (each with seafood), and a spicy zuppa di pesce (fish soup). Antipasti di pesce Cavana is an assortment of just about every sea creature. The food is authentic and seems prepared for the Venetian palate—not necessarily for the glitzy foreign visitor's.

INEXPENSIVE

Ristorante al Mondo Novo. Salizzada di San Lio, Castello 5409. ☎ **041/520-0698.** Reservations recommended. Main courses 15,000–35,000L ($9–$20); fixed-price lunch 23,000–39,000L ($13–$23). AE, MC, V. Daily 11:30am–11:30pm. Vaporetto: Rialto or San Marco. VENETIAN/SEAFOOD.

In a building from the Renaissance, with a dining room outfitted in a regional style, this well-established restaurant offers professional service and a kindly staff. Plus, it stays open later than many of its nearby competitors. Menu items include a selection of seafood, prepared as frittura misto dell'Adriatico or charcoal grilled. Other items are macaroni alla verdura (with fresh vegetables and greens), an antipasti of fresh fish, and beef filets with pepper sauce and rissole potatoes. Locals who frequent the place always order the fresh fish, knowing that the owner is a wholesaler in the Rialto fish market.

Rôsticceria San Bartolomeo. Calle della Bissa, San Marco 5424. ☎ **041/522-3569.** Main courses 12,000–25,000L ($7–$15); fixed-price menus 32,000–42,000L ($19–$24). AE, MC, V. Tues–Sun 9am–2:30pm and 4:30–9:30pm. Vaporetto: Rialto; take an underpass on your left (with your back facing the bridge); this passageway is labeled Sottoportego della Bissa. The restaurant will be at the first corner, off Campo San Bartolomeo. VENETIAN/ITALIAN.

This rôsticceria is Venice's most frequented fast-food place and has long been a haven for cost-conscious travelers. Downstairs is a tavola calda where you can eat standing up, but upstairs is a restaurant with waiter service. Typical dishes are baccalà alla vicentina (codfish simmered in herbs and milk), deep-fried mozzarella (which the Italians call in carrozza), and seppie con polenta (squid in its own ink sauce, served with polenta). Everything is washed down with typical Veneto wine.

Tiziano Bar. Campo SS. San Giovanni Cristostomo, midway between San Giovanni Cristostomo and the Teatro Mulibran, Cannaregio. ☎ **041/523-5544.** Main dishes 8,000–14,000L ($4.65–$8). Daily 8am–10:30pm. Vaporetto: Rialto. SANDWICHES/PASTA/PIZZA.

Tiziano Bar is a tavola calda ("hot table"). There's no waiter service—you eat standing at a counter or sitting on one of the high stools. The place is known in Venice for selling pizza by the yard. From noon to 3pm it serves hot pastas such as rigatoni and cannelloni. But throughout the day you can order sandwiches or perhaps a plate of mozzarella.

IN CANNAREGIO
MODERATE

Il Milion. Corte Prima al Milion, Cannaregio 5841. ☎ **041/522-9302.** Reservations recommended. Main courses 20,000–29,000L ($12–$17). No credit cards. Thurs–Tues noon–2pm and 6:30–11pm. Closed Aug. Vaporetto: Rialto. VENETIAN.

With a tradition of feeding patrons extending back more than 300 years and a location near the rear of San Giovanni Crisostomo, this is one of Venice's oldest restaurants. It's named after the book written by Marco Polo, *Il Milion,* describing his travels. In fact, it occupies a town house owned long ago by members of the explorer's family. The bar, incidentally, is a favorite with some of the gondoliers of Venice. Menu items include what reads like a who's who of well-recognized Venetian platters, each fresh and well prepared. Examples are veal kidneys, calves' liver with fried onions, grilled sardines, spaghetti with clams, risotto flavored with squid ink, and a fritto misto of fried fish. The staff is charming and friendly.

INEXPENSIVE

✪ **Ai Tre Spiedi.** Salizzada San Cazian, Cannaregio 5906. ☎ **041/520-8035.** Main courses 16,000L–26,000L ($9–$15). MC, V. Tues–Sat noon–2:30pm and 7–9:30pm, Sun 12:30–3:30pm. Vaporetto: Rialto. VENETIAN.

Venetians bring their visiting friends here to make a good impression without breaking the bank, then swear them to secrecy. Rarely will you find as pleasant a setting and as appetizing a meal as in this casually elegant trattoria with exposed beam ceilings and some of the most reasonably priced fresh-fish dining that'll keep meat-eaters happy as well. If you order à la carte, ask the English-speaking waiters to estimate the cost of your fish entree, since it'll typically appear priced by the *etto* (200 grams).

IN SAN POLO
MODERATE

✪ **Osteria da Fiore.** Calle del Scaleter, San Polo 2202. ☎ **041/721-308.** Reservations required. Main courses 36,000–42,000L ($21–$24). AE, DC, MC, V. Tues–Sat 12:30–2:30pm and 8–10:30pm. Closed 3 weeks in Aug and Dec 25–Jan 12. Vaporetto: San Tomà. SEAFOOD.

The breath of the Adriatic seems to blow through this place, though how the wind finds this little restaurant tucked away in a labyrinth is a mystery. An imaginative, changing fare is offered, depending on the availability of fresh fish and produce. If you have a love of maritime foods, you'll find everything from scampi (a sweet Adriatic prawn, cooked in as many ways as there are chefs) to granzeola, a type of spider crab. In days gone by, we've sampled fried calamari (cuttlefish), risotto with scampi, tagliata with rosemary, masenette (tiny green crabs you eat shell and all), and canoce (mantis shrimp). For your wine, we suggest Prosecco, which has a distinctive golden-yellow color and a bouquet that's refreshing and fruity. The proprietors extend a hearty welcome to match their fare.

IN SANTA CROCE
MODERATE

Trattoria Antica Besseta. Campo SS. de Ca' Zusto, Santa Croce 1395. ☎ **041/721-687.** Reservations required. Main courses 30,000–35,000L ($17–$20). AE, MC, V. Thurs–Mon noon–2:30pm and 7–10:30pm. Vaporetto: Rive di Biasio. VENETIAN.

If you manage to find the place (go with a good map), you'll be rewarded with true Venetian cuisine at its most unpretentious. Head for Campo San Giacomo dell'Orio, then negotiate your way across infrequently visited piazzas and winding alleys. Push through saloon doors into a bar area filled with modern art. The dining room in back is ringed with paintings and illuminated with wagon-wheel chandeliers. Nereo Volpe and his wife, Mariuccia, and one of their sons are the guiding force, the chefs, the buyers, and even the "talking menus." The food depends on what looked good in the market that morning, so the menu could include roast chicken, fried scampi, fritto misto, spaghetti in sardine sauce, various roasts, and a selection from the day's catch. The Volpe family produces two kinds of their own wine, a pinot blanc and a cabernet.

IN DORSODURO
MODERATE

La Furatola. Calle Lunga San Barnaba, Dorsoduro 2869. ☎ **041/520-8594.** Reservations recommended for dinner. Main courses 25,000–45,000L ($15–$26). AE, DC, MC, V. Fri–Tues noon–3pm and 7–10:30pm. Closed Aug, 2 weeks in Jan, and Mon lunch. Vaporetto: Ca' Rezzonico. SEAFOOD.

La Furatola (an old Venetian word meaning "restaurant") is very much a Dorsoduro neighborhood hangout, but it has captured the imagination of local foodies. It occupies a 300-year-old building, along a narrow flagstone-paved street you'll need a good map and a lot of patience to find. Perhaps you'll have lunch here after a visit to San Rocco, only a short distance away. In the simple dining room, the specialty is fish brought to your table in a wicker basket so you can judge its size and freshness by its bright eyes and red gills. A display of seafood antipasti is set out near the entrance. A standout is the baby octopus boiled and eaten with a drop of red-wine vinegar. Eel comes with a medley of mixed fried fish, including baby cuttlefish, prawns, and squid rings.

Linea d'Ombra. Fondamente delle Zattere, Dorsoduro 19. ☎ **041/528-5259.** Reservations not necessary. Main courses 30,000–50,000L ($17–$29). AE, DC, MC, V. Thurs–Tues noon–3:30pm and Thurs–Sat and Mon–Tues 7:30–10:30pm. Vaporetto: Salute. VENETIAN.

This popular bar/pub that spills onto a panoramic terrace during clement weather doubles as an informal trattoria featuring traditional recipes. You can order dishes that include Venetian-style risotto with octopus and squid ink; Venetian-style calves' liver; a wide selection of fish; piquant grilled scampi; and the most popular pasta in Venice, *bigoli in salsa.* The inspiration for the name of this restaurant, Linea d'Ombra, derives from the fascination of a former owner for Joseph Conrad's novella called *The Shadow Line.*

Locanda Montin. Fondamenta di Borgo, Dorsoduro 1147. ☎ **041/522-7151.** Reservations recommended. Main courses 20,000–30,000L ($12–$17). AE, DC, MC, V. Tues 12:30–2:30pm, Thurs–Mon 12:30–2:30pm and 7:30–9:30pm. Closed 10 days mid-Aug and 20 days Jan. Vaporetto: Accademia. INTERNATIONAL/ITALIAN.

The Montin is the kind of rapidly disappearing inn that nearly every literary and artistic figure in Venice has visited since it opened just after World War II. Famous patrons have included Ezra Pound, Jackson Pollock, Mark Rothko, and many of the assorted artist friends of the late Peggy Guggenheim. It's owned and run by the Carretins, who have covered the walls with paintings donated by or bought from their many friends and guests. The arbor-covered garden courtyard of this 17th-century building is filled with regulars, many of whom allow their favorite waiter to select most of the items for their meal. The frequently changing menu includes a variety of salads, grilled meats, and fish caught in the Adriatic. Dessert might be semifreddo di fragoline, a tempting chilled liqueur-soaked cake, capped with whipped cream and wild strawberries.

ON ISOLA DELLA GUIDECCA
VERY EXPENSIVE

✪ **Ristorante Cipriani.** In the Hotel Cipriani, Isola della Giudecca 10. ☎ **041/520-7744.** Reservations required. Main courses 23,000–66,000L ($13–$38). AE, DC, MC, V. Daily 12:30–3pm and 8–10:30pm. Closed Nov–Mar. Vaporetto: Zitelle. ITALIAN.

The grandest of the hotel restaurants, the Cipriani offers a sublime but relatively simple cuisine, depending on the freshest of ingredients perfectly prepared by one of the best-trained staffs along the Adriatic. This isn't a family favorite though, and children under six years old aren't allowed; however, a baby-sitter can be arranged. You can dine in the more formal room with Murano chandeliers and Fortuny curtains when the weather is nippy or out on the extensive terrace overlooking the lagoon. Freshly made pasta is a specialty, and it's among the finest we've ever sampled. Try the taglierini verdi with noodles and ham au gratin. Chef's specialties include mixed fried scampi and squid with tender vegetables and sautéed veal filets with spring artichokes. Come to Risorante Cipriani in October for the last Bellinis of the white peach season and the first white truffles of the season served in a champagne risotto.

EXPENSIVE

Harry's Dolci. Fondamenta San Biago 773, Isola della Giudecca 30133. ☎ **041/520-8337.** Reservations recommended, especially Sat–Sun. Main courses 30,000–40,000L ($17–$23); fixed-price menu 75,000L ($44). AE, MC, V. Wed–Mon noon–3pm and 7–10:30pm. Closed Nov–March 30. Vaporetto: S. Eufemia. INTERNATIONAL/ITALIAN.

The people at the famed Harry's Bar have established their latest enclave far from the maddening crowds of Piazza Sam Marco on this little-visited island. From the quay-side windows of this chic place, you can watch seagoing vessels, including everything from yachts to lagoon-based barges. White napery and uniformed waiters grace a modern room, where no one minds if you order only coffee and ice cream or perhaps a selection from the large pastry menu (the zabaglione cake is divine). Popular items are carpaccio Cipriani, chicken salad, club sandwiches, gnocchi, and house-style cannelloni. Dishes are deliberately kept simple, but each is well prepared.

ON THE LIDO
MODERATE

Favorita. Via Francesco Duodo 33, Lido di Venezia. ☎ **041/526-1626.** Main courses 23,000–70,000L ($13–$41). AE, DC, MC, V. Tues–Sun 12:30–2:30pm and 7:30–10:30pm. Vaporetto: Lido di Venezia. SEAFOOD.

Occupying two dining rooms and a garden that has thrived here since the 1920s, this place was reputedly named after Gabriella, wife (and presumably "the favorite") of Vittorio Emanuele, who occasionally stopped in for refreshment during her stops on the Lido. It's operated by the Pradel family, now in their third generation of ownership. Their years of experience contribute to flavorful, impeccably prepared seafood and shellfish, many of them grilled, served in the rustically beamed interior or at tables amid the flowering vines of the garden. Try the trenette (spaghetti-like pasta) with baby squid and eggplant; potato-based gnocchi with crabs from the Venetian lagoon; and grilled versions of virtually every fish in the Adriatic, including eel, sea bass, turbot, and sole.

Ristorante Belvedere. Piazzale Santa Maria Elisabetta 4, Lido di Venezia. ☎ **041/526-0115.** Reservations recommended. Main courses 12,000–50,000L ($7–$29); fixed-price menu 33,000L ($19). AE, DC, MC, V. Tues–Sun noon–2:30pm and 7–9:30pm. Closed Nov 4 to Easter. Vaporetto: Lido. VENETIAN.

Outside the big hotels, the best food on the Lido is served at the Belvedere. Don't be put off by its location, across from where the vaporetto from Venice stops. In such a location, you might expect a touristy place. Actually, the Belvedere attracts some of the finest people of Venice. They often come here as an excursion, knowing they can get some of the best fish along the Adriatic. Tables are placed outside, and there's a glass-enclosed portion for windy days. The main dining room is attractive, with cane backed bentwood chairs and big windows. In back, reached through a separate entrance, is a busy cafe. Main dishes include the chef's special sea bass, along with grilled dorade (or sole), and fried scampi. You might begin with the special fish antipasti or spaghetti en papillote (cooked in parchment).

5 Seeing the Sights

Venice appears to have been created specifically to entertain its legions of callers. Ever since the body of St. Mark was smuggled out of Alexandria and entombed in the basilica, the city has been host to a never-ending stream of visitors—famous, infamous, and otherwise. Venice has perpetually captured the imagination of poets and artists. Wordsworth, Byron, and Shelley addressed poems to the city, and it has been written about or used as a setting by many contemporary writers.

In the pages ahead, we'll explore the city's great art and architecture. But, unlike Florence, Venice would reward its guests with treasures even if they never ducked inside a museum or church. In the city on the islands, the frame eternally competes with the picture it contains. "For all its vanity and villainy," wrote Lewis Mumford, "life touched some of its highest moments in Venice."

ST. MARK'S SQUARE (PIAZZA SAN MARCO)

✪ **Piazza San Marco** was the heartbeat of La Serenissima in the heyday of its glory as a seafaring republic, the crystallization of the city's dreams and aspirations. If you have only 1 day for Venice, you need not leave the square, as the city's major attractions, like the Basilica of St. Mark and the Doge's Palace, are centered here or nearby.

The traffic-free square, frequented by visitors and pigeons and sometimes even by Venetians, is a source of bewilderment and interest. If you rise at dawn, you can almost have the piazza to yourself, and as you watch the sun come up, the sheen of gold mosaics glistens with a mystical beauty. At around 9am, the overstuffed pigeons are fed by the city (if you're caught under the whir, you'll think you're witnessing a remake of Hitchcock's *The Birds*). At midafternoon the tourists reign supreme, and it's not surprising in July to witness a scuffle over a camera angle. At sunset, when the two Moors in the Clock Tower strike the end of another day, lonely sailors begin a usually frustrated search for those hot spots that characterized the Venice of yore. Deeper into the evening, the strollers parade by or stop for an espresso at the fashionable Caffè Florian and sip while listening to a band concert.

Thanks to Napoléon, the square was unified architecturally. The emperor added the Fabbrica Nuova facing the basilica, thus bridging the Old and New Procuratie on either side. Flanked with medieval-looking palaces, Sansovino's Library, elegant shops, and colonnades, the square is now finished—unlike Piazza della Signoria in Florence.

If Piazza San Marco is Europe's drawing room, then the piazza's satellite, **Piazzetta San Marco,** is Europe's antechamber. Hedged in by the Doge's Palace, Sansovino's Library, and a side of St. Mark's, the tiny square faces the Grand Canal. Two tall granite columns grace the square. One is surmounted by a winged lion, representing St. Mark. The other is topped by a statue of a man taming a dragon, supposedly the dethroned patron saint Theodore. Both columns came from the East in the 12th century.

A St. Mark's Warning

A dress code for men and women prohibiting shorts, bare arms and shoulders, and skirts above the knee is strictly enforced at all times in the basilica. You *will* be turned away. In addition, you must remain silent and cannot take photographs.

During Venice's heyday, dozens of victims either lost their heads or were strung up here, many of them first being subjected to torture that would've made the Marquis de Sade flinch. One, for example, had his teeth hammered in, his eyes gouged out, and his hands cut off before being strung up. Venetian justice became notorious throughout Europe. If you stand with your back to the canal, looking toward the south facade of St. Mark's, you'll see the so-called *Virgin and Child* of the poor baker, a mosaic honoring Pietro Fasiol (also Faziol), a young man unjustly sentenced to death on a charge of murder.

To the left of the entrance to the Doge's Palace are four porphyry figures, which, for want of a better description, the Venetians called "Moors." These puce-colored fellows are huddled close together, as if afraid. Considering the decapitations and tortures that have occurred on the piazzetta, it's no wonder.

✪ **St. Mark's Basilica (Basilica di San Marco).** Piazza San Marco. ☎ **041/522-5205.** Basilica, free; treasury, 4,000L ($2.30); presbytery, 3,000L ($1.75); Marciano Museum, 3,000L ($1.75). Basilica (including baptistery and presbytery), Apr–Sept–Mon–Sat 9:30am–5:30pm, Sun 2–5:30pm; Oct–Mar Mon–Sat 9:30am–5pm, Sun 1:30–4:30pm. Treasury, Mon–Sat 9:30am–5pm, Sun 2–5pm. Marciano Museum, Apr–Sept Mon–Sat 10am–5:30pm, Sun 2–4:30pm; Oct–Mar Mon–Sat 10am–4:45pm. Vaporetto: San Marco.

Dominating Piazza San Marco is the so-called Church of Gold, one of the world's greatest and most richly embellished churches. In fact, it looks as if it had been moved intact from Istanbul. The basilica is a conglomeration of styles, though it's particularly indebted to Byzantium. Like Venice, St. Mark's is adorned with booty from every corner of the city's once far-flung mercantile empire—capitals from Sicily, columns from Alexandria, porphyry from Syria, and sculpture from old Constantinople.

The basilica is capped by a dome that—like a spider plant—sends off shoots, in this case a quartet of smaller-scale cupolas. Spanning the facade is a loggia, surmounted by replicas of the four famous St. Mark's horses, the Triumphal Quadriga. The facade's rich marble slabs and mosaics depict scenes from the lives of Christ and St. Mark. One of the mosaics re-creates the entry of the evangelist's body into Venice: St. Mark's body, hidden in a pork barrel, was smuggled out of Alexandria in 828 and shipped to Venice. The evangelist dethroned Theodore, the Greek saint who up until then had been the patron of the city that had outgrown him.

In the **atrium** are six cupolas with mosaics illustrating scenes from the Old Testament, including the story of the Tower of Babel. The interior of the basilica, once the private chapel and pantheon of the doges, is a stunning wonderland of marbles, alabaster, porphyry, and pillars. You'll walk in awe across the undulating multicolored ocean floor, patterned with mosaics.

To the right is the **baptistery,** dominated by the Sansovino-inspired baptismal font, upon which John the Baptist is ready to pour water. If you look back at the aperture over the entry, you can see a mosaic of the dance of Salome in front of Herod and his court. Salome, wearing a star-studded russet-red dress and three white fox tails, is dancing under a platter holding John the Baptist's head. Her glassy face is that of a Madonna, not an enchantress.

After touring the baptistery, proceed up the right nave to the doorway to the oft-looted **treasury** *(tesoro).* Here you'll find the inevitable skulls and bones of some

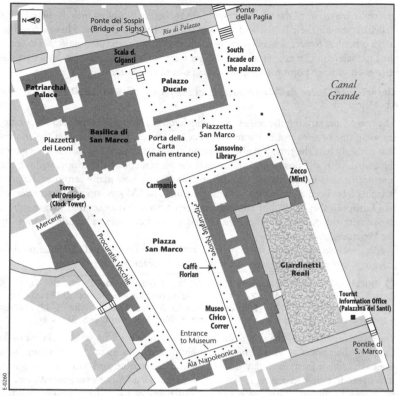

ecclesiastical authorities under glass, plus goblets, chalices, and Gothic candelabra. The entrance to the **presbytery** is nearby. In it, on the high altar, the alleged sarcophagus of St. Mark rests under a green marble blanket and is held by four sculptured Corinthian-style alabaster columns. The Byzantine-style **Pala d'Oro,** from Constantinople, is the rarest treasure at St. Mark's—made of gold and studded with precious stones.

On leaving the basilica, head up the stairs in the atrium to the **Marciano Museum** and the **Loggia dei Cavalli.** The star of the museum is the world-famous *Triumphal Quadriga,* four horses looted from Constantinople by Venetian crusaders during the sack of that city in 1204. These horses once surmounted the basilica but were removed because of pollution damage and subsequently restored. This is the only *quadriga* (which means a quartet of horses yoked together) to have survived from the classical era, believed to have been cast in the 4th century. Napoléon once carted these much-traveled horses off to Paris for the Arc de Triomphe du Carrousel, but they were returned to Venice in 1815. The museum, with its mosaics and tapestries, is especially interesting, but also be sure to walk out onto the loggia for a view of Piazza San Marco.

Bell Tower of St. Mark's (Campanile di San Marco). Piazza San Marco. ☎ 041/ 522-4064. Admission 8,000L ($4.65) for adults, 3,000L ($1.80) for children. May–Oct daily 9am–8pm; Nov–Apr daily 9:30am–3:45pm. Vaporetto: San Marco.

One summer night in 1902, the bell tower of St. Mark's, suffering from years of rheumatism in the damp Venetian climate, gave out a warning sound that sent the fashionable coffee drinkers in the piazza scurrying for their lives. But the campanile gracefully waited until the next morning, July 14, before tumbling into the piazza. The Venetians rebuilt their belfry, and it's now safe to climb to the top. However, unlike Italy's other bell towers, where you have to brave narrow, steep spiral staircases to reach the top, here you can take an elevator to get a pigeon's view of the city. It's a particularly good vantage point for viewing the cupolas of the basilica.

Clock Tower (Torre dell'Orologio). Piazza San Marco. ☎ **041/523-1879.** Vaporetto: San Marco.

The two Moors striking the bell atop this clock tower, soaring over the Old Procuratie, represent one of the most characteristic Venetian scenes. The clock under the winged lion not only tells the time but also is a boon to the astrologer: It matches the signs of the zodiac with the position of the sun. If the movement of the Moors striking the hour seems slow in today's fast-paced world, remember how many centuries the poor wretches have been at their task without time off. The "Moors" originally represented two European shepherds, but after having been reproduced in bronze, they've grown darker with the passing of time. As a consequence, they came to be called Moors by the Venetians.

Alas, because of continuing restoration, authorities have decided that interior visits are dangerous and you can view the tower only from the outside.

✪ Ducal Palace and Bridge of Sighs (Palazzo Ducale and Ponte dei Sospiri). Piazzetta San Marco. ☎ **041/522-4951.** Admission (including admission to Museo Civico) 17,000L ($10) adults, 10,000L ($6) students with ID, 6,000L ($3.50) children 6–13; children 5 and under free. Apr–Oct daily 9am–7pm (to 5pm Nov–Mar). Vaporetto: San Marco.

You enter the Palace of the Doges through the magnificent 15th-century **Porta della Carta** at the piazzetta. This Venetian Gothic palazzo gleams in the tremulous light somewhat like a frosty birthday cake in pinkish-red marble and white Istrian stone. Italy's grandest civic structure, it dates to 1309, though a 1577 fire destroyed much of the original building. That fire made ashes of many of the palace's greatest masterpieces and almost spelled doom for the building itself, as the new architectural fervor of the post-Renaissance was in the air. However, sanity prevailed. Many of the greatest Venetian painters of the 16th century contributed to the restored palace, replacing the canvases or frescoes of the old masters.

If you enter from the piazzetta, past the four porphyry Moors, you'll be in the splendid Renaissance courtyard, one of the most recent additions to a palace that has benefited from the work of many architects with widely varying tastes. You can take the "giants' stairway" to the upper loggia—so called because of the two Sansovino statues of mythological figures.

After climbing the Sansovino stairway of gold you'll enter some get-acquainted rooms. Proceed to the **Sala di Anti-Collegio,** housing the palace's greatest works—notably Veronese's *Rape of Europa,* to the far left on the right wall. Tintoretto is well represented with his *Three Graces* and his *Bacchus and Ariadne.* Some critics consider the latter his supreme achievement. The ceiling in the adjoining **Sala del Collegio** bears allegorical paintings by Veronese. As you proceed to the right, you'll enter the **Sala del Senato o Pregadi,** with its allegorical painting by Tintoretto in the center of the ceiling.

It was in the **Sala del Consiglio dei Dieci,** with its gloomy paintings, that the dreaded Council of Ten (often called the Terrible Ten for good reason) used to assemble to decide who was in need of decapitation. In the antechamber, bills of accusation were dropped in the lion's mouth.

The excitement continues downstairs. You can wander through the once-private apartments of the doges to the grand **Maggior Consiglio,** with Veronese's allegorical

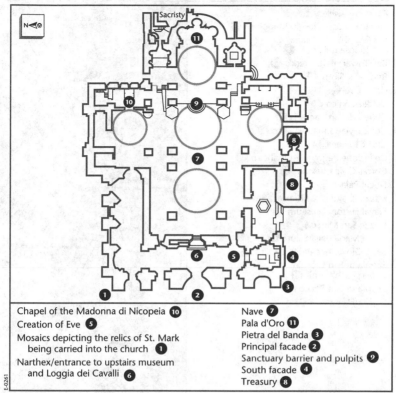

Chapel of the Madonna di Nicopeia **10**

Creation of Eve **5**

Mosaics depicting the relics of St. Mark being carried into the church **1**

Narthex/entrance to upstairs museum and Loggia dei Cavalli **6**

Nave **7**

Pala d'Oro **11**

Pietra del Banda **3**

Principal facade **2**

Sanctuary barrier and pulpits **9**

South facade **4**

Treasury **8**

Triumph of Venice on the ceiling. The most outstanding feature, however, is Tintoretto's *Paradise,* over the Grand Council chamber—said to be the world's largest oil painting. Paradise seems to have an overpopulation problem, perhaps reflecting Tintoretto's too-optimistic point of view (he was in his 70s when he began this monumental work and died 6 years later). The second grandiose hall, which you enter from the grand chamber, is the **Sala dello Scrutinio,** with paintings telling of Venice's past glories.

Reentering the Maggior Consiglio, follow the arrows on their trail across the **Bridge of Sighs (Ponte dei Sospiri),** linking the Doge's Palace with the Palazzo delle Prigioni. Here you'll see the cell blocks that once lodged the prisoners who felt the quick justice of the Terrible Ten. The "sighs" in the bridge's name stem from the sad laments of the numerous victims forced across it to face certain torture and possible death. The cells are somber remnants of the horror of medieval justice.

THE LIDO & THE GRAND CANAL
THE LIDO

Along the white sands of the **Lido** strolled Eleonora Duse and Gabriele d'Annunzio (*Flame of Life*), Goethe in Faustian gloom, a clubfooted Byron trying to decide with whom he was in love that day, Alfred de Musset pondering the fickle ways of George Sand, Thomas Mann's Gustave von Aschenbach with his eye on Tadzio in *Death in Venice,* and Evelyn Waugh's Sebastian Flyte and Charles Ryder with their eye on each

Venice Attractions

Church †

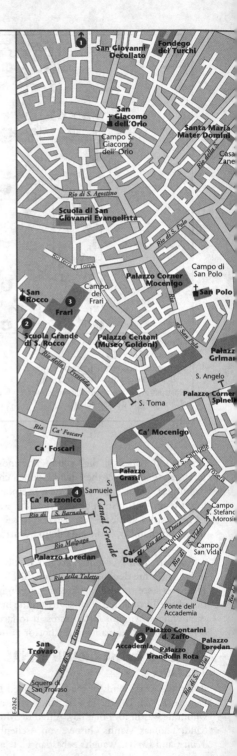

other in *Brideshead Revisited*. But gone is the relative isolation of yore. The de Mussets of today aren't mooning over lost loves—they're out chasing bikini-clad new ones.

Near the turn of the century, the Lido began to blossom into a fashionable beachfront resort, complete with deluxe hotels and its Casino Municipale (see "Venice After Dark," later in this chapter). However, as at other beachfront resorts throughout the world, you'll find that Lido prices are usually stratospheric.

The Lido is past its heyday. The chic of the world still patronize the Excelsior Palace and Hotel des Bains, but the beach strip is overrun with tourists and opens onto polluted waters. It's not just the beaches around Venice that are polluted but reputedly the entire Adriatic. For swimming, guests use the pools of their hotels instead. They can, however, still enjoy the Lido sands.

Even if you aren't planning to stay in this area, you should still come over and explore for an afternoon. If you don't want to tread on the beachfront property of the rarefied hotels (which have huts lining the beach like those of some tropical paradise), you can try the **Lungomare G. d'Annunzio (Public Bathing Beach)** at the end of the Gran Viale (Piazzale Ettore Sorger), a long stroll from the vaporetto stop. You can book cabins (*camerini*) and enjoy the sand. Rates change seasonally.

To reach the Lido, take vaporetto no. 1, 6, 52, or 82 (the ride takes about 15 minutes). The boat departs from a landing stage near the Doge's Palace.

✪ THE GRAND CANAL (CANAL GRANDE)

Peoria may have its Main Street, Paris its Champs-Elysées, New York City its Fifth Avenue—but Venice, for uniqueness, tops them all with its Canal Grande. Lined with palazzi (many in the Venetian Gothic style), this great road of water is filled with vaporetti, motorboats, and gondolas. The boat moorings are like peppermint sticks. The canal begins at Piazzetta San Marco on one side and Longhena's Salute Church opposite. At midpoint it's spanned by the Rialto Bridge. Eventually, the canal winds its serpentine course to the rail station.

Some of the most impressive buildings along the Grand Canal have been converted into galleries and museums. Others have been turned into cooperative apartments, but often the lower floors are now deserted. Venetian housewives aren't as incurably romantic as foreign visitors. A practical lot, these women can be seen stringing up their laundry to dry in front of thousands of tourists.

On one foggy day, Amandine Lucie Aurore Dudevant, née Dupin (otherwise known as George Sand), and her effete young lover, poet Alfred de Musset, arrived via this canal. John Ruskin debunked and exposed it in *The Stones of Venice*. Robert Browning, burnt out from the loss of his beloved Elizabeth and his later rejection at the hands of Lady Ashburton, settled down in a palazzo here, in which he eventually died. Eleonora Duse came this way with the young poet to whom she had given her heart, Gabriele d'Annunzio. Even Shakespeare came here in his fantasies. Intrepid guides will point out the "Palazzo de Desdemona."

The best way to see the Grand Canal is to board vaporetto no. 1 (push, shove, and gouge until you secure a seat at the front of the vessel). Settle yourself in, make sure you have your long-distance viewing glasses, and prepare yourself for a view that has thrilled even the hard-to-impress Ernest Hemingway, as well as millions of other visitors down through the ages.

MUSEUMS & GALLERIES

Venice is a city of art. Decorating its palazzi and adorning its canvases were artists like Giovanni Bellini, Carpaccio, Titian, Giorgione, Lotto, Tintoretto, Veronese, Tiepolo, Guardi, Canaletto, and Longhi, to name just the important ones. In the museums and galleries to follow, important works by all these artists are exhibited, as well as a number of modern surprises, such as those in the Guggenheim Collection.

✪ **Academy Gallery (Galleria dell'Accademia).** Campo della Carità, Dorsoduro. ☎ **041/522-2247.** Admission 12,000L ($7) adults; children 17 and under/seniors 60 and over free. Mon–Sat 9am–7pm, Sun 9am–2pm. Vaporetto: Accademia.

The pomp and circumstance, the glory that was Venice, lives on in this remarkable collection of paintings spanning the 13th to the 18th century. The hallmark of the Venetian school is color and more color. From Giorgione to Veronese, from Titian to Tintoretto, with a Carpaccio cycle thrown in, the Accademia has samples—often their best work—of its most famous sons. We highlight only some of the most-renowned masterpieces for the first-timer in a rush.

You'll first see works by such 14th-century artists as Paolo and Lorenzo Veneziano, who bridged the gap from Byzantine art to Gothic (see the latter's *Annunciation*). Next, you'll view Giovanni Bellini's *Madonna and Saint* (poor Sebastian, not another arrow) and Carpaccio's fascinating yet gruesome work of mass crucifixion. As you move on, head for the painting on the easel by the window, attributed to the great Venetian artist Giorgione. On this canvas he depicted the Madonna and Child, along with the mystic St. Catherine of Siena and John the Baptist (a neat trick for Catherine, who seems to have perfected transmigration to join the cast of characters).

Two of the most important works with secular themes are Mantegna's armored St. George, with the slain dragon at his feet, and Hans Memling's 15th-century portrait of a young man. A most unusual *Madonna and Child* is by Cosmé Tura, the master of Ferrara, who could always be counted on to give a new twist to an old subject.

The Madonnas and bambini of Giovanni Bellini, an expert in harmonious color blending, are the focus of another room. None but the major artists could stand the test of a salon filled with the same subject, but under Bellini's brush each Virgin achieves her individual spirituality. Giorgione's Tempest, displayed here, is the single most famous painting at the Accademia. It depicts a baby suckling from the breast of its mother, while a man with a staff looks on. What might've emerged as a simple pastoral scene by a lesser artist comes forth as rare and exceptional beauty. Summer lightning pierces the sky, but the tempest seems to be in the background—far away from the foreground figures, who are menaced without knowing it.

You can see the masterpiece of Lorenzo Lorto, a melancholy portrait of a young man, before coming to a room dominated by Paolo Veronese's *The Banquet in the House of Levi*. This is really a "Last Supper" but was considered a sacrilege in its day, so Veronese was forced to change its name to indicate a secular work. Impish Veronese caught the hot fire of the Inquisition by including dogs, a cat, midgets, Huns, and drunken revelers in the mammoth canvas. Four large paintings by Tintoretto—noted for their swirling action and powerful drama—depict scenes from the life of St. Mark. Finally, painted in his declining years (some have suggested in his 99th year, before he died from the plague) is Titian's majestic *Pietà*.

After an unimpressive long walk, search out Canaletto's *Porticato*. Yet another room is heightened by Gentile Bellini's stunning portrait of St. Mark's Square, back in the days (1496) when the houses glistened with gold in the sun. All the works in this salon are intriguing, especially the re-creation of the Ponte de Rialto and a covered wood bridge by Carpaccio.

Plan of the Accademia

Room	What You'll Find There
1	Venetian painters; 14th century
2	Giovanni Bellini and Cima da Conegliano
3	Late 15th century to early 16th century
4	Italian painters; 15th century
5	Giovanni Bellini and Giorgione
6	16th century
7	Lorenzo Lotto and GG Savoldo
8	Palma the Elder
9	16th-century schools of painting
10	Titian, Veronese, and Tintoretto
11	Veronese, Tintoretto, and GB Tiepolo
12	18th-century landscape painters
13	Tintoretto and Bassano
14	Renovators of the 17th century
15	Minor painters of the 18th century
16	Giambattista Piazzetta
17	Longhi, Camaletto, Carriera, and Guardi
18	18th-century painters and engravers
19	15th-century painters
20	Gentile Bellini and Vittorio Carpaccio
21	Vittorio Carpaccio
22	Bookshop
23	Venetian painters; 15th century
24	Albergo Room and Titian

Also displayed is the cycle of narrative paintings that Vittore Carpaccio did of St. Ursula for the Scuola of Santa Orsola. The most famous is no. 578, showing Ursula asleep on her elongated bed, with a dog nestled on the floor nearby, as the angels come for a visitation. Finally, on the way out, look for Titian's *Presentation of the Virgin*, a fit farewell to this galaxy of great Venetian art.

Correr Civic Museum (Museo Civico Correr). In the Procuratie Nuove, Piazza San Marco. ☎ **041/522-5625.** Admission (including admission to Ducal Palace) 17,000L ($10) adults, 10,000L ($6) students with ID, 6,000L ($3.50) children 6–13; children 5 and under free. Apr– Oct daily 9am–7pm (to 5pm Nov–Mar). Vaporetto: San Marco.

This museum traces the development of Venetian painting from the 14th to the 16th century. On the second floor are the red-and-maroon robes once worn by the doges, plus some fabulous street lanterns and an illustrated copy of *Marco Polo in Tartaria*. You can see Cosmé Tura's *Pietà*, a miniature of renown from the genius in the Ferrara School. This is one of his more gruesome works, depicting a bony, gnarled Christ sprawled on the lap of the Madonna. Farther on, search out Schiavone's *Madonna and Child* (no. 545), our candidate for ugliest bambino ever depicted on canvas (no wonder his mother looks askance).

A Note on Museum Hours

As throughout Italy, visiting hours in Venice's museums are often subject to major variations. Many visitors who have budgeted only 2 or 3 days for Venice often express disappointment when, for some unknown reason, a major attraction closes abruptly. When you arrive, check with the tourist office for a list of the latest open hours.

One of the most important rooms boasts three masterpieces: a *Pietà* by Antonello da Messina, a *Crucifixion* by Flemish Hugo van der Goes, and a *Madonna and Child* by Dieric Bouts, who depicted the baby suckling his mother in a sensual manner. The star attraction of the Correr is the Bellini salon, which includes works by founding padre Jacopo and his son, Gentile. But the real master of the household was the other son, Giovanni, the major painter of the 15th-century Venetian school (look for his *Crucifixion* and compare it with his father's treatment of the same subject). A small but celebrated portrait of St. Anthony of Padua by Alvise Vivarini is here, plus works by Bartolomeo Montagna. The most important work is Vittore Carpaccio's *Two Venetian Ladies*, though their true gender is a subject of much debate. In Venice they're popularly known as "The Courtesans." A lesser work, *St. Peter*, depicting the saint with the daggers in him, hangs in the same room.

The entrance is under the arcades of Ala Napoleonica at the western end of the square.

Ca' d'Oro. Calle Cadolo, Cannaregio 3934. ☎ **041/523-8790.** Admission 4,000L ($2.30); children 16 and under free. Daily 9am–1:30pm. Closed Jan 1, May 1, and Dec 25. Vaporetto: Ca' d'Oro.

The only problem with the use of this building as an art museum is the fact that the Ca' d'Oro is so opulent its architecture and decor compete with the works. It was built in the early 1400s, and its name translates as "House of Gold," though the gilding that once covered its facade eroded away long ago, leaving softly textured pink and white stone carved into lacy Gothic patterns. Historians compare its majesty to that of the Ducal Palace. The building was meticulously restored in the early 20th century by philanthropist Baron Franchetti, who attached it to a smaller nearby palazzo (Ca' Duodo), today part of the Ca' d'Oro complex. The interconnected buildings contain the Baron's valuable private collection of paintings, sculpture, and furniture, all donated to the Italian government during World War I.

You enter into a stunning courtyard, 50 yards from the vaporetto stop. The courtyard has a multicolored patterned marble floor and is filled with statuary. Proceed upstairs to the lavishly appointed palazzo. One of the gallery's major paintings is Titian's voluptuous *Venus*. She coyly covers one breast, but what about the other?

In a special niche reserved for the masterpiece of the Franchetti collection is Andrea Mantegna's icy-cold *St. Sebastian*, the central figure of which is riddled with what must be a record number of arrows. You'll also find works by Carpaccio. If you walk onto the loggia, you'll have one of the grandest views of the Grand Canal, a panorama that even inspired Lord Byron when he could take his eyes off the ladies.

Ca' Rezzonico. Fondamenta Rezzonico, Dorsoduro 3136. ☎ **041/241-0100.** Admission 12,000L ($7) adults, 8,000L ($4.65) children 12–18, 4,000L ($2.30) children 11 and under. Oct–Apr Sat–Thurs 10am–4pm (to 5pm May–Sept). Vaporetto: Ca' Rezzonico.

This 17th- and 18th-century palace along the Grand Canal is where Robert Browning set up his bachelor headquarters and eventually died in 1889. Pope Clement XIII also stayed here. It's a virtual treasure house, known for its baroque paintings and furniture. First you enter the Grand Ballroom with its allegorical ceiling, then proceed through lavishly embellished rooms with Venetian chandeliers, brocaded walls, portraits of patricians, tapestries, gilded furnishings, and touches of chinoiserie. At the end of the first walk is the Throne Room, with its allegorical ceilings by Giovanni Battista Tiepolo.

On the first floor you can walk out onto a balcony for a view of the Grand Canal as the aristocratic tenants of the 18th century saw it. Another group of rooms follows, including the library. In these salons, look for a bizarre collection of paintings: One, for example, depicts half-clothed women beating up a defenseless naked man (one Amazon is about to stick a pitchfork into his neck, another to crown him with a violin). In the adjoining room, another woman is hammering a spike through a man's skull.

Upstairs is a survey of 18th-century Venetian art. As you enter the main room from downstairs, head for the first salon on your right (facing the canal), which contains the best works, paintings from the brush of Pietro Longhi. His most famous work, *The Lady and the Hairdresser,* is the first canvas to the right on the entrance wall. Others depict the life of the idle Venetian rich. On the rest of the floor are bedchambers, a chapel, and salons—some with badly damaged frescoes, including a romp of satyrs.

✪ Collezione Peggy Guggenheim. In the Palazzo Venier dei Leoni, Calle San Cristoforo, Dorsoduro 701. ☎ **041/520-6288.** Admission 12,000L ($7) adults, 8,000L ($4.65) students/children 16 and under. Wed–Mon 11am–6pm. Vaporetto: Accademia.

This is one of the most comprehensive and brilliant modern-art collections in the Western world and reveals both the foresight and the critical judgment of its founder. The collection is housed in an unfinished palazzo, the former Venetian home of Peggy Guggenheim, who died in 1979. In the tradition of her family, Peggy Guggenheim was a lifelong patron of contemporary painters and sculptors. In the 1940s, she founded the Art of This Century Gallery in New York in the 1940s, one of the most avant-garde galleries for the works of contemporary artists. Critics were impressed not only by the high quality of the artists she sponsored but also by her methods of displaying them.

As her private collection increased, she decided to find a larger showcase and selected Venice, long a haven for artists. While the Solomon R. Guggenheim Museum was going up in New York City according to Frank Lloyd Wright's specifications, she was creating her own gallery here. You can wander through and enjoy art in an informal and relaxed way. Max Ernst was one of Peggy Guggenheim's early favorites (she even married him), as was Jackson Pollock (she provided a farmhouse where he could develop his painting technique). Displayed here are works not only by Pollock and Ernst but also by Picasso (see his 1911 cubist *The Poet*), Duchamp, Chagall, Mondrian, Brancusi, Delvaux, and Dalí, plus a garden of modern sculpture with works by Giacometti, some of which he struggled to complete while resisting the amorous intentions of Marlene Dietrich. Temporary modern-art shows may be presented during winter. Since Peggy Guggenheim's death, the collection has been administered by the Solomon R. Guggenheim Foundation, which also operates New York's Guggenheim Museum. In the new wing are a museum shop and a cafe, overlooking the sculpture garden.

Naval History Museum (Museo Storico Navale). Campo San Biasio, Castello 2148. ☎ **041/520-0276.** Admission 3,500L ($2.05). Mon–Sat 8:45am–1:30pm. Closed holidays. Vaporetto: Arsenale.

This museum is filled with cannons, ships' models, and fragments of old vessels dating to the days when Venice was supreme in the Adriatic. The prize exhibit is a gilded model of the *Bucintoro,* the great ship of the doge that surely would've made Cleopatra's barge look like an oil tanker. In addition, you'll find models of historic and modern fighting ships, local fishing and rowing craft, and a collection of 24 Chinese junks, as well as a number of maritime *ex voto* from churches of Naples.

If you walk along the canal as it branches off from the museum, you'll arrive at (about 270 yards from the museum and before the wooden bridge) the **Ships' Pavilion,** where historic vessels are displayed. Proceeding along the canal, you'll soon reach the **Arsenale,** Campo dell'Arsenale, guarded by stone lions, Neptune with a trident, and other assorted ferocities. You'll spot it readily enough because of its two towers flanking the canal. In its day, the Arsenale turned out galley after galley at speeds usually associated with wartime production.

CHURCHES & GUILD HOUSES

Much of the great art of Venice lies in its churches and *scuole* (guild houses or fraternities). Most of the guild members were drawn from the rising bourgeoisie. The guilds were said to fulfill both the material and the spiritual needs of their (male) members, who often engaged in charitable works in honor of the saint for whom their scuola was named. Many of Venice's greatest artists, including Tintoretto, were commissioned to decorate these guild houses. Some created masterpieces you can still see today. Narrative canvases that depicted the lives of the saints were called *teleri.*

✪ **Scuola di San Rocco.** Campo San Rocco, San Polo 3058. ☎ **041/523-4864.** Admission 8,000L ($4.65) adults, 6,000L ($3.50) students under 26, 3,000L ($1.75) children. Mar 28–Nov 2 daily 9am–5:30pm; Nov 3–Mar 27 Mon–Fri 10am–1pm, Sat–Sun 10am–4pm. Closed Easter and Dec 25–Jan 1. Vaporetto: San Tomà; from the station, walk straight onto Ramo Mondoler, which becomes Larga Prima; then take Salizzada San Rocco, which opens into Campo San Rocco.

Of all Venice's scuole, none is as richly embellished as this, filled with epic canvases by Tintoretto. Born Jacopo Robusti in 1518, he became known for paintings of mystical spirituality and phantasmagoric light effects. By a clever trick he won the competition to decorate this darkly illuminated early 16th-century building. He began painting in 1564, and the work stretched on until his powers as an artist waned; he died in 1594. The paintings sweep across the upper and lower halls, mesmerizing you with a kind of passion play. In the grand hallway they depict New Testament scenes, devoted largely to episodes in the life of Mary (the *Flight into Egypt* is among the best). In the top gallery are works illustrating scenes from the Old and New Testaments, the most renowned being those devoted to the life of Christ. In a separate room is Tintoretto's masterpiece: his mammoth *Crucifixion.* In it he showed his dramatic scope and sense of grandeur as an artist, creating a deeply felt scene that fills you with the horror of systematic execution, thus transcending its original subject matter.

Scuola di San Giorgio degli Schiavoni. Calle Furiani, Castello 3253A. ☎ **041/522-8828.** Admission 5,000L ($2.90). Tues–Sat 10am–12:30pm and 3–6pm, Sun 10am–12:30pm. Vaporetto: San Zaccaria.

At the St. Antonino Bridge (Fondamenta dei Furlani) is the second important guild house to visit. Between 1502 and 1509, Vittore Carpaccio painted a pictorial cycle here of exceptional merit and interest. Of enduring fame are his works of St. George and the dragon—these are our favorite art in all Venice and certainly the most delightful. For example, in one frame St. George charges the dragon on a field littered with half-eaten bodies and skulls. Gruesome? Not at all. Any moment you expect the director to call "Cut!" The pictures relating to St. Jerome are appealing but don't compete with St. George and his ferocious dragon.

Basilica di Santa Maria Gloriosa dei Frari. Campo dei Frari, San Polo. ☎ **041/ 522-2637.** Admission 3,000L ($1.75); free Sun. Mon–Sat 9–6pm, Sun 3–6pm. Vaporetto: San Tomà.

Known simply as the Frari, this Venetian Gothic church is only a short walk from the Scuola di San Rocco and is filled with some great art. The best work is Titian's *Assumption* over the main altar—a masterpiece of soaring beauty depicting the ascension of the Madonna on a cloud puffed up by floating cherubs. In her robe, but especially in the robe of one of the gaping saints below, "Titian red" dazzles as never before.

On the first altar to the right as you enter is Titian's second major work here—a *Madonna Enthroned,* painted for the Pesaro family in 1526. Although lacking the power and drama of the *Assumption,* it nevertheless is brilliant in its use of color and light effects. But Titian surely would turn redder than his Madonna's robes if he could see the latter-day neoclassical tomb built for him on the opposite wall. The kindest word for it: large.

Facing the tomb is a memorial to Canova, the Italian sculptor who led the revival of classicism. To return to more enduring art, head to the sacristy for a 1488 Giovanni Bellini triptych on wood; the Madonna is cool and serene, one of Bellini's finest portraits of the Virgin. Also see the almost primitive-looking wood carving by Donatello of St. John the Baptist.

Chiesa Madonna dell'Orto. Campo dell'Orto, Cannaregio 3512. ☎ **041/719-933.** Admission 2,000L ($1.15). Mon–Sat 10am–5:30pm, Sun 3–5:30pm. Vaporetto: Madonna dell'Orto.

This church provides a good reason to walk to this fairly remote northern district. At the church on the lagoon you'll be paying your final respects to Tintoretto. The brick structure with a Gothic front is famed not only because of its paintings by that artist but also because the great master is buried in the chapel to the right of the main altar. At the high altar are his *Last Judgment* (on the right) and *Sacrifice of the Golden Calf* (left)—monumental paintings curving at the top like a Gothic arch. Over the doorway to the right of the altar is Tintoretto's superb portrayal of the presentation of Mary as a little girl at the temple. The composition is unusual in that Mary isn't the focal point; rather, a pointing woman bystander dominates the scene.

The first chapel to the right of the main altar contains a masterly work by Cima de Conegliano, showing the presentation of a sacrificial lamb to the saints (the plasticity of St. John's body evokes Michelangelo). In first chapel on the left, as you enter, notice the large photo of Giovanni Bellini's *Madonna and Child.* The original, which was especially noteworthy for its depiction of the eyes and mouths of the mother and child, was stolen as part of a well-publicized 1994 theft, and pending the possibility of its hoped-for return, the photograph was installed in its place. Two other pictures in the apse are *The Presentation of the Cross to St. Peter* and *The Beheading of St. Christopher.*

Chiesa di San Zaccaria. Campo San Zaccaria, Castello. ☎ **041/522-1257.** Admission 2,000L ($1.15). Mon–Sat 10am–noon; daily 4–6pm. Vaporetto: San Zaccaria.

Behind St. Mark's Basilica is this Gothic church with a Renaissance facade. The church is filled with works of art, notably Giovanni Bellini's restored *Madonna Enthroned,* painted with saints (second altar to the left). Many have found this to be one of Bellini's finest Madonnas, and it does have beautifully subdued coloring, though it appears rather static. Many worthwhile works lie in the main body of the church, but for a view of even more of them, apply to the sacristan for entrance to the church's museum, housed in an area once reserved exclusively for nuns. Here you'll find works by Tintoretto, Titian, Il Vecchio, Anthony van Dyck, and Bassano. The paintings aren't labeled, but the sacristan will point out the names of the artists. In the Sisters' Choir are five armchairs in which the Venetian doges of yore sat. And if you save the best for last, you can see the faded frescoes of Andrea del Castagno in the shrine honoring San Tarasio.

Basilica di San Giorgio Maggiore. San Giorgio Maggiore, across from Piazzetta San Marco. ☎ **041/522-7827.** Free admission. Apr–Oct daily 9:30am–12:30pm and 2:30–6pm; Nov–Mar daily 10am–12:30pm and 2:30–4:30pm. Closed for Mass on Sunday and feast days 10:45am–noon. Vaporetto: Take the Giudecca-bound vaporetto (no. 82) on Riva degli Schiavoni and get off at the first stop, right in the courtyard of the church.

This church sits on the little island of San Giorgio Maggiore. The building was designed by Palladio, the great Renaissance architect—perhaps as a consolation prize since he wasn't chosen to rebuild the burnt-out Doge's Palace. The logical rhythm of the Vicenza architect is played here on a grand scale. But inside it's almost too stark since Palladio wasn't much on gilded adornment. The chief art hangs on the main altar: two epic paintings by Tintoretto, the *Full of Manna* to the left and the far more successful *Last Supper* to the right. It's interesting to compare Tintoretto's *Cena* with that of Veronese at the Accademia. Afterward you may want to take the elevator (for 3,000L/$1.75) to the top of the belfry for a view of the greenery of the island itself, the lagoon, and the Doge's Palace across the way. It's unforgettable.

Santa Maria della Salute. Campo della Salute, Dorsoduro. ☎ **041/523-7951.** Free admission (but offering is expected); sacristy 2,000L ($1.15). Mar–Nov daily 9am–noon and 3–6pm (to 5pm Dec–Feb). Vaporetto: Salute.

Like the proud landmark it is, La Salute—the pinnacle of the baroque movement in Venice—stands at the mouth of the Grand Canal overlooking Piazzetta San Marco and opening onto Campo della Salute. One of Venice's most historic churches, it was built by Longhena in the 17th century (work began in 1631) as an offering to the Virgin for delivering the city from the plague. Longhena, almost unknown when he got the commission, dedicated half a century to working on this church and died 5 years before the long-lasting job was completed. Surmounted by a great cupola, the octagonal basilica makes for an interesting visit, as it houses a small art gallery in its sacristy (tip the custodian), which includes a marriage feast of Cana by Tintoretto, allegorical paintings on the ceiling by Titian, a mounted St. Mark, and poor St. Sebastian with his inevitable arrow.

Santi Giovanni e Paolo Basilica. Campo SS. Giovanni e Paolo, Castello 6363. ☎ **041/ 523-5913.** Free admission. Daily 7:30am–12:30pm and 3–7:15pm. Vaporetto: Rialto or Fondamenta Nuove.

This church, also known as Zanipolo, is called the unofficial pantheon of Venice since it houses the tombs of many doges. The great Gothic church was built during the 13th and 14th centuries. Inside it contains work by many of the most noted Venetian painters. As you enter (right aisle), you'll find a retable by Giovanni Bellini (which includes a St. Sebastian filled with arrows). In the Rosary Chapel are ceilings by Veronese depicting New Testament scenes, including *The Assumption of the Madonna*. To the right of the church is one of the world's best-known equestrian statues—that of Bartolomeo Colleoni (paid for by the condottiere), sculpted in the 15th century by Andrea del Verrochio. The bronze has long been acclaimed as his masterpiece, though it was completed by another artist. The horse is far more beautiful than the armored military hero, who looks as if he had just stumbled on a three-headed crocodile.

To the left of the pantheon is the **Scuola di San Marco,** with a stunning Renaissance facade (it's now run as a civic hospital). The church requests that Sunday visits be of a religious nature, rather than for aesthetic purposes.

THE GHETTO

The Ghetto of Venice, called the ✪ **Ghetto Nuovo,** was instituted in 1516 by the Venetian Republic in the Cannaregio district. It's considered to be the first ghetto in the world and also the best kept. The word *geto* comes from the Venetian dialect and means "foundry." Originally there were two iron foundries here where metals were fused. The Ghetto stands in what's now the northwestern corner of Venice. Once Venetian Jews were confined to a walled area and obliged to wear distinctive red or yellow marks sewn onto their clothing and distinctive-looking hats. The walls that once enclosed and confined the Ghetto were torn down long ago, but much remains of the past.

There are five synagogues in Venice, each built during the 16th century and each representing a radically different aesthetic and cultural difference among the groups of Jews who built them. The oldest is the **Scola Tedesca** (German synagogue), restored after the end of World War II with funds from Germany. Others are the **Spanish** (the oldest continuously functioning synagogue in Europe), the **Italian,** the **Levantine-Oriental** (also known as the Turkish Synagogue), and the **Scuola Canton.**

The best way to visit the synagogues is to take one of the guided tours departing from the **Museo Comunità Ebraica,** Campo di Ghetto Nuovo 2902B (☎ 041/715-359). It contains a small but worthy collection of artifacts pertaining to the Jewish community of Venice but is by no means the focal point of your experience here: More worthwhile are the walking tours that begin and end at its premises. Tours last for 45 to 50 minutes each, incorporating a brisk commentary and stroll through the neighborhood and visits to the interior of three of the five synagogues. (The ones you visit depend on a series of factors like the scheduling of religious services, the availability of a rabbi, and the progress of renovations at the time of your visit.) Guided tours cost 12,000L ($7) adults and 9,000L ($5) students; children under 7 are free. They depart Sunday to Friday hourly between 10:30am and 3:30pm October to May and hourly between 10:30am and 5:30pm June to September. Participation in one of the tours includes free entrance to the museum.

If you want to visit just the museum (which is a lot less informative than participation in one of the tours), it will cost 5,000L ($2.90) adults and 3,000L ($1.75) students; children under 7 are free. The museum is open Sunday to Friday: June to September 10am to 7pm and October to May 10am to 4:30pm.

6 Organized Tours

Tours through the streets and canals of Venice are distinctly different from tours through other cities of Italy because of the complete absence of traffic. You can always wander at will through the labyrinth of streets, but many visitors opt for a guided tour to at least familiarize themselves with the geography of the city.

American Express, Calle San Moisè, San Marco 1471 (☎ 041/520-0844), which operates from a historic building a few steps from St. Mark's Square, offers an array of guided city tours. It's open for tours and travel arrangements Monday to Friday 9am to 5:30pm and Saturday 9am to 12:30pm. Here are some of the most popular offerings:

Daily at 9:10am, a 2-hour guided tour of the city departs from the front of the American Express building, costing 40,000L ($23). Sights include St. Mark's Square, the basilica, the Doge's Palace, the prison, and in some cases a demonstration of the art of Venetian glassblowing.

Daily between 3 and 5pm, a 2-hour guided tour incorporates visits to the exteriors of several palaces along Campo San Benetto and other sights of the city. The tour eventually crosses the Grand Canal to visit Santa Maria dei Frari (which contains the *Assumption* by Titian). The tour continues by gondola down the canal and eventually ends at the Rialto Bridge. The afternoon tour is 45,000L ($26), and the combined price for both tours is just 75,000L ($44).

The "Evening Serenade Tour," 50,000L ($29) per person, allows a nocturnal view of Venice accompanied by the sound of singing musicians in gondolas. From May to October there are two daily departures, 7 and 8pm, leaving from Campo Santa Maria del Giglio. Five to six occupants fit in each gondola. The experience lasts 50 minutes.

A "Tour of the Islands of the Venetian Lagoon," 25,000L ($15), departs twice daily, 9:30am and 2:30pm, and lasts 3 hours. You'll pass (but not land at) the islands of San Giorgio and San Francesco del Deserto and eventually land at Burano, Murano, and Torcello for brief tours of their churches and landmarks. This trip departs from and returns to the pier at Riva degli Schiavoni.

If you'd like more personalized tours, contact the **Venice Travel Advisory Service,** 22 Riverside Dr., New York, NY 10023 (☎ and fax **212/873-1964,** or 041/523-2379 in Venice). Born in New York City, Samantha Durell is a professional photographer who has lived and worked in Venice as a private tour guide for more than 10 years. Some locals claim she knows Venice far better than they do. She conducts orientation sessions and private walking tours day or night. She also assists with advance planning services and is an expert in making wedding arrangements for those who want to get married in Venice. Her expertise also includes advice on how to find out-of-the-way trattorie, where you can enjoy typical Venetian cuisine far away from the tourist hordes. In addition, she has a wealth of details about shopping, sightseeing, art, history, dining, and entertainment. Private guided tours are individually tailored to your needs.

Morning and afternoon tours, for a maximum of four people, last at least 4 to 5 hours and are $225 for two people, $50 for each additional adult, and $25 for each additional child.

For information on all-day boat tours of the villas along the **Brenta Canal,** see "The Riviera del Brenta & Its Villas" section in chapter 10.

7 Shopping

THE SHOPPING SCENE

Venetian glass and lace are known throughout the world. However, selecting quality products in either craft requires a shrewd eye, as there's much that's tawdry and shoddily crafted. Some of the glassware hawked isn't worth the cost of shipping it home. Yet other pieces represent some of the world's finest artistic and ornamental glass. Murano is the island famous for its handmade glass. However, you can find little glass animal souvenirs in shops all over Venice.

For lace, head out to Burano, where the last of a long line of women put in painstaking hours to produce some of the finest lace in the world.

TIPS ON SHOPPING FOR GLASS   Venice is literally crammed with glass shops: It's estimated there are at least 1,000 in the sestiere of San Marco alone. Unless you go to an absolutely top-quality reliable dealer, such as those we recommend, you'll find that most stores sell both shoddy and high-quality glassware and only the most trained eye can sometimes tell the difference. Note that a lot of so-called Venetian glass isn't from Venice at all but from former Eastern Bloc countries, like the Czech Republic. Of course, the Czech Republic has some of the finest glassmakers in Europe, so that may not be bad either. It boils down to this: If you like an item, buy it. It may not be high quality, but then high-quality glassware can cost thousands. If you're looking for an heirloom, stick to award-winning houses like Pauly & Co. and Venini. Even buyers of glassware for distribution in other parts of the world have been fooled by the vast array of glass for sale in Venice. And if even a buyer can be tricked, the layperson has only his or her own good instincts to follow.

TIPS ON SHOPPING FOR LACE   Most lace vendors center around Piazza San Marco. Although high, the prices of handmade Venetian lace are still reasonable considering the painstaking work that goes into the real thing. However, much of the lace is shoddy, and some of it—a lot of it, really—isn't lace handmade in Venice but machine-made lace done in who knows what country. The top name in Venetian lace is Jesurum (below), with its own lacemakers and even a school to teach apprentices how to make lace. It offers the most expensive, but also the highest quality, lace in Venice. At other places you just have to take your chances. The lace shops are like the glassware outlets, selling the whole gamut from the shoddy to the exquisite. Sometimes only the trained eye can tell the difference. However, even if a piece is handmade, you can never be sure exactly where it was handmade. Maybe China.

SHOPPING STROLLS   All the main shopping streets, even the side streets, are touristy and overrun. The greatest concentration of shops is around **Piazza San Marco** and the **Rialto Bridge.** Prices are much higher at San Marco, but the quality of merchandise is also higher. There are two major shopping strolls in Venice.

First, from **Piazza San Marco** you can stroll toward spacious **Campo Morosini.** You just follow one shop-lined street all the way to its end (though the name will change several times). You begin at Salizzada San Moisè, which becomes Via 22 Marzo, and then Calle delle Ostreghe, before it opens onto Campo Santa Maria Zobenigo. The street then narrows and changes to Calle Zaguri before widening once more into Campo San Maurizio, finally becoming Calle Piovan before reaching Campo Morosini. The only deviation from this tour is a detour down Calle Vallaressa, between San Moisè and the Grand Canal, which is one of the major shopping arteries with some of the biggest designer names in the business.

The other great shopping stroll wanders from Piazza San Marco to the Rialto in a succession of streets collectively known as the **Mercerie.** It's virtually impossible to get lost because each street name is preceded by the word *merceria,* like Merceria dell'Orologio, which begins near the clock tower in Piazza San Marco. Many commercial places, mainly shops, line the Mercerie before it reaches the Rialto, which then explodes into one vast shopping emporium.

SHOPPING A TO Z

ANTIQUES   Antichita Santomanco, Frezzeria, San Marco 1504 (☎ 041/523-6643), is for the specialist only—especially the well-heeled specialist. It deals in antique furniture, jewels, silver, prints, and old Murano glasses. Of course, the merchandise is ever-changing, but you're likely to pick up some little heirloom item in the midst of the clutter. Many of the items date from the Venetian heyday of the 1600s.

BOOKSTORES   The most centrally located is the **Libreria Sansovino,** Bacino Orseolo, San Marco 84 (☎ 041/522-2623), to the north of Piazza San Marco. It carries both hard- and softcover books in English. Near the American Express office is the **Libreria San Giorgio,** Calle Larga XXII Marzo, San Marco 2087 (☎ 041/523-8451), one of whose specialties is books on Venetian art, including Tiepolo.

BRASS   Founded in 1913, ✪ **Valese Fonditore,** Calle Fiubera, San Marco 793 (☎ 041/522-7282), serves as a showcase for one of the most famous of the several foundries with headquarters in Venice. Many of the brass copies of 18th-century chandeliers produced by this company grace fine homes in the United States, becoming valuable family heirlooms. One of the most appealing objects are the 50 or 60 replicas of the brass seahorses that grace the sides of many of the gondolas. A pair of medium-sized ones, each about 11 inches tall, begins at 320,000L ($186).

DOLLS The studio/shop **Bambole di Frilly,** Foundamenta dell'Osmarin, Castello 4974 (☎ 041/521-2579), offers dolls with meticulously painted porcelain faces (they call it a "biscuit") and hand-tailored costumes, including dressy pinafores. The reasonably priced low-end dolls are made with the same painstaking care, offering a real souvenir value. Prices begin at 28,000L ($16) and can go as high as 1,500,000L ($870).

FASHION **Belvest Boutique,** Calle Vallaresso, San Marco 1305, near Harry's Bar (☎ 041/528-7933), is one of Venice's finest boutiques, specializing in clothing for women and men, handmade and ready-to-wear. Fabric from some of the world's leading clothmakers is used in the designs. Linked with Vogini, the famous purveyor of leatherwork, the boutique is a bastion of top-quality craftsmanship and high-fashion style. In need of some new threads for the film festival? Then **La Bottega di Nino,** Mercerie dell'Orologio, San Marco 223 (☎ 041/522-5608), is the place for elegant cutting-edge male attire as stylish as anything you'll find in Milan's emporiums. It features the work of many European designers, even some from England, but shines brightest in its Italian names, such as Nino Cerruti and Zenia. The prices are also better for Italian wear.

Despite the similarity of its name, **La Fenice,** Calle Larga XXII Marzo, San Marco 2255 (☎ 041/523-1273), with one of Venice's most visible theaters, this is a large and well-stocked outlet for a stylish assortment of designers from throughout Europe. The most visible of several members of a city-wide chain, it sells women's clothing from designers like Mosquino, Thierry Mügler, German Rena Lang, and the well-received Turkish-born designer Osbek.

GIFTS If you never considered paper and stationery as a high art form, think again: **Il Papiro,** Campo San Maurizio, San Marco 2764 (☎ 041/522-3055), an upscale purveyor of the raw ingredients needed for elegant correspondence, is among the most sought-after in the world. Regardless of your personal literary style, whatever you compose is bound to look better (and make you feel better) if it's recorded on the high-fiber handprinted pages sold here. There's also a full supply of gift items, including photo albums, address books, picture frames, diaries, and boxes covered in artfully printed paper whose manufacturing techniques in some cases are hundreds of years old.

GLASS One of the oldest (founded in 1866) and largest purveyors of traditional Venetian glass is ✪ **Pauly & Co.,** Ponte Consorzi, San Marco 4392 (☎ 041/520-9899), whose labyrinth of showrooms—more than two dozen of them—is a highly visible part of Venice's commercial texture. Part of the premises is devoted to something akin to a museum, where past successes (now antiques) are displayed. Antique items are only rarely offered for sale, but they can be copied and shipped to virtually anywhere, and in the case of chandeliers, electrified in accordance with whatever electrical standards happen to be the norm. Chandeliers manufactured here range from the tasteful but conventional, beginning at about 2,000,000L ($1,160), but have frequently spiraled to as much as 1,000,000,000L ($580,000) in the case of some Saudi emirs who designed entire throne rooms around them.

The art glass sold by ✪ **Venini,** Piazzetta Leoncini, San Marco 314 (☎ 041/522-4045), has caught the attention of collectors from all over the world. Many of their pieces, including anything-but-ordinary lamps, bottles, and vases, are works of art representing the best of Venetian craftsmanship. Its best-known glass has a distinctive swirl pattern in several colors, called a venature. This shop is known for the refined quality of its glass, some of which appears almost transparent. Much of it is very fragile, but they learned long ago how to ship it anywhere safely. To visit the furnace, call ☎ 041/739-955.

Harking back to the days when they were used for trade in Venetian colonies, **Anticlea,** Campo San Provolo, Castello 4719 (☎ 041/528-6949), offers scores of antique and reproduction glass beads, strung or unstrung, in many sizes, shapes, and colors. **L'Isola,** Campo San Moisè, San Marco 1468 (☎ 041/523-1973), is the shop of Carlo Moretti, one of the world's best-known contemporary artisans working in glass. You'll find all his signature designs in decanters, drinking glasses, vases, bowls, and, of course, paperweights. On the island of Murano, home of the actual glassworks, the **Domus,** Fondamenta dei Vetrai 82, Murano (☎ 041/739-215), sells a good selection of designs by the island's top artisans. Prevalent are smaller objects like jewelry, vases, bowls, bottles, and drinking glasses. Here you'll find designs by Carlo Moretti.

Don't come to the **Galleria Marina Barovier,** Salizzada San Samuele, San Marco 3216 (☎ 041/523-6748), hoping to find a Murano-style glass trinket similar to the thousands of others sold around Venice, as it's the repository for some of the most creative modern glass sculptures in Italy. Since it was opened in the early 1980s by its namesake, Marina Barovier, in the unlikely Venetian suburb of Mestre, it has grown until today it's viewed by connoisseurs as one of the most glamorous art galleries in the world of contemporary glassmaking. Especially sought after are sculptures by master glassmakers Lino Tagliapietra and Dale Chihuely, whose chandeliers represent amusing and/or dramatic departures from traditional Venetian forms. Don't despair if you're on a budget, as some simple items begin as low as 20,000L ($12). Anything sold can be shipped. At **Vetri d'Arte,** Piazza San Marco 140 (☎ 041/520-0205), you can find moderately priced glass jewelry for souvenirs and gifts, as well as a selection of pricier crystal jewelry and porcelain bowls.

GRAPHICS   Bac Art Studio, Campo San Maurizio, San Marco 2663 (☎ 041/522-8171), sells paper goods, but it's mainly a graphics gallery, noted for its selection of engravings, posters, and lithographs representing Venice at Carnevale time. Items for the most part are reasonably priced, and it's clear that a great deal of care and selection have gone into the gallery's choice of merchandise. Head to **Osvaldo Böhm,** San Moisè, San Marco 1349–1350 (☎ 041/522-2255), for that just the right—and light—souvenir of Venice. Osvaldo Böhm has a rich collection of photographic archives specializing in Venetian art as well as original engravings and maps, lithographs, watercolors, and Venetian masks. You can also see modern serigraphs by local artists and some fine handcrafted bronzes.

HANDCRAFTS   In one showroom, **Veneziartigiana,** Calle Larga, San Marco 412–413 (☎ 041/523-5032), assembles the artisanal production of at least 11 local craftspeople, whose creations in silver, glass, ceramics, wood, and copper. Look for well-executed dolls, Carnevale masks, picture frames, and posters, any of which would make a well-received gift for relatives or friends back home.

JEWELRY   Since 1846, ✪ **Missiaglia,** Piazza San Marco 125 (☎ 041/522-4464), has been the private supplier to rich Venetians and savvy shoppers from around the world seeking the best in gold and jewelry. Go here for that special classic piece. But, as the family-owners keep a sharp watch on the latest developments in international jewelry design, something a little more cutting edge might catch your eye. Their specialty is colored precious and semiprecious gemstones set in white or yellow gold settings.

Venetian Carnevale Masks

Venetian masks, considered collectors' items, originated during Carnevale, which takes place the week before the beginning of Lent. In the old days there was a good reason to wear masks during the riotous Carnival, as they helped wives and husbands be unfaithful to one another and priests break their vows of chastity. Things got so out of hand that Carnevale was banned in the late 18th century. But it came back—and the masks went on again.

You can find shops selling masks practically on every corner. As with glass and lace, however, quality varies. Many masks are great artistic expressions, whereas others are shoddy and cheap. The most sought-after mask is the *Portafortuna* (luck bringer), with its long nose and birdlike visage. *Orientale* masks evoke the heyday of the Serene Republic and its trade with the Far East. The *Bauta* was worn by men to assert their macho qualities, and the *Neutra* blends the facial characteristics of both sexes. The list of masks and their origins seem endless.

The best place to buy Carnevale masks is the **Laboratorio Artigiano Maschere,** Castello 6657, Barbaria delle Tole (☎ **041/522-3110**), which sells handcrafted masks in papier-mâché or leather. This well-established store has a particularly good selection, including masks depicting characters of the Commedia dell'Arte. The shop also sells a variety of other handcrafted papier-mâché items, like picture and mirror frames, pots, consoles, and boxes in the shape of pets.

Also good is **Mondonovo,** Rio Terrà Canal, Dorsoduro 3063 (☎ **041/ 528-7344**), where talented artisans labor to produce copies of both traditional and more modern masks, each of which is one-of-a-kind and richly nuanced with references to Venetian lore and traditions. Prices range from 30,000L ($17) for a fairly basic model to 3,000,000L ($1,740) for something you might display on a wall as a piece of sculpture.

LACE   For serious purchases, ✪ **Jesurum,** Mercerie del Capitello, San Marco 4857 (☎ **041/520-6177**), is tops. This elegant shop, a center of noted lacemakers and fashion creators, has been located in a 12th-century church since 1868. You'll find Venetian handmade or machine-made lace and embroidery on table, bed, and bath linens as well as hand-printed swimsuits. Quality and originality are guaranteed and special orders accepted. The exclusive linens created here are expensive, but the inventory is large enough to accommodate many budgets. Staff members insist that everything sold is made in or around Venice in traditional patterns, with almost no emphasis on imports from China or other parts of Asia.

LEATHER   ✪ **Marforio,** Campo San Salvador, San Marco 5033 (☎ **041/ 522-5734**), was founded in 1875 and is Italy's oldest and largest leather-goods retail outlet, run by the same family for five generations. It's known for the quality of its leather products, and the outlet here has an enormous assortment, with all the famous European labels—Valentino, Armani, Ferré, and Cardin, among others. **Bottega Veneta,** Calle Vallaresso, San Marco 1337 (☎ **041/520-2816**), is primarily known for its woven leather bags. They're sold elsewhere, but the prices are said to be less at the company's flagship outlet in Venice. The shop also sells women's shoes, suitcases, belts, and a wide array of high-fashion accessories. Men will enjoy the assortment of leather wallets.

Furla, Mercerie del Capitello, San Marco 4954 (☎ 041/523-0611), is a specialist in women's leather bags but sells belts and gloves as well. Many of the bags are stamped with molds, creating alligator- and lizard-like textures. These bags come in a varied choice of colors, including what the Austrians call "Maria Theresa ocher." You'll also find a varied selection of costume jewelry, plus silk scarves, briefcases, and wallets. Every kind of leather work is offered at **Vogini,** Ascensione, San Marco 1291, 1292, and 1301, near Harry's Bar (☎ 041/522-2573), especially women's handbags, which are exclusive models. There's also a large assortment of handbags in petit-point embroideries and in crocodile, plus an assortment of men's and women's shoes. Brand names include works by Armani, Mosquino, and Versace, plus products designed and manufactured by Vogini itself. The travel-equipment department contains trunks and both hard- and soft-sided suitcases, as well as makeup cases.

MARKETS If you're looking for some bargain-basement buys, head not for any basement but to one of the little shops lining the **Rialto Bridge.** The shops there branch out to encompass fruit and vegetable markets as well. The Rialto isn't the Ponte Vecchio in Florence, but for what it offers it isn't bad, particularly if your lire are running short. You'll find a wide assortment of merchandise, from angora sweaters to leather gloves. The quality is likely to vary widely, so plunge in with the utmost discrimination.

PAPER Florence is still the major center in Italy for artistic paper—especially marbleized paper. However, craftspeople in Venice still make marble paper by hand, sheet by sheet. Except for France, marbling had largely disappeared with the coming of the Industrial Revolution, but it was revived in Venice in the 1970s. The technique offers unlimited decorative possibilities and the widest range of possible colors (craftspeople are called "color alchemists"). Each sheet of handmade marbleized paper is one of a kind.

One of Venice's most stylish purveyors of paper and writing supplies is **Piazzesi,** Campieillo della Feltrina, San Marco 2511 (☎ 041/522-1202), claiming to be the oldest purveyor of writing paper in Italy. Established in 1900, it sells elegant versions of stationery that require as many as 13 artisans to produce. Most of the production is hand-blocked, marbleized, stenciled, and/or accented with dyes that are blown onto each of the sheets with a breath-operated tube. In other words, if you want impressive paper for your social thank-you notes or wedding invitations, Piazzesi will undoubtedly have it in stock. Also look for papier-mâché masks and Commedia dell'Arte–style statues representing age-old professions like architects, carpenters, doctors, glassmakers, church officials, and notaries. Seeking for something more modern? Consider any of the whimsically decorated containers for CDs and computer disks.

8 Venice After Dark

For such a fabled city, Venice's nightlife is pretty meager. Who wants to hit the nightclubs when strolling the city at night is more interesting than any spectacle staged inside? Ducking into a cafe or bar for a brief interlude, however, is a good way to break up your evening walk. Although it offers gambling and a few other diversions, Venice is pretty much an early-to-bed town. Most restaurants close at midnight.

The best guide to what's happening is **"Un Ospite di Venezia,"** a free pamphlet (part in English, part in Italian) distributed by the tourist office every 15 days. It lists any music and opera or theatrical presentations, along with art exhibits and local special events.

At least 10 of Venice's historic churches are used for the presentation of **musical concerts,** according to a schedule that varies according to whatever musical group wishes to be heard. Foremost among the churches that present concerts are the Chiesa di Vivaldi, the Chiesa della Pietà, and the Chiesa Santa Maria Formosa. Many concerts are free; others charge an admission that rarely exceeds 20,000L ($12). For information about what might be playing at the time of your visit, call ☎ 041/520-8722.

THE PERFORMING ARTS

In January 1996, a dramatic fire left the fabled **Teatro de La Fenice** at Campo San Fantin, the city's main venue for performing arts, a blackened shell and a smoldering ruin. Opera lovers around the world, including Luciano Pavarotti, mourned its loss. The Italian government has pledged $12.5 million for its reconstruction. The theater's neoclassical facade survived the blaze and is the subject of sightseeing interest today. Optimistic predictions suggest that the theater will reopen around the millennium.

Despite the tragic loss of La Fenice, cultural events have continued, in a less glamorous form, in a temporary theater built as a short-term substitute. Designed in the form of a big circus-style tent, within walking distance of Piazzale Roma, is the **Teatro Temporaneo de La Fenice** (also known as **PalaFenice**), Isola Tronchetto (☎ 041/521-0161). For a list of other cultural performances in Venice, contact either the tourist office or City Hall, **Comunale Municipio di Venezia** at ☎ 041/274-8200.

The **Teatro Goldoni,** Calle Goldoni, near Campo San Luca, San Marco 4650B (☎ 041/520-7583), close to the Ponte di Rialto, honors Carlo Goldoni (1707 to 1793), the most prolific and one of the best Italian playwrights. The theater presents a changing repertoire of productions, often plays in Italian, but musical presentations as well. The box office is open Monday to Saturday 10am to 1pm and 4:30 to 7pm, and tickets are 18,000L to 66,000L ($10 to $38).

CAFES

Venice's most famous is ✪ **Caffè Florian,** Piazza San Marco 56–59 (☎ 041/528-5338), built in 1720. It remains romantically decorated—pure Venetian salons with red plush banquettes, elaborate murals under glass, and art nouveau lighting. It's the most fashionable rendezvous in Venice: The Florian roster of customers has included Casanova, Lord Byron, Goethe, Canova, de Musset, and Mme de Staël. Light lunch is served noon to 3pm, costing 20,000L ($12) and up, and an English tea 3 to 6pm, when you can select from a choice of pastries, ice creams, and cakes. It's open Thursday to Tuesday 9:30am to 11:30pm.

Previously recommended as a restaurant, ✪ **Quadri,** Piazza San Marco 120–124 (☎ 041/522-2105), stands on the opposite side of the square from the Florian and is as elegantly decorated in antique style. It should be, as it was founded in 1638. Wagner used to drop in for a drink when he was working on *Tristan und Isolde*. The bar was a favorite with the Austrians during their long-ago occupation. It's open Wednesday to Sunday noon to 2:30pm and 7 to 10:30pm.

The 18th-century **Gran Caffè Lavena,** Piazza San Marco 133–134 (☎ 041/522-4070), is a popular but intimate cafe under the arcades of Piazza San Marco. During his stay in Venice, Richard Wagner was a frequent customer; he composed some of his greatest operas here. It has one of the most beautifully ornate glass chandeliers in town. The most interesting tables are near the plate-glass window in front, though there's plenty of room at the stand-up bar as well. It's open daily 9:30am to

12:30am (closed for a few days in January and in November and on Thursday in winter).

BARS & PUBS

Want more in the way of nightlife? All right, but be warned: The Venetian bar owners may sock it to you when they present the bill.

The single most famous of all the watering holes of Ernest Hemingway, ❂ **Harry's Bar,** Calle Vallaresso, San Marco 1323 (☎ **041/528-5777**), is known for inventing its own drinks and exporting them around the world. It's also said that carpaccio, the delicate raw-beef dish, was invented here. Fans say that Harry's makes the best Bellini in the world, yet many old-time visitors still prefer a vodka martini. Harry's Bar is now found around the world, but this is the original. Except for a restaurant, Harry Cipriani, in New York City, the other bars are unauthorized knockoffs. Celebrities frequent the place during the various film and art festivals. Harry's is open daily 10:30am to 1am April to October, to 11pm in winter.

Bar ai Speci, in the Hotel Panada, Calle dei Specchieri, San Marco 646 (☎ **041/520-9088**), is a charming corner bar only a short walk from St. Mark's. Its richly grained paneling is offset by dozens of antique mirrors, each different, whose glittering surfaces reflect the rows of champagne and scotch bottles and the clustered groups of Biedermeier chairs. It's open Tuesday to Sunday 5:30pm to midnight. **Bar Ducale,** Calle delle Ostreghe, San Marco 2354 (☎ **041/521-0002**), occupies a tiny corner of a building near a bridge over a narrow canal. Customers stand at the zinc bar facing the carved 19th-century Gothic-reproduction shelves. Mimosas are the specialty, but tasty sandwiches are also offered. It's ideal for an early-evening aperitif as you stroll about. The ebullient owner learned his craft at Harry's Bar before going into business for himself. Bar Ducale is open daily 9am to 9pm.

A stone's throw from the Rialto Bridge, **Devil's Forest,** Calle Stagneri, San Marco 5185 (☎ **041/520-0623**), is an authentic Irish pub where you'll find a comfortable balance between the English- and Italian-speaking worlds. There's a comfortingly predictable roster of beers and ales on tap (Guinness, Harp, Kilkenny, and a line of German beers) and platters of food at about 8,000L to 12,000L ($4.65 to $7). Don't expect bangers and mash or steak-and-kidney pie, as things are more Mediterranean than that, with an emphasis on sandwiches, pastas, and simple grills. It's open daily 10am to 1am. Five minutes from the Rialto Bridge, **Fiddler's Elbow,** Corte dei Pali, Cannaregio 3847 (☎ **041/523-9930**), is called the "Irish pub" by the Venetians and is run by the same people who operate the equally popular Fiddler's Elbow in Florence and Rome. It has the only satellite TV in Venice with all channels—Sky, American, sports, music, whatever. In summer, there's live outdoor music. It's open daily 5pm to 12:30am.

Do Leoni is in the Londra Palace hotel, Riva degli Schiavoni, Castello 4171 (☎ **041/520-0533**). The interior is a rich blend of scarlet-and-gold carpeting with a lion motif, English pub-style furniture, and Louis XVI–style chairs, along with plenty of exposed mahogany. While sipping your cocktail, you'll enjoy a view of a 19th-century bronze statue, the lagoon, and the foot traffic along the Grand Canal. A piano player entertains Monday to Saturday. Do Leoni is open daily noon to 3pm and 7:30 to 11pm, bar open 10am to 1am. Venice's oldest pastry shop, **Guanotto,** Ponte del Lovo, San Marco 4819 (☎ **041/520-8439**), is a gelateria/pasticceria/bar. It's said to have virtually invented the spritzer, a combination of soda water, bitters, and white wine. Its drinks and cocktails are renowned, though enjoying a cappuccino here can take the chill off a rainy day in Venice as well. Guanotto is open Monday to Saturday 7:30am to 9:30pm.

WINE BARS

The historic **Cantina do Spade,** Calle do Spade, San Polo 860 (☎ **041/521-0574**), beneath an arcade near the main fish-and-fruit market, dates from 1475 and was once frequented by Casanova. The place is completely rustic and bare-bones, but devotees come to order chicchetti, the equivalent of Spanish tapas. Though there's no menu, the kitchen will occasionally turn out typical Venetian fare. Many diners prefer to order one of the 250 sandwiches the kitchen is usually willing to prepare. Venetians delight in the 220 types of wine; glasses begin at 1,500L (85¢). Don't come looking for glamour; head for Harry's Bar (see above) if that's what you're after. Cantina do Spade is open daily 7am to 3pm and 5pm to 1:30am.

Mascareta, Calle Lunga Santa Maria Formosa, Castello 5138 (☎ **041/523-0744**), opened in 1995 as a showcase for the rich assortment of Italian wines. Especially prevalent are reds and whites from the Veneto, Sicily, Apulia, and Tuscany, beginning at 2,000L ($1.15) per glass. There's only room for about 20 people at the cramped tables in this antique building. No hot food is served, but if you're hungry, you can order simple platters of cold food, from 12,000L to 18,000L ($7 to $10). It's open daily 6:30pm to 1am (closed mid-December to mid-January).

At **Vino Vino,** Calle del Caffettier, San Marco 2007A (☎ **041/523-7027**), you can choose from more than 250 Italian and imported wines. This place is loved by everyone from snobs to young people to almost-broke tourists. It offers wines by the bottle or glass, including Italian grappas. Popular Venetian dishes are served, including pastas, beans, baccalà (codfish), and polenta. The two rooms are always jammed like a vaporetto in rush hour, and there's takeout service if you can't find a place. Main courses are priced around 15,000L ($9). It's open daily noon to 11pm.

DINING & DANCING

Near the Accademia, **Il Piccolo Mondo,** Calle Contarini Corfu, Dorsoduro 1056A (☎ **041/520-0371**), is open during the day and at night features disco dancing and organized parties. The crowd is often young, and dance music prevails. It's open Thursday to Tuesday 10pm to 4am, but the action actually doesn't begin until after midnight. Cover, including the first drink, is 12,000L ($7) Thursday and Friday and 18,000L ($10) Saturday.

The **Martini Scala Club,** Campo San Fantin, San Marco 1980 (☎ **041/ 522-4121**), is an elegant restaurant with a piano bar. You can enjoy its food and wine until 2am—it's the only kitchen that stays open late. Dishes include smoked goose breast with grapefruit and arugula, fresh salmon with black butter and olives, or gnocchi (dumplings) with butter and sage. The piano bar gets going after 10pm. It's possible to order drinks without having food. The restaurant is open Thursday to Monday noon to 2:30pm and 7 to 11:30pm and Wednesday 7 to 11:30pm. Main courses begin at 36,000L ($21); a fixed-price dinner is 72,000L ($42) for four courses. The bar, which offers a piano bar and food, is open Wednesday to Monday 10pm to 3:30am.

Early every evening except Wednesday, **Paradiso Perduto,** Fondamenta della Misericordia, Cannaregio 2540 (☎ **041/720-581**), functions as a likable tavern, serving well-prepared platters of seafood. If you're interested in dining (the frittura mista of fish with polenta is wonderful), main courses are 8,000L to 25,000L ($4.65 to $15) and are served Thursday to Tuesday 7 to 10:30pm. But the place's real heart and soul emerge after 11pm, when a mix of soft recorded music and live piano music creates a backdrop for animated dialogues between the neighborhood crowd and visitors. The chitchat continues until at least 2am.

GAY CLUBS

There isn't much gay nightlife in Venice, certainly nothing conspicuous. There is, however, a local division of a government-affiliated agency, **ArciGay ArciLesbica,** Campo S. Giacomo dell'Orio, Santa Croce 1507 (☎ 041/721-197). It serves as a kind of home base for the gay community, with info on AIDS services, gay-friendly accommodations, and such. The best hours to call (it's hard to find) are Wednesday, Thursday, and Saturday 6 to 10pm.

CASINOS

Venice is home to two casinos, at least one of which is operational according to the changing seasons. The larger and busier of the two, the Casino Municipale, lies beside the flat, sandy expanses of the Lido, an isolated island in the Venetian lagoon that's almost deserted in winter and mobbed in summer. As cold winds descend on Venice from the Alps in winter, the action moves back to the center of town, to a smaller, cozier venue known as the Vendramin-Calergi Palace.

Regardless of where you might happen to drop your lire, know in advance that a jacket (but not a tie) is requested for men, and basketball sneakers and/or shorts are forbidden. Both contain slot machines, but more interesting are the roulette wheels, where minimum bets are 10,000L ($6) and maximum wagers 360,000L ($209).

If you want to risk your luck and your lire, take a vaporetto ride on the Casino Express, which leaves from stops at the rail station, Piazzale Roma, and Piazzetta San Marco and delivers you to the landing dock of the **Casino Municipale,** Lungomare G. Marconi 4, Lido (☎ 041/529-7111). The Italian government wisely forbids its nationals to cross the threshold unless they work here, so bring your passport. The building itself is foreboding, looking as if it had been inspired by Mussolini-era architects. Don't worry—the mood changes once you step inside. You can try your luck at blackjack, roulette, baccarat, or whatever. You can also dine, drink at the bar, or enjoy a floor show. Admission is 18,000L ($10), and it's open May to October, daily 3pm to 2:30am.

November to April, the casino action moves to the 15th-century **Vendramin-Calergi Palace,** Strada Nuova, Cannaregio 2040 (☎ 041/529-7111). Incidentally, in 1883 Wagner died in this house, which opens onto the Grand Canal. Admission is 18,000L ($10), and it's open September to mid-May, daily 3pm to 2:30am. Only slot machines are maintained during summer, at the same hours.

9 Side Trips from Venice: Murano, Burano & Torcello

MURANO

Murano is the island where for centuries glassblowers have turned out those fantastic chandeliers Victorian ladies used to prize so highly. They also produce heavily ornamented glasses so ruby-red or so indigo-blue you can't tell if you're drinking blackberry juice or pure grain alcohol. Happily, the glassblowers are still plying their trade, though increasing competition (notably from Sweden) has compelled a greater degree of sophistication in design.

Murano remains the chief expedition from Venice, but it's not the most beautiful nearby island. (Burano and Torcello are far more attractive.)

You can combine a tour of Murano with a trip along the lagoon. To reach it, take vaporetto no. 12 or 13 at Riva degli Schiavoni, a short walk from Piazzetta San Marco. The boat docks at the landing platform at Murano where the first furnace awaits conveniently. It's best to go Monday to Friday 10am to noon if you want to see some glassblowing action.

Touring the Glass Factories & Other Sights

As you stroll through Murano, you'll find that the factory owners are only too glad to let you come in and see their age-old crafts. While browsing through the showrooms, you'll need stiff resistance to keep the salespeople at bay. Bargaining is expected. Don't—repeat *don't*—pay the marked price on any item. That's merely the figure at which to open negotiations.

However, the prices of made-on-the-spot souvenirs aren't negotiable. For example, you may want to buy a horse streaked with blue. The artisan takes a piece of incandescent glass, huffs, puffs, rolls it, shapes it, snips it, and behold—he has shaped a horse. The showrooms of Murano also contain a fine assortment of Venetian crystal beads, available in every hue. You may find some of the best work to be the experiments of apprentices.

While on the island, you can visit the Renaissance palazzo housing the **Museo Vetrario di Murano,** Fondamenta Giustinian (☎ 041/739-586), which contains a spectacular collection of Venetian glass. It's open Monday, Tuesday, and Thursday to Saturday: April to October 10am to 5pm (to 4pm November to March). Admission is 8,000L ($4.65) adults and 5,000L ($2.90) students; children under 10 are free.

If you're looking for a respite from the glass factories, head to **San Pietro Martire,** Fondamente Vetrai (☎ 041/739-704), which dates from the 1300s but was rebuilt in 1511 and is richly decorated with paintings by Tintoretto and Veronese. Its proud possession is a *Madonna and Child Enthroned* by Giovanni Bellini, plus two superb altarpieces by the same master. The church lies right before the junction with Murano's Grand Canal, about 250 yards from the vaporetto landing stage. It's open daily 9am to noon and 3 to 6pm; closed for Mass on Sunday morning.

Even more notable is **Santa Maria e Donato,** Campo San Donato (☎ 041/739-056), open daily 9am to noon and 4 to 6pm with time variations for Sunday Mass. This building is a stellar example of Venetian Byzantine style, despite its 19th-century restoration. It dates from the 7th century but was reconstructed in the 1100s. The interior is known for its mosaic floor—a parade of peacocks and eagles, as well as other creatures—and a 15th-century ship's-keel ceiling. Over the apse is an outstanding mosaic of the Virgin against a gold background from the early 1200s.

Dining

Ai Vetrai. Fondamenta Manin 29. ☎ **041/739-293.** Reservations recommended. Main courses 17,000–30,000L ($10–$17). DC, MC, V. Fri–Wed 1–4pm. Closed Dec 15–Jan 5. Vaporetto: No. 52 from Central Venice. VENETIAN.

Ai Vetrai entertains and nourishes its guests in a large room not far from the Canale dei Vetrai. If you're looking for fish prepared in the local style, with what might be called the widest selection on Murano, this is it. Most varieties of crustaceans and gilled creatures are available on the spot. However, if you phone ahead and order food for a large party, as the Venetians sometimes do, the owners will prepare what they call "a noble fish." You might begin with spaghetti in green clam sauce and follow with griglia misto di pesce, a dish that combines all the seafood of the Adriatic or other types of grilled or baked fish accented with vegetables.

Al Corallo. Fondamenta dei Vetrai 73. ☎ **041/739-080.** Main courses 15,000–25,000L ($9–$15); fixed-price menu 18,000L ($10). AE, DC, MC, V. Wed–Mon noon–3pm and 7–10pm. Closed mid-Dec to mid-Jan (dates vary). Vaporetto: 52 to Murano from central Venice. VENETIAN.

Intimate and unpretentious and somewhat isolated from the hustle and bustle of the larger islands, the Al Corallois is family-run. Very little English is spoken, but the place is usually filled with a wide variety of patrons. Specialties are typically Venetian, like roasted veal and deep-fried mixed fish, and the service is polite. Locals, many of them workers at the nearby glass factories, choose this for a well-deserved meal after a morning of hard physical labor. The menu changes daily, according to whatever's available in the markets.

BURANO

Burano became world famous as a center of lacemaking, a craft that reached its pinnacle in the 18th century (recall Venetian point?). The visitor who can spare a morning to visit this island will be rewarded with a charming fishing village far removed in spirit from the grandeur of Venice but only half an hour away by ferry. Boats leave from Fondamente Nuove, overlooking the Venetian graveyard (which is well worth the trip all on its own). To reach Fondamente Nuove, take vaporetto no. 12 or 52 from Riva degli Schiavoni.

EXPLORING THE ISLAND

Once at Burano, you'll discover that the houses of the islanders come in varied colors—sienna, robin's-egg or cobalt blue, barn red, butterscotch, grass green. If you need a focal point for your excursion, it should be the **Scuola di Merletti di Burano,** "Museo del Merletto," S. Martino Destra 183 (☎ 041/730-034), in the center of the village at Piazza Baldassare Galuppi. The museum is open Wednesday to Monday: November to March 10am to 4pm and April to October 10am to 5pm. Admission is 5,000L ($2.90) adults and 3,000L ($1.75) students 6-12; children 5 and under are free. The Burano School of Lace was founded in 1872 as part of a movement aimed at restoring the age-old craft that had earlier declined, giving way to such lacemaking centers as Chantilly and Bruges. On the second floor you can see the lacemakers, mostly young women, at their painstaking work and can purchase hand-embroidered or handmade lace items.

After visiting the lace school, walk across the square to the **Duomo** and its leaning campanile (inside, look for the *Crucifixion* by Tiepolo). However, do so at once, because the bell tower is leaning so precariously it looks as if it may topple at any moment.

DINING

Ostaria ai Pescatori. Piazza Baldassare Galuppi 371. ☎ **041/730-650.** Reservations recommended. Main courses 22,000–30,000L ($13–$17). AE, MC, V. Thurs–Tues noon–3pm and 6–9:30pm. Closed Dec 25–Jan 25. Vaporetto: Line 12 or 52. SEAFOOD.

One of the most idiosyncratic restaurants on Burano, it opened 200 years ago in a building that was antique even then. Today, Paolo Torcellan and his wife are the gracious owners, serving a cuisine prepared with gusto by his stalwart mother, Iolanda, a matriarch in her 70s. The place has gained a reputation as the preserver of a type of simple restaurant unique to Burano. Locals in dialect call it a *buranello.* Patrons often take the vaporetto from other sections of Venice (the restaurant lies close to the boat landing) to eat at the plain wooden tables set up indoors or on the small square in front. Specialties feature all the staples of the Venetian seaside diet, like fish soup, risotto di pesce, pasta seafarer style, tagliolini in squid ink, and a wide range of crustaceans, plus grilled, fried, and baked fish. Dishes prepared with local game are also available, but you must request them well in advance. Your meal might include a bottle of fruity wine from the region.

Trattoria de Romano. Via Baldassare Galuppi 221. ☎ **041/730-030.** Reservations recommended. Main courses 18,000–25,000L ($10–$15). AE, MC, V. Wed–Mon noon–3pm and 7–9:30pm. Closed Dec 15–Jan 31. Vaporetto: Line 12 or 52. VENETIAN.

You may want to join a long line of people who enjoy this rather simple-looking trattoria, around the corner from the lace school. It was founded in 1920 by the Nono family, whose grandchildren continue to manage it. Your superb dinner might consist of risotto di pesce (the Italian version of the Valencian paella), followed by fritto misto di pesce, a mixed fish fry from the Adriatic, with savory bits of mullet, squid, and shrimp or risotto nero de seppia (risotto flavored with squid ink).

TORCELLO

Of all the islands of the lagoon, **Torcello**—the so-called Mother of Venice—offers the most charm. If Burano is behind the times, Torcello is positively antediluvian. You can follow in the footsteps of Hemingway and stroll across a grassy meadow, traverse an ancient stone bridge, and step back into that time when the Venetians first fled from invading barbarians to create a city of Neptune in the lagoon.

To reach Torcello, take vaporetto no. 12 from Fondamenta Nuova on Murano. The trip takes about 45 minutes.

Warning: If you go to Torcello on your own, don't listen to the gondoliers who hover at the ferry quay. They'll tell you that the cathedral and the locanda are miles away. Actually, they're both reached after a leisurely 12- to 15-minute stroll along the canal.

EXPLORING THE ISLAND

Torcello has two major attractions: a church with Byzantine mosaics good enough to make Empress Theodora at Ravenna turn as purple with envy as her robe, and a locanda (inn) that converts day-trippers into inebriated angels of praise. First the spiritual nourishment, then the alcoholic sustenance.

The **Cattedrale di Torcello,** also called **Santa Maria Assunta Isola di Torcello** (☎ 041/730-084), was founded in A.D. 639 and subsequently rebuilt. It stands in a lonely grassy meadow beside an 11th-century campanile. The stars here are its Byzantine mosaics. Clutching her child, the weeping Madonna in the apse is a magnificent sight, and on the opposite wall is a powerful *Last Judgment.* Byzantine artisans, it seems, were at their best in portraying hell and damnation. In their *Inferno,* they have re-created a virtual human stew with the fires stirred by wicked demons. Reptiles slide in and out of the skulls of cannibalized sinners. The church is open daily: April to October 10am to 12:30pm and 2:30 to 6:30pm (to 5pm November to March). Admission is 1,500L (85¢).

DINING & ACCOMMODATIONS

Locanda Cipriani. Piazza San Fosca 29, Torcello, 30012 Burano. ☎ **041/730-150.** Reservations recommended. Main courses 30,000–40,000L ($17–$23). AE, DC, MC, V. Wed–Mon noon–3pm; Fri–Sat 7–10pm. Closed Jan 15–Feb 15. Vaporetto: Line 12 and 14 to Torcello. VENETIAN.

It's operated by the same folks who bring you some of the grandest and most paralyzingly expensive hangouts in Venice. Throughout the years it has stayed in the family, now owned by the very cosmopolitan Bonifacio Brass, nephew of Harry Cipriani (Hotel Cipriani, Harry's Bar). But this artfully simple locanda is low-key, deliberately

---

Impressions

An overcrowded little island where the women make splendid lace and the men make children.

—Ernest Hemingway, on Burano

rustic, and light-years removed from the family's grander venues. You'll reach the place after a boat ride from other parts of the city, across from the island's landmark church. Menu items are uncompromisingly classic, with deep roots in family tradition. A good example is filleto di San Pietro alla Carlina (filet of John Dory in the style of Carla, a late and much-revered matriarch, who made the dish for decades using tomatoes and capers). Also look for carpaccio Cipriani; risotto alla Torcellano (with fresh vegetables and herbs from the family's garden); fish soup; tagliolini verdi gratinati; and a traditional roster of veal, liver, fish, and beef dishes.

Here you'll also find half a dozen charming but simple guest rooms, each outfitted like what you might have expected in an isolated country villa during the 1950s. With minibars, TVs, phones, and air-conditioning, they rent for 250,000L ($145) per person year-round, half board included.

The Veneto & the Dolomites

Tearing yourself away from Venice's Piazza San Marco is a task requiring an iron will. However, Venice doesn't have a monopoly on art or architectural treasures. Of the cities of interest you can easily reach from Venice, in the area known as the **Veneto,** three tower above the rest: Verona, home of the eternal lovers Romeo and Juliet; Padua, the city of Mantegna, with frescoes by Giotto; and Vicenza, the city of Palladio, with streets of Renaissance palazzi and villa-studded hills. If time remains, you can also explore the Riviera del Brenta with its Venetian palazzi and such historic old cities as Treviso and Bassano del Grappa. The miracle of these cities is that, even though Venice dominated them for centuries, the Serene Republic didn't siphon off their creative drive completely.

Those with even more time can venture farther afield to explore the limestone **Dolomites (Dolomiti),** one of Europe's greatest natural attractions. Some of the peaks of this peculiar mountain formation in the northeastern Italian Alps soar to 10,500 feet. The Dolomiti are a year-round pleasure destination, with two high seasons: midsummer and winter, when the skiers slide in. At times, the Dolomiti form fantastic shapes, combining to create a primordial landscape, with mountain chains resembling a giant dragon's teeth. Clefts descend precipitously along jagged rocky walls, and at other points a vast flat tableland—spared by nature's fury—emerges.

The provinces of Trent and Bolzano (Bozen in German) form the **Trentino–Alto Adige** region. The area is rich in health resorts, attracting many German-speaking visitors to its alpine lakes and mountains. Many of its waters—some of which are radioactive—are said to have curative powers.

The Alto Adige province around Bolzano was until 1919 known as South Tyrol and was part of Austria. And even though today it belongs to Italy, it's still very much Tyrolean in character, both in its language (German) and in its dress. Today, the Trentino–Alto Adige region functions with a great deal of autonomy from the national government.

Readers with an extra day or so to spare may first want to postpone their Dolomite adventure for a detour to **Trieste,** the unofficial capital of Friuli–Venezia Guilia. It was Venice's main rival in the Adriatic from the 9th to the 15th century. Though it doesn't boast Venice's charm, Trieste is still one of Italy's most interesting ports, with Hapsburg monuments at its core and the world's largest accessible cave on its outskirts.

The serious wine connoisseur contemplating a visit to the Veneto and the Dolomites might consider a stop at a winery or two. The addresses and phones of the best ones appear under "The Best Wine-Growing Regions" in chapter 1. Refer to "The Veneto" and "Trentino–Alto Adige" sections and be prepared to call in advance for reservations and directions from wherever you're staying. See also "The Wine Roads from Treviso" section under "Treviso" later in this chapter.

1 The Riviera del Brenta & Its Villas

The **Brenta Canal,** running from Fusina to Padua, functioned as a mainland extension of Venice during the Renaissance, when wealthy merchants began using the area as a retreat from the city's summer heat—this remained popular until the 19th century. Dubbed the **Riviera del Brenta,** the 10½-mile stretch along the banks of the canal from Malcontenta to Stra is renowned for the gracious villas to which Venetians escaped, 44 of which are still visible.

The region's primary architect was **Andrea di Pietro,** known as **Palladio** (1508 to 1580), who designed 19 of the villas. Inspired by ancient Roman architecture, Palladio's singular design—square, perfectly proportioned, functionally elegant—became the standard by which villas were judged. His designs are familiar to Americans as the basis for most state capitals as well as Jefferson's Monticello and to the British as the most common design for country estates. The importance of villa life to the Venetians was such that it gained immortality in *The Merchant of Venice,* in which Portia's home is a villa at Belmont along the Brenta.

ESSENTIALS
GETTING THERE   Consider an all-day guided excursion by **boat** along the Brenta Canal as far as Padua, including many of the most important Renaissance monuments en route. **American Express** (☎ 041/520-0844) will sell you tickets aboard the Burchiello Excursion Boat. Excursions depart from the piers at Piazza San Marco every Tuesday, Thursday, and Saturday at 9am for a boat ride that includes running bilingual commentary from an on-board host. The price is 114,000L ($66) per person, plus a supplement of 40,000L ($23) for an optional lunch in the historic town of Oriago. You get glimpses of the elegant villas that seem to cling to the shorelines, guided visits through the evocative villas at Malcontenta and Oriago, and a somewhat rushed tour through the most spectacular sights of Padua after the boat docks. At 6:10pm, you board a bus for transit back to Venice.

You can tour the Brenta Riviera by **buses** leaving from Venice headed for Padua. The buses, operated by the local **ACTV** line (☎ 041/528-7886), depart from the Venetian company's ticket office in Piazzale Roma Monday to Saturday 8am to 2:30pm. A one-way ticket to Villa Foscari is 1,400L (80¢), and a one-way fare to the Villa Pisano is 5,000L ($2.90).

If you've got a **car,** note that all villas open to the public are on the north bank of the canal directly along Route S11 headed west out of Venice toward Padua. The road follows the canal, offering you a chance to glimpse the other villas, situated on both banks. At the APT in Venice, you can pick up the visitor's guide "Riviera del Brenta Venezia," offering background info on the villas and a map of their locations between Malcontenta and Stra.

The most opulent way to tour the villas is by **personal guide.** Rates depend on where you want to go and how much you want to take in during a day. A list of guides along with their fixed fees is available from the principal **APT tourist office** at the

Palazzetto Selva, right off Piazza San Marco in Venice (☎ 041/522-6356). You can also contact the **Guides Association** in Venice at Calle San Antonio, Castello 5448A (☎ 041/520-9038).

VISITOR INFORMATION   Contact the **APT tourist office** of Riviera del Brenta, Via Don Minzoni 26, 30034 Mira Porte, Venezia (☎ 041/424-973). April to September, it's open Tuesday to Saturday 8:30am to 1:30pm and 2 to 4pm; October to March, hours are Monday to Saturday 8am to 2pm.

TOURING THE VILLAS

Among the villas you can tour, the one closest to Venice is the **Villa Foscari (Villa La Malcontenta)** (☎ 041/520-3966), on Route S11 about 2½ miles west of where the canal empties into the Venetian Lagoon. It was constructed by Palladio for the Foscari family in 1560. A Foscari wife was exiled here for some alleged misdeed to her husband, and the unhappiness surrounding the incident gave the name Malcontenta (unhappy one) to both the villa and its village. It's open only Tuesday and Saturday 9am to noon, with an admission of 10,000L ($6); you can call and make reservations to see it on other days, when admission is 15,000L ($9).

In Stra, 20 miles west of Venice on Route S11, stands the **Villa Pisani (Villa Nazionale)** (☎ 049/502-074). Built in 1720 as a palatial retreat for Doge Alvise Pisani, it became the Italian home of Napóleon and later served as the initial meeting site of Mussolini and Hitler. Given this historical context, it's no surprise the villa is the largest and grandest of them all. A reflecting pool out front gives added dimension, and a small army of statues stands guard over the premises. The highlights of a visit are the magnificent Giambattista Tiepolo frescoes, painted on the ballroom ceiling to depict the *Glory of the Pisani Family*, in which family members are surrounded by hovering angels and saints. The villa is open Monday to Saturday 9am to 6pm (Sunday and holidays to 1pm). Admission is 8,000L ($4.65).

There are other villas you can visit along the Riviera, each with looking like a stately private home whose owners recognize, appreciate, and fiercely protect the unique nature of their property. Although each welcomes the occasional well-intentioned and appropriately respectful visitor, call in advance before you drop in. Don't expect structures following the gracefully symmetrical rhythms of Palladio: Each is evocative of larger versions of the palazzi lining Venice's Grand Canal.

They include the **Villa Sagredo,** Via Sagredo (☎ 049/503-174; after hours, call 041/412-967), half a mile northwest of the hamlet of Vigonovo. In a suitably gnarled garden, it was built on ancient Roman foundations, and the form it has today dates from around 1700, the result of frequent rebuildings. You must reserve in advance, and they prefer scheduled visits Tuesday to Friday 6 to 10pm or Saturday and Sunday 2 to around 8pm. There's a bar and a restaurant on the premises, serving simple food and drink. Admission is free.

Also appealing, but without any public facilities, is the private home of **Dr. Bruno Bellemo,** Villa Gradenigo, Riviera San Pietro 75 in Oriago (☎ 041/429-631). Set adjacent to the pier where boats from Venice and Padua are moored, it's a pure 16th-century adaptation of a Venetian palazzo whose interior is noted for a series of frescoes executed by the brothers of Veronese, Paolo and Benedetto Caliari. Look for a small but verdant garden around it, and all the grace notes that accompany its role as a private home. Well-intentioned visitors and art students, if it's convenient for the owners, are welcomed inside, usually for free or a donation of 10,000L ($6), but only Tuesday to Friday 9am to noon and 2:30 to 6pm and Saturday and Sunday 10am to 6pm. Unless you're traveling with a group, it's best to call ahead.

The Veneto & the Dolomites

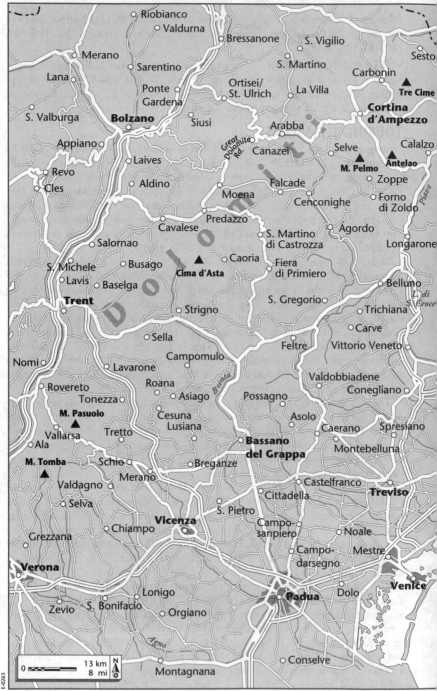

ACCOMMODATIONS

Dolo, only 15 minutes by car from Venice or Padua, is at the midpoint of the Brenta Canal. It contains several villas from the 17th and 18th centuries, most of which are still inhabited by families. Mira is 10 minutes from Venice and 20 from Padua at the most scenic bend of the Brenta—it's no wonder that several villas lie in the immediate area. While here, drop a card in the mail at the post office in the former Palazzo Foscarini, where Lord Byron lived and worked on *Childe Harold* from 1817 to 1819.

Villa Ducale. Riviera Martiri della Libertà 75, 30031 Dolo. ☎ **041/560-8020.** Fax 041/560-8004. 12 units. A/C MINIBAR TV TEL. 220,000–260,000L ($128–$151) double; 280,000L ($162) suite. Rates include breakfast. Free parking in lot. AE, DC, MC, V.

This villa, built in 1884 by Count Giulio Rocca, has been turned into a hotel. Restored to its original grandeur, it's graced with Murano glass chandeliers, elaborate frescoes, luxurious fabrics, and antique furnishings. The beautifully furnished guest rooms overlook the statue-filled grounds. Besides being large and comfortable, they're equipped with a safe-deposit box, trouser press, and hair dryer. The restaurant, La Colonne, specializes in Venetian seafood dishes.

Villa Margherita. Via Nazionale 416–417, 30030 Mira, Venezia. ☎ **041/426-5800.** Fax 041/426-5838. 19 units. A/C MINIBAR TV TEL. 290,000–340,000L ($168–$197) double. Rates include buffet breakfast. AE, DC, MC, V.

This 17th-century villa is on a particularly scenic bend of the Brenta River, and the beauty of its interiors justifies its setting. Features include marble columns and fireplaces, marble and terra-cotta floors, immaculate frescoes and stucco work, a sunny breakfast room, and guest rooms that blend individualized traditional elegance with modern comfort. An immense park opens up behind the villa, and a stroll of 100 yards brings you to the Ristorante Margherita, preparing the freshest Venetian seafood specialties, available with a large selection of fine wines and champagnes.

DINING

Ristorante Nalin. Via Nuovissimo 29, Mira. ☎ **041/420-083.** Reservations recommended. Main courses 18,000–22,000L ($10–$13); 3-course fixed-price menus 40,000–80,000L ($23–$46). AE, DC, MC, V. Tues–Sun noon–2:30pm, Tues–Sat 7:30–10pm. Closed Aug and Dec 26–Jan 6. VENETIAN/SEAFOOD.

Most of the Riviera del Brenta's restaurants focus on seafood, and this one is no exception. In a century-old building that was once a private home, the restaurant has flourished as a family-run enterprise since the 1960s. It's adjacent to the canal, near the town center, and you'll probably gravitate to the terrace, where potted shrubs and flowers bloom throughout summer. The specialties vary with whatever happens to be in season but are likely to include tagliatelle con salsa di calamaretti (with squid sauce), spaghetti al nero (with octopus ink), crabs culled from the Venetian lagoon, and seasonal variations on polenta and risotto.

2 Padua & Giotto's Frescoes

25 miles W of Venice, 50 miles E of Verona, 145 miles E of Milan

Padua (Padova) no longer looks as it did when Richard Burton's Petruchio tamed Elizabeth Taylor's Katerina in the Zeffirelli adaptation of *The Taming of the Shrew.* However, it remains a major art center of the Veneto. Shakespeare called Padua a "nursery of arts."

Padua is sometimes known as *La Città del Santo* (City of the Saint), a reference to St. Anthony of Padua, who's buried at a basilica the city dedicated to him. Il Santo was an itinerant Franciscan monk—not to be confused with St. Anthony of Egypt, the hermit who could resist all the temptations of the Devil. Many visitors stay in the cheaper Padua and commute to Venice. Of course, it doesn't have Venice's beauty and has been defaced by high-rises and urban blight, but its inner core has a wealth of attractions. Its university, the second oldest in Italy, adds life and vibrancy, though visitors and professors like Dante and Galileo haven't been seen here in a while.

ESSENTIALS

GETTING THERE   The **train** is best if you're coming from Venice, Milan, or Bologna. Trains depart for and arrive from Venice once every 30 minutes (trip time: 30 minutes), costing 4,000L ($2.30) one-way. Trains to and from Milan run every hour (trip time: 2½ hours) for 20,000L ($12) one-way. For information and schedules, call ☎ 049/875-1800 or 1478/88-088 toll free in Italy only. The main rail terminus is at Piazza Stazione, north of the historic core and outside the 16th-century walls. A bus will connect you to the center.

Buses from Venice arrive every 30 minutes (trip time: 45 minutes), costing 7,000L ($4.05) one-way. There are also connections from Vicenza every 30 minutes (trip time: 30 minutes) at 5,000L ($2.90) one-way. The bus station is at Via Trieste 40 (☎ 049/820-6844), near Piazza Boschetti, 5 minutes from the rail station.

If you've got a **car,** take A4 west from Venice.

VISITOR INFORMATION   The **tourist office** is at the train station (☎ 049/875-2077). April to October, it's open Monday to Saturday 9am to 7pm and Sunday 9am to noon; November to March, hours are Monday to Saturday 9:15am to 5:45pm and Sunday 9am to noon.

Tickets valid for admission to all Padua museums are 15,000L ($9) adults and 10,000L ($6) students/children at the tourist office or at any of the city's museums.

SEEING THE SIGHTS

A university that grew to fame throughout Europe was founded here as early as 1222 (poet Tasso attended). The **University of Padua** has remained one of the great centers for learning in Italy. The physics department counts Galileo among its past professors, and Petrarch lectured here. Today its buildings are scattered around the city. The historic main building is called **Il Bo,** after an inn on the site that used an ox as its sign. The chief entrance is on Via Otto Febbraio. Of particular interest is an anatomy theater, which dates from 1594 and was the first of its kind in Europe. For 5,000L ($2.90), you can join a guided tour of the university on Tuesday 9 to 11am, Wednesday and Thursday 9 to 11am and 3 to 5pm, and Friday 3 to 5pm. For information, contact the **Associazione Guide di Padova** at ☎ 049/820-9711.

If you're on a tight schedule, concentrate on the Cappella degli Scrovegni (Giotto frescoes) and the Basilica di San Antonio.

✪ **Chapel of the Scrovegni (Cappella degli Scrovegni, also Arena Chapel).** Piazza Ermitani, off Corso Garibaldi. ☎ 049/820-4550. Admission (including entry to Musei Civici) 10,000L ($6) adults, 5,000L ($2.90) children 6–17; children 5 and under free. Feb–Oct daily 9am–7pm (to 6pm Nov–Jan). Bus: 3, 8, 12, or 18.

This modest chapel is the best reason for visiting Padua. Sometime around 1305 and 1306, Giotto did a cycle of more than 35 remarkably well-preserved frescoes inside, which, along with those at Assisi, form the basis of his claim to fame. Like an illustrated storybook, the frescoes unfold biblical scenes. The third bottom panel (lower level on the right) depicts Judas kissing a most skeptical Christ and is the most reproduced and widely known panel. On the entrance wall is Giotto's *Last Judgment,* in which hell wins out for sheer fascination. The master's representation of the *Vices and Virtues* is bizarre; it reveals the depth of his imagination in personifying nebulous evil and elusive good. One of the most dramatic panels depicts the raising of Lazarus from the dead: This is a masterfully balanced scene, rhythmically ingenious for its day. The swathed and cadaverous Lazarus, however, looks indecisive as to whether or not he'll rejoin the living.

Civic Museum (Museo Civico di Padova). Piazza Eremitani 8. ☎ **049/820-4550.** Admission included with entry to Cappella degli Scrovegni (above). Apr–Oct Tues–Sun 9am–7pm (to 6pm Nov–Mar). Bus: 3, 8, 12, or 18.

This picture gallery is filled with minor works by major Venetian artists, some dating from the 14th century. Look for a wooden Crucifix by Giotto and two miniatures by Giorgione. Other works are Giovanni Bellini's *Portrait of a Young Man* and Jacopo Bellini's miniature *Descent into Limbo,* with its childlike devils. The 15th-century Arras tapestry is also on display. Other works are Veronese's *Martyrdom of St. Primo and St. Feliciano,* plus Tintoretto's *Supper in Simone's House* and *Crucifixion,* probably the finest single painting in the gallery.

Chiesa degli Eremitani. Piazza Eremitani 9. ☎ **049/875-6410.** Free admission (donations accepted). Apr–Sept Mon–Sat 8:15am–noon and 4–6:30pm, Sun and religious holidays 9:30am–noon and 4–6pm. Closes 30 min earlier rest of the year. Bus: 3, 8, 12, or 18.

One of Padua's tragedies was when this church was bombed on March 11, 1944. Before that, it housed one of the greatest treasures in Italy, the **Ovetari Chapel,** with the first significant cycle of frescoes by Andrea Mantegna (1431 to 1506). The church was rebuilt, but, alas, you can't resurrect 15th-century frescoes. To the right of the main altar are the fragments left after the bombing. The most interesting fresco saved is a panel depicting the dragging of St. Christopher's body through the streets. Note also the *Assumption of the Virgin.* Like Leonardo, the artist had a keen eye for architectural detail.

✪ Basilica di Sant'Antonio. Piazza del Santo 11. ☎ **049/824-2811.** Free admission. Apr–Sept daily 7am–7:30pm; Oct–Mar daily 7:30am–7pm. Bus: 8, 12, 18, 22, M, or T.

This basilica was built in the 13th century and dedicated to St. Anthony of Padua, who's interred within. It's a synthesis of styles, with mainly Romanesque and Gothic features. Campaniles and minarets combine to give it an Eastern appearance. Inside it's richly frescoed and decorated, filled with pilgrims devoutly touching the saint's marble tomb. One of the more unusual relics is in the treasury—the 7-centuries-old, still-uncorrupt tongue of St. Anthony.

The great art treasurers are the Donatello bronzes at the main altar, with a realistic Crucifix towering over the rest. Seek out as well the Donatello relief depicting the removal of Christ from the cross (at the back of the high altar), a unified composition expressing in simple lines and with an unromantic approach the tragedy of Christ and the sadness of the mourners.

Among his other innovations, Donatello restored the lost art of the equestrian statue with the well-known example in front of the basilica. Though the man it honors (Gattamelata) is of little interest to art lovers, the 1453 statue is of prime importance. The large horse is realistic, as Donatello was a master of detail. He cleverly directs the eye to the commanding face of the Venetian military hero, nicknamed "Spotted Cat." Gattamelata was a dead ringer for the late Lord Laurence Olivier.

Palace of Law (Palazzo della Ragione). Via VIII Febbraio, between Piazza delle Erbe and Piazza dell Frutta. ☎ **049/820-5006.** Admission 7,000L ($4.05) adults, 4,000L ($2.30) children under 18. Feb–Oct Tues–Sun 9am–7pm (to 6pm Nov–Jan). Bus: 8 or A.

Savoring a Cappuccino in the Elegance of 19th-Century Padua

Caffè Pedrocchi, Piazzetta Pedrocchi 15 (☎ 049/876-2576), off Piazza Cavour, is a neoclassical landmark. Hailed as Europe's most elegant coffeehouse when it opened in 1831 under Antonio Pedrocchi, its green, white, and red rooms reflect the national colors. On sunny days, you might want to sit out on one of the two stone porches; in winter, you'll have plenty to distract you inside. The sprawling bathtub-shaped travertine bar has a brass top and brass lion's feet, and the velvet banquettes have maroon upholstery, red-veined marble tables, and Egyptian Revival chairs. And if you tire of all this 19th-century outrageousness, you can retreat to a more conservatively decorated English-style pub, whose entrance is under a covered arcade a few steps away. Coffee is 1,400L (80¢) at the stand-up bar or 2,800L ($1.60) at a table. Though drinks cost more than they would in a lesser cafe, you haven't heard the heartbeat of Padua until you've been at the Pedrocchi. It's open Tuesday to Sunday 9:30am to 12:30pm and 3:30 to 8pm.

This palazzo, dating from the early 13th century, is among the most remarkable buildings of northern Italy. Ringed with loggias and with a roof shaped like the hull of a sailing vessel, it sits in the marketplace. Climb the steps and enter the grandiose Salone, a 270-foot assembly hall containing a gigantic 15th-century wooden horse. The walls are richly frescoed with symbolic paintings that replaced the frescoes by Giotto and his assistants destroyed by a 1420 fire.

SHOPPING

Padua is an elegant town with a rich university life, a solid industrial base, and an economy too diversified to rely exclusively on tourism. Therefore, you'll find a wide roster of upscale consumer goods and luxury items and less emphasis on souvenirs and handcrafts. For insights into the good life *alla Padovese*, trek through the neighborhood around the landmark **Piazza Insurrezione,** especially the **Galleria Borghese,** a conglomeration of shops off Via San Fermo.

Droves of shoppers head to the **Prato delle Valle** on the third Sunday of every month, when more than 200 antiques and collectibles vendors set up shop for the day. The square, one of the largest in all Europe, also hosts a smaller weekly market on Saturday. Shoes from nearby Brenta factories are the prevalent product, but the range of goods offered remains eclectic.

ACCOMMODATIONS

✪ **Albergo Leon Bianco.** Piazzetta Pedrocchi 12, 35122 Padova. ☎ **049/657-225.** Fax 049/875-0814. E-mail: tosanel@intercity.shiny.it. 22 units. A/C TV TEL. 160,000L ($93) double. Breakfast 15,000L ($9). AE, MC, V. Parking 25,000L ($15). Bus: 18.

This is the most nostalgic hotel in Padua, built "sometime after 1850." At the time, this "White Lion" was much, much larger that it is today, but during the economic uncertainties and conflicts of the 20th century, it was whittled away to only 22 rooms. In 1985, a major renovation added bright, sometimes jarring colors, a rather odd-looking modern entrance set into the massive arch of the front, and a cafe/breakfast area to the panoramic rooftop. (Throughout the warm-weather months, it blossoms with an exotic collection of geraniums.) Breakfast is the only meal served, and the staff is much more articulate and charming than at similar hotels in the region.

Hotel al Fagiano. Via Locatelli 45, 35123 Padova. ☎ **049/875-0073.** Fax 049/875-3396. 32 units. A/C TV TEL. 120,000L ($70) double. Breakfast 4,000L ($2.40). AE, MC, V. Bus: 8, 12, or 18.

In 1988, the owners of this 18th-century town house completed a radical restoration and opened their doors to a growing trade of business and pleasure travelers. Its location less than 100 yards from the bascilica is among its most appealing assets. Despite its age, don't expect too many baroque trappings. The ceilings in some of the rooms are higher than those in a modern building, but otherwise the place is modern and streamlined. A replica of a Renaissance fresco in the reception area adds one of the few historic touches, and the staff, not all of whom speak English, is particularly helpful. Breakfast is the only meal served.

Hotel Donatello. Piazza del Santo 102–104, 35123 Padova. ☎ **049/875-0634.** Fax 049/875-0829. 53 units. A/C MINIBAR TV TEL. 238,000–262,000L ($138–$152) double; 318,000–423,000L ($184–$245) suite. Breakfast 19,000L ($11). AE, DC, MC, V. Closed Dec 15–Jan 15. Parking 28,000L ($16). Bus: 3, 8, or 12.

The Donatello is a renovated hotel with an ideal location near the basilica—though the Plaza has more amenities and is better equipped. The Donatello's terraced restaurant is its most alluring feature. The hotel's buff-colored facade is pierced by an arched arcade, and the oversized chandeliers of its lobby combine with the checkerboard marble floor for a hospitable ambience. The guest rooms are well maintained and reasonably comfortable, yet furnished in a standard uninspired style.

Hotel Europa-Zaramella. Largo Europa 9, 35137 Padova. ☎ **049/661-200.** Fax 049/661-508. 59 units. A/C MINIBAR TV TEL. 210,000L ($122) double. Rates include breakfast. AE, DC, MC, V. Parking 25,000L ($15).

The Europa-Zaramella was built in the 1960s and looks its age but is a recommendable choice because of its fairly modest rates. The tasteful rooms, compact and serviceable, have pastel walls and simple built-in furnishings and open onto small balconies. The public rooms are enhanced by cubist murals, free-form ceramic plaques, and furniture placed in conversational groupings. The American bar is popular, as is the dining room. The Zaramella Restaurant features a good Paduan cuisine, with an emphasis on seafood dishes from the Adriatic.

Hotel Plaza. Corso Milano 40, 35139 Padova. ☎ **049/656-822.** Fax 049/661-117. E-mail: plazapd@gpneet.it. 147 units. A/C MINIBAR TV TEL. 280,000L ($162) double; from 380,000L ($220) suite. Rates include buffet breakfast. AE, DC, MC, V. Parking 20,000L ($12). Bus: 5, 7, or 10.

The Plaza is Padua's leading inn, a business hotel with brown ceramic tiles and concrete-trimmed square windows. The entrance is under a modern concrete arcade leading into a contemporary lobby. Its angular lines are softened with an unusual Oriental needlework tapestry, brown leather couches, and a pair of gilded baroque cherubs. The rooms are comfortable and well decorated. The bar, which you reach through a stairwell and an upper balcony dotted with modern paintings, is a relaxing place for a drink. The restaurant serving a Venetian and international cuisine is open Monday to Saturday 7:30 to 10:30pm.

Majestic Hotel Toscanelli. Piazzetta dell'Arco 2, 35122 Padova. ☎ **049/663-244.** Fax 049/876-0025. 32 units. A/C MINIBAR TV TEL. 180,000–280,000L ($104–$162) double; from 280,000L ($162) suite. Rates include buffet breakfast. AE, DC, MC, V. Parking 25,000L ($15). Bus: 8.

This four-star hotel has wrought-iron balconies that protect the stone-edged French windows on this pastel-pink building fronting a cobblestone square. A Renaissance well and dozens of potted shrubs are in front. The breakfast room is surrounded by a garden of green plants, and the lobby has white marble floors, Oriental rugs, an upper balcony, and a mishmash of old and new furniture. The guest rooms were completely overhauled in 1992. Elegant cherrywood furniture crafted by Tuscan artisans was added, along with mahogany and white marble. Pastel colors predominate, with traditional Louis XV or Louis XVI styles. On-site is a budget pizzeria that makes some of the best pies in town and serves several savory and freshly made pastas as well.

DINING

✪ **Antico Brolo.** Corso Milano 22. ☎ **049/664-455.** Reservations recommended. Main courses 25,000–40,000L ($15–$23). AE, DC, MC, V. Tues–Sun 12:30–2:30pm and 7:30 to 10:30pm. Bus: 5, 7, or 10. ITALIAN.

Across from the ornate Teatro de Padova (Civic Theater), this is acknowledged by every hotelier as the city's best restaurant. Even though the 16th-century dining room evokes the Renaissance, many diners prefer a candlelit table in the carefully cultivated terrace garden. The cuisine follows the tenets of most of Italy, with special emphasis on seasonal ingredients and the traditions of the Veneto and Emilia-Romagna. Especially delicious are the homemade garganelli (similar to penne) with garlic sauce, appetite-inducing onion soup baked in a crust, chateaubriand with balsamic vinegar, and grilled fish. The perfect dessert is zuppa inglese, a cream-enriched dessert similar to zabaglione.

✪ **Belle Parti–Toulà.** Via Belle Parti 11. ☎ **049/875-1822.** Reservations required. Main courses 25,000–32,000L ($15–$19). AE, DC, MC, V. Mon–Sat 12:30–2:30pm and 8–10:30pm. Closed first 3 weeks in Aug. Bus: 10. INTERNATIONAL/ITALIAN.

Toulà opened in 1982 under ceiling beams more than 500 years old. The age of the place, however, didn't stop a team of designers from creating a sensual decor showcasing Italian style at its best. The ground floor includes a slick black bar, and the main dining area offers the excellent service this most sophisticated of nationwide restaurant chains is eager to provide. The palate-pleasing menu changes monthly but might include crayfish salad with artichokes; scampi salad with fennel, orange slices, and olives; a salad of radicchio with bacon; a savory salad of bottargha fish, beans, and celery; or filet of beef with a sauce of rosemary and balsamic vinegar. The cookery isn't always as refined as that of its sibling in Rome but is first-rate nonetheless.

Osteria Speroni. Via Speroni 32–36. ☎ **049/875-3370.** Reservations recommended. Main courses 15,000–25,000L ($9–$15). AE, MC, V. Mon–Sat noon–3pm and 7–11pm. SEAFOOD.

Occupying a 16th-century building a 3-minute walk from Padua's cathedral, this is an affordable well-managed fish restaurant. You'll dine in any of three antique-looking rooms, each with lots of exposed stone. Don't expect a lot of meat on the menu, as everything is focused on seafood. The best way to begin is with a selection of antipasti from the buffet table, where fried calamari, marinated octopus, garlic-marinated shrimp, and a wide assortment of fried or marinated vegetables proclaim the agrarian bounty of Italy. A special pasta here is spaghetti alla busara, with shrimp, cubed tomatoes, and copious amounts of garlic. Also look for sea bass roasted in a salt crust.

Taverna del Teatro. Corso Milano 22. ☎ **049/664-455.** Main courses 20,000–30,000L ($12–$17). AE, DC, MC, V. Tues–Sun 7pm–1am. Bus: 5, 7, or 10. ITALIAN.

This is the unpretentious counterpart to Antico Brolo (above), with which it shares the same management. Set in Antico Brolo's stone-sided cellar, it combines many of the functions of beer tavern and wine bar. No one will mind if you descend into its depths just for a beer, priced at around 5,000L ($2.90), or some of the local wine, priced from 18,000L ($10) a bottle. But if you're hungry, there's a wide medley of pizzas, pastas, simple platters, and ice creams awaiting your pleasure.

PADUA AFTER DARK

You can network with students in town at any of the crowded cafes along **Via Cavour** or walk over to the wine and beer dives around **Piazza delle Frutte** to find out where most of the college crowd is being cool. But other than a quiet stroll through the town's historic core, there's little happening in the city.

For dancing in Padua, try **Disco-Bar Limbo,** Via San Fermo 44 (☎ 049/ 656-882), where electronic games alternate with recorded and (occasionally) live music. However, the most popular discos lie outside the city along the road between Padua and the spa town of Abano Terme, where the music is louder and the lights are dimmer. An example is **King's Club,** in Abano Terme, 10 miles from Padua (☎ 049/ 667-895). En route, about 2 miles west of Padua, are **Disco Extra Extra,** Via Ciamician 5 (☎ 049/620-044), and its neighbor **Disco P1,** Viale Giusti (☎ 049/ 860-1633).

3 Palladio's Vicenza

126 miles E of Milan, 42 miles W of Venice, 32 miles NE of Verona

In the 16th century, **Vicenza** was transformed into a virtual laboratory for the architectural experiments of Andrea di Pietro, known as Palladio (1508 to 1580). One of the greatest architects of the High Renaissance, he was inspired by the classical art and architecture of ancient Greece and Rome. Palladio peppered the city with palazzi and basilicas and the surrounding hills with villas for patrician families.

The architect was particularly important to England and America. In the 18th century, Robert Adam was inspired by him, as reflected by many country homes in England. Then, through the influence of Adam and others even earlier, the spirit of Palladio was brought to America (examples are Jefferson's Monticello and plantation homes in the antebellum South). Palladio even lent his name to this architectural style, Palladianism—identified by regularity of form, imposing size, and an adherence to lines established in the ancient world. Visitors arrive in Vicenza today principally to see the works left by Palladio, and it's for this reason the city was designated a UNESCO World Heritage Site in 1994.

Vicenza isn't entirely living off its former glory. Dubbed the Venice of Terra Firma, Vicenza is ringed with light industry on its outskirts, its citizens earning one of the highest average incomes in the country. Federico Faggin, inventor of the silicon chip, was born here, and many local computer component industries are prospering. Gold manufacturing is another traditional and rich industry.

ESSENTIALS

GETTING THERE   Most visitors arrive from Venice via the **train** (trip time: 1 hour), costing 5,700L ($3.30) one-way. Trains also arrive frequently from Padua (trip time: 25 minutes), charging 3,400L ($1.95) one-way. There are also frequent connections from Milan (trip time: 2½ hours), at 15,500L ($9) one-way. For information and schedules, call ☎ 0444/325-045 or 1478/88-088 toll free in Italy only. The rail station lies at Piazza Stazione (Campo Marzio), at the southern edge of Viale Roma.

It's best to arrive by train. Once at Vicenza, however, you'll find good **bus** connections for the province of Vicenza if you'd like to tour the environs. The service is operated by FTV, Viale Milano 138 (☎ 0444/223-115), to the left as you exit from the rail station.

If you've got a **car** and are in Venice, take A4 west toward Verona, bypassing Padua.

VISITOR INFORMATION The tourist office is at Piazza Matteotti 12 (☎ 0444/ 320-854), open Monday to Saturday 9am to 1pm and 2:30 to 6pm and Sunday 9am to 1pm.

EXPLORING THE WORLD OF PALLADIO

To introduce yourself to the world of Palladio, head for **Piazza dei Signori.** In this classical square stands the **Basilica Palladiana,** partially designed by Palladio. The loggias rise on two levels, the lower tier with Doric pillars, the upper with Ionic. In its heyday, this building was much frequented by the Vicentino aristocrats, who lavishly spent their gold on villas in the neighboring hills. They met here in a kind of social fraternity, perhaps to talk about the excessive sums being spent on Palladio-designed or -inspired projects. The original basilica was done in the Gothic style and served as the Palazzo della Ragione (hall of justice). The roof collapsed following a 1945 bombing but has been subsequently rebuilt. Though there aren't any treasures inside, two or three times a year art exhibits are held here. The basilica is open Tuesday to Saturday 9:30am to noon and 2:30 to 5pm and Sunday 9:30am to noon. Admission is free. Beside the basilica is the 13th-century **Torre Bissara,** soaring almost 270 feet. Across from the basilica is the **Loggia del Capitanio** (captain of the guard), designed by Palladio in his waning years.

✪ Olympic Theater (Teatro Olimpico). Piazza Matteotti. ☎ **0444/323-781.** Admission 5,000L ($2.90) adults, 3,000L ($1.75) students. Mon–Sat 9:30am–12:30pm and 2:15–5pm, Sun 9:30am–12:30pm.

Palladio's masterpiece and last work—ideal for performances of classical plays—is one of the world's greatest theaters still in use. It was completed in 1585, 5 years after Palladio's death, by Vincenzo Scamozzi, and the curtain went up on the Vicenza premiere of Sophocles's *Oedipus Rex.* The arena seating area, in the shape of a half moon, is encircled by Corinthian columns and balustrades. The simple proscenium is abutted by the arena. What's ordinarily the curtain in a conventional theater is here a permanent facade, U-shaped, with a large central arch and a pair of smaller ones flanking it. The permanent stage set represents the ancient streets of Thebes, combining architectural detail with trompe l'oeil. Above the arches (to the left and right) are rows of additional classic statuary on pedestals and in niches. Over the area is a dome, with trompe l'oeil clouds and sky, giving the illusion of an outdoor Roman amphitheater.

Civic Museum (Museo Civico). In the Palazzo Chiericati, Piazza Matteotti 37–39. ☎ **0444/321-348.** Admission 5,000L ($2.90) adults, 3,000L ($1.75) children under 14/ seniors over 60. Tues–Sat 9am–12:30pm and 2:15–5pm, Sun 9:30am–12:30pm.

This museum is housed in one of the most outstanding buildings by Palladio. Begun in the mid-16th century, it wasn't finished until the late 17th, during the baroque period. Visitors come chiefly to view its excellent collection of Venetian paintings on the second floor. Works by lesser-known artists—Paolo Veneziano, Bartolomeo Montagna, and Jacopo Bassano—hang alongside paintings by giants like Tintoretto (*Miracle of St. Augustine*), Veronese (*The Cherub of the Balustrade*), and Tiepolo (*Time and Truth*).

Tempio di Santa Corona. Via Santa Corona. ☎ **0444/323-644.** Free admission. Daily 8:30am–noon and 2:30–6:30pm.

This much-altered Gothic church was founded in the mid-13th century. Visit it to see Giovanni Bellini's *Baptism of Christ* (fifth altar on the left). In the left transept, a short distance away, is another of Vicenza's well-known artworks—this one by Veronese— depicting the three Wise Men paying tribute to the Christ child. The high altar with

La Città del Palladio

His name was Andrea di Pietro, but his friends called him **Palladio.** In time, he become the most prominent architect of the Italian High Renaissance, living and working in his beloved Vicenza. This city remains, despite the destruction of 14 of his buildings during World War II air raids (luckily, they were photographed and documented before their demise), a living museum of his architectural achievements. In time, Vicenza became known as *La Città del Palladio.* Palladio was actually born in Padua in 1508, where he was apprenticed to a stone carver but fled in 1523 to Vicenza, where he lived for most of his life, dying here in 1580.

In his youth, Palladio journeyed to Rome to study the architecture of the Roman Vitruvius, who had a profound influence on him. Returning to Vicenza, Palladio perfected the "Palladian style," with its use of pilasters and a composite structure on a gigantic scale. The "attic" in his design was often surmounted by statues. One critic of European architecture wrote, "The noble design, the perfect proportions, the rhythm, and the logically vertical order invites devotion." Palladio's treatise on architecture, published in four volumes, is required reading for aspiring architects.

By no means was Palladio a genius, in the way the Florentine Brunelleschi was. No daring innovator, Palladio was more like an academician who went by the rules. Although all his buildings are harmonious, there are no surprises in them. One of his most acclaimed buildings is the **Villa Rotonda** in Vicenza, a cube with a center circular hall crowned by a dome. On each external side is a pillared rectangular portico. The classic features, though dry and masquerading as a temple, captured the public's imagination. This same type of villa soon reappeared all over England and America.

The main street of Vicenza, **Corso Andrea Palladio,** honors its most famous hometown boy, who spent much of his life building villas for the wealthy. The street is a textbook illustration of the great architect's work (or that of his pupils), and a walk along the Corso is one of the most memorable in Italy.

its intricate marble work is also worth a look. A visit to Santa Corona is more rewarding than a trek to the Duomo, which is only of passing interest.

✪ **Villa Rotonda.** Via della Rotonda 25. ☎ **0444/321-793.** Admission 10,000L ($6) to interior; 5,000L ($2.90) to grounds. Interior, Wed 10am–noon and 3–6pm; grounds, Tues–Thurs 10am–noon and 3–6pm. Closed Nov 5–Mar 14.

This is Palladio's most famous villa, featuring his trademark design inspired by the Roman temples. The interior lacks the grand decor of many lesser-known villas, but the exterior is the focus anyway, having inspired Christopher Wren's English country estates, Jefferson's Monticello, and the work of a slew of lesser-known architects designing U.S. state capitols and Southern antebellum homes. On the World Heritage List of UNESCO, it was begun by Palladio in 1567, though he didn't live to see it finished. The final work was carried out by Scamozzi between Palladio's death in 1580 and 1592. If you aren't here during the limited open hours, you can still view it clearly from the road.

Villa Valmarana dei Nani. Via San Bastiano 8. ☎ **0444/543-976,** or 0444/544-546 for winter appointments. Admission 10,000L ($6) adults, 8,000L ($4.65) students/children. May–Sept Wed–Sat 10am–noon and 3–6pm; call for off-season hours, which vary.

The most magnificent thing about this 17th-century villa, built by Palladio disciple Mattoni, is the series of frescoes by Giambattista Tiepolo that, taken together, create an elaborate mythological world. In the garden, you'll find miniature statues, which are the *nani* (dwarves) referred to in its name. Winter tours, available by appointment, require a group of 10 or more and have an increased fee of 11,000L ($7) per person.

SHOPPING

Shopping and tourism-industry insiders note a lackluster number of shops in Vicenza devoted to sales of one of the region's biggest industries, goldsmithing. Likewise, most of Vicenza's shops, conscious of the city's role as an aesthetic style-setter since the days of the Renaissance, devote most of their energies to distributing high-fashion products.

Your best bet in Vicenza is pursuing the good life, Italian style, as defined by such high-style emporiums as **Max Mara,** Corso Palladio 141 (☎ **0444/543-058**), selling stylish upscale garments for women; and two other outfits with both men's and women's departments, **Duca d'Este,** Contrà Santa Barbara (☎ **0444/320-846**), and **EMO,** Contrà Cavour 22 (☎ **0444/545-939**).

ACCOMMODATIONS

Hotel Campo Marzio. Viale Roma 21, 36100 Vicenza. ☎ **0445/529-900.** Fax 445/528-134. 35 units. A/C MINIBAR TV TEL. 230,000–340,000L ($133–$197) double. Rates include breakfast. AE, DC, MC, V. Parking 15,000L ($9).

This contemporary hotel is ideally situated in a peaceful part of the historic center, adjacent to a park. The rooms have undergone complete renovation, and the sunny lobby has a conservatively comfortable decor that extends into the rooms. A cozy restaurant offers regional dining Monday to Friday.

Hotel Continental. Viale G.G. Trissino 89, 36100 Vicenza. ☎ **0444/505-478.** Fax 0444/513-319. 55 units. A/C MINIBAR TV TEL. 225,000L ($131) double. Rates include breakfast. AE, DC, MC, V.

The Continental is among the best choices for an overnight stop in a town not known for its hotels. It has been renovated in a modern style and offers comfortably appointed rooms. The hotel has a good restaurant; however, there's no meal service on Saturday or Sunday or in August or around Christmas. There's a solarium on the premises.

Hotel Cristina. Corso San Felice e Fortunato 32, 36100 Vicenza. ☎ **0444/323-751.** Fax 0444/543-656. 34 units. A/C MINIBAR TV TEL. 170,000–195,000L ($99–$113) double. Rates include buffet breakfast. AE, DC, MC, V. Parking 12,000L ($7).

The well-maintained contemporary Cristina is a cozy place near the city center, with an inside courtyard where you can park. The recently refurbished decor consists of large amounts of marble and parquet flooring and lots of exposed paneling, coupled with comfortable furniture in the public rooms. The high-ceilinged guest rooms are also well furnished, though some are small. A breakfast buffet is the only meal served.

Jolly Hotel Europa. Strada Padana Verso Verona 11, 36100 Vicenza. ☎ **800/221-2626** in the U.S., or 0444/564-111 in Italy. Fax 0444/564-382. 127 units. A/C MINIBAR TV TEL. 340,000L ($197) double. Rates include buffet breakfast. AE, DC, MC, V. Free parking.

Outside of town, the Jolly is the area's finest hotel—though it doesn't face much competition. It's a somewhat sterile but well-run place flying the flags of many nations. It's geared to the business traveler, as it lies in the Exhibition Center with easy access to the autostrada; however, it can also serve the leisure visitor. The rooms are done in a jazzy Italian style and are medium-sized, each with a small safe and a hair dryer. Some rooms are set aside for nonsmokers. Le Ville restaurant offers both international dishes and regional food of the Veneto.

DINING

Antica Trattoria Tre Visi. Corso Palladio 25. ☎ **0444/324-868.** Reservations required. Main courses 20,000–30,000L ($12–$17). AE, DC, MC, V. Tues–Sun 12:30–2:30pm; Tues–Sat 7:30–10:30pm. Closed July. VICENTINO/INTERNATIONAL.

This restaurant opened as a simple tavern in the early 1600s. After many variations, it was named "The Three Faces" more than a century ago after the rulers of Austria, Hungary, and Bavaria, whose political influence was powerful in the Veneto. The decor is rustic, with a fireplace, ceramic wall decorations, baskets of fresh fruit, tavern chairs, and an open kitchen. Along with the good selection of regional wines, you can enjoy a rich choice of international dishes like baccalà (salt codfish) alla vicentina, roast goat, zuppa di fagioli (bean soup), and spaghetti with duck sauce. Another specialty is capretto alla gambalaro (kid marinated for 4 days in wine, vinegar, and spices, then roasted). The best-known dessert is the traditional pincha alla vicentina, made with yellow flour, raisins, and figs.

✪ **Cinzia e Valerio.** Piazzetta Porta Padova 65–67. ☎ **0444/505-213.** Reservations recommended. Main courses 15,000–35,000L ($9–$20); fixed-price menu 65,000L ($38). AE, DC, V. Tues–Sun noon–2:30pm; Tues–Sat 7:30–9:30pm. Closed Aug 4–25. SEAFOOD.

This is the best and most elegant restaurant in Vicenza. You'll be greeted by a polite staff and views of masses of seasonal flowers. The house fish specialties are time-tested recipes from the Adriatic coast. Your meal might begin with mollusks and shellfish arranged into an elegant platter. Other dishes are risotto flavored with squid, a collection of crab and lobster that might surprise you by its size and weight, and an endless procession of fish cooked any way you prefer.

Ristorante Grandcaffè Garibaldi. Piazza dei Signori 2. ☎ **0444/542-455.** Main courses 10,000–20,000L ($6–$12). AE, DC, MC, V. Restaurant, daily 12:30–3pm and 7:30–11:30pm. Cafe, Thurs–Tues 8am–midnight. VICENTINO/ITALIAN/MEDITERRANEAN.

The most impressive cafe/restaurant in the town center has a design worthy of the city of Palladio. It has a wide terrace and an ornate ceiling, marble tables, and a long glass case of sandwiches from which you can make a selection before you sit down (the waitress will bring them to your table). In the cafe, panini (sandwiches) cost 4,000L to 5,000L ($2.30 to $2.90) and a cappuccino 3,000L ($1.75). Prices are slightly lower if you stand at the bar. There's also an upstairs restaurant with trays of antipasti and arrangements of fresh fruit set up on a central table. The menu's array of familiar Italian specialties is among the best in town.

VICENZA AFTER DARK

Faithful to its role as a staid town with a distinct bourgeois overcast, Vicenza places great emphasis on musical expressions in settings whose architectural splendor enhances (and sometimes dominates) the music. Two important series of concerts define the cultural context of the town. The more comprehensive of the two series revolves around the **Teatro Olimpico,** where, thanks to its outdoor venue, cultural events are scheduled only April to late September. Look for a changing program of classical Greek tragedy (*Oedipus Rex* is an enduring favorite), Shakespeare plays (sometimes translated into Italian), chamber music concerts, and dance recitals. You can pick up schedules and buy tickets either at the gate or from the series' administrative headquarters near Vicenza's basilica at **Agenzia Viaggi Palladio,** Contrà Cavour 16 (☎ **0444/546-111**). Tickets are 20,000L to 40,000L ($12 to $23), though in rare instances some nosebleed seats go for 12,000L ($7).

More esoteric, and with a shorter season, is a series of concerts scheduled in June, the **Concerti in Villa.** Every year, the venue changes to include performances of chamber music performed in or near often privately owned villas in the city's outskirts. Look for orchestras set up on loggias or under formal pediments and audiences sitting on chairs in gardens or inside. Note that these depend on the whims of both local musicians and villa owners. Contact the tourist office (above) for details.

4 Verona: City of Juliet & Her Romeo

71 miles W of Venice, 312 miles NW of Rome, 50 miles W of Padua

Verona was the setting for the most famous love story in the English language, Shakespeare's *Romeo and Juliet.* A long-forgotten editor of an old volume of the Bard's plays once wrote: "Verona, so rich in the associations of real history, has even a greater charm for those who would live in the poetry of the past." It's not known if a Romeo or a Juliet ever existed, but the remains of Verona's recorded past are much in evidence today. Its Roman antiquities are unequaled north of Rome.

In its medieval golden age under the despotic Scaligeri princes, Verona reached the pinnacle of its influence and prestige, developing into a town that, even today, is among the great cities of Italy. The best-known member of the ruling Della Scala family, Cangrande I, was a patron of Dante. His sway over Verona has often been compared to that of Lorenzo the Magnificent over Florence.

Verona stands in contrast to Venice, even though both are tourist towns. At least in Verona you can put your feet on solid land—not on water. It overflows with visitors and often lives off a glorious past. But most of the people walking the streets of Verona are actually residents and not visitors. For a city that hit its peak in the 1st century A.D., Verona is doing admirably well. However, stick to the inner core and not the newer sections, which are blighted by industry and tacky urban development.

ESSENTIALS

GETTING THERE   A total of 37 **trains** a day make the 2-hour run between Venice and Verona, at 10,100L ($6) one-way. If you're in the west—say, at Milan—there are even more connections, some 40 trains a day, taking 2 hours to reach Verona at 12,100L ($7) one-way. Six daily trains arrive from Rome, a 6-hour trip, costing 40,500L ($24) one-way. Rail arrivals are at the **Stazione Porta Nuova,** Piazza XXV Aprile (☎ **045/590-688**), south of the centrally located Arena and Piazza Brà; call ☎ 1478/88-099 toll free in Italy only for information. At least six bus lines service the area, taking you frequently into the core.

APT **buses** arrive and depart from the bus station at Piazza XXV Aprile (☎ **045/ 800-4129**), across from the main rail station (above). Buses serve the province and fan out to such cities as Brescia, Mantua, and Riva del Garda. Mid-June to mid-September, you can go from Venice to Verona without changing buses (though it's still better to take the train).

If you've got a **car** and are in Venice, take A4 west to the signposted cutoff for Verona—marked Verona Sud. If you're reaching Verona from the south or north, take A22 and get off at the exit marked Verona Nord.

VISITOR INFORMATION   The main tourist office is adjacent to the Arena at via Leoncino 61 (☎ **045/806-8680**). Summer hours are Monday to Saturday 8am to 8pm and Sunday 9am to noon; off-season hours are Monday to Saturday 8am to 7pm and Sunday 9am to noon. There's another information office at Piazza delle Erbe (☎ **045/800-0065**), open in summer Monday to Saturday 9am to 12:30pm and 2:30

to 7pm. Finally, there's a small office at the Porta Nuova rail station (☎ 045/800-0861), open Monday to Saturday 8am to 7:30pm and Sunday 9am to noon.

EXPLORING THE CITY

Verona lies along the Adige River. The city is most often visited on a quick half-day excursion but deserves more time—it's meant for wandering and contemplation. If you're rushed, head first to the old city. In addition to the sights listed below, there are other attractions that might merit a visit.

Opening onto **Piazza dei Signori,** the handsomest in Verona, is the **Palazzo del Governo,** where Cangrande extended the shelter of his hearth and home to the fleeing Florentine Dante Alighieri. A marble statue of the "divine poet" stands in the center of the square, with an expression as cold as a Dolomite icicle, but unintimidated pigeons perch on his pious head. Facing Dante's back is the late 15th-century **Loggia del Consiglio,** frescoed and surmounted by five statues. Five arches lead into Piazza dei Signori.

The **Arche Scaligere** are outdoor tombs surrounded by highly decorative wrought iron that form a kind of open-air pantheon of the Scaligeri princes. One tomb, that of Cangrande della Scala, rests directly over the door of the 12th-century **Santa Maria Antica.** The mausoleum contains many Romanesque features and is crowned by a copy of an equestrian statue (the original is now at the Castelvecchio). The tomb nearest the door is that of Mastino II; the one behind it—and the most lavish of all—is that of Cansignorio.

✪ **Piazza delle Erbe** ("Square of the Herbs") is a lively palace-flanked square that was formerly the Roman city's forum. Today it's the fruit-and-vegetable market milling with Veronese shoppers and vendors. In the center is a fountain dating from the 14th century and a Roman statue dubbed *The Virgin of Verona.* The pillar at one end of the square, crowned by a chimera, symbolizes the many years Verona was dominated by Venice. Important buildings include the early 14th-century **House of Merchants (Casa di Mercanti);** the **Torre Gardello,** built by one of the Della Scala princes; the restored former **city hall** and the **Torre Lamberti,** soaring about 260 feet; the baroque **Palazzo Maffei;** and the **Casa Mazzanti.**

From the vegetable market, you can walk down **Via Mazzini,** the most fashionable street in Verona, to **Piazza Brà,** with its neoclassical town hall and Renaissance palazzo, the **Gran Guardia.**

Arena di Verona. Piazza Brà. ☎ **045/800-3204.** Admission 6,000L ($3.50) adults, 4,000L ($2.30) children; free the first Sun of each month. Tues–Sun 8am–6:30pm (on performance days, 8am–1:30pm).

The elliptical amphitheater on Piazza Brà, resembling Rome's Colosseum, dates from the 1st century A.D. Four arches of the "outer circle" and a complete "inner ring" still stand, which is rather remarkable since in the 12th century an earthquake hit. From mid-July to mid-August it's the setting for an opera house, where more than 20,000 people are treated to Verdi and Mascagni. The acoustics are perfect, even after all these centuries, and performances are still able to be conducted without microphones. Attending an outdoor evening performance (see "Verona After Dark") can be one of highlights of your visit to Italy. In one season alone, you might be able to hear *Macbeth, Madama Butterfly, Aida, Carmen, Rigoletto,* and Verdi's *Requiem.*

✪ **Castelvecchio.** Corso Castelvecchio 2. ☎ **045/594-734.** Admission 6,000L ($3.50) adults, 2,000L ($1.15) students; free first Sun of each month. Tues–Sun 7:45am–6:30pm.

Built on the order of Cangrande II in the 14th century, the Old Castle stands beside the Adige River (head out Via Roma) near the Ponte Scaligero, a bridge bombed by

Verona

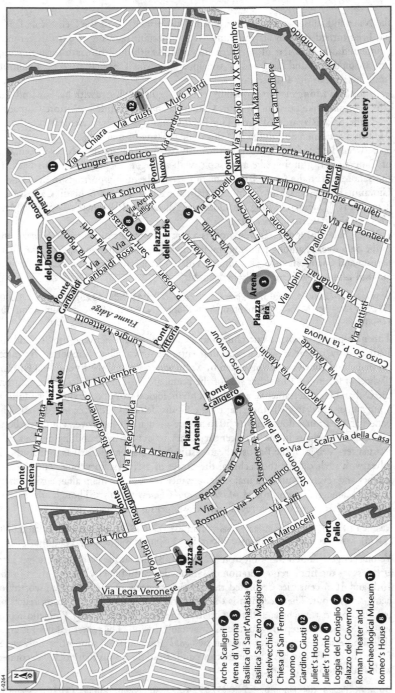

Cemetery

Via E. Torbido
Via S. Paolo Via XX Settembre
Via Mazza
Via Campofiore
Lungre Porta Vittoria
Via Filippini
Lungre Canuléti
Via del Pontiere
Ponte Aleardi
Via Navi
Ponte Nuovo
Via S. Chiara Via Giusti Muro Pardi
Via Carducci
Lungre Teodorico
Dottre Pietra
Via Sottoriva
Via Arche Scaligeri
Via Anastasia
Via Cappello
Via Pigna
Via Forti
Via Rosa
Sant'Anastasia
Plazza del Duomo
Garibaldi
Ponte Garibaldi
P. Bosari
Plazza delle Erbe
Via Stella
Via Mazzini
Stradone S. Fermo
Via Leoncino
Via Pallone
Via Alpini
Via Montanari
Via Battisti
Arena
Plazza Brà
Lungre Matteotti
Fiume Adige
Ponte Vittoria
Corso Cavour
Via Manin
Corso So. p. ta Nuova
Via Valverde
Via C. Marconi
Plazza Via Veneto
Via IV Novembre
Via Farinata
Via Risorgimento
Via Te Repubblica
Ponte Scaligero
Via C. Scalzi Via della Casa
Ponte Catena
Ponte Risorgimento
Plazza Arsenale
Via Arsenale
Regaste San Zeno
Via Rosmini
Via S. Bernardino
Stradone A. Provoeo
Stradone P. ta Palio
Via Saffi
Porta Palio
Via da Vico
Cir. ne Maroncelli
Plazza S. Zeno
Via Pontida
Via Lega Veronese

E-0264

N

Arche Scaligeri 7
Arena di Verona 3
Basilica di Sant'Anastasia 9
Basilica San Zeno Maggiore 1
Castelvecchio 2
Chiesa di San Fermo 5
Duomo 10
Giardino Giusti 12
Juliet's House 6
Juliet's Tomb 4
Loggia del Consiglio 7
Palazzo del Governo 7
Roman Theater and
  Archaeological Museum 11
Romeo's House 8

453

the Nazis and subsequently reconstructed. This former seat of the Della Scala family has been turned into an art museum, with important paintings from the Veronese school and other masters of northern Italy. Fourteenth- and fifteenth-century sculpture are on the ground floor, and on the upper floor you'll see masterpieces of painting from the 15th to the 18th century.

In the **Sala Monga** is Jacopo Bellini's *St. Jerome,* in the desert with his lion and crucifix. Two sisterlike portraits of Saint Catherina and Veneranda by Vittore Carpaccio grace the **Sala Rizzardi Allegri.** The Bellini family is also represented by a lyrical *Madonna con Bambino* painted by Giovanni, a master of that subject.

Between the buildings is the most provocative equestrian statue we've ever seen, that of Cangrande I, grinning like a buffoon, with a dragon sticking out of his back. In the **Sala Murari dalla Corte Brà** is one of the most beguiling portraits in the castle— Giovanni Francesco Caroto's smiling red-haired boy. In the **Sala di Canossa** are Tintoretto's *Madonna Nursing the Child* and *Nativity* and Veronese's *Deposition from the Cross* and *Pala Bevilacqua Lazise.*

In the **Sala Bolognese Trevenzuoli** is a rare self-portrait of Bernardo Strozzi, and in the **Sala Avena,** among paintings by the most famous Venetian masters, like Gianbattista and Giandomenico Tiepolo and Guardi, hangs an almost satirical portrait of an 18th-century patrician family by Longhi.

Basilica San Zeno Maggiore. Piazza San Zeno. ☎ **045/800-4325.** Admission 3,000L ($1.75). Mar–Oct Mon–Sat 9am–6pm, Sun 1–6pm; Nov–Feb Mon–Sat 10am–4pm, Sun 1–4pm.

This near-perfect Romanesque church and campanile built between the 9th and the 12th century is graced with a stunning entrance—two pillars supported by pucecolored marble lions and surmounted by a rose window called the Ruota della Fortuna ("wheel of fortune"). On either side of the portal are bas-reliefs depicting scenes from the Old and New Testaments, as well as a mythological story portraying Theodoric as a huntsman lured to hell (the king of the Goths defeated Odoacer in Verona). The panels on the bronze doors, nearly 50 in all, are a remarkable achievement of medieval art, sculpted perhaps in the 12th century. They reflect a naive handling of their subject matter—see John the Baptist's head resting on a platter. The artists express themselves with such candor they achieve the power of a child's storybook. The interior, somber and severe, contains a major Renaissance work at the main altar, a triptych by Andrea Mantegna, an enthroned *Madonna and Child* with saints. Though not remarkable in its characterization, it reveals the artist's genius for perspective.

Basilica di Sant'Anastasia. Piazza Sant'Anastasia. ☎ **045/800-4325.** Admission 3,000L ($1.75). Mar–Oct Mon–Sat 9:30am–6:30pm, Sun 1–6pm; Nov–Mar daily 10am–4pm.

Verona's largest church was built from 1290 to 1481. Its facade isn't complete, yet nevertheless it's the finest representation of Gothic design in the city. Many artists in the 15th and 16th centuries decorated the interior, but few of the works are worthy of being singled out. The exception is the **Pellegrini Chapel,** with terra-cotta reliefs by the Tuscan artist Michele, and the **Giusti Chapel,** with a fresco by Pisanello representing St. George preparing to face his inevitable dragon. The patterned floor is especially impressive. As you enter, look for two *gobbi* (hunchbacks) supporting holy water fonts. The church also has a beautiful campanile from the 1300s that's richly decorated with sculpture and frescoes.

Duomo. Piazza del Duomo. ☎ **045/595-627.** Admission 3,000L ($1.75). Mar–Oct Mon–Sat 9:30am–6pm, Sun 1–6pm; off-season Mon–Sat 10am–4pm, Sun 1:30–4pm.

Verona's cathedral is less interesting than San Zeno Maggiore but still merits a visit. It was begun in the 12th century but not completed until the 17th. A blend of

Romanesque and Gothic, its facade contains (lower level) 12th-century sculptured reliefs by Nicolaus depicting scenes of Roland and Oliver, two of the legendary dozen knights attending Charlemagne. In the left aisle (first chapel) is Titian's *Assumption,* the stellar work of the Duomo. The other major work is the rood screen in front of the presbytery, with Ionic pillars, designed by Samicheli.

Chiesa di San Fermo. Stradone San Fermo. ☎ **045/800-7287.** Admission 3,000L ($1.75). Apr–Oct Mon–Fri 9:30am–6pm, Sat noon–6pm; Nov–Mar Mon–Fri 10am–5pm, Sat noon–5pm.

This Romanesque church from the 11th century forms the foundation of the 14th-century Gothic building surmounting it. Through time it has been used by both the Benedictines and the Franciscans. The interior is unusual, with a single nave and a splendid roof constructed of wood and exquisitely paneled. The most important work inside is Pisanello's frescoed *Annunciation,* to the left of the main entrance (at the Brenzoni tomb). Delicate and graceful, the work reveals the artist's keen eye for architectural detail and his bizarre animals.

✪ Roman Theater (Teatro Romano) and Archeological Museum (Museo Archeologico). Rigaste Redentore 2. ☎ **045/800-0360.** Admission 5,000L ($2.90) adults, 2,000L ($1.15) students/children; free the first Sun of each month. Tues–Sun 8am–6:30pm (to 1:30pm in winter).

The **Teatro Romano,** built in the 1st century A.D., now stands in ruins at the foot of St. Peter's Hill. For nearly a quarter of a century a Shakespearean festival has been staged here in July and August, and, of course, a unique theater-going experience is to see *Romeo and Juliet* or *Two Gentlemen of Verona* in this setting. The theater is across the Adige River (take the Ponte di Pietra). After seeing the remains of the theater, you can take a rickety elevator to the 10th-century **Santi Siro e Libera** church towering over it. In the cloister of St. Jerome is the **Archaeological Museum,** with interesting mosaics and Etruscan bronzes.

Giardino Giusti. Via Giardino Giusti 2. ☎ **045/803-4029.** Admission 5,000L ($2.90) adults, 2,000L ($1.15) students/children. Apr–Sept daily 9am–8pm (to sunset off-season).

One of Italy's oldest and most famous gardens, the Giardino Giusti was created at the end of the 14th century. These well-manicured Italian gardens, studded with cypress trees, form one of the most relaxing and coolest spots in Verona for strolls. You can climb up to the "monster balcony" for an incomparable view of the city.

The layout was given to the gardens by Agostino Giusti. All its 16th-century characteristics—the grottoes, statues, fountains, box-enclosed flower garden, and maze—have remained intact. In addition to the flower displays, you can admire statues by Lorenzo Muttoni and Alessandro Vittoria, Roman remains, and the great cypress mentioned by Goethe. The gardens, with their adjacent 16th-century palazzo, form one of Italy's most interesting urban complexes. The maze, constructed with myrtle hedges, faithfully reproduces the 1786 plan of the architect Trezza. Its complicated pattern and small size make it one of the most unusual in Europe. The gardens lie near the Roman Theater, only a few minutes' walk from the heart of the city.

Juliet's Tomb (Tomba di Giulietta). Via del Pontiere 5. ☎ **045/800-0361.** Admission 5,000L ($2.90) adults; 2,000L ($1.15) students/children; free the first Sun of each month. Tues–Sun 7:45am–7pm.

The so-called Juliet's tomb is sheltered in a Franciscan monastery you enter on Via Luigi da Porto, off Via del Pontiere. "A grave? O, no, a lantern. . . . For here lies Juliet, and her beauty makes this vault a feasting presence full of light." Don't you believe it! Still, the cloisters, near the Adige River, are graceful. Adjoining the tomb is a museum of frescoes, dedicated to G. B. Cavalcaselle.

Juliet's House (Casa di Giulietta). Via Cappello 23. ☎ **045/803-4303.** Admission 6,000L ($3.50) adults, 2,000L ($1.15) students/children. Tues–Sun 7:45am–6:30pm.

"Juliet's house" is a small home with a balcony and a courtyard. There's no evidence any family named Capulet lived here, but it was acquired by the city in 1905 and turned into this contrived sight. So powerful is the legend of Juliet that millions flock to this house, not seeming to care whether Juliet lived here or not. Tradition calls for visitors to rub the right breast of a bronze statue of Juliet that's now brightly polished by millions of hands. With a little bit of imagination, it's not difficult to hear Romeo say: "But, soft! What light through yonder window breaks? It is the east, and Juliet is the sun!"

SHOPPING

The byword for shopping in Verona is elegance, and shops feature the fashion being touted in Milan and Rome. Consequently, don't look for touristy products or rustic crafts and souvenirs, but rather for more upscale versions of all-Italian fashion and accessories. A worthwhile shop for men is **Class Uomo,** Via San Rocchetto 13B (☎ **049/595-775**). Every Veronese knows the allure for both genders of **Armani,** Via Cappello 25 (☎ **049/594-727**).

If you yearn for a Veronan antique to haul back to your private world, look for a dense concentration of vendors selling antiques or old bric-a-brac in the streets around **Sant'Anastasia** or head for **Piazza delle Erbe** for a more or less constant roster of merchants in flea market–style kiosks selling the dusty, and often junkier, collectibles of yesteryear, along with aromatic herbs, fruits, and vegetables.

ACCOMMODATIONS

Hotel rooms tend to be scarce during the County Fair in March and the opera and theater season in July and August.

VERY EXPENSIVE

✪ **Due Torri Hotel Baglioni.** Piazza Sant'Anastasia 4, 37121 Verona. ☎ **045/595-044.** Fax 045/800-4130. E-mail: duetorri.verona@baglionipalacehotel.it. 91 units. A/C MINIBAR TV TEL. 410,000–650,000L ($238–$377) double; from 1,000,000L ($580) suite. Rates include breakfast. AE, DC, MC, V. Parking 45,000L ($26).

Now owned by the upscale Cogeta Palace Hotels chain, this was the 1400s home of the Scaligeri dynasty. During the 18th and 19th centuries it hosted VIPs like Mozart, Goethe, and Tsar Alexander I. In the 1950s, legendary hotelier Enrico Wallner transformed the palace into a hotel with a stunning collection of antiques. Despite the 1990 takeover by Cogeta, which richly restored the entire hotel over 4 years, many of these antiques remain in the public areas and guest rooms—a splendid range of Directoire, Empire, Louis XVIII, and Biedermeier. There are also many old oil paintings, a large lobby in the palace's old courtyard, and a series of well-upholstered salons serviced by a discreet staff.

Dining/Diversions: The hotel's Ristorante All'Aquila serves typical local and light cuisine. This is one of the most distinguished restaurants of Verona (see "Dining" below). There's also an elegant bar.

Amenities: 24-hour room service, baby-sitting, laundry/valet.

✪ **Hotel Gabbia d'Oro.** Corso Porta Borsari 4A, 37121 Verona. ☎ **045/800-3060.** Fax 045/590-293. 27 units. A/C MINIBAR TV TEL. 350,000–450,000L ($203–$261) double; 650,000–800,000L ($377–$464) suite. Rates include breakfast except in July–Aug. AE, DC, MC, V. Valet parking 50,000L ($29) 1st day, 40,000L ($23) each extra day.

This upscale hotel in an 18th-century palazzo opened in 1990, the first hotel in years to give the Baglioni serious competition. It has a more romantic Romeo-and-Juliet atmosphere than the more fabled hostelry. Small, discreet, and devoted to the privacy of its guests, it contains many of the building's original grandiose frescoes, its beamed ceiling, and (in the cozy bar area) much of the original carved paneling. The interior courtyard contains potted plants, flowering shrubs, and tables devoted to drinking and dining in clement weather. The guest rooms boast framed engravings, antique furniture, and (in some cases) narrow balconies with wrought-iron detailing overlooking the street or the courtyard.

Dining: The hotel offers a rich setting for meals, which are available only to guests. A regional and international cuisine is served.

Amenities: Concierge, room service, dry cleaning/laundry, newspaper delivery on request, in-room massage, twice-daily maid service, baby-sitting, secretarial services.

EXPENSIVE

Hotel Accademia. Via Scala 12, 37121 Verona. ☎ and fax **045/596-222.** 95 units. A/C MINIBAR TV TEL. 240,000–395,000L ($139–$229) double; 335,000–570,000L ($194–$331) suite. Rates include buffet breakfast. AE, DC, MC, V. Parking 25,000L ($15).

This is one of Verona's few older hotels that was custom built as a hotel rather than having been transformed from a monastery or palazzo. Dating from the late 1800s, it contains Oriental carpets, a medieval tapestry, and a pair of grandiose marble columns flanking the polished stone stairwell leading to the three floors of guest rooms. The rooms are conservatively traditional and high-ceilinged.

Dining/Diversions: There's a paneled modern bar and a restaurant (the Accademia) that operates under a separate management. Guests receive a 10% discount on meals.

Amenities: Concierge, room service, baby-sitting, laundry/dry cleaning.

MODERATE

Colomba d'Oro. Via C. Cattaneo 10, 37121 Verona. ☎ **045/595-300.** Fax 045/594-974. 51 units. A/C MINIBAR TV TEL. 270,000–320,000L ($157–$186) double; 320,000–386,000L ($186–$224) suite. Rates include buffet breakfast. AE, DC, MC, V. Parking 26,000L ($15).

The Colomba d'Oro was built as a villa during the 1600s and later transformed into a monastery. During the 18th and 19th centuries it served as an inn for travelers and employees of the postal service and eventually grew into the large hotel it is today. The building is efficiently organized and has an atmosphere somewhere between semitraditional and contemporary. The rooms are nicely furnished with matching fabrics and comfortable furniture. Breakfast is the only meal served, but there are many restaurants nearby.

INEXPENSIVE

Hotel Aurora. Piazza delle Erbe, 37121 Verona. ☎ **045/594-717.** Fax 045/801-0860. 32 units. A/C TV TEL. 150,000–190,000L ($87–$110) double. Rates include breakfast. AE, MC, V. Parking free on street; 20,000L ($12) in public lot (a 10-minute walk).

The foundations of this tall and narrow hotel were already at least 400 years old when the building was constructed in the 1500s. In 1994, its owners completed a radical renovation that improved all the hidden systems (structural beams, electricity, and plumbing) but retained hints of the building's antique origins. It's set behind a sienna-colored facade on a square that's transformed every morning, beginning around 7:30am, into Verona's busiest emporium of fruits and vegetables. Views from all but a few of the simply furnished rooms encompass a full or partial look at the activity in the square. You have to climb a flight of steps to reach the reception area, but after that there's a cramped but serviceable elevator. The hotel's bar is open 24 hours.

Hotel de' Capuleti. Via del Pontiere 26, 37122 Verona. ☎ **045/800-0154.** Fax 045/803-2970. www.bestwestern.com. E-mail: capulet@easy1.easynet.it. 42 units. A/C MINIBAR TV TEL. 240,000L ($139) double. Rates include breakfast. AE, DC, MC, V. Closed Dec 22–Jan 10.

Hotel de' Capuleti is an attractively pristine little place, conveniently a few steps from Juliet's (supposed) tomb and the chapel where she's said to have married Romeo. The reception area has stone floors and leather couches, along with a tastefully renovated decor that's reflected upstairs in the comfortable guest rooms.

Hotel Giulietta e Romeo. Vicolo Tre Marchetti 3, 37121 Verona. ☎ **045/800-3554.** Fax 045/801-0862. www2.easynet.it/gr. E-mail: giuliettaeromeo@easynet.it. 32 units. A/C MINIBAR TV TEL. 140,000–260,000L ($81–$151) double. Rates include breakfast. Add 30% to these rates during trade fairs. AE, MC, V.

This place is permeated with a slightly saccharine replay of Shakespeare's great love affair, and most of the rooms in this once-stately palazzo look out over the Roman arena. In honor of the maiden Juliet, the hotel maintains at least one marble balcony that might be appropriate in a modern-day revival of the great play. The rooms are tastefully modernized, not overly large, and have marble-sheathed baths, touches of burnished hardwoods, comfortable furnishings, and lighting you can actually read by.

Hotel Torcolo. Vicolo Listone 3, 37121 Verona. ☎ **045/800-7512.** Fax 045/800-4058. 19 units. A/C MINIBAR TV TEL. 188,000L ($109) double. Rates include breakfast. MC, V. Parking 15,000–20,000L ($9–$12) in nearby public lot.

The setting is modest but, thanks to the devoted efforts of its trio of hardworking owners (Silvia Pomari and her colleagues, Marina and Diana), it's spotless. You'll find the Torcolo near both the Roman arena and Piazza Brà, in a building erected around 1825. The plain guest rooms' furnishings run the gamut from modern and banal to simple but antique. The staff speaks English.

DINING
EXPENSIVE

✪ **Arche.** Via Arche Scaligere 6. ☎ **045/800-7415.** Reservations required. Main courses 30,000–45,000L ($17–$26); fixed-price menus 80,000–90,000L ($46–$52). AE, DC, MC, V. Mon 7:30–9:30pm, Tues–Sat 12:30–2:30pm and 7:30–9:30pm. Closed Jan. ITALIAN.

This classic restaurant is acclaimed by some critics as the finest in Verona. We'd give that honor to Il Desco (below), but Arche is a close runner-up. Owners Giancarlo and Paola Gioco insist on market-fresh fish from nearby Chioggia. The restaurant was founded in 1879 by Giancarlo's great-grandfather, and the seafood dishes are based on recipes passed down from generation to generation, including some discovered in ancient cookbooks. Sole, sea bass with delectable porcini mushrooms, and scampi are among the eternal favorites. Baked "sea scorpion" with black olives and ravioli stuffed with sea bass and served with clam sauce are the chef's finest specialties. The furnishings in this 1420 building are Liberty style, enhanced by candlelight and fresh flowers.

Ristorante All'Aquila. In the Due Torri Hotel Baglioni, Piazza Sant'Anastasia 4. ☎ **045/595-044.** Reservations recommended. Main courses 29,000–35,000L ($17–$21); set-price menu 65,000L ($39). AE, DC, MC, V. Daily 12:30–2:30pm and 7:30–10pm. ITALIAN/INTERNATIONAL.

Verona's most appealing upscale restaurant benefits from a sophisticated and impeccably trained staff headed by Sr. Mattia, who trained at Claridge's in London. Boasting in an art-nouveau decor of pink and apple green, it offers one of the most gracefully orchestrated dining experiences in Verona. The menu is almost completely rewritten every 6 months but is likely to include rarities like smoked horsemeat served with arugula and shaved parmigiano, marinated trout with citrus sauce, and tartare of fish with fresh cucumber. Pastas include ravioli with a medley of soft cheeses, spinach, and watercress sauce and subtly flavored tagliatelle with cream, herb, and egg-yolk sauce. Main course could include braised arugula and eggplant and filets of perch prepared with sage. Dessert might be tiramisu or ricotta mousse. The list of mostly Italian wine is as comprehensive as that at any other restaurant in town.

○ **Ristorante il Desco.** Via Dietro San Sebastiano 7. ☎ **045/595-358.** Reservations recommended. Main courses 42,000–45,000L ($24–$26); *menu degustazione* 135,000L ($78). AE, DC, MC, V. Mon–Sat 12:30–2pm and 7:30–10pm. Closed Jan 1–7 and Dec 25–26. ITALIAN.

The tops in Verona, Il Desco is a handsome restaurant occupying a tastefully renovated palazzo that's one of the civic prides of the city. The menu steers closer to the philosophy of cuisine moderne than anything else in town. Specialties make use of the freshest ingredients—shrimp purée; potato pie with mushrooms and black truffles; calamari salad with shallots; tortellini with sea bass; risotto with radicchio and truffles; and tagliolini with fresh mint, lemon, and oranges. The wine cellar is superb, and the sommelier will help if you're unfamiliar with regional vintages. The cheese selection is wide-ranging, featuring choices from France.

MODERATE

Nuovo Marconi. Via Fogge 4. ☎ **045/591-910.** Reservations required. Main courses 15,000–30,000L ($9–$17). AE, DC, MC, V. Mon–Sat 12:30–2:45pm and 8–10:30pm. ITALIAN.

Nuovo Marconi is glamorous, in an ocher-colored villa on a narrow street around the corner from Piazza dei Signori. The doors are covered with an art nouveau wrought-iron grill, and the interior has stone columns, silk-shaded lamps, and framed paintings. The menu, reflecting the best traditional and regional dishes, changes daily depending on the availability of ingredients. The kitchen uses only fresh products, whether it be pasta, fish, or meat. In season, the chef likes to specialize in game dishes, and the fish antipasti are reason enough to visit. The wine list is updated every 6 months.

Ristorante 12 Apostoli. Vicolo Corticella San Marco 3. ☎ **045/596-999.** Reservations recommended. Main courses 25,000–30,000L ($15–$17). AE, DC, MC, V. Tues–Sun 12:30–2:30pm; Tues–Sat 7:30–10pm. Closed June 15–July 5. ITALIAN.

Operated by the two Gioco brothers, this is Verona's oldest restaurant, in business for 250 years. It's a festive place, steeped in tradition, with frescoed walls and two dining rooms separated by brick arches. Giorgio, the artist of the kitchen, changes his menu daily in the best tradition of great chefs, while Franco directs the dining room. Just consider salmon baked in a pastry shell (the fish is marinated the day before, seasoned with garlic, and stuffed with scallops) or chicken stuffed with shredded vegetables and cooked in four layers of paper. To begin, we recommend the tempting antipasti alla Scaligera. For dessert, try the homemade cake.

INEXPENSIVE

Ristorante Re Teodorico. Piazzale di Castel San Pietro 1. ☎ **045/834-9990.** Reservations required. Main courses 25,000–30,000L ($15–$17). AE, DC, MC, V. Thurs–Tues noon–3pm and 7–10pm. Closed Jan. REGIONAL/INTERNATIONAL.

Ristorante Re Teodorico is perched high on a hill at the edge of town, with a panoramic view of Verona and the Adige. From its entrance, you descend a cypress-lined road to the ledge-hanging restaurant suggestive of a lavish villa. Tables are set out on a wide flagstone terrace edged with classical columns and an arbor of red, pink, and yellow vines. Specialties are homemade pasta, always delectable; swordfish with tomatoes, capers, and fresh basil; and chateaubriand with béarnaise sauce. The dessert specialty is crêpes Suzette.

VeronAntica. Via Sottoriva 10. ☎ **045/800-4124.** Reservations recommended. Main courses 13,000–25,000L ($8–$15). AE, DC, MC, V. Sept–June Wed–Mon noon–2:30pm and 7–10:45pm; July–Aug Wed–Mon 6–10:45pm. INTERNATIONAL.

VeronAntica is a distinguished local restaurant on the ground floor of a town house a short block from the river, across from a cobblestone arcade similar to the ones used in Zeffirelli's *Romeo and Juliet.* This place attracts the locals—not just tourists. It's made even more romantic at night by a hanging lantern that dimly illuminates the street. The chef knows how to prepare all the classic Italian dishes as well as some innovative ones. Try bretelline (tagliatelle made with flower of rice) with rughetta salad and asparagus or salmon in papillote with fresh mussels, seafood, and tomatoes. June to September, you can dine on an open-air terrace.

VERONA AFTER DARK

Opera festivals on a scale more human and accessible than those in cities like Milan are presented in Verona annually between July and August. The setting is the ancient **Arena di Verona,** a site that's grand enough to include as many elephants as might be needed for a performance of *Aïda.* Schedules vary every year, so for more information and tickets call ☎ **045/800-51-51.** Prices of tickets vary with view lines and whatever is being staged but usually are 40,000L to 250,000L ($23 to $145).

For tickets and information on the opera or ballet in Verona, **Edwards & Edwards** has a U.S. office from which you can buy tickets before you go: 1270 Ave. of the Americas, Suite 2414, New York, NY 10020 (☎ **800/223-6108** or 914/328-2150; fax 914/328-2752). A personal visit isn't necessary, and they can mail vouchers or fax a confirmation to allow you to pick up the tickets half an hour prior to curtain call.

Looking for a break from too much Verdi? Head for **Disco Berfis Club,** Via Lussemburgo (☎ **045/508-024**), or **Bar/Disco Tribu,** Via Calderara 17 (☎ **045/566-470**), where rhythms echo what's being broadcast in New York and Milan. More closely linked to Verona's historic core is **Bar Campidoglio,** Piazza Tira Bosco (☎ **045/594-448**), which is more subdued, less frenzied and electronic, and more evocative of the Italy of long ago.

Gays and lesbians can call **Circolo Pink,** Via Scriminari 7 (☎ **045/801-2854**), to get details on gay cultural activities, parties, or newly opened bars. You can call the hot line only Monday to Wednesday 9 to 11pm and Sunday 6 to 9pm.

5 Treviso

19 miles N of Venice

A city of sweets and art, **Treviso** is known to culinary fans for cherries and the creation of tiramisu ("pick me up")—a delicious blend of ladyfingers, mascarpone cheese, eggs, cocoa, liqueur, and espresso. Art aficionados know it for its many works by Tomaso da Modena.

ESSENTIALS

GETTING THERE   There are four **trains** per hour from Venice, a trip of 30 minutes costing 2,800L ($1.60) one-way, and hourly trains from Udine, a trip of 1 hour 30 minutes for 10,000L ($6) one-way. Treviso's station (☎ **0422/655-111** or 1478/88-088 toll-free in Italy only) is at Piazza Duca d'Aosta on the southern end of town.

The station at Lungosile Mattei 21 receives **buses** on the La Marca bus line (☎ 0422/412-222) from Bassano del Grappa nine times daily, a trip of 1 hour costing 5,800L ($3.35) one-way, and every 30 minutes from Padua, a 1-hour 10-minute excursion for 3,800L ($2.20) one-way. The ACT line (☎ 0422/541-821) runs two buses an hour from Venice, a 30-minute trip for 3,800L ($2.20).

If you've got a **car** and are in Venice, take A11 through Mestre, a distance of 6 miles; head northeast on A4 for 3 miles, then take Route S13 for 10 miles north to Treviso.

VISITOR INFORMATION   The tourist office, Via Toniolo 41 (☎ 0422/ 547-632), is open Monday to Friday 9am to noon and 3 to 6pm, and Saturday 8:30am to noon.

SEEING THE SIGHTS

Tommaso da Modena painted 40 portraits in the **Capitolo dei Dominicani** of the **Seminario Vescovile,** Via San Nicolò (☎ 0422/3247). They capture the diverse personalities of a series of Dominican monks seated at their desks. There's no admission fee, and daily hours are 8am to noon and 3:30 to 7pm (to 5:30pm in winter).

No longer a church, the **Chiesa di Santa Caterina,** Piazzetta Mario Botter, houses the frescoes comprising Modena's depiction of the Christian legend of the Ursula Cycle, with its 11,000 virgins all accounted for. Alas, a restoration program may keep the church closed until the end of 1999. Call the **Civic Museum (Museo Civico),** Borgo Cavour 24 (☎ 0422/658-442), for hours or an appointment. The museum houses the strange *Il Castragatti* (The Cat Fixer) by Sebastiano Florigero, a *Crucifixion* by Bassano, and the fresco *San Antonio Abate* by Pordenone. Hours are Tuesday to Saturday 9am to 12:30pm and 2:30 to 5pm and Sunday 9am to noon. Admission is 4,000L ($2.30).

You can visit the **Duomo,** Piazza del Duomo at Via Canoniche 2 (☎ 0422/ 545-720), Monday to Saturday 8 to noon and 3:30 to 7pm and Sunday 7:30am to 1pm and 3:30 to 8pm. It contains more frescoes by Pordenone as well as an *Annunciation* by Titian. The crypt is open after 10:30am. A stroll through Piazza dei Signori offers views of several interesting Romanesque buildings, like the municipal **bell tower,** the **Palazzo Trecento,** and the nearby **Loggia dei Cavalieri** on Via Martiri della Libertà.

SHOPPING

The city is known for its production of wrought iron and copper utensils, and the best places to find these goods are **Prior,** Via Palesto 12 (☎ 0422/545-886) and **Morandin,** Via Palestro 50 (☎ 0422/543-651).

ACCOMMODATIONS

Ca' del' Galletto. Via Santa Bona Vecchia 30, 31100 Treviso. ☎ 0422/432-550. Fax 0422/ 432-510. 60 units. A/C MINIBAR TV TEL. 220,000–270,000L ($128–$157) double; 300,000L ($174) suite. Rates include buffet breakfast. AE, DC, MC, V. Free parking.

This thoroughly modern hotel offers comfortable soundproof rooms with safe-deposit boxes, trouser presses, and hair dryers. Deluxe accommodations also include Jacuzzis. An enclosed garden allows you outdoor privacy in the city. The lobby bar is open 24 hours for your convenience, and the Ristorante Albertini next door serves rich Venetian seafood and other traditional specialties. The hotel is currently constructing a pool, with an expected completion date of mid- to late 1999.

✪ **Hotel Al Fogher.** Viale della Repubblica 10, 31100 Treviso. ☎ 800/528-1234 in the U.S., or 0422/432-950. Fax 0422/430-391. www.bestwestern.com. 56 units. A/C TV TEL. 240,000L ($139) double; 280,000L ($162) suite. Rates include breakfast. AE, DC, MC, V.

We especially recommend this business favorite of wine merchants, just north of the medieval fortifications of Treviso. The decor contrasts antique statuary with modern art prints and marble with glass bricks. The guest rooms are done in cool pastels and floral prints and outfitted in an internationally modern style. The top floor has a panoramic terrace where guests congregate for views over the countryside, and the well-regarded basement restaurant serves seasonal Venetian dishes made from the market's freshest ingredients (it's popular, so reservations are suggested). Meals are highlighted with real silver service and a substantial wine list. The restaurant is closed in August and the first week of January.

Hotel Continental. Via Roma 16, 31100 Treviso. ☎ **0422/411-216.** Fax 0422/55-054. 80 units. A/C MINIBAR TV TEL. 235,000L ($136) double. Rates include breakfast. AE, DC, MC, V. Parking 25,000L ($15).

Close to the sights in the old city walls, this four-star hotel has since 1958 provided dependable service and comfortable accommodations. The building itself, though only about 40 years old, pays homage to Italian design of various eras, mixing and matching antique furnishings so each room gains an individuality that's elegantly highlighted by beautiful fabrics and Oriental rugs. There's no restaurant or parking, but a number of eateries and parking lots are close by.

NEARBY ACCOMMODATIONS

✪ **Villa Condulmer.** Via Zermanese 1, 31021 Zerman di Mogliano Veneto. ☎ **041/457-100.** Fax 041/457-134. www.tsi.it/condulmer. 42 units. A/C MINIBAR TEL. 300,000L ($174) double; 340,000–380,000L ($197–$220) junior suite; 420,000L ($244) apt. Rates include breakfast. AE, DC, MC, V. Drive 7 miles south on S13 to Zerman, just outside Mogliano Veneto.

The finest place to stay is outside Treviso. Giuseppe Verdi fled here in 1853 after the Venetian debut of *La Traviata* was met with catcalls. This illustrious house was built in 1743 by the Condulmer family, whose wealth and power can be traced to 14th-century ancestor Pope Eugene IV. It passed from the family's hands in the early 19th century, when frescoes by Moretti Laresi were added. The kind of luxury Ronald Reagan found here in 1987 includes elaborate stuccowork, marble floors, crystal chandeliers, Oriental carpets, period furnishings, and large guest rooms located in the main house as well as in two annexes with lofts. The back garden houses a private chapel, and beyond it stretches a park with a small lake, hillocks, ruins, a pool, a 27-hole golf course, a tennis court, and riding grounds. There's also a piano bar and a restaurant, which grows its own produce to supplement the market's fresh fish and game.

DINING

Beccherie. Piazza Ancilotto 10. ☎ **0422/56-601.** Reservations recommended. Main courses 18,000–30,000L ($10–$17). AE, DC, MC, V. Tues–Sun 12:30–2pm; Tues–Sat 7:30–10pm. Closed July 15–31. VENETIAN.

Despite the prevalence of the car park, this stone-sided building still evokes the era of its construction (1830). The cuisine and the flavorings of the dishes vary with the seasons and include such midwinter game dishes as faraona in salsa peverada (guinea hen in peppery sauce) and a spring/summer favorite, pasticcio di melanzane (eggplant casserole). In between, look for enduring traditions like fried crabs from the Venetian lagoon, served with herb-flavored polenta; salt cod Vicenza style; osso bucco; fiery hot pastas; and roasted chicken.

El Toulà da Alfredo. Via Collalto 26. ☎ **0422/540-275.** Reservations required. Sat–Sun. Main courses 15,000–40,000L ($9–$23). AE, DC, MC, V. Tues–Sun noon–2:30pm and 7:30–11pm. Closed Aug 8–24. INTERNATIONAL/VENETIAN.

This is the upscale restaurant that launched what's now a nine-member chain known throughout Italy for its food and service. It offers Veneto-based dishes whose inspiration varies with the seasonality of the ingredients and the chef's intelligent takes on local traditions. In a pair of dining rooms built in 1790 and outfitted in an upscale art nouveau style, you can order superb versions of risotto with baby peas, pappardelle pasta studded with baby asparagus tips and herbs, Venetian-style calves' liver, veal kidneys in mustard sauce, risotto con funghi (rice with mushrooms), and blinis with caviar. The lengthy dessert roster includes light sweet sorbets, often made from local fruit. The service is impeccable.

THE WINE ROADS FROM TREVISO

Many travelers indelibly associate wine and the cultivation of grapes with the gently rolling foothills of the Dolomites around Treviso. For a view of the ancient vines that have produced thousands of gallons of the region's most drinkable wine, take a drive along the two local highways whose adjacent vineyards are the most respected in the region. Together, they're known as the **Strade dei Vini del Piave** in honor of the nearby Piave River, and both begin at the medieval town of **Conegliano,** where the tourist office is at Via Columbo 45 (☎ 0438/21-230), open Tuesday to Friday 9am to 1pm and 3 to 6pm and Saturday 9am to 1pm.

You won't find route numbers associated with either of these wine roads, but each is clearly signposted en route, beginning in central Conegliano. The less interesting is the **Strada del Vino Rosso (Red Wine Road),** running through 25 miles of humid flatlands southeast of Conegliano. Significant points en route include the scenic hamlets of Oderzo, Motta, and Ponte di Piave, a site on the outskirts of the province of Treviso.

Much more scenic and evocative is the **Strada del Vino Bianco (White Wine Road),** or, more specifically, the **Strada del Prosecco,** meandering through the foothills of the Dolomites for about 24 miles northwest of Conegliano, ending at Valdobbiadene. En route, it passes through particularly prestigious regions famous for their sparkling Prosecco, a quality white meant to be drunk young, with the characteristic taste and smell of ripe apples, wisteria, and acacia honey. The most charming of the many hamlets you'll encounter (blink an eye and you'll miss them) are San Pietro di Feletto, Follina, and Pieve di Soligno. Each is awash with family-run cantinas, kiosks, and roadside stands, all selling the fermented fruits of the local harvest and offering platters of prosciutto, local cheese, and crusty bread.

Don't expect mega-agriculture here, as the low-slung stone buildings baking in the sun amid verdant vines look virtually unchanged since they were built. The Strada del Vino Bianco was the first wine road established by the Italian government, in 1966, and the designation immediately prompted equivalent regions throughout Italy to apply for official recognition.

The two best hotels for establishing a base here are in Conegliano. The three-star **Canon d'Oro,** Via XX Settembre 129, 31015 Conegliano (☎ and fax **0438/34-246**), occupies a 15th-century building near the rail station and charges 140,000L ($81) double. The four-star **Hotel Città de Conegliano,** Via Parrilla 1 (☎ **0438/21-445;** fax 0438/410-950), is the best in town, an elegant landmark with unusual frescoes on the facade and doubles for 108,000L to 130,000L ($63 to $75).

FOOD & DRINK EN ROUTE

IN CONEGLIANO   Among the many country-comfortable sites dotting the area, our favorite is **Tre Panoce,** Via Vecchia Trevigiano 50 (☎ **0438/60-071**). Occupying a 16th-century (or perhaps older) stone building, it charges around 50,000L ($29) for full meals that include a culinary celebration for whatever is in season (wine isn't included). Your pasta may be flavored with radicchio, fresh mushrooms, wild herbs, or local cheese, depending on the whim of the chef, but will always be a suitable foil for the local wines. Tre Panoce is in the hills above Conegliano, half a mile from the town center. It's open Tuesday to Sunday noon to 2:30pm and Tuesday to Saturday 8 to 10pm. Closed August.

More formal (indeed, the most formal restaurant in town), is **Al Salisà,** Via XX Settembre 2 (☎ **0438/24-288**), which occupies a stone building with 12th-century foundations. Excellent food, complemented by the authentically old-fashioned setting, attracts the best-heeled visitors in town. Menu items include roasted veal prepared with wild herbs, sea bass with seasonal vegetables and basil-flavored white-wine sauce, and fettuccine with wild duck. Expect to spend 45,000L ($26) and up for a full meal. It's open Thursday to Tuesday noon to 3pm and Thursday to Monday 7:30 to 10:30pm.

IN VALDOBBIADENE You might not be too hungry by the time you reach this hamlet because of the many edible temptations you're likely to have sampled en route. But if you're in the mood for a meal, the two most appealing restaurants are **Al Pesce,** Via Erizza 287 (☎ **0423/980-296**), and **Valle Mariana,** Via Cal Vecchia del Col 8 (☎ **0423/972-616**). Both feature the region's seasonal produce, fresh fowl, fish, and meat. Al Pesce is open Wednesday to Monday noon to 3pm and Wednesday to Sunday 7 to 11pm; Valle Mariana is open Friday to Tuesday noon to 2pm and 7:30 to 10pm.

If you do decide to stop and take a look around, **Altamarca** (☎ **0423/972-655**), a small tour group, provide English-speaking tours of the various vineyards along the wine route between Conegliano and Valdobbiadene. Call for tour times and admission prices.

6 Asolo: Town of a Hundred Horizons

11 miles E of Marostica, 7 miles E of Bassano, 20 miles NW of Treviso

Known as the "Town of a Hundred Horizons" because of its panoramic views, **Asolo** entered the mainstream of Renaissance politics in the late 1400s, when Caterina Cornari, daughter of a prominent Venetian family, became a pawn in a strategic treaty between Venice and the king of Cyprus. After the king's death, Queen Caterina struggled unsuccessfully, with Venetian help, to keep the Turks off Cyprus. When they conquered the island and ousted the Venetians, Caterina was given this hamlet as a consolation prize.

Between 1498 and her death in 1510, she shuttled between Venice and her country estate in Asolo, building up the local economy and supporting the arts, creating the village you see today. Partly because of her patronage of music, literature, and painting, the town's reputation as a centerpiece for the arts flourished through the turn of this century as home to both English poet Robert Browning and Italy's grande dame of the stage, Eleonora Duse, a figurehead of the art-nouveau movement.

ESSENTIALS

GETTING THERE There's daily **bus** service from Bassano, Treviso, and Venice. For information, call ☎ **0422/412-222** in Treviso. If you've got a **car** and are in Treviso, take Route 348 for 16 miles northwest to Cornuda, then follow Route 248 for 5½ miles west to Asolo. From Bassano, take Route 248 for 7 miles east to reach the town.

VISITOR INFORMATION The **APT tourist office** is at Piazza Gabriele d'Annunzio 1 (☎ **0423/529-046**), open Monday to Saturday 8:30am to 1pm and 3 to 6pm.

EXPLORING CATERINA'S TOWN

Most of Asolo's allure comes from its well-preserved Renaissance architecture and timeless agrarian charm, but there are a handful of monuments worth visiting. Queen Caterina's rebuilt home is the **Castello Cornaro,** Via Regina Cornaro. Of its former grandeur, only the tower is original, and in the late 1800s, much of its interior was transformed into a municipal theater, the **Teatro Municipio Eleonora Duse.** This castle is currently being restored, but the theater may reopen by the time of your visit. When it is up and running, it's the setting for chamber music concerts and light Italian-language comedies. For its current status, check with the tourist office.

Brooding over the eastern edge of town, less than a quarter-mile from the center, is **La Rocca.** Built as a medieval stronghold by the Venetians and now only a weathered rampart with a panoramic view, it can be visited only Saturday 2 to 6pm and Sunday 10am to sunset, for an entrance fee of 3,000L ($1.75).

Asolo's only museum, the **Museo Civico,** Piazza Garibaldi 207 (☎ 0423/ 952-313), has been closed for renovation but may be reopened during the lifetime of this edition. Call or ask anyone in town prior to your visit and expect lots of memorabilia devoted to Caterina Cornaro, Robert Browning, Eleonora Duse, and her lover, romantic poet Gabriele d'Annunzio. In the town's **Cimiterio di Sant'Anna,** Via Sant'Anna, you can find the gravestones of Duse and Robert Browning's son, Pen. The oft-renovated **Duomo,** Via Browning (☎ 0423/952-376), houses *Assumptions* by Bassano and Lorenzo Lotto.

Regardless of what you see and do in Asolo, you'll pass several times through the landmark **Piazza Maggiore,** lined with Renaissance palaces and turn-of-the-century cafes where Browning, Duse, and other greats gathered for refreshment, socializing, and/or gossip.

ACCOMMODATIONS

Hotel Duse. Via Browning 190, 31001 Asolo. ☎ **0432/55-241.** Fax 0432/950-404. 14 units. A/C MINIBAR TV TEL. 200,000–300,000L ($116–$174) double, 300,000–400,000L ($174–$232) suite. AE, MC, V.

Opposite the Duomo on Asolo's main square, this hotel occupies a stone building that's at least a century old and is named for the great stage actress Eleonora Duse. Staffed by a charming, partly English-speaking staff, it contains cozy rooms with art nouveau–style accessories and bright colors. Breakfast is the only meal served, but nearby are many restaurants.

✪ Hotel Villa Cipriani. Via Canova 298, 31001 Asolo. ☎ **800/325-3535** or 0423/ 952-166. Fax 0423/952-095. www.ittsheraton.com. 31 units. A/C TV TEL. 407,000L ($236) deluxe double, 517,000L ($300) superior double. AE, DC, MC, V. Valet parking 20,000L ($12).

Once the home of actress Eleonora Duse and poet Robert Browning, this 18th-century villa is now part of the ITT Sheraton chain. The individualized rooms are in either the main house or a garden house and feature wood-beamed ceilings, period furnishings, Oriental carpets, and incredible views of the grounds, town, and surrounding hills. There's abundant plant life everywhere, from ivy creeping down an internal balcony or scaling the exterior walls, to the bright blossoms of window boxes, potted plants, and the garden, often riotous with the bloom of azaleas and roses.

Dining: The two restaurants, Sala Contarini and Veranda, even grow the vegetables that are combined with fresh market fish and game in creative seasonal Venetian and international dishes. There's an American-style bar and a terrace for enjoying the weather while partaking of meals and drinks.

Amenities: Concierge, room service, dry cleaning/laundry, newspaper delivery, twice-daily maid service; hotel guests have access to nearby Asolo Golf Club; car rentals and tours arranged on request, jogging track, conference rooms.

DINING

Ca' Derton. Piazza d'Annunzio 11. ☎ **0423/529-648.** Reservations recommended. Main courses 20,000–25,000L ($12–$15). AE, MC, V. Tues–Sun noon–2pm and 7:30–10pm. Closed July 15–31. VENETIAN.

It's hard to miss this family-run restaurant, as it occupies a white-fronted palace built in the early 1700s near the fountain in the center of town. Run by members of the Baggio family since 1978, it has room for only 45 diners, who admire the venerable paintings and antiques and consume large quantities of dishes like potato-based gnocchi, oven-roasted lamb with rosemary and herbs, and fettuccine with asparagus. Especially delicious are the various risotto dishes with peas, mushrooms, or whatever else happens to be seasonal—when it's available, try the succulent version with local cheeses and braised radicchio. Also look for the roast duckling marinated in balsamic vinegar and bigoli (a local pasta) flavored with tomatoes, herbs, and duck meat.

OFF THE BEATEN PATH: A PALLADIAN VILLA

Take SS248 for 4½ miles northeast of Asolo to the ✪ **Villa Barbaro,** Via Cornuda 2 (☎ **0423/923-004**), in Maser. Built in 1559, it is Palladio's second-greatest Renaissance villa, after La Rotonda in Vicenza. It's still in private hands, and the owners will make you put scuffs over your shoes so you won't mark up their polished floors. Once inside, you can admire beautiful stuccos and frescoes by Paolo Veronese and an ornate grotto by Alessandro Vittorio in the back garden. April to September, the villa is open Tuesday, Saturday, and Sunday 3 to 7pm; October to March, hours are Saturday and Sunday 2:30 to 5pm. Admission is 9,000L ($5).

7 Bassano del Grappo

23 miles N of Venice

At the foot of Mount Grappa in the Valsugana Valley, this hideaway along the Brenta River draws Italian vacationers because of its proximity to the mountains and its panoramic views. **Bassano** is best known for its liquor, grappa, a brandy usually made from grape pomace left in a winepress, but is also known for pottery, porcini mushrooms, white asparagus, and radicchio.

ESSENTIALS

GETTING THERE　There's direct **train** service from Trento 8 times a day, a 2-hour journey costing 8,300L ($4.80) one-way. There are also trains requiring a change at Castelfranco from Padua and Venice. The former is a 1-hour trip arriving 12 times daily for 4,400L ($2.55); the latter, 16 trains daily taking 1 hour 20 minutes for 6,000L ($3.50). Contact the train station (☎ **0424/525-034**) for information and schedules.

There are many more **buses** to Bassano than trains. The FTV bus line (☎ **0424/ 30-850**) offers service hourly from Vicenza (trip time: 1 hour) for 5,700L ($3.30) one-way. **CO.APT** (☎ **0424/820-68-11**) arrives from Padua every 30 minutes, the trip taking 1 hour and costing 6,000L ($3.50).

If you've got a **car** and are in Asolo, take Route 248 for 7 miles west.

VISITOR INFORMATION　The **tourist office** is at Largo Corona d'Italia 35, off Via Jacopo del Ponte (☎ **0424/524-351**); it hands out the *Bassano News*, a monthly information/accommodation guide with a town map. It's open Monday to Friday 9am to 12:30pm and 2 to 5pm and Saturday 9am to 12:30pm.

EXPLORING THE TOWN

The village is lovely and the liquor is strong, but there aren't a lot of specific sights. Bassono's best-known landmark is the **Ponte dei Alpini,** a covered wooden bridge over the Brenta, which has been replaced numerous times because of flooding, but each version is faithful to the original 1209 design.

Housing numerous paintings by Bassano, the **Museo Civico,** in Piazza Garibaldi at Via Museo 12 (☎ **0424/522-235**), also has works by Canova, Tiepolo, and others. It's open Tuesday to Saturday 10am to 6:30pm and Tuesday to Sunday 3:30 to 6:30pm, with an admission of 7,000L ($4.05) adults or 4,000L ($2.30) children under 18/seniors. That ticket will also admit you to the **Palazzo Sturm,** Via Schiavonetti (☎ **0424/522-235**), home of the Ceramics Museum, featuring 4 centuries of finely crafted regional pottery. Summer hours are the same as the Civic Museum's; off-season hours are Friday 9am to 12:30pm and Saturday and Sunday 3:30 to 6:30pm.

SHOPPING

If you don't get sick from overindulging on grappa, you may want to pick some up to take home. The best-known distillery is the 18th-century **Nardini,** Via Madonna Monte Berico 4 (☎ **0424/567-040**), next to the Ponte degli Alpini, where juniper, pear, peach, and plum versions supplement the grape standard. Other grappa shops are **Poli,** Via Gamba (☎ **0424/524-426**), and **Bassanina,** Via Angarano (☎ **0424/ 502-140**). Because you're in the heart of grappa country, you can also find good smaller labels like Folco Portinari, Maschio, Jacopo de Poli, Rino Dal Tosco, Da Ponte, and Carpene Malvolti.

ACCOMMODATIONS

Al Castello. Piazza Terraglio 19, 36061 Bassano del Grappa. ☎ or fax **0424/228-665.** 11 units. A/C TV TEL. 120,000L ($70) double. Breakfast 10,000L ($6). AE, MC, V.

Opened by the Cattapan family more than 25 years ago, this is a small simple hotel outfitted to provide you with a comfortable stay at a bargain rate. Conveniently in the heart of town near the medieval Civic Tower, this antique town house was renovated in 1992 but retains classical style. Each comfortably furnished room has a shower. There's no restaurant, but at a cafe/bar with a sidewalk terrace you can relax over coffee or a drink.

Hotel Belvedere. Piazzale Generale Giardino 14, 36061 Bassano del Grappa. ☎ **0424/ 529-845.** Fax 0424/529-849. www.bonotto.it. E-mail: belvederehotel@bonotto.it. 91 units. A/C MINIBAR TV TEL. 230,000L ($133) double. Rates include breakfast. AE, DC, MC, V. Parking 20,000L ($12).

The first inn in the village, the Belvedere opened in the 15th century as a place to rest and change horses before traveling to Venice. The third-floor rooms attest to the hotel's age with rustic exposed beams. All rooms incorporate classical, Venetian, and Bassanese styles in a blend of antiquity and comfort. The public rooms are luxurious, with Oriental rugs and tapestries, fresh-cut flowers, and curvaceous wooden furniture covered with rich fabrics. The lounge houses a baby grand piano, a fireplace, and a wooden balcony overhung with ivy. The chandeliered Del Buon Ricordo specializes in baccalà alla vicentina, and you get to take your plate, illustrated with a drawing of the Bassano bridge, home as a souvenir. The restaurant is shared with the Palladio Bassano, 500 yards away, whose gym facilities are open to Belvedere guests.

Hotel Palladio Bassano. Via Gramsci 2, 36061 Bassano del Grappa. ☎ **0424/523-777.**
Fax 0424/524-050. E-mail: paladiohotel@bonotto.it. 66 units. A/C MINIBAR TV TEL. 240,000L
($139) double; 270,000L ($157) junior suite. Rates include breakfast. AE, DC, MC, V. Parking
20,000L ($12).

This is a sibling to the Belvedere—they're 500 yards apart and share a restaurant, gym,
and parking facilities—but you'd never guess they were related. This hotel's facade is
modern with cut stone and stepped glass panels. The interior is contemporary as well,
and the lobby boasts a curved wood and brass counter and modern recessed lighting.
They do have common interior elements though, mainly in the form of mottled
marble floors and Oriental rugs. The furniture runs the gamut from curved wood with
richly patterned fabrics to overstuffed black leather and tasseled velveteen. The guest
rooms are modern and streamlined, painted in pastels and off-whites. Three golf
courses are within a 10- to 20-mile drive. Step over to the Belvedere to partake in
meals at Del Buon Ricordo.

Villa Palma. Via Chemin Palma 30, 36065 Mussolente. ☎ **0424/577-407.** Fax 0424/
87-687. 21 units. A/C MINIBAR TV TEL. 300,000L ($174) double; 420,000L ($244) junior
suite; 480,000L ($278) suite. Rates include breakfast. AE, DC, MC, V.

Just 3 miles from Bassano del Grappa, this 18th-century villa was opened as a hotel in
1991 after renovations that carefully preserved features like its beamed and vaulted
brick ceilings. The guest rooms are spread across three floors and individualized by
mixing antiques, carpets, and tapestries to create a comfortable yet elegant atmosphere. Some baths have sauna showers or Jacuzzis. The hotel restaurant, La Loggia, is
closed on Monday and for 2 weeks in August and 1 week following New Year's, but at
other times it creates wonderful regional meals.

DINING
Al Sole. Via Jacopo Vittorelli 41. ☎ **0424/523-206.** Main courses 15,000–25,000L ($9–
$15). AE, DC, MC, V. Tues–Sun noon–3pm and 7:30–10pm. Closed July. VENETIAN.

Gian-Franco Chiurato's successful restaurant opened nearby in 1949, then moved into
this cavernous early 19th-century palazzo, where both dining rooms are decorated
with local ceramics. The cuisine is rooted in the Veneto's traditions and celebrates two
annual crops: In springtime, look for the region's distinctive white asparagus blended
into pastas and risottos, as a garnish for main courses, and often featured as a
refreshing course on its own. In autumn and winter, look for similar variations on
mushrooms, especially porcini, which its fans claim is absolutely addictive with game
birds and venison. The rest of the year, expect polenta with codfish, puff pastry layered with local cheeses and mushrooms, homemade bigoli pasta drenched with duck
meat and mushrooms, and baked lamb with herbed polenta.

✪ Birreria Ottone. Via Matteoti 48–50. ☎ **0424/522-206.** Reservations recommended
Fri–Sat. Main courses 12,000–25,000L ($7–$15). AE, DC, MC, V. Wed–Mon 10am–3:15pm;
Wed–Sun 7pm–midnight. AUSTRIAN/ITALIAN/VENETO.

Occupying a 13th-century building across from Bassano's City Hall, this is the best
established and most appealing beer hall in the region. Thanks to generous portions
and copious amounts of beer, the site is preferred by extended families and groups of
friends, some of whom actually dine. Look for two dining rooms encircled with chiseled stone, marble accents, and ceramic tiles and food items that include such favorites
as goulash, Wiener schnitzel, frankfurters, roasted lamb, and Venetian-style calves'
liver. In spring, look for savory local asparagus. The beer focus is on Dutch-brewed
Amstel, though because the suppliers change from time to time, the featured brew
might be something else by the time of your visit.

OFF THE BEATEN PATH: A HUMAN CHESS GAME

Four-and-a-half miles west of Bassano del Grappa on Route 248, **Marostica** hosts the **Game of Life,** a reminder of how far sexual relations have actually progressed. The second week of September in even-numbered years, the town square in front of the Castello da Basso is used as a chessboard and costumed townspeople become its pieces in order to re-create the medieval practice of playing scacchi to claim the hand of the kingdom's most beautiful woman (the loser got a homelier maiden). For more information, contact the **Associazione Pro Marostica,** Piazza Castello 1 (☎ **0424/ 72-127;** fax 0424/72-800). While you're here, you might want to indulge in the wonderful cherries that is the town's other claim to fame.

8 Far Afield to Trieste

72 miles NE of Venice, 414 miles NE of Rome, 253 miles E of Milan

Remote **Trieste,** a shimmering, bright city with many neoclassical buildings, is perched on the half-moon Gulf of Trieste, which opens into the Adriatic. Trieste has had a long history, with many changes of ownership. The Habsburg emperor Charles VI declared it a free port in 1719, but by the 20th century it was an ocean outlet for the Austro-Hungarian Empire. After the war and a secret deal among the Allies, Trieste was ceded to Italy in 1918. In 1943, Trieste again fell to foreign troops—this time the Nazis, who were ousted by Tito's Yugoslav army in 1945. In 1954, after much hassle, the American and British troops withdrew as the Italians marched in, with the stipulation that the much-disputed Trieste would be maintained as a free port. Today that status continues. Politics, as always, dominates the agenda here. There's racial tension, and many Italian Fascists and anti-Slav parties are centered in Trieste.

Trieste has known many glamorous literary associations, particularly in the pre–World War II years. As a stop on the Orient Express, it became a famed destination. Dame Agatha Christie came this way, as did Graham Greene. James Joyce, eloping with Nora Barnacle, arrived in Trieste in 1904. Out of money, Joyce got a job teaching at the Berlitz School and lived here for nearly 10 years. He wrote *A Portrait of the Artist as a Young Man* here and may have begun his masterpiece *Ulysses* here as well. Poet Rainer Maria Rilke also lived in the area. Author Richard Burton, known for his Arabian Nights translations, lived in Trieste from 1871 until he died about 20 years later.

Trieste, squashed between Slovenia and the Adriatic, has been more vulnerable to conditions following the collapse of Yugoslavia than any other city in Italy. Civil war and turmoil have halted the flow of thousands who used to cross the border to buy merchandise—mainly jeans and household appliances. The port has also suffered from crises in the shipbuilding and steel industries. Trieste remains Italy's insurance capital, and one-fourth of its population of 150,000 residents is retired (it has the highest per capita pensioner population in Italy).

ESSENTIALS

GETTING THERE   Trieste is serviced by an **airport** at **Ronchi dei Legionari** (☎ **0481/7731** for information), 21½ miles northwest of the city. Daily flights on Alitalia connect it with Linate airport in Milan (trip time: 50 minutes), Franz Josef Strauss airport in Munich (1 hour 10 minutes), and Leonardo da Vinci airport in Rome (1 hour 10 minutes).

Trieste lies on a direct **rail** link from Venice. Trip time to Venice is 2½ hours, and a one-way ticket is 14,000L ($8). The station is on Piazza della Libertà (☎ **040/ 418-207** or 1478/88-088 toll free in Italy only), northwest of the historic center. It's better to fly, drive, or take the train to Trieste. Once here, you'll find a network of **local buses** servicing the region from Corso Cavour (☎ **040/336-0300** for schedules).

If you've got a **car** and you're coming from Venice, continue northeast along A4 until reaching the end of the line at Trieste.

VISITOR INFORMATION   The **tourist office** is at Via San Nicolò 20 (☎ **040/ 679-611**), open Monday to Friday 8:30am to 7pm and Saturday 8:30am to 1pm. A second office is in Stazione Centrale (☎ **040/420-182**), open Monday to Saturday 9am to 7pm and Sunday 10am to 1pm and 4 to 7pm.

EXPLORING THE CITY

The heart of Trieste is the neoclassic ✪ **Piazza dell'Unità d'Italia,** Italy's largest square that fronts the sea. Opening onto the square is the town hall with a clock tower, the Palace of the Government, and the main office of the Lloyd Triestino ship line. Flanking it are numerous cafes and restaurants, popular at night with locals who sip an aperitif, then promenade along the seafront esplanade.

After visiting the main square, you may want to view Trieste from an even better vantage point. Head up the hill for another cluster of attractions—you can take an antiquated tram leaving from Piazza Oberdan and get off at Obelisco. At the **belvedere,** the city of the Adriatic will spread out before you.

Cattedrale di San Giusto. Piazza Cattedrale, Colle Capitolino. ☎ **040/302-874.** Free admission. Daily 8:30am–noon and 4–7pm.

Dedicated to the patron saint (St. Just) of Trieste, who was martyred in A.D. 303, this basilica was consecrated in 1330, incorporating a pair of churches that had been separate until then. The front is in the Romanesque style, enhanced by a rose window. Inside, the nave is flanked by two pairs of aisles. To the left of the main altar are the best of the Byzantine mosaics in Trieste (note especially the blue-robed Madonna and Child). The main altar and the chapel to the right contain less interesting mosaics. To the left of the basilica entrance is a small campanile from the 14th century, which you can scale for a view of Trieste and its bay. At its base are preserved the remains of a Roman temple from the 1st century. You may prefer to take a taxi up to the cathedral, then walk a leisurely 15 minutes back down. From the basilica you can also stroll to the nearby Castle of San Giusto.

Castello di San Giusto. Piazza Cattedrale 3. ☎ **040/309-362.** Castle, 2,000L ($1.15); museum, 3,000L ($1.75). Castle, daily 9am–sunset; museum, Tues–Sun 9am–1pm.

Constructed in the 15th century by the Venetians on the site of a Roman fort, this fortress maintained a sharp eye on the bay, watching for unfriendly visitors arriving by sea. From its bastions, panoramic views of Trieste unfold. Inside is a **museum** (☎ 040/313-636) with a collection of arms and armor. The castle's **open-air theater** hosts a film festival in July and August.

✪ **Castello di Miramare.** Viale Miramare, Grignano (4½ miles northwest of town). ☎ **040/224-143.** Castle, 8,000L ($4.65) adults; children 18 and under/seniors 60 and over free. Castle, Apr–Sept daily 9am–6pm; Oct–Mar daily 9am–1pm. Grounds, Apr–Sept daily 9am–7pm; Oct–Mar daily 9am–5pm. Bus: 36.

Overlooking the Bay of Grignano, this castle was built by Archduke Maximilian, the brother of Franz Josef, the Habsburg emperor of Austria. Maximilian, who married Princess Charlotte of Belgium, was the commander of the Austrian navy in 1854. In an ill-conceived move, he and "Carlotta" sailed to Mexico in 1864, where he became the emperor in an unfortunate brief reign. He was shot in 1867 in Querétaro, Mexico. His wife lived until 1927 in a château outside Brussels, driven insane by the Mexican episode. (If you're a fan of old movies, you may remember *Juárez*, starring Brian Aherne and Bette Davis as Maximilian and Carlotta.) On the ground floor, you can visit Maximilian's bedroom (built like a ship's cabin) and Charlotte's, as well as an impressive receiving room and more parlors, including a chinoiserie salon.

Enveloping the castle are magnificently designed grounds (the **Parco di Miramare**), ideal for pleasant strolls. In July and August, a **sound-and-light presentation** in the park depicts Maximilian's tragedy in Mexico. Tickets begin at 15,000L ($9).

A ROOM WITH NO VIEW: THE GROTTA GIGANTE

In the heart of the limestone plateau called Carso surrounding the city, you can visit the ✪ **Grotta Gigante** (☎ 040/327-312), an enormous cavern that's one of the most interesting phenomena of speleology. First explored in 1840 via the top ceiling entrance, this huge room, some 380 feet deep, was opened to the public in 1908. It's the biggest single-room cave ever opened to visitors and one of the world's largest underground rooms. You can visit only with a guide on a 40-minute tour. Near the entrance is the Man and Caves Museum, unique in Italy.

Tours of the cave are given Tuesday to Sunday: March and October, they're offered every 30 minutes 9am to noon and 2 to 5pm; November to February, every hour 10am to noon and 2:30 to 4:30pm; April to September, every 30 minutes 9am to noon and 2 to 7pm. Tours cost 13,000L ($8) adults and 9,000L ($5) children 6 to 12. If you're driving, take Strada del Friuli beyond the white marble Victory Lighthouse as far as Prosecco. On the freeway you can take the exit at Prosecco. By public transport, take the tram from Piazza Oberdan and then bus no. 45 to Prosecco.

SHOPPING

The city's industrial base and sense of sophistication have discouraged shopkeepers from emphasizing the kitsch, the folkloric, or the merely touristic. Instead, the city has traded on its polyglot of former regimes and cultures and developed into one of the most interesting centers of the antiques trade in this corner of Europe. Look for examples of both Biedermeier and Liberty (Italian art nouveau) furniture and accessories and wander at will through the city's densest collection of antiques dealers, the neighborhood around **Piazza dell'Unità d'Italia.** Dealers to look out for are **Davia,** Via dell'Annunziata 6 (☎ 040/304-321) specializing in antique engravings; **Jésu,** Via Felice Venezian 9 (☎ 040/300-719), dealing in small art objects and furniture; and **Dr. Fulvio Rosso,** Via Diaz 13 (☎ 040/306-226) specializing in crystal and porcelain from the turn of the 20th century.

If the sense of the old-fashioned and deep patinas don't appeal to you, you might want one of the wood carvings from Trieste's most comprehensive collection of half-Austrian, half-Italian accessories, **Paolo Hrovatin,** Borgo Grotte Gigante (☎ 040/327-077).

Fine leather and suede goods fill **Christine Pellettrie,** Piazza della Borso 15 (☎ 040/366-212), where women can find well-crafted shoes, bags, and pants. A chic boutique, **Fendi,** Capo di Piazza 1 (☎ 040/366-464), sells upscale clothing and leather goods for women and well-crafted belts, wallets, and ties for men. Offering both casual and formal attire, **Max Mara,** Via Carducci 23 (☎ 040/636-723), features impeccable women's designs, plus shoes and bags. From classic to contemporary, formal to casual, **Le Monde,** Passo San Giovanni 1 (☎ 040/636-343), offers fashionable clothing for men and women. A waterfront shop, **Spangher,** Riva Gulli 8 (☎ 040/305-158), sells trendy sportswear and Italianized version of Abercrombie and Finch.

The 130-year-old **La Bomboniera,** Via XXX Ottobre 3 (☎ **040/632-752**), is a sweets shop as beautifully wrapped as the chocolates it sells, with etched glass, carved walnut shelves, and an elaborate glass chandelier. Besides fine chocolates, it offers traditional sweets and pastries of the region, as well as a few Austro-Hungarian specialties.

ACCOMMODATIONS

✪ **Grand Hotel Duchi d'Aosta.** Piazza dell'Unità d'Italia 2, 34124 Trieste. ☎ **040/ 760-0011.** Fax 040/366-092. 54 units. A/C MINIBAR TV TEL. 340,000L ($197) double; from 585,000L ($339) suite. Rates include breakfast. AE, DC, MC, V. Parking 37,000L ($21).

This now-glamorous hotel began about 200 years ago as a restaurant for the dock workers who toiled nearby. In 1873, one of the most beautiful facades in Trieste—a white neoclassical shell with delicate carving, arched windows, and a stone crown of heroic sculptures—was erected over the existing building. The design is very much that of an 18th-century palace, an effect enhanced by views over the fountains and lamps of the square and the sea beyond it, while the Victorian-style public rooms give it a 19th-century ambience. The interior was practically rebuilt in the 1970s, and each room boasts a well-stocked minibar, antiqued walls, and tasteful furniture.

Dining: The Ristorante Harry's Grill is so good we've reviewed it under "Dining."

Amenities: Concierge, room service, twice-daily maid service, dry cleaning/laundry.

Hotel al Teatro. Capo di Piazza G. Bartoli 1, 34124 Trieste. ☎ **040/366-220.** Fax 040/ 366-560. 45 units, 35 with bathroom. TEL. 115,000L ($67) double without bathroom, 150,000L ($87) double with bathroom. Rates include breakfast. AE, MC, V.

The theatrical mask carved into the stone arch above the entrance is an appropriate symbol of this hotel, a favorite with many of Trieste's visiting opera stars. It's a few steps from the seaside panorama of Piazza dell'Unità d'Italia and about a 10-minute walk from the station. The simply furnished and slightly old-fashioned rooms have parquet floors, lots of space, and comfortable but minimal furniture. The hotel was built in 1830 as a private house and later served as headquarters of the British army in the aftermath of World War II.

Novo Hotel Impero. Via Sant'Anastasio 1, 34132 Trieste. ☎ **040/364-242.** Fax 040/ 365-023. 50 units. TV TEL. 220,000L ($128) double; 350,000L ($203) suite. Rates include breakfast. AE, DC, MC, V.

This completely restored hotel occupies a neoclassic building just in front of the rail station. Next to the historical center and the business area, it offers tastefully, albeit sparsely, furnished rooms. This member of Fenice hotels is well run and has completely modernized baths. The building still retains much of the original glamour of its facade.

DINING

Ai Due Triestini. Via Cadorna 10. ☎ **040/303-759.** Main courses 15,000–22,000L ($9–$13). No credit cards. Mon–Sat noon–3pm. Closed Sept. AUSTRIAN/INTERNATIONAL/ TRIESTINO.

For one of the best lunch bargains in Trieste, we suggest this tavern behind Piazza dell'Unità d'Italia. Run by a husband-and-wife team, this little trattoria covers its tablecloths with plastic and doesn't bother to print a menu. Some of the cookery is heavily influenced by neighboring Austria. Try spezzatino, chunks of beef in a goulash ragoût, with fresh peas and potatoes. The Hungarian goulash is quite good, as is a rich strudel in the tradition of Budapest. Fresh fish, calamari, and octopus lend an Italian flavor.

Al Bragozzo. Riva Nazario Sauro 22. ☎ **040/303-001.** Reservations required. Main courses 16,000–45,000L ($9–$26); fixed-price all-you-can-eat menu 60,000L ($35). AE, DC, MC, V. Tues–Sat 11am–3pm and 7–10pm. Closed June 22–July 10 and Dec 25–Jan 10. SEAFOOD.

This is the best-known restaurant at the port, opened in the late 1960s in a Jugenstil building. If you're a steak lover, you've come to the wrong place—only fish and pasta are served. Simply yet creatively prepared meals pay homage to the sea and its heritage by combining the elements of Italian cuisine and riches of the Mediterranean. Specialties include spaghetti al' Giorgio (with tomatoes and herbs); ravioli stuffed with herbs; monkfish braised with artichokes and cooked with white wine; spaghetti with lobster; and many preparations of salmon and shrimp. If you visit in summer, you can dine at the outdoor tables sheltered by a canopy.

Al Granzo. Piazza Venezia 7. ☎ **040/306-788.** Reservations recommended. Main courses 16,000–35,000L ($9–$20); fixed-price menu 29,000L ($17). AE, DC, MC, V. Thurs–Tues 12:30pm–3pm; Mon–Tues and Thurs–Sat 7:30–10pm. SEAFOOD.

This restaurant was opened in 1923 by the ancestors of the three brothers who run it today. It's one of Trieste's leading seafood restaurants, serving flavorful versions of that curious mix of Italian, Austrian, and Yugoslav cuisines known as Triestino. Menu items include brodetto, a traditional bouillabaisse spiced with saffron and other herbs; vermicelli with black mussels; and risotto with seafood. Fresh fish are displayed on a bed of crushed ice in a wagon, and there's an impressive selection of fresh contorni (vegetables, sold individually). A suitable wine would be a local Tocai Friulano, aromatic and somewhat tart, lemon yellow to pale green in color. Dessert might be homemade strudel.

Antica Trattoria Suban. Via Comici 2, at San Giovanni. ☎ **040/54-368.** Reservations recommended. Main courses 20,000–26,000L ($12–$15). AE, DC, MC, V. Wed–Sun 12:30–2:30pm; Wed–Mon 7:30–10pm. Closed Aug 1–20. ITALIAN/CENTRAL EUROPEAN.

This country tavern is 2½ miles north of Trieste in the district of San Giovanni, on a spacious terrace opening onto a view of the hills. The surrounding landscape contains glimpses of the Industrial Age, but the brick and stone walls, the terrace, and the country feeling are still intact. The restaurant is run by descendants of the founding family, and the cuisine is both hearty and delicate. It draws its inspiration from northeastern Italian, Slavic, Hungarian, and Germanic traditions. Dishes include a flavorful risotto with herbs, basil-flavored crêpes, beef with garlic sauce, a perfectly prepared chicken Kiev, and veal croquettes with parmigiano and egg yolks, crêpes stuffed with basil and roasted veal, and haunch of veal with roasted potatoes. The chef's handling of grilled meats is adept, and the rich pastries, such as the honey strudel, are worth the extra calories.

Ristorante Harry's Grill. In the Hotel Duchi d'Aosta, Piazza dell'Unità d'Italia 2. ☎ **040/365-646.** Reservations required. Main courses 30,000–38,000L ($17–$22); Sun brunch 40,000L ($23). AE, DC, MC, V. Daily 12:15–3pm and 7:15–10:30pm. INTERNATIONAL.

In Trieste's most upscale hotel, this restaurant manages to be both elegant and relaxed, a place where you can have an American-style martini followed by a simple plate of pasta or a complete sumptuous meal. The big lace-covered curtains complement the paneling, the polished brass, and the blue Murano chandeliers. In summer, tables are set up in the traffic-free Piazza dell'Unità d'Italia. The outdoor terrace, which is sheltered by a canopy, has a separate area for bar patrons. The Mediterranean-inspired cuisine is good but not great and includes fresh shrimp with oil and lemon, pasta and risotto dishes, boiled salmon in sauce, butter-fried calves' liver with onions, bigoli (fat spaghetti) pasts with duck meat, and an array of beef and fish dishes, such as a filet of beef with red-wine sauce. The adjoining bar (not related to Italy's other famed Harry's Bars) is one of the most popular rendezvous spots in town, particularly for the business community.

TRIESTE AFTER DARK

If you're interested in an exposure to Trieste's particular blend of Italian and Teutonic cultural blend, head for its most visible and impressive theater, the **Teatro Verdi,** Corso Cavour (☎ 040/672-2111), an opera house that has been compared to a blend of the Vienna State Opera and Milan's La Scala. Built in 1801 and massively renovated in the mid-1990s, it presents classical concerts and operas throughout the year. Tickets range from 20,000L to 120,000L ($12 to $70).

The town's most evocative cafe, conveniently located almost adjacent to the above-mentioned theater, is the **Caffè Tommaseo,** Riva III Novembre 3 (☎ 040/366-765). If you're interested in dancing the night away, the neighborhood around Piazza dell'Unita d'Italia offers the town's most animated disco: **Mandracchio,** Passo di Piazza (☎ 040/366-292), which is rivaled by **Disco Machiavelli,** Viale Miramare 285 (☎ 040/44-104), a crowded see-and-be-seen dance hall whose only drawback is its location 4 miles north of Piazza dell'Unità d'Italia. Catering to a more mature crowd is **Bar Jamin,** a woodsy-looking hideaway in the Il Giulia Shopping Center, Via Giulia 75 (☎ 040/569-306).

9 Cortina d'Ampezzo: Gateway to the Dolomites

100 miles N of Venice, 82 miles E of Bolzano, 255 miles NE of Milan

This fashionable resort is your best center for exploring the snowy Dolomiti. Its reputation as a tourist mecca dates back to before World War I, but its recent growth has been phenomenal, spurred by the 1956 Olympics held here. **Cortina d'Ampezzo** draws throngs of nature lovers in summer and both Olympic-caliber and neophyte skiers in winter. It's a hotel owner's Shangrila, charging maximum prices in July and August as well as in the 3 months of winter.

A public-relations signora once insisted, "Just say Cortina has everything." Such statements of propaganda, even when they come from charming Italian ladies, are suspect—but in this case she's nearly right. First and foremost, "everything," in the Cortina context, means people of every shape and hue. New York socialites rub elbows in late-night spots with frumpy Bremen hausfraus. Young Austrian men, clad in Loden jackets and stout leather shorts, walk down the streets with feathers in their caps and gleams in their eyes. Frenchwomen in red ski pants sample Campari at cafe tables, and the tweedy English sit at rival places drinking "tea like mother made."

Second, "everything" means location. Cortina is in the middle of a valley ringed by enough Dolomite peaks to cause Hannibal's elephants to throw up their trunks and flee in horror. Regardless of which road you choose for a drive, you'll find the scenery rewarding. Third, "everything" means good food. Cortina sets an excellent table, inspired by the cuisine of both Venice and Tyrol. Fourth, "everything" means summer and winter sporting facilities—chiefly golf, horseback riding, curling, tennis, fishing, mountain climbing, skiing, skating, and swimming. The resort has an Olympic ice stadium, bobsled track, and ski jump. In addition, it has a skiing school, a large indoor pool, an Olympic downhill track, and a cross-country track.

Finally, "everything" means top-notch hotels, pensioni, private homes, and even mountain huts. The locations, facilities, types of service, price structures, and decor vary considerably, but we've never inspected an accommodation that wasn't clean. Most of the architecture of Cortina, incidentally, seems more appropriate to Zell am See, Austria, than to an Italian town.

ESSENTIALS

GETTING THERE   Frequent **trains** run between Venice and Calalzo di Cadore (trip time: 2½ hours), 19 miles south of Cortina. You proceed the rest of the way by bus. For information about schedules, call ☎ **01478/88-088** in Calalzo. About 14 to 16 **buses** a day connect Calalzo di Cadore with Cortina. Buses arrive at the Cortina bus station on Viale Marconi (☎ **0436/2741** for information about schedules). If you've got a **car,** take A27 from Venice to Pian de Vedoia, continuing north along S51 all the way to Cortina d'Ampezzo.

VISITOR INFORMATION   The tourist office is at Piazzetta San Francesco 8 (☎ **0436/3231**), open Monday to Friday 9am to 12:30pm and 4 to 7pm, Saturday 10am to 12:30pm and 4 to 7pm, and Sunday 10am to 12:30pm.

CLIMBING TO THE STARS

One of the main attractions in Cortina is to take a **cable car** "halfway to the stars," as the expression goes. On one of them, at least, you'll be just a yodel away from the pearly gates. It's the **Freccia nel Cielo** ("Arrow of the Sky"). Beginning at 9am, from the base behind Cortina's Olympic Stadium, cars depart every 20 minutes, July 12 to September 28 and December 16 to May 1 (call ☎ **0436/5052** for departure information the rest of the year). A round-trip is 50,000L ($29). An ascent to the cable-car's summit requires two changes en route, and an uphill ride through three separate cable-car segments. The first station is Col Druscie at 5,752 feet; the second, Ra Valles, stands at 8,027 feet; and the top station, Tofana di Mezzo, is at 10,543 feet. At Tofana on a clear day, you can see as far as Venice.

SKIING & OTHER OUTDOOR ACTIVITIES

DOWNHILL SKIING   The **Faloria-Cristallo area** surrounding Cortina is known for its 18½ miles of slopes and 10 miles of fresh-snow runs. At 4,014 feet above sea level, Cortina's altitude isn't particularly forbidding, at least compared to that of other European ski resorts, and though snowfall is usually abundant from late December to early March, a holiday in November or April might leave you stranded without adequate snow. Die-hard Cortina enthusiasts usually compensate for that, at least during the tail end of the season, by remaining only at the surrounding slopes' higher altitudes (there's lots of skiability at 9,000 feet) and traversing lower-altitude snow-fields by cable car.

As Italy's premier ski resort, Cortina boasts more than 50 cable cars and lifts spread out across the valley of the Boite River. The surrounding mountains also contain about two dozen restaurants, about 90 miles of clearly designated ski trails, and, at least in theory, a virtually unlimited number of off-piste trails for cross-country enthusiasts. Cortina's ample sunshine, relative lack of crowding, and array of slopes well suited to intermediate, advanced intermediate, and novice skiers can pay off handsomely. During winter, ski lifts are open daily 9am to between 4 and 5pm, depending on the time of sunset.

Cortina boasts eight distinct ski areas, each with its own challenges and charms. Regrettably, because they sprawl rather disjointedly across the terrain, they're not always easy to interconnect. The most appealing of the ski areas are the **Tofana-Promedes, Forcella Rossa,** and **Faloria-Tondi** complexes. The **Pocol, Mietres,** and **Socepres** areas are specifically for novices, the **Cinque Torre** is valuable

Exploring the Peaks of the Dolomiti

The very existence of the high, snowy peaks of the **Dolomiti** comes as a surprise to foreigners who assume Italy is an exclusively maritime country of rolling hills, steamy flatlands, and sun-flooded harbors. The Dolomiti contribute a distinctive high-altitude wealth and Germanic overtones to Italy. Both the rock of which they're composed (dolomitic limestone) and the peaks themselves are named after an 18th-century French geologist, Déodat Guy Silvani Trancrède Gratet de Domolieu, who spent most of his life analyzing their mineral content.

Part of the eastern Alps, the Dolomiti stretch along the northwestern tier of Italy, following the line of the Austrian border between the valleys of the Adige and Brenta rivers. Though the highest peak is the Marmolada (a few feet shy of 11,000 feet above sea level), the range contains an additional 17 peaks in Italian territory that rise above 10,000 feet. Escaping from the often intense heat of other parts of their country, Italians travel here to breathe the Dolomiti's cool mountain air and to ski and play in such glittering resorts as Cortina.

The mountains' mixture of limestone and porphyry, combined with the angle of the rising and setting sun, contributes to the dramatic coloration of the peaks. Most pronounced in the morning and at dusk, their colors range from soft pinks to brooding tones of russet. When the sun shines directly overhead, the hues fade to a homogenized and rather dull gray. Fortunately for tourists, trekkers, and skiers, the climate isn't as bone-chillingly cold as it is in the alpine regions of western Italy and in the Alps of the Tyrol, farther north.

As you explore the Dolomiti, don't expect lush vegetation. When not camouflaged with snow, the slopes tend to be stony and relatively bare of groundcover. And don't rush out to gather hillside bouquets for your beloved, as many of the wildflowers (including the Austrian national flower, the edelweiss) are endangered species. Picking flowers or destroying vegetation is punishable by stiff fines.

Throughout the Dolomiti, networks of hiking trails are clearly marked with painted signs, and local tourist offices (as well as most hotel reception staffs) are well versed in the length, duration, and degree of difficulty of most treks in their neighborhood. Maps of hiking trails are broadly distributed, and any local tourist office can refer you to the nearest branch of whatever Associazione Guide Alpine proliferates in the region.

If you decide to ramble across the Dolomiti for a day or two, stout shoes, warm clothing, and a waterproof jacket (storms erupt quickly at these altitudes) would be prudent. Chairlifts, cog railways, and alpine gondolas usually operate in both summer and winter, offering an alternative means of enjoying sweeping views over ferociously beautiful mountain scenery. Rustically charming *refugi* (mountain huts) offer the opportunity for an overnight stay or just a rest.

---

for intermediates, and the outlying **Falzarego** is a long, dramatic, and sometimes terrifying downhill jaunt not recommended for anyone except a very competent skier.

Despite the availability of dozens of cable cars originating outside the town center along the valley floor, Cortina's most dramatic cable cars are the **Freccia nel Cielo** ("Arrow to the Sky"), the region's longest and most panoramic (see above), and the **Funivia Faloria** (Faloria chairlift), which begins 200 yards east of town, adjacent to the Olympic ice Stadium. Both of these cable cars are patronized even by visitors who'd never dream of skiing. A single round-trip ticket on either is 45,000L ($26), though if you plan on spending time in Cortina it's almost always more economical to buy a ski pass (see below).

Ski passes are issued in increments of 1 to 21 days. They can include access to either just the lifts around Cortina (about 50) or to all the ski lifts in the Dolomiti (around 464). By far the better value is the more comprehensive pass. This Dolomiti Super Ski Pass allows you unlimited access to a vast network of chairlifts and gondolas stretching over Cortina and the mountains flanking at least 10 other resorts. The single-day pass is 58,000L ($34), but the daily cost goes down as you increase the days of the pass. For example, a 7-day pass is 303,000L ($176) (43,285L/$25 per day) and a 21-day pass 691,000L ($401) (32,904L/$19 per day). The Cortina-only pass sells for about 10% less, but few people opt for it. Children born after January 1, 1990, ski for free.

Included in any pass is free transport on any of Cortina's bright yellow ski buses that run the length of the valley in season, connecting the many cable cars. Depending on snowfall, the two ski lifts mentioned above, as well as most of the other lifts in Cortina, are closed from around April 20 to July 15 and September 15 to around December 1. For information, call ☎ **0436/862-171.**

CROSS-COUNTRY SKIING   The trails start about 2 miles north of town. Some, but not all, run parallel to the region's roads and highways. For information about their location, instruction, and rental of equipment, contact the **Scuola Italiana Sci Fondo Cortina** in Fiames at ☎ **0436/867-088.**

CURLING   When the weather is cold enough, the center for this sport is at the **Stadio Olimpico del Ghiaccio,** Via dello Stadio (☎ **0436/2661**).

FISHING   If you opt to fish in the cold, clear waters of the River Boite, you should first arrange with the tourist office for a permit, costing 10,000L ($6) per day. Many visitors, however, prefer to fish in any of the three lakes around Cortina, the best stocked of which is the Lago di Aial. For fishing in any of the lakes, you won't be charged for a permit until you actually catch something—lake access roads leading from Cortina have checkpoints with the Italian equivalent of a park ranger, who charges you a small fee based on the size and weight of your catch. For information on fishing in Cortina and the surrounding region, contact the tourist office at ☎ **0436/3231.**

ICE SKATING   In winter, the town's main outlet for the sport is the two rinks in the **Stadio Olimpico del Ghiaccio,** Via dello Stadio (☎ **0436/2661**). One of the two remains frozen throughout summer, but the other is converted to a concrete surface suitable for in-line skating. Regardless of the season, you'll pay 15,000L ($9), with skates rented for an additional fee.

MOUNTAIN CLIMBING   No one should head into the Dolomiti for a spate of rock climbing or mountain climbing without consulting local authorities on climbing conditions, local bylaws, and well-intentioned advice about safety. The center for all this information, as well as a repository of local guides and teachers, is the **Scuola di Roca Cortina,** Corso Italia (☎ **0436/4740**).

ACCOMMODATIONS

The tourist office has a list of all the private homes in town that take in paying guests. It's a good opportunity to live with a Dolomite family in comfort and informality. However, the office won't personally book you into a private home. Even though there are nearly 4,700 hotel beds available, it's best to reserve ahead, especially in August and December 20 to January 7.

⊘ **Hotel Ancora.** Corso Italia 62, 32043 Cortina d'Ampezzo. ☎ **0436/3261.** Fax 0436/3265. 74 units. TV TEL. 460,000L ($267) double; 430,000L ($249) per person suite. Rates include breakfast. AE, DC, MC, V. Closed after Easter to June and Sept 15–Dec 20. Valet parking 40,000L ($23).

This "Romantik Hotel" (one of a chain of hotels known for their nostalgic architecture) is the domain of that hearty empress of the Dolomiti, Flavia Bertozzi, who believes in her guests having a good time. It attracts sporting guests from all over the world and hosts modern art exhibits and classical concerts. The antique sculptures and objets d'art filling the place were gathered from Signora Flavia's trips throughout Italy. Hers is a revamped hotel flanked by terraces with outdoor tables and umbrellas—the town center for sipping and gossiping. Garlanded wooden balconies encircle the five floors. Most rooms open directly onto these sunny porches, and all are well furnished, comfortable, and especially pleasant—many with sitting areas. The suites boast Jacuzzis.

Dining/Diversions: The cuisine served in the dining room is reason enough to check in or at least pay to visit even if you're not a guest. Signora Bertozzi demands that the chefs keep topping themselves year after year. If they don't quite succeed, they continue to maintain their culinary standards and continue to delight. The cuisine is creatively prepared and exquisitely presented. The Petite Fleur is a chic piano bar, even attracting royalty now and then.

Amenities: Concierge, room service, laundry, newspaper delivery, in-room massage, baby-sitting, twice-daily maid service, secretarial services, game rooms, nearby sauna and jogging track, golf arrangements nearby, business center, tennis courts nearby, sun deck.

Hotel Corona. Via Val di Sotto 12, 32040 Cortina d'Ampezzo. ☎ **0436/3251.** Fax 0436/867-339. E-mail: hcorona@sunrise.it. 44 units. TV TEL. 260,000–360,000L ($151–$209) double. Rates include half board. MC, V. Closed Apr 2–July and Sept–Dec 20.

Dating from 1935, the Corona was one of the first hotels built at Cortina. For anyone interested in modern Italian art, a stop here is an event—the walls are hung with dozens of carefully inventoried works. Many of the most important artists of Italy (and a few from France) from 1948 to 1963 are represented by paintings, sculptures, and ceramic bas-reliefs acquired by manager Luciano Rimoldi. The guest rooms are cozy, done in the style of the high Alps, with lots of varnished pine and local artifacts. Rimoldi is also a ski instructor (he once coached Princess Grace in her downhill technique) and was head of the Italian ice-hockey team during the 1988 Winter Olympics, at which one of his pupils, Alberto Tomba, began his Olympic domination of alpine events. The hotel prefers guests to take half board (breakfast and dinner).

Hotel Dolomiti. Via Roma 118, 32043 Cortina d'Ampezzo. ☎ **0436/861-400.** Fax 0436/862-140. 42 units. TV TEL. 100,000–200,000L ($58–$116) double. Rates include breakfast. AE, DC, MC, V. Parking 10,000L ($6).

This hotel offers many amenities, though it's a sterile choice after the other atmospheric places we list. But if you're watching your lire, this isn't a bad place. It's also a good bet if you arrive in Cortina in the off-season, when virtually everything else is closed. Its convenient location on the main road just outside the center of town—coupled with its clean, comfortable, and no-nonsense format—has gained it increasing favor with visitors. The rooms are predictably furnished and fairly quiet, and the management is helpful. The restaurant serves good food, featuring regional specialties.

⊘ **Hotel Menardi.** Via Majon 110, 32043 Cortina d'Ampezzo. ☎ **0436/2400.** Fax 0436/86-2183. www.sunrise.it/cortina/alberghi/menardi. 51 units. TEL. 230,000–460,000L ($133–$267) double. Rates include half board. AE, MC, V. Closed Apr 10–June 20 and Sept 20–Dec 20. Parking 15,000L ($9).

This eye-catcher in the upper part of Cortina looks like a great country inn, with wooden balconies and shutters. Its rear windows open onto a flowery meadow a view of the rough Dolomite crags. The inn is 100 years old and run by the Menardi family, who still know how to speak the old Dolomite tongue, Ladino. Decorated in the Tyrolean fashion, each room has its distinct personality. Considering what you get—the quality of the facilities, the reception, and the food—we'd rate this as one of the best values here. The living rooms and dining rooms have lots of knickknacks, pewter, antlers, and spinning wheels.

✪ **Miramonti Majestic Grand Hotel.** Via Pezzie 103, 32043 Cortina d'Ampezzo. ☎ **0436/4201.** Fax 0436/867-019. www.assaritaliani.it/atahotels. 108 units. MINIBAR TV TEL. 540,000–740,000L ($313–$429) double; 500,000–800,000L ($290–$464) per person suite. Rates include half board. AE, DC, MC, V. Closed Apr–June and Sept–Nov. Parking 30,000L ($17) in garage, free outside. Hotel shuttle bus to/from town center every 30 minutes.

Built in 1893, this hotel, one of the grandest in the Dolomiti, is a short distance from the center of town. It consists of two ocher-colored buildings with alpine hipped roofs and dignified facades. The rustic interior is filled with warm colors, lots of exposed timbers, and the most elegant crowd in Cortina. The well-furnished guest rooms look like those of a private home, complete with matching accessories, built-in closets, and all the modern amenities.

Dining/Diversions: In a sumptuous setting, the hotel serves a refined cuisine, both regional and international specialties. Many owners of winter villas come here for special occasions to enjoy the refined setting and market-fresh ingredients. There's always a roaring fire in the cozy bar on winter nights.

Amenities: Concierge, room service, dry cleaning/laundry, baby-sitting, car-rental desk; sports facility with an indoor pool, exercise and massage equipment, sauna, hydrotherapy, and physical therapy; other sports facilities for winter and summer exercises are nearby, including golf and tennis.

DINING

Da Beppe Sello. Via Ronco 68. ☎ **0436/3236.** Reservations recommended. Main courses 22,000–36,000L ($13–$21). AE, DC, MC, V. High season, daily 12:30–2pm and 7:30–10pm; low season, Wed–Sun 12:30–2pm and 7:30–10pm. Closed Easter–May 15 and Sept 30–Oct 31. ALPINE/INTERNATIONAL/ITALIAN.

When you tire of the sometimes oppressive glamour of the more expensive restaurants, head for this charming Tyrolean-style place in a hotel at the edge of the village. Named after the double nicknames of the hotel's founder, Joseph (Beppe) Menardi (Sello) and run by his multilingual niece, Elisa, it's a bastion of superb regional cuisine. Menu items include filet of venison with pears, polenta, and marmellata di mirtilli (marmalade made from an alpine berry resembling a huckleberry or blueberry); pappardelle with rabbit sauce; tagliolini with porcini mushrooms; roast chicken with bay leaves; and filet steak flavored with bacon. You get to keep your plate as a souvenir.

El Toulà. Località Ronco 123. ☎ **0436/3339.** Reservations required. Main courses 36,000–42,000L ($21–$24). AE, DC, MC, V. Tues–Sun 12:30–2:30pm and 8–11pm. Closed Easter to late July and Sept–Christmas. ITALIAN/VENETIAN.

Located 2 miles east of Cortina toward Pocol, this was the first El Toulà, today a chain of 11 restaurants scattered throughout Italy and the world. It's a wood-framed structure with picture windows and a terrace. You get excellently prepared dishes, like grilled squab with an expertly seasoned sauce and veal braised with white truffle sauce. Try the frittata of sea crabs "Saracen" style, pasta e fagioli (pasta and beans) Veneto style, pasticcio of eggplant, or Venetian-style calves' liver. In the 1960s, this place was terribly chic, reserved for Cortina's jet set. In the 1990s, the rich and flavorful cuisine is appreciated by a more down-to-earth crowd.

✪ **Ristorante Tivoli.** Località Lacedel. ☎ **0436/866-400.** Reservations required. Main courses 22,000–36,000L ($13–$21). AE, DC, MC, V. High season daily 12:30–2:30pm and 7:30–10pm; off-season, closed Mon. Closed May–June and Oct–Nov. ALPINE.

The low-slung alpine chalet whose rear seems almost buried in the slope of the hillside is Cortina's best restaurant and one of the area's finest. About a mile from the resort's center, Tivoli is beside the road leading to the hamlet of Pocol. It derives its excellence from the hardworking efforts of the gracious Calderoni family, who use only the freshest of ingredients. Try the stuffed rabbit in onion sauce, wild duck with honey and orange, veal filet with basil and pine nuts, or salmon flavored with saffron. The pastas are made fresh daily. For dessert, you might try an aspic of exotic fruit.

CORTINA AFTER DARK

In true European alpine resort style, Cortina's bar and disco scene does a roaring business in winter, virtually closes down in spring and autumn, and reopens rather half-heartedly in midsummer. Most clubs lie off or along the pedestrian-only Corso Italia, and by the time you read this, the nightlife landscape will probably feature two or three newcomers. Anyway, the popularity rating of any of them is about as fleeting as the mountain snow in June. Here are a few of the more enduring places.

Area, Via Ronco (☎ **0436/867-393**), keeps up-to-date with the latest nightlife trends of Rome, Milan, and London. You enter a bar on the street level but go down to the basement to dance. A rocking competitor popular with mostly Europeans is the **Bilbo Club,** Galleria Nuovo Centro 7 (☎ **0436/5599**), whose interior is dark, woodsy, and just battered enough so no one minds if you spill your beer. More dancing is available in the cellar of the **Hyppo Dance Hall,** Largo Poste (☎ **0436/ 2333**), where you can preface your boogying with a drink in the street-level bar. Better synchronized to a wider spectrum of ages is **Limbo,** Corso Italia 97 (☎ **0436/ 860-026**), whose restaurant is open later than virtually anything else in town (until 3am).

A less frenetic setting that features an esoteric roster of wines from every region of Italy is **Enoteca Cortina,** Via del Mercato 5 (☎ **0436/862-040**). Its owners claim it's the first wine bar here, with a success story going back to 1964 and a carefully polished interior that might remind you of an English pub. Locals happily mingle with skiers in winter and mountain climbers in summer. An equivalent kind of calm is available at the **Piano Bar** in the lobby of the Splendid Hotel Venezia, Corso Italia 209 (☎ **0436/5527**), with soothing music during midwinter and midsummer from dusk until midnight.

EN ROUTE TO BOLZANO VIA THE GREAT DOLOMITE ROAD

Stretching from Cortina d'Ampezzo in the east to Bolzano in the west, the ✪ **Great Dolomite Road** follows a circuitous route of about 68 miles and ranks among the grandest scenic drives in all Europe. The first panoramic pass you'll cross is Falzarego, about 11 miles from Cortina and 6,900 feet above sea level. The next great pass is Pordoi, at about 7,350 feet above sea level, the loftiest point. (You can get out of your car and ride a cable car—the Funiculare Porta Vescovo—between the roadside parking lot and the mountain's summit. At both ends, you'll find alpine-style restaurants, hotels, and cafes. Cable cars depart at 30-minute intervals throughout daylight hours. For fares and more information, contact the tourist office in Cortina.) In spring, edelweiss grows in the surrounding fields; in winter, virtually everything except the surface of the road is blanketed in snow. After crossing the pass, you'll descend to the little resort of Canazei, then much later pass by sea-blue Carezza Lake.

10 Bolzano

177 miles NE of Milan, 298 miles N of Rome, 95 miles N of Verona

The terminus of the Great Dolomite Road (or the gateway, depending on your approach), **Bolzano** is a town of mixed blood, reflecting the long rule that Austria enjoyed until 1919. Many names, including that of the town (Bozen), appear in German. As the recipient of considerable Brenner Pass traffic (55 miles north), the city is a melting pot of Italians and both visitors and residents from the Germanic lands. Bolzano lies in the center of the Alto Adige region and is traversed by two rivers, the Isarco and Talvera, one of which splits the town in two.

ESSENTIALS

GETTING THERE   Bolzano is a 1¼-hour **train** ride north of Verona; a one-way fare is 12,100L ($7). For information and schedules, call ☎ **0471/974-292** or 1478/88-088 toll free in Italy only. The Austrian city of Innsbruck, reached via the Brenner Pass, lies about a 95-minute train ride north of Bolzano. Trains arrive at Piazza Stazione in the center of town, 300 feet up Viale Stazione is the very heart of the city, Piazza Walther.

Four **buses** a day make the 1-hour trip from Merano, costing 4,000L ($2.30) one-way. For information about schedules, call ☎ **0471/974-292.** If you've got a **car** and are coming from Trent (below), continue north to Bolzano on A22; if you're in Cortina d'Ampezzo, head west along Route 48 until reaching the signposted junction with Route 241, which covers the final circuitous lap into Bolzano.

VISITOR INFORMATION   The **tourist office** is at Piazza Walther 8 (☎ **0471/307-000**), open Monday to Friday 9am to 6pm and Saturday 9am to 12:30pm.

EXPLORING BOLZANO & THE DOLOMITES

Bolzano is a modern industrial town yet a worthwhile sightseeing attraction in its own right. On **Piazza Walther,** the main square in town, is a 15th-century Gothic **Duomo** with a colorful roof. The most interesting street is the colonnaded **Via dei Portici.** You can begin your stroll down this street of old buildings at either **Piazza Municipio** or **Piazza delle Erbe,** the latter a fruit market for the orchards of the province. There are many **esplanades** for promenading along the river.

Bolzano makes a good headquarters for exploring the Dolomiti and the scenic surroundings, like **Monte Renon** (Ritten in German) on the alpine plateau, with its cog train; the village of **San Genesio,** reached by cable car north of Bolzano; and **Salten,** 4,355 feet up, an alpine tableland. If you have time for only one of these excursions, we advise you make it Monte Renon, whose summit is connected to Bolzano by a cable car operating daily 7:10am to 7:25pm (to 8:25pm July and August). Round-trip passage is 7,200L ($4.20) for a ride of 12 scenic minutes each way. The cable cars leave from a station on Via Renon, a 15-minute walk northwest from the rail station (take bus no. 1 from the station). You'll ride 3,000 feet up to the hamlet of Soprabolzano, where you'll find a simple restaurant, a cafe or two, and a panorama over the Dolomites.

SHOPPING

You'll get a whiff of what's being produced in the mountains of western Austria after a quick perusal of Bolzano's folkloric shops, many of which lie beneath the vaulted arcades around and between **Piazza Walther** and **Piazza della Erbe.** One of the town's biggest and best-stocked is **Tschager,** Piazza Municipio (☎ 0471/973-674), where three floors of wood carvings include depictions of everything from a panoply of saints to rifle-toting huntsmen. Also look for ceramics, pottery, metalwork, and fabrics. A worthy competitor is **Artigiani Atesini,** Via Portici 39 (☎ 0471/978-590).

Looking for outdoor food and/or flea markets? Check out the *frutta e verdura* (fruits and vegetables) sold every Monday to Saturday 8am to around 5:30pm in **Piazza delle Erbe.** The first Saturday of every month, there's a **flea market** held in the streets between Piazza Walther and Piazza delle Erbe. Lots of used clothing but only the occasional genuine heirloom draw buyers, collectors, and curiosity-seekers. If you happen to visit during December and want to be pulled into the German-inspired spirit of Christmas, replete with Tannenbaums and evergreen boughs, attend the **Christkindl-markt,** held November 28 to December 23 in Piazza Walther, adjacent to the Duomo. From a series of temporary kiosks you can buy wooden toys, decorative ornaments, and alpine handcrafts that evoke the traditions of Austria more than those of Italy.

ACCOMMODATIONS

Hotel Alpi. Via Alto Adige 35, 39100 Bolzano. ☎ **0471/970-535.** Fax 0471/971-929. 110 units. A/C MINIBAR TV TEL. 260,000L ($151) double. Rates include breakfast. AE, DC, MC, V. Parking 15,000L ($9).

The exterior of this tastefully contemporary hotel—the second-best choice in town—is dotted with recessed balconies, large aluminum-framed windows, and the flags of many nations. The spacious public rooms boast paneling, exposed stone, and ceramic wall sculptures and contain upholstered seating areas. The hotel is in the commercial center of town and has a bar, a restaurant, a well-trained staff, and cozy guest rooms.

✪ **Park Hotel Laurin.** Via Laurin 4, 39100 Bolzano. ☎ **800/223-5652** in the U.S. or 0471/311-000 in Italy. Fax 0471/311-148. 106 units. A/C MINIBAR TV TEL. 285,000–415,000L ($165–$241) double; from 440,000L ($255) suite. Rates include breakfast. AE, MC, V. Parking 19,000L ($11).

The town's best address, the Park Laurin captures the glamour of the past. It was built in 1910 and is set on landscaped grounds, and its rooms and suites have been refurbished, with baths in Italian marble. In fact, the Park Hotel is among the top first-class hotels in the Dolomiti. The private garden is dominated by old shade trees and a flagstone-enclosed pool.

Dining/Diversions: The garden terrace is ideal for lunches or dinners, or you can try the elegant Ristorante Belle Epoque, serving the most refined international and regional cuisine in Bolzano (see "Dining" below). The refurbished bar is decorated with frescoes and daily piano music is featured, enlivened by occasional jazz fests.

Amenities: Concierge, room service, dry cleaning/laundry, baby-sitting, secretarial services.

✪ **Scala Hotel Stiegl.** Via Brennero 11 (Brennerstrasse 11), 39100 Bolzano. ☎ **0471/ 976-222.** Fax 0471/981-141. www.exinet.com/scalahot. E-mail: info@scalahot.com. 65 units. MINIBAR TV TEL. 220,000L ($128) double; 400,000L ($232) suite. Rates include breakfast. AE, DC, MC, V. Closed Dec 27–Jan 12. Parking 15,000L ($9) in garage, free outside.

The Scala is the best of the middle-bracket hotels. Its trilingual staff speaks fluent English and keeps the interior spotless. The neobaroque yellow-and-white facade is well maintained, with plenty of ornamentation. There are two kinds of guest rooms: those renovated in the early 1990s, in soothing dark colors, and those renovated around 1996, with lighter color schemes. All rooms have touches of varnished pine and contemporary furnishings. The hotel affords easy access to the train station and the historic center of town.

Dining/Diversions: The restaurant serves an excellent cuisine, worth a visit even if you're not staying here. We prefer it in summer, when you can dine in the garden. There's also a bar.

Amenities: Concierge, room service, laundry, baby-sitting, outdoor pool, car-rental desk.

DINING

Da Abramo. Piazza Gries 16 (Grieserplatz 16). ☎ **0471/280-141.** Reservations recommended. Main courses 21,000–29,000L ($12–$17); fixed-price menu 38,000L ($22). AE, DC, MC, V. Mon–Sat noon–2:15pm and 7–9:45pm. Closed Jan 6–13 and 3 weeks in Aug. MEDITERRANEAN/SEAFOOD.

In a century-old Liberty-style villa, the best and most elegant restaurant in Bolzano took great pains to introduce a chic modern airiness to its decor. Across the river from the historic center of town, Da Abramo offers a summer garden covered with vine arbors, plus a labyrinthine arrangement of rooms. Full meals cost upward of 50,000L ($29) and might include, depending on the mood of the chef, veal in a sauce of tuna and capers, roast quail with polenta, fish soup, warm seafood antipasti, codfish Venetian style, shellfish with seafood, tagliatelle with prosciutto, and beefsteak flambé with cognac. Flavors are robust, some thanks to the best of herbs and spices.

⭐ **Ristorante Belle Epoque.** In the Park Hotel Laurin, Via Laurin 4. ☎ **0471/311-000.** Reservations recommended. Main courses 30,000–45,000L ($18–$27); fixed-price menus 42,000–82,000L ($25–$49). AE, DC, MC, V. Daily noon–2pm and 7–10pm. ITALIAN.

Bolzano's most glamorous restaurant occupies a Liberty-style dining room near the lobby of the previously recommended Park Hotel Laurin. Between May and September, you can ask for an outdoor table below a large pergola extending into the hotel garden. The chefs have a real flair, and their food is perfectly cooked, with full, harmonious flavors. The antipasti is the town's best, everything from smoked carpaccio of fish with a salad of small white beans and tomatoes to vine-ripened melon with prosciutto. Every day, the chefs make a primi piatti (first plate) of three types of pasta along with a risotto selection. The fish is wonderful, and you may opt for the pesce misto di mare, a selection of the day's best offerings. Meat eaters will also find comfort, with tender veal steaks and herb-flavored lamb from the Dolomites.

Zur Kaiserkron. Piazza della Mostra 1 (Mustergasse 1). ☎ **0471/970-770.** Reservations recommended. Main courses 25,000–35,000L ($15–$20). AE, DC, MC, V. Mon–Fri noon–2:30pm and 7–9:30pm, Sat noon–2:30pm. SOUTH TYROLEAN/FRENCH/INTERNATIONAL.

The food is excellent and the decor appealing, and the multilingual management preserves the bicultural ambience for which Bolzano is known. The restaurant is a block from the Duomo in a yellow-and-white baroque building. For warm-weather dining, there's a canopy-covered wooden platform in front surrounded with greenery. Inside are tables under vaulted ceilings and wrought-iron chandeliers. Favorite dishes include an assortment of alpine-dried charcuterie; pâté of minced pheasant and duck liver; ravioli stuffed with spinach and minced beef; homemade tagliatelle with truffles; a traditional recipe of grüstl made from minced veal fried together with onions, eggs, and potatoes; home-smoked salmon; filet of venison with rosemary, pine nuts, and sweet-and-sour sauce; roast lamb or kid; and beef goulash with polenta.

BOLZANO AFTER DARK

The high altitudes and vestiges of alpine gemütlich from its days as an Austrian possession help contribute to good times and high energy after dark. Three discos (only one of which lies in the town center) are ready for you. The cellar-level **Club Miro,** Piazza Dominicani 3B (☎ **0471/976-464**), is the smallest but most central and convivial of the three. It features a piano bar, a disco, lots of beer and wine from the German-speaking world, and the occasional live concert.

Within the city's less evocative industrial zone are the town's biggest and flashiest discos, **Disco Pathos,** Via Siemens 14 (☎ **0471/201-188**), featuring dancing and drinking on two floors; and **Disco Big,** Via Galvani (☎ **0471/931-810**), the city's biggest, most imaginative, and most widely publicized. Both emulate New York and Milan more aggressively than they do the evergreen folklore of the Italian Dolomiti.

11 Trent: Capital of Trentino–Alto Adige

36 miles S of Bolzano, 144 miles NE of Milan, 63 miles N of Verona

A northern Italian city that basks in its former glory, the medieval **Trent (Trento)** on the left bank of the Adige is famous as the host of the Council of Trent (1545 to 1563). Beset with difficulties, such as the rising tide of "heretics," the Ecumenical Council convened at Trent, leading to the Counter-Reformation. Trent lies on the main rail line from the Brenner Pass, and many visitors like to stop off here before journeying farther south into Italy.

Although it has an alpine aura, Trento is much more Italian in flavor than Bolzano. As capitals of provinces go, Trent is rather sleepy and provincial. It hasn't been overly commercialized and is still richly imbued with a lot of architectural charm, with a small array of attractions—none to get too excited about. Nonetheless, it makes a good refueling stop for those exploring this history-rich part of Italy.

ESSENTIALS

GETTING THERE   Trent enjoys excellent **rail** connections. It lies on the Bologna-Verona-Brenner Pass-Munich rail line, and trains pass through day and night. The trip from Milan takes 2¾ hours and from Rome 7 hours. Trains also connect Trent with Bolzano once every hour. Seven trains per day make the 3½-hour run from Venice. For rail information and schedules, call ☎ **0461/234-545** or 1478/88-088 toll free in Italy only.

Both the train and the bus stations lie between the Adige River and the public gardens of Trent. The heart of town is to the east of the Adige. From the station, turn on Via Pozzo, which becomes Via Orfane and Via Cavour before reaching the heartbeat Piazza del Duomo.

It's better to take the train to Trent and then rely on local **buses** once you get there. The local bus station is next to the train station (☎ **0461/821-000** for schedules) and serves such places as Riva del Garda (see chapter 11).

If you've got a **car,** Trent lies on A22, south of Bolzano and north of Verona.

VISITOR INFORMATION   The **tourist office** is on Via Alfieri 4 (☎ **0461/983-880**). July and August, it's open Monday to Saturday 9am to noon and 3 to 6pm and Sunday 10am to noon; the rest of the year, hours are Monday to Friday 9am to noon and 3 to 6pm and Saturday 9am to noon.

EXPLORING THE CITY

Trent has much old charm. For a quick glimpse of the old town, head for **Piazza del Duomo,** dominated by the **Cattedrale di San Vergilio.** Built in the Romanesque style and much restored over the years, it dates from the 12th century. A medieval crypt under the altar holds a certain fascination, and the ruins of a 6th-century Christian basilica were recently discovered beneath the church. You can visit these remains along with your admission to the **Museum of the Diocese (Museo Diocesano),** facing the cathedral (☎ **0461/234-419**), with its religious artifacts on display relating to the Council of Trent, which met in the Duomo from 1545 to 1563. The museum is open Monday to Saturday 9:30am to 12:30pm and 2:30 to 6pm, costing 5,000L ($2.90). The Duomo is open daily 8:30am to noon and 2:30 to 8pm. In the center of the square is a mid–18th-century **Fountain of Neptune.**

The ruling prince-bishops of Trent, who held sway until they were toppled by the French in the early 19th century, resided at the medieval **Castello del Buonconsiglio** (☎ **0461/233-770**), reached from Via Bernardo Clesio 3. Now the old castle has been turned into a **Museum of Provincial Art (Museo Provincale d'Arte),** with a collection of paintings and fine art, some quite ancient, including early medieval mosaics. Its most interesting art is a fresco cycle from the 1400s, *Cico dei Mesi* (Cycle of the Months). The **Museum of Italian National Unity (Museo del Risorgimento),** also at the castle, contains mementos related to the period of national unification between 1796 and 1948. The museums are open Tuesday to Sunday: September to May 9am to noon and 2 to 5pm (to 5:30pm June to August. Admission is 7,000L ($4.05) adults and 3,000L ($1.75) children under 18/seniors 60 and over; children under 12 are free.

Trent makes a good base for exploring **Monte Bondone,** a sports resort about 22 miles from the city center; **Paganella,** slightly more than 12 miles from Trent (the summit is nearly 7,000 feet high); and the **Brenta Dolomiti.** The last excursion, which will require at least a day for a good look, will reward you with some of the finest mountain scenery in Italy. En route from Trent, you'll pass by **Lake Toblino,** then travel a winding road past jagged boulders. A 10-minute detour from the main road at the turnoff to the Genova valley offers untamed scenery. Take the detour at least to the thunderous **Nardis waterfall.** A good stopover point is the little resort of **Madonna di Campiglio.**

SHOPPING

Hoping to carry home some of the abundant agrarian bounty of the Trentino region? The most memorable food-and-wine shop in town is **Enoteca de Corso,** Corso 3 Novembre 54 (☎ **0471/916-424**), with wines from the region and everywhere else in Italy, as well as the salamis, olives, cheeses, and other salty tidbits that go well with them. Another outlet for the reds and whites produced through the Trentino and the rest of Italy as well is **Enoteca Lunelli,** Largo Carducci 12 (☎ **0471/982-496**). If you're in doubt about any aspect of the wine trade in this region, just ask. If you're looking for handcrafts, ceramics, woodcarvings, and metal work, head for the largest store of its type in town, **Artigianato Trentino,** Via Manchi 62 (☎ **0471/234-892**).

ACCOMMODATIONS

Albergo Accademia. Vicolo Colico 6, 38100 Trento. ☎ **0461/233-600.** Fax 0461/ 230-174. 43 units. A/C MINIBAR TV TEL. 250,000L ($145) double; from 310,000–445,000L ($180–$258) suite. Rates include breakfast. AE, DC, MC, V. Parking 20,000L ($12).

This alpine inn in the center of town behind the Renaissance Santa Maria Maggiore is made up of three buildings that have been joined to create a comfortable and attractive hostelry. One of the structures is believed to be of 11th- or 12th-century origin, based on a brick wall similar to the city walls found during renovation work. According to legend, the older part of the Accademia housed church leaders who attended the Council of Trent in the 16th century. The rooms are done in light natural wood, and a suite at the top of the house has a terrace with a view of the town and mountains. The alpine influence is carried over to the bar and the restaurant (closed Monday).

Hotel Buonconsiglio. Via Romagnosi 16–18, 38100 Trento. ☎ **0461/272-888.** Fax 0461/ 272-889. 46 units. A/C MINIBAR TV TEL. 180,000–255,000L ($104–$148) double; 280,000L ($162) suite. AE, DC, MC, V. Rates include breakfast. Parking 10,000L ($6).

Built shortly after World War II as the Hotel Alessandro Vittorio and renamed the Buonconsiglio in 1990 at the time of a massive renovation, this is an immaculate hotel with pleasant rooms and an English-speaking staff. It's located on a busy street near the rail station and has a slight edge over the Accademia (above). In the lobby is a collection of abstract modern paintings. Each guest room has a personal safe and soundproofing against traffic noise.

DINING

La Cantinota. Via San March 24. ☎ **0461/238-527.** Reservations recommended. Main courses 15,000–25,000L ($9–$15). AE, DC, MC, V. Fri–Wed noon–3pm and 8pm–midnight. TRENTINO/INTERNATIONAL.

Occupying a 13th-century building a short walk from the historic zone's Castello Bonconsiglio, this is an attractive restaurant where reasonably priced food has been served since the 1920s. You'll dine in one of two dining rooms or (more appealingly, if weather allows) a verdant garden. Menu items, flavorful and linked to Trento traditions, may include gnocchi with a mushroom-flavored cream sauce; potato-and-herb tarts; grilled beef filet with a hearty red-wine sauce; and a medley of freshwater fish from the nearby lake, either grilled or prepared with balsamic vinegar sauce. Before or after your meal, you might enjoy the artist performing in the piano bar.

Orso Grigio. Via degli Orti 19. ☎ **0461/984-400.** Reservations recommended. Main courses 16,000–25,000L ($9–$15). AE, DC, MC, V. Mon–Sat 12:30–2:30pm and 7:30–10pm. ITALIAN/TRENTINE.

This spacious elegant restaurant lies about 30 yards from Piazza Fiera, in a building whose origins may go back to the 1500s. When you see the immaculate table linen, well-cared-for plants, and subdued lighting, you know something is going right. Menus are seasonally adjusted to take in the finest fresh produce. The place enjoys local popularity—a good sign, since the Trentino is noted for a refined palate. Rufioli, a green tortellini, is a specialty. Another good regional dish is squazzet con polenta, Trentine-style fried tripe. Finish with chocolate mousse. Wines of the province are a special feature here.

⭐ **Restaurant Chiesa.** Via San Marco 64. ☎ **0461/238-766.** Reservations recommended. Main courses 14,000–26,000L ($8–$15); fixed-price "apple menu" 75,000L ($44). AE, DC, MC, V. Mon–Sat noon–2:30pm and 7–10pm. TRENTINE.

Restaurant Chiesa offers the largest array of dishes we've ever seen made with apples. Owners Allesandro and Alberto recognized that Eve's favorite fruit, which grows more abundantly around Trent than practically anywhere else, was the base of dozens of traditional recipes. Specialties include risotto with apple, liver pâté with apple, filet of perch with apple, and a range of other well-prepared specialties (a few of which, believe it or not, don't contain apples).

TRENT AFTER DARK

Trent enjoys a reputation as an industrial workhorse, with an early-to-bed/early-to-rise philosophy that has never fostered an emphasis on nighttime carousing. Your most appealing option might be an after-dark stroll around **Piazza del Duomo,** where three bars offer conviviality.

Still in the town center but farther afield, you might be attracted to **Bar Picaro,** Via San Giovanni 36 (☎ **0461/230-145**), where live loud music attracts the under-30 crowd. More soothing is the hideaway piano bar in the previously recommended **La Cantinota,** Via San Marco 24 (☎ **0461/238-527**). Every night from 10pm to around 4am, you'll find a singer, usually an Italian who speaks and sings goodly amounts of English, will perform stylish songs, including any you might request.

If you want to dance (something the bishops who convened here during the Council of Trent would find highly irreverent), head for the hamlet of Pergine, 6 miles east of Trent, to the region's most popular disco, **Paradisi,** Via al Lago (☎ **0461/532-694**). There are at least two bars, and one side of the place is devoted to amusing versions of such old-fashioned dances as the waltz and jitterbug, the other to the more exuberant kinds of boogying of conventional discos.

11 Milan, Lombardy & the Lake District

The vicissitudes of Italy's history are reflected in **Lombardy** as perhaps in no other region. Conquerors from barbarians to Napoléon have marched across its plain, and even Mussolini came to his end here. He and his mistress (both already dead) were strung up in a Milan square as war-weary residents vented their rage.

Among the most progressive of all the Italians, the Lombards have charted an industrial empire unequaled in Italy. Often the dream of the underfed and jobless in the south is to go to Milano for the high wages and the good life, though thousands end up finding neither. Lombardy isn't all manufacturing, however. **Milan** is filled to the brim with important attractions, and nearby are old Lombard art cities like Bergamo, Cremona, and Mantua.

The **Lake District,** with its flower-bedecked promenades, lemon trees, villas, parks and gardens, and crystal-clear blue waters, may sound a bit dated, but the lakes—notably Garda, Como, and Maggiore—continue to form one of the most enchanting splashes of scenery in northern Italy. They've attracted poets and writers, everybody from Goethe to Gabriele d'Annunzio. But after World War II, the Italian lakes seemed to be largely the domain of matronly English and German types. In our more recent swings through the district, however, we've noticed an increasing joie de vivre and a rising influx of the 25-to-40 age group, particularly at resorts like Limone on Lake Garda. Even if your time is limited, you'll want to have at least a look at Lake Garda.

The serious wine connoisseur might want to schedule a visit to one of Italy's largest wineries, lying in the Po Valley. For details about making an appointment, refer to the Lombardy entry under "The Best Wine-Growing Regions" in chapter 1.

1 Milan: High Fashion, La Scala & More

355 miles NW of Rome, 87 miles NE of Turin, 88 miles N of Genoa

Southern Italians, perhaps resentful of the north's hard-earned prosperity, sometimes declare the Milanese are like the nearby no-nonsense Swiss. With 2 million inhabitants, **Milan (Milano)** doesn't evoke the languor and garrulousness of the rest of Italy, doesn't muck about with excessive manners, and doesn't snooze somnolently in the midday heat. It works, moves, bustles. Milan is Italy's window on

Lombardy & the Lake District

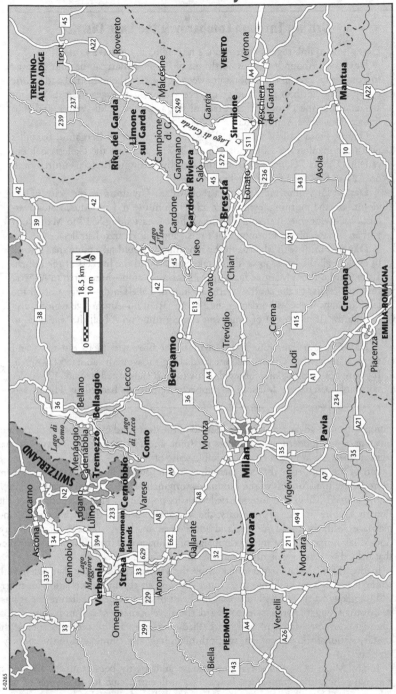

Driving Through Lombardy & the Lake District

Here's how to link together the region's highlights if you have a car.

Days 1–2: About 360 miles northwest of Rome, **Milan** can be your gateway to Lombardy. Take in the panoramic sweep of the city, the industrial and artistic center of the north of Italy, and go on several shopping binges. Visit such major attractions as the Duomo, Pinacoteca di Brera, Museo Poldi-Pezzoli, and Biblioteca-Pinacoteca Ambrosiana.

Day 3: From Milan, take A4 (E64) east for a visit to **Bergamo,** 31 miles northeast. Explore its Città Alta (Upper Town) and visit the Galleria dell'Accademia Carrara. Continue east on the autostrada toward Brescia, cutting south on A21 to Cremona for the night.

Day 4: Fifty-nine miles southeast of Milan, **Cremona** is the "city of the violin." In the morning, explore Piazza del Comune and the Museo Stradivariano. Enjoy lunch at Ceresole. For the night, cut east along SS10 to **Mantua.** If you arrive late, plan a morning visit to its Museo di Palazzo Ducale.

Day 5: Finish with Mantua in the morning. It would take more than a week to explore all the lakes, so we'll just take you around the liveliest of the bunch, **Lake Garda.** From Mantua, head up A22 toward Verona, but switch to A4 west toward Brescia, to the southwestern corridor of Lake Garda—largest of all the lakes in Italy, it shores bordering the Veneto, Trentino–Alto Adige regions, and Lombardy. (If you're out of time, you can continue on A4 all the way back to Milan.)

Day 6: Begin your tour at **Desenzano del Garda,** with its old town and scenic harbor. Most visitors take the road along the western shore (S572) north. If you're not running late, follow the first turnoff signposted to Salò, 12½ miles north of Desenzano. Mussolini's puppet government, backed by Hitler, was

---

Europe, its most advanced showcase, devoid of the dusty and musty history that sometimes paralyzes modern developments in Rome and Florence or the watery rot that seems to pervade Venice with an inevitable sense of decay.

Part of the work ethic that has catapulted Milan toward the 21st century may stem from the Teutonic origins of the Lombards (originally from northwestern Germany), who occupied Milan and intermarried with its population after the collapse of the Roman Empire. In the 14th century, the Viscontis, through their wits, wealth, and marriages with the royalty of England and France, made Milan Italy's strongest city. And Milan initiated a continuing campaign of drainage and irrigation of the Po Valley that helped to make it one of the most fertile regions in the world.

In the 1700s, Milan was dominated by the Habsburgs, a legacy that left it with scores of neoclassical buildings in its inner core and an abiding appreciation for music and (perhaps) work. In 1848, it was at the heart of the northern Italian revolt against its Austro-Hungarian rulers, encouraged the development of a Pan-Italian dialect (through novelist Manzoni) and, with Piedmont, was at the center of the 19th-century nationalistic passion that swept through Italy and culminated in the country's unification.

Today, Milan is a commercial powerhouse and, partly because of its 400 banks and major industrial companies, Italy's most influential city. It's the center of publishing, silk, TV and advertising, and design and lies close to the densest collection of automobile-assembly plants, rubber and textile factories, and chemical plants. Milan also boasts La Scala, one of Europe's most prestigious opera houses, and a major

established here in September 1943. **Gardone Riviera,** with its memories of Gabriele d'Annunzio, who died there in 1938, lies just 3 miles north of Salò. Anchor in at this lakeside resort for an overnight stay.

Day 7: SS45B continues for 7½ miles north to **Gargnano,** where Mussolini occupied a villa, the Feltrinelli (closed to the public). From here, another 12 miles leads you to one of the most charming spots along the lake, **Limone sul Garda,** named for its lemon groves, where you may want to stop for lunch and explore the town. In the days when Goethe frequented the place it was accessible only by boat. After Limone, continue on SS45B north to **Riva del Garda,** as the road passes through tunnel after tunnel blasted out of rock. Overnight in Riva, at the top of the lake.

Day 8: Leave Riva, but this time drive along the less touristy side of the lake, the eastern shore bordering the Veneto. This route is called **Gardesana Orientale** (S249). It passes through **Malcesine,** 11 miles south of Riva, a favorite holiday target for Greta Garbo, who called herself Harriet Browne when visiting. At the town of **San Vigilio** you can stop for lunch at the Locanda San Vigilio, which Churchill chose as a spot to paint and hibernate.

From here drive south for 14 miles to **Peschieta del Garda,** joining S11 for a 6-mile drive to Colombare, where you can follow the signposts heading north on a promontory jutting out into the lake and leading you to the little walled resort town of **Sirmione.** The next morning, continue on SS11 until it runs into SS572 for the quick jaunt south to A4 headed west toward Milan. If you're out of time, you can return all the way to Milan, or you can turn north outside the city onto S36 toward Como to explore **Lake Como** and **Lake Maggiore** on your own.

commercial university (the alma mater of most of Italy's corporate presidents). It is also the site of several world-renowned annual trade fairs.

With unashamed capitalistic style, Milan has purchased more art than it has produced and lured to its borders an energetic and hardworking group of creative intellects. To make it in Milan, in either business or the arts, is to have made it to the top of the pecking order. If you came to Italy to find sun-flooded piazzas and somnolent afternoons, you won't find them amid the fogs and rains of Milan. You will, however, have placed your finger on the pulse of modern Italy.

ESSENTIALS

GETTING THERE   Milan is serviced by two airports, the **Aeroporto di Linate,** 4½ miles east of the inner city, and the **Aeroporto della Malpensa,** 31 miles northwest. Malpensa is used for most transatlantic flights, and Linate is for flights within Italy and Europe. For general flight information, call ☎ **02/7485-2200.** Buses for Linate leave from the **Porta Garibaldi station** every 20 minutes 5:40am to 7pm and every 30 minutes 7 to 9pm. Buses for Malpensa leave from the **Stazione Centrale** 2½ hours before all international and intercontinental flights. (Buses run in both directions, so they're the best bet for new arrivals to come into town.) This is much cheaper than taking a taxi.

Milan is serviced by the finest **rail connections** in Italy. The main rail station for arrivals is Mussolini's mammoth **Stazione Centrale,** Piazza Duca d'Aosta (☎ **1478/ 675-001** or 1478/88-088 toll free in Italy only), where you'll find the National

Railways information office open daily 7:30am to 9:30pm. One train per hour arrives from both Genoa and Turin (trip time: 1½ to 2 hours), costing 22,000L ($13) one-way. Twenty-five trains arrive daily from Venice (trip time: 3 hours), costing 36,000L ($21) one-way; and one train per hour arrives from Florence (trip time: 2½ hours), costing 38,000L ($22) one-way. Trains from Rome arrive every hour, taking 5 hours for the journey and costing 68,000L ($39) one-way. The station is directly northeast of the heart of town; trams, buses, and the metro link the station to Piazza del Duomo in the very center.

Buses link Milan with Pavia, Bergamo, and other cities of Lombardy. Some of these companies are privately owned and others are under the control of Regione Lombardia. For information about various routings in the province, ask at the **ATM Information Office,** on the departures floor of Stazione Centrale, at Piazza Duca d'Aosta (☎ 02/669-70-32), open daily 8am to 8pm.

If you're arriving by **car,** A4 is the principal east-west route for Milan, with A8 coming in from the northwest, A1 from the southeast, and A7 from the southwest. A22 is another major north-south artery, running just east of Lake Garda.

VISITOR INFORMATION You'll find the **Azienda di Promozione Turistica del Milanese,** Piazza del Duomo at Via Marconi 1 (☎ 02/7252-4300), particularly helpful, dispensing free maps and whatever advice they can. There's also a branch at the Stazione Centrale (☎ 02/7252-4370). The offices are open Monday to Friday 8:30am to 7pm and Saturday, Sunday, and holidays 9am to 1pm and 2 to 5pm.

CITY LAYOUT With its spired cathedral, **Piazza del Duomo** lies at the heart of Milan. The city is encircled by three "rings," one of which is the **Cerchia dei Navigli,** a road more or less following the outline of the former medieval walls. The road runs along what was formerly a series of canals—hence the name navigli. The second ring, known both as **Bastioni** and **Viali,** follows the outline of the Spanish Walls from the 16th century. It's now a tram route (no. 29 or 30). A much more recent ring is the **Circonvallazione Esterna,** connecting with the main roads coming into Milan.

If you're traveling within the relatively small Cerchia dei Navigli, you can do so on foot. We don't recommend you attempt to drive in this circle unless you're heading for a garage. All the major attractions, including Leonardo's *Last Supper,* La Scala, and the Duomo, lie in this ring.

One of Milan's most important streets, **Via Manzoni,** begins near the Teatro alla Scala and will take you to **Piazza Cavour,** a key point for the traffic arteries. The **Arch of Porta Nuova,** a remnant of the medieval walls, marks the entrance to Via Manzoni. To the northwest of Piazza Cavour is the **Giardini Pubblici,** and to the northwest of these gardens is **Piazza della Repubblica.** From this square, Via Vittorio Pisani leads into **Piazza Duca d'Aosta,** site of the cavernous Stazione Centrale.

At Piazza Cavour, you can head west on Via Fatebenefratelli into the **Brera** district, whose major attraction is the Pinacoteca di Brera. This district in recent years has become a major center in Milan for offbeat shopping and after-dark diversions.

GETTING AROUND The tourist office sells a **travel pass** costing 5,000L ($2.90) for 1 day or 9,000L ($5) for 2 days, good for unlimited use on the city's tram, bus, and subway network. Those planning a longer stay can purchase a **weekly pass,** costing 20,000L ($12) and requiring a photo.

The city **bus** system covers most of Milan, and regular tickets costs 1,500L (85¢), as does the **subway** at the same fare. Some subway tickets are good for continuing trips on city buses at no extra charge, but they must be used within 75 minutes of purchase.

To phone a **taxi,** dial ☎ 02/6767, 02/5353, 02/8585, or 02/8388; fares start at 6,000L ($3.50), with a nighttime surcharge of 5,000L ($2.90).

FAST FACTS **American Express** The office is at Via Brera 3 (☎ **02/7200-3693** or 02/8646-0930), open Monday to Friday 9am to 5pm.

Consulates The **U.S. Consulate,** Via Principe Amedeo 2/10 (☎ **02/2903-5141**), is open Monday to Friday 9 to 11am. The **Canadian Consulate** is at Via Vittorio Pisani 19 (☎ **02/67-581**), open Monday to Friday 9am to 12:30pm and 1:30 to 5pm. The **U.K.** **Consulate** is at Via San Paolo 7 (☎ **02/723-001**), open Monday to Friday 9:15am to 12:15pm and 2:30 to 4:30pm. The **Australian Consulate** is at Via Borgogna 2 (☎ **02/777-041**), open Monday to Thursday 9am to noon and 2 to 4pm and Friday 9am to noon. Citizens of **New Zealand** should contact their consulate in Rome.

Emergencies For the **police,** call ☎ **62261;** for an **ambulance,** ☎ **118;** for any **emergency,** ☎ **113.**

Hospital About a 5-minute ride from the Duomo, the **Ospedale Maggiore Policlinico,** Via Francesco Sforza 35 (☎ **02/55-031**), has English-speaking doctors.

Pharmacies You can find an all-night pharmacy by phoning ☎ **192.** The pharmacy (☎ **02/669-0735**) at the Stazione Centrale never closes.

Post Offices Most branches are open Monday to Saturday 8:30am to 1:30pm. The **Central Post Office** is at Via Cordusio 4 (☎ **02/805-6812**), open Monday to Friday 8:30am to 7:15pm and Saturday 8:30am to 3:30pm. You can also call the Information Office at Piazza Cordusio (☎ **02/805-6812**).

SEEING THE SIGHTS
THE TOP ATTRACTIONS

Despite its modern architecture and industry, Milan is still a city of great art. The serious sightseer should give it at least 2 days for exploration. If your schedule is frantic, see the Duomo; the Brera Picture Gallery; and one of the most important galleries of northern Italy, the Biblioteca-Pinacoteca Ambrosiana.

✪ **Il Duomo.** Piazza del Duomo. ☎ **02/8646-3456.** Cathedral, free; roof, 6,000L ($3.50) stairs, 8,000L ($4.65) elevator; crypt, 2,000L ($1.15); baptistery, 3,000L ($1.75). Cathedral, daily 7:15am–6:45pm. Roof, daily 9am–4:30pm. Crypt, daily 9am–noon and 2:30–6pm. Baptistery, Tues–Sun 10am–noon and 3–5pm. Metro: Duomo.

In Milan's center is Piazza del Duomo. Its impressive lacy Gothic cathedral, 479 feet long and 284 feet wide at the transepts, ranks with St. Peter's in Rome and the cathedral at Seville, Spain, as among the world's largest. It was begun in 1386 and has seen numerous architects and builders. The conqueror of Milan, Napoléon, even added his own decorating ideas to the facade. The imposing structure of marble is the grandest and most flamboyant example of the Gothic style in Italy.

Built in the shape of a Latin cross, the Duomo is divided by soaring pillars into five naves. The overall effect is like a marble-floored Grand Central Terminal (that is, in space), with far greater dramatic intensity. In the **crypt** rests the tomb of San Carlo Borromeo, the cardinal of Milan. To experience the Duomo at its most majestic, you must ascend to the **roof,** on which you can walk through a forest of pinnacles, turrets, and marble statuary—like a promenade in an early Cocteau film. Alfred, Lord Tennyson, rhapsodized about the panorama of the Alps as seen from this roof. A gilded Madonna towers over the tallest spire.

If you're interested in antiquity, you may want to explore the **Baptistery (Battistero Paleocristiano),** which you enter through the cathedral. This is a subterranean ruin going back to the 4th century and lying beneath the cathedral's piazza. It's believed that this is the site where Ambrose, first bishop and patron saint of the city, baptized Augustine.

Duomo Museum (Museo del Duomo) and Civic Museum of Contemporary Art (Museo Civico d'Arte Contemporaneau). In the Palazzo Reale, Piazza del Duomo 12 and 14. ☎ **02/860-358** (Duomo Museum) or ☎ 02/62-08-39-14 (Contemporary Art Museum). Duomo Museum, 10,000L ($6) adults, 8,000L ($4.65) children/seniors 60 and over. Contemporary Art Museum, free admission. Duomo Museum, Tues–Sun 9:30am–12:30pm and 3–6pm. Contemporary Art Museum, Tues–Sat 9am–5:30pm. Metro: Duomo.

Housed in the Palazzo Reale (Royal Palace), the **Duomo Museum** is like a picture storybook of the cathedral's 6 centuries of history. It has exhibits of statues and decorative sculptures, some of which date from the 14th century. There are also antique art objects, stained-glass windows (some from the 15th century), and ecclesiastical vestments, many as old as the 16th century.

The palazzo also houses the **Civic Museum of Contemporary Art.** Contemporary as interpreted by this museum could mean anything painted in the 20th century, even a work executed in 1900. You're often greeted with some of the best modern art exhibits in Italy here, often the works of contemporary artists who are either world class or the mere daring of the avant-garde. However, permanent works include those by Picasso, De Chirico, and Modigliani. There's also a fine collection of Italian Futurist art.

✪ **Ambrosiana Library and Pictury Gallery (Biblioteca-Pinacoteca Ambrosiana).** Piazza Pio XI no. 2. ☎ **02/806-921.** Admission 12,000L ($7). Tues–Sun 10am–5:30pm. Metro: Duomo–Cordusio.

Near the Duomo, the Ambrosiana Library and Picture Gallery were founded in the early 17th century by Cardinal Federico Borromeo. On the second floor, the **Pinacoteca** contains a remarkable collection of art, mostly from the 15th to the 17th century. Most notable are a *Madonna and Angels* by Botticelli; works by Brueghel (which have impressive detail and are among the best pieces); paintings by Lombard artists, including Bramantino's *Presepe,* in earthy primitive colors; a curious miniature *St. Jerome with Crucifix* by Andrea Solario; and works by Bernardino Luini. The museum owns a large sketch by Raphael on which he labored before painting *The School of Athens* for the Vatican. The most celebrated treasures are the productions of Leonardo da Vinci's *Codice Atlantico.* (In Milan, the master had as a patron the powerful Ludovico Sforza, known as "The Moor.") After seeing the sketches (in facsimile), you can only agree with Leonardo's evaluation of himself as a genius without peer. Attributed to him is a portrait of a musician, believed to have been Franchino Gaffurio. The **Library** contains many medieval manuscripts, which are shown for scientific examination only.

✪ **Chiesa di Santa Maria delle Grazie (*The Last Supper*).** Piazza Santa Maria delle Grazie (off Corso Magenta). ☎ **02/498-7588.** Church, free; *The Last Supper,* 12,000L ($7). Church, Mon–Sat 7:30am–noon and 3–7pm, Sun 3:30–6:30pm; *The Last Supper,* Tues–Sun 8am–1pm. Metro: Cadorna or Conciliazione.

This Gothic church was erected by the Dominicans in the mid-15th century, and a number of its more outstanding features, such as the cupola, were designed by the great Bramante. But visitors from all over the world flock here to gaze on a mural in the convent next door. In what was once a refectory, the incomparable Leonardo da Vinci adorned one wall with *The Last Supper.*

Commissioned by Ludovico the Moor, the 28- by 15-foot mural was finished about 1497, began to disintegrate almost immediately, and was totally repainted in the 1700s and the 1800s. Its gradual erosion makes for one of the most intriguing stories in art.

Milan

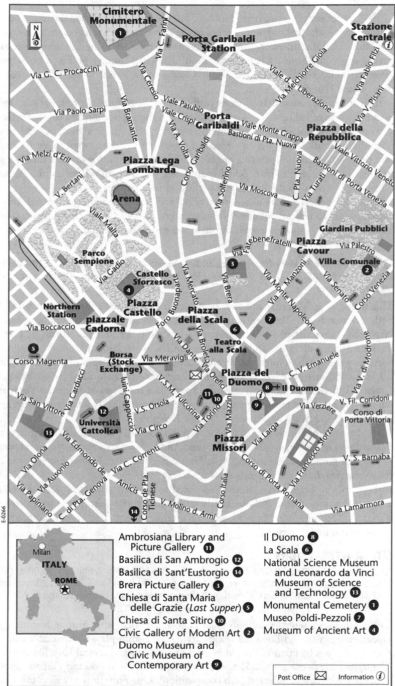

Ambrosiana Library and
  Picture Gallery **11**
Basilica di San Ambrogio **12**
Basilica di Sant'Eustorgio **14**
Brera Picture Gallery **3**
Chiesa di Santa Maria
  delle Grazie (*Last Supper*) **5**
Chiesa di Santa Sitiro **10**
Civic Gallery of Modern Art **2**
Duomo Museum and
  Civic Museum of
  Contemporary Art **9**

Il Duomo **8**
La Scala **6**
National Science Museum
  and Leonardo da Vinci
  Museum of Science
  and Technology **13**
Monumental Cemetery **1**
Museo Poldi-Pezzoli **7**
Museum of Ancient Art **4**

Post Office ✉   Information ⓘ

495

In 1943, it narrowly escaped being bombed, but the bomb demolished the roof, and—astonishingly—the painting was exposed to the elements for 3 years before a new roof was built. The current restoration has been controversial, drawing fire from some art critics, as did the Sistine Chapel restoration. The chief restorer of *The Last Supper*, Pinin Brambilla Barcilon, said the Sistine Chapel was a "simple window wash" compared to the Leonardo.

It has been suggested that all that's really left of the original *Last Supper* is a "few isolated streaks of fading color"—everything else is the application and color of artists and restorers who followed. What remains, however, is Leonardo's "outline," and even it is suffering badly. As an Italian newspaper writer put it: "If you want to see *Il Cenacolo*, don't walk—run!" A painting of grandeur, the composition portrays Christ at the moment he announces to his shocked apostles that one of them will betray him. Vasari called the portrait of Judas "a study in perfidy and wickedness."

Only 25 viewers are admitted at a time, and you're required to pass through antechambers to remove pollutants from your body. After viewing the painting—for 10 minutes only—you must walk through two additional filtration chambers as you exit.

✪ **Brera Picture Gallery (Pinacoteca di Brera).** Via Brera 28. ☎ **02/867-518.** Admission 8,000L ($4.65). Tues–Sat 9am–5pm, Sun 9am–12:15pm. Metro: Cairoli, Lanza, or Montenapoleone.

This is one of Italy's finest galleries, boasting an exceptional collection of works by both Lombard and Venetian masters. Like a Roman emperor, Canova's nude Napoléon—a toga draped over his shoulder—stands in the courtyard (fittingly, a similar statue ended up in the Duke of Wellington's house in London).

Among the notable pieces, the *Pietà* by Lorenzo Lotto is a work of great beauty, as is Gentile Bellini's *St. Mark Preaching in Alexandria* (it was finished by his brother, Giovanni). Seek out Andrea Mantegna's *Virgin and the Cherubs*, from the Venetian school. Three of the most important prizes are Mantegna's *Dead Christ*, Giovanni Bellini's *La Pietà*, and Carpaccio's *St. Stephen Debating*.

Other paintings include Titian's *St. Jerome*, as well as such Lombard art as Bernardino Luini's *Virgin of the Rose Bush* and Andrea Solario's *Portrait of a Gentleman*. One of the greatest panels is Piero della Francesca's *Virgin and Child Enthroned with Saints and Angels* and the *Kneeling Duke of Urbino in Armor*. Another work to seek out is the *Christ* by Bramante. One wing, devoted to modern art, offers works by such artists as Boccioni, Carrà, and Morandi. One of our favorite paintings in the gallery is Raphael's *Wedding of the Madonna*, with a dancelike quality. The moving *Last Supper at Emmaus* is by Caravaggio.

OTHER ATTRACTIONS

✪ **Museo Poldi-Pezzoli.** Via Manzoni 12. ☎ **02/794-889.** Admission 10,000L ($6) adults; 5,000L ($2.90) children under 17/seniors over 60. Tues–Sun 9:30am–12:30pm and 2:30–6pm (to 7:30pm on Sat). Closed Sun afternoon Apr–Sept. Metro: Duomo or Montenapoleone.

This fabulous museum is done in great taste and is rich with antique furnishings, tapestries, frescoes, and Lombard wood carvings. It also displays a remarkable collection of paintings by many of the old masters of northern and central Italy, like Andrea Mantegna's *Madonna and Child*, Giovanni Bellini's *Cristo Morto*, and Filippo Lippi's *Madonna, Angels, and Saints* (superb composition). One portrait that enjoys the same fame in Milan that the *Mona Lisa* does worldwide is Antonio Pollaiolo's *Portrait of a Lady*, a work of haunting originality. One buyer from Paris's garment district says he comes here on every trip to Milan—regardless of how rushed—just to gaze in wonder at this stunning portrait. One room is devoted to Flemish artists, and there's a collection of ceramics and also one of clocks and watches. The museum grew out of a private collection donated to the city in 1881.

Museum of Ancient Art (Museo d'Arte Antica). In the Castello Sforzesco, Piazza Castello. ☎ **02/7600-2378.** Free admission. Tues–Sun 9am–5:45pm. Metro: Cairoli.

The Castle Sforzesco is an ancient fortress rebuilt by Francesco Sforza, who launched another governing dynasty. It's believed that both Bramante and Leonardo contributed architectural ideas to the fortress. Following extensive World War II bombings, it was painstakingly restored and continues its activity as a Museum of Ancient Art. On the ground floor are sculptures from the 4th century A.D., medieval art mostly from Lombardy, and armor. The most outstanding exhibit, however, is Michelangelo's *Rondanini Pietà,* on which he was working the week he died. In the rooms upstairs, besides a good collection of ceramics, antiques, and bronzes, is the important picture gallery, rich in paintings from the 14th to the 18th century. Included are works by Lorenzo Veneziano, Mantegna, Lippi, Bellini, Crivelli, Foppa, Bergognone, Cesare da Sesto, Lotto, Tintoretto, Cerano, Procaccini, Morazzone, Guardi, and Tiepolo.

National Science Museum and Leonardo da Vinci Museum of Science and Technology (Museo Nazionale della Scienza e della Tecnica Leonardo da Vinci). Via San Vittore 21. ☎ **02/4801-0040.** Admission 10,000L ($6) adults; 6,000L ($3.50) children 18 and under/seniors 60 and over. Tues–Fri 9:30am–5pm, Sat–Sun 9:30am–6:30pm. Metro: S. Ambrogio.

If you're a fan of Leonardo da Vinci, as we are, you'll want to visit this vast museum complex where you could practically spend a week. For the average visitor, the most interesting section is the Leonardo da Vinci Gallery, displaying copies and models from the Renaissance genius. There's a reconstructed convent pharmacy, a monastic cell, and collections of antique carriages and even sewing machines. You'll also see exhibits relating to astronomy, telecommunications, watchmaking, goldsmithery, motion pictures, and the subjects of classic physics.

Civic Gallery of Modern Art (Civica Galleria d'Arte Moderna). In the Villa Reale (Ville Comunale), Via Palestro 16. ☎ **02/7600-2819.** Free admission. Tues–Sun 9am–5:45pm. Metro: Palestro.

Housed in one of the historic core's most prestigious palaces, this is Milan's most important collection of late 19th- and early 20th-century art, mostly from 1850 to 1918. The palace was built from 1790 to 1793 by noted architect Leopold Pollack and served as the Milanese home of both Napoléon and Eugène de Beauharnais. This is also the site of many weddings, whose participants appreciate the building's sense of history and its ornate decor. The exhibit space is divided into three collections (the Carlo Grassi, the Vismara, and the Marino Marini), all showing the development of impressionism and modernism as defined by Italian, and especially Lombard, painters. Most visible of these is the collection of Marino Marini, a 20th-century sculptor whose artworks (more than 200) were donated to the museum in 1973. Other artists whose works are displayed are Picasso, Matisse, Rouault, Renoir, Modigliani, Corot, Millet, Manet, Cézanne, Bonnard, and Gauguin.

Basilica di Sant'Eustorgio. Piazza Sant'Eustorgio 1. ☎ **02/5810-1583.** Basilica, free; chapel, 5,000L ($2.90). Daily 8:30am–noon and 3–6:30pm. Metro: Genova.

The bell tower of this 4th-century basilica dates from the 13th century; it was built in the romantic style by patrician Milanese families. It has the first tower clock in the world, made in 1305. Originally this was the tomb of the Three Kings (4th century A.D.). Inside, its greatest treasure is the **Capella Portinari,** designed by the Florentine Michelozzo in Renaissance style. The chapel is frescoed and contains a bas-relief of angels at the base of the cupola. In the center is an intricately carved tomb containing the remains of St. Peter Martyr, supported by 13th-century marble statuary by Balduccio of Pisa. The basement has a Roman crypt.

Basilica di San Ambrogio. Piazza San Ambrogio 15. ☎ **02/8645-0895.** Basilica, free; museum, 3,000L ($1.75). Basilica, Mon–Sat 9:30am–noon and 2:30–6:30pm; museum, Mon–Sat 10am–noon; daily 3–5pm. Closed Aug. Metro: San Ambrogio.

This church was first built by St. Ambrose in the later years of the 4th century A.D., but the present structure was built in the 12th century in the Romanesque style. The remains of St. Ambrose rest in the crypt. The church, entered after passing through a quadrangle, is rather stark and severe, in the style of its day. The atrium is its most distinguishing feature. In the apse are interesting mosaics from the 12th century. The Lombard tower at the side dates from 1128, and the facade, with its two tiers of arches, is impressive. In the church is the **Museo della Basilica di S. Ambrogio,** containing some frescoes, 15th-century wood paneling, silver and gold objects originally for the altar, paintings, sculpture, and Flemish tapestries.

Monumental Cemetery (Cimitèro Monumentale). Piazzale Cimitèro Monumentale 1. ☎ **02/659-9938.** Free admission. Tues–Fri 8:30am–5:15pm, Sat–Sun 8:30am–5:45pm. Metro: Garibaldi. Tram: 3, 4, 11, 12, 14, 29, 30, or 33.

This cemetery has catered for more than 100 years to the whims of Milan's elite. The only requirements for burial here are that you're dead and that when you were alive you were able to buy your way into a plot. Some families have paid up to 200,000,000L ($116,000) just for the privilege of burying their dead here. The graves are marked not only with brass plates or granite markers but also with Greek temples, elaborate obelisks, or such original works as an abbreviated version of Trajan's Column.

This outdoor museum has become such an attraction that a superintendent has compiled an illustrated guidebook—a sort of "Who Was Who." Among the cemetery's outstanding sights is a sculpted version of *The Last Supper.* Several fine examples of art-nouveau sculpture dot the hillside, and there's a tasteful example of Liberty-style architecture (Italy's version of art nouveau) in a tiny chapel designed to hold the remains of Arturo Toscanini's son, who died in 1906. Among the notables buried here are Toscanini himself and novelist Alessandro Manzoni. In the Memorial Chapel is the tomb of Salvatore Quasimodo, who won the 1959 Nobel prize in literature. Here also rest the ashes of Ermann Einstein, father of the scientist. In the Palanti Chapel is a monument commemorating the 800 Milanese citizens slain in Nazi concentration camps. (A model of this monument is displayed in New York's Museum of Modern Art.) It's a few blocks east of Stazione Porta Garibaldi, in the urban congestion of Milan, 2 miles north of Il Duomo.

SHOPPING

Milan is blessed with one of the most unusual concentrations of shopping possibilities in Europe. Most of the boutiques are infused with the style, humor, and sophistication that has made Milan the dynamo of the Italian fashion industry, a place where the sidewalks sizzle with the hard-driving entrepreneurial spirit that has been part of the northern Italian textile industry for centuries. The shops say it all—Dolce & Gabbana, Ferré, Krizia, Moschino, Prada, Armani, and Versace have all catapulted to international stardom from design studios based here.

THE SHOPPING SCENE

THE GOLDEN TRIANGLE   One well-heeled shopper from Florida recently spent the better part of her vacation in Italy shopping for what she called "the most unbelievable variety of shoes, clothes, and accessories in the world." A walk on the fashion subculture's focal point, **Via Montenapoleone,** heart of the "Golden Triangle," will quickly confirm that impression. It's one of Italy's three great shopping streets.

Note carefully that beauty doesn't come cheaply in the garment industry, and the attention you receive will often be based directly on the salesperson's impression of how much money you plan to spend.

CORSO BUENOS AIRES   Bargain hunters leave the Golden Triangle and head for a 1-mile stretch of Corso Buenos Aires, where today's Evita on a budget shops for style at affordable prices. What to look for? Virtually everything. Saturday is the worst time to go because of overcrowding. Most self-guided shopping tours begin at **Piazza Oberdan,** the square closest to the heart of Milan. Clothing abounds on Corso Buenos Aires, especially casual wear. But you'll find a vast array of merchandise, from scuba-diving equipment to soft luggage. Some shops hawk rip-offs of designer merchandise, especially clothing. You get the look but not the craftsmanship.

THE BRERA DISTRICT   You'll find more bargains in the Brera, the name given to a sprawling shopping district around the Brera Museum. This area is far more attractive than Corso Buenos Aires and has often been compared to New York's Greenwich Village because of its cafes, shops, antiques stores, and art students. Skip the main street here, **Via Brera,** and concentrate on the side streets, especially **Via Solferino, Via Madonnina,** and **Via Fiori Chiari.** To reach the district, you can start by the La Scala opera house and continue to walk along Via Verdi, which becomes Via Brera. Running off from Via Brera to the left is the pedestrian-only Via Fiori Chiari, good for bric-a-brac and even some fine art deco and art nouveau pieces. Via Fiori Chiari will lead to another traffic-free street, Via Madonnina, which has some excellent buys in store after store in clothing. Some well-made leather goods are also hawked. Via Madonnina connects with Corso Garibaldi, a busy thoroughfare. This will take you to Via Solferino, the third-best shopping street. In addition to traditional clothing and styling, a lot of eye-catching but eccentric modern clothing is sold here.

The best time to visit the Brera area is for the **Mercantone dell'Antiquariato,** which takes place on the third Saturday of each month (it's especially hectic at Christmastime) along Via Brera in the shadow of La Scala. Artists and designers, along with antiques dealers and bric-a-brac peddlers, turn out in droves.

SHOPPING HOURS   Early-morning risers will be welcomed only by silent streets and closed gates. Most shops are closed all day Sunday and Monday (though some open on Monday afternoon). Some stores open at 9am unless they're very chic, and then they're not likely to open until 10:30am. They remain open, for the most part, until 1pm, reopening again between 3:30 and 7:30pm.

SHOPPING A TO Z

BOOKS   There are bigger and flashier bookstores in Rome, but the **American Bookstore,** Via Camperio 16 (☎ 02/878-920), will probably stock that paperback novel you're looking for or the scholarly exegesis of Milanese artwork you should've reviewed before your trip. They only stock English-language books and periodicals. Milan has one gay bookstore, **Libreria Babele,** Via Sammartini (☎ 02/669-2986).

A DEPARTMENT STORE & A MALL   La Rinascente, Piazza del Duomo (☎ 02/88-521), bills itself with accuracy as Italy's largest fashion department store. In addition to clothing, the basement carries a wide variety of giftware, including handwork from all regions of Italy. There's an information desk on the ground floor,

Italian Design: From Retro to the Restless

Since the laissez-faire indulgences of *La Dolce Vita,* no one has denied the whimsy, allure, and sheer intelligence of Italian design. Many people born after Sputnik know how Olivetti used to win awards for designs of everything from typewriters to office calculators, and there isn't a red-blooded star or wanna-be in Hollywood who wouldn't experience a meltdown at the possibility of acquiring a Lamborghini whose air-streamed lines are more alluring in some circles than (dare we admit it) sex?

Why is Italian design so wonderful? Murry Moss, owner of Moss, a design store in New York's SoHo that's made a living bringing the real Italian McCoy to the Anglo-Saxon world, says, "The Italians are good at taking something simple, like a plain white tile, and making a big deal out of it. The point is that everyone who looks at it, goes, 'Ah.'"

Consumers began to say "Ah!" to Italian objects during the belle epoque, when Liberty style carried art nouveau to more serpentine limits. In 1918, Adele Fendi, matriarch of the worldwide empire, convinced thousands of chic Italians they'd be underdressed without a wardrobe of fur coats—hardly a necessity in steamy Italy. In 1920, Elsa Schiaparelli elevated a simple black sweater with a trompe l'oeil bow into high chic. Within a decade, her "pagoda sleeve" hats, inspired by the shape of a veal cutlet, and "Schiaparelli pink" entered the mainstream of chic. In 1925, an obscure Neapolitan shoemaker named Salvatore Ferragamo emigrated to Hollywood, where Greta Garbo, Marion Davies, and Gloria Swanson quickly became visibly devoted to his products; the divine Ms. Crawford wore his wedge heels more glamorously than any other woman before or since. (Later clients, after the maestro's return to Italy, included Queen Elizabeth II—who did not wear wedgies—and her more fashionable sister, Margaret.)

In 1948, Ottavio Missoni, later part-owner of the knitwear empire, installed zippers along the length of his track suits, revolutionizing the design of form-fitting ski suits. (In 1978, the Whitney Museum exhibited his geometric designs as artworks in their own right.) In 1950, Emilio Pucci—a designer who elevated Italian temperament to heights not known since Nero—introduced what's now proclaimed as the precursor of psychedelic fashion. In 1951, the Fontana sisters raised their mother's small dressmaking shop to the level of haute couture, scoring their biggest success with their design for the wedding dress of Margaret (daughter of Harry) Truman. In 1957, Mariuccia Mandeli, an ex-elementary school teacher, elevated photo-printed fabric to worldwide notoriety. Her corporate logo (Krizia) was inspired from a line in an essay by Plato on the nature of women's vanity.

and on the seventh, a bank, a travel agency, a hairdresser, an Estée Lauder Skincare Center, a coffee bar, and the Brunch and Bistro restaurants.

One of Milan's most famous landmarks, the huge ✪ **Galleria Vittorio Emanuele II,** Corso Vittorio Emanuelle II, is reminiscent of a rail station, and the architectural details may impress you as much as—or even more than—any shop in it. Its features include vaulted glass ceilings merging in a huge central dome, decorative window and door casings, elaborate bas-reliefs, huge arched frescoes, wrought-iron globe lamps, and a decorative tile floor. You can browse in shops that include a Prada boutique and a Rizzoli bookstore or grab a coffee from one of the bistros or

In 1968, Jacqueline Kennedy wore a Valentino dress during her much-photographed marriage to "the Greek." In a buying spree that had never before happened in the rarefied world of haute couture, the same dress was then ordered by 38 women. And who can remember the Reagan years without flashes of the Valentino red outfits so beloved by First Lady Nancy Reagan? From 1970 to 1985, Giorgio Armani, Gianfranco Ferré (later the artistic director of Dior), Moschino, Versace, Domenico Dolce and Stefano Gabbana (founders of Dolce & Gabbana), and Trussari all burst on the world's fashion scene. In 1996, in honor of the 50th anniversary of the bikini, Italian designers "reinvented" the two-piece bathing suit.

The ever-so-stylish darling of Hollywood, Armani (lately the most visible designer at the Academy Awards) continues to produce artfully simple suits and jackets for men and women that seem to conform gracefully to the bodies of the young, the beautiful, the restless, and those rich enough to afford it. In 1998, a surge in the number of new mono-label stores took Milan by storm, including Dolce & Gabbana, Christian Lacroix, and Gianfranco Ferré. Arriving soon will be Mandarina Duck and Jil Sander among countless others. There's an exciting new energy, and major designers want to appear as savvy retailers as well.

What about utilitarian objects? In the recent past, Italian design has been identified by a coolly calculated minimalism and graceful references to American corporate culture. Furniture was well considered and elegant, patterned after the High Temple of the style as exemplified in Philip Johnson's Seagram Building in New York, reflecting overscale proportions, smoothly rectangular but not very dramatic forms, high gloss, and a sophisticated mix of natural and synthetic materials. Adam Tihany, well-known decorator of the most recent version of Le Cirque in Manhattan, referred to Milan's recent design trends as "sophisticated American corporate retro."

Chairs identified by their designers as "swinging divans" might combine uncomfortable-looking metal spikes with a single piece of triple-thick felt and be marketed directly to people relaxing during "downtime off the Internet." Lots of the new look in furniture is designed as cost-conscious furniture for nomadic apartment dwellers and can be disassembled and rolled into an easy-to-transport bundle—presumably for setup near another Internet station.

How can you identify a cutting-edge piece of Italian design? In the words of one designer, "I hope that if someone digs up one of the season's best designs in someone's garden a century from now, it will be instantly recognized as coming from right now."

---

restaurants (see review for Savini under "Dining," below) and relax while people-watching. It's worth a stop even if shopping isn't your top priority.

FASHION   In the Brera district, **Accademia,** Via Solferino 11 (☎ 02/659-5961), is the store for men's and women's outdoor clothing, carrying a variety of classical and casual styles. This is also the store to go to for men who need clothes in hard-to-find dimensions because you can order an item made-to-measure; however, it takes more than 1 month and to have alterations, it takes 4 to 5 extra days. Also in the Brera, **Drogheria Solferino,** Via Solferino, at the corner of Via Pontaccio (☎ 02/878-740), is a quite affordable store stocking a wide range of clothing. Look especially for the

A Note About Sales

The best time for the savvy shopper to visit Milan is for the January sales, when SALDI ("sale") signs appear in the windows. Sales usually begin in mid-January and in some cases extend all the way through February. Prices in some emporiums are cut by as much as 50% (but don't count on it). Of course, items offered for sale are most often last season's merchandise, but many good buys are possible. Items bought on sale can't be returned.

line of knitwear and the cotton or silk blouses. You can find rather elegant men's and women's ready-to-wear clothing and shoes.

Despite its name, **Il Drug Store,** Corso Buenos Aires 28 (☎ 02/2951-5592), sells men's and women's clothing for the young and the young at heart. "It's cheap, but trendy," one young customer told us. There's an interesting selection of sweaters both embroidered and ornamented. Knits and dresses with that young look are always sold, but there's a fast turnover. After searching the shops in Milan's fabled Golden Triangle, you may decide you can't afford anything. Don't despair. There's always **Il Salvagente,** 16 Via Fratelli Bronzetti (☎ 02/7611-0328), for the fashion conscious with a bargain basement purse. On the second floor is the selection of men's clothing, and the womenswear, including sweaters, clothes, shoes, and belts, is on the main floor. Here you'll find Versace gowns at cut-rate prices. Of course, it'll be last year's style or something that didn't sell, but who'll ever know? Another place for affordable stylish clothes is **Primavera,** Via Torino 47 (☎ 02/874-565).

Darsena, Corso Buenos Aires 16 (☎ 02/2952-1535), which has far better prices than competitors in the Golden Triangle, carries very high-quality men's clothing that's both casual and elegant. Most items are the store brand, but they also sell items with such names as Armani, Valentino, and Trussardi. **Ermenegildo Zenga,** Via Pietro Verri 3 (☎ 02/7600-6437), offers a complete range of menswear, beginning with the Sartorial line of suits, jackets, trousers, and accessories. The "soft line" is dedicated to a younger customer, and the sportswear collection and yachting line allow you to wander the globe with the right apparel. The shop also offers a "made-to-measure" service with a selection of 300 fabrics per season. They can make an outfit in about 4 weeks, then ship it to any destination.

✪ **Giorgio Armani,** Via San Andrea 9 (☎ 02/7600-3234), houses the style we've come to expect in a large showroom vaguely reminiscent of an upscale aircraft hangar. Armani's trademark look incorporates loose-fitting, unstructured, and unpadded clothing draped loosely over firm bodies. Though there's a bit more structure to the clothes since Richard Gere made the look popular in *American Gigolo,* Armani still creates elegant upholstery for elegant people. At **Mila Schön,** Via Montenapoleone 2 (☎ 02/781-190), the sophisticated look is casually chic, hip, and expensive. If you're male and relatively muscular, you'll look terrific. Mila's women's line is on the ground floor. Even the somewhat flippant accessories are stratospherically expensive.

✪ **Gianfranco Ferré,** Via della Spiga 11–13 (☎ 02/7600-0385), is the only outlet in Milan for the famous designer whose fashions are worn by some of the world's most elegant women. The range is wide—perfect tailleurs and soft knitwear, organza shirts, or sensual evening dresses, along with refined leather accessories, bijoux, and foulards. Next door to the women's shop is an outlet for the designer's men's clothing. It's closed in August. ✪ **Prada,** Via della Spiga 1 (☎ 02/7600-2019), has the best leather goods and other stylish accessories for women in Milan. *Travel & Leisure* called it "a fashion industry phenomenon." The black nylon backpack is the most popular item.

GIFTS   In the tiny **G. Lorenzi,** Via Montenapoleone 9 (☎ 02/7602-2848), you'll find everything you were looking for in the way of small gifts—and a lot of stuff you've never seen before. Many are one-of-a-kind items.

JEWELRY   At ✪ **Mario Buccellati,** Via Montenapoleone 4 (☎ 02/7600-2153), you'll find Italy's best-known—and most expensive—silver and jewels. The designs of the cast-silver bowls, tureens, and christening cups are nothing short of rhapsodic, and the quality is among the finest in the world. In the Brera district, ✪ **Meru,** Via Solferino 3 (☎ 02/8646-0700), sells consciously avant-garde jewelry, rumored to have been worn and privately publicized by beautiful young European film stars. Many of the pieces are set into enameled backgrounds and often include unusual types of gemstones like rose quartz, coral, and amber. Leather-and-gold combinations are also used. All pieces are made by Meru craftspeople. It's closed July 30 to September 10.

LACE   ✪ **Jesurum,** Via Verri 4 (☎ 02/7601-5045), is the Milanese outlet of a Venice-based lace company that has been famous since 1870. On a very short street where none of the buildings has an obvious street number, it sells all-lace or lace-edged tablecloths, doilies, and all the handmade textiles a bride might like to add to her trousseau. It also sells lace blouses and even a swimsuit, plus lace by the meter for trimming curtains or whatever.

LEATHER GOODS & SHOES   The prices on the merchandise at **Alfonso Garlando,** Via Madonnina 2 (☎ 02/8646-3733), range up to the very expensive, but the shop's size and lack of concern for a stylish showroom guarantee a reasonable choice at a reasonable price. It sells shoes for men and women but not children. At ✪ **Beltrami,** Via Montenapoleone 16 (☎ 02/7602-3422), the prices are chillingly high, but the leather goods for men and women are among the best you'll find in the world. The showroom is glamorous and the merchandise chic. Beltrami has another shop at Piazza San Babila 4A (☎ 02/7600-0546).

The factory outlet **Calzaturificio di Parabiago,** Corso Buenos Aires 52 (☎ 02/2940-6851), carries classical and casual shoes for men and women. The prices vary from relatively inexpensive to expensive. But most of the merchandise is sold at discount prices along this "street of bargains." Parabiago is one of the major shoe-manufacturing areas of the country. **Gucci,** Via Montenapoleone 5 (☎ 02/7601-3050), is the Milanese headquarters for the most famous leather-goods distributor in Italy. Its shoes, luggage, and wallets for men and women, handbags, and leatherware accessories usually have the colors of the Italian flag (olive and crimson) stitched in the form of a more-or-less discreet ribbon across the front.

At ✪ **Salvatore Ferragamo,** Via Montenapoleone 3 (☎ 02/7600-6660), the label is instantly recognizable and the quality high. Rigidly controlled by an extended second generation of the original founders, it's still a leader in style and allure. The store contains inventories of shoes, luggage, and accessories for women and men. Also for sale are Ferragamo leather jackets, pants, and a small selection of clothing. **Sebastian,** Via Borgospesso 18 (☎ 02/780-532), sells excellent shoes for men and women from a ready-made stockpile of more than 150 fashionable models, which Sebastian makes in its own factories. For almost the same price (if you don't mind waiting 2 months or more) you can order custom-made shoes, shipped anywhere (they're usually available only in women's styles). This place is a boon for those with wide, narrow, large, or small feet.

LINENS   You'll find some great buys (as much as 50% off) in linens at the company headquarters of **Frette,** Via Visconti di Modrone (☎ 02/777-091). Frette is one of the finest names in Italian linens, so this is an exceptional deal, especially if you're looking for damask tablecloths in the vibrant colors of Italy, everything from apple green to sunflower yellow. If you've got the time and are a dedicated shopper, you can head for the **Spaccio Frette** shop at 45 Via Vittorio Veneto in Concorezzo (☎ 039/604-93-90), in the northeastern outskirts. Remainders from hotel and restaurant orders are sold at even greater discounts than at the main headquarters.

PAPER & STATIONERY In the Brera district, **I Giorni di Carta,** Corso Garibaldi 81 (☎ 02/655-2514), is one of the city's most unusual outlets for stationery, with dozens of colors, textures, and weights. Much of the inventory is made from recycled paper. It also sells briefcases, pens and ink, notebooks, lamps, dishes, dolls, and ornamental paperweights. **Papier,** 4 Via San Maurilio (☎ 02/865-221), is the premier address for stationery. The paper here would be called haute couture in the fashion world. Three former schoolteachers in the late 1980s banded together to open this shop specializing in "extreme paper" (plasticized and plaited paper given a metallic sheen evoking fabric). Banana-leaf pages from Thailand and Nepal are sold, even hairy coconut sheets resembling their namesake. History buffs can order the parchment paper.

PERFUME In the Brera district, **Profumo,** Via Brera 6 (☎ 02/7202-3334), sells some of Italy's most exotic perfumes for women, plus cologne and aftershave lotions for men. Some Italian scents are exclusively distributed here near the American Express office.

PORCELAIN & CRYSTAL Since 1735, **Richard-Ginori,** Corso Buenos Aires 1 (☎ 02/2951-6611), has manufactured and sold porcelain to dukes, duchesses, and ordinary bourgeois consumers, who seek out the best deals along the street of affordable merchandise. A household word in Italy, Ginori sells ovenproof porcelain in both modern and traditional themes, as well as crystal and silverware they either make themselves or inventory from other manufacturers, such as Baccarat and Wedgwood.

PRINTS & ENGRAVINGS **Raimondi di Pettinaroli,** Corso Venezia 6 (☎ 02/7600-2412), is the finest shop in Milan for antique prints and engravings, plus reprints of old engravings made from the original copper plates. Of particular interest are the engravings of Italian cityscapes during the 19th century and the many treasures worth framing after you return home.

ACCOMMODATIONS

In Milan, you'll find some deluxe hotels and an abundance of first- and second-class hotels, most big on comfort but short on romance. In the third- and fourth-class bracket and on the pensione (boardinghouse) level are dozens of choices—many ranking at the bottom of the totem pole of comparably classed places in all Italy's major cities, except Naples. In several places, men sit around in the lobby in their bathrobes watching soccer games on TV. Some places are even outright dangerous.

Our recommendation is—if you can afford it—to stay in a better grade of hotel here and to leave your serious budgeting to such tourist meccas as Rome, Florence, and Venice, which have clean, comfortable, and often architecturally interesting third- and fourth-class hotels and pensioni. However, for the serious economizer we've included the best of the budget lot.

VERY EXPENSIVE

✪ **Four Seasons Hotel Milano.** Via Gesù 8, 20121 Milano. ☎ **02/77-088.** Fax 02/7708-5000. www.fshr.com/locations/milan/main.html. 98 units. A/C MINIBAR TV TEL. 852,500–1,094,500L ($494–$635) double; from 1,550,000L ($899) suite. Breakfast 45,000L ($27). AE, DC, MC, V. Parking 70,000L ($41). Metro: Montenapoleone or San Babila.

Milan's most exciting five-star hotel started in 1993 on a side street opening onto Via Montenapoleone's concentration of upscale boutiques. Its acquisition was a real-estate coup by Four Seasons. The building was the residence of the Habsburg-appointed governor of northern Italy in the 1850s and later housed luxury apartments. The medieval facade, many of the frescoes and columns, and the original monastic details were incorporated into a modern edifice flooded with sun and accented with bronze, stone floors, glass, pearwood cabinetry, Murano chandeliers, and acres of Fortuny fabrics. The guest rooms are cool, conservative, spacious, and discreetly outfitted in tones of beige and pale green, always with a sense of understated luxury.

Dining: The hotel lounge contains the architectural renderings for stage sets used at the nearby La Scala. Il Teatro serves dinner daily 8pm to midnight (see "Dining," below). Less formal, La Veranda serves meals daily 11am to 11pm.

Amenities: Concierge, 24-hour room service, same-day valet/laundry, high-tech fitness center/spa, business center.

Hotel Principe di Savoia. Piazza della Repubblica 17, 20124 Milano. ☎ **800/325-3535** in the U.S. and Canada, or 02/62301. Fax 02/653-799. www.ittsheraton.com (click on "luxury collection"). 299 units. A/C MINIBAR TV TEL. 693,000–891,000L ($402–$517) double; from 1,320,000L ($766) suite. Breakfast 36,300L ($22). AE, DC, MC, V. Parking 60,000L ($35) and up. Metro: Repubblica.

The Principe was built in 1927 to fill the need for a luxurious hotel near the Stazione Centrale. It was completely restored in 1991. Substantial and luxurious, the six stories offer solid comfort amid crystal, detailed plasterwork, fine carpets, and polished marble. The rooms are spacious and modern, decorated in a 19th-century Lombard style. Many are paneled in hardwoods, and all contain leather chairs and other stylish furniture. The front rooms face the hysterical traffic of Piazza della Repubblica, but the ones in back are more tranquil, opening onto the Alps.

Dining/Diversions: There's a spacious bar area off the main lobby. The hotel has a notable restaurant, Galleria, serving both regional and international dishes. It also offers the popular Doney cafe (see "Dining" below).

Amenities: Room service, baby-sitting, laundry/valet, sauna, health club, solarium, indoor pool, limited facilities for the disabled.

Palace Hotel. Piazza della Repubblica 20, 20124 Milano. ☎ **800/325-3589** in the U.S., 800/955-2442 in Canada, or 02/63361. Fax 02/654-485. 221 units. A/C MINIBAR TV TEL. 561,000–660,000L ($325–$383) double; from 990,000L ($574) suite. Breakfast 32,000L ($19). E, DC, MC, V. Parking 50,000–75,000L ($29–$44). Metro: Repubblica.

The Palace, blithely ignoring the noisy commercial world around it, stands aloof on a hill near the rail station; it has a formal car entrance and a facade of 14 floors with tiers of balconies. Though primarily a business hotel, the Palace also welcomes tourists and occasional entertainers. The Principe di Savoia, its sibling across the street, is superior to the Palace in sheer old-world opulence—and the Four Seasons leaves both properties behind. The guest rooms are furnished with pastel upholstery and reproductions of Italian antiques. Modern conveniences include heated towel racks and minibars concealed behind mahogany chests.

Dining/Diversions: The hotel bar attracts an international crowd, and the Grill Casanova is acclaimed as one of the finest in Milan, offering both regional and international dishes.

Amenities: Room service, baby-sitting, laundry/valet, fitness center.

EXPENSIVE

Hotel Excelsior Gallia. Piazza Duca d'Aosta 9, 20124 Milano. ☎ **800/225-5843** in the U.S. and Canada, or 02/67851. Fax 02/6671-3239. E-mail: 106340.2331@compuserve.com.

250 units. A/C MINIBAR TV TEL. 400,000–700,000L ($232–$406) double; from 720,000L ($418) suite. Breakfast 28,000L ($17). AE, DC, MC, V. Parking 20,000–40,000L ($12–$23). Metro: Stazione Centrale. Tram: 33 or 59.

This Liberty-style (art nouveau) monument was built by the Gallia family in 1933. Near Stazione Centrale, it's one of the most visible in Milan and was once one of Italy's top hotels—but today it's more of an upmarket rail station hotel. The 1994 renovations combined some of the smaller rooms into larger and more comfortable accommodations. The rooms are in two categories: modern and comfortable in the newer wing and graciously old-fashioned and charming in the original core. All are soundproofed against the roar of traffic in the piazza.

Dining/Diversions: The noted Gallia's serves haute Lombard and international dishes. The Baboon Bar is stylish, and a piano player sometimes performs in the lobby.

Amenities: Room service, laundry/valet, baby-sitting, business center, fitness club/massage center, gym, whirlpool, sauna.

MODERATE

Casa Svizzera. Via San Raffaele 3, 20121 Milano. ☎ 02/869-2246. Fax 02/7200-4690. 45 units. A/C MINIBAR TV TEL. 280,000L ($162) double. Rates include breakfast. AE, DC, MC, V. Parking 50,000L ($29). Metro: Duomo.

Casa Svizzera, right off Piazza del Duomo, is one of the most serviceable hotels in the city, following a reconstruction in 1970. Two elevators service five floors of well-maintained rooms. Features include paneled double windows and soundproofing to keep out the noise. The homelike rooms have air-conditioning that can be independently regulated.

Hotel Galles-Milano. Via Ozanam 1 (Corso Buenos Aires), 20129 Milano. ☎ 800/ 528-1234 in the U.S. and Canada, or 02/204-841. Fax 02/204-8422. www.galles.it. E-mail: gallesmi@mbox.it.net. 120 units. A/C MINIBAR TV TEL. 220,000–550,000L ($128–$319) double; from 260,000–750,000L ($151–$435) suite. Rates include breakfast. AE, DC, MC, V. Parking 40,000L ($23). Metro: Lima.

This hotel was built in 1901 as one of the then-most-glamorous hotels in Milan. In 1990, a consortium of Italian investors poured millions of lire into an elegant rehabilitation, producing an aggressively marketed hotel that's much favored by businesspeople, conventioneers, and visitors looking for comfortable unpretentious lodgings. The interior lacks the art-nouveau glamour of many of its competitors, but this doesn't seem to bother the many guests who approve of the building's functional lines and conservatively modern rooms. The hotel contains a big-windowed rooftop restaurant (La Terrazza) with additional seating on a canopy-covered terrace as well as a cocktail bar. In spring and summer there's a roof garden with a solarium and Jacuzzi.

INEXPENSIVE

✪ **Antica Locanda dei Mercanti.** Via San Tomaso 6, 20123 Milano. ☎ 02/ 805-4080. Fax 02/805-4090. E-mail: locanda@iol.it. 10 units. TEL. 180,000–250,000L ($104–$145) double. Parking 25,000–35,000L ($15–$20). Breakfast 12,000L ($7). AE, DC, MC, V. Tram: 1, 14, or 24.

The building containing this reasonably priced but sophisticated hotel was built in the late 1800s by a wealthy merchant who used it as a pied-à-terre. In 1996, a former model for Milan Schön, the charming Paola Ora, gutted the second floor and installed a streamlined hotel, custom designing each room and naming each after a successful Milanese mercantile family. The furnishings are upholstered in top-echelon Milanese fabrics with embroidered floral designs or pale monochromes and the baths sheathed in slabs of marble. Don't be startled by the severe-looking monumental entrance or the businesslike appearance of three of the building's four floors, most of which are occupied by crafts studios for the jewelry industry. Breakfast—in bed—is the only meal served. The neighborhood was intricately described in Alessandro Manzoni's 19th-century classic *I Promessi Sposi* (The Promised Spouse).

✪ **Antica Locanda Solferino.** Via Castelfidardo 2, 20121 Milano. ☎ **02/657-0129.** Fax 02/657-1361. 10 units. TV TEL. 200,000–250,000L ($116–$145) double. Rates include breakfast. AE, DC, MC, V. Parking 25,000–30,000L ($15–$17) nearby. Metro: Moscova or Repubblica.

When this country-style hotel opened in 1976, the neighborhood was a depressed backwater of downtown Milan. Today it's an avant-garde community of actors, writers, and poets, and this inn deserves some of the credit for that. It got off to a fortuitous start soon after it opened when editors from *Gentleman's Quarterly* stayed here while working on a fashion feature. Since then, celebrities have become guests, either staying in one of the old-fashioned rooms or dining at the ground-floor restaurant (see "Dining" below). Each guest room is unique, reflecting the 19th-century floor plan of the building; there are no singles. The furnishings include Daumier engravings and art nouveau or late 19th-century bourgeois pieces. But the baths are modern. Since the hotel is small and often fully booked, reserve as far in advance as possible.

Hotel Gran Duca di York. Via Moneta 1A (Piazza Cordusio), 20123 Milano. ☎ **02/ 874-863.** Fax 02/869-0344. 33 units. TV TEL. 230,000L ($133) double; 280,000L ($162) triple. Rates include breakfast. AE, V. Closed Aug. Parking 35,000L ($20). Metro: Cordusio.

When it was built by the Catholic Church in the 1890s, this Liberty-style palace housed dozens of priests from the nearby Duomo. Among them was the cardinal of Milan, who later became Pope Pius XI. Today anyone can rent one of the pleasantly furnished and well-kept rooms, each with a bath sheathed in patterned tiles. Behind the ocher-and-stone facade, you'll find a bar in an alcove of the severely elegant lobby, where a suit of armor and leather-covered armchairs contribute to the restrained tone.

Hotel Manzoni. Via Santo Spirito 20, 20121 Milano. ☎ **02/7600-5700.** Fax 02/784-212. 52 units. TEL. 235,000L ($136) double. Breakfast 20,000L ($12). AE, DC, MC, V. Parking 22,000–50,000L ($13–$29). Metro: Montenapoleone or San Babila.

The Manzoni, built around 1910 and renovated frequently since, charges reasonable prices considering its location near the most fashionable shopping streets. It lies behind a facade of stone slabs on a fairly quiet one-way street. Each of its rooms is outfitted with color-coordinated comfortable furniture and carpeting; many have TVs. A brass-trimmed winding staircase leads from the lobby into a bar and TV lounge. The English-speaking staff is cooperative.

Hotel Star. 5 Via dei Bossi, 20121 Milano. ☎ **02/801-501.** Fax 02/861-787. www. starhotel.it. E-mail: information@starhotel.it or reservation@starhotel.it. 30 units. A/C MINIBAR TV TEL. 260,000L ($151) double. Rates include buffet breakfast. AE, MC, V. Closed Aug and Christmas. Parking 35,000–40,000L ($20–$23). Metro: Cordusio or Duomo.

The Ceretti family welcomes guests to their well-run little hotel on a narrow street a few blocks from La Scala and the Duomo. The lobby has been refurbished, making it brighter than before, and the guest rooms are comfortable but a bit dour. Amenities like hair dryers have been installed in the baths, and double-glass windows cut down on street noise. The buffet breakfast includes jams, pâté, yogurts, cheese, eggs, ham, and fruit salad, along with cereal, croissants, and various teas, juices, and coffee.

Hotel Valgauna. Via Vare 32, 20158 Milano. ☎ **02/3931-0089.** Fax 02/3931-2566. www. traveleurope.it/mil78.htm. E-mail: hotel.valganna@traveleurope.it. 40 units. A/C MINIBAR TV TEL. 100,000–240,000L ($58–$139) double. Rates include buffet breakfast. AE, DC, MC, V. Parking 10,000L ($6). Bus: 82 or 92.

This hotel is tasteful, modern, and centrally located. It offers amenities like satellite TV and piped music in each renovated and tastefully furnished room. Some, however, are a bit cramped. For the grand buffet, there's the breakfast lounge, and for later in the day a refined bar to welcome you. For sunbathing, there's a spacious terrace, and the reception staff is happy to assist you with transportation tickets to get to the nearby lakes of Como and Maggiore.

DINING
VERY EXPENSIVE

✪ **Giannino.** Via Amatore Sciesa 8. ☎ **02/5519-5582.** Reservations required. Main courses 55,000–75,000L ($32–$44); fixed-price menus 110,000–130,000L ($64–$75). AE, DC, MC, V. Mon–Sat 12:30–3pm and 7:30pm–midnight. Tram: 60 or 73. MILANESE/SEAFOOD/TUSCAN.

Giannino enchants its loyal patrons and wins new fans every year. It's one of the top restaurants in all of Lombardy and has been since 1899. You have a choice of several attractive rooms, and eyes rivet on the tempting underglass offerings of the specialità gastronomiche milanesi. The choice is excellent, including such Lombard dishes as breaded veal cutlet and risotto simmered in broth and coated with parmigiano. We have special affection for tagliolini con scampi al verde, fresh homemade noodles with prawn tails in herb sauce. Also superb are the cold fish and seafood salad and the beautifully seasoned orata al cartoccio (fish baked in a paper bag with shrimp butter and fresh herbs).

EXPENSIVE

Il Teatro. In the Four Seasons Hotel Milano, Via Gesù 8. ☎ **02/7708-1435.** Reservations recommended. Main courses 30,000–40,000L ($17–$23); fixed-price meal 85,000–150,000L ($49–$87). AE, DC, MC, V. Mon–Sat 7:30pm–midnight. Closed Aug. Metro: Montenapoleone or San Babila. MEDITERRANEAN.

This is the culinary showcase of the shopping district's newest and most glamorous hotel. Favored since its 1993 opening by such luminaries as Calvin Klein and members of the Agnelli family, the restaurant is in a 1400s Milanese palazzo. The patio overlooks a garden, and the dining room is sheathed in burnished paneling and nut-colored leather under a ceiling of tented champagne silk. The prices are lower than you might think. The menu changes at least four times a year but might include a tantalizing involtini of eggplant with ricotta and mint, crispy crayfish with a purée of tomatoes, and red mullet filet with essence of tomato and black truffles. Everything tastes as fresh as the day it was picked, harvested, or caught. Dessert might be a mille-feuille croquante layered with walnuts, chocolate mousse, and raspberries.

St. Andrews. Via Sant'Andrea 23. ☎ **02/798-236.** Reservations required. Main courses 35,000–70,000L ($20–$41). AE, DC, MC, V. Mon–Sat 1–3:30pm and 8pm–1am. Closed Aug. Metro: Montenapoleone or San Babila. LOMBARD/INTERNATIONAL.

This restaurant has given much pleasure to many people for many years, offering one of the finest kitchens in Lombardy. The menu includes an unusual appetizer of steak tartare mixed with caviar and seasonings, John Dory in a salt crust, and rack of lamb Provençal style. The dessert specialty is a tartatelli, composed of pastry with a honey-and-strawberry sauce. At lunch it seems like a private club and is apt to be filled with businesspeople. The armchairs are covered in black leather, the paneling is dark wood, and the lighting is discreet from hooded lamps. The formally attired waiters give superb service.

✪ **Savini.** In the Galleria Vittorio Emanuele II. ☎ **02/7200-3433.** Reservations required. Main courses 25,000–45,000L ($15–$26); fixed-price lunch (with wine) 70,000L ($41);

fixed-price dinner (with wine) 115,000–140,000L ($67–$81). AE, DC, MC, V. Mon–Fri noon–3pm and 7:30–11pm, Sat 7:30–11pm. Closed Dec 24–Jan 2 and Aug 10–25. Metro: Duomo. LOMBARD/INTERNATIONAL.

Savini provides a heavenly introduction to the cookery of Lombardy and has attracted everybody from Puccini to Pavarotti. Perched in the heart of the great glass-enclosed arcade opposite the Duomo, the classico restaurant draws both the out-of-towner and the discriminating local. You sit on the terrace or dine in the old-world room with its crystal chandeliers and glittering silverware. Waiters in black jackets hover over you to see you enjoy every mouthful. Many of the most memorable dishes are unassuming, like the Lombardy specialty costoletta alla milanese, tender veal coated with egg batter and bread crumbs, then fried a rich brown. The pièce de résistance of Milan, most often ordered before the main course, is risotto alla milanese—rice simmered in a broth and dressed with whatever the artiste in the kitchen selects. The restaurant is excellently stocked with wines (the staff will gladly assist you).

MODERATE

Al Chico. Via Sirtori 24, ☎ 02/2953-0280. Reservations recommended. Main courses 35,000–40,000L ($20–$23). AE, DC, MC, V. Mon–Sat noon–2:30pm and 7–10:30pm. Closed Aug 3–27. Metro: Porta Venezia. TUSCAN/ITALIAN.

Al Chico, a good neighborhood restaurant specializing in such fare as onion soup and fondue bourguignonne, opened in the 1970s in a much-renovated century-old building. Tuscan specialties such as Florentine beefsteak are also featured, and portions are tasty and satisfying. The chef is rightly proud of his pappardelle pasta with porcini mushrooms, branzini (sea bass) cooked in a salt crust, and spaghetti with mushrooms and spring onions. The place is usually crowded, but it's worth the wait. The service is good, and the ingredients are fresh and well selected at the market. They stock good house wines from Tuscany, including the classic Chianti. In summer you can eat on the veranda.

Alfio-Cavour. Via Senato 31. ☎ 02/7600-9671. Reservations recommended. Main courses 25,000–45,000L ($15–$26). AE, DC, MC, V. Mon–Fri 12:30–3pm and 7:30–11pm, Sun 7:30–11pm. Closed Aug. Metro: Montenapoleone or San Babila. ITALIAN/INTERNATIONAL.

There's a luminous quality to this family-run restaurant. It stems partly from the Tahitian-style decor, where trees grow through the glass panels of a greenhouselike roof and vines entwine themselves among bamboo lattices. The restaurant is best known for its serve-yourself display of antipasti, where the polite but sharp-eyed staff bills you for what you select. A pasta specialty is the flavorful spaghetti pescatore, with bits of seafood. You might follow with large grilled shrimp, a gran misto fish fry, or one of the many excellent beef or veal dishes.

Al Porto. Piazzale Generale Cantore. ☎ 02/832-1481. Reservations required. Main courses 28,000–40,000L ($16–$23). AE, DC, MC, V. Tues–Sat 12:30–2:30pm; Mon–Sat 7:30–10:30pm. Closed Dec 24–Jan 3 and Aug. Metro: Porta Genova or S. Agostino. SEAFOOD.

Opened in 1907, this is among the most popular seafood restaurants in Milan. As you enter, you pass by tanks of "demons of the deep." The glassed-in garden room is the most sought after by loyals. It's especially popular among business patrons; you may need to reserve several days in advance. Menu items include orata (dorado) with pink peppercorns and branzini (sea bass) with white Lugurian wine and olives. Many come here just for risotto ai frutti di mare, the classic Lombard dish served with an assortment of "sea creatures." One of the staff confided that the best patrons begin with a warm antipasto, then follow with a risotto, and then order the traditional fritto misto (almost anything that swims is likely to turn up on the plate)—though some find this far too much food. Everything tastes better with a Friuli wine.

A Santa Lucia. Via San Pietro all'Orto 3. ☎ **02/7602-3155.** Reservations recommended. Main courses 25,000–35,000L ($15–$20). V. Tues–Sun 12:30–3pm and 7:30pm–midnight. Closed Aug. Metro: San Babila. MEDITERRANEAN/SEAFOOD.

A Santa Lucia pulls out hook, line, and sinker to lure you with some of the best fish dinners in Milan. A festive place, it's decked out with photographs of pleased celebs, who attest to the skill of its kitchen. You can order such specialties as a savory fish soup, a meal in itself; fried baby squid; or good-tasting sole. Spaghetti alla vongole evokes the tang of the sea with its succulent clam sauce. Pizza also reigns supreme: Try either the calzone of Naples or the pizza alla napoletana.

Bistrot di Gualtiero Marchesi. In the Rinescente Center, Via San Raffaele 2. ☎ **02/ 877-120.** Reservations required. Main courses 30,000–35,000L ($17–$20); fixed-price menu 45,000–60,000L ($26–$35). AE, DC, MC, V. Tues–Sat 12:30–2:30pm; Mon–Sat 7:30–10:30pm. Closed 2 weeks in Aug. Metro: Duomo. LOMBARD/ITALIAN.

This bistro was created by Signor Gualtiero Marchesi, the patron saint of *cucina nuova* in Italy. Once hailed by *Time* magazine as among the world's 10 top chefs, he operated a very expensive restaurant in another part of town that moved to Erbusco, near Brescia; but this bistro was left as a love token to Milan. It boasts one of the best views of the Duomo in the city, for it's on the top floor of the Rinascente Center, which rises seven stories across a narrow street from the cathedral. The bistro has big walls of glass for you to better admire the view. The menu depends on the inspiration of the chef, but in the past we've enjoyed an unusual form of half-opened ravioli and crayfish cooked very al dente with cucumbers. You're almost certain to find a perfect veal cutlet milanese.

Boeucc Antico Ristorante. Piazza Belgioioso 2. ☎ **02/7602-0224.** Reservations required. Main courses 25,000–35,000L ($15–$20). AE. Mon–Fri 12:40–2:30pm; Sun–Fri 7:40–10:40pm. Closed Aug, Easter, and Christmas. Metro: Duomo, Montenapoleone, or San Babila. INTERNATIONAL/MILANESE.

This restaurant, opened in 1696, is a trio of rooms in a severely elegant old palace, within walking distance of the Duomo and the major shopping streets. Throughout you'll find soaring stone columns and modern art. In summer, guests gravitate to a terrace for open-air dining. The hearty specialties come from regions of Italy. You might enjoy a spaghetti in clam sauce, a salad of shrimp with arugula and artichokes, or grilled liver, veal, or beef with aromatic herbs. In season, sautéed zucchini flowers accompany some dishes.

Doney. In the Prìncipe di Savoia Hotel, Piazza della Repubblica 17. ☎ **02/62301.** Main courses 17,000–30,000L ($10–$17); fixed-price menu 75,000–120,000L ($44–$70); afternoon tea 25,000L ($15). AE, DC, MC, V. Daily noon–12:30am (afternoon tea 4–7pm). Metro: Repubblica. Tram: 1, 4, 11, 29, or 30. LIGHT INTERNATIONAL/AFTERNOON TEA/LOMBARD/ VEGETARIAN.

Its burnished paneling, plush upholstery, and soaring frescoed ceiling are some of the high points of one of Milan's most recent (and most expensive) hotel restorations. Doney borrowed its name from a historic cafe in Rome and much of its decorative allure from the turn-of-the-century Liberty style. Its menu features elegant but simple preparations of salads (lobster, artichokes, and pear), sandwiches (smoked salmon on brown bread), and steaks. During teatime you can select from nine kinds of tea and pastries and finger sandwiches from a trolley. At any hour, the place is a popular meeting point.

✪ **Peck's Restaurant.** Via Victor Hugo 4. ☎ **02/876-774.** Reservations required. Main courses 30,000–45,000L ($17–$26); fixed-price menu 70,000–90,000L ($41–$52). AE, DC,

MC, V. Mon–Sat 12:15–2:30pm and 7:15–10:30pm. Closed 10 days in Jan and July 1–21. Metro: Duomo. MILANESE/ITALIAN.

Peck's is owned by the famous delicatessen of Milan, which gastronomes view as the Milanese equivalent of Fauchon's in Paris. It was opened by Francesco Peck, who came to Milan from Prague in the 19th century. His small restaurant eventually became a food empire. In an environment filled with shimmering marble and modern Italian paintings, an alert staff serves an elegant cuisine. The fresh specialties include a classic version of risotto milanese, rack of lamb with fresh rosemary, ravioli alla fonduata, and lombo di vitello (veal) with artichokes, followed by chocolate meringue for dessert. Its cured meats are said to be the richest in Italy. There's also a less-expensive Peck's (see below).

Taverna del Gran Sasso. Piazza Principessa Clotilde 10. ☎ **02/659-7578.** All-you-can-eat meal 60,000L ($35). MC, V. Mon–Sat 12:30–2pm and 7:30–10:30pm. Closed Jan 1 and Aug. Metro: Repubblica. ABRUZZI.

This tavern is filled with lots of sentimental baubles, its walls crowded ceiling to floor with copper molds, ears of corn, strings of pepper and garlic, and cart wheels. A tall open hearth burns with a charcoal fire, and a Sicilian cart is laden with baskets of bread, dried figs, nuts, and kegs of wine. As you enter, you'll find a mellowed wooden keg of wine with a brass faucet (you're supposed to help yourself, using glass mugs). The cuisine features a number of specialties from the Abruzzi—like maccheroni alla chitarra, a distinctively shaped macaroni with savory meat sauce. Meals are an all-you-can-eat feast.

✪ **Trattoria Bagutta.** Via Bagutta 14. ☎ **02/7600-2767.** Reservations required. Main courses 19,000–45,000L ($11–$26). AE, DC, MC, V. Mon–Sat 12:30–2:30pm and 7:30–10:30pm. Closed Dec 24 and Jan 6. Metro: San Babila. INTERNATIONAL.

Patronized by artists, this restaurant is Milan's most celebrated trattoria. From 1927, the Bagutta is known for the caricatures (framed and frescoed) covering its walls. Of the many bustling dining rooms, the rear one with its picture windows is most enticing. The tempting food draws on the kitchens of Lombardy, Tuscany, and Bologna for inspiration. On offer are assorted antipasti, and main-dish specialties include fried squid and scampi, lingua e purè (tongue with mashed potatoes), linguine with shrimp in tomato-cream sauce, and scaloppine alla Bagutta.

INEXPENSIVE

Al Tempio d'Oro. Via delle Leghe 23. ☎ 02/2614-5709. Main courses 8,000–19,000L ($4.65–$11). No credit cards. Mon–Sat 8pm–2am. Closed 2 weeks in mid-Aug. Metro: Pasteur. ITALIAN/INTERNATIONAL.

This restaurant, near the central rail station, offers inexpensive well-prepared meals. The chef is justifiably proud of his fish soup, Spanish paella, and North African couscous. The crowd scattered among the ceiling columns is relaxed, and they contribute to an atmosphere somewhat like that of a beer hall. No one will mind if you stop by just for a drink.

La Magolfa. Via Magolfa 15. ☎ **02/832-1696.** Reservations required. Main courses 18,000L ($10); fixed-price meal from 35,000L ($20). AE, DC, MC, V. Tues–Sun 8pm–1am. Closed Sat in July–Aug. Metro: Porta Genova. LOMBARD/INTERNATIONAL.

La Magolfa, one of the city's dining bargains, offers a gargantuan fixed-price meal. The building is a country farmhouse whose origins go back to the 1500s, though the restaurant opened only in 1960. It's likely to be crowded, as is every other restaurant in Milan that offers such value. If you don't mind its location away from the center of town, in Zona Ticinese in the southern part of the city, you'll be treated to some very good regional cookery that emerges fresh from battered pots and pans. A general air of conviviality reigns, and there's music of local origin nightly.

✪ **Peck.** Via Victor Hugo 4. ☎ **02/876-774.** Reservations required. Main courses 18,000–22,000L ($10–$13). AE, DC, MC, V. Mon–Sat 7:30am–9pm. Closed 10 days in Jan and July 1–21. Metro: Duomo. MILANESE/LOMBARD.

Peck offers one of the best values in Milan—food served in a glamorous cafeteria associated with the most famous delicatessen in Italy (the higher-priced restaurant in the basement is listed above). Only a short walk from the Duomo, Peck has a stand-up bar and well-stocked display cases of specialties fresh from their treasure trove of produce. Armed with a plastic tray, you can sample such temptations as artichoke-and-Parmesan salad, marinated carpaccio, slabs of tender veal in herb sauce, risotto marinara, and selections from a carving table laden with a juicy display of roast meats.

MILAN AFTER DARK

As in Rome, many of the top nightclubs in Milan shut down for the summer, when the cabaret talent and the bartenders pack their bags and head for the hills or the seashore. However, Milan is a big city, and there are always plenty of after-dark diversions. This sprawling metropolis is also one of Europe's cultural centers.

THE PERFORMING ARTS   The most complete list of cultural events appears in the large Milan newspaper, the left-wing *La Repubblica.* Try for a Thursday edition, usually with the most complete listings.

Alas, the world-famous ✪ **Teatro alla Scala,** Piazza della Scala (☎ **02/809-126,** or 02/861-772 for tickets Tuesday to Sunday noon to 3pm), will be closed for restorations through the lifetime of this edition until sometime after 2000. Check with the box office about their current temporary home, which may vary.

The **Conservatorio,** Via del Conservatorio 12 (☎ **02/762-1101** or 02/7600-1755), in the San Babila sector, features the finest in classical music. Year-round, a cultured Milanese audience enjoys high-quality programs of widely varied classical concerts. Tickets are 30,000L to 60,000L ($17 to $35). The **Piccolo Teatro,** Via Rivoli 2, near Via Dante (☎ **02/862-771**), became a socialist theater after World War II, but now the city of Milan is the landlord. Programs are varied today, and performances are in Italian. Its director, Giorgio Strehler, is acclaimed as one of the most avant garde and talented in the world. The theater lies between the Duomo and the Castle of the Sforzas. It's sometimes hard to obtain seats. Performances are Tuesday to Sunday at 8:30pm (closed August). Tickets are 50,000L ($29).

LIVE-MUSIC CLUBS   The **Ca' Bianca Club,** Via Lodovico il Moro 117 (☎ **02/8912-5777**), has a changing offering of live music and dancing on Wednesday night, from folk music to cabaret to Dixieland jazz. This is a private club, but no one at the door will prevent nonmembers from entering. The show—whatever it may be—begins at 11pm. The club is open daily 8:30pm to 1am (closed in August). Cover is 30,000L ($17) including the show and the first drink or 90,000L to 100,000L ($52 to $58) with dinner. Since opening in the 1970s, **Capolinea,** Via Lodovico II Moro 119 (☎ **02/8912-2024**), has been one of the most appealing jazz clubs in town, with an ongoing roster of jazz acts of every imaginable ilk. Doors open nightly at 8pm and music is performed 10:30pm to 1 or 1:30am. There's no cover.

Le Scimmie, Via Ascanio Sforza 49 (☎ **02/8940-2874**), echoes with applause and approval for the various types of live music that are the norm. Depending on the venue, bands play everything from funk to blues to creative jazz to an appreciative audience that shows up every night except Tuesday. Doors open around 8pm, and music is presented 10pm to around 12:30am. There's no cover. **Rolling Stone,** Corso XXII Marzo 32 (☎ **02/733-172**), was opened for the Beat Generation of the 1950s and then attracted la dolce vita crowd in the 1960s. In 1984, it adopted its present rock preoccupation, featuring heavy metal and other aggressively energetic groups in their 20s. Its open every night, usually 10:30pm to 4am, but don't even consider showing up until at least midnight. For some concerts, the place doesn't open until 1am. Closed in July and August. Cover for men on Friday is 20,000L ($12), on Saturday 25,000L ($15), and other days 12,000L ($7); cover for women is 15,000L ($9) on Friday and Saturday only.

CAFES   Every city in Italy seems to have a cafe or two filled with 19th-century detailing and memories of Verdi or some such famous person. It usually offers a wide variety of pastries and a particular kind of crowd who gossips, sips espresso, munches snacks, and compares notes on shopping. All service at the tables is more expensive, as is the rule in Europe.

As its name implies, the decor of the **Berlin Café**, Via Gian Giacomo Mora 9 (☎ **02/839-2605**), emulates a cafe in turn-of-the-century Berlin; the ambience is enhanced with etched glass and marble-topped tables. It's a great spot for coffee or a drink. A variety of simple snack food is available, primarily during the day. One drawback is the surly staff. It's open Tuesday to Sunday 10am to 2am. Boasting a chic crowd of garment-district personnel and shoppers, **Café Cova**, Via Montenapoleone 8 (☎ **02/7600-0578**), follows a routine established in 1817. This involves making gallons of heady espresso and dispensing staggering amounts of pralines, chocolates, brioches, and sandwiches. The more elegant sandwiches contain smoked salmon and truffles. Patrons drink their espresso from fragile gold-rimmed cups at one of the small tables in an elegant inner room or while standing at the prominent bar. It's open Monday to Saturday 8am to 8pm; closed in August.

Opened in 1910, **Pasticceria Taveggia,** Via Visconti di Modrone 2 (☎ **02/ 7602-1257**), is one of Milan's oldest and most historic cafes. Behind ornate glass doors set into the 19th-century facade, Taveggia makes the best cappuccino and espresso in town. To match this quality, a variety of brioches, pastries, candies, and tortes is offered. You can enjoy them while standing at the bar or seated in the Victorian tearoom. It's open Tuesday to Sunday 7:30am to 8:30pm; closed in August.

BARS & PUBS   Decorated a bit like a bohemian parlor of the last century, **Al Teatro,** Corso Garibaldi 16 (☎ **02/864-222**), is a popular bar across from the Teatro Fossati. It opens for morning coffee Tuesday to Sunday at 2pm and closes (after several changes of ambience) at 3am. There's sometimes musical entertainment at night, but most of the time the crowd seems perfectly happy to drink, gossip, and flirt. In addition to coffee and drinks, it serves toasts and tortes. In fine weather tables are set out on Corso Garibaldi.

Bar Giamaica, Via Brera 32 (☎ **02/876-723**), is loud and bustling and seats its customers with a no-nonsense kind of gruff humor. That, however, is part of the allure of a bar that's one of the mainstays of the Milanese night scene. The personalities who work here haven't changed in years. If you want only a drink, you'll have lots of company among the office workers who jostle around the tiny tables, often standing because of the lack of room. It's open as a restaurant Monday to Saturday noon to 2:30pm and 7:30 to 10pm. Meals range from 10,000L ($6) for a salad and a beer to as much as 45,000L ($26) for a full Italian regalia. Reservations aren't accepted. The bar opens at 9am Monday to Saturday and remains open until around 12:30am or later. Closed 1 week in mid-August.

Despite its name, **Grand Hotel Pub,** Via Ascanio Sforza 75 (☎ 02/8951-1586), doesn't rent rooms or even pretend to be grand. Instead, it's a large animated restaurant/pub with frequent live music or cabaret. In summer, the crowds can move quickly from the smoky interior into a sheltered garden. Friday and Saturday, entertainment is live jazz and rock music. Most visitors come here only for a drink, but if you're hungry, the restaurant charges around 50,000L ($29) for a full meal. The place is open Tuesday to Sunday 8pm to 2am. Entrance is usually free.

DANCE CLUBS & NIGHTCLUBS **Killer Plastic,** Viale Umbria 120 (☎ 02/733-996), is Milan's most oft-changed disco and the most often cited as everybody's favorite. Your experience will depend largely on the night you show up. Thursday is gay night, welcoming gay men (and to a lesser extent, lesbians) onto the high-tech dance floors, and Saturday is crammed with the crème of the city's alta moda night crowd. Other nights, the site is animated, high-energy, and exhibitionistic. Doors usually open Thursday to Sunday 10:30pm to around 3am or later, depending on the crowd. The cover is 15,000L ($9) but rises to 18,000L ($11) on Saturday.

Rock Hollywood, Corso Como 15 (☎ 02/659-8996), is small and has a sound system that's so good you might get swept up in the animated fun of it all. Let your hair down, dress whimsically or in your best party-down costume, and dance, dance, dance. No matter how attractive you might think you are, be assured that there'll be dozens of contenders here. It's open Tuesday to Sunday 10:30pm to at least 3am. Cover is 25,000L to 30,000L ($15 to $17) and includes the first drink. The popular **Club Astoria,** Piazza Santa Maria Beltrade 2 (☎ 02/8646-3710), is one of the most frequented nightclubs in town, especially by the expense-account-junket crowd. When there's a floor show, drinks might cost around 50,000L ($29), taking the place of a cover; otherwise, they begin at 30,000L ($17). It's open Monday to Saturday 10:30pm to 4am, and there's no cover.

Coquetel, Via Vetere 14 (☎ 02/836-0688), is loud and wild and celebrates the American-style party-colored cocktail with a whimsy that could only be all Italian. The action around here, coupled with babble from dozens of regulars, ain't exactly sedate, and you might just get swept away by the energy. It's open Monday to Saturday 8pm to 2am. **Facsimile,** Via Tallone 11 (☎ 02/738-0635), is a popular bar/birreria where Milanese rockers can commune with their favorite video stars in living color. The decor is almost entirely gray and red, and there are outdoor tables for stargazing. The bar is open Tuesday to Sunday 9am to 1am. There's no cover but a one-drink minimum.

GAY & LESBIAN CLUBS **Nuova Idea International,** Via de Castillia 30 (☎ 02/6900-7859), is the largest, oldest, most active, and most fun gay disco in Italy, very much tied to Milan's urban bustle. It prides itself on mimicking the large all-gay discos of northern Europe and draws a patronage of young and not-so-young men, many of whom are film or theater actors. There's a large video screen and occasional live entertainment. It's open Thursday to Sunday 9:30pm to 2:30am. Cover is 15,000L ($9) on Thursday, Friday, and Sunday and 25,000L ($15) on Saturday, including the first drink.

Zip, Corso Sempione 76, at Via Salvioni (☎ 02/331-4904), is one of the most deliberately raunchy gay clubs in southern Europe. It's a *club privato,* though non-Italian newcomers can enter on presentation of a passport. This dive contains a labyrinth of inner rooms devoted to a disco packed with gay males, a late-night cafeteria, a screen showing gay porn, and a dark room where the action is uninhibited. The disco opens Wednesday to Sunday at 12:30am, but no one arrives before 2:30 or 3am. It shuts down for a much-needed rest at 6am (to 8am Saturday). The club lies in back of Castello Sforzesco. If you attend, be alert to the neighborhood at this late hour and exercise caution once you're inside. Cover is 30,000L to 40,000L ($17 to $23) and includes the first drink.

Recycle, Via Calabria 5 (☎ 02/376-1531), is a lesbian bar popular with not only locals but also expats, including some high-fashion models. It's open Thursday to Sunday 9pm to anywhere from 2 to 5am, depending on business.

A SIDE TRIP FROM MILAN

The ✪ **Certosa (Charter House) of Pavia,** Via Monumento 4 (☎ 0382/925-613), marks the pinnacle of the Renaissance statement in Lombardy. The Carthusian monastery is 5 miles north of the town of Pavia and 19 miles south of Milan. It was founded in 1396 but not completed until years afterward and is one of the most harmonious structures in Italy. The facade, studded with medallions and adorned with colored marble and sculptural work, was designed in part by Amadeo, who worked on it in the late 15th century. Inside, much of its rich decoration is achieved by frescoes reminiscent of an illustrated storybook. You'll find works by Perugino (*The Everlasting Father*) and Bernardino Luini (*Madonna and Child*). Gian Galeazzo Visconti, the founder of the Certosa, is buried in the south transept.

Through an elegantly decorated portal you enter the cloister, noted for its exceptional terra-cotta decorations and continuous chain of elaborate "cells," attached villas with their own private gardens and loggia. Admission is free, but donations are requested. May to August, it's open daily 9 to 11:30am and 2:30 to 6pm; March, April, September, and October, hours are Tuesday to Sunday 9 to 11:30am and 2:30 to 5pm; November to February, hours are Tuesday to Sunday 9 to 11:30am and 2:30 to 4:30pm.

Buses run between Milan and Pavia daily every hour 5am to 10pm, taking 50 minutes and costing 4,500L ($2.60) one-way. Trains leave Milan bound for Pavia once every hour, costing 3,600L ($2.10) one-way. Motorists can take Route 35 south from Milan or A7 to Binasco and continue on Route 35 to Pavia and its Certosa.

2 Bergamo

31 miles NE of Milan, 373 miles NW of Rome

Known for its defenses and wealth since the Middle Ages, **Bergamo** is one of the most characteristic Lombard hill towns. Many of the town's stone fortifications were built on Roman foundations by the medieval Venetians, who looked on Bergamo as one of the gems of their trading network during several centuries of occupation. Set on a hilltop between the Seriana and the Brembana valleys, Bergamo lies in the alpine foothills.

The Old Town, 900 feet above sea level, is buttressed by and terraced on the original Venetian fortifications. About half a mile downhill is the New Town (usually identified by residents simply as "Bergamo"), with many 19th- and early 20th-century buildings. A settlement of wide streets and northern Italian bourgeois prosperity, this modern metropolis and industrial center contains the bus and rail stations, most hotels, and the town's commercial and administrative center. The two-in-one aspect of Bergamo, as well as its role in Lombardy's mercantile history, was analyzed and praised by one of its strongest champions, 19th-century French novelist Stendhal.

Bergamo has many famous native sons, including the maestro of bel canto, composer Gaetano Donizetti. The great Venetian painters Palma Vecchio and Lorenzo Lotto were actually from Bergamo, as was the master of the portrait, Gian Battista

Moroni. Bergamo even gave the world the "Bergomask," the peasant dance at the end of *A Midsummer's Night Dream.*

ESSENTIALS

GETTING THERE **Trains** arrive from Milan once every hour, depositing passengers in the center of the new town. The trip takes an hour, costing 7,200L ($4.20) one-way. For information about rail connections in Bergamo, call ☎ 035/247-624 or 1478/88-088 toll free in Italy only. The **bus station** in Bergamo is across from the train station. For information or schedules, call ☎ **035/248-150.** Buses arrive from Milan once every 30 minutes, costing 7,200L ($4.20) one-way. If you've got a **car** and are coming from Milan, head east on A4.

VISITOR INFORMATION The **tourist office** is on Piazzale Marconi, Vicolo Aquila Nera 2 (☎ 035/242-226), open April to September daily 9am to 12:30pm and 2:30 to 5:30pm.

EXPLORING THE UPPER TOWN

For the sightseer, the higher you climb, the more rewarding the view will be. The ✪ **Città Alta** is replete with narrow circuitous streets, old squares, splendid monuments, and imposing and austere medieval architecture that prompted d'Annunzio to call it "a city of muteness." To reach the Upper Town, take bus no. 1 or 3 then take a 10-minute walk up Viale Vittorio Emanuele.

The heart of the Upper Town is **Piazza Vecchia,** which has witnessed most of the town's upheavals and a parade of conquerors ranging from Attila to the Nazis. On the square is the Palazzo della Ragione (town hall), an 18th-century fountain, and the Palazzo Nuovo of Scamozzi (town library).

A vaulted arcade connects Piazza Vecchia with **Piazza del Duomo.** Opening onto the latter is the cathedral of Bergamo, which has a baroque overlay.

Basilica di Santa Maria Maggiore. Piazza del Duomo. Free admission. Mon–Sat 8am–noon and 3–6pm, Sun 9am–12:45pm and 3–6pm.

D'Annunzio said of this basilica that it seemed "to blossom in a rose-filtered light." Built in the Romanesque style, the church was founded in the 12th century. Much later it was baroqued on its interior and given a disturbingly busy ceiling. Displayed are exquisite Flemish and Tuscan tapestries incorporating such themes as the Annunciation and the Crucifixion. The choir, designed by Lotto, dates from the 16th century. In front of the main altar is a series of inlaid panels depicting themes like Noah's Ark and David and Goliath.

Facing the cathedral is the **baptistery,** dating from Giovanni da Campione's design in the mid-14th century, but it was rebuilt at the end of the 19th century.

✪ **Colleoni Chapel.** Free admission. Mar–Oct Tues–Sun 9am–noon and 2–6:30pm; off-season Tues–Sun 9am–noon and 2:30–4:30pm.

Also opening onto Piazza del Duomo is this chapel, honoring the inflated ego of the Venetian military hero. The Renaissance chapel, with an inlaid marble facade reminiscent of Florence, was designed by Giovanni Antonio Amadeo, who's chiefly known for his creation of the Certosa in Pavia. For the condottiere, Amadeo built an elaborate tomb, surmounted by a gilded equestrian statue (Bartolomeo Colleoni (1400–75), who was once the ruler of the town, and under whose watch thetown fell to the Republic of Venice which he then served, was also the subject of one of the world's most famous equestrian statues, now standing on a square in Venice). The tomb sculpted for his daughter, Medea, is much less elaborate. Giovanni Battista Tiepolo painted most of the frescoes on the ceiling.

EXPLORING THE NEW TOWN

✪ **Academy Gallery (Galleria dell'Accademia Carrara).** Piazza Giacomo Carrara 82A. ☎ **035/399-643.** Admission 5,000L ($2.90) adults; children 17 and under/seniors 60 and over free. Wed–Mon 9:30am–12:15pm and 2:30–5:15pm.

Filled with a wide-ranging collection of the works of homegrown artists, as well as Venetian and Tuscan masters, the academy draws art lovers from all over the world. The most important works are on the top floor—head here first if your time is limited. The Botticelli portrait of Giuliano di Medici is well known, and one room contains three versions of Giovanni Bellini's favorite subject, the *Madonna and Child*. It's interesting to compare his work with that of his brother-in-law, Andrea Mantegna, whose *Madonna and Child* is also displayed, as is Vittore Carpaccio's *Nativity of Maria,* seemingly inspired by Flemish painters.

Farther along, you encounter a most original treatment of the old theme of the Madonna and Child—this one by Cosmé Tura of Ferrara. Also displayed are three tables of a predella by Lotto and his *Holy Family with St. Catherine* (wonderful composition) and Raphael's *St. Sebastian.* The entire wall space of another room is taken up with paintings by Moroni (1523–78), a local artist who seemingly did portraits of everybody who could afford it. In the salons to follow, foreign masters, like Rubens, van der Meer, and Jan Brueghel, are represented, along with Guardi's architectural renderings of Venice and Longhi's continuing parade of Venetian high society.

ACCOMMODATIONS

Hotel Agnello d'Oro. Via Gombito 22, 24100 Bergamo. ☎ **035/249-883.** Fax 035/235-612. 20 units. TV TEL. 125,000L ($73) double. Breakfast 10,000L ($8). AE, DC, V.

The Agnello d'Oro is an intimate old-style country inn in the heart of the Città Alta. It's an atmospheric background for good food or an adequate room, all refurbished in 1995. When you enter the cozy reception lounge, ring an old bell to bring the owner away from the kitchen. You dine at wooden tables and sit on carved ladderback chairs. Among the à la carte offerings are three worthy regional specialties. Try casoncelli alla bergamasca, a succulent ravioli dish, or quaglie farcite (quail stuffed and accompanied by slices of polenta). The room becomes a tavern lounge between meals. The restaurant is closed Sunday night and Monday.

Hotel Cappello d'Oro. Viale Papa Giovanni XXIII 12, 24100 Bergamo. ☎ **035/232-503.** Fax 035/242-946. 110 units. MINIBAR TV TEL. 201,000L ($117) double. Rates include breakfast. AE, DC, MC, V. Parking 30,000L ($17).

The Cappello d'Oro is a renovated 150-year-old corner building on a busy street in the center of the New Town, at Porta Nuova near the rail station. The 19th-century facade has been stuccoed, and the public rooms and the guest rooms are functional, high-ceilinged, and clean. The rooms are adequately but rather plainly furnished, and 80 of them are air-conditioned. If you need a parking space, reserve it along with your room.

Hotel Excelsior San Marco. Piazza della Repubblica 6, 24122 Bergamo. ☎ **035/366-111.** Fax 035/223-201. 166 units. A/C MINIBAR TV TEL. 310,000L ($180) double; 450,000L ($261) suite. Rates include breakfast. AE, DC, MC, V. Parking 30,000L ($17) indoors, 20,000L ($12) outdoors.

This 36-year-old place at the edge of a city park is about midway between the old and new towns, both of which might be visible from the balcony of your room. The lobby contains a small bar, reddish stone accents, and low-slung leather chairs. The most prominent theme of the ceiling frescoes is the lion of St. Mark. The rooms are attractively furnished and comfortable.

DINING

✪ **Ristorante da Vittorio.** Viale Papa Giovanni XXIII 21. ☎ **035/218-060.** Reservations required. Main courses 35,000–40,000L ($20–$23); fixed-priced menus 60,000–150,000L ($35–$87). AE, DC, MC, V. Thurs–Tues noon–3pm and 7:30–10:30pm. Closed 3 weeks in Aug. INTERNATIONAL.

This restaurant on the main boulevard in the New Town serves a cuisine almost better than anything found in Milan. The menu offers more than a dozen risottos, more than 20 pastas, and around 30 meat dishes, as well as just about every kind of fish that swims in Italy's waters. Examples include grilled "fantasy of the sea" with fresh seasonal vegetables, breast of goose with a tapenade of black olives, and tartare of salmon with avocado. The service is efficient, directed by members of the Cerea family, who by now are among the best-known citizens of Bergamo.

Taverna del Colleoni dell'Angelo. Piazza Vecchia 7. ☎ **035/232-596.** Reservations required. Main courses 25,000–38,000L ($15–$22); fixed-price lunch 50,000L ($29); fixed-price dinner 95,000L ($55); fixed-price Sunday meal 75,000L ($44). AE, DC, MC, V. Tues–Sun noon–2:30pm; Tues–Sat 7:45–10:30pm. Closed Aug 12–25. LOMBARDO/NORTH ITALIAN.

In the heart of the Città Alta, this restaurant is known to many a gourmet who journeys here to try regional dishes of exceptional merit. The building dates from the 14th century and is the most historic restaurant in Bergamo. The sidewalk tables are popular in summer, and the view is part of the reward of dining here. The decor suggests medievalism but with a fresh approach. The ceiling is vaulted, the chairs are leather, and there's a low-floor dining room with a wood-burning fireplace. Known for its creative interpretations of Lombard cuisines, the restaurant features such dishes as a casserole of jumbo shrimp with polenta, homemade flat pasta with a delicate ragoût of wild duck, and Adriatic turbot on a bed of crispy potatoes.

BERGAMO AFTER DARK

The citizens are passionate about opera, the season lasting from September to November with a drama being staged from then until April at the **Donizetti Theater,** Piazza Cavour (☎ **035/416-0611**). A program of free events, **Viva La Tua Città,** is staged every summer. The tourist office (above) will provide a pamphlet.

If visiting a birreria (beer hall) is what you want, head for **Via Gombito** in the upper city. It's lined with places to drink. One of the most popular joints is **Papageno Pub,** Via Colleoni (☎ 035/236-624), which makes the best sandwiches and bruschetta in town. In Città Bassa, the young people's favorite is **Capolinea,** Via Giacomo Quarenghi 29 (☎ **035/320-981**), with an active bar up front.

3 Cremona: City of the Violin

59 miles SE of Milan, 61 miles S of Bergamo

This city of the violin is on the Po River plain. Music lovers from all over the world flock to the birthplace of Monteverdi (the father of modern opera) and Stradivari (latinized to Stradivarius), who made violin making an art. Born in Cremona in 1644, Antonio Stradivari became the most famous name in the world of violin crafting, far exceeding the skill of his teacher, Nicolò Amati. The third great family name associated with the craft, Giuseppe Guarneri, was also of Cremona. Today students still flock here to the International School for Violin Making. Graduates of the school have opened some 60 workshops all over town.

ESSENTIALS

GETTING THERE   At least nine **trains** per day run between Milan and Cremona (trip time: 1½ hours), costing 7,400L ($4.30) one-way. Call the rail station in Cremona, at Via Dante 68 (☎ 0372/22-237). Arrivals are in the north of town. Via Palestro leads south to Piazza Cavour, which connects with the heartbeat Piazza del Comune and the adjoining Piazza del Duomo. One **bus** a day makes the run from Milan to Cremona, costing 9,300L ($5) one-way. The bus station is on Via Dante (☎ 0372/29-212 for schedules and information). If you've got a **car** and are in Milan, take Route 415 southeast.

VISITOR INFORMATION   The **tourist office** is at Piazza del Comune 5 (☎ 0372/21-722), open Monday to Saturday 9:30am to 12:30pm and 3 to 6pm and Sunday 9:45am to 12:15pm.

EXPLORING CREMONA

Most of the attractions of the city are centered on the harmonious **Piazza del Comune.**

The Romanesque cathedral dates from 1107, though over the centuries, Gothic, Renaissance, and even baroque elements were incorporated. In the typical Lombard style, the pillars of the main portal rest on lions, a detail matched in the nearby octagonal 13th-century baptistery. Surmounting the portal are some marble statues in the vestibule, with a Madonna and Bambino in the center. The rose window over it, from the 13th century, is inserted in the facade like a medallion.

Inside, the pillars are draped with Flemish tapestries. Five arches on each side of the nave are admirably frescoed by such artists as Boccaccio Boccaccino (see his *Annunciation* and other scenes from the life of the Madonna, painted in the early 16th century). Other artists who worked on the frescoes were Gian Francesco Bembo (*Adoration of the Wise Men* and *Presentation at the Temple*), Gerolamo Romanino (scenes from the life of Christ), and Altobello Melone (a *Last Supper*). The cathedral is open Monday to Saturday 7am to noon and 3 to 7pm and Sunday 7am to 1pm and 3:30 to 7pm. Admission is free.

Beside the cathedral is the Torrazzo, dating from the late 13th century and enjoying a reputation as the tallest campanile (bell tower) in Italy, soaring to 353 feet. It's open Monday to Saturday 10:30am to noon and 3 to 6pm and Sunday 10:30am to 12:30pm and 3 to 7pm; from November to Easter, however, it's open only Sunday and holidays. Admission is 5,000L ($2.90) adults and 3,000L ($1.75) children.

From the same period and also opening onto the piazza are the Loggia dei Militi and the Palazzo Comunale in the typical Lombardy Gothic style. The **Palazzo Comunale** (☎ 0372/4071-31971) displays a collection of violins crafted by the Armatis, Guarneri, and, of course, Stradivari. It also exhibits antiques and paintings, some from the 17th century. Hours are Tuesday to Saturday 8:30am to 6pm and Sunday 9am to 12:15pm and 3 to 6pm. Admission is 6,000L ($3.50).

At the **Museo Stradivariano,** Via Palestro 17 (☎ 0372/461-886), you can see a collection of models, designs, and shapes and tools of Stradivari (1644 to 1737). This Italian violin maker produced more than 1,000 string instruments, many of which are among the best ever made. Admission is 6,000L ($3.50) adults and 3,000L ($1.75) children. It's open Tuesday to Saturday 8:15am to 6pm and Sunday 9:15am to 12:15pm and 3 to 6pm.

SHOPPING

Cremona is famous for bars of torrone, a nougat made with honey, egg, and nuts. The best ones are sold at Spelari, Via Solferino 25 (☎ 0372/22-346), in business since 1836. The torrone made at Pasticceria Duomo, Via Boccaccino 6 (☎ 0372/22-273), are shaped like violins. This is a pastry shop from the past century, following recipes the owner calls "legendary."

ACCOMMODATIONS

Hotel Agip. Località San Felice, 26100 Cremona. ☎ 0372/450-490. Fax 0372/451-097. 77 units. A/C MINIBAR TV TEL. 180,000L ($104) double. Rates include breakfast. AE, DC, MC, V. Motorists exit A21 at Casello and drive 1½ miles.

This motel, part of a nationwide chain, is at the San Felice exit of the superhighway between Piacenza and Brescia. It's a modern place offering comfortable rooms outfitted with hair dryers and soundproofed against the noise of the highway. A good restaurant on the premises serves copious amounts of food, with a fixed-price menu as well as a self-service area.

Hotel Continental. Piazza della Libertà 26, 26100 Cremona. ☎ 0372/434-141. Fax 0372/454-873. 64 units. A/C MINIBAR TV TEL. 190,000L ($110) double; from 240,000L ($139) suite. Rates include breakfast. AE, DC, MC, V.

Roads from many parts of northern Italy converge on the busy piazza where the comfortable 1980s Continental stands. It's the best choice in town, having more atmosphere and personality than the Agip. The staff show an obvious pride in the musical history of Cremona as they eagerly point out their collection of early 20th-century copies of violins by Amati and Stradivari housed in illuminated glass cases. There are also instruments made by master luthiers of Cremona, some of whom seem to be on a first-name basis with the management. A bronze bust of Claudio Monteverdi, the 17th-century composer, looks out over the lobby, and there's a restaurant that can seat 500. Each of the hotel's comfortably furnished rooms has sound-insulated windows.

DINING

✪ **Ceresole.** Via Ceresole 4. ☎ 0372/30-990. Reservations required. Main courses 28,000–32,000L ($16–$19). DC, MC, V. Tues–Sat noon–2:30pm and 8–10:30pm. Closed Jan 1–10 and Aug 6–28. ITALIAN.

Near the Duomo, Ceresole is an elegant culinary institution in a century-old building. It's the finest restaurant in the entire surrounding area and is richly deserving of its star. Specialties include rice with rhubarb, a wide array of delicately seasoned fish (some served with fresh seasonal mushrooms and truffles), and the most delectable grilled baby piglet this side of Segovia. Some of the dishes are based on time-honored regional recipes, like spaghetti alla marinara, straccotto di manzo (beef stew), and grilled filets of eel.

CREMONA AFTER DARK

The prospect is a bit bleak unless you're here in May or June. At that time, classical music is performed at the **Teatro Ponchielli,** Corso Vittorio Emanuele (for tickets, call the tourist office at ☎ 0372/23-233). Tickets range from 25,000L to 30,000L ($15 to $17). The opera season, also at the Teatro Ponchielli, runs mid-October to early December, with tickets beginning at 25,000L ($15). All that jazz is heard at **Cremona Jazz** in March and April, with tickets costing 15,000L ($9) and up. Call the tourist office for tickets to all these events.

If you'd like a bar that overflows with local life, patronize **Ristorante Centrale,** Via Pertusio 4, off Via Solferino (☎ 0372/28-701). If you get hungry, you can dine on

Cremonese cuisine at its restaurant. Bollito misto, a medley of boiled meats, is the specialty.

4 Mantua: Domain of the Gonzagas

25 miles S of Verona, 95 miles SE of Milan, 291 miles NW of Rome, 90 miles SW of Venice

Once a duchy, **Mantua (Mantova)** had a flowering of art and architecture under the Gonzaga dynasty that held sway over the city for nearly 4 centuries. Originally an Etruscan settlement and then a Roman colony, it has known many conquerors, including the French and Austrians in the 18th and 19th centuries. Virgil, the great Latin poet, has remained its most famous son (he was born outside the city in a place called Andes), Verdi set *Rigoletto* here, Romeo (Shakespeare's creation, that is) took refuge here, and writer Aldous Huxley called Mantua "the most romantic city in the world."

Mantua is an imposing and at times even austere city, despite its position near three lakes—Superiore, di Mezzo, and Inferiore. It's very much a city of the past and is within easy reach of a number of cities in northern Italy. The historic center is traffic-free.

ESSENTIALS

GETTING THERE   Mantua has excellent **train** connections, lying on direct lines to Milan, Cremona, Modena, and Verona. Nine trains a day arrive from Milan, taking 2¼ hours and costing 30,400L ($18) one-way. From Cremona, trains arrive every hour (trip time: 1 hour), costing 6,000L ($3.50) one-way. The train station is on Piazza Don Leoni (☎ **0376/321-647**). Take bus no. 3 from outside the station to get to the center of town.

Most visitors arrive by train, but Mantova has good **bus** connections with Brescia; 17 buses a day make a 1¾-hour journey at a cost of 9,300L ($5) one-way. The bus station is on Piazza Mondadori (☎ **0376/327-237**).

If you've got a **car** and are in Cremona, continue east along Route 10.

VISITOR INFORMATION   The **tourist office** is at Piazza Andrea Mantegna 6 (☎ **0376/328-253**), open Monday to Saturday 8:30am to 12:30pm and 3 to 6pm.

EXPLORING THE PALACES & THE BASILICA

✪ **Museo di Palazzo Ducale.** Piazza Sordello 40. ☎ **0376/320-283.** Admission 12,000L ($7) adults; children 17 and under/seniors 60 and over free. Mon–Sat 9am–1pm and 2:30–6pm, Sun 9am–2pm.

The ducal apartments of the Gonzagas, with more than 500 rooms and 15 courtyards, are the most remarkable in Italy—certainly when judged from the standpoint of size. Like Rome, the compound wasn't built in a day . . . or even in a century. The earlier buildings, erected to the specifications of the Bonacolsi family, date from the 13th century. The 14th and early 15th centuries saw the rise of the **Castle of St. George**, designed by Bartolino da Novara. The Gonzagas also added the **Palatine Basilica of Santa Barbara** by Bertani.

Over the years, the historic monument of Renaissance splendor has lost many of the art treasures collected by Isabella d'Este during the 15th and 16th centuries in her efforts to turn Mantua into "La Città dell'Arte." Her descendants, the Gonzagas, sold the most precious objects to Charles I of England in 1628, and 2 years later most of the remaining rich collection was looted during the sack of Mantua. Even Napoléon did his bit by carting off some of the objects still there.

What remains of the painting collection is still superb, including works by Tintoretto and Sustermans and a "cut-up" Rubens. The display of classical statuary is impressive, gathered mostly from the various Gonzaga villas at the time of Maria Theresa of Austria. Among the more inspired sights are the **Zodiac Room,** the **Hall of Mirrors** (with a vaulted ceiling from the beginning of the 17th century), the **River Chamber,** the **Apartment of Paradise,** the **Apartment of Troia** (with frescoes by Giulio Romano), and a scale reproduction of the **Holy Staircase** in Rome. The most interesting and best-known room in the castle is the **Camera degli Sposi (Bridal Chamber),** frescoed by Andrea Mantegna. Winged cherubs appear over a balcony at the top of the ceiling. Look for a curious dwarf and a mauve-hatted portrait of Christian I of Denmark. There are many paintings by Domenico Fetti, along with a splendid series of nine tapestries woven in Brussels and based on cartoons by Raphael. A cycle of frescoes on the age of chivalry by Pisanello has recently been discovered. A guardian takes visitors on a tour to point out the many highlights.

Basilica di Sant'Andrea. Piazza Mantegna. ☎ **0376/328-504.** Free admission. Mon–Sat 8am–noon; daily 3–6pm.

Built to the specifications of Leon Battista Alberti, this church opens onto Piazza Mantegna, just off Piazza delle Erbe, where you'll find fruit vendors. The actual work was carried out by a pupil of Alberti's, Luca Fancelli. However, before Alberti died in 1472, it's said that, architecturally speaking, he knew he had "buried the Middle Ages." The church wasn't completed until 1782, when Juvara crowned it with a dome.

As you enter, the first chapel to your left contains the tomb of the great Mantegna (the paintings are by his son, except for the *Holy Family* by the old master himself). The sacristan will light it for you. In the crypt, you'll encounter a representation of one of the more fanciful legends in the history of church relics: St. Andrew's claim to possess the blood of Christ, "the gift" of St. Longinus, the Roman soldier who's said to have pierced His side. Beside the basilica is a 1414 campanile (bell tower).

Palazzo Te. Viale Te 13. ☎ **0376/323-266.** Admission 12,000L ($7) adults, 10,000L ($6) seniors 60 and over, 5,000L ($2.90) children 12–18; children under 12 free. Tues–Sun 9am–6pm, Mon 1–6pm.

This Renaissance palace from the 16th century is known for its frescoes by Giulio Romano and his pupils. Fun-loving Federigo II, one of the Gonzagas, had it built as a place where he could slip away to see his mistress, Isabella Boschetto. The name, Te, is said to have been derived from the word *tejeto,* which in the local dialect means "a cut to let the waters flow out." This was once marshland drained by the Gonzagas for their horse farm.

The frescoes in the various rooms, dedicated to everything from horses to Psyche, rely on mythology for subject matter. The **Room of the Giants (Sala dei Gigante),** the best known, has a scene depicting heaven venting its rage on the giants who had moved threateningly against it. Federico's motto was, "What the lizards lack is that which tortures me," an obscure reference to the reptile's cold blood as opposed to his hot blood. The **Banquet Hall (Sala di Amore e Psiche)** forever immortalizes the tempestuous love affair of these swingers—decorated with erotic frescoes on the theme of the marriage of Cupid and Psyche, two other "hot bloods."

SHOPPING

The best shopping is at the **open-air market** that operates only on Thursday morning at Piazza delle Erbe and Piazza Sordello. Here you can find a little bit of everything—from cheap clothing (often designer rip-offs) to bric-a-brac. The place is like an outdoor traveling department store.

ACCOMMODATIONS

✪ **Albergo San Lorenzo.** Piazza Concordia 14, 46100 Mantova. ☎ **0376/220-500.** Fax 0376/327-194. 32 units. A/C MINIBAR TV TEL. 160,000–320,000L ($93–$186) double; 185,000–370,000L ($107–$215) suite. Rates include breakfast. AE, DC, MC, V. Parking 30,000L ($17).

Your best bet is this four-star hotel in the historic center. The building is ancient but received a careful 1996 restoration. Restorers paid great attention to the architectural details and the furnishings, most of which are antique, with marble floors, oil paintings, and Oriental carpets. The great service makes you feel at home in a pleasant, intimate atmosphere. The guest rooms, painted mostly in soft muted whites and blues, are furnished with dark woods (antique reproductions) and gilded mirrors; the baths are up-to-date, and (a godsend in steamy Mantua) the air-conditioning is individually adjustable. Breakfast is the only meal served, but the hotel offers a panoramic terrace with a view of the city.

Hotel Dante. Via Corrado 54, 46100 Mantova. ☎ **0376/326-425.** Fax 0376/221-141. 40 units. A/C MINIBAR TV TEL. 150,000L ($87) double. Breakfast 13,000L ($8). AE, DC, MC, V. Parking 20,000L ($12).

This boxy modern hotel from 1969 is your best bet when funds are low. On a narrow street in the busy commercial center, it has a recessed entrance area and a marble-accented interior, parts of which look out over a flagstone-covered courtyard. Some of the simply furnished but clean rooms have air-conditioning and minibars.

Mantegna Hotel. Via Fabio Filzi 10B, 46100 Mantova. ☎ **0376/328-019.** Fax 0376/368-564. 40 units. A/C TV TEL. 160,000L ($93) double; 200,000L ($116) suite. Breakfast 15,000L ($9). AE, DC, MC, V. Closed Dec 24–Jan 5.

The Mantegna is in a commercial section, a few blocks from one of the entrances to the old city. The lobby is accented with gray and red marble slabs, along with enlargements of details of paintings by (as you probably guessed) Mantegna. About half the units look out over a sunny rear courtyard, though the rooms facing the street are fairly quiet as well. The hotel is a good value for the rates charged.

Rechigi Hotel. Via P. F. Calvi 30, 46100 Mantova. ☎ **0376/320-781.** Fax 0376/220-291. 65 units. A/C TV TEL. 240,000L ($139) double; 290,000L ($168) suite. Breakfast 20,000L ($12). AE, DC, MC, V. Parking 30,000L ($17).

Near the center of the old city stands the Rechigi, a comfortable modern hotel, rivaled only by the San Lorenzo. It's a cozy nest but short on style. The lobby is warmly decorated with modern paintings and contains an alcove bar. The owners maintain the property well and have decorated the attractively furnished rooms in good taste. Breakfast is the only meal served.

DINING

The local specialty is donkey stew (stracotto di asino). Legend claims you'll never be a man until you've sampled it.

Il Cigno Trattoria dei Martini. Piazza Carlo d'Arco 1. ☎ **0376/327-101.** Reservations recommended. Main courses 20,000–25,000L ($12–$15). DC, MC, V. Wed–Sun 12:30–1:45pm and 8–9:45pm. Closed Jan 7–14 and Aug 1–22. MANTOVANO.

This trattoria overlooks a cobblestone square in the old part of Mantua. The exterior is a faded ocher, with wrought-iron cross-hatched window bars within sight of the easy parking on the piazza outside. After passing through a large entrance hall studded with frescoes, you'll come to the bustling dining rooms. The menu offers both freshwater and saltwater fish and dishes like agnoli (a form of pasta) in a light sauce or risotto.

Bollito misto (a medley of boiled meats) is served with various sauces, including one made of mustard. One excellent pasta, tortelli di zucca, is stuffed with pumpkin.

✪ **L'Aquila Nigra (The Black Eagle).** Vicolo Bonacolsi 4. ☎ **0376/327-180.** Reservations recommended. Main courses 22,000–25,000L ($13–$15). AE, DC, MC, V. Tues–Sat noon–2pm and 8–10pm (also Sun noon–2pm Apr–May and Sept–Oct). Closed Jan 1–15 and Aug. MANTOVANO/ITALIAN.

This restaurant is in a Renaissance mansion on a narrow passageway by the Bonacolsi Palace. The foundations were laid in the 1200s, but the restaurant dates from 1984. In the elegant rooms, you can choose from such dishes as pike from the Mincio River (luccio), served with salsa verde (green sauce) and polenta, as well as other specialties of the region. You also might order gnocchi alle ortiche (potato dumplings tinged with puréed nettles), eel marinated in vinegar (one of the most distinctive specialties of Mantua), or tortelli di zucca (with a pumpkin base).

Ristorante Pavesi. Piazza delle Erbe 13. ☎ **0376/323-627.** Reservations recommended. Main courses 20,000–35,000L ($12–$20). AE, DC, MC, V. Fri–Wed 12:30–2:30pm and 7:30–9:30pm. Closed Jan 25–Feb 14. MANTOVANO.

The Pavesi has the advantage of being located under an ancient arcade on Mantua's most beautiful square. The walls partially date from the 1200s, though the restaurant goes back only before World War II. It's an intimate family-run place with hundreds of antique copper pots hanging randomly from the single-barrel vault of the plaster ceiling; tables spill out into the square in summer. The antipasti table is loaded with delicacies, and specialties include agnolotti (a form of tortellini) with meat, cheese, sage, and butter, as well as risotto alla mantovana (with pesto). Also try the roast filet of veal (deboned and rolled) and a well-made blend of fagioli (white beans) with onions.

MANTUA AFTER DARK

The major cultural venue is the **Teatro Sociale di Mantova,** Piazza Cavallotti (☎ **0376/323-860**), lying off Corso Vittorio Emanuele. They put on operas in October, followed by a season of Italian dramas November to May. Tickets begin at 20,000L ($12). In lieu of any other major entertainment, locals depend on **festivals,** with **chamber music series** in April and May and the **Mantua Jazz Festival** at the end of July. The tourist office (above) has details.

If you're just looking for a place to drink and meet some companions, head for **Leoncino Rosso,** Via Giustiziati 33 (☎ **0376/323-277**), behind Piazza Erbe. This osteria opened in 1750 and hasn't changed some of its recipes (such as tortellini with nuts or pumpkin) since then. It stays open until 10pm except Sunday and is the best place for drinking and general carousing. It's closed August and 2 weeks in January. The best selection of beer in town is at **Oblo,** Via Arrivabene 50 (☎ **0376/360-676**), which also has a good offering of reasonably priced wine, such as the fizzy red Lambrusco.

5 Lake Garda

The easternmost of the northern Italian lakes, **Lake Garda** is also the largest, 32 miles long and 11½ miles at its widest. Sheltered by mountains, its scenery, especially the part on the western shore that reaches from Limone to Salo, has been compared to that of the Mediterranean; you'll see olive, orange, and lemon trees and even palms. The almost-transparent lake is ringed with four art cities: Trent to the northeast, Brescia to the west, Mantua to the south, and Verona to the east.

The lake's eastern side is more rugged and less trampled, but the resort-studded western strip is far more glamorous to the first-timer. On the western side, a circuitous road skirts the lake through one molelike tunnel after another. You can park your car at several secluded belvederes for a panoramic lakeside view. In spring, the scenery is splashed with color, everything from wild poppies to oleander. Garda is well served by buses, or you can traverse the lake on steamers or motorboats. The lake, once a mandatory stop on the Grand Tour, has attracted everyone from the Romans to Mussolini.

ESSENTIALS

GETTING THERE   Eight **buses** a day make the 1-hour trip from Trent to Riva del Garde, costing 5,200L ($3) one-way. For information and schedules, call the **Autostazione on Viale Trento** in Riva (☎ **0365/821-000**). The nearest **train** station is at Roverto, a 20-minute ride from Riva. Frequent buses make the 20-minute trip from the train station to Riva, costing 3,200L ($1.85) one way. For getting around Lake Garda, you'll need a car. If you've got a **car** and are coming from Milan or Brescia, A4 east runs to the southwestern corner of the lake. From Mantua, take A22 north to A4 west. From Verona and points east, take A4 west.

GETTING AROUND   Most **drivers** take the road along the western shore, S572, north to Riva di Garda. For a less-touristed jaunt, try heading back down the lake along its eastern shore on the Gardesana Orientale (S249). S11 runs along the south shore.

Both **ferries** and **hydrofoils** operate on the lake from Easter to September. For schedules and information, contact **Navigazione Lago di Garda** (☎ **030/914-951** for its main office in Desenzano, or 0464/55-26-25 for its Riva del Garda branch). Ferries connect Riva's harbor, Porto San Nicolò, with the major lakeside towns, like Gardone (trip time: 2½ hours), costing 9,200L ($5) one-way; Sirmione (trip time: 4 hours), 12,900L ($8) one-way; and Desenzano (trip time: 4 hours 20 minutes), 15,400L ($9) one-way.

These ferries provide the best opportunity for leisurely admiring the shorelines and the lake's beauty and are also the most affordable way to see the lake. Following the same routes, at more or less the same times, are a battalion of hydrofoils, which cut the travel time to each of the above destinations in half. Transit on any of them requires a supplement of 1,800L to 5,000L ($1.05 to $2.90), depending on the distance you intend to travel. If you want to admire the lake from a waterside vantage, a well-recommended mode of attack is traveling in one direction via conventional ferry and returning to Riva del Garda by hydrofoil. Between early November and late February, there's no transportation offered in and out of Riva del Garda's port or anywhere else along the lake's northern tier, and only very limited transportation options are available from Desenzano, in the south.

RIVE DEL GARDA

Some 195 feet above sea level, **Riva del Garda** is the lake's oldest and most traditional resort. It consists of both an expanding new district and an old town, the latter centered at **Piazza III Novembre.**

GETTING THERE   Riva del Garda is linked to the Brenner–Modena motorway (Rovereto Sud/Garda Nord exit) and to the railway (Rovereto station) and is near Verona's Airport.

VISITOR INFORMATION   Go to the **Palazzo dei Congressi,** Giardini di Porta Orientale 8 (☎ **0464/554-444**). Mid-September to Easter, it's open Monday to Friday 9am to noon and 2 to 7pm; Easter to mid-September, hours are Monday to

A Driving Warning

The twisting roads following the shores of Lake Garda would be enough to rattle even the most experienced driver. Couple the frightening turns, dimly lit tunnels, and emotional local drivers with convoys of tour buses and trucks that rarely stay in their lane and you have one of the more frightening drives in Italy. Use your horn around blind curves and be warned that Sunday is especially risky, since everyone on the lake and from the nearby cities seems to take to the roads after a long lunch with lots of heady wine.

Saturday 9am to noon and 2 to 7pm; mid-June to mid-September, it's also open Sunday 10am to noon and 4 to 6:30pm.

SEEING THE SIGHTS

On the harbor, at Piazza III Novembre, you'll see the town's highest building, a 13th-century watchtower, the **Torre d'Apponale (Tower of Apponale).** It isn't open for visits, but the angelic-looking trumpeter adorning its pinnacle has been adopted as the symbol of the town itself. There's also a severe-looking castle, **La Rocca,** Piazza Battisti 3 (☎ **0464/57-38-69**). Built in 1124 and owned at various times by both the ruling Scaligeri princes of Verona and the Viennese Hapburgs (who used it as a prison), La Rocca has been turned into a **Civic Museum (Museo Civico La Rocca),** which you might visit on a rainy day, as it exhibits local artworks and attractions reflecting local traditions. Admission is 4,000L ($2.30) adults; those under 18 are free. It's open Tuesday to Sunday: September to June 9:30am to 5:30pm and July and August 9am to 10pm.

On the northern banks of the lake, between the Benacense plains and towering mountains, Riva offers the advantages of the Riviera and the Dolomites. Its climate is classically Mediterranean—mild in winter and moderate in summer. Vast areas of rich vegetation combine with the deep blue of the lake. Many people come for health cures; others for business conferences, meetings, and fairs. Riva is popular with tour groups from the Germanic lands and from England.

OUTDOOR ACTIVITIES

Riva is the windsurfing capital of Italy. Windsurfing schools offer lessons and also rent equipment. The best one is **Nautic Club Riva,** Viale Rovereto 132 (☎ **0464/552-453**), closed November to Easter. It has full rentals, including life jackets, wet suits, and boards, for 45,000L ($26) per day. If you'd like to explore the lake by bike, go to **Girelli Mountain Bike,** Viale Damiano Chiesa 15–17 (☎ **0464/554-719**), where rentals are 20,000L ($12) per day.

SHOPPING

Retailers mainly peddle souvenirs of only passing interest; however, a large **open-air market,** the best on Lake Garda, comes to town on the second and fourth Wednesday of every month. It mainly sprawls along Viale Dante, Via Prati, and Via Pilati. You can buy virtually anything, from alpine handcrafts to busts of Mussolini. While shopping, drop in to **Pasticceria Copat di Fabio Marzari,** Viale Dante 27 (☎ **0464/551-885**), for delectable pastries.

ACCOMMODATIONS

✪ **Hotel du Lac et du Parc.** Viale Rovereto 44, 38066 Riva del Garda. ☎ **0464/551-500.** Fax 0464/555-200. 178 units. MINIBAR TV TEL. 190,000–430,000L ($110–$249) double; from 490,000L ($284) suite. Rates include breakfast. AE, DC, MC, V. Closed Oct 20–Mar 20. Parking 25,000L ($15).

This deluxe Spanish-style hotel, the best in town, is set back from the busy road behind a shrub-filled parking lot dotted with stone cherubs. The interior of the main building is freshly decorated, with arched windows and lots of spacious comfort. The hotel has a comfortably sprawling format, giving the impression of being part of a large private home. The well-trained staff speaks a variety of languages and seems genuinely concerned with the well-being of their guests. The guest rooms are well furnished, and 54 are air-conditioned.

Dining: There's a huge dining room and an attractive bar, plus two more informal restaurants, each serving international and regional specialties.

Amenities: Concierge, room service, baby-sitting, laundry/dry cleaning; garden with two pools, lakeside beach, two tennis courts; sauna, fitness room, beauty salon.

Hotel Sole. Piazza III Novembre 35, 38066 Riva del Garda. ☎ **0464/552-686.** Fax 0464/552-811. 55 units. MINIBAR TV TEL. 230,000–270,000l ($133–$157) double; from 350,000L ($203) suite. Rates include breakfast. AE, DC, MC, V. Closed Jan 8–Mar and Nov–Dec 25. Parking 10,000L ($6).

The medium-priced Sole had far-sighted founders who snared the best position on the waterfront. The hotel has amenities worthy of a first-class rating. It's an overgrown villa with arched windows and colonnades, and the interior has time-clinging traditional rooms. The lounge has a beamed ceiling and centers around a hooded fireplace. The character and quality of the guest rooms vary considerably according to their position (most have lake views). Some are almost suites, with living-room areas; the smaller ones are less desirable. Nevertheless, all rooms are comfortable and spotless. You can dine in the formal interior room or on the flagstone lakeside terrace. There's a sauna and a solarium.

Hotel Venezia. Viale Rovereto 62, 38066 Riva del Garda. ☎ **0464/552-216.** Fax 0464/556-031. 24 units. TV TEL. 115,000–175,000L ($67–$102) double. Rates include breakfast. AE, V. Closed Nov–Easter.

The Hotel Venezia is one of the most attractive budget hotels in town. The main section of the Venezia's angular modern building is raised on stilts above a private parking lot set back from the lakefront promenade. The complex is surrounded by trees on a quiet street bordered with flowers and private homes. The reception area is at the top of a flight of red marble steps. There's a private pool surrounded by palmettos, and a clean and sunny dining room with Victorian reproduction chairs. The guest rooms are pleasantly furnished and well maintained.

DINING

Ristorante San Marco. Viale Roma 20. ☎ **0464/554-477.** Reservations recommended. Main courses 18,000–32,000L ($10–$19). AE, DC, MC, V. Tues–Sun noon–2:30pm and 7–10pm. Closed Feb. ITALIAN/SEAFOOD.

Set back from the lake on one of the main shopping streets of the resort, San Marco was built in the 19th century as a hotel and converted into a restaurant in 1979. If you arrive early for your reserved table, you can enjoy an aperitif at the bar. The superb food is classically Italian and the service excellent. You might begin with pasta, such as spaghetti with clams or tortellini with prosciutto. They serve many good fish dishes, including sole and grilled scampi. Among the meat selections, try the tournedos opera or veal cutlet bolognese. During summer, you may dine in the open-air garden.

RIVA AFTER DARK

Begin your evening with a drink at **Pub al Gallo,** Via San Rocca 11 (☎ 0464/551-177), which stays open until 3am. The best disco is **Discoteca Tiffany,** Giardini di Porta Orientale (☎ 0464/552-512), open only Thursday to Sunday. You can also shake it at **Après Club,** Via Monte d'Oro 14 (☎ **0464/552-187**), open most of the year Wednesday to Sunday 9pm to 2:30am (though the owners will often cut hours to just Friday and Saturday in spring and autumn).

LIMONE SUL GARDA

Limone sul Garda lies 6 miles south of Riva on the western shore of Lake Garda. Taking its name from the fruit of the abundant local lemon tree, Limone is one of the liveliest resorts on the lake, once praised by Goethe and D. H. Lawrence.

Limone snuggles close to the water at the bottom of a narrow, steep road, so its shopkeepers, faced with no building room, dug right into the rock. There are 2½ miles of beach from which you can bathe, sail, or surf. The only way to get about is on foot, but at Limone you can enjoy tennis, soccer, and other sports, as well as discos.

If you're bypassing Limone, you may still want to make a detour south of the village to the turnoff to Tignale, in the hills. You can climb a modern highway to the town for a sweeping vista of Garda, one of the most scenic spots on the entire lake.

VISITOR INFORMATION   April to September, a **tourist office** is operated at Via Comboni 15 (☎ **0365/954-070**), open Monday to Friday 8:30am to noon and 2:30 to 6pm.

ACCOMMODATIONS & DINING

Hotel Capo Reamol. Via IV Novembre 92, 25010 Limone sul Garda. ☎ **0365/954-040.** Fax 0365/954-262. E-mail: hcreamol@anthesi.com. 60 units. MINIBAR TV TEL. 236,000–278,000L ($137–$161) double. Rates include half board. AE, MC, V. Closed Nov–Mar.

You won't even get a glimpse of this 1960s hotel from the main highway because it nestles on a series of terraces well below road level. Pull into a roadside area indicated 1¼ miles north of Limone, then follow the driveway down a steep narrow hill. The guest rooms are well furnished and freshly decorated. The bar, restaurant, and sports facilities are on the lowest level, sheltered from the lakeside breezes by windbreaks. You can swim in the lake or the pool and rent Windsurfers and take a Windsurfing class on the graveled beach. The restaurant serves an Italian cuisine and many fine Italian wines, with live music on weekends. A tavern profits, like everything else in the hotel, from views of the water. A new beauty farm (spa/fitness facility) may remind you of the spas of France but on a lesser scale.

Hotel Le Palme. Via Porto 36, 25010 Limone sul Garda. ☎ **0365/954-028.** Fax 0365/954-120. E-mail: lepalme@limone.com. 28 units. TEL. 140,000–200,000L ($81–$116) double. Rates include breakfast. AE, MC, V. Closed Nov–Mar 15.

Completely renovated, this Venetian-style villa with period furniture stands in the shade of 2-centuries-old palm trees in the historic center, opening directly onto Lake Garda. It offers well-furnished rooms, each individually decorated. The second floor has a comfortable reading room with a TV and the third floor a wide terrace. The ground floor contains a large dining room with decorative sculpture, opening onto a wide terrace where in fair weather you can order meals and drinks. The cuisine, backed up by a good wine list, is excellent. Because of the popularity of the hotel, it's best to make reservations.

GARDONE RIVIERA

On Lake Garda's western shore 60 miles east of Milan, Gardone Riviera is well equipped with a number of good hotels and sporting facilities. Its lakeside promenade attracts a wide range of predominantly European tourists for most of the year. When it used to be chic for patrician Italian families to spend their holidays by the lake, many of the more prosperous built elaborate villas not only in Gardone Riviera but also in neighboring Fasano (some have been converted to receive guests). The town also has the major attraction along the lake, d'Annunzio's Villa Vittoriale.

GETTING THERE   The resort lies 26 miles south of Riva on the west coast. During the day, buses from Brescia arrive every 30 minutes, the trip takes 1 hour and costing 4,800L ($2.80) one-way. Two buses make the 3-hour trip from Milan, costing 15,100L ($9) one-way. For schedule information, call ☎ **0365/21-061.**

VISITOR INFORMATION   The **tourist office** is at Corso della Repubblica 35 (☎ **0365/20-347**). April to October, it's open Monday to Saturday 9am to 12:30pm and 4 to 7pm; November to March, hours are Monday to Friday 9am to 12:30pm and 3 to 6pm and Saturday 9am to 12:30pm.

VISITING GABRIELE D'ANNUNZIO'S VILLA

The ✪ **Villa Vittoriale,** Via Vittoriale 12 (☎ **0365/20-130**), was the home of Gabriele d'Annunzio (1863 to 1938), the poet and military adventurer, another Italian who believed in la dolce vita, even when he couldn't afford it. Most of the celebrated events in d'Annunzio's life occurred before 1925, including his love affair with Eleonora Duse and his bravura takeover as a self-styled commander of a territory being ceded to Yugoslavia. In the later years of his life, until he died in the winter before World War II, he lived the grand life at his private estate on Garda.

The furnishings and decor passed for avant garde in their day but now evoke the Radio City Music Hall of the 1930s. D'Annunzio's death mask is of morbid interest, and his bed with a "Big Brother" eye adds a curious touch of Orwell's *1984* (over the poet's bed is a faun casting a nasty sneer). The marble bust of Duse—"the veiled witness" of his work—seems sadly out of place, but the manuscripts and old uniforms perpetuate the legend. In July and August, d'Annunzio plays are presented at the amphitheater on the premises. Villa Vittoriale is a bizarre monument to a hero of yesteryear.

North of the town, Vittoriale is open Tuesday to Sunday: winter 9am to 12:30pm and 2 to 6pm (to 5pm spring and autumn) and summer 8:30am to 8pm. Admission is 8,000L ($4.65) to the grounds only or 16,000L ($9) to the grounds and the villa. To reach it, head out Via Roma, connecting with Via Colli.

ACCOMMODATIONS

Bellevue Hotel. Via Zanardelli 81, 25083 Gardone Riviera. ☎ **0365/290-088.** Fax 0365/ 290-080. 33 units. TEL. 135,000L ($81). Rates include breakfast. V. Closed Oct 10–Mar 27.

This villa perched up from the main road has many terraces surrounded by trees and flowers—and an unforgettable view. You can stay here even on a budget, enjoying the advantages of lakeside villa life complete with a pool. The lounges are comfortable, and the dining room affords a view through the arched windows and excellent meals (no skimpy helpings here). In fair weather you can dine in a large garden.

✪ **Grand Hotel.** Via Zanardelli 84, 25083 Gardone Riviera. ☎ **0365/20-261.** Fax 0365/ 22-695. www.grangardone.it. 200 units. MINIBAR TV TEL. 270,000–320,000L ($157–$186) double; 350,000–400,000L ($203–$232) junior suite. Rates include buffet breakfast. Half board 35,000L ($20) per person. AE, DC, MC, V. Closed Oct 18–Mar 31. Parking 20,000L ($12).

When it was built in 1881, this was the most fashionable hotel on the lake and one of the biggest resorts of its kind in Europe. Famous guests have included Winston Churchill, Gabriele d'Annunzio, and Somerset Maugham. It's only a rumor that Vladimir Nabokov was inspired to write *Lolita* after spotting a young girl here. The main salon's sculpted ceilings, parquet floors, and elegantly comfortable chairs make it an ideal spot for reading or watching the lake. The guest rooms for the most part are spacious and traditionally furnished, always inviting and comfortable.

Dining/Diversions: The piano bar (see Winnie's Bar under "Gardone After Dark," below) has the appropriate romantic atmosphere to put you in the mood for the refined cuisine served in the old-world dining room, with its menu of international and regional dishes. In summer, dining is possible on the lakeside terrace.

Amenities: Concierge, room service, dry cleaning/laundry, twice-daily maid service, baby-sitting, in-room massage; series of garden terraces, private beach, pool. The staff can arrange horse riding in the hills, tennis at courts within a 5-minute walk, and golf within a radius of 8 miles.

NEARBY ACCOMMODATIONS

Fasano del Garda is a satellite resort of Gardone Riviera, 1¼ miles to the north. Many prefer it to Gardone.

✪ **Hotel Villa del Sogno.** Via Zanardelli 107, Fasano del Garda, 25083 Gardone Riviera. ☎ **0365/290-181.** Fax 0365/290-230. 38 units. TV TEL. 300,000–480,000L ($174–$278) double; 490,000L–640,000L ($294–$384) suite. Rates include breakfast. AE, DC, MC, V. Closed Oct 20–Apr 1.

This 1920s re-creation of a Renaissance villa offers sweeping views of the lake and spacious old-fashioned guest rooms (nine are air-conditioned). This "Villa of the Dream" resort is far superior to anything in the area, having long ago surpassed the Grand (above). The baronial stairway of the interior, as well as many of the ceilings and architectural details, were crafted from wood.

Dining/Diversions: The hotel serves the finest food among the area's hotel dining rooms, offering international and regional specialties. There are two formal restaurants, though many guests prefer to dine on the summer terrace when possible. The terrace overlooks the lake where in summer both a buffet breakfast and a romantic evening dinner are served.

Amenities: Concierge, dry cleaning/laundry, room service; private beach, pool.

DINING

Most visitors to this resort take their meals at their hotels. However, there are some good independent choices.

Ristorante La Stalla. Strade per Il Vittoriale. ☎ **0365/21-038.** Reservations recommended. Main courses 15,000–30,000L ($9–$17); fixed-price menu 25,000L ($15). AE, DC, MC, V. Wed–Mon 12:30–2:30pm and 7:30–9:30pm. Closed Jan 8–20. INTERNATIONAL.

This charming restaurant, set in a garden ringed with cypresses on a hill above the lake, is frequented by local families. It occupies a handcrafted stone building with a brick-columned porch, outdoor tables, and an indoor room loaded with rustic artifacts and crowded tables. To get here, follow the signs toward Il Vittoriale (the building was commissioned by d'Annunzio as a horse stable) to a quiet residential street. Depending on the shopping that day, the specialties might include a selection of freshly prepared antipasti, risotto with cuttlefish, or crêpes fondue. Polenta is served with Gorgonzola and walnuts, or you may prefer beef filet in beer sauce. Sunday afternoon can be crowded.

✪ **Villa Fiordaliso.** Via Zanardelli 150. ☎ **0365/20-158.** Reservations required. Main courses 25,000–55,000L ($15–$32); fixed-price menu 85,000L ($49) for 5 courses, 120,000L ($7) for 7 courses. AE, DC, MC, V. Tues–Sun 12:30–2pm; Wed–Sun 7:30–10:30pm. Closed Jan–Feb. ITALIAN.

This deluxe restaurant is a Liberty-style (art nouveau) villa from 1924 with gardens stretching down to the edge of the lake. It's not only the most scenic and beautiful on Lake Garda but also serves the finest cuisine. This is personalized by the chef and likely to include a terrine of eel and salmon in herb-and-onion sauce, a timbale of rice and shellfish with curry, and several fish and meats grilled over a fire. Other specialties are ravioli with Bergoss (a salty regional cheese), sardines from a nearby lake baked in an herb crust, and scampi in a sauce of tomatoes and wild onions. This little bastion of fine food has impeccable service to match.

GARDONE AFTER DARK

Though we agree with Goethe that "it is not possible to express in words the enchantment of this luxuriant riviera," there's time when even scenery is tiring. If so, make your way to **Winnie's Bar** in the previously recommended Grand Hotel, Via Zanardelli 74 (☎ 0365/20-261), named after its most famous guest, Sir Winston Churchill, who preferred a bottle of cognac a day. Here you can drink and dance.

SIRMIONE

Perched at the tip of a narrowing strip on the southern end of Lake Garda, **Sirmione** juts out 2½ miles into the lake. Noted for its thermal baths (used to treat deafness), the town is a major resort, just north of the autostrada connecting Milan and Verona, that blooms in spring and wilts in late autumn.

GETTING THERE   Sirmione lies 3½ miles from the A4 exit and 5 miles from Desanzano. Buses run from Brescia and from Verona to Sirmione every hour (trip time from either, depending on traffic: 1 hour). A one-way ticket from Brescia is 5,400L ($3.15) and from Verona 4,600L ($2.65). There's no rail service. The nearest train terminal is at Desanzano, on the Venice-Milan rail line. From here, there's frequent bus service to Sirmione; the bus trip takes 30 minutes, costing 2,100L ($1.20) one-way.

VISITOR INFORMATION   The **tourist office** is at Viale Marconi 2 (☎ 030/916-245). April to October, it's open daily 9am to 12:30pm and 3 to 6pm; November to March, hours are Monday to Friday 9am to 12:30pm and 3 to 6pm and Saturday 9am to 12:30pm.

SEEING THE SIGHTS

The resort was a favorite of Giosuè Carducci, the Italian poet who won the Nobel Prize for literature in 1906. In Roman days it was frequented by still another poet, the hedonistic Catullus, who died in 54 B.C. Today the **Grotte di Catullo,** on Via Catullo (☎ 030/916-157), is the chief sight, an unbeatable combination of Roman ruins and a panoramic lake view. You can wander through the remains of this once-great villa April to September on Tuesday to Sunday 9am to 6pm and October to March on Tuesday to Sunday 9am to 4pm. Admission is 8,000L ($4.65) adults; children 17 and under/seniors 60 and over are free.

At the entrance to the town stands the moated 13th-century **Castello Scaligera,** Piazza Castello (☎ 030/916-468), which once belonged to the powerful Scaligeri princes of Verona. You can climb to the top and walk the ramparts April to September daily 9am to 6pm and October to March Tuesday to Sunday 9am to 1pm. Admission is 8,000L ($4.65).

OUTDOOR ACTIVITIES

Known for its beaches (invariably overcrowded in summer), Sirmione is Garda's major lakeside resort. The best beach is **Lido delle Bione,** which you reach by taking Via

Dante near the castle. Here vendors will rent you a chaise longue with an umbrella for 10,000L ($6). If you're feeling more athletic, other vendors will hook you up with a **pedal boat** at 12,000L ($7) per hour or a **kayak** at 8,000L ($4.65) per hour. If you'd like to go biking in the area, head for **Bar Chocolat,** Via Verona 47 (☎ 030/990-5297), with rentals at 5,000L ($2.90) per hour.

SHOPPING

The resort is filled with souvenir shops, many hawking cheaply made trinkets aimed at the day-tripper. However, the best buys are on Friday 8am to 1pm when an **outdoor market** blossoms in Piazza Montebaldo. Vendors bring their wares here (likely to be anything) not only from nearby lake villages but also from towns and villages to the south.

ACCOMMODATIONS

During the peak summer season, motorists need a hotel reservation to take their vehicles into the crowded town. However, there's a large parking area at the town entrance. Accommodations are plentiful.

Flaminia Hotel. Piazza Flaminia 8, 25019 Sirmione. ☎ **030/916-078.** Fax 030/916-193. 45 units. A/C TV TEL. 170,000–220,000L ($99–$128) double. Rates include breakfast. AE, DC, MC, V.

This is one of the best little hotels in Sirmione, recently renovated with a number of modern facilities and amenities. It's right on the lakefront, with a terrace extending into the water. The guest rooms are made attractive by French doors opening onto private balconies, and the lounges are furnished in a functional modern style. Breakfast is the only meal served.

Grand Hotel Terme. Viale Marconi 1, 25019 Sirmione. ☎ **030/916-261.** Fax 030/916-568. 74 units. A/C MINIBAR TV TEL. 420,000L ($244) double; 500,000L ($290) junior suite; 900,000L ($522) suite. Rates include breakfast. AE, DC, MC, V. Closed Oct 27–Mar 21.

This rambling hotel at the entrance of the old town is on the lake next to the Scaligeri Castle. After Villa Cortine (below), it's the second-best choice, known especially for its lake-bordering garden. The wide marble halls and stairs lead to well-furnished balconied rooms. Constructed in 1948, the hotel has contemporary furnishings, plus a number of spa and physical-therapy facilities.

Dining: The traditional Italian cuisine served in the indoor/outdoor dining room is excellent, with such offerings as prosciutto and melon, risotto with snails, fettuccine with fresh porcini, and a wide choice of salads and fruits.

Amenities: Concierge, room service, dry cleaning/laundry, solarium, gym, pool, Jacuzzi, sauna, car-rental desk.

Hotel Olivi. Via San Pietro 5, 25019 Sirmione. ☎ **030/990-5365.** Fax 030/916-472. 60 units. A/C TV TEL. 180,000–240,000L ($104–$139) double. Rates include breakfast. AE, DC, MC, V. Closed Dec–Jan.

A creation of sun-loving owner Cerini Franco, this hotel has an excellent location on the rise of a hill in a grove of olive trees at the edge of town. The all-glass walls of the major rooms never let you forget you're in a garden spot of Italy. Even the compact and streamlined guest rooms have walls of glass leading onto open balconies. The hotel serves typically Italian meals. Sometimes live music is featured—even country music when the hotel stages a barbecue. The hotel offers an outdoor pool, a solarium, and laundry and room service.

✪ **Villa Cortine Palace Hotel.** Via Grotte 12, 25019 Sirmione. ☎ **030/990-5890.** Fax 030/916-390. E-mail: vcortine@gardanet.it. 49 units. A/C TV TEL. 480,000–620,000L

($278–$360) double; 700,000–1,100,000L ($406–$638) suite. Rates include breakfast. AE, DC, MC, V. Closed end of Oct–Easter.

This first-class choice is luxuriously set apart from the town center, surrounded by sumptuous gardens. For serenity, atmosphere, professional service, and even good food, there's nothing to equal it in Sirmione. The hotel was built in 1905, though in 1957 a new wing greatly increased its amenities and capacities. Today all but a handful of its guest rooms are in this new wing, with the bar and reception area in the original building. Some rooms offer a minibar. The interior has one formal drawing room, with much gilt and marble—it's positively palatial.

Dining/Diversions: There's an informal restaurant and a more formal dining room serving Italian and international cuisine, with an excellent selection of wines. There's also an elegant cocktail bar. At lunch, the hotel often offers a barbecue, mainly with fresh fish from the lake.

Amenities: Concierge, room service, laundry/dry cleaning, baby-sitting, pool, clay tennis court, private beach.

DINING

La Rucola. Vicolo Strentelle 5. ☎ **030/916-326.** Reservations recommended. Main courses 25,000–28,000L ($15–$16); fixed-price menu 85,000L ($49). AE, MC, V. Fri–Wed 12:30–2:30pm and 7:30–10:30pm. Closed Jan–Feb 9. ITALIAN.

This restaurant lies on a small alley a few steps from the main gate leading into Sirmione. The building looks like a vine-laden, sienna-colored country house and was a stable 150 years ago. Full meals could include fresh salmon, langoustines, mixed grilled fish, and a more limited meat selection. Meats are most often grilled or flambéed, like Florentine beefsteak. More innovative items include gnocchetti di riso with baby squid and squid ink and filet of turbot with potatoes and zabaglione of spinach. A good pasta dish is spaghetti with clams. Many of the desserts are made for two, including crêpes Suzette and banana flambé.

Ristorante Grifone da Luciano. Via delle Bisse 5. ☎ **030/916-097.** Main courses 12,000–20,000L ($7–$12). AE, DC, MC, V. Thurs–Tues noon–2:30pm and 7–10:30pm. Closed Nov–Easter. INTERNATIONAL.

One of the most attractive restaurants in town is separated from the castle by a row of shrubbery, a low stone wall, and a moat. From your seat on the flagstone terrace, you'll have a view of the crashing waves and the plants ringing the dining area. The main building is an old stone house surrounded with olive trees, but many diners gravitate toward the low glass-and-metal extension. The staff is charming and fun and the chef talented, keeping quality high and prices moderate. The food includes many varieties of fish and many standard Italian dishes, like gnocchetti dragoncella (with tomatoes and aromatic herbs), risotto with shellfish, Venetian-style calves' liver with onions, beef filet flambéed with whisky, and beef cutlets (costello di Manzo).

6 Lake Como

Everything noble, everything evoking love—that was how Stendhal characterized **Lake Como.** Others have called it "the looking glass of Venus," and Virgil pronounced it "our greatest lake." More than 30 miles north of Milan, it's a shimmering deep blue, spanning 2½ miles at its widest point. With its flower-studded gardens, villas built for the wealthy of the 17th and 18th centuries, and mild climate, Larius (as it was known to the Romans) is among the most scenic spots in all Italy.

The scenery around Lake Como has been fabled since the days when residents of the flat, sometimes steamy fields of nearby Lombardy sought refuge from heat waves around its edges. The best way to admire the lake's many faces is taking a boat tour, pulling into selected ports of call en route for a meal, an espresso, a stroll, or some shopping or swimming. There's no service from Como between October and Easter.

The city of Como (below) is the best site for excursions of this nature, as boats departing from its piers make calls at every significant settlement along the lake. If the idea appeals to you, stroll down to the **Lungo Lario,** adjacent to the Piazza Cavour, for access to the ticket windows of the **Società Navigazione Lago di Como** (☎ 031/304-060). Between Easter and September, half a dozen ferries and almost as many high-speed hydrofoils embark for circumnavigations of the lake. One-way transit from Como to Colico at the northern end of the lake takes 4 hours by ferry and 90 minutes by hydrofoil and includes stops at each of the towns en route. Transit each way is 13,000 to 19,000L ($8 to $11) per person, depending on which boat you take. One-way transit between Como and Bellagio takes 2 hours by ferry and 45 minutes by hydrofoil and costs 9,600L to 15,000L ($6 to $9) per person.

Note: Be warned in advance that much of your view will be obscured by mists thrown up by the hydrofoils, so if you really want the view, the slower, cheaper boat is preferable, at least during one leg of your round-trip.

ESSENTIALS

GETTING THERE   **Trains** arrive daily at Como from Milan every hour. The trip takes 40 minutes, and a one-way fare is 7,800L ($4.50). The main station, **Stazione San Giovanni,** Piazzale San Gottardo (☎ 031/271-466), lies at the end of Viale Gallio, a 15-minute walk from the center (Piazza Cavour). If you've got a **car,** the city of Como is 25 miles north of Milan and is reached via A9. Once at the Como, a small road (S583) leads to the popular resort of Bellagio.

GETTING AROUND   **SPT,** Piazza Matteotti (☎ 031/304-744), offers bus service to the most important centers on the lake. A one-way fare to the most popular resort at Bellagio is 4,300L ($2.50). Travel time depends on the traffic.

COMO

At the southern tip of the lake, 25 miles north of Milan, **Como** is known for its silk industry. Most visitors pass through here to take a boat ride on the lake (see above). The lakeside **Piazza Cavour** is the center of local life.

Because Como is also an industrial city, we've generally shunned it for overnighting, preferring to anchor into one of the more attractive resorts along the lake, like Bellagio. However, train passengers who don't plan to rent a car may prefer Como (the city, that is) for convenience.

For centuries, the destiny of the town has been linked to that of Milan. Como is still called the world capital of silk, the silk makers of the city joining communal hands with the fashion designers of Milan. Como has been making silk since Marco Polo first returned with silkworms from China (since the end of World War II Como has left the cultivating of silk to the Chinese and just imported the thread to weave into fabrics). Designers like Giorgio Armani and Bill Blass come here to discuss the patterns they want with silk manufacturers.

VISITOR INFORMATION   The **tourist office** is at Piazza Cavour 17 (☎ 031/269-712), open Monday to Saturday 9am to 12:30pm and 2:30 to 6pm.

EXPLORING THE TOWN

Before rushing off on a boat for a tour of the lake, you may want to visit the **Cattedrale di Como,** Piazza del Duomo (☎ 031/265-244). Construction began in the 14th century in the Lombard Gothic style and continued on through the Renaissance until the 1700s. The exterior, frankly, is more interesting than the interior. From 1487, it's lavishly decorated with statues, including those of Pliny the Elder (A.D. 23 to 79) and the Younger (A.D. 62 to 113), who one writer once called "the beautiful people of ancient Rome." Look for the 16th-century tapestries depicting scenes from the Bible. The cathedral is open Monday to Saturday 7am to noon and 3 to 6:30pm.

On the other side of the Duomo lie the colorfully striped **Brolette** (town hall), and adjoining it, the **Torre del Comune.** Both are from the 13th century.

If time remains, head down the main street, **Via Vittorio Emanuele,** where, 2 blocks south of the cathedral, rises the five-sided **San Fedele,** a church from the 12th century standing on Piazza San Fedele. It's known for its unusual pentagonal apse and a doorway carved with "fatted" figures from the Middle Ages. Farther along, you come to the **Garibaldi National Unity Civic Museum (Museo Civico del Risorgimento Garibaldi),** Piazza Medaglie d'Oro Comasche (☎ 031/271-343), the virtual "attic" of Como, displaying artifacts collected by the city from prehistoric times through World War II. It's open Tuesday to Sunday 9:30am to 12:30pm and Tuesday to Saturday 2 to 5pm. Admission is 4,000L ($2.30).

The art museum of Como is of passing interest: The small **Pinacoteca Palazzo Volpi** at Via Diaz 84 (☎ 031/269-869) has several old and quite wonderful paintings from the Middle Ages, most of which were taken here from the monastery of Santa Margherita del Broletto. Two of the museum's best paintings are anonymous— that of St. Sebastian riddled with arrows (though appearing quite resigned to the whole thing) and a moving *Youth & Death.* The museum is open Monday to Saturday 9:30am to 12:30pm and 2 to 5pm and Sunday 10am to 1pm. Admission is 4,000L ($2.30) adults and 2,500L ($1.45) students/children.

After the museum, continue down Via Giovio until you come to the **Porta Vittoria,** a gate dating from 1192 with five tiers of arches. A short walk away, passing through a dreary commercial area leads you to Como's most interesting church, the 11th-century **Sant'Abbondio,** a Romanesque gem. From Porta Vittoria, take Viale Cattaneo to Viale Roosevelt, turning left onto Via Sant'Abbondio on which the church stands. Because of its age, it was massively restored in the 19th century. Heavily frescoed, the church has five aisles.

The heartbeat of life in Como is **Piazza Cavour** with its hotels, cafes, and steamers departing for lakeside resorts. Immediately to the west, the **Public Gardens (Giardini Pubblici)** make for a pleasant stroll, especially if you're heading for the **Tempio Voltiano,** Viale Marconi (☎ 031/574-705), honoring native son Alessandro Volta, the physicist and pioneer of electricity. The temple contains memorabilia of his life and experiments. It's open Tuesday to Sunday: April to September 10am to noon and 3 to 6pm and October to March 10am to noon and 2 to 4pm. Admission is 5,000L ($2.90).

To bid adieu to Como, take the funicular at Lungolario Trieste (near the main beach at Villa Genio) to the top of **Brunante,** a hill overlooking Como and providing a panoramic view. Departures are every 30 minutes daily, costing 6,800L ($3.95) round-trip.

OUTDOOR ACTIVITIES

The best swimming is at the **Lido Villa Olmo,** Via Cantoni (☎ 031/570-968), a pool adjoining a sandy stretch of beach for sunbathing. Admission is 7,500L ($4.35), and it's open daily 10am to 6pm.

SHOPPING

This lakeside city has been known throughout Europe as a focal point of the silk industry since the era of Marco Polo. Slinky fashion accessories, especially scarves blouses, pillows, and neckties, are literally bursting the seams of many merchants here. Before you buy, you might be interested in viewing a museum devoted exclusively to the history and techniques of the silk industry, the **Museo Didactico delle Sete,** Via Vallegio 3 (☎ 031/303-180). Maintained by a local trade school, it displays antique weaving machines and memorabilia going back to the Renaissance concerning the world's most elegant fabric. Entrance, 15,000L ($9), is relatively expensive. It's open Tuesday to Friday 9am to noon and 3 to 6pm.

Not all the silk factories will sell retail to individuals, but the best of those that do are these: One of the largest outlets is **Seterie Ratti,** Via Cernobbio 10 (☎ 031/ 269-053). On the premises of an antique villa, accessible via a formal-looking gate on the periphery of town (follow the signs to Cernobbio), you'll find a duet of rooms stuffed with retail goods of a local producer. Look for yard goods and ties that look very similar to the high-fashion accessories of some of the world's most prestigious names, at extremely reasonable prices. Within Como, two somewhat smaller but eminently tasteful outlets are **Binda,** Viale Geno (☎ 031/303-440), and **Martinetti,** Via Torriani 41 (☎ 031/269-053).

ACCOMMODATIONS

Hotel Barchetta Excelsior. Piazza Cavour 1, 22100 Como. ☎ **031/261-817.** Fax 031/ 302-622. 84 units. A/C MINIBAR TV TEL. 220,000–270,000L ($128–$157) double; 350,000– 400,000L ($203–$232) suite. Rates include breakfast. AE, DC, MC, V. Parking 28,000L ($16).

This first-class hotel is at the edge of the main square in the commercial section of town. Major additions have been made to the 1957 structure, including the alteration of its restaurant and an upgrading of the guest rooms, which are comfortably furnished, often with a balcony overlooking this heartbeat square and the lake. All accommodations have radios, among other amenities, and most have lake views. There's a parking lot behind the hotel, plus a covered garage just over 50 yards away.

Hotel Metropole & Suisse. Piazza Cavour 19, 22100 Como. ☎ **031/269-444.** Fax 031/ 300-808. E-mail: suisse@galactica.it. 74 units. A/C MINIBAR TV TEL. 260,000L ($151) double; 300,000L ($174) suite. Breakfast 22,000L ($13). AE, DC, MC, V. Closed Dec 18–Jan 7. Parking 20,000L ($12).

This hotel offers good value and well-maintained convenient rooms. Near the cathedral and the major lake-fronting square, it's composed of three lower floors dating from around 1700, with upper floors added about 60 years ago. A photo of the Swiss creator of the hotel with his staff in 1892 hangs behind the reception desk. Each of the rooms is different, rich with character for the most part. A parking garage and the city marina are nearby. A popular restaurant, Imbarcadero, under separate management (below), fills most of the ground floor of the hotel.

DINING

Ristorante Imbarcadero. In the Hotel Metropole & Suisse, Piazza Cavour 20. ☎ **031/ 270-166.** Reservations recommended. Main courses 24,000–32,000L ($14–$19); fixed-price menu 40,000L ($23). AE, DC, MC, V. Daily 12:30–3:30pm and 7:30–10pm. Closed Jan 1–8. INTERNATIONAL/LOMBARD.

Opened more than a decade ago in a 300-year-old building near the edge of the lake, this restaurant is filled with a pleasing blend of carved Victorian chairs, panoramic windows with marina views, and potted palms. The summer terrace set up on the square is ringed with shrubbery and illuminated with evening candlelight. The restaurant attracts patrons with demanding tastes who take pleasure in the first-class ingredients deftly handled by the kitchen. The chef makes his own tagliatelle, or you may want to order spaghetti with garlic, oil, and red pepper. The fish dishes are excellent, especially slices of sea bass with braised leek and aromatic vinegar and sage-flavored Como lake whitefish. Try the breaded veal cutlet Milanese style or breast of pheasant flavored with port and shallots. Desserts might include a parfait of almonds, hazelnuts, and apple sorbet flavored with Calvados.

COMO AFTER DARK

The most fun is in July, when **Jazz & Co.** stages five concerts at Piazza San Federale. The tourist office (above) will supply details.

CERNOBBIO

Cernobbio, 3 miles northwest of Como and 33 miles north of Milan, is a small fashionable resort frequented by the wealthy of Europe for its deluxe hotel, the 16th-century Villa d'Este. But its idyllic anchor on the lake has also attracted a less affluent tourist, who'll find a number of third- and fourth-class accommodations as well.

VISITOR INFORMATION   The **tourist office** is at Via Regina 33B (☎ 031/ 510-198), open Monday to Saturday 9:30am to 12:30pm and 2:30 to 5:30pm; closed January.

ACCOMMODATIONS

✪ **Grand Hotel Villa d'Este.** 22010 Cernobbio. ☎ **031/3481.** Fax 031/348-844. www. villadeste.it. 166 units. A/C MINIBAR TV TEL. 775,000–935,000L ($450–$542) double; 1,155,000–2,200,000L ($670–$1,276) suite. Rates include breakfast. AE, DC, MC, V. Closed Nov 15–Mar 1.

One of Italy's most legendary hotels, the Villa d'Este was built in 1568 as a lakeside home/pleasure pavilion for Cardinal Tolomeo Gallio. One of the most famous Renaissance-era hotels in the world, designed in the neoclassical style by Pellegrino Pellegrini di Valsolda, it passed from owner to illustrious owner for 300 years until it was transformed into a hotel in 1873.

The hotel remains a kingdom unto itself, a splendid palace surrounded by 10 acres of some of the finest hotel gardens in Italy. The interior lives up to the enthralling beauty of the grounds. The silken wall coverings of the Salon Napoleone were embroidered especially for the emperor's visit; the Canova Room is centered around a statue of Venus by the room's namesake; and the Grand Ballroom is suitable for the most festive banquets. The frescoed ceilings, impeccable antiques, and attentive service create one of the world's most envied hotels. Each guest room has an individual decor and a roster of famous former occupants. Some 34 of the hotel's 166 accommodations are in the Queen's Pavilion, an elegant annex built in 1856.

Dining/Diversions: The hotel contains two restaurants, both of culinary merit serving formal à la carte dinners. The cookery is sublime. Lunches are less expensive, especially in summer, when light buffets are set on long tables within view of the gardens. Throughout the year there's always at least a live pianist on most nights, and in midsummer a small orchestra plays dance music three evenings a week.

Amenities: Concierge, room service, baby-sitting, laundry/valet, hairdresser, massage, pool floating atop Lake Como; access to the world-class golf course at nearby Montofano; red-clay tennis courts; gym, sauna, Turkish bath, squash court, water-skiing and other sports.

BELLAGIO

Sitting on a promontory at the point where Lake Como forks, 48 miles north of Milan and 18 miles northeast of Como, Bellagio is with much justification labeled the "Pearl of Larius." It has also been called "the prettiest town in Europe." A sleepy veil hangs over the arcaded streets and little shops. Bellagio is rich in memories, having attracted fashionable and even royal visitors, such as Leopold I of Belgium, who used to own the 18th-century Villa Giulia. Still going strong, though no longer the aristocratic address today that it was, Bellagio is a 45-minute drive north of Como.

VISITOR INFORMATION The **tourist office** is at Piazza della Chiesa 14 (☎ **031/950-204**). May to September, it's open daily 9am to 12:15pm and 3 to 6pm; October to April, hours are Monday and Wednesday to Saturday 8:30am to 12:15pm and 2:30 to 6pm.

EXPLORING THE LAKESIDE GARDENS

To reach many of the places in Bellagio, you must climb streets that are really stairways. Its lakeside promenade blossoms with flowering shrubbery. From the town, you can take tours of Lake Como and enjoy sports like rowing and tennis or just lounge at the Bellagio Lido (the beach).

Bellagio's most important attraction is the garden of the **Villa Melzi Museum and Chapel,** Lungolario Marconi (☎ **031/950-318**). The villa was built in 1808 for Duke Francesco Melzi d'Eril, vice-president of the Italian republic founded by Napoléon. Franz Liszt and Stendhal are among the illustrious guests who've stayed here. The park has many well-known sculptures, and if you're here in spring you can enjoy the azaleas. Today it's the property of Count Gallarti Scotti, who opens it March 22 to October, daily 9am to 6pm. The museum contains a not very distinguished collection of Egyptian sculptures. Admission is 5,000L ($2.90).

If time allows, try to explore the gardens of the **Villa Serbelloni,** Piazza della Chiesa (☎ **031/950-204**), the Bellagio Study and Conference Center of the Rockefeller Foundation (not to be confused with the Grand Hotel Villa Serbelloni by the waterside in the village). The landlord here used to be Pliny the Younger. The villa isn't open to the public, but you can visit the park on 1½-hour guided tours starting at 11am and 4pm. Tours are conducted mid-April to mid-October, Tuesday to Sunday, at a cost of 6,000L ($3.50); the proceeds go to local charities.

A NEARBY VILLA

From Como, car ferries sail back and forth across the lake to **Cadenabbia** on the western shore, another lakeside resort, with hotels and villas. Directly south of Cadenabbia on the run to Tremezzo, the **Villa Carlotta** (☎ **0344/40-405**) is the most-visited attraction of Lake Como—and with good reason. In a serene setting, the villa is graced with gardens of exotic flowers and blossoming shrubbery, especially rhododendrons and azaleas. Its beauty is tame, cultivated, much like a fairy tale that recaptures the halcyon life available only to the very rich of the 19th century. Dating from 1847, the estate was named after a Prussian princess, Carlotta, who married the duke of Sachsen-Meiningen. Inside are a number of art treasures, like Canova's *Cupid and Psyche,* and neoclassical statues by Bertel Thorvaldsen, a Danish sculptor who died in 1844. There are also neoclassical paintings, furniture, and a stone-and-bronze table ornament that belonged to Viceroy Eugene Beauharnais. It's open daily: March 15 to 31 and October 9am to 11:30am and 2 to 4:30pm and April to September 9am to 6pm. Admission is 8,000L ($4.65) adults and 5,000L ($2.90) children 7 to 14; children 6 and under are free.

ACCOMMODATIONS & DINING

✪ **Grand Hotel Villa Serbelloni.** Via Roma 1, 22021 Bellagio. ☎ **800/223-6620** in the U.S., or 031/950-216. Fax 031/951-529. 82 units. A/C MINIBAR TV TEL. 460,000–710,000L ($267–$412) double; 900,000–1,100,000L ($522–$638) suite. Rates include breakfast. AE, DC, MC, V. Closed Nov 1–Mar 27. Parking 25,000L ($15).

This lavish old hotel, surpassed on the lake only by the Villa d'Este, is for those born to the grand style of life. It stands proud and serene at the edge of town against a backdrop of hills, surrounded by beautiful gardens of flowers and semi-tropical plants. The public rooms rekindle the spirit of the baroque: a drawing room with a painted ceiling, marble columns, a glittering chandelier, and gilt furnishings and a mirrored neoclassical dining room. The guest rooms are wide-ranging, from elaborate suites with recessed tile baths, baroque furnishings, and lake-view balconies to more chaste quarters. The most desirable rooms open onto the lake. You can sunbathe on the waterside terrace or doze under a willow tree.

Dining: The great Royal Dining Room is the venue for a high standard of Italian and international cooking. In summer, guests prefer a table on the lakeside terrace.

Amenities: Concierge, room service, dry cleaning/laundry, in-room massage, twice-daily maid service, baby-sitting, secretarial services, children's center, business center; fitness and beauty center with four programs ranging from 2 to 6 days (prices are 550,000L to 2,450,000L/$319 to $1,421, which includes meals and treatments but not the hotel room); health and fitness center, outdoor heated pool, lakeside beach, Jacuzzi, sauna, jogging track, golf course nearby.

Hotel du Lac. Piazza Mazzini 32, 22021 Bellagio. ☎ **031/950-320.** Fax 031/951-624. www.fromitaly.it/bellagio/h3/dulac. E-mail: dulac@mbox.vol.it. 48 units. A/C MINIBAR TV TEL. 220,000–230,000L ($128–$133) double. Rates include breakfast. MC, V. Closed Nov–Mar 25. Parking 12,000L ($7).

The Hotel du Lac was built 150 years ago, when the waters of the lake came directly up to the front door. Landfill has since created Piazza Mazzini, and today there's a generous terraced expanse of flagstones in front with cafe tables and an arched arcade. The rooms are comfortably furnished, containing such amenities as satellite TV and hair dryers. On the second floor is a glassed-in terrace restaurant, and you can bask in the sun or relax in the shade on the rooftop garden, opening onto panoramic views of the lake.

✪ **Hotel Florence.** Piazza Mazzini 45, 22021 Bellagio. ☎ **031/950-342.** Fax 031/951-722. 36 units. TV TEL. 220,000–240,000L ($128–$139) double; 310,000–330,000L ($180–$191) suite. Rates include breakfast. AE, MC, V. Closed Oct 25–Apr 1.

The entrance to this green-shuttered villa is under a vaulted arcade near the ferry landing. Wisteria climbs over the iron balustrades of the lake-view terraces. The entrance hall's vaulted ceilings are supported by massive timbers and granite Doric columns; there's even a Tuscan fireplace. The main section of the hotel was built around 1720, though most of what you see today was added around 1880. For 150 years, the Florence has been run by the Ketzlar family, and you'll probably be welcomed by the charming Roberta Ketzlar, her brother Ronald, and their mother, Friedl. The guest rooms are scattered amid spacious sitting and dining areas and often have high ceilings, antiques, and lake views. In the 1990s the hotel was vastly improved, with the addition of a gourmet restaurant and an America Bar, which becomes a kind of jazz club on Sunday evening.

TREMEZZO

Reached by frequent ferries from Bellagio, **Tremezzo,** 48 miles north of Milan and 18 miles north of Como, is another popular west-shore resort that opens onto a panoramic view of Lake Como. Around the town is a district known as Tremezzina, with luxuriant vegetation like citrus trees, palms, cypresses, and magnolias. Tremezzo is the starting point for many excursions, but its accommodations are much more limited than those in Bellagio.

VISITOR INFORMATION The **tourist office** is at Via Regina 3 (☎ 0344/ 40-493). May to October, it's open Monday to Wednesday and Friday to Saturday 9am to noon and 3:30 to 6:30pm.

ACCOMMODATIONS

Grand Hotel Tremezzo Palace. Via Regina 8, 22019 Tremezzo. ☎ **0344/40-446.** Fax 0344/40-201. 100 units. MINIBAR TV TEL. 320,000–380,000L ($186–$220) double; from 360,000–420,000L ($209–$244) suite. Rates include breakfast. AE, DC, MC, V. Closed Nov–Mar 1.

Built in 1910 on a terrace several feet above the traffic of the lakeside road, this hotel is one of the region's best examples of the Italian Liberty style, and the unquestioned leading choice at this resort. In 1990, most of the hotel was discreetly modernized, and the rooms on two of the hotel's four floors received air-conditioning. (Many guests still reject the air-conditioning in favor of open-windowed access to lakefront breezes.) The rooms are comfortable, traditionally furnished, high-ceilinged, and priced according to views of either the lake (most expensive, often with balconies) or the rear park and garden.

Dining/Diversions: There are three restaurants and an outdoor dining terrace (closed during inclement weather). All serve regional and international cuisines. On a platform beside the lake is the Club l'Escale, a bar popular with residents of surrounding communities.

Amenities: Room service, baby-sitting, laundry/valet, very large park, two pools, tennis court, lido beside the lake, jogging track, billiard room, heliport, conference facilities.

Hotel Bazzoni & du Lac. Via Regina 26, 22019 Tremezzo. ☎ **0344/40-403.** Fax 0344/ 41-651. 123 units. TEL. 160,000–170,000L ($93–$99) double. Rates include breakfast. AE, DC, MC, V. Closed Oct 10–Apr 24. Ferry from Ballagio or hydrofoil from Como.

There was an older hotel on this spot during Napoléon's era, bombed by the British 5 days after the official end of World War II. Today the reconstructed hotel is a collection of glass-and-concrete walls, with prominent balconies at the edge of the lake. It's one of the best choices in a resort town filled with hotels of grander format but much less desirable rooms. The main restaurant has a baronial but unused fireplace, contemporary frescoes of the boats on the lake, and scattered carvings. The pleasantly furnished sitting rooms include antique architectural elements from older buildings. A summer restaurant near the hotel's entrance is constructed like a small island of glass walls.

NEARBY ACCOMMODATIONS

✪ **Grand Hotel Victoria.** Via Lungolago Castelli 7–11, 22017 Menaggio. ☎ 0344/ 32-003. Fax 0344/32-992. 54 units. A/C MINIBAR TV TEL. 320,000–370,000L ($186–$215) double; from 450,000L ($261) junior suite. Rates include breakfast. Half board 20,000L ($12) per person. AE, DC, MC, V.

This is one of the best hotels on the lake, built in 1806 along a lakeside road bordered with chestnut trees. It was luxuriously renovated in 1983, with attention paid to the preservation of the ornate plasterwork of the ceiling vaults. The modern furniture and amenities in the rooms include bathroom tiles designed by Valentino. The beach in front of the hotel is one of the best spots on Lake Como for windsurfing, especially between 3 and 7pm.

Dining: Guests enjoy drinks on the outdoor terrace near the stone columns of the tree-shaded portico or in the antique-filled public rooms. The restaurant has well-prepared food, art nouveau chandeliers, and an embellished ceiling showing the fruits of an Italian harvest and mythical beasts.

Amenities: Room service, baby-sitting, laundry/valet, pool, beach, tennis court, private boats.

DINING

Al Veluu. Via Rogaro 11, Rogaro di Tremezzo. ☎ **0344/40-510.** Reservations recommended. Main courses 20,000–35,000L ($12–$20). AE, MC, V. Wed–Mon noon–2pm and 7:30–9:30pm. Closed Nov–Mar 1. LOMBARD/INTERNATIONAL.

Al Veluu, 1 mile north of the resort in the hills, is an excellent regional restaurant with plenty of relaxed charm and personalized attention from owner Carlo Antonini and his son, Luca. The terrace tables offer a panoramic sweep of the lake, and the rustic dining room with its fireplace and big windows is a welcome refuge in inclement weather. Most of the produce comes freshly picked from the garden; even the butter is homemade, and the best cheeses come from a local farmer. The menu is based on the fresh, light, and flavorful cuisine of northern Italy. Examples are missoltini (dried fish from the lake, marinated, and grilled with olive oil and vinegar), penne al Veluu (with spicy tomato sauce), risotto al Veluu (with champagne sauce and fresh green peppers), and an unusual lamb pâté.

7 Lake Maggiore & the Borromean Islands

The waters of **Lake Maggiore** wash up on the banks of Piedmont and Lombardy in Italy, but its more austere northern basin (Locarno, for example) lies in the mountainous region of Switzerland. It stretches more than 40 miles and is 6½ miles at its widest. A wealth of natural beauty awaits you: mellowed lakeside villas, dozens of lush gardens, sparkling waters, and panoramic views. A veil of mist seems to hover at times, especially in early spring and late autumn. Such men as Hemingway, Flaubert, Goethe, and Wagner have cited its charms.

Maggiore is a most rewarding lake to visit from Milan, especially because of the Borromean Islands in its center (most easily reached from Stresa). If you have time, drive around the entire basin; on a more limited schedule, you may find the resort-studded western shore the most scenic.

ESSENTIALS

GETTING THERE   The major resort of the lake, Stresa, is just 1 hour by **train** from Milan on the Milan-Domodossola line. Service is every hour, costing 7,200L to 15,000L ($4.20 to $9) one-way, depending on the train. For information and schedules, call ☎ **0323/30-472.** There's no bus service to the lake. If you've got a **car** and are in Milan, take a 51-mile drive northwest along A8 (staying on E62 out of Gallarate until it joins SS33 up the western shore of the lake) to Stresa.

GETTING AROUND   If you're **driving,** S33 goes up the west side of the lake to Verbania, where it becomes S34 on its way to the Swiss town of Locarno, about 25 miles. If you want to encircle the lake you'll have to clear Swiss Customs before passing through such famed resorts as Ascona and eventually Locarno. From Locarno you can head south again along the eastern, less touristy shore, which becomes SS493 on the Italy side. At Luino, you can cut off on SS233, then A8 to return to Milan, or continue along the lake shore (the road becomes SS629) to the southern point again, where you can get E62 back toward Milan.

Cruising Lake Maggiore with modern **boats** and fast **hydrofoils** is great fun. There's a frequent ferry service for cars and passengers between Intra (Verbania) and Laveno.

Boats leave from Piazza Marconi along Corso Umberto I in Stresa. For boat schedules, contact the **Navigazione Sul Lago Maggiore,** Viale F. Baracca 1 (☎ **0322/46-651),** in the lakeside town of Arona.

STRESA

On the western shore, 407 miles northwest of Rome and 51 miles northwest of Milan, **Stresa** has skyrocketed from a simple village of fisherfolk to a first-class international resort. Its vantage on the lake is almost unparalleled, and its accommodations level is superior to that of other Maggiore resorts in Italy. Scene of sporting activities and an international **Festival of Musical Weeks** (beginning in late August), it swings into action in April, then dwindles in popularity at the end of October.

VISITOR INFORMATION The **tourist office** is at Via Prìncipe Tomaso 70–72 (☎ **0323/30-150).** May to September, hours are Monday to Saturday 8:30am to 12:30pm and 3 to 6:15pm and Sunday 9am to noon; October to April, hours are Monday to Saturday 8:30am to 12:30pm and Monday to Friday 3 to 6:15pm.

ACCOMMODATIONS

Albergo Ariston. Corso Italia 60, 28049 Stresa. ☎ and fax **0323/31-195.** 11 units. 140,000L ($81) double. Rates include breakfast. Half board 95,000L ($55) per person. AE, DC, MC, V. Closed Dec–Apr 1. Free parking.

Here's a good bargain. The hotel is listed as third class, but its comfort is superior. The rooms are well kept and attractively furnished. Nonguests can stop in for a meal, ordering lunch or dinner on the terrace, which has a panoramic view of the lake and gardens. Your hosts are the Balconi family.

✪ **Grand Hotel des Iles Borromées.** Corso Umberto I 67, 28049 Stresa. ☎ **0323/ 30-431.** Fax 0323/938-938. www.stresa.net/hotel/borromees. E-mail: borromees@isanet.it. 186 units. A/C MINIBAR TV TEL. 429,000–536,000L ($249–$311) double; from 690,000– 3,900,000L ($400–$2,262) suite. AE, DC, MC, V.

On the edge of the lake in a flowering garden, this is by far Stresa's leading resort hotel. You can see the Borromean Islands from many rooms, which are furnished in an Italian/French Empire style, including rich ormolu, burnished hardwoods, plush carpets, and pastel colors. The baths look as if every quarry in Italy was scoured for matched marble. The hotel opened in 1863, attracting titled notables and guests like J. P. Morgan. Hemingway had the hero of *A Farewell to Arms* stay here to escape World War I. The elegant public rooms, with two-tone ornate plasterwork and crystal chandeliers, once hosted a top-level meeting among the heads of state of Italy, Great Britain, and France in an attempt to stave off World War II. The hotel also operates a 27-room **Residenza** in a separate building, where the prices are 20% lower and the rooms decorated in a modern style, with air-conditioning, TVs, and minibars.

Dining: The restaurant serves specialties of Lombardy and Piedmont. Special dishes include filet of perch with sage and tenderloin cooked on a black stone.

Amenities: Room service, laundry, baby-sitting, medically supervised health/exercise program, two outdoor pools, tennis court, sauna.

Hotel Astoria. Corso Umberto I 31, 28049 Stresa. ☎ **0323/32-566.** Fax 0323/933-785. 99 units. MINIBAR TV TEL. 190,000–290,000L ($110–$168) double; 360,000L ($209) suite. Rates include breakfast. AE, DC, MC, V. Closed late Oct–Mar 27.

A 5-minute walk from either the rail station or the center of Stresa, this hotel fronting the lake was partially rebuilt in 1993, giving an even more modern gloss to an already contemporary hotel. It's expressly for sunseekers who want a heated pool, Turkish bath, small gym, roof garden, and Jacuzzi. It features triangular balconies—one to each guest room—jutting out for the view. The rooms are streamlined and spacious. The public lounges have walls of glass opening toward the lake view and the garden. The portion of the dining room favored by most guests is the open-air front terrace, where under shelter you dine on good Italian and international cuisine while enjoying a view of Maggiore.

Hotel Moderno. Via Cavour 33, 28838 Stresa. ☎ **0323/933-773.** Fax 0323/933-775. 52 units. MINIBAR TV TEL. 200,000L ($116) double. Rates include breakfast. AE, DC, MC, V. Closed Nov–Mar. Parking 15,000L ($9).

A block from the lake and boat-landing stage, the Moderno lies in the center of Stresa. It dates from the turn of the century, but subsequent modernization, most recently in 1989, has rendered the building's original lines unrecognizable. The rooms have a personalized decor and good beds. The Moderno has three restaurants, unusual for such a small hotel.

Regina Palace. Corso Umberto I 33, 28049 Stresa. ☎ **0323/933-777.** Fax 0323/933-776. 174 units. MINIBAR TV TEL. 380,000L ($220) double; from 700,000L ($406) suite. Rates include breakfast. AE, DC, MC, V. Closed Oct–Easter. Parking 15,000L ($9) in garage, free outside.

The Regina Palace was built in 1908 in a boomerang shape whose central curve faces the lakefront. The art deco illuminated-glass columns inside are capped with gilded Corinthian capitals, and a wide marble stairwell is flanked with carved oak lions. The guest roster has included George Bernard Shaw, Ernest Hemingway, Umberto I of Italy, and Princess Margaret. Lately, about half the guests are American, many with the tour groups that stream through Stresa. The rooms are equipped with all the modern comforts, and many have views of the Borromean Islands. Facilities include a pool, tennis and squash courts, a Jacuzzi, saunas, a health club, and a Turkish bath. The hotel also has two dining rooms, one reserved only for guests; the other is the Charleston, an à la carte restaurant.

DINING

Ristorante Pescatore. Vicolo del Poncivo 1. ☎ **0323/31-986.** Main courses 18,000–28,000L ($10–$16). MC, V. Fri–Wed noon–3pm and 6–10pm. SPANISH/ITALIAN SEAFOOD.

One of the smallest (only 30 seats) restaurants in Stresa occupies a single dining room in a simple building in the historic core. An additional trio of tables extend into a garden. The focus is on seafood that's fresh, generously portioned, and sometimes prepared in the national style of Spain, since the owners and some of the staff are from the province of Galicia. Look for succulent version of *zarzuela de pescada* (fish stew) and a *paella* you might have imagined came from Valencia, redolent as it is with shellfish, saffron-flavored rice, fish, chicken, and sausage. More authentically Italian are *zuppe di pesce* (fish soup) or any of a medley of grilled or braised fish, most of which were hauled out of the sea a few hours before you'll eat them. Favorite garnishes are garlic-and-wine sauce, lemon and oil, or a garlicky green sauce with pesto.

Taverna del Pappagallo. Via Principessa Margherita 46. ☎ **0323/30-411.** Reservations recommended. Main courses 15,000–20,000L ($9–$12); pizzas 8,000–16,000L ($4.65–$9). No credit cards. Thurs–Mon 11:30am–2:30pm and 6:30–10:30pm. ITALIAN/PIZZA.

This formal little garden restaurant and tavern is operated by the Ghiringhelli brothers, who turn out some of the least expensive meals in Stresa. Specialties include gnocchi, many types of scaloppine, scalamino allo spiedoc fagioli (grilled sausage with beans), and saltimbocca alla romana (a veal-and-prosciutto dish). At night, pizza is king (try the pizza Regina). The service has a personal touch.

THE BORROMEAN ISLANDS

The heart of Lake Maggiore is occupied by the **Borromean Islands,** a chain of tiny islands that were turned into sites of lavish villas and gardens by the Borromeo clan. Boats leave from Stresa about every 30 minutes in summer, and the trip takes 3 hours. The **navigation offices** at Stresa's center port (☎ 0323/30-393) are open daily 7am to 7pm. The best deal is to buy an excursion ticket for 13,500L ($8) entitling you to go back and forth to all three islands during the day.

EXPLORING THE ISLANDS

Dominating the **Isola Bella (Beautiful Island)** is the major stopover: the 17th-century **Borromeo Palazzo** (☎ 0323/30-556). From the front, the figurines in the garden evoke the appearance of a wedding cake. Napoléon slept here. On conducted tours, you're shown through the airy palace, whose views are remarkable. A special feature is the six grotto rooms, built piece by piece like a mosaic. In addition, there's a collection of quite good tapestries, with gory, cannibalistic animal scenes. Outside, the white peacocks in the garden enchant year after year. The palace and its grounds are open March 27 to October 24, daily 9am to noon and 1:30 to 5:30pm. Admission is 13,000L ($8) adults and 6,000L ($3.50) children 6 to 15; children 5 and under are free.

The largest of the chain, **Isola Madre (Mother Island)** is visited chiefly for its **Orto Botanico (Botanical Garden).** You wander through a setting ripe with pomegranates, camellias, wisteria, rhododendrons, bougainvillea, hibiscus, hydrangea, magnolias, and even a cypress tree from the Himalayas. You can also visit the 17th-century **palace** (☎ 0323/31-261), which contains a rich collection of 17th- and 18th-century furnishings. Of particular interest is a collection of 19th-century French and German dolls belonging to Countess Borromeo and the livery of the House of Borromeo. The unique 18th-century marionette theater, complete with scripts, stage scenery, and devices for sound, light, and other special effects, is on display. Peacocks, pheasants, and other birds live and roam freely on the grounds. Visits are March 27 to October 24, daily 9am to noon and 1:30 to 5:30pm. Admission to the palace and grounds is 13,000L ($8) adults and 6,000L ($3.50) children 6 to 15; children 5 and under are free.

The **Isola del Pescatori (Fisher's Island)** is without major sights or lavish villas, but in many ways it's the most colorful. Less a stage setting than its two neighbors, it's inhabited by fisherfolk who live in cottages that haven't been converted to souvenir shops. Good walks are possible in many directions.

VILLA TARANTO

Back on the mainland near the resort of Pallanza, north of Stresa, the **Giardini Botanici at Villa Taranto,** Via Vittorio Veneto 111, Verbania-Pallanza (☎ 0323/556-667), spread over more than 50 acres of the Castagnola Promontory jutting out into Lake Maggiore. In this dramatic setting between the mountains and the lake, more than 20,000 species of plants from all over the world thrive in a cultivated institution begun in 1931 by a Scotsman, Capt. Neil McEacharn. Plants range from rhododendrons and azaleas to specimens from such faraway places as Louisiana. Seasonal exhibits include fields of Dutch tulips (80,000 of them), Japanese magnolias, giant water lilies, cotton plants, and rare varieties of hydrangeas. The formal gardens are carefully laid out with ornamental fountains, statues, and reflection pools. Among the more ambitious creations is the elaborate irrigation system that pumps water from the lake to all parts of the gardens and the Terrace Gardens, complete with waterfalls and pool.

March 28 to October 31, the gardens are open daily 8:30am to 6:30pm. To arrange an hour-long guided tour (groups only), contact the **Palazzo dei Congressi di Stresa** (☎ **0323/30-389**). You may also take a round-trip boat ride from Stresa, docking at the Villa Taranto pier adjoining the entrance to the gardens. You pay an admission of 13,000L ($8) adults and 9,000L ($5) children 6 to 14; children 5 and under are free.

12 Piedmont & Valle d'Aosta

Towering snowcapped alpine peaks; oleander, poplar, and birch trees; sky-blue lakes; river valleys and flower-studded meadows; the chamois and the wild boar; medieval castles; Roman ruins and folklore; the taste of vermouth on home ground; Fiats and fashion—northwestern Italy is a fascinating area to explore.

Piedmont (Piemonte) is largely agricultural, though its capital, Turin, is one of Italy's front-ranking industrial cities (with more mechanics per square foot than any other location in Europe). The influence of France is strongly felt, both in the dialect and in the kitchen.

Valle d'Aosta (really a series of valleys) has traditionally been associated with Piedmont, but in 1948 it was given wide-ranging autonomy. Most of the residents in this least-populated district in Italy speak French. Closing in Valle d'Aosta to the north on the French and Swiss frontiers are the tallest mountains in Europe, including Mont Blanc (15,780 ft.), the Matterhorn (14,690 ft.), and Monte Rosa (15,200 ft.). The road tunnels of Great St. Bernard and Mont Blanc (opened in 1965) connect France and Italy.

Serious wine connoisseurs who explore the region may want to visit one of the outstanding wineries. To call for an appointment, refer to the "Piedmont" section under "The Best Wine-Growing Regions" in chapter 1.

1 Turin: Capital of Piedmont

140 miles SW of Milan, 108 miles NW of Genoa, 414 miles NW of Rome

In **Turin (Torino),** the capital of Piedmont, the Italian Risorgimento (unification movement) was born. While the United States was fighting its Civil War, Turin became the first capital of a unified Italy, a position it later lost to Florence. Turin was once the capital of Sardinia. Much of the city's history is associated with the House of Savoy, a dynasty that reigned for 9 centuries, even presiding over the kingdom of Italy when Victor Emmanuel II was proclaimed king in 1861. The family ruled, at times in name only, until the monarchy was abolished in 1946.

In spite of extensive bombings, Turin found renewed prosperity after World War II, largely because of the Fiat manufacturers based here (it has been called the Detroit of Italy). Many buildings were destroyed, but much of its 17th- and 18th-century look remains. Located on the Po River, Turin is well laid out, with wide streets,

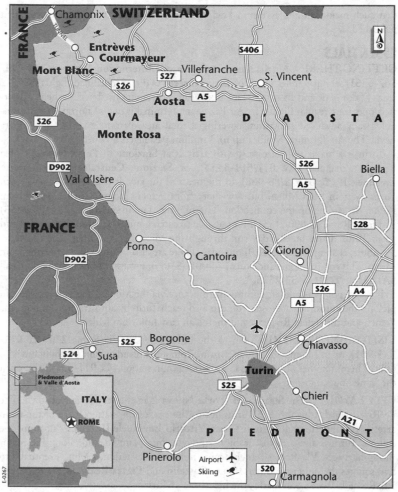

historic squares, churches, and parks. For years it has had a reputation as the least-visited and least-known of Italy's major cities.

Turin's biggest draw, the **Cattedrale di San Giovanni,** home to the **Shroud of Turin,** was damaged by fire in 1997. The Chapel of the Holy Shroud, where the silver reliquary that protects the controversial Christian symbol is usually on display, and the west wing of the neighboring Royal Palace sustained most of the damage. Luckily, the shroud had been moved into the cathedral itself because the dome of its chapel was being renovated.

Turin is one of Italy's richest cities, with some million Turinese, many of whom are immigrants who came here to get a piece of the pie. "Car Capital of Italy," Turin is surrounded by some hideous suburbs that are ever growing, but its Crocietta district is home to some of the most aristocratic residences in Italy and its inner core is one of grace and harmony. One of Italy's most feared and powerful men, Gianni Agnelli, lives here. It was once the home of Antonio Gramsci, who staged "occupations" of the Fiat factory and later helped found the Italian Communist Party before dying in a Fascist prison. On a cultural note, Turin is the center of modern Italian writing; it was here that such major authors as Primo Levi, Cesare Pavese, and Italo Calvino were first published.

ESSENTIALS

GETTING THERE   Alitalia flies into the **Caselle International Airport** (☎ 011/567-6361), about 9 miles north of Turin. It receives direct scheduled flights from 22 cities (7 domestic and 15 from major European centers); it's used by 13 scheduled carriers operating regular flights. Its Air Passenger Terminal is one of Europe's most technologically advanced structures, covering a total area of more than 43,000 square yards. The Air Terminal handles up to 3 million passengers a year.

Turin is a major **rail** terminus, with arrivals at **Stazione di Porta Nuova,** Corso Vittorio Emanuele (☎ 011/561-3333), or **Stazione Centrale,** Corso Vittorio Emanuele II (☎ 01478/88-088), in the heart of the city. It takes 1¼ hours to reach Turin by train from Milan, but anywhere from 9 to 11 hours to reach Turin from Rome, depending on the connection. The one-way fare from Milan is 14,000L ($8) and from Rome 53,000L ($31). It's possible to catch a **bus** in Chamonix (France) and go to Turin. Three buses a day run through the Mont Blanc Tunnel. The trip takes 3½ hours; costing 35,000L ($20) one-way. There are also 15 buses a day arriving from Milan. This trip is 2 hours and costs 17,200L ($10) one-way. For bus information, call **SATEM** at ☎ 011/433-2525.

If you've got a **car** and are coming from France via the Mont Blanc Tunnel, you can pick up the autostrada at Aosta. You can also reach Turin by autostrada from both the French and the Italian Rivieras, and there's an easy link from Milan.

VISITOR INFORMATION   Go to the office of **APT,** Via Roma 226 (☎ 011/535-901), open Monday to Friday 9am to 7pm and Saturday 9am to noon and 1 to 6pm. There's another office at the Porta Nuova train station (☎ 011/531-327), open the same hours.

CITY LAYOUT   The **Stazione di Porta Nuova** is in the very center of town. The Po River, which runs through Turin, lies to the east of the station. One of the main arteries running through Turin is **Corso Vittorio Emanuele II,** directly north of the station. Turin is also a city of fashion, and you may want to walk along the major shopping street, **Via Roma,** which begins north of the station, leading eventually to two squares that join each other, **Piazza Castello** and **Piazza Reale.** In the middle of Via Roma is **Piazza San Carlo,** the heartbeat of Turin.

SPECIAL EVENTS   Turin stages two major cultural fests every year: the **Sere d'Estate festival** in July, with programs devoted to dance, music, and theater; and the monthlong Settembre Musica in September, with classical music performances at various parts of the city. For details about these festivals, contact the **Assesorato per la Cultura,** Piazza San Carlo 161 (☎ 011/442-4715).

EXPLORING THE CITY

Begin your explorations at ✪ **Piazza San Carlo.** Although heavily bombed during World War II, it's still the loveliest and most unified square in the city. It was designed by Carlo di Castellamonte in the 17th century and covers about 3½ acres. The two churches are those of **Santa Cristina** and **San Carlo.** Some of the most prestigious figures in Italy once sat on this square, sipping coffee and plotting the unification of Italy.

✪ **Egyptian Museum (Museo delle Antichità Egizie) and Galleria Sabauda.** In the Palazzo dell'Accademia delle Scienze, Via Accademia delle Scienze 6. ☎ **011/561-7776** (Egyptian Museum) or ☎ **011/547-440** (Galleria Sabauda). Egyptian Museum, 12,000L ($7) adults; children under 18/seniors over 60 free. Galleria Sabauda, 8,000L ($4.65) adults; children 17 and under free. Egyptian Museum, Tues–Sat 9am–7pm, Sun and holidays 9am–2pm. Galleria Sabauda, guided tours Tues–Wed and Fri–Sat 9am–2pm, Thurs 9am–7pm, Sun 10am–10pm. Both closed Jan 1, May 1, Aug 15, and Dec 25.

Two interesting museums are housed in the Guarini-designed 17th-century Science Academy Building. The collection of the **Egyptian Museum** is so vast it's rated second only to the one at Cairo. Of the statuary, those of Ramses II and of Amenhotep II are best known. A room nearby contains a rock temple consecrated by Thutmose III in Nubia. In the crowded wings upstairs, the world of the pharaohs lives on (one of the prize exhibits is the Royal Papyrus, with its valuable chronicle of the Egyptian monarchs from the 1st to the 17th dynasty). The funerary art is exceptionally rare and valuable, especially the chapel built for Maia and his young wife and an entirely reassembled tomb (of Kha and Merit, 18th Dynasty), discovered in good condition at the turn of the century.

The **Galleria Sabauda** presents one of Italy's richest art collections, acquired over a period of centuries by the House of Savoy. The largest exhibit is of Piedmontese masters, but it has many fine examples of Flemish art as well. Of the latter, the best-known painting is Sir Anthony van Dyck's *Three Children of Charles I*. Other important works are Botticelli's *Venus*, Memling's *Passion of Christ*, Rembrandt's *Sleeping Old Man*, Duccio's *Virgin and Child*, Mantegna's *Holy Conversation*, Jan van Eyck's *The Stigmata of Francis of Assisi*, Veronese's *Dinner in the House of the Pharisee*, Bellotto's *Views of Turin*, intriguing paintings by Brueghel, and a section of the royal collections between 1730 and 1832.

✪ **Cattedrale di San Giovanni.** Piazza San Giovanni. ☎ **011/521-5960.** Free admission. Daily 9am–noon and 3–5pm.

This Renaissance cathedral, dedicated to John the Baptist, was swept by fire on April 12, 1997, with major damage sustained by Guarini's Chapel of the Holy Shroud, the usual resting place of the contested Christian relic—fortunately, the shroud itself was undamaged. The shroud made world headlines in 1998 when it was put on public display for the first time in 20 years. At its unveiling for the fourth time in this century on the occasion of the cathedral's 500th anniversary, some 3 million pilgrims and tourists traveled to Turin to see it. Alas, you won't be able to see it for yourself in 1999—however, the shroud will again be exhibited in 2000 to mark the beginning of the third millennium.

The authorities supervising the administration of the shroud maintain the **Holy Shroud Museum (Museo della Sindone),** Via San Domenico 28 (☎ 011/464-7999), a small, dusty library/research center near the cathedral. It's open to ecclesiastics and qualified scholars only on special request.

Royal Palace (Palazzo Reale). Piazza Castello. ☎ **011/436-1455.** Admission 8,000L ($4.65). Tues–Sun 9am–5pm.

The palace the Savoys called home was begun in 1645. The halls, the columned ballroom by Palagi, the tea salon, and the "Queen's Chapel" are richly baroque in style. The original architect was Amedeo de Castellamonte, but numerous builders supplied ideas and effort before the palazzo was completed. As in nearly all ducal residences of that period, the most bizarre room is the one bedecked with flowering chinoiserie.

The Throne Room is of interest, as is the tapestry-draped Banqueting Hall. Le Nôtre, the famous Frenchman, mapped out the gardens, which may also be visited along with the Royal Armory (Armeria Reale), containing a large collection of arms and armor and many military mementos. Guided tours are offered every 20 minutes.

The Mystery of Turin's Holy Shroud

One of the world's greatest mysteries, the **Santissima Sindone (Holy Shroud)** is the most famous and controversial religious artifact on earth, housed in Turin's Cattedrale di San Giovanni. The shroud is said to be the one that Joseph of Arimathea wrapped around the body of Christ when he was removed from the cross.

This 4-yard length of linen reveals the agonized features of a man who suffered crucifixion in almost photographic detail. The face of the bearded man is complete with a crown of thorns, and the marks of a thonged whip and bruises are compatible with the torment of carrying a cross. No one has successfully put forth a scientific explanation as to why the imprints of the man on the cloth exists or even how its image became impregnated in the threads. Photography, of course, was centuries from being invented.

Turin didn't always possess this relic. First mentioned in the Gospel of Matthew, it disappeared in history until it mysteriously "turned up" in Cyprus, centuries after the death of Christ. From Cyprus, it was taken to France, where it was first exhibited in 1354 and immediately denounced as a fraud by a French bishop. In 1578, it was acquired by Duke Emanuele Filiberto, of the House of Savoy, who took the shroud to Turin in 1578.

For centuries, the church didn't allow scientists to conduct dating tests of the shroud. The first scientific testing suggested it was a fraud, probably from the 12th century. In 1988, three teams of scientists (from the United States, Britain, and Italy) each announced that the shroud was a clever forgery, except they estimated the time frame of its fabrication as between 1260 and 1390. Recent findings, however, propose a much earlier dating. Using calculations based on the fact that the shroud was involved in a fire in the 16th century, scientists now purport that the shroud is roughly 1,800 years old—a date that could realistically make it the shroud of Christ. In 1997, Avinoam Danin, a plant expert at the University of Jerusalem, analyzed threads from the linen and detected traces of pollen in the flax. This pollen was believed to have dropped into the linen from flowers laid on the shroud. Danin stated that some of those species are found only in the Middle East.

The archbishop of Turin has presented the shroud to the Holy See, and the fact that the Vatican accepted it as a holy relic has increased some world belief in its validity. However, the Vatican has refrained from pronouncing it "the true shroud." The shroud remains encased in a silver casket. Only two keys can unlock the casket, one held by the archbishop of Turin and the other by the Palatine cardinals, church seniors based permanently in the Vatican. The key unlocks only the casket—not the mystery of the shroud.

The west wing of the palace was damaged when fire spread through the chapel of the neighboring cathedral on April 12, 1997. Restoration of this wing could take years.

SHOPPING

The most adventurous shopping is at the **Gran Balôn,** an old-fashioned flea market set up every second Sunday in Piazza della Repubblica. Some of the merchandise peddled here is from the home of various immigrants.

Some of the best-known drinks in the world are manufactured in Turin. For the best sampling, head for **Paissa,** Piazza San Carlo 196 (☎ 011/562-8364), where among the wine and food items available, you'll find the best deals on Cinzano and Martini & Rossi vermouths.

ACCOMMODATIONS

Like Milan, Turin is an industrial city first and a tourist center second. Most of its hotels were built after 1945 with an eye toward modern comfort but not necessarily style.

EXPENSIVE

✪ **Jolly Hotel Prìncipi di Piemonte.** Via Gobetti 15, 10123 Torino. ☎ **212/685-3700** in the U.S. or 011/562-9693. Fax 011/562-0270. www.travel2000.com/h/europe/italy/turin/jollyptu.it/1.htm. 115 units. A/C MINIBAR TV TEL. 450,000L ($261) double; from 750,000L ($435) suite. Rates include breakfast. AE, DC, MC, V. Parking 33,000L ($19). Bus: 9.

A favorite choice of Fiat executives, this 10-story hotel is in the center of the city, near the rail station. It's owned by Italy's Jolly chain and dates from 1939, but some of Italy's finest architects and designers were involved in its wholesale revamping. The public rooms are grand in style and furnishings, with bas-relief ceilings, gold wall panels, silk draperies, Louis XVI–style chairs, and baroque marble sideboards. The guest rooms are traditionally furnished and maintained in state-of-the-art condition.

Dining/Diversions: There are both formal and informal dining rooms serving Piedmontese food, as well as a fashionable drinking lounge.

Amenities: Concierge, room service, laundry/dry cleaning, baby-sitting, secretarial services, access to nearby health club.

✪ **Villa Sassi.** Via Traforo del Pino 47, 10132 Torino. ☎ **011/898-0556.** Fax 011/898-0095. 16 units. A/C MINIBAR TV TEL. 400,000L ($232) double; 500,000L ($290) suite. Rates include breakfast. AE, DC, MC, V. Closed Aug. Tram: 15. Bus: 61.

This classic 17th century–style estate lies 4 miles east of the town center and is surrounded by park grounds and approached by a winding driveway. If you want tranquillity, head here. The impressive original architectural details are still intact, including the wooden staircase in the entrance hall. The drawing room features an overscale mural and life-sized sculpted baroque figures holding bronze torchiers. Each guest room has been individually decorated with both antiques and reproductions. The manager sees that the hotel is run in a personal way. The intimate drinking salon features draped red-velvet walls, a bronze chandelier, and low seat cushions.

Dining: See "Dining" below for a recommendation of the hotel restaurant, El Toulà–Villa Sassi.

Amenities: Concierge, room service, laundry, secretarial services.

MODERATE

Hotel Due Mondi. Via Saluzzo 3, 10125 Torino. ☎ **011/650-5084.** Fax 011/669-9383. 45 units. A/C TV TEL. Mon–Fri 160,000–230,000L ($93–$133) double; weekends 120,000L ($70) double. Rates include buffet breakfast. AE, DC, MC, V. Closed Aug 10–20. Bus: 52. Tram: 1 or 9.

Off Corso Vittorio Emanuele and within walking distance of Stazione di Porta Nuova, this little hotel is near the top for those seeking old-fashioned grace at an affordable price. In a sea of characterless hotels, it has a real Italian aura—not deluxe by any means, but with traditional furnishings. Everything is smartly outfitted, often in dark patterns and woods. Breakfast is the only meal served, but there are many restaurants nearby. Amenities include a concierge, room service, dry cleaning/laundry, and secretarial services.

INEXPENSIVE

Hotel Genio. Corso Vittorio Emanuele II 47, 10125 Torino. ☎ **011/650-5771.** Fax 011/650-8264. www.hotelres.it. E-mail: hotel.genio@torino.alpcom.it. 109 units. A/C MINIBAR TV TEL. Mon–Thurs 220,000L ($128) double; Fri–Sun 170,000L ($99) double. Rates include breakfast. AE, DC, MC, V. Parking 20,000L ($12).

Built at the end of the 19th century, this four-story hotel in the center of town was renovated into a streamlined modern format in 1990. Set close to the rail station, its accommodations contain a comfortable blend of contemporary and early 20th-century furniture and have double-paned windows for soundproofing.

Hotel Piemontese. Via Berthollet 21, 10125 Torino. ☎ **011/669-8101.** Fax 011/669-0571. www.hotelres.it. E-mail: hotel.piemontese@torino.alpcom.it. 40 units. A/C MINI-BAR TV TEL. Mon–Thurs 220,000L ($128) double; 280,000L ($162) suite. Fri–Sun 150,000L ($87) double; 180,000L ($104) suite. Rates include breakfast. AE, DC, MC, V. Parking 15,000L ($9). Tram: 1, 9, or 18.

The Piemontese is in a 19th-century building near Stazione Centrale. The facade is covered with iron balconies and ornate stone trim. The restructured interior is well maintained, and the comfortable rooms and public places have undergone a complete restoration. Breakfast, taken in a sunny room, is the only meal served, but nearby restaurants are willing to offer ample fixed-price menus to guests of the Piemontese. Laundry and 24-hour room service are available. Guests can patronize a nearby sports center with a pool.

DINING

EXPENSIVE

Del Cambio. Piazza Carignano 2. ☎ **011/546-690.** Reservations required. Main courses 31,000–38,000L ($18–$22); fixed-price menu 95,000L ($55). AE, DC, MC, V. Mon–Sat 12:30–2:30pm and 8–10:30pm. PIEDMONTESE/MEDITERRANEAN.

Del Cambio is a classic restaurant where you dine amid a grand setting of white-and-gilt walls, crystal chandeliers, and gilt mirrors. Opened in 1757, it's the oldest restaurant in Turin—perhaps in all Italy. Statesman Camillo Cavour was a loyal patron, and his much-frequented corner is immortalized with a bronze medallion. The chef has received many culinary honors, and white truffles are featured in many of his specialties. The assorted fresh antipasti are excellent; the best pasta dish is the regional agnolotti piemontesi. Among the main dishes, the Agnolotti with truffles and the beef braised in Barolo wine deserve special praise. Some trademark specialties derive from very old recipes of the southwestern Alps: artichokes stewed with bone marrow and truffles; girello aromatizzato alla piemontese (flank steak marinated in sugar, salt, and aromatic herbs, sliced paper thin, and served with parmigiano and vegetables); and tonno di coniglio à la manière antica (rabbit).

✪ **El Toulà–Villa Sassi.** In the Villa Sassi hotel, Via Traforo del Pino 47. ☎ **011/898-0556.** Reservations required. Main courses 25,000–40,000L ($15–$23); fixed-price menu 90,000L ($52). AE, DC, MC, V. Mon–Sat noon–2pm and 8–10:30pm. Closed Aug, Dec 24, and Jan 6. Tram: 15. Bus: 61. PIEDMONTESE/INTERNATIONAL.

This spacious 17th-century villa is on the rise of a hill 4 miles east of the town center. The stylish antique-decorated place has seen the addition of a modern dining room, with glass walls extending toward the gardens (most of the tables have an excellent view). Some of the basic foodstuff is brought in from the villa's own farm—not only the vegetables, fruit, and butter but also the beef. For an appetizer, try the frog's legs cooked with broth-simmered rice, or fonduta (a Piedmont fondue with Fontina cheese and local white truffles). If it's featured, you may want to sample the prized specialty: camoscio in salmi—chamois (a goatlike antelope) prepared in a sauce of olive oil, anchovies, and garlic, laced with wine, and served with polenta. Other menu items worth noting are agnolotti pasta with a sauce of roasted veal and fresh tomatoes; *nodino di vitello* (roasted filet of veal) with rosemary and sage; monkfish baked in a crust of salt; and braised slices of sturgeon with orange-pepper-cinnamon sauce.

✪ **Vecchia Lanterna.** Corso Re Umberto 21. ☎ **011/537-047.** Reservations required. Main courses 20,000–40,000L ($12–$23); fixed-price menu 70,000–100,000L ($41–$58). DC, MC, V. Mon–Fri noon–3pm and 8pm–midnight, Sat 8pm–midnight. Closed Aug 10–20. Bus: 5, 61, or 67. PIEDMONTESE/INTERNATIONAL.

This is one of Turin's most popular upper-bracket restaurants and usually proves to be a rewarding experience. It's housed in a building from 1740. The bar area near the entrance has belle-epoque lighting fixtures, heavy gilt mirrors, ornate 19th-century furniture, and Oriental rugs over carpeting. The dining room evokes old Venice. The antipasti selection is a treat—king crab Venetian style, asparagus flan, pâté de foie gras, grilled snails on a skewer, and marinated trout. This could be followed by ravioli stuffed with duck and served with truffle sauce, your choice of risotto, or snail soup. Main courses change seasonally but often include goose-liver piccata on fresh mushrooms, sea bass Venetian style, or garnished frog's legs. The seafood grill is especially delectable—each element is prepared individually and then assembled.

MODERATE

✪ **Ristorante C'Era una Volta.** Corso Vittorio Emanuele II 41. ☎ **011/655-498.** Reservations required. Fixed-price menus 38,000–48,000L ($22–$28). AE, DC, MC, V. Mon–Sat 8:30pm–midnight. Closed Aug. PIEDMONTESE.

Near the Porta Nuova train station, this restaurant is entered from the busy street through carved doors; you take an elevator one floor above ground level. Because it adheres to classic Piedmontese cuisine, it's a good introduction to the food of the Italian alpine regions. The decor is in the typical Piedmontese style, with hanging copper pots and thick walls of stippled plaster. Fixed-price meals feature an aperitif, a choice of seven or eight antipasti, and two first and two main courses, with vegetables, dessert, and coffee. The fare includes polenta, crêpes, rabbit, and guinea fowl. The restaurant's name means "Once upon a time."

INEXPENSIVE

Caffè Torino. Piazza San Carlo 204. ☎ **011/545-118.** Main courses 18,000–25,000L ($10–$15). AE, DC, MC, V. Daily 7am–1am. Bus: 61. ITALIAN.

Opened in 1903, this famous coffeehouse is the best re-creation in Turin of the days of Vittorio Emanuele, set on one of the most elegant squares in northern Italy. It's decorated with faded frescoes, brass and marble inlays, and a somewhat battered 19th-century formality. The staff adheres to a confusing series of rules about where and when guests can and should be seated. There's a stand-up bar near the entrance, a rather formal dining room off to the side, and a cafe area with tiny tables and unhurried service.

Da Mauro. Via Maria Vittoria 21. ☎ **011/817-0604.** Reservations not accepted. Main courses 10,000–18,000L ($6–$10). No credit cards. Tues–Sun noon–2:30pm and 7:30–10pm. Closed July. Bus: 61. ITALIAN/TUSCAN.

Within walking distance of Piazza San Carlo, this place, the best of the town's affordable trattorie, is generally packed (everybody loves a bargain). The food is conventional but does have character; the chef borrows freely from most of the gastronomic centers of Italy, though the cuisine is mainly Tuscan. An excellent pasta specialty is the cannelloni. Most main dishes consist of well-prepared fish, veal, and poultry. The desserts are consistently enjoyable.

TURIN AFTER DARK

This city of Fiat is also the cultural center of northwestern Italy. Turin is a major stopover for concert artists performing between Genoa and Milan. The daily newspaper of Piedmont, *La Stampa,* lists complete details of current cultural events.

Classical music concerts are presented at the **Auditorium della RAI,** Via Rossini 15 (☎ 011/8800), throughout the year, though mainly in winter. Tickets are 30,000L to 55,000L ($17 to $32), depending on the production. Turin is also home to one of the country's leading opera houses, the **Teatro Regio,** Piazza Castello 215 (☎ 011/88-151). Concerts and leading ballets are also presented here. The box office (☎ 011/881-5241 or 011/881-5242) is open Tuesday to Sunday 10:30am to 6pm; closed in August. Tickets cost 20,000L to 250,000L ($12 to $145).

Opera and other classical productions are presented in summer outside the gardens of the **Palazzo Reale.** The last remaining government-subsidized (RAI) orchestra performs at Via Nizza 294. The **orchestra hall** (☎ 011/664-4111) is part of the extensive Lingotto exhibition/conference center that grew out of Fiat's first large-scale automobile assembly plant. Ticket prices vary for each performance.

The city's other nightlife is like a smaller version of urbanized Milan, with one of the most diverse collections of electronic options in northern Italy. **Alcatraz,** Manzani Po (☎ 011/836-900), is a hypermodern patchwork of avant-garde design and late-breaking music from virtually everywhere. An important competitor is **Discoteca Atlantide,** Via Monginevro 10 (☎ 011/936-7783), and a somewhat corny contender, **II Scoppiato,** Via Villarbasse 26 (☎ 011/338-567), where karaoke contests from local wanna-bes might intrigue or repel you. Another karaoke club worth a mention is **Luca's,** Via Fredour 26 (☎ 011/776-4604), where sports talk and karaoke contests bring out the exhibitionism of cinematic hopefuls. **Ziegfild Follies,** Via Pomba 7 (☎ 011/812-7395), offers disco music, restaurant service, and a bar where you might strike up a dialogue. The more punkish **Exit,** Via Barge 4C (☎ 011/434-8233), describes itself as a pub devoted to "trend music." Some (but not all) music here is performed by a roster of north Italian punkers, techno artists, and rockers.

2 Aosta: Capital of Valle d'Aosta

114 miles NW of Milan, 78 miles N of Turin, 463 miles NW of Rome

Founded by the Emperor Augustus, who called it Augusta Praetoria, the capital of Valle d'Aosta has lost much of its quaintness today. It's called the "Rome of the Alps," but that's just tourist propaganda. Aostanas today number about 40,000 and live in the shadow of the peaks of Mont Blanc and San Bernardo. The economy is increasingly dependent on tourism.

Lying as it does on a major artery, **Aosta** makes for an important stop, either for overnighting or as a base for exploring Valle d'Aosta or taking the cable car to the Conca di Pila, the mountain that towers over the town.

ESSENTIALS

GETTING THERE   Thirteen **trains** per day run directly from Turin to Aosta (trip time: 2 hours), costing 12,000L ($7) one-way. From Milan, the trip takes 4½ hours and costs 18,000L ($10) one-way; you must change trains at Chivasso. For information and schedules, call ☎ 0165/262-057 or 1478/88-088 toll free in Italy only. The train station is at Piazza Manzetti, only a 5-minute stroll over to the Piazza Chanoux, the very core of Aosta. Ten **buses** a day travel between Turin and Aosta (trip time: 2 hours), costing 12,500L ($7) one-way. There's another bus that departs at 9am that doesn't make a direct route, making for a slightly longer trip at 3½ hours. There are seven buses a day arriving from Milan (3½ hours), costing 20,500L ($12) one-way. For schedules and information, call ☎ **0165/262-027.**

If you've got a **car** and are coming from Turin, continue north along A5, which comes to an end just east of Aosta.

VISITOR INFORMATION   The **tourist office** is at Piazza Chanoux 8 (☎ **0165/ 236-627**), open Monday to Saturday 9am to 1pm and 3 to 8pm and Sunday 9am to 1pm.

EXPLORING AOSTA

The town's Roman ruins include the **Arch of Augustus,** built in 24 B.C., the date of the Roman founding of the town. Via Sant'Anselmo, part of the old city from the Middle Ages, leads to the arch. Even more impressive are the ruins of a **Roman theater,** reached by the Porta Pretoria, a major gateway built of huge blocks that dates from the 1st century B.C. The ruins are open year-round Monday to Friday 9am to 7pm; entrance is free. A **Roman forum** is today a small park with a crypt, lying off Piazza San Giovanni near the cathedral.

The town is also enriched by its medieval relics. The Gothic **Collegiata dei Santi Pietro e Orso,** directly off Via Sant'Anselmo (☎ **0165/262-026**), was founded in the 12th century and is characterized by its landmark Romanesque steeple. You can explore the crypt, but the cloisters, with capitals of some three dozen pillars depicting biblical scenes, are more interesting. The church is open Tuesday to Sunday: April to September 9am to 7pm and October to March 9:30am to noon and 2 to 5:30pm.

A SIDE TRIP TO A GREAT NATIONAL PARK

Aosta is a good base for exploring the ✪ **Parco Nazionale di Gran Paradiso,** five lake-filled valleys that in 1865 were a royal hunting ground of Vittorio Emanuele II. Even back then, long before the term *endangered species* was common, he awarded that distinction to the ibex, a nearly extinct species of mountain goat. In 1919, Vittorio Emanuele III gave the property to the Italian state, which established a national park in 1922. The park encompasses some 1,400 square miles of forest, pastureland, and alpine meadows, filled with not only ibex but also the chamois and other animals who roam wild.

The main gateway to the park is **Cogne,** a popular resort. The best time to visit is in June, when the wildflowers are at their most spectacular. You can get a sampling of this rare alpine fauna by visiting the **Giardino Alpino Paradiso,** near the village of Valnontey, a mile south of Cogne. It's open June 10 to September 10, daily 9:30am to 12:30pm and 2:30 to 6:30pm, charging an admission of 3,000L ($1.75) (free for children under 10). For information about the park, visit the **park headquarters** at Via Losanna 5 in Aosta (☎ **0165/44-126** or 011/817-1187). Cogne lies about 18 miles south of Aosta, reached along S35 and S507.

SHOPPING

Valle d'Aosta is known for its wood carvings and wrought-iron work. For a sampling, head for the permanent craft exhibits in the arcades of **Piazza Chanoux,** the center of Aosta. You're not expected to pay the first price quoted, so test your bargaining power. The big explosion of handcrafts, however, takes place the last 2 days in January, when alpine dwellers appear en masse to sell their handcrafts, mostly carved wood and stonework. Count yourself lucky if you pick up some handmade lace from neighboring Cogne. It's highly valued for its workmanship.

Valdostan handcrafts can be found at **IVAT,** Via Xavier de Maistre 1 (☎ 0165/41-462), where sculpture, bas-relief, and wrought iron are offered for sale. The shop owners can also provide you with a list of local furniture makers. Antique furniture and paintings are the domain of **Bessone,** Via Edouard Aubert 53 (☎ 0165/40-853), while **New Gallery,** Via Sant'Anselmo 115 (☎ 0165/40-929), features a more diverse selection of antiquated goods.

ACCOMMODATIONS

Hotel Le Pageot. Via Giorgio Carrel 31, 11100 Aosta. ☎ **0165/32-433.** Fax 0165/33-217. 18 units. TV TEL. 130,000L ($75) double. Breakfast 10,000L ($6). AE, DC, MC, V. Parking 10,000L ($6).

Built in 1985, this is one of the best-value hotels in town. It has a modern angular facade of brown brick with big windows and floors crafted from carefully polished slabs of mountain granite. The rooms are clean and functional, and the well-lit public areas include a breakfast room and a TV room (but no restaurant). The hotel's name is antiquated local dialect for "bed."

Hotel Roma. Via Torino 7, 11100 Aosta. ☎ **0165/41-000.** Fax 0165/32-404. 33 units. TV TEL. 106,000–135,000L ($62–$78) double. Breakfast 10,000L ($6). AE, DC, MC, V. Parking 10,000L ($6).

Silvio Lepri and Graziella Nicoli are the owners of this hotel, which is on a peaceful alley in a cubist-style white stucco building; it's surrounded by the balconies and windows of what appear to be private apartments. The rooms are well maintained, modern, and simple, with touches of varnished pine and modern tiled baths. The entrance is at the top of an exterior concrete stairwell. The public rooms include a warmly paneled bar area, big windows, and a homelike decor filled with bright colors and rustic accessories.

Hotel Valle d'Aosta. Corso Ivrea 146, 11100 Aosta. ☎ **0165/41-845.** Fax 0165/236-660. 104 units. MINIBAR TV TEL. 170,000–230,000L ($99–$133) double. Rates include breakfast. AE, DC, MC, V. Closed Dec 1–27. Free garage parking.

This modern hotel with its zigzag concrete facade is one of Aosta's leading choices. Located on a busy road leading from the old town to the entrance of the autostrada, it's a prominent stop for motorists using the Great St. Bernard and Mont Blanc tunnels into Italy. The sunny lobby has beige stone floors, paneled walls, deep leather chairs, and an oversized bar. All guest rooms have double windows and views angled toward the mountains. The Ristorante Le Foyer on the premises, under a different management, is reviewed under "Dining," below. The hotel also offers room service, baby-sitting, and laundry.

DINING

Ristorante Le Foyer. Corso Ivrea 146. ☎ **0165/32-136.** Reservations recommended. Main courses 17,000–30,000L ($10–$17); fixed-price menu 38,000L ($22). AE, DC, MC, V. Wed–Mon 12:15–1:50pm; Wed–Sun 7:30–9:30pm. Closed Jan 8–25 and July 5–20. VALDOSTAN/INTERNATIONAL.

This restaurant sits beside a traffic artery on the outskirts of town. The full Valdostan meals you get are both flavorful and affordable. In a wood-paneled dining room illuminated by a wall of oversized windows, you can dine on specialties like salmon trout, beef tagliata with balsamic vinegar, vegetable flan with fondue, or fresh noodles with smoked salmon and asparagus. There's also a good selection of French and Italian wines.

Ristorante Piemonte. Via Porta Pretoria 13. ☎ **0165/40-111.** Main courses 22,000–40,000L ($13–$23); fixed-price menu 22,000–50,000L ($13–$29). MC, V. Sat–Thurs noon–3pm and 7–10pm. Closed Feb. VALDOSTAN/INTERNATIONAL.

On a relatively traffic-free street, this is a charming unpretentious trattoria with all the authenticity of its 250-year-old premises. It's a staple of the town's restaurant scene, known for its savory versions of age-old mountain recipes. Surrounded by vaulted ceilings and terra-cotta floors, you can order at least four set menus, all featuring either truffles or mushrooms, when they're in season. Other tried-and-true favorites are heaping platters of charcuterie, cannelloni in the style of the chef, several versions of fondue, risotto with roasted pork, and an array of desserts that could include fresh strawberries from local suppliers. Especially interesting is roast chamoix prepared with a red-wine Barolo sauce.

Vecchia Aosta. Piazza Porta Pretoria 4. ☎ **0165/361-186.** Reservations recommended. Main courses 18,000–32,000L ($10–$19); fixed-price menus 40,000–70,000L ($23–$41). AE, DC, MC, V. Thurs–Tues noon–3pm and 7:30–10pm. Closed Feb 15–30 and Nov 15–30. VALDOSTAN/INTERNATIONAL.

The most unusual restaurant in Aosta lies in the narrow niche between the inner and outer Roman walls of the Porta Pretoria. It's in an old structure that, though modernized, still bears evidence of the superb building techniques of the Romans, whose chiseled stones are sometimes visible between patches of modern wood and plaster. Full meals are served on at least two levels in a labyrinth of nooks and isolated crannies and may include homemade ravioli, beef filet with mushrooms, pepperoni flan, eggs with cheese fondue and truffles, tournedos Rossini, roasted duck with tomatoes and orange sauce, and a cheese-laden version of Valdostan fondue.

AOSTA AFTER DARK

You won't lack for diversions in this alpine capital. The town's leading disco is **La Compagnia dei Motori,** Piazza Arco d'Augusto (☎ **0165/363-484**), where a partially metallic interior includes a network of dance floors, bars, and a deserved self-image as the trendiest and most happening disco-of-the-minute. The **Sweet Rock Café,** Via Piccolo St. Bernardo 18 (☎ **0165/553-251**), caters to a 25-to-45 crowd, featuring rock and jazz with live music on Mondays. At the **Old Distillery Pub,** Via Prés Fossés 7 (☎ **0165/230-511**), taps dispense foaming mugs full of lager and stout in a room whose decor and ambience was inspired by Olde England and its pub traditions.

3 Courmayeur & Entrèves: Skiing & Alpine Beauty

COURMAYEUR

Courmayeur, a 22-mile drive northwest of Aosta, is Italy's best all-around ski resort, with two "high seasons," attracting alpine excursionists in summer and ski enthusiasts in winter. Its popularity was given a considerable boost with the opening of the Mont Blanc road tunnel, feeding traffic from France into Italy (estimated trip time: 20 minutes). The cost for an average car is 43,000L ($25) one-way or 145L (10¢) from the French side.

With Europe's highest mountain in the background, Courmayeur sits snugly in a valley. Directly to the north of the resort is the alpine village of Entrèves, sprinkled with a number of chalets (some of which take in paying guests).

ESSENTIALS

GETTING THERE   Proceed to Aosta by **rail.** In Aosta, you can take any of 11 **buses** leaving daily for Courmayeur from the bus terminal, Piazza Narbonne (☎ **0165/841-305**), adjacent to the train station. There's a bus every hour, costing 4,800L ($2.80) each way or 8,200L ($4.75) round-trip. Transit time is 1 hour. Departures are daily, beginning in the early morning, with the last departure from

Aosta scheduled for 10:15pm. **Motorists** should continue west from Aosta on Route 26 heading toward Monte Bianco.

VISITOR INFORMATION   The **tourist office**r for Courmayeur is on Piazzale Monte Bianco (☎ **0165/842-060**), open Monday to Friday 9am to 12:30pm and 3 to 6:30pm and Saturday to Sunday 9am to 7:15pm.

RIDING ACROSS THE GLACIERS

In the vicinity of Courmayeur, you can take a cable-car lift—one of the most unusual in Europe—across Mont Blanc all the way to Chamonix, France. It's a ride across glaciers that's altogether frightening and thrilling and is for steel-nerved adventure seekers only. Departures on the **Funivie Monte Bianco** are from La Palud, near Entrèves. The three-stage cable car heads for the intermediate stations, Pavillon and Rifugio Torino, before reaching its peak at Punta Helbronner at 11,254 feet. At the latter, you'll be on the doorstep of the glacier and the celebrated 11½-mile Vallée Blanche ski run to Chamonix, France, usually opened at the beginning of February every year. The round-trip price for the cable ride is 48,000L ($28), plus 290L (15¢) from the French side. Departures are every 20 minutes, and service is daily 8am to 1pm and 2 to 5pm. At the top is a terrace for sunbathing, a bar, and a snack bar. Bookings are possible at **Esercizio Funivie,** Frazione La Palud 22 (☎ **0165/89-925**).

ACCOMMODATIONS

Courmayeur has a number of attractive hotels, many of which are open seasonally. Always reserve ahead in high season, either summer or winter.

Expensive

Grand Hotel Royal e Golf. Via Roma 87, 11013 Courmayeur. ☎ **0165/846-787.** Fax 0165/842-093. 91 units. A/C MINIBAR TV TEL. 300,000–600,000L ($174–$348) double; 500,000–1,000,000L ($290–$580) suite. Rates include breakfast. AE, DC, MC, V. Closed Apr 27–June 20 and Sept 20–Nov. Parking 18,000L ($10) inside, free outside.

Built in 1950, this hotel is in a dramatic location above the heart of the resort between the most fashionable pedestrian walkway and a heated outdoor pool. As a hotel, it's tops except for the more tranquil and elegant Pavillon (below). Much of its angular facade is covered with rocks, so it fits in neatly with the mountainous landscape. The rooms are generally large, with built-in furnishings and streamlined baths.

Dining/Diversions: A large comfortable lounge is flanked by a bar and a dais with a pianist nightly in season. The deluxe dining room, La Grill dell'Hotel Royal e Golf, is reviewed under "Dining." There's also a regular dining room open daily.

Amenities: Room service, baby-sitting, laundry/valet, hydromassage, pool, sauna, Jacuzzi, solarium, Turkish bath.

Hotel Pavillon. Strada Regionale 60, 11013 Courmayeur. ☎ **0165/846-120.** Fax 0165/846-122. 60 units. MINIBAR TV TEL. 370,000–620,000L ($215–$360) double; 520,000–820,000L ($302–$476) suite for two. Rates include half board. AE, DC, MC, V. Closed May–June 15 and Oct 2–Dec 2. Valet parking 12,000L ($7).

This is easily the swankest and most important hotel at the resort, despite its small size. Many of the guests warming themselves around the stone fireplace are from England, Germany, and France, which adds a continental allure. Built in 1965, renovated in 1990, and designed like a chalet, the hotel is a 4-minute walk south of Courmayeur's inner-city pedestrian zone. The rooms, entered through leather-covered doors, feature built-in furniture and a conservative decor; all but two have private balconies. The hotel is only a short walk from the funicular that goes to Plan Checrouit.

Dining/Diversions: The half-board requirement is no hardship, as the hotel serves market-fresh ingredients deftly prepared by a skilled kitchen staff in its Grill Le Bistroquet (winter only) or its regular year-round restaurant. Skiers and others are also fond of gathering at its chic rendezvous, the American Bar.

Amenities: Concierge, room service, laundry/dry cleaning, twice-daily maid service, baby-sitting, secretarial services; hydrotherapy facilities, solarium, covered pool.

Moderate

✪ **Palace Bron.** Località Plan Gorret 41, 11013 Courmayeur. ☎ **0165/846-742.** Fax 0165/844-015. 27 units. TV TEL. 260,000–360,000L ($151–$209) double; 550,000–690,000L ($319–$400) suite. AE, DC, MC, V. Closed Easter–July 1 and mid-Sept to Dec 8.

About 1¼ miles from the heart of the resort, this tranquil oasis is one of the plushest addresses in town. The white-walled chalet is the most noteworthy building on the pine-studded hill, and it has a commanding view over Courmayeur and the mountains beyond. Guests are made to feel like members of a baronial household. The rooms are handsomely furnished and well maintained. Winter visitors appreciate its proximity to the many ski lifts. Walking from the chalet to the center of town is a good way to exercise after formal dining on the kitchen's filling international cuisine. The hotel's piano bar is especially lively in winter, hosting skiers from all over Europe and America. Also offered are room service, baby-sitting, laundry, and valet.

Inexpensive

Hotel Bouton d'Or. Strada Traforo del Monte Bianco 10 (off Piazzale Monte Bianco), 11013 Courmayeur. ☎ **0165/846-729.** Fax 0165/842-152. 35 units. TV TEL. 150,000–190,000L ($87–$110) double. AE, DC, MC, V. Rates include breakfast. Closed June and Nov.

Named after the buttercups that cover the surrounding hills in summer, this hotel is owned by the Casale family, who built it in 1970 and renovated it in 1990. It features an exterior painted yellow and gray, stone trim, and a flagstone roof. French windows lead from the well-maintained, comfortable rooms onto small balconies. The hotel is about 100 yards (toward the Mont Blanc Tunnel) from the most popular restaurant in Courmayeur, Le Vieux Pommier, which is owned by the same family. The hotel also has a garage, sauna, solarium, and garden.

Hotel Courmayeur. Via Roma 158, 11013 Courmayeur. ☎ **0165/846-732.** Fax 0165/845-125. 26 units. TV TEL. 90,000–170,000L ($52–$99) per person double. Rates include half board. AE, DC, V. Closed Apr 6–June 21 and Oct–Nov.

The Hotel Courmayeur, in the center of the resort, was built so most of its rooms would have unobstructed views of the nearby mountains. It's a small, unpretentious hotel with immaculate rooms and low prices. A number of the rooms, furnished in the mountain chalet style, also have wooden balconies. Even nonguests can dine on regional food in the hotel restaurant.

Hotel del Viale. Viale Monte Bianco 74, 11013 Courmayeur. ☎ **0165/846-712.** Fax 0165/844-513. www.valdigne.com/courmayeur/viale. E-mail: viale@courmayeur.valdigne.com. 23 units. MINIBAR TV TEL. 120,000–210,000L ($70–$122) per person double. Rates include half board. AE, DC, MC, V. Closed May and Nov. Parking 10,000L ($6) inside, free outside.

This old-style mountain chalet at the edge of town is a good place to enjoy the indoor/outdoor life. There's a front terrace with tables set under trees in fair weather, and the rooms inside are cozy and pleasant in the chillier months. In winter, guests can gather in the taproom to enjoy après-ski life, drinking at pine tables and warming their feet before the open fire. The clean and comfortable guest rooms, with natural wood, have a rustic air.

DINING

Expensive

✪ **La Grill dell'Hotel Royal e Golf.** In the Grand Hotel Royal e Golf, Via Roma 87. ☎ **0165/846-787.** Reservations required in winter. Fixed-price menus 75,000–85,000L ($44–$49). AE, DC, MC, V. Tues–Sun 8–9:30pm. Closed Apr 27–June 20 and Sept 20–Dec 1. VALDOSTAN.

On the lobby level of this previously recommended hotel is the most fashionable (and most expensive) restaurant in town. It has only 30 places for diners interested in the cultivated cuisine inspired by the legacy of Harry Cipriani, of Harry's Bar fame. It's sparsely decorated, with a carved Gothic screen from an English church standing against one wall. The relatively simple but fresh and well-prepared dishes include pasta e fagioli, carpaccio, risotto with radicchio, and rosettes of veal Cipriani style. The hotel's foie gras—served on a brioche—is rumored to be the best anywhere. The menu changes daily.

Inexpensive

✪ **Cadran Solaire.** Via Roma 122. ☎ **0165/844-609.** Reservations required. Main courses 20,000–35,000L ($12–$20). AE, DC, MC, V. Wed–Sun 12:30–2pm and 7:30–11pm. Closed May and Oct. VALDOSTAN.

In the center of town is its most interesting restaurant, named after the sundial (cadran solaire) embellishing the upper floor of its chalet facade and owned by Leo Garin, whose La Maison de Filippo (see under Entrèves, below) is Valle d'Aosta's most popular restaurant. Try to come for a before-dinner drink in the vaulted bar; its massive stones were crafted into almost alarmingly long spans in the 16th century using construction techniques the Romans perfected. A few steps away, the rustically elegant dining room has its own stone fireplace, a beamed ceiling, and wide plank floors. Specialties change with the season but are likely to include warm goat cheese blended with a salad, noodles with seasonal vegetables, a baked cheese and spinach casserole, and duck breast with plums. The desserts are sumptuous.

Leone Rosso. Via Roma 73. ☎ **0165/846-726.** Reservations recommended. Main courses 20,000–38,000L ($12–$22); fixed-price menus 35,000–60,000L ($20–$35). AE, MC, V. and Oct–May Sat–Sun noon–2:30pm and 7–10pm; June–Sept Tues–Sun noon–2:30pm and 7–10pm. VALDOSTAN.

Leone Rosso is in a stone- and timber-fronted house in a slightly isolated courtyard, a few paces from the busy pedestrian traffic of Via Roma. It serves well-prepared Valdostan specialties, like fondues, a thick and steaming regional version of minestrone, tagliatelle with mushrooms and en papillote, and a selection of rich, creamy desserts. Some meats you grill yourself at your table. This place is not to be confused with the Red Lion pub.

Le Vieux Pommier. Piazzale Monte Bianco 25. ☎ **0165/842-281.** Reservations recommended. Main courses 23,000–28,000L ($13–$16); fixed-price menu 28,000L ($16). AE, DC, MC, V. Tues–Sun noon–2pm and 7–9:30pm. Closed Oct and 10–15 days in May. VALDOSTAN/INTERNATIONAL.

The hacked-up trunk of the "old apple tree" that was cut down to build this place was re-erected inside and serves as the sculptural focal point of the restaurant, located on the main square. Filmmaker Ingmar Bergman, like everyone else, has appreciated the exposed stone, the copper-covered bar, and the thick pine tables arranged in an octagon. Today Alessandro Casale, the son of the founder, directs the kitchen assisted by his wife, Lydia. Your meal might consist of three kinds of dried alpine beef, followed by noodles in ham-studded cream sauce or an arrangement of three pastas or four fondues, including a regional variety with Fontina, milk, and egg yolks. Then it's on to chicken suprême en papillote (parchment) or four or five unusual meat dishes cooked mountain style, right at your table.

Courmayeur After Dark

Not to be confused with a less desirable bar of the same name at the end of the same street, the **American Bar,** Via Roma 43 (☎ **0165/846-707**), is one of the most popular bars on the après-ski circuit. It's rowdy and sometimes outrageous but most often a lot of fun. Most guests end up in one of the two rooms, beside either an open fireplace or a long crowded bar. The place is open in winter daily 9am to 1:30am; it's sometimes closed on Tuesday, but never in ski season. The **Café della Posta,** Via Roma 51 (☎ **0165/842-272**), the oldest cafe in Courmayeur, is as sedate as its neighbor, the American Bar, is unruly. Many guests prefer to remain in the warmly decorated bar area, never venturing into the large salon with a glowing fireplace. The place changes its stripes throughout the day, opening as a morning cafe at 8:30am.

ENTRÈVES

Even older than Courmayeur, **Entrèves** is an ancient community that's small and compact, really a mountain village of wood houses. Many discriminating visitors prefer its alpine charm to the more bustling resort of Courmayeur. It's reached by a steep and narrow road. Many gourmets book in here just to enjoy the regional fare, for which the village is known.

Just outside Entrèves on the main highway lies the **Val Veny cable car,** which skiers take in winter to reach the Courmayeur lift system.

Entrèves is 2 miles north of Courmayeur (signposted off Route 26). Buses from the center of Courmayeur run daily to Entrèves. For more information, contact Courmayeur's tourist office (above).

Accommodations

✪ **La Grange.** Strada La Brenva 1, 11013 Courmayeur–Entrèves. ☎ **0165/869-733.** Fax 0165/869-744. 23 units. MINIBAR TV TEL. 200,000L ($116) double; from 400,000L ($232) suite. Rates include breakfast. AE, DC, MC, V. Closed May–June and Oct–Nov.

This will be one of the first buildings you'll see as you enter this rustic alpine village. A few foundation stones date from the 1300s, when this was a barn. What you'll see today is a stone building whose balconies and gables are outlined against the steep hillside into which it's constructed. The Berthod family transformed a dilapidated property into a rustic and comfortable hotel in 1979, surrounding it with summer flower beds. It's enthusiastically managed by Bruna Berthod Perri and her nephew, Stefano Pellin. The unusual decor includes a collection of antique tools and a series of thick timbers, stucco, and exposed stone walls. There's a piano in the bar, plus an exercise room and sauna. A rich breakfast is the only meal served, but several restaurants are nearby.

Dining

La Maison de Filippo. Frazione Entrèves di Courmayeur. ☎ **0165/869-797.** Reservations required. Fixed-price menu 50,000–60,000L ($29–$35). MC, V. Wed–Mon 12:30–2:30pm and 7:30–10:30pm. Closed June and Nov–Dec 20. VALDOSTAN.

This colorful tavern, the creation of Leo Garin, is for those who enjoy a festive atmosphere and bountiful regional food. The three-story open hallway seems like a rustic barn, with an open worn wooden staircase leading to the various dining nooks. You pass casks of nuts, baskets of fresh fruits, bowls of salad, fruit tarts, and loaves of freshly baked bread. The outdoor summer beer garden has a full view of Mont Blanc. Mr. Garin features local specialties on an all-you-can-eat basis, earning the place the nickname "Chalet of Gluttony." A typical meal might begin with a selection of antipasti, followed by a 2-foot-long platter of about 60 varieties of sausage. Next comes a parade of pasta dishes. For a main course, you can pick everything from fondue to camoscio (chamois meat) to trout with almond-butter sauce. Huge hunks of coarse country bread are served from a wicker basket the size of a laundry bin.

Dining & Accommodations

La Brenva. La Palud 12, Frazione Entrèves di Courmayeur, 11013 Courmayeur–Entrèves. ☎ **0165/869-780.** Fax 0165/869-726. Reservations required. Main courses 25,000–32,000L ($15–$19); fixed-price menus 30,000–45,000L ($17–$26). AE, MC, V. Tues–Sun 12:30–2pm and 7:30–10:30pm. Closed May and Oct. VALDOSTAN/FRENCH.

Many skiers make a special trek to Entrèves just for a drink at the old-fashioned bar of this hotel and restaurant. The copper espresso machine topped by a brass eagle and many of the other decorative accessories are at least a century old. The core of the building was constructed in 1884 as a hunting lodge for Victor Emmanuel. In 1897 it became a hotel, and in 1980 the owners enlarged its stone foundations with the addition of extra rooms and a larger eating area. The restaurant consists of exposed stone walls, wide flooring planks, hunting trophies, copper pots, and straw-bottomed chairs. Fires burn in winter, and many diners prefer an apéritif in the unusual salon, within view of the well-chosen paintings. On any given day the menu could include prosciutto, fonduta for two, carbonada with polenta, scaloppine with fresh mushrooms, Valle d'Aostan beefsteak, and zabaglione for dessert.

Each of the 12 simple and comfortable guest rooms has a bath, TV, phone, and lots of peace and quiet. Many have covered loggias. With breakfast included, they rent for 100,000L to 150,000L ($58 to $87) per person. The inn takes a vacation in either May or June.

Genoa & the Italian Riviera

13

For years the retreat of the wintering wealthy, the **Italian Riviera** now enjoys a broad base of tourism. Even in winter (the average January temperature hovers around 50°F) the Riviera is popular, though not for swimming. The protection provided by the Ligurian Apennines looming in the background makes the balmy weather possible.

The winding coastline of the Rivieras, particularly the one stretching from the French border to San Remo, is especially familiar to moviegoers as the background for countless flicks about sports-car racing, jewel thieves, and spies. Over the years Italy's northwestern coast has seen the famous and the infamous, especially literary figures: Percy Shelley (who drowned off the shore), Gabriele d'Annunzio, Lord Byron, Katherine Mansfield, George Sand, and D. H. Lawrence.

The Mediterranean vegetation is characterized by pines, olives, citrus trees, and cypresses. The western Riviera—the **Riviera di Ponente,** from the border to Genoa—is sometimes known as the Riviera of Flowers because of its profusion of blossoms. Starting at the French border, Ventimiglia is the gateway city to Italy. Along the way you'll encounter the first big resort, Bardighera, followed by San Remo, the major center of Riviera tourism.

Genoa, dividing the Riviera in two, is the capital of Liguria. It's a big bustling port that has charm for those willing to take the time to seek out its treasures. On the western Riviera—the **Riviera di Levante**—are three dramatically situated small resorts, Rapallo, Santa Margherita, and Portofino (the favorite of the yachting set).

The Ligurians are famous for ceramics, lace, silver and gold filigree, marble, velvet, olive wood, and macramé, and all the towns and villages of the region hold outdoor markets either in the main square or on the waterfront. Haggling is a way of life, so good deals do exist, but English speakers be warned that prices may not fall as low as they would if you were negotiating in the local dialect.

1 San Remo: A Mini-Vegas by the Sea

10 miles E of the French border, 85 miles SW of Genoa, 397 miles NW of Rome

The reputation of **San Remo** has grown ever since Emperor Frederick William wintered in a villa here. In time, Empress Maria Alexandrova, wife of Czar Alexander II, showed up, trailed by a Russian colony that included Tchaikovsky, who composed the Fourth Symphony here

Driving Through the Italian Riviera

Here's how to link together the region's highlights if you have a car.

Day 1: Let **San Remo,** east of Monaco and the French resort of Menton, be your gateway to the Italian Riviera. The capital of the Riviera di Fiori (Riviera of Flowers), San Remo evokes an Edwardian aura and has been fashionable since the turn of the century, when it attracted German and Russian aristocrats. Visit its Mercato dei Fiori (Flower Market), test your luck at its Municipal Casino, and explore the old town. For a panoramic view of the coast (sometimes you can see as far as Cannes), take the funicular to Monte Bignone. Overnight in San Remo.

Day 2: Leave San Remo and head for **Genoa.** A good stop en route would be **Savona,** the largest town on the Riviera di Ponente. From Savona it's a 29-mile drive to Genoa, Italy's major port. Overnight there.

Day 3: Since you'll have had little time to explore the port, spend this day taking in its attractions, including a stroll down Via Garibaldi and a visit to its most important museums, like the Galleria Nazionale. Take a boat tour of the port and spend another night.

Day 4: From Genoa, drive south along the coast for about 17 miles until reaching **Rapallo,** one of the most fashionable resorts. Take a cable car to the Sanctuary of Montallegro and walk along Monte Rosa for one of the most panoramic views of the Ligurian coastline available. Consider a summer boat trip to Portofino.

Day 5: To avoid checking in and out of another hotel, you can base in Rapallo and use it as a center for exploring **Santa Margherita Ligure,** only 19 miles east of Genoa. It's a rival of Rapallo, opening onto the Gulf of Tigullio. After exploring the town, drive about 4 miles south to **Portofino,** where you'll want to spend the entire day, exploring the village and its hillsides and then dining in a local restaurant before returning to Rapallo for the night.

during a stay in 1878. Alfred Nobel, the father of dynamite and the founder of the famous prizes in Stockholm, died here in 1896.

The flower-filled resort today has been considerably updated, and its casino, race track, 18-hole golf course, and deluxe Royal Hotel still attract the fashionable on occasion. But mostly it's a "mini-Vegas by the sea." Its climate is the mildest on the western Riviera, and the town offers miles on miles of cultivated beaches.

ESSENTIALS

GETTING THERE   Since San Remo lies on the coast between Ventimiglia and Imperia—6 miles from each—it's a major stop for many **trains.** A train leaves Genoa heading for the French border once per hour, stopping in San Remo. Rome is 8 hours by train from San Remo. For train information and schedules, call ☎ **01478/88-088** toll free in Italy only.

If you've arrived in Italy from France in the gateway town of Ventimiglia, you'll find a **bus** leaving for San Remo about every 15 minutes. The trip takes 30 minutes and costs 3,000L ($1.80) one-way. On Saturday a bus departs Milan for San Remo at 8am, arriving at 1:45pm. For information, call ☎ **0184/502-030.**

If you've got a **car,** A10, running east-west along the Riviera, is the fastest way to reach San Remo from either the French border or Genoa.

The Italian Riviera

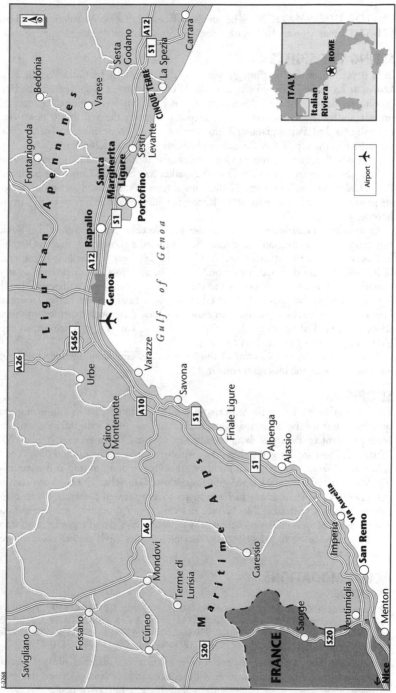

VISITOR INFORMATION   The **tourist office** is on Corso Nuvoloni (☎ 0184/ 571-571), open Monday to Saturday 8am to 7pm and Sunday 9am to 1pm.

SEEING THE SIGHTS

Even if you're just passing through, you might want to visit **La Città Vecchia** (also known as **La Pigna**), the old city atop the hill. Far removed in spirit from the burgeoning sterile-looking town down near the water, old San Remo blithely ignores the present, and its tiny houses on narrow, steep lanes capture the past. In the new town, the palm-flanked **Passeggiata dell'Imperatrice** attracts promenaders. For a scenic view, drive to the top of **San Romolo** and **Monte Bignone** (4,265 feet).

Daily 6 to 8am from October to June, you can visit the most famous flower market in Italy, the **Mercato di Fiori,** held in the market hall between Corso Garibaldi and Piazza Colombo. You'll see some 20,000 tons of roses, mimosa, and carnations, which are grown in the balmy climate of the Riviera in winter before shipment to all parts of Europe.

As an offbeat excursion you can visit **Bussana Vecchia,** 5 miles west of San Remo (signposted). Too well inhabited to really be considered a ghost town, Bussana Vecchia is, however, a rather unofficial town. A substantial 1887 earthquake killed thousands of its residents and destroyed many buildings. The survivors, too frightened to stay, started a new Bussana 1¼ miles closer to the sea. The original town, with several buildings still standing, has gradually been taken over by artist/squatters who've revamped interior spaces—but not exteriors, no reason to draw that much attention to themselves—and hooked up water, electricity, and phones. They live off their art, so haggling can get you a good deal on a painting.

As a bit of trivia, one survivor of the 1887 quake, Giovanno Torre detto Merlo, went on to invent the ice-cream cone in 1902.

SHOPPING

Frankly, San Remo is too sophisticated a resort to assume that its sun-loving and sybaritic guests will be interested in acquiring a suitcase filled with folkloric artifacts. More prevalent are the stylish boutiques that line the town's busiest thoroughfare, **Via Matteotti.** Most are devoted to high-style Milan-inspired beachwear and slinky cocktail dresses. Wander up and down the street, making it a point to stop at **Annamoda,** Via Matteotti 141 (☎ 0184/505-550), or **Moro Gabrielle,** Corso Matteotti 126 (☎ 0184/531-614), both of which sell sporty-looking as well as formal garments for men and women, with labels like Versace and YSL. If you absolutely can't live without another piece of local craft, one noteworthy shop sells crystal and ceramics: **Pon Pon,** Via Matteotti 140 (☎ 0184/509-069), which prides itself on its collection of Svarowski crystal.

ACCOMMODATIONS
EXPENSIVE

✪ **Royal Hotel.** Corso dell'Imperatrice 80, 18038 San Remo. ☎ 0184/5391. Fax 0184/ 661-445. www.lhw.com/sanremo/royal.htm. 146 units. A/C MINIBAR TV TEL. 320,000– 525,000L ($186–$305) double; 565,000–990,000L ($328–$574) suite. Rates include buffet breakfast. AE, DC, MC, V. Closed Oct 10–Dec 18. Parking 17,000–30,000L ($10–$17).

Though long past its heyday, this resort hotel is still a formidable challenger because of its size and facilities. It's complete with terraces and gardens, a heated free-form saltwater pool, a forest of palms, bright flowers, and hideaway nooks for shade. Activity centers around the garden terrace—little emphasis is put on the public lounges decked out in grand old dowager style. The guest rooms vary considerably:

Some are tennis-court size with private balconies, many have sea views, and others face the hills. The furnishings range from traditional to modern. The luxurious fifth-floor rooms have the best views and are more expensive.

Dining/Diversions: There's an American bar with piano music nightly. Lunch is served in fair weather on the veranda. The more formal restaurant features regional and international cuisine.

Amenities: Room service, baby-sitting, laundry/valet, heated pool, sauna, solarium, minigolf, gym, tennis court, facilities for children, hairdresser, 18-hole golf course and horseback riding nearby.

MODERATE

✪ **Grand Hotel Londra.** Corso Matuzia 2, 18038 San Remo. ☎ **0184/668-000.** Fax 0184/668-073. 145 units. MINIBAR TV TEL. 290,000–310,000L ($168–$180) double. Rates include breakfast. AF, DC, MC, V. Closed Sept 30–Dec 18. Free parking.

Built around 1900 as a two-story hotel, this place was later expanded into the imposing structure you see today. Located within a 10-minute walk of the commercial district, it's in a park with a sea view. Like the Royal, it continues to coast on its past glory. The well-furnished interior is filled with framed engravings, porcelain in illuminated cases, gilt mirrors, and brass detailing. Many of the guest rooms have wrought-iron balconies, and some are air-conditioned. There's also a bar and an outdoor pool.

Hotel Méditerranée. Corso Cavallotti 76, 18038 San Remo. ☎ **0184/571-000.** Fax 0184/541-106. 65 units. A/C MINIBAR TV TEL. 250,000–300,000L ($145–$174) double; 400,000L ($232) suite. Rates include breakfast. Children staying in parents' room receive a 30% discount. AE, DC, MC, V. Parking 35,000L ($20) in garage, free outside.

The traffic in front of this steel-and-glass structure can be profuse, especially in peak season, but once you're inside or in the rear garden with its Olympic-sized pool, you'll scarcely be aware of it. Built about a century ago, the hotel received its present appearance in 1974 during a tasteful modernization. Today it competes effectively with the Grand Hotel. Some of the public rooms retain signs of their turn-of-the-century grandeur and are filled with potted plants, polished floors, and modern sculptures. The guest rooms are modernized and well furnished.

Hotel Miramare Continental Palace. Corso Matuzia 9, 18038 San Remo. ☎ **0184/667-601.** Fax 0184/667-655. 66 units. TEL. 270,000–330,000L ($157–$191) double; 430,000–600,000L ($249–$348) suite. Full board 100,000L ($58) per person. AE, DC, MC, V. Free parking.

A curved drive leads past palmettos to this traditional building set behind semitropical gardens bordering a busy thoroughfare. After passing through the well-appointed public rooms, you'll discover a seaside garden with sculptures and plenty of verdant hideaways. The guest rooms are clean and comfortable; some are in a neighboring annex with views of the garden. The hotel has a good restaurant specializing in Ligurian seafood. A covered saltwater pool is in one of the outbuildings, and there's also a sauna, solarium, and gym.

Suite Hotel Nyala. Strada Solaro 134, 18038 San Remo. ☎ **0184/667-668.** Fax 0184/666-059. www.nyalahotel.com. E-mail: nyala@sistel.it. 80 units. A/C TV TEL. 210,000–320,000L ($122–$186) double; 230,000–420,000L ($133–$244) suite. Rates include breakfast. AE, DC, MC, V. Closed Nov 3–Dec 23. Free parking.

Built in 1984 and doubled in size in 1993, this comfortable modern hotel lies among the venerable trees of what was a century ago the English-style park of a since-demolished villa. Though it's in a residential neighborhood with some impressive antique villas, this is San Remo's most modern hotel. The accommodations are divided among three buildings interconnected with corridors. It's a good choice for those who prefer a more up-to-date atmosphere than that offered at the previous selections. Most rooms have a view over the sea and a sun-filled terrace; about half are junior suites, with a separate sitting area and larger balconies. On the premises are a dining room, a palm-fringed outdoor pool, and a bar.

INEXPENSIVE

Hotel Belsoggiorno Juana. Corso Matuzia 41, 18038 San Remo. ☎ **0184/667-631.** Fax 0184/667-471. 43 units. TV TEL. 140,000L ($81) double. Rates include breakfast. Half board 100,000L ($58) per person. DC, MC, V. Parking 10,000L ($6) in garage, free outside.

This centrally located hotel is near the Corso dell'Imperatrice, the main sea promenade, and the beaches. Attractively furnished and inviting, it contains a large reception area, plenty of living rooms for lounging, and TV rooms. The guest rooms are contemporary and functional, not very stylish. Manager Luciana Maurizi de Benedetti has also provided a pleasant garden in which to sit and enjoy the sun and plants. Because the food is good, you may prefer to order the fixed-price menu if you're not staying on half board.

Hotel Eletto. Corso Matteotti 44, 18038 San Remo. ☎ **0184/531-548.** Fax 0184/531-506. 29 units. TV TEL. 140,000L ($81) double. Half board 120,000L ($70) per person. AE, MC, V.

This hotel is on the main artery of town, near more expensive hotels. It has a 19th-century facade with cast-iron balconies and ornate detailing. The rear of the hotel is set in a small garden with perhaps the biggest tree in San Remo casting a welcome shade over the flower beds. This pleasant stop has public rooms filled with carved panels, old mirrors, and antique furniture. The guest rooms are old-fashioned and comfortable. The sunny dining room serves inexpensive meals, and the hotel also provides a cabana on the beach.

Hotel Mariluce. Corso Matuzia 3, 16038 San Remo. ☎ **0184/667-805.** Fax 0184/667-655. 23 units, 19 with bathroom. 70,000–100,000L ($41–$58) double without bathroom, 80,000–120,000L ($46–$70) double with bathroom. V. Closed Nov–Dec 20.

As you're walking along the flowered promenade away from the commercial center, you'll notice a flowering garden enclosed on one side by the neighboring walls of a Polish church; one of the walls is emblazoned with a gilded coat-of-arms. Behind the garden is the building that until 1945 was a refugee center that Poles throughout Europe used for finding friends and relatives. Today it's one of the most reasonably priced hotels in the resort, a bargain for San Remo, offering simply furnished but comfortable guest rooms and sunny public rooms. A passage under the street leads from the garden to the beach.

DINING
EXPENSIVE

✪ **Paolo e Barbara.** Via Roma 47. ☎ **0184/531-653.** Reservations recommended. Main courses 35,000–87,000L ($20–$50); fixed-price lunch (with wine) 75,000L ($44); menu degustazione (without wine) 120,000L ($70). AE, DC, MC, V. Fri–Tues 12:30–2pm and Thurs–Tues 8–10pm. LIGURIAN/ITALIAN.

Named after the husband-and-wife team who owns it (the Masieris), this restaurant near the casino has caught the imagination of San Remo since it opened in 1987. It specializes in traditional regional recipes, as well as a handful of innovative dishes created by its staff. Meals tend to be drawn-out affairs, so allow adequate time. Depending on the season, the menu might feature a tartare of raw marinated mackerel with garlic mousse and a potato-tomato and basil-flavored garnish, trenette (a regional pasta) with freshly pulverized pesto, or grilled crayfish on onion purée with fresh herbs, olive oil, and pine nuts.

MODERATE

✪ **Da Giannino.** Lungomare Trento e Trieste 23. ☎ **0184/504-014.** Reservations recommended. Main courses 30,000–45,000L ($17–$26); fixed-price menus 70,000–120,000L ($41–$70). AE, DC, MC, V. Tues–Sat 12:30–2:30pm and 7:30–10pm, Sun 12:30–2:30pm. LIGURIAN/SEAFOOD.

This is still acclaimed San Remo's finest restaurant, though Paolo e Barbara is closing in fast. In a conservatively elegant setting, you can enjoy such specialties as warm seafood antipasti, a flavorful risotto laced with cheese and a pungently aromatic green sauce, and a selection of main courses that changes with the availability of ingredients. An exotic selection is marinated cuttlefish gratinée. The wine list features many of the better vintages of both France and Italy.

Il Bagatto. Via Matteotti 145. ☎ **0184/531-925.** Reservations required. Main courses 25,000–38,000L ($15–$22); fixed-price menus 45,000–65,000L ($26–$38). MC, V. Mon–Sat noon–3pm and 7:30–10pm. Closed July. LIGURIAN/SEAFOOD.

Il Bagatto provides good meals in the 16th-century home of an Italian duke, with dark beams and provincial chairs. It's located in the shopping district of the town, about 2 blocks from the sea. Our most recent dinner began with a choice of creamy lasagne and savory hors d'oeuvres. The scaloppine with artichokes and asparagus was especially pleasing, as was (on another occasion) a mixed grill of Mediterranean fish. All orders were accompanied by potatoes and a choice of vegetables, then followed by crème caramel for dessert. They serve many kinds of Ligurian fish, including filet of sea bass in a sauce made with fresh peppers, and a gallinella, the quintessential white-flesh Ligurian fish, roasted with potatoes and olives.

La Lanterna. Via Molo di Ponente al Porto 16. ☎ **0184/506-855.** Reservations required Sat–Sun. Main courses 17,000–40,000L ($10–$23); fixed-price menu 50,000L ($29). AE, DC, MC, V. Fri–Wed 12:30–2:30pm and 7:30–10pm. Closed Dec–Jan. SEAFOOD.

Many locals recommend this place, a nautically decorated enclave of good seafood in a building near the harbor. Opened around 1917, it's one of the few restaurants that has survived in San Remo from the heady days of its Edwardian grandeur. The crowd can get very fashionable, especially in summer, when outdoor tables are set within view of the harbor. Meals might include an excellent fish soup (brodetto di pesce con crostini), a Ligurian fish fry, or a meat dish like scaloppine in marsala wine sauce. Sea bass and red snapper are readily available and might be grilled; fried with olive oil, herbs, and lemon; or baked with artichokes, olives, and white-wine sauce.

SAN REMO AFTER DARK

The high life holds forth at the **San Remo Casino,** Corso Inglesi 18 (☎ **0184/5951**), in the center of town. For decades, fashionable visitors have dined in high style in the elegant restaurant, reserved tables at the roof garden's cabaret, or tested their luck at the gaming tables. Like a white-walled palace, the pristine-looking casino stands at the top of a steep flight of stone steps above the main artery of town.

Today you can attend a variety of shows, fashion parades, concerts, and theatrical presentations staged throughout the year. The entrance fee is 15,000L ($9) for the French and American gaming rooms, open Sunday to Friday 2:30pm to 3am and Saturday 2:30pm to 4am. Presentation of a passport is required, and a jacket and tie are requested for men. For the slot machines section, open Sunday to Friday 10am to 2:30am and Saturday 2:30pm to 3am, entrance is free and there's no particular dress code. The casino restaurant is open nightly 7pm to 1:30am, charging 60,000L to

100,000L ($35 to $58) per person for dinner. The restaurant has an orchestra playing everything from waltzes to rock. The roof-garden cabaret is open June to September on Friday and Saturday nights, with shows beginning at 10:30pm. If you visit for drinks only (not dinner), the cost is 35,000L ($20) per drink.

At least part of your nocturnal adventures will transpire in the lobby of your hotel or one of the grand palaces (especially the Royal, recommended above) whose bars are always open to well-dressed nonguests. You can always strike out for the cafes along the town's main artery, **Via Matteotti,** which serve drinks until late at night, then drop into the resort's most elegant and whimsical disco, a favorite for everyone except the most hard-core crowd, **Discoteca Nifa Igaria,** Via Matteotti 178 (☎ **0184/ 509-009**). Don't even think of showing up before 10pm.

2 Genoa: Italy's Premier Port

88 miles SW of Milan, 311 miles NW of Rome, 120 miles NE of Nice

It was altogether fitting that "Genova the Proud" (Repubblica Superba) gave birth to Christopher Columbus. Its link with the sea dates back to ancient times. However, Columbus did his hometown a disservice. By blazing the trail to the New World, he dealt a devastating blow to Mediterranean ports in general, as the balance of trade shifted to newly developing centers on the Atlantic.

Even so, **Genoa (Genova)** today is Italy's premier port and ranks with Marseille in European importance. In its heyday (the 13th century), Genoa's empire, extending from colonies on the Barbary Coast to citadels on the Euphrates, rivaled that of Venice. Apart from Columbus, its most famous son was Andrea Doria (yes, the ill-fated ocean liner was named after him), who wrested his city from the yoke of French domination in the early 16th century.

With a population of some 820,000, Genoa is the capital of Liguria and one of the richest cities in Italy. Though shipping remains its major business, other industries have become highly developed in recent years, including insurance, communications, banking, and electronics.

Like a half moon, the port encircles the Gulf of Genoa. Its hills slope down to the water, so walking is an up- and downhill affair. Because of the terrain, the Christopher Columbus Airport opened quite late in Genova's development. The center of the city's maritime life, the harbor makes for an interesting stroll, particularly in the part of the old town bordering the water. Sailors from many lands search for adventure and women in the little bars and cabarets occupying the back alleyways. Often the streets are merely medieval lanes, with foreboding buildings closing in.

The present harbor is the result of extensive rebuilding, following massive World War II bombardments that crippled its seaside installations. The best way to view the overall skyline is from a **harbor cruise.** Tours depart from Stazione Marittima daily every half hour and cost 10,000L ($6) adults and 7,000L ($4.05) children 9 and under/seniors 60 and over.

ESSENTIALS

GETTING THERE   Alitalia and other carriers fly into the **Aeroporto Internazionale de Genova Cristoforo Colombo,** 4 miles west of the city center in Sestri Ponente (☎ **010/601-51** for flight information).

Genoa has good **rail** connections with the rest of Italy; it lies only 1½ hours from Milan, 3 hours from Florence, and 1½ hours from the French border. Genoa has two major rail stations, **Stazione Prìncipe** and **Stazione Brignole.** Chances are you'll arrive at the Prìncipe, Piazza Acquaverde, nearest to the harbor and the old part of the

A Harbor Warning

The harbor, particularly after dark, isn't for the squeamish. If you go wandering, don't go alone and don't carry valuables. Genoa is rougher than Barcelona, more comparable to Marseille. Not only in the harbor area but also on any side street running downhill, a woman is likely to lose her purse if she doesn't take precautions.

city. Brignole, on Piazza Verde, lies in the heart of the modern city. Both trains and municipally operated buses run between the two stations. For train information, call ☎ 1478/88-088 toll free in Italy only.

If you've got a **car,** Genoa is right along the main autostrada (A10) that begins at the French border and continues along the Ligurian coastline.

There's a 22-hour **ferry** service to Genoa originating in Palermo (Sicily), costing from 98,000L ($57) per person. Ferries also leave Porto Torres (Sardinia) for Genoa, costing from 90,000L ($52). The number to call in Genova for information is the Stazione Marittima (☎ 010/256-682).

VISITOR INFORMATION   The **Azienda di Promozione Turistica** is on Via al Porto Antico (☎ 010/248-711), open daily 8:30am to 6:30pm. You'll also find information booths dispensing tourist literature at the rail stations and the airport. The rail station office at Prìncipe (☎ 010/246-2633) is open Monday to Saturday 8am to 8pm and Sunday 9am to noon; the airport office (☎ 010/60-151) is open Monday to Saturday 8am to 8pm.

CITY LAYOUT   Genoa opens onto the **Porto di Genova,** and most of the section of interest lies between the two rail stations, **Stazione Prìncipe,** on the western fringe of the town near the port, and **Stazione Brignole,** to the northeast, opening onto Piazza Verdi. A major artery is **Via XX Settembre,** running between Piazza Ferrari in the west and Piazza della Vittoria in the east. **Via Balbi** is another major artery, beginning east of Stazione Prìncipe, off Piazza Acquaverde. Via Balbi ends at Piazza Nunziata. From here, a short walk along Via Cairola leads to the most important tourist street in Genoa, the palazzo-flanked **Via Garibaldi** (but more about that later).

FAST FACTS   Currency Exchange   You can exchange money at **Basso,** via Gramsci 245 (☎ 010/26-10-67), open Monday to Friday 8am to 7pm and Saturday 8am to 1pm. There are also exchange offices in both the Brignole and the Prìncipe rail stations, open daily 7am to 10pm.

Drugstores   At least one of Genoa's pharmacies remains open 24 hours, based on a revolving schedule that changes from week to week. One of the largest of the city's pharmacies, **Pescetto,** via Balbi 185R (☎ 010/246-2696), across from the entrance to the Prìncipe rail station, is often selected for all-night duty.

Emergencies   For assistance in a medical or police emergency, dial ☎ 113 at any time, from any phone in Genoa. If it's automobile trouble, call ACI, Soccorso Stradale (☎ 116).

Medical Care   If you're in need of any medical service, the city's largest hospital, **Ospedale San Martino,** Viale Benedetto XV 10 (☎ 010/5551), maintains a roster of emergency services and can link you with an appropriate medical specialist.

Police   Dial ☎ 113.

Post Office   Genoa's **main post office,** at Via Dante and Piazza de Ferrari (☎ 010/593-811), maintains telex and fax facilities but no phones. You might find it more convenient to have your hotel send a fax for you, but if you really want to involve the post office, it'll send your fax or telex at rates that are a bit cheaper than your hotel will charge. The post office is open Monday to Saturday 8:15am to 7:20pm (telex service stays open till 10pm).

Taxi To call a radio taxi, dial ☎ 010/5966.

Telephone Long-distance calls are the least expensive when they're placed at the headquarters for **Telecom Italia,** Via San Vicenzo 2 (☎ 010/5971), open Monday to Saturday 9am to 7pm. There are also public phone services offered in the Brignole and the Principe rail stations, but it's a lot more convenient, despite the surcharge, to phone from your hotel, using a credit card from such well-respected outfits as ATT Direct.

SEEING THE SIGHTS

In the heart of the city, you can stroll down ✪ **Via Garibaldi,** the street of patricians, on which noble Genovese families erected splendid palazzi in late Renaissance times. The guiding hand behind the general appearance and most of the architecture was Alessi, who grew to fame in the 16th century (he studied under Michelangelo).

Civic Gallery of the Red Palace (Civica Galleria di Palazzo Rosso). Via Garibaldi 18. ☎ 010/557-4141. Admission 6,000L ($3.50) adults; children 17 and under/seniors 60 and over free. Tues and Thurs–Fri 9am–1pm, Wed and Sat 9am–7pm, Sun 10am–6pm.

This 17th-century palace was once the home of the Brignole-Sale, a local aristocratic family who founded a Genovese dynasty. It was restored after having been bombed in World War II and now contains a good collection of paintings, with such exceptional works as *Giuditta* by Veronese, *St. Sebastian* by Guido Reni, and *Cleopatra* by Guercino. The best-known works are Sir Anthony van Dyck's portrait of Pauline and Anton Giulio Brignole-Sale from the original collection and the magnificent frescoes by Gregorio de Ferrari (*Spring* and *Summer*) and Domenico Piola (*Autumn* and *Winter*). There are also collections of ceramics and sculpture and a display of gilded baroque statuary. Across from this red palace is the white palace, the Palazzo Bianco (below).

Civic Museum of the White Palace (Museo Civico di Palazzo Bianco). Via Garibaldi 11. ☎ 010/557-3499. Admission 6,000L ($3.50) adults; children 17 and under free. Tues and Thurs–Fri 9am–1pm, Wed and Sat 9am–7pm, Sun 10am–6pm.

The duchess of Gallier donated this palace, along with her art collection, to the city. Although the palace dates from the 16th century, its appearance today is the work of later architects and reflects the most recent advances in museum planning. The most significant paintings—from the Dutch and Flemish schools—include Gerard David's *Polittico della Cervara* and Memling's *Jesus Blessing the Faithful,* as well as works by Sir Anthony van Dyck and Peter Paul Rubens. A wide-ranging survey of European and local artists is presented, with paintings by Caravaggio, Zurbarán, and Murillo and works by Bernardo Strozzi (a whole room) and Alessandro Magnasco (an excellent painting of a scene in a Genovese garden).

National Gallery (Galleria Nazionale). In the Palazzo Spinola, Piazza della Pellicceria 1. ☎ 010/270-5300. Admission 8,000L ($4.65) adults; children under 18 free. Mon 9am–1pm, Tues–Sat 9am–7pm, Sun 2–7pm.

This gallery houses a major painting collection. Its notable works include Joos van Cleve's *Madonna in Prayer,* Antonello da Messina's *Ecce Homo,* and Giovanni Pisano's *Giustizia.* The gallery is also known for its decorative arts collection (furniture, silver, and ceramics, among other items). The palace itself was designed for the Grimaldi family in the 16th century as a private residence, though the Spinolas took it over eventually.

Genoa

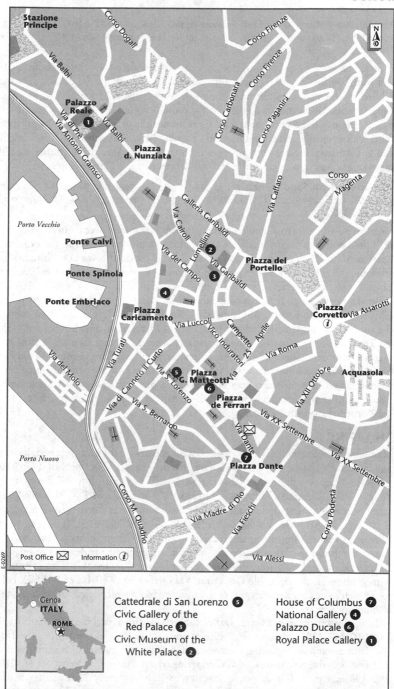

Stazione Principe

Corso Dogali

Corso Firenze

Corso Firenze

Via Balbi

Palazzo Reale ❶

Via di Pre

Via Balbi

Via Antonio Gramsci

Piazza d. Nunziata

Corso Carbonara

Corso Paganiri

Galleria Garibaldi

Corso Magenta

Porto Vecchio

Ponte Calvi

Via Caffaro

Via Cairoli

Via del Campo

Lomellini

❷

Via Garibaldi

❸

Piazza del Portello

Ponte Spinola

Ponte Embriaco

❹

Piazza Caricamento

Via Luccoli

Via Turati

Vico Indoratori

Campetto

25 Aprile

Via Roma

Piazza Corvetto ⓘ

Via Assarotti

Via del Molo

Via di Canneto il Curto

Via S. Lorenzo

❺ Piazza G. Matteotti

❻

Piazza de Ferrari

Acquasola

Via XII Ottobre

Via S. Bernardo

Via Dante

Via XX Settembre

❼ Piazza Dante

Via XX Settembre

Porto Nuovo

Corso M. Quadrio

Via Madre di Dio

Via Fieschi

Corso Podestà

Via Alessi

Post Office ✉   Information ⓘ

Genoa
ITALY

ROME ★

Cattedrale di San Lorenzo ❺
Civic Gallery of the Red Palace ❸
Civic Museum of the White Palace ❷

House of Columbus ❼
National Gallery ❹
Palazzo Ducale ❻
Royal Palace Gallery ❶

573

Royal Palace Gallery (Galleria di Palazzo Reale). Via Balbi 10. ☎ **010/27-101.** Admission 8,000L ($4.65) adults; children 18 and under free. Sun–Tues 9am–1:30pm, Wed–Sat 9am–7pm.

A 5-minute walk from Stazione Prìncipe, the Royal Palace was started about 1650, and work continued until the early 18th century. It was built for the Balbi family, was sold to the Durazzos, and became one of the royal palaces of the Savoias in 1824. King Charles Albert modified many of the rooms around 1840. As in all Genovese palazzi, some of these subsequent alterations marred the original designs. Its gallery is filled with paintings and sculpture, works by van Dyck, Tintoretto, G. F. Romanelli, and L. Giordano. Frescoes and antiques from the 17th to the 19th centuries are displayed. Seek out, in particular, the Hall of Mirrors and the Throne Room.

✪ **Cattedrale di San Lorenzo.** Piazza San Lorenzo, Via Tommaso Reggio 17. ☎ **010/ 311-269.** Admission 9,000L ($5) adults; 7,000L ($4.05) students/children. Mon–Sat 9am–noon and 3–6pm.

Genoa is noted for its medieval churches, and this one towers over them all. A British shell fired during World War II almost spelled its doom—miraculously, the explosion never went off. The cathedral is distinguished by its bands of black and white marble adorning the facade in the Pisan style. In its present form, it dates from the 13th century, though it was erected on the foundation of a much earlier structure. Alessi designed the dome, and the campanile (bell tower) dates from the 16th century. The Chapel of John the Baptist, with interesting Renaissance sculpture, is said to contain the remains of the saint for whom it's named. Off the nave and in the vaults, the cathedral treasury contains a trove of artifacts acquired during Genoa's heyday as a mercantile empire. Some of the claims are a bit hard to believe, however—a crystal dish reputed to have been used for dinner service at the Last Supper and a blue chalcedony platter on which the head of John the Baptist was rested for its delivery to Salome. Other treasures include an 11th-century arm reliquary of St. Anne and a jewel-studded Byzantine Zaccaria Cross.

SHOPPING

Shopping in Genoa includes a good selection of apparel, all things antiquated, jewelry, and foodstuff. Classic but contemporary, **Berti,** Via XII Ottobre 94R (☎ **010/ 540-026**), carries a line of Burberry items, as well as British-inspired creations by designers like Valentino and Pedroni. **Lucarda,** Via Sottoripa 61 (☎ **010/297-963**), offers nautically inspired clothing for men and women; it doesn't, however, carry beachwear. **Le Mimose,** Via XXV Aprile 58R (☎ **010/292-615**), is a small room filled with women's lingerie of impeccable quality and design. Elegant **Pescetto,** Via Scurreria 8 Rosso (☎ **010/247-3433**), offers men's and women's designer outfits and fragrances, coupled with accessories like leather bags and wallets. On a street overrun with goldsmiths, the reputable **Codevilla,** Via Orefici 53 (☎ **010/247-2567**), fashions jewelry and small objects out of gold, silver, and a wide variety of precious and semiprecious stones.

In the historic center of town, **Dallai Libreria Antiquaria,** Piazza de Marini 11R (☎ **010/247-2338**), handles first editions and rare books and prints from the 18th and 19th centuries. Displaying their wares in a 16th-century chapel featuring elaborate frescoes, the proprietors of **Galleria Imperiale,** Piazza Campetto 8 (☎ **010/ 299-290**), are estate liquidators, specializing in 19th- and early 20th-century household goods, including objets d'art, all types of furniture, and paintings.

With bakers working around the clock, **Il Fornaio di Sattanino,** Via Fiasella 18r (☎ **010/580-972**), turns out versions of the region's famous focaccia filled with almost any ingredient available at the market. It also offers other types of bread and various pastries. A death-by-chocolate lover's dream, **Pietro Romanengo fu Stefano,** Via Soziglia 74 Rosso (☎ 010/297-869), allows you to indulge your sweet tooth on handmade confections coated, sprinkled, glazed, or composed of the dark sugary concoction. When your hunger turns to thirst, the retail-only **Vinoteca Sola,** Piazza Colombo 13 (☎ 010/561-329), offers a huge selection of wines from all over the world.

Combining Old World beliefs with New Age enthusiasm, **Antica Erboristeria San Giorgio,** Via Luccoli 47R (☎ 010/206-888), prepares and sells herbs, teas, and natural personal-care products. **Pecchiolo,** Via Pisa 13 (☎ 010/362-5082), sells upscale dinner- and cookware of ceramic, crystal, and silver; and if you'd rather just have a one-stop shopping excursion, **La Rinascente,** Via Vernazza 1 (☎ 010/586-995), and **Coin,** Via XII Ottobre 4 (☎ 010/570-5821), are the two biggest department stores in town.

ACCOMMODATIONS

Generally, hotels in Genoa are second rate, but some good finds await those who search diligently.

Warning: Some of the cheap hotels and pensions in and around the waterfront are to be avoided. Our recommendations, however, are suitable even for women traveling alone.

EXPENSIVE

Bristol Palace. Via XX Settembre 35, 16121 Genova. ☎ **010/592-541.** Fax 010/561-756. 133 units. A/C MINIBAR TV TEL. 340,000–430,000L ($197–$249) double; 520,000L ($302) suite. Rates include breakfast. AE, DC, MC, V. Parking 40,000L ($23).

The Bristol Palace, from the late 19th century, boasts a number of features that will make your stay in Genoa special, even though it's in the grimy heart of old town. Its obscure entrance behind colonnades on a commercial street is misleading; the salons and drawing rooms are decorated nicely with traditional pieces, though both the fabrics and the furnishings are beginning to show their age. The larger of the guest rooms have an old-fashioned elegance and are tastefully furnished, often with chandeliers, Queen Anne desks, and padded headboards. All the rooms contain at least one antique and often several. The hotel's stairway is one of the most stunning in Genova.

Dining/Diversions: The English bar is a favorite rendezvous point, and the small but elegant Caffè de Bristol offers daily lunches and dinners.

Amenities: Concierge, room service, laundry/dry cleaning, baby-sitting.

City Hotel. Via San Sebastiano 6, 16123 Genova. ☎ **010/5545.** Fax 010/586-301. www. bestwestern.com/thisco/bw/98097/98097_b.html. 69 units. A/C MINIBAR TV TEL. 380,000L ($220) double; 700,000L ($406) suite. Rates include breakfast. AE, DC, MC, V. Valet parking 40,000L ($23).

One of the best hotels in its category, last renovated in 1990, occupies a starkly angular stucco-and-travertine postwar building, surrounded by a crumbling series of town houses. The convenient location, near Piazza Corvetto and Via Garibaldi, is one of the best features. Other pluses are a welcoming staff, a comfortable wood-and-granite lobby, and guest rooms with parquet floors, specially designed furniture, and up-to-date amenities.

Dining/Diversions: The cocktail bar serves snacks, and the first-class restaurant offers many regional specialties. A short list of cold and hot foods is served room service style during the day and early evening.

Amenities: Concierge, room service, laundry/dry cleaning, twice-daily maid service.

Hotel Savoia Majestic. Via Arsenale di Terra 5, 16126 Genova. ☎ **010/261-641.** Fax 010/261-883. 128 units. MINIBAR TV TEL. 290,000–340,000L ($168–$197) double; from 410,000L ($238) suite. Rates include breakfast. AE, DC, MC, V. Valet parking 30,000L ($18).

Across from Piazza Prìncipe, the 1887 Savoia Majestic still contains some of its original accessories, though its heyday when it entertained dukes and duchesses has long since passed. These days, guests tend to be European businesspeople. The decor of the high-ceilinged guest rooms ranges from modern to conservatively old-fashioned. Try for a room on the sixth floor for the best harbor views. All but 20 of the rooms are air-conditioned. Some of the baths are unusually large, with pink marble surfaces, whereas others are extremely cramped. Because the rooms vary so widely from good to bad, your experience will depend entirely on where you're stashed for the night. The lobby and reception area is shared with the **Hotel Londra & Continentale** (same phone as above), where doubles are 220,000L/$132.

Dining: The restaurant is so routine you'll want to seek better fare at one of the nearby trattorie.

Amenities: Concierge, room service, dry cleaning/laundry, newspaper delivery, twice-daily maid service, baby-sitting, secretarial services, courtesy car.

Jolly Hotel Plaza. Via Martin Piaggio 11, 16122 Genova. ☎ **800/221-2626** in the U.S., 800/237-0319 in Canada, or 010/839-3641. Fax 010/839-1850. 146 units. A/C MINIBAR TV TEL. 330,000–400,000L ($191–$232) double; 900,000L ($522) suite. Rates include breakfast. AE, DC, MC, V. Parking 36,000L ($21).

A four-star member of the Jolly chain, this hotel is newer than its modified classic facade would suggest. Centrally located near Piazza Corvetto, it was built in 1950 to replace an older hotel destroyed during an air raid in World War II. In 1992, the hotel was renovated, upgraded, and enlarged, linking two former hotels, the Baglioni Eliseo and the Plaza. The rooms in the old Eliseo are generally more spacious than those in the Plaza (and better decorated). Elegant touches include mother-of-pearl inlay in the doors and marble baths.

Dining: On the premises are an American-style bar and a grill room, La Villetta di Negro. When business is slow, the management sometimes opts not to open the restaurant on weekends.

Amenities: Concierge, room service, dry cleaning/laundry.

MODERATE

Columbus Sea Hotel. Via Milano 63, 16126 Genova. ☎ **010/265-051.** Fax 010/255-226. 87 units. A/C MINIBAR TV TEL. 265,000–330,000L ($154–$191) double; 350,000–430,000L ($203–$249) junior suite. Rates include buffet breakfast. AE, DC, MC, V. Valet parking 36,000L ($21).

One of the best moderate hotels in town, the Columbus Sea Hotel looks out at the new cruise-ship terminal and is close to Genoa's World Trade Center. The city center and old town lie only a mile away. The hotel is warmer and more inviting inside than its cold boxy exterior suggests. The guest rooms are spacious for the most part, furnished in muted colors with Oriental carpeting. The public rooms are more gracious, outfitted with a certain taste and flair. A popular rendezvous point in Genova is Il Mandraccio, the hotel's American bar. The hotel's restaurant, La Lanterna, serves excellent Ligurian specialties and treats diners to a panoramic view of the harbor and city. The Columbus Sea Hotel offers many of the amenities of far more expensive hotels, like a concierge, room service, dry cleaning/laundry, secretarial services, a courtesy car, and baby-sitting on request.

INEXPENSIVE

✪ **Albergo Viale Sauli.** Viale Sauli 5, 16121 Genova. ☎ **010/561-397.** Fax 010/590-092. 56 units. A/C MINIBAR TV TEL. 170,000L ($99) double. Rates include breakfast. AE, DC, MC, V.

This hotel is on the second floor of a modern concrete office building, just off a busy shopping street. It's scattered over three floors, each reachable by elevator from the lobby. The high-ceilinged public rooms include a bar, a breakfast room, and a reception area, all with big windows and lots of comfort. Enore Sceresini is the opera-loving owner, and his guests usually include businesspeople who appreciate cleanliness and comfort. Each of the units has marble floors and a spacious bath.

Hotel Agnello d'Oro. Vico delle Monachette 6, 16126 Genova. ☎ **010/246-2084.** Fax 010/246-2327. 38 units. TV TEL. 150,000L ($87) double. Breakfast 10,000L ($6). AE, DC, MC, V.

When the Doria family owned this structure and everything around it in the 1600s, they carved their family crest on the walls near the top of the alley so all of Genoa would know the point at which their property began. The symbol was a golden lamb, and you can still see one at the point where the narrow street joins the busy boulevard leading to Stazione Prìncipe. The hotel, named after the animal on the crest, is a 17th-century building that includes vaulted ceilings and paneling in the lobby. About half the units are in a newer wing, but if you want the oldest accommodations, ask for room no. 6, 7, or 8. Today the hotel is maintained by a family who has installed a small bar and restaurant off the lobby.

Hotel Astoria. Piazza Brignole 4, 16122 Genova. ☎ **010/873-316.** Fax 010/831-7326. 69 units. TV TEL. 220,000L ($128) double. Rates include breakfast. AE, DC, MC, V. Parking 25,000L ($15).

Built in the 1920s but opened as a hotel only in 1978, this place has lots of polished paneling, wrought-iron accents, beige marble floors, and a baronial carved fireplace in one of the public rooms. The guest rooms are comfortably furnished and well maintained. The hotel sits on an uninspiring square that contains a filling station, and its view encompasses a traffic hub and many square blocks of apartment buildings. There's a bar but no restaurant.

Hotel Vittoria Orlandi. Via Balbi 33–45, 16126 Genova. ☎ **010/261-923.** Fax 010/246-2656. 47 units. A/C TV TEL. 100,000–140,000L ($58–$81) double. Breakfast 10,000L ($6). AE, DC, MC, V. Parking 25,000L ($15).

Since this hotel is built on one of the hillsides for which Genoa is famous, its entrance is under a tunnel opening at a point about a block from Stazione Prìncipe. An elevator will take you up to the reception area. It welcomes a wide variety of guests to its simple but clean rooms. Many rooms have balconies, and about half are air-conditioned and contain a minibar. Best of all, the hotel is quiet because of the way it's sheltered from the boulevards by other buildings.

DINING

Genoa, which has been praised for its cuisine, has lots of restaurants and trattorie, many strung along the harbor. The following recommendations will give you several opportunities to judge it for yourself.

MODERATE

✪ **Da Giacomo.** Corso Italia 1R. ☎ **010/362-9647.** Reservations required. Main courses 25,000–45,000L ($15–$26); fixed-price menu 80,000L ($46). DC, V. Mon–Sat 12:30–2:30pm and 7:30–11pm. Closed 1 week in Aug. LIGURIAN.

Many food critics regard Da Giacomo the premier restaurant of Genoa. The service is deluxe, as is the dining room, decorated in an elegant modern style and graced with plants. Ligurian cooking is dominated by the sea, and the menu begins with superb seafood antipasti, some of which is raw but cut and carved with the exquisite care you find in Tokyo. Meat, fish, and poultry dishes are prepared with unusual flair. Pesto sauce accompanies many dishes, especially the pasta. (During the Crusades it was reported that the Genovese contingent could always be identified by the aroma of pesto surrounding them.) They offer some of the finest regional wines in Italy, and the desserts are made fresh daily. There's also a piano bar where you can dance.

✪ **Gran Gotto.** Viale Brigate Bisagno 69R. ☎ 010/583-644. Reservations recommended. Main courses 30,000–40,000L ($17–$23); fixed-price menu 90,000L ($52). AE, MC, V. Daily 12:30–2:30pm and 7:30–10:30pm. Closed Aug 12–31. SEAFOOD.

Though it opened in 1937 and has been in the same family since, this restaurant moved to new quarters in 1995. We consider it the top restaurant in Genoa. The emphasis is on seafood, but the meat and pasta dishes aren't neglected. In fact, the most typical offering, trenette al pesto, is quite famous, a pasta of paper-thin noodles served with the characteristic pesto. The delicately simmered risotto is also tempting. The main dishes are reasonably priced and of high standard, including the mixed fish fry and the French baby squid. The zuppa di pesce (fish soup) has made many a luncheon for many a gourmet. The rognone al cognac is another superb choice—tender calves' kidneys that have been cooked and delicately flavored in cognac.

Ristorante Saint Cyr. Piazza Marsala 4. ☎ 010/886-897. Reservations required. Main courses 30,000–35,000L ($17–$20). AE, DC, MC, V. Mon–Fri noon–2:30pm and 7:30–10pm, Sat 7:30–10pm. Closed Dec 23–Jan 7 and 2 weeks in Aug. LIGURIAN/PIEDMONTESE.

Our favorite time to come to this restaurant is at night, when some of the most discriminating palates in Genoa might be seen enjoying dishes generously adapted from regional recipes. Menu items change daily, though recent offerings featured rice with truffles and cheese, a timbale of fresh spinach, a charlotte of fish, and a variety of braised meats, each delicately seasoned and perfectly prepared. Specialties include scamone (a certain cut of beef) cooked in Barolo wine and ravioli al sugo di carne (ravioli with sauce made from meat juices). The restaurant is also open for lunch, when the patrons are likely to be conservatively dressed businesspeople discussing shipping contracts.

Ristorante Zeffirino. Via XX Settembre 20. ☎ 010/591-990. Reservations recommended. Main courses 30,000–60,000L ($17–$35); fixed-price menus 60,000–98,000L ($35–$57). AE, DC, MC, V. Daily noon–midnight. LIGURIAN.

In a cul-de-sac just off one of the busiest boulevards, this place has hosted everyone from Frank Sinatra to Luciano Pavarotti and Pope John Paul II to Liza Minnelli. Opened in the 1930s, it moved to its present location in the 1950s. At least 14 members of the Zeffirino family prepare the best pasta in the city, using recipes collected from all over Italy. These include lesser-known varieties like quadrucci, pettinati, and cappelletti, as well as the more familiar tagliatelle and lasagne. Next, you can select from a vast array of meat and fish, along with 1,000 kinds of wine. Ligurian specialties, including risotto alla pescatore and beef stew with artichokes, are featured. Try a wide array of shellfish—either baked or steamed—served with seasonal vegetables.

GENOA AFTER DARK

Warning: Be alert to the unsavory aspects of nightlife in Genoa, especially within the labyrinthine alleys of the medieval core. Equally inadvisable are the dubious neighborhoods around the bus station and Piazza Matteotti, where drug sales and commercial sex are only two of the preoccupations.

You'll find enough discos to keep you fully occupied every night. The best of them is **Caffè Nessundorma,** Via Porta d'Arci 74 (☎ **010/561-773**), where live music, beginning at 10:30pm, usually segues into recorded music, often from the 1970s and 1980s; the place combines aspects of a singles bar and a hip cafe. Somewhat more elegant is **Mako,** Corso Italia 28 (☎ **010/367-652**), which has a piano bar, a disco, and a restaurant. Two other centrally located contenders for the bar/disco trade are **Vanilla,** Via Brigata Salerno (☎ **010/399-0872**), and **Eccentrica,** Via Ceccardi 24 (☎ **010/ 570-2809**), which are neither as vanilla nor as eccentric as their names. **M&M,** Piazza Fontana Marose, Salita Santa Caterina (☎ **010/586-787**), is either intimate or cramped, depending on who happens to be here at the time. It features recorded music, and, after the evening brings rock, some live jazz and blues as well.

Looking for a simple pint of beer, some pub grub, and access to a dose of English humor? Head for the **Brittania Pub,** Vico Calzana, near Piazza de Ferrari, where groups of friends fill a woodsy-looking setting that evokes Winston Churchill with an Italian accent.

The most popular gay spot is **La Cage,** Via Sampierdarena 167R (☎ **010/ 645-4555**), attracting mainly males 21 to 40. There's no cover, and it's open Tuesday to Saturday 10pm to 3:30am.

3 Rapallo

296 miles NW of Rome, 17 miles SE of Genoa, 100 miles S of Milan

A top seaside resort—known for years to the chic crowd who live in the villas on the hillside—**Rapallo** occupies a remarkable site overlooking the Gulf of Tigullio. In summer, the crowded heart of Rapallo takes on a carnival air, as hordes of bathers occupy the rocky sands along the beach. In the area is an 18-hole golf course, as well as an indoor pool, a riding club, and a modern harbor. You can also take a cable car to the **Sanctuary di Montallegro,** then walk to **Monte Rosa** for one of the finest views of the Ligurian coast. There are many opportunities for summer **boat trips,** not only to Portofino but also to the Cinque Terre.

Rapallo's long history is often likened to Genoa's. It became part of the Repubblica Superba in 1229, but Rapallo had existed long before that. Its **cathedral** dates from the 6th century when it was founded by the bishops of Milan. Walls once enclosed the medieval town, but now only the **Saline Gate** remains. Rapallo has also been the scene of many an international meeting, the most notable of which was the 1917 conference of wartime allies.

Today Rapallo is a bit past its heyday, though it was once known as one of Europe's most fashionable resorts, numbering among its residents Ezra Pound and D. H. Lawrence. Other artists, poets, and writers have been drawn to its natural beauty, which has been marred in part by an uncontrolled building boom brought on by tourism. At the innermost corner of the Gulf of Tiguillio, Rapallo is still the most famous resort on the Riviera di Levante, a position it owes to its year-round mild climate.

ESSENTIALS

GETTING THERE   Three **trains** from Genoa stop here each hour 4:30am to midnight, costing 2,800L ($1.60) one-way. A train also links Rapallo with Santa Margherita every 30 minutes, costing 1,500L (85¢) one-way. For more information, dial ☎ **1478/88-088** toll free in Italy only. From Santa Margherita, a **bus** operated by Tigullio runs every 30 minutes to Rapallo, costing 1,400L (80¢) one-way and taking half an hour. The bus information office is at Piazza Vittorio Veneto in Santa Margherita (☎ **0185/288-834**). If you've got a **car** and are coming from Genoa, go southeast along A12.

VISITOR INFORMATION   The **tourist office** is at Via Diaz 9 (☎ **0185/230-346**), open Monday to Saturday 9am to 12:30pm and 2:30 to 5:30pm and Sunday 9am to 12:30pm.

ACCOMMODATIONS

Grand Hotel Bristol. Via Aurelia Orientale 369, 16035 Rapallo. ☎ **0185/273-313.** Fax 0185/55-800. 91 units. A/C MINIBAR TV TEL. 280,000–380,000L ($162–$220) double; from 800,000L ($464) suite. Rates include breakfast. AE, MC, V. Parking 22,000L ($13) in garage, free outdoors.

This hotel, one of the Riviera's grand old buildings, is still a viable choice despite falling standards. Built in 1908, it was reopened in 1984 and the pink-and-white facade, with surrounding shrubbery and iron gates, was spruced up but basically unchanged. The interior, however, was gutted. Some guest rooms have private terraces, and all contain electronic window blinds, lots of mirrors, and oversized beds. The inviting waters of a pool are visible from many rooms, and the kitchens are about the most modern anywhere.

Dining/Diversions: The hotel has several restaurants, including a rooftop restaurant that's often closed when it's too hot. If business is slow, only one restaurant might be open.

Amenities: Room service, baby-sitting, laundry/valet, hairdresser, beautician, massage salon, free-form pool, conference rooms.

Hotel Eurotel. Via Aurelia di Ponente 22, 16035 Rapallo. ☎ **0185/60-981.** Fax 0185/50-635. 65 units. A/C MINIBAR TV TEL. 192,000–234,000L ($111–$136) double. Rates include buffet breakfast. AE, MC, V. Parking 20,000L ($12) in garage, free outdoors.

With seven floors and three elevators, this vivid sienna-colored structure is one of the tallest hotels in town, set above the port at the top of a winding road where you'll have to negotiate the oncoming traffic with care. (Many of the units, though, are privately owned condominiums.) The lobby has marble floors and a helpful staff. All guest rooms contain built-in cabinets, arched loggias with views over the gulf of Rapallo, and beds that fold, Murphy style, into the walls.

Dining/Diversions: A bar and a second-floor panoramic restaurant, Antica Aurelia, are on the premises.

Amenities: Concierge, room service, laundry/dry cleaning, massage, baby-sitting, small rectangular pool.

Hotel Giulio Cesare. Corso Cristoforo Colombo 52, 16035 Rapallo. ☎ **0185/50-685.** Fax 0185/60-896. 33 units. TV TEL. 140,000L ($81) double; 100,000L ($58) per person double with half board. AE, DC, MC, V. Closed Nov 6–Dec 20. Free parking in low season, 15,000L ($9) in high season.

This modernized villa is a bargain for the Italian Riviera. When the genial owner skillfully renovated it, he kept expenses down to keep room rates lower. The hotel, on the coast road about 90 feet from the sea, offers rooms with a homelike atmosphere, featuring good views of the Gulf of Tigullio and furnished with tasteful reproductions (most have sunny balconies). Ask for the rooms on the top floor if you want a better view and quieter surroundings. The meals are prepared with fine ingredients (the fresh fish dishes are superb).

Hotel Miramare. Lungomare Vittorio Veneto 27, 16035 Rapallo. ☎ **0185/230-261.** Fax 0185/273-570. 28 units. MINIBAR TV TEL. 140,000–160,000L ($81–$93) double; 150,000–180,000L ($87–$104) suite. Half board 110,000–140,000L ($66–$84) per person. AE, DC, MC, V. Closed Nov. Parking 20,000L ($12).

On the water near a stone gazebo is this 1929 re-creation of a Renaissance villa, with exterior frescoes that have faded in the salt air. The gardens in front have been replaced by a glass extension that contains a contemporary restaurant (see "Dining" below). The accommodations are clean and simple, comfortable, and high-ceilinged; many have iron balconies that stretch toward the harbor.

DINING

Ristorante da Monique. Lungomare Vittorio Veneto 6. ☎ **0185/50-541.** Reservations required. Main courses 20,000–30,000L ($12–$17); fixed-price menu 35,000L ($20). AE, DC, MC, V. Wed–Mon 12:30–2:30pm and 7:30–10pm. Closed Jan 7–Feb 15. SEAFOOD.

This is one of the most popular seafood restaurants along the harbor, especially in summer. It features a nautical decor and big windows overlooking the boats in the marina. As you'd expect, fish is the specialty, including seafood salad, fish soup, risotto with shrimp, spaghetti with clams or mussels, grilled fish, and both tagliatelle and scampi "Monique." Some of these dishes may not always hit the mark, but you'll rarely go wrong ordering the grilled fish.

Ristorante Elite. Via Milite Ignoto 19. ☎ **0185/50-551.** Main courses 20,000–40,000L ($12–$23); fixed-price menu 35,000L ($20). AE, MC, V. Thurs–Tues noon–2:30pm and 7:30–11pm. Closed several days in Nov. SEAFOOD.

This restaurant is set back from the water on a busy commercial street in the center of town. Mainly fish is served; the offering depends on the catch of the day. Your dinner might consist of mussels marinara, minestrone Genovese style, risotto marinara, trenette al pesto, scampi, zuppa di pesce, sole meunière, turbot, or a mixed fish fry from the Ligurian coast. A limited selection of the standard meat dishes is available too. At the peak of the midsummer invasion, the restaurant is likely to remain open every day.

Ristorante Miramare. In the Hotel Miramare, Lungomare Vittorio Veneto 27. ☎ **0185/230-261.** Reservations recommended. Main courses 16,000–35,000L ($9–$20); fixed-price menu 45,000L ($26). AE, DC, MC, V. Daily 12:30–2pm and 7:30–9:30pm. SEAFOOD/LIGURIAN.

In a previously recommended hotel, this restaurant serves well-prepared unpretentious food in a modern dining room overlooking the sea. Your dinner might include fried calamari, spaghetti with clams, sea bass or turbot baked with potatoes and artichokes, veal in marsala sauce, or flavorful versions of fish soup.

4 Santa Margherita Ligure

19 miles E of Genoa, 3 miles S of Portofino, 296 miles NW of Rome

A resort rival to Rapallo, **Santa Margherita Ligure** also occupies a beautiful position on the Gulf of Tigullio. Its attractive harbor is usually thronged with fun seekers, and the resort offers the widest range of accommodations in all price levels on the eastern Riviera. It has a festive appearance, with a promenade, flower beds, and palm trees swaying in the wind. As is typical of the Riviera, its beach combines rock and sand. Santa Margherita Ligure is linked to Portofino by a narrow road. The climate is mild, even in winter, when many elderly guests visit the resort.

The town dates back to A.D. 262. The official name of Santa Margherita Ligure was given to the town by Victor Emmanuel II in 1863. Before that it had many other names, including Porto Napoleone, an 1812 designation from Napoléon.

You can visit the richly embellished **Sanctuary of Santa Maria della Rosa** (☎ 0185/286-555), Piazza Caprera, with its Italian and Flemish paintings, along with relics of the saint for whom the town was named. Admission is free, and it's open daily 7am to 6pm.

ESSENTIALS

GETTING THERE   Three **trains** per hour arrive from Genoa daily 4:30am to midnight, costing 2,800L ($1.60) one-way. The train station is at Piazza Federico Raoul Nobili. For more information, call ☎ 1478/88-088 toll free in Italy only. **Buses** run frequently between Portofino and Santa Margherita Ligure daily, costing 1,700L ($1) one-way. You can also catch a bus in Rapallo to Santa Margherita; during the day one leaves every 30 minutes. For information, call ☎ 010/231-108. If you've got a **car,** take Rte. 227 southeast from Genoa.

VISITOR INFORMATION   The **tourist office** is at Via 25 Aprile 2B (☎ 0185/ 287-485), open Monday to Saturday 9am to 12:30pm and 2:30 to 5:30pm and Sunday 9am to 12:30pm.

ACCOMMODATIONS
VERY EXPENSIVE
Imperiale Palace Hotel. Via Pagana 19, 16038 Santa Margherita Ligure. ☎ 0185/ **288-991.** Fax 0185/284-223. 113 units. A/C MINIBAR TV TEL. 400,000–560,000L ($232– $325) double; from 720,000–820,000L ($418–$476) suite. Rates include breakfast. AE, DC, MC, V. Closed Dec–Mar. Parking: 35,000L ($20).

The Imperiale looks like an ornate gilded palace, and many guests, attracted to its faded grandeur, choose to spend their "season on the Riviera" here. Though still regal, it's fading a bit, and the Miramare (below) has overtaken it. It's built against a hillside at the edge of the resort, surrounded by semitropical gardens. The time-worn public rooms live up to the hotel's name—old courtly splendor dominates, with vaulted ceilings, satin-covered antiques, ornate mirrors, and inlaid marble floors. The guest rooms vary widely, from royal suites to simple singles away from the sea. Many have elaborate ceilings, balconies, brass beds, chandeliers, and white antique furniture, but others are rather sparse.

Dining/Diversions: The formal dining room serves Ligurian and international meals, and there's a two-decker open-air restaurant. Most inviting is a music room, with a grand piano and satin chairs, for teatime. In summer, live music is presented on the terrace.

Amenities: Room service, laundry/valet, festive recreation center with oval flagstone pool, extended stone wharf, cabanas.

EXPENSIVE
✪ **Grand Hotel Miramare.** Via Milite Ignoto 30, 16038 Santa Margherita Ligure. ☎ 800/ **223-6800** in the U.S., or 0185/287-013. Fax 0185/284-651. E-mail: miramare@pn.itnet.it. 92 units. A/C MINIBAR TV TEL. 390,000–500,000L ($226–$290) double; 630,000–860,000L ($365–$499) suite. Rates include breakfast. Reduced rates available for children under 12 in parents' room. AE, DC, MC, V. Parking 30,000–35,000L ($17–$20).

Now the prestige address of the resort, this old-world choice, a palatial 1929 building, has kept more up with the times than has the Imperiale. It was on the terrace of this hotel in 1933 that Marconi succeeded in transmitting for the first time telegraph and telephone signals a distance of more than 90 miles. Separated from a stony beach by a busy boulevard, it's a 3-minute walk from the center of town. The hotel building has a festive confectionery look, surrounded by meticulous gardens. To one side is a curved outdoor pool with heated seawater, adjoining a raised sun terrace dotted with parasols and iron tables. The guest rooms are classically furnished, and many of the baths are spacious and packed with amenities from hair dryers to makeup mirrors. Even some of the standard rooms have large terraces with sea views.

Dining: The hotel restaurant has many Victorian touches, including fragile chairs and blue-and-white porcelain set into the plaster walls.

Amenities: Room service, baby-sitting, laundry/valet, heated saltwater outdoor pool, private beach, Miramare Skywater School.

MODERATE

Hotel Continental. Via Pagana 8, 16038 Santa Margherita Ligure. ☎ **0185/286-512.** Fax 0185/284-463. 76 units. A/C MINIBAR TV TEL. 250,000–310,000L ($145–$180) double, including breakfast; 160,000–215,000L ($93–$125) per person double with half board. AE, DC, MC, V. Parking 15,000–25,000L ($9–$15).

You'll see this hotel's grandiose facade from the winding road into town. The high-ceilinged public rooms give a glimpse of the terraced gardens stretching down to a private beach. The Continental is the only hotel directly on the water. In fair weather, it operates a snack bar here, where guests enjoy views of Santa Margherita bay. The guest rooms are filled with comfortable, conservative, if somewhat fading furnishings and often have French windows opening onto wrought-iron balconies. Try for a room on the top floor; the annex contains very lackluster lodgings. The view from the restaurant encompasses the curved harbor in the center of town, a few miles away. Since the turn of the century the Ciana family has managed this property, along with the Regina Elena and Metropole and Laurin. With such a command of rooms, they can almost always accommodate you in any season.

Hotel Regina Elena. Lungomare Milite Ignoto 44, 16038 Santa Margherita Ligure. ☎ **0185/287-003.** Fax 0185/284-473. 103 units. A/C MINIBAR TV TEL. 232,000–294,000L ($135–$171) double, including breakfast; 298,000–390,000L ($173–$226) double with half board. AE, DC, MC, V. Parking: 25,000L ($15).

This pastel-painted hotel is along the scenic thoroughfare leading to Portofino. The well-maintained rooms are furnished with modern styling, and most open onto a balcony with a sea view. An annex in the garden contains additional rooms. The hotel was built in 1908 and many turn-of-the-century details remain, including a marble staircase. It's operated by the Ciana family, which has been receiving guests for almost a hundred years. They also operate the Continental (above) and the Metropole and Laurin. The dining room is a 12-sided glass-walled structure serving excellent cuisine. The hotel offers room service, baby-sitting, and laundry/valet. There's also a conference center and a roof garden pool with a Jacuzzi.

Park Hotel Suisse. Via Favale 31, 16038 Santa Margherita Ligure. ☎ **0185/289-571.** Fax 0185/281-469. 85 units. TV TEL. 140,000–360,000L ($81–$209) double, 100,000–260,000L ($58–$151) suite. Rates include continental breakfast. No credit cards.

Set in a garden above the town center, the Suisse features a panoramic view of the sea and harbor. It has seven floors, all modern in design, with deep private balconies that are like alfresco living rooms for some of the guest rooms. On the lower terrace is a free-form saltwater pool surrounded by semitropical vegetation. A modernistic water chute, diving boards, and a cafe with parasol tables for refreshments all give one the advantages of seaside life and then some. The comfortable guest rooms that open onto the rear gardens, without sea view, cost slightly less. You have to cross a small street to reach the water.

INEXPENSIVE

Albergo Conte Verde. Via Zara 1, 16038 Santa Margherita Ligure. ☎ **0185/287-139.** Fax 0185/284-211. 35 units, 26 with bathroom. 80,000–95,000L ($46–$55) double without bathroom, 130,000–150,000L ($75–$87) double with bathroom. Rates include breakfast. AE, DC, MC, V. Closed Mar 1–15 and Dec 1–25. Parking 20,000L ($12).

This place offers one of the warmest welcomes in town to the budget traveler. Only 2 blocks from the sea, this third-class hotel has been revamped, and its rooms are simple but adequate. The front terrace has swing gliders and the lounge period furnishings, including rockers. All is consistent with the villa exterior of shuttered windows, flower boxes, and a small front garden and lawn where tables are set out for refreshments.

Hotel Jolanda. Via Luisito Costa 6, 16038 Santa Margherita Ligure. ☎ **0185/287-513.** Fax 0185/284-763. E-mail: jolanda@promix.it. 40 units. TV TEL. 138,000–178,000L ($80–$103) double, including breakfast; 85,000–120,000L ($49–$70) per person with half board. AE, MC, V. Parking 15,000L ($9) in garage, free outdoors.

Since the 1940s, the Pastine family has been welcoming visitors to their little hotel, a short walk from the sea. A patio serves as a kind of open-air living room. The pensione lies on a peaceful little street, away from traffic noise. The rooms are comfortably furnished. Guests often gather in the bar before proceeding to the restaurant, where an excellent Ligurian cuisine is served.

DINING
MODERATE

Ristorante La Ghiaia. In the Lido Palace Hotel, Via Andrea Doria 5. ☎ **0185/283-708.** Reservations recommended. Main courses 12,000–35,000L ($7–$20); fixed-price menu 45,000L ($26). AE, DC, MC, V. Thurs–Tues 12:30–2pm and 8–10pm. Closed Nov. SEAFOOD.

This name means "sea rocks," and that's precisely what you'll see from the windows overlooking the water. The restaurant occupies the ground floor of one of the town's most central hotels, and the modern decor includes paintings throughout the sunny dining rooms. Outdoor tables are shielded from pedestrians by rows of shrubbery. Your meal might begin with antipasti di mare, tagliolini al pesto, zuppa di pesce (fish soup), risotto di mare (rice with seafood), or spaghetti with lobster sauce. Fresh fish, including turbot, scampi, gamberini, and sea bass, is priced by the gram. This restaurant, though not particularly distinguished, is still one of the best in town.

Trattoria Cesarina. Via Mameli 2C. ☎ **0185/286-059.** Reservations recommended, especially in midsummer. Main courses 15,000–35,000L ($9–$20); fixed-price menu 80,000L ($46). AE, DC, MC, V. Wed–Mon 12:30–2:30pm and 7:30–10pm. Closed Dec. SEAFOOD.

This is the best of the trattorie, beneath the arcade of a short but monumental street running into Piazza Fratelli Bandiere. In an atmosphere of bentwood chairs and discreet lighting, you can enjoy a variety of Ligurian dishes. Specialties include meat, vegetables, and seafood antipasti, along with such classic Italian dishes as taglierini with seafood and pappardelle in a fragrant sausage sauce, plus seasonal fish like red snapper or dorado, best when grilled.

SANTA MARGHERITA LIGURE AFTER DARK

Nightlife here seems geared to sipping wine or cocktails on terraces with sea views, flirting with sunburned strangers, and flip-flopping through the town's sand-strewn beachfront promenades looking for whatever you're looking for. But if a day in the sun has activated your dancing shoes, head for either of the town's most appealing discos, **Covo di Nortest,** Via Rossetti 1 (☎ **0195/286-558**), or **Disco Carillon,** Localitá Paragi (☎ **0185/286-721**). Both cater to dance and music lovers aged 20 to 40.

Looking for something completely unpretentious where you can show your skill as a pool jockey? Head for the **Old Inn Bar,** Piazza Mazzini 40 (☎ **0185/286-041**), where you can play pool for 8,000L ($4.65) per person per hour, drink bottled beers, and generally hang out with a crowd of locals, many of them under 20.

5 Portofino: Villas, Yachts & Tour Buses

22 miles SE of Genoa, 106 miles S of Milan, 301 miles NW of Rome

✪ **Portofino** is about 4 miles south of Santa Margherita Ligure, along one of the most beautiful coastal roads in all Italy. Favored by the yachting set, the resort is in an idyllic location on a harbor, where the water reflects all the pastel-washed little houses running along it. In the 1930s, it enjoyed a reputation with artists; later, a chic crowd moved in—and they're still here, occupying villas in the hills and refusing to surrender completely to the tourists who pour in by the busloads during the day.

The thing to do in Portofino: **Take a walk,** preferably before sunset, leading toward the tip of the peninsula. You'll pass the entrance to an old castle (where a German baron once lived), old private villas, towering trees, and much vegetation before you reach the lighthouse. Allow an hour at least. When you return to the main piazza, proceed to one of the two little drinking bars on the left side of the harbor that rise and fall in popularity.

Before beginning that walk to the lighthouse, however, you can climb the steps from the port leading to the little parish church of **San Giorgio.** From here you'll get a panoramic view of the port and bay. In summer, you can also take **boat rides** around the coast to such points as San Fruttuoso.

ESSENTIALS

GETTING THERE   Take the **train** first to Santa Margherita Ligure (above), then continue the rest of the way by bus. Tigullio **buses** leave Santa Margherita Ligure once every 30 minutes bound for Portofino, costing 1,700L ($1) one-way, and you can buy tickets aboard the bus. Call ☎ **0185/288-8334** for information and schedules. If you've got a **car** and are in Santa Margherita Ligure, continue south along the only road, hugging the promontory, until you reach Portofino. In summer, traffic is likely to be heavy.

VISITOR INFORMATION   The **tourist office** is at Via Roma 35 (☎ **0185/ 269-024**). It's open daily: summer 9:30am to 1pm and 1:30 to 6:30pm and off-season 9:30am to 12:30pm and 2:30 to 5:30pm.

ACCOMMODATIONS

Portofino is severely limited in hotels. In July and August, you may be forced to book a room in nearby Santa Margherita Ligure or Rapallo.

✪ **Albergo Nazionale.** 16034 Portofino. ☎ **0185/269-575.** Fax 0185/269-578. 16 units. MINIBAR TV TEL. 300,000–450,000L ($174–$261) double; 450,000–500,000L ($261–$290) suite. MC, V. Closed Nov 20–Mar 20.

At stage center right on the harbor, this old villa is modest yet well laid out. It was restored and renovated in the mid-1980s. The suites are tastefully decorated, and the little lounge has a brick fireplace, a coved ceiling, antique furnishings, and good reproductions. Most of the guest rooms, furnished in a mix of styles (hand-painted Venetian in some rooms), open onto a view of the harbor.

✪ **Albergo Splendido.** Viale Baratta 13, 16034 Portofino. ☎ **800/237-1236** in the U.S., or 0185/269-551. Fax 0185/269-614. E-mail: splendido@pn.itnet.it 67 units. A/C MINIBAR TV

The Pearl of the Italian Riviera

Even though now overrun by tourists slurping ice cream, **Portofino** has gone down in the annals of world chicdom as a haven for the elite who arrive by yacht and occupy villas in the hills. They appear at the portside bars and piazzetta of Portofino only when the day-trippers have mercifully departed. The locals call the visitors "barbarians," though most working people in Portofino live exclusively off them.

No one seems to know for sure who launched this tiny fishing village into fashion, making it known worldwide as the "Pearl of the Italian Riviera." Perhaps it was Guy de Maupassant, who arrived in 1889 aboard his sailboat *Bel-Ami*, named after the French author's frivolous but successful novel.

However, it was the British—not the French—who have been enraptured with Portofino, at least since the 19th century. Their connection goes back even earlier, as Richard the Lion-Hearted sailed from here in 1190 on the Third Crusade. In the 1960s, British actor Rex Harrison, famed for *My Fair Lady*, invited the world's most notorious lovers (at the time), Elizabeth Taylor and Richard Burton, to visit him at Portofino. The three were recovering from the debacle called *Cleopatra*, in which they had starred. Taylor's visit is long remembered. Villagers crowded around her as she emerged from various boutiques, holding up their babies for her to admire, often aggressively thrusting them in her face. It soon became apparent they were actually trying to sell their babies to the fabled star and were quoting amounts in lire. Taylor didn't purchase any babies that night but did spend more than $5,000 in one boutique alone.

Such are the happenings and events likely to occur at the harbor of Portofino and in the Splendido on the hill, one of the most famous and expensive hotels in Italy. The hotel, too, would have its stories to tell, especially after such illustrious guests as the duke and duchess of Windsor, Ernest Hemingway, Greta Garbo, Ingrid Bergman, Aristotle Onassis, Clark Gable, John Wayne, and even Larry Hagman had come to call.

Today a lot of villas in the hills around Portofino remain unoccupied. Continuing corruption scandals in Italy have meant that some of the powerful elite are lying low and avoiding such high-profile paparazzi-packed resorts.

TEL. 1,120,000–1,380,000L ($650–$800) double; 1,820,000–2,500,000L ($1,056–$1,450) suite for two. Rates include half board. AE, DC, MC, V. Closed Jan 3–Mar 20. Parking 35,000L ($20).

This Relais & Châteaux property, reached by a steep and winding road from the port, provides a luxury base for those who moor their yachts in the harbor or have closed down their Palm Beach residences for the summer and can afford its outrageous prices. The four-story structure was built as a monastery during the Middle Ages, but pirates attacked so frequently that the monks abandoned it. Later it became a family summer home. The building opened as a hotel in 1901, set on 4 acres of semitropical gardens, and has attracted the likes of Winston Churchill. The rambling villa offers several levels of public rooms, terraces, and "oh, that view" guest rooms. Each room is furnished in a personal way—no two alike.

Dining: The dining room is divided by arches and furnished with Biedermeier chairs, flower bouquets, and a fine old tapestry. The restaurant terrace enjoys a fine view and serves traditional Ligurian and international specialties.

Amenities: Room service, baby-sitting, laundry/valet, massage, hotel speedboat, heated saltwater pool, beauty center, solarium, sauna.

Hotel Eden. Vico Dritto 18, 16034 Portofino. ☎ **0185/269-091.** Fax 0185/269-047. 9 units. MINIBAR TV TEL. 250,000–330,000L ($145–$191) double. Rates include breakfast. AE, DC, MC, V. Closed Dec 1–20. Public parking 30,000L ($17).

Just 150 feet away from the harbor in the heart of the village and set in a garden (hence its name), this albergo is a budget holdout in an otherwise high-fashion resort. Though it doesn't have a view of the harbor, there's a winning vista from the front veranda, where breakfast is served. The hotel is run by Mr. Ferruccio, and life here is decidedly casual.

DINING

Da U'Batti. Vico Nuovo 17. ☎ **0185/269-379.** Reservations recommended. Main courses 45,000–50,000L ($26–$29); fixed-price menu 75,000L ($44). AE, DC, MC, V. Tues–Sun noon–3pm and 8–11pm. Closed Dec–Jan. SEAFOOD.

Informal and colorful, this place is on a narrow cobblestone-covered piazza a few steps above the port. A pair of barnacle-encrusted anchors hanging above the arched entrance hint at the seafaring specialties that have become this place's trademark. Owner/sommelier Giancarlo Foppiano serves delectable dishes, which might include a soup of "hen clams," rice with shrimp or crayfish, or fish alla Battista. It has a good selection of grappa, as well as French and Italian wines.

Delfino. Piazza Martiri delli Olivetta 40. ☎ **0185/269-081.** Reservations recommended Sat. Main courses 30,000–90,000L ($17–$52). AE, DC, MC, V. Apr–Oct daily noon–3pm and 7–11pm; Nov–Mar Tues–Sun noon–2:30pm and 7–10:30pm. SEAFOOD.

Opened in the 1800s on the village square that fronts the harbor, Delfino is Portofino's most fashionable dining spot (along with Il Pitosforo, below). It's both nautically rustic and informally chic and offers virtually the same type of food as Il Pitosforo, including lasagne al pesto. The fish dishes are the best bets: zuppa di pesce (a soup made of freshly caught fish with a secret spice blend) and risotto with shrimp, sole, squid, and other sea creatures. The chef also prides himself on his sage-seasoned vitello all'uccelletto, roast veal with a gamey taste. Try to get a table near the front so you can enjoy (or at least be amused by) the parade of visitors and villagers.

Il Pitosforo. Molo Umberto I 9. ☎ **0185/269-020.** Reservations required. Main courses 45,000–70,000L ($26–$41). AE, DC, MC, V. Wed–Sun 7:30–11pm. Closed from the end of Nov to Feb and for lunch Apr–Oct. LIGURIAN/ITALIAN.

You have to climb some steps to reach this place, which draws raves when the meal is served and, most likely, wails when the tab is presented. While not blessed with an especially distinguished decor, its position right on the harbor gives it all the native chic it needs. Zuppa di pesce is a delectable Ligurian fish soup, or you may prefer the bouillabaisse, which is always reliable. The pastas are especially tasty and include lasagne al pesto, wide noodles prepared in typical Genovese sauce. Fish dishes feature mussels alla marinara and paella valenciana for two, saffron-flavored rice studded with seafood and chicken. Some meat and fish dishes are grilled over hot stones, others over charcoal.

Ristorante da Puny. Piazza Martiri dell'Olivetta. ☎ **0185/269-037.** Reservations required. Main courses 28,000–38,000L ($16–$22). No credit cards. Fri–Wed noon–3pm and 7–11pm. Closed Dec 15–Feb 20. SEAFOOD.

Da Puny is set up on the stone square that opens onto the harbor. Because of its location, it's practically in the living room of Portofino, within sight of the evening activities of the oh-so-chic and oh-so-tan yachting set. Green-painted tables are set under trees at night on a slate-covered outdoor terrace. The menu includes pappardelle Portofino, antipasto of the house, spaghetti with clams, baked fish with potatoes and olives, fried zucchini flowers, and an array of freshly caught fish.

PORTOFINO AFTER DARK

La Gritta American Bar, Calata Marconi 20 (☎ 0185/269-126), vies for business with its rival a few storefronts away (below). It's said that Rex Harrison, while drinking here with the duke of Windsor, excused himself to go and buy a package of cigarettes. He never came back—on the way for the cigarettes, he ran into actress Kay Kendal and the two eloped. These celebrities have intermingled with dozens of tourists and a collection of U.S. Navy personnel in the small well-appointed restaurant. As James Jones, author of *From Here to Eternity,* noted: "This is the nicest waterfront bar this side of Hong Kong." That's true, but it's always wise to check your bar tab carefully before you stagger out looking for a new adventure. It's open Friday to Wednesday 8:30pm to 3am.

Scafandro American Bar, Calata Marconi 10 (☎ 0185/269-105), is one of the village's chic rendezvous points, a place that has attracted a slew of yachting guests. The three-quarter-round banquettes inside contribute to the general feeling of well-being. If some international celebrity doesn't happen to come in while you're here, you can always study one of the series of unusual nautical engravings adorning the walls. It's open Wednesday to Monday 10:30am to 3am.

6 The Cinque Terre

Monterosso: 56 miles E of Genoa, 6 miles W of La Spezia

Among olive and chestnut groves on steep, rocky terrain overlooking the gulf of Genoa, the communities of Corniglia, Manarola, Riomaggiore, and Vernazza offer a glimpse into another time. These rural villages, inaccessible by car, are an agricultural belt where garden and vineyard exist side-by-side. Together with their "city cousin" Monterosso, they're known as the **Cinque Terre** ("five lands"). The northernmost town, Monterosso, is the tourist hub of the region, with traffic, crowds, and the only notable glimpse of contemporary urban life here.

The area is best known for its culinary delights, culled from forest, field, and sea. Here the land yields an incredible variety of edible mushrooms, and oregano, borage, rosemary, and sage grow abundantly. The pine nuts essential to pesto are easily collected from the forests, as are chestnuts for making flour and olives for the oil at the base of all dishes. Garlic and leeks flavor sautéed dishes, whereas beets turn up unexpectedly in ravioli and other dishes. Fishing boats add their rich hauls of anchovies, mussels, squid, octopus, and shellfish, and to wash it all down, vineyards produce Sciacchetra, a DOC wine, rarer than many other Italian varieties because of the low 25% yield characteristic of the Vermentino, Bosco, and Albarola grapes from which it's derived.

Most visitors explore the villages by excursion boat. To avoid these crowds and really get to know the region, you may want to stroll along its renowned walking paths that meander scenically for miles across the hills and through the forests.

ESSENTIALS

GETTING THERE   Hourly **trains** run from Genoa to La Spezia, a trip of 1½ hours, where you must backtrack by rail to any of the five towns you wish to visit. Once in the Cinque Terre, local trains, which run frequently between the five stops, offer daily unlimited travel at a cost of 5,000L ($2.90). For more information, dial ☎ 1478/88-088 toll free in Italy only.

If you've got a **car** and you're coming from Genoa, take A12 and exit at Monterosso—the only town of the five you can actually approach by car. A gigantic parking lot accommodates visitors, who then travel between the towns by rail, boat, or foot. **Navagazione Golfo dei Porto** (☎ 0185/967-676) plies the waters between Monterosso and Manarola or Riomaggiore five times daily, whereas Motobarca Vernazza runs hourly to Vernazza.

VISITOR INFORMATION The **APT office** for the five villages is in Monterosso, Via Fegina 38 (☎ 0185/817-506). April to October, it's open Monday to Saturday 10am to noon and 5 to 7:30pm and Sunday 10am to noon.

EXPLORING THE COAST

There are 14 **walking trails** laid out for exploring the wilds of the area, as well as functioning as a viable way of going from town to town. The APT office above offers a brochure, "Footpaths Along the Cinque Terre and the Eastern Riviera," which defines and maps out routes ranging as far north as Deiva Marina and as far south as Portovenere but suggests several within the boundaries of the Cinque Terre as well. Each hike takes from 1 to 5 hours. Some turn inland, emphasizing the hills and forests of the region. The longest and most scenic, highlighting both coast and forest, is the Sentieri Azzurri ("azure path along the coast"), running from Monterosso, starting near the town hall, to Riomaggiore, ending along the Via dell'Amore. En route, you pass through Vernazza, Corniglia, and Manarola.

Good walking shoes, long pants, and a rain jacket are suggested gear for even the least strenuous of the routes, along with a water bottle and snacks. Many routes are steep and some include hazards like frequent landslides. A walking companion is recommended, and in case of accident the **local emergency telephone number** is ☎ 115.

ACCOMMODATIONS
In Monterosso

Hotel Baia. Via Fegina 72, 19016 Monterosso. ☎ **0187/817-512.** Fax 0187/818-322. 29 units. TV TEL. 200,000L ($116) double. Rates include breakfast. MC, V. Closed Nov–Feb.

Opened in 1911, this hotel features a private beach and comfortable rooms where the whitewashed furniture lends an illusion of size and space. The restaurant serves regional seafood specialties, and patio dining is available overlooking the beach. What it doesn't offer is air-conditioning or shuttle service—but the train station is only 110 yards away.

Hotel Jolie. Via Gioberti 1, 19016 Monterosso. ☎ **0187/817-539.** Fax 0187/817-273. 31 units. TV TEL. 200,000–325,000L ($116–$189) double. Rates include breakfast. MC, V. Closed Jan 10–Feb 7.

This pleasant inn only 160 yards to the beach features well-furnished and soundproofed rooms, a solarium, a garden, and a restaurant serving local and national cuisine prepared by the owner himself. Don't expect a lot of excitement if you stay here, but you can be moved by scenes on local life: a rainbow of laundry flapping in the wind, grandmothers sitting in ancient doorways watching life drift by, and kids playing soccer on the breakwater.

Hotel Palme. Via IV Novembre 18, 19016 Monterosso. ☎ **0187/829-013.** Fax 0187/829-081. 49 units. A/C MINIBAR TEL. 210,000–260,000L ($122–$151) double. Rates include breakfast. AE, DC, MC, V. Closed Nov–Mar.

One street away from the beach, this 30-year-old hotel was renovated 15 years ago. The decor leaves something to be desired: bright abstract fabrics looking gaudy in contrast to dark wood furniture and unflattering fluorescent lighting in the dining room. Nevertheless, it's comfortable, with a conscientious staff. Actually, the guest rooms are more inviting than the public areas, relying more on muted blues and whites to create a relaxed atmosphere. There's a game room, bar, and shaded garden. Although the hotel doesn't have its own restaurant, the staff recommends one adjacent to it.

Hotel Pasquale. Via Fegina 4, 19016 Monterosso. ☎ **0187/817-477.** Fax 0187/817-056. www.pasini.com. E-mail: pasquale@pasini.com. 15 units. A/C TV TEL. 170,000L ($99) double. Rates include breakfast. MC, V.

This small hotel sits right by the beach, offering both intimacy and privacy since its small number of guests are spread out across four floors. It was built and opened as a hotel 36 years ago and updated in 1994. It's modern and has been decorated in the manner of a private Genovan home. The bar/restaurant is reminiscent of an Italian coffee shop, with gleaming marble floors, glass cases, dark wood wainscoting, window frames, and a service counter accented with a brass rail and foot guard.

✪ **Hotel Porto Roca.** Via Corone 1, 19016 Monterosso. ☎ **0187/817-502.** Fax 1087/817-692. 43 units. A/C MINIBAR TV TEL. 250,000–320,000L ($145–$186) double. Rates include breakfast. AE, MC, V. Closed Nov–Mar.

You give up direct beach access to stay here, but it's a small price to pay for accommodations as gracious as these. The hotel is set on a cliff offering panoramic views of the village and harbor, and every corner is filled with eclectic antiques, knickknacks, and art, mixing Oriental rugs with wooden furniture ranging from the simple to the ornate. The terrace, hemmed in by a curvaceous wrought-iron railing and lit by matching globe lamps, is alive with lush greenery and an assortment of white-blossomed flowers that complement the blue of the bay. The restaurant serves local seafood, and its large dining room offers privacy through the placement of columns and Liberty-style glass screens. The bar also allows privacy, clustering furniture to create cozy pockets in which to relax and converse. Its fanciful fireplace adds warmth on cool off-season days.

IN MANAROLA

Hotel Ca' d'Andrean. Via Lo Scalo 101, 19010 Manarola. ☎ **0187/920-040.** Fax 0187/920-652. 10 units. TEL. 105,000L ($61) double. Breakfast 9,000L ($5). No credit cards. Closed Nov.

A small garden is the nicest feature of this bare-bones three-story hotel, which opened in a former private home in 1988. The building that contains it was owned a century ago by the grandparents of the present owners. The guest rooms, each with a simple white-walled decor, are clean, uncomplicated, and straightforward. There is a bar, but no restaurant, on the premises.

Hotel Marina Piccola. Via Lo Scalo 16, 19010 Manarola. ☎ **0187/920-103.** Fax 0187/920-966. 10 units. TEL. 110,000L ($64) per person double. Rates include half board. AE, DC, MC, V. Closed Jan.

With 10 rooms spread across 5 floors, this former home is a hotel as vertical as the town that houses it. Opened in 1981, there's a rustic charm to the small rooms, which feature wrought-iron beds. There's no bar, but the restaurant, as simply decorated as the hotel, offers a great view of the harbor. The cuisine is typical of the region (see "Dining," below).

IN VERNAZZA

Locanda Barbara. Piazza Marconi 21, 19018 Vernazza. ☎ and fax **0187/812-398.** 9 units, none with bathroom. 70,000–80,000L ($41–$46) double. AE. Closed Dec–Jan.

Offering small, simple rooms with no amenities, this is the economical way to sample the simplicity of life in this undeveloped region. Your room will lie on the street level of the circa 1965 modern building that also, under separate management, contains the town's most appealing restaurant, the Taverna del Capitano (see "Dining," below).

IN RIOMAGGIORE

Villa Argentina. Via de Gaspari 187, 19017 Riomaggiore. ☎ **0187/920-213.** 15 units. TV. 110,000–125,000L ($66–$73) double. Rates include breakfast. AE, DC, MC, V. Closed Nov.

This 21-year-old hotel has a maritime theme, and its greatest asset is its quiet country setting just outside town. If you don't feel like walking, an efficient shuttle service will transport you into the village. There's no air-conditioning, but each room has a ceiling fan—somewhat more effective than it would be in the heart of the village. There's a small restaurant and a bar on the premises. Although it's a simple choice, its prices evoke Italy of the late 1960s.

DINING
IN MONTEROSSO

Il Gigante. Via IV Novembre 9. ☎ **0187/817-401.** Reservations recommended on holidays. Main courses 16,000–30,000L ($9–$17). AE, DC, MC, V. Daily noon–3pm and 6:30–10pm. Closed some Mon. LIGURIAN.

This traditional trattoria is one of the best places to introduce yourself to the flavorful cuisine of Liguria, and there's no better introduction than the zuppa di pesce. Actually the fish soup is enough for a main course, but locals are rarely satisfied with just soup. Another pleasing first course—and one most typical of the area—is minestrone alla genovese, a bean-and-vegetable soup flavored with the inevitable pesto. Waiters cite the daily specials, none more delectable than a risotto made with freshly plucked shellfish. To go truly Ligurian, opt for the spaghetti with octopus sauce. The mixed grill is another savory offering. Though the restaurant in theory is open daily, watch for erratic and unannounced closings on Monday.

IN MANAROLA

Aristide. Via Lo Scalo 138. ☎ **0187/920-000.** Reservations recommended. Main courses 18,000–25,000L ($10–$15); fixed-price menus Mon–Fri 15,000–35,000L ($9–$20); Sat–Sun 50,000–60,000L ($29–$35). No credit cards. Tues–Sun and holidays noon–2:30pm and 7–10pm. LIGURIAN.

This comfortable old trattoria showcases the simplicity of the region's cuisine, combining a few key ingredients in tasty combinations. The weekday fixed-price menu includes wine with the meal, and the weekend version also features antipasto and coffee. House specialties include lasagne al pesto, penne all'aragosta, and zuppa di pesce, one of the most savory kettles of fish in the "five lands." Traditional recipes have never been forgotten and are always part of the menu.

Marina Piccola. Via Lo Scalo 16. ☎ **0187/920-103.** Reservations recommended. Main courses 18,000–29,000L ($10–$17). AE, DC, MC, V. Wed–Mon noon–3pm and 7–10pm. LIGURIAN.

This simple restaurant is next to the inn of the same name (see above). Gruff but well-meaning, this eatery is imbued with a maritime, almost naval matter-of-factness that's absolutely void of any pretensions. For a Ligurian palate tantalizer, try cozze ripiene, mussels cooked in white wine and served with butter sauce. Squid in its own ink tastes best when combined with homemade spaghetti. Fresh sardines are a local crowd pleaser, and another homemade pasta, trenette, comes flavored with some of the best-tasting pesto along the coast. Grilled fish is the invariable favorite for a main dish. It's always fresh and perfectly prepared, though seasoned simply, as is the Ligurian style.

IN VERNAZZA

Gianni Franzi. Via Visconti 2. ☎ **0187/812-228.** Reservations recommended. Main courses 20,000–32,000L ($12–$19). AE, DC, MC, V. Closed Wed from Jan 10–Mar 8. LIGURIAN.

Don't expect high-blown manners or even too strong an allegiance to old-fashioned protocol. Much of the activity revolves around the active bar area, where patrons seem to know one another well. Expect high noise volumes, hysterical waiters, and—on bad days—a staff that's been somewhat jaded. But overall, the cuisine is better than you might think and served in large portions. The mixed grill of fish is a sure-fire palate pleaser, as are the white sardines of the area that might appear on a platter, garnished with lemon and Mediterranean herbs.

Il Gambero Rosso. Piazza Marconi 7. ☎ **0187/812-265.** Reservations recommended Sat–Sun. Main courses 20,000–38,000L ($12–$22); fixed-price menu 55,000L ($32). AE, DC, MC, V. Tues–Sun 12:30–3pm and 7:30–10:30pm. Closed mid-Dec to Mar 1. LIGURIAN.

Opened 108 years ago, this restaurant is high up on a rocky cliff overlooking the sea. Ask for a table on the terrace to make the most of this setting. The food is typically Ligurian, and house specialties include ravioli stuffed with fresh fish. The wonderful porcini mushrooms that are harvested in the area figure into some dishes. Many of the recipes were passed by word of mouth from mother to daughter. A lot of the flavoring is based on the use of herbs and other ingredients that grow in the hills. The pesto sauce is made with the best olive oil and mixed with basil, grated cheese, pine nuts, and fresh marjoram.

✳ Taverna del Capitano. Piazza Marconi 21, in the Locanda Barbara. ☎ **0187/812-224.** Reservations recommended. Main courses 14,000–25,000L ($8–$15). MC, V. Thurs–Tues 7:30am–3pm and 7–10pm. Closed Dec–Jan. LIGURIAN.

This tavern is on the top floor of a two-story hotel whose street level contains the Locanda Barbara, under separate management. It's one of the best eateries in all the Cinque Terre, seating 60 in three informal and nautically rustic dining rooms. Its most popular dishes are grilled prawns, grilled beef filet, potato-based gnocchi, pasta with pesto sauce, and linguine flavored with crabmeat.

Naples, the Amalfi Coast & Capri

14

Campania is in many ways Italy's most eerie, memorable, and beautiful region. It forms a fertile crescent around the bays of Naples and Sorrento and stretches inland into a landscape of limestone rocks dotted with patches of fertile soil. It was off the shores of Campania that Ulysses ordered his crew to tie him to the mast of his ship, ears unstopped, so he alone would hear the songs of the sirens without throwing himself overboard to sample their pleasures. Today the siren song of Campania still lures, with a chemistry that some visitors insist is an aphrodisiac.

The geological oddities of Campania include a smoldering and dangerous volcano (already famous for having destroyed Pompeii and Herculaneum), sulfurous springs that belch steam and smelly gases, and lakes that ancient myths refer to as the gateway to Hades. Its seaside highway is the most beautiful, and probably the most treacherous, in the world, combining danger at every hairpin turn with some of Italy's most reckless drivers. Despite such dark images, Campania is a most captivating region, sought out by native Italians and visitors alike for its combination of earth, sea, and sky. Coupled with this are Europe's densest collection of ancient ruins, each celebrated by classical scholars as among the very best of its kind.

The ancient Romans dubbed the land Campania Felix, which may reflect their satisfaction with the district that inspired the construction of hundreds of private villas. In some ways, the beauty of Campania contributed to the decay of the Roman Empire, as emperors, their senators, and their courtiers spent more and more time pursuing its pleasures and abandoning the cares of Rome's administrative problems. Even today, seafront land here is so desirable that hoteliers have poured their life savings into buildings that are sometimes bizarrely cantilevered above rock-studded cliffs. Despite their numbers, these hotels tend to be profitably overbooked in summer.

Although residents of Campania sometimes stridently extol the virtues of its cuisine, it's not the most renowned in Italy. The region's produce, however, is superb, its wine is heady, and its pizzas are highly memorable.

Today Campania typifies the conditions that northern Italians label "the problem of the south." Although the inequities are the most pronounced in **Naples,** the entire region, outside the resorts along the coast, has a lower standard of living and education and higher crime rates, plus less developed standards of health care, than the more affluent north.

When the English say "see Naples and die," they mean the city and the bay, with majestic Vesuvius in the background. When the Germans use the expression, they mean the **Amalfi Drive.** Indeed, several motorists do die each year on the dangerous coastal road, too narrow to accommodate the heavy stream of summer traffic, especially the large tour buses that almost sideswipe one another as they try to pass. Moreover, when driving along the coast you sometimes find it difficult to concentrate on the road because of the view. The drive, remarked André Gide, "is so beautiful that nothing more beautiful can be seen on this earth."

The island of **Capri** has long been known to international travelers. But the popularity of the resort-studded Amalfi Coast is a more recent phenomenon. It was discovered by German officers during World War II, then later by American and English servicemen (Positano was a British rest camp in the last months of the war). When the war was over, many of these servicemen returned, often bringing their families. The fishing villages in time became major tourism centers, with hotels and restaurants in all categories.

Sorrento and Amalfi are in the vanguard, with the widest range of facilities; Positano has more snob appeal and is popular with artists; Ravello is still the choice of the discriminating few, such as Gore Vidal, who desire relative seclusion. To cap off an Amalfi adventure, you can take a boat from Sorrento to Capri, which needs no advance booking. Three sightseeing attractions in this area—in addition to the towns and villages—are worthy of a special pilgrimage: the Emerald Grotto between Amalfi and Positano, the Blue Grotto of Capri, and the Greek temples of the ancient Sybarite-founded city of Paestum.

Wine connoisseurs traveling through the area might want to call for an appointment at one of the best wineries in the district. Refer to the "Campania" entry under "The Best Wine-Growing Regions" in chapter 1.

1 Naples: Gateway to Campania

136 miles SE of Rome, 162 miles W of Bari

Naples (Napoli) is Italy's most controversial city: You'll either love it or hate it. Is it paradiso or the inferno? It's louder, more intense, more unnerving, but perhaps ultimately more satisfying than almost anywhere else in Italy.

Naples has changed a lot since the 1973 cholera outbreak, when the world discovered it had no sewers and was basking on the edge of a picturesque but poisoned bay. New civic centers have been planned and some of the city's baroque palaces restored. But to foreigners unfamiliar with the complexities of the multifarious "Italys" and their regional types, the Neapolitan is still the quintessence of the country and easy to caricature ("O Sole Mio," "Mamma Mia," bel canto). If Sophia Loren (a native who moved elsewhere) evokes the Italian woman for you, you'll find more of her look-alikes here than in any other city. Naples also gave the world Enrico Caruso.

More visible are the city's children. In one of the most memorable novels to come out of World War II, *The Gallery* by John Horne Burns, there's this passage: "But I remember best of all the children of Naples, the *scugnizzi*. Naples is the greatest baby

The Amalfi Coast

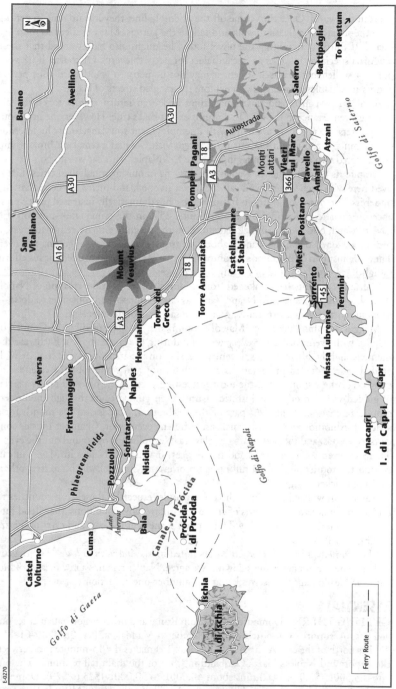

E-0270

Ferry Route ———

plant in the world. Once they come off the assembly line, they lose no time in getting onto the streets. They learn to walk and talk in the gutters. Many of them seem to live there." If Burns were writing the novel today, he might also have warned that these scugnizzi specialize in *lo scippo* (local dialect for petty thievery). Of course, if it's your purse or wallet that has been stolen, it may not be petty to you. Guard your person and your valuables carefully as you explore the tangled streets of Naples.

A lot a newspapers and travel magazines and even return visitors to Naples are touting a renaissance in the city. To a minor extent that's true. However, the notorious pickpockets are as busy as ever, and with unemployment still dangerously high, crime is very much a real factor. On our most recent visit, we had a rental car broken into and suffered two attempted muggings, so we feel Naples has a far way to go.

Despite its many problems, Naples remains one of our favorite Italian cities. Life is lived here with such vivacity you can fall under its spell, and there's a renewed vitality under its current mayor, Antonio Bassolino. He has dramatically increased police presence on the streets, leading to a drop of some 25% in the crime rate—but you still have to watch out. He has also closed streets in the magnificent city center to create a pedestrian zone, so you can wander about sightseeing without fear of getting run over. These are just two of Bassolino's accomplishments. He's to be applauded for his efforts in lighting a candle instead of cursing the darkness.

Culturally, the city has awakened from a long slumber with the creation of Napoli '99. This group of concerned Neapolitans has raised funds—and continues to do so—to maintain the city's art treasures, many in a sad state of deterioration.

Maggio dei Monumenti, or "May of Monuments," is sponsored by the Council of Naples, with events occurring every weekend during the entire month. Each year the theme is slightly different, most recently focusing on the ancient gates of the city with guided tours. Musical presentations and exhibitions also round out the calendar of events. For the visitor, one of the most interesting parts of the observations is a series of guided walks through the historic district, even guided tours through the underground passages of Naples. As part of the celebration, May is also the month for a series of exhibitions and fairs, which are different every year. Chamber music, concerts, operettas, and the performing of classical Neapolitan songs round out the event. There are even soccer matches and horse races. If you're in Naples in May, you can consult the tourist office for a full program of events, some of which are free, others carrying a ticket charge.

Naples is now gaining favor with young people, especially those from countries to the north. Undeterred by reports of crime and unfavorable conditions, they flood into the city and lend it a new vitality. The hippest scene is at the bars and cafes on Piazza Bellini, near Piazza Dante.

"The comedy is broad," Herbert Kubly noted in his *American in Italy.* "The tragedy violent. The curtain never rings down." We agree. Naples remains a raw theater of life, with the Neapolitans themselves being the number-one attraction.

ESSENTIALS

GETTING THERE Domestic flights from Rome and other major Italian cities put you into **Aeroporto Capodichino,** Via Umberto Maddalena (☎ **081/789-61-11**), 4 miles north of the city. A city ATAN bus (no. 14) makes the 15-minute run between the airport and Naples's Piazza Garibaldi in front of the main rail terminus. The bus fare is 3,500L ($2.05); a taxi runs about 40,000L to 50,000L ($23 to $29). Domestic flights are available on Alitalia, Alisarda, and Ati. Flying time from Milan is 1½ hours, from Palermo 1¼ hours, from Rome 50 minutes, and from Venice 1¼ hours.

Frequent **trains** connect Naples with the rest of Italy. One or two trains per hour arrive from Rome, taking 2½ hours and costing from 18,000L ($10) one-way. It's also possible to reach Naples from Milan in about 8 hours, costing from 64,000L ($37) one-way.

The city has two main rail terminals: **Stazione Centrale,** at Piazza Garibaldi, and **Stazione Mergellina,** at Piazza Piedigrotta. For general rail information, call ☎ 081/147-88-80-88 or 1478/88-088 toll free in Italy only.

Alitalia, in collaboration with FS, the Italian State Railways, links Naples with Rome's Leonardo da Vinci International Airport without intermediate stops. Twice a day, the "Alitalia Airport Train by FS" departs from Stazione Mergellina, heading north to Rome and the airport. To travel on the airport train, you must have an Alitalia airline ticket.

In the old days the custom was to sail into the Bay of Naples, but today's traveler is more likely to **drive** here, heading down the autostrada from Rome. The Rome-Naples autostrada (A2) passes Caserta 18 miles north of Naples and the Naples-Reggio di Calabria autostrada (A3) runs by Salerno, 33 miles north of Naples.

From Sicily, you can go on a **ferry** to Naples from Palermo on **Tirrenia Lines,** Molo Angionio, Stazione Marritima (☎ 091/333-300), in the port area of Palermo. A one-way ticket is 60,000L ($35) armchair and 90,000L ($52) first-class cabin per person for the 10½-hour trip.

VISITOR INFORMATION   The **Ente Provinciale per il Turismo,** at Stazione Centrale (☎ 081/268-779), is open daily 8:30am to 8:30pm. There's another office at Piazza del Gesù Nuovo 7 (☎ 081/552-3328), open Monday to Saturday 9am to 2:30pm and 3:30 to 7:30pm and Sunday 9am to 2pm.

CITY LAYOUT   If you arrive by train at Stazione Centrale, in front of **Piazza Garibaldi,** you'll want to escape from that horror by taking one of Naples's major arteries, **Corso Umberto,** in the direction of the Santa Lucia district. Along the water, many boats, such as those heading for Capri and Ischia, leave from **Porto Beverello.**

Many people confine their visit to the bayside **Santa Lucia** area and perhaps venture into another section to see an important museum. Most of the major hotels lie along **Via Partenope,** which looks out not only to the Gulf of Naples but also to the Castel dell'Ovo. To the west is the **Mergellina** district, site of many restaurants and dozens of apartment houses. The far western section of the city is known as **Posillipo.**

One of the most important squares is **Piazza del Plebiscito,** north of Santa Lucia. The Palazzo Reale opens onto this square. A satellite is **Piazza Trento y Trieste,** with its Teatro San Carlo and entrance to the famed Galleria Umberto I. To the east is the third most important square, **Piazza Municipio.** From Piazza Trento y Trieste, you encounter the main shopping street, **Via Toledo/Via Roma,** on which you can walk as far as Piazza Dante. From that square, take Via Enrico Pessina to the most important museum, located on **Piazza Museo Nazionale.**

GETTING AROUND   The **Metropolitana** line will deliver you from Stazione Centrale in the east all the way to Stazione Mergellina and even beyond to the suburb of Pozzuoli. Get off at Piazza Piedigrotta if you wish to take the funicular to Vómero. The Metro uses the same tickets as buses and trams.

It's dangerous to ride **buses** at rush hours—never have we seen such pushing and shoving. Many people prefer to leave the buses to the battle-hardened Neapolitans and take the subway or **tram** no. 1 or 4, running from Stazione Centrale to Stazione Mergellina. (It'll also let you off at the quayside points where the boats depart for Ischia and Capri.) For a ticket valid for 90 minutes with unlimited transfers during that time, the cost is 1,200L (70¢). However, for a full day of unlimited travel, you can buy a ticket for 4,000L ($2.30).

If you survive the **taxi** driver's reckless driving, you'll only have to do battle over the bill. Many cab drivers claim that the meter is broken and assess the cost of the ride, always to your disadvantage. Some legitimate surcharges are imposed, like night drives and extra luggage. However, many drivers deliberately take you "the long way there" to run up costs. In repeated visits to Naples, we've never yet been quoted an honest fare. We no longer bother with the meter; we estimate what the fare should be, negotiate with the driver, and take off into the night. If you want to take a chance, you can call a radio taxi at ☎ **081/556-4444,** 081/556-0202, or 081/570-7070.

Regarding getting around Naples by **car,** we have one word: Don't.

Funiculars take passengers up and down the steep hills of Naples. The **Funicolare Centrale** (☎ **081/714-5583**), for example, connects the lower part of the city to Vómero. Departures, daily 7am to 10pm, are from Piazzetta Duca d'Aosta, just off Via Roma. Watch that you don't get stranded by missing the last car back. The same tickets valid for buses and the Metro are good for the funicular.

FAST FACTS   American Express   American Express business is handled by Every Tours, Piazza Municipo 5 (☎ **081/551-8564**), open Monday to Saturday 9am to 1:30pm and 3:30 to 6:30pm.

Consulates   You'll find the **U.S. Consulate** on Piazza della Repubblica (☎ **081/583-8111**). Its consular services are open Monday to Friday 8am to noon. The **U.K. Consulate** is at Via Francesco Crispi 122 (☎ **081/663-511**), open Monday to Friday 8am to 1:30pm. Citizens of **Canada, Australia,** and **New Zealand** will need to go to the embassies or consulates in Rome (see "Fast Facts: Rome" in chapter 4).

Drugstore   Try **Farmacia Helvethia,** Piazza Garibaldi 11, near Stazione Centrale (☎ **081/554-8894**).

Emergencies   If you have an emergency, dial ☎ **113.** To reach the police or carabinieri, call ☎ **112.** For an ambulance, call ☎ **113** or **752-0696.**

Medical Care   Try the **Guarda Medica Permanente,** located in each area of town, or call ☎ **113** or ask for directions to the nearest Guarda Medica Permanente at your hotel.

Post Office   The main post office is on Piazza G. Matteotti (☎ **081/551-1456**). Look for the POSTA TELEGRAFO sign. It's open Monday to Friday 8:15am to 7:30pm and Saturday and Sunday 8:15am to 7:30pm.

Telephone   If you need to make a long-distance call, you can do so at Stazione Centrale, where an office is open 24 hours; if you make calls from your hotel, you'll likely be hit with an excessive surcharge.

SEEING THE SIGHTS

Before striking out for Pompeii or Capri, you should try to see some of the sights inside Naples. If you're hard-pressed for time, then settle for the first three museums of renown.

THE TOP MUSEUMS

Note: Reconfirm any museum hours before going there. A guidebook issued annually can't keep up with the changes—they've been known to change from month to month, depending on how little money is in the city treasury. Even the posted opening hours seem more ornamental than reliable.

۞ National Archaeological Museum (Museo Archeologico Nazionale). Piazza Museo Nazionale 18–19. ☎ **081/440-166.** Admission 12,000L ($7) adults; children 18 and under free. Wed–Mon 10am–10pm, Sun 9am–8pm. Metro: Piazza Cavour.

With its Roman and Greek sculpture, this museum contains one of Europe's most valuable archaeological collections—particularly notable are the select Farnese acquisitions and the mosaics and sculpture excavated at Pompeii and Herculaneum. The building dates from the 16th century and was turned into a museum 2 centuries later by Charles and Ferdinand IV Bourbon.

On the ground floor is one of the treasures of the Farnese collections: The nude statues of Armodio and Aristogitone are the most outstanding in the room. A famous bas-relief (from a 5th-century B.C. original) in a nearby salon depicts Orpheus and Eurydice with Mercury.

The nude statue of the spear-bearing *Doryphorus,* copied from a work by Polyclitus the Elder and excavated at Pompeii, enlivens another room. Also see the gigantic but weary *Hercules,* a statue of remarkable boldness that's a copy of an original by Lysippus, the 4th-century B.C. Greek sculptor for Alexander the Great, and was discovered in Rome's Baths of Caracalla. On a more delicate pedestal is the decapitated but exquisite *Venus* (Aphrodite). The *Psyche of Capua* shows why Aphrodite was jealous. The *Group of the Farnese Bull* presents a pageant of violence from the days of antiquity; a copy of a 2nd- or a 3rd-century B.C. Hellenistic statue—one of the most frequently reproduced—it too was discovered at the Baths of Caracalla. The marble group depicts a scene in the legend of Amphion and Zethus, who tied Dirce, wife of Lycus of Thebes, to the horns of a rampaging bull.

The mezzanine galleries are devoted to mosaics excavated from Pompeii and Herculaneum. These include scenes of cockfights, dragon-tailed satyrs, an aquarium, and *Alexander Fighting the Persians,* the finest of all. On the top floor are some of the celebrated bronzes dug out of the Pompeii volcanic mud and Herculaneum lava. Of particular interest are a Hellenistic portrait of Berenice, a comically drunken satyr, a statue of a sleeping satyr, and Mercury on a rock.

۞ National Museum and Gallery of the Capodimonte (Museo e Gallerie Nazionali di Capodimonte). In the Palazzo Capodimonte, Parco di Capodimonte (off Amedeo di Savoia), Via Milano 2. ☎ **081/744-1307.** Admission 14,000L ($8) adults; children 8 and under free. Tues–Sat 10am–10pm, Sun 10am–8pm. Bus: 22 or 23.

This museum and gallery, one of Italy's finest, are housed in the 18th-century Capodimonte Palace, built in the time of Charles III and set within a park. Seven Flemish tapestries, made according to the designs of Bernart van Orley, show grand-scale scenes from the Battle of Pavia (1525), in which the forces of François I of France—more than 25,000 strong—lost to those of Charles V. Van Orley, who lived in a pre-*Guernica* day, obviously considered war not a horror but a romantic ballet.

One of the picture gallery's greatest possessions is Simone Martini's *Coronation,* depicting the brother of Robert of Anjou being crowned king of Naples by the bishop of Toulouse. You'll want to linger over the great Masaccio's *Crucifixion,* a bold expression of grief. The most important room is literally filled with the works of Renaissance

---

Impressions

The museum is full, as you know, of lovely Greek bronzes. The only bother is that they all walk about the town at night.

—Oscar Wilde, letter to Ernest Dowson (October 11, 1897)

masters, notably an *Adoration of the Child* by Luca Signorelli, a *Madonna and Child* by Perugino, a panel by Raphael, a *Madonna and Child with Angels* by Botticelli, and—the most beautiful—Fillipino Lippi's *Annunciation and Saints.*

Look for Andrea Mantegna's *St. Eufemia* and portrait of Francesco Gonzaga, his brother-in-law Giovanni Bellini's *Transfiguration,* and Lotto's *Portrait of Bernardo de Rossi* and *Madonna and Child with St. Peter.* In one room is Raphael's *Holy Family and St. John* and a copy of his celebrated portrait of Pope Leo X. Two choice sketches are Raphael's *Moses* and Michelangelo's *Three Soldiers.* Displayed farther on are the Titians, with Danae taking the spotlight from Pope Paul III.

Another room is devoted to Flemish art: Pieter Brueghel's *Blind Men* is outstanding, and his *Misanthrope* is devilishly powerful. Other foreign works include Joos van Cleve's *Adoration of the Magi.* You can climb the stairs for a panoramic view of Naples and the bay, a finer landscape than any you'll see inside.

The State Apartments downstairs deserve inspection. Room after room is devoted to gilded mermaids, Venetian sedan chairs, ivory carvings, a porcelain chinoiserie salon, tapestries, the Farnese armory, and a large glass and china collection.

National Museum of San Martino (Museo Nazionale di San Martino). Largo San Martino 5 (in the Vómero district). ☎ 081/578-1769. Admission 8,000L ($4.65) adults; children 17 and under free. Tues–Sun 9am–2pm. Funicular: Centrale from Via Toledo.

Magnificently situated on the grounds of the Castel Sant'Elmo, this museum was founded in the 14th century as a Carthusian monastery but fell into decay until the 17th century, when it was reconstructed by architects in the Neapolitan baroque style. Now a museum for the city of Naples, it displays stately carriages, historic documents, ship replicas, china and porcelain, silver, Campagna paintings of the 19th century, military costumes and armor, and the lavishly adorned crib by Cuciniello. A balcony opens onto a panoramic view of Naples and the bay, as well as Vesuvius and Capri. Many people come here just to drink in the view. The colonnaded cloisters have curious skull sculptures on the inner balustrade.

MORE ATTRACTIONS

Royal Palace (Palazzo Reale). Piazza del Plebiscito 1. ☎ 081/580-8216. Admission 10,000L ($6) adults; children 17 and under free. Tues–Sun 9am–2pm. Bus: 106 or 150.

This palace was designed by Domenico Fontana in the 17th century, and the eight statues on the facade are of Neapolitan kings. In the heart of the city, the square on which the palace stands is one of Naples's most architecturally interesting, with a long colonnade and a church, San Francesco di Paolo, that evokes the style of the Pantheon in Rome. Inside the Palazzo Reale you can visit the royal apartments, adorned in the baroque style with colored marble floors, paintings, tapestries, frescoes, antiques, and porcelain. Charles de Bourbon, son of Philip IV of Spain, became king of Naples in 1734. A great patron of the arts, he installed a library here, one of the greatest in the south, with more than 1,250,000 volumes.

New Castle (Castel Nuovo). Piazza del Municipo. ☎ 81/795-2003. Admission 10,000L ($6) adults; children under 12/seniors over 65 free. Mon–Sat 8am–7pm. Tram: 1 or 4.

The New Castle, housing municipal offices, was built in the late 13th century on orders from Charles I, king of Naples, as a royal residence for the House of Anjou. It was badly ruined and virtually reconstructed in the mid-15th century by the House of Aragón. The castle is distinguished by a trio of imposing round battle towers at its front, and between two of the towers, guarding the entrance, is a triumphal arch designed by Francesco Laurana to commemorate the 1442 expulsion of the Angevins

Naples

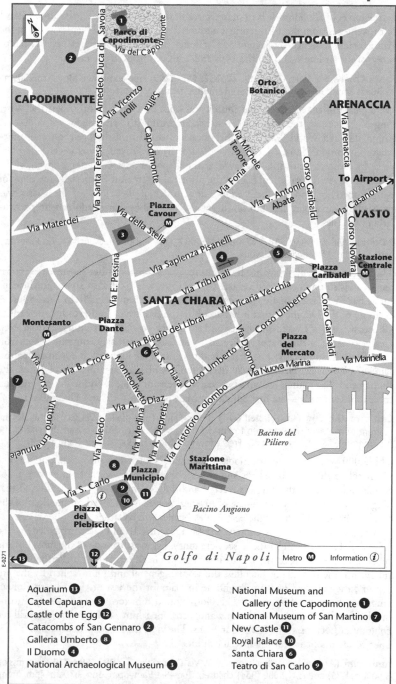

Metro **Ⓜ**   Information **ⓘ**

Aquarium **⑬**
Castel Capuana **⑤**
Castle of the Egg **⑫**
Catacombs of San Gennaro **②**
Galleria Umberto **⑧**
Il Duomo **④**
National Archaeological Museum **③**

National Museum and
   Gallery of the Capodimonte **①**
National Museum of San Martino **⑦**
New Castle **⑪**
Royal Palace **⑩**
Santa Chiara **⑥**
Teatro di San Carlo **⑨**

by the forces of Alphonso I. It's a masterpiece of the Renaissance. The Palatine Chapel in the center is from the 14th century, and the city commission of Naples meets in the Barons' Hall, designed by Segreta of Catalonia. You'll find some frescoes and sculptures (of minor interest) from the 14th and 15th centuries in the castle.

Santa Chiara. Via Santa Chiara 49. ☎ **081/552-6209.** Free admission. Mon–Sat 8:30am–12:30pm and 3:30–6pm, Sun 8:30am–12:30pm. Metro: Montesanto.

On a palazzo-flanked street, this church was built on orders from Robert the Wise, king of Naples, in the early 14th century. It became the church for the House of Anjou. Though World War II bombers heavily blasted it, it has been restored somewhat to its original look, a Gothic style favored by the Provençal architects. The altarpiece by Simone Martini is displayed at the Capodimonte Galleries (above), which leave the Angevin royal sarcophagi as the principal art treasures, especially the tomb of King Robert, behind the main altar. The Cloister of the Order of the Clares was restored by Vaccaro in the 18th century and is marked by ornate adornment, particularly in the tiles.

Il Duomo. Via del Duomo 147. ☎ **081/449-097.** Free admission. Daily 8am–12:30pm and 4:30–7:15pm. Metro: Piazza Cavour.

The Duomo of Naples may not be as impressive as some in other Italian cities, but it merits a visit nonetheless. Consecrated in 1315, it was Gothic in style, but the centuries have witnessed many changes; the facade, for example, is from the 1800s. A curiosity of the Duomo is that it has access to the Basilica of St. Restituta, the earliest Christian basilica erected in Naples and goes back to the 4th century. But an even greater treasure is the chapel dedicated to St. Januarius (San Gennaro), which you enter from the south aisle. The altar is said to contain the blood of St. Gennaro, patron saint of Naples. St. Gennaro may have been a Christian assimilation of Janus, the Roman god. The church contains two vials of the saint's blood, said to liquefy and boil three times annually—the first Sunday in May, September 19, and December 16.

Castle of the Egg (Castel dell'Ovo). Porto Santa Lucia (follow Via Console along the seafront from Piazza del Plebiscito to Porto Santa Lucia; Castel dell'Ovo is at the end of the promontory). ☎ **081/764-5688.** Free admission. Mon–Sat 9am–3pm. Tram: 1 or 4.

This 2,000-year-old fortress overlooks the Gulf of Naples. The site was important centuries before the birth of Christ and was fortified by early settlers. In time a major stronghold to guard the bay was erected and duly celebrated by Virgil. It's said that Virgil built it on an enchanted egg of mystical powers submerged on the floor of the ocean. Legend has it that if the egg breaks, Naples will collapse.

Actually, most of it was constructed by Frederick II and later expanded by the Angevins. Though there's little to see here today, Egg Castle is one of the most historic spots in Naples, perhaps the site of the original Greek settlement of Parthenope. In time it became the villa of Lucullus, the Roman general and philosopher. By the 5th century, the villa had become the home in exile for the last of the western Roman emperors, Romulus Augustulus. The Goths found him too young and stupid to be much of a threat to their ambitions and pensioned him off here. You can still see columns of Lucullus's villa in the dungeons. The view from here is panoramic. It's not open to the public except for special exhibits.

Aquarium (Acquario). Villa Comunale 1, Via Caracciolo. ☎ **081/583-3111.** Admission 3,000L ($1.75) adults, 1,500L (85¢) children. Tues–Sat 9am–6pm, Sun 9:30am–7pm. Tram: 1 or 4.

The Aquarium is in a municipal park, Villa Comunale, between Via Caracciolo and the Riviera di Chiaia. Established by a German naturalist in the 1800s, it's the oldest aquarium in Europe and displays about 200 species of marine plants and fish, all found in the Bay of Naples (they must be a hardy lot).

Catacombe di San Gennaro (St. Januarius). In the Chiesa del Buon Consiglio, Via di Capodimonte 13. ☎ **081/741-1071.** Admission 5,000L ($2.90); children free. Tours daily 9:30am–12:30pm. Tram: 1 or 4.

A guide will show you through this two-story underground cemetery, dating back to the 2nd century and boasting many interesting frescoes and mosaics. You enter the catacombs on Via di Capodimonte (head down an alley going alongside the Madre del Buon Consiglio Church).

SHOPPING

Naples is hardly the shopper's paradise Milan, Venice, Florence, and Rome are. Nevertheless, there are some good buys for those willing to seek them out. The finest shopping area lies around **Piazza dei Martiri** and along such streets as **Via dei Mille, Via Calabritto,** and **Via Chiaia.** There's more commercial shopping between Piazza Trieste e Trento and Piazza Dante along **Via Toledo/Via Roma.**

Coral is much sought after by collectors. Much of the coral is now sent to Naples from Thailand, but it's still shaped into amazing jewelry at one of the workrooms at **Torre del Greco,** on the outskirts of Naples, off the Naples-Pompeii highway. Cameos are also made there.

ACCOMMODATIONS

The accommodations in Naples are generally a sad lot. Most of the large hotels are in the popular (also dangerous) district of Santa Lucia, and many of the so-called first-class places line Via Partenope along the water. In and around the central rail station are other clusters, many built in the late 1950s (some seemingly haven't been changed since).

Regardless of your price range, there's a bed waiting for you in Naples. Regrettably, that bed may not always be clean or comfortable. We present a selection of what are generally conceded to be the "best" hotels, but know that with an exception or two, none of the other candidates leaves us with much enthusiasm. Many of the innkeepers we've encountered seem indifferent at best.

EXPENSIVE

Grande Albergo Vesuvio. Via Partenope 45, 80121 Napoli. ☎ **800/223-6800** in the U.S. or 081/764-0044. Fax 081/764-4483. www.prestigehotels.it. E-mail: info@prestigehotels.it. 183 units. A/C MINIBAR TV TEL. 470,000L ($273) double; from 700,000L ($406) suite. Rates include breakfast. AE, DC, MC, V. Parking 35,000–40,000L ($20–$23). Bus: 104, 140, or 150.

Built in 1882, the Vesuvio was restored about 50 years later and features a marble-and-stucco facade with curved balconies extending toward the Castel dell'Ovo. It was—and, with the decline of the Excelsior, again is—the foremost hotel along the fabled bay; many aristocratic English flocked here, to be followed later by Bogie and Errol Flynn. The 1930s-style guest rooms have lofty ceilings, cove moldings, parquet floors, renovated tiled baths with lots of space, and large closets. Traditionalists should request rooms on the second floor, decorated in a 1700s style. You'll also find a scattering of antiques throughout the echoing halls.

Dining/Diversions: The hotel has a first-class restaurant, Caruso; a roof garden; and a comfortable bar evoking the most stylish decor of the 1950s.

Amenities: Concierge, room service, dry cleaning/laundry, baby-sitting, secretarial services, health club, Jacuzzi, sauna, tennis court a 5-minute walk away.

Hotel Excelsior. Via Partenope 48, 80121 Napoli. ☎ **800/325-3535** in the U.S. or 081/764-0111. Fax 081/764-9743. www.prestigehotels.it. E-mail: info@prestigehotels.it. 62 units. A/C MINIBAR TV TEL. 390,000–470,000L ($226–$273) double; 700,000–1,100,000L ($406–$638) suite. Rates include breakfast. AE, DC, MC, V. Parking 35,000L ($20). Bus: 104, 140, or 150.

The Excelsior occupies a most dramatic position right on the waterfront, with views of Santa Lucia and Vesuvius. The standards are slipping here, and it has lost its number-one position to the Vesuvio (above). Nevertheless, there are many elegant details, such as Venetian chandeliers, Doric columns, wall-sized murals, and bronze torchiers. Most of the guest rooms are bed/sitting rooms, furnished in a heavy Empire style; others are much less grand.

Dining: Both Neapolitan and international dishes are served in a windowless room. Breakfast can be ordered on a covered roof terrace.

Amenities: Concierge, room service, baby-sitting, laundry/valet.

Hotel Santa Lucia. Via Partenope 46, 80121 Napoli. ☎ **081/764-0666.** Fax 081/764-8580. www.santalucia.it. E-mail: slucia@tin.it. 101 units. A/C MINIBAR TV TEL. 380,000–440,000L ($220–$255) double; from 540,000L ($313) suite. Rates include breakfast. AE, DC, MC, V. Parking 30,000L ($17). Bus: 104, 140, or 150.

The Santa Lucia, whose neoclassical facade overlooks a sheltered marina on the bay, competes with the nearby Royal and is better maintained. From the windows of about half the rooms you can watch motorboats and yachts bobbing at anchor, fishermen repairing nets, and all the waterside life Naples is famous for. But beware of muggers if you go wandering around the area at night. The interior has undergone extensive renovations and is decorated in a family-friendly Neapolitan style, with terrazzo floors and lots of upholstered chairs scattered throughout the lobby. The rooms are large and high-ceilinged, with French doors opening onto tiny verandas. The noisier rooms overlook the traffic of Via Santa Lucia.

Dining/Diversions: There's an American-inspired bar, plus the Restaurant Jardin, serving a superb Mediterranean cuisine.

Amenities: Concierge, room service, baby-sitting.

MODERATE

Grand Hotel Parker's. Corso Vittorio Emanuele 135, 80121 Napoli. ☎ **081/761-2474.** Fax 081/663-527. www.bcedit.it. E-mail: cmbosco@tin.it. 83 units. A/C TV TEL. 310,000–370,000L ($180–$215) double; from 750,000L ($435) suite. Rates include breakfast. AE, DC, MC, V. Parking 20,000L ($12). Metro: Piazza Amedeo.

This 1870 hotel sits up and away from the harbor commotion on one of the better hillside avenues, and many guests check in just to enjoy the view of Naples. It has been fully restored and reclaimed its position as one of the finest hotels in Naples, topped only by the Vesuvio. The hotel was created when architects cared about the beauty of their work—neoclassic walls, fluted pilasters, and ornate ceilings. The guest rooms are traditionally furnished, some quite formal; each is in a different style, including Louis XVI, Directoire, Empire, and Charles X. The roof garden restaurant offers a fine view along with an international/Mediterranean cuisine. The hotel provides laundry/valet, baby-sitting, and room service and operates a currency exchange and business center.

Hotel Majestic. Largo Vasto a Chiaia 68, 80121 Napoli. ☎ **081/416-500.** Fax 081/410-145. www.prestigehotels.it. E-mail: info@prestigehotels.it. 135 units. A/C MINIBAR TV TEL. 270,000L ($157) double; 370,000–420,000L ($215–$244) suite. Rates include breakfast. AE, DC, MC, V. Parking 28,000–32,000L ($16–$19). Metro: Piazza Amedeo.

The four-star Majestic was built in 1959 and is one of the most up-to-date hotels in a city filled with decaying mansions. A favorite with the conference crowd, it's in the antiques district, so at your doorstep will be dozens of boutiques. Reservations are important, as this hotel is often fully booked. There's a cozy bar, and the Lagiara restaurant serves Neapolitan dishes and international specialties Monday to Saturday. The garage is small, so reserve parking space with your room.

Hotel Miramare. Via Nazario Saura 24, 80132 Napoli. ☎ **081/764-7589.** Fax 081/ 764-0775. www.hotelmiramare.com. E-mail: hotelmiramare@tin.it. 31 units. A/C MINIBAR TV TEL. Mon–Thurs 310,000–390,000L ($180–$226) double; Fri–Sun 250,000–340,000L ($145–$197) double. Rates include breakfast. AE, DC, MC, V. Parking 30,000L ($17). Bus: 104, 140, or 150.

In a superb location, seemingly thrust out toward the harbor on a dockside boulevard, the Miramare is central and sunny. Originally an aristocratic villa, it was transformed into a hotel in 1944 after serving for a short period as the American consulate. Its lobby evokes a little Caribbean hotel with a semitropical look. The guest rooms have been renovated and are pleasantly furnished and decently maintained, with sound-proof windows. An American bar and a roof garden are on the premises.

Hotel Paradiso. Via Catullo 11, 80122 Napoli. ☎ **800/528-1234** in the U.S. or 081/ 761-4161. Fax 081/761-3449. 74 units. A/C MINIBAR TV TEL. 280,000L ($162) double; from 450,000L ($261) suite. Rates include breakfast. AE, DC, MC, V. Parking 25,000L ($15).

This hotel might be paradise, but only after you reach it. It's only 3½ miles from the central station, but one irate driver claimed it takes about 3½ hours to get here. Once you arrive, however, your nerves are soothed by the view, one of the most panoramic of any hotel in Italy. The Bay of Naples unfolds before you, and in the distance Mt. Vesuvius looms menacingly. The hotel is one of the best in Naples, with well-furnished rooms. Should you elect not to go out at night, you can patronize the fine hotel restaurant, serving Neapolitan and Italian specialties.

Hotel Royal. Via Partenope 38, 80121 Napoli. ☎ **081/764-4800.** Fax 081/764-5707. 282 units. A/C MINIBAR TV TEL. 230,000–380,000L ($133–$220) double; 560,000L ($325) suite. Rates include breakfast. AE, DC, MC, V. Parking 26,000L ($15). Tram: 1.

The 10-story Royal, built in 1955, is in a desirable location on this busy but dangerous street beside the bay in Santa Lucia. A very commercial aura prevails, and the hotel is often filled with groups. You enter a greenery-filled vestibule, where the stairs leading to the modern lobby are flanked by a pair of stone lions. Each of the guest rooms has a balcony and aging modern furniture; some offer a water view. A seawater pool with an adjacent flower-dotted sun terrace is on the roof—the pool is vastly preferred over the polluted bay. The restaurant has panoramic views but only mediocre food.

INEXPENSIVE

Albergo San Germano. Via Beccadelli 41, 80125 Napoli. ☎ **800/528-1234** in the U.S. or 081/570-5422. Fax 081/570-1546. 105 units. A/C MINIBAR TV TEL. 270,000L ($157) double. Rates include breakfast. AE, DC, MC, V. Bus: C52.

Designed like an Italian version of a Chinese pagoda, this brick-and-concrete hotel is ideal for late-arriving motorists reluctant to negotiate the traffic of Naples. A terraced pool and garden are welcome respites after a day of sightseeing. The guest rooms are clean but simple. There's a lobby bar and a modern restaurant. From the autostrada, follow the signs to Tangenziale Napoli; exit 8 miles later at Agnano Terme. The hotel is on your right less than a mile from the toll booth.

Hotel Rex. Via Palepoli 12, 80132 Napoli. ☎ **081/764-9389.** Fax 081/764-9227. 40 units. A/C TV TEL. 170,000L ($99) double. Rates include breakfast. AE, DC, MC, V. Parking 30,000L ($17). Bus: 104.

Santa Lucia's most famous budget hotel, the Rex has played host to lire-watchers around the world since 1938. Some like it and others don't, but proof of its popularity is that its rooms are often fully booked when other hotels have vacancies. The building itself is lavishly ornate architecturally, but the rooms are simple and some very cramped. Breakfast is the only meal served.

Hotel Serius. Viale Augusto 74, 80125 Napoli. ☎ **081/239-4844.** Fax 081/239-9251. 69 units. A/C MINIBAR TV TEL. 175,000–200,000L ($102–$116) double. Rates include breakfast. AE, MC, V. Metro: Piazza Leopardi. Tram: 1 or 4.

Built in 1974, this hotel is on a palm-lined street of a relatively calm neighborhood known as Fuorigrotto, a short bus ride north of the center. The paneled split-level lobby contains an intimate bar and several metal sculptures of horses and birds. The guest rooms are simply furnished with boldly patterned fabrics and painted furniture. The dining room is pleasantly contemporary.

DINING

Naples is the home of pizza and spaghetti. If you're mad for either or both, then you'll delight in sampling the authentic versions. However, if you like subtle cooking and have an aversion to olive oil or garlic, you won't fare as well.

Warning: A major Naples dining problem is overcharging. It's not uncommon for four foreigners to have a meal in a restaurant, particularly those once-famous ones in Santa Lucia, and be billed for five dinners. Service in many restaurants tends to be poor. As with the hotels, we give you the best of the lot.

EXPENSIVE

✪ **Giuseppone a Mare.** Via Ferdinando Russo 13. ☎ **081/575-6002.** Reservations required. Main courses 16,000–36,000L ($9–$21). AE, DC, MC, V. Tues–Sun 12:30–3:30pm and 8pm–midnight. Closed Aug 16–31. SEAFOOD.

At this restaurant known for serving the best and freshest seafood in Campania, you can dine in Neapolitan sunshine on an open-air terrace with a view of the bay. The only better restaurant is La Cantinella (below). Diners make their selections from a trolley likely to include everything from crabs to eels. You might precede your fish dinner with some fritters (a batter whipped up with seaweed and fresh squash blossoms). Naturally, they serve linguine with clams—the chef adds squid and mussels. Much of the day's catch is deep-fried a golden brown. The pièce de résistance is an octopus casserole. If the oven's going, you can order a pizza. They stock some fine southern Italian wines too, especially from Ischia and Vesuvio.

Il Gallo Nero. Via Torquato Tasso 466. ☎ **081/643-012.** Reservations recommended. Main courses 45,000–55,000L ($26–$32); fixed-price menu 65,000L ($38) meat, 75,000L ($44) fish. AE, DC, MC, V. Tues–Sat 7pm–midnight, Sun 12:30–3pm. Closed Aug. Metro: Mergellina. PASTA/NEAPOLITAN.

Dinner here is almost like a throwback to the mid-19th century. Gian Paolo Quagliata, with a capable staff, maintains his hillside villa with its period furniture and accessories. In summer, the enthusiastic crowd is served on an elegant terrace. Many of the dishes are based on 100-year-old recipes, though a few are more recent inventions. You might enjoy the Neapolitan linguine with pesto, rigatoni with fresh vegetables, tagliatelle primavera, or macaroni with peas and artichokes. The fish dishes are usually well prepared, grilled, broiled, or sautéed. The meat dishes include slightly more exotic creations, like prosciutto with orange slices and veal cutlets with artichokes.

✪ **La Cantinella.** Via Cuma 42. ☎ **081/764-8684.** Reservations required. Main courses 20,000–30,000L ($12–$17). AE, DC, MC, V. Mon–Sat 12:30–3pm and 7:30pm–midnight. Closed 1–2 weeks mid-Aug. Bus: 104, 140, or 150. SEAFOOD.

You get the impression of 1920s Chicago as you approach this place, where speakeasy-style doors open after you ring. The restaurant is on a busy street skirting the bay in Santa Lucia. You'll find a well-stocked antipasto table and—get this—a phone on each table. We consistently find high-quality meals here. The chefs have a deft way of handling the region's fresh produce and turn out both Neapolitan classics and more imaginative dishes. The menu includes four preparations of risotto (including one with champagne), many kinds of pasta (including penne with vodka and linguine with scampi and seafood), and most of the classic beef and veal dishes of Italy. Best known for its fish, Cantinella serves grilled seafood at its finest.

MODERATE

Don Salvatore. Strada Mergellina 4A. ☎ **081/681-817.** Reservations recommended. Main courses 12,000–28,000L ($7–$16); fixed-price menu 65,000L ($38). AE, DC, MC, V. Thurs–Tues 1–4pm and 8pm–1am. Metro: Mergellina. SEAFOOD.

This is the creative statement of a serious restaurateur who directs his waterfront place with passion and dedication. Antonio Aversano takes his wine as seriously as his food. The latter is likely to include linguine with shrimp or squid, an array of fish, and a marvelous assortment of fresh Neapolitan vegetables grown in the countryside. The fish, priced according to weight, comes right out of the Bay of Naples, which may, but possibly may not, be a plus. Rice comes flavored in a delicate fish broth, and you can get a reasonably priced bottle from the wine cellar, said to be the finest in Campania. The restaurant is on the seafront near the departure point of hydrofoils for Capri.

La Sacrestia. Via Orazio 116. ☎ **081/761-1051.** Reservations required. Main courses 18,000–60,000L ($10–$35); fixed-price menu 80,000L ($46). AE, DC, MC, V. Tues–Sun 12:30–4:30pm and Mon–Sat 7:40–11pm. Closed 2 weeks mid-Aug. Funicular: From Mergellina. PASTA/SEAFOOD.

The trompe-l'oeil frescoes on the two-story interior and the name La Sacrestia vaguely suggest the ecclesiastical, but that's not the case. One of the best restaurants in Naples, this bustling place is sometimes called "the greatest show in town." It's perched near the top of a seemingly endless labyrinth of streets winding up from the port (take a taxi or go by funicular). In summer, a terrace with its flowering arbor provides a view over the harbor lights. Meals emphasize well-prepared dishes with strong doses of Neapolitan drama. You might try what's said to be the most luxurious macaroni dish in Italy ("Prince of Naples"), concocted with truffles and mild cheeses. Less ornate selections are a full array of pastas and dishes composed of octopus, squid, and shellfish.

Rosolino. Via Nazario Sauro 2–7. ☎ **081/764-9873.** Reservations required. Main courses 12,000–25,000L ($7–$15); fixed-price menu 50,000–70,000L ($29–$41). AE, DC, MC, V.

A Sweet Shop & a Grand Cafe

Giovanni Scaturchio, at Piazza San Domenico Maggiore 19 (☎ 081/551-6944), offers the most caloric collection of pastries in Naples and is famous for both satisfying and fattening locals since around 1900. Pastries include the entire selection of Neapolitan sweets, cakes, and candies, like brioches soaked in liqueur, cassate (pound cake) filled with layered ricotta, Moor's heads, and cheesy ricotta pastries known as sfogliatelle. Another specialty is ministeriale, a chocolate cake filled with liqueur and chocolate cream. Pastries start at 2,000L ($1.15) if consumed standing up or at 3,000L ($1.75) if enjoyed at a table. It's open Wednesday to Monday 7:20am to 8:40pm; closed 2 to 3 weeks in August.

The decor of the **Gran Caffè Gambrinus,** Via Chiaia 1, near the Galleria Umberto (☎ 081/417-582), Naples's oldest cafe, dating from 1860, would fit easily into a grand Bourbon palace. Along the vaulted ceiling of an inner room, Empire-style caryatids spread their togas in high relief above frescoes of mythological playmates. The cafe is known for its espresso and cappuccino, as well as pastries and cakes whose variety dazzles the eye. These pastries are the most famous in Naples. You can also order potato-and-rice croquettes and fried pizzas for a light lunch. Tea costs 4,000L ($2.30); cappuccino goes for 4,000L ($2.30) at a table. The cafe is open daily 8am to midnight.

Mon–Sun 12:30–3:30pm; Mon–Sat 8pm–midnight. Tram: 1 or 4. INTERNATIONAL/ITALIAN/SEAFOOD.

This stylish place isn't defined as a nightclub by its owners but rather as a restaurant with dancing. Set on the waterfront, it's divided into two areas: On Saturday evenings there's a piano bar near the entrance, where you might have a drink before passing into a much larger dining room. Here, in interiors ringed with stained glass set into striking patterns, you can dine within sight of a bandstand reminiscent of the Big Band Era. Live music is only on Saturday night, except for Wednesdays, which feature a light guitar in the style of Naples. The food is traditional, not very imaginative but well prepared with fresh vegetables. Dishes include rigatoni with zucchini and meat sauce, Pusillo (a locally made pasta), an impressive array of fresh shellfish, and such beef dishes as tournedos and veal scaloppine. Most fresh fish is priced according to weight. There are three wine lists, including one for French wines and champagne.

INEXPENSIVE

Dante e Beatrice. Piazza Dante 44–45. ☎ 081/549-9438. Reservations recommended. Main courses 20,000–30,000L ($12–$17); fixed-price menu 25,000–45,000L ($15–$26). No credit cards. Thurs–Tues 1:30–4pm and 8–midnight. Closed Aug 15–30. Tram: 1 or 4. NEAPOLITAN.

Gregarious and unpretentious and named after the players in one of the great romantic tragedies of the Middle Ages, Dante e Beatrice opened in 1956 and remains one of the best restaurants in its neighborhood. It specializes in all the staples of the Neapolitan cuisine, serving flavorful portions of lasagne, minestrone, spaghetti with clams, tagliatelle, pasta e fagiole, and grilled fish. Other notable items are maccheroni or spaghetti with seafood and "frittata" of spaghetti, with a sauce made of mozzarella, prosciutto, and salami, bound together with tomatoes.

Ristorante La Fazenda. Via Marechiaro 58A. ☎ 081/575-7420. Reservations required. Main courses 20,000–40,000L ($12–$23); fixed-price menu 50,000L ($29). AE, MC, V.

Tues–Sat 1–4pm and 7:30pm–12:30am; Sun 1–4pm; Mon 7:30pm–12:30am. Closed 1 week in mid-Aug. Bus: 106 or 150. SEAFOOD.

It'd be hard to find a more typically Neapolitan restaurant than this, offering a panoramic view that on a clear day can include Capri. The decor is rustic, loaded with agrarian touches and an assortment of Neapolitan families, lovers, and visitors who have made it one of their preferred places since it opened in 1973. In summer, the overflow from the dining room spills onto the terrace. Menu specialties include linguine with scampi, fresh grilled fish, sautéed clams, a mixed Italian grill, savory stews, and many chicken dishes, along with lobster with fresh grilled tomatoes. Look for "Mr. Nappo," allegedly "the largest pizza ever."

Umberto. Via Alabardieri 30. ☎ **081/418-555.** Reservations required. Main courses 9,000–30,000L ($5–$17). AE, DC, MC, V. Thurs–Tues 12:30–3:30pm and 7:30–10:30pm. Closed Aug. Bus: 106 or 150. NEAPOLITAN.

Off Piazza dei Martiri, Umberto is one of the most atmospheric places to dine, where there's likely to be a dance band playing at dinner. The tasteful dining room has been directed for many a year by the same interconnected family. The excellent Italian specialties include pizzas, gnocchi with potatoes, and grilled meats and fishes, as well as savory stews and a host of pasta dishes. The bel canto era lives on here.

Vini e Cucina. Corso Vittorio Emanuele 762. ☎ **081/660-302.** Reservations not accepted. Main courses 6,000–10,000L ($3.50–$6). No credit cards. Mon–Sat noon–4:30pm and 7pm–midnight. Closed Aug 10–26. Metro: Mergellina. NEAPOLITAN.

The best ragù sauce in all Naples is said to be made at this trattoria, with only 20 tables. You can get a really satisfying meal, but we must warn you—it's almost impossible to get in. Dedicated diners might do as we do: Arrive early and wait for a table. The cooking is the best home-style version of Neapolitan cuisine we've been able to find in this tricky city. The spaghetti, along with that fabulous sauce, is served al dente. The restaurant is in front of the Mergellina station.

A HISTORIC PIZZERIA

Pizzaria Brandi. Salita S. Anna di Palazzo. ☎ **081/416-928.** Reservations required. Main courses 10,000–22,000L ($6–$13); pizza from 5,000L ($2.90). No credit cards. Tues–Sun noon–3pm and 6:30pm–midnight. Bus: 106 or 150. NEAPOLITAN/PIZZA.

The most historic pizzeria in Italy, Brandi was opened by Pietro Colicchio in the 19th century. His successor, Raffaele Esposito, who enjoyed the reputation his hard work had earned, was requested one day to prepare a banquet for Margherita di Savoia, the queen of Italy. So successful was the reception of the pizza made with tomato, basil, olive oil, and mozzarella (the colors of the newly united Italy's flag) that the queen accepted the honor of having it named after her. Thus was pizza Margherita born from the kitchens of Naples's Restaurant Brandi. Today you can order the pizza that pleased a queen, as well as linguine with scampi, fettuccine "Regina d'Italia," and a full array of seafood dishes. Even Chelsea Clinton approved of the fare here.

NAPLES AFTER DARK

A **sunset walk through Santa Lucia** and along the waterfront never seems to dim in pleasure, even if you've lived in Naples for years. Visitors are also fond of riding around town in one of the *carrozzelle* (horse-drawn wagons).

Or you can stroll by the glass-enclosed **Galleria Umberto,** off Via Roma across from the Teatro San Carlo. The 19th-century gallery is still standing today, though a little the worse for wear. It's a kind of social center for Naples. John Horne Burns used it for the title of his novel *The Gallery,* in which he wrote: "In August 1944, everyone in Naples sooner or later found his way into this place and became like a picture on the wall of the museum."

OPERA The ✪ **Teatro San Carlo,** Via San Carlo 98F, across from the Galleria Umberto (☎ **081/797-2331**), is one of the largest opera houses in Italy, with some of the best acoustics. Built in only 6 months' time for King Charles's birthday in November 1737, it was restored in a gilded neoclassical style. Grand-scale productions are presented on the main stage. The box office is open December to June, Tuesday to Sunday 10am to 1pm and 4:30 to 6:30pm. Tickets are 80,000L to 160,000L ($46 to $93).

THE CLUB SCENE On its nightclub/cabaret circuit, Naples offers more sucker joints than any other port along the Mediterranean. If you're starved for action, you'll find plenty of it—and you're likely to end up paying for it dearly.

Chez Moi, Via dei Parco Margherita 13 (☎ **081/407-526**), is one of the city's best-managed nightclubs, strictly refusing entrance to anyone who looks like a trouble-maker. This is appreciated by the designers, government ministers, and visiting socialites who enjoy the place. The crowd tends to be over 25. You'll be ushered to a table amid a decor of soft blues and greens. The place is open Friday and Saturday 10:30pm to 4 or 5am. Occasionally there's a cabaret act or a live pianist at the bar, but more frequently the music is disco. The cover is 25,000L ($15).

Madison Street, Via Sgambati 47 (☎ **081/546-6566**), is the largest disco in Naples. The youngish crowd, usually between 18 and 25, mingles and dances and gen-erally has an uninhibited good time. If you tire of the human melee going on at the several bars or on the dance floor, you can watch video movies or videotaped rock con-certs on one of several screens. The place is open Tuesday and Thursday to Saturday 10pm to 3am and Sunday 8pm to 2am. The Friday crowd tends to be older and slightly more sedate. The cover ranges from 15,000L to 20,000L ($9 to $12).

A leading Naples hot spot is **Piazza di Spagna,** Via Petrarca 101 (☎ **081/575-48-82**), in Vomero. It features dancing Friday to Sunday from September to July; go after 10pm and expect a 15,000L to 20,000L ($9 to $12) cover. The best local jazz is often heard at **Riot,** Via San Biagio 38 (☎ **081/552-32-31**), open Thursday to Tuesday 10:30am to 3am. If you're mature and want a piano bar ambiance, head for **Airone,** Via Petrarca 123 (☎ **081/575-0175**).

Looking for gay action? Head for **Tongue,** Via Mazonik 207 (☎ **081/769-0800**), which has a mixed crowd, a large part of whom are gay, dancing to techno music. It's open only weekends 9pm to 3am, charging a cover of 10,000L to 20,000L ($6 to $12). There are no all-exclusive lesbian or gay clubs, but **ARCI-Gay/Lesbica** (☎ **081/551-8293**), is a well-meaning support group whose function is referring gay and les-bian problems to the correct public or private entity. They operate during limited hours, usually three evenings a week, 7 to 10pm. Some of the volunteers speak English.

2 The Environs of Naples: The Phlaegrean Fields & Herculaneum

THE PHLAEGREAN FIELDS

One of the bizarre attractions of southern Italy, the **Phlaegrean Fields (Campi Flegrei)** form a backdrop for a day's exploring west of Naples and along its bay. An explosive land of myth and legend, the fiery fields contain the dormant volcano Solfatara, the cave of the Cumaean Sibyl, Virgil's gateway to the "Infernal Regions," the ruins of thermal baths and amphitheaters built by the Romans, deserted colonies left by the Greeks, and lots more.

If you're depending on public transport, the best center for exploring the area is **Pozzuoli,** reached by Metropolitana (subway) from Stazione Centrale in Naples. The fare is 1,500L (85¢). Once in Pozzuoli, you can catch one of the SEPSA buses at any bus stop and can be in Baia in 20 minutes. You can also go to Cumae on one of these buses or to Solfatara or Lago d'Averno.

✪ **SOLFATARA**   About 7½ miles west of Naples, near Pozzuoli, is the ancient **Vulcano Solfatara,** Via Solfatara 161 (☎ **081/854-3060**). It hasn't erupted since the final year of the 12th century but has been threatening ever since. It gives off sulfurous gases and releases scalding vapors through cracks in the earth's surface. In fact, Solfatara's activity (or inactivity) has been observed for such a long time that the crater's name is used by Webster's dictionary to define any "dormant volcano" emitting vapors.

You can visit the crater daily 8:30am to 1 hour before sunset at a cost of 7,000L ($4.05) adults and 4,000L ($2.30) children. From Naples, take bus no. 152 or the Metropolitana from Stazione Centrale. Once you get off at the train station, you can board one of the city buses that go up the hill or can walk to the crater in about 20 minutes.

POZZUOLI   Just 1½ miles from Solfatara, the port of Pozzuoli opens onto a gulf screened from the Bay of Naples by a promontory. The ruins of the **Anfiteatro Flavio,** Via Nicola Terracciano (☎ **081/526-6007**), built in the last part of the 1st century, testify to past greatness. One of the finest surviving ancient arenas, it's particularly distinguished by its "wings"—which, considering their age, are in good condition. You can see the remains where exotic beasts from Africa were caged before being turned loose in the ring to test their jungle skill against a gladiator. The amphitheater is said to have entertained 40,000 spectators at the height of its glory. You can visit it June to August daily 9am to 6pm (to 4pm September to March and to 5pm April and May). Admission is 4,000L ($2.30).

In another part of town, the **Tempio di Serapide** was really the Macellum (market square), and some of its ruined pillars still project upward. It was erected during the reign of the Flavian emperors. You can reach Pozzuoli by subway from Stazione Centrale in Naples.

BAIA   In the days of Imperial Rome, the emperors—everybody from Julius Caesar to Hadrian—came here to frolic in the sun while enjoying the comforts of their luxurious villas and Roman baths. It was here that Emperor Claudius built a grand villa for his first wife, Messalina, who spent her days and nights reveling in debauchery and plotting to have her husband replaced by her lover (for which she was beheaded). And it was here that Claudius was poisoned by his last wife, Agrippina, the controlling mother of Nero. Nero is said to have had Agrippina murdered at nearby Bacoli, with its Pool of Mirabilis—after she survived his first attempt on her life, a collapsing boat meant to send her to a watery rest. Parts of Baia's illustrious past have been dug out, including both the **Temple of Baiae** and the **Thermal Baths,** among the greatest erected in Italy.

You can explore this archaeological district (☎ **081/868-7592**) daily 9am to 2 hours before sunset. Admission is 6,000L ($3.50). Ferrovia Cumana trains depart from Stazione Centrale for the 15-minute trip from Naples.

LAGO D'AVERNO   About 10 miles west of Naples, a bit north of Baia, is a lake occupying an extinct volcanic crater. Known to the ancients as the **Gateway to Hades,** it was for centuries shrouded in superstition. Its vapors were said to produce illness and even death, and Lake Averno could well have been the source of the expression "Still waters run deep." Facing the lake are the ruins of what has been known as the **Temple of Apollo** from the 1st century A.D. and what was once thought to be the Cave of the

Treading Lightly on Mount Vesuvius

Stand at the bottom of the great market-place of Pompeii, and look up at the silent streets . . . over the broken houses with their inmost sanctuaries open to the day, away to Mount Vesuvius, bright and snowy in the peaceful distance; and lose all count of time, and heed of other things, in the strange and melancholy sensation of seeing the Destroyed and the Destroyer making this quiet picture in the sun.

—Charles Dickens, *Pictures from Italy*

A volcano that has struck terror in Campania, the towering, pitch-black **Mount Vesuvius** looms menacingly over the Bay of Naples. August 24, A.D. 79, is the infamous date when Vesuvius burst forth and buried Pompeii, Herculaneum, and Stabiae under its mass of ash and volcanic mud. What many fail to realize is that Vesuvius has erupted periodically ever since (thousands were killed in 1631): The last major spouting of lava occurred in this century (it blew off the ring of its crater in 1906). The last spectacular eruption was on March 31, 1944. The approach to Vesuvius is dramatic, with the terrain growing foreboding as you near the top. Along the way you'll see villas rising on its slopes and vineyards— the grapes produce an amber-colored wine known as Lacrimae Christi (Tears of Christ); the citizens of Pompeii enjoyed wine from here, as excavations revealed). Closer to the summit, the soil becomes colored puce and an occasional wild-flower appears.

Though it may sound like a dubious invitation (Vesuvius, after all, is an active volcano), it's possible to visit the rim—or lips, so to speak—of the crater's mouth. As you look down into its smoldering core, you may recall that Spartacus, in a century before the eruption that buried Pompeii, hid in the hollow of the crater, which was then covered with vines.

To reach Vesuvius from Naples, take the Circumvesuviana Railway or (summer only) a motorcoach service from Piazza Vittoria, which hooks up with bus connections at Pugliano. You get off the train at the Ercolano station, the 10th stop. Six SITA buses per day go from Herculaneum to the crater of Vesuvius, costing 4,000L ($2.30) round-trip. Once at the top, you must be accompanied by a guide, costing 5,000L ($2.90).

Cumaean Sibyl (below). According to legend, the Sibyl is said to have ferried Aeneas, son of Aphrodite, across the lake, where he traced a mysterious spring to its source, the River Styx. In the 1st century B.C., Agrippa turned it into a harbor for Roman ships by digging out a canal. Take the Napoli-Torre Gaveta bus from Baia to reach the site.

CUMA   Cuma was one of the first outposts of Greek colonization in what's now Italy. Located 12 miles west of Naples, it's of interest chiefly because it's said to have contained the **Cave of the Cumaean Sibyl.** The cave of the oracle, really a gallery, was dug by the Greeks in the 5th century B.C. and was a sacred spot to them. Beloved by Apollo, the Sibyl is said to have written the *Sibylline Oracles,* a group of books of prophecy bought, according to tradition, by Tarquin the Proud. You may visit not only the caves but also the ruins of temples dedicated to Jupiter and Apollo (later converted into Christian churches), daily 9am to 1 hour before sunset; admission is 8,000L ($4.65) adults (children under 18 free). On Via Domitiana, to the east of Cuma, you'll pass the **Arco Felice,** an arch about 64 feet high, built by Emperor

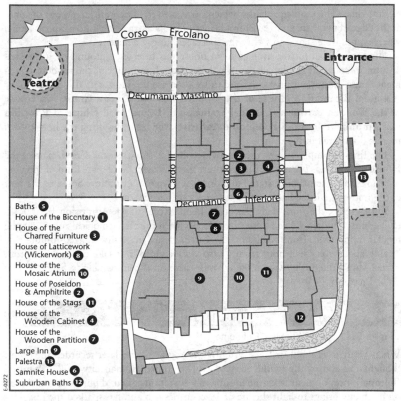

Baths **5**
House of the Bicentary **1**
House of the
   Charred Furniture **3**
House of Latticework
   (Wickerwork) **8**
House of the
   Mosaic Atrium **10**
House of Poseidon
   & Amphitrite **2**
House of the Stags **11**
House of the
   Wooden Cabinet **4**
House of the
   Wooden Partition **7**
Large Inn **9**
Palestra **13**
Samnite House **6**
Suburban Baths **12**

Domitian in the 1st century A.D. Ferrovia Cumana trains run here, departing from Stazione Centrale in Naples.

HERCULANEUM

The builders of ✪ **Herculaneum (Ercolano)** were still working to repair the damage caused by an A.D. 62 earthquake when Vesuvius erupted on that fateful August day in A.D. 79. Herculaneum, about one-fourth the size of Pompeii, didn't start to come to light again until 1709, when Prince Elbeuf launched the unfortunate fashion of tunneling through it for treasures, more intent on profiting from the sale of objets d'art than in uncovering a dead Roman town.

Subsequent excavations at the site, the **Ufficio Scavi di Ercolano,** Corso Resina, Ercolano (☎ **081/739-0963**), have been slow and sporadic. In fact, Herculaneum, named after Hercules, is not completely dug out today. One of the obstacles has been that the town was buried under lava, much heavier than the ash and pumice stone that piled onto Pompeii. Of course, this formed a greater protection for the buildings buried underneath—many of which were more elaborately constructed than those at Pompeii, as Herculaneum was a seaside resort for patricians. The complication of having the slum of Resina resting over the yet-to-be-excavated district has further impeded progress and urban renewal.

Although all the streets and buildings of Herculaneum hold interest, some ruins merit more attention than others. The **baths (*terme*)** are divided between those at the forum and the **Suburban Baths (Terme Suburbane)** on the outskirts, near the more elegant villas. The municipal baths, which segregated the sexes, are larger, but the ones at the edge of town are more lavishly adorned. The **Palestra** was a kind of sports arena, where games were staged to satisfy the spectacle-hungry denizens.

The typical plan for the average town house was to erect it around an uncovered atrium. In some areas, Herculaneum possessed the forerunner of the modern apartment house. Important private homes to seek out are the **House of the Bicentenary (Casa del Bicentario), House of the Wooden Cabinet (Casa a Graticcio), House of the Wooden Partition (Casa del Tramezzo di Legno),** and **House of Poseidon and Amphitrite (Casa di Poseidon e Anfitrite),** the last containing the best-known mosaic discovered in the ruins.

The finest example of how the aristocracy lived is the **Casa dei Cervi,** named the **House of the Stags** because of the sculpture found inside. Guides are fond of showing their males on their tours a statue of a drunken Hercules urinating. Some of the best of the houses are locked and can be seen only by permission.

You can visit the ruins daily 9am to 1 hour before sunset. Admission is 12,000L ($7) adults; children 17 and under are free. To reach the archaeological zone, take the regular train service from Naples on the Circumvesuviana Railway, a 20-minute ride leaving about every half hour from Corso Garibaldi 387; or take bus no. 255 from Piazza Municipio. Otherwise, it's a 4½-mile drive on the autostrada to Salerno (turn off at Ercolano).

3 Pompeii & Its Amazing Ruins

15 miles S of Naples, 147 miles SE of Rome

When Vesuvius erupted in A.D. 79, Pliny the Younger, who later recorded the event, thought the end of the world had come. The ruined Roman city of ✪ **Pompeii (Pompei),** now dug out from the inundation of volcanic ash and pumice stone rained on it, vividly brings to light the life of 19 centuries ago and has sparked the imagination of the world.

Numerous myths have surrounded Pompeii, one of which is that a completely intact city was rediscovered. Actually the Pompeiians (that is, those who escaped) returned to their city when the ashes had cooled and removed some of the most precious treasures from the thriving resort. But they left plenty behind to be uncovered at a later date and carted off to museums throughout Europe and America.

After a long medieval sleep, Pompeii was again brought to life in the late 16th century, quite by accident, by architect Domenico Fontana. However, it was in the mid-18th century that large-scale excavations were launched. Somebody once remarked that Pompeii's second tragedy was its rediscovery, that it really should've been left to slumber for another century or two, when it might've been better excavated and maintained.

ESSENTIALS

GETTING THERE The **Circumvesuviana Railway** departs Naples every half hour from Piazza Garibaldi. However, be sure you get on the train headed toward *Sorrento* and get off at Pompeii/Scavi (*scavi* means "ruins"). If you get on the Pompeii train you'll end up in the town of Pompeii and have to transfer there to the Sorrento train to get to the ruins. A round-trip costs 2,700L ($1.55); trip time is 45 minutes each way. Circumvesuviana trains leave Sorrento several times during the day for Pompeii, costing 2,000L ($1.20) one-way. There's an entrance about 50 yards from the rail station at Villa dei Misteri. At the rail station in the town of Pompeii, **bus** connections take you to the entrance to the excavations. To reach Pompeii by **car** from Naples, take

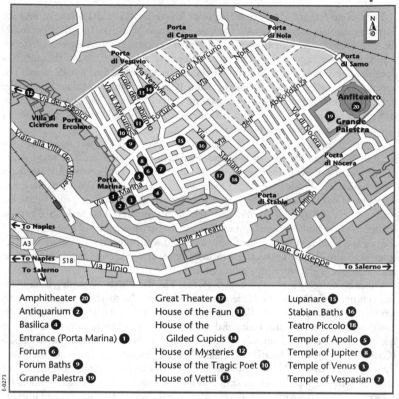

Amphitheater **20**	Great Theater **17**	Lupanare **15**
Antiquarium **2**	House of the Faun **11**	Stabian Baths **16**
Basilica **4**	House of the	Teatro Piccolo **18**
Entrance (Porta Marina) **1**	Gilded Cupids **14**	Temple of Apollo **5**
Forum **6**	House of Mysteries **12**	Temple of Jupiter **8**
Forum Baths **9**	House of the Tragic Poet **10**	Temple of Venus **3**
Grande Palestra **19**	House of Vettii **13**	Temple of Vespasian **7**

the 13½-mile drive on the autostrada to Salerno. If you're coming from Sorrento, head east on SS145, where you can connect with A3 (marked Napoli). Then take the sign-posted turnoff for Pompeii.

VISITOR INFORMATION   The **tourist office** is at Via Sacra 1 (☎ **081/ 850-7255**). October to March, it's open Monday to Friday 8am to 3:40pm and Saturday 8am to 2pm; April to September, hours are Monday to Friday 8am to 7pm and Saturday 8am to 2pm.

EXPLORING THE RUINS
Most of the curious visit the ✪ **Ufficio Scavi di Pompei,** Piazza Esedra (☎ **081/ 861-0744**), the best preserved 2,000-year-old ruins in Europe, on a day trip from Naples (allow at least 4 hours for even a superficial look at the archaeological site). The ruins are open daily 9am to 1 hour before sunset. Admission is 12,000L ($7) adults; children under 18 are free.

The most elegant of the patrician villas is the **House of Vettii (Casa dei Vettii),** boasting a courtyard, statuary (such as a two-faced Janus), paintings, and a black-and-red Pompeiian dining room known for its frescoes of delicate cupids. The house was occupied by two brothers named Vettii, both of whom were wealthy merchants. As you enter the vestibule, you'll see a painting of Priapus resting his gargantuan phallus on a pair of scales. The guard will reveal other erotic fertility drawings and statuary, though most such material has been removed to the Archaeological Museum in Naples. This house is the best example of a villa and garden that's been restored.

The second important villa, the **House of Mysteries (Villa dei Misteri),** near the Porto Ercolano, is outside the walls (go along Viale alla Villa dei Misteri). What makes the villa exceptional, aside from its architectural features, are its remarkable frescoes, depicting scenes associated with the sect of Dionysus (Bacchus), one of the cults that flourished in Roman times. Note in some of the backgrounds the Pompeiian red. The largest house, called the **House of the Faun (Casa del Fauno)** because of a bronze statue of a dancing faun found here, takes up a city block and has four dining rooms and two spacious peristyle gardens. It sheltered the celebrated *Battle of Alexander the Great* mosaic that's now in a Naples museum.

In the center of town is the **Forum (Foro)**—rather small, it was nonetheless the heart of Pompeiian life, known to bakers, merchants, and the aristocrats who lived in the villas. Parts of the Forum were severely damaged in an earthquake 16 years before the eruption of Vesuvius and hadn't been repaired when the final destruction came. Three buildings surrounding the Forum are the **basilica** (the city's largest single structure) and the **Temple of Apollo** and **Temple of Jupiter.** The **Stabian Thermae** (baths)—where both men and women lounged in between games of knucklebones— are in good condition, among the finest to come down from antiquity. Here you'll see some skeletons. In the **Lupanare (brothel)** are some erotic paintings (these frescoes are the source of the fattest tips to the guides).

Other buildings of interest include the **Great Theater (Teatro Grande),** built in the 5th century B.C. During the Hellenistic period from 200 to 150 B.C., it was vastly rebuilt, as it was again by the Romans in the 1st century A.D. This open-air theater could hold 5,000 spectators, many of them bloodthirsty as they screamed for death in the battles between wild animals and gladiators. The **House of the Gilded Cupids (Casa degle Amorini Dorati)** was a flamboyant private home, its owner unknown, though he probably lived during the reign of Nero. Obviously he had theatrical flair, attested to by the gilded and glass cupids known as *amorini.* Though badly ruined, the house still contains a peristyle with one wing raised almost like a stage. The **House of the Tragic Poet (Casa del Poeta Tragico)** gets its name from a mosaic discovered here (later sent to Naples): It depicts a chained watchdog on the doorstep with this warning—Cave Canem ("beware of the dog").

ACCOMMODATIONS

Accommodations appear to be for earnest archaeologists only. The Villa Laura is the only really suitable hotel; the other choices are barely passable and suggested only as emergency stops. Some hotels in Pompeii aren't considered safe because of robberies. Protect your valuables and your person and don't wander the streets at night. Most visitors look at the excavations, then seek better accommodations at either Naples or Sorrento.

Hotel del Santuario. Piazza Bartolo Longo 2–6, 80045 Pompei. ☎ **081/850-6165.** Fax 081/850-2822. 51 units. TEL. 100,000–120,000L ($58–$70) double. Rates include breakfast. AE, MC, V. Free limited parking.

This hotel is in the very center and opens onto the major square across from the basilica. It rents simply furnished rooms, very basic, and offers a ristorante, pizzeria, gelateria, and tearoom. The restaurant serves reasonably priced meals. You can enjoy such dishes as beefsteak pizzaiola or a mixed fry of shrimp and squid.

Hotel Villa dei Misteri. Via Villa dei Misteri 11, 80045 Pompei-Scavi. ☎ **081/861-3593.** Fax 081/862-2983. www.ptn.pandora.it/hmisteri. 41 units. 80,000L ($46) double. Breakfast 7,500L ($4.50). DC, MC, V. From the Naples rail station Circum-Vesviana, take the Sorrento train and get off at the Villa dei Misteri stop.

Located 250 yards from the Scavi Station, this 1930s hotel is suitable for motorists. About 1½ miles south of the center of town, it features a pool, a little garden, and a place to park your car. The family-style welcome may compensate for a certain lack of facilities and amenities. The place could stand a face-lift, but many readers have expressed their fondness for it. The only rooms are bare-bones doubles.

Villa Laura. Via della Salle 13, 80045 Pompei. ☎ **081/863-1024.** Fax 081/850-4893. 24 units. A/C TV TEL. 125,000L ($73) double. Breakfast 9,000L ($5). AE, DC, MC, V. Parking 9,000L ($5).

The Villa Laura is the best hotel in town, which isn't saying a lot. On a somewhat hidden street, it escapes a lot of the noise that plagues Pompeii hotels. It's mercifully air-conditioned, and the rooms are comfortably but not spectacularly furnished. Try for one with a balcony. There's a breakfast room with a bar in the basement. The breakfasts are a bit dull, but for lunch and dinner you can escape to many trattorie nearby or patronize one of the restaurants below. The hotel also has a garden.

DINING

✪ **Il Prìncipe.** Piazza Bartolo Longo 8. ☎ **081/850-5566.** Reservations required. Main courses 25,000–35,000L ($15–$20); fixed-price menu 50,000L ($29). AE, DC, MC, V. Summer daily 12:30–3pm and 7:30–11:30pm; off-season Tues–Sun 12:30–3pm and 7:30–11:30pm. CAMPANIAN/MEDITERRANEAN.

Pompeii's leading restaurant, Il Prìncipe is also acclaimed one of the best restaurants in Campania. The decor incorporates the best decorative features of ancient Pompeii, including a scattering of brightly colored frescoes and mosaics. You can dine in its beautiful interior or at a sidewalk table on the most important square in Pompeii, with views of the basilica. You might start with carpaccio or a salad of porcini mushrooms, then follow with one of the pastas, perhaps spaghetti vongole (with baby clams). You can also order superb fish dishes, like sea bass and turbot; saltimbocca (sage-flavored veal with ham); or steak Diane.

Zi Caterina. Via Roma 20. ☎ **081/850-7447.** Reservations recommended. Main courses 15,000–30,000L ($9–$17). AE, DC, MC, V. Daily noon–11pm. SEAFOOD/NEAPOLITAN.

This good choice is in the center of town near the basilica, with two spacious dining rooms. The antipasto table may tempt you with its seafood, but don't rule out the pasta e fagioli (pasta and beans) with mussels. The chef's special rigatoni, with tomatoes and prosciutto, is tempting, as is the array of fish or one of the live lobsters fresh from the tank.

POMPEII AFTER DARK

The hot spot in town used to be the Lupanare (brothel), but Vesuvius ended those nocturnal adventures long ago. Today you must settle for the **Panatenee Pompeiane,** a festival of the performing arts with a series of classical plays in July and August. For more information, contact the tourist office in Pompeii or Naples.

4 The Emerald Island of Ischia

21 miles W of Naples

Dramatically situated in the Gulf of Gaeta, the island of **Ischia** is of volcanic origin. Some of its beaches are radioactive, and its thermal spas claim cures for most anything that ails you—be it "gout, retarded sexual development, or chronic rheumatism." Called the Emerald Island, Ischia is studded with pine groves, bathed in brilliant light, and surrounded by sparkling waters that wash up on many sandy beaches (a popular one is Sant'Angelo). In Greek mythology, it was the home of Typhoeus (Typhon), who created volcanoes and fathered the three-headed canine Cerberus, guardian of the gateway to Hades, and the incongruous Chimera and Sphinx. The island covers just over 18 square miles, and its prominent feature is **Monte Epomeo,** near the center, a volcano that was a powerful force and source of worry for the Greek colonists who settled here in the 8th century B.C.

Today, the 2,590-foot peak is dead, having last erupted in the 14th century, but it's still responsible for warming the island's thermal springs. Ischia slumbered for centuries after its early turbulence, though many discerning visitors knew of its charms. Ibsen, for example, lived in a villa near Casamicciola to find the solitude necessary to complete *Peer Gynt.* However, in the 1950s, Ischia was discovered, this time by wealthy Italians who built a slew of first-class hotels in the process of trying to avoid the overrun resorts of Capri.

The island is known for its sandy beaches, health spas (which utilize the hot springs for hydromassage and mud baths), and vineyards producing a red and white Monte Epomeo, a red and white Ischia, and the white Biancolella. The largest community is at Ischia Porto on the eastern coast, a circular town seated in the crater of an extinct volcano that functions as the island's main port of call. The most lively settlement is Forio on the western coast, with its many bars along tree-lined streets. The other major communities are Lacco Ameno and Casamicciola Terme, on the north shore, and Serrara Fontana and Barano d'Ischia, inland and to the south.

ESSENTIALS

GETTING THERE   The easiest and most frequent route of access is from Naples, from which both **hydrofoils** (passengers only) and **ferries** (passengers with their cars) make frequent runs throughout the year. With departures three to seven times a day, depending on the season, the hydrofoil is the most convenient option, charging 18,000L ($10) per person each way. Transit by hydrofoil takes about 40 minutes each way; transit by ferry takes about 1 hour 20 minutes each way but costs only 9,500L ($6) for foot passengers. On the ferry, a medium-sized vehicle, with as many passengers as will fit inside, costs from 70,000L ($41) each way. Both ferries and hydrofoils depart from Naples's Mergellina Pier, near the Hotel Vesuvio, whereas only ferries leave from Molo Beverello, near Piazza Municipio. Two companies maintain both hydrofoils and ferries: **Caremar** (☎ **081/761-3688** in Naples or 081/991-781 in Ischia) and **Linee Lauro** (☎ **081/552-2838** in Naples or 081/837-7577 in Ischia). Caremar is somewhat more upscale, with better-maintained ships and a more cooperative staff.

VISITOR INFORMATION   In Porto d'Ischia, the **Azienda di Turismo** has two offices, one right by the docks on Via Jasolino (☎ **081/991-146**), open Monday to Saturday 9am to noon and 1:30 to 5pm.

ISCHIA PORTO

This harbor actually emerged from the crater of a long-dead volcano. Most of the population and the largest number of hotels are centered in **Ischia Porto.** The **Castello Aragonese** (☎ **081/992-834**) once guarded the harbor from raids. At the castle lived poetess Vittoria Colonna, the confidante of Michelango, to whom he wrote the celebrated letters.

References to a fortress on this isolated rock date from as early as 474 B.C. Today it's the symbol of Ischia, jutting like a Mediterranean version of France's Mont-St-Michel from the sea surrounding it. It's connected to the oldest part of town by the Ponte d'Ischia, a narrow bridge barely wide enough for a car. If you're driving, park on the "mainland" side of the bridge and cross on foot. The fortress is privately owned, and you pay 10,000L ($6) to get inside. It's closed January to March, but open daily otherwise 9:30am to 6pm.

ACCOMMODATIONS

✪ **Grand Hotel Excelsior.** Via Emanuele Gianturco 19, 80077 Ischia Porto. ☎ **081/ 991-020.** Fax 081/984-100. 74 units. A/C MINIBAR TV TEL. 460,000–640,000L ($267–$371) double; from 700,000L ($406) suite. Rates include half board. AE, DC, MC, V. Closed Nov 3–Apr 23. Free valet parking.

The superior accommodation on Ischia, this palatial hotel, the private retreat of English nobleman James Nihn at the end of the 19th century, was opened by the counts of Micangeli early in this century. The decor is a bit ostentatious but never lets you forget you're relaxing in the lap of luxury. The public spaces contain huge multitiered chandeliers, terra-cotta tile floors, Oriental carpets, and thickly padded furniture. In the guest rooms, curvaceous wrought-iron headboards rise above loudly colorful bedspreads matched to the lampshades, curtains, and sheers. Each room has a private patio beyond French doors.

Dining: There's a small but fastidious bar, and dining is indoors or on a covered terrace, where rich specialty dishes of seafood are served with local and international wines.

Amenities: Concierge, room service, dry cleaning/laundry, newspaper delivery, twice-daily maid service, baby-sitting; covered and outdoor pools, fitness room, minigolf course.

Grand Hotel Punta Molino Terme. Lungomare Cristoforo Colombo 23, 80070 Ischia Porto. ☎ **081/991-544.** Fax 081/991-562. www.puntomolino.it. E-mail: pmolino@ pointel.it. 84 units. A/C MINIBAR TV TEL. 450,000–650,000L ($261–$377) double; from 990,000L ($574) suite. Rates include half board. AE, DC, MC, V. Closed Nov–Apr 14. Parking 35,000L ($20).

Standing in the midst of cliffs of olive groves, this large modern hotel combines comfort with excellent service and a full health spa. The public areas feature a mix of contemporary with 17th- and 18th-century furnishings, with reproductions in the guest rooms, and are floored with stone, marble, or terra-cotta—some tiles of which are painted. Fresh-cut flowers and living plants add life and color, unifying the interior with the lush grounds.

Dining: Candlelit dining in the restaurant offers a wide selection of Italian dishes, like succulent seafood specialties. Meals taken on the terrace feature regional barbecued specialties. Both offer views of the sea and a lengthy wine list.

Amenities: Concierge, room service, dry cleaning/laundry, baby-sitting, secretarial services, courtesy car, car-rental desk, solarium, gym; indoor and outdoor pools heated by thermal springs, freshwater outdoor pool; sauna, tennis courtyards nearby.

Hotel Continental Terme. Via M. Mazzella 74, 80077 Ischia Porto. ☎ **081/991-588.** Fax 081/982-929. www.ischia.it/contiterme. A/C MINIBAR TV TEL. 310,000–350,000L ($180–$203) double; from 470,000L ($273) suite. Rates include half board. AE, DC, MC, V. Closed Nov–Mar. Free valet parking.

The thermal springs at this sprawling complex are among the largest and most fully equipped on the island. There are five thermal water pools, three covered, surrounded by the exotic greenery of 32,700 square yards of gardens. The public spaces feature polished marble and terra-cotta floors, contemporary Italian seating, and wicker-and-glass tables, accented by cut flowers and plant life. The guest rooms are well decorated and rather luxuriously furnished, set in a diverse collection of town-house villas scattered throughout the grounds.

Dining/Diversions: There's a bar lounge, a poolside bar, and a piano bar that provides evening entertainment. Meals, which you can enjoy in the dining room or on the terrace, feature the island's bountiful seafood offered with a lengthy list of wines.

Amenities: Concierge, room service, dry cleaning/laundry, baby-sitting, twice-daily maid service, secretarial services; boutiques, pool; spa facilities with a gym, thermal pools, advanced physiotherapy equipment, and full-service beauty salon offering thermal mud treatments.

Hotel Il Moresco. Via Emanuele Gianturo 16, 80077 Ischia Porto. ☎ **081/981-355.** Fax 081/992-338. www.ischia.it/moresco. 76 units. 210,000–350,000L ($122–$203) per person. Rates include half board. AE, DC, MC, V. Closed Nov–Feb. Valet parking 35,000L ($20).

This hotel's spa facilities and health/beauty center are so complete some guests check in for the entire duration of their vacation. It sits in a sun-dappled park whose pines and palmettos grow close to the arched loggias of its thick concrete walls. From some angles, the Moorish-inspired exterior looks almost like a cubist fantasy. Inside, the straightforward design re-creates a modern oasis in the southern part of Spain—matador-red tiles couple with stark-white walls and Iberian furniture. Each of the well-furnished guest rooms has a terrace or balcony.

Dining/Diversions: The hotel attracted a chic crowd, especially to its piano bar. In the restaurant overlooking the pool you can dine on a savory Mediterranean cuisine with a scattering of well-prepared international specialties—all served by a highly professional staff.

Amenities: Concierge, room service, dry cleaning/laundry, newspaper delivery, twice-daily maid service, baby-sitting, secretarial services; large Spa and Fitness Center; Beauty Center, with heated pool in natural cave; Physiotherapy Center with indoor thermal pool with whirlpool.

✪ **Hotel La Villarosa.** Via Giacinto Gigante 5, 80077 Ischia Porto. ☎ **081/991-316.** Fax 081/992-425. 37 units. TV TEL. 240,000–310,000L ($139–$180) double per person half board. AE, MC, V. Closed Nov–Mar.

This is Ischia's finest pensione. Set in a garden of gardenias, banana, eucalyptus, and fig trees, it's like a private villa, charmingly furnished with antiques. The dining room is in the informal country style, with terra-cotta tiles, lots of French windows, and antique chairs. The meals are a delight, served with a variety of offerings, including the local specialties. And what looks like a carriage house in the garden has been converted into an informal tavern with more antiques. The staff is selected to maintain the personal atmosphere. The bright and airy guest rooms are well kept, conveying a homelike flavor.

DINING

Ristorante Damiano. Via Nuova Circumvallazione/Highway SS-270. ☎ **081/983-032.** Reservations recommended. Main courses 40,000–80,000L ($23–$46). MC, V. Daily 8pm–midnight. Apr–June and Sept, Sun 1–3pm. Closed Oct–Mar. ISCHIAN.

In a circa 1980 building that was angled for maximum exposure to the coastline, this charming restaurant is about a mile southwest of the ferry terminal at Ischia Porto. Its guiding spirit is culinary entrepreneur Damiano Caputo, who infuses his seafood with zest and very fresh ingredients. In the consciously rustic setting that includes long communal tables and fresh flowers, you can select from an array of antipasti arranged on a sturdy buffet; linguine that might be studded with lobster, shrimp, or clams; steamy bowls of minestrone; at least four kinds of seafood salad, including a version with mussels; and grilled fresh fish or lobster. Desserts include tiramisu and a soothing assortment of gelati.

LACCO AMENO

Jutting up from the water, a rock named **Il Fungo (The Mushroom)** is the landmark natural sight of **Lacco Ameno.** The spa is the center of the good life (and contains some of the best and most expensive hotels on the island). People come from all over the world either to relax on the beach and be served top-level food or to take the cure. The radioactive waters at Lacco Ameno have led to the development of a modern spa with extensive facilities for thermal cures, everything from underwater jet massages to mud baths.

ACCOMMODATIONS

Hotel La Reginella. Piazza Santa Restituta 1, 80076 Lacco Ameno d'Ischia. ☎ 081/994-300. Fax 081/980-481. 90 units. A/C MINIBAR TV TEL. 260,000–500,000L ($151–$290) double. Rates include half board. AE, DC, MC, V. Closed Nov 3–Mar 26. Parking 35,000L ($20).

Set in a lush garden typical of the island's accommodations, this hotel boasts a Mediterranean decor combining printed tile floors with light woods and pastel or floral fabrics to create a relaxed atmosphere. The guest rooms are so well maintained and comfortably furnished that the hotel draws a large number of discriminating repeat visitors annually.

Dining: Indoor and outdoor meal service is provided by the hotel restaurant, where fresh seafood dishes and a selection of wines will revitalize you from the activities of the day.

Amenities: Concierge, room service, dry cleaning/laundry, baby-sitting, car-rental desk; solarium, gym, tennis courts; spa facilities with Finnish saunas, outdoor thermal pool, indoor version with underwater jet massage and against-current swimming; use of private beach at nearby Regina Isabella.

Hotel Regina Isabella e Royal Sporting. 80076 Lacco Ameno d'Ischia. ☎ 081/994-322. Fax 081/900-190. 134 units. A/C MINIBAR TV TEL. 220,000–500,000L ($128–$290) double; from 570,000L ($331) suite. Rates include half board. AE, DC, MC, V. Valet parking 35,000L ($20).

Requiring a minimum stay of 3 days, this resort offers the finest accommodations and service available in Lacco Ameno, in a refined setting that successfully contrasts contemporary furnishings with rococo and less ornate antique styles. In the guest rooms, serene blues and greens prevalent in the upholstery and draperies, and some printed tile floors are offset by earthy brown tiles and woodwork.

Dining/Diversions: You can take a break in the piano bar. The hotel restaurant features a dining room and a terrace, serving seafood specialties and eclectic wines with a view over the gardens to the sea beyond.

Amenities: Concierge, room service, baby-sitting, twice-daily maid service, secretarial services; outdoor freshwater pool, indoor thermal pool, private beach with windsurfing and motorboat rental; spa offerings like regimented stretching and walking programs, various types of massages and mud baths, and "cures" for almost anything.

Hotel Terme di Augusto. Viale Campo 128, 80076 Lacco Ameno d'Ischia. ☎ 081/994-944. Fax 081/980-244. 118 units. A/C MINIBAR TV TEL. 240,000–340,000L ($139–$197) double. Rates include half board. AE, DC, MC, V. Closed Dec 1–27. Parking 35,000L ($20).

This hotel, some 50 yards from the shore, provides comfortable accommodations and excellent service in a setting that's less ostentatious than that of many competing resorts. It combines prominent arched ceilings, patterned tile floors, and floral drapery and upholstery to create the light, airy spaces typical of Mediterranean style.

Dining: The dining room and terrace restaurants offer local, national, and international cuisine and wines, served with great attention to detail.

Amenities: Concierge, room service, dry cleaning/laundry, baby-sitting, health club with Jacuzzi and sauna, tennis courts, car-rental desk, beauty salon; freshwater outdoor pool, fully equipped gym; indoor pool with a temperature range up to 96.8°F; thermal beauty center offering mud packs, massage, and "cures" for symptoms ranging from dandruff to vaginal infections.

✪ **Hotel Terme San Montano.** Via Monte Vico, 80076 Lacco Ameno d'Ischia. ☎ **081/994-033.** Fax 081/980-242. 65 units. A/C MINIBAR TV TEL. 440,000–620,000L ($255–$360) double. Rates include half board. AE, DC, MC, V. Closed Nov–Apr 26. Parking 40,000L ($23).

Man Ray was once a faithful guest, as were opera stars Mario del Monaco and Giuseppi di Stefano. The grounds spread out around the hotel in a luxuriant garden. Aged woods, leather, and brass are combined in furnishings, and marine lamps shed light on almost every room. The headboards resemble a ship's helm, windows are translated as portholes, and miniature ships and antiquated diving gear are decoratively scattered about.

Dining/Diversions: The roof restaurant offers a panoramic view of the island, or you can dine indoors in grand comfort. The cuisine is typically Mediterranean, with only the freshest ingredients. The Neapolitan pastry specialties are especially delectable. Every week, evening galas or barbecues with Neapolitan guitar music are presented. After dinner, guests retreat to the piano bar with its soft music.

Amenities: Room service, baby-sitting, secretarial services, boat and car rental; full gym, solarium, natural sauna, thermal and freshwater pools, spa/beauty center, private beach; tennis, squash, or water-skiing lessons, massage, mud baths, full range of health-related treatments.

FORIO

A short drive from Lacco Ameno, **Forio** stands on the west coast of Ischia opening onto the sea near the Bay of Citara. Long a favorite with artists—filmmaker Lucchino Visconti maintains a villa here—it's now developing a broader base of tourism. Locals produce some of the finest wines on the island. On the way from Lacco Ameno, stop at the **beach of San Francesco,** with its sanctuary. At sunset, many visitors head for a rocky spur on which sits the church of **Santa Maria del Soccorso.** The lucky ones get to witness the famous "green flash" over the Gulf of Gaeta. It appears on occasion immediately after the sun sets.

ACCOMMODATIONS

✪ **Grande Albergo Mezzatorre.** Via Mezzatorre, 80075 Forio d'Ischia. ☎ **081/986-111.** Fax 081/986-015. 55 units. A/C MINIBAR TV TEL. 300,000–420,000L ($174–$244) double; 450,000–570,000L ($261–$331) suite. Rates include half board. AE, DC, MC, V. Closed Nov–Apr. Parking 40,000L ($23).

The best hotel in Forio, this complex is built around a 16th-century villa whose stone tower once guarded against invaders; now it houses the least expensive of the doubles. The five postmodern buildings run a few hundred feet downhill to a waterfront bluff. The setting is placid and romantic, with matching rough stone sea walls and paths under tall twisted evergreens. A casual airiness prevails in the public spaces, which contrast soft lighting with terra-cotta floors. Recurring elements are woven straw mats, vaulted ceilings, and round and lancet arched doorways and nooks. The decor in the guest rooms is bright and contemporary, with wooden furniture and brightly upholstered seating, mimicked in the fabrics of bedspreads and drapery.

Dining/Diversions: A delightful Mediterranean cuisine, one of the finest on the island, is served in the hotel dining room. Fresh seafood is the chef's specialty. Many nonguests dine here, including some of the rich island set themselves. You can also enjoy terraces and an elegant bar.

Amenities: Concierge, room service, dry cleaning/laundry, baby-sitting, health club, Jacuzzi, sauna, car-rental desk, beauty salon, tennis courts, seaside outdoor pool, private dock, thermal baths.

DINING

La Romantica. Via Marina 46. ☎ **081/997-345.** Reservations recommended. Main courses 8,000–16,000L ($4.80–$10). AE, DC, MC, V. Daily noon–3pm and 7pm–midnight. Closed Wed from Nov–Mar. NEAPOLITAN/ISCHIAN.

Near the dry-docked fishing vessels of Forio's old port, this is the most appealing non-hotel restaurant. It occupies a Neapolitan-style building whose facade has been enlarged with a jutting wooden extension that has welcomed everyone from Josephine Baker to heart surgeon Christian Barnard. Your meal may include linguine with clams or scampi or a house specialty, "penne 92," garnished with artichoke hearts and shrimp. Swordfish, grilled and served with lemon sauce or with herb-flavored green sauce, is delicious, as are the baked spigola and several risotto and veal dishes. You might prefer, weather permitting, a seat on the outdoor terrace.

SANT'ANGELO

The most charming settlement on Ischia, **Sant'Angelo** juts out on the southernmost tip. The village of fishers is joined to the "mainland" of Ischia by a 300-foot-long lava-and-sand isthmus. Driving into the town is virtually impossible. In summer, you may have to park a long way away and walk. Its **beach** is among the best on the island.

ACCOMMODATIONS

Park Hotel Miramare. 80070 Sant'Angelo d'Ischia. ☎ **081/999-219.** Fax 081/999-325. 50 units. MINIBAR TV TEL. 284,000–316,000L ($165–$183) double. Rates include breakfast. DC, V. Closed Nov–Feb.

Right on the sea, this hotel has no beach to speak of, but there's a concrete terrace with chairs and umbrellas and a stairway that clears the rocky shore, leading into the water. Within the hotel, boldly patterned floor tiles and contemporary furnishings favor hues of blue. Curved wrought-iron balconies, white wickerwork, and canopied iron bed frames are recurring decorative elements. The hotel's health spa isn't on the premises but is only a short walk away, down a flower-lined path. Among its offerings are 12 thermal pools, mud treatments, massage, sauna, and designated nudist areas. The hotel's dining room features the seafood the island is known for, and a snack bar offers an informal and inexpensive option.

5 Sorrento: City of the Sirens

31 miles S of Naples, 159 miles SE of Rome, 31 miles W of Salerno

Borrowing from Greek mythology, the Romans placed the legendary abode of the sirens—those wicked mermaids who lured seamen to their deaths with their sweet songs—at **Sorrento (Surrentum).** Ulysses resisted their call by stuffing the ears of his crew with wax and having himself bound to the mast of his ship. Perched on high cliffs overlooking the bays of Naples and Salerno, Sorrento has been sending out its siren call for centuries—luring everybody from Homer to Lord and Lady Astor. It's the birthplace of Torquato Tasso, author of *Jerusalem Delivered.* Some aging locals still get wet-eyed hearing Vic Damone sing "Come Back to Sorrento."

The streets in summer tend to be as noisy as a carnival. And the traffic is horrendous (no traffic signals in such a bustling city!). The hotels on the "racing strip," **Corso Italia,** need to pass out earplug kits when they tuck you in for the night. Perhaps you'll

Driving Along the Amalfi Coast

If you wish to brave the harrowing twists and turns and assorted other perils of the Amalfi Drive, here's how to link together the region's highlights if you have a car.

Day 1: Begin your tour of the Amalfi Drive in **Sorrento,** 31 miles south of Naples. Subject of song and legend as the home of the sirens, the town stands on a cliff overlooking the Bay of Naples. Its shopping is the best along the coast, so you can easily spend a day here (more if you have time).

Day 2: A narrow, curvy, and twisting highway stretches for 11 miles around the Amalfi peninsula to the enchanting little resort of **Positano.** Although the scenery is panoramic, this drive may be too scary for most. In that case you can reach Positano another way: From Sorrento, head back toward Naples on Route S145. At Meta you can get on Route S163, which cuts across mountainous terrain until you're delivered to the Costa Amalfitana on the south side of the peninsula. Route S163 continues its hellish way all the way to Salerno. Follow this treacherous drive until coming to Positano. This holiday town deserves an overnight or a lot more time if your schedule permits. At least stop for lunch.

Day 3: Figure on an hour to make the twisting 10-mile drive to **Amalfi.** Pause to take in the views from the villages of **Vettica Maggiore** and **Praiano.** The cliffside corniche takes you through the gorges of the **Valley of the Furies (Vallone di Furore).** Along the way, visit the **Emerald Grotto (Grotta di Smeraldo),** the major attraction along the coast. Reach Amalfi for a late-afternoon stroll of exploration and dine in a trattoria along the water.

Day 4: In the morning, drive up to **Ravello,** a distance of 4 miles, and spend the morning exploring this hilltop village where "poets go to die," taking in the panoramic vistas. In the afternoon you can return to the Amalfi Drive and continue along the coast toward Salerno, where you can hook up with autostrada E45 going south. Take it until the turnoff onto Route SS18 leading directly south to **Paestum,** 25 miles south of Salerno. Here you can explore the ancient Sybarite city of Poseidonia, dating back to 600 B.C. These ruins, including a Doric temple (the basilica) and the Temple of Neptune, are among the more evocative in Italy.

---

have a hotel on a cliffside in Sorrento with a view of the "sea of the sirens." If you want to swim in that sea, you'll find both paths and private elevators to take you down.

To enjoy the beauty of the Amalfi Drive and avoid its perils, don't drive it yourself. Take a blue SITA bus that runs between Sorrento and Salerno or Amalfi. In Sorrento, bus stations with timetables are outside the rail station and in the central piazza.

ESSENTIALS

GETTING THERE   Sorrento is served by frequent express **trains** from Naples (trip time: 1 hour). The high-speed train, called Ferrovia Circumvesuviana, leaves from one floor underground at Stazione Centrale. If you've got a **car** and are in Naples, head south on Route 18, cutting west at the junction with Route S145.

VISITOR INFORMATION   The **tourist office** is at Via de Maio 35 (☎ 081/807-4033), which winds down to the port where ships headed for Capri (see "The Isle of Capri," later in this chapter) and Naples anchor. It's open Monday to Saturday 8am to 6pm.

EXPLORING THE CITY

For such a famous beach resort, Sorrento's actual beaches are limited—most of them just bathing piers extending into the water. Chaise longues and umbrellas line these decks along the rock-strewn coastline. The best beach is **Punta del Capo,** reached by going along Corso Italia to Via del Capo. If you'd like to go hiking, you can explore the green hills above Sorrento. Many of the trails are marked, and the tourist office will advise.

Although few visitors come to Sorrento to look at churches and monuments, there are some worth exploring. The **Chiesa di San Francesco,** Via San Francesco (☎ 081/878-1269), dates from the 14th century. This cloister is a pocket of beauty in over-crowded Sorrento, with delicate archways and a garden studded with flowering vines. The convent is also an art school offering exhibits, and in July and August jazz and classical music are performed almost nightly in the outdoor atrium. Show time is 9pm, with an admission of 18,000L to 25,000L ($10 to $15) adults or 15,000L ($9) for those under 26. The cloister is otherwise open daily 9am to 6pm, and admission is free.

If time remains, visit the **Museo Correale di Terranova,** Via Correale (☎ 081/878-1846), north of Piazza Tasso. A former palace, it has displays of ancient statues, antiques, and Italian art. Here's a chance to introduce yourself to *intarsia,* a technique of making objects with paper-thin pieces of patterned wood. Neapolitan bric-a-brac and other curiosities finish off the exhibits. After a visit to the museum, you can stroll through the gardens. April to September, it's open Monday and Wednesday to Saturday 9am to 12:30pm and 5 to 7pm and Sunday 9am to 12:30pm. Off-season, hours are Monday and Wednesday to Saturday 9 to 11:30pm and 3 to 5pm and Sunday 9 to 11:30am. Admission is 8,000L ($4.65) to the museum and gardens.

SHOPPING

The tradition of handcrafts and artisanship is more deeply entrenched in Sorrento than anywhere else along the Amalfi Drive. The city's cobbled alleyways and flower-ringed piazzas encourage strolls, and the best ones for window-shopping are **Piazza Tasso** and **Via San Cesareo,** densely packed with shoppers on weekend afternoons.

Noteworthy is **Gargiulo & Jannuzzi,** Piazza Tasso (☎ 081/878-1041), the region's best-known maker of marquetry furniture. Opened in 1863, the shop demonstrates the centuries-old technique in the basement, where an employee will combine multihued pieces of wood veneer to create patterns of arabesques and flowers. The sprawling showrooms feature an array of card tables, clocks, and partners' desks, each inlaid with patterns of elmwood, rosewood, bird's-eye maple, and mahogany. Upstairs is a collection of embroidered napery and table linen, and the outlet has its own ceramic factory. The pottery can be shipped anywhere.

Embroidery and lace are two of the best shopping bargains in Sorrento, and **Luigia Gargiulo,** Corso Italia 48 (☎ 081/878-1081), comes recommended for embroidered sheets and tablecloths but also offers children's clothing. In **Cuomo's Lucky Store,** Piazza Antica Mura 2–7 (☎ 081/878-5649), you'll find a little bit of everything made in the area, including displays of porcelain dating back to the 1700s.

One of the most appealing assortments of cameos, meticulously hand-carved from seashells, is available at the reasonably priced **Ciro Bimonte,** Via Guiliani 61 (☎ 081/807-1880). And if you're feeling underdressed or underaccessorized, consider checking out **Coin,** Via San Cesareo 39 (☎ 081/807-1747), or **Max & Co.,** Corso Italia 62 (☎ 081/807-4529), both selling clothing of all degrees of formality for men, women, and children.

ACCOMMODATIONS

In its first- and second-class hotels, Sorrento is superior to almost any resort in the south and offers accommodations in all price ranges.

EXPENSIVE

✪ **Grand Hotel Excelsior Vittoria.** Piazza Tasso 34, 80067 Sorrento. ☎ **081/807-1044.** Fax 081/877-1206. 118 units. MINIBAR TV TEL. 415,000–536,000L ($241–$311) double; from 683,000L ($396) suite. Rates include breakfast. AE, DC, MC, V. Free parking.

This luxury bastion, built between 1834 and 1882 on the edge of a cliff overlooking the Bay of Naples and surrounded by semitropical gardens with lemon and orange trees, combines 19th-century glamour with modern amenities. The terrace theme predominates, especially on the water side, where you can enjoy the cold drinks served at sunset while gazing at Vesuvius. Three elevators take bathers down to the harbor. Inside, the atmosphere is old-worldish, especially in the mellow dining room. In 1921, Enrico Caruso stayed in the suite now named for him. The huge guest rooms boast their own drama, some with balconies opening onto the cliffside drop; they have a wide mix of furnishings, with many antique pieces.

Dining/Diversions: The dining room is formal, with hand-painted ceilings and a panoramic view. You'll sit in ivory-and-cane provincial chairs while enjoying topnotch Sorrento cuisine. In summer, you can dine in the open air. Live entertainment is presented twice a week.

Amenities: Concierge, room service, baby-sitting, laundry/dry cleaning, twice-daily maid service, large pool.

Hotel Imperial Tramontano. Via Vittorio Veneto 1, 80067 Sorrento. ☎ **081/878-2588.** Fax 081/807-2344. 116 units. A/C TV TEL. 360,000L ($209) double. Half board 240,000L ($139) per person. AE, MC, V. Closed Jan–Feb.

Although outclassed by the Vittoria (above), this pocket of posh in a semitropical garden is still one of the leading hotels along the Amalfi Drive. It was the birthplace of poet Torquato Tasso, yet he'd hardly recognize the palatial villa as it has been much altered. When approached by boat from Naples, the hotel seems like an integral part of the high cliff to which it's attached. The spacious guest rooms, with tile floors, are well furnished, and some have balconies opening onto panoramic sea views. The drawing room, with English and Italian antiques, modifies its spaciousness by its informal treatment of furnishings. In the garden, you can inhale the aroma of sweet-smelling trees and walk down paths of oleanders, hydrangea, acacia, coconut palms, and geraniums.

Dining/Diversions: The bar and drinking lounge are spiked with period pieces—many of them mahogany, Victorian style. The restaurant is a worthy choice if you don't want to go out in the evening, serving a flavorful Mediterranean cuisine.

Amenities: Concierge, room service, twice-daily maid service, laundry/dry cleaning, baby-sitting.

MODERATE

Grand Hotel Ambasciatori. Via Califano 18, 80067 Sorrento. ☎ **081/878-2025.** Fax 081/807-1021. 109 units. A/C TV TEL. 240,000–340,000L ($139–$197) double; 345,000–445,000L ($200–$258) suite. Rates include breakfast. AE, MC, V. Free parking.

The heavily buttressed foundation that prevents this cliffside hotel from plunging into the sea looks like something from a medieval monastery. Built in a style reminiscent of a private villa, it was landscaped to include several rambling gardens along the precipice. A set of steps and a private elevator lead to the wooden deck of a bathing wharf. Inside, a substantial collection of Oriental carpets, marble floors, and armchairs provide plush comfort. The restaurant offers regional and international fare; there's a snack bar by the pool and live Neapolitan songs twice a week.

Hotel Bristol. Via del Capo 22, 80067 Sorrento. ☎ **081/878-4522.** Fax 081/807-1910. 135 units. A/C TV TEL. 280,000–360,000L ($168–$216) double; 300,000–400,000L ($174–$232) suite. Rates include breakfast. AE, DC, MC, V. Free parking.

The Bristol was built pueblo style on a hillside at the edge of town, and all but 15 rooms have a view of Vesuvius and the Bay of Naples. The hotel lures with its contemporary decor and spaciousness and with well-appointed public and private rooms. The guest rooms are warm and inviting, with bright covers and built-in niceties. Most have balconies overlooking the sea, and some contain minibars. The hotel also has two panoramic restaurants, a pool, mini-golf, an American bar, a solarium, and a Finnish sauna. In summer, you can dine on the terrace.

INEXPENSIVE

Hotel Désirée. Via del Capo 31 bis, 80067 Sorrento. ☎ and fax **081/878-1563.** 22 units. TEL. 120,000L ($70) double. Rates include breakfast. No credit cards. Closed Nov–Mar 10.

The Désirée is half a mile from the town center at the beginning of the Amalfi Drive. This tranquil hotel, directed by the Gargiulo family, is ringed with terraces whose flowered masonry overlooks the Bay of Naples and nearby trees. This used to be an upper-class private home before it was transformed into a good-value hotel. Many attractive personal touches remain. You'll recognize the hotel by its green glass lanterns in front and the awning over the entrance. An elevator leads to the private beach, and there's a solarium.

Hotel Regina. Via Marina Grande 10, 80067 Sorrento. ☎ **081/878-2722.** Fax 081/878-2721. 36 units. TEL. 280,000L ($163) double. Rates include half board. AE, DC, DISC, MC, V. Closed Nov 15–Mar. Parking 10,000L ($6).

Evenly spaced rows of balconies jut out over the Regina's well-tended garden. On its uppermost floor, a glassed-in dining room and a terrace encompass views of the Mediterranean extending as far as Naples and Vesuvius. The clean, functional rooms have tile floors and private terraces; a dozen open onto views from private balconies and are the most requested as they're the same price as units sans the panorama. Only 10 rooms are air-conditioned. The hotel employs a helpful staff who provide road maps and offer hints about sightseeing. Though small, the inn does provide some amenities found in first-class hotels, like a concierge, room service, baby-sitting, and laundry service.

Villa di Sorrento. Via Fuorimura 4, 80067 Sorrento. ☎ **081/878-1068.** Fax 081/807-2679. 20 units. TEL. 205,000L ($119) double. Rates include breakfast. AE, DC, MC, V.

This is a pleasant villa in the center of town. Architecturally romantic, the Sorrento attracts travelers with its petite wrought-iron balconies, tall shutters, and vines climbing the facade. The comfortably furnished and well maintained rooms have such small niceties as bedside tables and lamps, and some contain terraces.

DINING
EXPENSIVE

✪ **Don Alfonso.** Piazza Sant'Agata, Sant'Agata, 6 miles south of Sorrento. ☎ **081/878-0026.** Reservations recommended. Main courses 37,000–40,000L ($22–$24); set-price menus 100,000–130,000L ($60–$78). AE, DC, MC, V. Wed–Mon 12:30–2:30pm and 8–10:30pm. Closed Mon Oct–May. By car, follow the signs to Sant'Agata; by bus, take the blue-and-white SITA bus marked "sant'agata" from the piazza in front of Sorrento's rail station. SOUTHERN ITALIAN.

One of southern Italy's most highly recommended restaurants occupies a turn-of-the-century faux-Pompeian building adjacent to Santa Maria delle Grazie, the centerpiece of the hamlet of Sant'Agata, perched more than 1,200 feet above sea level. This Relais & Châteaux member is unusual in that its chef/co-owner, Alfonso Laccarino, makes it a point to hire as many international assistants as possible, many of whom spend a year here from such homelands as Sweden, Austria, Switzerland, Japan, and the United States. Alfonso's wife, Okivia, directs the dining room and maintains the award-winning wine cellars.

The menu items include lots of organic vegetables and greens from the family's sprawling gardens in a neighboring village, adding tremendously to the appeal of a Mediterranean diet of fish and shellfish. Free-range chicken with garlic and home-grown herbs is particularly wonderful, as is the mixed fish fry, where everything seems ultra-fresh and flavorful. An ongoing favorite (prepared only for two) is a Neapolitan casseruolla of lobster, squid, clams, mussels, and assorted saltwater fish.

Don Alfonso also offers three suites, two with kitchens and all with air-conditioning, TVs, and phones. They rent for 250,000L ($150), including breakfast.

MODERATE

L'Antica Trattoria. Via P. R. Giuliani 33. ☎ 081/807-1082. Reservations recommended. Main courses 20,000–40,000L ($12–$23); fixed-price menu 40,000–90,000L ($23–$52). AE, MC, V. Tues–Sun noon–3:30pm and 6pm–midnight. Closed Jan 10–Feb 10. CAMPANESE/INTERNATIONAL.

Inside the weather-beaten walls of what was built 300 years ago as a stable, this 200-year-old restaurant is charming, polite, and one of the best recommended in Sorrento. Although all its food is well prepared, its real virtue is its antipasti. You'll find several varieties of fish cooked in a salt crust, which transforms the dish into a sweetly scented, firm but flaky delicacy, and a daunting array of pastas from lasagne to ravioli (the best is stuffed with seafood). The house special pasta, spaghetti alla ferrolese, is made with fish roe, shrimp, red cabbage, and cream. A particularly delicious specialty is seafood pezzogna, made with pulverized cherry tomatoes, olive oil, garlic, parsley, crushed red pepper, and shellfish. The assortment of ice creams is especially tempting, some of the best in town.

INEXPENSIVE

La Favorita—O'Parrucchiano. Corso Italia 71. ☎ 081/878-1321. Main courses 12,000–24,000L ($7–$14). MC, V. Daily noon–3:30pm and 7pm–11:30pm. Closed Wed Nov 15–Mar 15. NEAPOLITAN/SORRENTINE.

This is a good choice on the busiest street in town. The building is like an old tavern, with an arched ceiling in the main dining room. On the terrace you can dine in a garden of trees, rubber plants, and statuary. Among the à la carte dishes, classic Italian fare is offered, like ravioli Caprese (filled with fresh cheese and covered with tomato sauce), cannelloni, a mixed fish fry from the Bay of Naples, and veal cutlet Milanese. The chef will also prepare a pizza for you.

SORRENTO AFTER DARK

At the **Taverna dell' 800,** Via dell'Accademia 29 (☎ 081/878-5970), owner Tony Herculano dispenses flavorful house-style maccheroni (pink-tinged, it combines tomatoes with ham, cream, and bacon) and good cheer. From 9pm to midnight, the music of a guitar and a piano duet enlivens a cozy bar with flickering candles and a cross-cultural polyglot of languages. There's no cover charge, and main courses are 6,000L to 14,000L ($3.50 to $8). The joint is open Tuesday to Sunday 8am to 4:30am and does lots of business throughout the day as a cafe and pub.

For a dose of Neapolitan-style folklore, head for the **Circolo de Forestière,** Via Luigi de Maio 35 (☎ **081/877-3012**), a bar/cafe whose views extend out over a flowering terrace and the wide blue bay. Music from the live pianist is interrupted only for episodes of folkloric dancing and cheerful music from a troupe of players. The town's central square, **Piazza Tasso,** is the site of two worthwhile nightclubs. The one that's more closely geared to folkloric music is **Fauno** (☎ **081/878-1021**), where you can slug down a beer or two during the sporadic performances of tarantella. Brief but colorful, they interrupt a program otherwise devoted to recorded dance (usually disco) music. There's usually no cover. Less nostalgic is **The Club** (☎ **081/878-4052**), where dance music blares out to a youngish crowd from throughout Europe and North America. The cover is 30,000L ($17) and includes the first drink. It's open daily 10pm to 3am (depending on the crowd).

6 Positano: Boutiques, Bikinis & More

35 miles SE of Naples, 10 miles E of Sorrento, 165 miles SE of Rome

A Moorish-style hillside village on the southern strip of the Amalfi Drive, **Positano** opens onto the Tyrrhenian Sea with its legendary Sirenuse Islands, Homer's siren islands in the *Odyssey,* which form the mini-archipelago of Li Galli (The Cocks). Still privately owned, these islands were once purchased by Leonid Massine, the Russian-born choreographer who became Diaghilev's favorite after Nijinsky left him. It's said that the town was "discovered" after World War II when Gen. Mark Clark stationed troops in nearby Salerno. It has jackrabbited along the classic postwar route of many a European resort: a sleeping fishing village that was visited by painters and writers (Paul Klee, Tennessee Williams) and then was taken over by bohemia-sampling visitors. You may recognize Positano if you've seen the film *Only You,* starring Marisa Tomei and Robert Downey, Jr.

Once Positano was part of the powerful Republic of the Amalfis, a rival of Venice as a sea power in the 10th century. Today smart boutiques dot the village, and bikinis add vibrant colors to the mud-gray beach where you're likely to get pebbles in your sand castle. Prices have been rising sharply over the past few years. The 500-lire-a-night rooms popular with sunset-painting artists have gone the way of your baby teeth.

The topography of the village, you'll soon discover, is impossibly steep. Wear comfortable walking shoes—no heels! But, as John Steinbeck once wrote, "Positano bites deep. It is a dream place that isn't quite real when you are there and becomes beckoningly real after you have gone."

If you make reservations the day before with **Alicost** (☎ **089/875-092**), you can take a hydrofoil or a ferry to Capri. There are three hydrofoil departures per day, costing 18,000L ($11) one-way, and three ferry departures, costing 12,000L ($7) one-way.

ESSENTIALS

GETTING THERE SITA **buses** leave from Sorrento frequently throughout the day, more often in summer than winter, for the rather thrilling ride to Positano; a one-way fare is 4,300L ($2.50). For information, call SITA at ☎ **089/871-016.** If you've got a **car,** Positano lies along Route 145, which becomes Route 163 at the approach to the resort.

VISITOR INFORMATION   The **tourist office** is at Via del Saracino 4 (☎ 089/ 875-067), open Monday to Friday 8:30am to 2pm and Saturdays June to September 8:30am to noon.

SHOPPING
In a town famous for beach and casual wear, **La Brezza,** Via del Brigantino 1 (☎ 089/ 875-811), on the shore, has the perfect location for selling its swimsuits, beach towels, and summer clothes. Clothing that's a bit more formal, and better suited to a glamorous dinner on one of Positano's flowering terraces, is **Nadir,** Piazza dei Mulini (☎ 089/875-975). Another fashion option, with merchandise inspired by the *alta-moda* boutiques of faraway Milan, is **Carro Fashion,** Viale Pasitea (☎ 089/875-780). And if you're in the market for brightly colored, intricately patterned regional pottery, consider a visit to **Umberto Carro,** Via Pasitea 90 (☎ 089/811-596), where the focus is on dishes, cookware, and ceramic tiles.

ACCOMMODATIONS
VERY EXPENSIVE
✪ **Hotel Le Sirenuse.** Via Christoforo Colombo 30, 84017 Positano. ☎ **089/875-066.** Fax 089/811-798. www.sirenuse.it. E-mail: sirenuse@macronet.it. 60 units. A/C MINIBAR TV TEL. 400,000–900,000L ($232–$522) double; from 1,265,000L ($734) suite. Rates include breakfast. AE, DC, MC, V. Parking 40,000L ($23).

A feel of the 1950s still lingers around this candy box of a hotel, and Jean Cocteau could've (but didn't) designed some of the decor. The sophisticated crowd includes numerous artists and writers. The hotel, an old villa only a few minutes' walk up from the bay, is owned by the Marchesi Sersale family and was their residence until 1951. The marchesa selects all furnishings, which include fine carved chests, 19th-century paintings and old prints, a spinet piano, upholstered pieces in bold colors, and a Victorian cabinet from an old jewelry shop. The guest rooms, many with Jacuzzis, are varied, and all have terraces overlooking the village. Your room may have an iron bed, high and ornate and painted red, as well as a carved chest and refectory tables.

Dining: Meals are well served on one of the three terraces, and the chef caters to the international palate with a regional cuisine. The hotel boasts one of the best dining rooms along the coast (see "Dining," below).

Amenities: Room service, baby-sitting, laundry/valet, narrow pool, sauna, gym.

✪ **San Pietro.** Via Laurito 2, 84017 Positano. ☎ **089/875-455.** Fax 089/811-449. 59 units. A/C MINIBAR TV TEL. 620,000–700,000L ($360–$406) double; 800,000–1,100,000L ($464–$638) suite. Rates include breakfast. AE, DC, MC, V. Closed Nov 3–Easter. Free parking.

A mile from Positano toward Amalfi, San Pietro is signaled only by a miniature 17th-century chapel projecting out on a high cliff. The hotel opened in 1970 and has been renovated virtually every winter since. An elevator takes you down to the cliff ledges of the choicest resort along the Amalfi Coast and one of the grandest resort hotels in Europe. The suitelike rooms are superglamorous, many with a picture window beside the bathtub (there's even a huge sunken Roman bath in one suite). Bougainvillea from the terraces reaches into the ceilings of many living rooms filled with antiques and reproductions. Guests have included Lord Laurence Olivier, Rudolf Nureyev, Gregory Peck, Julia Roberts, and Sting.

Dining/Diversions: Guests gather at sunset in the piano bar. A dining room cut into the cliff features picture windows and a refined international cuisine. There's also a lovely tiled terrace on which you can sip drinks while enjoying the view.

Amenities: Room service, baby-sitting, laundry/valet, pool, private beach, tennis court.

EXPENSIVE

✪ **Hotel Poseidon.** Via Pasitea 148, 84017 Positano. ☎ **089/811-111.** Fax 089/875-833. www.starnet.it/poseidon. E-mail: poseidon@starnet.it. 51 units. A/C MINIBAR TV TEL. 310,000–390,000L ($180–$226) double; 510,000–680,000L ($296–$394) suite. Rates include breakfast. AE, DC, MC, V. Closed Nov 4–Mar 29. Parking 35,000L ($20).

This hotel, among the very finest in Positano, was built in 1950 by the Aonzo family as their summer residence. In 1955, it was enlarged and transformed into a hotel, still owned and managed by the hospitable Aonzos. Centrally located, it's charming, discreet, and elegant, with tastefully selected antique furniture and objects. The rooms are traditionally furnished and beautifully maintained.

Dining: Along with its terraces and garden, the hotel offers both indoor and outdoor dining; its chefs feature regional and continental cuisine.

Amenities: Concierge, room service, dry cleaning/laundry, twice-daily maid service, secretarial services, baby-sitting; freshwater pool, health club (the first and only in Positano) with sauna, hydromassage spa, and gym with professional trainer.

MODERATE

Albergo L'Ancora. Via Colombo 36, 84017 Positano. ☎ **089/875-318.** Fax 089/811-784. 18 units. MINIBAR TV TEL. 200,000–240,000L ($116–$139) double. Rates include breakfast. AE, DC, MC, V. Closed Nov–Apr 1. Free parking.

This is a stand-out choice, a hillside villa turned hotel with the atmosphere of a private club. It's fresh and sunny—each room, 11 of them air-conditioned, is like a bird's nest on a cliff, with a private terrace. The hotel is a 5-minute climb from the beach. Its main lounge has clusters of club chairs, tile floors, and teardrop chandeliers. But the guest rooms (all doubles) are the stars, with their individualized treatments. Well-chosen antiques, such as fine inlaid desks, are mixed with contemporary pieces. Only guests can dine on the informal terrace under a vine-covered sun shelter. Note the hotel will be closed for renovations from January to April 1999.

Albergo Miramare. Via Trara Genoino 31, 84017 Positano. ☎ **089/875-002.** Fax 089/ 875-219. 18 units. A/C TEL. 220,000–330,000L ($128–$191) double; 270,000–380,000L ($157–$224) triple. Rates include breakfast. AE, MC, V. Closed Nov 15–Mar 15. Parking 35,000L ($20)

The Miramare is for those who like the personalized touch only a small inn can provide. On a cliff in the town center, it attracts a discriminating crowd who appreciates the terraces where you can sip a Campari and soda and contemplate the sea. Guests stay in one of two tastefully furnished buildings amid citrus trees and flamboyant bougainvillea. Your bed will most likely rest under a vaulted ceiling, and the white walls will be thick. The baths have a sense of kitsch: What might seem like questionable taste in Los Angeles—a pink porcelain clamshell as a wash basin—becomes charming here, even when the water rushes from a sea-green ceramic fish with coral-pink gills. The conversation piece is room 210's glass bathtub (once an aquarium) on a flowery terrace. The beach is a 3-minute walk away down a series of stairs.

Albergo Ristorante Covo dei Saraceni. 84017 Positano. ☎ **089/875-400.** Fax 089/ 875-878. 58 units. A/C MINIBAR TV TEL. 230,000–340,000L ($133–$197) double; 350,000–450,000L ($203–$261) junior suite. Rates include buffet breakfast. AE, DC, MC, V. Closed Jan 10–Mar 31. Parking 30,000L ($17).

You'll find this rambling yellow-ochre building a few steps above the port, a desirable choice for those who want to be in the swim of the summer action. The side closest to the water culminates in a rounded tower of rough-hewn stone, inside of which is an appealing restaurant open to the breezes and a firsthand view of the crashing waves. The guest rooms are comfortably furnished.

Buca di Bacco. Via Rampa Teglia 8, 84017 Positano. ☎ **089/875-699.** Fax 089/875-731. 53 units. A/C MINIBAR TV TEL. 250,000–300,000L ($145–$174) double. Rates include breakfast. AE, DC, MC, V. Closed Oct 31–Mar. Parking 30,000–35,000L ($17–$20).

This is one of the best moderately priced hotels, with one of the best restaurants in the area (see "Dining," below). The main beach of Positano often draws guests who patronize only its bar, one of the best-known rendezvous points along the Amalfi Drive. A large terrace opens onto the beach, and you can enjoy a cocktail while still in your swimsuit. The oldest and most expensive part, the Buca Residence, was an old seaside mansion at the dawn of the 19th century. The guest rooms are well furnished, with many facilities, like balconies facing the sea.

INEXPENSIVE

Casa Albertina. Via Tavolozza 4, 84017 Positano. ☎ **089/875-143.** Fax 089/811-540. 20 units. A/C MINIBAR TV TEL. 220,000–260,000L ($128–$151) double with breakfast; 340,000–360,000L ($197–$209) double with half board. Half board compulsory Apr–Oct. AE, DC, MC, V. Parking 25,000–30,000L ($15–$17).

This villa guesthouse, up a steep and winding road, offers a view of the coast from its hillside perch. The guest rooms are gems, color coordinated in mauve or blue; they're furnished with well-selected pieces, such as gilt mirrors, fruitwood end tables, and bronze bed lamps. Each has wide French doors leading out to a private balcony, and a few have Jacuzzis. You can breakfast on the terra-cotta-tile terrace and enjoy lunch and dinner in the good restaurant specializing in fresh grilled fish. Laundry service and a baby-sitter are available on request, and the hotel has both a bar and a solarium.

✪ **Palazzo Murat.** Via dei Mulini 23, 84017 Positano. ☎ **089/875-177.** Fax 089/811-419. 28 units. MINIBAR TV TEL. 290,000–390,000L ($168–$226) double. Rates include breakfast. AE, DC, MC, V. Closed Jan 1–one week before Easter. Parking 35,000L ($20).

For nostalgic atmosphere and baroque style, this place has no equal in Positano. The jasmine and bougainvillea are so profuse in its garden they spill over their enclosing wall onto the arbors of the narrow street. Once this was the sumptuous retreat of Napoléon I's brother-in-law, the king of Naples, who was notorious for confiscating some of the statuary and church art that had belonged to the former occupants, an order of Benedictine monks. Shell designs cap the villa windows, which look out over a cluster of orange trees and the wrought-iron tendrils of the gate that leads into the garden. To enlarge the property, a previous owner erected a comfortable annex compatible with the original villa. Breakfast is the only meal served. Many of the guest rooms contain their original stucco ornamentation from the late 17th century, and each boasts one or several antiques, often in the baroque style; nineteen are air-conditioned.

DINING
EXPENSIVE

✪ **Ristorante La Sirenuse.** In the Hotel La Sirenuse, Via Christoforo Colombo 30. ☎ **089/875-066.** Reservations imperative. Main courses 30,000–70,000L ($18–$42); set-price menu 90,000L ($54). AE, DC, MC, V. Daily 1–2:30pm and 8–10pm. Closed Jan 6–Mar 15. SOUTHERN ITALIAN.

One of Italy's most stylish hotel restaurants occupies the third floor of the previously recommended hotel. Waiters will tell you its terrace is "just 80 steps above the level of the sea." Bougainvillea, geraniums, hibiscus, and lemon trees are artfully massed in the terrace corners, and during clement weather the inside dining room closes completely in favor of the alfresco experience. The menu items revolve around what's available at the seafood markets and include dishes like linguine le Sirenuse, with lobster, scampi, and crayfish; linguine with artichoke hearts and scampi that's been cooked en papillote; fresh salads and antipasti; and a grilled medley of fish and shellfish prepared only for two or more. Expect lots of Mediterranean herbs, mozzarella, and home-made pastries.

MODERATE

Buca di Bacco. Via Rampa Teglia 8. ☎ **089/875-699.** Reservations required. Main courses 25,000–30,000L ($15–$17). AE, DC, MC, V. Daily 12:30–3:30pm and 8–11pm. Closed Oct 31–Mar. CAMPANIA/ITALIAN.

Right on the beach you'll find one of Positano's top restaurants, opened just days after the end of World War II. Guests often stop for a drink in the bar before heading up to the dining room on a big covered terrace facing the sea. On display are fresh fish, special salads, and fruit, like luscious black figs and freshly peeled oranges soaked in caramel. An exciting opener is a salad made with fruits of the sea, or you may prefer the zuppa di cozze (mussels), prepared with flair in a tangy sauce. Other items not to miss are linguine with lobster and grillata del Golfo, a unique mixed fish fry. The pasta dishes are homemade and the meats well prepared with fresh ingredients. Finish off with the chic after-dinner drink, limoncello, the lemon liqueur celebrated along the Amalfi Drive.

Chez Black. Via del Brigantino 19–21. ☎ **089/875-036.** Reservations required in summer. Main courses 15,000–35,000L ($9–$20). AE, DC, MC, V. Apr–Oct daily 12:30–3pm and 7:30–11pm; Nov–Mar daily 12:30–3pm. Closed Jan 7–Feb 20. SEAFOOD.

The owner is Salvatore Russo, but for his restaurant he uses the suntan-inspired name his friends gave him in college. Founded after World War II, the restaurant occupies a desirable position near the beach, and in summer it's in the "eye of the hurricane" of action. The interior emulates an expensive yacht with varnished ribbing, a glowing sheath of softwood and brass, and semaphore symbols, making it one of the most beautiful restaurants in town. A stone-edged aquarium holds fresh lobsters, and rack on rack of local wines give you a vast choice. Seafood is the specialty, as well as a wide selection of pizzas. The best-known dish is the spaghetti with crayfish, but you might be tempted by linguine with fresh pesto, grilled swordfish, sole, or shrimp, plus an array of veal, liver, chicken, and beef dishes. Don't underestimate the spicy and heady *zuppe di pesce* (fish soup): A meal in itself and brimming with succulent finned creatures whose composition changes according to the catch of the day, it's one of the most prized and sought-after dishes. The staff will be quick to tell you it's not to be confused with bouillabaisse.

✪ Da Adolfo. Via Laurito, Località Laurito. ☎ **089/875-022.** Reservations not necessary. Main courses 11,000–24,000L ($7–$14)). No credit cards. Late May–June and Sept–Oct 14 daily 1–4pm; July–Aug also Sat 8pm–midnight. SOUTHERN ITALIAN.

Don't even think of going here via car or taxi, as you'd have to descend around 450 rugged stone steps from the highway above. The husband/wife team of Sergio (Italian) and Amanda (Australian) provides a 25-passenger motorboat to take you from Positano's main jetty across the water to the restaurant. (You'll recognize the boat by the large red fish on its side.) During the season Da Adolfo is open, the boat departs daily every 30 minutes 10am to 1pm and 4pm to whenever the last customer has left the beach, usually sometime between 6:30 and 8pm or even later on Saturdays in July and

August, the only time dinner is served. The shuttle service is free, as is the use of the sands, changing rooms, and freshwater showers maintained by the restaurant. The only things you'll pay for are whatever you eat and drink in the restaurant and the optional rental of a beach chair (7,000L/$4.20) and an umbrella (4,000L/$2.40).

Fans of Da Adolfo compare it to a beachfront restaurant in Greece, where pungent summery food, a casual attitude toward toplessness, an utter lack of pretension, and sun and fun are featured. Menu items focus on the fish, herbs, mozzarella, and zest of Mediterranean Italy. Especially appealing are the heaping bowl of mussel soup, slices of fresh mozzarella wrapped in lemon leaves, and scialetti, pasta with stewed clams and mussels.

POSITANO AFTER DARK

Virtually anyone in town will agree that Positano and the nearby coast contain only two nightclubs that appeal to visitors' sense of style and whimsy. More convenient to Positano is **Music on the Rocks,** Spiaggia Grande (☎ 089/875-874), designed on two levels, one of which contains a contemplative piano bar. It's owned by the same man who owns the très chic Chez Black (above). Similar in its choice of music, crowd, and setting is **L'Africana,** Vettica Maggiore (☎ 089/874-042), in the satellite resort of Praiano, about 2 miles from Positano. Local fishers come in during the most frenzied peak of the dancing and dredge a sinkhole at the edge of the dance floor with nets, pulling up a bountiful catch of seafood for consumption in local restaurants. The contrast of new-age music with old-world folklore is as riveting as it is bizarre. Many chic guests from Positano often arrive here by boat. Both clubs are open nightly June to August, but only Friday and Saturday in May and September, and they're closed the rest of the year.

7 Amalfi & the Emerald Grotto

38 miles SE of Naples, 11 miles E of Positano, 21 miles W of Salerno, 169 miles SE of Rome

From the 9th to the 11th century, the seafaring Republic of Amalfi rivaled the great maritime powers of Genoa and Venice. Its maritime code, the Tavole Amalfitane, was followed in the Mediterranean for centuries. But raids by Saracens and a flood in the 14th century devastated the city. Amalfi's power and influence weakened, until it rose again in modern times as the major resort on the Amalfi Drive.

From its position at the slope of the steep Lattari hills, it overlooks the Bay of Salerno. The approach to **Amalfi** is dramatic, whether you come from Positano or from Salerno. Today Amalfi depends on tourist traffic, and the hotels and pensioni are right in the milling throng of holiday makers. The finest and most highly rated accommodations are on the outskirts.

ESSENTIALS

GETTING THERE   SITA **buses** run every 2 hours during the day from Sorrento, costing 4,000L ($2.30) one-way. There are also SITA bus connections from Positano, costing 2,000L ($1.15) one-way. Information about schedules is available in Amalfi by calling the bus terminal at the waterfront on Piazza Flavio Gioia (☎ 089/871-009). If you've got a **car,** from Positano continue east along the Amalfi Drive (S163) with its narrow hairpin turns.

VISITOR INFORMATION   The **tourist office** is at Corso delle Repubbliche Marinare 19–21 (☎ 089/871-107), open Monday to Friday 8am to 2pm and Saturday 8am to noon.

EXPLORING THE CATHEDRAL & THE EMERALD GROTTO

The ✪ **Duomo,** Piazza del Duomo (☎ **089/871-059**)—named in honor of St. Andrew (Sant'Andrea), whose remains are said to be buried inside the crypt (see below)—evokes Amalfi's rich past. Reached by climbing steep steps, the cathedral is characterized by its black-and-white facade and mosaics. The one nave and two aisles are all richly baroqued. The cathedral dates from the 11th century, though the present structure has been rebuilt. Its bronze doors were made in Constantinople and its campanile (bell tower) is from the 13th century, erected partially in the Romanesque style. The Duomo is open daily 7:30am to 8pm and charges no admission.

You can also visit the **Cloister of Paradise (Chiostro del Paradiso),** to the left of the Duomo, originally a necropolis for members of the Amalfitan "establishment." This graveyard dates from the 1200s and contains broken columns and statues, as well as sarcophagi. The aura is definitely Moorish, with a whitewashed quadrangle of interlaced arches. One of the treasures is fragments of Cosmatesque work—brightly colored geometric mosaics that once formed parts of columns and altars, a specialty of this region. The arches create an evocative setting for concerts, both piano and vocal, held on Friday nights July to September, with tickets at 5,000L ($2.90). The cloister is open daily 9am to 7pm and charges 5,000L ($2.90) admission. You reach the crypt from the cloister. Here lie the remains of St. Andrew—that is, everything except his face. The Pope donated his face to St. Andrew's in Patras, Greece, but the back half of his head remained here.

A minor attraction, good for that rainy day, is the **Civic Museum (Museo Civico),** Piazza Municipio (☎ **089/871-001**), which displays original manuscripts of the Tavoliere Amalfitane. This was the maritime code that governed the entire Mediterranean until 1570. Some exhibits relate to Flavio Gioia, Amalfi's most famous merchant adventurer. Amalfitani claim he invented the compass in the 12th century. "The sun, the moon, the stars and—Amalfi," locals used to say. What's left from the "attic" of their once great power is preserved here. The museum is free and open Monday to Saturday 9am to 1pm.

For your most **scenic walk** in Amalfi, start at Piazza del Duomo and head up Via Genova. The classic stroll will take you to the **Valley of the Mills (Valle dei Mulini),** so called because of the paper mills along its rocky reaches (the seafaring republic is said to have acquainted Italy with the use of paper). You'll pass by fragrant gardens and scented citrus groves. If the subject interests you, you can learn more details about the industry at the **Museum of Paper (Museo della Carta),** Via Valle dei Mulini (☎ **089/872-615**), filled with antique presses and yellowing manuscripts from yesterday. It's open Tuesday to Thursday and Saturday and Sunday 9am to 1pm. Admission is 2,000L ($1.15).

For the biggest attraction of all, head west to the ✪ **Emerald Grotto (Grotta di Smeraldo).** This ancient cavern, known for its light effects, is a millennia-old chamber of stalagmites and stalactites. Three miles west of Amalfi, the grotto is reached from the coastal road via a descent by elevator and then a boat ride traversing the eerie world of the grotto. The elevator and boat ride cost 5,000L ($2.90). The stalagmites are unique in that some are underwater. You can visit daily 9am to 4pm, provided the seas are calm enough not to bash boats to pieces as they try to land. The SITA bus (traveling toward Amalfi) departs from Piazza Flavio Gioia at 30-minute intervals throughout the day. En route to Sorrento, it stops at the Emerald Grotto. For more information about SITA buses, call ☎ **089/871-009.** The best way to go is by boat from Amalfi's docks; it costs 10,000L ($6) round-trip, plus the 5,000L ($2.90) entry fee.

HITTING THE BEACH

Amalfi lays some claim to being a beach resort, and narrow public beaches flank the harbor. In addition, between rocky sections of the coast, many of the first-class and deluxe hotels have carved out small stretches of sand reserved for their guests. However, better and more expansive beaches are adjacent to the nearby villages of **Minori** and **Maiori,** a short drive along the coast. Those beaches enjoy access to a scattering of cafes, souvenir kiosks, and restaurants that thrive mostly during the warm-weather months. You can reach the villages by buses leaving from Amalfi's Piazza Flavio Gioia at 30-minute intervals during the day. Expect to pay 2,000L ($1.15) each way.

If you're adventurous and good with machinery, you might consider renting a motorboat from either of two entrepreneurs located beside or near Amalfi's port: **Raffaele Florio,** Al Porto de Amalfi (☎ 089/871-009), or **Lido delle Sirene,** Piazza dei Protontini (☎ 089/871-489). Both maintain about five to ten 15-foot motorboats, available May to October. Depending on the size of their engines, they rent for 25,000L to 40,000L ($15 to $23) per hour, with a 2-hour minimum. A full-day rental is 100,000L to 180,000L ($58 to $104). Lido delle Sirene also offers waterskiing for groups of friends or relatives who want to practice the sport together. An hour's access to a high-powered boat, an operator and all water-skiing equipment included, begins at 120,000L ($70). During these activities, we urge you to exercise reasonable caution and all the tenets of water safety.

SHOPPING

The coast has long been known for its ceramics, and the area at **Piazza del Duomo** is filled with hawkers peddling "regional" ware. However, that region today often means Asia. But the real thing is still made at nearby Vietri sul Mare, 8 miles west of Amalfi. The pottery made in Vietri is distinguished by its florid colors and sunny motifs. Vietri's best outlet is **Ceramica Solimene,** Via Madonna degli Angeli 7 (☎ 089/ 210-243), which has been producing quality terra-cotta ceramics for centuries. It's fabled for its production of lead-free surface tiles, dinner and cookware, umbrella holders, and stylish lamps. You might also check out **La Taverna Paradiso,** Via Diego Taiani 1 (☎ 089/212-509), and **La Sosta,** Via Costiera 6 (☎ 089/211-790).

In Amalfi itself, the town's two most famous products involve drinking and writing. Limoncello, a sweet lemon-derived liqueur that tastes best chilled, is manufactured most visibly in town by the **Luigi Aceto** factories. You can drop by their headquarters on Salita Chiarito 5 to buy a bottle or two (call ☎ 089/873-288 or 089/873-211 for information). The Aceto Group's product is marketed under the **Limoncello Cata** label and sold at many outlets around town. A bottle of Limoncello costs 15,000L ($9).

Looking for fancy paper whose design and high rag content have been perfected in and around Amalfi for longer than anyone can remember? You can visit the showroom at the **Amatruda** group, one of the town's larger manufacturers, on Via Fiume, near the corner of the Valle dei Mulini (☎ 089/971-315). A worthy competitor, who manufactures the luxury items on a smaller scale, is **Antonio Cavaliere,** Via Fiume (☎ 089/871-954). Both sell traditional cream-colored, high-fiber versions that seem appropriate for invitations to a royal wedding, as well as versions that amalgamate dried flowers, faintly visible through the surface, into the manufacturing process.

If items other than paper appeal to you, head for one of Amalfi's best retail outlets, **Criscuolo,** Largo Scario 2 (☎ 089/871-089). Established by the ancestors of the present owners in 1935 as a site selling only cigarettes and newspapers, it has expanded to specialize in jewelry, including a charming collection of cameos; locally crafted ceramics; and general memorabilia commemorating your visit to Amalfi.

ACCOMMODATIONS
VERY EXPENSIVE

✪ **Hotel Santa Caterina.** Strada Amalfitana, 84011 Amalfi. ☎ **089/871-012.** Fax 089/871-351. 86 units. A/C MINIBAR TV TEL. 340,000–560,000L ($197–$325) double; 680,000–780,000L ($394–$452) suite. Rates include breakfast. Half board 75,000L ($44) per person. AE, DC, MC, V. Parking 25,000L ($15) in garage, free outside.

Perched atop a cliff, the Santa Caterina has an elevator that'll take you down to a private beach. This "saint" is one of the most scenic hotels around. Built in 1880, the structure was destroyed by a rockslide on Christmas Eve 1902, prompting a rebuilding on a "safer" site in 1904, though the look today is more from the 1930s. You're housed in the main structure or one of the small "villas" in the citrus groves along the hill slopes. The guest rooms are furnished in good taste, with an eye toward comfort; most have private balconies facing the sea. The furniture respects the tradition of the house, and in every room is an antique piece. The baths are spacious, with luxurious fittings, and each has a hair dryer.

Dining/Diversions: The food here is among the best at Amalfi. Many of the vegetables are grown in the hotel's garden, and the fish tastes so fresh we suspect the chef has an agreement with local fishers to bring in the "catch of the day." Once or twice a week there's a special evening buffet accompanied by music.

Amenities: Room service, baby-sitting, laundry/valet, saltwater pool.

EXPENSIVE

Hotel Luna Convento. Via Pantaleone Comite 33, 84011 Amalfi. ☎ **089/871-002.** Fax 089/871-333. www.amalficoast.it/hotel/luna. E-mail: luna@amalficoast.it. 45 units. TV TEL. 240,000L ($139) double including breakfast; half board (compulsory in summer) 360,000–440,000L ($209–$255) per person. AE, DC, MC, V. Valet parking 20,000L ($12).

This hotel (the best in Amalfi except for the Santa Caterina, above) boasts a 13th-century cloister said to have been founded by St. Francis of Assisi. Most of the building, however, was rebuilt in 1975. The long corridors, where monks of old (and in time Wagner and Ibsen) used to tread, are lined with sitting areas used by the most unmonastic guests seeking a tan. The guest rooms have sea views, terraces, and modern furnishings, though many are uninspired in decor.

Dining/Diversions: The rather formal dining room has a coved ceiling, high-backed chairs, arched windows opening toward the water, and good food (Italian and international). The hotel has a nightclub that projects toward the sea, and in summer dancing is offered in the piano bar.

Amenities: Concierge, room service, laundry/dry cleaning, newspaper delivery, in-room massage, baby-sitting, free-form pool.

MODERATE

Excelsior Grand Hotel. Via Pogerola, 84011 Amalfi. ☎ **089/830-015.** Fax 089/830-255. 97 units. TEL. 110,000–155,000L ($64–$90) per person. Rates include full board. AE, DC, MC, V.

Two miles north of Amalfi at Pogerola, the Excelsior is a modern first-class hotel on a high mountain perch. It's structure is unconventional—an octagonal glass tower rising above the central lobby, with exposed mezzanine lounges and an open stairs. All its guest rooms are angled toward the view so you get the first glimmer of dawn and the last rays of sunset. They're individually designed, with lots of space and good reproductions, some antiques, king-size beds, and tile floors. The private balconies, complete with garden furniture, are the most important feature. The social center is the terrazzo-edged pool filled with filtered mountain spring water. The dignified dining room serves Italian cuisine with Gallic overtones, and at the Bar del Night, musicians play for dancing on weekends. Transportation to and from the private beach is provided by boat and bus for 15,000L ($9).

Hotel Belvedere. Via Smeraldo, Conca dei Marini, 84011 Amalfi. ☎ **089/831-282.** Fax 089/831-439. 36 units. TEL. 145,000–180,000L ($84–$104) per person double. Rates include half board. AE, DC, MC, V. Closed Oct 15–Apr 15. Free parking.

Lodged below the coastal road outside Amalfi on the drive to Positano, the aptly named Belvedere has one of the best pools in the area. The house originated as a private villa in the 1860s and was transformed by its present owners into a hotel in 1962. It's in a prime location, just 2 miles from the center of Amalfi, hidden from the view and noise of the heavily traveled road. The guest rooms have terraces overlooking the water, and some offer air-conditioning. Signor Lucibello, who owns the hotel, sees to it that guests are content, and there's a shuttle bus into Amalfi. You can dine on well-prepared Italian meals either inside (where walls of windows allow for views of the coast) or on the terrace. There's also a cocktail bar.

INEXPENSIVE

✪ **Hotel Lidomare.** Largo Duchi Piccolomini 9, 84011 Amalfi. ☎ **089/871-332.** Fax 089/871-394. 15 units. A/C MINIBAR TV TEL. 90,000–100,000L ($52–$58) double. Rates include breakfast. AE, DC, MC, V. Parking 15,000L ($9).

This pleasant small hotel is just a few steps from the sea, in a building from the 13th century. The high-ceilinged rooms are airy and clean and contain a scattering of modern furniture mixed with Victorian-era antiques; most are air-conditioned. The Camera family extends a warm welcome to their never-ending stream of foreign visitors. Breakfast is the only meal served, but you can order it until 11:30am. This hotel is one of the best bargains in Amalfi.

Hotel Marina Riviera. Via Comite 9, 84011 Amalfi. ☎ **089/872-394.** Fax 089/871-024. 20 units. A/C MINIBAR TV TEL. 220,000–240,000L ($128–$139) double. Rates include breakfast. AE, MC, V. Closed Oct 31–Mar. Parking 15,000L ($9).

Just 50 yards from the beach, this hotel offers rooms with terraces overlooking the sea. Directly on the coastal road, it rises against the foot of the hills, with side verandas and balconies. Two adjoining public lounges are traditionally furnished, and a small bar provides drinks whenever you want them. The newly refurbished rooms are comfortable, with a balcony and such amenities as a hair dryer. There's a gracious dining room, but we suggest you dine alfresco. A restaurant called Eolo is right below the hotel and under the same management.

Hotel Miramalfi. Via Quasimodo 3, 84011 Amalfi. ☎ **089/871-588.** Fax 089/871-287. 47 units. A/C MINIBAR TV TEL. 190,000–240,000L ($110–$139) double; 290,000–340,000L ($168–$197) suite. Rates include breakfast. Half board 130,000–180,000L ($75–$104) per person. AE, DC, MC, V. Parking 15,000L ($9).

On the western edge of Amalfi, the Miramalfi lies below the coastal road on its own beach. The rooms are wrapped around the curving contour of the coast and have unobstructed sea views. The stone swimming pier—used for sunbathing, diving, and boarding motor launches for waterskiing—is down a winding cliffside path, past terraces of grapevines. The dining room has glass windows and some semitropical plants; the food is good and served in abundant portions. Breakfast is served on one of the main terraces or your own balcony. Each room is well equipped, with built-in headboards, fine beds, cool tile floors, and efficient maintenance. There's a pool and an elevator to the private beach.

DINING
MODERATE

✪ **Da Gemma.** Via Frà Gerardo Sassi 9. ☎ **089/871-345.** Reservations required. Main courses 20,000–50,000L ($12–$29). AE, DC, MC, V. Thurs–Tues 12:45–2pm and 7:45–10:30pm. Closed Jan. SEAFOOD/MEDITERRANEAN.

Occupying a stone-sided building constructed in 1872 a short walk from the cathedral, Da Gemma is one of Amalfi's best restaurants, with a strong emphasis on fresh seafood. It has been directed by members of the Grimaldi family for many generations, a fact that caused a lot of fuss when Princess Caroline of Monaco (whose family name is also Grimaldi, but with a family link that's very distant) came to dine. The kitchen sends out plateful after plateful of savory spaghetti, grilled or sautéed fish, succulent casseroles, and an enduring favorite—*zuppe di pesce* (fish soup), a full meal in its own right and prepared only for two. In summer, the size of the intimate dining room more than doubles because of its expansion onto a terrace.

La Caravella–Amalfi. Via Matteo Camera 12. ☎ **089/871-029.** Reservations required. Main courses 15,000–45,000L ($9–$26). AE, DC, MC, V. Daily 12:30–2:30pm and 7:30–11pm. Closed Nov and Tues Sept 1–July 31. CAMPANIA.

The stone-sided building containing this restaurant was a boatyard and marine warehouse during the 1400s, when the Republic of Amalfi used it to store supplies critical to its survival. Today, it functions as one of the most visible restaurants in town, with a name commemorating the caravelles that used to be built nearby and a menu featuring authentic Italian specialties. Examples are spaghetti Caravella with seafood sauce and fresh fish with lemon. Scaloppine alla Caravella is served with a tangy clam sauce, and a healthy portion of zuppa di pesce (fish soup) is also ladled out. You can have a platter of the mixed fish fry, with crisp bits of shrimp and squid, followed by an order of fresh fruit served at your table in big bowls.

Ristorante Luna Convento. In the Hotel Luna Convento, Via Panteleone Comite 33. ☎ **089/871-002.** Reservations recommended. Main courses 25,000–32,000L ($15–$19). AE, DC, MC, V. Daily 1–2pm and 7:30–9pm. ITALIAN.

If you're unable to reserve a table at dinner, try for a sunflooded lunch at this stylish place, as there's likely to be less of a crowd and the view over the town and the sea will be clearer. The restaurant is half indoor/half outdoor and staffed by consummate professionals. The menu items are usually based on seafood and include fresh seafood salad, seafood pastas, baked slices of sea bass or monkfish with herbs and garlic, and risotto alla pescatore (fisherman's rice); other choices are chicken, veal, beef, and pork. The antipasti are particularly tantalizing.

If you can't get a reservation even for lunch, perhaps try the restaurant's sibling, the **Ristorante Torre Saracena,** a very short walk away; any staff member will contact it for you. The prices, menu, and hours there are more or less the same as here.

8 Ravello: A Posh Retreat

171 miles SE of Rome, 41 miles SE of Naples, 18 miles W of Salerno

Known to long-ago personages ranging from Richard Wagner to Greta Garbo—even D. H. Lawrence, who wrote *Lady Chatterley's Lover* here—✪ **Ravello** is the choice spot along the Amalfi Drive. It's where "poets go to die," or so it is said. Ravello's reigning celebrity at the moment is Gore Vidal, who purchased a villa as a writing retreat. Other writers have also been inspired by the spot, including André Gide. William Styron set his novel *Set This House on Fire* here. Boccaccio dedicated part of the *Decameron* to Ravello, and John Huston used it as a location for his film *Beat the Devil*, with Bogie.

The sleepy village seems to hang 1,100 feet up, between the Tyrrhenian Sea and some celestial orbit. You approach from Amalfi, 4 miles southwest, by a wickedly curving road cutting through the villa- and vine-draped hills that hem in the Valley of the Dragone. Celebrated in poetry, song, and literature are Ravello's major attractions, two villas.

ESSENTIALS

GETTING THERE   **Buses** from Amalfi leave for Ravello from the terminal at the waterfront at Piazza Flavio Gioia (☎ **089/871-016** for schedules and information) every hour 7am to 10pm, costing 1,500L (85¢) one-way. If you've got a **car** and are in Amalfi, take a circuitous mountain road north of the town (the road is signposted to Ravello).

VISITOR INFORMATION   The **tourist office** is at Piazza del Duomo 10 (☎ **089/857-096**), open May to September, Monday to Saturday 8am to 8pm (to 7pm October to April).

TWO FABULOUS VILLAS & THE DUOMO

Villa Cimbrone. Via Santa Chiara 26. ☎ **089/857-459.** Admission 6,000L ($3.50) adults, 4,000L ($2.30) children under 12. Daily 9am–7pm.

One of Ravello's most aristocratic-looking palaces is the Villa Cimbrone. A 10-minute walk uphill from the main square, it's accessible only via a signposted footpath punctuated with steps and stairs. Built in the 15th century, it was occupied by a wealthy and eccentric Englishman, Lord Grimthorpe, who renovated it to its present status. During his tenure, he entertained such luminaries as Edvard Grieg, Henrik Ibsen, D. H. Lawrence, Virginia Woolf, Graham Greene, Greta Garbo and her then-lover Leopold Stokowsky, and Tennessee Williams. Lord Grimthorpe died in London in 1917, but his heirs followed his orders and buried his remains near his replica of the Temple of Bacchus. On reaching the villa's entrance, ring the bell to summon the attendant. You'll be shown vaulted cloisters, evocative architecture, ruined chapels, and panoramic views over the Bay of Salerno. The view from some of the platforms in the garden is one the devout might claim was the spot where Satan took Christ to tempt him with the world. Gore Vidal, a nearby resident, referred to the view as "the most beautiful in the world." You can also stay at the villa, as it's now a hotel (see "Accommodations," below).

Villa Rufolo. Piazza Vescovado. ☎ **089/857-657.** Admission 5,000L ($2.90) adults, 3,000L ($1.75) children. Oct–Apr daily 9am–6pm; May–Sept daily 9am–8pm.

The Villa Rufolo was named for the patrician family who founded it in the 11th century. Once the residence of kings and popes, such as Hadrian IV, it's now remembered chiefly for its connection with Richard Wagner. He composed an act of *Parsifal* here in a setting he dubbed the "Garden of Klingsor." He also lived and composed at Palazzo Sasso (see "Accommodations," below). Boccaccio was so moved by the spot he included it as background in one of his tales. The Moorish-influenced architecture evokes Granada's Alhambra. The large tower was built in what's known as the "Norman-Sicilian" style. You can walk through the flower gardens leading to lookout points over the memorable coastline.

Duomo. Piazza Vescovado. Duomo, free; museum, 2,000L ($1.15). Duomo, daily 8am–7pm. Museum, May–Sept daily 9am–7:30pm (to 5pm Oct–Apr).

It's unusual for such a small place to have a cathedral, but Ravello boasts one because it was once a major bishopric. The building itself dates from the 11th century, but its bronze doors are the work of Barisano da Trani, crafted in 1179. Its campanile (bell tower) was erected in the 13th century. One of its major treasures is the pulpit of the Rufolo family, decorated with intricate mosaics and supported by spiral columns resting on the backs of half a dozen white marble lions. This is the work of Nicolò di Bartolomeo da Foggia in 1272. Another less intricate pulpit from 1130 features two large mosaics of Jonah being eaten and regurgitated by a dragonlike green whale. To the left of the altar is the Chapel of San Pantaleone, the patron saint of Ravello to whom the cathedral is dedicated. His "unleakable" blood is preserved in a cracked vessel. The saint was beheaded at Nicomedia on July 27, A.D. 290. When Ravello holds a festival on that day every year, the saint's blood is said to liquefy. A minor museum of religious artifacts is also on site.

ACCOMMODATIONS

The choice of accommodations at Ravello is limited in number but large on charm. The **Ristorante Garden** (see "Dining," below) also rents rooms.

VERY EXPENSIVE

✪ **Hotel Palumbo/Palumbo Residence.** Via San Giovanni del Toro 16, 84010 Ravello. ☎ **089/857-244.** Fax 089/858-133. www.hotelpalumbo.it. 30 units. A/C MINIBAR TV TEL. Hotel, 780,000–880,000L ($452–$510) double; from 1,040,000L ($603) suite. Residence, 520,000–580,000L ($302–$336) double. Rates include half board. AE, DC, MC, V. Parking 20,000L ($12).

This elite retreat on the Amalfi Coast, a 12th-century palace, has been favored by the famous since composer Richard Wagner persuaded the Swiss owners, the Vuilleumiers, to take in paying guests. If you stay you'll understand why Humphrey Bogart, Henry Wadsworth Longfellow, Ingrid Bergman, Zsa Zsa Gabor, Tennessee Williams, Richard Chamberlain, and a young John and Jacqueline Kennedy found it ideal. D. H. Lawrence even wrote part of *Lady Chatterley's Lover* while staying here.

The hotel offers gracious living in its drawing rooms, furnished with English and Italian antiques. Most of the snug but elegantly decorated guest rooms have their own terrace. The original Hotel Palumbo contains by far the more glamorous and better-accessorized accommodations; seven functional rooms are in the modern annex (1950s vintage) in the garden, but a few have sea views.

Dining: Meals are served in a 17th-century dining room with baroque accents and a panoramic terrace. The cuisine, the finest in Ravello, shows the influence of the Swiss-Italian ownership. It's worth visiting just for the lemon and chocolate soufflés. The Palumbo also produces its own Episcopio wine, stored in 50,000L casks in a vaulted cellar.

Amenities: Room service, baby-sitting, laundry/valet, solarium overlooking the Gulf of Salerno.

✪ **Palazzo Sasso.** Via San Giovanni del Toro 28, 84010 Ravello. ☎ **089/818-181.** Fax 089/858-900. www.palazzosasso.com. E-mail: info@palazzosasso.com. 43 units. A/C MINIBAR TV TEL. 450,000–680,000L ($261–$394) double; 850,000–1,200,000L ($493–$696) suite. Rates include continental breakfast. AE, DC, MC, V. Park your car in the free municipal parking lot just below Ravello and call the hotel for a porter, who'll carry your luggage and guide you along the 2-minute walk downhill to the hotel.

Built in the 1100s as the stately home for an aristocratic family, this palace began functioning as a hotel in 1880. Richard Wagner composed parts of *Parsifal* here. And Ingrid Bergman found a snug retreat here with producer Roberto Rossellini back in the days when their affair was the scandal of the world. The hotel fell into ruin in 1978, but in 1997 it reopened thanks to a flood of money from new owners (Virgin Airlines Holding Co., of which Richard Branson is the most visible owner), who welcomed Plácido Domingo as their first guest. The Sasso is perched 1,000 feet above the Amalfi Coast and evokes a Moorish pavilion. The guest rooms are luxurious, even if not overly large, but the views of the Mediterranean compensate for the lack of space. Ask for room no. 1, 201, 204, or 301 or the grand suite, 304, as they have the most all-encompassing views. Comfort and state-of-the-art housekeeping are the rule throughout.

Dining: The Rossellini Restaurant (named after Roberto, Ingrid, and Isabella) serves savory Mediterranean cuisine in an undeniably chic venue that charges an average of 120,000L ($70) per person, without drinks. Meals are served daily noon to 2pm and 7:30 to 10:30pm. Antonio Genovese, who honed his culinary skills in London, presides over the dining room and is proud that his cuisine matches the panorama from the terrace, which seats 100. A well-recommended specialty is the platter of prawns, bell peppers, tomatoes, and vegetable mousse.

Amenities: Concierge, room service, baby-sitting, laundry/dry cleaning, twice-daily maid service, two plunge pools, hydromassage.

Villa Cimbrone. Via Santa Chiara 26, 84010 Ravello. ☎ **089/857-459.** Fax 089/857-777. 11 units. MINIBAR TV TEL. 350,000–450,000L ($203–$261) double; 550,000L ($319) suite. Rates include breakfast. AE, DC, MC, V. Closed Nov–Mar. From the main square of Ravello, walk uphill along a well-marked footpath for an arduous 10 minutes.

You'll find no restaurant and none of the glossy modern amenities offered by more modern hotels. In fact, you can't even drive to its entrance, as there's no road leading up to it. But despite the inconvenience, few connoisseurs of art and literature would pass up the chance to stay in one of the most historically evocative villas in Ravello (see above). Amid gardens dotted with statuary, ancient ruins, and late 19th-century re-creations of Greek and Roman temples, it contains only a handful of rooms, giving the impression that's more akin to that of a museum than a hotel. The rooms are high-ceilinged, gracefully furnished with antiques and fine fabrics, and most enjoy views sweeping over the countryside. If you arrive by car, park it in the municipal parking lot, a short walk downhill from Ravello's main square, then call the hotel for a porter who, with a rolling trolley, will haul your luggage up the winding paths to the villa. Though it charges high rates because of its romantic ambience and position, it doesn't offer the service and facilities of a hotel like the Palumbo. Breakfast is the only meal served.

EXPENSIVE

Hotel Caruso Belvedere. Via San Giovanni del Toro, 84010 Ravello. ☎ **089/857-111.** Fax 089/857-372. 26 units. TEL. Jan–May and Oct–Dec 22 200,000–340,000L ($116–$197) double; June–Sept and Christmas 240,000–380,000L ($139–$220) double. Rates include breakfast. AE, DC, MC, V. Parking 20,000L ($12) in garage, free outside.

This spacious clifftop hotel, built into the remains of an 11th-century palace, is operated by the Caruso family, descended from the great Enrico himself. Some of the most famous people of the 20th century, including Greta Garbo, have stayed here. This property has semitropical gardens and a belvedere that looks over terraced rows of grapes, used to make their "Grand Caruso" wine, to the Bay of Salerno. Although antiques appear here and there, many rooms are rather plain, about on the same level as some of the town's economy-minded inns. The best ones have sunrooms for breakfast and open onto "oh, that view" terraces.

Dining: The dining room retains its original coved ceiling, plus tile floors. It opens onto a wide terrace where meals are served under a canopy. Naturally, the locally produced wines are touted.

Amenities: Room service, baby-sitting, laundry/valet.

MODERATE

Hotel Giordano e Villa Maria. Piazza del Duomo, Via S. Chiara 2, 84010 Ravello. ☎ **089/857-255.** Fax 089/857-071. 48 units. A/C TV TEL. Hotel Giordano: 170,000–180,000L ($99–$104) double; Villa Maria: 220,000–260,000L ($128–$151) double; 320,000–480,000L ($186–$278) suite. Rates include breakfast. AE, DC, MC, V. Parking 20,000L ($12).

The older, but more obviously modernized, of these two hotels is the Giordano, built in the late 1700s as a private manor house of the family who runs it today. In the 1970s, the owners bought the neighboring 19th-century Villa Maria. The two operate as quasi-independent hotels with shared facilities. Accommodations in the Villa Maria are more glamorous than those in the Giordano and usually contain high ceilings, a scattering of antiques, and sea views. The Giordano's rooms have garden views and conservative reproductions of traditional furniture. You'll find a large heated pool near the Giordano, two bars, and two restaurants. (Unlike its twin, the Villa Maria's restaurant remains open throughout the winter and has a panoramic sea view.) The beach is a 15-minute walk along ancient pathways (you can also take a public bus from Ravello's central square every hour).

Hotel Parsifal. Via G. D'Anna 5, 84010 Ravello. ☎ **089/857-144.** Fax 089/857-972. 19 units. TV TEL. 105,000–115,000L ($61–$67) per person double. Rates include half board. AE, DC, MC, V. Closed Oct 15–Easter. Free parking.

This little hotel incorporates part of a convent founded in 1288 by Augustinian monks, who had an uncanny instinct for picking spots with inspiring views. The cloister, with stone arches and a tile walk, has a multitude of potted flowers and vines, and the garden spots, especially the one with a circular reflection pool, are the favorites of all. There are chairs placed for watching the setting sun. Dining is on the terrace where bougainvillea and wisteria scents mix with that of lemon blossoms. The living rooms have bright and comfortable furnishings, set against pure white walls. The guest rooms, though small, are tastefully arranged, and a few have terraces.

Hotel Rufolo. Via San Francesco 3, 84010 Ravello. ☎ **089/857-133.** Fax 089/857-935. 32 units. A/C MINIBAR TV TEL. 280,000–320,000L ($162–$186) double; 500,000–550,000L ($290–$319) suite. Rates include breakfast. AE, DC, MC, V. Parking 10,000L ($6).

This little gem housed D. H. Lawrence for a long while in 1926. The view from the sun decks is superb, and chairs are placed on a wide terrace and around the pool. The guest rooms are cozy and immaculate, some with air-conditioning, and the suites have Jacuzzis. Recently enlarged and modernized, the hotel lies in the center between cloisters of pine trees of the Villa Rufolo, from which the hotel takes its name, and the road leading to the Villa Cimbrone. Mr. Schiavo and his family take good care of their guests. The restaurant is quite good and the service efficient.

INEXPENSIVE

Albergo Toro. Viale Wagner 3, 84010 Ravello. ☎ and fax **089/857-211.** 9 units. TEL. 125,000L ($73) double, including breakfast; 85,000L ($49) per person double with half board. AE, MC, V. Closed Nov 6–Mar.

This real bargain is a charming small villa that has been converted to receive paying guests. The Toro—entered through a garden—lies just off the village square with its cathedral. It has semimonastic architecture, boasting deeply set arches, long colonnades, and a tranquil character. The rooms are decent and comfortably furnished but a bit plain. The owner is especially proud of the Mediterranean meals he serves.

DINING

Most guests take meals at their hotels. But try to escape the board requirement at least once to sample the goods at the following places.

Cumpa' Cosimo. Via Roma 44–46. ☎ **089/857-156.** Reservations recommended. Main courses 15,000–45,000L ($9–$26); fixed-price menus 18,000–25,000L ($10–$15). AE, DC, MC, V. Daily noon–3:45pm and 6:30–10pm. Closed Mon Nov–Dec and mid-Jan to mid-Mar. CAMPANIA.

You're likely to find here everyone from the electrician down the street to a movie star looking for the best home-cooking in town. Gore Vidal, who often dines here, recommends it to his visiting guests. It was established as an offshoot to a nearby butcher shop in 1929 by a patriarch known affectionately as Cumpa' (godfather) Cosimo and his wife, Cumma' (godmother) Chiara. Today their daughter, the kindly Netta Bottone, runs the place, turning out well-flavored regional food in generous portions. Menu items include homemade versions of seven pastas, served with your choice of seven sauces. Any of these might be followed by a mixed grill of fish, giant prawns, roasted lamb seasoned with herbs, zuppe di pesce (fish soup), fritta di pesce (fish fry), veal scallopine, or beefsteak with garlic and wine sauce. The seasonal availability of vegetables is respected, as the restaurant offers artichokes, asparagus, or mushrooms. Certain fish dishes are priced according to weight based on daily market quotations.

Ristorante Garden. Via Boccacio 4, 84010 Ravello. ☎ **089/857-226.** Main courses 14,000–23,000L ($8–$13). AE, MC, V. Apr–Sept daily noon–3pm and 7:30–10pm; Nov–Mar Wed–Mon noon–3pm and 7:30–10pm. CAMPANIA.

This pleasant restaurant's greatest claim to fame occurred in 1962, when Jacqueline Kennedy came from a villa where she was staying to dine here with the owner of Fiat. Today some of that old glamour is still visible on the verdant terrace, which was designed to cantilever over the cliff below. The Mansi family offers well-prepared meals that might include one of four kinds of spaghetti, cheese crêpes, and an array of soups, a well-presented antipasto table, brochettes of grilled shrimp, a mixed fish fry, and sole prepared in several ways. One of the local wines will be recommended.

The restaurant also rents 10 well-scrubbed doubles, each with its own phone, bath, and terrace with a view, for 100,000L to 125,000L ($58 to $73), including breakfast.

RAVELLO AFTER DARK

The hilltop town is known for its summer **classical music festivals.** Sometimes internationally famed artists appear. The venues range from the Duomo to the gardens of Villa Rufolo. Tickets, which you can buy at the tourist office, start at 30,000L ($17).

9 Paestum & Its Greek Temples

25 miles S of Salerno, 62 miles SE of Naples, 189 miles SE of Rome

The ancient city of ✪ **Paestum (Poseidonia)** dates back to 600 B.C., founded by colonists from the Greek city of Sybaris, which was located in today's Calabria (the "toe" of Italy's boot). It was abandoned for centuries and fell to ruins. But the remnants of its past, excavated in the mid-18th century, are glorious—the finest heritage left from the Greek colonies that settled in Italy. The roses of Paestum, praised by the ancients, bloom two times yearly, splashing the landscape of the city with scarlet, a good foil for the salmon-colored temples that still stand in the archeological garden.

ESSENTIALS

GETTING THERE   Paestum is within easy reach of Salerno, an hour away. Wherever you are in the area, you must go to Salerno to get to Paestum. You can catch a southbound **train,** which departs Salerno with a stop at Paestum about every 2 hours. For schedules, call ☎ **089/255-005** in Salerno, or 1478/88-088 toll free in Italy only. A one-way fare is 4,300L ($2.50), and the journey takes an hour. The **bus** from Salerno leaves from Piazza Concordia (near the rail station) about every 30 minutes. Call ☎ **089/226-604** for information. A one-way fare is 4,300L ($2.50). If you've got a **car,** from Salerno take S18 south.

VISITOR INFORMATION   The **tourist office** is at Via Magna Grecia 151–156 (☎ **0828/811-016**), in the archaeological zone, open Monday to Saturday 8am to 2pm.

EXPLORING THE TEMPLES

The ✪ **basilica** is a Doric temple from the 6th century B.C., Italy's oldest temple from the ruins of the Hellenic world. The basilica is characterized by 9 Doric pillars in front and 18 on the sides (they're about 5 feet in diameter). The walls and ceiling long ago gave way to decay. Animals were sacrificed to the gods on the altar.

The **Temple of Neptune (Tempio di Netuno)** is the most impressive of the Greek ruins at Paestum. It and the Temple of Haphaistos ("Theseum") in Athens remain the best-preserved Greek temples in the world, both from around 450 to 420 B.C. Six columns in front are crowned by an entablature, and there are 14 columns on each side. The **Temple of Ceres (Tempio di Cerere),** from the 6th century B.C., has 34 columns still standing and a large altar for sacrifices to the gods.

You can visit the temple zone daily 9am to sunset for 8,000L ($4.65) adults; children under 18 are free. Using the same ticket, you can visit the **National Archaeological Museum of Paestum (Museo Archeologico Nazionale di Paestum),** Via Magna Grecia 169 (☎ **0828/811-023**), across from the Ceres Temple. It displays the metopes removed from the treasury of the Temple of Hera (Juno) and some of southern Italy's finest tomb paintings from the 4th century B.C. The Diver's Tomb is an extraordinary example of painting from the first half of the 5th century B.C. The museum is open 9am to 7pm daily (closed the first and third Monday of every month).

New discoveries have revealed hundreds of Greek tombs, which have yielded many Greek paintings. Archaeologists have called the finds astonishing. In addition, other excavated tombs were found to contain clay figures in a strongly impressionistic vein.

ACCOMMODATIONS

Strand Hotel Schuhmann. Via Laura Mare, 84063 Paestum. ☎ **0828/851-151.** Fax 0828/851-183. www.schuhman.paestum.peoples.it. E-mail: hotelsch@paestum.peoples.it. 53 units. A/C MINIBAR TV TEL. 95,000–155,000L ($55–$90) per person double. Rates include half board. AE, DC, MC, V. Free parking.

If you'd like to combine serious looks at Italy's archaeological past with the first-class amenities of a beachside resort, try the Strand. Set in a pine grove removed from traffic noises, it has a large terrace with a view of the sea and a subtropical garden that overlooks the Gulf of Salerno and the Amalfi Coast to Capri. Its rooms are well furnished and maintained, each with a balcony or terrace. Guests get use of the beach facilities and deck chairs. The hotel restaurant serves a savory Mediterranean cuisine.

DINING

Nettuno Ristorante. Zona Archeologica. ☎ **0828/811-028.** Main courses 15,000–40,000L ($9–$23). AE, DC, MC, V. July–Aug daily noon–3:30pm and 7:30–10pm; Sept–June daily noon–3:30pm. CAMPANESE.

The only drawback is that throughout most of the year, this place is open only for lunch. At the edge of Paestum's ruins, it's built from the same beige-colored limestone blocks that were used by the ancient Romans. Its core consists of an ancient tower built in the 2nd century B.C. Seated in the dining room or garden ringed with vines, oleander, and pines, you can order *crespolina,* a savory crêpe stuffed with mozzarella and Mediterranean herbs; succulent pastas; a wide selection of fish; and veal, chicken, and beef dishes.

10 The Isle of Capri

3 miles off the tip of the Sorrentine peninsula

The broiling dog-day July and August sun that beats down on ✪ **Capri** illuminates a circus of humanity. The parade of visitors would give Ripley's "Believe It or Not" material for years. In the upper town, a vast snakelike chain of tourists of every ilk promenades through the narrow quarters (many of the lanes evoke the casbahs of North Africa).

The Greeks called Capri (pronounced *Cap*-ry in the British manner, not Ca-*pree*) "the island of the wild boars." Before the big season rush, Easter to the end of October, Capri is an island of lush Mediterranean vegetation (olives, vineyards, flowers) encircled by emerald waters, an oasis even before Emperor Tiberius moved the seat of the empire here. Writers like D. H. Lawrence have in previous decades found Capri a haven. Some have written of it, including Axel Munthe (*The Story of San Michele*) and Norman Douglas (*Siren Land*). The latter title is a reference to Capri's reputation as the "island of the sirens" that tempted Ulysses. Other distinguished visitors have included Mendelssohn, Dumas, and Hans Christian Andersen.

Don't visit Capri, incidentally, for great beaches. The mountainous landscape doesn't make for long sandy beaches. There are some spots for bathing, but many of these have been turned into clubs called *stabilimenti balneari,* which you must pay to visit.

Touring the island is relatively simple. You dock at unremarkable **Marina Grande,** the port area. You can then take the funicular to the town of **Capri** above, site of the major hotels, restaurants, cafes, and shops. From Capri, a short bus ride will deliver you to **Anacapri,** at the top of the island near Monte Solaro. The only other settlement you might want to visit is **Marina Piccola,** on the south side of the island with the major beach. There are also beaches at **Punta Carnea** and **Bagni di Tiberio.** The tourist office will pinpoint these on a map for you.

ESSENTIALS

GETTING THERE   You can go from Naples's Molo Beverello dock (not near the train station—take a taxi) by **hydrofoil** in just 45 minutes. The hydrofoil (*aliscafo*) leaves several times daily (some stop at Sorrento). A one-way trip is 18,000L ($10). It's cheaper but takes longer (about 1½ hours) to go by regularly scheduled **ferry** (*traghetto*), costing 9,500L to 11,000L ($5 to $6) one-way. For ferry and hydrofoil schedules, call ☎ **081/761-3688** in Naples.

If you're coming from Sorrento, go to the dock right off Piazza Tasso, where you can board one of the **ferries** run by Linee **Marittime Veloci** (☎ **081/878-1430**) or **Caremar** (☎ **081/807-3077**). Departures are several times per day from 7am (last

Swinging in Siren Land

Over the centuries, artists and writers have been drawn to the **Isle of Capri,** which Emperor Augustus called Capri Apragopolis ("city of sweet idleness"). The island's first big-time "swinger" was another emperor, Tiberius, who spent the last decade of his licentious life at his Villa Jovis, wandering from bed to bed in search of erotic amusement. He's said to have inspired a long line of hedonists over the centuries, ranging from munitions king Baron Von Krupp to the acerbic Oscar Wilde, who appreciated the golden Mediterranean youth of the island.

There's definitely a live-and-let-live attitude on Capri—perhaps that's why even Maxim Gorky settled here from 1907 to 1913, running a school for revolutionaries that's said to have been attended by Lenin and Stalin.

English writers, especially, have been fond of the island. Noël Coward pronounced it "the most beautiful operetta stage in the world." His visits here were noted by playwright Tennessee Williams, who notoriously satirized him in the play *The Milk Train Doesn't Stop Here Any More,* in which the "witch of Capri" was played by Mildred Dunnock. Rather ironically, when the play was rewritten as a movie, *Boom,* starring Richard Burton and Elizabeth Taylor, the part of the "witch of Capri" was recast as a man and Coward played himself. A very different writer, Graham Greene, found Capri an island of inspiration for his writing and returned to his villa here frequently.

The English writer most identified with the island was Norman Douglas (1868 to 1952). Capri provided the inspiration for his best-known novel, *South Wind* (1917). He later told friends he'd fallen in love with Capri when he first saw it in full bloom in the spring of 1888. At the age of only 28, Douglas had been forced into retirement from the Foreign Office in London because of an impending scandal. With what money he had, he purchased a villa along the Posillipo peninsula overlooking the Bay of Naples. Calling it Villa Maya, he lived there for 4 years in a disastrous marriage to his cousin, Elsa Fitzgibbon, finally divorcing her in 1904.

It was then he moved to Capri, purchasing Villa Daphne. In about 3 years he'd spent all his money and told friends he'd been forced into writing because of "sheer poverty." His first book, *Siren Land* (1911), was followed by *Fountains in the Sand* (1912) and *Old Calabria* (1915). Critics hailed these now-almost-forgotten books as among the best travel books ever penned, but the public wasn't buying until the publication of the novel *South Wind,* with Capri as a setting.

Other works were to follow: *They Went* (1920), *Alone* (1921), *Together* (1923), *Paneros* (1931), *Looking Back* (1933), and *Late Harvest* (1946). Douglas died in 1952 after writing *Footnote on Capri.* He spent the postwar years of his life at the Villa Tuoro on Capri (owned by friend), and you can visit his tomb in the Capri cemetery.

departure back at 7:45pm), costing 7,000L ($4.20) one-way. It's much faster to take one of the **hydrofoils** operated by **Alilauro** (☎ 081/807-3024), departing every 20 minutes daily 7am to 4pm, taking only 15 minutes and costing 10,000L ($6) one-way.

VISITOR INFORMATION   Get in touch with the **Tourist Board,** Piazza Umberto I 19 (☎ 081/370-686), at Capri. June to September, it's open Monday to

Saturday 8:30am to 8:30pm and Sunday 8:30am to 2:30pm; and October to May, Monday to Saturday 9am to 1pm and 3:30 to 6:45pm.

GETTING AROUND   There's no need to have a car on tiny Capri with its impossible hairpin roads. The island is serviced by funiculars, taxis, and buses. Many of Capri's hotels are remotely located, especially those at Anacapri, and we strongly recommend you bring as little luggage as possible. If you need a porter, you'll find their union headquarters in a building connected to the jetty at Marina Grande. Here you can cajole, coddle, coerce, or connive your way through the hiring process where the only rule seems to be that there are no rules. But your porter will know where to find the hotel among the winding passageways and steep inclines of the island's arteries. Your best defense during your pilgrimage might be a sense of humor.

MARINA GRANDE

The least attractive of the island's communities, **Marina Grande** is the port, bustling daily with the comings and goings of hundreds of visitors. It has a little sand-cum-pebble beach, on which you're likely to see American sailors (on shore leave from Naples) playing ball, occasionally upsetting a Coca-Cola over mamma and bambino.

If you're just spending the day on Capri, you should leave at once for the island's biggest attraction, the ✪ **Grotta Azzurra (Blue Grotto),** open daily 9am to 1 hour before sunset. In summer, boats leave frequently from the harbor at Marina Grande to transport passengers to the entrance of the grotto for 10,000L ($6) round-trip. Once at the grotto, you'll pay 15,000L ($9) for the small rowboat that takes you inside.

The Blue Grotto is one of the best-known natural sights of the region, though the way passengers are hustled in and out of it makes it a tourist trap. It's truly beautiful, however. Known to the ancients, it was later lost to the world until an artist stumbled on it in 1826. Inside the cavern, light refraction (the sun's rays entering from an opening under the water) achieves the dramatic Mediterranean cerulean color. The effect is stunning, as thousands testify yearly.

If you wish, you can take a trip around the entire island, passing not only the Blue Grotto but also the **Baths of Tiberius,** the **Palazzo al Mare** built in the days of the empire, the **Green Grotto** (less known), and the much-photographed rocks called the **Faraglioni.** Motorboats circle the island in about 1½ hours at 25,000L ($15) per person.

Connecting Marina Grande with the town of Capri is a frequently running **funicular** charging 1,500L (85¢) one-way. However, the funicular, really a cog railway, doesn't operate off-season. Instead, you take a bus from Marina Grande to Capri (same price).

SWIMMING & SUNNING

The coastline surrounding Capri is punctuated with jagged rocks that allow for very few sandy beaches. So most swimmers patronize the **Bagni Nettuno,** Via Grotta Azzurra 46 (☎ **081/837-1362**), a short distance from the Blue Grotto in Anacapri. Surrounded by scenic cliffsides, with an undeniable drama, it charges 15,000L ($9) adults and 12,000L ($7) children under 12. The price includes use of a cabana, towels, and deck chairs. It's open mid-March to mid-November, daily 9am to sunset. From a point nearby, you can actually swim into the narrow, rocky entrance guarding the Blue Grotto, but this is advisable only after 5pm, once the boat services into the grotto have ended for the day, and only during relatively calm seas.

Another possibility for swimming is the **Bagni di Tiberio,** a sandy bathing beach a short walk from the ruins of an ancient Roman villa. To reach it, you have to board a motorboat departing from Marina Grande for the 15-minute ride to the site. Passage

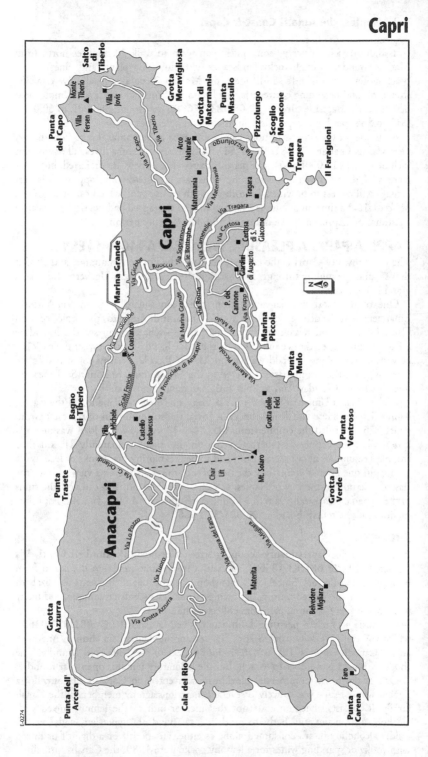

costs 8,000L ($4.65) per person, unless you want to walk 30 minutes north from Marina Grande, through rocky landscapes with flowering plants and vineyards. A beach closer to the island's south side is the **Marina Piccola,** a usually overcrowded stretch of sand extending between jagged lava rocks. You can rent a small motorboat here from the **Bagni le Sirene** (☎ 081/837-7688), for around 30,000L to 60,000L ($17 to $35) per hour, depending on its size and amenities.

A number of watersports options can be arranged at **Sercomar,** Largo Fontana 64, near Marina Grande (☎ 081/837-8781), where one-tank scuba dives, all equipment included, cost 110,000L ($64) per person. Experienced divers are preferred, but new-comers, if they have strong swimming skills, are accepted. More appealing is Sercomar's willingness to provide a motorboat, with an operator, which can haul groups of up to six at a time on circumnavigations around the jagged and poetically evocative coastlines of Capri. The price is around 10,000L ($6) per person.

CAPRI: A PARK, A PLEASURE PALACE & A MONASTERY

The main town of **Capri** is the center of most of the hotels, restaurants, and elegant shops—and the milling throngs. The heart of the resort, **Piazza Umberto I,** is like a grand living room.

One of the most popular walks from the main square is down Via Vittorio Emanuele, past the deluxe Quisisana, to the **Giardini di Augusto,** the choice spot on Capri for views and relaxation. From this park's perch, you can see the legendary **I Faraglioni,** the rocks once inhabited by the "blue lizard." At the top of the park is a belvedere overlooking emerald waters and Marina Piccola. Nearby you can visit the **Certosa,** a Carthusian monastery erected in the 14th century to honor St. James. It's open Tuesday to Sunday 9am to 2pm and charges no admission.

Back at Piazza Umberto I, head up Via Longano, then Via Tiberio, all the way to Monte Tiberio. Here you'll find the **Villa Jovis,** the splendid ruin of the estate from which Tiberius ruled the empire from A.D. 27 to 37. Actually, the Jovis was one of a dozen villas the depraved emperor erected on the island. Apparently Tiberius had trouble sleeping, so he wandered from bed to bed, exploring his "nooks of lechery," a young girl one hour, a young boy the next. From the ruins there's a view of both the Bay of Salerno and the Bay of Naples, as well as of the island. You can visit the ruins of the imperial palace daily 9am to 1 hour before sunset for 4,000L ($2.30). For infor-mation, call the tourist board at ☎ 081/370-686.

SHOPPING

A little shop on Capri's luxury shopping street, **Carthusia-Profumi di Capri,** Via Camerelle 10 (☎ 081/837-0368), specializes in perfume made on the island from local herbs and flowers. Since 1948 this shop has attracted such clients as Elizabeth Taylor, before she started touting her own perfume. The scents are unique, and many women consider Carthusia perfumes collector's items.

Carthusia also has a **perfume laboratory,** Via Matteotti 2 (☎ 081/837-0368), which you can visit daily 9am to 7pm. There's another **Carthusia shop** in Anacapri, at Via Capodimonte 26 (☎ 081/837-3668), next to the Villa Axel Munthe. The shops are closed November to March, but the laboratory remains open year-round.

One of the recent commercial blockbusters invented on Capri is **Limoncello,** a liqueur whose recipe was conceived several generations ago by members of the Canali family. It consists of lemon zest (not the juice or pith of the lemon) mixed with alcohol, sugar, water, and herbs to produce a tart kind of "hyper-lemonade" with a mildly alcoholic lift. It's consumed alone as either an aperitif or a digestif or mixed with vodka or sparkling wines for a lemony cocktail. In 1989, the Canalis formalized their family recipe, established modern distilleries on Capri and in nearby Sorrento, and hired professionals to promote the product as far away as the United States and Japan. Today you can buy half-liter bottles at this factory store for 15,000L ($9) each.

Shoppers here also look for deals on sandals, cashmere, and jewelry, the town's big bargains. The cobblers at **Canfora,** Via Camerelle 3 (☎ 081/837-0487), make all the sandals found in their shop. If you don't find what you need, you can order custom-made footwear. They also sell shoes but don't make those themselves. You can find a good selection of men's cashmere pullovers at **Russo Uomo,** Piazzetta Quisisina 8–10 (☎ 081/838-8208). But for cashmere pullovers for the whole family, go to **Russo Donna,** Via Vittorio Emanuele 55 (☎ 081/838-8207). The eight talented jewelers at **La Perla,** Piazza Umberto 10–21 (☎ 081/837-0641), work exclusively with gold and gems and can design and create anything you want.

ACCOMMODATIONS

Finding a bed for the night can be a real problem if you arrive in July or August without a reservation. Capri is also an exclusive enclave of the wealthy, and even the lesser accommodations are able to charge high prices. Many serious economizers find that they have to return to the mainland for the night.

Very Expensive

✪ **Grand Hotel Quisisana Capri.** Via Camerelle 2, 80073 Capri. ☎ **081/837-0788.** Fax 081/837-6080. 165 units. A/C MINIBAR TV TEL. 400,000–800,000L ($232–$464) double; from 900,000L ($522) suite. Rates include breakfast. AE, DC, MC, V. Closed Nov 1 to mid-Mar.

The deluxe choice on the island, this is the favorite of a regular international crowd. Opened as a sanitorium in 1845, it became a resort in 1880 and was an R&R site for American GIs in the final months of World War II. The sprawling premises are painted a distinctive yellow and accented with vines and landscaping. Its rooms range from cozy singles to spacious suites—all opening onto wide arcades with a view of the coast. They vary greatly in decor, with traditional and conservatively modern furnishings. The hotel terrace is where everybody who is anybody goes for cocktails before dinner.

Dining/Diversions: The hotel has two restaurants, both under famed chef Gualtiero Marchesi. The Colombaia (lunch only) is proud of its fresh-tasting and attractively displayed fish dishes, as well as its lush fruits and vegetables. The Quisi (dinner only) is alluring with candlelight, serving a creative Mediterranean and local cuisine. The American bar overlooks the pool on the lower terrace.

Amenities: Room service, baby-sitting, laundry/valet; sauna, Turkish bath/massage facilities, indoor and outdoor pools, beauty shop, gymnasium, tennis courts, two golf courses.

La Scalinatella (Little Steps). Via Tragara 8, 80073 Capri. ☎ **081/837-0633.** Fax 081/837-8291. 30 units. A/C MINIBAR TV TEL. 480,000–700,000L ($278–$406) suite. Rates include breakfast. AE, MC, V. Closed Nov–Easter.

One of the most delightful hotels in Capri is constructed like a private villa above terraces offering a panoramic view of the water and a nearby monastery. Many former Quisisana guests have deserted to this more intimate and exclusive pair of 200-year-old houses, with a vaguely Moorish design, run by the Morgano family. The ambience is one of unadulterated luxury; all units are junior suites that include a phone beside the bathtub, beds set into alcoves, elaborate wrought-iron accents ringing both the inner stairwell and the ornate balconies, and a sweeping view over the gardens and pool.

Dining/Diversions: The hotel contains a restaurant open only at lunchtime, where a flavorful Mediterranean cuisine is served on a terrace beside the pool.

Amenities: Concierge, room service, dry cleaning/laundry, pool, Jacuzzi, sauna, access to health club and tennis courts nearby.

Expensive

Hotel Luna. Viale Matteotti 3, 80073 Capri. ☎ **081/837-0433.** Fax 081/837-7459. 54 units. A/C TV TEL. 260,000–490,000L ($151–$284) double. Rates include breakfast. AE, DC, MC, V. Closed Oct 1–Easter.

This first-class hotel stands on a cliff overlooking the sea and the rocks of Faraglioni. It's set almost between the Gardens of Augustus and the Carthusian monastery of St. James. The building is nondescript, the furnishings reproductions of antiques. The guest rooms, a mix of contemporary Italian pieces and Victorian decor, incorporate wood and padded headboards and gilt mirrors over the desk. Some have recessed terraces overlooking the garden of flowers and semitropical plants.

Dining/Diversions: There's a clubby drinking lounge, and the dining room lures with good cuisine.

Amenities: Concierge, dry cleaning/laundry, newspaper delivery, twice-daily maid service, secretarial services, baby-sitting, pool, access to nearby health club and jogging track, Jacuzzi.

Hotel La Palma. Via Vittorio Emanuele 39, 80073 Capri. ☎ **081/837-0133.** Fax 081/837-6966. 70 units. A/C MINIBAR TV TEL. 360,000–430,000L ($209–$249) double. Rates include breakfast. AE, DC, MC, V.

This hotel was opened a century ago as one of the first symbols of modern tourism on the island. Right in the center of Capri town, it caters to guests who seek first-class amenities and comforts and are willing to pay the piper for the privilege. Restored and renovated in an appealing style that blends modern and traditional styles, the hotel has a white-walled exterior and a forecourt with palms and potted shrubs. Each guest room is handsomely furnished.

Dining/Diversions: Its Relais la Palma is one of the finest on Capri (but it operates only Easter to late September).

Amenities: Concierge, room service, laundry/dry cleaning, baby-sitting, solarium, in-room massage, access to a nearby health club and tennis courts, car-rental desk.

Hotel Punta Tragara. Via Tragara 57, 80073 Capri. ☎ **081/837-0844.** Fax 081/837-7790. 47 units. A/C MINIBAR TV TEL. 380,000–520,000L ($220–$302) double; 530,000–630,000L ($307–$365) suite. Rates include breakfast. AE, DC, MC, V. Closed Nov–Easter.

This former private villa—designed by Le Corbusier—stands above rocky cliffs at the tip of the most desirable panorama on Capri. Its sienna-colored walls and Andalusian-style accents are designed so that each unit is subtly different. It ranks just under the Quisisana and Scalinatella but far above the Luna. With mottled carpeting, big windows, substantial furniture, and all the modern comforts, each unit opens onto a terrace or balcony studded with flowers and vines, plus a sweeping view. The premises include quiet retreats near a baronial fireplace. An often-debated point involves this hotel's isolation from the other island activities, though many guests consider this a virtue.

Dining/Diversions: At the characteristic open-air Bussola you can dine on the veranda by candlelight. It offers a savory Mediterranean cuisine prepared by the chefs with flair and served by friendly, efficient waiters. There's also a nightclub built entirely in the rocks.

Amenities: Concierge, room service, laundry, newspaper delivery, twice-daily maid service, pool, Jacuzzi, sundeck, beauty salon.

Moderate

Hotel La Vega. Via Occhio Marino 10, 80073 Capri. ☎ **081/837-0481.** Fax 081/837-0342. 24 units. A/C MINIBAR TV TEL. 200,000–380,000L ($116–$220) double. Rates include breakfast. AE, DC, MC, V. Closed Nov–Easter.

Hotel Palatium, Via Marina Grande 225, 80073 Capri (☎ **081/837-6144;** fax 081/837-6150). *"The Hotel Palatium sits on a bluff and is painted a striking Pompeian red. Having breakfast by the beautiful pool, surrounded by statuary and the view of the bay beyond, gave us a sense of peace. An on-call minibus whisks you to the main square at a moment's notice, and the staff was quite obliging and made our stay a real pleasure. We paid around 258,000L ($150) for a great room."*
—Richard Fox and Matthew X. Kiernan, New York, NY

This hotel originated in the 1930s as the private home of the family that continues to run it today. Renovated in 1993, it has a clear view of the sea and is nestled amid trees against a sunny hillside. The oversized rooms have decoratively tiled floors and Jacuzzis, and some beds have wrought iron headboards; each room has a private balcony overlooking the water. Below is a garden of flowering bushes, and on the lower edge is a free-form pool with a grassy border for sunbathing and a bar for refreshments. Breakfast is served on a terrace surrounded by trees and large potted flowers or on your balcony.

Hotel Regina Cristina. Via Serena 20, 80073 Capri. ☎ **081/837-0744.** Fax 081/837-0550. 55 units. A/C MINIBAR TV TEL. 200,000–350,000L ($116–$203) double; 450,000L ($261) suite. Rates include breakfast. Midwinter discounts up to 45%. AE, DC, MC, V.

The white facade of the Regina Cristina rises four stories above one of the most imaginatively landscaped gardens on Capri. It was built in 1959 and renovated in 1993 in a sun-flooded design of open spaces, sunken lounges, cool tiles, and la dolce vita armchairs. Each room has its own balcony and is very restful; most have Jacuzzis. In general, for what you get this hotel appears overpriced. But on Capri in July and August you're sometimes lucky to find a room at any price.

Villa Brunella. Via Tragara 24, 80073 Capri. ☎ **081/837-0122.** Fax 081/837-0430. 20 units. A/C MINIBAR TV TEL. 380,000L ($220) double; 495,000L ($287) suite. Rates include breakfast. AE, DC, MC, V. Closed Nov 6–Mar 20.

A 10-minute walk from many of Capri's largest hotels, the Brunella was built in the late 1940s as a private villa. In 1963, it was transformed into a well-appointed comfortable hotel by its present owner, Vincenzo Ruggiero, who named it after his hard-working wife. The hotel has been completely renovated and competes with most hotels with its sea views and flowery terrace. All the doubles have balconies or terraces and views of the sea. There's also a carefully landscaped pool, a bar, and a cozy restaurant.

Inexpensive
Villa Krupp. Via Matteotti 12, 80073 Capri. ☎ **081/837-0362.** Fax 081/837-6489. 15 units. TEL. 180,000–240,000L ($104–$139) double. Rates include breakfast. MC, V. Closed Nov 4–Mar 15.

During the early 20th century, Russian revolutionaries Gorky and Lenin called this villa home. Surrounded by shady trees, it offers panoramic views of the sea and the Gardens of Augustus from its lofty terraces. At this family-run place, the front parlor is all glass with views of the seaside and semitropical plants set near Hong Kong chairs, intermixed with painted Venetian-style pieces. Your room may be large, with a fairly good bath. Many of the rooms have a terrace. Breakfast is the only meal offered.

Villa Sarah. Via Tiberio 3A, 80073 Capri. ☎ **081/837-7817.** Fax 081/837-7215. 20 units. MINIBAR TV TEL. 220,000–280,000L ($128–$162) double. Rates include breakfast. AE, MC, V. Closed late Oct–Mar 19.

The modern Sarah, though far removed from the day-trippers from Naples, is still very central. A steep walk from the main square, it seems part of another world with its Capri garden and good views. All it lacks is a pool. One of the bargains of the island, it's often fully booked, so reserve ahead in summer. The sea is visible only from the upper floors. Some rooms have terraces. Breakfast, the only meal, is sometimes served on the terrace.

DINING
Moderate
'Ai Faraglioni. Via Camerelle 75. ☎ **081/837-0320.** Reservations required. Main courses 15,000–35,000L ($9–$20). AE, DC, V. Mid-Mar to Oct daily noon–3pm and 7:30pm–11:30pm. Closed Nov to mid-Mar. SEAFOOD/CONTINENTAL.

Some locals say the food is only a secondary consideration to the social ferment of this popular restaurant where tables are set out onto the main street in clement weather. Stylish and appealing and occupying a stone-sided building at least 150 years old, it has a kitchen that turns out a well-prepared collection of European specialties, usually based on seafood from the surrounding waters. Examples are linguine with lobster, seafood crêpes, rice Creole, fisherman's risotto, grilled or baked fish of many varieties, and a wide assortment of meat dishes like pappardelle with rabbit. For dessert, try one of the regional pastries mixed with fresh fruit.

✪ **La Capannina.** Via Le Botteghe 12B–14. ☎ **081/837-0732.** Reservations required for dinner. Main courses 20,000–28,000L ($12–$16). AE, DC, MC, V. Apr–Sept daily noon–3pm and 7:30–midnight; Oct and Mar Thurs–Tues noon–3pm and 7:30–midnight. Closed Nov–Feb 28, except New Year's week. CAMPANA/ITALIAN.

This restaurant is patronized by a host of glamorous people who appreciate it for its lack of pretentiousness. Part of its charm derives from the American-born wife, Aurelia de Angelis, of the fifth-generation owner, who's always on hand to translate or help with menu selections. A trio of rooms is decorated in a tavern manner, though the main draw in summer is the inner courtyard, with ferns and hanging vines. At a table covered with a colored cloth, you can select from baby shrimp au gratin, pollo (chicken) alla Capannina, or scaloppine Capannina. If featured, a fine opener is Sicilian macheroni. The most savory skillet of goodies is the zuppa di pesce, a soup made with fish from the bay. Some of the dishes were obviously inspired by the nouvelle cuisine school. Wine is from vineyards owned by the restaurant.

La Pigna. Via Roma 30. ☎ **081/837-0280.** Reservations recommended. Main courses 20,000–36,000L ($12–$21). AE, DC, MC, V. Aug daily noon–3pm and 8pm–2am; July and Sept Tues 8pm–2am, Wed–Mon noon–3pm and 8pm–2am; Apr–June and Oct Wed–Mon noon–3pm and 8pm–2am; Nov–Mar daily noon–3pm. NEAPOLITAN.

La Pigna serves the finest meals for the money on the island. Dining here is like attending a garden party, and this has been true since 1875. It isn't as chic as it once was, but the food is as good as ever. The owner loves flowers almost as much as good food, and the greenhouse ambience includes purple petunias, red geraniums, bougainvillea, and lemon trees. Much of the produce comes from the restaurant's gardens in Anacapri. Try in particular the penne tossed in eggplant sauce, the chicken suprème with mushrooms, or the herb-stuffed rabbit. The dessert specialty is an almond-and-chocolate torte. Another specialty is the homemade liqueurs, one of which is distilled from local lemons. The waiters are courteous and efficient, and the atmosphere is nostalgic, as guitarists stroll by singing sentimental Neapolitan ballads.

Inexpensive

✪ **Casanova.** Via Le Botteghe 46. ☎ **081/837-7642.** Reservations required at dinner in summer. Main courses 14,000–40,000L ($8–$23). AE, DC, MC, V. Mar–Nov daily noon–3pm and 7–11pm. Closed Dec to mid-Mar. NEAPOLITAN/CAPRESE/SEAFOOD.

Run by the D'Alessio family and only a short walk from Piazza Umberto I, this is one of the finest dining rooms on Capri. Its cellar offers a big choice of Italian wines, with most of the favorites of Campania, and its cooks turn out a savory blend of Neapolitan and Italian specialties. You might begin with cheese-filled ravioli, then go on to veal Sorrento or red snapper "crazy waters" (with baby tomatoes). The seafood is always fresh and well prepared. A tempting buffet of antipasti is at hand. In a small wine cellar you can enjoy a good selection of Italian and foreign wines with a variety of cheeses. Most meals are inexpensive, but some exotic dishes and specialties that appear infrequently can cause your check to soar. Lunch offers some lighter choices such as simple pizzas and salads.

Da Gemma. Via Madre Serafina 6. ☎ **081/837-7113.** Reservations recommended. Main courses 12,000–25,000L ($7–$15). AE, DC, MC, V. Daily noon–3pm and 7pm–midnight. CAPRESE/SEAFOOD.

Relatively inexpensive when compared to many of its competitors, Da Gemma is reached by passing through a vaulted tunnel beginning at Piazza Umberto 1 and winding through dark underground passages. The cuisine includes authentic versions of Caprese favorites, with an emphasis on fish, to more modern dishes like pizzas. You might begin with a creamy version of mussel soup, followed by one of many kinds of grilled fish, as well as filets of veal or chicken prepared with lemon and garlic or with marsala wine. A specialty is a *fritta alla Gemma*, a succulent medley of fried foods that include fish, fried zucchini blossoms, potato croquettes, fried mozzarella, and a miniature pizza. During warm weather, the site expands from its cramped 14th-century core onto a covered open-air terrace with sweeping views of the Gulf of Naples. (To reach the terrace, you'll have to wander through the same labyrinth of covered passages, then cross the street.)

La Cantinella di Capri. In the Giardini Augusto, Viale Matteotti 8. ☎ **081/837-0616.** Reservations recommended. Main courses 18,000–30,000L ($10–$17). AE, DC, MC, V. Tues–Sun 12:30–3pm and 7:30pm–12:30am. Closed Nov–Mar. NEAPOLITAN/FRENCH.

One of the most scenically located restaurants, it occupies a circa-1750 villa in a verdant park a short but soothing distance from the town center. It was acquired in 1996 by the owners of a popular restaurant in Naples, who shuttle between Naples and Capri, thereby catering to as broad-based a crowd as possible. Menu items include lots of pungent sauces and fresh seafood that's sometimes combined into pastas like linguine Sant Lucia (with octopus, squid, whitefish, and tomato sauce). Try the veal scaloppine prepared with lemon and white wine or parmigiana style. The pasta fagiole (beans and pasta) is hearty, and such desserts as tiramisu are invariably velvety smooth.

La Cisterna. Via Madre Serafina 5. ☎ **081/837-5620.** Reservations required. Main courses 11,000–22,000L ($6–$13). AE, DC, MC, V. Fri–Wed noon–3:30pm and 7pm–midnight. Closed mid-Nov to mid-Mar. SEAFOOD.

This excellent small restaurant is run by brothers Francesco and Salvatore Trama, who extend a warm welcome. Ask what the evening specials are. They might be mamma's green lasagne or whatever fish was freshest that afternoon, marinated in wine, garlic, and ginger and broiled. You could also try the lightly breaded and deep-fried baby squid and octopus, a mouth-watering saltimbocca, spaghetti with clams, and a filling zuppa di pesce (fish soup). Pizza begins at 6,000L ($3.50). La Cisterna is only a short walk from Piazza Umberto I via a labyrinth of covered "tunnels."

Ristorante al Grottino. Via Longano 27. ☎ **081/837-0584.** Reservations required for dinner. Main courses 16,000–28,000L ($9–$16). AE, MC, V. Daily noon–3pm and 7pm–midnight. Closed Nov 3–Mar 30. SEAFOOD/NEAPOLITAN.

Founded in 1937, this was the retreat of the rich and famous during its 1950s heyday. Ted Kennedy, Ginger Rogers, the Gabor sisters, and Princess Soraya of Iran once dined here, and the place is now popular among ordinary folk. To reach it you must walk down a narrow alley branching off from Piazza Umberto I. Bowing to the influence of the nearby Neapolitan cuisine, the chef offers four different dishes of fried mozzarella, any one highly recommended. Try a big plate of the mixed fish fry from the seas of the Campania. The zuppa di cozze (mussel soup) is a savory opener, as is the ravioli alla caprese. The linguine with scampi is truly wonderful.

CAPRI AFTER DARK

You'll find an amusing roster of nightclubs on the island, all of which you can enter without a cover. Foremost among them is **Number Two,** Via Camerelle 1 (☎ **081/837-7078**), rivaled closely by **Disco New Pentothal,** Via Vittorio Emmanuele 45 (☎ **081/837-6793**). Both cater to all ages and all nationalities, but only between May and September.

The presence of these electronicized clubs doesn't detract from the allure of dozens of cafes, bars, and taverns scattered through the narrow streets of Capri's historic center. Among the most appealing is **Taverna Guarracino,** Via Castello 7 (☎ **081/837-0514**), where bouts of convivial beer and wine drinking might be interrupted by quasi-spontaneous performances of Neapolitan songs. More consciously stylish and aloof is **The Blue Bar,** Via Camerelle 85 (☎ **081/837-6650**), where music from a live pianist amuses and distracts crowds from window-shopping and people-watching along the main street.

One of the major pastimes in Capri is occupying an outdoor table at one of the cafes on Piazza Umberto I. Even some permanent residents (and this is a good sign) patronize **Bar Tiberio,** Piazza Umberto I (☎ **081/837-0268**), open daily 7am to 2am (sometimes to 4am). Larger and a little more comfortable than some of its competitors, this cafe has tables both inside and outside that overlook the busy life of the square.

ANACAPRI

Capri is the upper town of Marina Grande. To see the upper town of Capri, you have to get lost in the clouds of **Anacapri**—more remote, secluded, and idyllic than the main resort and reached by a daring 3,000L ($1.75) round-trip bus ride more thrilling than any roller coaster. One visitor once remarked that all bus drivers to Anacapri "were either good or dead." At one point in island history, Anacapri and Capri were connected only by the Scala Fenicia, the Phoenician Stairs (reconstructed a zillion times).

When you disembark at **Piazza della Victoria,** you'll find a Caprian Shangri-la, a village of charming dimensions.

To continue your ascent to the top, you then hop aboard a chair lift (Segiovia) to **Monte Solaro,** the loftiest citadel on the island at 1,950 feet. The ride takes about 12 minutes; operates winter, spring, and fall 9:30am to sunset; and charges 7,500L

($4.35) round-trip. At the top, the panorama of the Bay of Naples is spread before you.

You can head out on Viale Axel Munthe from Piazza Monumento for a 5-minute walk to the **Villa San Michele**, Capodimonte 34 (☎ 081/837-1401). This was the home of Axel Munthe, the Swedish author (*The Story of San Michele*), physician, and friend of Gustav V, king of Sweden, who visited him several times on the island. The villa is as Munthe (who died in 1949) furnished it, in a harmonious and tasteful way. From the rubble and ruins of an imperial villa built underneath by Tiberius, Munthe purchased several marbles, which are displayed inside. You can walk through the gardens for another in a series of endless panoramas of the island. Tiberius used to sleep out here alfresco on hot nights. You can visit the villa daily: May to September 9am to 6pm, April and October 9:30am to 5pm, March 9:30am to 4:30pm, and November to February 10:30am to 3:30pm. Admission is 6,000L ($3.50) adults; children 12 and under are free.

ACCOMMODATIONS
Expensive
Europa Palace. Via Capodimonte 2, 80071 Anacapri. ☎ 081/837-3800. Fax 081/837-3191. 116 units. A/C MINIBAR TV TEL. 370,000–530,000L ($215–$307) double; from 850,000–1,050,000L ($493–$609) suite. Rates include breakfast. AE, DC, MC, V. Closed Nov 15–Easter.

On the slopes of Monte Solaro, the first-class Europa sparkles with moderne and turns its back on the past to embrace the semiluxury of today. Its bold designer obviously loved wide open spaces, heroic proportions, and vivid colors. The landscaped gardens with palm trees and plenty of bougainvillea have a large pool, which most guests use as their outdoor living room. Although lacking the intimate charms of Scalinatella, it's alluring because of its setting and its Capri Beauty Farm, offering spa treatments. Each of the guest rooms is attractively and comfortably furnished, and from some on a clear day you can see smoking Vesuvius. Each of the four special suites has a private pool.

Dining/Diversions: The hotel restaurant is known for its fine cuisine with Neapolitan and other Mediterranean specialties, even with some nouvelle cuisine. A snack bar with light lunches is in the pool area.

Amenities: Room service, baby-sitting, laundry/valet, pool, beauty spa.

Moderate
Hotel Bella Vista. Via Orlandi 10, 80071 Anacapri. ☎ 081/837-1821. Fax 081/837-0957. 15 units. TEL. 105,000–135,000L ($61–$78) per person double. Rates include half board. AE, MC, V. Closed Nov 1–Easter.

Only a 2-minute walk from the main piazza, this is a modern holiday retreat with a panoramic view and a distinct sense of a family-run regional inn. Lodged into a mountainside, the hotel is decorated with primary colors and has large living and dining rooms and terraces with sea views. The breakfast and lunch terrace has garden furniture and a rattan-roofed sun shelter, and the cozy lounge features an elaborate tile floor and a hooded fireplace. The guest rooms are pleasingly contemporary (a few have a bed mezzanine, a sitting area on the lower level, and a private entrance). The restaurant is open daily.

Hotel San Michele di Anacapri. Via Orlandi 1–3, 80071 Anacapri. ☎ 081/837-1427. Fax 081/837-1420. 56 units. TV TEL. 200,000–240,000L ($116–$139) double. Rates include breakfast. AE, DC, MC, V. Closed Nov 5–Mar 31.

This well-appointed contemporary hotel has spacious cliffside gardens and unmarred views as well as enough shady or sunny nooks to please everybody. It also has the largest pool on Capri. Guests linger peacefully in its private gardens, where the green trees are softened by splashes of color from hydrangea and geraniums. The view for diners includes the Bay of Naples and Vesuvius. The rooms carry out the same theme, with a respect for the past but also with sufficient examples of today's amenities, such as a tile bath in most rooms, good beds, and plenty of space.

Inexpensive

Hotel Loreley. Via Orlandi 12, 80071 Anacapri. ☎ **081/837-1440.** Fax 081/837-1399. 18 units. TEL. 120,000–150,000L ($70–$87) double. Rates include breakfast. AE, MC, V. Closed Oct 15–Mar 30.

The Loreley has more to offer than economy: It's a cozy immaculate place, with a genial homelike atmosphere. It features an open-air veranda with a bamboo canopy, rattan chairs, and a good view. The rooms overlook lemon-bearing trees that have (depending on the season) either scented blossoms or fruit; they're quite large, with unified colors and enough furniture to make for a sitting room. Each has a balcony. You approach the hotel through a white iron gate, past a stone wall. It lies off the road toward the sea and is surrounded by fig trees and geraniums.

DINING

La Rondinella. Via Orlandi 245. ☎ **081/837-1223.** Reservations recommended. Main courses 15,000–25,000L ($9–$15). AE, DC, MC, V. Daily noon–3pm and 7:30pm–1am. SOUTHERN ITALIAN.

Despite the competition from the more formal restaurants in some of Anacapri's hotels, this is the most appealing place, thanks to the likable staff, garden view, and a location adjacent to Santa Sophia, Anacapri's most visible church. The menu items are tried-and-true versions of classics, yet the chefs manage to produce everything in copious amounts and with lots of robust flavors. Look for succulent homemade ravioli stuffed with cheese and tomatoes, a mixed grill of fresh seafood, braised radicchio and/or artichokes, and filet of veal or chicken slathered with mozzarella, tomatoes, and fresh herbs. For dessert, you might try the sugary version of Sicilian tiramisu.

MARINA PICCOLA

You can reach the little south-shore fishing village and beach of **Marina Piccola** by bus (later you can take a bus back up the steep hill to Capri). The village opens onto emerald-and-cerulean waters, with the Faraglioni rocks of the sirens jutting out at the far end of the bay. Treat yourself to lunch at **La Canzone del Mare,** Marina Piccola (☎ **081/837-0104**), daily noon to 4pm. Seafood and Neapolitan cuisines are served.

Known to the Italians as **La Puglia,** the district of **Apulia** encompasses the southeasternmost section of Italy, the heel of the boot. It's the country's gateway to the Orient, and for many travelers it's the gateway to Greece from the port of Brindisi. Apulia is little known but fascinating, embracing some of Italy's most poverty-stricken areas and some of its most interesting sections (like the Trulli District). Many signs of improved living conditions are in the air, however.

The land is rich in archaeological discoveries, and some of its cities were shining sapphires in the crown of Magna Graecia (Greater Greece). The Ionian and Adriatic Seas wash up on its shores, which have seen the arrival of cross-currents of civilizations and of the armies of tribes and countries seeking to conquer this access route to Rome. The Goths, Germanic hordes, Byzantines, Spanish, and French sought to possess it. Saracen pirates and Turks came to see what riches they might find.

Apulia offers the beauty of marine grottoes and caverns as well as turquoise seas and sandy beaches. Forests of wind-twisted pines, huge old carob trees, junipers, sage, and rosemary grow near the sea, while orchards, vineyards, fields of grain, and vegetable gardens grow inland. Flocks of sheep and goats dot the landscape.

In recent years, Apulia has been caught in the eye of the "Albanian Hurricane." Political turmoil and economic upheaval have sent tens of thousands of Albanians to commandeer yachts, ferries, and tugboats and cross the narrow Strait of Otranto into this region. This has adversely affected tourism, leading to massive hotel booking cancellations, presumably because of the fear that this massive deluge has made the region undesirable.

Regional officials stress that there's nothing to worry about and promise that Apulia is now "more of a bargain than ever." The Albanian presence in most tourist zones is barely noticeable, if at all. Actually, most of the refugees are moved elsewhere or housed in discreet camps away from the mainstream attractions. The regional tourist commissioner, Rossana Di Bello, assured us, "You have only to impress upon potential visitors that they can visit our land and find peace and tranquillity."

1 Foggia

60 miles W of Bari, 108 miles NE of Naples, 225 miles SE of Rome

Foggia, the capital of Capitanata, which is Apulia's northernmost province. A history of tragedy, including a serious earthquake in 1731 and extensive bombing during World War II, has left Foggia with little in the way of attractions, though it's a good base for exploring nearby attractions like Lucera and Troia. The city is also used by many motorists as a base for a day's motor tour of the Gargano Peninsula. A 12th-century cathedral remains; the rest of the city is pleasant but thoroughly modern. Foggia is clean and has parks and wide boulevards lined with a decent selection of hotels and restaurants. This is a good place to take care of business—rent a car, exchange money, mail postcards, or whatever, because it's relatively safe, easy to get around, and in a central location.

ESSENTIALS

GETTING THERE   Foggia is at the crossroads of the Lecce-Bologne **rail** line and the Bari-Naples run, so it's easy to get here from just about anywhere in Italy. Trains from Naples arrive four times daily; the trip lasts about 3 hours and costs 16,000L ($9) one way. Trains arrive from Bari every hour during the day, taking 1½ hours and costing 10,500L ($6) one way. There are also three trains daily from Rome, taking 4 hours and costing 45,000L ($26). Train arrive at the **Stazione Centrale** in the center of Piazza Vittorio Veneto (☎ 0881/608-234).

Because of inconvenience, **bus** travel to the city is usually not recommended. However, once you're here you can ride ATAF and SITA buses to many towns in the area. Tickets and information are provided by the train station (above). There are hourly buses to Lucera, taking 30 minutes and costing 2,500L ($1.45) one way, and service to Manfredonia on the Gargano Peninsula, taking 45 minutes and costing 4,000L ($2.30) each way.

If you've got a **car,** follow Route 90 from Naples directly to Foggia. From Bari, take A14.

VISITOR INFORMATION   The **tourist office** is at Via Senatore Emilio Perrone 17 (☎ 0881/776-864), open Monday to Friday 8am to 1:30pm.

SEEING THE SIGHTS

The 12th-century **Cattedrale della Santa Maria Icona Vetere** (☎ 0881/773-482) lies off Piazza del Lago. The province's largest cathedral, it was constructed in an unusual Norman and Apulian Baroque style. Today, after extensive repairs and expansions, the Duomo is an eclectic mix of styles. The present campanile (bell tower) was built to replace the one destroyed in the 1731 quake. The crypt was built in the Romanesque style, and some of its "excavation" was compliments of Allied bombers in 1943. The cathedral is open daily 9am to noon and 5 to 8pm; admission is free.

The other notable attraction is the **Civic Museum (Museo Civico),** Piazza Nigri (☎ 0881/771-823), featuring exhibits on Apulia's archaeology and ethnography. It's housed in the remains of the residence of Frederick II and is open Monday to Friday 9am to 1pm and 5 to 7pm and Sunday 9am to 1pm. Admission is 1,200L (70¢).

ACCOMMODATIONS

Grand Hotel Cicolella. Viale XXIV Maggio 60, 71100 Foggia. ☎ 0881/688-890. Fax 0881/778-984. 108 units. A/C MINIBAR TV TEL. 260,000–290,000L ($151–$168) double; from 320,000L ($186) suite. Breakfast 15,000L ($9). AE, DC, V. Parking 10,000–15,000L ($6–$9).

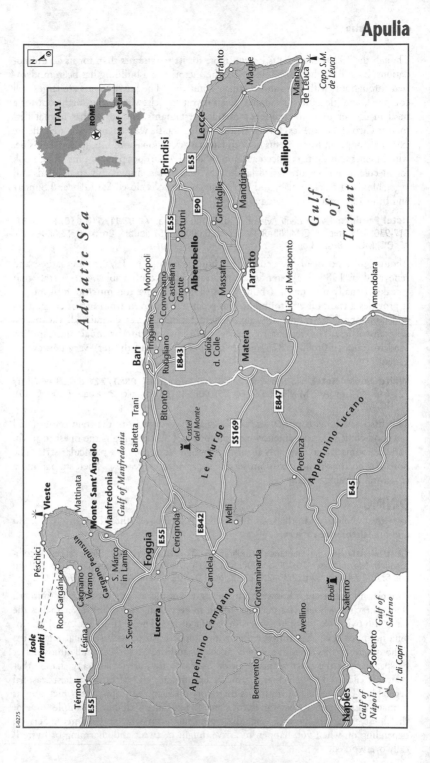

Though the 1920s Cicolella is known more for its restaurants than for its accommodations, it's still the best hotel in town. The Victorian-era building has been modernized throughout, with glass and marble dominating. The guest rooms are large, well equipped, and pleasantly decorated. Even if you stay elsewhere, you might opt for a meal in one of the two well-recommended restaurants, the somewhat formal Ristorante Cicolello or the less formal Ristorante Infiera. Be warned, however, that they're extremely popular. Menu items in both emphasizes regional and international cuisine, with lunches and dinners priced at about 45,000L ($26) per person, plus wine. Look for succulent versions of roasted lamb, as well as pastas, impeccably fresh salads and vegetables, and chicken, fish, and beef dishes. Ciolello is closed Saturday and Sunday and Infiera Monday and Tuesday.

Hotel President. Viale degli Aviatori 130, 71100 Foggia. ☎ **0881/618-010.** Fax 0881/617-930. 125 units. A/C MINIBAR TV TEL. 130,000L ($75) double. Breakfast 10,000L ($6). AE, DC, MC, V. Bus: 18 or 19.

About a mile north of the center, this hotel was built in 1970 and enlarged and renovated in 1985. Unpretentious and reasonably comfortable, with a staff that speaks virtually no English (though this shouldn't prove too much of a problem), it provides a tranquil environment that seems far removed from urban congestion and concerns. The rooms are angular and functional yet contain all the necessary amenities. The restaurant serves well-prepared international and Apulian food for about 40,000L ($23) per person, at lunch and dinner every day except Friday.

White House Hotel. Via Sabotino 24, 71100 Foggia. ☎ **0881/721-644.** Fax 0881/721-646. 40 rms. A/C MINIBAR TV TEL. 290,000L ($168) double. Breakfast 15,000L ($9). AE, DC, MC, V.

This first-class hotel is in the heart of Foggia, a few steps from the train station, and is a good choice for convenience and comfort. Its housekeeping is the finest in town, and the rooms are comfortably furnished though lacking in any particular style. The hotel has no restaurant, but room service is provided on request. There's a bar and a comfortable lounge area.

DINING

Two great choices are in the Grand Hotel Cicolella (above): the **Ristorante Cicolello** and the **Ristorante Infiera.**

✪ **Il Ventaglio.** Via Gaetano Postiglione 6. ☎ **0881/661-500.** Reservations recommended. Main courses 20,000–25,000L ($12–$15). AE DC MC, V. Tues–Sat 12:30–2:45pm and 8:30–10:45pm, Sun 12:30–2:45pm. Closed Dec 23–31 and Aug 13–31. ITALIAN.

This elegant restaurant is known for its inventive cuisine, among the finest in southern Italy. The chef, who adds a personal touch to everything, says she "never makes the same dish twice." Some of her specialties are fagottino di pesce (fish) and agnolotti ripieni, her pasta specialty stuffed either with chopped fish or with seasonal vegetables. (Though the pasta comes in a variety of shapes and sizes, be assured it'll almost never be spaghetti, as the place seems to pride itself on offering virtually any shape other than that cliché.) The orecchiette come in a clam sauce and with the freshest seasonal vegetables. The area is known for its migratory birds and swamp game, which appear in many dishes with a great variety of sauces. Here's also a chance to sample some of the finest cheese in the area, including pecorino, scamorza, and manteca. Service, depending on when you happen to arrive, might be sweet and charming or hysterically overworked.

A SIDE TRIP TO LUCERA & TROIA

From Foggia, you can take an hourly bus, a 30-minute trip costing 2,000L ($1.15), or drive 12 miles west to the small medieval town of **Lucera.** Its hilltop site opens onto the Tavoliere, the largest tract of flat country in Italy. Its large castello dominates the terrain for miles around. Once it was a city of Saracens who carried out a thriving trade after their banishment from Sicily. Frederick II resettled about 20,000 of these Arabs here in the early 13th century on the site of a long-abandoned Roman town.

A bus from Foggia will deposit you at **Piazza del Popolo,** and then you can walk up Via Gramsci to the ✪ **Duomo,** at Piazza del Duomo (☎ **0881/941-705**), the heart of the old walled town of the Middle Ages. Today's building was constructed over the site of a mosque the Angevins destroyed when they massacred the Arab residents in the early 1300s. One of the major architectural treasures of southern Italy, the Byzantine-Gothic cathedral was built by Charles III of Anjou in 1305. The Arabic layout of Lucera is said to still exist, though the Islamic buildings have long turned to dust. The Duomo is open daily 7am to noon and 4:30 to 8pm, and admission is free.

Near the Duomo, you can visit the **Civic Museum (Museo Civico G. Fiorelli)** by heading down Via de Nicastri to no. 36 (☎ **0881/547-041**). The building housing the museum was the ancestral home of Baroness de Nicastri, and some of her antiques are still here. Otherwise, exhibits are the area's archaeological finds, like old Arab teapots and some mosaics from Roman times. It's open Tuesday to Friday: May to August 9am to 1pm and 3 to 6pm and September to April 9am to 1pm and 5 to 7pm. Admission is 1,500L (85¢) adults and 1,000L (60¢) children/seniors.

Northwest of town are the ruins of a **Roman amphitheater,** Viale Augusto (☎ **0881/549-214**), constructed in 27 B.C. It was dedicated to the Emperor Augustus, and the site is open Tuesday to Sunday 8am to 1:30pm and 2:30 to 8pm. From the amphitheater, you can walk to the **castle** (no phone), Apulia's largest, topped with two dozen towers. This fortress was built for Frederick II in 1230 and measures more than a kilometer in circumference. It's open Tuesday to Sunday 9am to 1pm, charging no admission. From Piazza del Duomo, head out Via Bovio and Via Frederico II to Piazza Matteotti. Follow the CASTELLO signs.

If time remains, you can make an offbeat excursion to the small town of **Troia,** 12 miles due south of Lucera. If you're driving, take Rte. 160. Frequent buses make the run from both Foggia and Lucera. No one seems to know the origins of the town's name *(troia* in Italian means "bitch"). That bizarre twist sets the stage for one of the strangest towns in Apulia, a village time forgot. Once the Roman town of Aecae, Troia was refounded in 1017. It's now a dusty place visited by those wishing to see its **Duomo,** an 11th-century medley of many styles, from Romanesque to Byzantine, even Saracen, but with a distinctive Apulian flavor and a baroque interior. Look for the bronze doors decorated with biblical characters and animals like apes and elephants; they're surmounted by a rose window.

DINING IN LUCERA

Ristorante Alhambra. Via De Nicastri 10–14. ☎ **0881/547-066.** Reservations recommended. Main courses 12,000–22,000L ($7–$13). AE, DC, MC, V. Daily noon–3pm and Mon–Sat 7:30–11pm. Closed 2 weeks in late Aug. APULIAN/ITALIAN.

This is the most historic and best recommended restaurant in town, a stone's throw from the Duomo. The well-prepared Apulian and classic Italian cuisine is served in a setting that was the palace of an Arab patriarch, built in the 1300s. Menu items include a sprawling selection of seafood antipasti; a savory version of clam soup or another version combining a medley of shellfish; pasta flavored with mushrooms or fresh clams; grilled lamb; and a wide selection of fish (like spigola and brodetto) served as grilled filets or oven baked with herbs and vegetables.

2 The Gargano Peninsula

Called the **Gargano,** this mountainous wooded promontory is the "spur" of Italy. The best time to come is autumn, when you can enjoy the colors of the Umbra Forest, featuring maples, ashes, cedars, and chestnuts. The world here has a timeless quality. Unspoiled salt-lake areas are at Lesina and Varano, and bathing and water sports are prevalent because of the mild climate and calm seas. The coast is a series of cliffs, rocks, caves, islets, and beaches, and vegetable gardens grow inland on a landscape dotted with flocks of sheep and goats. In addition to nature's wild and varied landscape, the promontory is rich in historic interest, boasting monuments that are Byzantine, Romanesque, Norman, and medieval.

It'll take a leisurely 7 hours to drive around the Gargano (perhaps longer depending on your stops), staying on Rte. 89. We consider this sometimes difficult route among the most scenically rewarding in Italy. In ancient times, the peninsula was an island, until the sediment from a river eventually formed a "bridge" linking it to the mainland. Train service into the peninsula is limited to a private spur along the northwestern coast, so for travelers who wish to fully explore the area by bus or car, the gateway will be Manfredonia.

ESSENTIALS

GETTING THERE   From Foggia, make a **train** connection to San Severo, 24 miles north, an hourly trip of 25 minutes costing 3,800L ($2.20), and transfer to the Ferrovia del Gargano (☎ **0882/221-414**), Gargano's private rail, traveling the northwestern edge of the peninsula to Rodi Garganico and a point near Peschici six times daily. You can also take an hourly train to Manfredonia, 27 miles northeast of Foggia, for 3,750L ($2.20); here buses depart to explore the peninsula. For rail information in Manfredonia, call ☎ **0884/581-015.**

Bus services are provided by the ATAF and SITA lines, which overlap, with hourly buses running from Foggia to Manfredonia, a 45-minute trip costing 4,000L ($2.30) each way. In Manfredonia, you can make connections 7 times daily to Vieste, a 2-hour trip costing 5,000L ($2.90); 16 times daily to Mattinata, a 30-minute trip costing 1,800L ($1.05); and 17 times daily to Monte Sant'Angelo, a 45-minute trip costing 3,200L ($1.85). Buses also leave from the parking lot of Camping Sports, Via Montesanto 34–40 (☎ **0884/964-015**) in Peschici, following the coastal Rte. 89 to Vieste, a 40-minute trip costing 3,200L ($1.85).

From Vieste, contact **Gargano Viaggi,** Piazza Roma 7 (☎ **0884/708-501**), or **Viaggi Sol,** Via Tripicione 5 (☎ **0881/773-117**), for participation in a somewhat rushed 4-hour bus tour of the peninsula costing 20,000L ($12).

If you've got a **car,** you'll note that three roads dissect the peninsula and connect its major sights. Rte. 89 runs an 81-mile circuit around the coast; Rte. 528 cuts through the heart of the peninsula, starting 5 miles west of Peschici on the northern coast and running south through the Umbra Forest before ending at Rte. 272 just west of Monte Sant'Angelo; Rte. 272 slices east to west through the southern part of the region, from San Marco in Lamis in the west through San Giovanni Rotondo and over to Monte Sant'Angelo, ending on the coast near Punta Rossa.

VISITOR INFORMATION   The **tourist office** in Manfredonia, Corso Manfredi 26 (☎ **0884/581-998**), is open Monday to Saturday 9am to 1:30pm. Here you can pick up a map and get data about touring the Gargano district, including bus and train schedules—especially since in most towns there are no actual bus stations. In Vieste, the **tourist office,** Piazza Kennedy 1 (☎ **0884/708-806**), will give you information about the many excursion possibilities in the area, especially the excellent beaches along the southern shore. June 20 to September 20, hours are Monday to Saturday 8:30am to 1pm and 3 to 8pm and Sunday 8:30am to 1pm; off-season hours are Monday to Saturday 8:30am to 1:30pm and 3 to 8pm.

MANFREDONIA

27 miles NE of Foggia, 74 miles NW of Bari, 135 miles NE of Naples

If you approach Gargano from the south, your first stop, perhaps at lunchtime, will be **Manfredonia,** a small port known for its castle. It was named for Manfred, illegitimate son of Frederick II. In the heyday of the Crusades, this was a bustling port, with knights and pilgrims leaving for the Levant. Much later, the town was noted in World War I documents as the place where the first blow of the conflict was launched—the Austrians bombed the rail station in 1915. Manfredonia is on a rail route from Foggia.

After arriving in town, turn right and go along Viale Aldo Moro to Piazza Marconi. Across the square, Corso Manfredi leads to the **Manfredonia Castello,** built for Manfred and later enlarged by the Angevins. Other bastions were constructed in 1607 by the Spanish fearing an invasion from Turkey. Regrettably, it didn't do the job, as the Turks arrived in 1620 and destroyed a lot of Manfredonia, leaving some of its former walls standing. Today the castle is home to the **National Museum of Manfredonia (Museo Nazionale di Manfredonia)** (☎ **0884/587-838**), open Tuesday to Sunday 8:30am to 1:30pm and 3:30 to 7:30pm and charging 4,000L ($2.30) admission. The archaeological remnants and finds include a collection of Stone Age objects from area villages, the most striking of which are the Daunian stelae, stone slabs decorated like human torsos and topped with stone heads, the legacy of the Daunian civilization that settled in the region around the 9th century B.C.

Two miles outside town is **Santa Maria di Siponto,** a church in a setting of pine woods that once was the site of the ancient city of Siponte, abandoned after being ravaged by an earthquake and a plague. The church, dating from the 11th century, is in the Romanesque style, showing both Tuscan and Arabic influences.

ACCOMMODATIONS

Hotel Gargano. Viale Beccarini 2, 71043 Manfredonia. ☎ and fax **0884/586-021.** 46 units. A/C TV TEL. 160,000L ($93) double. MC, V. Closed Jan. Parking 20,000L ($12).

This is the largest and most appealing hotel in town, a four-star place that isn't horrendously expensive. The rooms have simple summery furnishings, with monochromatic color schemes of blue or white. Each faces the sea from a private terrace or veranda. A seawater pool is close to a dance bar whose recorded music floats over chairs and tables angled for the best panorama of sea and shore. There's no room service, but the bar is open 24 hours.

DINING

Il Barrocchio. Corso Roma 38. ☎ **0884/583-874.** Reservations recommended. Main courses 25,000–50,000L ($15–$29). AE, DC, MC, V. Fri–Wed 12:30–2:30pm and 7:30–10:30pm. APULIAN/SEAFOOD.

In a turn-of-the-century building very close to Piazza Municipio, this is the most appealing restaurant in town. It attracts civic and business leaders at lunch and groups of friends for dinners accompanied with a great roster of antipasti (mostly seafood and vegetarian). Pasta dishes include spaghetti and orecchiette, prepared in simple versions of tomatoes, pesto, and local cheese; with garlic, olive oil, and fresh broccoli; or more elaborately garnished with seafood, especially octopus. Look for grilled baby lamb as savory and aromatic as the nearby hills on which the animals were raised.

MONTE SANT'ANGELO

37 miles NE of Foggia, 84 NW of Bari, 145 miles NE of Naples

Motorists will find the interior's principal town, **Monte Sant'Angelo,** 10 miles north of Manfredonia in the great Umbra Forest, to be a good starting point for a tour. From here you can venture into a landscape of limes, laurels, towering yews, and such animal life as foxes and gazelles. Narrow passages, streets that are virtually stairways, and little houses washed a gleaming white characterize the town.

The site of Monte Sant'Angelo, standing on a spur, commands panoramic views of the surrounding terrain. Before leaving town, you may want to visit the **Sanctuary of San Michele (Santuario di San Michele),** Via Reale Basilica, built in the Romanesque-Gothic style. The campanile is octagonal, dating from the last years of the 13th century. The sanctuary commemorates the legend of St. Michael, who's said to have left his red cloak after he appeared to some shepherds in a grotto in 490. You can also visit the grotto—to enter from the church, go through some bronze doors, made in Constantinople in the 11th century. Crusaders stopped here to worship before going to the Holy Land. The sanctuary is open daily 7:30am to 12:30pm and 2:30 to 6:30pm, charging no admission.

Opposite the campanile (bell tower) is the **Tomb of Rotharis (Tomba di Rotari).** The tomb is said to hold the bones of the king of the Lombards, Rotharis, though it's a baptistery dating from as early as the 12th century.

Past the sanctuary leads to the semirestored ruins of the **Norman Swabian Aragonese Castle,** Piazzale Fere, with a second entrance on the Corso Manfredi (☎ **0884/565-444**); it's open daily 8:30am to 1:30pm, charging 4,000L ($2.30) admission. Its Torre dei Giganti was constructed in 837, though most of the castle dates from the Middle Ages. From its ramparts is one of the most sweeping views in the Gargano.

You can also visit the **Museo Tancredi,** Piazza San Francesco d'Assisi (☎ **0884/ 562-098**), exhibiting artifacts that local farmers and vintners used in their trade. May to September, it's open Monday 8:30am to 2pm, Tuesday to Saturday 8:30am to 2pm and 2:30 to 8pm, and Sunday 10am to 12:30pm and 3:30 to 7pm; off-season hours are Monday to Saturday 8am to 2pm. Admission is 4,000L ($2.30).

SHOPPING

As you wander about, look for local shops selling wrought-iron goods, which are among the finest in Italy. It's been a long tradition here with sons following in their father's footsteps. The locals also make wooden furniture and utensils. Most shops are located in an area called Juno, in the exact center of town.

ACCOMMODATIONS

Hotel Rotary. Via per Pulsano km 1, 71037 Monte Sant'Angelo. ☎ and fax **0884/562-146.** 24 units. TV TEL. 105,000–115,000L ($61–$67) double. Rates include breakfast. AE, MC, V.

You'll find this 1981 hotel half a mile west of town, amid a sloping terrain with ancient olive groves and almond trees. Many visitors appreciate it for the panoramas of the Adriatic, about 6 miles southeast, sweeping across the landscape from many of the windows. There aren't many amenities; none of the simple rooms is air-conditioned, but because of the hotel's location in relative high altitudes, ocean breezes usually keep the temperatures comfortable. The restaurant serves a cuisine based on local culinary traditions, usually with competency and generosity.

DINING

Ristorante Medioevo. Via Castello 21. ☎ **0884/565-356.** Reservations recommended. Main courses 10,000–25,000L ($6–$15). AE, MC, V. June–Sept daily 12:30–2:30pm and 7:30–11pm; the rest of the year Tues–Sun 12:30–2:30pm and 7:30pm–11pm. CONTADINA.

In the heart of this medieval town, the Medioevo's dining room takes its name from the weather-beaten but historic neighborhood surrounding it. Though it has served countless numbers of diners from other parts of Europe, there remain vague hints of suspicion toward newcomers. The cuisine is firmly entrenched in recipes rehearsed by countless generations of contadine (peasant women). Examples are *zuppe di panne cotte*, a savory soup made of chicory and fava beans, homemade pasta (especially orecchiette), and a wide roster of meat or fish and roasted lamb from rocky nearby meadows. The kitchen is particularly proud of its orecchiette Medioevo—ear-shaped pasta with a sauce made from roasted lamb, braised arugula, and fresh tomatoes.

THE ISOLE TREMITI

7 miles NW of Gargano

While in the area, consider visiting the jewel-like cluster of the **Isole Tremiti (Tremiti Islands),** northwest of the Gargano Peninsula in the Adriatic. These small limestone islands boast lovely reefs, gin-clear waters, and towering peaks.

June to September, **boats** and **hydrofoils** travel from Vieste, Manfredonia, and Peschici to the Tremiti Islands, and you should make advance reservations in the peak weeks of summer, when the vessels get crowded. In Vieste, contact **Motonave Vieste,** Corso Fazzini 33 on the dock (☎ **0884/707-489**), about boat service, a 1⅓-hour trip costing 20,000L ($12), or **Adriatica,** Piazza Roma 7 at the Gargano Viaggi office (☎ **0884/708-501**), providing 1-hour hydrofoil service from Vieste for 20,000L ($12), as well as a 2-hour trip from Manfredonia for 32,000L ($19), leaving from the dock a 3-minute walk south along Piazza Marconi toward Siponto. In Peschici, **Onda Azzurra,** Corso Umberto I 16 (☎ **0884/964-234**), makes daily boat runs to the islands, a trip of just over an hour costing 18,000L ($10). Departures from all ports leave at 9:05am daily, with a return at 6pm.

EXPLORING THE TREMITI

By boat or hydrofoil, you'll arrive at the docks of **San Nicola,** the smaller of the two inhabited islands, where you can explore the **castle** from the 15th century (it's not much of a sight, but the view is spectacular). You might also want to visit **Santa Maria a Mare (Church of Santa Maria),** which grew out of a 9th-century abbey, one of many monasteries that once stood in the Tremiti. It has been largely rebuilt over the years, retaining only an intricate mosaic floor and early Byzantine cross from its early history. All its treasures were plundered by pirates in 1321.

Between the islands of San Nicola and **San Domino,** the other inhabited island, you can take a shuttle boat running every 15 minutes at 2,000L ($1.15). San Domino is the largest island of the group, with a rock-strewn shoreline. It's best known for its grottoes—**Grotta del Bue Marino, Grotta di Sale,** and **Grotta delle Viole.** The only beaches of the Tremiti are found here, and the **Cala delle Arene,** near the dock, is generally crowded, but you can also make your way to the west and south sides of the island, where the only other approachable beaches (most are at the foot of treacherous cliffs) offer stretches of solitude. As a historical footnote, Charlemagne's quarrelsome Italian father-in-law was exiled on the island, and this is where Augustus banished his daughter, Julia, because of her "excesses" (like sleeping with nearly every man in Rome).

ACCOMMODATIONS

Hotel Gabbiano. Isola San Domino, 71040 San Nicola di Tremiti. ☎ and fax **0882/ 463-410.** 40 units. A/C MINIBAR TV TEL. 95,000–150,000L ($55–$87) per person double. Rates include full board. AE, DC, MC, V.

Built in 1973 and radically renovated in 1992, this is the best-managed and most appealing hotel on the island. It lies about half a mile from the port, on San Domino's most beautiful stretch of coastline, in a palm garden that, after the sun-baked terrain around it, seems like a lush oasis. Most of the ground floor is devoted to a bar, a restaurant open to nonguests, a solarium, and the reception area. The guest rooms are airy, painted in pastel shades that go well with the sunshine streaming through the big windows. The restaurant is one of the most sought-after on the island, and specialties include fish and pastas, with main courses at 20,000L to 30,000L ($12 to $17).

Hotel San Domino. Isola San Domino, 71040 San Nicola di Tremiti. ☎ **0882/463-404.** Fax 0882/463-220. 24 units. TV TEL. 95,000–149,000L ($55–$86) per person double. Rates include full board. MC, V.

Less elegant than the Gabbiano (above), this is a simple three-star hotel built in 1976 about a mile from the port. It's within a 5-minute walk from the nearest beach and contains serviceable but simple white-walled rooms designed for escapist holidays near the beach. There's a restaurant and a bar, but few other amenities.

VIESTE

57 miles NE of Foggia, 111 miles NW of Bari, 170 miles NE of Naples

At **Vieste,** on the far eastern shore of the Gargano, a legendary monolith stands firmly rooted in the sea. The rock is linked to the woeful tale of Vesta, a beautiful girl supposedly held prisoner on the stone by jealous sirens.

In recent years, the town has blossomed as a summer resort, as it offers some of the beast beaches in the south. If you're just passing through, take time out to walk through the charming medieval quarter, with its whitewashed houses built on terraces overlooking the sea. Vieste is a good center from which to explore the other excellent sandy beaches along the southern shoreline.

ACCOMMODATIONS

✪ **Pizzomunno Vieste Palace Hotel.** Lungomare Enrico Mattei, 71019 Vieste. ☎ **0884/ 708-741.** Fax 0884/707-325. 216 units. 500,000–810,000L ($290–$470) double; 780,000– 1,390,000L ($452–$806) junior suite for two. Rates include full board. AE, DC, MC, V. Closed late Oct to mid-Mar. Free valet parking.

This five-star hotel is much better than any other contender in Gargano and proud of its 80% Italian clientele. Its Mediterranean architecture, with five stories growing smaller as they rise, allows lots of private terraces on the fourth and fifth floors. The rooms are airy and relatively spacious, with big windows. Within 30 yards is the companion La Pineta, with which it shares the same management and the same prices. Even the staff is charming.

Dining/Diversions: Ristorante Trabucco is the best hotel dining room in the region, with delectable main courses like roast lamb with fresh herbs, baked or grilled fish, and seafood like sea wolf, lobster, and fresh shrimp. Salads are freshly made with crisp ingredients, and pastas come with a wide variety of sauces. There's also the less formal Il Ristorante sulla Spiaggia, serving a regional cuisine, and a pizzeria, Al Pozzo, in a 19th-century house. Bars are found in the hotel disco, at the beach, at pool side, and in the pizzeria.

Amenities: Concierge, room service, dry cleaning/laundry, newspaper delivery, in-room massage, twice-daily maid service, baby-sitting, secretarial services, courtesy car, huge playground for kids; two tennis courts, two pools (one for children), swimming courses, sailing and windsurfing classes, motorboats for water skiing, sail boats, beach rafts, archery, fitness trail, basketball court; health, beauty, and diet center; hairdresser, boutique, perfumery.

Hotel Seggio. Piazza del Seggio/Via Vieste 7, 71019 Vieste. ☎ **0884/708-123.** Fax 0884/708-727. 28 units. A/C TV TEL. 138,000–270,000L ($80–$157) double. Rates include breakfast. AE, DC, MC, V. Free parking.

This is the best affordable hotel in town, with a historic pedigree more impressive than any of the grander palaces. It occupies a civic monument that between its construction in the 1600s and around 1910 was the town's city hall. In 1983, it was renovated to become a hotel, with comfortable but basic rooms. One edge of it abuts the seafront, the other one of the town's keynote squares. There's a smallish pool on an outdoor terrace as well as a restaurant, open to nonguests, charging 12,000L to 17,000L ($7 to $10) for main courses.

DINING

Al Dragone. Via Duomo 8. ☎ **0884/701-212.** Reservations recommended. Main courses 14,000–28,000L ($8–$16). AE, DC, MC, V. Daily noon–3pm and 7–11:30pm. Closed Nov to mid-Mar. APULIAN.

Its name derives from the dragon you'd expect to emerge from the primeval cave housing it. Near the cathedral, it's usually the first restaurant anyone mentions when honeymooners are looking for a secluded romantic hideaway. The decor includes flickering candles and raffia-sheathed Chianti bottles, and the cuisine is based on the folkloric traditions of old Apulia. Look for seafood pastas, antipasti buffets, lamb roasted with herbs and potatoes in the oven, and flavors lush with garlic, rosemary, and pesto. The owners pride themselves on their comprehensive collection of red and white Apulian wines, which they inventory and decant with style and panache. An excellent example is Patrilione.

Box 19. Via Santa Maria di Merino 13. ☎ **0884/705-229.** Reservations recommended. Main courses 9,000–28,000L ($5–$16). MC, V. Daily noon–3pm and 7pm–midnight. Closed Mon Oct–Mar. APULIAN.

Box 19 makes less of an attempt to capitalize on local folklore than some other competitors and offers a more culturally neutral and relatively sophisticated dining experience. Despite that, the cuisine is characteristically Apulian, with an emphasis on fresh fish, tomato-based pastas, roasted lamb with potatoes, and antipasti offerings that might wow you with their pungent fresh fish (especially anchovies and sardines) and fresh marinated vegetables. It opened in the early 1980s in a former car repair shop—its post office box was no. 19.

3 Bari: Capital of Apulia

162 miles SE of Naples, 281 miles SE of Rome

The teeming seaport of **Bari,** the capital of Apulia and often called the "doorway to the Orient," has been an important port since ancient times. Because of the central location of the city, almost every one of the major European powers has made use of the port. The crusaders passed through on their way to the Holy Land. In more recent times, planes and ships departed from Bari during World War II to stage attacks on Yugoslavia and Greece.

ESSENTIALS

GETTING THERE   Until recently, several international airlines flew into Bari from the great cities of Europe, but at this writing, only two Italy-based airlines service Bari, **Alitalia** (☎ 01478/868-641 for reservations and information) flies into Bari from both Rome and Milan and **Air One** (☎ 01478/488-80) conducts twice-per-day flights from Rome. Although plans had been inaugurated for a new airport (which might be in service by the time of your visit), flights at press time land at the **Bari Palese Airport** (☎ 080/538-5320), less than 15 miles west of the city. A shuttle bus will take you to the bus station in Bari for 6,000L ($3.50). Otherwise, any of the taxis that queue up outside the arrivals terminal will drive you from the airport to the town's commercial center for around 35,000L ($20).

The main FS **train** network has seven trains per day that leave Rome for the 6-hour trip to Bari, arriving at the city station in Piazza Aldo Moro (☎ 080/521-6801) in the center. The one-way fare is 37,000L ($21). More frequent trips between Bari and some of the larger towns in the region are also provided by FS. The 2-hour ride from Brindisi or Taranto will cost 9,800L ($6); a 2½-hour trip from Lecce goes for 11,700L ($7). Several private lines also use the station.

Several **bus** companies serve the Bari area. Of these, the companies with the most convenient service are **SITA** (☎ 080/574-1800) and **Marozzi** (☎ 080/521-0365), which maintains a bus that travels between Bari and Rome at least once a day as part of a 4½-hour transit that costs 65,000L ($38) each way.

If you've got a **car**, take A14, coming down Italy's Adriatic coast and passing by Foggia, to Bari. A16 from Naples meets up with A14 about 72 miles west of Bari.

VISITOR INFORMATION   The **tourist office** is at Piazza Aldo Moro 32 (☎ 080/524-2244). It's open Monday to Friday 8:30am to 1pm; during summer, the hours are extended Monday to Friday 3 to 7pm and Saturday 8:30am to 1pm.

EXPLORING BARI

Bari is divided into two parts. The **modern section** dates from the 19th century, with wide palm-lined streets following a strict grid pattern. The area is home to the best restaurants, along with the more upscale hotels and shops.

In contrast, a twisting maze of narrow lanes characterizes the other section, called the **Città Vecchia (old city).** Buildings here date from Byzantine times, though the present look is medieval. This area is definitely worth a visit—the streets are filled with shops, old women in black hanging laundry out to dry, and hordes of children, many of whom bathe in the public fountains. Alas, the old town is also peopled with petty thieves and pickpockets who target tourists. Don't let fear keep you from enjoying the area—just guard your belongings closely and be very aware of your s urroundings.

To reach the old city from Stazione Centrale, head north to Piazza Umberto I and continue along one of several streets, perhaps Via Andrea da Bari, until you come to it. In the southwestern corner of the Città Vecchia is **Piazza Garibaldi,** a heartbeat center of the area. From here you can head west along Corso Vittorio Emanuele to the **Porto Vecchia (old port).** The pedestrians-only **Via Sparano** is the major shopping street. Finally, you may want to either drive or walk along one of the most scenic streets, **Lungomare Nazario Sauro,** running along the Porto Vecchia.

Basilica di San Nicola. Via Palazzo di Città. ☎ **080/521-1205.** Free admission. Daily 8am–noon and 3:30–7pm.

Bari's most famous attraction is this basilica, built during the 11th and 12th centuries to house the bones of the city's patron saint, known to many as Santa Claus. The saint was known for his kindness for children; in fact, he's said to have raised three from the dead after a butcher had sliced them up and preserved their bodies in brine. A painting depicting the resurrection of the children fills the back wall of the church. The bones of the saint, which legend says in 1087 were brought home from Mira in Asia Minor (now part of Turkey) by Barese sailors, are housed in an underground crypt. The church's other chief treasure is the white-marble bishop's throne in the upper part. The basilica itself was built in the Apulian-Romanesque style and incorporates parts of a palace once occupied by Byzantine rulers.

Cattedrale di Bari. Piazza dell'Odegitria. ☎ **080/521-1269.** Free admission. Daily 9am–noon and 5–7pm.

The narrow Strada di Carmine in back of the basilica leads to this cathedral, in much the same style. It's primarily from the 12th century but has been rebuilt and restored many times. A big rose window "protected" by monsters and grotesques, along with a squat bell tower, dominate the exterior. The interior is rather austere.

Swabian Castle (Castello Svevo). Piazza Federico di Svevia. ☎ **080/521-4361.** Admission 4,000L ($2.30). Mon–Sat 8:30am–1pm and 3:30–7pm, Sun 8:30am–1pm.

Looming behind the cathedral, this castle was built on a Roman fort but later redesigned by Frederick II. During the 16th century, Queen Isabella of Spain held court here. Though the castle is often closed to allow archaeologists to excavate mementos from Roman and Byzantine times, you can sometimes pass under the Gothic portal into the harmonious courtyard.

Archaeological Museum (Museo Archeologico). In the Palazzo dell'Anteneo, Piazza Umberto I. ☎ **080/521-1559.**

The most complete collection of Apulian archaeological material in Italy is shown here. Greek and Roman artifacts found in excavations in Bari province, including a rich collection of ancient vases and a remarkable array of bronzes, are displayed. The museum has been closed for renovations but should reopen late in 1999.

Provincial Picture Gallery (Pinacoteca Provinciale). Via Spalato 19. ☎ **080/521-2422.** Free admission. Tues–Sat 9:30am–1pm and 4–7pm, Sun 9am–1pm.

On the seaside promenade Lungomare Nazario Sauro, this gallery presents a rather dull collection of Italian art, covering late medieval to present times and including several paintings by well-known artists. Among these, works by Bellini, Veronese, and Tintoretto are the major attractions, though they're minor.

A CASTLE NEARBY
Castel del Monte. Atop a hill 35 miles from Bari. Admission 4,000L ($2.30). Apr–Sept Mon–Sat 9:30am–7pm, Sun 9am–1pm; Oct–Mar Mon–Sat 8:30am–1pm and 2pm–sunset, Sun 9am–1pm. Take the Bari–Nord train to Andria, then a bus to Spinazzola (10,000L/$6 round-trip). To drive, follow Rte. 96 toward Modugno; after 6 miles, transfer to A98 west for 17 miles, passing Bitonto and Terlizzi. Just past Ruvo di Puglia, get on Rte. 170 west for 12 miles.

Built for Frederick II from 1240 to 1250, this impressive and somewhat mysterious castle is arranged in a perfect octagon, with eight corner towers and eight trapezoidal rooms on each floor. Theories abound as to why it was erected. Scholars have ruled out its use as a military defense, and rumors of its construction as a prison have gone unproved. It's known that the castle was used as a hunting lodge at some point and may have served as an observatory. Although fully restored, many of the sculptures and decoration that characterized the interior were lost before the 18th century. Today the castle is mostly visited for its unique architecture and the views the upper levels provide of the Tavoliere and the surrounding countryside.

ACCOMMODATIONS

The **Stop-Over Bari** program (☎ 080/521-4538; e-mail stopover@inmedia.it), a cooperative effort between the city government and grassroots organizations to make Bari more attractive to backpackers headed for Greece, offers those under 30 a free campsite and other assistance. If you're older or just not willing to rough it but are still on a budget, Bari is probably not the place for you. Medium-priced or first-class lodgings are your best bet here.

Grand Hotel Ambasciatori. Via Omodeo 51, 70125 Bari. ☎ **080/501-0077.** Fax 080/502-1678. 191 units. A/C MINIBAR TV TEL. 220,000–290,000L ($128–$168) double; 500,000L ($290) suite. Rates include breakfast. AE, DC, MC, V. Parking 20,000L ($12).

This is a comfortable first-class facility on the outskirts. Equipped with its own rooftop heliport, the hotel also has panoramic elevators that provide sweeping views of the gardens and cityscape. The rooms are soundproof, attractively furnished, and well kept.

Dining: The hotel's well-appointed La Mongolfiera serves both classic Italian dishes and occasional specialties of Puglia.

Amenities: Concierge, room service, dry cleaning/laundry, secretarial service, baby-sitting, car-rental desk, solarium, gym nearby; heated pool.

Hotel Boston. Via Piccinni 155, 70122 Bari. ☎ **800/528-1234** in the U.S. or 080/521-6633 in Italy. Fax 080/524-6802. www.bestwestern.com. 70 units. A/C MINIBAR TV TEL. 150,000–210,000L ($87–$122) double. Rates include breakfast. AE, DC, MC, V. Parking 25,000L ($15).

The Boston is a modern hotel near the center of town, the port, and the rail station. It's on a major street, just off of Piazza Garibaldi and a short walk from the Bari's major attractions. A member of the Best Western chain, the Boston is one of the best middle-bracket hotels in Bari, with comfortable but uninspired bedrooms.

Dining/Diversions: The hotel doesn't offer a restaurant, serving only a buffet breakfast. However, it does offer an elegant bar where you can have aperitifs or drinks throughout the day—even a quick coffee.

Amenities: Concierge, room service, dry cleaning/laundry, newspaper delivery.

Jolly Hotel. Via Giulio Petroni 15, 70124 Bari. ☎ **080/556-4366.** Fax 080/556-5219. www.jollyhotels.com.it. 164 units. A/C MINIBAR TV TEL. 210,000L ($122) double. Rates include breakfast. AE, DC, MC, V. Parking 25,000L ($15).

Part of one of Italy's top four-star hotel groups, the Jolly is an up-to-date place. Built in 1974 about 1½ miles from the harbor, the hotel is convenient to most of Bari's important attractions. The rooms are spacious and well furnished and provide a comfortable respite from touring sticky Bari.

Dining: The hotel restaurant is open daily for lunch and dinner, serving a variety of local Italian main courses along with international cuisine.

Amenities: Concierge, room service, baby-sitting, dry cleaning/laundry.

Palace Hotel. Via Lombardi 13, 70122 Bari. ☎ **080/521-6551.** Fax 080/521-1499. E-mail: palaceh@tin.it. 207 units. A/C MINIBAR TV TEL. 270,000–310,000L ($157–$180) double; from 390,000L ($226) suite. Rates include breakfast. AE, DC, MC, V. Parking 20,000L ($12).

This first-class hotel offers the best accommodations in Bari, and the severe exterior lines belie the comfortable luxury of the interior. Antique furniture and reproductions of classic Italian art characterize the decor; each floor is furnished in a different style, from Louis XVI to Liberty of London.

Dining/Diversions: The Murat, an exclusive rooftop dining room, is well known for its sophisticated cuisine and city view. Also popular is the hotel's piano bar.

Amenities: Concierge, room service, dry cleaning/laundry, newspaper delivery, baby-sitting, courtesy car to the airport. jogging track, bike rentals.

Villa Romanazzi Carducci-Mercure. Via Giuseppe Capruzzi 326, 70124 Bari. ☎ **080/ 542-7400.** Fax 080/556-0297. 89 units. A/C MINIBAR TV TEL. 260,000–360,000L ($151– $209) double. Rates include breakfast. AE, DC, MC, V. Parking 20,000L ($12).

Old meets new in this hotel as structures of metal and glass rise from century-old Italian gardens complete with fountains and exotic plants. Although the rooms are a bit austere, the villa provides comfortable accommodations, and it's more intimate than the Palace, attracting a chic crowd.

Dining: An inviting dining room serves Italian and international dishes relying on market-fresh ingredients. The restaurant mainly attracts businesspeople and isn't especially lively in spite of its often superb offerings.

Amenities: Concierge, room service, baby-sitting, laundry/dry cleaning, pool.

DINING

Even if you're here for only a short time, try to visit one of the old town's restaurants, serving authentic Apulian cuisine at reasonable prices. However, these places often don't provide menus or itemized checks, so be careful—you may end up with something you can't eat that costs more than you'd bargained for. Most of the modern restaurants are in the commercial center of town.

Ai Due Ghiottoni. Via Putignani 11. ☎ **080/523-2240.** Reservations recommended. Main courses 20,000–28,000L ($12–$17). AE, DC, MC, V. Mon–Sat 12:30–3:30pm and 7:30pm– midnight. Closed Sun and Aug. ITALIAN/INTERNATIONAL.

This well-decorated restaurant is in the commercial center, near the burnt out Petruzzelli Theater. The cuisine includes both international and northern-Italian specialties as well as those from Puglia. Risotto ai frutti di mare, pasta with a variety of seafood, is a favorite. Also deservedly popular are the grilled lamb and the pappardelle (wide noodles) ai Due Ghiottoni. You might also try a local favorite, fava bean purée with chicory leaves. Various Adriatic fish are available, and the chef will prepare it as you like it.

✪ **La Nuova Vecchia Bari.** Via Dante Alighieri 47. ☎ **080/521-6496.** Reservations recommended. Main courses 18,000–32,000L ($10–$19); menu degustazione 70,000L ($41). AE, DC, MC, V. Sat–Thurs noon–3:30pm and 7:30–11pm. Closed Aug. BARESE.

This restaurant serves the best food in Bari. Concentrating on regional cuisine, menu items include spicy meats, fish, pastas, and seasonal vegetables. The restaurant is most known for its antipasti trolley, whose wide selection includes local mortadella and sausages and focaccia with anchovy, ricotta, onion, and olives. Desserts often use almonds as a base. The decor is strictly regional, and a meal here is a bit Rabelaisian. Locals really know how to tuck it in.

La Pignata. Via Melo 9. ☎ **080/523-2481.** Reservations recommended. Main courses 16,000–28,000L ($9–$16); fixed-price menu 50,000L ($29). AE, DC, MC, V. Tues–Sun noon– 3:30pm and 7:30pm–12:30am. Closed Aug. ITALIAN/APULIAN.

The modern setting and traditional food of this restaurant combine to create a pleasant dining experience. The varieties of homemade pasta are favorites, especially when accompanied by fresh local seafood. Other specialties are the Tiella alla barese (a kind of Italian paella) and a purée of fava beans and chicory leaves. The chefs offer a style of cookery that adheres to the ancient concepts of the Pugliese cuisine.

BARI AFTER DARK

Bari is home to two of southern Italy's most historic theaters. Badly destroyed in a 1991 fire, the **Teatro Petruzzelli**, Corso Cavour (☎ **080/521-3717**), remains under restoration with no opening date in sight. However, performances of drama, opera, and ballet are staged to appreciative audiences at the other historic theater, the **Teatro Piccini,** Corso Emmanuele 42 (☎ 080/521-1882). Theatrical performances are often staged at the **Teatro TEAM,** Via Caldarolla at the corner of Via Lapira (☎ 080/554-7730), a less imposing theater.

After dark, most of the young people gather on the streets between **Piazza Armando Diaz** and **Largo Eroi del Mare.** You may want to stop in for a drink in this area at **Baraonda,** 71 Largo G. Bruno (☎ 080/524-8382), or **Reiff,** Largo Adua 1 (no phone), which has live music and American food. **Night & Day,** Via Gentile 67 (☎ 080/549-2178), attracts lots of enthusiasts under 30 for dancing Wednesday to Saturday after 10pm. If you're looking for a more authentic Italian good time, catch a bus to Bisceglie, 24 miles from Bari. Here you'll find **Divanae Follie,** Via Ponte Lama 3 (☎ 080/958-0033), a dance club packed with sweaty patrons. The cover is 25,000L ($15). Closer, but not as popular, is **Arena,** Via Tridente 15/21 (no phone). The mix of Italian, American, and English music keeps dancers grooving into the night.

During summer, festivals keep the air in Bari filled with music. The **Fest della Musica** brings an eclectic mix of locals and visitors into the streets to enjoy free concerts that last all day and part of the night. The **Bari Rock Contest** at the Pineta San Francesco is held every year in August.

The largest fair in southern Italy, the **Levante Fair** attracts vendors from all over the world. Held adjacent to the municipal stadium, the event runs for 10 days in mid-September. The **Festival of San Nicola,** mid-April to early June, celebrates the city's patron saint. The tourist office will supply information and details about all these festivals.

4 Alberobello & the Trulli District

45 miles NW of Brindisi, 37 miles SE of Bari, 28 miles N of Taranto

The center of a triangle made up by Bari, Brindisi, and Taranto, the Valley of Itria has long been known for olive cultivation and the beehive-shaped houses dotting its landscape. These curious structures, called *trulli*, were built at least as early as the 13th century. Their whitewashed limestone walls and conical fieldstone roofs utilize the materials available in the area in such a way that mortar isn't used to keep the pieces together. Theories abound as to why they aren't built with mortar—the most popular being that the trulli, considered substandard peasant dwellings, had to be easily dismantled in case of a royal visit. See the box "The Mystery of the Trulli" for more speculation.

The center of the **Trulli District,** and home to the greatest concentration of trulli, is **Alberobello.** Here the streets are lined with some 1,000 of the buildings. You may feel as if you've entered into some page of a child's storybook as you walk through the maze of cobbled streets curving through Italy's most fantastic village. The crowds of visitors will quickly relieve you of any such thoughts, however. Many of the trulli have been converted into souvenir shops where you can buy everything from postcards to miniature models of the dwellings. Be careful though: If you enter you're expected to buy something—and the shop owners will let you know it.

ESSENTIALS

GETTING THERE   FSE **trains** leave Bari every hour (every 2 hours on Sunday) heading to Alberobello. The trip takes about 1¾ hours and costs 5,700L ($3.30). To

The Mystery of the Trulli

The architectural mystery of southern Italy, the igloo-shaped *trulli* are the country's most idiosyncratic habitations, built of local limestone without mortar. A hole in the top allows smoke to escape. Southwest of Bari, in an area roughly hemmed in by Gioia del Colle to the west, Ostuni to the south, and the Adriatic coast to the east, these strange whitewashed buildings are roofed with tall spiraling cones of a stone prevalent in the region. Trulli are found nowhere else in the entire country.

The structures look somewhat primitive, giving them an air of being ancient, though most of the existing buildings are less than 2 centuries old. Many are new constructions, since the people of the area are attached to their unique architectural form, using it to house businesses as well as homes. The trulli are of a uniformly small size. If more space is needed, local custom dictates the construction of several connected trulli rather than a single larger one. In fact, only one trullo in the entire area dared expand into a two-story structure (see below).

Some locals call trulli signalmen's houses, and others refer to them as monuments and point out obscure symbols that adorn the most traditional ones. These symbols were copied over the centuries from the emblems that embellish the few remaining ancient structures. One of the most puzzling things is that, despite the great attachment to the buildings, no one in the region can tell you why the form came into favor in the first place, what the traditional emblems symbolize, or even why they're called by any of the names associated with them.

The people of Alberobello don't seem to care where the trulli came from. Only a few scholars have tackled the problem, in the end making half-hearted suggestions that perhaps they're of Saracenic or Greek origin—theories that have been neither proved nor disproved. One line of logic points out that limestone, a calcareous rock found in abundant stratification throughout the region, is easily separated into thin layers that can readily be shaped into crude bricks that don't require mortar when relayered. The dome design also allows heat to rise, perhaps slightly cooling the living space, a significant factor in the region's brutal summer heat. Given that the area has long been impoverished, perhaps the design is nothing but good old ingenuity, a means of cheaply constructing homes and businesses with the materials at hand—but that still doesn't explain the hieroglyphics.

One suggestion is that the origin of the trulli had to do with outwitting Ferdinand I of Aragón. This king ordered that Apulians couldn't build permanent dwellings. That way, he could move the labor force around as he chose. Apulians constructed these houses so they could be dismantled when they spotted the king's agents. Another theory suggests that during Spanish rule a tax was levied on individual homes, except for unfurnished homes, for which the trulli qualified when their roofs were removed.

Other theories link them with similar structures in Mycenae and suggest their origins may be as old as 3000 B.C. Apulia was part of Magna Graecia and could've come under the influence. Similarities have been noted between the trulli of Apulia and the "sugarloaf" houses of Syria. It's been suggested that this idea, traveling west, influenced builders in southern Italy who initially used the trulli as tombs. It's also been noted that soldiers returning from the Crusades may have brought the architectural curiosity to Alberobello.

find the trulli, follow Via Mazzini, which turns into Via Garibaldi, until you reach Piazza del Popolo. Turn left on Largo Martellotta, which will take you to the edge of the popular tourist area. If you've got a **car,** head south of Bari on S100, then east (signposted) on S172.

VISITOR INFORMATION   The **tourist office** in Alberobello is off of the central square, Piazza del Popolo, at Piazza Ferdinando IV (☎ **080/932-3171**), open daily 9am to noon and 4 to 8pm.

SEEING THE SIGHTS

The most well-known of the trulli is the **trullo sovrano (soverreign trullo)** in Alberobello at Piazza Sacramento. The 50-foot structure, the only true two-story trullo, was built during the 19th century to serve as headquarters for a religious confraternity and carbonari sect. To find it, head down Corso Vittorio Emanuele until you get to the church, then take a right. The trullo sovrano is open daily 10am to 1pm and 3 to 7pm, charging no admission.

On the outskirts of Alberobello, you can also visit the small town of **Castellana,** home to a series of caverns that have been carved out over the centuries by water streaming through the rocky soil. A wide stairway leads you down through a tunnel into a cavern called the Grave. From here, a series of paths winds through other underground rooms filled with the strange shapes of stalagmites and stalactites. The culmination of the journey into the earth ends with the majestic Grotta Bianca, where alabaster concretions are the result of centuries of Mother Nature's work. You can visit the Grotte di Castellana only on guided tours, usually one per hour until early afternoon at 15,000L to 30,000L ($9 to $17); call ☎ **080/896-5511** for a schedule. Be sure to bring a sweater—the average underground temperature is 59°F, even on hot summer days.

SHOPPING

Most popular among visitors to the Trulli District are the hand-painted clay figurines that abound in every souvenir shop. You can also find a good assortment of fabrics and rugs at reasonable prices.

One of the most evocative souvenirs would be a miniature re-creation of the region's legendary trulli. Crafted in the same type of stone that was used by the ancient builders, they're small-scale duplicates of the originals, ranging in size from a simple rendering to a replica of an entire village. The artisan is **Giuseppe Maffei,** and he works out of his workshop at 741 Via Duca d'Aosta, in Alberobello (☎ **080/432-5471**). Prices range from 15,000L to 100,000L ($9 to $58), depending on the size and intricacy of the model you select.

ACCOMMODATIONS

Most visitors visit the area for a 1-day excursion; Alberobello's hotels are limited. You may be able to find individual renovated trulli that are rented to two to eight people for a relatively cheap rate. Call the tourist office for information. Otherwise, the accommodations here are usually more expensive than those in Bari and other nearby towns.

Hotel Colle del Sole. Via Indipendenza 63, 70011 Alberobello. ☎ **080/721-814.** Fax 080/ 721-370. E-mail: decarlo@mailbox.media.it. 24 units. TV TEL. 80,000L ($46) double. AE, DC, MC, V. Parking 10,000L ($6).

On the edge of town, a few minutes walk from the trulli zone, this hotel is a modern two-story structure. The rooms are basic yet comfortable and have small balconies. A friendly staff is eager to make your stay a pleasant one. The hotel also has a restaurant serving both local and international dishes. Further grace notes are a music cafe, a coffee bar, gardens, and a lounge with TV.

Hotel Dei Trulli. Via Cadore 32, 70011 Alberobello. ☎ **080/432-3555.** Fax 080/432-3560. E-mail: htrulli@inmedia.it. 19 units. MINIBAR TV TEL. 170,000L ($99) per person double with half board. AE, MC, V.

In what's almost a village unto itself, Dei Trulli offers the experience of living in one of the unique beehive-shaped trulli. Each mini-apartment may have one, two, or three cones—circular buildings wedged together in the Siamese fashion. Most have a bedroom with a bath, a small sitting room with a fireplace, and a patio. The complex also has a pool and attractively landscaped grounds. In the restaurant, the cuisine is mostly regional, presented in individual ceramic pots. The pignata (veal stew) with a glass of red Primotivo wine from Turi makes a good meal.

✪ **Hotel Il Melograno.** Contrada Torricella, 70043 Monopoli. ☎ **080/690-9030.** Fax 080/747-908. www.melograno.com. E-mail: melograno@melograno.com. 37 units. 180,000–300,000L ($104–$174) per person double; 270,000–465,000L ($157–$270) per person suite. Rates include breakfast. AE, DC, MC, V. From Alberobello, follow the signs to Monopoli and drive 11 miles east.

This is the most elegant hotel in Apulia and the only Relais & Châteaux south of Naples. Occupying what was the centerpiece for a large farm and estate during the 16th century and enlarged with a discreet modern wing in the mid-1900s, it sits less than a mile from the hamlet of Monopoli. The creative force behind the place is a hard-working Bari-based antiques dealer, Camillo Gurra. His polite staff spends long hours maintaining a roster of important antiques and paintings that decorate the comfortable and artfully rustic premises of this charming country inn.

Dining: In the main hotel, lunches at about 60,000L ($35) are served beside the pool, and dinners at about 80,000L ($46) are served on a flowering terrace or in a formal dining room. The cuisine is the very finest in the area, both in its preparation (only top chefs are employed) and in its elegant presentation. At the beach club, simple lunches are available.

Amenities: Concierge, room service, twice-daily maid service, dry cleaning/laundry, baby-sitting; pool, shuttle bus (June to September) taking guests at frequent intervals to/from private beach club 3 miles away.

DINING

✪ **Il Poeta Contadino.** Via Indipendenza 21. ☎ **080/432-1917.** Reservations recommended. Main courses 28,000–32,000L ($16–$19). AE, DC, MC, V. June–Sept daily noon–3pm an 7–11pm; Oct–May Tues–Sun noon–3pm and 7–11pm. ITALIAN/APULIAN.

In the center of Alberobello, beneath the arched and vaulted stone ceilings of what was built in the 1700s as a barn, this is the region's most elegant restaurant. It's managed by Leonardo Marco and his Canadian-born wife, Carol, who together prepare and serve an array of sophisticated dishes mostly based on seafood. Their menu changes with the season but is likely to include such culinary staples as *involtini* of eggplant, monkfish, and prawns with mussel sauce. A signature dish is *pesce alla Leonardo*, sea bass that's steamed in a mix of water, wine, and oil and served with a chilled sauce made from fine-chopped cherry tomatoes, chives, olive oil, black olives, and vinegar. Also look for roasted lamb on a bed of braised chicory. The wine list is one of the most comprehensive in the region and was the winner of a *Wine Spectator* award in 1997.

Trullo d'Oro. Via Cavallotti 27. ☎ **080/432-1820.** Reservations required Sat–Sun. Main courses 15,000–40,000L ($9–$23). AE, DC, MC, V. Tues–Sun noon–3pm and 8–11pm. Closed Jan.

Housed in several linked trulli, this rustic restaurant is one of the town's best. The cuisine consists mainly of well-prepared local and regional dishes. Specialties are purée of fava beans and chicory leaves, roast lamb with lampasciuni (a wild onion from the region), and the chef's special pasta, orecchiette served with bitter greens or tomatoes, olive oil, garlic, and arugula. Southern desserts, like ricotta cooked with marmalade, are also served.

5 Brindisi

563 miles SE of Rome, 45 miles E of Taranto

Known to the Romans as Brundisium, **Brindisi** was the terminus of the Appian Way. Many famous Romans passed through: Augustus, Marc Antony, Cicero, and Virgil to name a few. An important seaport throughout its history, Brindisi figured in many of Europe's historical movements, including the Crusades. More recently, the town was a strategic Adriatic port during both world wars.

Though the Italian word *brindisi* has come into the language of the world as a toast, at first you may not want to raise your glass to this town. It is today, as it has always been, an embarkation point for those crossing the Adriatic to Greece. This means that the place is filled with backpackers and students waiting to catch a boat across. Get away from the main streets, though, and you'll find a pleasant if not overly exciting city.

ESSENTIALS

GETTING THERE The **FS train line** (☎ 01831/521-975) has service to the main station in Piazza Crispi, about 1½ miles from the ferry port. Four trains per day leave Rome for the 7-hour trip; towns closer to Brindisi, such as Taranto and Lecce, have more frequent service. During summer, two trains daily go all the way to the Brindisi Marittima station at the port. **Miccolis,** Corso Garibaldi 109 (☎ 0831/560-678), has three buses a day running between Naples and Brindisi. The trip takes 5 hours and costs 40,000L ($23) one-way.

If you have a **car** and are in Naples, it's 233 miles to Brindisi. Take A3 for 30 miles to E45/A3, driving toward Salerno, where you get E847/SS407 east. Drive past Potenza and continue another 62 miles to E90/Route 106. Head north on this road for 30 miles, curving around the Gulf of Taranto. At Taranto, veer northwest on E90/Route 7 to drive into Brindisi.

VISITOR INFORMATION The **tourist office** is at Piazza Dionisi (☎ 0831/521-944), open Monday to Friday 8am to 2pm (Tuesday also 4 to 7pm).

SEEING THE SIGHTS

While waiting for your ferry to Greece, you may want to explore some of Brindisi. Most of the sights of interest are close to the port, so you won't have to go far and risk missing the boat. Start by heading toward the **Duomo** at Piazza del Duomo; you'll be able to find it by the steeple poking out from the surrounding cityscape. A mosaic

A Brindisi Warning

Because of the constant flow of people through the town, Brindisi has more than its share of petty thieves; guard your money and passport closely. If you're not heading straight to Greece, it's best to store your bags—lone backpackers are considered easy targets.

Gateway to Greece

Many parts of southern Italy, including Brindisi, were colonized by settlers from ancient Greece, so for an insight into the travel and trade that once flourished between the two regions, you might want to hop over to Greece for a quick visit. Transit between the two countries involves a baffling array of options, with departures originating in Brindisi as well as Bari, Venice, and Ancona. Greek ports include Piraeus (the seaport servicing Athens), the island of Crete, and the busy ports of Patras and Izmir (Turkey). At least half a dozen Italian operators and as many Greek operators maintain ferries with a labyrinth of routes and a changing roster of seasonal schedules.

The easiest and quickest way to visit Greece is taking a **hydrofoil** from Brindisi to the island of Corfu, a youth-oriented site loaded with discos, bars, and beaches. It departs daily at 2pm, takes 3 hours of transit time, and can't transport cars. Depending on the season, the price is 90,000L to 130,000L ($52 to $75) each way. The busiest route from Brindisi, however, is a **ferry** service to Patras, gateway to Athens, and site of most of the truck and lorry passages transiting the Adriatic. Transit aboard one of the car-ferries takes 12 hours and costs 50,000L ($29) for a car with one driver. Each additional person in the car pays 50,000L ($29). If you want access to a cramped private cabin that'll be yours for 12-hour trip, you'll pay a per-person supplement that begins between 65,000L to 100,000L ($38 to $58), depending on the season. In addition to the prices above, each person pays a port tax of 10,000L ($6).

One of the best ways to book a ticket to the glories of Greece is contacting any of the travel agencies lining the side of Corso Garibaldi. Basically, you can take your pick, as they all offer, with slight variations, access to basically the same things. But one of the best is **Italia Ferry,** Corso Garibaldi 96 (☎ 0831/509-305), which, though brusque during periods of heavy demand, enjoys a wide access to the products offered by each of the ferry lines. If you prefer to contact the lines directly, you'll run the risk of being steered only toward the products offered by that individual line. Three of the biggest are **Adriatica,** Corso Garibaldi 85–87 (☎ 0831/523-825); **Fragline,** Corso Garibaldi 88 (☎ 0831/590-310); and **Medlink,** Corso Garibaldi 56 (☎ 0831/527-667).

floor from the 12th century is worth seeing, though the rest of the structure was rebuilt in the 18th century and is unremarkable.

To the left of the Duomo, near steep stairs leading to the water, is a **Roman column** crowned with carvings of several deities—Neptune, Jove, Mars, and eight tritons tower on the marble cylinder marking the end of the ancient Appian way. Nearby, a small **Archaeological Museum (Museo Archeologico),** Piazza del Duomo 8 (☎ 0831/221-401), presents numerous finds from excavations along with pottery and sculpture. It's open Monday, Wednesday, and Friday 9am to 1pm (Tuesday also 3:30 to 6:30pm). Admission is free.

Also in the area is the **Castello Svevo,** a defense fortification built by Frederick II in the 13th century. It's not open to the public, but from the harborfront side you can look back at the oldest part of Brindisi and the Roman column.

If you just want a break from Roman ruins and artifacts, you may want to take a good book and head to the **Cloister of San Benedetto.** A short walk down Via Tarantini takes you to the cloister, where a peaceful courtyard awaits those looking for a place to relax before boarding their ferries to Greece.

To see Brindisi's greatest attraction, you'll have to leave the harbor area: **Santa Maria del Casale** lies just north of the city, on the way to the airport (follow Via Provinciale S. Vito around the harbor; it becomes Via E. Ciciriello, then Via Benedetto Brin, then Via U. Maddalena before heading toward the airport; the church is near a sports complex). Started in the 1320s, the structure cannot be confined to one particular period style or cultural influence. The two-toned sandstone facade consists of delicate patterns that contrast with the vertical lines and severe arches. Inside, Byzantine-inspired frescoes adorn the walls. Most notable is the brightly colored portrayal of the *Last Judgment*. Painted by Rinaldo, from Taranto, the work graphically depicts saints and sinners as they're judged and meet their fate. Sadly, many of the other frescoes are faded and in disrepair, though they're still of interest to those who take time to examine them. It's open daily 9am to 4pm but is often closed for no apparent reason.

For a different kind of experience, you may want to visit the **open-air market** off Corso Umberto on Via Battisti. Here you can join the locals as they search for the best ingredients for their meals. You may come here to wander through just for fun, but the massive quantities of fresh fruit overflowing from the stalls and scent of fresh pizza and focaccia drifting through the air will probably tempt you to buy at least a snack.

ACCOMMODATIONS

Most travelers spend only a few hours in Brindisi; few choose to stay overnight. So owners are reluctant to invest in their hotels—most are dull and uninspired. The one exception is the Masseria San Domenico outside of town (below).

✪ **Masseria San Domenico.** Litoranea 379, 72010 Savelletri di Fasano. ☎ **080/ 482-7990.** Fax 080/482-7978. www.albert.net/masseria. E-mail: masseriasdomenico@albert. net. 32 units. A/C MINIBAR TV TEL. 320,000–520,000L ($186–$302) double; 1,000,000– 1,400,000L ($580–$812) suite. AE, DC, MC, V. From Brindisi, drive 28 miles north, following the signs to Bari.

One of the region's most historically important hotels sits in an olive grove about half a mile from the harborfront of an obscure fishing village of Savelletri, more or less midway between Bari and Brindisi. Though its foundations date back to the 1100s, when it was a stronghold of the semimonastical order of the Knights of Malta, the building you'll see is a 17th-century construction loosely based on a severe interpretation of baroque models as developed in other parts of Italy. Until 1996, it was a stately private home, but today, a native son, Francesco Pellegrino, serves as manager, bringing to the job the experience and polish he gathered after years of living and working in Milan. The decor is evocative of an aristocratic residence in the 19th century, with paintings, antiques, and objets d'art. Views from the guest rooms encompass either the sea or the surrounding olive groves.

Dining: There's an elegant bar and a dignified restaurant serving excellent dinners to guests and to nonguests who phone in advance. Meals average 70,000L ($41).

Amenities: Concierge, room service, dry cleaning/laundry, baby-sitting; large pool.

Hotel Majestic. Corso Umberto I, 151, 72100 Brindisi. ☎ **0831/222-941.** Fax 0831/ 524-071. 68 units. A/C MINIBAR TV TEL. 220,000L ($128) double. Rates include buffet breakfast. AE, DC, MC, V. Parking 20,000L ($12).

In the late 1970s, this was a member of the nationwide Jolly chain, but it broke away to become an independent entity in its own right. Inside, you'll find a family-run hotel directly across from the rail station; it provides comfortable accommodations for spending the night before or after a boat ride across the Adriatic. If you don't want to venture into the crowded streets to search for a place to dine, the hotel also has a restaurant and bar, but the cuisine is only standard.

Hotel Mediterraneo. Via Aldo Moro 70, 72100 Brindisi. ☎ **0831/582-811.** Fax 0831/ 587-858. 65 units. A/C TV TEL. 190,000L ($110) double. Rates include continental breakfast. AE, DC, MC, V. Parking 20,000L ($12).

This modern and fairly comfortable hotel just outside the city center is ranked immediately after the Majestic in standards of comfort. The rooms are rather blandly furnished, but many have balconies and look over the city toward the sea. The hotel's restaurant serves an international menu centered around well-prepared seafood. Service is prompt and friendly. An added bonus is the private minibus, offering service throughout the city on request.

DINING

Tourist menus are served by most restaurants on the main street. These are best avoided—though they're low in price, the portions are so small you'll need to eat twice to get your fill. Depending on the strength of your stomach, there are also some Brindisi dishes you may want to stay away from—like *gnummarieddi* (spit-cooked goat entrails) and *stacchiodde* (pig ears in tomato sauce).

La Lanterna. Via Tarantini 14. ☎ **0831/564-026.** Reservations recommended. Main courses 16,000–24,000L ($9–$14); fixed-price menu 45,000L ($26). AE, DC, MC, V. Mon–Sat 12:30–2:30pm and 8–11:30pm. Closed Aug 10–30. ITALIAN/APULIAN.

Near Piazza Vittoria, this restaurant is elegant, occupying a building constructed as an inn during the 1400s; it has a garden where diners can enjoy meals during summer. Along with a well-chosen collection of wines, La Lanterna specializes in seafood. The pasta is all homemade with whole wheat and is served in rich sauces. The ravioli ripieni di pesce made with fresh seafood is savory and filling. Also good is the maccheroncini alla contadina, the old-fashioned "housewife" style of cooking macaroni.

BRINDISI AFTER DARK

A citywide celebration, the **City of Brindisi Festival** is held throughout summer. Folklore, art, and music can be enjoyed most nights. The tourist office has complete details.

6 Lecce: The Florence of the South

25 miles SE of Brindisi, 54 miles E of Taranto, 562 miles SE of Rome

Often called "the Florence of the South," **Lecce** lies in the heart of the Salento Peninsula—the "heel" of the Italian boot. The town was founded before the time of the ancient Greeks, but it's best known for the architecture, barocco leccese (Lecce Baroque), that defines many of its buildings. Dating from Lecce's heyday in the 16th, 17th, and 18th centuries, these structures are made mostly of fine-grained yellow limestone. Masons delighted in working with the golden material; their efforts turned the city into what one architectural critic called a "gigantic bowl of overripe fruit." Alas, recent restorations have taken away much of the color as workers have whitewashed the buildings.

For centuries, Lecce has been neglected by tourists. Perhaps it's for this reason that many of the baroque-style buildings have remained intact—progress hasn't overrun the city with modern development. Lecce's charm lies in these displays of the lighter baroque (though many buildings are now in dire need of repair).

ESSENTIALS

GETTING THERE   Lecce is connected to Brindisi by hourly **train** service on the state-run FS line. For service from points east and south, you'll have to take the FSE line—which isn't known for its speed. Several trains coming from Otranto and Gallipoli enter Lecce each day. The train station is about a 1½ miles from Piazza Sant'Oronzo, in the center of the old quarter. Call ☎ **1478/88-088** in Italy only for schedules and information. STP **buses** provide service to Lecce from areas not serviced by train. The tourist office has schedules. Or call **Sud-Est** at ☎ **0832/347-634.** If you've got a **car,** take Rte. 613 from Brindisi.

VISITOR INFORMATION   The **tourist office** is at Via 25 Luglio (☎ **0832/ 248-092**), open Monday to Saturday 9am to 1pm (Monday to Friday also 5 to 7pm).

SEEING THE SIGHTS

Piazza Sant'Oronzo is a good place to begin a stroll through Lecce. The 2nd-century A.D. Roman column, **Colonna Romana,** erected here once stood near its mate in Brindisi and together served to mark the end of the Appian Way. Lightning toppled this column in 1528, and the Brindisians left it lying on the ground until 1661, at which time Lecce purchased it and set the pillar up in their home town. St. Oronzo, for whom the square is named, now stands atop it guarding the area. At the southern side of the piazza are the remains of a **Roman amphitheater.** Dating from the 1st century B.C., it accommodated 20,000 fans who came to watch bloody fights between gladiators and wild beasts.

North of the piazza, Via Umberto I leads to the **Basilica di Santa Croce** (☎ **0832/ 261-957**). This ornate display of Leccese Baroque architecture took almost 1½ centuries to complete. Architect Gabriele Riccardo began work in the mid-15th century; the final touches weren't added until 1680. The facade bears some similarity to the Spanish Plateresque style and is peopled by guardian angels, grotesque demons, and a variety of flora and fauna. St. Benedict and St. Peter are also depicted. The top part of the facade— the flamboyant part—is the work of Antonio Zimbalo, who was called Zingarello (gypsy). The interior is laid out in a Latin cross plan and is in a simple Renaissance style. The basilica is open daily 7am to 12:30pm and 4 to 7pm. Admission is free.

Down Via Vittorio Emanuele, the **Duomo,** Piazza del Duomo (☎ **0832/ 308-557**), stands in a closed square. The building, which has two facades, was reconstructed between 1659 and 1670 by Zingarello. To the left of the duomo, the campanile towers 210 feet above the piazza. The cathedral is open daily 7:30am to 12:30pm and 4 to 7pm, and admission is free. On the opposite side of the cathedral is the **Bishop's Place (Palazzo Vescovile),** where Lecce's archbishop still lives today. Also in the courtyard is a seminary, built between 1694 and 1709 by Giuseppe Cino, who was a student of Zimbalo. Its decorations have been compared to those of a wedding cake. A baroque well, extraordinarily detailed with garlands and clusters of flowers and fruit, stands in the seminary's courtyard.

The collection of bronze statuettes, Roman coins, and other artifacts at the **Provincial Museum (Museo Provinciale),** Viale Gallipoli (☎ **0832/247-025**), will keep your interest for a while. It's worth the time to stop by to have a look at the ornately decorated 13th-century gospel cover. Inlaid with enamel of blue, white, and gold, it's a rare treasure. There's also a small picture gallery here. It's open Monday to Friday 9am to noon and 4:30 to 7:30pm. Admission is free.

SHOPPING

The hot, arid landscapes of southern Italy have fostered some of Europe's finest metalworkers. For an example of the wrought-iron goods (trivets, ornamental grills, and the like) that have traditionally derived from Lecce, visit **Salvatore Mancarella,** Via Fanteria 95 (☎ **0832/634-218**). For a different selection of local crafts, including cartapesta (papier-mâché), ceramics, and terra-cotta, go to **Mostra dell' Artigianato,** Via Rubichi 21 (☎ **0832/246-758**). And if you're interested in any of the wines and foodstuffs on the region, head for a food emporium that's been here as long as anyone can remember, **Enoteca,** Via Cesare Battisti 23 (☎ **0832/302-832**). Usually, they'll let you taste a glass of whatever wine you're interested in before you buy a bottle.

ACCOMMODATIONS

The baroque architecture that Lecce is famous for is lacking in its hotels. Most are modern structures built to accommodate large numbers of visitors who care more about seeing the town and surrounding area than spending time in their rooms.

Albergo Delle Palme. Via di Leuca 90, 73100 Lecce. ☎ and fax **0832/347-171.** 96 units. A/C TV TEL. 150,000–180,000L ($87–$104) double. Rates include breakfast. AE, DC, MC, V. Free parking.

This is the best hotel of the middle-bracket choices, within easy walking distance of the major baroque monuments. The public rooms, with their overstuffed leather furniture and paneled walls, are warm and inviting. The guest rooms are comfortably decorated with painted iron beds and small sitting areas. The hotel also operates a good restaurant, serving both regional and national cuisine.

Hotel Cristal. Via Marinosci 16, 73100 Lecce. ☎ **0832/372-314.** Fax 0832/315-109. 64 units. A/C TV TEL. 170,000L ($99) double. Rates include breakfast. AE, DC, MC, V. Parking 16,000L ($9).

This metal-and-glass high-rise is a good choice for comfort at a reasonable price. The glossy marble lobby and lounge area is severe but not sterile and offers a pleasant place to sit and enjoy a drink. The guest rooms vary in size and are decorated monochromatically in purples, pinks, or blues; a small refrigerator and a safe are standard. The hotel also has tennis courts and a large garage.

Hotel President. Via Salandra 6, 73100 Lecce. ☎ **0832/311-881.** Fax 0832/372-283. 154 units. A/C MINIBAR TV TEL. 240,000L ($139) double; from 300,000L ($174) suite. Rates include buffet breakfast. AE, DC, MC, V. Parking 10,000L ($6).

Although this hotel lies near the historical baroque center, it's a severely modern structure. The rooms are decorated in the browns and oranges that were the rage during the 1970s but are large and comfortable. Luckily, the service here makes up for the not-so-appealing decor.

Dining: Fresh pastries and breads are the highlights of the breakfast buffet. The restaurant serves good regional and international dishes at lunch and dinner.

Amenities: Concierge, room service, dry cleaning/laundry, newspaper delivery, twice-daily maid service, baby-sitting, car-rental desk, tour desk.

DINING

During your stay, be sure to sample some of the specialties of the Salento region, like a tasty combination of mozzarella and tomato wrapped in a light pastry shell.

I Tre Moschettieri. Via Paisiello, 73100 Lecce. ☎ **0832/308-484.** Main courses 8,000–20,000L ($4.65–$12). DC, MC, V. Mon–Sat noon–3pm and 7pm–midnight. ITALIAN/PIZZA/APULIAN.

Although this restaurant has two rooms, most visitors choose to have their meal on the alfresco patio. The tables throughout the restaurant are widely spaced and allow for easy conversation. Offerings from the cucina rustica here include a variety of fresh seafood dishes and a vast selection of made-to-order pizzas. Local politicians often frequent this place, where formal service at moderate prices is the rule.

Ristorante Villa G.C. della Monica. Via SS. Giacomo e Fillippo 40. ☎ **0832/458-432.** Reservations recommended. Main courses 8,000–20,000L ($4.80–$12). AE, DC, MC, V. Wed–Mon 12:30–3pm and 8–10:30pm. SOUTHERN ITALIAN/INTERNATIONAL.

The charming Valenti family will tell you that their restaurant's name is a shortened version of the name of the villa's builder, Giovanni Camillo della Monica. This is one of Lecce's most stately villas, built of chiseled stone between 1550 and 1600. There are four dining rooms (one of which is a palatial showcase for more than 400 diners and another available only for private parties) and a flower-strewn terrace overlooking a historic neighborhood near Piazza Mazzini. The menu items are steeped in local culinary traditions and emphasize a regional tubular pasta called strozzapetti (a bit smaller than penne), usually served with clams, mussels, crabmeat, and squid. Other specialties are well-seasoned filet steak al tartufo (with black truffles) and fresh fish that seems to taste better when baked in a salt crust to seal in the moisture.

LECCE AFTER DARK

Because of the large student population at the University of Lecce, there's usually something to keep night owls entertained. Nightfall usually sees the emergence of young people who flock to the main piazza to join friends for a drink. **Piazzetta del Duca d'Atena** is an especially popular hangout. For a more active night, you may want to head to **Corto Maltese,** Via Giusti 23 (no phone). Wednesday to Monday 9pm to 2am, crowds gather to dance the night away.

July and August are good times to come to Lecce if you're interested in enjoying authentic Italian nightlife. During these months the **Estate Musicale Leccese** has nightly festivals of music and dance. Tamer tourists may want to visit the public gardens of the city during July when **plays** (and sometimes operas) are performed for the public. In September, the churches of Lecce are venues for a **festival of baroque music.** The tourist office (above) will provide complete details.

A SIDE TRIP TO GALLIPOLI

Twenty-three miles southwest of Lecce, on the Gulf of Taranto side of the Salento Peninsula, lies **Gallipoli.** This isn't the Gallipoli infamous in history books as the sight of one of the bloodiest battles ever fought; that World War I landmark is part of Turkey. The Italian town has a much quieter and less tragic past. Originally named Kallipolis (beautiful city) by the Greeks, the present town still has a distinct Greek look. The medieval quarter, once a small island, is especially inviting to explore, with its twisting lanes and plain whitewashed houses.

It's best to rent a car for this trip; train service to Gallipoli from Lecce is extremely slow and public transportation in the area limited. It's a quick 25-minute drive down to the town from Lecce, perfect for a day trip to the beach.

SEEING THE SIGHTS

Many people who come to Gallipoli head straight for the beaches. **Baia Verde,** just south of the town, is especially popular. However, if you take the time to drive down from Lecce, you might as well see what the town has to offer.

One of the most interesting places to visit is the **Civic Museum (Museo Civico),** Via De Pace (☎ **0833/264-224**). There's a little of everything here; it's almost as if the townspeople had cleaned out their closets and made what they found into a museum. The collection covers several centuries and many aspects of life—from unexploded sea mines to clothing from the 18th century. The museum is open Sunday to Tuesday, Thursday, and Friday 8:30am to 1pm and 4 to 6pm.

The Greek **nymphaion,** a fountain elaborately decorated with mythological scenes, can be found in the new town near the bridge. It's the only fountain of this type left in Italy, though there are a few still left in Greece.

The town also has a **cathedral** from the 1400s and a **castle** jutting out into the Ionian sea. The circular fortress has protected the city for centuries; locals fought off Charles of Anjou's men for 7 months here and troops from England attacked the castle in 1809.

If you drive to Gallipoli, you can continue on to discover the tip of the Salento Peninsula, often called **Finibus Terrae (Land's End).** The Temple of Minerva that was once used by ancient sailors to trace their course has been replaced with the church of Santa Maria di Leuca, though stones and dolmens that stand in the area are reminders of the long-ago civilization.

Also nearby is **Casarano,** the birthplace of Boniface IX, who was pope from 1339 to 1404. The small church of Casaranello is here; early Christian mosaics adorn the walls.

ACCOMMODATIONS

Grand Hotel Costa Brada. Strada Litoranea, 73014 Gallipoli. ☎ **0833/202-551.** Fax 0833/202-555. www.kronos.clio.it/costab/costa.htm. E-mail: costabrada@mail4.clio.it. 80 units. A/C TV TEL. 250,000L ($145) double. AE, DC, MC, V. Free parking.

With two pools, tennis courts, a private beach, and its own nightclub, the Costa Brada is more of a resort than a hotel, a modern building with typical Mediterranean styling. It's outside Gallipoli, about 4 miles down a scenic seaside road. This is the area's best place to stay, with attractively furnished and well-maintained rooms, each with a balcony opening onto a view of the sea. The hotel attracts an international crowd who can be seen in its elegant public rooms.

Dining: The chefs are the best around, expert at preparing both an international and a regional Apulian cuisine. There's also an American snack bar. When the weather's right, terrace dining alfresco is possible.

Amenities: Room service, laundry/dry cleaning, concierge, baby-sitting; two pools, tennis courts, private beach; Jacuzzi, sauna, Turkish baths, solarium, gym, massages, beauty center, bike rentals, water-skiing facilities, hairdresser, heliport.

DINING

Ristorante Marecaro. Lungomare Marconi. ☎ **0833/266-143.** Reservations recommended. Main courses 15,000–25,000L ($9–$15). AE, DC, MC, V. Daily noon–4pm and 7pm–midnight. Closed Tues in winter. GALLIPOLI/ITALIAN.

The Marecaro, in a circa-1900 villa on a small island connected to the mainland by a bridge, is a popular favorite of locals. In any of the three dining rooms or on a flowering terrace with a view of the sea you'll enjoy the cuisine of Antonio Giungato, who serves dishes immersed in the cuisine of Gallipoli. Fish dishes are a staple, with emphasis on a spicy version of *zuppe di pesce* (fish soup), *risotto alla pescatora* (rice flavored with seafood), linguine with seafood and a creamy white sauce; and sophisticated combinations of calamarfi, octopus, sea bass, and other fish culled from nearby waters. Each dessert is homemade.

7 Taranto: Birthplace of the Tarantella

44 miles W of Brindisi, 62 miles SE of Bari, 331 SE of Rome

Taranto, known to the ancient Greeks as Taras, is said to have been named for a son of Poseidon who rode into the harbor on a dolphin's back. A less fantastic theory, trumpeted by historians, is that a group of Spartans was sent here in 708 B.C. to found a colony. Taranto was once a major center of Magna Graecia and continued as an important port on the Ionian coast throughout the 4th century. A long period of rule under Archytas, a Pythagorean mathematician/philosopher, was the high point in the city's history. According to some, Plato himself came to Taranto during this time to muddle through the mysteries of life with the wise and virtuous ruler.

Ten years of war with the Romans in the 3rd century ended in defeat for Taranto. Although the city lost much of the power and prestige it had been known for, it did survive through the dark ages and became an important port once more during the time of the Crusades.

Taranto did lend its name to the tarantula, but don't be alarmed; the only spiders here are rather small, harmless brown ones. The dance known today as the tarantella also takes its name from this city. Members of various dancing cults believed that individuals who'd been bitten by spiders should dance wildly to rid their bodies of the poison; the inflicted person would sometimes dance for days. In modern times, the tarantella is characterized by hopping and foot tapping and is one of the most popular folk dances of southern Italy.

Taranto is a modern industrial city many visitors pass by. The once prosperous old city has begun to crumble and the economy of the town has hit a slump, in part because of the scaling back of naval forces stationed in Taranto. However, the new city, with its wide promenades and expensive shops, still draws crowds. Come here if only to taste some of Italy's best seafood. Taranto's location on a peninsula between two seas, the Mare Piccolo and Mare Grande, is perfect for cultivation of oysters, mussels, and other shellfish.

ESSENTIALS

GETTING THERE   Regular service from both Bari and Brindisi is provided by the FS and FSE **train** lines. Trains leave Bari about once an hour for Taranto; the trip takes 1½ to 2 hours and costs 8,500L ($4.95). For 5,700L ($3.30), you can take the hour ride from Brindisi; trains leave every 2 hours. Arrivals are on the western outskirts of town, from which you can proceed into the center by bus or taxi. For information and schedules, call ☎ **01478/88-088.**

Three **bus** companies, FSE, SITA, and CTP, provide service to Taranto. From Bari, take the FSE bus, departing every 2 hours. The trip takes from 1 to 2 hours and costs 8,500L ($4.95). The tourist office has schedules. Call ☎ **099/732-4201** for information and schedules.

If you've got a **car,** take A14 here from Bari; E90 comes in from Brindisi; and Route 7ter makes the trek west from Lecce.

VISITOR INFORMATION   The **tourist office** is at Corso Umberto I, 113 near Piazza Garibaldi (☎ **099/453-2392**), open Monday to Friday 9am to 1pm and 4:30 to 6:30pm and Saturday 9am to noon.

SEEING THE SIGHTS

For the best view of the city, walk along the waterfront promenade, **Lungomare Vittorio Emanuele.** The heart of the old town, **Città Vecchia,** lies on an island, separating the Mare Piccolo from the Mare Grande. The modern city, or **Città Moderna,** lies to the north of Lungomare Vittorio Emanuele.

Evidence of Taranto's former glory as an important city in Magna Graecia can be found at the ✪ **National Museum of Taranto (Museo Nazionale di Taranto),** Corso Umberto 41 (☎ **099/453-2112**), where an assortment of artifacts documenting Pugliese civilization from the Stone Age to modern times is displayed. Most of the items are the results of archaeological digs in the area, especially the excavated

---

Tracking Down the Sheik of Araby

For years, movie buffs have visited the town of **Castellaneta,** birthplace of Rudolph Valentino, the silent-screen actor known for starring roles in *The Sheik* (1921), *Blood and Sand* (1922), and *Four Horsemen of the Apocalypse* (1921). Valentino was born in 1895 at Via Roma 114; for decades, the town's young men modeled themselves, heavily oiled hair and all, after the star. The town still sells mementos of the matinee idol and souvenir photos. In the town piazza stands a statue of Valentino in the full costume as the Sheik of Araby.

Castellaneta is also known for its "cave churches" and views of the Gulf of Taranto and the Basilicata mountains. Set high in a ravine, the village isn't easily accessible except by car. From Taranto, take S7 to the turnoff for Castellaneta.

---

necropolis. The museum boasts the world's largest collection of terra-cotta figures, along with a glittering array of Magna Grecian art such as vases, goldware, marble and bronze sculpture, and mosaics. The designs of many of these works would be considered sophisticated even by today's standards. The museum is open daily 9am to 1:30pm; admission is 8,000L ($4.65).

SHOPPING

If the ornate vases at the National Museum enchanted you, you may want to visit **Grottaglie,** a nearby small town that's the ceramics capital of southeast Italy. Modern styles are crafted here, but most shoppers prefer to purchase traditional pieces, such as the giant vases that originally held laundry or the glazed wine bottles that mimic those of the ancient Greeks. You can buy pieces for a standard 50% discount over what you'd pay anywhere else for Grottaglie pottery, which is sold all over Italy. The whole village looks like one great china shop. Plates and vases are stacked on the pavements and even on the rooftops. Just walk along looking to see what interests you—then bargain, bargain, bargain.

ACCOMMODATIONS

The choices here are limited. Inexpensive accommodations, in fact, may be impossible to find. Many third- or fourth-class hotels, especially around the waterfront, are unsafe. Proceed with caution. Make reservations in advance—the good hotels, though expensive, fill up fast.

Grand Hotel Delfino. Viale Virgilio 66, 74100 Taranto. ☎ **099/732-3232.** Fax 099/730-4654. 204 units. A/C MINIBAR TV TEL. 180,000L ($104) double; 250,000–300,000L ($145–$174) suite. Rates include breakfast. AE, DC, MC, V. Parking 20,000L ($12).

Built in the 1960s and radically renovated in 1994, the Delfino stands on the waterfront, much like a beach club, and is the best place to stay in Taranto. The well-furnished rooms are modern and beachy, with tile floors, wooden furniture, and small balconies.

Dining/Diversions: The restaurant serves regional cuisine, including excellent fish dishes. The seaview dining room is a perfect setting in which to try such specialties as Taranto oysters. There's also a cozy country-style drinking lounge and bar with ladderback chairs and wood paneling.

Amenities: Concierge, room service, dry cleaning/laundry, baby-sitting, pool.

Hotel Palace. Biale Virilio 10, 74100 Taranto. ☎ **099/459-4771.** Fax 099/459-4771. 73 units. A/C MINIBAR TV TEL. 243,000L ($141) double. Rates includes breakfast. AE, MC, V. Parking 12,000L ($7).

The Palace is the Delfino's nearest rival but is often preferred by visitors. A first-class hotel, it lies at the eastern end of Lungomare Vittorio Emanuele III, opening onto the Mare Grande. The modern building offers good rooms, all with balconies. A restaurant, bar, and cafe are operated on the premises. Garage parking is available; the peace of mind it provides is worth the extra charge.

Hotel Plaza. Via d'Aqhino 46, 74100 Taranto. ☎ 099/459-0775. Fax 099/459-0675. 119 units. A/C TV TEL. 160,000L ($93) double; 210,000L ($122) suite. Rates include breakfast. AE, DC, MC, V.

This is the choice hotel for those who want style along with comfort. The modern hotel opens onto a main square; each well-furnished guest room has a balcony overlooking it. Inside, glossy marble and classic furnishings give the place a dignified and contemporary feeling.

DINING

Taranto is blessed with a bountiful supply of seafood; it's fresh from the water, delicious, and best of all inexpensive. However, avoid anything raw—the locals may like some fish dishes this way, but you don't want to risk spending your vacation in the hospital.

Al Gambero. Via del Ponte 4. ☎ 099/471-1190. Reservations not necessary. Main courses 25,000–30,000L ($15–$17). AE, DC, MC, V. Tues–Sun noon–3pm and 7–10pm. ITALIAN/ SEAFOOD.

This restaurant has thrived since 1952 in a modern-looking building near the rail station, a short walk northwest of the island that contains Taranto's Città Vecchia. It's devoted to the fish dishes for which Taranto is famous, with an emphasis on shellfish, fresh fish, and such signature dishes as pappardelle pasta with herbs and a lobster-flavored cream sauce and risotto with shellfish. You have a choice of enjoying your meal alfresco or in one of the rooms overlooking the harbor and the old city fish market. The view is supplemented by a collection of colorful contemporary paintings. To start your meal, try the antipasti frutti di mare—an assortment of seafood hors d'oeuvres. Main courses include spaghetti al Gambero; grilled or braised versions of veal, beef, or pork; and a filling orecchiette alla Pugliese, the most known pasta dish of Apulia.

L'Assassino. Lungomare Vittorio Emanuele II, 29. ☎ 099/459-3447. Reservations recommended. Main courses 15,000–50,000L ($9–$29); fixed-price menu 40,000–55,000L ($23– $32). AE, DC, MC, V. Sat–Thurs noon–4pm and 9pm–midnight. Closed Christmas and Aug. ITALIAN/INTERNATIONAL.

Described by its owners as "normal but nice," this restaurant is exactly that—nothing too fancy but a pleasant place for a good affordable meal. The dining area offers a panoramic view of the water and a wide range of Italian dishes. Of course, L'Assassino has a variety of fresh fish dishes, including risotto al frutti di mare (rice with the "fruits of the sea"). Other specialties are orecchiette and spaghetti marinara. The proprietors, who've run the place for more than 30 years, are friendly and provide good service.

Sicily 16

Sicily is a land unto itself, proudly different from the rest of Italy in customs and traditions. On the map, the toe of the Italian boot appears poised to kick Sicily away from the mainland, as if it didn't belong to the rest of the country. The largest of the Mediterranean islands, it's separated from Italy by a 2½-mile channel that's a dangerously unstable earthquake zone, making the eventual construction of a bridge doubtful.

While the island's economy and, consequently, its social habits are moving closer to those of Europe and the rest of Italy, its culture is still very much its own. The aura of its Arab past reminds us that Sicily broke away from the mainland of Africa—not Italy—millions of years ago. Its Greek heritage still lives. Though there are far too many cars in Palermo and parts of the island are heavily polluted by industrialization, this is still a different country. Life is slower, tradition is respected, and the myths and legends of the past aren't yet forgotten.

Sicily has been inhabited since the Ice Age, and its history is full of natural and political disasters. It has been conquered and occupied over and over: by the Greeks in the 6th to 5th centuries B.C., then the Romans, the Vandals, the Arabs (who created a splendid civilization), the Normans, the Swabians, the fanatically religious House of Aragon, and the French Bourbons. When Garibaldi landed at Marsala in 1860, he brought an illusion of freedom, soon dissipated by the patronage system of the Mafia. Besides the invaders, a series of plagues, volcanic eruptions, earthquakes, and economic hardships has threatened the interwoven culture of Sicily through the centuries.

Too long neglected by travelers wooed by the art-rich cities of the north, Sicily today is attracting greater numbers of foreign visitors. This land has a deep archaeological heritage and is full of sensual sights and experiences: vineyards and fragrant citrus groves, horses with plumes and bells pulling gaily painted carts, masses of blooming almond and cherry trees in February, Greek temples, ancient theaters, complex city architecture, and the aromatic fragrance of a glass of Marsala. In summer, the sirocco whirling out of the Libyan deserts dries the island's fertile fields, crisping the harvest into a sun-blasted palette of browns.

Like its landscape, Sicily is a hypnotic place of dramatic turbulence, as intense as a play by native son Luigi Pirandello. Luigi Barzini, in *The Italians,* wrote: "Sicily is the schoolroom model of Italy for beginners, with every Italian quality and defect magnified, exasperated, and

Driving Around Sicily

Here's how to link together the region's highlights if you have a car.

Day 1: Arrive in tacky **Messina,** often by car ferry from the mainland. The third-largest city in Sicily (and the setting of Shakespeare's *Much Ado About Nothing*), it doesn't invite lingering. Take A18 down the eastern coast about 30 miles to ✪ **Taormina,** where one night will be all too brief. Set atop Monte Tauro, overlooking the Ionian Sea, this is the most majestic resort in Sicily.

Day 2: A18 continues south to **Catania,** Sicily's second-largest city and a busy seaport, where you might want to have lunch. Continue south from Catania for 36 miles to Syracuse and stay overnight.

Day 3: Plan on a full day exploring the ruins and monuments of **Syracuse.** In ancient times it was the capital of Magna Graecia (Greater Greece) and was one of the greatest cities on earth. You can spend hours exploring its archaeological zone and such attractions as a steep-walled quarry known as the Latomia del Paradiso. Spend another night in Syracuse.

Day 4: South of Syracuse, the autostrada soon ends and Route SS115 takes over. It leads to **Noto,** about 12½ miles from Syracuse, with its Sicilian baroque architecture. Most of the city's monuments are on the main street, Corso Vittorio Emanuele. Back on SS115, proceed to **Ragusa,** encircled by large chemical plants. Hurry on for another 70 miles, passing Gela, until you reach your goal for the night: Agrigento.

Day 5: While based in **Agrigento,** explore the ✪ **Valley of the Temples,** one of the highlights of your tour. See them at dawn, when they're hauntingly beautiful, and again at twilight when floodlights create a spectacle.

Day 6: The route west (SS115) leads to **Sciacca,** 39 miles from Agrigento. Sciacca is known for its ceramics and its thermal baths. Continue along SS115 for 25 miles to **Selinunte.** This ancient town, founded in 682 B.C., was one of the most prosperous Greek colonies in Italy. After exploring the incredible ruins, continue on SS115 north to Castelvetrano, then head west for 22 miles to Marsala. **Marsala** is known for its fortified wine, often compared to sherry. This is where Garibaldi landed with a thousand men to launch his campaign to liberate Sicily from Bourbon rule. From Marsala, take SS115 north 19 miles to Trápani and spend the night.

Day 7: In the morning explore **Trápani,** the westernmost Sicilian town. After passing through its dreary suburbs, head for the narrowing promontory to explore the most interesting part of this colorful port. From Trápani continue to **Érice,** 9 miles northeast. This was ancient Eryx, founded by the Elymnians and mentioned in Virgil's *Aeneid.* With its fortified castles, it owes much of its present look to its Norman conquerors. Take S113 directly out of Érice east for 12 miles to Segesta. A rival of Selinunte, **Segesta** was founded in the 12th century B.C. It contains one of the world's great Doric temples. From Segesta follow the autostrada signs (A29) and head east to Palermo for the night.

Days 8–9: In **Palermo,** you'll be busy day and night with the many attractions. You need the 9th day to explore the sights in the environs, including Cefalù and Monreale. Try to work in some time at the beach at Mondello Lido, 7½ miles east of Palermo.

brightly colored. . . . Everywhere in Italy, life is more or less slowed down by the exuberant intelligence of the inhabitants: In Sicily it is practically paralyzed by it."

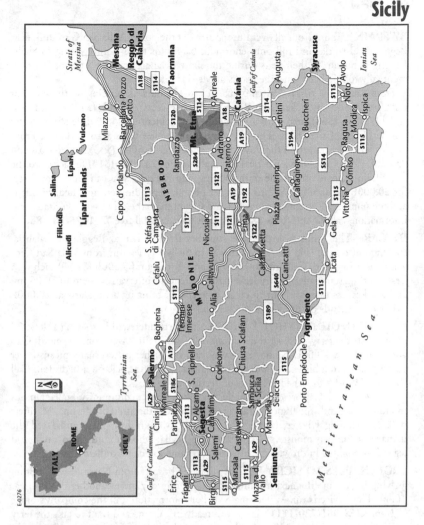

GETTING TO SICILY

BY PLANE   **Alitalia** (☎ **800/223-5730** or 800/625-4825 in the U.S.; toll free in Italy 1478/656-41 for domestic flights, or 1478/656-42 for international reservations) operates at least six flights a day to Palermo from Rome and about half a dozen from Milan (nonstop or with stops in Naples or Rome). From Turin, Venice, Pisa, Genoa, and Bologna, Palermo receives at least one nonstop flight a day and several with a stop at Rome or Naples. Charter flights occasionally land in Trápani, but all other major flights to Sicily land at Catania, with at least one flight a day from Milan, Pisa, Rome, and Turin.

Meridiana (☎ **201/798-7000** in the U.S., 06/478-041 in Rome, 091/323-141 in Palermo), once the Aga Khan's Alisarda line, shares some of its flights and reservation functions with Alitalia. Most of the carrier's Sicilian flights operate between Rome and Palermo and can be booked separately or as part of a transatlantic itinerary through Alitalia. Regardless of how you opt to fly, it's cheaper to have your sojourn in Palermo written into your ticket when you book your flight from North America. Flying time from Rome to Palermo is 1 hour.

BY TRAIN Trains from all over Europe arrive at the port at Villa San Giovanni, near Reggio di Calabria, and roll onto enormous barges for the 1-hour crossing to Sicily. Passengers remain in their seats during the short voyage across the Strait of Messina, eventually rolling back onto the tracks at Messina, Sicily.

From Rome, the trip to Palermo takes 11 to 13 hours, depending on the speed of the train. A one-way ticket from Rome to Palermo costs 70,000L ($41) second class and 117,000L ($68) first, with a per-person supplement of 25,000L ($15) for rides on the fastest of the trains. The rail route from Naples takes 9 to 11 hours. From Naples, one-way transit on the slowest of the trains is 56,500L ($33) second class and 93,000L ($54) first, with a per-person supplement of 23,000L ($13) for access to the faster train. Aboard any of the trains pulling into Palermo, you can rent a couchette for 20,000L to 30,500L ($12 to $18) per person, depending on how luxurious it is and the number of persons (between 4 and 6) you share the cabin with. For fares and information, call ☎ 091/616-1806. Within Italy, call toll free ☎ 1478/880-88.

BY CAR The Autostrada del Sole stretches from Milan to Reggio di Calabria, sticking out on the "big toe," the gateway to Sicily. Ferries run from Villa San Giovanni, near Reggio di Calabria, to Messina, and cost around 5,000L ($2.90) each way. Vessels of the state railway ferry leave daily at frequent intervals 3:20am to 10:05pm, and it takes less than an hour to cross. The cost of bringing a car starts at 20,000L ($12) and depends on the size of the vehicle.

BY HYDROFOIL (WITHOUT A CAR) If you're interested in shaving at least 22 minutes off the ferry crossing time, an *aliscafo* (hydrofoil) leaves from Reggio di Calabria. You'll pay 8,000L ($4.65) each way, and the higher price usually means fewer passengers—and a bit less crowding. You can't take your vehicle on a hydrofoil. Call ☎ 0965/295-68 for schedules and connections.

Near Reggio di Calabria, incidentally, is a much smaller community, Scilla, famous in Homeric legend. You'll spot it during your transit of the Strait of Messina. Mariners of old, including Ulysses, crossed the Strait of Messina from here and faced the menace of the two monsters, Charybdis and Scylla, who—according to myth and legend—delighted in drowning mariners who came too close to their lairs.

FROM NAPLES TO SICILY BY SEA The night ferry from Naples leaves at 8pm, arriving in Palermo the next morning at 7am. On Friday there's another departure at 10pm. The service is run by Tirrenia S.A. For information, call the company's office in Naples (☎ 081/720-1111). If you're already in Palermo and want to take the ferry to Naples, dial ☎ 091/333-300; alas, you won't always find someone who speaks English. Passage from Naples without a car begins at 150,000L ($87) per person, each way. Passage for a car with a driver and one passenger starts at 225,000L ($131). There's a supplement of about 60,000L ($35) per person for use of a cabin, double occupancy. Cabins are sometimes booked many days in advance, and there might be space available only on deck.

1 Taormina: A Sicilian Oasis

33 miles N of Catania, 33 miles S of Messina, 155 miles E of Palermo

Runaway bougainvillea, silvery olive branches, a cerulean sky, cacti like modern sculpture adorning the hills, pastel-plastered walls, garden terraces of geraniums, trees laden with oranges and lemons, ancient ruins—all that and more is **Taormina,** Sicily's most desirable oasis.

Dating from the 4th century B.C., Taormina hugs the edge of a cliff overlooking the Ionian Sea. Writers rave about its unspoiled charms and enchantment. The sea, even the railroad track, lies below, connected by bus routes. Looming in the background is Mount Etna, an active volcano. Noted for its mild climate, the town enjoys a year-round season.

A lot of people contributed to putting Taormina on the tourist map. First inhabited by a tribe known as the Siculi, it has known many conquerors, including the Greeks, Carthaginians, Romans, Saracens, French, and Spanish. Its first tourist is said to have been Goethe, who arrived in 1787. He recorded his impressions in his *Journey to Italy*. Other Germans followed over the centuries, including a red-haired Prussian, Otto Geleng. Arriving at the age of 20 in Taormina, he recorded its beauties in his painted landscapes, which were exhibited in Paris. They caused much excitement—people had to go themselves to find out if Taormina was all that beautiful.

Another German, Wilhelm von Gloeden, arrived to photograph not only the town but also nude boys crowned with laurel wreaths. His pictures sent European high society flocking to Taormina. Von Glocden's photographs, some of which are printed in official tourist literature to this day, form one of the most enduring legends of Taormina. Souvenir shops still sell his pictures, which, though considered scandalous in their day, are tame—even innocent—by today's standards.

In von Gloeden's footsteps came a host of celebrities hoping to see what all the excitement was about: Truman Capote, Tennessee Williams, Marlene Dietrich, Joan Crawford, Rita Hayworth, and Greta Garbo. Always in disguise, sometimes as Harriet Brown, Garbo used Taormina as a vacation retreat from 1950 until her last mysterious arrival in 1979. Many stars, including Garbo, stayed at a villa on the road to Castel Mola owned by Gayelord Hauser, the celebrated dietitian to Hollywood stars of the golden age. In time another wave of stars arrived, including Elizabeth Taylor and Richard Burton, Cary Grant, and the woman who turned him down, Sophia Loren.

The rich and famous still come here, along with a lot of middle-class visitors. Taormina remains chic.

ESSENTIALS

GETTING THERE You can make **rail** connections on the Messina line from Syracuse. Call ☎ 0942/51-026 in Taormina for schedules. There are 29 trains a day each from Messina and Catania; both take 45 to 50 minutes and cost 4,200L ($2.45) one-way. The train station at Taormina is a mile from the heart of the resort. Buses run up a hill every 15 to 45 minutes (schedules vary throughout the year), daily 9am to 9pm; a one-way ticket costs 2,500L ($1.45).

Most visitors arrive in Messina, where you can board a Taormina-bound **bus.** There are 14 a day, taking 1½ hours and costing 5,100L ($2.95) one-way. More details are available by calling **SAIS,** the bus company, at ☎ 090/625-301.

By **car** from Messina, head south along A18. From Catania, continue north along A18.

VISITOR INFORMATION The **tourist office** is in the Palazzo Corvaja, Piazza Santa Caterina (☎ 0942/23-243), open Monday to Saturday 8am to 2pm and 4 to 7pm.

SEEING THE SIGHTS

The ✪ **Teatro Greco,** Via Teatro Greco (☎ 0942/23-220), is the most visited monument, offering a view of rare beauty of Mount Etna and the seacoast. At an unrecorded time the Greeks hewed the theater out of the rocky slope of Mount Tauro, and the Romans remodeled and modified it greatly. The conquering Arabs, who seemed intent on devastating the town, slashed away at it in the 10th century. On the premises is an antiquarium containing artifacts from the classical and early Christian

Mighty Mount Etna

Looming menacingly over the coast of eastern Sicily, **Mount Etna** is the highest and largest active volcano in Europe—and we do mean active! The peak changes in size over the years but is currently in the neighborhood of 10,800 feet. Etna has been active in modern times (in 1928 the little village of Mascali was buried under its lava), and eruptions in 1971 and 1992 rekindled Sicilians' fears.

Etna has figured in history and in Greek mythology. Empedocles, the 5th-century B.C. Greek philosopher, is said to have jumped into its crater as a sign that he was being delivered directly to Mount Olympus to take his seat among the gods. It was under Etna that Zeus crushed the multiheaded, viper-riddled dragon Typhoeus, thereby securing domination over Olympus. Hephaestus, the god of fire and blacksmiths, made his headquarters in Etna, aided by the single-eyed Cyclops.

The Greeks warned that whenever Typhoeus tried to break out of his prison, lava erupted and earthquakes cracked the land. That must mean the monster nearly escaped on March 11, 1669, the date of one of the most violent eruptions ever recorded—it destroyed Catania, about 17 miles away.

Always get the latest report from the tourist offices before contemplating a trip to Mount Etna, because adventurers have been killed by a surprise "belch" (volcanic explosion).

For a good view of the ferocious lava-spewing mountain, take one of the trains operated by Ferrovia Circumetnea that circumnavigate the base of the volcano. Board at the **Stazione Borgo,** Via Caronda 350 (☎ **095/541-24**), in Catania, off Viale Leonardo da Vinci. A 5-hour tour from Catania costs 15,000L ($9).

If you'd prefer not to attempt this rather cumbersome do-it-yourself means of seeing Etna, consider a package tour from Taormina. Contact **CIT,** Corso Umberto I, 101 (☎ **0942/23-301**), to see if any tours are being offered. CIT organizes tours to Etna about twice a week in summer. They cost around 75,000L ($44). There are no plans to offer winter tours.

periods. The theater is open Tuesday to Sunday 9am to 2 hours before sunset. Admission is 2,000L ($1.15) adults; children under 18/seniors over 59 are free.

Behind the tourist office, on the other side of Piazza Vittorio Emanuele, is the **Roman Odeon,** a small theater partly covered by the church of Santa Caterina next door. The Romans constructed this theater around A.D. 21, when Taormina was under their rule. Much smaller than the Greek theater and with very similar architecture, it was discovered in 1892 by a blacksmith digging in the area. A peristyle (colonnade) was discovered here, perhaps all that was left of a Greek temple dedicated to Aphrodite.

Next door you can visit **Santa Caterina,** whose exact consecration date is unknown. Opposite the Palazzo Corvaja, the church, consecrated to St. Catherine of Alexandria, lies in the center of town. It may have been built in the mid-17th century, and the sacristy may have been constructed even earlier. The facade of the sacristy contains two small windows decorated with sea shells, the same motif used on the architrave of its doors. The church's open hours are erratic.

Farther along the main drag, **Corso Umberto I,** you arrive at Piazza del Duomo and the **Duomo (cathedral)** of Taormina. Built around 1400 on the ruins of a church from the Middle Ages, this is a fortress cathedral with a Latin cross plan and a trio of aisles. The nave is held up by half a dozen monolithic columns—three on each side—in pink marble. A fish-scale decoration graces their capitals. The ceiling of the nave is an attraction, with its wooden beams held up by carved corbels decorated with Arabian scenes. The main portal was reconstructed in 1636, with a large Renaissance-inspired rosette sculpted on it. The cathedral is often open in the early morning or early evening, but is likely to be closed during the day. The monsignor apparently opens it when he feels in the mood.

The other thing to do in Taormina is to walk through the **Public Garden (Giardino Pubblico),** Via Bagnoli Croce. The flower-filled garden overlooking the sea is a choice spot for views as well as a place to relax. At a bar in the park you can order drinks.

OTHER ACTIVITIES

Many visitors to Taormina come for the **beach,** though the sands aren't exactly at the resort. For the best and most popular beach, **Lido Mazzarò,** you have to go south of town. From Taormina, you can reach the beach by cable car, which leaves from Via Pirandello every 15 minutes. A one-way ticket costs 2,000L ($1.15) until 8:15pm, then 2,500L ($1.45).

The most popular excursion, other than to Mount Etna (see the box "Mighty Mount Etna"), is to the **Gole Alcantara** (☎ 0942/985-010), a series of beautiful gorges, complete with rapids and waterfalls. Uncharacteristically for Sicily, the waters are extremely cold—but quite refreshing in August. To reach the Alcantara, take one of the SAIS buses (a 20-minute trip) running from Taormina at 9:15am, 12:15pm, and 2pm. There's only one bus back, leaving at 2:20pm. The round-trip fare is 7,300L ($4.25).

SHOPPING

Shopping is easy in Taormina—just find **Corso Umberto I** and go. The trendy shops here sell everything upscale, from lacy linens and fashionable clothing to antique furniture and jewelry.

Hand-embroidered lace is the draw at **Galeano** (also known as **Concetta**), Corso Umberto I 233 (☎ 0942/625-144), where bedspreads and tablecloths are meticulously crafted from fine cotton and linen. If it's old, wearable, and gold, it's at **Gioielleria Giuseppe Stroscio,** Corso Umberto I 169 (☎ 0942/24-865), where the collection of antique gold jewelry dates from 1500 to the turn of this century. Favoring aesthetics over utility, the jewelers at **Estro,** Corso Umberto I 205 (☎ 0942/24-991), sell contemporary adornments, including rings, necklaces, and bracelets.

One of the most appealing clothing stores in Taormina is **Naramaglie,** Corso Umberto I 83 (☎ 0942/242-18). Catering to both men and women, its inventory is a bit more stylish, and a lot more cosmopolitan in focus and selection, than those at some of the more locally minded emporiums nearby. Everything from formal wear to beach outfits is available. Women's fashions are the focus at **Mazzullo,** Corso Umberto I 35 (☎ 0942/23-152), which does, however, offer upscale clothing and accessories for both sexes.

Mixing the new and the old, **Carlo Panarello,** Corso Umberto I, 122 (☎ 0942/23-910), offers Sicilian ceramics (from pots to tables), and also deals in eclectic antique furnishings, paintings, and engravings. A small shop filled with a bounty of national treasures, **Casa d'Arte M. Forin,** Corso Umberto I 148 (☎ 0942/23-060), sells Italian antiques, ranging from furniture to prints, silver, and bronze, with an emphasis on Sicilian and Venetian pieces. From curios to furniture, **Giovanni Panarello,** Corso Umberto I 110 (☎ 0942/23-823), offers one of the best selections of antiques in town.

ACCOMMODATIONS

The hotels in Taormina are the best in Sicily—in fact, the finest in Italy south of Amalfi. All price levels and accommodations are available, from sumptuous suites to army cots.

VERY EXPENSIVE

✪ **Palazzo San Domenico.** Piazza San Domenico 5, 98039 Taormina. ☎ **0942/23-701.** Fax 0942/625-506. 110 units. A/C MINIBAR TV TEL. 630,000–720,000L ($365–$418) double; 1,155,000–1,244,250L ($670–$722) suite. Rates include breakfast. AE, DC, MC, V. Parking 30,000L ($17).

This is one of Europe's great old hotels, converted from a 14th-century Dominican monastery. In 1996, it was used for meetings of top NATO officials. Past guests have included François Mitterrand and Winston Churchill. In 1997, it was discreetly renovated. For sheer luxury, it has no equal in Sicily. Its position is legendary high up from the coast, on different levels surrounded by terraced gardens of almond, orange, and lemon trees.

The large medieval courtyard is planted with semitropical trees and flowers. The encircling enclosed loggia—the old cloister—is decorated with potted palms and ecclesiastical furnishings (high-backed carved choir stalls, wooden angels and cherubs, oil paintings). Off the loggia are great refectory halls turned into sumptuously furnished lounges. Though antiques are everywhere, the atmosphere is gracious rather than museumlike. Ornate ceilings climb high, and arched windows show off the view. The guest rooms, opening off the cloister, would impress a cardinal. They're filled with one-of-a-kind furniture, including elaborate carved beds, provincial pieces, Turkish rugs, and Venetian chairs and dressers.

Dining: The cuisine, supervised by a masterful chef and the most refined in Taormina, is a combination of Sicilian and Italian dishes. Dining in the main hall is an event. Meals are served around the pool in summer.

Amenities: Room service, baby-sitting, laundry/valet, pool.

MODERATE

Bristol Park Hotel. Via Bagnoli Croce 92, 98039 Taormina. ☎ **0942/23-006.** Fax 0942/24-519. 52 units. A/C MINIBAR TV TEL. 250,000–300,000L ($145–$174) double; 380,000L ($220) suite. Rates include breakfast. Half board 40,000L ($23) per person. AE, DC, MC, V. Closed Dec–Feb. Parking 20,000L ($12) in garage.

This four-star hotel is one of the town's all-out comfort destinations. Constructed high on the cliffside at the edge of Taormina, close to the public gardens of Duca di Cesaro, it offers a panoramic view of the coastline and Mount Etna from most of its private sun balconies. The interior decor is amusing, with tufted satin, plush and ornate. In contrast, the guest rooms are decorated in traditional style. The dining room, with arched windows framing the view, offers international meals with an occasional Sicilian dish. There's a private beach with free deck chairs and parasols, plus bus service to the beach (June to October), where the hotel maintains a full-service bar. There's also a pool.

Hotel Monte Tauro. Via Madonna delle Grazie 3, 98039 Taormina. ☎ **0942/24-402.** Fax 0942/24-403. 70 units. A/C MINIBAR TV TEL. 300,000L ($174) double; from 350,000L ($203) junior suite. Rates include breakfast. AE, DC, MC, V. Closed Jan 15–Mar.

This hotel is built into the side of a scrub-covered hill rising high above the sea, within view of the coastline. Though not as good as the Palazzo San Domenico and Bristol Park, it does compete successfully against the Hotel Villa Diodoro (below). Renovated in the early 1990s, each room has a circular balcony with a sea view, often festooned with flowers. The social center is the many-angled swimming pool, whose cantilevered platform is ringed with a poolside bar and dozens of plants. The velvet-covered chairs of the modern, tile-floored interior are upholstered in the same blues, grays, and violets of the sunny guest rooms, where Mondrian-style rectangles and stripes decorate the bedspreads and accessories.

Hotel Villa Diodoro. Via Bagnoli Croce 75, 98039 Taormina. ☎ **0942/23-312.** Fax 0942/ 23-391. 102 units. A/C MINIBAR TV TEL. 240,000–340,000L ($139–$197) double with breakfast; 180,000–220,000L ($104–$128) per person double with half board. AE, DC, MC, V.

This is one of the most luxurious of the first-class hotels. The design of everything is tasteful and well coordinated. The dining room, with tall windows on three sides, faces the sea and Mount Etna. The outdoor pool is a sun trap; you can sunbathe, swim, and enjoy the view of mountains, trees, and flowers. The rooms are elegant and comfortable, with well-designed furniture and the latest gadgets. Many rooms are angled toward the sea, with wide-open windows. A shuttle bus makes a half-dozen runs per day (June to October) to the beach at nearby Lido Caparena.

✪ **Villa Ducale.** 60 Via Leonardo da Vinci, 98039 Taormina. ☎ **0942/281-53.** Fax 0942/ 287-10. 13 units. A/C MINIBAR TV TEL. 270,000–340,000L ($157–$197) double; 380,000L ($220) suite. Rates include breakfast. AE, DC, MC, V.

Villa Ducale sits in a panoramic position on a hillside above Taormina, a 10-minute uphill walk from the center. The public areas look like slightly streamlined versions of spaces that several generations of the same Sicilian family might have shared. Painted depictions of local landscapes are scattered throughout the salons and accommodations. There's a tile-floored terrace, where afternoon tea and breakfast are served; the view encompasses the bay, the historic core of Taormina, and the upward thrust of Mount Etna. The well-trained staff does everything except prepare meals. (Breakfast is the only meal.) Each guest room has a safe, a veranda with a sea view, a handful of antiques, and an artfully idiosyncratic decor.

✪ **Villa Fiorita.** Via Pirandello 39, 98039 Taormina. ☎ **0942/24-122.** Fax 0942/625-967. 26 units. A/C MINIBAR TV TEL. 175,000L ($102) double; from 225,000L ($131) suite. Rates include breakfast. AE, MC, V. Parking 15,000L ($9).

One of the most charming hotels in its category, Villa Fiorita stretches toward the town's Greek theater from its position beside the road leading to the top of this cliff-hugging town. Its imaginative decor includes a handful of ceramic stoves, which the owner delights in collecting. A well-maintained flower garden with a pool lies alongside an empty but ancient Greek tomb whose stone walls have been classified as a national treasure. The rooms are arranged in a steplike labyrinth of corridors and stairwells, some of which bend to correspond to the rocky slope on which the hotel was built. Each unit contains a piece of antique furniture, and most have flowery private terraces.

Villa Paradiso. Via Roma 2, 98039 Taormina. ☎ **0942/23-922.** Fax 0942/625-800. 35 units. A/C TV TEL. 230,000–280,000L ($133–$162) double. Rates include breakfast. AE, DC, MC, V. Parking 20,000L ($12).

This charming hotel is at one end of the town's main street, near the Greek theater and overlooking the public gardens and tennis courts. The creation of Signore Salvatore Martorana, it's a reasonably priced choice for those who want to live well. He loves his establishment, and that attitude is reflected in the personal manner in which the living room is furnished, with antiques and reproductions. Each individually decorated room has a balcony. Guests spend many sunny hours in the rooftop solarium, the TV room, or the informal drinking bar and lounge, open 24 hours. Late May to late

October, the hotel offers free access to the private Paradise Beach Club 4 miles east in the hamlet of Letojanni, beside the coastal road as you drive toward Messina. It contains an outdoor pool, a beach, changing rooms, a tennis court, and a Jacuzzi.

INEXPENSIVE

Hotel Ariston. Via Bagnoli Croce 168, 98039 Taormina. ☎ **0942/23-838.** Fax 0942/21-137. 176 units. A/C MINIBAR TV TEL. 88,000–140,000L ($51–$81) per person with half board. AE, MC, V.

Substantial and cost-conscious, this modern hotel rises 4 stories above a verdant park about 400 yards from the center of Taormina. It's a favorite with families from Italy and the rest of Europe. The well-maintained rooms are airy, streamlined, and comfortable. About 36 rooms are in a low-rise garden annex nearby. The hotel is inland, a short walk from the sea. On the premises are a pool, a piano bar, and a restaurant with efficient service that offers Sicilian and international specialties. Dinner is served on a poolside terrace in summer.

Hotel La Campanella. Via Circonvallazione 3, 98039 Taormina. ☎ **0942/23-381.** Fax 0942/625-248. 12 units. TEL. 120,000L ($70) double. Rates include breakfast. No credit cards.

This hotel is rich in plants, paintings, and hospitality. It sits at the top of a seemingly endless flight of stairs, which begin at a sharp curve of the main road leading into town. You climb past terra-cotta pots and the dangling tendrils of a terraced garden, eventually arriving at the house. The owners maintain clean and uncluttered guest rooms, each containing potted plants and the kind of accessories you might expect in a private home.

Pensione Svizzera. Via Pirandello 26, 98039 Taormina. ☎ **0942/23-790.** Fax 0942/625-906. 26 units. TEL. 100,000L ($58) double; 120,000L ($70) triple; 136,000L ($79) quad. Rates include breakfast. AE, DC, MC, V. Closed Jan. Free parking for 5 cars.

This pleasant hotel is about an eighth of a mile from the center of town. Formerly a private home, it's run by third-generation innkeeper Antonino Vinciguerra and his German-born wife, both of whom speak English. Try to get a room overlooking the sea and Isola Bella. All rooms have hair dryers, and 12 offer sea views. There's also a garden with shady palm trees where breakfast is served in summer. The funicular to the beach at Mazzarò is a little more than 100 yards from the pensione, as is the bus terminal.

Villa Belvedere. Via Bagnoli Croci 79, 98039 Taormina. ☎ **0942/23-791.** Fax 0942/625-830. E-mail: hotelbelve@tao.it. 30 units. TEL. 150,000–215,000L ($87–$125) double. Rates include breakfast. MC, V. Closed Nov 15–Dec 15 and Jan 15–Mar 15. Parking 8,000L ($4.65).

This hotel near the Giardino Pubblico offers the same view enjoyed by guests at the more expensive first-class hotels nearby. The building was constructed as a private villa in 1904 and soon thereafter transformed into a charming hotel. In its garden is a heated pool. From the cliffside terrace in the rear—a social center for guests—is that view: the clear blue sky, the gentle Ionian Sea, the cypress-studded hillside, and menacing Mount Etna. Potted plants and wall-covering vines enhance the formal entrance, and the interior is captivating. The guest rooms have been restored, and 30 are air-conditioned. There are two bars. A snack bar by the pool serves lunch.

Villa Nettuno. Via Pirandello 33, 98039 Taormina. ☎ **0942/23-797.** Fax 0942/626-035. 13 units. 110,000L ($64) double. Rates include breakfast. MC, V. Parking 8,000L ($4.65).

A favorite budget accommodation in town is this geranium-colored villa with Renaissance-style stone trim. It lies near the city center, opposite a cableway that transports passengers down to the sea. You must climb several flights of steps after leaving the main street, passing beneath an archway whose keystone is carved with a grotesque stone face. The villa was built in 1860 and acquired by the Sciglio family in 1887. In 1955 it became a well-managed hotel run by the warm-hearted but highly discerning Maria Sciglio and her son, Antonio. Guests enjoy breakfast in a garden with hibiscus and night-blooming jasmine. The dining room is like the rococo living quarters of an elegant Sicilian family. Each of the attractive, well-scrubbed guest rooms has a terrace or balcony, in most cases with views out to sea.

Villa Schuler. Piazzetta Bastione, Via Roma, 98039 Taormina. ☎ **0942/23-481.** Fax 0942/ 23-522. www.cys.it/schuler. E-mail: schuler@cys.it. 27 units. TEL. 150,000L ($87) double. Rates include breakfast. AE, MC, V. Parking 15,000L ($9) in garage, free outside.

Surrounded by gardens and filled with the fragrance of bougainvillea and jasmine, this hotel is an ideal retreat. Family-owned and -run, it sits high above the Ionian Sea, with views of snow-capped Mount Etna and the Bay of Naxos. The hotel is only a 2-minute stroll from the central Corso Umberto I, and about a 15-minute walk from the cable car to the beach below. It's also near the ancient theater of Taormina. The rooms are comfortably furnished, and many have a small balcony or terrace with a view of the sea. Breakfast can be served in your room or taken on a terrace with a panoramic view of the coast. Facilities and services include a roof terrace solarium, a small library, 24-hour bar and room service, and laundry.

NEARBY ACCOMMODATIONS

If you visit Taormina in summer, you may prefer to stay at **Mazzarò,** about 3 miles from the more famous resort. This is the major beach of Taormina and has some fine hotels. A bus for Mazzarò leaves from the center of Taormina every 30 minutes daily from 8am to 9pm. The one-way fare is 1,500L (85¢).

Grande Albergo Capotaormina. Via Nazionale 105, 98039 Taormina. ☎ **0942/ 572-111.** Fax 0942/625-467. 203 units. A/C MINIBAR TV TEL. 350,000L ($203) double; from 500,000L ($290) suite. Rates include buffet breakfast. AE, DC, MC. V. Closed Oct 30–Feb. Parking 15,000L ($9).

The Grande Albergo is a world unto itself, nestled atop a rugged cape projecting into the Ionian Sea. It was designed by one of Italy's most famous architects, Minoletti. There are 5 floors with wide sun terraces, plus a saltwater swimming pool at the edge of the cape. Elevators take you through 150 feet of solid rock to the beach below. The rooms are handsomely furnished and well proportioned, with wide glass doors opening onto private terraces. The lobby blends the cultures of Rome, Carthage, and Greece, and an open atrium reaches skyward through the center.

Dining/Diversions: The hotel has a simple outdoor cafe. In the more intimate indoor venue, the food is lavishly presented and effectively enhanced by Sicilian wines. There are two bars—one cozy, the other more expansive, with an orchestra for dancing.

Amenities: Concierge, room service, dry cleaning/laundry, solarium, saltwater pool.

✪ **Mazzarò Sea Palace.** Via Nazionale 147, 98030 Mazzarò. ☎ **0942/24-004.** Fax 0942/626-237. 84 units. A/C MINIBAR TV TEL. 250,000–520,000L ($145–$302) double; 680,000L ($394) suite for 2. Rates include half board. AE, DC, MC, V.

The Sea Palace is a leading four-star hotel in this little satellite resort of Taormina. It opens onto the most beautiful bay in Sicily and has a private beach. Completed in 1962, it has been renovated frequently since, most recently in the mid-1990s. Big windows let in cascades of light and offer views of the coast. The rooms are well furnished, and most have panoramic views.

Dining/Diversions: The elegant restaurant opens onto a terrace and offers excellent food and service. The menu, which changes daily, emphasizes seafood and fresh produce. The piano bar is a popular nighttime spot.

Amenities: Concierge, room service, baby-sitting, and dry cleaning/laundry; private beach.

Villa Sant'Andrea. Via Nazionale 137, 98030 Taormina Mare. ☎ **0942/23-125.** Fax 0942/24-838. 67 units. A/C MINIBAR TV TEL. 310,000–530,000L ($180–$307) double. Rates include breakfast. AE, DC, MC, V. Parking 22,000L ($13).

This hotel lies at the base of the mountain, directly on the sea, and has a private beach. It enjoys one of the most idyllic positions at the resort, set in the midst of subtropical gardens with palms and banana plants. A stay here is like going to a house party at a pretty home. The atmosphere and tasteful refurbishment draw return visits by artists, painters, and other discriminating guests. Rooms are well maintained and comfortable, although size and décor vary. Many have sea-facing balconies or terraces. A cable car, just outside the front gates of the hotel, runs into the heart of Taormina.

Dining/Diversions: Oliviero's, which opens onto delightful views across the bay, serves some of the finest cuisine on the island. The restaurant Sant'Andrea offers international and Sicilian cuisine. A garden terrace is another summer dining venue. A piano bar keeps the evenings lively.

Amenities: Concierge, room service, baby-sitting, dry cleaning/laundry; private beach next to hotel; changing facilities; sports activities such as windsurfing; sailboats, motorboats, and pedalos to rent; nearby tennis courts and golf.

DINING
MODERATE

Giova Rosy di Turi Salsa. Corso Umberto I 38. ☎ **0942/24-411.** Reservations recommended. Main courses 18,000–60,000L ($10–$35). AE, DC, V. Daily noon–3pm and 7–midnight. Closed Jan–Feb. SICILIAN.

One of the oldest restaurants in Taormina (since 1960), this old-fashioned rustic place serves a variety of local specialties, including an array of linguine and risotto dishes. Seafood offerings include spiedini with shrimp and lobster dosed with a generous shot of cognac, tagliolini with seafood, and swordfish cooked *in cartoccio* (in a paper bag). You might also enjoy Sicilian antipasti or eggplant with ricotta. The restaurant overlooks the ancient theater.

Ristorante da Lorenzo. Via Roma, near Via Michele Amari. ☎ **0942/23-480.** Reservations required. Main courses 16,000–40,000L ($9–$23); fixed-price menus from 40,000L ($23). AE, DC, MC, V. Thurs–Tues noon–3pm and 6:30–11pm. Closed Nov 15–Dec 15. SICILIAN/ITALIAN.

This is a bright restaurant on a quiet street near the landmark Palazzo San Domenico hotel, in front of the town hall. The restaurant has a terrace shaded by an 850-year-old tree—the botanical pride of the town—and oil paintings decorating its white walls. Your meal might include a fresh selection of antipasti, spaghetti with sea urchins, scaloppine mozzarella, grilled swordfish, or filet of beef with Gorgonzola.

INEXPENSIVE

Il Ciclope. Corso Umberto I 203. ☎ **0942/23-263.** Reservations not accepted. Main courses 18,000–30,000L ($10–$17). AE, MC, V. Thurs–Tues 12:30–3pm and 7:30–10pm. Closed Jan 10–Feb 10, and Tues Oct–June. SICILIAN/ITALIAN.

This is one of the best of Taormina's low-priced trattorie. Set back from the main street, it opens onto the pint-sized Piazzetta Salvatore Leone. In summer, try for an outside table if you'd like both your food and yourself inspected by the passing parade. Meals are fairly simple, but the ingredients are fresh and the dishes well prepared. Try the fish soup or Sicilian squid. If those don't interest you, then go for entrecôte Ciclope or grilled shrimp. Most diners begin their meal with a selection from the antipasti di mare, a savory assortment of seafood hors d'oeuvres.

Ristorante La Griglia. Corso Umberto I 54. ☎ **0942/23-980.** Reservations recommended. Main courses 12,000–25,000L ($7–$15). AE, DC, MC, V. Wed–Mon 12:30–2:30pm and 7:30–11:30pm. Closed Nov 20–Dec 20. SICILIAN/INTERNATIONAL.

This restaurant has been one of the best in town since it opened in 1974. The vestibule that opens off the main street contains a bubbling aquarium and a menagerie of carved stone lions. The masses of plants inside almost conceal the terra-cotta floors and big windows with views over feathery trees. Your meal might include a selection from the antipasto display, fresh fish carpaccio, and *involtino* of spaghetti and eggplant.

Ristorante Luraleo. Via Bagnoli Croce 27. ☎ **0942/24-279.** Reservations recommended. Main courses 16,000–60,000L ($9–$35). DC, MC, V. Summer daily noon–3pm and 7–11pm; winter closed Wed. SICILIAN/INTERNATIONAL.

Acclaimed by a handful of residents as the best place in town, Ristorante Luraleo offers excellent value for an attractive price. Many diners prefer the flowery terrace, where pastel tablecloths are shaded by a vine-covered arbor. If you prefer to dine indoors, there's a rustic dining room with tile accents, flowers, evening candlelight, racks of wine bottles, and a richly laden antipasto table. Grilled fish is good, as are pastas— such as house-made maccheroni with tomato, eggplant, and basil—regional dishes, and herb-flavored steak. Risotto with salmon and pistachio nuts is a specialty, as is the house tortellini.

Ristorante U'Bossu. Via Bagnoli Croce 50. ☎ **0942/23-311.** Reservations required. Main courses 8,000–12,000L ($4.65–$7); fixed-price menu 20,000L ($12). MC, V. Tues–Sun noon–3pm and 7–11pm. Closed Jan 10–May 10. SICILIAN/MEDITERRANEAN.

Vines twine around the facade of this small crowded restaurant in a quiet part of town. Amid fresh flowers, wagon-wheel chandeliers, prominently displayed wine bottles, and burnished wooden panels, you can enjoy a meal pungent with the aromas of an herb garden. Start with the complimentary bruschetta (grilled bread with oil and garlic or tomato). Specialties include pasta *con la sarde* (with fish) and *involtini di pesce spada* (swordfish stew), and there's a groaning antipasti table. The restaurant is decorated with a folkloric scene from *Cavalleria Rusticana,* and the chef has paid homage to the famed opera by naming his best pasta dish *maccheroni alla Turiddu,* after the principal character (it contains tuna, olives, capers, onions, wild herbs, fresh tomatoes, and fennel). For dessert, nothing can top the zabaglione with fresh strawberries.

NEARBY DINING

Ristorante Angelo a Mare–Il Delfino. Via Nazionale. ☎ **0942/23-004.** Main courses 14,000–40,000L ($8–$23). AE, DC, MC, V. Daily noon–3pm and 7pm–midnight. Closed Nov–Mar. MEDITERRANEAN/ITALIAN.

This late 19th-century structure is in Mazzarò, about 3 miles from Taormina and a 2-minute walk from the cable-car station. From the flower-filled terrace, there's a view over the bay. The decor and the menu items are inspired by the sea and carefully supervised by the chef and owner. Mussels *delphio* (cooked with garlic, parsley, olive oil, and lemons) and house-style steak (with fresh tomatoes, onions, garlic, capers, and parsley) are specialties. Other good choices are *involtini* of fish, cannelloni, risotto marinara (fisher's rice), and anchovies roasted with basil.

TAORMINA AFTER DARK

Begin your evening at the **Caffè Wunderbar,** Piazza IX Aprile 7, Corso Umberto I (☎ **0942/625-302**), a popular spot that was once a favorite watering hole of Tennessee Williams and his longtime companion, Frank Merlo. It's on the most delightful square in town. Beneath a vine-covered arbor, the outdoor section is perched as close to the edge of the cliff as safety allows. We prefer one of the Victorian armchairs beneath chandeliers in the elegant interior. There's a well-stocked bar, as well as a piano bar. An espresso costs 4,200L ($2.45), and a cappuccino 5,200L ($3) if you sit. It's open daily 8:30am to 2:30am; closed Tuesday in December and January.

The entire town is geared to holiday-making, and a healthy roster of nightclubs is scattered among Taormina's medieval masonry. **Bella Blu,** Guardiola Vecchia (☎ **0942/24-239**), caters to high-energy, dance-a-holic patrons from throughout Europe. At the **Club Septimo,** Via San Pancrazio 50 (☎ **0942/625-522**), a sweeping view of the town and sea is framed with reproductions of ancient Roman columns, and the interior has all the strobe and ultraviolet lights you might want. More elegant than either of these is **La Jarra,** Via La Floresta 1, off Corso Umberto (☎ **0942/ 23-360**), the only one of the three that's open year-round. A bar with recorded music and occasional bouts of dancing is **Le Perroquet,** Piazza San Domenico de Guzman, at Via Roma (☎ **0942/24-462**), a spot more closely geared to gay life than any of the others here.

Taormina also has a cultural side. The Greek and Roman theater (see above) offers regular **theatrical performances** July to September. In addition, churches and other venues are the settings for a **summer festival of classical music,** staged from May to September. Each July the resort sponsors an **international film festival** in its amphitheater. For more information on cultural events, contact the tourist office or call ☎ **0942/23-243.**

2 Syracuse

35 miles SE of Catania

Of all the Greek cities of antiquity that flourished on the coast of Sicily, **Syracuse (Sir- acusa)** was the most important, a formidable competitor of Athens. In its heyday, it dared take on Carthage, even Rome. At one time its wealth and size were unmatched by any other city in Europe.

Colonists from Corinth founded the city on the Ionian Sea in about 735 B.C. Much of its history was linked to despots, beginning in 485 with Gelon, the tyrant of Gela, who subdued the Carthaginians at Himera. Syracuse came under attack from Athens in 415, but the main Athenian fleet was destroyed and the soldiers on the mainland captured. They were herded into the Latomia di Cappuccini at Piazza Cappuccini, a stone quarry. The "jail," from which there was no escape, was particularly horrid—the defeated soldiers weren't given food and were packed together like cattle and allowed to die slowly.

Dionysius I was one of the greatest despots, reigning over the city during its greatest glory, in the 4th century B.C., when it extended its influence as a sea power. But in A.D. 212 the city fell to the Romans under Marcellus, who sacked its riches and art. In that attack, Syracuse lost its most famous son, the Greek physicist and mathemati- cian Archimedes, who was slain in his study by a Roman soldier.

Before you go, you might want to read Mary Renault's novel *The Mask of Apollo,* set in Syracuse of the 5th century B.C. As one critic put it, "It brings the stones to life."

Today the city's harborfront is lined with a distinguished collection of brightly painted 18th- and 19th-century town houses, making up one of the most charming vistas in Sicily.

Syracuse is a cauldron in summer. You can do as the locals do and head for the sea. The finest beach is about 12 miles away at **Fontane Bianche;** buses nos. 21 and 22 leave from the Syracuse post office, Piazza delle Poste 15. The same buses will take you to Lido Arenella, only 5 miles away but not as good.

ESSENTIALS

GETTING THERE   From other major cities in Sicily, Syracuse is best reached by **train.** It's 1½ hours from Catania, 2 from Taormina, and 5 from Palermo. Usually you must transfer in Catania. For information, call ☎ **095/531-625.** Trains arrive in Syracuse at the station on Via Francesco Crispi, centrally located midway between the archaeological park and Ortygia.

From Catania, 12 SAIS **buses** daily make the 1¼-hour trip to Syracuse. The one-way fare is 6,100L ($3.55). Phone **SAIS** (☎ **0931/66-710** in Syracuse or 095/536-168 in Catania) for information and schedules.

By **car** from Taormina, continue south along Rte. 114, past Catania.

VISITOR INFORMATION   The **tourist office** is at Largo Paradiso (☎ **0931/605-10**), facing San Giovanni, and there's a branch office at the entrance to the archaeological park. Both offices are open Monday to Saturday 8:30am to 2pm and 4:30 to 7:30pm.

SEEING THE ANCIENT SIGHTS

✪ **Archaeological Zone (Zona Archeologica).** Via Augusto (off intersection of Corso Gelone and Viale Teocrito). ☎ **0931/66-206.** Admission 4,000L ($2.30). Apr–Oct daily 9am–6pm; Nov–Mar daily 9am–3pm.

Syracuse's archaeological park contains the town's most important attractions: the Greek theater (Teatro Greco), the Roman Amphitheater (Anfiteatro Romano), and the Latomia del Paradiso.

On the Temenite Hill, the ✪ **Teatro Greco** was one of the great theaters of the classical period. Hewn from rock during the reign of Hieron I in the 5th century B.C., the ancient seats have been largely eaten away by time. You can, however, still stand on the remnants of the stone stage where plays by Euripedes were mounted. The theater was much restored in the time of Hieron II in the 3rd century B.C. In the spring of even-numbered years (and in Segesta in the summer of odd-numbered years), the Italian Institute of Ancient Drama presents classical plays by Euripedes, Aeschylus, and Sophocles. (In other words, the show hasn't changed much in 2,000 years!)

Outside the entrance to the Greek theater is the most famous of the ancient quarries, the **Latomia del Paradiso,** one of four or five from which stones were hauled to erect the great monuments of Syracuse in its glory days. On seeing the cave in the wall, Caravaggio is reputed to have dubbed it "The Ear of Dionysius," because of its unusual shape. But what an ear—it's nearly 200 feet long. You can enter the inner chamber of the grotto, where the tearing of paper sounds like a gunshot. Although dismissed by some scholars as fanciful, the story goes that the despot Dionysius used to force prisoners into the "ear" at night, where he was able to hear every word they said. Nearby is the Grotta dei Cordari, where ropemakers plied their craft.

The ✪ **Anfiteatro Romano** was created at the time of Augustus. It ranks among the top five amphitheaters left by the Romans in Italy. Like the Greek theater, part of it was carved from rock. Unlike the Greek theater and its classical plays, the Roman amphitheater tended toward gutsier fare. Gladiators—prisoners of war and "exotic" blacks from Africa—faced each other with tridents and daggers, or naked slaves were whipped into the center of a battle to the death between wild beasts. Either way the victim lost. If his opponent, man or beast, didn't do him in, the crowd would often scream for the ringmaster to slit his throat. The amphitheater is near the entrance to the park, but you can also view it in its entirety from a belvedere on the road.

✪ **Paolo Orsi Regional Archaeological Museum (Museo Archeologico Regionale Paolo Orsi).** In the gardens of the Villa Landolina in Akradina, Viale Teocrito 66. ☎ **0931/464-022.** Admission 8,000L ($4.65). Tues–Sat 9am–1pm.

One of the most important archaeological museums in southern Italy surveys the Greek, Roman, and early Christian epochs in sculpture and fragments of archeological remains. The museum also has a rich coin collection. The best known of the several excellent statues here is the headless *Venus Anadyomene* (rising from the sea), from the Hellenistic period in the 2nd century B.C. One of the earliest works is of an earth mother suckling two babes, from the 6th century B.C. The pre-Greek vases have great style and elegance.

✪ **Catacombs of St. John (Catacombe di San Giovanni).** Piazza San Giovanni, at end of Viale San Giovanni. ☎ **0931/67-955.** Admission 4,000L ($2.30) adults, 2,000L ($1.15) children under 11. Mar 15–Nov 14 daily 9am–6pm; Nov 15–Mar 14 daily 9am–1pm and 3–6pm.

These honeycombed tunnels of empty coffins evoke the catacombs along the Appian Way in Rome. You enter the world below from the Chiesa di San Giovanni, established in the 3rd century A.D. (the present building is much more recent). Included in the early Christian burial grounds is the crypt of St. Marcianus, which lies under what was reportedly the first cathedral erected in Sicily. *Warning:* Make sure you exit in plenty of time before closing. Two readers who entered the catacombs after 5pm were accidentally locked in and managed to escape only after a harrowing ordeal of wandering around in the dark.

EXPLORING ORTYGIA ISLAND

Ortygia, inhabited for many thousands of years, is also called Città Vecchia ("old city"). It contains the town's Duomo, many rows of houses spanning 500 years of building styles, most of the city's medieval and baroque monuments, and some of the most charming vistas in Sicily. Pindar praised the beauties of the island. In Greek mythology, it's said to have been ruled by Calypso, daughter of Atlas, the sea nymph who detained Ulysses (Odysseus) for 7 years. The island, reached by crossing the Ponte Nuova, is about a mile long and half again as wide.

Heading out the Foro Italico, you'll come to the **Fonte Arethusa,** also famous in mythology. The river god Alpheius, son of Oceanus, is said to have fallen in love with the sea nymph Arethusa. The nymph turned into this spring or fountain, but Alpheius became a river and "mingled" with his love. According to legend, the spring ran red when bulls were sacrificed at Olympus.

At Piazza del Duomo is the **Duomo** of Syracuse, which was built over the ruins of the Temple of Minerva and employs the same Doric columns; 26 of the originals are still in place. The temple was erected after Gelon the Tyrant defeated the Carthaginians at Himera in the 5th century B.C. The Christians converted it into a basilica in the 7th century A.D. It's open daily 8am to noon and 4 to 7pm.

The **Palazzo Bellomo,** Via Capodieci 14, off Foro Vittorio Emanuele II, dates from the 13th century, with many alterations, and is today the home of the **Galleria**

Regionale (☎ 0931/69-617). The palace is fascinating, with its many arches, doors, and stairs, and also has a fine collection of paintings. The most notable is an *Annunciation* by Antonello da Messina from 1474. There's also a noteworthy collection of antiques and porcelain. It's open Monday to Saturday 9am to 1:30pm and Sunday 9am to 12:30pm. Admission is 2,000L ($1.15).

ACCOMMODATIONS
MODERATE

Hotel Forte Agip. Viale Teracati 30–32, 96100 Siracusa. ☎ **0931/463-232.** Fax 0931/ 67-115. 87 units. A/C MINIBAR TV TEL. 227,000L ($132) double. Rates include buffet breakfast. AE, DC, MC, V. Free parking.

A short drive inland from the medieval Città Vecchia, near the ancient Greek theater and most of the city's classical monuments, this branch of a national hotel chain is designed for easy access and convenience to motorists. Each monochromatic room is simple and streamlined. The in-house restaurant attracts locals, who consider the generous portions, unpretentious service, and flavorful specialties worth the trip. Menu items include pastas, stuffed veal, American-style tournedos, salads, and a changing array of fresh fish.

Jolly Hotel. Corso Gelone 45, 96100 Siracusa. ☎ **800/221-2626** in the U.S., 800/ 237-0319 in Canada, or 0931/461-1111 in Italy. Fax 0931/461-126. 100 units. A/C MINIBAR TV TEL. 260,000L ($151) double. Rates include breakfast. AE, DC, MC, V. Parking 20,000L ($12).

A major group stop, the 6-story Jolly is part of the chain that's the Holiday Inn of Italy. You get no surprises here—just clean, modern, tropical-style rooms, short on soul but good on comfort, though a bit worn. At least the view of Mount Etna and the sea is panoramic. The hotel restaurant is better than the hotel, offering a standard lunch or dinner of Sicilian or international cuisine.

INEXPENSIVE

Hotel Bellavista. Via Diodoro Siculo 4, 96100 Siracusa. ☎ **0931/411-355.** Fax 0931/ 37-927. 45 units, 42 with bathroom. TV TEL. 94,000L ($55) double without bathroom, 148,000L ($86) double with bathroom. Rates include breakfast. AE, MC, V.

Family owned and -run, this hotel lies in the commercial center, close to the archaeological zone. There's an annex in the garden for overflow guests. The spacious main lounge has leather chairs and semitropical plants. The guest rooms are informal and comfortable, often furnished with traditional pieces. Most rooms feature a sea-view balcony. There's a restaurant serving Sicilian cuisine for hotel guests and groups only.

Hotel Panorama. Via Necropoli Grotticelle 33, 96100 Siracusa. ☎ **0931/412-188.** Fax 0931/412-527. 51 units. TV TEL. 130,000L ($75) double. Rates include continental breakfast. AE, MC, V. Free parking.

Near the entrance to the city, on a rise of Temenite Hill, this bandbox-modern hotel sits on a busy street about 5 minutes from the Greek theater and Roman amphitheater. It's not a motel, but it does provide parking. Inside, contemporary accommodations await you. The rooms are pleasant and up-to-date, with comfortable but utilitarian furniture. The dining room serves breakfast only.

DINING
MODERATE

Arlecchino. Via dei Tolomei 5. ☎ **0931/66-386.** Reservations recommended. Main courses 17,000–20,000L ($10–$12). AE, DC, MC, V. Daily 12:30–3:30pm and 7:30pm–midnight. Closed Sun Apr–Sept. SEAFOOD/PIZZA.

This restaurant occupies the street level of a 250-year-old palace in the heart of the Città Vecchia, a short walk from the cathedral. Despite its understated decor and inexperienced staff, it serves a memorable cuisine. Many specialties emerge from the fragrant kitchen, including a wide array of homemade pastas, a cheese-laden crespelline of the house, pasta with sardines, spiedini with shrimp, and a selection of pungent beef, fish, and veal dishes. There's also a pizzeria on site.

Gambero Rosso. Via Eritrea 2. ☎ **0931/68-546.** Reservations recommended. Main courses 15,000–25,000L ($9–$15). AE, DC, MC, V. Wed–Mon noon–3:30pm and 7:30–11pm. SICILIAN/MEDITERRANEAN/SEAFOOD.

Near the bridge to the Città Vecchia, this restaurant is in an old tavern. It's a mellow building, close to the fishing boats, where you can sample the best of Sicilian dishes. A reliable choice is *zuppa di pesce* (fish soup). An agreeable alternative is *zuppa di cozze*, a plate brimming with fresh mussels in a tasty marinade. The Sicilian cannelloni are good too. The meat dishes feature a number of choices from the kitchens of Lazio, Tuscany, and Emilia-Romagna. The dining room extends from the restaurant onto a terrace dotted with potted flowers and shrubs that faces the port. Getting a table shouldn't be a worry—the restaurant can seat 120.

✪ **Ristorante Jonico-a Rutta e Ciauli.** Riviera Dionisio il Grande 194. ☎ **0931/65-540.** Reservations recommended. Main courses 18,000–28,000L ($10–$16); pizza 5,000–12,000L ($2.90–$7). AE, MC, V. Wed–Mon noon–3pm and 7–10:30pm. SICILIAN.

This is one of the best restaurants on the island for the typical cuisine and local wines of Sicily. It's right on the sea, with a panoramic view, about 100 yards from the Piazzale dei Cappuccini. The decoration is firmly rooted in the turn-of-the-century Liberty (art nouveau) style. The antipasti array is dazzling, and the homemade pasta dishes are superb—try pasta rusticana with eggplant, cheese, ham, and herbs (ask one of the English-speaking waiters to explain the many variations) or spaghetti with fresh tuna and herbs. One of the most interesting fish dishes we recently sampled was *spada a pizzaiola* (swordfish in a savory, garlic-flavored sauce). Meat specialties include *bistecca siciliana* (tender beef with pulverized tomatoes, eggplant, onions, white wine, and local cheese); sliced veal with eggplant, tomatoes, onions, and slices of local cheese; and delicious fish stew. The dessert specialty is *cassatine siciliana* (mocha-chocolate ice cream capped with sprinkles of coffee-flavored chocolate, all floating in a lake of English custard). There's also a roof garden with a pizzeria serving typical Sicilian pizza.

Ristorante Rossini. Via Savoia 6. ☎ **0931/24-317.** Reservations recommended. Main courses 18,000–25,000L ($10–$15). AE, DC, MC, V. Wed–Mon noon–2pm and 7–10pm. Closed Dec 25. MEDITERRANEAN.

The Rossini is a homelike and comfortable enclave of regional gastronomy, offering meals to 50 fortunate diners a night. Pasqualino Guidice is one of the most respected chefs in Sicily, with a fame that derives from many international cooking demonstrations conducted throughout the Americas. Occupying a building from the 1920s, the restaurant offers an amply stocked buffet table of antipasti, including fish mousse garnished with shrimp, shellfish risotto with roasted peppers and tomato purée, *pesce alla matelote* (roasted fish with a sauce of capers, tomatoes, olives, herbs, and white wine), and an age-old Sicilian recipe for *pesce alla stimpirata* (with olive oil, garlic, mint, and vinegar). Twice-roasted swordfish is also a specialty.

SYRACUSE AFTER DARK

If you tire of the spectacular vista beside the ancient harbor, you might want to stray farther afield for an evening of dancing. The region's most appealing disco is **Fontana**

Bianca, Via Dei Lidi (☎ 0931/790-611), 11 miles southwest of the town center. It contains a walled garden, a pool that at night seems mostly ornamental, and a clientele that's older and better established than you'll find at the student hangouts closer to the town center. Another option is the **Discotecca Malibu,** Via Elorina (☎ 0931/ 721-888), about 3½ miles southwest of town on the SS115, where a younger crowd seems full of the energy it takes to dance all night at a seaside pavilion that evokes its California namesake.

Malibu's most visible competitor is **La Nottola,** Via Gargallo 61 (☎ 0931/ 60-009). On a small street near Via Maestanza, it conveys a sense of restrained style and, at times, even glamour. Mingling aspects of a jazz club, piano bar, and disco, it attracts a crowd that's usually better dressed than the norm. If you ask anyone in town where to go, this is the place they'll probably recommend. If you should happen to arrive in midsummer, head for the **Sporting Cub Terrauzza** (☎ 0931/714-505), centerpiece of the hamlet of Terrauzza, about 6 miles southwest of Syracuse, where whoever happens to be vacationing on the local beaches shows up to mingle with local 20-somethings.

Some of the most evocative cultural events in Sicily are presented in May and June of even-numbered years, when actors from the Istituto Nazionale del Dramma Antico present a repertoire of **classical plays** by Aeschylus, Euripides, and their contemporaries. The setting is the ancient Greek theater (Teatro Greco) in the archaeological park, beneath the open sky. Tickets are 25,000L to 70,000L ($15 to $41). For information, schedules, and tickets, write or call **INDA,** Corso G. Matteotti 29, 96100 Siracusa (☎ 0931/674-15 or, within Italy, ☎ 1478/822-11).

3 Agrigento: A Great Classical Site

80 miles S of Palermo, 109 miles SE of Trápani, 135 miles W of Syracuse

Greek colonists from Gela (Caltanissetta) called this area Akragas when they established a beachhead here in the 6th century B.C. In time, the settlement grew to become one of the most prosperous cities in Magna Graecia. A great deal of that growth is attributed to the despot Phalaris, who ruled from 571 to 555 B.C. and is said to have roasted his victims inside a brass bull. He eventually met the same fate.

Empedocles (ca. 490 to 430 B.C.), the Greek philosopher and politician (also considered by some the founder of medicine in Italy), was the most famous son of Akragas. He formulated the theory that matter consists of four elements (earth, fire, water, and air), modified by the agents love and strife. In modern times the town produced playwright Luigi Pirandello (1867 to 1936),who won the Nobel Prize for literature in 1934.

Like nearby Selinunte, the city was attacked by war-waging Carthaginians, beginning in 406 B.C. In the 3rd century B.C. the city changed hands between the Carthaginians and Romans until it finally succumbed to Roman domination by 210 B.C. It was then known as Agrigentium.

The modern part of **Agrigento** (in 1927 the name was changed from Girgenti to Agrigento) occupies a hill. The narrow casbahlike streets show to the influence of the conquering Saracens. Heavy Allied bombing during World War II necessitated much rebuilding. The result is for the most part uninspired and not helped by all the cement factories in the area.

Below the town stretch the long reaches of the ✪ **Valley of the Temples (La Valle dei Templi),** containing some of the greatest Greek ruins in the world. See "Wandering Among the Ruins," below.

You visit Agrigento for its past—it's one of the most impressive classical sites in all of Italy—and not for the modern incarnation. It's been a long time since Pindar called it "man's finest city." However, once you've been awed by the ruined temples, you can visit the *centro storico*, with its tourist boutiques hawking postcards and T-shirts, and enjoy people-watching at a cafe along Via Atenea. When it gets too hot (as it so often does), flee to a beach at nearby San Leone.

ESSENTIALS

GETTING THERE   The **train** trip from Palermo takes 1½ hours and costs 12,100L ($7) each way. There are 11 trains daily. The main rail station, **Stazione Centrale,** Piazza Marconi (☎ **0922/29-007**), is just downhill from Piazzale Aldo Moro and Piazza Vittorio Emanuele, both landmark squares in the center of town. From Syracuse by rail, you must first take one of nine daily trains to Ragusa, a 2½-hour trip costing 10,500L ($6) each way. Three trains a day make the 3½-hour trip from Ragusa to Agrigento, costing 15,500L ($9) each way.

Capolinea, Via Ragazzi del 99, 10 (☎ **0922/596-490**), runs four **buses** per day from Palermo to Argirento. The trip takes 2½ hours and costs 11,000L ($6) one-way. **SAIS** buses, Via Favara Vecchia (☎ **0922/595-260**), make the 2½-hour trip from Catania 11 times a day. The one-way fare is 16,500L ($10).

By **car** from Syracuse, take SS115 through Gela. From Palermo, cut southeast along S121, which becomes S188 and S189 before it finally reaches Agrigento and the Mediterranean.

VISITOR INFORMATION   The **tourist office** is at Via Cesare Battisti, 15 (☎ **0922/20-454**). There's another office at Via Empedocle 73 (☎ **0922/20-391**). Both are open Monday to Saturday 8:30am to 1:45pm and 4 to 7pm.

WANDERING AMONG THE RUINS

Many writers are fond of suggesting that the Greek ruins in the **Valle dei Templi** be viewed at dawn or sunset. Indeed, their mysterious aura is heightened then. But for details, search them out under the bright cobalt-blue Sicilian sky. The backdrop is idyllic, especially in spring when the striking almond trees blossom into pink.

Board a bus or climb into your car to investigate. Riding out the Strada Panoramica, you'll first approach (on your left), the ✪ **Temple of Juno (Tempio di Giunone).** This temple was erected sometime in the mid–5th century B.C., at the peak of a construction boom honoring the deities. Many of its Doric columns have been restored. As you climb the blocks, note the remains of a cistern as well as a sacrificial altar in front. The temple affords good views of the entire valley.

The ✪ **Temple of the Concordia (Tempio della Concordia),** which you'll come to next, ranks along with the Temple of Hephaestos (the Theseion) in Athens as the best-preserved Greek temple in the world. With 13 columns on its side, 6 in front and 6 in back, the temple was built in the peripheral hexastyle. You'll see the clearest example in Sicily of what an inner temple was like. In the late 6th century A.D. the pagan structure was transformed into a Christian church, which may have saved it for posterity, though today it has been stripped down to its classical purity.

The **Temple of Hercules (Tempio di Ercole)** is the oldest, dating from the 6th century B.C. Badly ruined (only eight pillars are standing), it once ranked in size with the Temple of Zeus. At one time the temple sheltered a celebrated statue of Hercules. The infamous Gaius Verres, the Roman magistrate who became an especially bad governor of Sicily, attempted to steal the image as part of his temple-looting tear on the island. Astonishingly, you can still see signs of black searing from fires set by long-ago Carthaginian invaders.

The ✪ **Temple of Jove or Zeus (Tempio di Giove)** was the largest in the valley, similar in some respects to the Temple of Apollo at Selinunte, until it was ruined by an earthquake. It even impressed Goethe. In front of the structure was a large altar. The giant on the ground was one of several telamones (atlases) used to support the edifice. Carthaginian slave labor built what was then the largest Greek temple in the world, and one of the most remarkable.

The so-called **Temple of Castor and Pollux (Tempio di Dioscuri),** with four Doric columns intact, is a pasticcio—it's composed of fragments from different buildings. At various times it has been designated as a temple honoring Castor and Pollux, the twin sons of Leda and deities of seafarers; Demeter (Ceres), the goddess of marriage and of the fertile earth; or Persephone, the daughter of Zeus who became the symbol of spring. Note that on some maps this temple is called Tempio di Castore e Polluce.

The temples can usually be visited daily 9am until 1 hour before sunset. City bus nos. 8, 9, 10, and 11 run to the valley from the train station in Agrigento.

OTHER ATTRACTIONS

The **Regional Archaeological Museum (Museo Regionale Archeologico),** near San Nicola, on Contrada San Nicola at the outskirts of town on the way to the Valle dei Templi (☎ 0922/401-565), is open daily 8am to 1pm. Admission is free. Its single most important exhibit is a head of the god Telamon from the Tempio di Giove. The collection of Greek vases is also impressive. Many of the artifacts on display were dug up when Agrigento was excavated. Take bus no. 8, 9, 10, or 11.

Pirandello's House (Casa di Pirandello), Contrada Kaos, Frazione Kaos (☎ 0922/511-102), is the former home of the 1934 Nobel Prize winner, known worldwide for his plays *Six Characters in Search of an Author* and *Enrico IV.* He died 2 years after winning the prize and its attendant world acclaim. Though Agrigentans back then might not have liked his portrayal of Italy, all is forgiven now, and Pirandello is the local boy who made good. In fact, the Teatro Luigi Pirandello at Piazza Municipio bears his name. His "casa natale" is now a museum devoted to memorabilia pertaining to the playwright's life, including his study and murals he painted. His tomb lies under his favorite pine tree ("One night in June I dropped down like a firefly beneath a huge pine tree in the garden"). The tomb lies a few hundred yards from the house and the admission-free grounds, which are open Monday to Saturday 9am to 1:30pm (Monday to Friday also 3 to 5:45pm). The birthplace lies outside of town in the village of Kaos (catch bus no. 11 from Piazza Marconi), just west of the temple zone.

The **Settimana Pirandelliana** is a weeklong festival of plays, operas, and ballets staged in Piazza Kaos at the end of July and August. The tourist office can supply details; tickets cost 10,000L to 20,000L ($6 to $12).

ACCOMMODATIONS

Hotel Tre Torri. Strada Statale 115, Viale Canatello, Villaggio Mosè, 92100 Agrigento. ☎ 0922/606-733. Fax 0922/607-839. 118 units. A/C TV TEL. 160,000L ($93) double. Rates include breakfast. AE, MC, V. Free parking.

Though it's near an unattractive commercial district 4½ miles south of Agrigento in Villaggio Mosè, this is among the best hotels in the area. Sheltered behind a mock-medieval facade of white stucco, chiseled stone blocks, false crenellations, and crisscrossed iron balconies, the hotel, which opened in 1982, is a favorite with Italian business travelers. The guest rooms are comfortable, with modern furnishings. A pool in the terraced garden is visible from the restaurant. There are also an indoor swimming pool, sauna, and fitness center. The hotel also contains a bar, sometimes with live piano music, and a disco.

Hotel Villa Athena. Via dei Templi 33, 92100 Agrigento. ☎ **0922/596-288.** Fax 0922/ 402-180. 40 units. A/C TV TEL. 250,000–300,000L ($145–$174) double. Rates include breakfast. AE, DC, MC, V. Free parking.

A former private villa, this 18th-century structure rises from the landscape in the Valley of the Temples, less than 2 miles from town. It's the best place to stay in the area. The rooms are modern, with Italian styling. No. 205 frames a perfect view of the Temple of Concord. The grounds are planted with fruit trees that bloom in January. During the day guests sit in the paved courtyard, enjoying a drink and the fresh breezes. At night you have a view of the floodlit temples, a string of Doric ruins, from one of the windows. There's a pool in a setting of gardenia bushes and flowers. The dining room is in a separate building, serving both regional specialties and international dishes. In summer, make a reservation about 2 weeks in advance.

DINING
Le Caprice. Strada Panoramica dei Templi 51. ☎ **0922/26-469.** Reservations required. Main courses 20,000–32,000L ($12–$19). AE, DC, MC. V. Sat–Thurs 12:30–3pm and 7:30–11pm. Closed July 1–15. SEAFOOD/SICILIAN.

Loyal customers return to this well-directed restaurant for special celebrations and every-day fun. Le Caprice is the only restaurant of any consequence in Agrigento; the rest are simple trattorie. Specialties of the house include an antipasto buffet, a mixed fry of fish from the gulf, and rolled pieces of veal in a flavorful sauce. The chef takes justifiable pride in his local specialty, stuffed swordfish. One German visitor came here seven nights in a row and ordered the dish each time.

Trattoria del Vigneto. Via Cavalleri Magazzeni 11. ☎ **0922/414-319.** Main courses 8,000–20,000L ($4.65–$12); fixed–price menu 25,000–30,000L ($15–$17). V. Wed–Mon noon–2:30pm and 7pm–midnight. Closed Nov. SICILIAN.

This is a simple place to go for a Sicilian meal after a visit to the nearby Valley of the Temples. You might try homemade pasta flavored with sardines, pine nuts, and balsamic vinegar; pasta alla Norma, with eggplant, ricotta, tomatoes, and fresh basil; or *bistecca vignolo* (steak garnished with prosciutto, mozzarella, and tomatoes). The welcome is sincere and the food perfectly acceptable and often quite flavorful.

4 Selinunte

76 miles SW of Palermo, 70 miles W of Agrigento, 55 miles SE of Trápani

One of the lost cities of ancient Sicily, ✪ **Selinunte** traces its history to the 7th century B.C., when immigrants from Megara Hyblaea (Syracuse) set out to build a new colony. They succeeded, erecting a city of power and prestige adorned with many temples. But that was calling attention to a good thing. Much of Selinunte's history concerns seemingly endless conflicts with the Elymi people of Segesta (see below). Siding with Selinunte's rival, Hannibal virtually leveled the city in 409 B.C. The city never recovered its former glory and ultimately fell into decay.

ESSENTIALS
GETTING THERE   From Palermo, Trápani, or Marsala, you can make **rail** connections to Castelvetrano. Once at Castelvetrano, you must board a bus for Selinunte. Most passengers reach Selinunte from Palermo (call ☎ 091/616-1806 in Palermo for rail information); the trip takes 2 hours and costs 5,200L ($3.10) each way.

From Agrigento, take one of the four daily **buses** to Castelvetrano, a 2¼-hour trip that costs 9,600L ($6) one-way. Buses (about five per day) depart for Selinunte from in front of the rail terminal at Castelvetrano. The one-way fare is 2,000L ($1.15) for the 20-minute trip. For information, call ☎ **091/617-5411.**

Selinunte is on the southern coast of Sicily and is best explored by **car,** because public transportation is awkward. From Agrigento, take Route 115 northwest into Castelvetrano, then follow the signposted secondary road marked SELINUNTE, which leads south to the sea.

VISITOR INFORMATION   There are no tourist offices in the area.

EXPLORING THE ARCHAEOLOGICAL GARDEN

Today Selinunte's temples lie in scattered ruins, the honey-colored stone littering the ground as if an earthquake had struck (as one did in ancient times). From 9am to dusk daily you can walk through the monument zone, exploring such relics as the remains of the **Acropolis,** the heart of old Selinunte. Parts of it have been partially excavated and reconstructed, as much as is possible with the bits and fragments remaining. Admission is 2,000L ($1.15).

The temples, in varying states of preservation, are designated by letters. They're dedicated to such mythological figures as Apollo and Hera (Juno); most date from the 6th and 5th centuries B.C. The Doric **Temple E** contains fragments of an inner temple. Standing on its ruins before the sun goes down, you can look across the water that washes up on the shores of Africa, from which the Carthaginian fleet emerged to destroy the city. **Temple G,** in scattered ruins, was one of the largest erected in Sicily and was also built in the Doric style.

ACCOMMODATIONS & DINING NEARBY

The site of the ruins of Selinunte contains virtually no hotels, restaurants, or watering holes of note. Most visitors stop at the temple for a daylight visit, heading on to other locales at night. There are a handful of overnight accommodations in the little seafront village of Marinella, about a mile east of Selinunte. To reach Marinella, you'll travel along a narrow country road.

Hotel Alceste. Via Alceste 23, 91020 Marinella di Selinunte. ☎ **0924/46-184.** Fax 0924/ 46-143. 26 units. A/C TV TEL. 130,000–140,000L ($75–$81) double. Breakfast 10,000L ($6). AE, DC, MC, V.

This hotel, most busy in summer (and occasionally closed for periods in winter), is about a 15-minute walk from the ruins. The recently renovated rooms have new furniture. Most visitors, however, stop only for a meal in the plant-filled courtyard. They enjoy a regional Sicilian dinner; the price of a meal starts at 25,000L ($15). In summer, there's musical entertainment, dancing, cabaret, and theater in the garden in front of the hotel, which is only 300 yards from the sea.

At press time, the owners were planning a second hotel, the 50-room **Alceste II,** a short walk from the original hotel. Rates and amenities were expected to be roughly equivalent to those at the Alceste.

5 Segesta

24 miles SW of Palermo, 91 miles NW of Agrigento

✪ **Segesta** was the ancient city of the Elymi, a people of mysterious origin linked by some to the Trojans. As the major city in western Sicily, it was brought into a series of conflicts with the rival power nearby, Selinus (Selinunte). From the 6th through the

5th centuries B.C. there were near-constant hostilities. The Athenians came from the east to aid the Segestans in 415 B.C., but the expedition ended in disaster, eventually forcing the city to turn for help to Hannibal of Carthage.

Twice in the 4th century B.C. Segesta was besieged and conquered, once by Dionysius and again by Agathocles (a particularly brutal victor who tortured, mutilated, or made slaves of most of the citizenry). Segesta in time turned on its old but dubious ally, Carthage. Like all Greek cities of Sicily, it ultimately fell to the Romans.

ESSENTIALS

GETTING THERE   One **train** a day runs between Palermo and Segesta. It departs at the inconvenient hour of 6:42am, returning to Palermo at 1pm. The ride takes about 30 minutes each way and costs 9,000L ($5).

There's **bus** service between Palermo and the ancient theater, but it's scheduled only in conjunction with the presentation of plays. As many as half a dozen buses leave from Palermo's Piazza Politeama, beginning around 2 hours before the scheduled beginning of any performance. For information, contact either the tourist office or **Noema Viaggi,** Via di Marzo 13 (☎ **091/625-4221**). A round-trip ticket is around 8,500L ($4.95).

By **car,** drive west from Palermo along autostrada A29, branching onto the A29dir past Álcamo. From Selinunte, head to Castelvetrano to connect to the A29 headed north, branching onto the A29dir.

VISITOR INFORMATION   Consult the **tourist office** in Palermo (see below).

EXPLORING ANCIENT RUINS & ATTENDING CLASSICAL PLAYS

Visit Segesta for its remarkable ✪ **Doric temple** from the 5th century B.C. Although never completed, it's in an excellent state of preservation (the entablature still remains). The temple was far enough away from the ancient town to have escaped leveling during the "scorched earth" days of the Vandals and Arabs.

From its position on a lonely hill, the Doric temple commands a majestic setting. Though you can scale the hill on foot, you're likely to encounter boys trying to hustle you for a donkey ride (we advise against it—some of the animals have saddle sores and seem to be in pain when ridden). From mid-July until the first of August in odd-numbered years, **classical plays** are performed at the temple. (In the spring of even-numbered years, equivalent performances take place at the ancient theater at Syracuse.) Ask at the tourist information office in Palermo for details. Travel agents in Palermo sell tickets for 15,000L to 25,000L ($9 to $15).

In another spot on Mount Barbaro, a **theater,** built in the Greek style into the rise of the hill, has been excavated. It was erected in the 3rd century B.C.

There's a cafe in the parking area leading to the temple; otherwise, Segesta is bereft of dining or accommodation selections.

6 Palermo: Sicily's Capital

145 miles W of Messina, 448 miles S of Naples, 580 miles S of Rome

As the ferry docks in the Bay of Palermo and you start spotting blond, blue-eyed *bambini* all over the place in **Palermo,** don't be surprised. If fair-haired children don't fit your concept of what a Sicilian should look like, remember that the Normans landed here in 1060, 6 years before William the Conqueror put in at Hastings, and launched a campaign to wrest control of the island from the Arabs. Today you can see elements of both cultures, notably in Palermo's architecture—a unique style, Norman-Arabic.

Impressions

I have heard it said that Sicilians can't use the telephone because they need both hands to talk with.

—Anonymous

The city is the largest port of Sicily, its capital, and the meeting place of a regional parliament granted numerous autonomous powers in postwar Italy. Against a backdrop of the citrus-studded Conca d'Oro plain and Monte Pellegrino, it's a city of wide boulevards, old quarters in the legendary Sicilian style (laundry lapping against the wind, smudge-faced kids playing in the street), town houses, architecturally harmonious squares, baroque palaces, and modern buildings (many erected after Allied bombings in 1943). It also has the worst traffic jams in Sicily.

Palermo was founded by the Phoenicians, but it has known many conquerors. Some (Frederick II) established courts of great splendor; others (the Angevins) brought decay.

Today the city of 900,000 is *la brutta e la bella,* the ugly and the beautiful. Overcrowded, decaying in parts, and with unemployment and poverty rampant, it's nevertheless a historically significant showcase of artistic treasures. It has the dubious reputation of being the home turf of the Mafia, sheltering some of the world's most powerful dons (none of whom looks like Marlon Brando). As you make your way through the city—occasionally seeing an armor-plated Alfa Romeo pass by—avoid Vespa-riding bag snatchers and some of the most brilliant pickpockets in the world and you should have a fine time.

ESSENTIALS

GETTING THERE   If you **fly** from Rome or Naples, you'll land at **Cinisi–Punta Raisi** (☎ 091/601-9333 for domestic flights, 091/702-0111 for international), 19 miles west of Palermo. It's best to catch a local airport bus from the airport to Piazza Castelnuovo; the fare is 4,500L ($2.60). For the same trip a taxi is likely to charge at least 65,000L ($38)—more if the driver thinks he can get away with it.

For information about traveling by **train,** see "Getting to Sicily," at the beginning of this chapter. After a 3½-hour ride from Messina across the north coast, you arrive at Palermo's station at **Piazza Giulio Césare** (☎ 091/616-1806), which lies on the east side of town and is linked to the center by buses and taxis.

Palermo has **bus** connections with other major cities, operated by **SAIS,** Via Balsamo 16 (☎ 091/616-6028). Some 23 buses a day make the 2½-hour trip from Catania; the one-way cost is 18,000L ($10). One bus a day (except Sunday) arrives from Syracuse; the trip lasts 4 hours and costs 16,000L ($9) one-way. The bus terminal is near the rail station.

After you arrive by **car** from mainland Italy at Messina, head west on autostrada A20, which becomes Route 113, then A20 again, and finally A19 before its final approach to Palermo.

VISITOR INFORMATION   There are **tourist offices** at strategic points, including the **Palermo airport** (☎ 091/591-698). The principal office is the **Azienda Autonoma Turismo,** Piazza Castelnuovo 34 (☎ 091/583-847), open Monday to Friday 8am to 8pm and Saturday 8am to 2pm.

GETTING AROUND   One municipal bus ticket costs 1,500L (85¢), or you can buy a full-day ticket for 5,000L ($2.90). For information and schedules, call **AMAT,** Via Borrelli (091/321-333). Most passengers purchase their tickets at tobacco shops (*tabacchi*) before boarding. Otherwise, keep some 100L coins handy.

A Crime Warning

Be especially alert. Palermo is home to some of the most skilled pickpockets on the continent. Keep your gems locked away (in other words, don't flaunt any sign of wealth). Women who carry handbags are especially vulnerable to purse-snatchers on Vespas (wear the strap over one shoulder and across your chest with the purse hanging on the wall side of the sidewalk). Don't leave valuables in your car. In fact, we almost want to say don't leave your car alone, even knowing how impossible that is unless you put it in a garage (highly recommended). Police squads operate mobile centers through the town to help combat street crime.

EXPLORING THE OLD TOWN

The "four corners" of the city, **Quattro Canti di Città,** is in the heart of the old town, at the junction of Corso Vittorio Emanuele and Via Maqueda. The ruling Spanish of the 17th century influenced the design of this grandiose baroque square, replete with fountains and statues. From here you can walk to **Piazza Bellini,** the most attractive square of the old city. In an atmosphere reminiscent of the setting for an operetta, you're likely to hear strolling singers with guitars entertaining pizza eaters. Opening onto it is **Santa Maria dell'Ammiraglio** (also known as "La Martorana"), Piazza Bellini 3 (☎ **091/616-1692**). Erected in 1143 by an admiral to Roger II, it has a Byzantine cupola. Its decaying but magnificent bell tower was built from 1146 to 1185. The church is open Monday to Saturday 9:30am to 1pm and 3:30 to 7pm and Sunday 8:30am to 1pm. Admission is free.

Also fronting the square is **San Cataldo** (1160), in the Arab-Byzantine style with a trio of faded pink cupolas. In a 12th-century building constructed in a cubic form, it belonged to the order of the Knights of the Holy Sepulchre. Also opening onto Piazza Bellini is **Santa Caterina,** attached to a vast Dominican monastery constructed in 1310. The church is late 16th century and contains interesting 18th-century multicolored marble ornamentation.

Adjoining the square is **Piazza Pretoria,** dominated by a fountain designed in Florence in 1554 for a villa but acquired by Palermo about 20 years later. A short walk will take you to the cathedral of Palermo.

Il Duomo. Piazza di Cattedrale, Corso Vittorio Emanuele. ☎ **091/334-376.** Free admission (donation appreciated). Apr–Oct daily 7am–7pm; Nov–Mar daily 7am–noon and 4–6pm.

East meets West in this cathedral, a curious spectacle. It was built in the 12th century on the foundation of an earlier basilica that the Arabs had converted into a mosque. The cathedral—much altered over the centuries—was founded by an English archbishop known as Walter of the Mill. The impressive gothic "porch" on the southern front was built in the 15th century. But the cupola, added in the late 18th century, detracts from the overall appearance, and the interior was revamped unsuccessfully at the same time, resulting in a glaring incongruity in styles. The pantheon of royal tombs includes that of the Holy Roman Emperor Frederick II, in red porphyry under a canopy of marble.

San Giovanni degli Eremiti. Via dei Benedettini Bianchi 3. ☎ **091/651-5019.** Free admission. Daily 9am–12:30pm; Mon and Thurs 3–6pm.

The other church (now deconsecrated) worthy of note is St. John of the Hermits. In an atmosphere appropriate for the recluse it honors, this little church with its twin-columned cloister is one of the most idyllic spots in all of Palermo. A medieval veil hangs heavy in the gardens, with their citrus blossoms and flowers, especially on

Checking Out La Kalsa

Although it's a bit dangerous, especially at night, the crumbling **La Kalsa** is the most interesting district of Palermo. In the southwestern sector of the old city, it was built by the Arabs as a walled seaside residence for their chief ministers. It's bounded by the port and Via Garibaldi and Via Paternostro to the east and west and by Corso Vittorio Emanuele and Via Lincoln to the north and south. Later, much of the Arabs' fine work was destroyed when the Spanish viceroys took over, adding their own architectural interpretations. One of the neighborhood's most dramatic churches (though not necessarily the oldest) is the fancifully baroque **Santa Teresa,** Piazza Kalsa (☎ **091/617-1658**).

La Kalsa, one of whose main thoroughfares is the Via Butero, has been called one of the least restored, most authentically battered historic neighborhoods in Europe. To reach it, begin at the Quattro Canti di Città (above), and walk eastward along the **Corso Vittorio Emanuele,** which locals usually refer to simply as "Il Corso." Cross over the bustling Via Roma, then turn right onto the Via Paternostro until you reach **San Francesco d'Assisi,** a church from the 13th century on Piazza San Francesco d'Assisi (☎ **091/616-2819**). Visit the church if for no other reason than to see its magnificent Cappella Mastrotonio, carved in 1468. Don't count on the church's being open, however.

From Piazza San Francesco d'Assisi, follow Via Merlo to the **Palazzo Mirto,** Via Merlo 2 (☎ **091/616-4751**), to see how nobility lived in the days when this was an upmarket neighborhood. The palace, a splendid example of a princely residence of the early 20th century, contains its original 18th- and 19th-century furnishings. It's open Monday to Friday 9am to 1pm and 3 to 6pm and Saturday and Sunday 9am to 12:30pm. Admission is 4,000L ($2.30).

Via Merlo leads into the landmark **Piazza Marina,** one of the most evocative parts of Palermo. The port of La Cala was here, but it silted up the 1100s. Like something out of the American Deep South, a garden is found at the Villa Garibaldi in the center of the square. The square is dominated by the Palazzo Chiaramonte on the southeast corner, dating from the early 14th century. Renaissance churches occupy the other three corners of this historic square.

---

a hot summer day as you wander around in the cloister. Built on the order of Roger II in 1132, the church exhibits its Arabic influence, surmounted by pinkish cupolas, while showing the Norman style as well.

Palace of the Normans (Palazzo dei Normanni). Piazza del Parlamento. ☎ **091/ 705-4317.** Free palace tours by advance reservation only. Chapel Mon–Sat 9am–noon; Mon–Fri 3–5pm; Sun 9–10am and noon–1pm.

The Palace of the Normans contains one of the greatest art treasures in Sicily, the **Palatine Chapel (Cappella Palatina).** Erected at Roger II's command in the 1130s, it's the finest example of the Arabic-Norman style of design and building. The effect of the lushly colored mosaics inside is awe-inspiring. Almond-eyed biblical characters from the Byzantine art world create a panorama of epic pageantry, illustrating such Gospel scenes as the Nativity. The overall picture is further enhanced by inlaid marble and mosaics as well as by pillars made of granite shipped from the East. For a look at still more mosaics, this time in a more secular vein depicting scenes of the hunt, head upstairs to the **Hall of Roger II,** the seat of the Sicilian Parliament, where security is likely to be tight.

Regional Gallery (Galleria Regionale della Sicilia). Via Alloro 4. ☎ **091/616-4317.** Admission 8,000L ($4.65) adults, free for children under 18. Mon–Sat 9am–1:30pm; Tues, Thurs 3–7:30pm; and Sun 9am–12:30pm.

The Gothic-Renaissance Palazzo Abatellis houses the Regional Gallery, which shows the evolution of art in Sicily from the 13th to the 18th century. On the ground floor is the most famous work, the 15th-century fresco *Triumph of Death,* in all its gory magnificence. A horseback-riding skeleton, representing Death, tramples his victims. Worthy of mention are three majolica plates, valuable specimens of *Loza dorada* manufactured in the workshops of Manises, and the *Giara* produced in the workshops of Málaga at the end of the 13th century.

Francesco Laurana's slanty-eyed *Eleonora d'Aragona* is worth seeking out, as are seven grotesque D'Roleries painted on wood. On the second floor, *L'Annunziata* by Antonello da Messina, a portrait of the Madonna executed with depth and originality, is one of the most celebrated paintings in Italy. The 13th room contains a very good series of Flemish paintings from the 15th and 16th centuries; the best is the *Trittico Malvagna* by Jean Gossaert (known as Mabuse).

Regional Archaeological Museum (Museo Archeologico Regionale). Piazza Olivella 4. ☎ **091/662-0220.** Admission 2,000L ($1.15). Mon–Sat 9am–2pm, Sun 9am–1pm; Tues, Fri 3–6:30pm.

In a former residence for Philippine friars, this is one of the greatest archeological collections in southern Italy, where the competition's stiff. Many works displayed here were excavated at Selinunte, once one of the major towns in Magna Graecia. See, in particular, the Sala di Selinunte, displaying the celebrated metopes that adorned the classical temples, as well as slabs of bas-relief. The gallery also owns important sculpture from the Temple of Himera. The collection of bronzes is exceptional, including the athlete and the stag discovered in the ruins of Pompeii (a Roman copy of a Greek original) and a bronze ram that came from Syracuse, dating from the 3rd century B.C. Among the Greek sculpture is *The Pouring Satyr,* excavated at Pompeii (a Roman copy of a Greek original by Praxiteles).

Catacombs of the Capuchins (Catacombe dei Cappuccini). Piazza Cappuccini 1. ☎ **091/212-117.** Free admission (donations accepted). Tours Mon–Sat 9am–noon and 3–6pm; closed holidays.

The final attraction, on the outskirts of the city, is the most bizarre. The fresco you might have seen in the Regional Gallery, *Triumph of Death,* dims in comparison to the real thing. These catacombs contained a preservative that helped to mummify the dead. Sicilians—from nobles to maids—were buried here in the 19th century, and it was the custom on Sunday to visit Uncle Luigi and see how he was holding together. If he fell apart, he was wired together or wrapped in burlap sacking. In 1920 the last person buried in the catacombs was laid to rest—a little girl almost lifelike in death. Many 19th-century Sicilians are in fine shape, considering—with eyes, hair, and even clothing fairly intact. Some of the expressions on the faces of the skeletons take the fun out of Halloween—a grotesque ballet.

SHOPPING

The most colorful place to shop, even if you don't buy anything, is **Vucciria,** off Via Roma in the rear of San Domenico. This is one of the great casbahlike markets of Europe. Here are mountains of food, from fish to meat and vegetables. The array of wild fennel, long-stemmed artichokes, and blood oranges, as well as giant octopus and squid, calls for a painter at least. In Sicilian dialect, *vucciria* means "hubbub," and that's an apt name for this market. As an offbeat adventure, try dining at **Shangai,**

Vicolo Mezzani 34 (☎ 091/589-702), which cooks virtually anything that is sold in the market. You can sample several fish specialties, including eel, by ordering the mixed fish fry. The market is open Monday to Saturday 8am to 4pm; Shangai stays open to 11pm. You can also sample the wares offered at various food stalls, including chickpea-flour fritters or deep-fried meat- or cheese-filled pockets of dough (*calzoni*). To go really local, ask for *guasteddi*—a fresh bun stuffed with narrow strips of calf's spleen and ricotta, dished up with a fiery hot sauce. Everything shuts down on Sunday.

Two shops in one, **Battaglia,** Via Ruggero Settimo 74/M (☎ 091/580-224), sells womenswear. Within it, Hermès offers upscale men's and women's apparel, including prêt-à-porter and alta moda collections. There's also a limited selection of casual and sports shoes, as well as leather accessories, but this shop is really about clothing.

If it comes in linen, **Frette,** Via Ruggero Settimo 12 (☎ 091/585-166) and Via G. Sciutti 85 (☎ 091/343-288), sells it. The shop offers sheets, tablecloths, towels, bedspreads, pajamas, nightgowns, curtains, and tapestries. Call for an appointment at **Miroslava Tasic,** Largo Cavalieri di Malta 2 (☎ 091/588-126), if you're interested in purchasing handmade sheets, curtains, towels, tablecloths, or upholstery fabrics in fine cottons, silks, and linens, adorned with embroidery or lace trim.

For jewelry in silver or gold, plain or inlaid with the gems of your choice, check out **Ma Gi,** Via Ruggero Settimo 45 (☎ 91/611-1513). It also carries dishes and cutlery in silver. If you can afford it, they can make it. For sterling and Sheffield silver pieces from various eras, **Fecarotta,** Via Principe di Belmonte 103/B (☎ 091/331-518), is a market leader. It also sells English and Italian antique furniture and paintings, as well as English silver, antique jewelry, and Sheffield silver plates.

You'll find traditional fruit-filled tarts as well as *cassata siciliana* (tarts with ricotta-based filling) at **Fratelli Magri,** Via Isidoro Carini 42 (☎ 091/584-788). The shop also makes other types of sweets, and in the summer offers gelato, but come here for the authentic high-calorie pastries.

A meat-eater's fantasy shop, **Mangia Charcuterie,** Via Principe di Belmonte 104/D (☎ 091/587-651), stocks all the meats and meat products produced in Sicily. It's a baffling compendium of sausages, pâtés, mortadellas, and every possible kind of sausage, as well as a worthy selection of meats and sausages imported from Austria. There are also pâtés either imported from France or crafted in the French style. You can carry these products away as part of a picnic or arrange to have items shipped.

A celebration of local and national confections, **I Peccatucci di Mamma Andrea,** Via Principe di Scordia 67 (☎ 091/334-835), tempts newcomers with the bounty of Sicily's traditional fattening desserts. Named after a legendary and formidable matriarch whose reputation as a pastry maker was almost celestial (at least in her family), the shop sells desserts that are very, very sweet and very, very Italian. Examples are pralines, *torrone, panetoni,* segments of fruit dripping with Sicilian honey, marzipan, and an age-old specialty known as *ghirlande di croccantini* (a hazelnut torte). Get ready for sugar shock and lots of local color.

One of the most comprehensive bookstores in Palermo is the **Libreria Flaccovio,** Via Ruggero Settimo 37 (☎ 091/589-442). Most of the inventory is in Italian, with good numbers of art books that celebrate the historic legacies of Sicily; a few volumes (but more than any other outfit in Palermo) are in English.

Four generations have handcrafted tortoiseshell picture frames at **Meli,** Via Dante 294 (☎ 091/682-4213), where you can also find a selection of stylish prints, etchings, and engravings from the 16th through 19th centuries. One of the best-established emporiums for Sicilian versions of majolica-style stoneware is **De Simone,** which has been making the stuff in a family-run setup since at least the 1920s. There's a shop at Via Gaetano Daita 13B (☎ 091/584-876), and both a shop and a factory (which can be visited) at Via Principe de Scalea 698 (☎ 091/671-1005). The shops are open Monday to Saturday, but the factory can be visited only Monday to Friday 8am to 5pm. No reservations are necessary.

Sicilian potters have artfully merged influences from the Arab and Christian world in their brightly painted trademark stoneware. One of Palermo's most visible outlets is **Verde Italiano,** Via Principe di Villafranca 42 (☎ 091/320-282). The store sells artfully crafted dinner plates, coffee cups, garden ornaments, jardinieres, and chandeliers, any of which can be insured and shipped to wherever you specify. There's also a factory on the premises, which you can tour without an appointment.

ACCOMMODATIONS

Generally you'll find a poor lot of hostelries, with only a few fine choices. Hunt and pick carefully.

EXPENSIVE

Centrale Palace Hotel. Corso Vittorio Emanuele 327 (at Via Maqueda), 91039 Palermo. ☎ **091/336-666.** Fax 091/334-881. www.bestwestern.com. E-mail: cphotel@tin.it. 63 units. A/C TV TEL. 310,000L ($180) double; 388,500L ($225) junior suite. Rates include buffet breakfast. AE, MC, V. Parking 15,000L ($9).

One of the city's most appealing hotels occupies the premises of a structure built in the 1600s as an opulent private home in the historic core. About a century ago, it became a hotel and in the early 1990s was thoroughly renovated into a plush and comfortable favorite of traveling business executives. You'll find flowers in the public rooms, a congenial, well-informed staff, and enough comforts (including airconditioning) to make you appreciate the amenities of the modern age. Guests gather in the bar before heading for the formal dining room. The chef specializes in Sicilian and international dishes.

Villa Igiea Grand Hotel. Salita Belmonte 43, 90142 Palermo. ☎ **091/543-744.** Fax 091/547-654. 116 units. A/C MINIBAR TV TEL. 367,000L ($213) double; 800,000L ($464) suite. Rates include breakfast. AE, DC, MC, V. Free parking.

The Villa Igiea was built at the turn of the century as one of Sicily's great aristocratic estates, and today it's the second-best luxury hotel on the island (it lags behind the San Domenico in Taormina). The exterior resembles a medieval Sicilian fortress whose carefully chiseled walls include crenellated battlements and forbidding watchtowers. It was constructed of the same buff-colored stone Greek colonists used during the Punic Wars. They erected a circular temple that, heavily buttressed with modern scaffolding, still stands in the garden. Nearby, in a grove of pines and palms, is an art nouveau statue of Igiea, goddess of flowers. Everywhere are clusters of antiques. The accommodations vary from sumptuous suites with private terraces to smaller, less glamorous rooms. The hotel, reached by passing through an industrial port area north of Palermo, sits on a cliff with a view of the open sea.

Dining/Diversions: The hotel's bar is baronial, with a soaring stone vault. You dine on Sicilian and classic Italian meals in a grand, glittering room against a backdrop of paneled walls, ornate ceilings, and chandeliers.

Amenities: Room service, baby-sitting, laundry/valet; terrace overlooking the water, pool, tennis court.

MODERATE

Grande Albergo Sole. Corso Vittorio Emanuele 291, 90133 Palermo. ☎ **091/581-811.** Fax 091/611-0182. 150 units. A/C MINIBAR TV TEL. 200,000–210,000L ($116–$122) double. Rates include breakfast. AE, DC, MC, V. Parking 10,000L ($6).

This pleasant, second-class hotel lies in the busy historic center of Palermo. A 1960s remake of a century-old building, it has a helpful staff and simple guest rooms, with radios and modern furniture, often reproductions of Sicilian 19th-century pieces. There's a lounge, a bar, a simple restaurant, and a roof garden terrace for sunbathing.

Jolly Hotel del Foro Italico. Via Foro Italico 22, 90133 Palermo. ☎ **800/221-2626** in the U.S., 800/247-1277 in Canada, or 091/616-5090 in Italy. Fax 091/616-1441. 218 units. A/C MINIBAR TV TEL. 210,000–250,000L ($122–$145) double; 250,000–296,000L ($145–$172) suite. Rates include breakfast. Half board 43,000L ($25) per person. AE, DC, MC, V. Parking 20,000L ($12).

Off a busy boulevard facing the Gulf of Palermo, this aging 1960s chain hotel is one of the best in town, especially popular for wedding receptions. The well-organized guest rooms contain lots of built-in pieces and comfortable beds. Try for the quieter rooms on the upper floors (which afford at least a glimpse of the Mediterranean) or at the rear. The Jolly also has a garden, a pool, a restaurant that serves Sicilian and Italian food, and an American bar.

President Hotel. Via Francesco Crispi 230, 90139 Palermo. ☎ **091/580-733.** Fax 091/611-1588. 129 units. A/C TV TEL. 200,000L ($116) double. Rates include breakfast. AE, DC, MC, V. Parking 9,000L ($5).

With an 8-story concrete-and-glass facade rising above the harborfront quays, this is one of the better and more up-to-date middle-bracket hotels in town. Built in 1978, it was renovated in the early 1990s. You'll pass beneath the soaring arcade before entering the informal stone-trimmed lobby. One of the most appealing coffee shop/bars in town lies at the top of a short flight of stairs next to the reception area. There's a restaurant on the top floor, plus a guarded parking garage in the basement. The guest rooms are comfortably furnished though short on style.

INEXPENSIVE

Albergo Cavour. Via Alessandro Manzoni 11, 90133 Palermo. ☎ **091/616-2759.** 10 units, 4 with bathroom. 45,000L ($26) double without bathroom, 55,000L ($32) double with bathroom. No credit cards. Parking 10,000L ($6).

Albergo Cavour is on the fifth floor of a Mussolini-modern-style 1930s building conveniently located 150 yards from the central station. The rooms are functional, unpretentious, and suitable for overnight stopovers; the manager sees to it that they're well kept and decently furnished, with comfortable mattresses. No meals are served, but many cafes are nearby.

Hotel Sausele. Via Vincenzo Errante 12, 90127 Palermo. ☎ **091/616-1308.** Fax 091/616-7525. 36 units. TEL. 125,000L ($73) double. Rates include breakfast. AE, DC, MC, V. Parking 15,000L ($9).

This hotel near the railway station is the best in a run-down area. Owned and managed efficiently by Swiss-born Signora Sausele, it's a modest but pleasant albergo, with rooms just adequate for a good night's rest. The hotel has an elevator, garage, bar, and TV room. The lounges are air-conditioned.

DINING
MODERATE

Gourmand's. Via della Libertà 37/A. ☎ **091/323-431.** Reservations recommended. Main courses 14,000–28,000L ($8–$16). AE, DC, MC, V. Mon–Sat 12:30–3pm and 7:30–11pm. Closed Aug 5–25. SICILIAN.

Gourmand's is among the best restaurants in Palermo for an introduction to the rich, aromatic cookery of Sicily. The cuisine is on par with Charleston's, though the atmosphere is less elegant. A corner restaurant in the commercial district, it's an air room filled with original paintings and Chinese-red ceiling lattices. You'll admire the richly laden antipasto table before you're ushered to your table. For a first course, try spaghetti Gourmand's (with fresh mozzarella, basil, and tomatoes) or an *involtino* of eggplant. Fresh fish is always available—try it grilled. The chef does many Italian dishes well, including veal escalope in the Valdostan style, pepper steak, and, if available, roast quail. Risotto with salmon is often featured on the menu, as is rigatoni Henry IV, made with mushrooms and ham in white sauce and tomato sauce.

La Scuderia. Viale del Fante 9. ☎ **091/520-323.** Reservations recommended. Main courses 22,000–35,000L ($13–$20). AE, DC, MC, V. Mon–Sat 12:30–3pm and 8:30pm–midnight. Closed 2 weeks in Aug. INTERNATIONAL/ITALIAN.

Dedicated professionals direct this appealing restaurant surrounded by trees at the foot of Monte Pellegrino, 3 miles north of the city center. It's the only restaurant in Palermo whose cuisine equals that of Gourmand's and Charleston. In summer, it has one of the prettiest flowery terraces in town, sought after by everyone from lovers to extended families to vacationing glamour queens. The imaginative cuisine includes a mixed grill of fresh vegetables with a healthy dose of a Sicilian cheese called *caciocavallo*, stuffed turkey cutlet, a wide array of beef and veal dishes, *involtini* of eggplant or veal, risotto with seafood, hake baked in saffron sauce, *maccheroni Nettuno* (studded with swordfish, sliced eggplant, and tomato sauce). Among the tempting desserts is one known as *pernice all'erotica* (vanilla ice cream with hot chocolate sauce).

Ristorante Charleston. Oct–May, Piazzale Ungheria 30, Palermo. June–Sept, Viale Regina Elena, Mondello. ☎ **091/321-366.** Main courses 15,000–60,000L ($9–$35). AE, DC, MC, V. Oct–May Mon–Sat 1–3:30pm and 8pm–midnight; June–Sept daily 1–4pm and 8pm–midnight. SICILIAN/INTERNATIONAL.

For years, the Charleston was regarded as the finest restaurant in Sicily. Although there's a lot more competition for that title today, it remains a national culinary monument, an appealing choice in Palermo—and, in summer, in nearby Mondello. The owners create a refined milieu for their renditions of Sicilian dishes, which naturally concentrate on fresh fish, especially roast swordfish. The kitchen prepares a number of international dishes as well, but we prefer to stick to the regional fare, especially if it's the chef's special spaghetti *all'aragosta* (with a delectable lobster sauce). Other specialties include pasta with sardines; eggplant Charleston, laden with tomatoes, cheese, and herbs; an *involtini* of swordfish; and torta Charleston, an oh-so-rich cake.

INEXPENSIVE

Al Vicolo. Cortile Scimecaz (off Piazza San Francesco Saverio). ☎ **091/651-2464.** Reservations recommended. Main courses 12,000–14,000L ($7–$8); fixed-price menu 26,000–32,000L ($15–$19). No credit cards. Mon–Sat 1–3pm and 8–11:30pm. Closed Aug 10–25. SICILIAN.

This is one of the most characteristic trattorie in the city, and deserves more acclaim than it receives. The dining rooms were converted from a produce warehouse. For antipasti, try *panelle* (chickpea or garbanzo fritters), *arancini* (rice croquettes), potato croquettes, or sardines *à beccafico* (stuffed and flavored with laurel). You'll have a choice of many of the most typical dishes of Sicily, including pasta mixed with sardines and wild fennel (an acquired taste for some; for the devotee of Sicilian cuisine, reason enough to visit the restaurant). Any pasta labeled "alla Norma" comes with vine-ripened tomatoes and eggplant. The local fish is fresh and abundant, and local meats including lamb and kid are always offered. You can wash down the meal—Sicilians say "irrigate"—with a selection of regional wines.

Friends' Bar. Via Filipo Brunelleschi 138, Borgo Nuovo. ☎ **091/201-401.** Reservations required. Main courses 21,000–35,000L ($12–$20). AE, DC, MC, V. Tues–Sun 12:30–2:30pm and 8–11:30pm. Closed 3 weeks in Aug. SICILIAN.

In a suburb of Palermo about 6 miles north of the city center, this is one of the finest restaurants in the region. Named after the four friends (*amici*) who established it in the 1970s, it features an air-conditioned dining room and a gazebo-like indoor-outdoor structure that rises from the premises of a lush garden lined with potted flowers and shrubs. A meal here is a sought-after event for many Sicilians, and a reservation (especially for a seat in the garden) is almost essential. Antipasti, rich with marinated vegetables and grilled fish, are loaded onto a buffet table, and pastas tend to be strong, aromatic, and laced with flavors like anchovies, fresh basil, and sardines. Grilled swordfish, calamari, and octopus are always worthwhile, and the house wine is redolent with the flavors and sunshine of southern Italy.

PALERMO AFTER DARK

We always like to begin our evening by heading to the century-old **Caffè Mazzara,** Via Generale Magliocco 15 (☎ **091/321-443**). You can sample Sicilian ice cream—among the best in the world—and order the richest coffee in all the country. Or perhaps you'll prefer to sit quietly, sipping the heady Sicilian wines in the corner where Giuseppe di Lampedusa wrote a great many chapters of his novel, *The Leopard,* in the late 1950s. Besides an espresso bar and pastry shop on the street level, the premises contain a piano bar and pub, a well as a well-recommended, somewhat more substantial restaurant. If you can't find a place to eat in Palermo on a Sunday, when virtually everything is shut, Mazzara is a good bet. It's open Sunday to Friday 7:30am to 11pm and Saturday 7:30am to 1am. Signature treats include *canoli* and *gelati.*

Palermo's three most popular dance clubs lie in the modern, commercial center of the city, and all feature current music and loudspeaker systems that encourage patrons to dance. **Il Dancing Club,** Viale Piemonte 16 (☎ 091/348-917), opens at 10:30pm Wednesday to Sunday. **Il Cherchio,** Viale Strasbourg 312 (☎ **091/688-5421**), and **Grant's Club,** Via Principe de Paterno 80 (☎ **091/346-7720**), are open only Friday and Saturday from 10:30pm to at least 3am, depending on the crowd. All of them charge 15,000L to 20,000L ($9 to $12), including one drink.

If you're looking for relief from Palermo's oppressive heat, consider a short trek north of the city to Mondello. There's an attractive piano bar in the **Mondello Palace Hotel,** Via Principe de Scalea 12 (☎ 091/450-001).

Palermo is also a cultural center of some note. The opera and ballet seasons last from January to June. The principal venue is the **Teatro Politeama Garibaldi,** Piazza Ruggero Séttimo (☎ **091/605-3315**). Tickets cost 30,000L to 45,000L ($17 to $26). The box office, across from the tourist office, is open Tuesday to Saturday 10am to 1pm and 5 to 7pm.

The city is known also for its puppet performances, the best of which are staged by **Compagnia Bradamante di Anna Cuticchio,** Via Lombardia 25 (☎ **091/625-9223** or 091/625/323-400). Tickets cost 20,000L to 25,000L ($12 to $15); the box office opens one hour before show time.

Ask at the tourist office about times and dates of performances for the major summer event, a **festival** at an open-air seaside theater, **Teatro di Verdura Villa Castelnuovo.** The month-long festival usually begins the first week of July, and encompasses classical music, jazz, and ballet performances. For more information or to purchase tickets, contact the **Teatro Politeama Garibaldi** (above).

SIDE TRIPS FROM PALERMO
MONREALE

The town of **Monreale** is 6 miles from Palermo, up Monte Caputo and on the edge of the Conca d'Oro plain. If you don't have a car, you can reach it by taking bus no. 389 from Piazza Indipendenza in Palermo.

The Normans under William II founded a Benedictine monastery at Monreale in the 1170s. Near the ruins of that monastery, a great cathedral was erected. Like the Alhambra in Granada, Spain, the ✪ **Chiostro del Duomo di Monreale,** Piazza Guglielmo il Buono (☎ 091/640-4403), has a relatively drab facade, giving little indication of the riches inside. The interior is virtually covered with shimmering mosaics illustrating scenes from the Bible. The artwork provides a distinctly original interpretation of the old, rigid Byzantine form of decoration. The mosaics have an Eastern look despite the Western-style robed Christ reigning over his kingdom. The ceiling is ornate, even gaudy. On the north and west facades are two bronze doors depicting biblical stories in relief. The cloisters are also of interest. Built in 1166, they consist of twin mosaic columns, and every other pair bears an original design (the lava inlay was hauled from Mount Etna). Admission to the cathedral is free; if you visit the cloisters, there's a charge of 2,000L ($1.15). The cathedral is open daily 8:30am to noon and 3:30 to 6pm. July to September, the cloister is open Monday to Saturday 9am to 1pm; Monday, Wednesday, and Friday 3 to 6pm; and Sunday 9am to 12:30pm. In the off-season, ask at the cathedral, because hours vary.

You can also visit the **treasury** and the **terraces;** each charges another 2,000L ($1.15) for admission. They're open daily 8:30am to 12:30pm and 3 to 6:30pm. The terraces are actually the rooftop of the church, from which you'll be rewarded with a view of the cloisters.

Accommodations
Park Hotel Carrubella. Corso Umberto I, 90046 Monreale. ☎ **091/640-2188.** Fax 091/640-2189. 30 units. A/C TEL. 130,000L ($75) double. AE, DC, MC, V.

The aging Park Hotel is one of the tallest buildings in town, and its terraces provide a sweeping view over the famous church, the surrounding valleys, and the azure coastline of faraway Palermo. To reach it, follow a one-lane road from the piazza near the church along a serpentine series of terraces; the hotel is 800 yards from the cathedral. The spacious but tattered interior is filled with mirrors and deep armchairs, along with scattered pieces of sculpture. In the public rooms, as in the guest rooms, the floors are covered with rows of hand-painted Sicilian tiles. The hotel offers comfortably furnished accommodations, each with its own balcony. Well-prepared meals are served in the conservatively elegant dining room.

Dining
La Botte. Contrada Lenzitti 20 (SS186). ☎ **091/414-051.** Reservations recommended. Main courses 14,000–24,000L ($80–$14). AE, DC, MC, V. Tues–Sun noon–3pm and 8–11pm. Closed June 20–Aug 30. SICILIAN/ITALIAN.

Charming and well managed, with a strong emphasis on meticulous adherence to traditional Sicilian recipes, this restaurant occupies a structure originally built as a wine press and farmhouse about a century ago. The present management has been in place since 1962, and has earned the respect of local residents who appreciate the trattoria's strong flavors and robust portions. It's 12 miles north of central Palermo, beside highway SS186 and uphill from the center of Monreale. Specialties include such time-tested dishes as *gnocchi alla barra* (stuffed with local cheeses and herbs); *delizia tre naccia* (fettuccine with ricotta, mozzarella, eggplant, tomatoes, and Sicilian herbs); and a succulent dish of veal layered with cheese, salami, basil, and herbs. By all means, try to begin a meal here with the savory offerings (marinated tuna, grilled sardines or anchovies, marinated red peppers) from the antipasto table.

MONDELLO LIDO

When the summer sun burns hot, old men on the square seek a place in the shade, and *bambini* tire of their toys, it's beach weather. For residents of Palermo, that means **Mondello,** 7½ miles east. Before this beachfront town started attracting the wealthy class of Palermo, it was a fishing village (as it still is), and you can see rainbow-colored fishing boats bobbing in the harbor. A good sandy beach stretches for about a mile and a half, and it's filled to capacity on a July or August day. Some women traveling alone find Mondello more inviting and less intimidating than the center of Palermo. In summer, an express bus (no. 6, "Beallo") leaves for Mondello from the central train station in Palermo.

Accommodations

✪ **Mondello Palace Hotel.** Viale Principe di Scalea 2, 90151 Mondello. ☎ **091/450-001.** Fax 091/450-657. 73 units. A/C MINIBAR TV TEL. 280,000L ($162) double; from 360,000L ($209) suite. Rates include breakfast. AE, DC, MC, V. Free parking.

Set in a garden of palms and semitropical shrubs across the coastal road from the beach, this is the best and most famous hotel in Mondello. Built in 1950 and renovated several times since, it offers airy, comfortable rooms in tones of blue, red, and white. All doubles have balconies and sea views. Guests of yesteryear have included Sophia Loren and Luchino Visconti; today the place might house families vacationing en masse from the hinterlands of Sicily or northern Europe. There's a large pool in the garden, a bar, and an indoor/outdoor restaurant with a sea view.

Splendid Hotel la Torre. Via Piano di Gallo 11, 90151 Mondello. ☎ **091/450-222.** Fax 091/450-033. 179 units. A/C MINIBAR TV TEL. 198,000L ($115) double; 268,000L ($155) triple. Rates include breakfast. AE, DC, MC, V. Free parking.

This beachside hotel lies half a mile north of Mondello's center. From your comfortable bed you can get up and walk out onto a private terrace overlooking the sea. Some of the well-furnished rooms are quite spacious; all are well maintained (the 1962 building was renovated in 1984). During the day many sports and recreational activities can occupy your time—there are swimming pools, a tennis court, a garden, and plenty of games for children. La Torre is very much a family resort, not a romantic retreat. It is crowded during the peak summer months, so reservations are important. It attracts some heavy drinkers as well—the bar opens at 9am and doesn't close until 1am. The place is not a gourmet haven, but we've enjoyed our meals here, especially the pasta and fish dishes. The cooking is quite good, the choice is ample, and the staff takes good care of you.

Dining

From June to September the famous restaurant **Charleston** moves here from Palermo. See "Dining" under Palermo for details.

CEFALÙ

For another day's excursion, we recommend a trek 50 miles east from Palermo to this fishing village. It's known all over Europe for its Romanesque cathedral, an outstanding achievement of the Arab-Norman architectural style.

From Palermo, 18 **trains** make the 1-hour trip daily, costing 5,700L ($3.30) one-way. For information and schedules, call ☎ **0921/21-169. SPISA,** Via Umberto I, 2 (☎ **0921/24-301**), runs **buses** between Palermo and Cefalù, costing 7,600L ($4.4

one-way for the 1½-hour trip. **Motorists** can follow Route 113 east from Palermo to Cefalù.

You'll find **the tourist office** at Corso Ruggero 77 (☎ 0921/21-050), open Monday to Saturday 8am to 2pm and Monday to Friday 4 to 7pm.

Seeing the Sights

✪ **Il Duomo.** Piazza di Duomo (off Corso Ruggero). ☎ 0921/922-021. Free admission. Daily 8:30am–noon and 3:30–6:30pm.

Resembling a military fortress, the Duomo was built by Roger II to fulfill a vow he'd made when faced with a possible shipwreck. Construction began in 1131, and in time two square towers dotted the landscape of Cefalù, curiously placed between the sea and a rocky promontory. The architectural line of the cathedral boasts a severe elegance that has earned it a position in many art-history books. Some critics have hailed it as Sicily's finest church from this era.

The interior, which took a century to complete, overwhelms you with a total of 16 Byzantine and Roman columns supporting towering capitals. The graceful horseshoe arches are one of the island's best examples of the Saracen influence on Norman architecture. The celebrated mosaic of Christ the Pantocrator—one of only three on Sicily—in the dome of the cathedral apse is alone worth the trip. The nearby mosaic of the Virgin with angels and the Apostles is a well-preserved work from 1148. In the transept is a marble statue of the Madonna. Roger's plan to have a tomb placed in the Duomo was derailed by the authorities at Palermo's cathedral, where he rests today.

Museo Mandralisca. Via Mandralisca 13. ☎ 0921/215-47. Admission 5,000L ($2.90). Daily 9:30am–12:30pm and 4–6pm.

Before leaving town, try to visit this museum opposite the cathedral. It has an outstanding art collection, including the 1470 portrait of an unknown by Antonello da Messina. Some art critics have journeyed all the way from Rome just to stare at this handsome work, and it's often featured on Sicilian tourist brochures.

Dining

Al Gabbiano da Saro. Viale Lungomare 17. ☎ 0921/421-495. Reservations recommended Sat–Sun. Main courses 12,000–30,000L ($7–$17). AE, DC, MC, V. Thurs–Tues noon–3pm and 7pm–midnight. Closed mid-Dec to mid-Jan. SEAFOOD/SICILIAN.

In a century-old building, this rustic seaside trattoria is typical of the area, attracting locals and visitors in almost equal measure. Fresh fish is the item to order, from a list of unpronounceable sea creatures. You might begin with *zuppa di cozze,* a luscious mussel soup. The vegetables and pastas are good, too, especially pennette alla Norma (with eggplant). Other specialties are *involtini* of swordfish, and Sicilian versions of a mixed-meat grill and a mixed-fish fry. The cooking is consistent, as is the service. If you speak a little Italian, it helps.

Da Nino al Lungomare. Viale Lungomare 11. ☎ 0921/422-582. Reservations required. Main courses 13,000–22,000L ($8–$13); fixed-price menu 21,000L ($12). AE, MC, V. June–Sept daily noon–3pm and 7–11pm; Oct and Dec–May, Wed–Mon noon–3pm and 7–11pm. Closed Nov. SOUTHERN ITALIAN/SICILIAN/PIZZA.

In a century-old salt warehouse, this is a reasonably good choice for southern Italian and Sicilian cuisine served al fresco in a seaside setting. The kitchen is in no way influenced by trends or food fads. Time-tested recipes are served here, including a delectable *risotto marinara* (fisher's rice), *involtini* of meat, and pasta with sardines. Fresh fish is featured, prepared almost any way you like it. You can also order delicious pizzas fresh from the oven.

7 Journeys Off the Beaten Path

If you want to spend more time in Sicily, the northwest corner offers scenic, historic towns and villages. Shaped by mythology, they reflect the multicultural influences of nearby Africa and the numerous civilizations that have dominated the territory over the centuries. From here, it's a short ferry ride to the remote Egadi Islands.

ÉRICE

Érice sits 2,300 feet above the sea on Mount Érice, 60 miles southwest of Palermo. A well-preserved medieval town composed of steep cobblestone streets and narrow twisted alleys, it has a long history as a mystical, mythic place. It is laid out in a triangle, with two outer walls built in the 11th century by the Normans over pre-existing walls that dated to at least the 4th century B.C. It was home of a long-standing temple dedicated to the reigning goddess of love. Cult worship evolved from the Phoenician Astarte to the Greek Aphrodite and finally to the Roman Venus. Details about sights and accommodations are available from the **tourist office,** Viale Conte Pepoli 11 (☎ 0923/869-388), open Monday, Wednesday, and Friday 8am to 2pm (Tuesday, Thursday, and Saturday also 4 to 8pm).

SEEING THE SIGHTS   At the western corner of town, the **Temple of Venus,** Viale Conte Pepoli, is represented only by its base and the Well of Venus, down which young girls were thrown in sacrifice after being deflowered. The Normans, outraged by such behavior, destroyed the pagan structure, which was also associated with orgies, prostitution, and self-castration rituals. Still standing at its side is the Norman castle they built to replace it, surrounded by the lush **Balio Gardens,** which make for a pleasant stroll. The grounds, including the temple, castle, and gardens, are open daily 8am to sunset; admission is free. The **Museo Communale Cordici,** Piazza Umberto I (☎ 0923/866-9258), houses artifacts that trace the town's long and varied history and contains a collection of works by the Gaginis, Sicily's leading family of sculptors. It's open Monday to Saturday 8:30am to 7:30pm and Sunday 8:30am to 1:30pm; admission is 2,000L ($1.15).

ACCOMMODATIONS & DINING   The best accommodations are at the **Hotel Elimo,** Via Vittorio Emanuele 75, 91016 Érice, Trápani (☎ 0923/869-377, fax 0923/869-252), a restored villa featuring original limestone masonry, beamed ceilings, and a decoratively tiled fireplace. A double is 250,000L ($145).

Serving regional Trápani cuisine in its romantic terrace garden, **Monte San Giuliano,** Vicolo San Rocco 7 (☎ 0923/869-595), offers meals at 28,000L to 55,000L ($16 to $32). One of the best dining rooms is in a hotel, **Moderno,** Via Vittorio Emanuele 63, 91016 Érice (☎ 0923/869-300; fax 0923/869-139). It rents functionally furnished, comfortable doubles for 200,000L ($116). Most patrons, however, come for the wonderful Sicilian meals—authentic regional cooking at its best. In a room with turn-of-the-century jewel-box decor, you can sample one of the island's best versions of *zuppa di pesce* (fish soup), made with small local fish and flavored with almonds. The *bisiati al pesto trapanese* is homemade fusilli-like pasta with an uncooked sauce of fresh tomato and basil, again flavored with almonds. The *involtini alla siciliana* is a splendid medley of grilled veal rolls stuffed with raisins, bread crumbs, pine nuts, and ham.

TRÁPANI

On the western coast of Sicily 64 miles southwest of Palermo and about 8 miles west of Érice, Trápani is blasted by the hot winds of nearby northern Africa. The Afric influence is evident in the local cuisine, which includes a seafood condiment made of cucumbers, celery, capers, and olives, as well as the staple couscous flavored with fish. You can get further information on the town at the **tourist office,** Via San Francesco d'Assisi 25 (☎ **0923/545-511**); August hours are daily 8am to 8pm, and hours from September to July are Monday to Saturday 8am to 8pm and Sunday 9am to noon.

SEEING THE SIGHTS   Trápani's inland growth has been as a bland modern town, but a charming historic district lies on its narrow western peninsula. On the northern perimeter, Via Torrearsa is home to the local fish markets; Viale Regina Elene, to the south, is the port serving the Égadi and other nearby islands. The main street of the peninsula is **Corso Vittorio Emanuele,** blocked off at its mainland end by the baroque **Palazzo Cavaretta.** From its balcony, the patriotic hero Giuseppe Garibaldi cried, "Rome or death!" in 1860, a reference to his exhausting efforts to unify the then-splintered nation.

Of the many churches in the town, **Santa Maria del Gesu,** behind the palace off Corso Italia, is certainly worth a visit. It has a marble canopy constructed by Antonello Gagini in 1521 to shelter Andrea della Robbia's enameled terra-cotta *Madonna of the Angels.* The small baroque **Santuario dell'Purgatorio,** Via Gen. Giglio, houses 21 wooden statues, dating mainly from the 18th century, that represent scenes from the Passion. On Good Friday, the statues are carried through the streets, but the rest of the year they can be viewed Monday, Wednesday, and Friday 9am to 1pm.

Moving into the mainland along Via Fardella, you can view the most important church in town, the 14th-century **Church of the Annunciation (Santuario dell'Annunziata).** It incorporates a Renaissance arch by the Gaginis and a statue of the Madonna of Trápani attributed to Nino Pisano.

Set in a 16th-century palace, the **Museo Nazionale Pepoli** (☎ **0923/553-269**), features art by Titian and Roberto di Oderisio, as well as archaeological remnants gathered from around the area. It's open Tuesday to Saturday 9am to 1pm; Tuesday, Thursday, and Friday 3 to 6pm; and Sunday 9am to 12:30pm. Admission is 2,500L ($1.45) except on Sunday, when it's free. Take SAU bus no. 24, 25, or 30 from Piazza Vittorio Emanuele to reach it.

ACCOMMODATIONS & DINING   The best place to stay is the new **Hotel Crystal,** Via San Giovanni Bosco 17, 91100 Trápani (☎ **0923/200-00; fax 0923/255-55**), which emphasizes creature comforts over atmosphere. A double runs 205,000L ($119).

The **Taverna Paradiso,** Lungo Mare Dante Aligheri 22 (☎ **0923/223-03**), offers the freshest fish in town, much of it recently plucked from the sea. Orders can be prepared to your specifications.

THE EGADI ISLANDS (THE ISOLE ÉGADI)

Lévanzo, Favignana, and Maréttimo, known for their solitude, caves, and calm, clear waters, make up the **Egadi Islands.** To get to the islands, just a few miles off Sicily's west coast, call **Siremar** (☎ **0923/277-80**) in Trápani, which runs ferries to all three islands several times a day from the docks at Viale Regina Elena. The trip to nearby Lévanzo takes 20 minutes and costs 5,500L ($3.20) each way. From there you can continue by ferry to the other two islands. Additional information on the Egadi can be obtained at the **tourist office** in Trápani (above).

The closest island to the mainland, **Lévanzo** lies 10 miles west of Trápani, with the only real community in the small port town of the same name. It's the smallest of the islands, with an area of just over 2 square miles, and its main attraction is the **Grotta del Genovese,** which holds skillfully rendered Paleolithic drawings of animals and humans (there are 33 figures) believed to be at least 10,000 years old. There are

Neolithic drawings, added 5,000 years later, but they aren't as impressive. The cave is owned by Giuseppe Castiglione, Via Calvario 11 (☎ 0923/924-032), who will take you from the dock to the cave for a fee of 20,000L ($12) per person—or less if you qualify for the group rate (eight or more people).

Sitting 3½ miles south of Lévanzo, larger, more populous **Favignana** occupies 7½ square miles of land mass. The port village shares the island's name, and is home to a well-developed tuna industry and a maximum-security prison housed in the Forte S. Giacomo, which dates from 1120. The oldest section of town, the **Rione Sant'Anna,** is worth a stroll just to look at the homes made entirely of tufa, but here, too, the main attraction is caves. They are found west of town on the Punta San Nicola. **Grotta del Pazzo** is inscribed with Punic and early Christian messages; **Grotta degli Archi** houses 4th- and 5th-century Christian tombs.

The most developed of the islands, Favignana offers the chain's only accommodations. The best of these is **Aegusa,** Via Garibaldi 11/17, Favignana, Égadi, Trápani (☎ 0923/922-430, fax 0923/922-440), an 11-room inn open April 10 to October 15. It charges 260,000L ($151) for a double with half board. Other meals can be taken at **Égadi,** Via Cristoforo Colombo 12 (☎ 0923/921-232), where the cost of a seafood-based meal ranges from 40,000L to 55,000L ($23 to $32).

Thirteen miles west of Favignana, **Maréttimo** is the most remote of the islands, with the smallest population and least activity. There's small fishing community in the village named after the island, and beaches extend north and south of the town. Follow the hiking trail that leads west into the island's interior and you'll come to the **Case Romane,** ruins of a late Roman fort. Head north out of the village, and you'll skirt the base of the island's highest peak, 2,243-foot **Monte Falcone,** on your way to the **Castello di Punta Troia.** It sits on a precipice 379 feet above the sea at the northeast corner of the island.

8 The Aeolian Islands

Lipari: 18½ miles N of Milazzo; Strómboli: 50 miles N of Milazzo; Vulcano: 12½ miles N of Milazzo

The **Aeolian Islands (Isole Eolie o Lipari)** have been inhabited for more than 3,000 years, in spite of volcanic activity that even now causes the earth to issue forth sulfuric belches, streams of molten lava, and hissing clouds of steam. Ancient Greek sailors believed these seven windswept islands were the home of Aeolus, god of the winds. He supposedly lived in a cave on Vulcano, keeping the winds of the world in a bag to be opened only with great caution.

Today, visitors seek out the limited accommodations at Lipari (14 square miles), the largest and most developed island; Strómboli (5 square miles), the most distant and volcanically active; and Vulcano (8 square miles), the closest island to the Sicilian mainland, with its brooding, potentially volatile cone and therapeutic mud baths. The other islands—Salina, Filicudi, Alicudi, and Panarea—offer only bare-bones facilities and are visited mainly by day-trippers.

In spite of the volcanoes, the area attracts tourists—mainly Germans and Italians—with crystalline waters that foster active snorkeling, scuba, and spear-fishing ind'' tries, and photogenic beaches composed of hot black sand and rocky outcropp'' jutting into the Tyrrhenian Sea. The volcanoes themselves offer hikers the thr'' peering into a bubbling crater.

ESSENTIALS

GETTING THERE   **Ferry** and **hydrofoil** service to Lipari, Strómboli, and'' is available in Milazzo, on the northeastern coast of Sicily 20 miles west o''

through **Societa Siremar,** Via Dei Mille (☎ **090/928-3242**). **Societa SNAV,** Via L. Rizzo 17 (☎ **090/928-4509**), offers hydrofoil service.

Siremar operates 2 ferry routes, which are cheaper and slower than the hydrofoils. The Milazzo-Vulcano-Lipari-Salina line leaves Milazzo 4 to 6 times daily 7am to 6:30pm. It takes 1½ hours to reach Vulcano, and a one-way ticket costs 10,800L ($6). Lipari is 2 hours from Milazzo; tickets cost 11,600L ($7) one-way. To reach Strómboli, take the Milazzo-Panarea-Strómboli line, which departs from Milazzo at 7am Friday to Wednesday, and at 2:30pm on Thursday. The Strómboli trip takes 5 hours and costs 18,500L ($11) one-way.

There are also two hydrofoil lines. The Milazzo-Vulcano-Lipari-Salina line reaches Vulcano in 40 minutes; a one-way ticket costs 18,400L ($11). It takes 55 minutes to reach Lipari, and costs 19,700L ($11) one-way. Siremar makes the trip 6 to 12 times daily 7:05am to 7pm; SNAV makes six runs daily between 7:30am and 7:30pm. To reach Strómboli, use the Milazzo-Panarea-Strómboli line, which takes 2½ hours and costs 28,700L ($17) one-way. Siremar trips leave 4 times daily 6:15am to 3pm; SNAV makes runs daily at 6:40am, 7:25am, and 2:20pm.

If you're **driving,** from Messina, take S113 west to Palermo until you come to the turnoff for Milazzo.

VISITOR INFORMATION   The **tourist office** in Lipari is at Via Vittorio Emanuele 202 (☎ **090/988-0095**). July and August, it's open daily 8am to 2pm (Monday to Saturday also 4:30 to 10pm); September to June, hours are Monday to Saturday 8am to 2pm and 4:30 to 7:30pm. There's no information center in Strómboli. The office in Vulcano, Via Porto do Levante (☎ **090/985-2028**), keeps the same hours as the Lipari office but is open only June to September.

LIPARI

Homer called it "a floating island, a wall of bronze and splendid smooth sheer cliffs." The offspring of seven volcanic eruptions, **Lipari** is the largest of the Aeolians. Lipari is also the name of the island's only real town. It's the administrative headquarters of the Aeolian Islands (except autonomous Salina). The town of Lipari sits on a plateau of red volcanic rock on the southeastern shore. It's framed by two beaches, Marina Lunga, which functions as the harbor, and Marina Corta.

Its dominant feature is a 16th-century Spanish castle, within the walls of which lie a 17th-century cathedral featuring a 16th-century Madonna and an 18th-century silver statue of San Bartolomeo. There's also an archaeological park where stratified clues about continuous civilizations dating to 1700 B.C. have been uncovered.

Excellent artifacts from the Stone and Bronze ages, as well as relics from Greek and Roman acropolises that once stood here, are housed next door in the former bishop's palace, now the **Museo Archeologico Eoliano** (☎ **090/988-0174**), one of Sicily's major archaeological museums. It houses one of the world's finest Neolithic collections. The oldest discoveries date from 4200 B.C. Lustrous red ceramics—known as "the Diana style"—come from the last Neolithic period, 3000 to 2500 B.C. Other ꭐhibits are reconstructed necropolises from the Middle Bronze Age and a 6th-century ꝛ. depiction of Greek warships. Some 1,200 pieces of 4th and 3rd century B.C. ᷼ted terra-cotta, including stone theatrical masks, are on exhibit. The museum also ᷼es the only Late Bronze Age (8th century B.C.) necropolis found in Sicily. It's ᷼Monday to Friday 9am to 2pm and 4 to 7pm. Admission is free.

ᷓmost popular **beaches** are at **Canneto,** about a 20-minute walk north of Lipari ᷓstern coast, and just north of it, **Spiaggia Bianca** (named for the white sand, ᷓ among the region's predominant black sands). At the latter nudists gather ᷓ the hot sun and sharp rocks. To reach the beach from Canneto, take the waterfront road, climb the stairs of Via Marina Garibaldi, then veer right down a narrow cobbled path for about 325 yards.

Acquacalda ("hot water") is the island's northernmost city, but nobody likes to go on its beaches (the sand is rocky and black and so unpleasant for walking or lying on). The town is also known for its obsidian and pumice quarries. West of Acquacalda at Quattropani, you can make a steep climb to the **Duomo de Chiesa Barca,** where the point of interest isn't the cathedral but the panoramic view from the church grounds. On the west coast, 2½ miles from Lipari, the island's other great view is available by making another steep climb to the **Quattrocchi Belvedere.**

Eighteen miles of road circle the island, connecting all its villages and attractions. Buses run by Lipari's **Autobus Urso Guglielmo,** Via Cappuccini (☎ 090/ 981-1262), make 10 circuits of the island per day. The trip to Quattropani and Acquacalda on the north coast costs 2,000L ($1.15); closer destinations cost 1,500L (85¢).

Agriculturally, Lipari yields capers, prevalent in the local cuisine, and Malvasia grapes, which produce a malmsey-like wine too acidic to compare favorably with many other Italian wines. Figs, ginger, rosemary, and wild fennel also manage to grow in the sulfuric soil.

ACCOMMODATIONS

Gattopardo Park Hotel. Via Diana, 98055 Lipari. ☎ **090/981-1035.** Fax 090/988-0207. E-mail: gattopardo@netnet.it. 40 units, 20 bungalows. 180,000–360,000L ($104–$209) double. Rates include half board. AE, DC, V.

The lobby of this hotel, in an 18th-century villa, has a rough log-beamed ceiling, white stucco walls, and a patterned tile floor of subdued gray and black. Flooded with sun from the big windows, the guest rooms feature very Sicilian color schemes (stark white walls with earth-toned upholsteries and accessories) and traditional wooden furniture; all are equipped with ceiling fans. There are also numerous flat-roofed bungalows that allow for some added privacy. The public rooms feature wood-framed furniture with canvas seats, and the dining area includes a covered terrace with ceiling fans to help fight the heat while you dine on regional seafood dishes. A flagstone terrace holds wrought-iron tables and chairs around a small fountain, and geraniums, palm trees, and other greenery create a lush oasis in the midst of the largely barren island. At night, ornate wrought-iron globe lamps illuminate this patio.

Giardino sul Mare. Via Maddalena 65, 98055 Lipari. ☎ **090/981-1004.** Fax 090/ 988-0150. www.netnet.it/hotel/giardino/index. E-mail: conti@netnet.it. 30 units. A/C TV TEL. 130,000–190,000L ($75–$110) double including breakfast; 180,000–320,000L ($104–$186) double including half board. AE, DC, MC, V. Closed Nov 16–Mar 14.

A short walk from the port at Marina Corta, this hotel stands on a rock outcropping overlooking the bay and the distant Sicilian coastline. It is a typical Mediterranean structure of white stucco with a red tile roof. The hotel pool mimics the bright blue waters of the sea just beyond it. Throughout the hotel there are bright tile floors, and public rooms feature padded white wicker furniture. The guest rooms have simple, comfortable dark hardwood furnishings. The restaurant terrace is protected from the brutal heat by a canopy of trees, allowing you to enjoy the sea view while dining on fresh seafood.

Hotel Carasco. A Porto delle Genti, 98005 Lipari. ☎ **090/981-1606.** Fax 090/981-182᾿ 88 units. TEL. 220,000–370,000L ($128–$215) double including breakfast; 240,00᾿ 390,000L ($139–$226) double including half board. AE, DC, MC, V. Closed Oct 19–Mar ᾿

This large hotel consists of two buildings connected by an addition, sitting on a ᾿ by the sea with a staircase leading down to the rocky coastline. The interior con᾿

with the bright heat of the outdoors; it has brown terra-cotta floors and dark wood furniture upholstered with fabrics striped in shades of brown. Each well-furnished guest room features a ceiling fan. Just above the sea, a terrace of tables with umbrellas surrounds a large seawater pool. The hotel offers its own limited nightlife, with a full bar and a piano bar. The restaurant serves Aeolian seafood typical of the islands.

DINING

E Pulera. Via Diana 51. ☎ **090/981-1158.** Reservations recommended. Main courses 15,000–28,000L ($9–$16). AE, DC, MC, V. Daily 7:30pm–2am. Closed June–mid-Oct. SICILIAN/AEOLIAN.

More than Filippino, owned by the same family, this restaurant stresses its Aeolian Island origins. Artifacts and maps of the islands fashioned from ceramic tiles are scattered throughout the premises. Some tables occupy a terrace with a view of a flowering lawn where you'll probably want to linger. Specialties include a delightful version of *zuppe di pesce alla pescatora* (fisher's soup), *bocconcini di pesce spada* (swordfish ragoût), and risotto with crayfish or squid in its own ink. Other good choices are a rich assortment of seafood antipasti that's usually laden with basil and garlic, *involtini* of eggplant, and herb-laden versions of roasted lamb. Desserts might include Sicilian cassata and tiramisù.

✪ **Filippino.** Piazza Municipio. ☎ **090/981-1002.** Reservations recommended. Main courses 15,000–50,000L ($9–$29). AE, DC, MC, V. Daily noon–2:30pm and 7:30–10:30pm. Closed Mon Oct–Mar. SICILIAN.

Surprisingly in such a remote outpost, this is one of the finest restaurants in Italy. It has thrived in the heart of town, near Town Hall, since 1910, when it was established by the ancestors of the family that runs it today. You'll dine in one of two large, airy rooms or on an outdoor terrace ringed with flowering shrubs and potted flowers that affords a view over the town and the sea. Menu items are based on old-fashioned Sicilian recipes and prepared with flair and gusto. Try ravioloni (large ravioli) stuffed with pulverized pork and served with salsa paysana made from tomatoes, capers, and herbs. Homemade maccheroni with mozzarella, prosciutto, and ricotta is baked in the oven. Veal scaloppine is especially tempting when cooked in Malvasina wine, and the array of fresh fish is broad. Culinary masterpieces are the *cupolette di pesce spada* (or "little dome" of swordfish) and the eggplant caponata. Another interesting dish is ravioloni stuffed with grouper and served with caper sauce. A plate of fresh anchovies is served whole, to be consumed bone and all.

STRÓMBOLI

The most distant island in the archipelago, **Strómboli** achieved notoriety and became a household word in the United States in 1950 with the release of the Rossellini cinéma vérité film starring Ingrid Bergman. The American public was far more interested in the "illicit" affair between Bergman and Rossellini than in the film. Though the affair seems tame by today's standards, it temporarily ended Bergman's American film career, and she was denounced on the Senate floor. Movie fans today are more likely to remember Strómboli from the film version of the Jules Verne novel *Voyage to the Center of the Earth*, starring James Mason. The volcanic island was used for the ʌeroes' exit.

The entire surface of Strómboli is the cone of a sluggish but active volcano. Puffs of ʌoke can be seen during the day. At night on the **Sciara del Fuoco** ("Slope of Fire"), ʌ glows red-hot on its way down to meet the sea with a loud hiss and a cloud of ʌn—a memorable vision that may leave you feeling a little too vulnerable.

In fact, the island can serve as a fantasyland for those who were bitten by Hollywood's 1997 volcano-mania. The main attraction is a steep, difficult climb to the lip of the 3,000-foot **Gran Cratere.** The view of bubbling pools of ooze (which glow with heat at night) is accompanied by rising clouds of steam and a sulfuric stench. The journey is a 3-hour hike best taken in early morning or late afternoon to avoid the worst of the brutal sunshine—and even then it requires plenty of sunscreen and water and a good pair of shoes. You'll be following in the footsteps of the sad characters who sloshed their way to trouble in Malcolm Lowry's *Under the Volcano.* A 1990 ordinance made it illegal to climb the slope without a guide, although many daring visitors defy this ban. The island's authorized guide company is **Guide Alpine Autorizzate** (☎ 090/986-211), which charges 20,000L ($12) per person. It leads groups on the 3-hour trip up the mountain at 6pm, returning at midnight (the trip down takes 2 hours, leaving you an hour at the rim).

In spite of the volcano and its sloped terrain, there are two settlements. **Ginostra** is on the southwestern shore, little more than a cluster of summer homes with only 15 year-round residents. **Strómboli** is on the northeastern shore, a conglomeration of the villages of Ficogrande, San Vincenzo, and Piscità, where the only in-town attraction is the black-sand beaches.

ACCOMMODATIONS & DINING

La Sirenetta–Park Hotel. Via Marina 33, 98050 Ficogrande, Strómboli. ☎ **090/986-025.** Fax 090/986-124. 43 units. 180,000–270,000L ($104–$157) double including breakfast; 260,000–420,000L ($151–$244) double including half board. AE, DC, MC, V. Closed Nov–Mar 22.

This is a well-maintained, uncluttered hotel, with white tile floors and walls offset by contemporary dark wood furniture and trim in the guest rooms. Natural wicker furnishings upholstered with blue floral prints grace the public areas. A large pool is on the terrace overlooking the sea. There's also an Italian fashion boutique, plus a full bar and a restaurant featuring Aeolian and Sicilian seafood dishes.

La Sciara Residence Hotel. Via Soldato Cincotta, 98050 Piscita, Strómboli. ☎ **090/986-0004.** Fax 090/986-284. 60 units, 4 apts with kitchens. 115,000–215,000L ($67–$125) per person, double occupancy, including half board; 2-person apt 800,000L ($464) per week, without meals; 5-person apt 1,650,000L ($957) per week, without meals. AE, DC, MC, V. Closed Oct 12–Easter.

One of the most appealing hotels on Strómboli was designed and built in 1971 as a replica of a Sicilian fishing village, with glaring white walls and terra-cotta roofs. Set less than 100 feet from a black-sand beach, it consists of seven 3-story buildings, each named after an Aeolian island. All guest rooms have a balcony and a sea view. There are a tennis court and a big rectangular swimming pool in the complex's center, and a collection of the striking modern paintings and murals of the German-born artist known as Jürgens. The staff is charming and friendly, and although the landscape is stark and arid, many plants fill the hotel compound, thanks to careful maintenance and an elaborate sprinkler system.

VULCANO

The island closest to the mainland, the ancient Thermessa figured heavily in the mythologies of the region. The still-active **Vulcano della Fossa** was thought to be not only the home of Vulcan, but also the gateway to Hades. Thucydides, Siculus, and Aristotle each recorded eruptions. Three dormant craters also exist on the island, but a climb to the rim of the active **Gran Cratere** ("Big Crater") draws the most attention. It hasn't erupted since 1890, but one look inside the sulfur-belching hole makes you understand how it could have inspired the hellish legends surrounding it. The 1,372-foot peak is an easier climb than the one on Stròmboli, taking just about an hour—though it's just as hot, and the same precautions prevail. Avoid midday, load up on sunscreen and water, and wear good hiking shoes.

Here the risks of mounting a volcano are not addressed by legislation, so you can make the climb without a guide. Breathing the sulfuric air at the summit has its risks, though, because the steam is tainted with numerous toxins. To get to the peak from Porto Levante, the main port, follow Via Piano away from the sea for about 220 yards until you see the first of the CRATERE signs, then follow the marked trail.

The **Laghetto di Fanghi,** famous free mud baths that reputedly cure every known ailment, are along Via Provinciale a short way from the port. Be warned that the mud discolors anything from cloth to jewelry, which is one explanation for the prevalent nudity. Within sight, the acquacalda features hot-water jets that act as a natural Jacuzzi. Either can scald you if you step or sit on the vents that release the heat, so take care if you decide to enter.

The island offers one of the few smooth beaches in the entire chain, the **Spiaggia Sabbie Nere** ("Black Sands Beach"), with dark sand so hot in the midday sun that thongs or wading shoes are suggested if you plan to while away your day along the shore. You can find the beach by following signs posted along Via Ponente.

A knowledge of street names is worthless, really, because there are no signs. Not to worry—the locals who gather at the dock are friendly and experienced at giving directions to tongue-tied foreign visitors, especially because all they ever have to point out are the paths to the crater, the mud baths, and the beach, the island's only attractions.

ACCOMMODATIONS

Hotel Conti. A Porto Ponente, 98050 Vulcano. ☎ 090/981-1004. Fax 090/988-0150. 63 units. TV TEL. 86,000–130,000L ($50–$75) per person, double occupancy, with half board. AE, DC, MC, V. Closed Nov–Apr.

Adjacent to Porto Ponente beach, this was the first conventional hotel built in Vulcano (in 1950). It proudly claims that it inaugurated the notion of tourism on an island previously inhabited only by fisherfolk. With a 2-story central core flanked by single-story wings that stretch around a landscaped courtyard, it's outfitted entirely in white, both inside and outside, with little concern for the niceties of cutting-edge fashion. There's no swimming pool on the premises, but because of the beach's proximity, no one seems to mind. On the premises is a well-managed restaurant, open daily for lunch and dinner, where main courses cost 20,000 to 35,000L ($12 to $20). At the less expensive Pizzeria Zamara, meal-sized pizzas cost 15,000L to 25,000L ($9 to $15).

DINING

Restaurant Vincencino. Vulcano Porto. ☎ 090/985-2016. Main courses 12,000–18,000L ($7–$10). AE, DC, MC, V. Daily noon–3:30pm and 7–9:30pm. SICILIAN.

This is the most appealing of the limited number of restaurants that are convenient to the ferry port. In a rustic setting less than 30 yards from the waterfront, you can order filling portions of local specialties. Good choices include house-style maccheroni (with ricotta, eggplant, fresh tomatoes, and herbs), spaghetti Vincencino (with crayfish, capers, and tomato sauce), grilled fish, including an *involtini* of swordfish, and seafood salad. October to March, the menu is limited to a simple array of platters served from the bar.

Appendix

A Basic Vocabulary

English	Italian	Pronunciation
Thank you	**Grazie**	*graht*-tzee-yey
You're welcome	**Prego**	*prey*-go
Please	**Per favore**	*pehr* fah-*vohr*-eh
Yes	**Sì**	see
No	**No**	noh
Good morning or Good day	**Buongiorno**	bwohn-*djor*-noh
Good evening	**Buona sera**	*Bwohn*-ah *say*-rah
Good night	**Buona notte**	*Bwohn*-ah *noht*-tay
How are you?	**Come sta?**	*koh*-may *stah*
Very well	**Molto bene**	*mohl*-toh *behn*-ney
Goodbye	**Arrivederci**	ahr-ree-vah-*dehr*-chee
Excuse me (to get attention)	**Scusi**	*skoo*-zee
Excuse me (to get past some- one on the bus)	**Permesso**	pehr-*mehs*-soh
Where is...?	**Dovè?...**	doh-*vey*
the station	**la stazione**	lah stat-tzee-*oh*-neh
a hotel	**un albergo**	oon ahl-*behr*-goh
a restaurant	**un ristorante**	oon reest-ohr-*ahnt*-eh
the bathroom	**il bagno**	eel *bahn*-nyoh
To the right	**A destra**	ah *dehy*-stra
to the left	**A sinistra**	ah see-*nees*-tra
straight ahead	**Avanti (or sempre diritto)**	ahv-vahn-tee (*sehm*-pray dee-*reet*-toh)
How much is it?	**Quanto costa?**	*kwan*-toh *coh*-sta?
The check, please	**Il conto, per favore**	eel kon-toh *pehr* fah-*vohr*-eh
When?	**Quando?**	*kwan*-doh
Yesterday	**Ieri**	ee-*yehr*-ree
Today	**Oggi**	*oh*-jee
Tomorrow	**Domani**	doh-*mah*-nee
Breakfast	**Prima colazione**	*pree*-mah coh-laht-tzee-*ohn*-ay
Lunch	**Pranzo**	*prahn*-zoh

Dinner	**Cena**	*chay*-nah
What time is it?	**Che ore sono?**	kay *or*-ay *soh*-noh
Monday	**Lunedì**	loo-nay-*dee*
Tuesday	**Martedì**	mart-ay-*dee*
Wednesday	**Mercoledì**	mehr-cohl-ay-*dee*
Thursday	**Giovedì**	joh-vay-*dee*
Friday	**Venerdì**	ven-nehr-*dee*
Saturday	**Sabato**	*sah*-bah-toh
Sunday	**Domenica**	doh-*mehn*-nee-kah

Numbers

1	**uno**	*oo*-noh
2	**due**	*doo*-ay
3	**tre**	tray
4	**quattro**	*kwah*-troh
5	**cinque**	*cheen*-kway
6	**sei**	say
7	**sette**	*set*-tay
8	**otto**	*oh*-toh
9	**nove**	*noh*-vay
10	**dieci**	dee-*ay*-chee
11	**undici**	*oon*-dee-chee
20	**venti**	*vehn*-tee
21	**ventuno**	vehn-*toon*-oh
22	**venti due**	*vehn*-tee *doo*-ay
30	**trenta**	*trayn*-tah
40	**quaranta**	kwah-*rahn*-tah
50	**cinquanta**	cheen-*kwan*-tah
60	**sessanta**	sehs-*sahn*-tah
70	**settanta**	seht-*tahn*-tah
80	**ottanta**	oht-*tahn*-tah
90	**novanta**	noh-*vahnt*-tah
100	**cento**	*chen*-toh
1,000	**mille**	*mee*-lay
5,000	**cinque milla**	*cheen*-kway *mee*-lah
10,000	**dieci milla**	dee-*ay*-chee *mee*-lah

B Menu Terms

Abbacchio   Roast haunch or shoulder of lamb baked and served in a casserole and sometimes flavored with anchovies.

Agnolotti   A crescent-shaped pasta shell stuffed with a mix of chopped meat, spices, vegetables, and cheese; when prepared in rectangular versions, the same combination of ingredients is identified as **ravioli.**

Amaretti   Crunchy, sweet almond-flavored macaroons.

Anguilla alla veneziana   Eel cooked in a sauce made from tuna and lemon.

Antipasti   Succulent tidbits served at the beginning of a meal (before the pasta), whose ingredients might include slices of cured meats, seafood (especially shellfish), and cooked and seasoned vegetables.

Aragosta   Lobster.

Arrosto   Roasted meat.

Baccalà   Dried and salted codfish.

Bagna cauda   Hot and well-seasoned sauce, heavily flavored with anchovies, designed for dipping raw vegetables; literally translated as "hot bath."

Bistecca alla fiorentina   Florentine-style steaks, coated before grilling with olive oil, pepper, lemon juice, salt and parsley.

Bocconcini   Veal layered with ham and cheese, then fried.

Bollito misto   Assorted boiled meats served on a single platter.

Braciola   Pork chop.

Bresaola   Air-dried spiced beef.

Bruschetta   Toasted bread, heavily slathered with olive oil and garlic and often topped with tomatoes.

Bucatini   Coarsely textured hollow spaghetti.

Busecca alla Milanese   Tripe (beef stomach) flavored with herbs and vegetables.

Cacciucco ali livornese   Seafood stew.

Calzone   Pizza dough rolled with the chef's choice of sausage, tomatoes, cheese, and so on, then baked into a kind of savory turnover.

Cannelloni   Tubular dough stuffed with meat, cheese, or vegetables, then baked in a creamy white sauce.

Cappellacci alla ferrarese   Pasta stuffed with pumpkin.

Cappelletti   Small ravioli ("little hats") stuffed with meat or cheese.

Carciofi   Artichokes.

Carpaccio   Thin slices of raw cured beef, sometimes in a piquant sauce.

Cassatta alla siciliana   A richly caloric dessert combining layers of sponge cake, sweetened ricotta cheese, and candied fruit, bound together with chocolate butter-cream icing.

Cervello al burro nero   Brains in black-butter sauce.

Cima alla genovese   Baked filet of veal rolled into a tube-shaped package containing eggs, mushrooms, and sausage.

Coppa   Cured morsels of pork filet encased in sausage skins, served in slices.

Costoletta alla milanese   Veal cutlet dredged in bread crumbs, fried, and sometimes flavored with cheese.

Cozze   Mussels.

Fagioli   White beans.

Fave   Fava beans.

Fegato alla veneziana   Thinly sliced calves' liver fried with salt, pepper, and onions.

Foccacia   Ideally, concocted from potato-based dough left to rise slowly for several hours, then garnished with tomato sauce, garlic, basil, salt, and pepper and drizzled with olive oil; similar to a deep-dish pizza most popular in the deep south, especially Bari.

Fontina   Rich cow's-milk cheese.

Frittata   Italian omelet.

Fritto misto   A deep-fried medley of whatever small fish, shellfish, and squid are available in the marketplace that day.

Fusilli   Spiral-shaped pasta.

Gelato (produzione propria)   Ice cream (homemade).

Gorgonzola   One of the most famous blue-veined cheeses of Europe—strong, creamy, and aromatic.

Gnocchi   Dumplings usually made from potatoes (*gnocchi alla patate*) or from semolina (*gnocchi alla romana*), often stuffed with combinations of cheese, spinach, vegetables, or whatever combinations strike the chef's fancy.

Granita   Flavored ice, usually with lemon or coffee.

Insalata di frutti di mare   Seafood salad (usually including shrimp and squid) garnished with pickles, lemon, olives, and spices.

Involtini   Thinly sliced beef, veal, or pork, rolled, stuffed, and fried.

Minestrone   A rich and savory vegetable soup usually sprinkled with grated parmigiano and studded with noodles.

Mortadella   Mild pork sausage, fashioned into large cylinders and served sliced; the original lunchmeat baloney (because its most famous center of production is Bologna).

Mozzarella   A nonfermented cheese, made from the fresh milk of a buffalo (or, if unavailable, from a cow), boiled and then kneaded into a rounded ball, served fresh.

Mozzarella con pomodori (also "**caprese**")   Fresh tomatoes with fresh mozzarella, basil, pepper, and olive oil.

Nervetti   A northern Italian antipasto made from chewy pieces of calves' foot or shin.

Osso buco   Beef or veal knuckle slowly braised until the cartilage is tender, then served with a highly flavored sauce.

Pancetta   Herb-flavored pork belly, rolled into a cylinder and sliced—the Italian bacon.

Panettone   Sweet yellow-colored bread baked in the form of a brioche.

Panna   Heavy cream.

Pansotti   Pasta stuffed with greens, herbs, and cheeses, usually served with a walnut sauce.

Pappardelle alle lepre   Pasta with rabbit sauce.

Parmigiano   Parmesan, a hard and salty yellow cheese usually grated over pastas and soups but also eaten alone; also known as *granna*. The best is parmigiano reggiano.

Peperoni   Green, yellow, or red sweet peppers (not to be confused with pepperoni).

Pesci al cartoccio   Fish baked in a parchment envelope with onions, parsley, and herbs.

Pesto   A flavorful green sauce made from basil leaves, cheese, garlic, marjoram, and (if available) pine kernels.

Piccata al marsala   Thin escalope of veal braised in a pungent sauce flavored with marsala wine.

Piselli al prosciutto   Peas with strips of ham.

Pizza   Specific varieties include *capricciosa* (its ingredients can vary widely depending on the chef's culinary vision and the ingredients at hand), *margherita* (with tomato sauce, cheese, fresh basil, and memories of the first queen of Italy, Marguerite di Savoia, in whose honor it was first made by a Neapolitan chef), *napoletana* (with ham, capers, tomatoes, oregano, cheese, and the distinctive taste of anchovies), *quatro stagione* (translated as "four seasons" because of the array of fresh vegetables in it; it also contains ham and bacon), and *siciliana* (with black olives, capers, and cheese).

Pizzaiola   A process whereby something (usually a beefsteak) is covered in a tomato-and-oregano sauce.

Polenta   Thick porridge or mush made from cornmeal flour.

Polenta de uccelli   Assorted small birds roasted on a spit and served with polenta.

Polenta e coniglio   Rabbit stew served with polenta.

Polla alla cacciatore   Chicken with tomatoes and mushrooms cooked in wine.

Pollo all diavola   Highly spiced grilled chicken.

Ragu   Meat sauce.

Ricotta   A soft bland cheese made from cow's or sheep's milk.

Risotto   Italian rice.

Risotto alla milanese   Rice with saffron and wine.

Salsa verde   "Green sauce," made from capers, anchovies, lemon juice and/or vinegar, and parsley.

Saltimbocca   Veal scallop layered with prosciutto and sage; its name literally translates as "jump in your mouth," a reference to its tart and savory flavor.

Salvia   Sage.

Scaloppina alla Valdostana   Escalope of veal stuffed with cheese and ham.

Scaloppine   Thin slices of veal coated in flour and sautéed in butter.

Semifreddo   A frozen dessert; usually ice cream with sponge cake.

Seppia   Cuttlefish (a kind of squid); its black ink is used for flavoring in certain sauces for pasta and also in risotto dishes.

Sogliola   Sole.

Spaghetti   A long, round, thin pasta, variously served: *alla bolognese* (with ground meat, mushrooms, peppers, and so on), *alla carbonara* (with bacon, black pepper, and eggs), *al pomodoro* (with tomato sauce), *al sugo/ragù* (with meat sauce), and *alle vongole* (with clam sauce).

Spiedini   Pieces of meat grilled on a skewer over an open flame.

Strangolaprete   Small nuggets of pasta, usually served with sauce; the name is literally translated as "priest-choker."

Stufato   Beef braised in white wine with vegetables.

Tagliatelle   Flat egg noodles.

Tiramisu   Richly caloric dessert containing layers of triple-crème cheeses and rum-soaked sponge cake.

Tonno   Tuna.

Tortelli   Pasta dumplings stuffed with ricotta and greens.

Tortellini   Rings of dough stuffed with minced and seasoned meat and served either in soups or as a full-fledged pasta covered with sauce.

Trenette   Thin noodles served with pesto sauce and potatoes.

Trippe alla fiorentina   Beef tripe (stomach).

Vermicelli   Very thin spaghetti.

Vitello tonnato   Cold sliced veal covered with tuna-fish sauce.

Zabaglione/zabaione   Egg yolks whipped into the consistency of a custard, flavored with marsala, and served warm as a dessert.

Zampone   Pig's trotter stuffed with spicy seasoned port, boiled and sliced.

Zuccotto   A liqueur-soaked sponge cake, molded into a dome and layered with chocolate, nuts, and whipped cream.

Zuppa inglese   Sponge cake soaked in custard sauce and rum.

Index

Page numbers in italics refer to maps.

FROMMER'S® COMPLETE TRAVEL GUIDES
(Comprehensive guides with selections in all price ranges—from deluxe to budget)

Alaska
Amsterdam
Arizona
Atlanta
Australia
Austria
Bahamas
Barcelona, Madrid & Seville
Belgium, Holland & Luxembourg
Bermuda
Boston
Budapest & the Best of Hungary
California
Canada
Cancún, Cozumel & the Yucatán
Cape Cod, Nantucket & Martha's Vineyard
Caribbean
Caribbean Cruises & Ports of Call
Caribbean Ports of Call
Carolinas & Georgia
Chicago
China
Colorado
Costa Rica
Denver, Boulder & Colorado Springs
England
Europe
Florida

France
Germany
Greece
Hawaii
Hong Kong
Honolulu, Waikiki & Oahu
Ireland
Israel
Italy
Jamaica & Barbados
Japan
Las Vegas
London
Los Angeles
Maryland & Delaware
Maui
Mexico
Miami & the Keys
Montana & Wyoming
Montréal & Québec City
Munich & the Bavarian Alps
Nashville & Memphis
Nepal
New England
New Mexico
New Orleans
New York City
Nova Scotia, New Brunswick & Prince Edward Island
Oregon
Paris
Philadelphia & the Amish Country

Portugal
Prague & the Best of the Czech Republic
Provence & the Riviera
Puerto Rico
Rome
San Antonio & Austin
San Diego
San Francisco
Santa Fe, Taos & Albuquerque
Scandinavia
Scotland
Seattle & Portland
Singapore & Malaysia
South Pacific
Spain
Switzerland
Thailand
Tokyo
Toronto
Tuscany & Umbria
USA
Utah
Vancouver & Victoria
Vermont, New Hampshire & Maine
Vienna & the Danube Valley
Virgin Islands
Virginia
Walt Disney World & Orlando
Washington, D.C.
Washington State

FROMMER'S® DOLLAR-A-DAY GUIDES
(The ultimate guides to comfortable low-cost travel)

Australia from $50 a Day
California from $60 a Day
Caribbean from $60 a Day
England from $60 a Day
Europe from $50 a Day
Florida from $60 a Day
Greece from $50 a Day
Hawaii from $60 a Day
Ireland from $50 a Day

Israel from $45 a Day
Italy from $50 a Day
London from $70 a Day
New York from $75 a Day
New Zealand from $50 a Day
Paris from $70 a Day
San Francisco from $60 a Day
Washington, D.C., from $60 a Day

FROMMER'S® MEMORABLE WALKS

Chicago
London

New York
Paris

San Francisco

FROMMER'S®PORTABLE GUIDES

Acapulco, Ixtapa/	Dublin	Puerto Vallarta, Manzanillo
Zihuatanejo	Las Vegas	& Guadalajara
Bahamas	London	San Francisco
California Wine	Maine Coast	Sydney
Country	New Orleans	Tampa Bay & St. Petersburg
Charleston & Savannah	New York City	Venice
Chicago	Paris	Washington, D.C.

FROMMER'S®NATIONAL PARK GUIDES

Grand Canyon	Yosemite & Sequoia/
National Parks of the American West	Kings Canyon
Yellowstone & Grand Teton	Zion & Bryce Canyon

THE COMPLETE IDIOT'S TRAVEL GUIDES
(The ultimate user-friendly trip planners)

Cruise Vacations	Las Vegas	New York City
Planning Your Trip to Europe	Mexico's Beach Resorts	San Francisco
Hawaii	New Orleans	Walt Disney World

SPECIAL-INTEREST TITLES

The Civil War Trust's Official Guide to	Outside Magazine's Adventure Guide
the Civil War Discovery Trail	to the Pacific Northwest
Frommer's Caribbean Hideaways	Outside Magazine's Guide to Family Vacations
Israel Past & Present	Places Rated Almanac
New York City with Kids	Retirement Places Rated
New York Times Weekends	Washington, D.C., with Kids
Outside Magazine's Adventure Guide	Wonderful Weekends from Boston
to New England	Wonderful Weekends from New York City
Outside Magazine's Adventure Guide	Wonderful Weekends from San Francisco
to Northern California	Wonderful Weekends from Los Angeles

THE UNOFFICIAL GUIDES®
(Get the unbiased truth from these candid, value-conscious guides)

Atlanta	Florida with Kids	Miami & the Keys	Skiing in the West
Branson, Missouri	The Great Smoky	Mini-Mickey	Walt Disney World
Chicago	& Blue Ridge	New Orleans	Walt Disney World
Cruises	Mountains	New York City	Companion
Disneyland	Las Vegas	San Francisco	Washington, D.C.

FROMMER'S®IRREVERENT GUIDES
(Wickedly honest guides for sophisticated travelers)

Amsterdam	London	New Orleans	San Francisco
Boston	Manhattan	Paris	Walt Disney World
Chicago			Washington, D.C.

FROMMER'S®DRIVING TOURS

America	Florida	Ireland	Scotland
Britain	France	Italy	Spain
California	Germany	New England	Western Europe